Social Theory

SECOND EDITION

Social
Theory

The Multicultural
and Classic Readings

edited by

Charles Lemert
WESLEYAN UNIVERSITY

Westview Press
A Member of the Perseus Books Group

In loving memory of
Florence Lyons Brown (1915?–1995),
who taught me to think and feel about these things,
and thus to read and speak of them

Copyright © 1999 by Charles Lemert

Published in 1999 in the United States of America by Westview Press, 5500 Central Avenue, Boulder, Colorado 80301-2877, and in the United Kingdom by Westview Press, 12 Hid's Copse Road, Cumnor Hill, Oxford OX2 9JJ

Library of Congress Cataloging-in-Publication Data
Social theory : the multicultural and classic readings / edited by
    Charles Lemert. — 2nd ed.
       p.   cm.
    Includes index.
    ISBN 0-8133-3472-1
    1. Sociology.   2. Sociology—History.   I. Lemert, Charles C.,
1937– .
HM51.S66235   1999
301—dc21   98-11803
                                                                               CIP

The paper used in this publication meets the requirements of the American National Standard for Permanence of Paper for Printed Library Materials Z39.48-1984.

10   9   8   7   6   5   4   3

Contents

Part Two
Social Theories and World Conflict: 1919–1945

Part Three
The Golden Moment: 1945–1963

Part Four
Will the Center Hold? 1963–1979
Charles Lemert

Experiments at Renewal and Reconstruction

Part Five
After Modernity, Since 1979
Charles Lemert

Part Six
Searching for the Millennium

Rethinking the Globalizing World

The New Social Formations

Social Theory:
Its Uses and Pleasures

CHARLES LEMERT

Social theory is a basic survival skill. This may surprise those who believe it to be a special activity of experts of a certain kind. True, there are professional social theorists, usually academics. But this fact does not exclude my belief that social theory is something done necessarily, and often well, by people with no particular professional credential. When it is done well, by whomever, it can be a source of uncommon pleasure.

When one of my sons was in elementary school, he came home one day with questions that led to some good social theory. After he spent his first two school years in an informal, somewhat countercultural school, we moved. He was then enrolled in a more traditional public school. Thus began a more lively and sociologically interesting line of dinner table talk. He observed, for example, that when his class marched from its classroom to the lunchroom, the boys were told to form one line, the girls another. The march itself was under a code of silence. Having grown accustomed to schools with few rules of any sort, my son found this strange. At dinner, he reported this exotic practice with the ironic question, "What was this for? Do they think we are going to attack the girls?"

Later, sometime in junior high school, he began to figure this out. After several years of close observation, he determined that schools impose arbitrary social rules, like walking silently in sex-segregated lines, because they are institutions concerned as much with civil discipline and authority as with learning. He used his own words, but he had developed a social theory congruent to his earlier questions. This he enjoyed because he felt the power of being able to say something persuasive about the world of people with whom he lived.

Most people—whatever their social class, age, gender, race, or sexual orientation—develop a good enough repertoire of social theories of this sort. Usually, one suspects, these theories come into some focus in childhood and early adolescence, often in reply to innocent questions about daily social practices. When such theories are stated, very often in ordinary language, innocence is already lost. The world as it is comes into being.

In *There Are No Children Here,* Alex Kotlowitz tells the story of two boys trying to survive in one of Chicago's most dangerous public housing projects. Lafeyette, then age ten, said: "If I grow up, I want to be a bus driver." The "if" suggests one of the reasons Kotlowitz took the book's title from an observation by Lafeyette's mother: "But you know, there are no children here. They've seen too much to be children." This, too, is a social theory. The boy and his mother both put into plain words the social world of the uncounted thousands of urban children whose lullaby is gunfire. If not pleasure, there must at least be some satisfaction in knowing and being able to describe one's place in a world. If you cannot say it, how can you deal with it? Between the experiences of the middle-class, white boy (my son) and a welfare-class, Black boy (Lafeyette), there is common ground. Both knew they knew something important about their social worlds, and they knew what they knew because they could put it into words.

Thus considered, social theory is the normal accomplishment of socially adept human creatures figuring out what other creatures of the same sort are doing with, to, or around them. Such theories are everywhere, though they are not easy to come by. David Bradley, in his novel *The Chaneysville Incident,* explains why:

> The key to the understanding of any society lies in the observation and analysis of the insignificant and the mundane. For one of the primary functions of societal institutions is to conceal the basic nature of the society, so that the individuals that make up the power structure can pursue the business of consolidating and increasing their power untroubled by the minor carpings of a dissatisfied peasantry. Societal institutions act as fig leaves for each other's nakedness. . . . And so, when seeking to understand the culture or the history of a people, do not look at the precepts of the religion, the form of the government, the curricula of the schools, or the operations of businesses; flush the johns.

Bradley then put into words what his readers all know but never have reason to say: The toilets on buses are foul, while those on airplanes are neat and well supplied, and it is no accident that poor people ride buses, while the less poor fly. It is, thus, a plausibly coherent social theory to say that such a society considers its poor filth, yet wishes to disguise this unpleasant attitude.

Social theory, Bradley might suggest, is about the mundane and the concealed—those hidden aspects of social life we sometimes encounter in the ordinary course of daily life. We don't always see them, thus we aren't always in a position to speak of them, for at least the following reasons: (1) the powers-that-be want them concealed (Bradley's idea). (2) Either the empowered or the weak may resist talking about them because they are too threatening (Kotlowitz's implicit idea that some people deny the reality of urban life because it's too much to deal with). Or (3) people need time and experience to learn how to put into words the reality they live with (but not everyone has the time to do this). Social theories don't just occur to us. Some we never get. Others come in time. Some we have to work to get at. But they are there to be known and said.

It could therefore be said that an individual survives in society to the extent he or she can say plausibly coherent things about that society. Our ability to endure, and on occasion to enjoy, the worlds of irrational lunch-line rules, of crack wars in the hallways, of clean airplane restrooms and much more depends on our knowing something about why things are as they are. And we only know such things well enough when we can talk about them.

Professional social theorists may find this too simple a definition of their stock-in-trade. Presumably, no one likes the idea that what he or she does for a living is but a specialized version of what any person on the street can do. Yet the evidence supports the idea that there is at best a difference of degree, not of kind, between lay and professional theories of social life. Professional social theorists, if they are honest, must admit that they encounter this truth whenever they teach students who invariably say in introductory courses: "Interesting stuff, but it sounds like jargon for what everyone knows." The comeback to the wisdom of these students should be: "Perhaps, but can they all say it?" Though professional social theorists sometimes get carried away with *how* they say what they know about the social world, they at least are skilled at coming up with something coherent to say.

From this uneasy balance of trade between lay and professional social theorists, I draw the justification for this collection of readings in social theory. Everyone can do it. Everyone should do more of it. Responsible lay members of society presumably would live better—with more power, perhaps more pleasure—if they could produce more social theories, that is, if they could use their already considerable practical sociologies to greater advantage. One of the ways lay members can learn to say more about their social worlds is to pay attention to what professional social theorists have said and are saying. This is not because the professionals are more likely to be right—only because they are more practiced.

The Origins of Social Theory

The surprising thing is that professional social theorists have not been practicing their trade for very long, at least not in great numbers. In fact, professional social theory has been around only for the past several hundred years, roughly since the beginning of modern times. Though it has been argued that earlier peoples did a type of social theory (the Greeks are usually cited in this regard), social theory as we know it really began only in the eighteenth century in the various expressions of Enlightenment culture. It did not become a popular activity among the urban intelligentsia until the middle of the nineteenth century, when there first were relatively free and open social spaces. The development of civil society in the eighteenth century, mostly in European (and a few North American) urban centers, permitted enough freedom of expression to encourage independent thinking. These were the circumstances in which a critical mass of literate citizens began to pose the questions social theory tries to answer.

It is even possible to say that the foundational categories with which social theory first began were themselves an attempt to account for what was then a striking difference between modern societies and the preceding traditional ones. The modern/traditional dichotomy became, therefore, a technical expression with innumerable variations. Max Weber wrote of a rational, future-oriented ethic as the distinctive feature of modern, capitalist societies and distinguished this ethic from traditionalism. Emile Durkheim wrote of different types of moral cohesiveness, the modern being a more complicated social division of labor in which individuals tended to become lost without the more immediate social controls of traditional societies. Karl Marx, of course, wrote of the uniquely subtle forms of alienation under the capitalist mode of production in which despotism, slavery, and feudal domination were replaced by less overt, but still exploitative, aggressions against the human spirit. Though these three, and many other nineteenth-century social theorists, held sharply different views on the actual state of the modern world, all began their social theories with an explicit theory of the modern world's differences from the traditional.

In the briefest of terms, they all believed what no thinking person could deny: Beginning with the cultural, political, and economic revolutions of the late eighteenth and nineteenth centuries, fewer and fewer people could avoid the responsibility to have something to say about the new society. This was not just because the society was new and changing. More importantly, it was because this society demanded, in effect, that its more urbanized and literate citizens participate. Little in early or later modernity was settled. Little remained the same for any period of time. As a result, in a world where change was everywhere, those who desired to have a public life and to participate in the economic and political activities of the new times had to make up their own minds about what was going on.

The contrast with the immediately preceding period must have been quite compelling, perhaps shocking. Few of us who live in the Europeanized, Northern world today have any inkling of what the change must have meant. Even those who come from rural areas can only catch a glimpse. I once lived in rural southern Illinois. On a Sunday's drive, one could visit small villages like Buncombe (pop. 850), where the boarded-up general store and the peeling paint told of the effect of the new Wal-Mart outlet in Carbondale, twelve miles to the north. There, the traditional rural world was still passing away. But today's passings of the pre-modern order in rural Illinois or Nebraska are but occasional glimpses of the early modern experience when *everywhere* the old life was disappearing.

Today, we can only imagine at some remove the traditional world the early social theorists saw fading. Consider a passage from R. W. Southern's *Making of the Middle Ages*:

> By the thirteenth century . . . the main features of village life were established as they were to exist for another five hundred years. Materially, there was probably remarkably little difference between the life of the peasant in the thirteenth century and the village before it was transformed by modern mechanisms: the produce of the land had increased sixfold or tenfold during these centuries, but very little of this increase went into the pocket or stomach of the individual peasant. Compared with the rest of the community, he remained immune from new wants, or the means of satisfying them. Everywhere the peasant kept himself alive on a diet whose scarcity and monotony was broken only by intermittent feastings, at harvest time, at pig-killing time, and when people got married or died. There were great differences in the fortunes of individual peasants: families rose and fell, holdings grew and withered away again, following laws similar to those which governed the rise and fall of kingdoms. Over the fortunes of all, high and low, there presided the unpredictable factors of marriage and child-birth. The rules of succession, infinitely various and complicated, often modified, but with the general authority of centuries of growth behind them, were the framework within which the pattern of village—as of national—life was woven.

Since R. W. Southern wrote these words (in 1953), social historians have learned a great deal more about the underlying strains and potential for rebellion and change in the traditional medieval world. Just the same, one can take this view of village life as a fair guide to the traditional, premodern world. Yes, there was change. But change was a "rise and fall" of fortune. Everything social was pressed under the "general authority of centuries of growth." For at least five hundred years, social life in these villages remained much the same. Hence, we have Max Weber's eloquent definition of traditional values as those adhering to the "eternal yesterday."

By contrast, read the description of modern life written in 1903 by a friend of Weber's, Georg Simmel, in "The Metropolis and Modern Life":

> The psychological foundation, upon which the metropolitan individual is erected, is the intensification of emotional life due to the swift and continuous shift of external and in-

ternal stimuli. Man is a creature whose existence is dependent on differences, i.e., his mind is stimulated by the difference between present impressions and those which have preceded. Lasting impressions, the slightness in their differences, the habituated regularity of their course and contrast between them, consume, so to speak, less mental energy than the rapid telescoping of changing images, pronounced differences within what is grasped at a single glance, and the unexpectedness of violent stimuli. To the extent that the metropolis creates these psychological conditions—with every crossing of the street, with the tempo and multiplicity of economic, occupational and social life—it creates in the sensory foundations of mental life, and the degree of awareness necessitated by our organization as creatures dependent on differences, a deep contrast with these lower, more habitual, more smoothly flowing rhythm of the sensory-mental phase of small town and rural existence.

Hardly anyone who lives in or has recently visited a modern metropolis could fail to understand intuitively what Simmel meant by the psychological individual who, even on crossing an urban street, must react differently from—and thus become some other sort of human individual than—a rural cousin or an ancestor in an early thirteenth-century village. But what is most interesting is that it would have been impossible for Simmel merely to describe the metropolitan mental life. He had to produce a theory. The passage is, of course, a sometimes abstract but clear enough social theory, not just of urban mentality but also of modern life itself. Few people in those earliest decades of the new urban society, even as late as 1903 when Simmel wrote, could have spoken of the new life without comparing it somehow to the traditional or the rural. This necessity was the first condition of social theory.

   Thus, we may say that the first professional theorists were individuals who could not have done social theory without the new society. At the same time, they were individuals who, having begun to think of that society, could not help but think about it theoretically. It was as though the open space and rapid pace of the new world meant one could best embrace it not with any act of the will or reflex of feeling but only with a theory. The first form of that theory was comparative. Simmel and the others writing a century and more ago thought the modern social world in comparison to the traditional.

   Today, these are no longer the necessary conditions for doing social theory. The social worlds in which people must now do their theories are sharply different from those in the late nineteenth century. Still, always in the background somewhere is that foundational condition of social theory: It would not have come into its own, certainly not as a professional activity, had it not been for the new modern society that encouraged and even required thoughtful talk about what was going on.

Thinking the New World Order

Today's changed conditions for doing social theory have disturbed the original balance of trade between lay and expert social theorists. Were we to compare, say, the end of the nineteenth century to the end of the twentieth, we would soon find two major differences in the circumstances affecting who thinks about social life and how they think. First, the number of people with ready access to a culture supportive of critical thinking has increased dramatically, especially after the hold of the European powers on their colonies came to a formal end, primarily during the 1950s and 1960s. Second, the people normally engaged in critical social thinking are no longer necessarily members of or identified with a dominant class of bourgeois intellectuals. Many of the new social theorists do not consider themselves bourgeois (even if they are), and many are visibly not anything like the white, male advocates of European culture who wrote the first, best-known social theories. These two differences—one of number, one of kind—make social theory today an enterprise largely, but not entirely, different from that of the nineteenth century. Among the more salient differences is that today's social theory is produced in more intimate intercourse with the lives of people who are not at all professional in the subject. Hence, the balance is different. At the end of the nineteenth century, social theory was chiefly done by experts; today, even the experts pay closer attention to what some might call everyday-life social theory.

Alvin W. Gouldner, a social theorist who wrote in the period when these differences became evident, would have referred to these as cultures of critical discourse—cultures that encourage large numbers of people to think critically about the social world *and* that provide these people with the tools with which to do the thinking. Gouldner himself thought of this change in what turned out to be overly general terms. He assumed there was one culture of critical discourse and that it was ready-made within the culture of modern life. In one important sense, Gouldner was correct. Modern life, in contrast to the traditional, did seem to encourage critical thinking. This was, in effect, the main point of the Enlightenment—that, in Immanuel Kant's famous definition, modern, enlightened people would "dare to know." Daring to know and daring to use that knowledge are attitudes toward life and the world that could only arise among people willing to break with tradition, thereby looking to new, future possibilities. In this sense, modernity was a culture of critical thinking and thus of social theory. Just the same, the present social world encourages a state of mind more complicated than an essential and universal humanistic attitude of critical reasoning. Increasingly in the last generation, the world seems to engender any number of different cultures, many of which in turn encourage critical social theories—theories that may each be in a different voice.

Very often, these differences are subtle, barely detectable. My son and Lafeyette were about the same age when each put into words a shrewd diagnosis of his worldly circumstances. On the surface, both boys might seem to have been producing social ideas appropriate to a certain level of male psychological development. On close inspection (whatever developmental psychology might teach us about when children can formulate cognitive or moral objects), the differences between the theories of the two boys are there to be seen. The white, middle-class boy who diagnoses the duplicitous and confusing functions of his school does so in a gesture of prowess. What he discovers and says about this aspect of his world is, to be sure, armament against a sometimes frightening, often goofy social arrangement. Yes, even members of the middle class have reason to fear the world. Some individuals make the journey to adult life with ease, some with great pain. And a few do not make it at all. But most do, somehow.

Lafeyette's real world was different. He said "if I grow up" in recognition of the factual world in which he lived. By the time he met Kotlowitz, Lafeyette had witnessed the murder of other children not much older than he. Like the middle-class boy in a safer, suburban life, he was a shrewd observer. Yet Lafeyette was expressing something that went well beyond keen observational sense. He was putting into words what every Black, male child growing up in urban projects knows to be true: Poor Black boys do not always grow up. Boys like my son can be enrolled in countercultural schools or private schools where, on occasion, the rules make more sense. They might have options. But boys like Lafeyette, whatever their options, cannot escape the simple, hard facts of their social situation. Their odds are different, and the difference is a complex result of powerful social forces that go well beyond anything Lafeyette and his brother and their mates could hope to manage. He was not using the technical language of social theory, but he was saying that he recognized the meaning of being poor, Black, male, American. These four social forces—class, race, gender, nationality—form a matrix that defines, and limits, at an early age, what and who boys like Lafeyette can be. Some may outrun the limits; some grow up; some grow up whole and well. But boys born into Lafeyette's social circumstances must, somehow, figure out who they are and what they want to be in relation to the limiting condition "*If I grow up.*" This makes his theory of his world different from my son's.

But what about this is new? Surely this is not the only world in which a generation of children, even a generation of children of a specific race and gender, has been under threat of extinction. No, but it may be a time when the culture in which children grow up believes that a person's social identity is fixed somehow in relation to the particulars of his or her life. The children themselves cannot be expected to grasp such abstractions, but a child like Lafeyette must, it seems, understand his concrete difference from others. "If I grow up, I want to be a bus driver." Lafeyette understood, and answered, the question asked of all children. The "if" was local knowledge of his reality.

The world today is less dominated than it once was by a single, unified dream of how things should be. People living in areas influenced by modern European culture have always exaggerated the truth of their dream. For several centuries, they and quite a few others were persuaded that theirs was also the world's dream. European modernity's idea of human history moving progressively toward a better world— one in which life everywhere would be more and more like life in some European or North American metropolis—was an ideology of global proportions and quite a successful one. But today, boys like Lafeyette are not alone in refusing to be taken in by such promises. Whatever is noble in it, the dream of one world or one America getting better all the time does not speak to them.

This is the big and recent change in social theory. The new social theories are no longer beholden to the West's ideology of human history. At the beginning, the classic social theorists accepted with modest reluctance the idea that European culture was the future for humankind. The great ones had their reservations, true. Still, Marx's *Manifesto* began with a famous line about the specter haunting Europe, then quickly shifted to a discussion of "the history of all hitherto existing society," which turned out to be a history of the West. Durkheim, likewise, wrote humbly of the foundations of knowledge in the most elementary and non-European religious societies; yet his primary scientific and political preoccupations were to explain and develop a thoroughly modern society, of which Third Republic France was the ideal. Weber, too, was restrained and judicious in his scholarly studies of non-Western religions, but his most famous book, *The Protestant Ethic and the Spirit of Capitalism,* has contributed mightily to the myth of the superiority of Western rationality over Eastern traditionalism. Certainly, Weber's doubts about the future of the West were severe—but not because he preferred some other civilization. He was vexed because he believed in the West. These three men, along with Sigmund Freud, are usually considered the greatest of the original social theorists, and surely their greatness is due in some part to their intuitive sense that something was wrong with the West's dream of having discovered the final solution to humanity's problem. Others before them (like Auguste Comte) and after them (like Talcott Parsons) dreamed the dream with much less caution.

Until the past generation, most of the recognized experts in social theory took for granted the parochial idea that the culture of a relatively small number of white people in the north explained the "is and ought" of the world. Because the modern culture that invented social theory also invented the various myths of the inherent superiority of the West, one can easily see the limitations built into the classic versions of the best-known social theories in the last century and a half. It is tempting to conclude that just as the late nineteenth century required its version of critical social theory to account for the startling emergence of the modern, so the late twentieth century required some other sort of social theory to reckon with the disturbances in the culture and political economy of the European and American spheres of influence. This is why the changes in social theory could first be detected with the collapse of Europe's hold on its colonial empires in the 1950s and the rebellions and revolutions within European and American societies that began in the 1960s. If social theory, whether lay or expert, is a theory of a kind of world, then the type of theory must change as the world turns.

At the very end of the twentieth century, hardly any public issue is more controversial than this, particularly in the United States. There are those who still insist that, whatever has changed, America and the world can still be unified around the original Western ideas that Arthur Schlesinger described as "still a good answer—still the best hope" in *The Disuniting of America.* Schlesinger—white, male, Harvard, liberal, intellectual, historian—is the most persuasive of those in this camp. Against them are others who say, "Enough. Whatever is useful in these ideas, they don't speak to me." Audre Lorde—black, feminist, lesbian, poet and social theorist—put this opposing view sharply in an often-quoted line: "The master's tools will never dismantle the master's house." Between these two views, there is more than enough controversy to go around. In large part, the controversy is between two different types of social theorists *and* over how social theory ought be done. It involves who has the right to say what about the social world. As the world turns more and more into an information age of uncertain globalizing effects, hardly anyone can refuse to say something about the social world. Social theory, thus, becomes ever more a virtual imperative of life in the global society. As the world turns more and more into an information age of uncertain globalizing effects, hardly anyone can refuse to say something about the social world. Social theory, thus, becomes ever more a virtual imperative of life in the global society. This is an odd turn. The change in social theory has brought social theory back full circle to at least one important aspect of its origins. Though the first social theorists were bourgeois intellectuals, they were also, for the most part, public figures. Marx stirred the masses, wrote for newspapers, and roused the suspicion of the authorities. In Paris a generation later, the public took note of what Durkheim had to say on any number of topics, from the innocence of Captain Alfred Dreyfus to the reform of French schools. At about the same time, Weber's public lectures were packed, and the early recruits of the Chicago School of sociology were reformers, journalists, settlement house workers, and clergy. Then, social theory was a public activity. Now, after a long exile in the guise of an academic science, social theory is slowly working its way back into the public sphere—as provocateur of social conscience, as object of ridicule and controversy, as source of new thinking about the social world.

The reason for this is plain. Everyone, from the politician to the common man or woman, is aware that there seems to be something different in the world, something that can reasonably be called a new world order. Few can define it. No one can be certain what it is. Some do not believe in it. Some consider it their best hope in a long while. Yet whatever one thinks, the changes in the world between the mid-1960s and the early 1990s seem gradually to have cumulated to the point where now hardly anyone refuses to speak of them.

What is meant by the new world order? What place will it allow for the old ways? What new demands will it put before human beings? Questions like these nag at us, whatever our politics or ethics or situation in life. In this respect, the end of the twentieth century is a time much like the end of the nineteenth. We are asked what to make of the new order. We are asked to think about the world in terms different from, and more serious than, those used before. This is why social theory has changed. This is why having something different to say about the world is of broad human interest—even, and especially, to those with no particular professional investment in social theory. Social theory has come back to its roots.

Multiculturalism and the New Social Theories

It would not be very far wrong to say that social theory sets root only in the soil of social disruption. This seems to be equally true for both lay and professional social theories. The evidence is reasonably clear.

Social theories arose in their classic form when Europe was most disrupted by the uncertain progress of the modern world. Marx and Engels wrote their *Manifesto* on the eve of the 1848 revolutions; Marx's *Capital* was written during the flood and ebb of economic confusion in the two decades that followed. Durkheim wrote during the bouleversements caused by France's attempts, during the Third Republic, to conclude its century-long revolution by founding a thoroughly modern social order. Weber and Simmel wrote during the social conflicts caused by Germany's transition from the traditionalism under Otto von Bismarck's reign to its role as a world industrial power under the ineffectual principles of the Weimar Republic. Each of these men, in their personal lives as in their published theories, reflected the tensions of their times.

Tensions expressed in the master concepts of the great white men—Marx's alienation, Weber's iron cage, Durkheim's anomie—were felt throughout their societies. What they sensed through the veil of their bourgeois culture was confirmed in other writings, repressed until recently, by social theorists who experienced more directly the brutalities visited on ordinary people for reason of their race or gender—and more. Charlotte Perkins Gilman's *The Yellow Wallpaper,* now understood to be a classic of feminist writing, is witness to more than the oppressive attitudes of the men in her life. Though fiction, it documented the way in which the female character's insanity was not a wholly inappropriate reaction to the modern world. Gilman's fictional character was modeled on her own experiences during a rest cure for a mental disorder, after the leading (male) specialist on "the nervous disorders of women" had prescribed complete abandonment of all work. Gilman's then husband enforced this cure, which only deepened her distress. The wallpaper in the room to which she was confined became a projective field for her character's (and her own) experiences of the world:

> He thought I was asleep first, but I wasn't, and lay there for hours trying to decide whether that front pattern and the back pattern really did move together or separately.

> On a pattern like this, by daylight, there is a lack of sequence, a defiance of law, that is a constant irritant to a normal mind.
> The color is hideous enough, and unreliable enough, and infuriating enough, but the pattern is torturing.

How different is this from the madness Max Weber saw in the superficially rational patterns of modern life? He spoke of this in the closing words of *The Protestant Ethic and the Spirit of Capitalism:* "Specialists without spirit, sensualists without heart; this nullity imagines that it has attained a level of civilization never before achieved." Was not his image of the iron cage of the modern world Weber's figure for the odd, disturbing effect of a world in which the rational front pattern moved irregularly against an irrational back pattern, in such defiance of reason that the normal mind was unsettled?

And what of W.E.B. Du Bois's now-famous figure of the twoness haunting and defining the American Negro? In *Souls of Black Folk,* Du Bois spoke of the social experience of his race in words that described what had to have been a widespread, if not universal, social experience of the earlier moderns—of a social world divided within, and against, itself:

> It is a peculiar sensation this double-consciousness, this sense of always looking at one's self through the eyes of others, of measuring one's soul by the tape of a world that looks on in amused contempt and pity. One ever feels his twoness,—an American, a Negro; two souls, two thoughts, two unreconciled strivings; two warring ideas in one dark body, whose dogged strength alone keeps it from being torn asunder.

Du Bois, like Gilman, wrote in the more autobiographical languages that gave them access to the conditions and dreams of ordinary life. The same languages were used by Anna Julia Cooper—writer, early Black feminist, educator. In *A Voice from the South* (published, like *The Yellow Wallpaper,* in 1892), Cooper spoke of the "colored woman's office," of the Black woman's responsibility to redeem America and the West by showing the moral path beyond the limitations of race and gender—a path between the good race-men (who could not understand women) and the good white feminists (who could not understand Blacks). Cooper, in her way, wrote of a double-consciousness, or perhaps a multiple consciousness, that was incumbent upon American Black women, who bore the several obligations of race and gender.

Writers like these, some only now coming into the public eye, help us see the deep, mysterious ties that bind all people thinking about their social worlds in times of change and turmoil. In many ways, the writings of Du Bois (especially his more personal books, *Souls of Black Folk* and *Dusk of Dawn*) are near-perfect repositories of the struggles of early modern social thinkers. They provide today's readers access to the trained thought of expert social theorists shaken by reverberations of the suffering and desires of ordinary folk. Du Bois's concept of double-consciousness could be said to be one of those rare ideas that entered both theoretical literature and the popular imagination because it resonated finely with both. This was its power. As the passage just quoted suggests, Du Bois, though trained at Harvard and educated in Europe, was very much in touch with the pathos of Black Americans during his lifetime. Born just after the Civil War, he lived for ninety-five years—from Reconstruction, through Jim Crow, Booker T. Washington, the founding of the National Association for the Advancement of Colored People (NAACP), Marcus Garvey, to the civil rights movement. Du Bois died in Ghana on the morning of August 27, 1963, just as Martin Luther King, Jr. was preparing to deliver his "I Have a Dream" speech the next day in Washington, D.C. In a certain sense, Du Bois's life embodied, even acted out, a good portion of the social history of race in modern America (which is why his *Dusk of Dawn* is subtitled *An Autobiography of the Race Concept*). Du Bois had been a student of both William James and Max Weber (though he was much closer to James). The formal aspect of his double-consciousness concept was reasonably close to James's idea of the social self. "A man has as many social selves," said James, "as there are individuals who recognize him and carry an image of him in their mind." Against this, compare Du Bois's "sense of always looking at one's self through the eyes of others." In addition to its apparent relation to James's social self, Du Bois's double-consciousness appeared in *Souls of Black Folk* in 1903, one year after Charles Horton Cooley defined the looking-glass self and just over a year before Max Weber wrote of the strangely double nature of the modern world—rational, yet irrational; freedom bound by the iron cage.

Men and women, both writers and ordinary people, reflecting on their world around the end of the nineteenth century seemed to have been thinking along similar lines. Whatever the subterranean passages connecting the professional and the amateur social theories, the similarities in the separate writings of Simmel, Weber, Du Bois, Gilman, James, Cooper, and Cooley are evident—not neatly linked and certified, but present nonetheless.

Perhaps because of the social disturbances of the present time, we are only now able to appreciate the complexity of classical social theory. The great white men—Weber, Marx, Durkheim—were great social thinkers because they did not buy the official story of the modern world uncritically. They were circumspect (Durkheim), conflicted (Weber), or passionate (Marx) in their reservations about the progressive glory claimed by modern European culture and industry. In this respect, they understood quite well the underside of progress, the destruction visited on ordinary people by a changing world. They understood, if vaguely and uncertainly, that no single dream of progress for all of humanity could soothe the just (if sometimes inarticulate) complaints of those living outside the security of bourgeois society. At the same time, the voices of people like Du Bois, Cooper, and Gilman were muffled by the prejudices of the times and for that reason were necessarily truer expressions of what those less able to put their words into a public voice might have been thinking.

Thus, by juxtaposing the writings of the great official social theorists and those of the great but ignored (though now rediscovered) theorists, today's reader can begin to see the many complex sides of social theory's contributions to survival in the social world. On one side, the expert social theorists themselves are always, in some sense, conflicted because their task is to be at critical odds with the world about which they are speaking. The more disturbed the social order, as in the late nineteenth century, the more open the social theories. But on another side, one can entertain a supposition for which there is now compelling evidence: that official, professional, expert social theories (by whatever name) ought not always be considered the most articulate expressions of the social thinking of inarticulate, ordinary people. One must *never* assume that those without a public voice are inarticulate. The arrogance of intellectuals lies in the assumption that they alone know and speak the truth. Even the most radical, most passionately critical of thinkers fails to escape this arrogance for long. Marx, for one, certainly did not. The oppressed people of any social world *always* have a voice and thus something to say. For very good and sensible reasons, those in the privileged position in any society seldom hear what the oppressed say—not because they are ignorant and inarticulate (though they may be) but often because the weak have the good sense not to tell us, in so many words, what they think. The weak know very well that their truth—their understanding of social arrangements—may be a weapon for their survival if kept hidden but a cause of deepening their misery if revealed to the wrong authorities. Thus, what they know, when written, is very often hidden under pseudonyms or otherwise kept at a secretive distance from those in a position to punish.

In 1861, Harriet Jacobs published (under the name Linda Brent) *Incidents in the Life of a Slave Girl,* which included an astute analysis of the plantation household in which she had been held. The following passage is from her analysis of the household's delicate political balance. It came just after she described with analytic precision her mistress's pained restraint on hearing the slave's confession of how the master, a physician, had made sexual advances to Harriet:

> I did as she ordered. As I went on with my account her color changed frequently, she wept, and sometimes groaned. She spoke in tones so sad, that I was touched by her grief. The tears came to my eyes; but I was soon convinced that her emotions arose from anger and wounded pride. . . . I pitied Mrs. Flint. . . . She was completely foiled and knew not how to proceed. She would gladly have had me flogged for my supposed false oath; but, as I have already stated, the doctor never allowed any one to whip me. The old sinner was politic. The application of the lash might have led to remarks that would have exposed him in the eyes of his children and grandchildren. How often did I rejoice that I lived in a town where all the inhabitants knew each other! If I had been on a remote plantation, or lost among the multitude of a crowded city, I should not be a living woman.

On the surface, the confrontation with her mistress put Harriet Jacobs at risk. Yet as the narrative suggests, she held the upper hand. Mrs. Flint was to be pitied. Harriet had the power of understanding more exactly than her mistress the complicated workings of the rural community and the power of protection it gave her. Narratives of this sort and their equivalent among women in the white community were the early resources for Anna Julia Cooper, W.E.B. Du Bois, and Charlotte Perkins Gilman. The original narratives may be described as lay social theories of a local world—the frank reflections of ordinary people forced to think through that world. The subsequent writings drew on this knowledge to fashion theories poised midway between the official theories that were salient in the eyes of the dominant culture and the reflex of pain and hope in the hearts of common, oppressed people.

This is the culture of social theory—any social world unsettled enough to disturb the natural tendency of social thought to relax, any social world that discomforts the easy acceptance of appearances as realities. Social theories, as distinct from the formal theories of social sciences and official policymaking, work in the tense, unreconciled spaces of social turmoil. Social theories require the energy and vision that come from those who are less comfortable in any society. *Social theory,* therefore, is simply a name for talk about the social world, talk rooted in the common experiences of those least able to avoid the consequences of social disruption. Were there ever a world in which all people were comfortable with whatever was, a world in which whatever appeared in daily life was a good enough reality, then social theory would slowly fade away, to be replaced by the confident pronouncements of enlightened science or well-intended policies. The most creative moments in the modern history of social theories were those when fewer and fewer of the privileged could relax as more and more of the disadvantaged could speak. The classic period of social theory, we now know, was one such moment. Not until the mid-1960s was there another quite the same.

Between the late nineteenth century and the 1960s, social theory remained more on the margins. In the interwar years, 1917 to 1945, social theory was preoccupied with the turmoil felt most acutely in the European sphere—political instability, depression, fascism, another world war. In this period, the disruption tested the ability of the West to believe in itself and to make that belief work in successful political and economic systems. Social theories of this time gave voice to the urban poor in new industrial cities, to the new marginal working class, to the dislocated in urban areas, to Jewish people suffering under Hitler, and to the first movements toward liberation among what were later called Third World people. These were the people whose suffering provoked social theories. Yet this period of world conflict ended in 1945 with the world order essentially the same as it had been at the end of the nineteenth century, with only one crucial difference: The Americans now reigned where once the British had.

For a moment in the 1950s and early 1960s in America, many thought they were within reach of a world order in which, indeed, one could relax in order to enjoy the benefits of an affluent society and the apparent reality of America showing just how good society could be. Then, social theory went underground. A newly confident social science dominated thinking about society, only slightly disturbed by the hedged bets of writers like Erik Erikson, Erving Goffman, and David Riesman. Riesman, principally, suggested (in *The Lonely Crowd*) that the old ideas of the world no longer suited as they once did. He described a change in the American and modern character from the inner-directed entrepreneur of early modernity to someone else: the other-directed conformist.

Still, this was before very many people in so comfortable a world understood the full force of what was coming. They thought the Communists were the problem. Little did they know. This was before those riding the wave of post–World War II affluence in the United States and recovery in Europe could ever have been expected to understand the final effects of the independence of India, the falling away of Europe's colonies in Africa, and the early civil rights movement in the United States. This was before even the best and brightest of liberal people could understand exactly what was happening before their eyes. In the 1950s, they were much too preoccupied with the Soviets' Sputnik, China's revolution, the Korean War, and Cuba's Fidel Castro. The real, long-lasting perturbations were just beginning to shake nearer to home.

In late October 1960, only days before the American electorate would decide between Richard Nixon and John F. Kennedy, Martin Luther King, Jr., was arrested in Georgia. His life was at risk. Taylor Branch, in *Parting the Waters,* described the moment when Robert Kennedy came face to face with a reality he could not yet understand. The account began with a campaign aide's report to Kennedy on King's situation:

"They took Dr. King out of Atlanta on an old traffic charge of driving without a license. Then they sentenced him to four months on the chain gang, denied bail, and took him off in the middle of the night to the state prison. All in one day."

"How could they do that?" Kennedy asked doubtfully. "Who's the judge? You can't deny bail on a misdemeanor." Martin [the campaign aide] decided that Kennedy may have lost sight of the essential fact that King was a Negro—a detail Southern politicians carefully avoided in their protests against interference in the King case. "Well, they just did it," said Martin. "They want to make an example of him as an uppity Negro."

Kennedy paused for a number of seconds and then said, "Uh, godammit," in a weary expletive that could have cut in many directions.

Without discussion, Robert Kennedy later called the judge. King was freed from danger, and the word spread through the Black community. John Kennedy won the election by a margin attributable to his unexpected voter strength among Blacks. Whatever Robert Kennedy's motivation may have been—political, legal, moral—this was a moment of foggy recognition of the true social circumstances of others about whom he then knew little. Though, like Kennedy's expletive, the experience cut in many directions among different people, it was of a sort encountered by many people— mostly white, mostly privileged—in Europe and North America through the 1960s.

This led to the second important time of creativity in social theory. As the Golden Age of America (what Henry Luce had called "the American Century") faded, there were signs that the movement of Blacks in the American South was not an isolated, regional event provoked by the Communists. Within the decade following the Montgomery, Alabama, bus boycott of 1955–1956, the first major event in the modern civil rights movement, it had become clear that the demands of American Blacks were close in content and form to those of other previously colonized people throughout the world. It is too seldom realized that many of the important intellectual resources for the Black rebellion in the United States were of Third World origin—Gandhi, Islam, and Africa.

Between 1956 and 1966, as Blacks eventually moved away from the civil rights movements and turned to Black consciousness, whites—including early feminists, students, antiwar protesters, and gays and lesbians—began to transform the ideas and political experiences (good and bad) of the civil rights movement into their own demands for change. C. Wright Mills's vision of the sociological imagination in 1959 was a direct inspiration for the early political philosophy of the Students for a Democratic Society (SDS) as expressed in their *Port Huron Statement* in 1962. One year later, Betty Friedan's *The Feminine Mystique* took up (without acknowledgment) the ideas of Simone de Beauvoir's *The Second Sex*. Friedan was read both by middle-class, white women suffering under the stultifying demands of suburban life and by younger women, often the daughters of suburban housewives, who had heard of Mary King and Casey Hayden's underground manifesto against the sexist treatment of women in the civil rights movement. Post–World War II feminism was thus born. In 1963, Blacks and whites also began to read Frantz Fanon, just one of a number of theorists critical of the colonial world. In 1964, following the march on Washington, Malcolm X delivered his stunning "Ballot or the Bullet" speech. At first, the social theories of these thinkers migrated slowly, initially among those young people already engaged in the dialogue and eventually spreading in wider and wider circles. More and more people—more and more white, middle-class people—came to that moment of recognition and turned as Robert Kennedy did—awkwardly, slowly, but definitely.

This was the beginning of the second great period in social theory, a period during which social theory itself changed. The greatest irony of the time was that the social theories of previously excluded and oppressed peoples came increasingly to the fore in large part because of the success of some very abstract philosophical doctrines taught in the most bourgeois and philosophical of world cities, Paris. The year

1966 was the year in which Stokely Carmichael is said to have used the term *Black Power* for the first time. It was also the year of the first influential pronouncements of the French philosophers, Jacques Derrida and Michel Foucault. Hence the irony: Doctrines that are to this day virtually unintelligible (even to trained academics) were somehow part and parcel of the movement that brought lay social theories their most influential public attention.

How could this be? One explanation (not necessarily the most satisfying) is that many people who were young revolutionaries in the 1960s crossed that magical age of thirty in the 1970s. They had to find work, and in the United States and parts of Europe, the universities were then still hiring. Academic work was consistent with their earlier revolutionary thinking, and it paid the rent. The French social theorists, like a different line of German critical thinkers (of which Jürgen Habermas is the most important), were academically respectable, in part because they were difficult to understand. The appropriation of the ideas of the European thinkers thus contributed to the building of academic careers without seriously compromising political and moral ideals. One of the deepest ironies in the aftermath of the 1960s is that the students who had once rebelled against the academic establishment now moved so directly to enter it. In the 1990s, many of them are part of that establishment. They teach and debate Habermas, Derrida, and Foucault or the ideas that evolved from the movements their writings encouraged. Many became deans, departmental chairs, international academic stars, editors, and worse. One might well appreciate their need to hold a job and the wider appeal of career success and fame. But even this does not explain the irony. The deeper explanation lies in the ideas themselves, the weird but true connection between a new wave of professional social theories and the real world experiences of many people who would never dream of inventing a word like *deconstruction*.

In 1966, in a now-famous talk at Johns Hopkins University in Baltimore, Jacques Derrida announced the beginning of poststructuralism, a theoretical movement in which the practice known as deconstructionism came to be well regarded. Also in 1966, Derrida spoke at the first international conference of academics interested in what was then considered the newest, most exciting method in humanistic studies. Although appreciative of the contributions of structuralism, Derrida devoted his talk to the argument that even structuralism's innovative spirit did not make it different from all prior, traditional forms of thought. His principal complaint against all philosophies up to that moment was that they limited the free play of social imagination. They were, he said, methods of thinking that so revolved around a principle of the Center that the freedom to explore and affirm differences was destroyed. Derrida believed he and those who shared his ideas were living in a revolutionary moment when that principle of the Center was giving way to, of all things, language:

> This was the moment when language invaded the universal problematic, the moment when, in the absence of a center or origin, everything became discourse—provided we can agree on this word—that is to say, a system in which the central signified, the original or transcendental signified, is never absolutely present outside a system of differences. The absence of the transcendental signified extends the domain and the play of signification infinitely.

Not, to be sure, the clearest of statements to the uninitiated. But certain key words are clear or clearly implied: *decentering, play, differences*.

Derrida's poststructuralist social theory uses these three terms in two ways. First, they propose an alternative way of thinking. Social theory, he argued, should reject overarching, limiting principles and open itself to the world of differences. Second, this was justified because only this method could make sense of the world of the mid-1960s—a world in which, in France and the United States, former colonial subjects, women, workers, and Blacks were asserting themselves by asserting their differences. It was, clearly, a time when neither the political nor the economic Center was holding against the play of cultural and political differences. Within two years, Paris and many of the Western capitals would shake with political protest. The complexity of his philosophy notwithstanding, Derrida was drawing the connection between very abstract social theory and political events in the social world. Theory, he argued, had to be decentered because the social world was decentering. Give up the West and its philosophy, he advised (though not in so many words), because the world all around—Algeria, Cuba, Vietnam, Alabama, Mississippi—was shifting rapidly out from under the sway of the cultural and political powers that had dominated the modern era.

Others, like Michel Foucault, said much the same thing. As their works were translated into the languages of the world, people coming into the universities from lives of political activism found the ideas persuasive, entirely suited to their own experiences, if not to their accustomed way of speaking. Today, the movements that Derrida and Foucault and others spawned in the mid-1960s are still at the center of controversy in the academy, though now they are widely known as postmodernism. To the amazement of those who bother to look into it, postmodernism bears a very close resemblance to other social theories rooted directly in the common language of people who are, in effect, following a lead much like that offered by Derrida. These are the theories of individuals asserting, for political and personal reasons, the authority of their previously suppressed cultures in order to define new ways of understanding themselves and their experiences without regard for the powers of the Center.

Gloria Anzaldúa, in *Borderlands/La Frontera,* an autobiographically based theory of the new mestiza, described this culture rediscovering its past and present life in the cultural and political borderland between the United States and Mexico:

> The U.S.-Mexican border *es una herida abierta* where the Third World grates against the first and bleeds. And before a scab forms it hemorrhages again, the lifeblood of two worlds merging to form a third country—a border culture. Borders are set up to define the places that are safe and unsafe, to distinguish *us* from *them.* A border is a dividing line, a narrow strip along a steep edge. . . . *Los atravesados* live here: the squint-eyed, the perverse, the queer, the troublesome, the mongrel, the mulatto, the half-breed, the half dead; in short, those who cross over go through the confines of the "normal." Gringos in the U.S. Southwest consider the inhabitants of the borderlands transgressors, aliens— whether they possess documents or not, whether they're Chicanos, Indians or Blacks. . . . The only "legitimate" inhabitants are those in power, the whites and those who align themselves with whites.

Anzaldúa claims these illegitimate people as her own. She is one of them—a people whose history reaches back before the United States appropriated these borderlands in 1848. Her theory is not really a theory in the usual sense. Its form is more in the tradition of Du Bois, Cooper, and Gilman. It transgresses the formal dependence of theory on prose. It plays with poetry, imagination, languages, and idioms. It rejects the gringo to affirm multiply cultured peoples who live and have lived against the oppressive force of American ambition.

Multiculturalism, like *social theory,* is a term without any definite denotation. One could say that the former term has come to represent the social theories of those who resist the usual classifications of thought and politics. Whichever terms are used, the evidence is clear that the latest period in social theory has produced theories that disturb tradition. They resist easy classification—neither lay and practical nor professional, neither poetry nor sociology, neither political nor academic, neither American nor Spanish nor African, and so on. Yet the new theories are social theories in every coherent sense of the term. They say something clear about the social world. They do so in words utterly different from anything that has gone before in the West. Oddly, however, they are not that far from the spirit and practice of social theory in its earliest days.

The longer the world lives in a multicultural environment, the more people accept, however grudgingly in some cases, that the unleashing of social differences in the arena of public politics is somehow aggravated by (perhaps even the result of) the odd shrinking of the world caused by new information technologies. The peoples of the multicultural world are a long way from understanding just exactly how, and why, these technologies have *simultaneously* made us aware of our differences *and* brought us into more intimate contact with each other. Yet the inhabitants of the globalizing world, as they strain against each other in this odd mix of social distance and intimacy, realize that they—that we, that is—must assume, at least in spirit, the moral imperatives of the earliest days of modern social theory. Though the structures of the social world of the end of the nineteenth century were light years distant from ours today at the end of the twentieth, we bear the same responsibilities as did our great-grandparents and grandparents in those days. We have no choice but to speak of our worlds, such as they are—and when we do, we become social theorists of a very practical and necessary sort.

Saying It, Reading It, and Getting By Better

When Derrida announced the beginning of his new social theory, he referred to an event in which "language entered the universal problematic." What?

Why has language become so much the preoccupation of social theorists in the last twenty years? Among academic social theorists, it is normal, almost necessary, to develop a theory of language, literature, or discourse early in one's career. Other, less traditionally professorial writers—like Gloria Anzaldúa, Toni Morrison, and Audre Lorde—tend to *use* language to disturb the world. What both types of social theorists have in common is one basic idea: If our way of thinking about the world has changed, so must our way of speaking and writing. Yet the new social theorists believe that we cannot escape the languages we have. The best course, they agree, is to use language to call attention to meanings. Anzaldúa gives *mestiza,* and *borderland* new meanings, just as other people have given *Black, Latina, woman, African, queer,* and *American* new political meanings.

The importance of these terms to those who define themselves in relation to them is very often beyond those who are seldom, if ever, called on to explain themselves. One of the unintended consequences of the modern world has been that the original Enlightenment principles have actually worked to better effect than the early moderns ever dreamed. At the end of the twentieth century, we live in a time of confusion wrought every bit as much by the successes of modernity as by its failures. True, by the formal measures of what was promised, the modern age has not paid off. War, poverty, human misery, and hunger recur as they always have, now along-side quite a few environmental and other miseries the modern world invented of its own accord. Remote telephones, MTV, Home Shopping Channel, and the other wonders of technology hardly balance this ledger. Just the same, it is unlikely that any of the bourgeois revolutionaries in the eighteenth century dreamed that human knowledge would be so widely and immediately communicated to every corner and level of global society as it is today. How could they have? Their world was so small. Kant, the author of the Enlightenment's slogan "dare to know," is also known to have been a racist by any standard. Few of the Enlightenment thinkers, political rev-olutionaries, or even early social theorists gave more than passing thought to the moral, political, or economic powers and rights of those outside their very narrow spheres of social experience.

Such observations may be considered cheap shots, insensitive to moral standards prevailing in the earliest days of the modern age—trendy indictments of white, mid-dle-class males everywhere. But this is the point: It is a fact of no minor importance that, until recently, the culture to which educated people have been expected to con-form was invented, and sustained, mostly by men who encountered little in their ex-perience that would or could broaden their horizons. They may be excused for their original innocence, if not for their clumsy attempt to hang on even at this late mo-ment. Thus, we can rightly conclude that the original idea of a culture in which knowl-edge would give human beings new power to define and move their world has en-joyed an unexpected success. Our forefathers had an excellent idea. Our criticism of them should be tempered with some forbearance. What they were not able to antici-pate a century ago was that this new knowledge would be held so widely, and used so powerfully and in such alarming ways, to criticize the very world they dreamed up.

This is where language entered the universal problematic. Language is the most important weapon of the weak (to borrow a phrase from James Scott). However much people are oppressed, however much they may be systematically deprived of the means to defend themselves or attack their opponents, people can always use words. The poor, the enslaved, the depressed, the illiterate, the imprisoned, and the abused can speak. Even those so disturbed by some primeval trauma in early life so as to lose their minds in later years can speak. They may speak only to themselves or to those who own or are wise to their condition. But they can speak. They may speak in some unusual code—of dreams, of a political underground, of the gang or the cell block, of the schizophrenic, of the therapist's office, of hushed conversations with others in like circumstance—but they do speak.

For some, this is a revolting idea. It is indeed. Of all the available human capaci-ties, Putting-it-into-words is the most powerful. Thinking-it, Feeling-it, or Seeing-it, by themselves, are nothing. It is only when people put what they think or sense or see into words that whatever is there to be thought, felt, or seen comes into play as a force in social life. The willingness to trust the language of things is what distin-guishes social theory from seemingly similar but often quite different activities—like, say, social *science*. The attitude of science in the modern world is Seeing-it, then Thinking-it. Thus, sociologists and other academics regularly can be overheard de-scribing their current research project in this way: "I'm *looking at* . . . such and such." The ideal of science is that of the enlightened thinker who peers sensitively and knowingly into the world in order to gather up its evidence that data, in turn, may be thought into truth.

Social theory, even in its original forms, tends to be skeptical of science's neat idea of truth—of a world offering up its evidence to the enlightened vision of the scientist. The great classic men—Freud, Marx, Ferdinand de Saussure, even Weber in his way—were largely preoccupied with finding some clever way around science. Freud based everything on the small, displaced clues to the unconscious life, clues that may appear in dreams and sneak out in the patient's talk on the couch. Saussure developed the original formal theory of the hidden, absent elements of language, the abstract system or grammars and terms that lie behind actual speech. Weber, always master of the tour de force, sought to invent a science of human things that saw the deepest truths of subjective meanings through the aesthetic trick of ideal types. And Marx believed the only good science was one that refused to take appearances for reality. The truth of the economic value of labor was found not in the marketplace but in the hidden secrets of production. Halfway through the first volume of *Capital*, he said that the social theorist who hopes to uncover this secret must leave the shop floor and the marketplace,

> this noisy sphere, where everything takes place on the surface and in the view of all men, and follow [Mr. Moneybags] into the hidden abode of production, on whose threshold there stares us in the face "No admittance except on business". Here we shall see, not only how capital produces, but how capital is produced. We shall at last force the secret of profit making.

Even Durkheim, in his last and greatest work, *Elementary Forms of the Religious Life*, seemed to set aside his earlier confident belief in scientific progress to explain that the secret of knowledge itself was not even the mind's ability to see the world but the human being's elementary dependence on the social group.

The classic social thinkers have been used to justify various types of sociologies and other social sciences. This is good. Science is good, important in its way. Sensible social theory need not set itself against science, from which it gathers a good bit of its descriptive information. Whether classic or new, social theory need only accept itself for what it is—that type of social knowledge concerned with putting into words whatever is there, especially whatever is most difficult to see on the surface. Those well trained in social theory do this for a living. Because they devote so much of their lives to it, they are more practiced in finding the words to say something sensible, critical, and revolting about the social world. This, however, does not make them different from any other social creature who, given the right degree of social disturbance and sufficient reason, finds a way to say, "If I grow up, I want to be a bus driver." Writers like Du Bois, Gilman, Anzaldúa, and Lorde—the other, and new, social theorists—would understand Lafeyette as standing somehow alongside the great original theorists.

The world is unevenly cruel. Whatever pleasures it offers are offered only to those who find a way to get by in it. Many, it would seem, are given such a head start that they would apparently have no use for social theory, no need for putting into words the deeper secrets. Yet those who are wise know this is not true. It would be absurd to suggest that Lafeyette and my son started from the same place; that a middle-class, white boy in America suffers as much as the boy in a city's failed project who must sleep, if at all, through threats of death. At the same time, it would be another kind of romance to believe that relatively well-off boys with all the necessary comforts do not struggle. The uneven cruelty of the world does not exempt any of us from the only real universal in human experience—that we encounter limits and injuries we must overcome; that survival is the prerequisite of pleasure.

Social theory is what we do when we find ourselves able to put into words what nobody seems to want to talk about. When we find those words, and say them, we begin to survive. For some, learning to survive leads to uncommon and exhilarating pleasures. For others, perhaps the greater number of us, it leads at least to the common pleasure—a pleasure rubbed raw with what is: the simple but necessary power of knowing that one knows what is there because one can say it.

This, whatever else, is what makes social theory worth reading,

C. L.

Notes

Footnotes are seldom at the foot anymore. Usually, they are at the end and difficult to find. Sometimes, they grow out of proportion to the text at the foot of which they claim to be humbly poised. The notes in Weber's *Protestant Ethic* are longer than the book itself! Notes, thus, can discourage reading. Yet the reader rightly desires some information, even if it is difficult to know how much and where. Because most of the references in this general introduction and the section introductions are to familiar sources, often to texts appearing elsewhere in the book, notes are kept to a bare minimum and located just after the introduction.

Page 1: Kotlowitz, *There Are No Children Here* (Doubleday, 1991), x.

Page 2: Bradley, *Chaneysville Incident* (Harper & Row, 1981), 6.

Page 4: Southern, *Making of the Middle Ages* (London: Arrow Books, 1953), 78.

Page 4: Simmel, in *On Individuality and Social Forms* (University of Chicago Press, 1971), 235.

Page 8: Schlesinger, *Disuniting of America* (Knoxville, TN, Whittle Books, 1991), 83.

Page 12: Jacobs, *Incidents* (Oxford University Press, 1988), 53.

Page 13: Branch, *Parting the Waters* (Simon and Schuster, 1988), 365.

Page 16: Anzaldúa, *Borderlands/La Frontera* (San Francisco, Spinsters, 1987), 3.

Quoted material not noted here is usually from a selection elsewhere in this book and acknowledged there.

PART ONE

Modernity's Classical Age: 1848–1919

A work of literature is considered a "classic" when, long after it was written, readers continue to read it. A famous example is Sophocles' dramatic telling of the story of Oedipus. This is so much a classic that one does not need to have read Sophocles, Shakespeare's *Hamlet,* or Freud to know something of the story. Most people recognize in themselves the truth told in this ancient Greek drama: that human beings are affected deeply by extreme feelings of love and hate for their parents. In most versions of the story, Oedipus loves his mother too much. Without knowing what he is doing or who the people involved really are, Oedipus kills his father and marries his mother. He rules his land with Jocasta, his mother-wife and queen. When a plague threatens the kingdom, Oedipus learns that his land can be saved only if his father's murder is avenged—and that he himself is the murderer! He blinds himself and goes into exile. Oedipus's actual blindness represents his deeper blindness to the effects of his desires on his behavior. His fate is tragically determined not because he had forbidden feelings of love and aggression for his parents but because he acted on them without knowing what he was doing. This story is a classic because people find in it some sort of standard for normal, if confusing, human experience. In literature, a writing is classic because it still serves as a useful reference or meaningful model for stories people tell of their own lives.

Hence, a period of historical time is considered classical because people still refer back to it in order to say things about what is going on today. Generally speaking, classical ages contain a greater number of classical writings for the obvious reason that literatures express their social times. Thus, at present, when people refer to the Oedipus story, they usually have in mind Freud's version, which still conveys much of drama of the modern world affecting people today. The Oedipus story figured prominently in one of Freud's classic writings, *The Interpretation of Dreams,* which was published in 1899. In this book, Freud made one of his most fundamental claims about dreams just after retelling the Oedipus story. Dreams, he explained, are always distorted stories of what the dreamer really wishes or feels. They can thus serve "to prevent the generation of anxiety or other forms of distressing affect."

Freud's telling of the Oedipus myth is a subject of controversy today because it is taken as a case in point for the feminist criticism that most classical writings in the social and human sciences systematically excluded and distorted women's reality. They did. In this case, Freud distorted reality by his preposterous inference from the Oedipus he saw in his patients to the claim that the major drama of early life is the little boy's desire to make love to his mother. Little girls were left out of this story, the crucial formative drama of early life. They were said to be driven by the trivial desire of envy for the visible instrument of true human development, the boy's penis. The feminist critique is to the point, but it does not destroy the classic status of Freud's writings. Feminists are among those who still find much else of interest in his ideas.

Freud's version of Oedipus also tells the deeper story of human blindness, of the natural tendency of most human beings to resist the full truth of their lives—to deny many deep feelings of love and hate that govern them and the world. Freud's Oedipus remains a classic today because, among other reasons, people still find in it two basic truths of their lives: (1) They have very mixed and strong feelings about the people around them, and (2) therefore, they tend to distort what they say and think about the world because what they feel below the surface is far too upsetting. People are blind to their own feelings because their worlds are too much to feel.

This would also be a reasonably good description of what many bourgeois Europeans at the turn of the century were feeling (but not saying) about the modern world in which they lived. They said it was a wonderful thing, filled with hope. They felt, but resisted saying it, that the modern world did a lot of harm and made them feel less than hopeful about the human condition. In other words, Freud told of Oedipus to help tell the story of dreams, which, in turn, helped tell the larger story of the late modern culture in which many people wanted to believe anything but the complicated reality of their worlds. Carl Schorske, in *Fin-de-siècle Vienna,* explained that in his theory of dreams, "Freud gave his fellow liberals an ahistorical theory of man and society that could make bearable a political world spun out of orbit and beyond control."

This, it turns out, is a good description of the modern world in the period from the revolutions of 1848 through at least the end of World War I. Contemporaries of those who visited Freud for psychoanalytic consultation in Vienna at the end of the nineteenth century were the children or grandchildren of people whose roots were in the traditional world. People who lived in a major city like Vienna may have enjoyed much of its cultural, political, and economic abundance. But it would be hard to believe that they did not also regret what was lost in these new cities. The political revolutions in America and France at the end of the previous century promised a new and better world, as did the dramatic economic revolution that was then spreading from England across modern Europe. Democracy in politics, capitalism in the marketplace, and science in culture offered much. On the surface, everything was expected to be better. For many it was.

For many more, and even for those whose material lives were better than anything their parents ever knew, life was filled with anxiety. For one thing, the modern world brought destruction. Throughout the century, lands were taken to build the railroads that fueled the factory system. In America, native civilizations were destroyed in the name of progress. Someone *must* have given this a second thought. If not, people surely saw what was happening closer to home. After 1853, Baron Georges Haussmann, often called the first city planner, ordered the destruction of much of old Paris to build the new boulevards and monuments that today's tourists mistakenly associate with tradition. The boulevards were allegedly built to allow a straight cannon shot into the working-class quarters, where rebellions like those in 1848 were most likely to recur. In Chicago in 1871, the great fire destroyed much of the city. The fire provided occasion for the rebuilding of Chicago as a modern city. Architectural historians claim that engineering advances necessary to construct the skyscraper were developed in order to rebuild Chicago vertically. Even today, everyone who lives in a city knows that modern "progress" entails the tearing down of much that is traditional. The skyscraper became the strong symbol of modern urban power, typically built on the site of perfectly good lands and homes. What met the eye in the cities was just the surface representation of what so many people felt about the modern world. In a different political sense, many still contend that the modern world destroys the old family and small-town values, as indeed it does.

Modernity could be defined as that culture in which people are promised a better life—one day. Until then, they are expected to tolerate contradictory lives in which the benefits of modernity are not much greater than its losses, if that. In Marx's famous line, the modern world was one in which "all that is solid melts into air"— nothing was quite what it appeared to be. No future payoff was ever quite assured for the vast majority of people. The first sign of the coming good society was always, it seemed, the destruction or loss of something familiar and dear. Many people in Europe and North America in the second half of the nineteenth century lived in an oedipal state, as Freud described it: affected by strong feelings of love and anger for their world but unable to give voice to the anger for fear of "saying the wrong thing." They were expected to love a world that was killing what was dear to them.

These were the cultural conditions prevailing in the modern West from 1848 into the first quarter of the twentieth century. This was the classic age of modernity, and of social theory. Whether practical or professional, social theory became a more acutely necessary skill in this period. Practically, ordinary people, many of them new to the strange and alien city, needed to learn to introduce and explain themselves to strangers who knew nothing of their family names. Professionally, there arose for the first time a class of writers, lecturers, teachers, and public intellectuals who devoted themselves to telling, in scientific language, the story of the modern West. Among them were the classic writers of modernity's classic age.

Karl Marx, Emile Durkheim, Max Weber, Georg Simmel, Sigmund Freud, and others are still considered classic writers because they told the story of modernity with a subtle regard for its two sides—for the official story of progress and the good society and for the repressed story of destruction, loss, and the terror of life without meaningful traditions. Their value to present-day readers is partly evident in the very fact that they are still read. This separates them from others: Those great writers of the nineteenth century who are no longer read seriously lacked the subtle grasp of both sides of the modern world. Auguste Comte is often considered to be a founding father of sociology, along with his mentor Saint-Simon. But few would read his works today in order to understand the modern world. Comte was too blind to the other side of that world. He believed too much in its progress and thus could say, in 1822: "A social system is in its decline, a new system arrived at maturity and approaching its completion—such is the fundamental character that the general progress of civilization has assigned to the present epoch." Simple, all too simple. Much the same can be said of the sociologist who has become for many the perfect illustration of the fallen classical god. Herbert Spencer, a more sober and scientific man than Comte, saw the world as progressing slowly but perfectly toward good and thus could say, in 1857: "Progress is not an accident, not a thing within human control, but a beneficent necessity."

Delicate is the line separating those no longer read and those who are. The difference is not so much in the ideas themselves as in the finer sensibilities with which certain nineteenth-century social theorists let on that they knew the world was complicated, while others did not. Emile Durkheim, heir apparent to Comte's faith in modern science, let it be known that scientific sociology was urgently needed not just because progress was at hand but also because the lawlessness of modern society had devastating effects on the weaker, more marginal individuals. And each of the writers who are still read wrote of concepts that described the dark side of modern life—Durkheim's anomie, Marx's alienation (or estrangement), Weber's overrationalization. Even Freud, who was not considered a social theorist until recently, hardly makes sense outside the social world for which he wrote. How else are we to interpret his compelling sense of psychological life as a wild disturbance in the hostile conflict between deep, natural desires to love and kill and the prudish, censorious forces of bourgeois manners? As much as Marx and Weber, Freud described the hidden irrational forces of social life. More perhaps than they, he described how the irrational is a given in the order of human things found just below the tranquil surface of reason.

These classic writers in a classical age are considered worthwhile because people continue to struggle with the confusing effects of modern life. There are some who would say, a century after social theory's classical age, that the modern world is coming to an end. This could be. But what remains true is that a great many people still find hard reality at moral odds with the promise of progress. Those who have no experience of this contradiction would not find these classic writers interesting, just as anyone who denies his or her experience of the deeper emotional forces would find Freud's Oedipus opaque.

It must be said, however, that a work can be considered classical for reasons other than the continuing appeal of its wisdom. Classics serve less lofty social purposes, as well. The process of canon formation is well understood today to be part of the social process whereby those in power (or some of those with some power) seek to perpetuate the authority of certain authors in order to enhance their own vested interests in a given view of social life.

The first condition of being read is to be published. Because publication involves commercial as well as literary judgments, decisions to publish are always and necessarily susceptible to the influence of editors, publishers, advisers, and critics whose interest in what is read is touched by an interest in the economics of literary and cultural life. Great works of literature can be excluded from an official canon for many reasons having nothing at all to do with their merit. Publishers think they won't sell. Editors think they serve no good purpose. Critics cannot understand why anyone would buy and read something by one of those people. Authors don't even try because they know what publishers will say. This is neither good nor bad. It is, however, a fact of cultural life that a literary work of great merit can be denied the status of a classic because it is excluded from the canon; conversely, a work can appear in the official canon of great writings even though it has no merit.

A writing that endures over time always encounters these two forces: To be classic, it must be readable to readers; to be a canonized classic, it must serve the interests of those who decide what readers will read. Great books like W.E.B. Du Bois's *Souls of Black Folk* were virtually unknown to the dominant, mostly white, literary establishment until recently. Other books, like Emile Durkheim's *Rules of Sociological Method*, have been canonized even though no one reads them. Herein lies a particularly interesting story. Durkheim's *Rules* is a book that made little or no sense, not even to Durkheim. When he tried to demonstrate his rules in his study of suicide, he was unable to make them work. Yet the young Durkheim wrote the book specifically so that it might one day be a classic. *Rules* began with a familiar locution: "*Up to now* sociologists have scarcely occupied themselves with the task of characterizing and defining the method they apply to the study of social facts." He then proceeded to attack the most widely known textbook on sociology, which just happened to have been Spencer's *Study of Sociology.* Durkheim thus used a familiar prophetic device—"Up to now . . . " / but, verily, I say unto you—to establish his little book as a classic. He was seeking a definite canonical market position. Today, as in his day, there are those who like the idea of keeping Durkheim's book on methods in the canon, so they assign it, students buy it, publishers print it. But does anyone read it? If so, can anyone honestly make sense of it? Has anyone ever actually used those rules? Not likely.

A classic must interest readers, whether or not it is in the official canon of classic works. Conversely, canonical status does not automatically make a book a classic. This awkward relation between the classical and canonical statuses of a writing is somewhat accidental and, in retrospect, of surprising importance to social theory. Today, it is well understood that a great number of social theories written during the classic age were, directly or indirectly, excluded from the list of officially approved great works. They were, therefore, denied the public availability that would have caused them to be read as classics. Until now. In addition to such powerful works as W.E.B. Du Bois's *Souls of Black Folk* (1903), Charlotte Perkins Gilman's *The Yellow Wallpaper* (1892), and Anna Julia Cooper's *Voice from the South* (1892), there are thousands of essays, novels, and narratives by women, freed slaves, workers, Native Americans, and others denied privilege of place in the public culture of their times. The discovery of these writings has encouraged a rethinking not only of some of the official classics of the modern era but also of the historical period itself. Once again, in a different way, the literature reveals the times.

If Marx, Weber, Durkheim, and Freud sketched theories of the contradictory nature of the modern world in the late nineteenth century, then these theories are painted in bolder, more passionate tones in the newly discovered classic texts. W.E.B. Du Bois wrote of the double-consciousness of American Blacks forced to live beyond the veil of racial degradations. Charlotte Gilman's *The Yellow Wallpaper* similarly described a woman's double-consciousness—expected (and desiring) to please the men who would heal her, knowing the irrationality of their condescending reasonableness. Anna Julia Cooper gave voice to the Black women in the South who knew (and know) that they must be doubly or multiply conscious of the good men of their own race and of the good whites of their own gender. These were the experiences of people cruelly oppressed by the dominant forces of modern culture. The traditionally oppressed were to serve the market and domestic purposes of the new capitalist world in field, factory, and home. Du Bois, Gilman, Cooper, and many others gave them voice.

But one might still ask: Were these degradations a cause or an effect of modern life? Was not, at least in some degree, the ugly oppression of people part and parcel of modernity's destructive force? If possible, one also ought to see borrowings and takings, back and forth, between the literature of those excluded and of those canonized in the classical era. People on several sides of the racial, class, and gender divides experienced the split life of the modern world. On the more oppressed side, the split tore at life in cruel ways; on the other, it tugged in ways that made people crazy. But its effect was evident. As a result, it is now possible to reread certain of the classic texts in the process of finding new ones. Perhaps the most striking example is the unexplored relation between Du Bois and William James. Among professional social theorists, it is customary to assume a line of theoretical influence from James, through Charles Horton Cooley, to George Herbert Mead, to modern-day theories of the social self. Viewed in the cool retrospect of the history of ideas, one can read William James's ideas as fertile, philosophical statements of the logic of social life, perhaps overlooking that his theories were themselves quite confusing and contradictory. If, as James explained, an individual develops a sense of personal identity when he recognizes that "I am the same self today that I was yesterday," then how is this important state to be reconciled with the experience of also "having as many social selves as there are individuals who recognize him"? In the cool wisdom of professional theory, there are ways to ease the contradictory demands of the personal and social selves on the individual. But the very idea of a social self takes on different, more compelling meanings when it is considered in relation to the writing of James's student, Du Bois. Is the double-consciousness of the American Black the social psychology of a particular social group with its own history? Or is it a special, if extreme, case of the social psychology of modernity? The questions change one's view of the theory.

Once the lines of canonical thinking are disturbed by such questions, theory is pushed in two directions at once: down closer to ordinary life and out from the canon of officially recognized experience. Could one, then, suggest that Charlotte Perkins Gilman's mental illness was every bit as much a result of her sensitivity to modern life as of her early feminist sensibilities? Or from the other side, was she treated with well-intended condescension by her husband and her male physician because she suffered what they considered a female malady, or did they do what they did because modern culture possessed no understanding of its effects on people? Is mental exhaustion a normal response to modern life? Were those who treated women as though they had female diseases really acting through their own denial of the other side of modern society? The answers are not clear, but the questions change everything. Reading the officially excluded writers causes one to rethink not just social theories but also the idea of modern life with which people still struggle.

This is not just a matter of a canonical fair play. Nor is it something so simple as revising the list of recommended classics in an appropriate response to demands for a multicultural attitude. It is more a matter of discovering in the exclusion of certain writings a disturbing fact about the modern world: Since the last century, modernity has obsessively denied its darker side. The exclusion of writings, like the oppression of people, is more than a passing aberration of an early, less-conscious time. It is a deep structural feature of the historical logic of modernity. Life in the modern world is a split life. Modern persons are torn—by their conflicting passions, by the contradictory messages of their culture, by the improbable divorce between what is promised and what is actually given. The hitherto excluded classic writers are worth reading today for a better understanding of the culture itself.

Reading the hitherto excluded in relation to those normally included can change one's literary and political sensitivities. If Du Bois changes what one sees in James, or even Weber, then Gilman's *Women and Economics* can alter what is found in Marx, just as Cooper's views on the moral duplicity of the post-Reconstruction South could add dimension to Durkheim's theory of modern morality. In one sense, this is not a strange process. Writings of all kinds, not just classics, are never read in isolation, as though the literary culture were not a complex field of influences. All that is changed now in reading the hitherto excluded is the way their works allow the reader to rethink the culture of exclusion, as well as the normally included classics. Both moves, taken together, enrich.

Social theories, like personal narratives, are ways of understanding social life by bringing its story out of memory, where it lies hidden and distorted. In "Remembering, Repeating, and Working-Through," Freud explained that the stories analytic patients tell in session allow them to work through the compulsion to repeat actions that prevent them from getting what they want. It might be that societies, too, must tell things through in order to move from their pasts to the present. For Freud, the idea was that the more we can tell a good listener of the story of our lives, the more we shall be able to remember and, thus remembering, to act less out of compulsion and more out of understanding. This, surely, is why Freud was so interested in his last years in the question of how a civilization recovers what it may have repressed, how it works through its compulsion to act out, rather than talk out, its aggression.

But Freud was far from the only classic social theorist to have such an idea. Marx began "The Eighteenth Brumaire of Louis Bonaparte" with the famous lines: "Hegel remarks somewhere that all great, world-historical facts and personages occur, as it were, twice. He had forgotten to add: the first time as tragedy, the second as farce." The essay following these words is, in effect, an interpretation of the revolutions of 1848 as a distorted repetition of the revolutions after 1789. It could be said that Marx's method, here and in *Capital,* was to retell the story of modern political and economic life in order to work through society's recurring tendency to act as though ownership and domination were more human than productive labor in cooperation with others.

All these classical writers told stories with such an effect. Weber's *Protestant Ethic* is more than the demonstration of an artful technique; it is the story of how the West invented itself to serve universal human truth, then found itself apprenticed to a machine it could not control. Even Durkheim returned to the most elementary traces of human society in order to tell the truth of Knowledge—in effect, to show that science was not some essence of Being but a palpable property of social life. Du Bois, like Frederick Douglass before him, told his autobiography four different times. Du Bois was not alone in using his own story to tell social theories. Cooper and Gilman did much the same. It might even be said that people in traditionally oppressed and excluded positions base the authority of their stories about the world on what they remember and can tell about their lives.

Social theory might be thought of as remembering in order to work through the distortions of the past. The classic social theorists are worth our attention because they did just this. At a time when others continued to deny the darker side of modern life, they spoke of it without lapsing into despair. In our day, near the end of the twentieth century, people across the globe, particularly in the West, need to work through their disappointment that the promises of early modernity have been paid so poorly. Social theory, beginning with these classic writings, is one of the ways this is done.

C. L.

Notes

Page 21: Freud, *Interpretation of Dreams* (Avon Books, 1965), 301.
Page 22: Schorske, *Fin-de-siècle Vienna* (Vintage, 1981), 203.
Page 23: Comte, in Gertrud Lenzer, ed., *Auguste Comte: Essential Writings* (Harpers, 1975), 9.
Page 23: Spencer, in *Illustrations of Universal Progress* (1857).
Page 24: Durkheim, *Rules* (Free Press, 1982), 48.

Other quotations are from material appearing in the selections that follow.

❖ The Two Sides of Society ❖

Karl Marx (1818–1883) lived the life of an independent intellectual and political activist. After his studies, he worked as a journalist before leaving his native Germany in 1843, initially for Paris. There, Marx met Friedrich Engels (1820–1895), his lifelong friend, collaborator, and benefactor. Marx's writings of this early period in Paris reflected his youthful philosophical interests in the then-popular debate over Hegel. *The Communist Manifesto*, written with Engels, appeared in 1848, on the eve of the revolutions of that year. The following year, he settled in London, where he began his scholarly labors in the public reading room of the British Museum. In 1867, the first volume of *Capital* was published. It is fashionable, and plausible, to describe the ideas in *Capital* as Marx's mature science, in contrast to his more humanistic philosophy in the 1840s. In the 1860s, Marx was the dominant intellectual and political force behind the working people's movement known as the International. Marx died, alone, in 1888, shortly after the deaths of his daughter and wife, both named Jenny.

Marxism as a political and social philosophy took many forms, with different effects—from the terror of Stalinism to the aesthetically subtle explorations of economic and cultural life by critical theorists and other students of culture today. The selections represent the full range of Marx's thinking. "Estranged Labour" is from the early, philosophical period. Readers should note that this translation uses *estrangement* where the term *alienation* might be expected. "Camera Obscura" is Marx's memorable metaphoric description of ideology's inverted relation to social reality. "Class Struggle" is from his best-known public tract, the *Manifesto*, in which he combined a commanding popular style with precise theoretical analysis. "The Eighteenth Brumaire," likewise, was a popular account of the 1851 coup in Paris, and it presented Marx's political theory through a careful, if passionate, interpretation of historical events. "On Imperialism in India" (1853) is comparable in tone and purpose, though here Marx turned his critique of bourgeois civilization against its colonial system. "The Values of Commodities" is the key section from Marx's important theory of value. Though it is offered as an argument in his critique of capital, the theory has been used as a general theory of value in society. (There are passages in Saussure's discussion of linguistic and social value that could have been lifted from Marx.) "The Fetishism of Commodities" (1867) might be compared to "Estranged Labour" (1844) to determine how some of Marx's ideas were unchanged in his more mature writings. "Labour-Power and Capital" is one of the most powerful examples of Marx's critical and structural method. Having led the reader, in the first half of *Capital* (vol. 1), through his technical theory of the relation between labor and economic value, Marx abruptly announced that the secret of capitalist profit cannot be seen in the visible marketplace. He then turned to the hidden logic of the capitalist and capitalism. The final selection, Engels's "Patriarchal Family," is a classic source for the outlines of a materialist feminism.

Estranged Labour

Karl Marx (1844*)

We have proceeded from the premises of political economy. We have accepted its language and its laws. We presupposed private property, the separation of labour, capital and land, and of wages, profit of capital and rent of land—likewise division of labour, competition, the concept of exchange-value, etc. On the basis of political economy itself, in its own words, we have shown that the worker sinks to the level of a commodity and becomes indeed the most wretched of commodities; that the wretchedness of the worker is in inverse proportion to the power and magnitude of his production; that the necessary result of competition is the accumulation of capital in a few hands, and thus the restoration of monopoly in a more terrible form; that finally the distinction between capitalist and land-rentier, like that between the tiller of the soil and the factory-worker, disappears and that the whole of society must fall apart into the two classes—the property-*owners* and the propertyless *workers*.

Political economy proceeds from the fact of private property, but it does not explain it to us. It expresses in general, abstract formulae the *material* process through which private property actually passes, and these formulae it then takes for *laws*. It does not *comprehend* these laws—i.e., it does not demonstrate how they arise from the very nature of private property. Political economy does not disclose the source of the division between labour and capital, and between capital and land. When, for example, it defines the relationship of wages to profit, it takes the interest of the capitalists to be the ultimate cause; i.e., it takes for granted what it is supposed to evolve. Similarly, competition comes in everywhere. It is explained from external circumstances. As to how far these external and apparently fortuitous circumstances are but the expression of a necessary course of development, political economy teaches us nothing. We have seen how, to it, exchange itself appears to be a fortuitous fact. The only wheels which political economy sets in motion are *avarice* and the *war amongst the avaricious—competition.*

Precisely because political economy does not grasp the connections within the movement, it was possible to counterpose, for instance, the doctrine of competition to the doctrine of monopoly, the doctrine of craft-liberty to the doctrine of the corporation, the doctrine of the division of landed property to the doctrine of the big estate—for competition, craft-liberty and the division of landed property were explained and comprehended only as fortuitous, premeditated and violent consequences of monopoly, the corporation, and feudal property, not as their necessary, inevitable and natural consequences.

Now, therefore, we have to grasp the essential connection between private property, avarice, and the separation of labour, capital and landed property; between exchange and competition, value and the devaluation of men, monopoly and competition, etc.; the connection between this whole estrangement and the *money*-system.

Excerpt from "Economic and Philosophic Manuscripts of 1844," Robert C. Tucker, ed., *The Marx-Engels Reader*, 2d ed. (New York: W. W. Norton, 1978), pp. 70–79.

*Dates following names usually refer to the first publication of the author's text. Where a work was composed over many years, those dates are given—for example, "Max Weber (1909–1920)" for texts from *Economy and Society*. In general, texts are identified by the dates considered important to their historical origin or impact—whichever is more significant to their interpretation. Explanatory notes are provided as needed.

Do not let us go back to a fictitious primordial condition as the political economist does, when he tries to explain. Such a primordial condition explains nothing. He merely pushes the question away into a grey nebulous distance. He assumes in the form of fact, of an event, what he is supposed to deduce—namely, the necessary relationship between two things—between, for example, division of labour and exchange. Theology in the same way explains the origin of evil by the fall of man: that is, it assumes as a fact, in historical form, what has to be explained.

We proceed from an *actual* economic fact.

The worker becomes all the poorer the more wealth he produces, the more his production increases in power and range. The worker becomes an ever cheaper commodity the more commodities he creates. With the *increasing value* of the world of things proceeds in direct proportion the *devaluation* of the world of men. Labour produces not only commodities; it produces itself and the worker as a *commodity*— and does so in the proportion in which it produces commodities generally.

This fact expresses merely that the object which labour produces—labour's product—confronts it as *something alien,* as a *power independent* of the producer. The product of labour is labour which has been congealed in an object, which has become material: it is the *objectification* of labour. Labour's realization is its objectification. In the conditions dealt with by political economy this realization of labour appears as *loss of reality* for the workers; objectification as *loss of the object* and *object-bondage;* appropriation as *estrangement,* as *alienation.*

So much does labour's realization appear as loss of reality that the worker loses reality to the point of starving to death. So much does objectification appear as loss of the object that the worker is robbed of the objects most necessary not only for his life but for his work. Indeed, labour itself becomes an object which he can get hold of only with the greatest effort and with the most irregular interruptions. So much does the appropriation of the object appear as estrangement that the more objects the worker produces the fewer can he possess and the more he falls under the dominion of his product, capital.

All these consequences are contained in the definition that the worker is related to the *product of his labour* as to an *alien* object. For on this premise it is clear that the more the worker spends himself, the more powerful the alien objective world becomes which he creates over-against himself, the poorer he himself—his inner world—becomes, the less belongs to him as his own. It is the same in religion. The more man puts into God, the less he retains in himself. The worker puts his life into the object; but now his life no longer belongs to him but to the object. Hence, the greater this activity, the greater is the worker's lack of objects. Whatever the product of his labour is, he is not. Therefore the greater this product, the less is he himself. The *alienation* of the worker in his product means not only that his labour becomes an object, an *external* existence, but that it exists *outside him,* independently, as something alien to him, and that it becomes a power of its own confronting him; it means that the life which he has conferred on the object confronts him as something hostile and alien.

Let us now look more closely at the *objectification,* at the production of the worker; and therein at the *estrangement,* the *loss* of the object, his product.

The worker can create nothing without *nature,* without the *sensuous external world.* It is the material on which his labour is manifested, in which it is active, from which and by means of which it produces.

But just as nature provides labor with the *means of life* in the sense that labour cannot *live* without objects on which to operate, on the other hand, it also provides the *means of life* in the more restricted sense—i.e., the means for the physical subsistence of the *worker* himself.

Thus the more the worker by his labour *appropriates* the external world, sensuous nature, the more he deprives himself of *means of life* in the double respect: first, that the sensuous external world more and more ceases to be an object belonging to his labour—to be his labour's *means of life;* and secondly, that it more and more ceases to be *means of life* in the immediate sense, means for the physical subsistence of the worker.

Thus in this double respect the worker becomes a slave of his object, first, in that he receives an *object of labour,* i.e., in that he receives *work;* and secondly, in that he receives *means of subsistence.* Therefore, it enables him to exist, first, as a *worker;* and, second, as a *physical subject.* The extremity of this bondage is that it is only as a *worker* that he continues to maintain himself as a *physical subject,* and that it is only as a *physical subject* that he is a *worker.*

(The laws of political economy express the estrangement of the worker in his object thus: the more the worker produces, the less he has to consume; the more values he creates, the more valueless, the more unworthy he becomes; the better formed his product, the more deformed becomes the worker; the more civilized his object, the more barbarous becomes the worker; the mightier labour becomes, the more powerless becomes the worker; the more ingenious labour becomes, the duller becomes the worker and the more he becomes nature's bondsman.)

Political economy conceals the estrangement inherent in the nature of labour by not considering the direct relationship between the worker (labour) *and production.* It is true that labour produces for the rich wonderful things—but for the worker it produces privation. It produces palaces—but for the worker, hovels. It produces beauty—but for the worker, deformity. It replaces labour by machines—but some of the workers it throws back to a barbarous type of labour, and the other workers it turns into machines. It produces intelligence—but for the worker idiocy, cretinism.

The direct relationship of labour to its produce is the relationship of the worker to the objects of his production. The relationship of the man of means to the objects of production and to production itself is only a *consequence* of this first relationship—and confirms it. We shall consider this other aspect later.

When we ask, then, what is the essential relationship of labour we are asking about the relationship of the *worker* to production.

Till now we have been considering the estrangement, the alienation of the worker only in one of its aspects, i.e., the worker's *relationship to the products of his labour.* But the estrangement is manifested not only in the result but in the *act of production*—within the *producing activity* itself. How would the worker come to face the product of his activity as a stranger, were it not that in the very act of production he was estranging himself from himself? The product is after all but the summary of the activity of production. If then the product of labour is alienation, production itself must be active alienation, the alienation of activity, the activity of alienation. In the estrangement of the object of labour is merely summarized the estrangement, the alienation, in the activity of labour itself.

What, then, constitutes the alienation of labour?

First, the fact that labour is *external* to the worker, i.e., it does not belong to his essential being; that in his work, therefore, he does not affirm himself but denies himself, does not feel content but unhappy, does not develop freely his physical and mental energy but mortifies his body and ruins his mind. The worker therefore only feels himself outside his work, and in his work feels outside himself. He is at home when he is not working, and when he is working he is not at home. His labour is therefore not voluntary, but coerced; it is *forced labour*. It is therefore not the satisfaction of a need; it is merely a *means* to satisfy needs external to it. Its alien character emerges clearly in the fact that as soon as no physical or other compulsion exists, labour is shunned like the plague. External labour, labour in which man alienates himself, is a labour of self-sacrifice, of mortification. Lastly, the external character of labour for the worker appears in the fact that it is not his own, but someone else's, that it does not belong to him, that in it he belongs, not to himself, but to another. Just as in religion the spontaneous activity of the human imagination, of the human brain and the human heart, operates independently of the individual—that is, operates on him as an alien, divine or diabolical activity—in the same way the worker's activity is not his spontaneous activity. It belongs to another; it is the loss of his self.

As a result, therefore, man (the worker) no longer feels himself to be freely active in any but his animal functions—eating, drinking, procreating, or at most in his dwelling and in dressing-up, etc.; and in his human functions he no longer feels himself to be anything but an animal. What is animal becomes human and what is human becomes animal.

Certainly eating, drinking, procreating, etc., are also genuinely human functions. But in the abstraction which separates them from the sphere of all other human activity and turns them into sole and ultimate ends, they are animal.

We have considered the act of estranging practical human activity, labour, in two of its aspects. (1) The relation of the worker to the *product of labour* as an alien object exercising power over him. This relation is at the same time the relation to the sensuous external world, to the objects of nature as an alien world antagonistically opposed to him. (2) The relation of labour to the *act of production* within the *labour* process. This relation is the relation of the worker to his own activity as an alien activity not belonging to him; it is activity as suffering, strength as weakness, begetting as emasculating, the worker's *own* physical and mental energy, his personal life or what is life other than activity—as an activity which is turned against him, neither depends on nor belongs to him. Here we have *self-estrangement*, as we had previously the estrangement of the *thing*.

We have yet a third aspect of *estranged labour* to deduce from the two already considered.

Man is a species being, not only because in practice and in theory he adopts the species as his object (his own as well as those of other things), but—and this is only another way of expressing it—but also because he treats himself as the actual, living species; because he treats himself as a *universal* and therefore a free being.

The life of the species, both in man and in animals, consists physically in the fact that man (like the animal) lives on inorganic nature; and the more universal man is compared with an animal, the more universal is the sphere of inorganic nature on which he lives. Just as plants, animals, stones, the air, light, etc., constitute a part of human consciousness in the realm of theory, partly as objects of natural science, partly as objects of art—his spiritual inorganic nature, spiritual nourishment which he must first prepare to make it palatable and digestible—so too in the realm of practice they constitute a part of human life and human activity. Physically man lives only on these products of nature, whether they appear in the form of food, heating, clothes, a dwelling, or whatever it may be. The universality of man is in practice manifested precisely in the universality which makes all nature his *inorganic* body—both inasmuch as nature is (1) his direct means of life, and (2) the material, the object, and the instrument of his life-activity. Nature is man's *inorganic body*— nature, that is, in so far as it is not itself the human body. Man *lives* on nature— means that nature is his *body*, with which he must remain in continuous intercourse if he is not to die. That man's physical and spiritual life is linked to nature means simply that nature is linked to itself, for man is a part of nature.

In estranging from man (1) nature, and (2) himself, his own active functions, his life-activity, estranged labour estranges the *species* from man. It turns for him the *life of the species* into a means of individual life. First it estranges the life of the species and individual life, and secondly it makes individual life in its abstract form the pur- pose of the life of the species, likewise in its abstract and estranged form.

For in the first place labour, *life-activity, productive life* itself, appears to man merely as a *means* of satisfying a need—the need to maintain the physical existence. Yet the productive life is the life of the species. It is life-engendering life. The whole character of a species—its species character—is contained in the character of its life- activity; and free, conscious activity is man's species character. Life itself appears only as *a means to life*.

The animal is immediately identical with its life-activity. It does not distinguish itself from it. It is *its life-activity*. Man makes his life-activity itself the object of his will and of his consciousness. He has conscious life-activity. It is not a determination with which he directly merges. Conscious life-activity directly distinguishes man from animal life-activity. It is just because of this that he is a species being. Or it is only because he is a species being that he is a Conscious Being, i.e., that his own life is an object for him. Only because of that is his activity free activity. Estranged labour reverses this relationship, so that it is just because man is a conscious being that he makes his life-activity, his *essential* being, a mere means to his *existence*.

In creating an *objective world* by his practical activity, in *working-up* inorganic na- ture, man proves himself a conscious species being, i.e., as a being that treats the species as its own essential being, or that treats itself as a species being. Admittedly an- imals also produce. They build themselves nests, dwellings, like the bees, beavers, ants, etc. But an animal only produces what it immediately needs for itself or its young. It produces one-sidedly, whilst man produces universally. It produces only under the do- minion of immediate physical need, whilst man produces even when he is free from physical need and only truly produces in freedom therefrom. An animal produces only itself, whilst man reproduces the whole of nature. An animal's product belongs imme- diately to its physical body, whilst man freely confronts his product. An animal forms things in accordance with the standard and the need of the species to which it belongs, whilst man knows how to produce in accordance with the standard of every species, and knows how to apply everywhere the inherent standard to the object. Man there- fore also forms things in accordance with the laws of beauty.

It is just in the working-up of the objective world, therefore, that man first really proves himself to be a *species being*. This production is his active species life. Through and because of this production, nature appears as *his* work and his reality. The object of labour is, therefore, the *objectification of man's species life*: for he dupli- cates himself not only, as in consciousness, intellectually, but also actively, in reality, and therefore he contemplates himself in a world that he has created. In tearing away from man the object of his production, therefore, estranged labour tears from him his *species life*, his real species objectivity, and transforms his advantage over an- imals into the disadvantage that his inorganic body, nature, is taken from him.

Similarly, in degrading spontaneous activity, free activity, to a means, estranged labour makes man's species life a means to his physical existence.

The consciousness which man has of his species is thus transformed by estrangement in such a way that the species life becomes for him a means.

Estranged labour turns thus:

(3) *Man's species being*, both nature and his spiritual species property, into a being *alien* to him, into a *means* to his *individual existence*. It estranges man's own body from him, as it does external nature and his spiritual essence, his *human* being.

(4) An immediate consequence of the fact that man is estranged from the product of his labour, from his life-activity, from his species being is the *estrangement of man* from *man*. If a man is confronted by himself, he is confronted by the *other* man. What applies to a man's relation to his work, to the product of his labour and to himself, also holds of a man's relation to the other man, and to the other man's labour and object of labour.

In fact, the proposition that man's species nature is estranged from him means that one man is estranged from the other, as each of them is from man's essential nature.

The estrangement of man, and in fact every relationship in which man stands to himself, is first realized and expressed in the relationship in which a man stands to other men.

Hence within the relationship of estranged labour each man views the other in accordance with the standard and the position in which he finds himself as a worker.

We took our departure from a fact of political economy—the estrangement of the worker and his production. We have formulated the concept of this fact—*estranged, alienated* labour. We have analysed this concept—hence analysing merely a fact of political economy.

Let us now see, further, how in real life the concept of estranged, alienated labour must express and present itself.

If the product of labour is alien to me, if it confronts me as an alien power, to whom, then, does it belong?

If my own activity does not belong to me, if it is an alien, a coerced activity, to whom, then, does it belong?

To a being *other* than me.

Who is this being?

The *gods*? To be sure, in the earliest times the principal production (for example, the building of temples, etc., in Egypt, India and Mexico) appears to be in the service of the gods, and the product belongs to the gods. However, the gods on their own were never the lords of labour. No more was *nature*. And what a contradiction it would be if, the more man subjugated nature by his labour and the more the miracles of the gods were rendered superfluous by the miracles of industry, the more man were to renounce the joy of production and the enjoyment of the produce in favour of these powers.

The *alien* being, to whom labour and the produce of labour belongs, in whose service labour is done and for whose benefit the produce of labour is provided, can only be *man* himself.

If the product of labour does not belong to the worker, if it confronts him as an alien power, this can only be because it belongs to some *other man than the worker*. If the worker's activity is a torment to him, to another it must be *delight* and his life's joy. Not the gods, not nature, but only man himself can be this alien power over man.

We must bear in mind the above-stated proposition that man's relation to himself only becomes *objective* and *real* for him through his relation to the other man. Thus, if the product of his labour, his labour *objectified*, is for him an *alien*, hostile, powerful object independent of him, then his position towards it is such that someone else is master of this object, someone who is alien, hostile, powerful, and independent of him. If his own activity is to him an unfree activity, then he is treating it as activity performed in the service, under the dominion, the coercion and the yoke of another man.

Every self-estrangement of man from himself and from nature appears in the relation in which he places himself and nature to men other than and differentiated from himself. For this reason religious self-estrangement necessarily appears in the relationship of the layman to the priest, or again to a mediator, etc., since we are here dealing with the intellectual world. In the real practical world self-estrangement can only become manifest through the real practical relationship to other men. The medium through which estrangement takes place is itself *practical*. Thus through estranged labour man not only engenders his relationship to the object and to the act of production as to powers that are alien and hostile to him; he also engenders the relationship in which other men stand to his production and to his product, and the relationship in which he stands to these other men. Just as he begets his own production as the loss of his reality, as his punishment; just as he begets his own product as a loss, as a product not belonging to him; so he begets the dominion of the one who does not produce over production and over the product. Just as he estranges from himself his own activity, so he confers to the stranger activity which is not his own.

Till now we have only considered this relationship from the standpoint of the worker and later we shall be considering it also from the standpoint of the non-worker.

Through *estranged, alienated labour*, then, the worker produces the relationship to this labour of a man alien to labour and standing outside it. The relationship of the worker to labour engenders the relation to it of the capitalist, or whatever one chooses to call the master of labour. *Private property* is thus the product, the result, the necessary consequence, of *alienated labour*, of the external relation of the worker to nature and to himself.❖

Camera Obscura

Karl Marx (1845–1846)

The fact is, therefore, that definite individuals who are productively active in a definite way enter into these definite social and political relations. Empirical observation must in each separate instance bring out empirically, and without any mystification and speculation, the connection of the social and political structure with production. The social structure and the State are continually evolving out of the life process of definite individuals, but of individuals, not as they may appear in their own or other people's imagination, but as they *really* are; i.e., as they operate, produce materially, and hence as they work under definite material limits, presuppositions and conditions independent of their will.

Excerpt from "The German Ideology," Robert C. Tucker, ed., *The Marx-Engels Reader*, 2d ed. (New York: W. W. Norton, 1978), p. 154.

The production of ideas, of conceptions, of consciousness, is at first directly inter-woven with the material activity and the material intercourse of men, the language of real life. Conceiving, thinking, the mental intercourse of men, appear at this stage as the direct efflux of their material behaviour. The same applies to mental production as expressed in the language of politics, laws, morality, religion, metaphysics, etc., of a people. Men are the producers of their conceptions, ideas, etc.—real, active men, as they are conditioned by a definite development of their productive forces and of the intercourse corresponding to these, up to its furthest forms. Consciousness can never be anything else than conscious existence, and the existence of men is their actual life-process. If in all ideology men and their circumstances appear upside-down as in a *camera obscura,* this phenomenon arises just as much from their historical life-process as the inversion of objects on the retina does from their physical life-process.❖

Class Struggle

Karl Marx and Friedrich Engels (1848)

The history of all hitherto existing society is the history of class struggles.

Freeman and slave, patrician and plebeian, lord and serf, guild-master and jour-neyman, in a word, oppressor and oppressed, stood in constant opposition to one another, carried on an uninterrupted, now hidden, now open fight, a fight that each time ended, either in a revolutionary re-constitution of society at large, or in the common ruin of the contending classes.

In the earlier epochs of history, we find almost everywhere a complicated arrange-ment of society into various orders, a manifold gradation of social rank. In ancient Rome we have patricians, knights, plebeians, slaves; in the Middle Ages, feudal lords, vassals, guild-masters, journeymen, apprentices, serfs; in almost all of these classes, again, subordinate gradations.

The modern bourgeois society that has sprouted from the ruins of feudal society has not done away with class antagonisms. It has but established new classes, new conditions of oppression, new forms of struggle in place of the old ones.

Our epoch, the epoch of the bourgeoisie, possesses, however, this distinctive fea-ture: it has simplified the class antagonisms: Society as a whole is more and more splitting up into two great hostile camps, into two great classes directly facing each other: Bourgeoisie and Proletariat.

From the serfs of the Middle Ages sprang the chartered burghers of the earliest towns. From these burgesses the first elements of the bourgeoisie were developed.

The discovery of America, the rounding of the Cape, opened up fresh ground for the rising bourgeoisie. The East-Indian and Chinese markets, the colonisation of America, trade with the colonies, the increase in the means of exchange and in com-modities generally, gave to commerce, to navigation, to industry, an impulse never before known, and thereby, to the revolutionary element in the tottering feudal soci-ety, a rapid development.

The feudal system of industry, under which industrial production was monopo-lised by closed guilds, now no longer sufficed for the growing wants of the new mar-kets. The manufacturing system took its place. The guild-masters were pushed on

Excerpt from "Manifesto of the Communist Party," Robert C. Tucker, ed., *The Marx-Engels Reader,* 2d ed. (New York: W. W. Norton, 1978), pp. 473–479.

one side by the manufacturing middle class; division of labour between the different corporate guilds vanished in the face of division of labour in each single workshop.

Meantime the markets kept ever growing, the demand ever rising. Even manufacture no longer sufficed. Thereupon, steam and machinery revolutionised industrial production. The place of manufacture was taken by the giant, Modern Industry, the place of the industrial middle class, by industrial millionaires, the leaders of whole industrial armies, the modern bourgeois.

Modern industry has established the world-market, for which the discovery of America paved the way. This market has given an immense development to commerce, to navigation, to communication by land. This development has, in its turn, reacted on the extension of industry; and in proportion as industry, commerce, navigation, railways extended, in the same proportion the bourgeoisie developed, increased its capital, and pushed into the background every class handed down from the Middle Ages.

We see, therefore, how the modern bourgeoisie is itself the product of a long course of development, of a series of revolutions in the modes of production and of exchange.

Each step in the development of the bourgeoisie was accompanied by a corresponding political advance of that class. An oppressed class under the sway of the feudal nobility, an armed and self-governing association in the mediaeval commune; here independent urban republic (as in Italy and Germany), there taxable "third estate" of the monarchy (as in France), afterwards, in the period of manufacture proper, serving either the semi-feudal or the absolute monarchy as a counterpoise against the nobility, and, in fact, corner-stone of the great monarchies in general, the bourgeoisie has at last, since the establishment of Modern Industry and of the world-market, conquered for itself, in the modern representative State, exclusive political sway. The execution of the modern State is but a committee for managing the common affairs of the whole bourgeoisie.

The bourgeoisie, historically, has played a most revolutionary part.

The bourgeoisie, wherever it has got the upper hand, has put an end to all feudal, patriarchal, idyllic relations. It has pitilessly torn asunder the motley feudal ties that bound man to his "natural superiors," and has left remaining no other nexus between man and man than naked self-interest, than callous "cash payment." It has drowned the most heavenly ecstasies of religious fervour, of chivalrous enthusiasm, of philistine sentimentalism, in the icy water of egotistical calculation. It has resolved personal worth into exchange value, and in place of the numberless indefeasible chartered freedoms, has set up that single, unconscionable freedom—Free Trade. In one word, for exploitation, veiled by religious and political illusions, it has substituted naked, shameless, direct, brutal exploitation.

The bourgeoisie has stripped of its halo every occupation hitherto honoured and looked up to with reverent awe. It has converted the physician, the lawyer, the priest, the poet, the man of science, into its paid wage-labourers.

The bourgeoisie has torn away from the family its sentimental veil, and has reduced the family relation to a mere money relation.

The bourgeoisie has disclosed how it came to pass that the brutal display of vigour in the Middle Ages, which Reactionists so much admire, found its fitting complement in the most slothful indolence. It has been the first to show what man's activity can bring about. It has accomplished wonders far surpassing Egyptian pyramids, Roman aqueducts, and Gothic cathedrals; it has conducted expeditions that put in the shade all former Exoduses of nations and crusades.

The bourgeoisie cannot exist without constantly revolutionising the instruments of production, and thereby the relations of production, and with them the whole relations of society. Conservation of the old modes of production in unaltered form, was, on the contrary, the first condition of existence for all earlier industrial classes. Constant revolutionising of production, uninterrupted disturbance of all social conditions, everlasting uncertainty and agitation distinguish the bourgeois epoch from all earlier ones. All fixed, fast-frozen relations, with their train of ancient and venerable prejudices and opinions, are swept away, all new-formed ones become antiquated before they can ossify. All that is solid melts into air, all that is holy is profaned, and man is at last compelled to face with sober senses, his real conditions of life, and his relations with his kind.

The need of a constantly expanding market for its products chases the bourgeoisie over the whole surface of the globe. It must nestle everywhere, settle everywhere, establish connexions everywhere.

The bourgeoisie has through its exploitation of the world market given a cosmopolitan character to production and consumption in every country. To the great chagrin of Reactionists, it has drawn from under the feet of industry the national ground on which it stood. All old-established national industries have been destroyed or are daily being destroyed. They are dislodged by new industries, whose introduction becomes a life and death question for all civilised nations, by industries that no longer work up indigenous raw material, but raw material drawn from the remotest zones; industries whose products are consumed, not only at home, but in every quarter of the globe. In place of the old wants, satisfied by the productions of the country, we find new wants, requiring for their satisfaction the products of distant lands and climes. In place of the old local and national seclusion and self-sufficiency, we have intercourse in every direction, universal inter-dependence of nations. And as in material, so also in intellectual production. The intellectual creations of individual nations become common property. National one-sidedness and narrow-mindedness become more and more impossible, and from the numerous national and local literatures, there arises a world literature.

The bourgeoisie, by the rapid improvement of all instruments of production, by the immensely facilitated means of communication, draws all, even the most barbarian, nations into civilisation. The cheap prices of its commodities are the heavy artillery with which it batters down all Chinese walls, with which it forces the barbarians' intensely obstinate hatred of foreigners to capitulate. It compels all nations, on pain of extinction, to adopt the bourgeois mode of production; it compels them to introduce what it calls civilisation into their midst, *i.e.*, to become bourgeois themselves. In one word, it creates a world after its own image.

The bourgeoisie has subjected the country to the rule of the towns. It has created enormous cities, has greatly increased the urban population as compared with the rural, and has thus rescued a considerable part of the population from the idiocy of rural life. Just as it has made the country dependent on the towns, so it has made barbarian and semi-barbarian countries dependent on the civilised ones, nations of peasants on nations of bourgeois, the East on the West.

The bourgeoisie keeps more and more doing away with the scattered state of the population, of the means of production, and of property. It has agglomerated population, centralised means of production, and has concentrated property in a few hands. The necessary consequence of this was political centralisation. Independent, or but loosely connected provinces, with separate interests, laws, governments and systems of taxation, became lumped together into one nation, with one government, one code of laws, one national class-interest, one frontier and one customs-tariff.

The bourgeoisie, during its rule of scarce one hundred years, has created more massive and more colossal productive forces than have all preceding generations together. Subjection of Nature's forces to man, machinery, application of chemistry to industry and agriculture, steam-navigation, railways, electric telegraphs, clearing of whole continents for cultivation, canalisation of rivers, whole populations conjured out of the ground—what earlier century had even a presentiment that such productive forces slumbered in the lap of social labour?

We see then: the means of production and of exchange, on whose foundation the bourgeoisie built itself up, were generated in feudal society. At a certain stage in the development of these means of production and of exchange, the conditions under which feudal society produced and exchanged, the feudal organisation of agriculture and manufacturing industry, in one word, the feudal relations of property became no longer compatible with the already developed productive forces; they became so many fetters. They had to be burst asunder; they were burst asunder.

Into their place stepped free competition, accompanied by a social and political constitution adapted to it, and by the economical and political sway of the bourgeois class.

A similar movement is going on before our own eyes. Modern bourgeois society with its relations of production, of exchange and of property, a society that has conjured up such gigantic means of production and of exchange, is like the sorcerer, who is no longer able to control the powers of the nether world whom he has called up by his spells. For many a decade past the history of industry and commerce is but the history of the revolt of modern productive forces against modern conditions of production, against the property relations that are the conditions for the existence of the bourgeoisie and of its rule. It is enough to mention the commercial crises that by their periodical return put on its trial, each time more threateningly, the existence of the entire bourgeois society. In these crises a great part not only of the existing products, but also of the previously created productive forces, are periodically destroyed. In these crises there breaks out an epidemic that, in all earlier epochs, would have seemed an absurdity—the epidemic of over-production. Society suddenly finds itself put back into a state of momentary barbarism; it appears as if a famine, a universal war of devastation had cut off the supply of every means of subsistence; industry and commerce seem to be destroyed; and why? Because there is too much civilisation, too much means of subsistence, too much industry, too much commerce. The productive forces at the disposal of society no longer tend to further the development of the conditions of bourgeois property; on the contrary, they have become too powerful for these conditions, by which they are fettered, and so soon as they overcome these fetters, they bring disorder into the whole of bourgeois society, endanger the existence of bourgeois property. The conditions of bourgeois society are too narrow to comprise the wealth created by them. And how does the bourgeoisie get over these crises? On the one hand by enforced destruction of a mass of productive forces; on the other, by the conquest of new markets, and by the more thorough exploitation of the old ones. That is to say, by paving the way for more extensive and more destructive crises, and by diminishing the means whereby crises are prevented.

The weapons with which the bourgeoisie felled feudalism to the ground are now turned against the bourgeoisie itself.

But not only has the bourgeoisie forged the weapons that bring death to itself; it has also called into existence the men who are to wield those weapons—the modern working class—the proletarians.

In proportion as the bourgeoisie, *i.e.*, capital, is developed, in the same proportion is the proletariat, the modern working class, developed—a class of labourers, who live only so long as they find work, and who find work only so long as their labour increases capital. These labourers, who must sell themselves piece-meal, are a commodity, like every other article of commerce, and are consequently exposed to all the vicissitudes of competition, to all the fluctuations of the market.

Owing to the extensive use of machinery and to division of labour, the work of the proletarians has lost all individual character, and consequently, all charm for the workman. He becomes an appendage of the machine, and it is only the most simple, most monotonous, and most easily acquired knack, that is required of him. Hence, the cost of production of a workman is restricted, almost entirely, to the means of subsistence that he requires for his maintenance, and for the propagation of his race. But the price of a commodity, and therefore also of labour, is equal to its cost of production. In proportion, therefore, as the repulsiveness of the work increases, the wage decreases. Nay more, in proportion as the use of machinery and division of labour increases, in the same proportion the burden of toil also increases, whether by prolongation of the working hours, by increase of the work exacted in a given time or by increased speed of the machinery, etc.

Modern industry has converted the little workshop of the patriarchal master into the great factory of the industrial capitalist. Masses of labourers, crowded into the factory, are organised like soldiers. As privates of the industrial army they are placed under the command of a perfect hierarchy of officers and sergeants. Not only are they slaves of the bourgeois class, and of the bourgeois State; they are daily and hourly enslaved by the machine, by the over-looker, and, above all, by the individual bourgeois manufacturer himself. The more openly this despotism proclaims gain to be its end and aim, the more petty, the more hateful and the more embittering it is.

The less the skill and exertion of strength implied in manual labour, in other words, the more modern industry becomes developed, the more is the labour of men superseded by that of women. Differences of age and sex have no longer any distinctive social validity for the working class. All are instruments of labour, more or less expensive to use, according to their age and sex.

No sooner is the exploitation of the labourer by the manufacturer, so far, at an end, that he receives his wages in cash, than he is set upon by the other portions of the bourgeoisie, the landlord, the shopkeeper, the pawnbroker, etc.❖

The Eighteenth Brumaire of Louis Bonaparte

Karl Marx (1852)

Hegel remarks somewhere that all great, world-historical facts and personages occur, as it were, twice. He has forgotten to add: the first time as tragedy, the second as farce. Caussidière for Danton, Louis Blanc for Robespierre, the Mountain of 1848 to 1851 for the Mountain of 1793 to 1795, the Nephew for the Uncle. And the same

Excerpt from Robert C. Tucker, ed., *The Marx-Engels Reader,* 2d ed. (New York: W. W. Norton, 1978), pp. 594–607.

caricature occurs in the circumstances in which the second edition of the Eighteenth Brumaire is taking place.

Men make their own history, but they do not make it just as they please; they do not make it under circumstances chosen by themselves, but under circumstances directly found, given and transmitted from the past. The tradition of all the dead generations weighs like a nightmare on the brain of the living. And just when they seem engaged in revolutionising themselves and things, in creating something entirely new, precisely in such epochs of revolutionary crisis they anxiously conjure up the spirits of the past to their service and borrow from them names, battle slogans and costumes in order to present the new scene of world history in this time-honoured disguise and this borrowed language. Thus Luther donned the mask of the Apostle Paul, the Revolution of 1789 to 1814 draped itself alternately as the Roman Republic and the Roman Empire, and the Revolution of 1848 knew nothing better to do than to parody, in turn, 1789 and the revolutionary tradition of 1793 to 1795. In like manner the beginner who has learnt a new language always translates it back into his mother tongue, but he has assimilated the spirit of the new language and can produce freely in it only when he moves in it without remembering the old and forgets in it his ancestral tongue.

Consideration of this world-historical conjuring up of the dead reveals at once a salient difference. Camille Desmoulins, Danton, Robespierre, Saint-Just, Napoleon, the heroes, as well as the parties and the masses of the old French Revolution, performed the task of their time in Roman costume and with Roman phrases, the task of releasing and setting up modern *bourgeois* society. The first ones knocked the feudal basis to pieces and mowed off the feudal heads which had grown from it. The other created inside France the conditions under which free competition could first be developed, the parcelled landed property exploited, the unfettered productive power of the nation employed, and outside the French borders he everywhere swept the feudal formations away, so far as was necessary to furnish bourgeois society in France with a suitable up-to-date environment on the European Continent. The new social formation once established, the antediluvian Colossi disappeared and with them the resurrected Romans—the Brutuses, Gracchi, Publicolas, the tribunes, the senators and Caesar himself. Bourgeois society in its sober reality had begotten its true interpreters and mouthpieces in the Says, Cousins, Royer-Collards, Benjamin Constants and Guizots; its real military leaders sat behind the office desks, and the hogheaded Louis XVIII was its political chief. Wholly absorbed in the production of wealth and in the peaceful struggle of competition, it no longer comprehended that ghosts from the days of Rome had watched over its cradle. But unheroic as bourgeois society is, yet it had need of heroism, of sacrifice, of terror, of civil war and of national battles to bring it into being. And in the classically austere traditions of the Roman Republic its gladiators found the ideals and the art forms, the self-deceptions that they needed in order to conceal from themselves the bourgeois limitations of the content of their struggles and to keep their passion at the height of the great historical tragedy. Similarly, at another stage of development, a century earlier, Cromwell and the English people had borrowed speech, passions and illusions from the Old Testament for their bourgeois revolution. When the real aim had been achieved, when the bourgeois transformation of English society had been accomplished, Locke supplanted Habakkuk.

The awakening of the dead in those revolutions therefore served the purpose of glorifying the new struggles, not of parodying the old; of magnifying the given tasks in imagination, not of taking flight from their solution in reality; of finding once more the spirit of revolution, not of making its ghost walk again.

From 1848 to 1851 only the ghost of the old revolution walked, from Marrast, the *republicain en gants jaunes* [Republican in yellow gloves], who disguised himself as the old Bailly, to the adventurer who hides his trivially repulsive features under the iron death mask of Napoleon. An entire people, which had imagined that by a revolution it had increased its power of action, suddenly finds itself set back into a dead epoch and, in order that no doubt as to the relapse may be possible, the old data again arise, the old chronology, the old names, the old edicts, which have long become a subject of antiquarian erudition, and the old henchmen, who had long seemed dead and decayed. The nation appears to itself like that mad Englishman in Bedlam, who fancies that he lives in the times of the ancient Pharaohs and daily bemoans the hard labour that he must perform in the Ethiopian mines as a gold digger, immured in this subterranean prison, a dimly burning lamp fastened to his head, the overseer of the slaves behind him with a long whip, and at the exits a confused mass of barbarian mercenaries, who understand neither the forced labourers in the mines nor one another, since they have no common speech. "And all this is expected of me," groans the mad Englishman, "of me, a free-born Briton, in order to make gold for the old Pharaohs." "In order to pay the debts of the Bonaparte family," sighs the French nation. The Englishman, so long as he was in his right mind, could not get rid of the fixed idea of making gold. The French, so long as they were engaged in revolution, could not get rid of the memory of Napoleon, as the election of December 10, 1848, proved. From the perils of revolution their longings went back to the flesh-pots of Egypt, and December 2, 1851, was the answer. They have not only a caricature of the old Napoleon, they have the old Napoleon himself, caricatured as he would inevitably appear in the middle of the nineteenth century.

The social revolution of the nineteenth century cannot draw its poetry from the past, but only from the future. It cannot begin with itself, before it has stripped off all superstition in regard to the past. Earlier revolutions required world-historical recollections in order to drug themselves concerning their own content. In order to arrive at its content, the revolution of the nineteenth century must let the dead bury their dead. There the phrase went beyond the content; here the content goes beyond the phrase.

The February Revolution was a sudden attack, a taking of the old society by *surprise*, and the people proclaimed this unhoped for *stroke* as a world-historic deed, opening the new epoch. On December 2 the February Revolution is conjured away by a card-sharper's trick, and what seems overthrown is no longer the monarchy; it is the liberal concessions that were wrung from it by century-long struggles. Instead of *society* having conquered a new content for itself, the *state* only appears to have returned to its oldest form, to the shamelessly simple domination of the sabre and the cowl. This is the answer to the *coup de main* of February 1848, given by the *coup de tête* of December 1851. Easy come, easy go. Meanwhile the interval has not passed by unused. During the years 1848 to 1851 French society has made up, and that by an abbreviated, because revolutionary, method, for the studies and experiences which, in a regular, so to speak, text-book development would have had to precede the February Revolution, if the latter was to be more than disturbance of the surface. Society now seems to have fallen back behind its point of departure; it has in truth first to create for itself the revolutionary point of departure, the situation, the relationships, the conditions, under which modern revolution alone becomes serious.

Bourgeois revolutions, like those of the eighteenth century, storm more swiftly from success to success; their dramatic effects outdo each other; men and things seem set in sparkling brilliants; ecstasy is the everyday spirit; but they are short lived; soon they have attained their zenith, and a long depression lays hold of society before it learns soberly to assimilate the results of its storm and stress period. Proletarian revolutions, on the other hand, like those of the nineteenth century, criticise themselves constantly, interrupt themselves continually in their own course, come back to the apparently accomplished in order to begin it afresh, deride with unmerciful thoroughness the inadequacies, weaknesses and paltrinesses of their first attempts, seem to throw down their adversary only in order that he may draw new strength from the earth and rise again more gigantic before them, recoil ever and anon from the indefinite prodigiousness of their own aims, until the situation has been created which makes all turning back impossible. . . .

For the rest, every fairly competent observer, even if he had not followed the course of French development step by step, must have had a presentiment that a terrible fiasco was in store for the revolution. It was enough to hear the self-complacent howl of victory with which Messieurs the Democrats congratulated each other on the gracious consequences of May 2, 1852. In their minds May 2, 1852, had become a fixed idea, a dogma, like the day on which Christ should reappear and the millennium begin, in the minds of the Chiliasts. As ever, weakness had taken refuge in a belief in miracles, had fancied the enemy overcome when he was only conjured away in imagination, and lost all understanding of the present in a passive glorification of the future that was in store for it and of the deeds it had *in petto,* but merely did not want to carry out as yet. Those heroes, who seek to disprove their demonstrated incapacity by mutually offering each other their sympathy and getting together in a crowd, had tied up their bundles, collected their laurel wreaths in advance and were just then engaged in discounting on the exchange market the republics *in partibus,* for which they had already thoughtfully organised the government personnel with all the calm of their unassuming disposition. December 2 struck them like a thunderbolt from a clear sky, and the peoples that in epochs of pusillanimous depression gladly let their inward apprehension be drowned by the loudest bawlers will perchance have convinced themselves that the times are past when the cackle of geese could save the Capitol.

The Constitution, the National Assembly, the dynastic parties, the blue and the red republicans, the heroes of Africa, the thunder from the platform, the sheet lightning of the daily press, the entire literature, the political names and the intellectual reputations, the civil law and penal code, the *liberté, egalité, fraternité* and the second of May 1852—all have vanished like a phantasmagoria before the spell of a man whom even his enemies do not make out to be a magician. Universal suffrage seems to have survived only for a moment, in order that with its own hand it may make its last will and testament before the eyes of all the world and declare in the name of the people itself: Everything that exists has this much worth, that it will perish.

It is not enough to say, as the French do, that their nation has been taken by surprise. A nation and a woman are not forgiven the unguarded hour in which the first adventurer that came along could violate them. The riddle is not solved by such terms of speech, but merely formulated in another way. It remains to be explained how a nation of thirty-six millions can be surprised and delivered unresisting into captivity by three high class swindlers.

Let us recapitulate in their general outlines the phases that the French Revolution has gone through from February 24, 1848, to December 1851.

Three main periods are unmistakable: the *February period;* the *period of the constituting of the republic or of the Constituent National Assembly,* May 4, 1848, to May 29, 1849; the *period of the constitutional republic or of the Legislative National Assembly,* May 29, 1849, to December 2, 1851.

The first period, from February 24, or the overthrow of Louis Philippe, to May 4, 1848, the meeting of the Constituent Assembly, the *February period proper,* may be described as the *prologue* of the Revolution. Its character was officially expressed in the fact that the government improvised by it declared itself to be *provisional* and, like the government, everything that was instigated, attempted or enunciated during this period, proclaimed itself to be *provisional.* Nothing and nobody ventured to lay claim to the right of existence and of real action. All the elements that had prepared or determined the Revolution, the dynastic opposition, the republican bourgeoisie, the democratic-republican petty bourgeoisie and the social-democratic workers, provisionally found their place in the February *government.*

It could not be otherwise. The February days originally intended an electoral reform, by which the circle of the politically privileged among the possessing class itself was to be widened and the exclusive domination of the aristocracy of finance overthrown. When it came to the actual conflict, however, when the people mounted the barricades, the National Guard maintained a passive attitude, the army offered no serious resistance and the monarchy ran away, the republic appeared to be a matter of course. Every party construed it in its own sense. Having been won by the proletariat by force of arms, the proletariat impressed its stamp on it and proclaimed it to be a *social republic.* There was thus indicated the general content of the modern revolution, which stood in most singular contradiction to everything that, with the material at hand, with the degree of education attained by the masses, under the given circumstances and relationships, could be immediately realised in practice. On the other hand, the claims of all the remaining elements that had participated in the February Revolution were recognised by the lion's share that they obtained in the government. In no period do we therefore find a more confused mixture of high-flown phrases and actual uncertainty and clumsiness, of more enthusiastic striving for innovation and more deeply rooted domination of the old routine, of more apparent harmony of the whole society and more profound estrangement of its elements. While the Paris proletariat still revelled in the vision of the wide prospects that had opened before it and indulged in seriously-meant discussions on social problems, the old powers of society had grouped themselves, assembled, reflected and found an unexpected support in the mass of the nation, the peasants and petty bourgeois, who all at once stormed on to the political stage, after the barriers of the July monarchy had fallen.

The second period, from May 4, 1848, to the end of May 1849, is the period of the *constitution,* of the *foundation of the bourgeois republic.* Directly after the February days the dynastic opposition had not only been surprised by the republicans, the republicans by the socialists, but all France had been surprised by Paris. The National Assembly, which had met on May 4, 1848, having emerged from the national elections, represented the nation. It was a living protest against the presumptuous aspirations of the February days and was to reduce the results of the Revolution to the bourgeois scale. In vain the Paris proletariat, which immediately grasped the character of this National Assembly, attempted on May 15, a few days after it met, forcibly to deny its existence, to dissolve it, to disintegrate once more into its constituent parts the organic form in which the proletariat was threatened by the reactionary spirit of the nation. As is known, May 15 had no other result save that of removing Blanqui and his comrades, that is, the real leaders of the proletarian party [the revolutionary communists], from the public stage for the entire duration of the cycle we are considering.

The *bourgeois monarchy* of Louis Philippe can only be followed by the *bourgeois republic,* that is, if a limited section of the bourgeoisie formerly ruled in the name of the king, the whole of the bourgeoisie will now rule in the name of the people. The demands of the Paris proletariat are utopian nonsense to which an end must be put. To this declaration of the Constituent National Assembly the Paris proletariat replied with the *June Insurrection,* the most colossal event in the history of European civil wars. The bourgeois republic triumphed. On its side stood the aristocracy of finance, the industrial bourgeoisie, the middle class, the petty bourgeois, the army, the *lumpenproletariat* organised as the Mobile Guard, the intellectual lights, the clergy, and the rural population. On the side of the Paris proletariat stood none but itself. More than three thousand insurgents were butchered after the victory, and fifteen thousand were transported without trial. With this defeat the proletariat passes into the background of the revolutionary stage. It attempts to press forward again on every occasion, as soon as the movement appears to make a fresh start, but with ever decreased expenditure of strength and always more insignificant results. As soon as one of the social strata situated above it gets into revolutionary ferment, it enters into an alliance with it and so shares all the defeats that the different parties suffer one after another. But these subsequent blows become steadily weaker, the more they are distributed over the entire surface of society. Its more important leaders in the Assembly and the press successively fall victims to the courts, and ever more equivocal figures come to the fore. In part it throws itself into *doctrinaire experiments, exchange banks and workers' associations, hence into a movement in which it renounces the revolutionising of the old world by means of its own great, combined resources, and seeks, rather, to achieve its salvation behind society's back, in private fashion, within its limited conditions of existence, and hence inevitably suffers shipwreck.* It seems to be unable either to rediscover revolutionary greatness in itself or to win new energy from the alliances newly entered into, until *all classes* with which it contended in June themselves lie prostrate beside it. But at least it succumbs with the honours of the great, world-historic struggle; not only France, but all Europe trembles at the June earthquake, while the ensuing defeats of the upper classes are so cheaply bought that they require bare-faced exaggeration by the victorious party to be able to pass for events at all and become the more ignominious the further the defeated party is removed from the proletariat.

The defeat of the June insurgents, to be sure, had now prepared and levelled the ground on which the bourgeois republic could be founded and built up, but it had shown at the same time that in Europe there are other questions involved than that of "republic or monarchy." It had revealed that here *bourgeois republic* signifies the unlimited despotism of one class over other classes. It had proved that in lands with an old civilisation, with a developed formation of classes, with modern conditions of production and with an intellectual consciousness into which all traditional ideas have been absorbed by the work of centuries, *the republic* signifies *in general only the political form of the revolution of bourgeois society* and not its *conservative form of life,* as, for example, in the United States of North America, where, though classes, indeed, already exist, they have not yet become fixed, but continually change and interchange their elements in a constant state of flux, where the modern means of production, instead of coinciding with a stagnant surplus population, rather supply the relative deficiency of heads and hands and where, finally, the feverishly youthful movement of material production, that has a new world to make its own, has left neither time nor opportunity for abolishing the old spirit world.

During the June days all classes and parties had united in the *Party of Order* against the proletarian class as the *party of anarchy*, of socialism, of communism. They had "saved" society from "*the enemies of society.*" They had given out the watchwords of the old society, "*property, family, religion, order,*" to their army as passwords and had proclaimed to the counter-revolutionary crusaders: "In this sign you will conquer!" From that moment, as soon as one of the numerous parties which had gathered under this sign against the June insurgents seeks to hold the revolutionary battlefield in its own class interests it goes down before the cry: "Property, family, religion, order." Society is saved just as often as the circle of its rulers contracts, as a more exclusive interest is maintained against a wider one. Every demand of the simplest bourgeois financial reform, of the most ordinary liberalism, of the most formal republicanism, of the most insipid democracy, is simultaneously castigated as an "attempt on society" and stigmatised as "socialism." And, finally, the high priests of "religion and order" themselves are driven with kicks from their Pythian tripods, hauled out of their beds in the darkness of night, put in prison-vans, thrown into dungeons or sent into exile; their temple is razed to the ground, their mouths are sealed, their pens broken, their law torn to pieces in the name of religion, of property, of family, of order. Bourgeois fanatics for order are shot down on their balconies by mobs of drunken soldiers, their domestic sanctuaries profaned, their houses bombarded for amusement—in the name of property, of family, of religion and of order. Finally the scum of bourgeois society forms *the holy phalanx of order* and the hero Crapulinsky installs himself in the Tuileries as the "*saviour of society.*" . . .

On the threshold of the February Revolution, the *social republic* appeared as a phrase, as prophecy. In the June days of 1848, it was drowned in the blood of the Paris proletariat, but it haunts the subsequent acts of the drama like a ghost. The *democratic republic* makes its appearance. On June 13, 1849, it is dissipated together with its *petty bourgeois*, who take to their heels, but in its flight it blows its own trumpet with redoubled boastfulness. The *parliamentary republic*, together with the bourgeoisie, takes possession of the entire stage; it lives out its existence to the full, but December 2, 1851, buries it to the accompaniment of the cry of terror of the royalists in coalition: "Long live the republic!"

The French bourgeoisie offered resistance to the domination of the working proletariat; it has brought the *lumpenproletariat* to domination, with the chief of the Society of December 10 at the head. The bourgeoisie kept France in breathless fear of the future terrors of red anarchy; Bonaparte discounted this future for it when, on December 4, he had the eminent bourgeois of the Boulevard Montmartre and the Boulevard des Italiens shot down at their windows by the army of order, whose enthusiasm was inspired by liquor. It apotheosised the sword; the sword rules it. It destroyed the revolutionary press; its own press has been destroyed. It placed public meetings under police supervision; its salons are under the supervision of the police. It disbanded the democratic National Guard; its own National Guard has been disbanded. It imposed the state of siege; the state of siege has been imposed on it. It supplanted the juries by military commissions; its juries are supplanted by military commissions; it subjected public education to the priests; the priests subject it to their own education. It transported people without trial; it is transported without trial. It suppressed every stirring in society by means of the state power; every stirring in its society is repressed by means of the state power. Out of enthusiasm for its purse, it rebelled against its own politicians and men of letters; its politicians and men of letters are swept aside, but its purse is plundered now that its mouth has been gagged and its pen broken. The bourgeoisie never wearied of crying out to the revolution what Saint Arsenius cried out to the Christians: "*Fuge, tace, quiesce!*" Flee, be silent, keep quiet! Bonaparte cries to the bourgeoisie: "*Fuge, tace, quiesce!*" Flee, be silent, keep quiet!

The French bourgeoisie had long since found the solution to Napoleon's dilemma: "*Dans cinquante ans l'Europe sera républicaine ou cosaque*" ["Within fifty years Europe will be republican or Cossack"]. It had found the solution to it in the "*république cosaque.*" No Circe, by means of black magic, has distorted that work of art, the bourgeois republic, into a monstrous shape. That republic has nothing but the semblance of respectability. The present-day France was contained in a finished state within the parliamentary republic. It only required a bayonet thrust for the bubble to burst and the monster to spring forth before our eyes. . . .

Why did not the Paris proletariat rise in revolt after December?

The overthrow of the bourgeoisie had as yet only been decreed; the decree had not been carried out. Any serious insurrection of the proletariat would at once have put fresh life into the bourgeoisie, would have reconciled it with the army and would have ensured a second June defeat for the workers.

On December 4 the proletariat was incited to fight by the bourgeois and the small shopkeepers. On the evening of that day several legions of the National Guard promised to appear, armed and uniformed, on the scene of action. For the bourgeois and the small shopkeepers had found out that in one of his decrees of December 2 Bonaparte abolished the secret ballot and enjoined them to record their "yes" or "no" in the official registers after their names. The resistance of December 4 intimidated Bonaparte. During the night he caused placards to be posted on all the street corners of Paris, announcing the restoration of the secret ballot. The bourgeois and the small shopkeepers believed that they had gained their end. Those who failed to appear next morning were the bourgeois and the small shopkeepers.

By a *coup de main* during the night of December 1 to 2, Bonaparte had robbed the Paris proletariat of its leaders, the barricade commanders. An army without officers, made disinclined to fight under the banner of the *Montagnards* by the memories of June 1848 and 1849 and May 1850, it left to its vanguard, the secret societies, the task of saving the insurrectionary honour of Paris, which the bourgeoisie had so spinelessly surrendered to the soldiers that, later on, Bonaparte could sneeringly give as his motive for disarming the National Guard—his fear that its arms would be turned against itself by anarchists!

"*C'est le triomphe complet et definitif du socialisme!*" ["This is the complete and final triumph of socialism"].

Thus Guizot characterised December 2. But if the overthrow of the parliamentary republic contains within itself the germ of the triumph of the proletarian revolution, its immediate and obvious result was *the victory of Bonaparte over parliament, of the executive power over the legislative power, of force without phrases over the force of phrases.* In parliament the nation made its general will the law, that is, it made the law of the ruling class its general will. Before the executive power it renounces all will of its own and surrenders itself to the superior orders of something alien, of authority. The executive power, in contrast to the legislative power, expresses the heteronomy of the nation, in contrast to its autonomy. France, therefore, seems to have escaped the despotism of a class only to fall back beneath the despotism of an individual and, what is more, beneath the authority of an individual without authority. The struggle seems to be settled in such a way that all classes, equally impotent and equally mute, fall on their knees before the club.

But the revolution is thorough-going. It is still in process of passing through purgatory. It does its work methodically. By December 2, 1851, it had completed one half of its preparatory work; it is now completing the other half. First it perfected the parliamentary power, in order to be able to overthrow it. Now that it has attained this, it perfects the *executive power,* reduces it to its purest expression, isolates it, sets it up against itself as the sole target, in order to concentrate all its forces of destruction against it. And when it has done this second half of its preliminary work, Europe will leap from her seat and exultantly exclaim: Well grubbed, old mole!

This executive power with its enormous bureaucratic and military organisation, with its artificial state machinery embracing wide strata, with a host of officials numbering half a million, besides an army of another half million, this appalling parasitic growth, which enmeshes the body of French society like a net and chokes all its pores, sprang up in the days of the absolute monarchy, with the decay of the feudal system, which it helped to hasten. The seigniorial privileges of the landowners and towns became transformed into so many attributes of the state power, the feudal dignitaries into paid officials and the motley pattern of conflicting mediaeval plenary powers into the regulated plan of a state authority, whose work is divided and centralised as in a factory. The first French Revolution, with its task of breaking all local, territorial, urban and provincial independent powers in order to create the bourgeois unity of the nation, was bound to develop what the absolute monarchy had begun—centralisation, but at the same time the extent, the attributes and the agents of governmental authority. Napoleon perfected this state machinery. The Legitimist monarchy and the July monarchy added nothing but a greater division of labour, growing in the same measure that the division of labour within bourgeois society created new groups of interests, and, therefore, new material for state administration. Every *common* interest was straightaway severed from society, counter-posed to it as a higher, *general* interest, snatched from the self-activity of society's members and made an object of governmental activity from the bridge, the school-house and the communal property of a village community to the railways, the national wealth and the national university of France. The parliamentary republic, finally, in its struggle against the revolution, found itself compelled to strengthen, along with the repressive measures, the resources and centralisation of governmental power. All the revolutions perfected this machine instead of smashing it. The parties that contended in turn for domination regarded the possession of this huge state edifice as the principal spoils of the victor.

But under the absolute monarchy, during the first revolution, and under Napoleon, bureaucracy was only the means of preparing the class rule of the bourgeoisie. Under the Restoration, under Louis Philippe and under the parliamentary republic, it was the instrument of the ruling class, however much it strove for power of its own.

Only under the second Bonaparte does the state seem to have made itself completely independent. As against bourgeois society, the state machine has consolidated its position so thoroughly that the chief of the Society of December 10 suffices for its head, an adventurer blown in from abroad, elevated on the shield by a drunken soldiery, which he has bought with liquor and sausages, and which he must continually ply with sausage anew. Hence the downcast despair, the feeling of most dreadful humiliation and degradation that oppresses the breast of France and makes her catch her breath. She feels herself dishonoured.❖

On Imperialism in India

Karl Marx (1853)

All the English bourgeoisie may be forced to do will neither emancipate nor materially mend the social condition of the mass of the people, depending not only on the development of the productive powers, but on their appropriation by the people. But what they will not fail to do is to lay down the material premises for both. Has the bourgeoisie ever done more? Has it ever affected a progress without dragging individuals and peoples through blood and dirt, through misery and degradation?

The Indians will not reap the fruits of the new elements of society scattered among them by the British bourgeoisie, till in Great Britain itself the now ruling classes shall have been supplanted by the industrial proletariat, or till the Hindoos themselves shall have grown strong enough to throw off the English yoke altogether. At all events, we may safely expect to see, at a more or less remote period, the regeneration of that great and interesting country, whose gentle natives are, to use the expression of Prince Soltykov, even in the most inferior classes, *"plus fins et plus adroits que les Italiens,"* whose submission even is counterbalanced by a certain calm nobility, who, notwithstanding their natural languor, have astonished the British officers by their bravery, whose country has been the source of our languages, our religions, and who represent the type of the ancient German in the *Jat* and the type of the ancient Greek in the Brahmin. . . .

The profound hypocrisy and inherent barbarism of bourgeois civilisation lies unveiled before our eyes, turning from its home, where it assumes respectable forms, to the colonies, where it goes naked. They are the defenders of property, but did any revolutionary party ever originate agrarian revolutions like those in Bengal, in Madras, and in Bombay? Did they not, in India, to borrow an expression of that great robber, Lord Clive himself, resort to atrocious extortion, when simple corruption could not keep pace with their rapacity? While they prated in Europe about the inviolable sanctity of the national debt, did they not confiscate in India the dividends of the *rajahs,* who had invested their private savings in the Company's own funds? While they combatted the French revolution under the pretext of defending "our holy religion," did they not forbid, at the same time, Christianity to be propagated in India, and did they not, in order to make money out of the pilgrims streaming to the temples of Orissa and Bengal, take up the trade in the murder and prostitution perpetrated in the temple of Juggernaut? These are the men of "Property, Order, Family, and Religion."

The devastating effects of English industry, when contemplated with regard to India, a country as vast as Europe, and containing 150 millions of acres, are palpable and confounding. But we must not forget that they are only the organic results of the whole system of production as it is now constituted. That production rests on the supreme rule of capital. The centralisation of capital is essential to the existence of capital as an independent power. The destructive influence of that centralisation upon the markets of the world does but reveal, in the most gigantic dimensions, the inherent organic laws of political economy now at work in every civilised town. The bourgeois period of history has to create the material basis of the new world—on the one hand the universal intercourse founded upon the mutual dependency of

Excerpt from Robert C. Tucker, ed., *The Marx-Engels Reader,* 2d ed. (New York: W. W. Norton, 1978), pp. 662–664.

mankind, and the means of that intercourse; on the other hand the development of the productive powers of man and the transformation of material production into a scientific domination of natural agencies. Bourgeois industry and commerce create these material conditions of a new world in the same way as geological revolutions have created the surface of the earth. When a great social revolution shall have mastered the results of the bourgeois epoch, the market of the world and the modern powers of production, and subjected them to the common control of the most advanced peoples, then only will human progress cease to resemble that hideous pagan idol, who would not drink the nectar but from the skulls of the slain.❖

The Values of Commodities
Karl Marx (1867)

The Two Factors of a Commodity: Use-Value and Value (The Substance of Value and the Magnitude of Value)

The wealth of those societies in which the capitalist mode of production prevails, presents itself as "an immense accumulation of commodities," its unit being a single commodity. Our investigation must therefore begin with the analysis of a commodity.

A commodity is, in the first place, an object outside us, a thing that by its properties satisfies human wants of some sort or another. The nature of such wants, whether, for instance, they spring from the stomach or from fancy, makes no difference. Neither are we here concerned to know how the object satisfies these wants, whether directly as means of subsistence, or indirectly as means of production.

Every useful thing, as iron, paper, &c., may be looked at from the two points of view of quality and quantity. It is an assemblage of many properties, and may therefore be of use in various ways. To discover the various uses of things is the work of history. So also is the establishment of socially-recognised standards of measure for the quantities of these useful objects. The diversity of these measures has its origin partly in the diverse nature of the objects to be measured, partly in convention.

The utility of a thing makes it a use-value. But this utility is not a thing of air. Being limited by the physical properties of the commodity, it has no existence apart from that commodity. A commodity, such as iron, corn, or a diamond, is therefore, so far as it is a material thing, a use-value, something useful. This property of a commodity is independent of the amount of labour required to appropriate its useful qualities. When treating of use-value, we always assume to be dealing with definite quantities, such as dozens of watches, yards of linen, or tons of iron. The use-values of commodities furnish the material for a special study, that of the commercial knowledge of commodities. Use-values become a reality only by use or consumption: they also constitute the substance of all wealth, whatever may be the social form of that wealth. In the form of society we are about to consider, they are, in addition, the material depositories of exchange-value.

Exchange-value, at first sight, presents itself as a quantitative relation, as the proportion in which values in use of one sort are exchanged for those of another sort, a relation constantly changing with time and place. Hence exchange-value appears to

Excerpt from "Capital, Vol. I," in Robert C. Tucker, ed., *The Marx-Engels Reader*, 2d ed. (New York: W. W. Norton, 1978), pp. 302–314.

be something accidental and purely relative, and consequently an intrinsic value, *i.e.*, an exchange-value that is inseparably connected with, inherent in commodities, seems a contradiction in terms. Let us consider the matter a little more closely.

A given commodity, *e.g.*, a quarter of wheat is exchanged for x blacking, y silk, or z gold, &c.—in short, for other commodities in the most different proportions. Instead of one exchange-value, the wheat has, therefore, a great many. But since x blacking, y silk, or z gold, &c., each represent the exchange-value of one quarter of wheat, x blacking, y silk, z gold, &c., must, as exchange-values, be replaceable by each other, or equal to each other. Therefore, first: the valid exchange-values of a given commodity express something equal; secondly, exchange-value, generally, is only the mode of expression, the phenomenal form, of something contained in it, yet distinguishable from it.

Let us take two commodities, *e.g.*, corn and iron. The proportions in which they are exchangeable, whatever those proportions may be, can always be represented by an equation in which a given quantity of corn is equated to some quantity of iron: *e.g.*, 1 quarter corn = x cwt. iron. What does this equation tell us? It tells us that in two different things—in 1 quarter of corn and x cwt. of iron, there exists in equal quantities something common to both. The two things must therefore be equal to a third, which in itself is neither the one nor the other. Each of them, so far as it is exchange-value, must therefore be reducible to this third.

A simple geometrical illustration will make this clear. In order to calculate and compare the areas of rectilinear figures, we decompose them into triangles. But the area of the triangle itself is expressed by something totally different from its visible figure, namely, by half the product of the base into the altitude. In the same way the exchange-values of commodities must be capable of being expressed in terms of something common to them all, of which thing they represent a greater or less quantity.

This common "something" cannot be either a geometrical, a chemical, or any other natural property of commodities. Such properties claim our attention only in so far as they affect the utility of those commodities, make them use-values. But the exchange of commodities is evidently an act characterised by a total abstraction from use-value. Then one use-value is just as good as another, provided only it be present in sufficient quantity. Or, as old Barbon says, "one sort of wares are as good as another, if the values be equal. There is no difference or distinction in things of equal value. . . . An hundred pounds' worth of lead or iron, is of as great value as one hundred pounds' worth of silver or gold." As use-values, commodities are, above all, of different qualities, but as exchange-values they are merely different quantities, and consequently do not contain an atom of use-value.

If then we leave out of consideration the use-value of commodities, they have only one common property left, that of being products of labour. But even the product of labour itself has undergone a change in our hands. If we make abstraction from its use-value, we make abstraction at the same time from the material elements and shapes that make the product a use-value; we see in it no longer a table, a house, yarn, or any other useful thing. Its existence as a material thing is put out of sight. Neither can it any longer be regarded as the product of the labour of the joiner, the mason, the spinner, or of any other definite kind of productive labour. Along with the useful qualities of the products themselves, we put out of sight both the useful character of the various kinds of labour embodied in them, and the concrete forms of that labour; there is nothing left but what is common to them all; all are reduced to one and the same sort of labour, human labour in the abstract.

Let us now consider the residue of each of these products; it consists of the same unsubstantial reality in each, a mere congelation of homogeneous human labour, of labour-power expended without regard to the mode of its expenditure. All that these things now tell us is, that human labour-power has been expended in their production, that human labour is embodied in them. When looked at as crystals of this social substance, common to them all, they are—Values.

We have seen that when commodities are exchanged, their exchange-value manifests itself as something totally independent of their use-value. But if we abstract from their use-value, there remains their Value as defined above. Therefore, the common substance that manifests itself in the exchange-value of commodities, whenever they are exchanged, is their value. The progress of our investigation will show that exchange-value is the only form in which the value of commodities can manifest itself or be expressed. For the present, however, we have to consider the nature of value independently of this, its form.

A use-value, or useful article, therefore, has value only because human labour in the abstract has been embodied or materialised in it. How, then, is the magnitude of this value to be measured? Plainly, by the quantity of the value-creating substance, the labour, contained in the article. The quantity of labour, however, is measured by its duration, and labour-time in its turn finds its standard in weeks, days, and hours.

Some people might think that if the value of a commodity is determined by the quantity of labour spent on it, the more idle and unskillful the labourer, the more valuable would his commodity be, because more time would be required in its production. The labour, however, that forms the substance of value, is homogeneous human labour, expenditure of one uniform labour-power. The total labour-power of society, which is embodied in the sum total of the values of all commodities produced by that society, counts here as one homogeneous mass of human labour-power, composed though it be of innumerable individual units. Each of these units is the same as any other, so far as it has the character of the average labour-power of society, and takes effect as such; that is, so far as it requires for producing a commodity, no more time than is needed on an average, no more than is socially necessary. The labour-time socially necessary is that required to produce an article under the normal conditions of production, and with the average degree of skill and intensity prevalent at the time. The introduction of power-looms into England probably reduced by one-half the labour required to weave a given quantity of yarn into cloth. The hand-loom weavers, as a matter of fact, continued to require the same time as before; but for all that, the product of one hour of their labour represented after the change only half an hour's social labour, and consequently fell to one-half its former value.

We see then that that which determines the magnitude of the value of any article is the amount of labour socially necessary, or the labour-time socially necessary for its production. Each individual commodity, in this connexion, is to be considered as an average sample of its class. Commodities, therefore, in which equal quantities of labour are embodied, or which can be produced in the same time, have the same value. The value of one commodity is to the value of any other, as the labour-time necessary for the production of the one is to that necessary for the production of the other. "As values, all commodities are only definite masses of congealed labour-time."

The value of a commodity would therefore remain constant, if the labour-time required for its production also remained constant. But the latter changes with every variation in the productiveness of labour. This productiveness is determined by various circumstances, amongst others, by the average amount of skill of the workmen, the state of science, and the degree of its practical application, the social organisation of production, the extent and capabilities of the means of production, and by physical conditions. For example, the same amount of labour in favourable seasons is embodied in 8 bushels of corn, and in unfavourable, only in four. The same labour extracts from rich mines more metal than from poor mines. Diamonds are of very rare occurrence on the earth's surface, and hence their discovery costs, on an average, a great deal of labour-time. Consequently much labour is represented in a small compass. Jacob doubts whether gold has ever been paid for at its full value. This applies still more to diamonds. According to Eschwege, the total produce of the Brazilian diamond mines for the eighty years, ending in 1823, had not realised the price of one-and-a-half years' average produce of the sugar and coffee plantations of the same country, although the diamonds cost much more labour, and therefore represented more value. With richer mines, the same quantity of labour would embody itself in more diamonds, and their value would fall. If we could succeed at a small expenditure of labour, in converting carbon into diamonds, their value might fall below that of bricks. In general, the greater the productiveness of labour, the less is the labour-time required for the production of an article, the less is the amount of labour crystallised in that article, and the less is its value; and *vice versa*, the less the productiveness of labour, the greater is the labour-time required for the production of an article, and the greater is its value. The value of a commodity, therefore, varies directly as the quantity, and inversely as the productiveness, of the labour incorporated in it.

A thing can be a use-value, without having value. This is the case whenever its utility to man is not due to labour. Such are air, virgin soil, natural meadows, &c. A thing can be useful, and the product of human labour, without being a commodity. Whoever directly satisfies his wants with the produce of his own labour, creates, indeed, use-values, but no commodities. In order to produce the latter, he must not only produce use-values, but use-values for others, social use-values. (And not only for others, without more. The mediaeval peasant produced quit-rent-corn for his feudal lord and tithe-corn for his parson. But neither the quit-rent-corn nor the tithe-corn became commodities by reason of the fact that they had been produced for others. To become a commodity a product must be transferred to another, whom it will serve as a use-value, by means of an exchange.) Lastly nothing can have value, without being an object of utility. If the thing is useless, so is the labour contained in it; the labour does not count as labour, and therefore creates no value.

The Two-fold Character of the Labour Embodied in Commodities

At first sight a commodity presented itself to us as a complex of two things—use-value and exchange-value. Later on, we saw also that labour, too, possesses the same two-fold nature; for, so far as it finds expression in value, it does not possess the same characteristics that belong to it as a creator of use-values. I was the first to point out and to examine critically this two-fold nature of the labour contained in commodities. As this point is the pivot on which a clear comprehension of Political Economy turns, we must go more into detail.

Let us take two commodities such as a coat and 10 yards of linen, and let the former be double the value of the latter, so that, if 10 yards of linen = W, the coat = 2W.

The coat is a use-value that satisfies a particular want. Its existence is the result of a special sort of productive activity, the nature of which is determined by its aim, mode of operation, subject, means, and result. The labour, whose utility is thus represented by the value in use of its product, or which manifests itself by making its product a use-value, we call useful labour. In this connexion we consider only its useful effect.

As the coat and the linen are two qualitatively different use-values, so also are the two forms of labour that produce them, tailoring and weaving. Were these two objects not qualitatively different, not produced respectively by labour of different quality, they could not stand to each other in the relation of commodities. Coats are not exchanged for coats, one use-value is not exchanged for another of the same kind.

To all the different varieties of values in use there correspond as many different kinds of useful labour, classified according to the order, genus, species, and variety to which they belong in the social division of labour. This division of labour is a necessary condition for the production of commodities, but it does not follow, conversely, that the production of commodities is a necessary condition for the division of labour. In the primitive Indian community there is social division of labour, without production of commodities. Or, to take an example nearer home, in every factory the labour is divided according to a system, but this division is not brought about by the operatives mutually exchanging their individual products. Only such products can become commodities with regard to each other, as result from different kinds of labour, each kind being carried on independently and for the account of private individuals.

To resume, then: In the use-value of each commodity there is contained useful labour, *i.e.*, productive activity of a definite kind and exercised with a definite aim. Use-values cannot confront each other as commodities, unless the useful labour embodied in them is qualitatively different in each of them. In a community, the produce of which in general takes the form of commodities, *i.e.*, in a community of commodity producers, this qualitative difference between the useful forms of labour that are carried on independently by individual producers, each on their own account, develops into a complex system, a social division of labour.

Anyhow, whether the coat be worn by the tailor or by his customer, in either case it operates as a use-value. Nor is the relation between the coat and the labour that produced it altered by the circumstance that tailoring may have become a special trade, an independent branch of the social division of labour. Wherever the want of clothing forced them to it, the human race made clothes for thousands of years, without a single man becoming a tailor. But coats and linen, like every other element of material wealth that is not the spontaneous produce of Nature, must invariably owe their existence to a special productive activity, exercised with a definite aim, an activity that appropriates particular nature-given materials to particular human wants. So far therefore as labour is a creator of use-value, is useful labour, it is a necessary condition, independent of all forms of society, for the existence of the human race; it is an eternal nature-imposed necessity, without which there can be no material exchanges between man and Nature, and therefore no life.

The use-values, coat, linen, &c., *i.e.*, the bodies of commodities, are combinations of two elements—matter and labour. If we take away the useful labour expended upon them, a material substratum is always left, which is furnished by Nature without the help of man. The latter can work only as Nature does, that is by changing the form of matter. Nay more, in this work of changing the form he is constantly helped by natural forces. We see, then, that labour is not the only source of material wealth, of use-values produced by labour. As William Petty puts it, labour is its father and the earth its mother.

Let us now pass from the commodity considered as a use-value to the value of commodities.

By our assumption, the coat is worth twice as much as the linen. But this is a mere quantitative difference, which for the present does not concern us. We bear in mind, however, that if the value of the coat is double that of 10 yds. of linen, 20 yds. of linen must have the same value as one coat. So far as they are values, the coat and the linen are things of a like substance, objective expressions of essentially identical labour. But tailoring and weaving are, qualitatively, different kinds of labour. There are, however, states of society in which one and the same man does tailoring and weaving alternately, in which case these two forms of labour are mere modifications of the labour of the same individual, and no special and fixed functions of different persons; just as the coat which our tailor makes one day, and the trousers which he makes another day, imply only a variation in the labour of one and the same individual. Moreover, we see at a glance that, in our capitalist society, a given portion of human labour is, in accordance with the varying demand, at one time supplied in the form of tailoring, at another in the form of weaving. This change may possibly not take place without friction, but take place it must.

Productive activity, if we leave out of sight its special form, viz., the useful character of the labour, is nothing but the expenditure of human labour-power. Tailoring and weaving, though qualitatively different productive activities, are each a productive expenditure of human brains, nerves, and muscles, and in this sense are human labour. They are but two different modes of expending human labour-power. Of course, this labour-power, which remains the same under all its modifications, must have attained a certain pitch of development before it can be expended in a multiplicity of modes. But the value of a commodity represents human labour in the abstract, the expenditure of human labour in general. And just as in society, a general or a banker plays a great part, but mere man, on the other hand, a very shabby part, so here with human labour. It is the expenditure of simple labour-power, *i.e.*, of the labour-power which, on an average, apart from any special development, exists in the organism of every ordinary individual. Simple average labour, it is true, varies in character in different countries and at different times, but in a particular society it is given. Skilled labour counts only as simple labour intensified, or rather, as multiplied simple labour, a given quantity of skilled being considered equal to a greater quantity of simple labour. Experience shows that this reduction is constantly being made. A commodity may be the product of the most skilled labour, but its value, by equating it to the product of simple unskilled labour, represents a definite quantity of the latter labour alone. The different proportions in which different sorts of labour are reduced to unskilled labour as their standard, are established by a social process that goes on behind the backs of the producers, and, consequently, appear to be fixed by custom. For simplicity's sake we shall henceforth account every kind of labour to be unskilled, simple labour; by this we do no more than save ourselves the trouble of making the reduction.

Just as, therefore, in viewing the coat and linen as values, we abstract from their different use-values, so it is with the labour represented by those values: we disregard the difference between its useful forms, weaving and tailoring. As the use-values, coat and linen, are combinations of special productive activities with cloth and yarn, while the values, coat and linen, are, on the other hand, mere homogeneous congelations of undifferentiated labour, so the labour embodied in these latter values does not count by virtue of its productive relation to cloth and yarn, but only as being expenditure of human labour-power. Tailoring and weaving are necessary factors in the creation of the use-values, coat and linen, precisely because these two kinds of labour are of different qualities, but only in so far as abstraction is made from their special qualities, only in so far as both possess the same quality of being human labour, do tailoring and weaving form the substance of the values of the same article.

Coats and linen, however, are not merely values, but values of definite magnitude, and according to our assumption, the coat is worth twice as much as the ten yards of linen. Whence this difference in their values? It is owing to the fact that the linen contains only half as much labour as the coat, and consequently, that in the production of the latter, labour-power must have been expended during twice the time necessary for the production of the former.

While, therefore, with reference to use-value, the labour contained in a commodity counts only qualitatively, with reference to value it counts only quantitatively, and must first be reduced to human labour pure and simple. In the former case, it is a question of How and What, in the latter of How much? How long a time? Since the magnitude of the value of a commodity represents only the quantity of labour embodied in it, it follows that all commodities, when taken in certain proportions, must be equal in value.

If the productive power of all the different sorts of useful labour required for the production of a coat remains unchanged, the sum of the values of the coats produced increases with their number. If one coat represents x days' labour, two coats represent 2x days' labour, and so on. But assume that the duration of the labour necessary for the production of a coat becomes doubled or halved. In the first case, one coat is worth as much as two coats were before; in the second case, two coats are only worth as much as one was before, although in both cases one coat renders the same service as before, and the useful labour embodied in it remains of the same quality. But the quantity of labour spent on its production has altered.

An increase in the quantity of use-values is an increase of material wealth. With two coats two men can be clothed, with one coat only one man. Nevertheless, an increased quantity of material wealth may correspond to a simultaneous fall in the magnitude of its value. This antagonistic movement has its origin in the two-fold character of labour. Productive power has reference, of course, only to labour of some useful concrete form, the efficacy of any special productive activity during a given time being dependent on its productiveness. Useful labour becomes, therefore, a more or less abundant source of products, in proportion to the rise or fall of its productiveness. On the other hand, no change in this productiveness affects the labour represented by value. Since productive power is an attribute of the concrete useful forms of labour, of course it can no longer have any bearing on that labour, so soon as we make abstraction from those concrete useful forms. However then productive power may vary, the same labour, exercised during equal periods of time, always yields equal amounts of value. But it will yield, during equal periods of time, different quantities of values in use; more, if the productive power rise, fewer, if it fall. The same change in productive power, which increases the fruitfulness of labour, and, in consequence, the quantity of use-values produced by that labour, will diminish the total value of this increased quality of use-values, provided such change shorten the total labour-time necessary for their production; and *vice versa*.

On the one hand all labour is, speaking physiologically, an expenditure of human labour-power, and in its character of identical abstract human labour, it creates and forms the value of commodities. On the other hand, all labour is the expenditure of human labour-power in a special form and with a definite aim, and in this, its character of concrete useful labour, it produces use-values.

The Form of Value or Exchange-Value

Commodities come into the world in the shape of use-values, articles, or goods, such as iron, linen, corn, &c. This is their plain, homely, bodily form. They are, however, commodities, only because they are something two-fold, both objects of utility, and, at the same time, depositories of value. They manifest themselves therefore as commodities, or have the form of commodities, only in so far as they have two forms, a physical or natural form and a value-form.

The reality of the value of commodities differs in this respect from Dame Quickly, that we don't know "where to have it." The value of commodities is the very opposite of the coarse materiality of their substance, not an atom of matter enters into its composition. Turn and examine a single commodity, by itself, as we will, yet in so far as it remains an object of value, it seems impossible to grasp it. If, however, we bear in mind that the value of commodities has a purely social reality, and that they acquire this reality only in so far as they are expressions or embodiments of one identical social substance, viz., human labour, it follows as a matter of course, that value can only manifest itself in the social relation of commodity to commodity. In fact we started from exchange-value, or the exchange relation of commodities, in order to get at the value that lies hidden behind it. We must now return to this form under which value first appeared to us.

Every one knows, if he knows nothing else, that commodities have a value-form common to them all, and presenting a marked contrast with the varied bodily forms of their use-values. I mean their money-form. Here, however, a task is set us, the performance of which has never yet even been attempted by *bourgeois* economy, the task of tracing the genesis of this money-form, of developing the expression of value implied in the value-relation of commodities, from its simplest, almost imperceptible outline, to the dazzling money-form. By doing this we shall, at the same time, solve the riddle presented by money.

The simplest value-relation is evidently that of one commodity to some one other commodity of a different kind. Hence the relation between the values of two commodities supplies us with the simplest expression of the value of a single commodity.

Elementary or Accidental Form of Value:
    x commodity A = y commodity B, or
    x commodity A is worth y commodity B.
    20 yards of linen = 1 coat, or
    20 yards of linen are worth 1 coat.

The Two Poles of the Expression of Value:
Relative Form and Equivalent Form

The whole mystery of the form of value lies hidden in this elementary form. Its analysis, therefore, is our real difficulty.

Here two different kinds of commodities (in our example the linen and the coat), evidently play two different parts. The linen expresses its value in the coat; the coat serves as the material in which that value is expressed. The former plays an active, the latter a passive, part. The value of the linen is represented as relative value, or appears in relative form. The coat officiates as equivalent, or appears in equivalent form.

The relative form and the equivalent form are two intimately connected, mutually dependent and inseparable elements of the expression of value; but, at the same time, are mutually exclusive, antagonistic extremes—*i.e.,* poles of the same expression. They are allotted respectively to the two different commodities brought into relation by that expression. It is not possible to express the value of linen in linen. 20 yards of linen = 20 yards of linen is no expression of value. On the contrary, such an equation merely says that 20 yards of linen are nothing else than 20 yards of linen, a definite quantity of the use-value linen. The value of the linen can therefore be expressed only relatively—*i.e.,* in some other commodity. The relative form of the value of the linen pre-supposes, therefore, the presence of some other commodity— here the coat—under the form of an equivalent. On the other hand, the commodity that figures as the equivalent cannot at the same time assume the relative form. That second commodity is not the one whose value is expressed. Its function is merely to serve as the material in which the value of the first commodity is expressed.

No doubt, the expression 20 yards of linen = 1 coat, or 20 yards of linen are worth 1 coat, implies the opposite relation: 1 coat = 20 yards of linen, or 1 coat is worth 20 yards of linen. But, in that case, I must reverse the equation, in order to express the value of the coat relatively; and, so soon as I do that, the linen becomes the equivalent instead of the coat. A single commodity cannot, therefore, simultaneously assume, in the same expression of value, both forms. The very polarity of these forms makes them mutually exclusive.

Whether, then, a commodity assumes the relative form, or the opposite equivalent form, depends entirely upon its accidental position in the expression of value—that is, upon whether it is the commodity whose value is being expressed or the commodity in which value is being expressed.❖

The Fetishism of Commodities
Karl Marx (1867)

A commodity appears, at first sight, a very trivial thing, and easily understood. Its analysis shows that it is, in reality, a very queer thing, abounding in metaphysical subtleties and theological niceties. So far as it is a value in use, there is nothing mysterious about it, whether we consider it from the point of view that by its properties it is capable of satisfying human wants, or from the point that those properties are the product of human labour. It is as clear as noon-day, that man, by his industry, changes the forms of the materials furnished by Nature, in such a way as to make them useful to him. The form of wood, for instance, is altered, by making a table out of it. Yet, for all that, the table continues to be that common, every-day thing, wood. But, so soon as it steps forth as a commodity, it is changed into something transcendent. It not only stands with its feet on the ground, but, in relation to all other com-

Excerpt from "Capital, Vol. I," in Robert C. Tucker, ed., *The Marx-Engels Reader,* 2d ed. (New York: W. W. Norton, 1978), pp. 319–322.

modities, it stands on its head, and evolves out of its wooden brain grotesque ideas, far more wonderful than "table-turning" ever was.

The mystical character of commodities does not originate, therefore, in their use-value. Just as little does it proceed from the nature of the determining factors of value. For, in the first place, however varied the useful kinds of labour, or productive activities, may be, it is a physiological fact, that they are functions of the human organism, and that each such function, whatever may be its nature or form, is essentially the expenditure of human brain, nerves, muscles, &c. Secondly, with regard to that which forms the groundwork for the quantitative determination of value, namely, the duration of that expenditure, or the quantity of labour, it is quite clear that there is a palpable difference between its quantity and quality. In all states of society, the labour-time that it costs to produce the means of subsistence, must necessarily be an object of interest to mankind, though not of equal interest in different stages of development. And lastly, from the moment that men in any way work for one another, their labour assumes a social form.

Whence, then, arises the enigmatical character of the product of labour, so soon as it assumes the form of commodities? Clearly from this form itself. The equality of all sorts of human labour is expressed objectively by their products all being equally valued; the measure of the expenditure of labour-power by the duration of that expenditure, takes the form of the quantity of value of the products of labour; and finally, the mutual relations of the producers, within which the social character of their labour affirms itself, take the form of a social relation between the products.

A commodity is therefore a mysterious thing, simply because in it the social character of men's labour appears to them as an objective character stamped upon the product of that labour; because the relation of the producers to the sum total of their own labour is presented to them as a social relation, existing not between themselves, but between the products of their labour. This is the reason why the products of labour become commodities, social things whose qualities are at the same time perceptible and imperceptible by the senses. In the same way the light from an object is perceived by us not as the subjective excitation of our optic nerve, but as the objective form of something outside the eye itself. But, in the act of seeing, there is at all events, an actual passage of light from one thing to another, from the external object to the eye. There is a physical relation between physical things. But it is different with commodities. There, the existence of the things *qua* commodities, and the value-relation between the products of labour which stamps them as commodities, have absolutely no connexion with their physical properties and with the material relations arising therefrom. There it is a definite social relation between men, that assumes, in their eyes, the fantastic form of a relation between things. In order, therefore, to find an analogy, we must have recourse to the mist-enveloped regions of the religious world. In that world the productions of the human brain appear as independent beings endowed with life, and entering into relation both with one another and the human race. So it is in the world of commodities with the products of men's hands. This I call the Fetishism which attaches itself to the products of labour, so soon as they are produced as commodities, and which is therefore inseparable from the production of commodities.

This Fetishism of commodities has its origin, as the foregoing analysis has already shown, in the peculiar social character of the labour that produces them.

As a general rule, articles of utility become commodities, only because they are products of the labour of private individuals or groups of individuals who carry on their work independently of each other. The sum total of the labour of all these private individuals forms the aggregate labour of society. Since the producers do not come into social contact with each other until they exchange their products, the specific social character of each producer's labour does not show itself except in the act of exchange. In other words, the labour of the individual asserts itself as a part of the labour of society, only by means of the relations which the act of exchange establishes directly between the products, and indirectly, through them, between the producers. To the latter, therefore, the relations connecting the labour of one individual with that of the rest appear, not as direct social relations between individuals at work, but as what they really are, material relations between persons and social relations between things. It is only by being exchanged that the products of labour acquire, as values, one uniform social status, distinct from their varied forms of existence as objects of utility. This division of a product into a useful things and a value becomes practically important, only when exchange has acquired such an extension that useful articles are produced for the purpose of being exchanged, and their character as values has therefore to be taken into account, beforehand, during production. From this moment the labour of the individual producer acquires socially a two-fold character. On the one hand, it must, as a definite useful kind of labour, satisfy a definite social want, and thus hold its place as part and parcel of the collective labour of all, as a branch of a social division of labour that has sprung up spontaneously. On the other hand, it can satisfy the manifold wants of the individual producer himself, only in so far as the mutual exchangeability of all kinds of useful private labour is an established social fact, and therefore the private useful labour of each producer ranks on an equality with that of all others. The equalisation of the most different kinds of labour can be the result only of an abstraction from their inequalities, or of reducing them to their common denominator, viz., expenditure of human labour-power or human labour in the abstract. The two-fold social character of the labour of the individual appears to him, when reflected in his brain, only under those forms which are impressed upon that labour in every-day practice by the exchange of products. In this way, the character that his own labour possesses of being socially useful takes the form of the condition, that the product must be not only useful, but useful for others, and the social character that his particular labour has of being the equal of all other particular kinds of labour, takes the form that all the physically different articles that are the products of labour, have one common quality, viz., that of having value.❖

Labour-Power and Capital
Karl Marx (1867)

The change of value that occurs in the case of money intended to be converted into capital, cannot take place in the money itself, since in its function of means of purchase and of payment, it does no more than realise the price of the commodity it buys or pays for; and, as hard cash, it is value petrified, never varying. Just as little can it originate in the second act of circulation, the re-sale of the commodity, which does not more than transform the article from its bodily form back again into its

Excerpt from "Capital, Vol. I," in Robert C. Tucker, ed., The Marx-Engels Reader, 2d ed. (New York: W. W. Norton, 1978), pp. 336–343.

money-form. The change must, therefore, take place in the commodity bought by the first act, M—C, but not in its value, for equivalents are exchanged, and the commodity is paid for at its full value. We are, therefore, forced to the conclusion that the change originates in the use-value, as such, of the commodity, *i.e.*, in its consumption. In order to be able to extract value from the consumption of a commodity, our friend, Moneybags, must be so lucky as to find, within the sphere of circulation, in the market, a commodity, whose use-value possesses the peculiar property of being a source of value, whose actual consumption, therefore, is itself an embodiment of labour, and consequently, a creation of value. The possessor of money does find on the market such a special commodity in capacity for labour or labour-power.

By labour-power or capacity for labour is to be understood the aggregate of those mental and physical capabilities existing in a human being, which he exercises whenever he produces a use-value of any description.

But in order that our owner of money may be able to find labour-power offered for sale as a commodity, various conditions must first be fulfilled. The exchange of commodities of itself implies no other relations of dependence than those which result from its own nature. On this assumption, labour-power can appear upon the market as a commodity, only if, and so far as, its possessor, the individual whose labour-power it is, offers it for sale, or sells it, as a commodity. In order that he may be able to do this, he must have it at his disposal, must be the untrammelled owner of his capacity for labour, *i.e.*, of his person. He and the owner of money meet in the market, and deal with each other as on the basis of equal rights, with this difference alone, that one is buyer, the other seller; both, therefore, equal in the eyes of the law. The continuance of this relation demands that the owner of the labour-power should sell it only for a definite period, for if he were to sell it rump and stump, once for all, he would be selling himself, converting himself from a free man into a slave, from an owner of a commodity into a commodity. He must constantly look upon his labour-power as his own property, his own commodity, and this he can only do by placing it at the disposal of the buyer temporarily, for a definite period of time. By this means alone can he avoid renouncing his rights of ownership over it.

The second essential condition to the owner of money finding labour-power in the market as a commodity is this—that the labourer instead of being in the position to sell commodities in which his labour is incorporated, must be obliged to offer for sale as a commodity that very labour-power, which exists only in his living self.

In order that a man may be able to sell commodities other than labour-power, he must of course have the means of production, as raw material, implements, &c. No boots can be made without leather. He requires also the means of subsistence. Nobody—not even "a musician of the future"—can live upon future products, or upon use-values in an unfinished state; and ever since the first moment of his appearance on the world's stage, man always has been, and must still be a consumer, both before and while he is producing. In a society where all products assume the form of commodities, these commodities must be sold after they have been produced, it is only after their sale that they can serve in satisfying the requirements of their producer. The time necessary for their sale is superadded to that necessary for their production.

For the conversion of his money into capital, therefore, the owner of money must meet in the market with the free labourer, free in the double sense, that as a free man he can dispose of his labour-power as his own commodity, and that on the other hand he has no other commodity for sale, is short of everything necessary for the realisation of his labour-power.

The question why this free labourer confronts him in the market, has no interest for the owner of money, who regards the labour-market as a branch of the general market for commodities. And for the present it interests us just as little. We cling to the fact theoretically, as he does practically. One thing, however, is clear—Nature does not produce on the one side owners of money or commodities, and on the other men possessing nothing but their own labour-power. This relation has no natural basis, neither is its social basis one that is common to all historical periods. It is clearly the result of a past historical development, the product of many economic revolutions, of the extinction of a whole series of older forms of social production.

So, too, the economic categories, already discussed by us, bear the stamp of history. Definite historical conditions are necessary that a product may become a commodity. It must not be produced as the immediate means of subsistence of the producer himself. Had we gone further, and inquired under what circumstances all, or even the majority of products take the form of commodities, we should have found that this can only happen with production of a very specific kind, capitalist production. Such an inquiry, however, would have been foreign to the analysis of commodities. Production and circulation of commodities can take place, although the great mass of the objects produced are intended for the immediate requirements of their producers, are not turned into commodities, and consequently social production is not yet by a long way dominated in its length and breadth by exchange-value. The appearance of products as commodities pre-supposes such a development of the social division of labour, that the separation of use-value from exchange-value, a separation which first begins with barter, must already have been completed. But such a degree of development is common to many forms of society, which in other respects present the most varying historical features. On the other hand, if we consider money, its existence implies a definite stage in the exchange of commodities. The particular functions of money which it performs, either as the mere equivalent of commodities, or as means of circulation, or means of payment, as hoard or as universal money, point, according to the extent and relative preponderance of the one function or the other, to very different stages in the process of social production. Yet we know by experience that a circulation of commodities relatively primitive, suffices for the production of all these forms. Otherwise with capital. The historical conditions of its existence are by no means given with the mere circulation of money and commodities. It can spring into life, only when the owner of the means of production and subsistence meets in the market with the free labourer selling his labour-power. And this one historical condition comprises a world's history. Capital, therefore, announces from its first appearance a new epoch in the process of social production.

We must now examine more closely this peculiar commodity, labour-power. Like all others it has a value. How is that value determined?

The value of labour-power is determined, as in the case of every other commodity, by the labour-time necessary for the production, and consequently also the reproduction, of this special article. So far as it has value, it represents no more than a definite quantity of the average labour of society incorporated in it. Labour-power exists only as a capacity, or power of the living individual. Its production consequently pre-supposes his existence. Given the individual, the production of labour-power consists in his reproduction of himself or his maintenance. For his maintenance he requires a given quantity of the means of subsistence. Therefore the labour-time requisite for the production of labour-power reduces itself to that necessary for the production of those means of subsistence; in other words, the value of labour-power is the value of the means of subsistence necessary for the maintenance of the labourer. Labour-power, however, becomes a reality only by its exercise; it sets itself in action only by working. But thereby a definite quantity of human muscle, nerve, brain, &c., is wasted, and these require to be restored. This increased expenditure demands a larger income. If the owner of labour-power works to-day, to-morrow he must again be able to repeat the same process in the same conditions as regards health and strength. His means of subsistence must therefore be sufficient to maintain him in his normal state as a labouring individual. His natural wants, such as food, clothing, fuel, and housing, vary according to the climatic and other physical conditions of his country. On the other hand, the number and extent of his so-called necessary wants, as also the modes of satisfying them, are themselves the product of historical development, and depend therefore to a great extent on the degree of civilization of a country, more particularly on the conditions under which, and consequently on the habits and degree of comfort in which, the class of free labourers has been formed. In contradistinction therefore to the case of other commodities, there enters into the determination of the value of labour-power a historical and moral element. Nevertheless, in a given country, at a given period, the average quantity of the means of subsistence necessary for the labourer is practically known.

The owner of labour-power is mortal. If then his appearance in the market is to be continuous, and the continuous conversion of money into capital assumes this, the seller of labour-power must perpetuate himself, "in the way that every living individual perpetuates himself, by procreation." The labour-power withdrawn from the market by wear and tear and death, must be continually replaced by, at the very least, an equal amount of fresh labour-power. Hence the sum of the means of subsistence necessary for the production of labour-power must include the means necessary for the labourer's substitutes, *i.e.*, his children, in order that this race of peculiar commodity-owners may perpetuate its appearance in the market.

In order to modify the human organism, so that it may acquire skill and handiness in a given branch of industry, and become labour-power of a special kind, a special education or training is requisite, and this, on its part, costs an equivalent in commodities of a greater or less amount. This amount varies according to the more or less complicated character of the labour-power. The expenses of this education (excessively small in the case of ordinary labour-power), enter pro tanto into the total value spent in its production.

The value of labour-power resolves itself into the value of a definite quantity of the means of subsistence. It therefore varies with the value of these means or with the quantity of labour requisite for their production.

Some of the means of subsistence, such as food and fuel, are consumed daily, and a fresh supply must be provided daily. Other such as clothes and furniture last for longer periods and require to be replaced only at longer intervals. One article must be bought or paid for daily, another weekly, another quarterly, and so on. But in whatever way the sum total of these outlays may be spread over the year, they must be covered by the average income, taking one day with another. If the total of the commodities required daily for the production of labour-power = A, and those required weekly = B, and those required quarterly = C, and so on, the daily average of these commodities = $(365A + 52B + 4C + \&c.)/365$. Suppose that in this mass of commodities requisite for the average day there are embodied six hours of social labour, then there is incorporated daily in labour-power half a day's average social labour, in other words, half a day's labour is requisite for the daily production of labour-power. This quantity of labour forms the value of a day's labour-power or the value of the labour-power daily reproduced. If half a day's average social labour is incorporated in three shillings, then three shillings is the price corresponding to the value of a day's labour-power. If its owner therefore offers it for sale at three shillings a day, its selling price is equal to its value, and according to our supposition, our friend Moneybags, who is intent upon converting his three shillings into capital, pays this value.

The minimum limit of the value of labour-power is determined by the value of the commodities, without the daily supply of which the labourer cannot renew his vital energy, consequently by the value of those means of subsistence that are physically indispensable. If the price of labour-power fall to this minimum, it falls below its value, since under such circumstances it can be maintained and developed only in a crippled state. But the value of every commodity is determined by the labour time requisite to turn it out so as to be normal quality.

It is a very cheap sort of sentimentality which declares this method of determining the value of labour-power, a method prescribed by the very nature of the case, to be a brutal method, and which wails with Rossi that, "To comprehend capacity for labour (*puissance de travail*) at the same time that we make abstraction from the means of subsistence of the labourers during the process of production, is to comprehend a phantom (*être de raison*). When we speak of labour, or capacity for labour, we speak at the same time of the labourer and his means of subsistence, of labourer and wages." When we speak of capacity for labour, we do not speak of labour, any more than when we speak of capacity for digestion, we speak of digestion. The latter process requires something more than a good stomach. When we speak of capacity for labour, we do not abstract from the necessary means of subsistence. On the contrary, their value is expressed in its value. If his capacity for labour remains unsold, the labourer derives no benefit from it, but rather he will feel it to be a cruel nature-imposed necessity that this capacity has cost for its production a definite amount of the means of subsistence and that it will continue to do so for its reproduction. He will then agree with Sismondi: "that capacity for labour . . . is nothing unless it is sold."

One consequence of the peculiar nature of labour-power as a commodity is, that its use-value does not, on the conclusion of the contract between the buyer and seller, immediately pass into the hands of the former. Its value, like that of every other commodity, is already fixed before it goes into circulation, since a definite quantity of social labour has been spent upon it; but its use-value consists in the subsequent exercise of its force. The alienation of labour-power and its actual appropriation by the buyer, its employment as a use-value, are separated by an interval of time. But in those cases in which the formal alienation by sale of the use-value of a commodity is not simultaneous with its actual delivery to the buyer, the money of the latter usually functions as means of payment. In every country in which the capitalist mode of production reigns, it is the custom not to pay for labour-power before it has been exercised for the period fixed by the contract, as for example, the end of each week. In all cases, therefore, the use-value of the labour-power is advanced to the capitalist: the labourer allows the buyer to consume it before he receives payment of the price; he everywhere gives credit to the capitalist. That this credit is no mere fiction, is shown not only by the occasional loss of wages on the bankruptcy of the capitalist, but also by a series of more enduring consequences. Nevertheless, whether money serves as means of purchase or as a means of payment, this makes no alteration in the nature of the exchange of commodities. The price of the labour-power is fixed by the contract, although it is not realised till later, like the rent of a house. The labour-power is sold, although it is only paid for at a later period. It will, therefore, be useful, for a clear comprehension of the relation of the parties, to assume provisionally, that the possessor of labour-power, on the occasion of each sale, immediately receives the price stipulated to be paid for it.

We now know how the value paid by the purchaser to the possessor of the peculiar commodity, labour-power, is determined. The use-value which the former gets in exchange, manifests itself only in the actual usufruct, in the consumption of the labour-power. The money-owner buys everything necessary for this purpose, such as raw material, in the market, and pays for it at its full value. The consumption of labour-power is at one and the same time the production of commodities and of surplus-value. The consumption of labour-power is completed, as in the case of every other commodity, outside the limits of the market or of the sphere of circulation. Accompanied by Mr. Moneybags and by the possessor of labour-power, we therefore take leave for a time of this noisy sphere, where everything takes place on the surface and in view of all men, and follow them both into the hidden abode of production, on whose threshold there stares us in the face "No admittance except on business." Here we shall see, not only how capital produces, but how capital is produced. We shall at last force the secret of profit making.

This sphere that we are deserting, within whose boundaries the sale and purchase of labour-power goes on, is in fact a very Eden of the innate rights of man. There alone rule Freedom, Equality, Property and Bentham. Freedom, because both buyer and seller of a commodity, say of labour-power, are constrained only by their own free will. They contract as free agents, and the agreement they come to, is but the form in which they give legal expression to their common will. Equality, because each enters into relation with the other, as with a simple owner of commodities, and they exchange equivalent for equivalent. Property, because each disposes only of what is his own. And Bentham, because each looks only to himself. The only force that brings them together and puts them in relation with each other, is the selfishness, the gain and the private interests of each. Each looks to himself only, and no one troubles himself about the rest, and just because they do so, do they all, in accordance with the preestablished harmony of things, or under the auspices of an all-shrewd providence, work together to their mutual advantage, for the common weal and in the interest of all.❖

The Patriarchal Family

Friedrich Engels (1884)

The pairing family, itself too weak and unstable to make an independent household necessary, or even desirable, did not by any means dissolve the communistic household transmitted from earlier times. But the communistic household implies the supremacy of women in the house, just as the exclusive recognition of a natural mother, because of the impossibility of determining the natural father with certainty, signifies high esteem for the women, that is, for the mothers. That woman was the slave of man at the commencement of society is one of the most absurd notions that have come

Excerpt from "The Origin of Family, Private Property, and State," in Robert C. Tucker, ed., *The Marx-Engels Reader*, 2d ed. (New York: W. W. Norton, 1978), pp. 735–736, 757–758.

down to us from the period of Enlightenment of the eighteenth century. Woman occupied not only a free but also a highly respected position among all savages and all barbarians of the lower and middle stages and partly even of the upper stage. Let Arthur Wright, missionary for many years among the Seneca Iroquois, testify what her place still was in the pairing family: "As to their family system, when occupying the old long houses [communistic households embracing several families] . . . it is probable that some one clan [gens] predominated, the women taking husbands from other clans [gentes]. . . . Usually the female portion ruled the house; the stores were in common; but woe to the luckless husband or lover who was too shiftless to do his share of the providing. No matter how many children or whatever goods he might have in the house, he might at any time be ordered to pack up his blanket and budge; and after such orders it would not be healthful for him to attempt to disobey. The house would be too hot for him; and he had to retreat to his own clan [gens]; or, as was often done, go and start a new matrimonial alliance in some other. The women were the great power among the clans [gentes], as everywhere else. They did not hesitate, when occasion required, to knock off the horns, as it was technically called, from the head of the chief and send him back to the ranks of the warriors." . . .

As wealth increased, it, on the one hand, gave the man a more important status in the family than the woman, and, on the other hand, created a stimulus to utilise this strengthened position in order to overthrow the traditional order of inheritance in favour of his children. But this was impossible as long as descent according to mother right prevailed. This had, therefore, to be overthrown, and it was overthrown; and it was not so difficult to do this as it appears to us now. For this revolution—one of the most decisive ever experienced by mankind—need not have disturbed one single living member of a gens. All the members could remain what they were previously. The simple decision sufficed that in the future the descendants of the male members should remain in the gens, but that those of the females were to be excluded from the gens and transferred to that of their father. The reckoning of descent through the female line and the right of inheritance through the mother were hereby overthrown and male lineage and right of inheritance from the father instituted. We know nothing as to how and when this revolution was effected among the civilised peoples. It falls entirely within prehistoric times. That it was actually *effected* is more than proved by the abundant traces of mother right which have been collected, especially by Bachofen. How easily it is accomplished can be seen from a whole number of Indian tribes, among whom it has only recently taken place and is still proceeding, partly under the influence of increasing wealth and changed methods of life (transplantation from the forests to the prairies), and partly under the moral influence of civilisation and the missionaries. Of eight Missouri tribes, six have male and two still retain the female lineage and female inheritance line. Among the Shawnees, Miamis and Delawares it has become the custom to transfer the children to the father's gens by giving them one of the gentile names obtaining therein, in order that they may inherit from him. "Innate human causuistry to seek to change things by changing their names! And to find loopholes for breaking through tradition within tradition itself, wherever a direct interest provided a sufficient motive!" (Marx) As a consequence, hopeless confusion arose; and matters could only be straightened out, and partly were straightened out, by the transition to father right. "This appears altogether to be the most natural transition." (Marx) As for what the experts on comparative law have to tell us regarding the ways and means by which this transition was effected among the civilised peoples of the Old World—almost mere hypotheses, of course—see M. Kovalevsky, *Outline of the Origin and Evolution of the Family and Property,* Stockholm, 1890.

The overthrow of mother right was the *world-historic defeat of the female sex.* The man seized the reins in the house also, the woman was degraded, enthralled, the slave of the man's lust, a mere instrument for breeding children. This lowered position of women, especially manifest among the Greeks of the Heroic and still more of the Classical Age, has become gradually embellished and dissembled and, in part, clothed in a milder form, but by no means abolished. . . .

Slavery was the first form of exploitation, peculiar to the world of antiquity; it was followed by serfdom in the Middle Ages, and by wage labour in modern times. These are the three great forms of servitude, characteristic of the three great epochs of civilisation; open, and, latterly, disguised slavery, are its steady companions.

The stage of commodity production, with which civilisation began, is marked economically by the introduction of 1) metal money and, thus, of money capital, interest and usury; 2) the merchants acting as middlemen between producers; 3) private ownership of land and mortgage; 4) slave labour as the prevailing form of production. The form of the family corresponding to civilisation and under it becoming the definitely prevailing form is monogamy, the supremacy of the man over the woman, and the individual family as the economic unit of society. The cohesive force of civilised society is the state, which in all typical periods is exclusively the state of the ruling class, and in all cases remains essentially a machine for keeping down the oppressed, exploited class. Other marks of civilisation are: on the one hand fixation of the contrast between town and country as the basis of the entire division of social labour; on the other hand, the introduction of wills, by which the property holder is able to dispose of his property even after his death. This institution, which was a direct blow at the old gentile constitution, was unknown in Athens until the time of Solon; in Rome it was introduced very early, but we do not know when. Among the Germans it was introduced by the priests in order that the good honest German might without hindrance bequeath his property to the Church.

With this constitution as its foundation civilisation has accomplished things with which the old gentile society was totally unable to cope. But it accomplished them by playing on the most sordid instincts and passions of man, and by developing them at the expense of all his other faculties. Naked greed has been the moving spirit of civilisation from the first day of its existence to the present time; wealth, more wealth and wealth again; wealth, not of society, but of this shabby individual was its sole and determining aim. If, in the pursuit of this aim, the increasing development of science and repeated periods of the fullest blooming of art fell into its lap, it was only because without them the ample present-day achievements in the accumulation of wealth would have been impossible.

Since the exploitation of one class by another is the basis of civilisation, its whole development moves in a continuous contradiction. Every advance in production is at the same time a retrogression in the condition of the oppressed class, that is, of the great majority. What is a boon for the one is necessarily a bane for the other; each new emancipation of one class always means a new oppression of another class. The most striking proof of this is furnished by the introduction of machinery, the effects of which are well known today. And while among barbarians, as we have seen, hardly any distinction could be made between rights and duties, civilisation makes the difference and antithesis between these two plain even to the dullest mind by assigning to one class pretty nearly all the rights and to the other class pretty nearly all the duties.

But this is not as it ought to be. What is good for the ruling class should be good for the whole of the society with which the ruling class identifies itself. Therefore, the more civilisation advances, the more it is compelled to cover the ills it necessarily creates with the cloak of love, to embellish them, or to deny their existence; in short, to introduce conventional hypocrisy—unknown both in previous forms of society and even in the earliest stages of civilisation—that culminates in the declaration: The exploiting class exploits the oppressed class solely and exclusively in the interest of the exploited class itself; and if the latter fails to appreciate this, and even becomes rebellious, it thereby shows the basest ingratitude to its benefactors, the exploiters. ❖

Emile Durkheim (1858–1917) was born in Lorraine in rural eastern France. His father and forefathers for generations were rabbis. Though Durkheim abandoned these roots in a provincial religious community, he devoted his intellectual life to studying, teaching, and advancing the sociology of moral life. After a brilliant student career at the École Normale Supérieure in Paris, Durkheim taught in Bordeaux. In the 1890s, he wrote *Division of Labor* (his doctoral thesis), *Rules of Sociological Method,* and *Suicide.* Though *Suicide* was meant, at least in part, to illustrate Durkheim's sociological method, it was every bit as much a social theory of the disorder of modern life. Here is where he refined his famous concept *anomie,* introduced in *Division of Labor* when Durkheim first compared the moral order of traditional and modern societies. In 1902, he was called to the Sorbonne in Paris, where he founded academic sociology in France and, just as importantly, influenced the future course of French public education through his teaching. Durkheim the sociologist was also a prominent public figure in Third Republic France. His sociological vision of the moral needs of modern society formed the basis of his political contributions to his native land. Some consider his last book, *The Elementary Forms of the Religious Life* (1912), a classic source for modern cultural studies. Durkheim was just fifty-nine when he died in 1917, seemingly from the emotional effects of his son's death two years earlier.

The first selection, "Anomie and the Modern Division of Labor," is from *Notes on Occupational Groups.* Durkheim attached this essay to the second edition of *Division of Labor* to recommend stronger occupational groups, like unions, to counter the effects of anomie in modern life. The selection plainly states Durkheim's critique of modern society. "Sociology and Sociology Facts" is a defense of sociology as Durkheim understood it. The argument that social facts are things is the scientific corollary to Durkheim's moral argument that society is a reality in its own right and thus must be morally powerful in order to guide the individual. "Suicide and Modernity"—from Durkheim's brilliant statistical study, *Suicide*—reveals both the precision of his scientific mind and his deep preoccupation with the effects of anomie on the modern individual. Durkheim's studies of religion were foundations for his lifelong conviction that society itself is the source of knowledge, including scientific knowledge. In "Primitive Classifications and Social Knowledge," written with Marcel Mauss, Durkheim examined the social organization of two tribal societies (the Sioux and the Wotjobaluk) in order to show that their bizarre methods for classifying the world were, in fact, sophisticated representations of the social order they experienced and lived by. From this, he argued that logical thought, whether tribal or modern, originates in the social experience of the group. "The Cultural Logic of Collective Representations" is from the conclusion to *Elementary Forms of the Religious Life*. Durkheim's ideas on religion, knowledge, and society are an implicit attack on the arrogance of Western culture's claim that modern science contains the essential truths of human life.

Anomie and the Modern Division of Labor
Emile Durkheim (1902)

We repeatedly insist in the course of this book upon the state of juridical and moral anomie in which economic life actually is found. Indeed, in the economic order, occupational ethics exist only in the most rudimentary state. There is a professional ethic of the lawyer and the judge, the soldier and the priest, etc. But if one attempted to fix in a little more precise language the current ideas on what ought to be the relations of employer and employee, of worker and manager, of tradesmen in competition, to themselves or to the public, what indecisive formulas would be obtained! Some generalizations, without point, about the faithfulness and devotion workers of all sorts owe to those who employ them, about the moderation with which employers must use their economic advantages, a certain reprobation of all competition too openly dishonest, for all untempered exploitation of the consumer; that is about all the moral conscience of these trades contains. Moreover, most of these precepts are devoid of all juridical character, they are sanctioned only by opinion, not by law; and it is well known how indulgent opinion is concerning the manner in which these vague obligations are fulfilled. The most blameworthy acts are so often absolved by success that the boundary between what is permitted and what is prohibited, what is just and what is unjust, has nothing fixed about it, but seems susceptible to almost arbitrary change by individuals. An ethic so unprecise and inconsistent cannot constitute a discipline. The result is that all this sphere of collective life is, in large part, freed from the moderating action of regulation.

It is this anomic state that is the cause, as we shall show, of the incessantly recurrent conflicts, and the multifarious disorders of which the economic world exhibits so sad a spectacle. For, as nothing restrains the active forces and assigns them limits they are bound to respect, they tend to develop haphazardly, and come into collision with one another, battling and weakening themselves. To be sure, the strongest succeed in completely demolishing the weakest, or in subordinating them. But if the conquered, for a time, must suffer subordination under compulsion, they do not consent to it, and consequently this cannot constitute a stable equilibrium. Truces, arrived at after violence, are never anything but provisional, and satisfy no one. Human passions stop only before a moral power they respect. If all authority of this kind is wanting, the law of the strongest prevails, and latent or active, the state of war is necessarily chronic.

That such anarchy is an unhealthy phenomenon is quite evident, since it runs counter to the aim of society, which is to suppress, or at least to moderate, war among men, subordinating the law of the strongest to a higher law. To justify this chaotic state, we vainly praise its encouragement of individual liberty. Nothing is

---

Excerpt from "Notes on Occupational Groups, Preface to the Second Edition," George Simpson, trans., *The Division of Labor in Society* (New York: Free Press, 1964), pp. 1–4. Reprinted with the permission of The Free Press, a Division of Macmillan, Inc. Copyright 1933, 1964 by The Free Press.

falser than this antagonism too often presented between legal authority and individual liberty. Quite on the contrary, liberty (we mean genuine liberty, which it is society's duty to have respected) is itself the product of regulation. I can be free only to the extent that others are forbidden to profit from their physical, economic, or other superiority to the detriment of my liberty. But only social rules can prevent abuses of power. It is now known what complicated regulation is needed to assure individuals the economic independence without which their liberty is only nominal.

But what brings about the exceptional gravity of this state, nowadays particularly, is the heretofore unknown development that economic functions have experienced for about two centuries. Whereas formerly they played only a secondary role, they are now of the first importance. We are far from the time when they were disdainfully abandoned to the inferior classes. In the face of the economic, the administrative, military, and religious functions become steadily less important. Only the scientific functions seem to dispute their place, and even science has scarcely any prestige save to the extent that it can serve practical occupations, which are largely economic. That is why it can be said, with some justice, that society is, or tends to be, essentially industrial. A form of activity which has assumed such a place in social life evidently cannot remain in this unruly state without resulting in the most profound disasters. It is a notable source of general demoralization. For, precisely because the economic functions today concern the greatest number of citizens, there are a multitude of individuals whose lives are passed almost entirely in the industrial and commercial world. From this, it follows that as that world is only feebly ruled by morality, the greatest part of their existence takes place outside the moral sphere. Now, for the sentiment of duty to be fixed strongly in us, the circumstances in which we live must keep us awake. Naturally, we are not inclined to thwart and restrain ourselves; if, then, we are not invited, at each moment, to exercise this restraint without which there is no ethic, how can we learn the habit? If in the task that occupies almost all our time we follow no other rule than that of our well-understood interest, how can we learn to depend upon disinterestedness, on self-forgetfulness, on sacrifice? In this way, the absence of all economic discipline cannot fail to extend its effects beyond the economic world, and consequently weaken public morality.

But, the evil observed, what is its cause and what can be its remedy?❖

Sociology and Social Facts

Emile Durkheim (1897)

Sociology has been in vogue for some time. Today this word, little known and almost discredited a decade ago, is in common use. Representatives of the new science are increasing in number and there is something like a public feeling favorable to it. Much is expected of it. It must be confessed, however, that results up to the present time are not really proportionate to the number of publications nor the interest which they arouse. The progress of a science is proven by the progress toward solution of the problems it treats. It is said to be advancing when laws hitherto unknown are discovered, or when at least new facts are acquired modifying the formulation of these

Excerpt from "Preface," George Simpson, ed., John A. Spaulding and George Simpson, trans., *Suicide: A Study in Sociology* (New York: Free Press, 1951), pp. 3–4. Reprinted with the permission of The Free Press, a Division of Macmillan, Inc. Copyright 1951, 1979 by The Free Press.

problems even though not furnishing a final solution. Unfortunately, there is good reason why sociology does not appear in this light, and this is because the problems it proposes are not usually clear-cut. It is still in the stage of system-building and philosophical syntheses. Instead of attempting to cast light on a limited portion of the social field, it prefers brilliant generalities reflecting all sorts of questions to definite treatment of any one. Such a method may indeed momentarily satisfy public curiosity by offering it so-called illumination on all sorts of subjects, but it can achieve nothing objective. Brief studies and hasty intuitions are not enough for the discovery of the laws of so complex a reality. And, above all, such large and abrupt generalizations are not capable of any sort of proof. All that is accomplished is the occasional citation of some favorable examples illustrative of the hypothesis considered, but an illustration is not a proof. Besides, when so many various matters are dealt with, none is competently treated and only casual sources can be employed, with no means to make a critical estimate of them. Works of pure sociology are accordingly of little use to whoever insists on treating only definite questions, for most of them belong to no particular branch of research and in addition lack really authoritative documentation.

Believers in the future of the science must, of course, be anxious to put an end to this state of affairs. If it should continue, sociology would soon relapse into its old discredit and only the enemies of reason could rejoice at this. The human mind would suffer a grievous setback if this segment of reality which alone has so far denied or defied it should escape it even temporarily. There is nothing necessarily discouraging in the incompleteness of the results thus far obtained. They should arouse new efforts, not surrender. A science so recent cannot be criticized for errors and probings if it sees to it that their recurrence is avoided. Sociology should, then, renounce none of its aims; but, on the other hand, if it is to satisfy the hopes placed in it, it must try to become more than a new sort of philosophical literature. Instead of contenting himself with metaphysical reflection on social themes, the sociologist must take as the object of his research groups of facts clearly circumscribed, capable of ready definition, with definite limits, and adhere strictly to them. Such auxiliary subjects as history, ethnography and statistics are indispensable. The only danger is that their findings may never really be related to the subject he seeks to embrace; for, carefully as he may delimit this subject, it is so rich and varied that it contains inexhaustible and unsuspected tributary fields. But this is not conclusive. If he proceeds accordingly, even though his factual resources are incomplete and his formulae too narrow, he will have nevertheless performed a useful task for future continuation. Conceptions with some objective foundation are not restricted to the personality of their author. They have an impersonal quality which others may take up and pursue; they are transmissible. This makes possible some continuity in scientific labor,— continuity upon which progress depends.

It is in this spirit that the work here presented has been conceived. Suicide has been chosen as its subject, among the various subjects that we have had occasion to study in our teaching career, because few are more accurately to be defined and because it seemed to us particularly timely; its limits have even required study in a preliminary work. On the other hand, by such concentration, real laws are discoverable which demonstrate the possibility of sociology better than any dialectical argument. The ones we hope to have demonstrated will appear. Of course we must have made more than one error, must have overextended the facts observed in our inductions. But at least each proposition carries its proofs with it and we have tried to make them as numerous as possible. Most of all, we have striven in each case to separate the argument and interpretation from the facts interpreted. Thus the reader can judge what is relevant in our explanations without being confused.

Moreover, by thus restricting the research, one is by no means deprived of broad views and general insights. On the contrary, we think we have established a certain number of propositions concerning marriage, widowhood, family life, religious society, etc., which, if we are not mistaken, are more instructive than the common theories of moralists as to the nature of these conditions or institutions. There will even emerge from our study some suggestions concerning the causes of the general contemporary maladjustment being undergone by European societies and concerning remedies which may relieve it. One must not believe that a general condition can only be explained with the aid of generalities. It may appertain to specific causes which can only be determined if carefully studied through no less definite manifestations expressive of them. Suicide as it exists today is precisely one of the forms through which the collective affection from which we suffer is transmitted; thus it will aid us to understand this.

Finally, in the course of this work, but in a concrete and specific form, will appear the chief methodological problems elsewhere stated and examined by us in greater detail [in *The Rules of Sociological Method*]. Indeed, among these questions there is one to which the following work makes a contribution too important for us to fail to call it immediately to the attention of the reader.

Sociological method as we practice it rests wholly on the basic principle that social facts must be studied as things, that is, as realities external to the individual. There is no principle for which we have received more criticism; but none is more fundamental. Indubitably for sociology to be possible, it must above all have an object all its own. It must take cognizance of a reality which is not in the domain of other sciences. But if no reality exists outside of individual consciousness, it wholly lacks any material of its own. In that case, the only possible subject of observation is the mental states of the individual, since nothing else exists. That, however, is the field of psychology. From this point of view the essence of marriage, for example, or the family, or religion, consists of individual needs to which these institutions supposedly correspond: paternal affection, filial love, sexual desire, the so-called religious instinct, etc. These institutions themselves, with their varied and complex historical forms, become negligible and of little significance. Being superficial, contingent expressions of the general characteristics of the nature of the individual, they are but one of its aspects and call for no special investigation. Of course, it may occasionally be interesting to see how these eternal sentiments of humanity have been outwardly manifested at different times in history; but as all such manifestations are imperfect, not much importance may be attached to them. Indeed, in certain respects, they are better disregarded to permit more attention to the original source whence flows all their meaning and which they imperfectly reflect. On the pretext of giving the science a more solid foundation by establishing it upon the psychological constitution of the individual, it is thus robbed of the only object proper to it. *It is not realized that there can be no sociology unless societies exist, and that societies cannot exist if there are only individuals.* Moreover, this view is not the least of the causes which maintain the taste for vague generalities in sociology. How can it be important to define the concrete forms of social life, if they are thought to have only a borrowed existence?

But it seems hardly possible to us that there will not emerge, on the contrary, from every page of this book, so to speak, the impression that the individual is dominated by a moral reality greater than himself: namely, collective reality. When each people is seen to have its own suicide-rate, more constant than that of general mortality, that its growth is in accordance with a coefficient of acceleration characteristic of each society; when it appears that the variations through which it passes at different times of the day, month, year, merely reflect the rhythm of social life; and that marriage, divorce, the family, religious society, the army, etc., affect it in accordance with definite laws, some of which may even be numerically expressed—these states and institutions will no longer be regarded simply as characterless, ineffective ideological arrangements. Rather they will be felt to be real, living, active forces which, because of the way they determine the individual, prove their independence of him; which, if the individual enters as an element in the combination whence these forces ensue, at least control him once they are formed. Thus it will appear more clearly why sociology can and must be objective, since it deals with realities as definite and substantial as those of the psychologist or the biologist. ❖

Suicide and Modernity

Emile Durkheim (1897)

No living being can be happy or even exist unless his needs are sufficiently proportioned to his means. In other words, if his needs require more than can be granted, or even merely something of a different sort, they will be under continual friction and can only function painfully. Movements incapable of production without pain tend not to be reproduced. Unsatisfied tendencies atrophy, and as the impulse to live is merely the result of all the rest, it is bound to weaken as the others relax.

In the animal, at least in a normal condition, this equilibrium is established with automatic spontaneity because the animal depends on purely material conditions. All the organism needs is that the supplies of substance and energy constantly employed in the vital process should be periodically renewed by equivalent quantities; that replacement be equivalent to use. When the void created by existence in its own resources is filled, the animal, satisfied, asks nothing further. Its power of reflection is not sufficiently developed to imagine other ends than those implicit in its physical nature. On the other hand, as the work demanded of each organ itself depends on the general state of vital energy and the needs of organic equilibrium, use is regulated in turn by replacement and the balance is automatic. The limits of one are those of the other; both are fundamental to the constitution of the existence in question, which cannot exceed them.

This is not the case with man, because most of his needs are not dependent on his body or not to the same degree. Strictly speaking, we may consider that the quantity of material supplies necessary to the physical maintenance of a human life is subject to computation, though this be less exact than in the preceding case and a wider margin left for the free combinations of the will; for beyond the indispensable minimum which satisfies nature when instinctive, a more awakened reflection suggests better conditions, seemingly desirable ends craving fulfillment. Such appetites, however, admittedly sooner or later reach a limit which they cannot pass. But how deter-

Excerpt from George Simpson, ed., John A. Spaulding and George Simpson, trans., *Suicide: A Study in Sociology* (New York: Free Press, 1951), pp. 246–258. Reprinted with the permission of The Free Press, a Division of Macmillan, Inc. Copyright 1951, 1979 by The Free Press.

mine the quantity of well-being, comfort or luxury legitimately to be craved by a human being? Nothing appears in man's organic nor in his psychological constitution which sets a limit to such tendencies. The functioning of individual life does not require them to cease at one point rather than at another; the proof being that they have constantly increased since the beginnings of history, receiving more and more complete satisfaction, yet with no weakening of average health. Above all, how establish their proper variation with different conditions of life, occupations, relative importance of services, etc.? In no society are they equally satisfied in the different stages of the social hierarchy. Yet human nature is substantially the same among all men, in its essential qualities. It is not human nature which can assign the variable limits necessary to our needs. They are thus unlimited so far as they depend on the individual alone. Irrespective of any external regulatory force, our capacity for feeling is in itself an insatiable and bottomless abyss.

But if nothing external can restrain this capacity, it can only be a source of torment to itself. Unlimited desires are insatiable by definition and insatiability is rightly considered a sign of morbidity. Being unlimited, they constantly and infinitely surpass the means at their command; they cannot be quenched. Inextinguishable thirst is constantly renewed torture. It has been claimed, indeed, the human activity naturally aspires beyond assignable limits and sets itself unattainable goals. But how can such an undetermined state be any more reconciled with the conditions of mental life than with the demands of physical life? All man's pleasure in acting, moving and exerting himself implies the sense that his efforts are not in vain and that by walking he has advanced. However, one does not advance when one walks toward no goal, or—which is the same thing—when his goal is infinity. Since the distance between us and it is always the same, whatever road we take, we might as well have made the motions without progress from the spot. Even our glances behind and our feeling of pride at the distance covered can cause only deceptive satisfaction, since the remaining distance is not proportionately reduced. To pursue a goal which is by definition unattainable is to condemn oneself to a state of perpetual unhappiness. Of course, man may hope contrary to all reason, and hope has its pleasures even when unreasonable. It may sustain him for a time; but it cannot survive the repeated disappointments of experience indefinitely. What more can the future offer him than the past, since he can never reach a tenable condition nor even approach the glimpsed ideal? Thus, the more one has, the more one wants, since satisfactions received only stimulate instead of filling needs. Shall action as such be considered agreeable? First, only on condition of blindness to its uselessness. Secondly, for this pleasure to be felt and to temper and half veil the accompanying painful unrest, such unending motion must at least always be easy and unhampered. If it is interfered with only restlessness is left, with the lack of ease which it, itself, entails. But it would be a miracle if no insurmountable obstacle were never encountered. Our thread of life on these conditions is pretty thin, breakable at any instant.

To achieve any other result, the passions first must be limited. Only then can they be harmonized with the faculties and satisfied. But since the individual has no way of limiting them, this must be done by some force exterior to him. A regulative force must play the same role for moral needs which the organism plays for physical needs. This means that the force can only be moral. The awakening of conscience interrupted the state of equilibrium of the animal's dormant existence; only conscience, therefore, can furnish the means to re-establish it. Physical restraint would be ineffective; hearts cannot be touched by physio-chemical forces. So far as the appetites are not automatically restrained by physiological mechanisms, they can be halted only by a limit that they recognize as just. Men would never consent to restrict their desires if they felt justified in passing the assigned limit. But, for reasons given above, they cannot assign themselves this law of justice. So they must receive it from an authority which they respect, to which they yield spontaneously. Either directly and as a whole, or through the agency of one of its organs, society alone can play this moderating role; for it is the only moral power superior to the individual, the authority of which he accepts. It alone has the power necessary to stipulate law and to set the point beyond which the passions must not go. Finally, it alone can estimate the reward to be prospectively offered to every class of human functionary, in the name of the common interest.

As a matter of fact, at every moment of history there is a dim perception, in the moral consciousness of societies, of the respective value of different social services, the relative reward due to each, and the consequent degree of comfort appropriate on the average to workers in each occupation. The different functions are graded in public opinion and a certain coefficient of well-being assigned to each, according to its place in the hierarchy. According to accepted ideas, for example, a certain way of living is considered the upper limit to which a workman may aspire in his efforts to improve his existence, and there is another limit below which he is not willingly permitted to fall unless he has seriously demeaned himself. Both differ for city and country workers, for the domestic servant and the day-laborer, for the business clerk and the official, etc. Likewise the man of wealth is reproved if he lives the life of a poor man, but also if he seeks the refinements of luxury overmuch. Economists may protest in vain; public feeling will always be scandalized if an individual spends too much wealth for wholly superfluous use, and it even seems that this severity relaxes only in times of moral disturbance. A genuine regimen exists, therefore, although not always legally formulated, which fixes with relative precision the maximum degree of ease of living to which each social class may legitimately aspire. However, there is nothing immutable about such a scale. It changes with the increase or decrease of collective revenue and the changes occurring in the moral ideas of society. Thus what appears luxury to one period no longer does so to another; and the well-being which for long periods was granted to a class only by exception and supererogation, finally appears strictly necessary and equitable.

Under this pressure, each in his sphere vaguely realizes the extreme limit set to his ambitions and aspires to nothing beyond. At least if he respects regulations and is docile to collective authority, that is, has a wholesome moral constitution, he feels that it is not well to ask more. Thus, an end and goal are set to the passions. Truly, there is nothing rigid nor absolute about such determination. The economic ideal assigned each class of citizens is itself confined to certain limits, within which the desires have free range. But it is not infinite. This relative limitation and the moderation it involves, make men contented with their lot while stimulating them moderately to improve it; and this average contentment causes the feeling of calm, active happiness, the pleasure in existing and living which characterizes health for societies as well as for individuals. Each person is then at least, generally speaking, in harmony with his condition, and desires only what he may legitimately hope for as the normal reward of his activity. Besides, this does not condemn man to a sort of immobility. He may seek to give beauty to his life; but his attempts in this direction may fail without causing him to despair. For, loving what he has and not fixing his desire solely on what he lacks, his wishes and hopes may fail of what he has happened to aspire to, without his being wholly destitute. He has the essentials. The equilibrium of his happiness is secure because it is defined, and a few mishaps cannot disconcert him.

But it would be of little use for everyone to recognize the justice of the hierarchy of functions established by public opinion, if he did not also consider the distribution of these functions just. The workman is not in harmony with his social position if he is not convinced that he has his deserts. If he feels justified in occupying another, what he has would not satisfy him. So it is not enough for the average level of needs for each social condition to be regulated by public opinion, but another, more precise rule, must fix the way in which these conditions are open to individuals. There is no society in which such regulation does not exist. It varies with times and places. Once it regarded birth as the almost exclusive principle of social classification; today it recognizes no other inherent inequality than hereditary fortune and merit. But in all these various forms its object is unchanged. It is also only possible, everywhere, as a restriction upon individuals imposed by superior authority, that is, by collective authority. For it can be established only by requiring of one or another group of men, usually of all, sacrifices and concessions in the name of the public interest.

Some, to be sure, have thought that this moral pressure would become unnecessary if men's economic circumstances were only no longer determined by heredity. If inheritance were abolished, the argument runs, if everyone began life with equal resources and if the competitive struggle were fought out on a basis of perfect equality, no one could think its results unjust. Each would instinctively feel that things are as they should be.

Truly, the nearer this ideal equality were approached, the less social restraint will be necessary. But it is only a matter of degree. One sort of heredity will always exist, that of natural talent. Intelligence, taste, scientific, artistic, literary or industrial ability, courage and manual dexterity are gifts received by each of us at birth, as the heir to wealth receives his capital or as the nobleman formerly received his title and function. A moral discipline will therefore still be required to make those less favored by nature accept the lesser advantages which they owe to the chance of birth. Shall it be demanded that all have an equal share and that no advantage be given those more useful and deserving? But then there would have to be a discipline far stronger to make these accept a treatment merely equal to that of the mediocre and incapable.

But like the one first mentioned, this discipline can be useful only if considered just by the peoples subject to it. When it is maintained only by custom and force, peace and harmony are illusory; the spirit of unrest and discontent are latent; appetites superficially restrained are ready to revolt. This happened in Rome and Greece when the faiths underlying the old organization of the patricians and plebeians were shaken, and in our modern societies when aristocratic prejudices began to lose their old ascendancy. But this state of upheaval is exceptional; it occurs only when society is passing through some abnormal crisis. In normal conditions the collective order is regarded as just by the great majority of persons. Therefore, when we say that an authority is necessary to impose this order on individuals, we certainly do not mean that violence is the only means of establishing it. Since this regulation is meant to restrain individual passions, it must come from a power which dominates individuals; but this power must also be obeyed through respect, not fear.

It is not true, then, that human activity can be released from all restraint. Nothing in the world can enjoy such a privilege. All existence being a part of the universe is relative to the remainder; its nature and method of manifestation accordingly depend not only on itself but on other beings, who consequently restrain and regulate it. Here there are only differences of degree and form between the mineral realm and the thinking person. Man's characteristic privilege is that the bond he accepts is not physical but moral; that is, social. He is governed not by a material environment brutally imposed on him, but by a conscience superior to his own, the superiority of which he feels. Because the greater, better part of his existence transcends the body, he escapes the body's yoke, but is subject to that of society.

But when society is disturbed by some painful crisis or by beneficent but abrupt transitions, it is momentarily incapable of exercising this influence; thence come the sudden rises in the curve of suicides which we have pointed out above.

In the case of economic disasters, indeed, something like a declassification occurs which suddenly casts certain individuals into a lower state than their previous once. Then they must reduce their requirements, restrain their needs, learn greater self-control. All the advantages of social influence are lost so far as they are concerned; their moral education has to be recommenced. But society cannot adjust them instantaneously to this new life and teach them to practice the increased self-repression to which they are unaccustomed. So they are not adjusted to the condition forced on them, and its very prospect is intolerable; hence the suffering which detaches them from a reduced existence even before they have made trial of it.

It is the same if the source of the crisis is an abrupt growth of power and wealth. Then, truly, as the conditions of life are changed, the standard according to which needs were regulated can no longer remain the same; for it varies with social resources, since it largely determines the share of each class of producers. The scale is upset; but a new scale cannot be immediately improvised. Time is required for the public conscience to reclassify men and things. So long as the social forces thus freed have not regained equilibrium, their respective values are unknown and so all regulation is lacking for a time. The limits are unknown between the possible and the impossible, what is just and what is unjust, legitimate claims and hopes and those which are immoderate. Consequently, there is no restraint upon aspirations. If the disturbance is profound, it affects even the principles controlling the distribution of men among various occupations. Since the relations between various parts of society are necessarily modified, the ideas expressing these relations must change. Some particular class especially favored by the crisis is no longer resigned to its former lot, and, on the other hand, the example of its greater good fortune arouses all sorts of jealousy below and about it. Appetites, not being controlled by a public opinion become disoriented, no longer recognize the limits proper to them. Besides, they are at the same time seized by a sort of natural erethism simply by the greater intensity of public life. With increased prosperity desires increase. At the very moment when traditional rules have lost their authority, the richer prize offered these appetites stimulates them and makes them more exigent and impatient of control. The state of deregulation or anomie is thus further heightened by passions being less disciplined, precisely when they need more disciplining.

But then their very demands make fulfillment impossible. Overweening ambition always exceeds the results obtained, great as they may be, since there is no warning to pause here. Nothing gives satisfaction and all this agitation is uninterruptedly maintained without appeasement. Above all, since this race for an unattainable goal can give no other pleasure but that of the race itself, if it is one, once it is interrupted the participants are left empty-handed. At the same time the struggle grows more violent and painful, both from being less controlled and because competition is greater. All classes contend among themselves because no established classification any longer exists. Effort grows, just when it becomes less productive. How could the desire to live not be weakened under such conditions?

This explanation is confirmed by the remarkable immunity of poor countries. Poverty protects against suicide because it is a restraint in itself. No matter how one acts, desires have to depend upon resources to some extent; actual possessions are partly the criterion of those aspired to. So the less one has the less he is tempted to extend the range of his needs indefinitely. Lack of power, compelling moderation, accustoms men to it, while nothing excites envy if no one has superfluity. Wealth, on the other hand, by the power it bestows, deceives us into believing that we depend on ourselves only. Reducing the resistance we encounter from objects, it suggests the possibility of unlimited success against them. The less limited one feels, the more intolerable all limitation appears. Not without reason, therefore, have so many religions dwelt on the advantages and moral value of poverty. It is actually the best school for teaching self-restraint. Forcing us to constant self-discipline, it prepares us to accept collective discipline with equanimity, while wealth, exalting the individual, may always arouse the spirit of rebellion which is the very source of immorality. This, of course, is no reason why humanity should not improve its material condition. But though the moral danger involved in every growth of prosperity is not irremediable, it should not be forgotten.

If anomie never appeared except, as in the above instances, in intermittent spurts and acute crisis, it might cause the social suicide-rate to vary from time to time, but it would not be a regular, constant factor. In one sphere of social life, however the sphere of trade and industry—it is actually in a chronic state.

For a whole century, economic progress has mainly consisted in freeing industrial relations from all regulation. Until very recently, it was the function of a whole system of moral forces to exert this discipline. First, the influence of religion was felt alike by workers and masters, the poor and the rich. It consoled the former and taught them contentment with their lot by informing them of the providential nature of the social order, that the share of each class was assigned by God himself, and by holding out the hope for just compensation in a world to come in return for the inequalities of this world. It governed the latter, recalling that worldly interests are not man's entire lot, that they must be subordinate to other and higher interests, and that they should therefore not be pursued without rule or measure. Temporal power, in turn, restrained the scope of economic functions by its supremacy over them and by the relatively subordinate role it assigned them. Finally, within the business world proper, the occupational groups by regulating salaries, the price of products and production itself, indirectly fixed the average level of income on which needs are partially based by the very force of circumstances. However, we do not mean to propose this organization as a model. Clearly it would be inadequate to existing societies without great changes. What we stress is its existence, the fact of its useful influence, and that nothing today has come to take its place.

Actually, religion has lost most of its power. And government, instead of regulating economic life, has become its tool and servant. The most opposite schools, orthodox economists and extreme socialists, unite to reduce government to the role of a more or less passive intermediary among the various social functions. The former wish to make it simply the guardian of individual contracts; the latter leave it the task of doing the collective bookkeeping, that is, of recording the demands of consumers, transmitting them to producers, inventorying the total revenue and distributing it according to a fixed formula. But both refuse it any power to subordinate other social organs to itself and to make them converge toward one dominant aim. On both sides nations are declared to have the single or chief purpose of achieving industrial prosperity; such is the implication of the dogma of economic materialism, the basis of both apparently opposed systems. And as these theories merely express the state of opinion, industry, instead of being still regarded as a means to an end transcending itself, has become the supreme end of individuals and societies alike. Thereupon the appetites thus excited have become freed of any limiting authority. By sanctifying them, so to speak, this apotheosis of well-being has placed them above all human law. Their restraint seems like a sort of sacrilege. For this reason, even the purely utilitarian regulation of them exercised by the industrial world itself through the medium of occupational groups has been unable to persist. Ultimately, this liberation of desires has been made worse by the very development of industry and the almost infinite extension of the market. So long as the producer could gain his profits only in his immediate neighborhood, the restricted amount of possible gain could not much overexcite ambition. Now that he may assume to have almost the entire world as his customer, how could passions accept their former confinement in the face of such limitless prospects?

Such is the source of the excitement predominating in this part of society, and which has thence extended to the other parts. There, the state of crisis and anomie is constant and, so to speak, normal. From top to bottom of the ladder, greed is aroused without knowing where to find ultimate foothold. Nothing can calm it, since its goal is far beyond all it can attain. Reality seems valueless by comparison with the dreams of fevered imaginations; reality is therefore abandoned, but so too is possibility abandoned when it in turn becomes reality. A thirst arises for novelties, unfamiliar pleasures, nameless sensations, all of which lose their savor once known. Henceforth one has no strength to endure the least reverse. The whole fever subsides and the sterility of all the tumult is apparent, and it is seen that all these new sensations in their infinite quantity cannot form a solid foundation of happiness to support one during days of trial. The wise man, knowing how to enjoy achieved results without having constantly to replace them with others, finds in them an attachment to life in the hour of difficulty. But the man who has always pinned all his hopes on the future and lived with his eyes fixed upon it, has nothing in the past as a comfort against the present's afflictions, for the past was nothing to him but a series of hastily experienced stages. What blinded him to himself was his expectation always to find further on the happiness he had so far missed. Now he is stopped in his tracks; from now on nothing remains behind or ahead of him to fix his gaze upon. Weariness alone, moreover, is enough to bring disillusionment, for he cannot in the end escape the futility of an endless pursuit.

We may even wonder if this moral state is not principally what makes economic catastrophes of our day so fertile in suicides. In societies where a man is subjected to a healthy discipline, he submits more readily to the blows of chance. The necessary effort for sustaining a little more discomfort costs him relatively little, since he is used to discomfort and constraint. But when every constraint is hateful in itself, how can closer constraint not seem intolerable? There is no tendency to resignation in the feverish impatience of men's lives. When there is no other aim but to outstrip constantly the point arrived at, how painful to be thrown back! Now this very lack of organization characterizing our economic condition throws the door wide to every sort of adventure. Since imagination is hungry for novelty, and ungoverned, it

TABLE [1]   Suicides per Million Persons of Different Occupations

	Trade	Transportation	Industry	Agriculture	Liberal[a] Professions
France (1878–87)[b]	440	.....	340	240	300
Switzerland (1876)	664	1,514	577	304	558
Italy (1866–76)	277	152.6	80.4	26.7	618[c]
Prussia (1883–90)	754	.....	456	315	832
Bavaria (1884–91)	465	.....	369	153	454
Belgium (1886–90)	421	.....	160	160	100
Wurttemberg (1873–78)	273	.....	190	206	...
Saxony (1878)		341.59[d]		71.17	...

[a]When statistics distinguish several different sorts of liberal occupations, we show as a specimen the one in which the suicide-rate is highest.

[b]From 1826 to 1880 economic functions seem less affected but were occupational statistics very accurate?

[c]This figure is reached only by men of letters.

[d]Figure represents Trade, Transportation and Industry combined for Saxony.

gropes at random. Setbacks necessarily increase with risks and thus crises multiply, just when they are becoming more destructive.

Yet these dispositions are so inbred that society has grown to accept them and is accustomed to think them normal. It is everlastingly repeated that it is man's nature to be eternally dissatisfied, constantly to advance, without relief or rest, toward an indefinite goal. The longing for infinity is daily represented as a mark of moral distinction, whereas it can only appear within unregulated consciences which elevate to a rule the lack of rule from which they suffer. The doctrine of the most ruthless and swift progress has become an article of faith. But other theories appear parallel with those praising the advantages of instability, which, generalizing the situation that gives them birth, declare life evil, claim that it is richer in grief than in pleasure and that it attracts men only by false claims. Since this disorder is greatest in the economic world, it has most victims there.

Industrial and commercial functions are really among the occupations which furnish the greatest number of suicides. (see Table [1]) Almost on a level with the liberal professions, they sometimes surpass them; they are especially more afflicted than agriculture, where the old regulative forces still make their appearance felt most and where the fever of business has least penetrated. Here is best recalled what was once the general constitution of the economic order. And the divergence would be yet greater if, among the suicides of industry, employers were distinguished from workmen, for the former are probably most stricken by the state of anomie. The enormous rate of those with independent means (720 per million) sufficiently shows that the possessors of most comfort suffer most. Everything that enforces subordination attenuates the effects of this state. At least the horizon of the lower classes is limited by those above them, and for this same reason their desires are more modest. Those who have only empty space above them are almost inevitably lost in it, if no force restrains them.

Anomie, therefore, is a regular and specific factor in suicide in our modern societies; one of the springs from which the annual contingent feeds. So we have here a new type to distinguish from the others. It differs from them in its dependence, not on the way in which individuals are attached to society, but on how it regulates them. Egoistic suicide results from man's no longer finding a basis for existence in life; altruistic suicide, because this basis for existence appears to man situated beyond life itself. The third sort of suicide, the existence of which has just been shown, results from man's activity's lacking regulation and his consequent sufferings. By virtue of its origin we shall assign this last variety the name of *anomic suicide.*

Certainly, this and egoistic suicide have kindred ties. Both spring from society's insufficient presence in individuals. But the sphere of its absence is not the same in both cases. In egoistic suicide it is deficient in truly collective activity, thus depriving the latter of object and meaning. In anomic suicide, society's influence is lacking in the basically individual passions, thus leaving them without a check-rein. In spite of their relationship, therefore, the two types are independent of each other. We may offer society everything social in us, and still be unable to control our desires; one may live in an anomic state without being egoistic, and vice versa. These two sorts of suicide therefore do not draw their chief recruits from the same social environments; one has its principal field among intellectual careers, the world of thought— the other, the industrial or commercial world.❖

Primitive Classifications and Social Knowledge
Emile Durkheim and Marcel Mauss (1903)

The foregoing permits the conclusion that the Zuñi system is really a development and a complication of the Australian system. But what finally demonstrates the reality of this relationship is that it is possible to discover the intermediate stages connecting these extremes, and thus to discern how the one developed from the other.

The Omaha tribe of the Sioux, described by Dorsey, are precisely in this mixed position: the classification of things by clans is still very clear, and was formerly even clearer, but the systematic idea of regions is only in process of formation.

The tribe is divided into two moieties, each containing five clans. These clans are recruited by exclusively patrilineal descent; which is to say that totemic organization, properly speaking, and the cult of the totem are in decline. Each of these is sub-divided in its turn into sub-clans which themselves are sometimes further subdivided. Dorsey does not say that everything in the world is divided among these different groups. But if the classification is not exhaustive, and perhaps never really was, certainly it must have been very comprehensive, at least in the past. This is shown by a study of the only complete clan which has been preserved for us; this is the Chatada clan, which is part of the first moiety. We shall leave on one side other accounts which are probably mutilated, and which in any case give us the same phenomena but with a lesser degree of complication.

The meaning of the word used to designate this clan is uncertain; but we have a fairly full list of the things which are connected with it. It comprises four sub-clans, which are themselves segmented.

The first sub-clan is that of the black bear. It comprises the black bear, the raccoon, the grizzly bear, and the porcupine, which seem to be totems of the segments.

Excerpt from Rodney Needham, ed. and trans., *Primitive Classifications* (Chicago: University of Chicago Press, 1967), pp. 55–62, 81–88. Copyright 1963 by Rodney Needham.

The second is 'they who do not eat (small) birds'. Under it come: (1) hawks; (2) blackbirds, which are themselves divided into those with white heads, red heads, and yellow heads, and those with red wings; (3) grey blackbirds, or 'Thunder people', who in turn are sub-divided into meadow larks and prairie chickens; and (4) owls, themselves divided into large, medium and small.

The third sub-clan is that of the eagle; it comprises in the first place three kinds of eagle; and a fourth segment which is called 'Workers' and appears not to be related to a particular order of things.

Lastly, the fourth sub-clan is that of the turtle. It is related to the fog, which its members have the power to stop. Four particular species of the same animal are subsumed under the genus turtle.

Since we may justifiably believe that this case was not unique, and that many other clans must have possessed similar divisions and sub-divisions, it is not a bold supposition that the system of classification still to be observed among the Omaha was once more complex than it is today. Now besides this distribution of things, analogous to that reported from Australia, we can see the apparition, though in a rudimentary form, of notions of orientation.

When the tribe camps, the encampment is made in a circular form; and within this circle each particular group has a fixed place. the two moieties are respectively to the right and the left of the route followed by the tribe, the ascription of sides being made with reference to the point of departure. Within the semicircle occupied by each moiety, the clans, in their turn, are clearly localized with respect to each other, and the same is the case with the sub-clans. The places thus assigned to them depend less on their relationships to each other than on their social functions, and consequently on the nature of the things subordinate to them and over which their influence is thought to be exercised. Thus in each moiety there is a clan which stands in a special relationship to thunder and war; one is the elk clan, the other that of the Ictasandas. They are placed facing each other at the camp entrance, more ritual than real, which they guard, and it is by relation to them that the other clans are disposed, still according to the same principle. Things are thus distributed in this way within the camp at the same time as the social groups to which they are attributed. Space is shared among the clans, and among beings, events, etc. which belong to these clans. But it is clear that what is divided in this way is not cosmic space, but only the space occupied by the tribe. Clans and things are orientated, not yet according to the cardinal points, but with reference to the centre of the camp. The divisions do not correspond to the quarters properly speaking, but to ahead and behind, right and left, with respect to this central point. Moreover, these particular divisions are attributed to the clans, rather than the clans being attributed to them as is the case among the Zuñi.

In other Sioux tribes the idea of orientation becomes more distinct. Like the Omaha, the Osage Indians are divided into two moieties, one situated to the right, the other to the left; but whereas among the former the functions of the two moieties merged at certain points (we have seen that each had a clan of war and the thunder), here they are clearly distinguished. One half of the tribe is in charge of war, the other of peace. This necessarily results in a more exact localization of things. We find the same organization among the Kansa Indians. Moreover, each of the clans and sub-clans stand in a definite relation to the four cardinal points. Lastly, among the Ponka we can go still further. As among the previous tribes, the circle formed by the tribe is divided into two equal halves corresponding to the two moieties. On the other hand, each moiety comprises four clans, but these are quite naturally reducible to two pairs;

for the same characteristic element is attributed to two clans at the same time. From this results the following disposition of people and things. The circle is divided into four parts. In the first, to the left of the entrance, are two fire clans (or thunder clans); in the part situated at the back, two wind clans; in the first to the right, two water clans; and beyond, two earth clans. Each of the four elements is thus localized exactly in one of the four arcs of the total circumference. Given this, it is only necessary for the axis of this circumference to coincide with one of the two axes of the compass for clans and things to be oriented with relation to the cardinal points. And we know that in these tribes the entrance to the camp generally faces west.

But this orientation (which is partly hypothetical) remains indirect. The secondary groups of the tribe, together with everything subject to them, are situated in quarters of the camp which are more or less clearly oriented; but in not one of these cases is it reported that the clan stands in a particular relationship to any part of space in general. It is still a question of tribal space alone; so we continue to be fairly far from the Zuñi situation. To get close to this we have to leave America and return to Australia. We shall find in an Australian tribe a part of what we lack among the Sioux, which is a new and particularly decisive proof that the differences between what we have so far called the American system and the Australian system are not matters of simply local causes and are in no way irreducible.

This tribe is the Wotjobaluk, which we have already examined. It is true that Howitt, to whom we owe our information, does not say that the cardinal points play any part in the classification of things; and we have no reason at all to suspect the exactitude of his observations on this point. But as far as the clans are concerned there is no doubt at all; each of them is connected with a particular spatial region which is entirely its own. And this time it is not a question of a quarter of the camp, but of a delimited portion of the horizon in general. Each clan can thus be situated on the compass-card. The relation between the clan and its spatial region is so intimate that its members must be buried in the direction thus determined. For example, a Wartwut, hot wind, is buried 'with the head a little to the west of north, that is, in the direction from which the hot wind blows in their country.' The sun-people are buried in the direction of the sunrise, and so on for the others.

This division into spatial regions is so closely linked to the essence of the social organization of this tribe that Howitt sees it as a 'mechanical method used by the Wotjobaluk to preserve and explain a record of their classes and totems, and of their relation to those and to each other.' Two clans cannot be related without being *ipso facto* connected with two neighbouring regions in space. This is shown in Figure [1], which Howitt constructed according to statements made by a highly intelligent native. The latter, in order to describe the organization of the tribe, began by laying a stick pointing exactly to the east, since Ngaui, the sun, is the principal totem and all the others are determined in relation to it. In other words, it is the clan of the sun and the east-west orientation which must have provided the general orientation of the two moieties Krokitch and Gamutch, the former being situated above the east-west line, the other below. In fact, it can be seen from the Figure that the Gamutch moiety is situated entirely to the south, the other almost entirely to the north. A single Krokitch clan, No. 9, crosses over the east-west line, and we have every reason to believe that this anomaly is due to an error of observation or to a more or less late alteration in the original system. This would give us a moiety of the north and a moiety of the south, completely analogous to such as we have seen in other societies. The north-south line is fixed very exactly in the northern part by the pelican clan of Krokitch moiety, and in

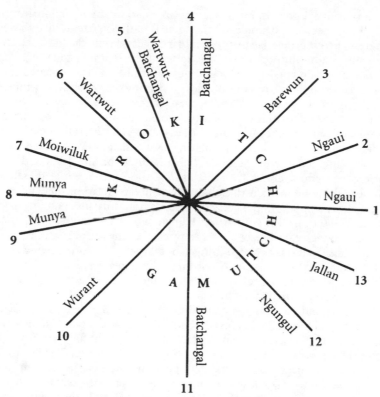

FIGURE [1] The following, so far as can be established, are the translations of the native terms designating the clans: 1 and 2 (Ngaui) mean 'sun'; 3 (Barewun), 'cave' (?); 4 and 11 (Batchangal), 'pelican'; 5 (Wartwut-Batchangal), 'hot wind-pelican'; 6 (Wartwut), 'hot wind'; 7 (Moi), 'carpet snake'; 8 and 9 (Munya), 'kangaroo' (?); 10 (Wurant), 'black cockatoo'; 12 (Ngungul), 'sea'; 13 (Jallan), 'death-adder.'

the southern part by the clan bearing the same name in Gamutch moiety. There are thus four sectors in which the other clans are located. As among the Omaha, the order in which they are arranged expresses relations of kinship between their totems. The spaces separating the clans bear the names of their primary clans, of which the others are segments. Thus clans 1 and 2 are described as 'men of the sun'; the space between them is 'wholly' of the white cockatoo. Since the white cockatoo is a synonym of the sun, as we have already shown, we may say that the whole of the sector between the east and the north is that of the sun. Similarly, the clans from 4 to 9, i.e. those going from north to west, are all segments of the pelican clan of the first moiety. It may be seen with what regularity, then, that things are oriented. . . .

Primitive classifications are therefore not singular or exceptional, having no analogy with those employed by more civilized peoples; on the contrary, they seem to be connected, with no break in continuity, to the first scientific classifications. In fact, however different they may be in certain respects from the latter, they nevertheless have all their essential characteristics. First of all, like all sophisticated classifications, they are systems of hierarchized notions. Things are not simply arranged by them in the form of isolated groups, but these groups stand in fixed relationships to each other and together form a single whole. Moreover, these systems, like those of science, have a purely speculative purpose. Their object is not to facilitate action, but to advance understanding, to make intelligible the relations which exist between things. Given certain concepts which are considered to be fundamental, the mind feels the need to connect to them the ideas which it forms about other things. Such classifications are thus intended, above all, to connect ideas, to unify knowledge; as such, they may be said without inexactitude to be scientific, and to constitute a first philosophy of nature. The Australian does not divide the universe between the totems of his tribe with a view to regulating his conduct or even to justify his practice; it is because, the idea of the totem being cardinal for him, he is under a necessity to place everything else that he knows in relation to it. We may therefore think that the conditions on which these very ancient classifications depend may have played an important part in the genesis of the classificatory function in general.

Now it results from this study that the nature of these conditions is social. Far from it being the case, as Frazer seems to think, that the social relations of men are based on logical relations between things, in reality it is the former which have provided the prototype for the latter. According to him, men were divided into clans by a pre-existing classification of things; but, quite on the contrary, they classified things because they were divided by clans.

We have seen, indeed, how these classifications were modelled on the closest and most fundamental form of social organization. This, however, is not going far enough. Society was not simply a model which classificatory thought followed; it was its own divisions which served as divisions for the system of classification. The first logical categories were social categories; the first classes of things were classes of men, into which these things were integrated. It was because men were grouped, and thought of themselves in the form of groups, that in their ideas they grouped other things, and in the beginning the two modes of grouping were merged to the point of being indistinct. Moieties were the first genera; clans, the first species. Things were thought to be integral parts of society, and it was their place in society which determined their place in nature. We may even wonder whether the schematic manner in which genera are ordinarily conceived may not have depended in part on the same influences. It is a fact of current observation that the things which they comprise are generally imagined as situated in a sort of ideational milieu, with a more or less clearly delimited spatial circumscription. It is certainly not without cause that concepts and their interrelations have so often been represented by concentric and eccentric circles, interior and exterior to each other, etc. Might it not be that this tendency to imagine purely logical groupings in a form contrasting so much with their true nature originated in the fact that at first they were conceived in the form of social groups occupying, consequently, definite positions in space? And have we not in fact seen this spatial localization of genus and species in a fairly large number of very different societies?

Not only the external form of classes, but also the relations uniting them to each other, are of social origin. It is because human groups fit one into another—the sub-clan into the clan, the clan into the moiety, the moiety into the tribe—that groups of things are ordered in the same way. Their regular diminution in span, from genus to species, species to variety, and so on, comes from the equally diminishing extent presented by social groups as one leaves the largest and oldest and approaches the more recent and the more derivative. And if the totality of things is conceived as a single system, this is because society itself is seen in the same way. It is a whole, or rather it is *the* unique whole to which everything is related. Thus logical hierarchy is only another aspect of social hierarchy, and the unity of knowledge is nothing else than the very unity of the collectivity, extended to the universe.

Furthermore, the ties which unite things of the same group or different groups to each other are themselves conceived as social ties. We recalled in the beginning that the expressions by which we refer to these relations still have a moral significance; but whereas for us they are hardly more than metaphors, originally they meant what they said. Things of the same class were really considered as relatives of the individuals of the same social group, and consequently of each other. They are of 'the same flesh,' the same family. Logical relations are thus, in a sense, domestic relations. Sometimes, too, as we have seen, they are comparable at all points with those which exist between a master and an object possessed, between a chief and his subjects. We may even wonder whether the idea of the pre-eminence of genus over species, which is so strange from a positivistic point of view, may not be seen here in its rudimentary form. Just as, for the realist, the general idea dominates the individual, so the clan totem dominates those of the sub-clans and, still more, the personal totems of individuals; and wherever the moiety has retained its original stability it has a sort of primacy over the divisions of which it is composed and the particular things which are included in them. Though he may be essentially Wartwut and partially Moiwiluk, the Wotjobaluk described by Howitt is above all a Krokitch or a Gamutch. Among the Zuñi, the animals symbolizing the six main clans are set in sovereign charge over their respective sub-clans and over creatures of all kinds which are grouped with them.

But if the foregoing has allowed us to understand how the notion of classes, linked to each other in a single system, could have been born, we still do not know what the forces were which induced men to divide things as they did between the classes. From the fact that the external form of the classification was furnished by society, it does not necessarily follow that the way in which the framework was used is due to reasons of the same origin. *A priori* it is very possible that motives of a quite different order should have determined the way in which things were connected and merged, or else, on the contrary, distinguished and opposed.

The particular conception of logical connexions which we now have permits us to reject this hypothesis. We have just seen, in fact, that they are represented in the form of familiar connexions, or as relations of economic or political subordination; so that the same sentiments which are the basis of domestic, social, and other kinds of organization have been effective in this logical division of things also. The latter are attracted or opposed to each other in the same way as men are bound by kinship or opposed in the vendetta. They are merged as members of the same family are merged by common sentiment. That some are subordinate to others is analogous in every respect to the fact that an object possessed appears inferior to its owner, and likewise the subject to his master. It is thus states of the collective mind (*âme*) which gave birth to these groupings, and these states moreover are manifestly affective. There are sentimental affinities between things as between individuals, and they are classed according to these affinities.

We thus arrive at this conclusion: it is possible to classify other things than concepts, and otherwise than in accordance with the laws of pure understanding. For in order for it to be possible for ideas to be systematically arranged for reasons of sentiment, it is necessary that they should not be pure ideas, but that they should themselves be products of sentiment. And in fact, for those who are called primitives, a species of things is not a simple object of knowledge but corresponds above all to a certain sentimental attitude. All kinds of affective elements combine in the representation made of it. Religious emotions, notably, not only give it a special tinge, but attribute to it the most essential properties of which it is constituted. Things are above all sacred or profane, pure or impure, friends or enemies, favourable or unfavourable, i.e. their most fundamental characteristics are only expressions of the way in which they affect social sensibility. The differences and resemblances which determine the fashion in which they are grouped are more affective than intellectual. This is how it happens that things change their nature, in a way, from society to society; it is because they affect the sentiments of groups differently. What is conceived in one as perfectly homogeneous is represented elsewhere as essentially heterogeneous. For us, space is formed of similar parts which are substitutable one for the other. We have seen, however, that for many peoples it is profoundly differentiated according to regions. This is because each region has its own affective value. Under the influence of diverse sentiments, it is connected with a special religious principle, and consequently it is endowed with virtues *sui generis* which distinguish it from all others. And it is this emotional value of notions which plays the preponderant part in the manner in which ideas are connected or separated. It is the dominant characteristic in classification.

It has quite often been said that man began to conceive things by relating them to himself. The above allows us to see more precisely what this anthropocentrism, which might better be called *sociocentrism,* consists of. The centre of the first schemes of nature is not the individual; it is society. It is this that is objectified, not man. Nothing shows this more clearly than the way in which the Sioux retain the whole universe, in a way, within the limits of tribal space; and we have seen how universal space itself is nothing else than the site occupied by the tribe, only indefinitely extended beyond its real limits. It is by virtue of the same mental disposition that so many peoples have placed the centre of the world, 'the navel of the earth,' in their own political or religious capital, i.e. at the place which is the centre of their moral life. Similarly, but in another order of ideas, the creative force of the universe and everything in it was first conceived as a mythical ancestor, the generator of the society.

This is how it is that the idea of a logical classification was so hard to form, as we showed at the beginning of this work. It is because a logical classification is a classification of concepts. Now a concept is the notion of a clearly determined group of things; its limits may be marked precisely. Emotion, on the contrary, is something essentially fluid and inconsistent. Its contagious influence spreads far beyond its point of origin, extending to everything about it, so that it is not possible to say where its power of propagation ends. States of an emotional nature necessarily possess the same characteristic. It is not possible to say where they begin or where they end; they lose themselves in each other, and mingle their properties in such a way that they cannot be rigorously categorized. From another point of view, in order to be able to mark out the limits of a class, it is necessary to have analysed the characteristics by which the things assembled in this class are recognized and by which they are distinguished. Now emotion is naturally refractory to analysis, or at least lends itself uneasily to it, because it is too complex. Above all when it has a collective origin it defies critical and rational examination. The pressure exerted by the group on each of its members does not permit individuals to judge freely the notions which society itself has elaborated and in which it has placed something of its personality. Such constructs are sacred for individuals. Thus the history of scientific classification is, in the last analysis, the history of the stages by which this element of social affectivity has progressively weakened, leaving more and more room for the reflective thought of individuals. But it is not the case that these remote influences which we have just studied have ceased to be felt today. They have left behind them an effect which survives and which is always present; it is the very cadre of all classification, it is the ensemble of mental habits by virtue of which we conceive things and facts in the form of co-ordinated or hierarchized groups.

This example shows what light sociology throws on the genesis, and consequently the functioning, of logical operations. What we have tried to do for classification might equally be attempted for the other functions or fundamental notions of the understanding. We have already had occasion to mention, in passing, how even ideas so abstract as those of time and space are, at each point in their history, closely connected with the corresponding social organization. The same method could help us likewise to understand the manner in which the ideas of cause, substance, and the different modes of reasoning, etc. were formed. As soon as they are posed in sociological terms, all these questions, so long debated by metaphysicians and psychologists, will at last be liberated from the tautologies in which they have languished. At least, this is a new way which deserves to be tried.❖

The Cultural Logic of Collective Representations
Emile Durkheim (1912)

The fundamental categories of thought, and consequently of science, are of religious origin. We have seen that the same is true for magic and consequently for the different processes which have issued from it. On the other hand, it has long been known that up until a relatively advanced moment of evolution, moral and legal rules have been indistinguishable from ritual prescriptions. In summing up, then, it may be said that nearly all the great social institutions have been born in religion. Now in order that these principal aspects of the collective life may have commenced by being only varied aspects of the religious life, it is obviously necessary that the religious life be the eminent form and, as it were, the concentrated expression of the whole collective life. If religion has given birth to all that is essential in society, it is because the idea of society is the soul of religion.

Religious forces are therefore human forces, moral forces. It is true that since collective sentiments can become conscious of themselves only by fixing themselves upon external objects, they have not been able to take form without adopting some of their characteristics from other things: they have thus acquired a sort of physical nature; in this way they have come to mix themselves with the life of the material world, and then have considered themselves capable of explaining what passes there. But when they are considered only from this point of view and this role, only their most superficial aspect is seen. In reality, the essential elements of which these collective sentiments are made have been borrowed by the understanding. It ordinarily seems that they should have a human character only when they are conceived under human forms; but even the most impersonal and the most anonymous are nothing else than objectified sentiments.

Excerpt from Joseph Ward Swain, trans., *The Elementary Forms of the Religious Life* (New York: Free Press, 1965), pp. 466–467, 469–472, 482–486, 488–496. Reprinted with the permission of The Free Press, a Division of Macmillan, Inc. Copyright 1965 by The Free Press.

It is only by regarding religion from this angle that it is possible to see its real significance. If we stick closely to appearances, rites often give the effect of purely manual operations: they are anointings, washings, meals. To consecrate something, it is put in contact with a source of religious energy, just as to-day a body is put in contact with a source of heat or electricity to warm or electrize it; the two processes employed are not essentially different. Thus understood, religious technique seems to be a sort of mystic mechanics. But these material manoeuvres are only the external envelope under which the mental operations are hidden. Finally, there is no question of exercising a physical constraint upon blind and, incidentally, imaginary forces, but rather of reaching individual consciousnesses of giving them a direction and of disciplining them. It is sometimes said that inferior religions are materialistic. Such an expression is inexact. All religions, even the crudest, are in a sense spiritualistic: for the powers they put in play are before all spiritual, and also their principal object is to act upon the moral life. Thus it is seen that whatever has been done in the name of religion cannot have been done in vain: for it is necessarily the society that did it, and it is humanity that has reaped the fruits. . . .

Men alone have the faculty of conceiving the ideal, of adding something to the real. Now where does this singular privilege come from? Before making it an initial fact or a mysterious virtue which escapes science, we must be sure that it does not depend upon empirically determinable conditions.

The explanation of religion which we have proposed has precisely this advantage, that it gives an answer to this question. For our definition of the sacred is that it is something added to and above the real: now the ideal answers to this same definition; we cannot explain one without explaining the other. In fact, we have seen that if collective life awakens religious thought on reaching a certain degree of intensity, it is because it brings about a state of effervescence which changes the conditions of psychic activity. Vital energies are over-excited, passions more active, sensations stronger; there are even some which are produced only at this moment. A man does not recognize himself; he feels himself transformed and consequently he transforms the environment which surrounds him. In order to account for the very particular impressions which he receives, he attributes to the things with which he is in most direct contact properties which they have not, exceptional powers and virtues which the objects of every-day experience do not possess. In a word, above the real world where his profane life passes he has placed another which, in one sense, does not exist except in thought, but to which he attributes a higher sort of dignity than to the first. Thus, from a double point of view it is an ideal world.

The formation of the ideal world is therefore not an irreducible fact which escapes science; it depends upon conditions which observation can touch; it is a natural product of social life. For a society to become conscious of itself and maintain at the necessary degree of intensity the sentiments which it thus attains, it must assemble and concentrate itself. Now this concentration brings about an exaltation of the mental life which takes form in a group of ideal conceptions where is portrayed the new life thus awakened; they correspond to this new set of psychical forces which is added to those which we have at our disposition for the daily tasks of existence. A society can neither create itself nor recreate itself without at the same time creating an ideal. This creation is not a sort of work of supererogation for it, by which it would complete itself, being already formed; it is the act by which it is periodically made and remade. Therefore when some oppose the ideal society to the real society, like two antagonists which would lead us in opposite directions, they materialize and oppose abstractions. The ideal society is not outside of the real society; it is a part of it. Far from being divided between them as between two poles which mutually repel each other, we cannot hold to one without holding to the other. For a society is not made up merely of the mass of individuals who compose it, the ground which they occupy, the things which they use and the movements which they perform, but above all is the idea which it forms of itself. It is undoubtedly true that it hesitates over the manner in which it ought to conceive itself; it feels itself drawn in divergent directions. But these conflicts which break forth are not between the ideal and reality, but between two different ideals, that of yesterday and that of to-day, that which has the authority of tradition and that which has the hope of the future. There is surely a place for investigating whence these ideals evolve; but whatever solution may be given to this problem, it still remains that all passes in the world of the ideal.

Thus the collective ideal which religion expresses is far from being due to a vague innate power of the individual, but it is rather at the school of collective life that the individual has learned to idealize. It is in assimilating the ideals elaborated by society that he has become capable of conceiving the ideal. It is society which, by leading him within its sphere of action, has made him acquire the need of raising himself above the world of experience and has at the same time furnished him with the means of conceiving another. For society has constructed this new world in constructing itself, since it is society which this expresses. Thus both with the individual and in the group, the faculty of idealizing has nothing mysterious about it. It is not a sort of luxury which a man could get along without, but a condition of his very existence. He could not be a social being, that is to say, he could not be a man, if he had not acquired it. It is true that in incarnating themselves in individuals, collective ideals tend to individualize themselves. Each understands them after his own fashion and marks them with his own stamp; he suppresses certain elements and adds others. Thus the personal ideal disengages itself from the social ideal in proportion as the individual personality develops itself and becomes an autonomous source of action. But if we wish to understand this aptitude, so singular in appearance, of living outside of reality, it is enough to connect it with the social conditions upon which it depends.

Therefore it is necessary to avoid seeing in this theory of religion a simple restatement of historical materialism: that would be misunderstanding our thought to an extreme degree. In showing that religion is something essentially social, we do not mean to say that it confines itself to translating into another language the material forms of society and its immediate vital necessities. It is true that we take it as evident that social life depends upon its material foundation and bears its mark, just as the mental life of an individual depends upon his nervous system and in fact his whole organism. But collective consciousness is something more than a mere epiphenomenon of its morphological basis, just as individual consciousness is something more than a simple efflorescence of the nervous system. In order that the former may appear, a synthesis *sui generis* of particular consciousnesses is required. Now this synthesis has the effect of disengaging a whole world of sentiments, ideas and images which, once born, obey laws all their own. They attract each other, repel each other, unite, divide themselves, and multiply, though these combinations are not commanded and necessitated by the condition of the underlying reality. The life thus brought into being even enjoys so great an independence that it sometimes indulges in manifestations with no purpose or utility of any sort, for the mere pleasure of affirming itself. We have shown that this is often precisely the case with ritual activity and mythological thought. . . .

The nature of the concept ... bespeaks its origin. If it is common to all, it is the work of the community. Since it bears the mark of no particular mind, it is clear that it was elaborated by a unique intelligence, where all others meet each other, and after a fashion, come to nourish themselves. If it has more stability than sensations or images, it is because the collective representations are more stable than the individual ones; for while an individual is conscious even of the slight changes which take place in his environment, only events of a greater gravity can succeed in affecting the mental status of a society. Every time that we are in the presence of a *type* of thought or action which is imposed uniformly upon particular wills or intelligences, this pressure exercised over the individual betrays the intervention of the group. Also, as we have already said, the concepts with which we ordinarily think are those of our vocabulary. Now it is unquestionable that language, and consequently the system of concepts which it translates, is the product of a collective elaboration. What it expresses is the manner in which society as a whole represents the facts of experience. The ideas which correspond to the diverse elements of language are thus collective representations.

Even their contents bear witness to the same fact. In fact, there are scarcely any words among those which we usually employ whose meaning does not pass, to a greater or less extent, the limits of our personal experience. Very frequently a term expresses things which we have never perceived or experiences which we have never had or of which we have never been the witnesses. Even when we know some of the objects which it concerns, it is only as particular examples that they serve to illustrate the idea which they would never have been able to form by themselves. Thus there is a great deal of knowledge condensed in the word which I never collected, and which is not individual; it even surpasses me to such an extent that I cannot even completely appropriate all its results. Which of us knows all the words of the language he speaks and the entire signification of each?

This remark enables us to determine the sense in which we mean to say that concepts are collective representations. If they belong to a whole social group, it is not because they represent the average of the corresponding individual representations; for in that case they would be poorer than the latter in intellectual content, while, as a matter of fact, they contain much that surpasses the knowledge of the average individual. They are not abstractions which have a reality only in particular consciousnesses, but they are as concrete representations as an individual could form of his own personal environment; they correspond to the way in which this very special being, society, considers the things of its own proper experience. If, as a matter of fact, the concepts are nearly always general ideas, and if they express categories and classes rather than particular objects, it is because the unique and variable characteristics of things interest society but rarely; because of its very extent, it can scarcely be affected by more than their general and permanent qualities. Therefore it is to this aspect of affairs that it gives its attention: it is a part of its nature to see things in large and under the aspect which they ordinarily have. But this generality is not necessary for them, and, in any case, even when these representations have the generic character which they ordinarily have, they are the work of society and are enriched by its experience.

That is what makes conceptual thought so valuable for us. If concepts were only general ideas, they would not enrich knowledge a great deal, for, as we have already pointed out, the general contains nothing more than the particular. But if before all else they are collective representations, they add to that which we can learn by our own personal experience all that wisdom and science which the group has accumulated in the course of centuries. Thinking by concepts is not merely seeing reality on its most general side, but it is projecting a light upon the sensation which illuminates it, penetrates it and transforms it. Conceiving something is both learning its essential elements better and also locating it in its place; for each civilization has its organized system of concepts which characterizes it. Before this scheme of ideas, the individual is in the same situation as the *voys* of Plato before the world of Ideas. He must assimilate them to himself, for he must have them to hold intercourse with others; but the assimilation is always imperfect. Each of us sees them after his own fashion. There are some which escape us completely and remain outside of our circle of vision; there are others of which we perceive certain aspects only. There are even a great many which we pervert in holding, for as they are collective by nature, they cannot become individualized without being retouched, modified, and consequently falsified. Hence comes the great trouble we have in understanding each other, and the fact that we even lie to each other without wishing to: it is because we all use the same words without giving them the same meaning.

We are now able to see what the part of society in the genesis of logical thought is. This is possible only from the moment when, above the fugitive conceptions which they owe to sensuous experience, men have succeeded in conceiving a whole world of stable ideas, the common ground of all intelligences. In fact, logical thinking is always impersonal thinking, and is also thought *sub species ternitatis*—as though for all time. Impersonality and stability are the two characteristics of truth. Now logical life evidently presupposes that men know, at least confusedly, that there is such a thing as truth, distinct from sensuous appearances. But how have they been able to arrive at this conception? We generally talk as though it should have spontaneously presented itself to them from the moment they opened their eyes upon the world. However, there is nothing in immediate experience which could suggest it; everything even contradicts it. Thus the child and the animal have no suspicion of it. History shows that it has taken centuries for it to disengage and establish itself. In our Western world, it was with the great thinkers of Greece that it first became clearly conscious of itself and of the consequences which it implies; when the discovery was made, it caused an amazement which Plato has translated into magnificent language. But if it is only at this epoch that the idea is expressed in philosophic formulae, it was necessarily pre-existent in the stage of an obscure sentiment. Philosophers have sought to elucidate this sentiment, but they have not succeeded. In order that they might reflect upon it and analyse it, it was necessary that it be given them, and that they seek to know whence it came, that is to say, in what experience it was founded. This is in collective experience. It is under the form of collective thought that impersonal thought is for the first time revealed to humanity; we cannot see by what other way this revelation could have been made. From the mere fact that society exists, there is also, outside of the individual sensations and images, a whole system of representations which enjoy marvellous properties. By means of them, men understand each other and intelligences grasp each other. They have within them a sort of force or moral ascendancy, in virtue of which they impose themselves upon individual minds. Hence the individual at least obscurely takes account of the fact that above his private ideas, there is a world of absolute ideas according to which he must shape his own; he catches a glimpse of a whole intellectual kingdom in which he participates, but which is greater than he. This is the first intuition of the realm of truth. From the moment when he first becomes conscious of these higher ideas, he sets himself to scrutinizing their nature; he asks whence these pre-eminent representations hold their prerogatives and, in so far as he believes that he has discovered their causes, he undertakes to put these causes into action for himself, in order that he may draw from them by his own force the effects which they produce; that is to say, he attributes to himself the right of making concepts. Thus the faculty of conception has individualized itself. But to understand its origins and function, it must be attached to the social conditions upon which it depends.

It may be objected that we show the concept in one of its aspects only, and that its unique role is not the assuring of a harmony among minds, but also, and to a greater extent, their harmony with the nature of things. It seems as though it had a reason for existence only on condition of being true, that is to say, objective, and as though its impersonality were only a consequence of its objectivity. It is in regard to things, thought of as adequately as possible, that minds ought to communicate. Nor do we deny that the evolution of concepts has been partially in this direction. The concept which was first held as true because it was collective tends to be no longer collective except on condition of being held as true: we demand its credentials of it before according it our confidence. But we must not lose sight of the fact that even to-day the great majority of the concepts which we use are not methodically constituted; we get them from language, that is to say, from common experience, without submitting them to any criticism. The scientifically elaborated and criticized concepts are always in the very slight minority. Also, between them and those which draw all their authority from the fact that they are collective, there are only differences of degree. A collective representation presents guarantees of objectivity by the fact that it is collective: for it is not without sufficient reason that it has been able to generalize and maintain itself with persistence. If it were out of accord with the nature of things, it would never have been able to acquire an extended and prolonged empire over intellects. At bottom, the confidence inspired by scientific concepts is due to the fact that they can be methodically controlled. But a collective representation is necessarily submitted to a control that is repeated indefinitely; the men who accept it verify it by their own experience. Therefore, it could not be wholly inadequate for its subject. It is true that it may express this by means of imperfect symbols; but scientific symbols themselves are never more than approximative. It is precisely this principle which is at the basis of the method which we follow in the study of religious phenomena: we take it as an axiom that religious beliefs, howsoever strange their appearance may be at times, contain a truth which must be discovered. . . .

Undoubtedly it will be easily understood that since they are themselves concepts, they are the work of the group. It can even be said that there are no other concepts which present to an equal degree the signs by which a collective representation is recognized. In fact, their stability and impersonality are such that they have often passed as being absolutely universal and immutable. Also, as they express the fundamental conditions for an agreement between minds, it seems evident that they have been elaborated by society.

But the problem concerning them is more complex, for they are social in another sense and, as it were, in the second degree. They not only come from society, but the things which they express are of a social nature. Not only is it society which has founded them, but their contents are the different aspects of the social being; the category of class was at first indistinct from the concept of the human group; it is the rhythm of social life which is at the basis of the category of time; the territory occupied by the society furnished the material for the category of space; it is the collective force which was the prototype of the concept of efficient force, an essential element in the category of causality. However, the categories are not made to be applied only to the social realm; they reach out to all reality. Then how is it that they have taken from society the models upon which they have been constructed?

It is because they are the pre-eminent concepts, which have a preponderating part in our knowledge. In fact, the function of the categories is to dominate and envelop all the other concepts; they are permanent moulds for the mental life. Now for them to embrace such an object, they must be founded upon a reality of equal amplitude.

Undoubtedly the relations which they express exist in an implicit way in individual consciousness. The individual lives in time, and, as we have said, he has a certain sense of temporal orientation. He is situated at a determined point in space, and it has even been held, and sustained with good reasons, that all sensations have something special about them.[1] He has a feeling of resemblances; similar representations are brought together and the new representation formed by their union has a sort of generic character. We also have the sensation of a certain regularity in the order of the succession of phenomena; even an animal is not incapable of this. However, all these relations are strictly personal for the individual who recognizes them, and consequently the notion of them which he may have can in no case go beyond his own narrow horizon. The generic images which are formed in my consciousness by the fusion of similar images represent only the objects which I have perceived directly; there is nothing there which could give me the idea of a class, that is to say, of a mould including the *whole* group of all possible objects which satisfy the same condition. Also, it would be necessary to have the idea of group in the first place, and the mere observations of our interior life could never awaken that in us. But, above all, there is no individual experience, howsoever extended and prolonged it may be, which could give a suspicion of the existence of a whole class which would embrace every single being, and to which other classes are only co-ordinated or subordinated species. This idea of *all*, which is at the basis of the classifications which we have just cited, could not have come from the individual himself, who is only a part in relation to the whole and who never attains more than an infinitesimal fraction of reality. And yet there is perhaps no other category of greater importance; for as the role of the categories is to envelop all the other concepts, the category *par excellence* would seem to be this very concept of *totality*. The theorists of knowledge ordinarily postulate it as if it came of itself, while it really surpasses the contents of each individual consciousness taken alone to an infinite degree.

For the same reasons, the space which I know by my senses, of which I am the centre and where everything is disposed in relation to me, could not be space in general, which contains all extensions and where these are co-ordinated by personal guide-lines which are common to everybody. In the same way, the concrete duration which I feel passing within me and with me could not give me the idea of time in general: the first expresses only the rhythm of my individual life; the second should correspond to the rhythm of a life which is not that of any individual in particular, but in which all participate. In the same way, finally, the regularities which I am able to conceive in the manner in which my sensations succeed one another may well have a value for me; they explain how it comes about that when I am given the first of two phenomena whose concurrence I have observed, I tend to expect the other. But this personal state of expectation could not be confounded with the conception of a universal order of succession which imposes itself upon all minds and all events.

---

[1]William James, *Principles of Psychology,* 1, p. 134.

Since the world expressed by the entire system of concepts is the one that society regards, society alone can furnish the most general notions with which it should be represented. Such an object can be embraced only by a subject which contains all the individual subjects within it. Since the universe does not exist except in so far as it is thought of, and since it is not completely thought of except by society, it takes a place in this latter; it becomes a part of society's interior life, while this is the totality, outside of which nothing exists. The concept of totality is only the abstract form of the concept of society: it is the whole which includes all things, the supreme class which embraces all other classes. Such is the final principle upon which repose all these primitive classifications where beings from every realm are placed and classified in social forms, exactly like men. But if the world is inside of society, the space which this latter occupies becomes confounded with space in general. In fact, we have seen how each thing has its assigned place in social space, and the degree to which this space in general differs from the concrete expanses which we perceive is well shown by the fact that this localization is wholly ideal and in no way resembles what it would have been if it had been dictated to us by sensuous experience alone. For the same reason, the rhythm of collective life dominates and embraces the varied rhythms of all the elementary lives from which it results; consequently the time which it expresses dominates and embraces all particular durations. It is time in general. For a long time the history of the world has been only another aspect of the history of society. The one commences with the other; the periods of the first are determined by the periods of the second. This impersonal and total duration is measured, and the guide-lines in relation to which it is divided and organized are fixed by the movements of concentration or dispersion of society; or, more generally, the periodical necessities for a collective renewal. If these critical instants are generally attached to some material phenomenon, such as the regular recurrence of such or such a star or the alternation of the seasons, it is because objective signs are necessary to make this essentially social organization intelligible to all. In the same way, finally, the causal relation, from the moment when it is collectively stated by the group, becomes independent of every individual consciousness; it rises above all particular minds and events. It is a law whose value depends upon no person. We have already shown how it is clearly thus that it seems to have originated.

Another reason explains why the constituent elements of the categories should have been taken from social life: it is because the relations which they express could not have been learned except in and through society. If they are in a sense immanent in the life of an individual, he has neither a reason nor the means for learning them, reflecting upon them and forming them into distinct ideas. In order to orient himself personally in space and to know at what moments he should satisfy his various organic needs, he has no need of making, once and for all, a conceptual representation of time and space. Many animals are able to find the road which leads to places with which they are familiar; they come back at a proper moment without knowing any of the categories; sensations are enough to direct them automatically. They would also be enough for men, if their sensations had to satisfy only individual needs. To recognize the fact that one thing resembles another which we have already experienced, it is in no way necessary that we arrange them all in groups and species: the way in which similar images call up each other and unite is enough to give the feeling of resemblance. The impression that a certain thing has already been seen or experienced implies no classification. To recognize the things which we should seek or from which we should flee, it would not be necessary to attach the effects of the two to their causes by a logical bond, if individual conveniences were the only ones in question. Purely empirical sequences and strong connections between the concrete representations would be as sure guides for the will. Not only is it true that the animal has no others, but also our own personal conduct frequently supposes nothing more. The prudent man is the one who has a very clear sensation of what must be done, but which he would ordinarily be quite incapable of stating as a general law.

It is a different matter with society. This is possible only when the individuals and things which compose it are divided into certain groups, that is to say, classified, and when these groups are classified in relation to each other. Society supposes a self-conscious organization which is nothing other than a classification. This organization of society naturally extends itself to the place which this occupies. To avoid all collisions, it is necessary that each particular group have a determined portion of space assigned to it: in other terms, it is necessary that space in general be divided, differentiated, arranged, and that these divisions and arrangements be known to everybody. On the other hand, every summons to a celebration, a hunt or a military expedition implies fixed and established dates, and consequently that a common time is agreed upon, which everybody conceives in the same fashion. Finally, the co-operation of many persons with the same end in view is possible only when they are in agreement as to the relation which exists between this end and the means of attaining it, that is to say, when the same causal relation is admitted by all the co-operators in the enterprise. It is not surprising, therefore, that social time, social space, social classes and causality should be the basis of the corresponding categories, since it is under their social forms that these different relations were first grasped with a certain clarity by the human intellect.

In summing up, then, we must say that society is not at all the illogical or a-logical, incoherent and fantastic being which it has too often been considered. Quite on the contrary, the collective consciousness is the highest form of the psychic life, since it is the consciousness of the consciousnesses. Being placed outside of and above individual and local contingencies, it sees things only in their permanent and essential aspects, which it crystallizes into communicable ideas. At the same time that it sees from above, it sees farther; at every moment of time, it embraces all known reality; that is why it alone can furnish the mind with the moulds which are applicable to the totality of things and which make it possible to think of them. It does not create these moulds artificially; it finds them within itself; it does nothing but become conscious of them. They translate the ways of being which are found in all the stages of reality but which appear in their full clarity only at the summit, because the extreme complexity of the psychic life which passes there necessitates a greater development of consciousness. Attributing social origins to logical thought is not debasing it or diminishing its value or reducing it to nothing more than a system of artificial combinations; on the contrary, it is relating it to a cause which implies it naturally. But this is not saying that the ideas elaborated in this way are at once adequate for their object. If society is something universal in relation to the individual, it is none the less an individuality itself, which has its own personal physiognomy and its idiosyncrasies; it is a particular subject and consequently particularizes whatever it thinks of. Therefore collective representations also contain subjective elements, and these must be progressively rooted out, if we are to approach reality more closely. But howsoever crude these may have been at the beginning, the fact remains that with them the germ of a new mentality was given, to which the individual could never have raised himself by his own efforts: by them the way was opened to a stable, impersonal and organized thought which then had nothing to do except to develop its nature.

Also, the causes which have determined this development do not seem to be specifically different from those which gave it its initial impulse. If logical thought tends to rid itself more and more of the subjective and personal elements which it still retains from its origin, it is not because a social life of a new sort is developing. It is this international life which has already resulted in universalizing religious beliefs. As it extends, the collective horizon enlarges; the society ceases to appear as the only whole, to become a part of a much vaster one, with indetermined frontiers, which is susceptible of advancing indefinitely. Consequently things can no longer be contained in the social moulds according to which they were primitively classified; they must be organized according to principles which are their own, so logical organization differentiates itself from the social organization and becomes autonomous. Really and truly human thought is not a primitive fact; it is the product of history; it is the ideal limit towards which we are constantly approaching, but which in all probability we shall never succeed in reaching.

Thus it is not at all true that between science on the one hand, and morals and religion on the other, there exists that sort of antinomy which has so frequently been admitted, for the two forms of human activity really come from one and the same source. Kant understood this very well, and therefore he made the speculative reason and the practical reason two different aspects of the same faculty. According to him, what makes their unity is the fact that the two are directed towards the universal. Rational thinking is thinking according to the laws which are imposed upon all reasonable beings; acting morally is conducting one's self according to those maxims which can be extended without contradiction to all wills. In other words, science and morals imply that the individual is capable of raising himself above his own peculiar point of view and of living an impersonal life. In fact, it cannot be doubted that this is a trait common to all the higher forms of thought and action. What Kant's system does not explain, however, is the origin of this sort of contradiction which is realized in man. Why is he forced to do violence to himself by leaving his individuality, and, inversely, why is the impersonal law obliged to be dissipated by incarnating itself in individuals? Is it answered that there are two antagonistic worlds in which we participate equally, the world of matter and sense on the one hand, and the world of pure and impersonal reason on the other? That is merely repeating the question in slightly different terms, for what we are trying to find out is why we must lead these two existences at the same time. Why do these two worlds, which seem to contradict each other, not remain outside of each other, and why must they mutually penetrate one another in spite of their antagonism? The only explanation which has ever been given of this singular necessity is the hypothesis of the Fall, with all the difficulties which it implies, and which need not be repeated here. On the other hand, all mystery disappears the moment that it is recognized that impersonal reason is only another name given to collective thought. For this is possible only through a group of individuals; it supposes them, and in their turn, they suppose it, for they can continue to exist only by grouping themselves together. The kingdom of ends and impersonal truths can realize itself only by the co-operation of particular wills, and the reasons for which these participate in it are the same as those for which they co-operate. In a word, there is something impersonal in us because there is something social in all of us, and since social life embraces at once both representations and practices, this impersonality naturally extends to ideas as well as to acts.

Perhaps some will be surprised to see us connect the most elevated forms of thought with society: the cause appears quite humble, in consideration of the value which we attribute to the effect. Between the world of the senses and appetites on the one hand, and that of reason and morals on the other, the distance is so considerable that the second would seem to have been able to add itself to the first only by a creative act. But attributing to society this preponderating role in the genesis of our nature is not denying this creation; for society has a creative power which no other observable being can equal. In fact, all creation, if not a mystical operation which escapes science and knowledge, is the product of a synthesis. Now if the synthesis of particular conceptions which take place in each individual consciousness are already and of themselves productive of novelties, how much more efficacious these vast synthesis of complete consciousnesses which make society must be! A society is the most powerful combination of physical and moral forces of which nature offers us an example. Nowhere else is an equal richness of different materials, carried to such a degree of concentration, to be found. Then it is not surprising that a higher life disengages itself which, by reacting upon the elements of which it is the product, raises them to a higher plane of existence and transforms them.

Thus sociology appears destined to open a new way to the science of man. Up to the present, thinkers were placed before this double alternative: either explain the superior and specific faculties of men by connecting them to the inferior forms of his being, the reason to the senses, or the mind to matter, which is equivalent to denying their uniqueness; or else attach them to some super-experimental reality which was postulated, but whose existence could be established by no observation. What put them in this difficulty was the fact that the individual passed as being the *finis natur*—the ultimate creation of nature; it seemed that there was nothing beyond him, or at least nothing that science could touch. But from the moment when it is recognized that above the individual there is society, and that this is not a nominal being created by reason, but a system of active forces, a new manner of explaining men becomes possible. To conserve his distinctive traits it is no longer necessary to put them outside experience. At least, before going to this last extremity, it would be well to see if that which surpasses the individual, though it is within him, does not come from this super-individual reality which we experience in society. To be sure, it cannot be said at present to what point these explanations may be able to reach, and whether or not they are of a nature to resolve all the problems. But it is equally impossible to mark in advance a limit beyond which they cannot go. What must be done is to try the hypothesis and submit it as methodically as possible to the control of facts. This is what we have tried to do.❖

Max Weber (1864–1920) was the ideal-type of the German university scholar. Master of several fields, Weber wrote classic works on music, economic and legal history, religion, and sociology. He was a founder of German academic sociology even though a debilitating mental breakdown ultimately forced him to abandon his own professorship. Weber's best-known book, *The Protestant Ethic and the Spirit of Capitalism,* appeared in 1905, just as he emerged from illness to enter the most productive period of his scholarly life. The book ended with his famous image of the iron cage of rationality, his most telling indictment of the dehumanizing effects of the modern world's overly rationalized social order. Today, Weber is still a source of original ideas in political theory, cultural and religious studies, and the sociologies of organizations and law, among other fields. His lasting importance as a social theorist is due, in large part, to the complexity of his thought. He sought to found a formal science that was also sensitive to subjective meaning in human life. He described the orderly evolution of capitalism and modern bureaucracy, yet he could bring to his scientific descriptions a powerful moral concern for the human spirit. In 1918, in Munich, he delivered his public lectures on *Politics as a Vocation* and *Science as a Vocation,* which together demonstrate Weber's grasp of the complex demands of the scientific life in politically troubled times. He was first and foremost a scientist, yet he was active in German public life. He died in 1920 in his fifty-sixth year, leaving his wife, Marianne, who had participated with him in the intellectual world centered in their home in Heidelberg.

"The Spirit of Capitalism and the Iron Cage" comprises two parts of Weber's *Protestant Ethic.* The "spirit of capitalism" is Weber's most famous ideal-type (a unique feature of his method). It is used here to present the ethical orientation, or disposition, of the modern capitalist. The iron cage metaphor at the end of *Protestant Ethic* is the best-known expression of Weber's doubts about the modern world, which are developed, in more technical terms, in his analysis of "The Bureaucratic Machine." The fragment "What Is Politics?" from Weber's *Politics as a Vocation,* outlines his theory of social domination, which is still used in contemporary critical theories. "Types of Legitimate Domination" illustrates the breadth of Weber's theory. Here, he touched on legal, political, and sociological insights to formulate his important theory of traditional, modern, and charismatic authority. At the same time, these selections show the extent to which his sociology attempted to solve the riddle of social life that becomes acute in the modern world: Why do people agree to obey authority? "Class, Status, Party," though difficult in places, is worth reading because it is one of Weber's most succinct attempts to supplement Marx's class analysis by demonstrating the importance of status groups, as well as political parties and class position, in determining how social power is distributed in modern societies. This selection, in particular, was an important model for C. Wright Mills's critique of post–World War II American society, *The Power Elite.*

The Spirit of Capitalism and the Iron Cage

Max Weber (1905)

In the title of this study is used the somewhat pretentious phrase, the *spirit* of capitalism. What is to be understood by it? The attempt to give anything like a definition of it brings out certain difficulties which are in the very nature of this type of investigation.

If any object can be found to which this term can be applied with any understandable meaning, it can only be an historical individual, i.e. a complex of elements associated in historical reality which we unite into a conceptual whole from the standpoint of their cultural significance.

Such an historical concept, however, since it refers in its content to a phenomenon significant for its unique individuality, cannot be defined according to the formula *genus proximum, differentia specifica,* but it must be gradually put together out of the individual parts which are taken from historical reality to make it up. Thus the final and definitive concept cannot stand at the beginning of the investigation, but must come at the end. We must, in other words, work out in the course of the discussion, as its most important result, the best conceptual formulation of what we here understand by the spirit of capitalism, that is the best from the point of view which interests us here. This point of view (the one of which we shall speak later) is, further, by no means the only possible one from which the historical phenomena we are investigating can be analysed. Other standpoints would, for this as for every historical phenomenon, yield other characteristics as the essential ones. The result is that it is by no means necessary to understand by the spirit of capitalism only what it will come to mean to *us* for the purposes of our analysis. This is a necessary result of the nature of historical concepts which attempt for their methodological purposes not to grasp historical reality in abstract general formulae, but in concrete genetic sets of relations which are inevitably of a specifically unique and individual character.

Thus, if we try to determine the object, the analysis and historical explanation of which we are attempting, it cannot be in the form of a conceptual definition, but at least in the beginning only a provisional description of what is here meant by the spirit of capitalism. Such a description is, however, indispensable in order clearly to understand the object of the investigation. For this purpose we turn to a document of that spirit which contains what we are looking for in almost classical purity, and at the same time has the advantage of being free from all direct relationship to religion, being thus, for our purposes, free of preconceptions.

> Remember, that *time* is money. He that can earn ten shillings a day by his labour, and goes abroad, or sits idle, one half of that day, though he spends but sixpence during his diversion or idleness, ought not to reckon *that* the only expense; he has really spent, or rather thrown away, five shillings besides.
>
> Remember, that *credit* is money. If a man lets his money lie in my hands after it is due, he gives me the interest, or so much as I can make of it during that time. This amounts to a considerable sum where a man has good and large credit, and makes good use of it.
>
> Remember, that money is of the prolific, generating nature. Money can beget money, and its offspring can beget more, and so on. Five shillings turned is six, turned again it is seven and threepence, and so on, till it becomes a hundred pounds. The more there is of it, the more it produces every turning, so that the profits rise quicker and quicker. He that kills a breeding-sow, destroys all her offspring to the thousandth generation. He that murders a crown, destroys all that it might have produced, even scores of pounds.
>
> Remember this saying, *The good paymaster is lord of another man's purse.* He that is known to pay punctually and exactly to the time he promises, may at any time, and on any occasion, raise all the money his friends can spare. This is sometimes of great use. After industry and frugality, nothing contributes more to the raising of a young man in the world than punctuality and justice in all his dealings; therefore never keep borrowed money an hour beyond the time you promised, lest a disappointment shut up your friend's purse for ever.
>
> The most trifling actions that affect a man's credit are to be regarded. The sound of your hammer at five in the morning, or eight at night, heard by a creditor, makes him easy six months longer; but if he sees you at a billiard-table, or hears your voice at a tavern, when you should be at work, he sends for his money the next day; demands it, before he can receive it, in a lump.
>
> It shows, besides, that you are mindful of what you owe; it makes you appear a careful as well as an honest man, and that still increases your credit.

Beware of thinking all your own that you possess, and of living accordingly. It is a mistake that many people who have credit fall into. To prevent this, keep an exact account for some time both of your expenses and your income. If you take the pains at first to mention particulars, it will have this good effect: you will discover how wonderfully small, trifling expenses mount up to large sums, and will discern what might have been, and may for the future be saved, without occasioning any great inconvenience.

For six pounds a year you may have the use of one hundred pounds, provided you are a man of known prudence and honesty.

He that spends a groat a day idly, spends idly above six pounds a year, which is the price for the use of one hundred pounds.

He that wastes idly a groat's worth of his time per day, one day with another, wastes the privilege of using one hundred pounds each day.

He that idly loses five shillings' worth of time, loses five shillings, and might as prudently throw five shillings into the sea.

He that loses five shillings, not only loses that sum, but all the advantage that might be made by turning it in dealing, which by the time that a young man becomes old, will amount to a considerable sum of money.

It is Benjamin Franklin who preaches to us in these sentences, the same which Ferdinand Kurnberger satirizes in his clever and malicious *Picture of American Culture* as the supposed confession of faith of the Yankee. That it is the spirit of capitalism which here speaks in characteristic fashion, no one will doubt, however little we may wish to claim that everything which could be understood as pertaining to that spirit is contained in it. Let us pause a moment to consider this passage, the philosophy of which Kurnberger sums up in the words, "They make tallow out of cattle and money out of men." The peculiarity of this philosophy of avarice appears to be the ideal of the honest man of recognized credit, and above all the idea of a duty of the individual toward the increase of his capital, which is assumed as an end in itself. Truly what is here preached is not simply a means of making one's way in the world, but a peculiar ethic. The infraction of its rules is treated not as foolishness but as forgetfulness of duty. That is the essence of the matter. It is not mere business astuteness, that sort of thing is common enough, it is an ethos. *This* is the quality which interests us. . . .

In fact, the *summum bonum* of this ethic, the earning of more and more money, combined with the strict avoidance of all spontaneous enjoyment of life, is above all completely devoid of any eudmonistic, not to say hedonistic, admixture. It is thought of so purely as an end in itself, that from the point of view of the happiness of, or utility to, the single individual, it appears entirely transcendental and absolutely irrational. Man is dominated by the making of money, by acquisition as the ultimate purpose of his life. Economic acquisition is no longer subordinated to man as the means for the satisfaction of his material needs. This reversal of what we should call the natural relationship, so irrational from a naive point of view, is evidently as definitely a leading principle of capitalism as it is foreign to all peoples not under capitalistic influence. At the same time it expresses a type of feeling which is closely connected with certain religious ideas. If we thus ask, *why* should "money be made out of men," Benjamin Franklin himself, although he was a colourless deist, answers in his autobiography with a quotation from the Bible, which his strict Calvinistic father drummed into him again and again in his youth: "Seest thou a man diligent in his business? He shall stand before kings" (Prov. xxii. 29). The earning of money within the modern economic order is, so long as it is done legally, the result and the expression of virtue and proficiency in a calling; and this virtue and proficiency are, as it is now not difficult to see, the real Alpha and Omega of Franklin's ethic, as expressed in the passages we have quoted, a well as in all his works without exception.

And in truth this peculiar idea, so familiar to us to-day, but in reality so little a matter of course, of one's duty in a calling, is what is most characteristic of the social ethic of capitalistic culture, and is in a sense the fundamental basis of it. It is an obligation which the individual is supposed to feel and does feel towards the content of his professional activity, no matter in what it consists, in particular no matter whether it appears on the surface as a utilization of his personal powers, or only of his material possessions (as capital)....

*   *   *

One of the fundamental elements of the spirit of modern capitalism, and not only of that but of all modern culture: rational conduct on the basis of the idea of the calling, was born—that is what this discussion has sought to demonstrate—from the spirit of Christian asceticism. One has only to re-read the passage from Franklin, quoted at the beginning of this essay, in order to see that the essential elements of the attitude which was there called the spirit of capitalism are the same as what we have just shown to be the content of the Puritan worldly asceticism, only without the religious basis, which by Franklin's time had died away. The idea that modern labour has an ascetic character is of course not new. Limitation to specialized work, with a renunciation of the Faustian universality of man which it involves, is a condition of any valuable work in the modern world; hence deeds and renunciation inevitably condition each other to-day. This fundamentally ascetic trait of middle-class life, if it attempts to be a way of life at all, and not simply the absence of any, was what Goethe wanted to teach, at the height of his wisdom, in the *Wanderjahren*, and in the end which he gave to the life of his *Faust*. For him the realization meant a renunciation, a departure from an age of full and beautiful humanity, which can no more be repeated in the course of our cultural development than can the flower of the Athenian culture of antiquity.

The Puritan wanted to work in a calling; we are forced to do so. For when asceticism was carried out of monastic cells into everyday life, and began to dominate worldly morality, it did its part in building the tremendous cosmos of the modern economic order. This order is now bound to the technical and economic conditions of machine production which to-day determine the lives of all the individuals who are born into this mechanism, not only those directly concerned with economic acquisition, with irresistible force. Perhaps it will so determine them until the last ton of fossilized coal is burnt. In Baxter's view the care for external goods should only lie on the shoulders of the "saint like a light cloak, which can be thrown aside at any moment." But fate decreed that the cloak should become an iron cage.

Since asceticism undertook to remodel the world and to work out its ideals in the world, material goods have gained an increasing and finally an inexorable power over the lives of men as at no previous period in history. To-day the spirit of religious asceticism—whether finally, who knows?—has escaped from the cage. But victorious capitalism, since it rests on mechanical foundations, needs its support no longer. The rosy blush of its laughing heir, the Enlightenment, seems also to be irretrievably fading, and the idea of duty in one's calling prowls about in our lives like the ghost of dead religious beliefs. Where the fulfilment of the calling cannot directly be related to the highest spiritual and cultural values, or when, on the other hand, it need not be felt simply as economic compulsion, the individual generally abandons the attempt to justify it at all. In the field of its highest development, in the United States, the pursuit of wealth, stripped of its religious and ethical meaning, tends to become associated with purely mundane passions, which often actually give it the character of sport.

No one knows who will live in this cage in the future, or whether at the end of this tremendous development entirely new prophets will arise, or there will be a great rebirth of old ideas and ideals, or, if neither, mechanized petrification, embellished with a sort of convulsive self-importance. For of the last stage of this cultural development, it might well be truly said: "Specialists without spirit, sensualists without heart; this nullity imagines that it has attained a level of civilization never before achieved."

But this brings us to the world of judgments of value and of faith, with which this purely historical discussion need not be burdened. The next task would be rather to show the significance of ascetic rationalism, which has only been touched in the foregoing sketch, for the content of practical social ethics, thus for the types of organization and the functions of social groups from the conventicle to the State. Then its relations to humanistic rationalism, its ideals of life and cultural influence; further to the development of philosophical and scientific empiricism, to technical development and to spiritual ideals would have to be analysed. Then its historical development from the mediaeval beginnings of worldly asceticism to its dissolution into pure utilitarianism would have to be traced out through all the areas of ascetic religion. Only then could the quantitative cultural significance of ascetic Protestantism in its relation to the other plastic elements of modern culture be estimated.

Here we have only attempted to trace the fact and the direction of its influence to their motives in one, though a very important point. But it would also further be necessary to investigate how Protestant Asceticism was in turn influenced in its development and its character by the totality of social conditions, especially economic. The modern man is in general, even with the best will, unable to give religious ideas a significance for culture and national character which they deserve. But it is, of course, not my aim to substitute for a one-sided materialistic an equally one-sided spiritualistic causal interpretation of culture and of history. Each is equally possible, but each, if it does not serve as the preparation, but as the conclusion of an investigation, accomplishes equally little in the interest of historical truth.❖

The Bureaucratic Machine

Max Weber (1909–1920)

Characteristics of Bureaucracy

Modern officialdom functions in the following specific manner:

I. There is the principle of fixed and official jurisdictional areas, which are generally ordered by rules, that is, by laws or administrative regulations.

Excerpt from "Bureaucracy" in Hans Gerth and C. Wright Mills, eds. and trans., *From Max Weber* (New York: Oxford University Press, 1946), pp. 196–198, 224–230. This selection is from *Economy and Society,* composed over many years and left uncompleted at Weber's death in 1920.

1. The regular activities required for the purposes of the bureaucratically governed structure are distributed in a fixed way as official duties.

2. The authority to give the commands required for the discharge of these duties is distributed in a stable way and is strictly delimited by rules concerning the coercive means, physical, sacerdotal, or otherwise, which may be placed at the disposal of officials.

3. Methodical provision is made for the regular and continuous fulfilment of these duties and for the execution of the corresponding rights; only persons who have the generally regulated qualifications to serve are employed.

In public and lawful government these three elements constitute 'bureaucratic authority.' In private economic domination, they constitute bureaucratic 'management.' Bureaucracy, thus understood, is fully developed in political and ecclesiastical communities only in the modern state, and, in the private economy, only in the most advanced institutions of capitalism. Permanent and public office authority, with fixed jurisdiction, is not the historical rule but rather the exception. This is so even in large political structures such as those of the ancient Orient, the Germanic and Mongolian empires of conquest, or of many feudal structures of state. In all these cases, the ruler executes the most important measures through personal trustees, table-companions, or court-servants. Their commissions and authority are not precisely delimited and are temporarily called into being for each case.

II. The principles of office hierarchy and of levels of graded authority mean a firmly ordered system of super- and subordination in which there is a supervision of the lower offices by the higher ones. Such a system offers the governed the possibility of appealing the decision of a lower office to its higher authority, in a definitely regulated manner. With the full development of the bureaucratic type, the office hierarchy is monocratically organized. The principle of hierarchical office authority is found in all bureaucratic structures: in state and ecclesiastical structures as well as in large party organizations and private enterprises. It does not matter for the character of bureaucracy whether its authority is called 'private' or 'public.'

When the principle of jurisdictional 'competency' is fully carried through, hierarchical subordination—at least in public office—does not meant that the 'higher' authority is simply authorized to take over the business of the 'lower.' Indeed, the opposite is the rule. Once established and having fulfilled its task, an office tends to continue in existence and be held by another incumbent.

III. The management of the modern office is based upon written documents ('the files'), which are preserved in their original or draught form. There is, therefore, a staff of subaltern officials and scribes of all sorts. The body of officials actively engaged in a 'public' office, along with the respective apparatus of material implements and the files, make up a 'bureau.' In private enterprise, 'the bureau' is often called 'the office.'

In principle, the modern organization of the civil service separates the bureau from the private domicile of the official, and, in general, bureaucracy segregates official activity as something distinct from the sphere of private life. Public monies and equipment are divorced from the private property of the official. This condition is everywhere the product of a long development. Nowadays, it is found in public as well as in private enterprises; in the latter, the principle extends even to the leading entrepreneur. In principle, the executive office is separated from the household, business from private correspondence, and business assets from private fortunes. The more consistently the modern type of business management has been carried through the more are these separations the case. The beginnings of this process are to be found as early as the Middle Ages.

It is the peculiarity of the modern entrepreneur that he conducts himself as the 'first official' of his enterprise, in the very same way in which the ruler of a specifically modern bureaucratic state spoke of himself as 'the first servant' of the state. The idea that the bureau activities of the state are intrinsically different in character from the management of private economic offices is a continental European notion and, by way of contrast, is totally foreign to the American way.

IV. Office management, at least all specialized office management—and such management is distinctly modern—usually presupposes thorough and expert training. This increasingly holds for the modern executive and employee of private enterprises, in the same manner as it holds for the state official.

V. When the office if fully developed, official activity demands the full working capacity of the official, irrespective of the fact that his obligatory time in the bureau may be firmly delimited. In the normal case, this is only the product of a long development, in the public as well as in the private office. Formerly, in all cases, the normal state of affairs was reversed: official business was discharged as a secondary activity.

VI. The management of the office follows general rules, which are more or less stable, more or less exhaustive, and which can be learned. Knowledge of these rules represents a special technical learning which the officials possess. It involves jurisprudence, or administrative or business management.

The reduction of modern office management to rules is deeply embedded in its very nature. The theory of modern public administration, for instance, assumes that the authority to order certain matters by decree—which has been legally granted to public authorities—does not entitle the bureau to regulate the matter by commands given for each case, but only to regulate the matter abstractly. This stands in extreme contrast to the regulation of all relationships through individual privileges and bestowals of favor, which is absolutely dominant in patrimonialism, at least in so far as such relationships are not fixed by sacred tradition. . . .

The Leveling of Social Differences

Bureaucratic organization has usually come into power on the basis of a leveling of economic and social differences. This leveling has been at least relative, and has concerned the significance of social and economic differences for the assumption of administrative functions.

Bureaucracy inevitably accompanies modern *mass democracy* in contrast to the democratic self-government of small homogeneous units. This results from the characteristic principle of bureaucracy: the abstract regularity of the execution of authority, which is a result of the demand for 'equality before the law' in the personal and functional sense—hence, of the horror of 'privilege,' and the principled rejection of doing business 'from case to case.' Such regularity also follows from the social preconditions of the origin of bureaucracies. The non-bureaucratic administration of any large social structure rests in some way upon the fact that existing social, material, or honorific preferences and ranks are connected with administrative functions and duties. This usually means that a direct or indirect economic exploitation or a 'social' exploitation of position, which every sort of administrative activity gives to its bearers, is equivalent to the assumption of administrative functions.

Bureaucratization and democratization within the administration of the state therefore signify and increase the cash expenditures of the public treasury. And this is the case in spite of the fact that bureaucratic administration is usually more 'economical' in character than other forms of administration. Until recent times—at least from the point of view of the treasury—the cheapest way of satisfying the need for administration was to leave almost the entire local administration and lower judicature to the landlords of Eastern Prussia. The same fact applies to the administration of sheriffs in England. Mass democracy makes a clean sweep of the feudal, patrimonial, and—at least in intent—the plutocratic privileges in administration. Unavoidably it puts paid professional labor in place of the historically inherited avocational administration by notables.

This not only applies to structures of the state. For it is no accident that in their own organizations, the democratic mass parties have completely broken with traditional notable rule based upon personal relationships and personal esteem. Yet such personal structures frequently continue among the old conservative as well as the old liberal parties. Democratic mass parties are bureaucratically organized under the leadership of party officials, professional party and trade union secretaries, et cetera. In Germany, for instance, this has happened in the Social Democratic party and in the agrarian mass-movement; and in England, for the first time, in the caucus democracy of Gladstone-Chamberlain, which was originally organized in Birmingham and since the 1870's has spread. In the United States, both parties since Jackson's administration have developed bureaucratically. In France, however, attempts to organize disciplined political parties on the basis of an election system that would compel bureaucratic organization have repeatedly failed. The resistance of local circles of notables against the ultimately unavoidable bureaucratization of the parties, which would encompass the entire country and break their influence, could not be overcome. Every advance of the simple election techniques, for instance the system of proportional elections, which calculates with figures, means a strict and interlocal bureaucratic organization of the parties and therewith an increasing domination of party bureaucracy and discipline, as well as the elimination of the local circles of notables—at least this holds for great states.

The progress of bureaucratization in the state administration itself is a parallel phenomenon of democracy, as is quite obvious in France, North America, and now in England. Of course one must always remember that the term 'democratization' can be misleading. The *demos* itself, in the sense of an inarticulate mass, never 'governs' larger associations; rather, it is governed, and its existence only changes the way in which the executive leaders are selected and the measure of influence which the *demos*, or better, which social circles from its midst are able to exert upon the content and the direction of administrative activities by supplementing what is called 'public opinion.' 'Democratization,' in the sense here intended, does not necessarily mean an increasingly active share of the governed in the authority of the social structure. This may be a result of democratization, but it is not necessarily the case.

We must expressly recall at this point that the political concept of democracy, deduced from the 'equal rights' of the governed, includes these postulates: (1) prevention of the development of a closed status group of officials in the interest of a universal accessibility of office, and (2) minimization of the authority of officialdom in the interest of expanding the sphere of influence of 'public opinion' as far as practicable. Hence, wherever possible, political democracy strives to shorten the term of office by election and recall and by not binding the candidate to a special expertness. Thereby democracy inevitably comes into conflict with the bureaucratic tendencies which, by its fight against notable rule, democracy has produced. The generally loose term 'democratiza-tion' cannot be used here, in so far as it is understood to mean the minimization of the civil servants' ruling power in favor of the greatest possible 'direct' rule of the *demos*, which in practice means the respective party leaders of the *demos*. The most decisive thing here—indeed it is rather exclusively so—is the *leveling of the governed* in opposi-tion to the ruling and bureaucratically articulated group, which in its turn may occupy a quite autocratic position, both in fact and in form.

In Russia, the destruction of the position of the old landed nobility through the regulation of the Mjeshtshitelstvo (rank order) and the permeation of the old nobil-ity by an office nobility were characteristic transitional phenomena in the develop-ment of bureaucracy. In China, the estimation of rank and the qualification for office according to the number of examinations passed mean something similar, but they have had consequences which, in theory at least, are still sharper. In France, the Revo-lution and still more Bonapartism have made the bureaucracy all-powerful. In the Catholic Church, first the feudal and then all independent local intermediary powers were eliminated. This was begun by Gregory VII and continued through the Council of Trent, the Vatican Council, and it was completed by the edicts of Pius X. The trans-formation of these local powers into pure functionaries of the central authority were connected with the constant increase in the factual significance of the formally quite dependent chaplains, a process which above all was based on the political party orga-nization of Catholicism. Hence this process meant an advance of bureaucracy and at the same time of 'passive democratization,' as it were, that is, the leveling of the gov-erned. The substitution of the bureaucratic army for the self-equipped army of nota-bles is everywhere a process of 'passive' democratization, in the sense in which every establishment of an absolute military monarchy in the place of a feudal state or of a republic of notables is. This has held, in principle, even for the development of the state in Egypt in spite of all the peculiarities involved. Under the Roman principate the bureaucratization of the provincial administration in the field of tax collection, for instance, went hand in hand with the elimination of the plutocracy of a capitalist class, which, under the Republic, had been all-powerful. Ancient capitalism itself was finally eliminated with this stroke.

It is obvious that almost always economic conditions of some sort play their part in such 'democratizing' developments. Very frequently we meet with the influence of an economically determined origin of new classes, whether plutocratic, petty bour-geois, or proletarian in character. Such classes may call on the aid of, or they may only call to life or recall to life, a political power, no matter whether it is of legitimate or of Caesarist stamp. They may do so in order to attain economic or social advan-tages by political assistance. On the other hand, there are equally possible and his-torically documented cases in which initiative came 'from on high' and was of a purely political nature and drew advantages from political constellations, especially in foreign affairs. Such leadership exploited economic and social antagonisms as well as class interests merely as a means for their own purpose of gaining purely po-litical power. For this reason, political authority has thrown the antagonistic classes out of their almost always unstable equilibrium and called their latent interest con-flicts into battle. It seems hardly possible to give a general statement of this.

The extent and direction of the course along which economic influences have moved, as well as the nature in which political power relations exert influence, vary widely. In Hellenic Antiquity, the transition to disciplined combat by Hoplites, and in

Athens, the increasing importance of the navy laid the foundation for the conquest of political power by the strata on whose shoulders the military burden rested. In Rome, however, the same development shook the rule of the office nobility only temporarily and seemingly. Although the modern mass army has everywhere been a means of breaking the power of notables, by itself it has in no way served as a leverage for active, but rather for merely passive, democratization. One contributing factor, however, has been the fact that the ancient citizen army rested economically upon self-equipment, whereas the modern army rests upon the bureaucratic procurement of requirements.

The advance of the bureaucratic structure rests upon 'technical' superiority. This fact leads here, as in the whole field of technique, to the following: the advance has been realized most slowly where older structural forms have been technically well developed and functionally adjusted to the requirements at hand. This was the case, for instance, in the administration of notables in England and hence England was the slowest of all countries to succumb to bureaucratization or, indeed, is still only partly in the process of doing so. The same general phenomenon exists when highly developed systems of gaslight or of steam railroads with large and fixed capital offer stronger obstacles to electrification than in completely new areas which are opened up for electrification.

The Permanent Character of the Bureaucratic Machine

Once it is fully established, bureaucracy is among those social structures which are the hardest to destroy. Bureaucracy is *the* means of carrying 'community action' over into rationally ordered 'societal action.' Therefore, as an instrument for 'societalizing' relations of power, bureaucracy has been and is a power instrument of the first order—for the one who controls the bureaucratic apparatus.

Under otherwise equal conditions, a 'societal action,' which is methodically or dered and led, is superior to every resistance of 'mass' or even of 'communal action.' And where the bureaucratization of administration has been completely carried through, a form of power relation is established that is practically unshatterable.

The individual bureaucrat cannot squirm out of the apparatus in which he is harnessed. In contrast to the honorific or avocational 'notable,' the professional bureaucrat is chained to his activity by his entire material and ideal existence. In the great majority of cases, he is only a single cog in an ever-moving mechanism which prescribes to him an essentially fixed route of march. The official is entrusted with specialized tasks and normally the mechanism cannot be put into motion or arrested by him, but only from the very top. The individual bureaucrat is thus forged to the community of all the functionaries who are integrated into the mechanism. They have a common interest in seeing that the mechanism continues its functions and that the societally exercised authority carries on.

The ruled, for their part, cannot dispense with or replace the bureaucratic apparatus of authority once it exists. For this bureaucracy rests upon expert training, a functional specialization of work, and an attitude set for habitual and virtuoso-like mastery of single yet methodically integrated functions. If the official stops working, or if his work is forcefully interrupted, chaos results, and it is difficult to improvise replacements from among the governed who are fit to master such chaos. This holds for public administration as well as for private economic management. More and more the material fate of the masses depends upon the steady and correct functioning of the increasingly bureaucratic organizations of private capitalism. The idea of eliminating these organizations becomes more and more utopian.

The discipline of officialdom refers to the attitude-set of the official for precise obedience within his *habitual* activity, in public as well as in private organizations. This discipline increasingly becomes the basis of all order, however great the practical importance of administration on the basis of the filed documents may be. The naive idea of Bakuninism of destroying the basis of 'acquired rights' and 'domination' by destroying public documents overlooks the settled orientation of *man* for keeping to the habitual rules and regulations that continue to exist independently of the documents. Every reorganization of beaten or dissolved troops, as well as the restoration of administrative orders destroyed by revolt, panic, or other catastrophes, is realized by appealing to the trained orientation of obedient compliance to such orders. Such compliance has been conditioned into the officials, on the one hand, and, on the other hand, into the governed. If such an appeal is successful it brings, as it were, the disturbed mechanism into gear again.

The objective indispensability of the once-existing apparatus, with its peculiar, 'impersonal' character, means that the mechanism—in contrast to feudal orders based upon personal piety—is easily made to work for anybody who knows how to gain control over it. A rationally ordered system of officials continues to function smoothly after the enemy has occupied the area; he merely needs to change the top officials. This body of officials continues to operate because it is to the vital interest of everyone concerned, including above all the enemy.

During the course of his long years in power, Bismarck brought his ministerial colleagues into unconditional bureaucratic dependence by eliminating all independent statesmen. Upon his retirement, he saw to his surprise that they continued to manage their offices unconcerned and undismayed, as if he had not been the master mind and creator of these creatures, but rather as if some single figure had been exchanged for some other figure in the bureaucratic machine. With all the changes of masters in France since the time of the First Empire, the power machine has remained essentially the same. Such a machine makes 'revolution,' in the sense of the forceful creation of entirely new formations of authority, technically more and more impossible, especially when the apparatus controls the modern means of communication (telegraph, et cetera) and also by virtue of its internal rationalized structure. In classic fashion, France has demonstrated how this process has substituted *coups d'état* for 'revolutions': all successful transformations in France have amounted to *coups d'état*.❖

What Is Politics?

Max Weber (1918)

This lecture, which I give at your request, will necessarily disappoint you in a number of ways. You will naturally expect me to take a position on actual problems of the day. But that will be the case only in a purely formal way and toward the end, when I shall raise certain questions concerning the significance of political action in the whole way of life. In today's lecture, all questions that refer to what policy and what content one should give one's political activity must be eliminated. For such

Excerpt from "Politics as a Vocation" in Hans Gerth and C. Wright Mills, eds. and trans., *From Max Weber* (New York: Oxford University Press, 1946), pp. 77–79.

questions have nothing to do with the general question of what politics as a vocation means and what it can mean. Now to our subject matter.

What do we understand by politics? The concept is extremely broad and comprises any kind of *independent* leadership in action. One speaks of the currency policy of the banks, of the discounting policy of the Reichsbank, of the strike policy of a trade union; one may speak of the educational policy of a municipality or a township, of the policy of the president of a voluntary association, and, finally, even of the policy of a prudent wife who seeks to guide her husband. Tonight, our reflections are, of course, not based upon such a broad concept. We wish to understand by politics only the leadership, or the influencing of the leadership, of a *political* association, hence today, of a *state*.

But what is a 'political' association from the sociological point of view? What is a 'state'? Sociologically, the state cannot be defined in terms of its ends. There is scarcely any task that some political association has not taken in hand, and there is no task that one could say has always been exclusive and peculiar to those associations which are designated as political ones: today the state, or historically, those associations which have been the predecessors of the modern state. Ultimately, one can define the modern state sociologically only in terms of the specific *means* peculiar to it, as to every political association, namely, the use of physical force.

'Every state is founded on force,' said Trotsky at Brest-Litovsk. That is indeed right. If no social institutions existed which knew the use of violence, then the concept of 'state' would be eliminated, and a condition would emerge that could be designated as 'anarchy,' in the specific sense of this word. Of course, force is certainly not the normal or the only means of the state—nobody says that—but force is a means specific to the state. Today the relation between the state and violence is an especially intimate one. In the past, the most varied institutions—beginning with the sib—have known the use of physical force as quite normal. Today, however, we have to say that a state is a human community that (successfully) claims the *monopoly of the legitimate use of physical force* within a given territory. Note that 'territory' is one of the characteristics of the state. Specifically, at the present time, the right to use physical force is ascribed to other institutions or to individuals only to the extent to which the state permits it. The state is considered the sole source of the 'right' to use violence. Hence, 'politics' for us means striving to share power or striving to influence the distribution of power, either among states or among groups within a state.

This corresponds essentially to ordinary usage. When a question is said to be a 'political' question, when a cabinet minister or an official is said to be a 'political' official, or when a decision is said to be 'politically' determined, what is always meant is that interests in the distribution, maintenance, or transfer of power are decisive for answering the questions and determining the decision or the official's sphere of activity. He who is active in politics strives for power either as a means in serving other aims, ideal or egoistic, or as 'power for power's sake,' that is, in order to enjoy the prestige-feeling that power gives.

Like the political institutions historically preceding it, the state is a relation of men dominating men, a relation supported by means of legitimate (i.e. considered to be legitimate) violence. If the state is to exist, the dominated must obey the authority claimed by the powers that be. When and why do men obey? Upon what inner justifications and upon what external means does this domination rest?

To begin with, in principle, there are three inner justifications, hence basic *legitimations* of domination.

First, the authority of the 'eternal yesterday,' i.e. of the mores sanctified through the unimaginably ancient recognition and habitual orientation to conform. This is 'traditional' domination exercised by the patriarch and the patrimonial prince of yore.

There is the authority of the extraordinary and personal *gift of grace* (charisma), the absolutely personal devotion and personal confidence in revelation, heroism, or other qualities of individual leadership. This is 'charismatic' domination, as exercised by the prophet or—in the field of politics—by the elected war lord, the plebiscitarian ruler, the great demagogue, or the political party leader.

Finally, there is domination by virtue of 'legality,' by virtue of the belief in the validity of legal statute and functional 'competence' based on rationally created *rules.* In this case, obedience is expected in discharging statutory obligations. This is domination as exercised by the modern 'servant of the state' and by all those bearers of power who in this respect resemble him.

It is understood that, in reality, obedience is determined by highly robust motives of fear and hope—fear of the vengeance of magical powers or of the power-holder, hope for reward in this world or in the beyond—and besides all this, by interests of the most varied sort. Of this we shall speak presently. However, in asking for the 'legitimations' of this obedience, one meets with these three 'pure' types: 'traditional,' 'charismatic,' and 'legal.'

These conceptions of legitimacy and their inner justifications are of very great significance for the structure of domination. To be sure, the pure types are rarely found in reality. But today we cannot deal with the highly complex variants, transitions, and combinations of these pure types, which problems belong to 'political science.' Here we are interested above all in the second of these types: domination by virtue of the devotion of those who obey the purely personal 'charisma' of the 'leader.' For this is the root of the idea of a *calling* in its highest expression.❖

The Types of Legitimate Domination

Max Weber (1909–1920)

Domination and Legitimacy

Domination was defined above as the probability that certain specific commands (or all commands) will be obeyed by a given group of persons. It thus does not include every mode of exercising "power" or "influence" over other persons. Domination ("authority") in this sense may be based on the most diverse motives of compliance: all the way from simple habituation to the most purely rational calculation of advantage. Hence every genuine form of domination implies a minimum of voluntary compliance, that is, an *interest* (based on ulterior motives or genuine acceptance) in obedience.

Not every case of domination makes use of economic means; still less does it always have economic objectives. However, normally the rule over a considerable number of persons requires a staff, that is, a *special* group which can normally be trusted to execute the general policy as well as the specific commands. The members of the adminis-

Excerpt from Guenther Roth and Claus Wittich, eds., *Economy and Society, Vol. I* (Berkeley: University of California Press, 1978), pp. 212–216. This selection from *Economy and Society* was left uncompleted at Weber's death in 1920.

trative staff may be bound to obedience to their superior (or superiors) by custom, by affectual ties, by a purely material complex of interests, or by ideal (*wertrationale*) motives. The quality of these motives largely determines the type of domination. *Purely material interests* and calculations of advantages as the basis of solidarity between the chief and his administrative staff result, in this as in other connexions, in a relatively unstable situation. Normally other elements, affectual and ideal, supplement such interests. In certain exceptional cases the former alone may be decisive. In everyday life these relationships, like others, are governed by custom and material calculation of advantage. But custom, personal advantage, purely affectual or ideal motives of solidarity, do not form a sufficiently reliable basis for a given domination. In addition there is normally a further element, the belief in *legitimacy*.

Experience shows that in no instance does domination voluntarily limit itself to the appeal to material or affectual or ideal motives as a basis for its continuance. In addition every such system attempts to establish and to cultivate the belief in its legitimacy. But according to the kind of legitimacy which is claimed, the type of obedience, the kind of administrative staff developed to guarantee it, and the mode of exercising authority, will all differ fundamentally. Equally fundamental is the variation in effect. Hence, it is useful to classify the types of domination according to the kind of claim to legitimacy typically made by each. In doing this, it is best to start from modern and therefore more familiar examples.

1. The choice of this rather than some other basis of classification can only be justified by its results. The fact that certain other typical criteria of variation are thereby neglected for the time being and can only be introduced at a later stage is not a decisive difficulty. The legitimacy of a system of control has far more than a merely "ideal" significance, if only because it has very definite relations to the legitimacy of property.

2. Not every claim which is protected by custom or law should be spoken of as involving a relation of authority. Otherwise the worker, in his claim for fulfilment of the wage contract, would be exercising authority over his employer because his claim can, on occasion, be enforced by order of a court. Actually his formal status is that of party to a contractual relationship with his employer, in which he has certain "rights" to receive payments. At the same time the concept of an authority relationship (*Herrschaftsverhältnis*) naturally does not exclude the possibility that it has originated in a formally free contract. This is true of the *authority* of the employer over the worker as manifested in the former's rules and instructions regarding the work process; and also of the *authority* of a feudal lord over a vassal who has freely entered into the relation of fealty. That subjection to military discipline is formally "involuntary" while that to the discipline of the factory is voluntary does not alter the fact that the latter is also a case of subjection to *authority*. The position of a bureaucratic official is also entered into by contract and can be freely resigned, and even the status of "subject" can often be freely entered into and (in certain circumstances) freely repudiated. Only in the limiting case of the slave is formal subjection to authority absolutely involuntary.

On the other hand, we shall not speak of formal domination if a monopolistic position permits a person to exert economic power, that is, to dictate the terms of exchange to contractual partners. Taken by itself, this does not constitute authority any more than any other kind of influence which is derived from some kind of superiority, as by virtue of erotic attractiveness, skill in sport or in discussion. Even if a big bank is in a position to force other banks into a cartel arrangement, this will not alone be sufficient to justify calling it an authority. But if there is an immediate relation of command and obedience such that the management of the first bank can give orders to the others with the claim that they shall, and the probability that they will, be obeyed regardless of particular content, and if their carrying out is supervised, it is another matter. Naturally, here as everywhere the transitions are gradual; there are all sorts of intermediate steps between mere indebtedness and debt slavery. Even the position of a "salon" can come very close to the borderline of authoritarian domination and yet not necessarily constitute "authority." Sharp differentiation in concrete fact is often impossible, but this makes clarity in the analytical distinctions all the more important.

3. Naturally, the legitimacy of a system of domination may be treated sociologically only as the probability that to a relevant degree the appropriate attitudes will exist, and the corresponding practical conduct ensue. It is by no means true that every case of submissiveness to persons in positions of power is primarily (or even at all) oriented to this belief. Loyalty may be hypocritically simulated by individuals or by whole groups on purely opportunistic grounds, or carried out in practice for reasons of material self-interest. Or people may submit from individual weakness and helplessness because there is no acceptable alternative. But these considerations are not decisive for the classification of types of domination. What is important is the fact that in a given case the particular claim to legitimacy is to a significant degree and according to its type treated as "valid"; that this fact confirms the position of the persons claiming authority and that it helps to determine the choice of means of its exercise.

Furthermore, a system of domination may—as often occurs in practice—be so completely protected, on the one hand by the obvious community of interests between the chief and his administrative staff (bodyguards, Pretorians, "red" or "white" guards) as opposed to the subjects, on the other hand by the helplessness of the latter, that it can afford to drop even the pretense of a claim to legitimacy. But even then the mode of legitimation of the relation between chief and his staff may vary widely according to the type of basis of the relation of the authority between them, and, as will be shown, this variation is highly significant for the structure of domination.

4. "Obedience" will be taken to mean that the action of the person obeying follows in essentials such a course that the content of the command may be taken to have become the basis of action for its own sake. Furthermore, the fact that it is so taken is referable only to the formal obligation, without regard to the actor's own attitude to the value or lack of value of the content of the command as such.

5. Subjectively, the causal sequence may vary, especially as between "intuition" and "sympathetic agreement." This distinction is not, however, significant for the present classification of types of authority.

6. The scope of determination of social relationships and cultural phenomena by virtue of domination is considerably broader than appears at first sight. For instance, the authority exercised in the schools has much to do with the determination of the forms of speech and of written language which are regarded as orthodox. Dialects used as the "chancellery language" of autocephalous political units, hence of their rulers, have often become orthodox forms of speech and writing and have even led to the formation of separate "nations" (for instance, the separation of Holland from Germany). The rule by parents and the school, however, extends far beyond the determination of such cultural patterns, which are perhaps only apparently formal, to the formation of the young, and hence of human beings generally.

7. The fact that the chief and his administrative staff often appear formally as servants or agents of those they rule, naturally does nothing whatever to disprove the quality of dominance. There will be occasion later to speak of the substantive features of so-called "democracy." But a certain minimum of assured power to issue commands, thus of domination, must be provided for in nearly every conceivable case.

The Three Pure Types of Authority

There are three pure types of legitimate domination. The validity of the claims to legitimacy may be based on:

1. Rational grounds—resting on a belief in the legality of enacted rules and the right of those elevated to authority under such rules to issue commands (legal authority).
2. Traditional grounds—resting on an established belief in the sanctity of immemorial traditions and the legitimacy of those exercising authority under them (traditional authority); or finally,
3. Charismatic grounds—resting on devotion to the exceptional sanctity, heroism or exemplary character of an individual person, and of the normative patterns or order revealed or ordained by him (charismatic authority).

In the case of legal authority, obedience is owed to the legally established impersonal order. It extends to the persons exercising the authority of office under it by virtue of the formal legality of their commands and only within the scope of authority of the office. In the case of traditional authority, obedience is owed to the *person* of the chief who occupies the traditionally sanctioned position of authority and who is (within its sphere) bound by tradition. But here the obligation of obedience is a matter of personal loyalty within the area of accustomed obligations. In the case of charismatic authority, it is the charismatically qualified leader as such who is obeyed by virtue of personal trust in his revelation, his heroism or his exemplary qualities so far as they fall within the scope of the individual's belief in his charisma.❖

Class, Status, Party
Max Weber (1909–1920)

Economically Determined Power and the Status Order

The structure of every legal order directly influences the distribution of power, economic or otherwise, within its respective community. This is true of all legal orders and not only that of the state. In general, we understand by "power" the chance of a man or a number of men to realize their own will in a social action even against the resistance of others who are participating in the action.

"Economically conditioned" power is not, of course, identical with "power" as such. On the contrary, the emergence of economic power may be the consequence of power

Excerpt from Guenther Roth and Claus Wittich, eds., *Economy and Society, Vol. II* (Berkeley: University of California Press, 1978), pp. 927–939. This selection was left uncompleted at Weber's death in 1920.

existing on other grounds. Man does not strive for power only in order to enrich himself economically. Power, including economic power, may be valued for its own sake. Very frequently the striving for power is also conditioned by the social honor it entails. Not all power, however, entails social honor: The typical American Boss, as well as the typical big speculator, deliberately relinquishes social honor. Quite generally, "mere economic" power, and especially "naked" money power, is by no means a recognized basis of social honor. Nor is power the only basis of social honor. Indeed, social honor, or prestige, may even be the basis of economic power, and very frequently has been. Power, as well as honor, may be guaranteed by the legal order, but, at least normally, it is not their primary source. The legal order is rather an additional factor that enhances the chance to hold power or honor; but it can not always secure them.

The way in which social honor is distributed in a community between typical groups participating in this distribution we call the "status order." The social order and the economic order are related in a similar manner to the legal order. However, the economic order merely defines the way in which economic goods and services are distributed and used. Of course, the status order is strongly influenced by it, and in turn reacts upon it.

Now: "classes," "status groups," and "parties" are phenomena of the distribution of power within a community.

Determination of Class Situation by Market Situation

In our terminology, "classes" are not communities; they merely represent possible, and frequent, bases for social action. We may speak of a "class" when (1) a number of people have in common a specific causal component of their life chances, insofar as (2) this component is represented exclusively by economic interests in the possession of goods and opportunities for income, and (3) is represented under the conditions of the commodity or labor markets. This is "class situation."

It is the most elemental economic fact that the way in which the disposition over material property is distributed among a plurality of people, meeting competitively in the market for the purpose of exchange, in itself creates specific life chances. The mode of distribution, in accord with the law of marginal utility, excludes the non-wealthy from competing for highly valued goods; it favors the owners and, in fact, gives to them a monopoly to acquire such goods. Other things being equal, the mode of distribution monopolizes the opportunities for profitable deals for all those who, provided with goods, do not necessarily have to exchange them. It increases, at least generally, their power in the price struggle with those who, being propertyless, have nothing to offer but their labor or the resulting products, and who are compelled to get rid of these products in order to subsist at all. The mode of distribution gives to the propertied a monopoly on the possibility of transferring property from the sphere of use as "wealth" to the sphere of "capital," that is, it gives them the entrepreneurial function and all chances to share directly or indirectly in returns on capital. All this holds true within the area in which pure market conditions prevail. "Property" and "lack of property" are, therefore, the basic categories of all class situations. It does not matter whether these two categories become effective in the competitive struggles of the consumers or of the producers.

Within these categories, however, class situations are further differentiated: on the one hand, according to the kind of property that is usable for returns; and, on the other hand, according to the kind of services that can be offered in the market. Ownership of dwellings; workshops; warehouses; stores; agriculturally usable land in large or small holdings—a quantitative difference with possibly qualitative consequences; ownership of mines; cattle; men (slaves); disposition over mobile instruments of production, or capital goods of all sorts, especially money or objects that can easily be exchanged for money; disposition over products of one's own labor or of others' labor differing according to their various distances from consumability; disposition over transferrable monopolies of any kind—all these distinctions differentiate the class situations of the propertied just as does the "meaning" which they can give to the use of property, especially to property which has money equivalence. Accordingly, the propertied, for instance, may belong to the class of rentiers or the class of entrepreneurs.

Those who have no property but who offer services are differentiated just as much according to their kinds of services as according to the way in which they make use of these services, in a continuous or discontinuous relation to a recipient. But always this is the generic connotation of the concept of class: that the kind of chance in the *market* is the decisive moment which presents a common condition for the individual's fate. Class situation is, in this sense, ultimately market situation. The effect of naked possession *per se*, which among cattle breeders gives the non-owning slave or serf into the power of the cattle owner, is only a fore runner of real "class" formation. However, in the cattle loan and in the naked severity of the law of debts in such communities for the first time mere "possession" as such emerges as decisive for the fate of the individual; this is much in contrast to crop-raising communities, which are based on labor. The creditor-debtor relation becomes the basis of "class situations" first in the cities, where a "credit market," however primitive, with rates of interest increasing according to the extent of dearth and factual monopolization of lending in the hands of a plutocracy could develop. Therewith "class struggles" begin.

Those men whose fate is not determined by the chance of using goods or services for themselves on the market, e.g., slaves, are not, however, a class in the technical sense of the term. They are, rather, a status group.

Social Action Flowing from Class Interest

According to our terminology, the factor that creates "class" is unambiguously economic interest, and indeed, only those interests involved in the existence of the market. Nevertheless, the concept of class-interest is an ambiguous one: even as an empirical concept it is ambiguous as soon as one understands by it something other than the factual direction of interests following with a certain probability from the class situation for a certain average of those people subjected to the class situation. The class situation and other circumstances remaining the same, the direction in which the individual worker, for instance, is likely to pursue his interests may vary widely, according to whether he is constitutionally qualified for the task at hand to a high, to an average, or to a low degree. In the same way, the direction of interests may vary according to whether or not social action of a larger or smaller portion of those commonly affected by the class situation, or even an association among them, e.g., a trade union, has grown out of the class situation, from which the individual may expect promising results for himself. The emergence of an association or even of mere social action from a common class situation is by no means a universal phenomenon.

The class situation may be restricted in its efforts to the generation of essentially *similar* reactions, that is to say, within our terminology, of "mass behavior." However, it may not even have this result. Furthermore, often merely amorphous social action emerges. For example, the "grumbling" of workers known in ancient Oriental ethics: The moral disapproval of the work-master's conduct, which in its practical significance was probably equivalent to an increasingly typical phenomenon of precisely the latest industrial development, namely, the slowdown of laborers by virtue of tacit agreement. The degree in which "social action" and possibly associations emerge from the mass behavior of the members of a class is linked to general cultural conditions, especially to those of an intellectual sort. It is also linked to the extent of the contrasts that have already evolved, and is especially linked to the transparency of the connections between the causes and the consequences of the class situation. For however different life chances may be, this fact in itself, according to all experience, by no means gives birth to "class action" (social action by the members of a class). For that, the real conditions and the results of the class situation must be distinctly recognizable. For only then the contrast of life chances can be felt not as an absolutely given fact to be accepted, but as a resultant from either (1) the given distribution of property, or (2) the structure of the concrete economic order. It is only then that people may react against the class structure not only through acts of intermittent and irrational protest, but in the form of rational association. There have been "class situations" of the first category (1), of a specifically naked and transparent sort, in the urban centers of Antiquity and during the Middle Ages; especially then when great fortunes were accumulated by factually monopolized trading in local industrial products or in foodstuffs; furthermore, under certain conditions, in the rural economy of the most diverse periods, when agriculture was increasingly exploited in a profit-making manner. The most important historical example of the second category (2) is the class situation of the modern proletariat.

Types of Class Struggle

Thus every class may be the carrier of any one of the innumerable possible forms of class action, but this is not necessarily so. In any case, a class does not in itself constitute a group (*Gemeinschaft*). To treat "class" conceptually as being equivalent to "group" leads to distortion. That men in the same class situation regularly react in mass actions to such tangible situations as economic ones in the direction of those interests that are most adequate to their average number is an important and after all simple fact for the understanding of historical events. However, this fact must not lead to that kind of pseudo-scientific operation with the concepts of class and class interests which is so frequent these days and which has found its most classic expression in the statement of a talented author, that the individual may be in error concerning his interests but that the class is infallible about its interests.

If classes as such are not groups, nevertheless class situations emerge only on the basis of social action. However, social action that brings forth class situations is not basically action among members of the identical class; it is an action among members of different classes. Social actions that directly determine the class situation of the worker and the entrepreneur are: the labor market, the commodities market, and the capitalistic enterprise. But, in its turn, the existence of a capitalistic enterprise presupposes that a very specific kind of social action exists to protect the possession of goods *per se,* and especially the power of individuals to dispose, in principle freely, over the means of production: a certain kind of legal order. Each kind of class situation, and above all when it rests upon the power of property *per se,* will become most clearly efficacious when all other determinants of reciprocal relations are, as far as possible, eliminated in their significance. It is in this way that the use of the power of property in the market obtains its most sovereign importance.

Now status groups hinder the strict carrying through of the sheer market principle. In the present context they are of interest only from this one point of view. Before we briefly consider them, note that not much of a general nature can be said about the more specific kinds of antagonism between classes (in our meaning of the term). The great shift, which has been going on continuously in the past, and up to our times, may be summarized, although at a cost of some precision: the struggle in which class situations are effective has progressively shifted from consumption credit toward, first, competitive struggles in the commodity market and then toward wage disputes on the labor market. The class struggles of Antiquity—to the extent that they were genuine class struggles and not struggles between status groups—were initially carried on by peasants and perhaps also artisans threatened by debt bondage and struggling against urban creditors. For debt bondage is the normal result of the differentiation of wealth in commercial cities, especially in seaport cities. A similar situation has existed among cattle breeders. Debt relationships as such produced class action up to the days of Catilina. Along with this, and with an increase in provision of grain for the city by transporting it from the outside, the struggle over the means of sustenance emerged. It centered in the first place around the provision of bread and determination of the price of bread. It lasted throughout Antiquity and the entire Middle Ages. The propertyless flocked together against those who actually and supposedly were interested in the dearth of bread. This fight spread until it involved all those commodities essential to the way of life and to handicraft production. There were only incipient discussions of wage disputes in Antiquity and in the Middle Ages. But they have been slowly increasing up into modern times. In the earlier periods they were completely secondary to slave rebellions as well as to conflicts in the commodity market.

The propertyless of Antiquity and of the Middle Ages protested against monopolies, pre-emption, forestalling, and the withholding of goods from the market in order to raise prices. Today the central issue is the determination of the price of labor. The transition is represented by the fight for access to the market and for the determination of the price of products. Such fights went on between merchants and workers in the putting-out system of domestic handicraft during the transition to modern times. Since it is quite a general phenomenon we must mention here that the class antagonisms that are conditioned through the market situations are usually most bitter between those who actually and directly participate as opponents in price wars. It is not the rentier, the share-holder, and the banker who suffer the ill will of the worker, but almost exclusively the manufacturer and the business executives who are the direct opponents of workers in wage conflicts. This is so in spite of the fact that it is precisely the cash boxes of the rentier, the share-holder, and the banker into which the more or less unearned gains flow, rather than into the pockets of the manufacturers or of the business executives. This simple state of affairs has very frequently been decisive for the role the class situation has played in the formation of political parties. For example, it has made possible the varieties of patriarchal socialism and the frequent attempts—formerly, at least—of threatened status groups to form alliances with the proletariat against the bourgeoisie.

Status Honor

In contrast to classes, *Stande* (*status groups*) are normally groups. They are, however, often of an amorphous kind. In contrast to the purely economically determined "class situation," we wish to designate as *status situation* every typical component of the life of men that is determined by a specific, positive or negative, social estimation of *honor*. This honor may be connected with any quality shared by a plurality, and, of course, it can be knit to a class situation: class distinctions are linked in the most varied ways with status distinctions. Property as such is not always recognized as a status qualification, but in the long run it is, and with extraordinary regularity. In the subsistence economy of neighborhood associations, it is often simply the richest who is the "chieftain." However, this often is only an honorific preference. For example, in the so-called pure modern democracy, that is, one devoid of any expressly ordered status privileges for individuals, it may be that only the families coming under approximately the same tax class dance with one another. This example is reported of certain smaller Swiss cities. But status honor need not necessarily be linked with a class situation. On the contrary, it normally stands in sharp opposition to the pretensions of sheer property.

Both propertied and propertyless people can belong to the same status group, and frequently they do with very tangible consequences. This equality of social esteem may, however, in the long run become quite precarious. The equality of status among American gentlemen, for instance, is expressed by the fact that outside the subordination determined by the different functions of business, it would be considered strictly repugnant—wherever the old tradition still prevails—if even the richest boss, while playing billiards or cards in his club would not treat his clerk as in every sense fully his equal in birthright, but would bestow upon him the condescending status-conscious "benevolence" which the German boss can never dissever from his attitude. This is one of the most important reasons why in America the German clubs have never been able to attain the attraction that the American clubs have.

In content, status honor is normally expressed by the fact that above all else a specific *style of life* is expected from all those who wish to belong to the circle. Linked with this expectation are restrictions on social intercourse (that is, intercourse which is not subservient to economic or any other purposes). These restrictions may confine normal marriages to within the status circle and may lead to complete endogamous closure. Whenever this is not a mere individual and socially irrelevant imitation of another style of life, but consensual action of this closing character, the status development is under way.

In its characteristic form, stratification by status groups on the basis of conventional styles of life evolves at the present time in the United States out of the traditional democracy. For example, only the resident of a certain street ("the Street") is considered as belonging to "society," is qualified for social intercourse, and is visited and invited. Above all, this differentiation evolves in such a way as to make for strict submission to the fashion that is dominant at a given time in society. This submission to fashion also exists among men in America to a degree unknown in Germany; it appears as an indication of the fact that a given man puts forward a *claim* to qualify as a gentleman. This submission decides, at least *prima facie,* that he will be treated as such. And this recognition becomes just as important for his employment chances in swank establishments, and above all, for social intercourse and marriage with "esteemed" families, as the qualification for dueling among Germans. As for the rest, status honor is usurped by certain families resident for a long time, and, of course, correspondingly wealthy, or by the actual or alleged descendants of the "Indian Princess" Pocahontas, of the Pilgrim fathers, or of the Knickerbockers, the members of almost inaccessible sects and all sort of circles setting themselves apart by means of any other characteristics and badges. In this case stratification is purely conventional and rests largely on usurpation (as does almost all status honor in its beginning). But the road to legal privilege, positive or negative, is easily traveled as soon as a certain stratification of the social order has in fact been "lived in" and has achieved stability by virtue of a stable distribution of economic power.

Ethnic Segregation and Caste

Where the consequences have been realized to their full extent, the status group evolves into a closed caste. Status distinctions are then guaranteed not merely by conventions and laws, but also by religious sanctions. This occurs in such a way that every physical contact with a member of any caste that is considered to be lower by the members of a higher caste is considered as making for a ritualistic impurity and a stigma which must be expiated by a religious act. In addition, individual castes develop quite distinct cults and gods.

In general, however, the status structure reaches such extreme consequences only where there are underlying differences which are held to be "ethnic." The caste is, indeed, the normal form in which ethnic communities that believe in blood relationship and exclude exogamous marriage and social intercourse usually associate with one another. As mentioned before, such a caste situation is part of the phenomenon of pariah peoples and is found all over the world. These people form communities, acquire specific occupational traditions of handicrafts or of other arts, and cultivate a belief in their ethnic community. They live in a diaspora strictly segregated from all personal intercourse, except that of an unavoidable sort, and their situation is legally precarious. Yet, by virtue of their economic indispensability, they are tolerated, indeed frequently privileged, and they live interspersed in the political communities. The Jews are the most impressive historical example.

A status segregation grown into a caste differs in its structure from a mere ethnic segregation: the caste structure transforms the horizontal and unconnected coexistences of ethnically segregated groups into a vertical social system of super- and subordination. Correctly formulated: a comprehensive association integrates the ethnically divided communities into one political unit. They differ precisely in this way: ethnic coexistence, based on mutual repulsion and disdain, allows each ethnic community to consider its own honor as the highest one; the caste structure brings about a social subordination and an acknowledgement of "more honor" in favor of the privileged caste and status groups. This is due to the fact that in the caste structure ethnic distinctions as such have become "functional" distinctions within the political association (warriors, priests, artisans that are politically important for war and for building, and so on). But even pariah peoples who are most despised (for example, the Jews) are usually apt to continue cultivating the belief in their own specific "honor," a belief that is equally peculiar to ethnic and to status groups.

However, with the negatively privileged status groups the sense of dignity takes a specific deviation. A sense of dignity is the precipitation in individuals of social honor and of conventional demands which a positively privileged status group raises for the deportment of its members. The sense of dignity that characterizes positively privileged status groups is naturally related to their "being" which does not transcend itself, that is, it is related to their "beauty and excellence" (*kaloka-gauia*). Their kingdom is "of this world." They live for the present and by exploiting their great past. The sense of dignity of the negatively privileged strata naturally refers to a future lying beyond the present, whether it is of this life or of another. In other words, it must be nurtured by the belief in a providential mission and by a belief in a specific honor before God. The chosen people's dignity is nurtured by a belief either that in the beyond "the last will be the first," or that in this life a Messiah will appear to bring forth into the light of the world which has cast them out the hidden honor of the pariah people. This simple state of affairs, and not the resentment which is so strongly emphasized in Nietzsche's much-admired construction in the *Genealogy of Morals,* is the source of the religiosity cultivated by pariah status groups; moreover, resentment applies only to a limited extent; for one of Nietzsche's main examples, Buddhism, it is not at all applicable.

For the rest, the development of status groups from ethnic segregations is by no means the normal phenomenon. On the contrary. Since objective "racial differences" are by no means behind every subjective sentiment of an ethnic community, the question of an ultimately racial foundation of status structure is rightly a question of the concrete individual case. Very frequently a status group is instrumental in the production of a thoroughbred anthropological type. Certainly status groups are to a high degree effective in producing extreme types, for they select personally qualified individuals (e.g. the knighthood selects those who are fit for warfare, physically and psychically). But individual selection is far from being the only, or the predominant, way in which status groups are formed: political membership or class situation has at all times been at least as frequently decisive. And today the class situation is by far the predominant factor. After all, the possibility of a style of life expected for members of a status group is usually conditioned economically.

Status Privileges

For all practical purposes, stratification by status goes hand in hand with a monopolization of ideal and material goods or opportunities, in a manner we have come to know as typical. Besides the specific status honor, which always rests upon distance and exclusiveness, honorific preferences may consist of the privilege of wearing special costumes, of eating special dishes taboo to others, of carrying arms—which is most obvious in its consequences—, the right to be a dilettante, for example, to play certain musical instruments. However, material monopolies provide the most effective motives for the exclusiveness of a status group; although, in themselves, they are rarely sufficient, almost always they come into play to some extent. Within a status circle there is the question of intermarriage: the interest of the families in the monopolization of potential bridegrooms is at least of equal importance and is parallel to the interest in the monopolization of daughters. The daughters of the members must be provided for. With an increased closure of the status group, the conventional preferential opportunities for special employment grow into a legal monopoly of special offices for the members. Certain goods become objects for monopolization by status groups, typically, entailed estates, and frequently also the possession of serfs or bondsmen and, finally, special trades. This monopolization occurs positively when the status group is exclusively entitled to own and to manage them; and negatively when, in order to maintain its specific way of life, the status group must *not* own and manage them. For the decisive role of a style of life in status honor means that status groups are the specific bearers of all conventions. In whatever way it may be manifest, all stylization of life either originates in status groups or is at least conserved by them. Even if the principles of status conventions differ greatly, they reveal certain typical traits, especially among the most privileged strata. Quite generally, among privileged status groups there is a status disqualification that operates against the performance of common physical labor. This disqualification is now "setting in" in America against the old tradition of esteem for labor. Very frequently every rational economic pursuit, and especially entrepreneurial activity, is looked upon as a disqualification of status. Artistic and literary activity is also considered degrading work as soon as it is exploited for income, or at least when it is connected with hard physical exertion. An example is the sculptor working like a mason in his dusty smock as over against the painter in his salon-like studio and those forms of musical practice that are acceptable to the status group.

Economic Conditions and Effects of Status Stratification

The frequent disqualification of the gainfully employed as such is a direct result of the principle of status stratification, and of course, of this principle's opposition to a distribution of power which is regulated exclusively through the market. These two factors operate along with various individual ones, which will be touched upon below.

We have seen above that the market and its processes knows no personal distinctions: "functional" interests dominate it. It knows nothing of honor. The status order means precisely the reverse: stratification in terms of honor and styles of life peculiar to status groups as such. The status order would be threatened at its very root if mere economic acquisition and naked economic power still bearing the stigma of its extra-status origin could bestow upon anyone who has won them the same or ever greater honor as the vested interests claim for themselves. After all, given equality of status honor, property *per se* represents an addition even if it is not overtly acknowledged to be such. Therefore all groups having interest in the status order react with special sharpness precisely against the pretensions of purely economic acquisition. In most cases they react the more vigorously the more they feel themselves threatened. Calderon's respectful treatment of the peasant, for instance, as opposed to Shakespeare's simultaneous ostensible disdain of the *canaille* illustrates the different way in which a firmly structured status order reacts as compared with a status order that has become economically precarious. This is an example of a state of affairs that recurs everywhere. Precisely because of the rigorous reactions against the claims of property *per se*, the "parvenu" is never accepted, personally and without reservation, by the privileged status groups, no matter how completely his style of life has been adjusted to theirs. They will only accept his descendants who have been educated in the conventions of their status group and who have never besmirched its honor by their own economic labor.

As to the general *effect* of the status order, only one consequence can be stated, but it is a very important one: the hindrance of the free development of the market. This occurs first for those goods that status groups directly withhold from free exchange by monopolization, which may be effected either legally or conventionally. For example, in many Hellenic cities during the "status era" and also originally in Rome, the inherited estate (as shown by the old formula for placing spendthrifts under a guardian) was monopolized, as were the estates of knights, peasants, priests, and especially the clientele of the craft and merchant guilds. The market is restricted, and the power of naked property *per se,* which gives its stamp to class formation, is pushed into the background. The results of this process can be most varied. Of course, they do not necessarily weaken the contrasts in the economic situation. Frequently they strengthen these contrasts, and in any case, where stratification by status permeates a community as strongly as was the case in all political communities of Antiquity and of the Middle Ages, one can never speak of a genuinely free market competition as we understand it today. There are wider effects than this direct exclusion of special goods from the market. From the conflict between the status order and the purely economic order mentioned above, it follows that in most instances the notion of honor peculiar to status absolutely abhors that which is essential to the market: hard bargaining. Honor abhors hard bargaining among peers and occasionally it taboos it for the members of a status group in general. Therefore, everywhere some status groups, and usually the most influential, consider almost any kind of overt participation in economic acquisition as absolutely stigmatizing.

With some over-simplification, one might thus say that classes are stratified according to their relations to the production and acquisition of goods; whereas status groups are stratified according to the principles of their *consumption* of goods as represented by special styles of life.

An "occupational status group," too, is a status group proper. For normally, it successfully claims social honor only by virtue of the special style of life which may be determined by it. The differences between classes and status groups frequently overlap. It is precisely those status communities most strictly segregated in terms of honor (viz. the Indian castes) who today show, although within very rigid limits, a relatively high degree of indifference to pecuniary income. However, the Brahmins seek such income in many different ways.

As to the general economic conditions making for the predominance of stratification by status, only the following can be said. When the bases of the acquisition and distribution of goods are relatively stable, stratification by status is favored. Every technological repercussion and economic transformation threatens stratification by status and pushes the class situation into the foreground. Epochs and countries in which the naked class situation is of predominant significance are regularly the periods of technical and economic transformations. And every slowing down of the change in economic stratification leads, in due course, to the growth of status structures and makes for a resuscitation of the important role of social honor.

Parties

Whereas the genuine place of classes is within the economic order, the place of status groups is within the social order, that is, within the sphere of the distribution of honor. From within these spheres, classes and status groups influence one another and the legal order and are in turn influenced by it. "*Parties*" reside in the sphere of power. Their action is oriented toward the acquisition of social power, that is to say, toward influencing social action no matter what its content may be. In principle, parties may exist in a social club as well as in a state. As over against the actions of classes and status groups, for which this is not necessarily the case, party-oriented social action always involves association. For it is always directed toward a goal which is striven for in a planned manner. This goal may be a cause (the party may aim at realizing a program for ideal or material purposes), or the goal may be personal (sinecures, power, and from these, honor for the leader and the followers of the party). Usually the party aims at all these simultaneously. Parties are, therefore, only possible within groups that have an associated character, that is, some rational order and a staff of persons available who are ready to enforce it. For parties aim precisely at influencing this staff, and if possible, to recruit from it party members.

In any individual case, parties may represent interests determined through class situation or status situation, and they may recruit their following respectively from one or the other. But they need be neither purely class nor purely status parties; in fact, they are more likely to be mixed types, and sometimes they are neither. They may represent ephemeral or enduring structures. Their means of attaining power may be quite varied, ranging from naked violence of any sort to canvassing for votes with coarse or subtle means: money, social influence, the force of speech, suggestion, clumsy hoax, and so on to the rougher or more artful tactics of obstruction in parliamentary bodies.

The sociological structure of parties differs in a basic way according to the kind of social action which they struggle to influence; that means, they differ according to whether or not the community is stratified by status or by classes. Above all else, they vary according to the structure of domination. For their leaders normally deal with its conquest. In our general terminology, parties are not only products of modern forms of domination. We shall also designate as parties the ancient and medieval ones, despite the fact that they differ basically from modern parties. Since a party always struggles for political control (*Herrschaft*), its organization too is frequently strict and "authoritarian." Because of these variations between the forms of domination, it is impossible to say anything about the structure of parties without discussing them first. Therefore, we shall now turn to this central phenomenon of all social organization.

Before we do this, we should add one more general observation about classes, status groups and parties: The fact that they presuppose a larger association, especially the framework of a polity, does not mean that they are confined to it. On the contrary, at all times it has been the order of the day that such association (even when it aims at the use of military force in common) reaches beyond the state boundaries. This can be seen in the [interlocal] solidarity of interests of oligarchs and democrats in Hellas, of Guelphs and Ghibellines in the Middle Ages, and with the Calvinist party during the age of religious struggles; and all the way up to the solidarity of landlords (International Congresses of Agriculture), princes (Holy Alliance, Karlsbad Decrees [of 1819]), socialist workers, conservatives (the longing of Prussian conservatives for Russian intervention in 1850). But their aim is not necessarily the establishment of a new territorial dominion. In the main they aim to influence the existing polity.❖

Sigmund Freud (1856–1939) lived to see the full effects of modern culture in the twentieth century: two world wars, depression, Hitler. In his last writings, particularly *Civilization and Its Discontents* (1930), Freud addressed his social concerns directly. Most of his writings, however, especially those following *Interpretation of Dreams* (1900), were devoted to the scientific and popular advancement of psychoanalysis. Like the other classic social theorists, he was a broadly educated man. His study of

Sophocles' *Oedipus* was just one of the many references he made to literature and the arts. He began his career in the 1880s as a medical doctor specializing in neurology. Before settling into life and marriage (to Martha Bernays), he spent a year, 1885–1886, in Paris. There, through the influence of Jean-Martin Charcot's clinical work on hypnosis, Freud began to think independently on the effects of unconscious life. Once his study of dreams established the general principles of psychoanalysis, Freud was irreversibly involved as the leader of the psychoanalytic movement. The path was not easy. He quarreled with members of the school (notably the Swiss analyst Carl Jung). He was not able to stop smoking, which aggravated the pain caused by his palate cancer. It seems, also, that he had his own trouble separating from his mother. Just the same, it was the humanity of the man, as well as his prodigious learning and creativity, that gave rise to psychoanalysis. Today, psychoanalytic thought serves equally the clinical practice of psychotherapy and social theorists who recognize the power of unconscious desire in shaping personal, cultural, and political life.

The first selections, "The Psychical Apparatus and the Theory of Instincts" and "Dream-Work and Interpretation," outline Freud's famous three-part division of the psyche, his mature theory of the instincts, and his view of dreams. Though his thinking changed over the years, these selections (from one of Freud's last works, left incomplete at his death) summarize the essentials of the theories. "Oedipus, the Child" is a text from his earliest work on dreams. It represents one of his many references to versions of Sophocles' *Oedipus, the King*. "Remembering, Repeating, and Working-Through" is one of Freud's numerous clinical writings, intended to instruct analysts in his therapeutic technique. "The Return of the Repressed in Social Life" (from *Moses and Monotheism*) and "Civilization and the Individual" (from *Civilization and Its Discontents*) are also late works, written during the period when he was most concerned to use his theory to reflect on Western civilization. Both show his attempt to link psychological theory to social life. The latter clearly indicates his reservations toward the alleged superiority of Western civilization. Indeed, the last sentence, added with Hitler in mind, reveals his concerns for the very future of that civilization.

The Psychical Apparatus and the Theory of Instincts

Sigmund Freud (1900–1939)

Psycho-analysis makes a basic assumption, the discussion of which is reserved to philosophical thought but the justification for which lies in its results. We know two kinds of things about what we call our psyche (or mental life): firstly, its bodily organ and scene of action, the brain (or nervous system) and, on the other hand, our acts of consciousness, which are immediate data and cannot be further explained by any sort of description. Everything that lies between is unknown to us, and the data do not include any direct relation between these two terminal points of our knowledge. If it existed, it would at the most afford an exact localization of the processes of consciousness and would give us no help towards understanding them.

Our two hypotheses start out from these ends or beginnings of our knowledge. The first is concerned with localization. We assume that mental life is the function of

Excerpt from James Stachey, ed. and trans., *An Outline of Psycho-Analysis*, standard ed., Vol. 23 (New York: W. W. Norton, 1949), pp. 13–21. Published posthumously, this selection is from one of Freud's last statements of psychoanalytic theory, developed throughout his career.

an apparatus to which we ascribe the characteristics of being extended in space and of being made up of several portions—which we imagine, that is, as resembling a telescope or microscope or something of the kind. Notwithstanding some earlier attempts in the same direction, the consistent working-out of a conception such as this is a scientific novelty.

We have arrived at our knowledge of this psychical apparatus by studying the individual development of human beings. To the oldest of these psychical provinces or agencies we give the name of *id*. It contains everything that is inherited, that is present at birth, that is laid down in the constitution—above all, therefore, the instincts, which originate from the somatic organization and which find a first psychical expression here [in the id] in forms unknown to us.

Under the influence of the real external world around us, one portion of the id has undergone a special development. From what was originally a cortical layer, equipped with the organs for receiving stimuli and with arrangements for acting as a protective shield against stimuli, a special organization has arisen which henceforward acts as an intermediary between the id and the external world. To this region of our mind we have given the name of *ego*.

Here are the principal characteristics of the ego. In consequence of the pre-established connection between sense perception and muscular action, the ego has voluntary movement at its command. It has the task of self-preservation. As regards *external* events, it performs that task by becoming aware of stimuli, by storing up experiences about them (in the memory), by avoiding excessively strong stimuli (through flight), by dealing with moderate stimuli (through adaptation) and finally by learning to bring about expedient changes in the external world to its own advantage (through activity). As regards *internal* events, in relation to the id, it performs that task by gaining control over the demands of the instincts, by deciding whether they are to be allowed satisfaction, by postponing that satisfaction to times and circumstances favourable in the external world or by suppressing their excitations entirely. It is guided in its activity by consideration of the tensions produced by stimuli, whether these tensions are present in it or introduced into it. The raising of these tensions is in general felt as *unpleasure* and their lowering as *pleasure*. It is probable, however, that what is felt as pleasure or unpleasure is not the *absolute* height of this tension but something in the rhythm of the changes in them. The ego strives after pleasure and seeks to avoid unpleasure. An increase in unpleasure that is expected and foreseen is met by a *signal of anxiety;* the occasion of such an increase, whether it threatens from without or within, is known as a *danger.* From time to time the ego gives up its connection with the external world and withdraws into the state of sleep, in which it makes far-reaching changes in its organization. It is to be inferred from the state of sleep that this organization consists in a particular distribution of mental energy.

The long period of childhood, during which the growing human being lives in dependence on his parents, leaves behind it as a precipitate the formation in his ego of a special agency in which this parental influence is prolonged. It has received the name of *super-ego*. In so far as this super-ego is differentiated from the ego or is opposed to it, it constitutes a third power which the ego must take into account.

An action by the ego is as it should be if it satisfies simultaneously the demands of the id, of the super-ego and of reality—that is to say, if it is able to reconcile their demands with one another. The details of the relation between the ego and the super-ego become completely intelligible when they are traced back to the child's attitude to its parents. This parental influence of course includes in its operation not only the personalities of the actual parents but also the family, racial and national traditions handed on through them, as well as the demands of the immediate social *milieu* which they represent. In the same way, the super-ego, in the course of an individual's development, receives contributions from later successors and substitutes of his parents, such as teachers and models in public life of admired social ideals. It will be observed that, for all their fundamental difference, the id and the super-ego have one thing in common: they both represent the influences of the past—the id the influence of heredity, the super-ego the influence, essentially, of what is taken over from other people—whereas the ego is principally determined by the individual's own experience, that is by accidental and contemporary events.

This general schematic picture of a psychical apparatus may be supposed to apply as well to the higher animals which resemble man mentally. A super-ego must be presumed to be present wherever, as is the case with man, there is a long period of dependence in childhood. A distinction between ego and id is an unavoidable assumption. Animal psychology has not yet taken in hand the interesting problem which is here presented. . . .

The Theory of the Instincts

The power of the id expresses the true purpose of the individual organism's life. This consists in the satisfaction of its innate needs. No such purpose as that of keeping itself alive or of protecting itself from dangers by means of anxiety can be attributed to the id. That is the task of the ego, whose business it also is to discover the most favourable and least perilous method of obtaining satisfaction, taking the external world into account. The super-ego may bring fresh needs to the fore, but its main function remains the limitation of satisfactions.

The forces which we assume to exist behind the tensions caused by the needs of the id are called *instincts*. They represent the somatic demands upon the mind. Though they are the ultimate cause of all activity, they are of a conservative nature; the state, whatever it may be, which an organism has reached gives rise to a tendency to re-establish that state so soon as it has been abandoned. It is thus possible to distinguish an indeterminate number of instincts, and in common practice this is in fact done. For us, however, the important question arises whether it may not be possible to trace all these numerous instincts back to a few basic ones. We have found that instincts can change their aim (by displacement) and also that they can replace one another—the energy of one instinct passing over to another. This latter process is still insufficiently understood. After long hesitancies and vacillations we have decided to assume the existence of only two basic instincts, *Eros* and *the destructive instinct*. (The contrast between the instincts of self-preservation and the preservation of the species, as well as the contrast between ego-love and object-love, fall within Eros.) The aim of the first of these basic instincts is to establish ever greater unities and to preserve them thus—in short, to bind together; the aim of the second is, on the contrary, to undo connections and so to destroy things. In the case of the destructive instinct we may suppose that its final aim is to lead what is living into an inorganic state. For this reason we also call it the *death instinct*. If we assume that living things came later than inanimate ones and arose from them, then the death instinct fits in with the formula we have proposed to the effect that instincts tend towards a return to an earlier state. In the case of Eros (or the love instinct) we cannot apply this formula. To do so would presuppose that living substance was once a unity which had later been torn apart and was now striving towards reunion.

In biological functions the two basic instincts operate against each other or combine with each other. Thus, the act of eating is a destruction of the object with the final aim of incorporating it, and the sexual act is an act of aggression with the purpose of the most intimate union. This concurrent and mutually opposing action of the two basic instincts gives rise to the whole variegation of the phenomena of life. The analogy of our two basic instincts extends from the sphere of living things to the pair of opposing forces—attraction and repulsion—which rule in the inorganic world.

Modifications in the proportions of the fusion between the instincts have the most tangible results. A surplus of sexual aggressiveness will turn a lover into a sex-murderer, while a sharp diminution in the aggressive factor will make him bashful or impotent.

There can be no question of restricting one or the other of the basic instincts to one of the provinces of the mind. They must necessarily be met with everywhere. We may picture an initial state as one in which the total available energy of Eros, which henceforward we shall speak of as 'libido,' is present in the still undifferentiated ego-id and serves to neutralize the destructive tendencies which are simultaneously present. (We are without a term analogous to 'libido' for describing the energy of the destructive instinct.) At a later stage it becomes relatively easy for us to follow the vicissitudes of the libido, but this is more difficult with the destructive instinct.

So long as that instinct operates internally, as a death instinct, it remains silent; it only comes to our notice when it is diverted outwards as an instinct of destruction. It seems to be essential for the preservation of the individual that this diversion should occur; the muscular apparatus serves this purpose. When the super-ego is established, considerable amounts of the aggressive instinct are fixated in the interior of the ego and operate there self-destructively. This is one of the dangers to health by which human beings are faced on their path to cultural development. Holding back aggressiveness is in general unhealthy and leads to illness (to mortification). A person in a fit of rage will often demonstrate how the transition from aggressiveness that has been prevented to self-destructiveness is brought about by diverting the aggressiveness against himself: he tears his hair or beats his face with his fists, though he would evidently have preferred to apply this treatment to someone else. Some portion of self-destructiveness remains within, whatever the circumstances; till at last it succeeds in killing the individual, not, perhaps, until his libido has been used up or fixated in a disadvantageous way. Thus it may in general be suspected that the *individual* dies of his internal conflicts but that the *species* dies of its unsuccessful struggle against the external world if the latter changes in a fashion which cannot be adequately dealt with by the adaptations which the species has acquired.

It is hard to say anything of the behavior of the libido in the id and in the super-ego. All that we know about it relates to the ego, in which at first the whole available quota of libido is stored up. We call this state absolute, primary *narcissism*. It lasts till the ego begins to cathect the ideas of objects with libido, to transform narcissistic libido into object-libido. Throughout the whole of life the ego remains the great reservoir from which libidinal cathexes are sent out to objects and into which they are also once more withdrawn, just as an amoeba behaves with its pseudopodia. It is only when a person is completely in love that the main quota of libido is transferred on to the object and the object to some extent takes the place of the ego. A characteristic of the libido which is important in life is its *mobility*, the facility with which it passes from one object to another. This must be contrasted with the *fixation* of the libido to particular objects, which often persists throughout life.

There can be no question but that the libido has somatic sources, that it streams to the ego from various organs and parts of the body. This is most clearly seen in the case of that portion of the libido which, from its instinctual aim, is described as sexual excitation. The most prominent of the parts of the body from which this libido arises are known by the name of '*erotogenic zones*,' though in fact the whole body is an erotogenic zone of this kind. The greater part of what we know about Eros—that is to say, about its exponent, the libido—has been gained from a study of the sexual function, which, indeed, on the prevailing view, even if not according to our theory, coincides with Eros. We have been able to form a picture of the way in which the sexual urge, which is destined to exercise a decisive influence on our life, gradually develops out of successive contributions from a number of component instincts, which represent particular erotogenic zones.❖

Dream-Work and Interpretation

Sigmund Freud (1900–1939)

An investigation of normal, stable states, in which the frontiers of the ego are safeguarded against the id by resistances (anti-cathexes) and have held firm, and in which the super-ego is not distinguished from the ego, because they work together harmoniously—an investigation of that kind would teach us little. The only thing that can help us are states of conflict and uproar, when the contents of the unconscious id have a prospect of forcing their way into the ego and into consciousness and the ego puts itself once more on the defensive against this invasion. It is only under these conditions that we can make such observations as will confirm or correct our statements about the two partners. Now, our nightly sleep is precisely a state of this sort, and for that reason psychical activity during sleep, which we perceive as dreams, is our most favourable object of study. In that way, too, we avoid the familiar reproach that we base our constructions of normal mental life on pathological findings; for dreams are regular events in the life of a normal person, however much their characteristics may differ from the productions of our waking life. Dreams, as everyone knows, may be confused, unintelligible or positively nonsensical, what they say may contradict all that we know of reality, and we behave in them like insane people, since, so long as we are dreaming, we attribute objective reality to the contents of the dream.

We find our way to the understanding ('interpretation') of a dream by assuming that what we recollect as the dream after we have woken up is not the true dream-process but only a *façade* behind which that process lies concealed. Here we have our distinction between the *manifest* content of a dream and the *latent* dream-thoughts. The process which produces the former out of the latter is described as the *dream-work*. The study of the dream-work teaches us by an excellent example the way in which unconscious material from the id (originally unconscious and repressed unconscious alike) forces its way into the ego, becomes preconscious and, as a result of the ego's opposition, undergoes the changes which we know as *dream-distortion*. There are no features of a dream which cannot be explained in this way.

Excerpt from James Stachey, ed. and trans., *An Outline of Psycho-Analysis*, standard ed., Vol. 23 (New York: W. W. Norton, 1949), pp. 38–46. This selection was published posthumously.

It is best to begin by pointing out that the formation of a dream can be provoked in two different ways. Either, on the one hand, an instinctual impulse which is ordinarily suppressed (an unconscious wish) finds enough strength during sleep to make itself felt by the ego, or, on the other hand, an urge left over from waking life, a preconscious train of thought with all the conflicting impulses attached to it, finds reinforcement during sleep from an unconscious element. In short, dreams may arise either from the id or from the ego. The mechanism of dream-formation is in both cases the same and so also is the necessary dynamic precondition. The ego gives evidence of its original derivation from the id by occasionally ceasing its functions and allowing a reversion to an earlier state of things. This is logically brought about by its breaking off its relations with the external world and withdrawing its cathexes from the sense organs. We are justified in saying that there arises at birth an instinct to return to the intra-uterine life that has been abandoned—an instinct to sleep. Sleep is a return of this kind to the womb. Since the waking ego governs motility, that function is paralysed in sleep, and accordingly a good part of the inhibitions imposed on the unconscious id become superfluous. The withdrawal or reduction of these 'anticathexes' thus allows the id what is now a harmless amount of liberty.

The evidence of the share taken by the unconscious id in the formation of dreams is abundant and convincing. (*a*) Memory is far more comprehensive in dreams than in waking life. Dreams bring up recollections which the dreamer has forgotten, which are inaccessible to him when he is awake. (*b*) Dreams make an unrestricted use of linguistic symbols, the meaning of which is for the most part unknown to the dreamer. Our experience, however, enables us to confirm their sense. They probably originate from earlier phases in the development of speech. (*c*) Memory very often reproduces in dreams impressions from the dreamer's early childhood of which we can definitely assert not only that they had been forgotten but that they had become unconscious owing to repression. That explains the help—usually indispensable—given us by dreams in the attempts we make during the analytic treatment of neuroses to reconstruct the dreamer's early life. (*d*) Furthermore, dreams bring to light material which cannot have originated either from the dreamer's adult life or from his forgotten childhood. We are obliged to regard it as part of the *archaic heritage* which a child brings with him into the world, before any experience of his own, influenced by the experiences of his ancestors. We find the counterpart of this phylogenetic material in the earliest human legends and in surviving customs. Thus dreams constitute a source of human prehistory which is not to be despised.

But what makes dreams so invaluable in giving us insight is the circumstance that, when the unconscious material makes its way into the ego, it brings its own modes of working along with it. This means that the preconscious thoughts in which the unconscious material has found its expression are handled in the course of the dream-work as though they were unconscious portions of the id; and, in the case of the alternative method of dream-formation, the preconscious thoughts which have obtained reinforcement from an unconscious instinctual impulse are brought down to the unconscious state. It is only in this way that we learn the laws which govern the passage of events in the unconscious and the respects in which they differ from the rules that are familiar to us in waking thought. Thus the dream-work is essentially an instance of the unconscious working-over of preconscious thought-processes. To take an analogy from history: invading conquerors govern a conquered country, not according to the judicial system which they find in force there, but according to their own. It is, however, an unmistakable fact that the outcome of the dream-work is a compromise. The ego-organization is not yet paralysed, and its influence is to be seen in the distortion imposed on the unconscious material and in what are often very ineffective attempts at giving the total result a form not too unacceptable to the ego (*secondary revision*). In our analogy this would be an expression of the continued resistance of the defeated people.

The laws that govern the passage of events in the unconscious, which come to light in this manner, are remarkable enough and suffice to explain most of what seems strange to us about dreams. Above all there is a striking tendency to *condensation*, an inclination to form fresh unities out of elements which in our waking thought we should certainly have kept separate. As a consequence of this, a single element of the manifest dream often stands for a whole number of latent dream-thoughts as though it were a combined allusion to all of them; and in general the compass of the manifest dream is extraordinarily small in comparison with the wealth of material from which it has sprung. Another peculiarity of the dream-work, not entirely independent of the former one, is the ease with which psychical intensities (cathexes) are *displaced* from one element to another, so that it often happens that an element which was of little importance in the dream-thoughts appears as the clearest and accordingly most important feature of the manifest dream, and, *vice versa,* that essential elements of the dream-thoughts are represented in the manifest dream only by slight allusions. Moreover, as a rule the existence of quite insignificant points in common between two elements is enough to allow the dream-work to replace one by the other in all further operations. It will easily be imagined how greatly these mechanisms of condensation and displacement can increase the difficulty of interpreting a dream and of revealing the relations between the manifest dream and the latent dream-thoughts. From the evidence of the existence of these two tendencies to condensation and displacement our theory infers that in the unconscious id the energy is in a freely mobile state and that the id sets more store by the possibility of discharging quantities of excitation than by any other consideration; and our theory makes use of these two peculiarities in defining the character of the primary process we have attributed to the id.

The study of the dream-work has taught us many other characteristics of the processes in the unconscious which are as remarkable as they are important; but we must only mention a few of them here. The governing rules of logic carry no weight in the unconscious; it might be called the Realm of the Illogical. Urges with contrary aims exist side by side in the unconscious without any need arising for an adjustment between them. Either they have no influence whatever on each other, or, if they have, no decision is reached, but a compromise comes about which is nonsensical since it embraces mutually incompatible details. With this is connected the fact that contraries are not kept apart but treated as though they were identical, so that in the manifest dream any element may also have the meaning of its opposite. Certain philologists have found that the same held good in the most ancient languages and that contraries such as 'strong-weak,' 'light-dark' and 'high-deep' were originally expressed by the same roots, until two different modifications of the primitive word distinguished between the two meanings. Residues of this original double meaning seem to have survived even in a highly developed language like Latin in its use of words such as '*altus*' ('high' and 'deep') and '*sacer*' ('sacred' and 'infamous').

In view of the complication and ambiguity of the relations between the manifest dream and the latent content lying behind it, it is of course justifiable to ask how it is at all possible to deduce the one from the other and whether all we have to go on is a lucky guess, assisted perhaps by a translation of the symbols that occur in the manifest dream. It may be said in reply that in the great majority of cases the problem can be satisfactorily solved, but only with the help of the associations provided by the dreamer himself to the elements of the manifest content. Any other procedure is arbitrary and can yield no certain result. But the dreamer's associations bring to light intermediate links which we can insert in the gap between the two [between the manifest and latent content] and by aid of which we can reinstate the latent content of the dream and 'interpret' it. It is not to be wondered at if this work of interpretation (acting in a direction opposite to the dream-work) fails occasionally to arrive at complete certainty.

It remains for us to give a dynamic explanation of why the sleeping ego takes on the task of the dream-work at all. The explanation is fortunately easy to find. With the help of the unconscious, every dream that is in process of formation makes a demand upon the ego—for the satisfaction of an instinct, if the dream originates from the id; for the solution of a conflict, the removal of a doubt or the forming of an intention, if the dream originates from a residue of preconscious activity in waking life. The sleeping ego, however, is focused on the wish to maintain sleep; it feels this demand as a disturbance and seeks to get rid of the disturbance. The ego succeeds in doing this by what appears to be an act of compliance: it meets the demand with what is in the circumstances a harmless *fulfilment of a wish* and so gets rid of it. This replacement of the demand by the fulfilment of a wish remains the essential function of the dream-work. It may perhaps be worth while to illustrate this by three simple examples—a hunger dream, a dream of convenience and a dream prompted by sexual desire. A need for food makes itself felt in a dreamer during his sleep: he has a dream of a delicious meal and sleeps on. The choice, of course, was open to him either of waking up and eating something or of continuing his sleep. He decided in favour of the latter and satisfied his hunger by means of the dream—for the time being, at all events, for if his hunger had persisted he would have had to wake up nevertheless. Here is the second example. A sleeper had to wake up so as to be in time for his work at the hospital. But he slept on, and had a dream that he was already at the hospital—but as a patient, who has no need to get up. Or again, a desire becomes active during the night for the enjoyment of a forbidden sexual object, the wife of a friend of the sleeper. He has a dream of sexual intercourse—not, indeed, with this person but with someone else of the same name to whom he is in fact indifferent; or his struggle against the desire may find expression in his mistress remaining altogether anonymous.

Naturally, every case is not so simple. Especially in dreams which have originated from undealt-with residues of the previous day, and which have only obtained an unconscious reinforcement during the state of sleep, it is often no easy task to uncover the unconscious motive force and its wish-fulfilment; but we may assume that it is always there. The thesis that dreams are the fulfilments of wishes will easily arouse scepticism when it is remembered how many dreams have an actually distressing content or even wake the dreamer in anxiety, quite apart from the numerous dreams without any definite feeling-tone. But the objection based on anxiety dreams cannot be sustained against analysis. It must not be forgotten that dreams are invariably the product of a conflict, that they are a kind of compromise-structure. Something that is a satisfaction for the unconscious id may for that very reason be a cause of anxiety for the ego.

As the dream-work proceeds, sometimes the unconscious will press forward more successfully and sometimes the ego will defend itself with greater energy. Anxiety dreams are mostly those whose content has undergone the least distortion. If the demand made by the unconscious is too great for the sleeping ego to be in a position to fend it off by the means at its disposal, it abandons the wish to sleep and returns to waking life. We shall be taking every experience into account if we say that a dream is invariably an *attempt* to get rid of a disturbance of sleep by means of a wish-fulfilment, so that the dream is a guardian of sleep. The attempt may succeed more or less completely; it may also fail, and in that case the sleeper wakes up, apparently woken precisely by the dream. So, too, there are occasions when that excellent fellow the night-watchman, whose business it is to guard the little township's sleep, has no alternative but to sound the alarm and waken the sleeping townspeople.❖

Oedipus, the Child

Sigmund Freud (1900)

In my experience, which is already extensive, the chief part in the mental lives of all children who later become psychoneurotics is played by their parents. Being in love with the one parent and hating the other are among the essential constituents of the stock of psychical impulses which is formed at that time and which is of such importance in determining the symptoms of the later neurosis. It is not my belief, however, that psychoneurotics differ sharply in this respect from other human beings who remain normal—that they are able, that is, to create something absolutely new and peculiar to themselves. It is far more probable—and this is confirmed by occasional observations on normal children—that they are only distinguished by exhibiting on a magnified scale feelings of love and hatred to their parents which occur less obviously and less intensely in the minds of most children.

This discovery is confirmed by a legend that has come down to us from classical antiquity: a legend whose profound and universal power to move can only be understood if the hypothesis I have put forward in regard to the psychology of children has an equally universal validity. What I have in mind is the legend of King Oedipus and Sophocles' drama which bears his name.

Oedipus, son of Laïus, King of Thebes, and of Jocasta, was exposed as an infant because an oracle had warned Laïus that the still unborn child would be his father's murderer. The child was rescued, and grew up as a prince in an alien court, until, in doubts as to his origin, he too questioned the oracle and was warned to avoid his home since he was destined to murder his father and take his mother in marriage. On the road leading away from what he believed was his home, he met King Laïus and slew him in a sudden quarrel. He came next to Thebes and solved the riddle set him by the Sphinx who barred his way. Out of gratitude the Thebans made him their king and gave him Jocasta's hand in marriage. He reigned long in peace and honour, and she who, unknown to him, was his mother bore him two sons and two daughters. Then at last a plague broke out and the Thebans made enquiry once more of the oracle. It is at this point that Sophocles' tragedy opens. The messengers bring back the reply that the plague will cease when the murderer of Laïus has been driven from the land.

Excerpt from James Stachey, ed. and trans., *The Interpretation of Dreams* (New York: Avon Books, 1965), pp. 294–301.

> But he, where is he? Where shall now be read
> The fading record of this ancient guilt?

The action of the play consists in nothing other than the process of revealing, with cunning delays and ever-mounting excitement—a process that can be likened to the work of a psycho-analysis—that Oedipus himself is the murderer of Laïus, but further that he is the son of the murdered man and of Jocasta. Appalled at the abomination which he has unwittingly perpetrated, Oedipus blinds himself and forsakes his home. The oracle has been fulfilled.

Oedipus Rex is what is known as a tragedy of destiny. Its tragic effect is said to lie in the contrast between the supreme will of the gods and the vain attempts of mankind to escape the evil that threatens them. The lesson which, it is said, the deeply moved spectator should learn from the tragedy is submission to the divine will and realization of his own impotence. Modern dramatists have accordingly tried to achieve a similar tragic effect by weaving the same contrast into a plot invented by themselves. But the spectators have looked on unmoved while a curse or an oracle was fulfilled in spite of all the efforts of some innocent man: later tragedies of destiny have failed in their effect.

If *Oedipus Rex* moves a modern audience no less than it did the contemporary Greek one, the explanation can only be that its effect does not lie in the contrast between destiny and human will, but is to be looked for in the particular nature of the material on which that contrast is exemplified. There must be something which makes a voice within us ready to recognize the compelling force of destiny in the *Oedipus,* while we can dismiss as merely arbitrary such dispositions as are laid down in [Grillparzer's] *Die Ahnfrau* or other modern tragedies of destiny. And a factor of this kind is in fact involved in the story of King Oedipus. His destiny moves us only because it might have been ours—because the oracle laid the same curse upon us before our birth as upon him. It is the fate of all of us, perhaps, to direct our first sexual impulse towards our mother and our first hatred and our first murderous wish against our father. Our dreams convince us that that is so. King Oedipus, who slew his father Laïus and married his mother Jocasta, merely shows us the fulfilment of our own childhood wishes. But, more fortunate than he, we have meanwhile succeeded, in so far as we have not become psychoneurotics, in detaching our sexual impulses from our mothers and in forgetting our jealousy of our fathers. Here is one in whom these primaeval wishes of our childhood have been fulfilled, and we shrink back from him with the whole force of the repression by which those wishes have since that time been held down within us. While the poet, as he unravels the past, brings to light the guilt of Oedipus, he is at the same time compelling us to recognize our own inner minds, in which those same impulses, though suppressed, are still to be found. The contrast with which the closing Chorus leaves us confronted—

> . . . Fix on Oedipus your eyes,
> Who resolved the dark enigma, noblest champion and most wise.
> Like a star has envied fortune mounted beaming far and wide:
> Now he sinks in seas of anguish, whelmed beneath a raging tide . . .

—strikes as a warning at ourselves and our pride, at us who since our childhood have grown so wise and so mighty in our own eyes. Like Oedipus, we live in ignorance of these wishes, repugnant to morality, which have been forced upon us by

Nature, and after their revelation we may all of us well seek to close our eyes to the scenes of our childhood.

There is an unmistakable indication in the text of Sophocles' tragedy itself that the legend of Oedipus sprang from some primaeval dream-material which had as its content the distressing disturbance of a child's relation to his parents owing to the first stirrings of sexuality. At a point when Oedipus, though he is not yet enlightened, has begun to feel troubled by his recollection of the oracle, Jocasta consoles him by referring to a dream which many people dream, though, as she thinks, it has no meaning:

> Many a man ere now in dreams hath lain
> With her who bare him. He hath least annoy
> Who with such omens troubleth not his mind.

Today, just as then, many men dream of having sexual relations with their mothers, and speak of the fact with indignation and astonishment. It is clearly the key to the tragedy and the complement to the dream of the dreamer's father being dead. The story of Oedipus is the reaction of the imagination to these two typical dreams. And just as these dreams, when dreamt by adults, are accompanied by feelings of repulsion, so too the legend must include horror and self-punishment. Its further modification originates once again in a misconceived secondary revision of the material, which has sought to exploit it for theological purposes. The attempt to harmonize divine omnipotence with human responsibility must naturally fail in connection with this subject-matter just as with any other.

Another of the great creations of tragic poetry, Shakespeare's *Hamlet*, has its roots in the same soil as *Oedipus Rex*. But the changed treatment of the same material reveals the whole difference in the mental life of these two widely separated epochs of civilization: the secular advance of repression in the emotional life of mankind. In the *Oedipus* the child's wishful phantasy that underlies it is brought into the open and realized as it would be in a dream. In *Hamlet* it remains repressed; and—just as in the case of a neurosis—we only learn of its existence from its inhibiting consequences. Strangely enough, the overwhelming effect produced by the more modern tragedy has turned out to be compatible with the fact that people have remained completely in the dark as to the hero's character. The play is built up on Hamlet's hesitations over fulfilling the task of revenge that is assigned to him; but its text offers no reasons or motives for these hesitations and an immense variety of attempts at interpreting them have failed to produce a result. According to the view which was originated by Goethe and is still the prevailing one today, Hamlet represents the type of man whose power of direct action is paralysed by an excessive development of his intellect. (He is 'sicklied o'er with the pale cast of thought.') According to another view, the dramatist has tried to portray a pathologically irresolute character which might be classed as neurasthenic. The plot of the drama shows us, however, that Hamlet is far from being represented as a person incapable of taking any action. We see him doing so on two occasions: first in a sudden outburst of temper, when he runs his sword through the eavesdropper behind the arras, and secondly in a premeditated and even crafty fashion, when, with all the callousness of a Renaissance prince, he sends the two courtiers to the death that had been planned for himself. What is it, then, that inhibits him in fulfilling the task set him by his father's ghost? The answer, once again, is that it is the peculiar nature of the task. Hamlet is able to do anything—except take vengeance on the man who did away with his father and took that father's place with his mother, the man who shows him the repressed wishes of his own childhood realized. Thus the loathing which should drive him on to revenge is replaced in him by self-reproaches, by scruples of conscience, which remind him that he himself is literally no better than the sinner whom he is to punish. Here I have translated into conscious terms what was bound to remain unconscious in Hamlet's mind; and if anyone is inclined to call him a hysteric, I can only accept the fact as one that is implied by my interpretation. The distaste for sexuality expressed by Hamlet in his conversation with Ophelia fits in very well with this: the same distaste which was destined to take possession of the poet's mind more and more during the years that followed, and which reached its extreme expression in *Timon of Athens*. For it can of course only be the poet's own mind which confronts us in Hamlet. I observe in a book on Shakespeare by Georg Brandes (1896) a statement that *Hamlet* was written immediately after the death of Shakespeare's father (in 1601), that is, under the immediate impact of his bereavement and, as we may well assume, while his childhood feelings about his father had been freshly revived. It is known, too, that Shakespeare's own son who died at an early age bore the name of 'Hamnet,' which is identical with 'Hamlet.' Just as *Hamlet* deals with the relation of a son to his parents, so *Macbeth* (written at approximately the same period) is concerned with the subject of childlessness. But just as all neurotic symptoms, and, for that matter, dreams, are capable of being 'over-interpreted' and indeed need to be, if they are to be fully understood, so all genuinely creative writings are the product of more than a single motive and more than a single impulse in the poet's mind, and are open to more than a single interpretation. In what I have written I have only attempted to interpret the deepest layer of impulses in the mind of the creative writer.

I cannot leave the subject of typical dreams of the death of loved relatives, without adding a few more words to throw light on their significance for the theory of dreams in general. In these dreams we find the highly unusual condition realized of a dream-thought formed by a repressed wish entirely eluding censorship and passing into the dream without modification. There must be special factors at work to make this event possible, and I believe that the occurrence of these dreams is facilitated by two such factors. Firstly, there is no wish that seems more remote from us than this one: 'we couldn't even *dream*'—so we believe—of wishing such a thing. For this reason the dream-censorship is not armed to meet such a monstrosity, just as Solon's penal code contained no punishment for parricide. Secondly, in this case the repressed and unsuspected wish is particularly often met half-way by a residue from the previous day in the form of a *worry* about the safety of the person concerned. This worry can only make its way into the dream by availing itself of the corresponding wish; while the wish can disguise itself behind the worry that has become active during the day. We may feel inclined to think that things are simpler than this and that one merely carries on during the night and in dreams with what one has been turning over in one's mind during the day; but if so we shall be leaving dreams of the death of people of whom the dreamer is fond completely in the air and without any connection with our explanation of dreams in general, and we shall thus be clinging quite unnecessarily to a riddle which is perfectly capable of solution.

It is also instructive to consider the relation of these dreams to anxiety-dreams. In the dreams we have been discussing, a repressed wish has found a means of evading censorship—and the distortion which censorship involves. The invariable concomitant is that painful feelings are experienced in the dream. In just the same way anxiety-dreams only occur if the censorship has been wholly or partly overpowered; and, on the other hand, the overpowering of the censorship is facilitated if anxiety has already been produced as an immediate sensation arising from somatic sources. We can thus plainly see the purpose for which the censorship exercises its office and brings about the distortion of dreams: it does so *in order to prevent the generation of anxiety or other forms of distressing affect.*❖

Remembering, Repeating, and Working-Through
Sigmund Freud (1919)

At this point I will interpolate a few remarks which every analyst has found confirmed in his observations. Forgetting impressions, scenes or experiences nearly always reduces itself to shutting them off. When the patient talks about these 'forgotten' things he seldom fails to add: 'As a matter of act I've always known it; only I've never thought of it.' He often expresses disappointment at the fact that not enough things come into his head that he can call 'forgotten'—that he has never thought of since they happened. Nevertheless, even this desire is fulfilled, especially in the case of conversion hysterias. 'Forgetting' becomes still further restricted when we assess at their true value the screen memories which are so generally present. In some cases I have had an impression that the familiar childhood amnesia, which is theoretically so important to us, is completely counterbalanced by screen memories. Not only *some* but *all* of what is essential from childhood has been retained in these memories. It is simply a question of knowing how to extract it out of them by analysis. They represent the forgotten years of childhood as adequately as the manifest content of a dream represents the dream-thoughts.

The other group of psychical processes—phantasies, processes of reference, emotional impulses, thought-connections—which, as purely internal acts, can be contrasted with impressions and experiences, must, in their relation to forgetting and remembering, be considered separately. In these processes it particularly often happens that something is 'remembered' which could never have been 'forgotten' because it was never at any time noticed—was never conscious. As regards the course taken by psychical events it seems to make no difference whatever whether such a 'thought-connection' was conscious and then forgotten or whether it never managed to become conscious at all. The conviction which the patient obtains in the course of his analysis is quite independent of this kind of memory.

In the many different forms of obsessional neurosis in particular, forgetting is mostly restricted to dissolving thought-connections, failing to draw the right conclusions and isolating memories.

There is one special class of experiences of the utmost importance for which no memory can as a rule be recovered. These are experiences which occurred in very early childhood and were not understood at the time but which were *subsequently* understood and interpreted. One gains a knowledge of them through dreams and one is obliged to believe in them on the most compelling evidence provided by the fabric of the neurosis. Moreover, we can ascertain for ourselves that the patient, after his resistances have been overcome, no longer invokes the absence of any memory of them (any sense of familiarity with them) as a ground for refusing to accept them.

Excerpt from James Stachey, ed. and trans., *The Standard Edition*, Vol. 12 (London: Hogarth, 1958), pp. 148–155. Reprinted by permission of Sigmund Freud Copyrights, The Institute of Psycho-Analysis, The Hogarth Press, and Basic Books.

This matter, however, calls for so much critical caution and introduces so much that is novel and startling that I shall reserve it for a separate discussion in connection with suitable material.

Under the new technique very little, and often nothing, is left of this delightfully smooth course of events. There are some cases which behave like those under the hypnotic technique up to a point and only later cease to do so; but others behave differently from the beginning. If we confine ourselves to this second type in order to bring out the difference, we may say that the patient does not *remember* anything of what he has forgotten and repressed, but *acts* it out. He reproduces it not as a memory but as an action; he *repeats* it, without, of course, knowing that he is repeating it.

For instance, the patient does not say that he remembers that he used to be defiant and critical towards his parents' authority; instead, he behaves in that way to the doctor. He does not remember how he came to a helpless and hopeless deadlock in his infantile sexual researches; but he produces a mass of confused dreams and associations, complains that he cannot succeed in anything and asserts that he is fated never to carry through what he undertakes. He does not remember having been intensely ashamed of certain sexual activities and afraid of their being found out; but he makes it clear that he is ashamed of the treatment on which he is now embarked and tries to keep it secret from everybody. And so on.

Above, the patient will *begin* his treatment with a repetition of this kind. When one has announced the fundamental rule of psycho-analysis to a patient with an eventful life-history and a long story of illness and has then asked him to say what occurs to his mind, one expects him to pour out a flood of information; but often the first thing that happens is that he has nothing to say. He is silent and declares that nothing occurs to him. This, of course, is merely a repetition of a homosexual attitude which comes to the fore as a resistance against remembering anything. As long as the patient is in the treatment he cannot escape from this compulsion to repeat; and in the end we understand that this is his way of remembering.

What interests us most of all is naturally the relation of this compulsion to repeat to the transference and to resistance. We soon perceive that the transference is itself only a piece of repetition, and that the repetition is a transference of the forgotten past not only on to the doctor but also on to all the other aspects of the current situation. We must be prepared to find, therefore, that the patient yields to the compulsion to repeat, which now replaces the impulsion to remember, not only in his personal attitude to his doctor but also in every other activity and relationship which may occupy his life at the time—if, for instance, he falls in love or undertakes a task or starts an enterprise during the treatment. The part played by resistance, too, is easily recognized. The greater the resistance, the more extensively will acting out (repetition) replace remembering. For the ideal remembering of what has been forgotten which occurs in hypnosis corresponds to a state in which resistance has been put completely on one side. If the patient starts his treatment under the auspices of a mild and unpronounced positive transference it makes it possible at first for him to unearth his memories just as he would under hypnosis, and during this time his pathological symptoms themselves are quiescent. But if, as the analysis proceeds, the transference becomes hostile or unduly intense and therefore in need of repression, remembering at once gives way to acting out. From then onwards the resistances determine the sequence of the material which is to be repeated. The patient brings out of the armoury of the past the weapons with which he defends himself against the progress of the treatment—weapons which we must wrest from him one by one.

We have learnt that the patient repeats instead of remembering, and repeats under the conditions of resistance. We may now ask what it is that he in fact repeats or acts out. The answer is that he repeats everything that has already made its way from the sources of the repressed into his manifest personality—his inhibitions and unserviceable attitudes and his pathological character-traits. He also repeats all his symptoms in the course of the treatment. And now we can see that in drawing attention to the compulsion to repeat we have acquired no new fact but only a more comprehensive view. We have only made it clear to ourselves that the patient's state of being ill cannot cease with the beginning of his analysis, and that we must treat his illness, not as an event of the past, but as a present-day force. This state of illness is brought, piece by piece, within the field and range of operation of the treatment, and while the patient experiences it as something real and contemporary, we have to do our therapeutic work on it, which consists in a large measure in tracing it back to the past.

Remembering, as it was induced in hypnosis, could not but give the impression of an experiment carried out in the laboratory. Repeating, as it is induced in analytic treatment according to the newer technique, on the other hand, implies conjuring up a piece of real life; and for that reason it cannot always be harmless and unobjectionable. This consideration opens up the whole problem of what is so often unavoidable—'deterioration during treatment'.

First and foremost, the initiation of the treatment in itself brings about a change in the patient's conscious attitude to his illness. He has usually been content with lamenting it, despising it as nonsensical and under-estimating its importance; for the rest, he has extended to its manifestations the ostrich-like policy of repression which he adopted towards its origins. Thus it can happen that he does not properly know under what conditions his phobia breaks out or does not listen to the precise wording of his obsessional ideas or does not grasp the actual purpose of his obsessional impulse. The treatment, of course, is not helped by this. He must find the courage to direct his attention to the phenomena of his illness. His illness itself must no longer seem to him contemptible, but must become an enemy worthy of his mettle, a piece of his personality, which has solid ground for its existence and out of which things of value for his future life have to be derived. The way is thus paved from the beginning for a reconciliation with the repressed material which is coming to expression in his symptoms, while at the same time place is found for a certain tolerance for the state of being ill. If this new attitude towards the illness intensifies the conflicts and brings to the fore symptoms which till then had been indistinct, one can easily console the patient by pointing out that these are only necessary and temporary aggravations and that one cannot overcome an enemy who is absent or not within range. The resistance, however, may exploit the situation for its own ends and abuse the licence to be ill. It seems to say: 'See what happens if I really give way to such things. Was I not right to consign them to repression?' Young and childish people in particular are inclined to make the necessity imposed by the treatment for paying attention to their illness a welcome excuse for luxuriating in their symptoms.

Further dangers arise from the fact that in the course of the treatment new and deeper-lying instinctual impulses, which had not hitherto made themselves felt, may come to be 'repeated.' Finally, it is possible that the patient's actions outside the transference may do him temporary harm in his ordinary life, or even have been so chosen as permanently to invalidate his prospects of recovery.

The tactics to be adopted by the physician in this situation are easily justified. For him, remembering in the old manner—reproduction in the psychical field—is the aim to which he adheres, even though he knows that such an aim cannot be achieved in the new technique. He is prepared for a perpetual struggle with his patient to keep in the psychical sphere all the impulses which the patient would like to direct into the motor sphere; and he celebrates it as a triumph for the treatment if he can bring it about that something that the patient wishes to discharge in action is disposed of through the work of remembering. If the attachment through transference has grown into something at all serviceable, the treatment is able to prevent the patient from executing any of the more important repetitive actions and to utilize his intention to do so *in statu nascendi* as material for the therapeutic work. One best protects the patient from injuries brought about through carrying out one of his impulses by making him promise not to take any important decisions affecting his life during the time of his treatment—for instance, not to choose any profession or definitive love-object—but to postpone all such plans until after his recovery.

At the same time one willingly leaves untouched as much of the patient's personal freedom as is compatible with these restrictions, nor does one hinder him from carrying out unimportant intentions, even if they are foolish; one does not forget that it is in fact only through his own experience and mishaps that a person learns sense. There are also people whom one cannot restrain from plunging into some quite undesirable project during the treatment and who only afterwards become ready for, and accessible to, analysis. Occasionally, too, it is bound to happen that the untamed instincts assert themselves before there is time to put the reins of the transference on them, or that the bonds which attach the patient to the treatment are broken by him in a repetitive action. As an extreme example of this, I may cite the case of an elderly lady who had repeatedly fled from her house and her husband in a twilight state and gone no one knew where, without ever having become conscious of her motive for decamping in this way. She came to treatment with a marked affectionate transference which grew in intensity with uncanny rapidity in the first few days, by the end of the week she had decamped from me, too, before I had had time to say anything to her which might have prevented this repetition.

The main instrument, however, for curbing the patient's compulsion to repeat and for turning it into a motive for remembering lies in the handling of the transference. We render the compulsion harmless, and indeed useful, by giving it the right to assert itself in a definite field. We admit it into the transference as a playground in which it is allowed to expand in almost complete freedom and in which it is expected to display to us everything in the way of pathogenic instincts that is hidden in the patient's mind. Provided only that the patient shows compliance enough to respect the necessary conditions of the analysis, we regularly succeed in giving all the symptoms of the illness a new transference meaning and in replacing his ordinary neurosis by a 'transference-neurosis' of which he can be cured by the therapeutic work. The transference thus creates an intermediate region between illness and real life through which the transition from the one to the other is made. The new condition has taken over all the features of the illness; but it represents an artificial illness which is at every point accessible to our intervention. It is a piece of real experience, but one which has been made possible by especially favourable conditions, and it is of a provisional nature. From the repetitive reactions which are exhibited in the transference we are led along the familiar paths to the awakening of the memories, which appear without difficulty, as it were, after the resistance has been overcome.❖

The Return of the Repressed in Social Life
Sigmund Freud (1937–1939)

There are a number of similar processes among those which the analytic investigation of mental life has made known to us. Some of them are termed pathological; others are counted among the varieties of the normal. This matters little, however, for the limits between the two are not strictly defined, and the mechanisms are to a certain extent the same. It is much more important whether the changes in question take place in the Ego itself or whether they confront it as alien; in the latter case they are called symptoms. From the fullness of the material at my disposal I will choose cases that concern the formation of character.

A young girl had developed into the most decided contrast to her mother; she had cultivated all the qualities she missed in her mother and avoided all those that reminded her of her mother. I may add that in former years she had identified herself with her mother—like any other female child—and had now come to oppose this identification energetically. When this girl married, however, and became a wife and mother in her turn, we are surprised to find that she became more and more like the mother towards whom she felt so inimical, until at last the mother-identification she had overcome had once more unmistakably won the day. The same thing happens with boys, and even the great Goethe, who in his *Sturm und Drang* period certainly did not respect his pedantic and stiff father very highly, developed in old age traits that belonged to his father's character. This result will stand out more strikingly where the contrast between the two persons is more pronounced. A young man, whose fate was determined by his having to grow up with a good-for-nothing father, developed at first—in spite of the father—into a capable, trustworthy, and honourable man. In the prime of life his character changed and from then on he behaved as if he had taken this same father as his example. So as not to lose the connection with our topic we must keep in mind that at the beginning of such a process there always exists an identification with the father from early childhood days. This gets repudiated, even over-compensated, and in the end again comes to light.

It has long since become common knowledge that the experience of the first five years of childhood exert a decisive influence on our life, one which later events oppose in vain. Much could be said about how these early experiences resist all efforts of more mature years to modify them, but this would not be relevant. It may not be so well known, however, that the strongest obsessive influence derives from those experiences which the child undergoes at a time when we have reason to believe his psychical apparatus to be incompletely fitted for accepting them. The fact itself cannot be doubted, but it seems so strange that we might try to make it easier to understand by a simile; the process may be compared to a photograph, which can be developed and made into a picture after a short or long interval. Here I may point out, however, that an imaginative writer, with the boldness permitted to such writers, made this disconcerting discovery before me. E. T. A. Hoffmann used to explain the wealth of imaginative figures that offered themselves to him for his stories by the quickly changing pictures and impressions he had received during a journey in a post-chaise, lasting for several weeks, while he was still a babe at his mother's breast.

What a child has experienced and not understood by the time he has reached the age of two he may never again remember, except in his dreams. Only through psychoanalytic treatment will he become aware of those events. At any time in later years, however, they may break into his life with obsessive impulsiveness, direct his actions, force him to like or dislike people, and often decide the choice of his love-object by a preference that so often cannot be rationally defended. The two points that touch on our problem are unmistakable. They are, first, the remoteness of time, which is considered here as the really decisive factor, as, for instance, in the special state of memory that in these childhood experiences we class as "unconscious." In this feature we expect to find an analogy with the state of mind that we ascribe to tradition when it is active in the mental emotional life of a people. It was not easy, it is true, to introduce the conception of the unconscious into mass psychology.

Contributions to the phenomena we are looking for are regularly made by the mechanisms that lead to a neurosis. Here also the decisive experiences in early childhood exert a lasting influence, yet in this case the stress falls not on the time, but on the process opposing that event, the reaction against it. Schematically expressed, it is thus: As a consequence of a certain experience there arises an instinctual demand which claims satisfaction. The Ego forgoes this satisfaction, either because it is paralysed by the excessiveness of the demand or because it recognizes in it a danger. The first of these reasons is the original one; both end in the avoidance of a dangerous situation. The Ego guards against this danger by repression. The excitation becomes inhibited in one way or another; the incitement, with the observations and perceptions belonging to it, is forgotten. This, however, does not bring the process to an end; either the instinct has kept its strength, or it will regain it, or it is reawakened by a new situation. It renews its claim and—since the way to normal satisfaction is barred by what we may call the scar tissue of repression—it gains at some weak point new access to a so-called substitutive satisfaction which now appears as a symptom, without the acquiescence and also without the comprehension of the Ego. All phenomena of symptom-formation can be fairly described as "the return of the repressed." The distinctive character of them, however, lies in the extensive distortion the returning elements have undergone, compared with their original form. Perhaps the objection will be raised here that in this last group of facts I have deviated too much from the similarity with tradition. I shall feel no regret, however, if this has led us nearer to the problems of instinctual renunciation.

The Historical Truth

I have made all these psychological digressions to make it more credible that the religion of Moses exercised influence on the Jewish people only when it had become a tradition. We have scarcely achieved more than a probability. Yet let us assume we have succeeded in proving this conclusively; the impression would still remain that we had satisfied only the qualitative factor of our task, not the quantitative as well. To all matters concerning the creation of a religion—and certainly to that of the Jewish one—pertains something majestic, which has not so far been covered by our explanations. Some other element should have part in it: one that has few analogies and nothing quite like it, something unique and commensurate with that which has grown out of it, something like religion itself.

Let us see if we can approach our subject from the reverse side. We understand that primitive man needs a god as creator of the world, as head of his tribe, and as one who takes care of him. This god takes his place behind the dead fathers of whom tradition still has something to relate. Man in later times—in our time, for instance—behaves similarly. He also remains infantile and needs protection, even when he is fully grown; he feels he cannot relinquish the support of his god. So much is indisputable, but it is not so easily to be understood why there must be only one god, why just the progress from henotheism to monotheism acquires such an overwhelming significance. It is true, as I have mentioned before, that the believer participates in the greatness of his god, and the more powerful the god, the surer the protection he can bestow. The power of a god, however, need not presuppose his being an only god: many peoples only glorified their chief god the more if he ruled over a multitude of inferior gods; he was not the less great because there were other gods than he. It also meant sacrificing some of the intimate relationship if the god became universal and cared equally for all lands and peoples. One had, so to speak, to share one's god with strangers and had to compensate oneself for that by believing that one was favoured by him. The point could be made that the conception of an Only God signifies a step forward in spirituality; this point, however, cannot be estimated so very highly.

The true believer knows of a way adequately to fill in this obvious gap in motivation. He says that the idea of an Only God has had this overwhelming effect on mankind because it is part of eternal truth, which, hidden for so long, has at last come to light and has swept all before it. We have to admit that at last we have an element of an order commensurate to the greatness of the subject as well as to that of the success of its influence.

I also should like to accept this solution. However, I have my misgivings. The religious argument is based on an optimistic and idealistic premiss. The human intellect has not shown itself elsewhere to be endowed with a very good scent for truth, nor has the human mind displayed any special readiness to accept truth. On the contrary, it is the general experience that the human intellect errs very easily without our suspecting it at all, and that nothing is more readily believed than what—regardless of the truth—meets our wishes and illusions half-way. That is why our agreement needs modifying. I too should credit the believer's solution with containing the truth; it is not, however, the material truth, but a historical truth. I would claim the right to correct a certain distortion which this truth underwent on its re-emergence. That is to say, I do not believe that one supreme great God "exists" today, but I believe that in primeval times there was one person who must needs appear gigantic and who, raised to the status of a deity, returned to the memory of men.

Our supposition was that the religion of Moses was discarded and partly forgotten and that, later on, it forced itself on the notice of the people as a tradition. I make the assumption that this process was the repetition of an earlier one. When Moses gave to his people the conception of an Only God it was not an altogether new idea, for it meant the reanimation of primeval experience in the human family that had long ago faded from the conscious memory of mankind. The experience was such an important one, however, and had produced, or at least prepared, such far-reaching changes in the life of man that, I cannot help thinking, it must have left some permanent trace in the human soul—something comparable to a tradition.

The psychoanalyses of individuals have taught us that their earliest impressions, received at a time when they were hardly able to talk, manifest themselves later in an obsessive fashion, although those impressions themselves are not consciously remembered. We feel that the same must hold good for the earliest experiences of mankind. One result of this is the emergence of the conception of one great God. It must be recognized as a memory—a distorted one, it is true, but nevertheless a memory. It has an obsessive quality; it simply must be believed. As far as its distortion goes, it may be called a delusion; in so far as it brings to light something from the past, it must be called truth. The psychiatric delusion also contains a particle of truth; the patient's conviction issues from this and extends to the whole delusional fabrication surrounding it.

. . . In 1912 I tried in my book *Totem and Taboo* to reconstruct the ancient situation from which all these effects issued. In that book I made use of certain theoretical reflections of Charles Darwin, J. J. Atkinson, and especially Robertson Smith, and combined them with findings and suggestions from psychoanalytic practice. From Darwin I borrowed the hypothesis that men originally lived in small hordes; each of the hordes stood under the rule of an older male, who governed by brute force, appropriated all the females, and belaboured or killed all the young males, including his own sons. From Atkinson I received the suggestion that this patriarchal system came to an end through a rebellion of the sons, who united against the father, overpowered him, and together consumed his body. Following Robertson Smith's totem theory, I suggested that this horde, previously ruled by the father, was followed by a totemistic brother clan. In order to be able to live in peace with one another the victorious brothers renounced the women for whose sake they had killed the father, and agreed to practise exogamy. The power of the father was broken and the families were regulated by matriarchy. The ambivalence of the sons towards the father remained in force during the whole further development. Instead of the father a certain animal was declared the totem; it stood for their ancestor and protecting spirit, and no one was allowed to hurt or kill it. Once a year, however, the whole clan assembled for a feast at which the otherwise revered totem was torn to pieces and eaten. No one was permitted to abstain from this feast; it was the solemn repetition of the father-murder, in which social order, moral laws, and religion had had their beginnings. The correspondence of the totem feast (according to Robertson Smith's description) with the Christian Communion has struck many authors before me.

I still adhere to this sequence of thought. I have often been vehemently reproached for not changing my opinions in later editions of my book, since more recent ethnologists have without exception discarded Robertson Smith's theories and have in part replaced them by others which differ extensively. I would reply that these alleged advances in science are well known to me. Yet I have not been convinced either of their correctness or of Robertson Smith's errors. Contradiction is not always refutation; a new theory does not necessarily denote progress. Above all, however, I am not an ethnologist, but a psychoanalyst. It was my good right to select from ethnological data what would serve me for my analytic work. The writings of the highly gifted Robertson Smith provided me with valuable points of contact with the psychological material of analysis and suggestions for the use of it. It cannot say the same of the work of his opponents. ❖

Civilization and the Individual
Sigmund Freud (1930)

The analogy between the process of civilization and the path of individual development may be extended in an important respect. It can be asserted that the community, too, evolves a super-ego under whose influence cultural development proceeds. It

Excerpt from James Stachey, ed. and trans., *Civilization and Its Discontents* (New York: W. W. Norton, 1961), pp. 88–92. Copyright 1961 by James Stachey. Reprinted by permission of W. W. Norton and Co. and Hogarth Press, Ltd.

would be a tempting task for anyone who has a knowledge of human civilizations to follow out this analogy in detail. I will confine myself to bringing forward a few striking points. The super-ego of an epoch of civilization has an origin similar to that of an individual. It is based on the impression left behind by the personalities of great leaders—men of overwhelming force of mind or men in whom one of the human impulsions has found its strongest and purest, and therefore often its most one-sided, expression. In many instances the analogy goes still further, in that during their lifetime these figures were—often enough, even if not always—mocked and maltreated by others and even despatched in a cruel fashion. In the same way, indeed, the primal father did not attain divinity until long after he had met his death by violence. The most arresting example of this fateful conjunction is to be seen in the figure of Jesus Christ—if, indeed, that figure is not a part of mythology, which called it into being from an obscure memory of that primal event. Another point of agreement between the cultural and the individual super-ego is that the former, just like the latter, sets up strict ideal demands, disobedience to which is visited with 'fear of conscience.' Here, indeed, we come across the remarkable circumstance that the mental processes concerned are actually more familiar to us and more accessible to consciousness as they are seen in the group than they can be in the individual man. In him, when tension arises, it is only the aggressiveness of the super-ego which, in the form of reproaches, makes itself noisily heard; its actual demands often remain unconscious in the background. If we bring them to conscious knowledge, we find that they coincide with the precepts of the prevailing cultural super-ego. At this point the two processes, that of the cultural development of the group and that of the cultural development of the individual, are, as it were, always interlocked. For that reason some of the manifestations and properties of the super-ego can be more easily detected in its behaviour in the cultural community than in the separate individual.

The cultural super-ego has developed its ideals and set up its demands. Among the latter, those which deal with the relations of human beings to one another are comprised under the heading of ethics. People have at all times set the greatest value on ethics, as though they expected that it in particular would produce especially important results. And it does in fact deal with a subject which can easily be recognized as the sorest spot in every civilization. Ethics is thus to be regarded as a therapeutic attempt—as an endeavour to achieve, by means of a command of the super-ego, something which has so far not been achieved by means of any other cultural activities. As we already know, the problem before us is how to get rid of the greatest hindrance to civilization—namely, the constitutional inclination of human beings to be aggressive towards one another; and for that very reason we are especially interested in what is probably the most recent of the cultural commands of the super-ego, the commandment to love one's neighbour as oneself. In our research into, and therapy of, a neurosis, we are led to make two reproaches against the super-ego of the individual. In the severity of its commands and prohibitions it troubles itself too little about the happiness of the ego, in that it takes insufficient account of the resistances against obeying them—of the instinctual strength of the id [in the first place], and of the difficulties presented by the real external environment [in the second]. Consequently we are very often obliged, for therapeutic purposes, to oppose the super-ego, and we endeavour to lower its demands. Exactly the same objections can be made against the ethical demands of the cultural super-ego. It, too, does not trouble itself enough about the facts of the mental constitution of human beings. It issues a command and does not ask whether it is possible for people to obey it. On the contrary, it assumes that a man's ego is psychologically capable of anything that is required of it, that his ego has unlimited mastery over his id. This is a mistake; and even in what are known as normal people the id cannot be controlled beyond certain limits. If more is demanded of a man, a revolt will be produced in him or a neurosis, or he will be made unhappy. The commandment, 'Love thy neighbour as thyself,' is the strongest defence against human aggressiveness and an excellent example of the unpsychological proceedings of the cultural super-ego. The commandment is impossible to fulfil; such an enormous inflation of love can only lower its value, not get rid of the difficulty. Civilization pays no attention to all this; it merely admonishes us that the harder it is to obey the precept the more meritorious it is to do so. But anyone who follows such a precept in present-day civilization only puts himself at a disadvantage *vis-à-vis* the person who disregards it. What a potent obstacle to civilization aggressiveness must be, if the defence against it can cause as much unhappiness as aggressiveness itself! 'Natural' ethics, as it is called, has nothing to offer here except the narcissistic satisfaction of being able to think oneself better than others. At this point the ethics based on religion introduces its promises of a better afterlife. But so long as virtue is not rewarded here on earth, ethics will, I fancy, preach in vain. I too think it quite certain that a real change in the relations of human beings to possessions would be of more help in this direction than any ethical commands; but the recognition of this fact among socialists has been obscured and made useless for practical purposes by a fresh idealistic misconception of human nature.

I believe the line of thought which seeks to trace in the phenomena of cultural development the part played by a super-ego promises still further discoveries. I hasten to come to a close. But there is one question which I can hardly evade. If the development of civilization has such a far-reaching similarity to the development of the individual and if it employs the same methods, may we not be justified in reaching the diagnosis that, under the influence of cultural urges, some civilizations, or some epochs of civilization—possibly the whole of mankind—have become 'neurotic'? An analytic dissection of such neuroses might lead to therapeutic recommendations which could lay claim to great practical interest. I would not say that an attempt of this kind to carry psycho-analysis over to the cultural community was absurd or doomed to be fruitless. But we should have to be very cautious and not forget that, after all, we are only dealing with analogies and that it is dangerous, not only with men but also with concepts, to tear them from the sphere in which they have originated and been evolved. Moreover, the diagnosis of communal neuroses is faced with a special difficulty. In an individual neurosis we take as our starting-point the contrast that distinguishes the patient from his environment, which is assumed to be 'normal.' For a group all of whose members are affected by one and the same disorder no such background could exist; it would have to be found elsewhere. And as regards the therapeutic application of our knowledge, what would be the use of the most correct analysis of social neuroses, since no one possesses authority to impose such a therapy upon the group? But in spite of all these difficulties, we may expect that one day someone will venture to embark upon a pathology of cultural communities.

For a wide variety of reasons, it is very far from my intention to express an opinion upon the value of human civilization. I have endeavoured to guard myself against the enthusiastic prejudice which holds that our civilization is the most precious thing that we possess or could acquire and that its path will necessarily lead to heights of unimagined perfection. I can at least listen without indignation to the critic who is of the opinion that when one surveys the aims of cultural endeavour and the means it employs, one is bound to come to the conclusion that the whole effort is not worth the trouble, and that the outcome of it can only be a state of affairs which the individual will be unable to tolerate. . . . Thus I have not the courage to rise up before my fellow-men as a prophet, and I bow to their reproach that I can offer them no consolation: for at bottom that is what they are all demanding—the wildest revolutionaries no less passionately than the most virtuous believers.

The fateful question for the human species seems to me to be whether and to what extent their cultural development will succeed in mastering the disturbance of their communal life by the human instinct of aggression and self-destruction. It may be that in this respect precisely the present time deserves a special interest. Men have gained control over the forces of nature to such an extent that with their help they would have no difficulty in exterminating one another to the last man. They know this, and hence comes a large part of their current unrest, their unhappiness and their mood of anxiety. And now it is to be expected that the other of the two 'Heavenly Powers,' eternal Eros, will make an effort to assert himself in the struggle with his equally immortal adversary. But who can foresee with what success and with what result?❖

Ferdinand de Saussure (1857–1913), a Swiss linguist, was a contemporary of Durkheim and Weber. His writings show signs of direct influence from Durkheim, as well as from Marx. Yet little is known of his direct connections to the other social theorists of his time. Though his theory of linguistics is technical and occasionally esoteric, many readers find in it the outlines of a general social theory. Saussure's theory of language as a silent reservoir of linguistic knowledges on which speakers draw was a major influence on early structuralism and poststructuralism in the two decades following World War II. One could even say that Saussure was discovered in this period in order to serve as a classic source for social theorists interested in remaking the social and human sciences with reference to language. This notion gains some credence from the fact that his best-known book, Course in General Linguistics, was composed by former students from notes they took in his classes in Geneva between 1906 and 1911. There were fewer public demands for Saussure's ideas during his lifetime.

The selections from *Course in General Linguistics* represent those aspects of Saussure's linguistics most frequently used in current social theory: the theory of signs, the social basis of language, and the theory of linguistic and social values. A careful reading will reveal the influences of Durkheim and Marx, which partly explain Saussure's later popularity among French structuralist social theorists.

Arbitrary Social Values and the Linguistic Sign
Ferdinand de Saussure (1906–1911)

Sign, Signified, Signifier

Some people regard language, when reduced to its elements, as a naming-process only—a list of words, each corresponding to the thing that it names. For example:

Excerpt from Charles Bally and Albert Sechenhaye, eds., and Wade Baskin, trans., *Course in General Linguistics* (1966) pp. 65–69, 71–72, 78–79, 111–117. Reprinted by permission of Philosophical Library, New York.

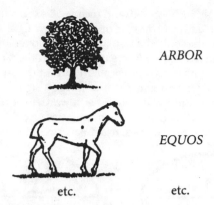

ARBOR

EQUOS

etc.   etc.

This conception is open to criticism at several points. It assumes that ready-made ideas exist before words; it does not tell us whether a name is vocal or psychological in nature (*arbor,* for instance, can be considered from either viewpoint); finally, it lets us assume that the linking of a name and a thing is a very simple operation—an assumption that is anything but true. But this rather naive approach can bring us near the truth by showing us that the linguistic unit is a double entity, one formed by the associating of two terms.

We have seen in considering the speaking-circuit that both terms involved in the linguistic sign are psychological and are united in the brain by an associative bond. This point must be emphasized.

The linguistic sign unites, not a thing and a name, but a concept and a sound-image. The latter is not the material sound, a purely physical thing, but the psychological imprint of the sound, the impression that it makes on our senses. The sound-image is sensory, and if I happen to call it "material," it is only in that sense, and by way of opposing it to the other term of the association, the concept, which is generally more abstract.

The psychological character of our sound-images becomes apparent when we observe our own speech. Without moving our lips or tongue, we can talk to ourselves or recite mentally a selection of verse. Because we regard the words of our language as sound-images, we must avoid speaking of the "phonemes" that make up the words. This term, which suggests vocal activity, is applicable to the spoken word only, to the realization of the inner image in discourse. We can avoid that misunderstanding by speaking of the *sounds* and *syllables* of a word provided we remember that the names refer to the sound-image.

The linguistic sign is then a two-sided psychological entity that can be represented by the drawing:

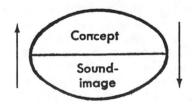

The two elements are intimately united, and each recalls the other. Whether we try to find the meaning of the Latin word *arbor* or the word that Latin uses to designate the concept "tree," it is clear that only the associations sanctioned by that language appear to us to conform to reality, and we disregard whatever others might be imagined.

Our definition of the linguistic sign poses an important question of terminology. I call the combination of a concept and a sound-image a *sign*, but in current usage the term generally designates only a sound-image, a word, for example (*arbor*, etc.). One tends to forget that *arbor* is called a sign only because it carries the concept "tree," with the result that the idea of the sensory part implies the idea of the whole.

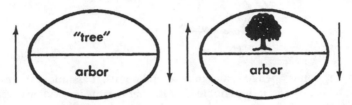

Ambiguity would disappear if the three notions involved here were designated by three names, each suggesting and opposing the others. I propose to retain the word *sign* [*signe*] to designate the whole and to replace *concept* and *sound-image* respectively by *signified* [*signifié*] and *signifier* [*signifiant*]; the last two terms have the advantage of indicating the opposition that separates them from each other and from the whole of which they are parts. As regards *sign*, if I am satisfied with it, this is simply because I do not know of any word to replace it, the ordinary language suggesting no other.

The linguistic sign, as defined, has two primordial characteristics. In enunciating them I am also positing the basic principles of any study of this type.

Principle I: The Arbitrary Nature of the Sign

The bond between the signifier and the signified is arbitrary. Since I mean by sign the whole that results from the associating of the signifier with the signified, I can simply say: *the linguistic sign is arbitrary.*

The idea of "sister" is not linked by any inner relationship to the succession of sounds *s-ö-r* which serves as its signifier in French; that it could be represented equally by just any other sequence is proved by differences among languages and by the very existence of different languages: the signified "ox" has as its signifier *b-ö-f* on one side of the border and *o-k-s* (*Ochs*) on the other.

No one disputes the principle of the arbitrary nature of the sign, but it is often easier to discover a truth than to assign to it its proper place. Principle I dominates all the linguistics of language; its consequences are numberless. It is true that not all of them are equally obvious at first glance; only after many detours does one discover them, and with them the primordial importance of the principle.

One remark in passing: when semiology becomes organized as a science, the question will arise whether or not it properly includes modes of expression based on completely natural signs, such as pantomime. Supposing that the new science welcomes them, its main concern will still be the whole group of systems grounded on the arbitrariness of the sign. In fact, every means of expression used in society is based, in principle, on collective behavior or—what amounts to the same thing—on convention. Polite formulas, for instance, though often imbued with a certain natural expressiveness (as in the case of a Chinese who greets his emperor by bowing down to the ground nine times), are nonetheless fixed by rule; it is this rule and not the intrinsic value of the gestures that obliges one to use them. Signs that are wholly arbitrary realize better than the others the ideal of the semiological process; that is why language, the most complex and universal of all systems of expression, is also the most characteristic; in this sense linguistics can become the master-pattern for all branches of semiology although language is only one particular semiological system.

The word *symbol* has been used to designate the linguistic sign, or more specifically, what is here called the signifier. Principle I in particular weighs against the use of this term. One characteristic of the symbol is that it is never wholly arbitrary; it is not empty, for there is the rudiment of a natural bond between the signifier and the signified. The symbol of justice, a pair of scales, could not be replaced by just any other symbol, such as a chariot.

The word *arbitrary* also calls for comment. The term should not imply that the choice of the signifier is left entirely to the speaker (we shall see below that the individual does not have the power to change a sign in any way once it has become established in the linguistic community); I mean that it is unmotivated, i.e. arbitrary in that it actually has no natural connection with the signified. . . .

The Sign and the Community

The signifier, though to all appearances freely chosen with respect to the idea that it represents, is fixed, not free, with respect to the linguistic community that uses it. The masses have no voice in the matter, and the signifier chosen by language could be replaced by no other. This fact, which seems to embody a contradiction, might be called colloquially "the stacked deck." We say to language: "Choose!" but we add: "It must be this sign and no other." No individual, even if he willed it, could modify in any way at all the choice that has been made; and what is more, the community itself cannot control so much as single word; it is bound to the existing language.

No longer can language be identified with a contract pure and simple, and it is precisely from this viewpoint that the linguistic sign is a particularly interesting object of study; for language furnishes the best proof that a law accepted by a community is a thing that is tolerated and not a rule to which all freely consent.

Let us first see why we cannot control the linguistic sign and then draw together the important consequences that issue from the phenomenon.

No matter what period we choose or how far back we go, language always appears as a heritage of the preceding period. We might conceive of an act by which, at a given moment, names were assigned to things and a contract was formed between concepts and sound-images; but such an act has never been recorded. The notion that things might have happened like that was prompted by our acute awareness of the arbitrary nature of the sign.

No society, in fact, knows or has ever known language other than as a product inherited from preceding generations, and one to be accepted as such. That is why the question of the origin of speech is not so important as it is generally assumed to be. The question is not even worth asking; the only real object of linguistics is the normal, regular life of an existing idiom. A particular language-state is always the product of historical forces, and these forces explain why the sign is unchangeable, i.e. why it resists any arbitrary substitution.

Nothing is explained by saying that language is something inherited and leaving it at that. Can not existing and inherited laws be modified from one moment to the next?

To meet that objection, we must put language into its social setting and frame the question just as we would for any other social institution. How are other social institutions transmitted? This more general question includes the question of immutability. We must first determine the greater or lesser amounts of freedom that the other institutions enjoy; in each instance it will be seen that a different proportion exists between fixed tradition and the free action of society. The next step is to discover why in a given category, the forces of the first type carry more weight or less weight than those of the second. Finally, coming back to language, we must ask why the historical factor of transmission dominates it entirely and prohibits any sudden widespread change.

There are many possible answers to the question. For example, one might point to the fact that succeeding generations are not superimposed on one another like the drawers of a piece of furniture, but fuse and interpenetrate, each generation embracing individuals of all ages—with the result that modifications of language are not tied to the succession of generations. One might also recall the sum of the efforts required for learning the mother language and conclude that a general change would be impossible. Again, it might be added that reflection does not enter into the active use of an idiom—speakers are largely unconscious of the laws of language; and if they are unaware of them, how could they modify them? Even if they were aware of these laws, we may be sure that their awareness would seldom lead to criticism, for people are generally satisfied with the language they have received. . . .

The linguistic sign is arbitrary; language, as defined, would therefore seem to be a system which, because it depends solely on a rational principle, is free and can be organized at will. Its social nature, considered independently, does not definitely rule out this viewpoint. Doubtless it is not on a purely logical basis that group psychology operates; one must consider everything that deflects reason in actual contacts between individuals. But the thing which keeps language from being a simple convention that can be modified at the whim of interested parties is not its social nature; it is rather the action of time combined with the social force. If time is left out, the linguistic facts are incomplete and no conclusion is possible.

If we considered language in time, without the community of speakers—imagine an isolated individual living for several centuries—we probably would notice no change; time would not influence language. Conversely, if we considered the community of speakers without considering time, we would not see the effect of the social forces that influence language. To represent the actual facts, we must then add to our first drawing a sign to indicate passage of time:

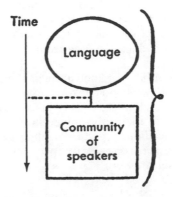

Language is no longer free, for time will allow the social forces at work on it to carry out their effects. This brings us back to the principle of continuity, which cancels freedom. But continuity necessarily implies change, varying degrees of shifts in the relationship between the signified and the signifier.

Linguistic and Social Values

Very few linguists suspect that the intervention of the factor of time creates difficulties peculiar to linguistics and opens to their science two completely divergent paths.

Most other sciences are unaffected by this radical duality; time produces no special effects in them. Astronomy has found that the stars undergo considerable changes but has not been obliged on this account to split itself into two disciplines. Geology is concerned with successions at almost every instant, but its study of strata does not thereby become a radically distinct discipline. Law has its descriptive science and its historical science; no one opposes one to the other. The political history of states is unfolded solely in time, but a historian depicting a particular period does not work apart from history. Conversely, the science of political institutions is essentially descriptive, but if the need arises it can easily deal with a historical question without disturbing its unity.

On the contrary, that duality is already forcing itself upon the economic sciences. Here, in contrast to the other sciences, political economy and economic history constitute two clearly separated disciplines within a single science; the works that have recently appeared on these subjects point up the distinction. Proceeding as they have, economists are—without being well aware of it—obeying an inner necessity. A similar necessity obliges us to divide linguistics into two parts, each with its own principle. Here as in political economy we are confronted with the notion of *value;* both sciences are concerned with *a system for equating things of different orders*—labor and wages in one and a signified and signifier in the other. . . .

To prove that language is only a system of pure values, it is enough to consider the two elements involved in its functioning: ideas and sounds.

Psychologically our thought—apart from its expression in words—is only a shapeless and indistinct mass. Philosophers and linguists have always agreed in recognizing that without the help of signs we would be unable to make a clear-cut, consistent distinction between two ideas. Without language, thought is a vague, uncharted nebula. There are no pre-existing ideas, and nothing is distinct before the appearance of language.

Against the floating realm of thought, would sounds by themselves yield prelimited entities? No more so than ideas. Phonic substance is neither more fixed nor more rigid than thought; it is not a mold into which thought must of necessity fit but a plastic substance divided in turn into distinct parts to furnish the signifiers needed by thought. The linguistic fact can therefore be pictured in its totality—i.e. language—as a series of contiguous subdivisions marked off on both the indefinite plane of jumbled ideas and the equally vague plane of sounds. . . .

Language can also be compared with a sheet of paper: thought is the front and the sound the back; one cannot cut the front without cutting the back at the same time; likewise in language, one can neither divide sound from thought nor thought from sound; the division could be accomplished only abstractedly, and the result would be either pure psychology or pure phonology.

Linguistics then works in the borderland where the elements of sound and thought combine; *their combination produces a form, not a substance.*

These views give a better understanding of what was said before about the arbitrariness of signs. Not only are the two domains that are linked by the linguistic fact shapeless and confused, but the choice of a given slice of sound to name a given idea is completely arbitrary. If this were not true, the notion of value would be compromised, for it would include an externally imposed element. But actually values remain entirely relative, and that is why the bond between the sound and the idea is radically arbitrary.

The arbitrary nature of the sign explains in turn why the social fact alone can create a linguistic system. The community is necessary if values that owe their existence solely to usage and general acceptance are to be set up; by himself the individual is incapable of fixing a single value.

In addition, the idea of value, as defined, shows that to consider a term as simply the union of a certain sound with a certain concept is grossly misleading. To define it in this way would isolate the term from its system; it would mean assuming that one can start from the terms and construct the system by adding them together when, on the contrary, it is from the interdependent whole that one must start and through analysis obtain its elements. . . .

When we speak of the value of a word, we generally think first of its property of standing for an idea, and this is in fact one side of linguistic value. But if this is true, how does *value* differ from *signification*? Might the two words be synonyms? I think not, although it is easy to confuse them, since the confusion results not so much from their similarity as from the subtlety of the distinction that they mark.

From a conceptual viewpoint, value is doubtless one element in signification, and it is difficult to see how signification can be dependent upon value and still be distinct from it. But we must clear up the issue or risk reducing language to a simple naming-process.

Let us first take signification as it is generally understood and as it was pictured. As the arrows in the drawing show, it is only the counterpart of the sound-image. Everything that occurs concerns only the sound-image and the concept when we look upon the word as independent and self-contained.

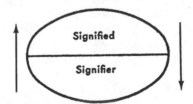

But here is the paradox: on the one hand the concept seems to be the counterpart of the sound-image, and on the other hand the sign itself is in turn the counterpart of the other signs of language.

Language is a system of interdependent terms in which the value of each term results solely from the simultaneous presence of the others, as in the diagram:

How, then can value be confused with signification, i.e. the counterpart of the sound-image? It seems impossible to liken the relations represented here by horizontal arrows to those represented above by vertical arrows. Putting it another way—and again taking up the example of the sheet of paper that is cut in two—it is clear that the observable relation between the different pieces A, B, C, D, etc. is distinct from the relation between the front and back of the same piece as in A/A, B/B, etc.

To resolve the issue, let us observe from the outset that even outside language all values are apparently governed by the same paradoxical principle. They are always composed:

1. of a *dissimilar* thing that can be *exchanged* for the thing of which the value is to be determined; and
2. of *similar* things that can be *compared* with the thing of which the value is to be determined.

Both factors are necessary for the existence of a value. To determine what a five-franc piece is worth one must therefore know: (1) that it can be exchanged for a fixed quantity of a different thing, e.g. bread; and (2) that it can be compared with a similar value of the same system, e.g. a one-franc piece, or with coins of another system (a dollar, etc.). In the same way a word can be exchanged for something dissimilar, an idea; besides, it can be compared with something of the same nature, another word. Its value is therefore not fixed so long as one simply states that it can be "exchanged" for a given concept, i.e. that it has this or that signification: one must also compare it with similar values, with other words that stand in opposition to it. Its content is really fixed only by the concurrence of everything that exists outside it. Being part of a system, it is endowed not only with a signification but also and especially with a value, and this is something quite different.

A few examples will show clearly that this is true. Modern French *mouton* can have the same signification as English *sheep* but not the same value, and this for several reasons, particularly because in speaking of a piece of meat ready to be served on the table, English uses *mutton* and not *sheep*. The difference in value between *sheep* and *mouton* is due to the fact that *sheep* has beside it a second term while the French word does not.

Within the same language, all words used to express related ideas limit each other reciprocally; synonyms like French *redouter* 'dread,' *craindre* 'fear,' and *avoir peur* 'be afraid' have value only through their opposition: if *redouter* did not exist, all its content would go to its competitors. Conversely, some words are enriched through contact with others: e.g. the new element introduced in *décrépit* (un vieillard *décrépit*) results from the co-existence of *décrépi* (un mur *décrépi*). The value of just any term is accordingly determined by its environment; it is impossible to fix even the value of the word signifying "sun" without first considering its surroundings: in some languages it is not possible to say "sit in the *sun*."

Everything said about words applies to any term of language, e.g. to grammatical entities. The value of a French plural does not coincide with that of a Sanskrit plural even though their signification is usually identical; Sanskrit has three numbers instead of two (*my eyes, my ears, my arms, my legs,* etc. are dual); it would be wrong to attribute the same value to the plural in Sanskrit and in French; its value clearly depends on what is outside and around it.

If words stood for pre-existing concepts, they would all have exact equivalents in meaning from one language to the next; but this is not true. French uses *louer* (*une maison*) 'let (a house)' indifferently to mean both "pay for" and "receive payment for," whereas German uses two words, *mieten* and *vermieten;* there is obviously no exact correspondence of values. The German verbs *schätzen* and *urteilen* share a number of significations, but that correspondence does not hold at several points.

Inflection offers some particularly striking examples. Distinctions of time, which are so familiar to us, are unknown in certain languages. Hebrew does not recognize even the fundamental distinctions between the past, present, and future. Proto-Germanic has no special form for the future; to say that the future is expressed by the present is wrong, for the value of the present is not the same in Germanic as in languages that have a future along with the present. The Slavic languages regularly single out two aspects of the verb: the perfective represents action as a point, complete in its totality; the imperfective represents it as taking place, and on the line of time. The categories are difficult for a Frenchman to understand, for they are unknown in French; if they were predetermined, this would not be true. Instead of preexisting ideas then, we find in all the foregoing examples *values* emanating from the system. When they are said to correspond to concepts, it is understood that the concepts are purely differential and defined not by their positive content but negatively by their relations with the other terms of the system. Their most precise characteristic is in being what the others are not.

Now the real interpretation of the diagram of the signal becomes apparent. This

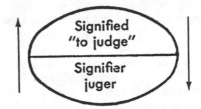

means that in French the concept "to judge" is linked to the sound-image *juger;* in short, it symbolizes signification. But it is quite clear that initially the concept is nothing, that is only a value determined by its relations with other similar values, and that without them the signification would not exist. If I state simply that a word signifies something when I have in mind the associating of a sound-image with a concept, I am making a statement that may suggest what actually happens, but by no means am I expressing the linguistic fact in its essence and fullness.❖

❖ Split Lives in the Modern World ❖

William James (1842–1910) was a psychologist in the days before the boundaries between psychology and philosophy were well formed. His writings, even including *Principles of Psychology* (1890), were, therefore, equally important to the early history of modern psychology in the United States and to the most indigenous American school of philosophy, pragmatism. James was born into America's literary elite. His father had been an intimate of Ralph Waldo Emerson, and his brother was Henry James, the novelist. Throughout most of his adult life, William James was associated with Harvard, where the building housing the social sciences now bears his name. The selection that follows describes his attempt to classify the dimensions of self. This is the classic formulation of the idea of a social self, described against three other parts of self. Though this is a formal scientific exposition, its manifest confusion over the parts of self reflect the ordinary life experience of individuals who feel themselves pulled in a number of directions.

The Self and Its Selves

William James (1890)

Let us begin with the Self in its widest acceptation, and follow it up to its most delicate and subtle form, advancing from the study of the empirical, as the Germans call it, to that of the pure, Ego.

The Empirical Self or Me

The Empirical Self of each of us is all that he is tempted to call by the name of *me*. But it is clear that between what a man calls *me* and what he simply calls *mine* the line is difficult to draw. We feel and act about certain things that are ours very much as we feel and act about ourselves. Our fame, our children, the work of our hands, may be as dear to us as our bodies are, and arouse the same feelings and the same acts of reprisal if attacked. And our bodies themselves, are they simply ours, or are they *us*? Certainly men have been ready to disown their very bodies and to regard them as mere vestures, or even as prisons of clay from which they should some day be glad to escape.

We see then that we are dealing with a fluctuating material; the same object being sometimes treated as a part of me, at other times as simply mine, and then again as if I had nothing to do with it at all. *In its widest possible sense,* however, *a man's Self is the sum total of all that he* CAN *call his,* not only his body and his psychic powers,

---

Excerpt from Frederick Burkhardt, general ed., and Fredson Bowers, textual ed., *The Principles of Psychology*, Vol. 1 (Cambridge: Harvard University Press, 1981 [1890]), pp. 279–283, 287–288, 314–316. Reprinted by permission of the publishers. Copyright 1981 by the President and Fellows of Harvard College.

but his clothes and his house, his wife and children, his ancestors and friends, his reputation and works, his lands and horses, and yacht and bank-account. All these things give him the same emotions. If they wax and prosper, he feels triumphant; if they dwindle and die away, he feels cast down—not necessarily in the same degree for each thing, but in much the same way for all. Understanding the Self in this widest sense, we may begin by dividing the history of it into three parts, relating respectively to—

1. Its constituents;
2. The feelings and emotions they arouse,—*Self-feelings;*
3. The actions to which they prompt,—*Self-seeking and Self-preservation.*

1. *The constituents of the Self* may be divided into two classes, those which make up respectively—

   a.   The material Self;
   b.   The social Self;
   c.   The spiritual Self; and
   d.   The pure Ego.

(*a*) The body is the innermost part of *the material Self* in each of us; and certain parts of the body seem more intimately ours than the rest. The clothes come next. The old saying that the human person is composed of three parts—soul, body and clothes—is more than a joke. We so appropriate our clothes and identify ourselves with them that there are few of us who, if asked to choose between having a beautiful body clad in raiment perpetually shabby and unclean, and having an ugly and blemished form always spotlessly attired, would not hesitate a moment before making a decisive reply. Next, our immediate family is a part of ourselves. Our father and mother, our wife and babes, are bone of our bone and flesh of our flesh. When they die, a part of our very selves is gone. If they do anything wrong, it is our shame. If they are insulted, our anger flashes forth as readily as if we stood in their place. Our home comes next. Its scenes are part of our life; its aspects awaken the tenderest feelings of affection; and we do not easily forgive the stranger who, in visiting it, finds fault with its arrangements or treats it with contempt. All these different things are the objects of instinctive preferences coupled with the most important practical interests of life. We all have a blind impulse to watch over our body, to deck it with clothing of an ornamental sort, to cherish parents, wife and babes, and to find for ourselves a home of our own which we may live in and 'improve.'

An equally instinctive impulse drives us to collect property; and the collections thus made become, with different degrees of intimacy, parts of our empirical selves. The parts of our wealth most intimately ours are those which are saturated with our labor. There are few men who would not feel personally annihilated if a lifelong construction of their hands or brains—say an entomological collection or an extensive work in manuscript—were suddenly swept away. The miser feels similarly towards his gold; and although it is true that a part of our depression at the loss of possessions is due to our feeling that we must now go without certain goods that we expected the possessions to bring in their train, yet in every case there remains, over and above this, a sense of the shrinkage of our personality, a partial conversion of ourselves to nothingness, which is a psychological phenomenon by itself. We are all at once assimilated to the tramps and poor devils whom we so despise, and at the same time removed farther than ever away from the happy sons of earth who lord it over land and sea and men in the full-blown lustihood that wealth and power can give, and before whom, stiffen ourselves as we will be appealing to anti-snobbish first principles, we cannot escape an emotion, open or sneaking, of respect and dread.

(*b*) *A man's Social Self* is the recognition which he gets from his mates. We are not only gregarious animals, liking to be in sight of our fellows, but we have an innate propensity to get ourselves noticed, and noticed favorably, by our kind. No more fiendish punishment could be devised, were such a thing physically possible, than that one should be turned loose in society and remain absolutely unnoticed by all the members thereof. If no one turned round when we entered, answered when we spoke, or minded what we did, but if every person we met 'cut us dead,' and acted as if we were non-existing things, a kind of rage and impotent despair would ere long well up in us, from which the cruellest bodily tortures would be a relief; for these would make us feel that, however bad might be our plight, we had not sunk to such a depth as to be unworthy of attention at all.

Properly speaking, *a man has as many social selves as there are individuals who recognize him* and carry an image of him in their mind. To wound any one of these his images is to wound him. But as the individuals who carry the images fall naturally into classes, we may practically say that he has as many different social selves as there are distinct *groups* of persons about whose opinion he cares. He generally shows a different side of himself to each of these different groups. Many a youth who is demure enough before his parents and teachers, swears and swaggers like a pirate among his 'tough' young friends. We do not show ourselves to our children as to our club-companions, to our customers as to the laborers we employ, to our own masters and employers as to our intimate friends. From this there results what practically is a division of the man into several selves; and this may be a discordant splitting, as where one is afraid to let one set of his acquaintances know him as he is elsewhere; or it may be a perfectly harmonious division of labor, as where one tender to his children is stern to the soldiers or prisoners under his command.

The most peculiar social self which one is apt to have is in the mind of the person one is in love with. The good or bad fortunes of this self cause the most intense elation and dejection—unreasonable enough as measured by every other standard than that of the organic feeling of the individual. To his own consciousness he *is* not, so long as this particular social self fails to get recognition, and when it is recognized his contentment passes all bounds.

A man's *fame*, good or bad, and his *honor* or dishonor, are names for one of his social selves. The particular social self of a man called his honor is usually the result of one of those splittings of which we have spoken. It is his image in the eyes of his own 'set,' which exalts or condemns him as he conforms or not to certain requirements that may not be made of one in another walk of life. Thus a layman may abandon a city infected with cholera; but a priest or a doctor would think such an act incompatible with his honor. A soldier's honor requires him to fight or to die under circumstances where another man can apologize or run away with no stain upon his social self. A judge, a statesman, are in like manner debarred by the honor of their cloth from entering into pecuniary relations perfectly honorable to persons in private life. Nothing is commoner than to hear people discriminate between their different selves of this sort: "As a man I pity you, but as an official I must show you no mercy"; "As a politician I regard him as an ally, but as a moralist I loathe him"; etc., etc. What may be called 'club-opinion' is one of the very strongest forces in life. The thief must not steal from other thieves; the gambler must pay his gambling debts, though he pay no other debts in the world. The code of honor of fashionable society has throughout history been full of permissions as well as of vetoes, the only reason for following either of which is that so we best serve one of our social selves. You must not lie in general, but you may lie as much as you please if asked about your relations with a lady; you must accept a challenge from an equal, but if challenged by an inferior you may laugh him to scorn: these are examples of what is meant.

(c) By the Spiritual Self, so far as it belongs to the Empirical Me, I mean a man's inner or subjective being, his psychic faculties or dispositions, taken concretely; not the bare principle of personal Unity, or 'pure' Ego, which remains still to be discussed. These psychic dispositions are the most enduring and intimate part of the self, that which we most verily seem to be. We take a purer self-satisfaction when we think of our ability to argue and discriminate, of our moral sensibility and conscience, of our indomitable will, than when we survey any of our other possessions. Only when these are altered is a man said to be *alienatus a se.* . . .

But when I forsake such general descriptions and grapple with particulars, coming to the closest possible quarters with the facts, *it is difficult for me to detect in the activity any purely spiritual element at all. Whenever my introspective glance succeeds in turning round quickly enough to catch one of these manifestations of spontaneity in the act, all it can ever feel distinctly is some bodily process, for the most part taking place within the head.* Omitting for a moment what is obscure in these introspective results, let me try to state those particulars which to my own consciousness seem indubitable and distinct.

In the first place, the acts of attending, assenting, negating, making an effort, are felt as movements of something in the head. In many cases it is possible to describe these movements quite exactly. In attending to either an idea or a sensation belonging to a particular sense-sphere, the movement is the adjustment of the sense-organ, felt as it occurs. I cannot think in visual terms, for example, without feeling a fluctuating play of pressures, convergences, divergences, and accommodations in my eyeballs. The direction in which the object is conceived to lie determines the character of these movements, the feeling of which becomes, for my consciousness, identified with the manner in which I make myself ready to receive the visible thing. My brain appears to me as if all shot across with lines of direction, of which I have become conscious as my attention has shifted from one sense-organ to another, in passing to successive outer things, or in following trains of varying sense-ideas.

When I try to remember or reflect, the movements in question, instead of being directed towards the periphery, seem to come from the periphery inwards and feel like a sort of *withdrawal* from the outer world. As far as I can detect, these feelings are due to an actual rolling outwards and upwards of the eyeballs, such as I believe occurs in me in sleep, and is the exact opposite of their action in fixating a physical thing. In reasoning, I find that I am apt to have a kind of vaguely localized diagram in my mind, with the various fractional objects of the thought disposed at particular points thereof; and the oscillations of my attention from one of them to another are most distinctly felt as alternations of direction in movements occurring inside the head.

In consenting and negating, and in making a mental effort, the movements seem more complex, and I find them harder to describe. The opening and closing of the glottis play a great part in these operations, and, less distinctly, the movements of the soft palate, etc., shutting off the posterior nares from the mouth. My glottis is like a sensitive valve, intercepting my breath instantaneously at every mental hesitation or felt aversion to the objects of my thought, and as quickly opening, to let the air pass through my throat and nose, the moment the repugnance is overcome. The feeling of the movement of this air is, in me, one strong ingredient of the feeling of assent. The movements of the muscles of the brow and eyelids also respond very sensitively to every fluctuation in the agreeableness or disagreeableness of what comes before my mind.

In *effort* of any sort, contractions of jaw-muscles and of those of respiration are added to those of the brow and glottis, and thus the feeling passes out of the head properly so called. It passes out of the head whenever the welcoming or rejecting of the object is *strongly* felt. Then a set of feelings pour in from many bodily parts, all 'expressive' of my emotion, and the head-feelings proper are swallowed up in this larger mass.

In a sense, then, it may be truly said that, in one person at least, *the 'Self of selves,' when carefully examined, is found to consist mainly of the collection of these peculiar motions in the head or between the head and throat.* I do not for a moment say that this is *all* it consists of, for I fully realize how desperately hard is introspection in this field. But I feel quite sure that these cephalic motions are the portions of my inner-most activity of which I am *most distinctly aware.* If the dim portions which I cannot yet define should prove to be like unto these distinct portions in me, and I like other men, *it would follow that our entire feeling of spiritual activity, or what commonly passes by that name, is really a feeling of bodily activities whose exact nature is by most men overlooked.* . . .

(*d*) *The Pure ego* [is the most puzzling aspect of the self—a transitional feature from the phenomenal self and pure personal identity—CL]. Having summed up the principal results of the chapter thus far, I have said all that need be said of the con-stituents of the phenomenal self, and of the nature of self-regard. Our decks are con-sequently cleared for the struggle with that pure principle of personal identity which has met us all along our preliminary exposition, but which we have always shied from and treated as a difficulty to be postponed. Ever since Hume's time, it has been justly regarded as the most puzzling puzzle with which psychology has to deal; and whatever view one may espouse, one has to hold his position against heavy odds. If, with the Spiritualists, one contends for a substantial soul, or transcendental princi-ple of unity, one can give no positive account of what that may be. And if, with the Humians, one deny such a principle and say that the stream of passing thoughts is all, one runs against the entire common-sense of mankind, of which the belief in a distinct principle of selfhood seems an integral part. Whatever solution be adopted in the pages to come, we may as well make up our minds in advance that it will fail to satisfy the majority of those to whom it is addressed. The best way of approaching the matter will be to take up first—

The Sense of Personal Identity

In the last chapter it was stated in as radical way as possible that the thoughts which we actually know to exist do not fly about loose, but seem each to belong to some one thinker and not to another. Each thought, out of a multitude of other thoughts of which it may think, is able to distinguish those which belong to its own Ego from those which do not. The former have a warmth and intimacy about them of which the latter are completely devoid, being merely conceived, in a cold and foreign fashion, and not appearing as blood-relatives, bringing their greetings to us from out of the past.

Now this consciousness of personal sameness may be treated either as a subjective phenomenon or as an objective deliverance, as a feeling, or as a truth. We may explain how one bit of thought can come to judge other bits to belong to the same Ego with itself; or we may criticise its judgment and decide how far it may tally with the nature of things.

As a mere subjective phenomenon the judgment presents no difficulty or mystery peculiar to itself. It belongs to the great class of judgments of sameness; and there is nothing more remarkable in making a judgment of sameness in the first person than in the second or the third. The intellectual operations seem essentially alike, whether I say 'I am the same,' or whether I say 'the pen is the same, as yesterday.' It is as easy to think this as to think the opposite and say 'neither I nor the pen is the same.'

This sort of *bringing of things together into the object of a single judgment* is of course essential to all thinking. The things are conjoined *in* the thought, whatever may be the relation in which they appear to the thought. The thinking them is *thinking* them together, even if only with the result of judging that they do not *belong* together. This sort of *subjective synthesis,* essential to knowledge as such (whenever it has a complex object), must not be confounded with *objective synthesis* or union instead of difference or disconnection, known among the things. The subjective synthesis is involved in thought's mere existence. Even a really disconnected world could only be *known* to be such by having its parts temporarily united in the Object of some pulse of consciousness.

The sense of personal identity is not, then, this mere synthetic form essential to all thought. It is the sense of a sameness perceived *by* thought and predicated of things *thought-about.* These things are a present self and a self of yesterday. The thought not only thinks them both, but thinks that they are identical. The psychologist, looking on and playing the critic, might prove the thought wrong, and show there was no real identity,—there might have been no yesterday, or, at any rate, no self of yesterday; or, if there were, the sameness predicated might not obtain, or might be predicated on insufficient grounds. In either case the personal identity would not exist as a *fact*; but it would exist as a *feeling* all the same; the consciousness of it by the thought would be there, and the psychologist would still have to analyze that, and show where its illusoriness lay. Let us now be the psychologist and see whether it be right or wrong when it says, *I am the same self that I was yesterday.*❖

William Edward Burghardt Du Bois (1868–1963) was born and grew up in Great Barrington, Massachusetts, where he experienced racial discrimination only obliquely. Yet he came to be the greatest American social theorist of race. Nearly every event in the history of race in America, from Reconstruction to the civil rights movement, was influenced by his ideas or his political actions. In his youth, Du Bois studied at Fisk University, then attended Harvard, where he received his Ph.D. in 1895 after two years of study in Germany. Early in his scholarly career, he single-handedly completed the first major, and still important, empirical sociological study of Negro life in the United States, *The Philadelphia Negro* (1899). But until recently, he was largely ignored by official sociology. Eventually, his work moved beyond social science into history, fiction, and essays. A chapter in his *Souls of Black Folk* (1903) sparked his battle with Booker T. Washington, then the dominant spokesman for Negro Americans. Du Bois organized the Niagara Movement (1905–1910) in opposition to Washington, who opposed the higher education of Blacks in favor of industrial training. From it came the NAACP, with which he was associated during much of the rest of his active life. In the 1920s, he was locked in controversy with Marcus Garvey over their differing views of Pan-Africanism. Though Du Bois's roots were in America, he was a leader in the world Pan-African movement, and in his last years, he was honored in China, the USSR, Africa, and Europe. In 1961, then ninety-three years old, Du Bois moved to Ghana to *begin* work on the *Encyclopedia Africana.* He died on the eve of the civil rights march on Washington, D.C.—August 27, 1963.

"Double-Consciousness and the Veil" is the opening chapter of *Souls of Black Folk,* in which Du Bois used poetry, autobiography, and history to make strong theoretical points. His concept of twoness, or double-consciousness, has been an enduring force in African-American social and literary theory. The book's title is meant precisely—two souls, one self. Du Bois's literary method reflected his theory, as in his practice of composing epigraphs that juxtaposed the classic literature of the West and unmarked bars of music from the American black tradition. "The Spirit of Modern Europe," published only recently, was the title of an address given in Louisville, Kentucky, in 1900, shortly after Du Bois returned from London, where he had organized and led the first international Pan-African conference. This is a clear example of what today might be called a multicultural social theory. Du Bois understated his attack on Europe's narrow cultural logic in order to define the global interests (and responsibilities) of the civilizations of Africa and other societies across the world.

Double-Consciousness and the Veil

W.E.B. Du Bois (1903)

> O water, voice of my heart, crying in the sand,
> All night long crying with a mournful cry,
> As I lie and listen, and cannot understand
> The voice of my heart in my side or the voice of the sea,
> O water, crying for rest, is it I, is it I?
> All night long the water is crying to me.
> Unresting water, there shall never be rest
> Till the last moon droop and the last tide fail,
> And the fire of the end begin to burn in the west;
> And the heart shall be weary and wonder and cry like the sea,
> All life long crying without avail,
> As the water all night long is crying to me.
>
> —Arthur Symons

Excerpt from *The Souls of Black Folk* (New York: Bantam, 1989 [1903]), pp. 1–9.

Between me and the other world there is ever an unasked question: unasked by some through feelings of delicacy; by others through the difficulty of rightly framing it. All, nevertheless, flutter round it. They approach me in a half-hesitant sort of way, eye me curiously or compassionately, and then, instead of saying directly, How does it feel to be a problem? they say, I know an excellent colored man in my town; or, I fought at Mechanicsville; or, Do not these Southern outrages make your blood boil? At these I smile, or am interested, or reduce the boiling to a simmer, as the occasion may require. To the real question, How does it feel to be a problem? I answer seldom a word.

And yet, being a problem is a strange experience,—peculiar even for one who has never been anything else, save perhaps in babyhood and in Europe. It is in the early days of rollicking boyhood that the revelation first bursts upon one, all in a day, as it were. I remember well when the shadow swept across me. I was a little thing, away up in the hills of New England, where the dark Housatonic winds between Hoosac and Taghkanic to the sea. In a wee wooden schoolhouse, something put it into the boys' and girls' heads to buy gorgeous visiting-cards—ten cents a package—and exchange. The exchange was merry, till one girl, a tall newcomer, refused my card,— refused it peremptorily, with a glance. Then it dawned upon me with a certain suddenness that I was different from the others; or like, mayhap, in heart and life and longing, but shut out from their world by a vast veil. I had thereafter no desire to tear down that veil, to creep through; I held all beyond it in common contempt, and lived above it in a region of blue sky and great wandering shadows. That sky was bluest when I could beat my mates at examination-time, or beat them at a foot-race, or even beat their stringy heads. Alas, with the years all this fine contempt began to fade; for the words I longed for, and all their dazzling opportunities, were theirs, not mine. But they should not keep these prizes, I said; some, all, I would wrest from them. Just how I would do it I could never decide: by reading law, by healing the sick, by telling the wonderful tales that swam in my head,—some way. With other black boys the strife was not so fiercely sunny: their youth shrunk into tasteless sycophancy, or into silent hatred of the pale world about them and mocking distrust of everything white; or wasted itself in a bitter cry. Why did God make me an outcast and a stranger in mine own house? The shades of the prison-house closed round about us all: walls strait and stubborn to the whitest, but relentlessly narrow, tall, and unscalable to sons of night who must plod darkly on in resignation, or beat unavailing palms against the stone, or steadily, half hopelessly, watch the streak of blue above.

After the Egyptian and Indian, the Greek and Roman, the Teuton and Mongolian, the negro is a sort of seventh son, born with a veil, and gifted with second-sight in this American world,—a world which yields him no true self-consciousness, but only lets him see himself through the revelation of the other world. It is a peculiar sensation, this double-consciousness, this sense of always looking at one's self through the eyes of others, of measuring one's soul by the tape of a world that looks on in amused contempt and pity. One ever feels his twoness,—an American, a Negro; two souls, two thoughts, two unreconciled strivings; two warring ideals in one dark body, whose dogged strength alone keeps it from being torn asunder.

The history of the American Negro is the history of this strife,—this longing to attain self-conscious manhood, to merge his double self into a better and truer self. In this merging he wishes neither of the older selves to be lost. He would not Africanize America, for America has too much to teach the world and Africa. He would not bleach his Negro soul in a flood of white Americanism, for he knows that

Negro blood has a message for the world. He simply wishes to make it possible for a man to be both a Negro and an American, without being cursed and spit upon by his fellows, without having the doors of Opportunity closed roughly in his face.

This, then, is the end of his striving: to be a co-worker in the kingdom of culture, to escape both death and isolation, to husband and use his best powers and his latent genius. These powers of body and mind have in the past been strangely wasted, dispersed, or forgotten. The shadow of a mighty Negro past flits through the tale of Ethiopia the Shadowy and of Egypt the Sphinx. Through history, the powers of single black men flash here and there like falling stars, and die sometimes before the world has rightly gauged their brightness. Here in America, in the few days since Emancipation, the black man's turning hither and thither in hesitant and doubtful striving has often made his very strength to lose effectiveness, to seem like absence of power, like weakness. and yet it is not weakness,—it is the contradiction of double aims. The double-aimed struggle of the black artisan—on the one hand to escape white contempt for a nation of mere hewers of wood and drawers of water, and on the other hand to plough and nail and dig for a poverty-stricken horde—could only result in making him a poor craftsman, for he had but half a heart in either cause. By the poverty and ignorance of his people, the Negro minister or doctor was tempted toward quackery and demagogy; and by the criticism of the other world, toward ideals that made him ashamed of his lowly tasks. The would-be black *savant* was confronted by the paradox that the knowledge of his people needed was a twice-told tale to his white neighbors, while the knowledge which would teach the white world was Greek to his own flesh and blood. The innate love of harmony and beauty that set the ruder souls of his people a-dancing and a-singing raised but confusion and doubt in the soul of the black artist; for the beauty revealed to him was the soul-beauty of a race which his larger audience despised, and he could not articulate the message of another people. This waste of double aims, this seeking to satisfy two unreconciled ideals, has wrought sad havoc with the courage and faith and deeds of ten thousand thousand people,—has sent them often wooing false gods and invoking false means of salvation, and at times has even seemed about to make them ashamed of themselves.

Away back in the days of bondage they thought to see in one divine event the end of all doubt and disappointment; few men ever worshipped Freedom with half such unquestioning faith as did the American Negro for two centuries. To him, so far as he thought and dreamed, slavery was indeed the sum of all villainies, the cause of all sorrow, the root of all prejudice; Emancipation was the key to a promised land of sweeter beauty than ever stretched before the eyes of wearied Israelites. In song and exhortation swelled one refrain—Liberty; in his tears and curses the God he implored had Freedom in his right hand. At last it came,—suddenly, fearfully, like a dream. With one wild carnival of blood and passion came the message in his own plaintive cadences:—

> "Shout, O children!
> Shout, you're free!
> For God has bought your liberty!"

Years have passed away since then,—ten, twenty, forty; forty years of national life, forty years of renewal and development, and yet the swarthy spectre sits in its accustomed seat at the Nation's feast. In vain do we cry to this our vastest social problem:—

"Take any shape but that, and my firm nerves
Shall never tremble!"

The Nation has not yet found peace from its sins; the freedman has not yet found in freedom his promised land. Whatever of good may have come in these years of change, the shadow of a deep disappointment rests upon the Negro people,—a disappointment all the more bitter because the unattained ideal was unbounded save by the simple ignorance of a lowly people.

The first decade was merely a prolongation of the vain search for freedom, the boon that seemed ever barely to elude their grasp,—like a tantalizing will-o'-the-wisp, maddening and misleading the headless host. The holocaust of war, the terrors of the Ku-Klux Klan, the lies of carpet-baggers, the disorganization of industry, and the contradictory advice of friends and foes, left the bewildered serf with no new watchword beyond the old cry for freedom. As the time flew, however, he began to grasp a new idea. The ideal of liberty demanded for its attainment powerful means, and these the Fifteenth Amendment gave him. The ballot, which before he had looked upon as a visible sign of freedom, he now regarded as the chief means of gaining and perfecting the liberty with which war had partially endowed him. And why not? Had not votes made war and emancipated millions? Had not votes enfranchised the freedmen? Was anything impossible to a power that had done all this? A million black men started with renewed zeal to vote themselves into the kingdom. So the decade flew away, the revolution of 1876 came, and left the half-free serf weary, wondering, but still inspired. Slowly but steadily, in the following years, a new vision began gradually to replace the dream of political power,—a powerful movement, the rise of another ideal to guide the unguided, another pillar of fire by night after a clouded day. It was the ideal of "book-learning"; the curiosity, born of compulsory ignorance, to know and test the power of the cabalistic letters of the white man, the longing to know. Here at last seemed to have been discovered the mountain path to Canaan; longer than the highway of Emancipation and law, steep and rugged, but straight, leading to heights high enough to overlook life.

Up the new path the advance guard toiled, slowly, heavily, doggedly; only those who have watched and guided the faltering feet, the misty minds, the dull understandings, of the dark pupils of these schools know how faithfully, how piteously, this people strove to learn. It was weary work. The cold statistician wrote down the inches of progress here and there, noted also where here and there a foot had slipped or some one had fallen. To the tired climbers, the horizon was ever dark, the mists were often cold, the Canaan was always dim and far away. If, however, the vistas disclosed as yet no goal, no resting-place, little but flattery and criticism, the journey at least gave leisure for reflection and self-examination; it changed the child of Emancipation to the youth with dawning self-consciousness, self-realization, self-respect. In those sombre forests of his striving his own soul rose before him, and he saw himself,—darkly as through a veil; and yet he saw in himself some faint revelation of his power, of his mission. He began to have a dim feeling that, to attain his place in the world, he must be himself, and not another. For the first time he sought to analyze the burden he bore upon his back, that dead-weight of social degradation partially masked behind a half-named Negro problem. He felt his poverty; without a cent, without a home, without land, tools, or savings, he had entered into competition with rich, landed, skilled neighbors. To be a poor man is hard, but to be a poor race in a land of dollars is the very bottom of hardships. He felt the weight of his ignorance,—not simply of letters, but of life, of business, of the humanities; the accumulated sloth and shirking and awkwardness of decades and centuries shackled his hands and feet. Nor was his burden all poverty and ignorance. The red stain of bastardy, which two centuries of systematic legal defilement of Negro women had stamped upon his race, meant not only the loss of ancient African chastity, but also the hereditary weight of a mass of corruption from white adulterers, threatening almost the obliteration of the Negro home.

A people thus handicapped ought not to be asked to race with the world, but rather allowed to give all its time and thought to its own social problems. But alas! while sociologists gleefully count his bastards and his prostitutes, the very soul of the toiling, sweating black man is darkened by the shadow of a vast despair. Men call the shadow prejudice, and learnedly explain it as the natural defence of culture against barbarism, learning against ignorance, purity against crime, the "higher" against the "lower" races. To which the Negro cries Amen! and swears that to so much of this strange prejudice as is founded on just homage to civilization, culture, righteousness, and progress, he humbly bows and meekly does obeisance. But before that nameless prejudice that leaps beyond all this he stands helpless, dismayed, and wellnigh speechless; before that personal disrespect and mockery, the ridicule and systematic humiliation, the distortion of fact and wanton license of fancy, the cynical ignoring of the better and the boisterous welcoming of the worse, the all-pervading desire to inculcate disdain for everything black, from Toussaint to the devil,—before this there rises a sickening despair that would disarm and discourage any nation save that black host to whom "discouragement" is an unwritten word.

But the facing of so vast a prejudice could not but bring the inevitable self-questioning, self-disparagement, and lowering of ideals which ever accompany repression and breed in an atmosphere of contempt and hate. Whisperings and portents came borne upon the four winds: Lo! we are diseased and dying, cried the dark hosts; we cannot write, our voting is vain; what need of education, since we must always cook and serve? And the Nation echoed and enforced this self-criticism, saying: Be content to be servants, and nothing more; what need of higher culture for half-men? Away with the black man's ballot, by force or fraud,—and behold the suicide of a race! Nevertheless, out of the evil came something of good,—the more careful adjustment of education to real life, the clearer perception of the Negroes' social responsibilities, and the sobering realization of the meaning of progress.

So dawned the time of *Sturm und Drang:* storm and stress to-day rocks our little boat on the mad waters of the world-sea; there is within and without the sound of conflict, the burning of body and rending of soul; inspiration strives with doubt, and faith with vain questionings. The bright ideals of the past,—physical freedom, political power, the training of brains and the training of hands,—all these in turn have waxed and waned, until even the last grows dim and overcast. Are they all wrong,—all false? No, not that, but each alone was over-simple and incomplete,—the dreams of a credulous race-childhood, or the fond imaginings of the other world which does not know and does not want to know our power. To be really true, all these ideals must be melted and welded into one. The training of the schools we need to-day more than ever,—the training of deft hands, quick eyes and ears, and above all the broader, deeper, higher culture of gifted minds and pure hearts. The power of the ballot we need in sheer self-defence,—else what shall save us from a second slavery? Freedom, too, the long-sought, we still seek,—the freedom of life and limb, the freedom to work and think, the freedom to love and aspire. Work, culture, liberty,—all these we need, not singly but together, not successively but together, each growing and aiding each, and all striving toward that vaster ideal that swims before the Negro people, the ideal of human brotherhood, gained through the unifying ideal of Race; the ideal of fostering and developing the traits and talents of the Negro, not in opposition to or contempt for other races, but rather in large conformity to the greater ideals of the American Republic, in order that some day on American soil two world-races may give each to each those characteristics both so sadly lack. We the darker ones come even now not altogether empty-handed: there are to-day no truer exponents of the pure human spirit of the Declaration of Independence than the American Negroes; there is no true American music but the wild sweet melodies of the Negro slave; the American fairy tales and folklore are Indian and African; and, all in all, we black men seem the sole oasis of simple faith and reverence in a dusty desert of dollars and smartness. Will America be poorer if she replace her brutal dyspeptic blundering with light-hearted but determined Negro humility? or her coarse and cruel wit with loving jovial good-humor? or her vulgar music with the soul of the Sorrow Songs?

Merely a concrete test of the underlying principles of the great republic is the Negro Problem, and the spiritual striving of the freedmen's sons is the travail of souls whose burden is almost beyond the measure of their strength, but who bear it in the name of an historic race, in the name of this land of their fathers' fathers, and in the name of human opportunity.❖

The Spirit of Modern Europe

W.E.B. Du Bois (1900)

What is the spirit of modern Europe?

Europe today represents in her civilization five leading ideas: Continuity of Organization, Authority of government, Justice between men, Individual Freedom and Systematic Knowledge.

Continuity of Organization conserves the civilization of the past and makes modern civilization possible: for what is civilization but the gathering and conserving of the ideas of different men and peoples? The great Graeco-Roman civilization borrowed and developed the culture of Africa and India and Judae. The mass of barbarism that reeled down golden haired and drunk from the blue north did not bring a new culture, did not quench the old, but doffing its ignorance and idolatry and donning Christianity, and the civilization it had well nigh destroyed, gave to that old Egyptian-Grecian-Roman civilization, through the Renaissance, a new birth into the world, which modern Europe has nurtured to manhood. To conserve this culture it was necessary that human society should never die and the eternal life of the organism of which you and I form a part is the vastest realization of modern times. Here is an eternity that must be conserved, must be striven for, must be made broader and around the idea of preserving intact the institutions of society from generation to generation from century to century modern Europe has built its first wall.

The second idea of authority is an acknowledgement of the fact of human inequality and difference of capacity. There are men born to rule, born to think, born

Excerpt from Herbert Aptheker, ed., *Against Racism: Unpublished Essays, Papers, Addresses, 1887–1961* (Amherst: University of Massachusetts Press, 1985), pp. 60–64. Copyright 1985 by The University of Massachusetts Press.

to contrive, born to persuade. To such as have special aptitude or special training for special work the principle of authority declares that they and not others should do that work; that tailors cannot build houses, nor carpenters make shoes, nor shoemakers run electric plants. The principle of authority declares that in the limited range of special ability or training men should be rendered implicit obedience by their fellow men: that we should bow to the rule of rulers, to the knowledge of students, to the skill of artisans and to the righteousness of Christ and that the refusal to do this is anarchy, revolution, ignorance and wickedness.

The third idea of European culture is Justice: that is the full free recognition of individual desert. It declares on the one hand that they who will not support the pillars of civilization must be forcibly restrained from tearing them down. This is its older and negative side: today justice also declares that we must distinguish between those who will not support human culture and those who cannot, and give moral training to the one and physical, and industrial and mental training to the other: and that, finally, there must be in the distribution of this help and encouragement, no prejudice, no discrimination; it must reach all alike, rich and poor, high and low, good and bad, black and white, Jew and Gentile, barbarian, Scythian, bond and free.

The fourth element of the Spirit of Europe is Freedom: not license, not absence of bonds, not even in all cases, abolition of slavery, but the right to choose the work of life according to individual bent and capacity, the right to carry on that work untrammelled by ignorance, prejudice or deviltry and the right to enjoy the unstolen fruit of striving—in short the Freedom to choose that life—slavery to an Ideal which through the Truth shall make you free.

The fifth element of European culture is Knowledge: woe to the coward of the 20th century, who dare not know, for the spirit of the 19th has proven that from the deep and modest search for Truth, neither Beauty nor Goodness have aught to fear, and that the only way in which the world can advance to higher culture, to more eternal Life, to more unquestioned authority—to more impartial Justice and to more devoted Freedom, is by means of a cultivation of Science, of that systematic knowing, in the future, with ever greater doggedness, insight and determination, than in the mighty past.

In short, then, Europe today stands for a systematic and continuous union of individual effort to promote Justice and Freedom by means of Knowledge and Authority.

It may easily be said that this is after all the end and striving of all civilization, no matter how imperfectly realized in particular societies. This is both true and false: true that the same ideals which Europe today clearly recognizes were more or less dimly seen in Egypt, Persia and Judea but it is false to think that ever before in human history these ideals of society ever stood in such clean light, or came so near realization. The inquiry therefore resolves itself into a question of method: What is the method and means by which Europe has attained its ends? The answer is the secret of the success of the culture of modern Europe. It is the thorough recognition of the fact that no army march faster than its rear guard, that the civilization of no community can outstrip that same community's barbarism, that knowledge is measured by the amount of ignorance abroad in the land, that the culture of every nation and city is measured by its slums. This idea of social solidarity and social responsibility, this recognition of the fact that human life is not an individual foot race where the devil takes the hindmost, is the central idea of the 20th century and woe to the race or individual that does not recognize its power.

Nevertheless the application of this idea is narrowed by sheer necessity: England may recognize the Social Responsibility of the English nation for every English man, woman and child: Germany for every German, France for every Frenchman but if the great Culture states should at a bound seek to assume Social Responsibility for all humanity—for China, India, Egypt and Central Africa, Borneo and the Fiji Islands, civilization would simply be swallowed up in Barbarism: the solution which Europe is going to give to this puzzling dilemma is the placing of the Social Responsibility of each race in the hands of that race and the allowing it with as little hindrance as possible to work out its own peculiar civilization. Thus the national and Race ideal has been set before the world in a new light—not as meaning subtraction but addition, not as division but as multiplication—not to narrow humanity to petty selfish ends, but to point out a practical open road to the realization in all the earth of a humanity broad as God's blue heavens and deep as the deepest human heart.

The modern theory of the world's races no longer looks upon them as antagonistic hatred-cultivating groups: the patriotism of the Italian does not preclude his honoring the Englishman. The race pride of the German did not suffer in bowing to the genius of the Slav. Races and Nations represent organized Human effort, striving each its own way, each in its own time to realize for mankind the Good, the Beautiful and the True. The German unites and strives in *his* way, and so long as they strive not *against*, but along *with* each other the results blend and harmonize into vast striving of *one humanity*

> One God, one law, one element
> And one far off divine event
> To which the whole creation moves.

What lesson, has all this to us? What part in this striving has any new race like this we represent here tonight that comes upon the world's stage in the morning twilight of the 20th century: Is there still a place in the world for more striving, for more race Ideals, for a broader Humanity? And if there be what are the new races doing? Some are rising: yonder where the whiteness of the north first begins to soften into the dark yellow come the Japanese—working, suffering and fighting, bullied and imposed upon but striving—ceaselessly striving and already in the mighty struggle now going on the European world reckons with a new factor, a new nation—a new Race, a larger humanity. Farther on lie an historic people rich with history but long dead—but even there is heard the faint crying of a new birth, the signs of new activity, the rise of new ideas. China some day will follow Japan and the world of modern culture will be larger. Farther on the world darkens—dark brown faces are seen, the scattered remains of an ancient civilization appear and in the millions of India the world is listening for the sign of the new birth which the Queen's Jubilee gave warning of. At last come that mighty and mysterious people, sons of the night

> "Whose visage is too bright
> To hit the sense of human sight
> And therefore to our weaker view
> O'er laid with Black staid Wisdom's Hire
> Black, but such as in esteem
> Prince Memnon's sister might beseem

Or that starr'd Ethiop queen that strove
To set her beauty's praise above the sea nymphs."

The African people sweep over the birth place of human civilization, they dot the islands of the sea, they swarm in South America, they teem in our own land.

The students of Louisville are a part of the advance guard of the new people; the teachers of Louisville are training the minds and forming the ideals that are to aid and guide their onward marching.

These ideals differ in no respect from the ideals of that European civilization of which we all today form a part. And therefore our watch word today must be Social Solidarity—Social Responsibility: Systematic and Continuous union of our individual effort to promote Justice and Freedom among ourselves and throughout this land by means of knowledge and authority.

Here justice means absolute honesty of purpose and action. Young Negroes are today peculiarly tempted to impose upon the ignorance of their people, to prey upon their weakness, to flatter their vanity. You must rise to a higher ideal, knowing that a lie in tongue or deed is a deadly thing whether it be for or against us. Freedom means not the right to loaf and squander money on luxuries, not aimless enjoyment of life but rather the right to work, to delve, to struggle, to save, to sweat for God and that Truth that brought our fathers out of the House of Bondage. Knowledge means the trained capacity for comprehending the truth: in this world men who can do nothing, get nothing to do. And men who can and will do must know how and what to do. Young men and women who would serve the Negro race must bravely face the facts of its condition: the ignorance, the immorality, the laziness, the waste, and the crime. Finally authority means the recognition of the fact that all cannot lead because all are not fit to lead but that we must listen to the noblest not to the loudest, to the workers rather than to the talkers, to the Right and not to the Wrong.

Here are the paths which civilization points out and in these paths we must plod. With the unfortunate surrounding prejudice we have little concern. Beyond a quiet and dignified protest we can do nothing but await the action of time and common sense. Meantime however within our own ranks lies work enough—a people who are training up far more than their proportion of criminals—who are scattering disease and death, whose ignorance threatens the foundations of democratic government—such a people have a task before them calculated to keep their hands busy and their eyes open for a century to come.

We are puzzled at times as to just how to begin so colossal a work and yet as it seems to me the opening paths are before us: and they are for the masses good common school training and industrial education; for the talented few the best higher training that suits them. And this aristocracy of learning and talent—the graduates of Spelman, Atlanta, Howard, Fisk, and Northern institutions, are not to be trained for their own sakes alone but to be the guides and servants of the vast unmoved masses who are to be led out of poverty, out of disease and out of crime. It is a vast undertaking and yet a noble one—one in which we need all the divine faith of our mothers to cheer us in victory or in defeat

"For how can man die better
Than facing fearful odds
For the ashes of his fathers
And the temples of his Gods." ❖

Charlotte Perkins Gilman (1860–1935) is best known today for *The Yellow Wallpaper* (1892), the fictionalized account of her nervous breakdown, which was most acute in the two years following April 1886. At that time, she was married to Charles Walter Stetson, who colluded in a treatment plan that called for her to withdraw from all intellectual labors. Charlotte eventually worked her way out of the illness by resuming her intellectual life. After her first marriage ended more or less amicably, she moved to California, where she rebuilt a life with her daughter. In these years, she earned her livelihood in large part through public lectures. Her feminism was undoubtedly shaped by these early experiences. While living the life of a public intellectual, reformer, and feminist, Charlotte Perkins Gilman wrote important scholarly works (including publications in academic journals such as the *American Journal of Sociology*). Her principal writings in social theory developed a sophisticated feminist interpretation of the effects and relations among economic life, the family, and gender roles. *Women and Economics* (1898) was widely read in its day. Other books, along with scholarly articles, brought her a degree of recognition from the literary and academic establishment; these include *The Home* (1903) and *Human Work* (1904). For seven years, beginning in 1909, she organized, edited, and wrote every word (including advertising copy) for *Forerunner,* a monthly magazine. By her own estimate, the total words involved equaled that of four major books each year. Her literary output—scholarly works, essays, lectures, fiction—was prodigious. After the *Forerunner* years, Gilman's influence lessened. Yet she continued to write and live with purpose and courage—after 1922, in Norwich, Connecticut. She took her own life in 1935, saying, "I have preferred chloroform to cancer."

The selection from *The Yellow Wallpaper* illustrates Gilman's ability to use fiction to rivet the reader's attention on what amounts to an implicit social theory of gender relations. Her utopian novel, *Herland* (1915), extends this method into a more complete feminist statement. The "Women and Economics" selection stands up well against more recent analyses of the family wage system and "second-shift" labor demands, whereby a society's economic interests are served at a cost to women.

The Yellow Wallpaper

Charlotte Perkins Gilman (1892)

It is very seldom that mere ordinary people like John and myself secure ancestral halls for the summer.

A colonial mansion, a hereditary estate, I would say a haunted house and reach the height of romantic felicity—but that would be asking too much of fate!

Still I will proudly declare that there is something queer about it.

Else, why should it be let so cheaply? And why have stood so long untenanted?

John laughs at me, of course, but one expects that.

John is practical in the extreme. He has no patience with faith, an intense horror of superstition, and he scoffs openly at any talk of things not to be felt and seen and put down in figures.

Excerpt from Ann J. Lane, ed., *The Charlotte Perkins Gilman Reader: "The Yellow Wallpaper" and Other Fiction* (New York: Pantheon Books, 1980), pp. 3–5.

John is a physician, and *perhaps*—(I would not say it to a living soul, of course, but this is dead paper and a great relief to my mind)—*perhaps* that is one reason I do not get well faster.

You see, he does not believe I am sick! And what can one do?

If a physician of high standing, and one's own husband, assures friends and relatives that there is really nothing the matter with one but temporary nervous depression—a slight hysterical tendency—what is one to do?

My brother is also a physician, and also of high standing, and he says the same thing.

So I take phosphates or phosphites—whichever it is—and tonics, and air and exercise, and journeys, and am absolutely forbidden to "work" until I am well again.

Personally, I disagree with their ideas.

Personally, I believe that congenial work, with excitement and change, would do me good.

But what is one to do?

I did write for a while in spite of them; but it *does* exhaust me a good deal—having to be so sly about it, or else meet with heavy opposition.

I sometimes fancy that in my condition, if I had less opposition and more society and stimulus—but John says the very worst thing I can do is to think about my condition, and I confess it always makes me feel bad.

So I will let it alone and talk about the house.

The most beautiful place! It is quite alone, standing well back from the road, quite three miles from the village. It makes me think of English places that you read about, for there are hedges and walls and gates that lock, and lots of separate little houses for the gardeners and people.

There is a *delicious* garden! I never saw such a garden—large and shady, full of box-bordered paths, and lined with long grape-covered arbors with seats under them.

There were greenhouses, but they are all broken now.

There was some legal trouble, I believe, something about the heirs and co-heirs; anyhow, the place has been empty for years.

That spoils my ghostliness, I am afraid, but I don't care—there is something strange about the house—I can feel it.

I even said so to John one moonlight evening, but he said what I felt was a draught, and shut the window.

I get unreasonably angry with John sometimes. I'm sure I never used to be so sensitive. I think it is due to this nervous condition.

But John says if I feel so I shall neglect proper self-control; so I take pains to control myself—before him, at least, and that makes me very tired.

I don't like our room a bit. I wanted one downstairs that opened onto the piazza and had roses all over the window, and such pretty old-fashioned chintz hangings! But John would not hear of it.

He said there was only one window and not room for two beds, and no near room for him if he took another.

He is very careful and loving, and hardly lets me stir without special direction.

I have a schedule prescription for each hour in the day; he takes all care from me, and so I feel basely ungrateful not to value it more.

He said he came here solely on my account, that I was to have perfect rest and all the air I could get. "Your exercise depends on your strength, my dear," said he, "and your food somewhat on your appetite; but air you can absorb all the time." So we took the nursery at the top of the house.

It is a big, airy room, the whole floor nearly, with windows that look all ways, and air and sunshine galore. It was nursery first, and then playroom and gymnasium, I should judge, for the windows are barred for little children, and there are rings and things in the walls.

The paint and paper look as if a boys' school had used it. It is stripped off—the paper—in great patches all around the head of my bed, about as far as I can reach, and in a great place on the other side of the room low down. I never saw a worse paper in my life. One of those sprawling, flamboyant patterns committing every artistic sin.

It is dull enough to confuse the eye in following, pronounced enough constantly to irritate and provoke study, and when you follow the lame uncertain curves for a little distance they suddenly commit suicide—plunge off at outrageous angles, destroy themselves in unheard-of contradictions.

The color is repellant, almost revolting: a smouldering unclean yellow, strangely faded by the slow-turning sunlight. It is a dull yet lurid orange in some places, a sickly sulphur tint in others.

No wonder the children hated it! I should hate it myself if I had to live in this room long.

There comes John, and I must put this away—he hates to have me write a word.❖

Women and Economics

Charlotte Perkins Gilman (1898)

The economic status of the human race in any nation, at any time, is governed mainly by the activities of the male: the female obtains her share in the racial advance only through him.

Studied individually, the facts are even more plainly visible, more open and familiar. From the day laborer to the millionaire, the wife's worn dress or flashing jewels, her low roof or her lordly one, her weary feet or her rich equipage,—these speak of the economic ability of the husband. The comfort, the luxury, the necessities of life itself, which the woman receives, are obtained by the husband, and given her by him. And, when the woman, left alone with no man to "support" her, tries to meet her own economic necessities, the difficulties which confront her prove conclusively what the general economic status of the woman is. None can deny these patent facts,—that the economic status of women generally depends upon that of men generally, and that the economic status of women individually depends upon that of men individually, those men to whom they are related. But we are instantly confronted by the commonly received opinion that, although it must be admitted that men make and distribute the wealth of the world, yet women earn their share of it as wives. This assumes either that the husband is in the position of employer and the wife as employee, or that marriage is a "partnership," and the wife an equal factor with the husband in producing wealth.

Excerpt from *Women and Economics* (New York: Source Book Press, 1970 [Boston: Small, Maynard, 1898]), pp. 9–21.

Economic independence is a relative condition at best. In the broadest sense, all living things are economically dependent upon others,—the animals upon the vegetables, and man upon both. In a narrower sense, all social life is economically interdependent, man producing collectively what he could by no possibility produce separately. But, in the closest interpretation, individual economic independence among human beings means that the individual pays for what he gets, works for what he gets, gives to the other an equivalent for what the other gives him. I depend on the shoemaker for shoes, and the tailor for coats; but, if I give the shoemaker and the tailor enough of my own labor as a house-builder to pay for the shoes and coats they give me, I retain my personal independence. I have not taken of their product, and given nothing of mine. As long as what I get is obtained by what I give, I am economically independent.

Women consume economic goods. What economic product do they give in exchange for what they consume? The claim that marriage is a partnership, in which the two persons married produce wealth which neither of them, separately, could produce, will not bear examination. A man happy and comfortable can produce more than one unhappy and uncomfortable, but this is as true of a father or son as of a husband. To take from a man any of the conditions which make him happy and strong is to cripple his industry, generally speaking. But those relatives who make him happy are not therefore his business partners, and entitled to share his income.

Grateful return for happiness conferred is not the method of exchange in a partnership. The comfort a man takes with his wife is not in the nature of a business partnership, nor are her frugality and industry. A housekeeper, in her place, might be as frugal, as industrious, but would not therefore be a partner. Man and wife are partners truly in their mutual obligation to their children,—their common love, duty, and service. But a manufacturer who marries, or a doctor, or a lawyer, does not take a partner in his business, when he takes a partner in parenthood, unless his wife is also a manufacturer, a doctor, or a lawyer. In his business, she cannot even advise wisely without training and experience. To love her husband, the composer, does not enable her to compose; and the loss of a man's wife, though it may break his heart, does not cripple his business, unless his mind is affected by grief. She is in no sense a business partner, unless she contributes capital or experience or labor, as a man would in like relation. Most men would hesitate very seriously before entering a business partnership with any woman, wife or not.

If the wife is not, then, truly a business partner, in what way does she earn from her husband the food, clothing, and shelter she receives at his hands? By house service, it will be instantly replied. This is the general misty idea upon the subject,— that women earn all they get, and more, by house service. Here we come to a very practical and definite economic ground. Although not producers of wealth, women serve in the final processes of preparation and distribution. Their labor in the household has a genuine economic value.

For a certain percentage of persons to serve other persons, in order that the ones so served may produce more, is a contribution not to be overlooked. The labor of women in the house, certainly, enables men to produce more wealth than they otherwise could; and in this way women are economic factors in society. But so are horses. The labor of horses enables men to produce more wealth than they otherwise could. The horse is an economic factor in society. But the horse is not economically independent, nor is the woman. If a man plus a valet can perform more useful service than he could minus a valet, then the valet is performing useful service. But, if the valet is the property of the man, is obliged to perform this service, and is not paid for it, he is not economically independent.

The labor which the wife performs in the household is given as part of her functional duty, not as employment. The wife of the poor man, who works hard in a small house, doing all the work for the family, or the wife of the rich man, who wisely and gracefully manages a large house and administers its functions, each is entitled to fair pay for services rendered.

To take this ground and hold it honestly, wives, as earners through domestic service, are entitled to the wages of cooks, housemaids, nursemaids, seamstresses, or housekeepers, and to no more. This would of course reduce the spending money of the wives of the rich, and put it out of the power of the poor man to "support" a wife at all, unless, indeed, the poor man faced the situation fully, paid his wife her wages as house servant, and then she and he combined their funds in the support of their children. He would be keeping a servant: she would be helping keep the family. But nowhere on earth would there be "a rich woman" by these means. Even the highest class of private housekeeper, useful as her services are, does not accumulate a fortune. She does not buy diamonds and sables and keep a carriage.

But the salient fact in this discussion is that, whatever the economic value of the domestic industry of women is, they do not get it. The women who do the most work get the least money, the women who have the most money do the least work. Their labor is neither given nor taken as a factor in economic exchange. It is held to be their duty as women to do this work; and their economic status bears no relation to their domestic labors, unless an inverse one. Moreover, if they were thus fairly paid,—given what they earned, and no more,—all women working in this way would be reduced to the economic status of the house servant. Few women—or men either—care to face this condition. The ground that women earn their living by domestic labor is instantly forsaken, and we are told that they obtain their livelihood as mothers. This is a peculiar position. We speak of it commonly enough, and often with deep feeling, but without due analysis.

In treating of an economic exchange, asking what return in goods or labor women make for the goods and labor given them,—either to the race collectively or to their husbands individually,—what payment women make for their clothes and shoes and furniture and food and shelter, we are told that the duties and services of the mother entitle her to support.

If this is so, if motherhood is an exchangeable commodity given by women in payment for clothes and food, then we must of course find some relation between the quantity or quality of the motherhood and the quantity and quality of the pay. This being true, then the women who are not mothers have no economic status at all; and the economic status of those who are must be shown to be relative to their motherhood. This is obviously absurd. The childless wife has as much money as the mother of many,—more; for the children of the latter consume what would otherwise be hers; and the inefficient mother is no less provided for than the efficient one. Visibly, and upon the face of it, women are not maintained in economic prosperity proportioned to their motherhood. Motherhood bears no relation to their economic status. Among primitive races, it is true,—in the patriarchal period, for instance,—there was some truth in this position. Women being of no value whatever save as bearers of children, their favor and indulgence did bear direct relation to maternity; and they had reason to exult on more grounds than one when they could boast a son. To-day, however, the maintenance of the woman is not conditioned upon this. A man is not allowed to discard his wife because she is barren. The claim of motherhood as a factor in economic exchange is false to-day. But suppose it were true. Are we willing to hold this ground, even in theory? Are we willing to consider motherhood as a business, a form of commercial exchange? Are the cares and duties of the mother, her travail and her love, commodities to be exchanged for bread?

It is revolting so to consider them; and, if we dare face our own thoughts, and force them to their logical conclusion, we shall see that nothing could be more repugnant to human feeling, or more socially and individually injurious, than to make motherhood a trade. Driven off these alleged grounds of women's economic independence; shown that women, as a class, neither produce nor distribute wealth; that women, as individuals, labor mainly as house servants, are not paid as such, and would not be satisfied with such an economic status if they were so paid; that wives are not business partners or co-producers of wealth with their husbands, unless they actually practise the same profession; that they are not salaried as mothers, and that it would be unspeakably degrading if they were,—what remains to those who deny that women are supported by men? This (and a most amusing position it is),—that the function of maternity unfits a woman for economic production, and, therefore, it is right that she should be supported by her husband.

The ground is taken that the human female is not economically independent, that she is fed by the male of her species. In denial of this, it is first alleged that she is economically independent,—that she does support herself by her own industry in the house. It being shown that there is no relation between the economic status of woman and the labor she performs in the home, it is then alleged that not as house servant, but as mother, does woman earn her living. It being shown that the economic status of woman bears no relation to her motherhood, either in quantity or quality, it is then alleged that motherhood renders a woman unfit for economic production, and that, therefore, it is right that she be supported by her husband. Before going farther, let us seize upon this admission,—that she *is* supported by her husband.

Without going into either the ethics or the necessities of the case, we have reached so much common ground: the female of genus homo is supported by the male. Whereas, in other species of animals, male and female alike graze and browse, hunt and kill, climb, swim, dig, run, and fly for their livings, in our species the female does not seek her own living in the specific activities of our race, but is fed by the male.

Now as to the alleged necessity. Because of her maternal duties, the human female is said to be unable to get her own living. As the maternal duties of other females do not unfit them for getting their own living and also the livings of their young, it would seem that the human maternal duties require the segregation of the entire energies of the mother to the service of the child during her entire adult life, or so large a proportion of them that not enough remains to devote to the individual interests of the mother.

Such a condition, did it exist, would of course excuse and justify the pitiful dependence of the human female, and her support by the male. As the queen bee, modified entirely to maternity, is supported, not by the male, to be sure, but by her co-workers, the "old maids," the barren working bees, who labor so patiently and lovingly in their branch of the maternal duties of the hive, so would the human female, modified entirely to maternity, become unfit for any other exertion, and a helpless dependant.

Is this the condition of human motherhood? Does the human mother, by her motherhood, thereby lose control of brain and body, lose power and skill and desire for any other work? Do we see before us the human race, with all its females segregated entirely to the uses of motherhood, consecrated, set apart, specially developed, spending every power of their nature on the service of their children?

We do not. We see the human mother worked far harder than a mare, laboring her life long in the service, not of her children only, but of men; husbands, brothers, fathers, whatever male relatives she has; for mother and sister also; for the church a little, if she is allowed; for society, if she is able; for charity and education and reform,—working in many ways that are not the ways of motherhood.

It is not motherhood that keeps the housewife on her feet from dawn till dark; it is house service, not child service. Women work longer and harder than most men, and not solely in maternal duties. The savage mother carries the burdens, and does all menial service for the tribe. The peasant mother toils in the fields, and the workingman's wife in the home. Many mothers, even now, are wage-earners for the family, as well as bearers and rearers of it. And the women who are not so occupied, the women who belong to rich men,—here perhaps is the exhaustive devotion to maternity which is supposed to justify an admitted economic dependence. But we do not find it even among these. Women of ease and wealth provide for their children better care than the poor woman can; but they do not spend more time upon it themselves, nor more care and effort. They have other occupation.

In spite of her supposed segregation to maternal duties, the human female, the world over, works at extra-maternal duties for hours enough to provide her with an independent living, and then is denied independence on the ground that motherhood prevents her working!❖

Anna Julia Cooper (1858–1964) was born in North Carolina, the daughter of Hannah Stanley Haywood, a slave, and her owner. After being widowed as a young woman, Cooper attended Oberlin College, where she was a classmate of Mary Church Terrell, another important black feminist of the classic age. Most of her career was devoted to teaching, principally at Washington, D.C.'s M Street School. She served the students at M Street off and on from 1887 until her retirement. In 1906, she was forced out of her position as principal of M Street by agents of Booker T. Washington, who favored industrial training over classical education for blacks. Cooper, who had helped students gain admission to the best universities, was considered too similar in her views to Washington's chief opponent, W.E.B. Du Bois.

Anna Julia Cooper's *A Voice from the South* (1892) was her most important book. Yet after returning to M Street in 1910, she lived a life of varied accomplishments as writer, lecturer, settlement house founder, adoptive mother of five children (at age fifty-seven), scholar (she received her Ph.D. from the Sorbonne at age sixty-seven), translator, and college president. Today, she is recognized as a major figure in the tradition of Black feminist social theory. She died in Washington, D.C., in 1964, having lived from the days of slavery and emancipation to the modern civil rights movement.

"The Colored Women's Office" represents Cooper's principal contribution to Black feminist social theory. In these selections from *A Voice from the South*, she argues that moral progress depends on the only person able to understand the deep connections of race and gender in America—the black woman.

The Colored Woman's Office

Anna Julia Cooper (1892)

Now the fundamental agency under God in the regeneration, the re-training of the race, as well as the ground work and starting point of its progress upward, must be the *black woman.*

With all the wrongs and neglects of her past, with all the weakness, the debasement, the moral thralldom of her present, the black woman of to-day stands mute and wondering at the Herculean task devolving upon her. But the cycles wait for her. No other hand can move the lever. She must be loosed from her bands and set to work.

Our meager and superficial results from past efforts prove their futility; and every attempt to elevate the Negro, whether undertaken by himself or through the philanthropy of others, cannot but prove abortive unless so directed as to utilize the indispensable agency of an elevated and trained womanhood.

A race cannot be purified from without. Preachers and teachers are helps, and stimulants and conditions as necessary as the gracious rain and sunshine are to plant growth. But what are rain and dew and sunshine and cloud if there be no life in the plant germ? We must go to the root and see that that is sound and healthy and vigorous; and not deceive ourselves with waxen flowers and painted leaves of mock chlorophyll.

We too often mistake individuals' honor for race development and so are ready to substitute pretty accomplishments for sound sense and earnest purpose.

A stream cannot rise higher than its source. The atmosphere of homes is no rarer and purer and sweeter than are the mothers in those homes. A race is but a total of families. The nation is the aggregate of its homes. As the whole is sum of all its parts, so the character of the parts will determine the characteristics of the whole. These are all axioms and so evident that it seems gratuitous to remark it; and yet, unless I am greatly mistaken, most of the unsatisfaction from our past results arises from just such a radical and palpable error, as much almost on our own part as on that of our benevolent white friends.

The Negro is constitutionally hopeful and proverbially irrepressible; and naturally stands in danger of being dazzled by the shimmer and tinsel of superficials. We often mistake foliage for fruit and overestimate or wrongly estimate brilliant results.

The late Martin R. Delany, who was an unadulterated black man, used to say when honors of state fell upon him, that when he entered the council of kings the black race entered with him; meaning, I suppose, that there was no discounting his race identity and attributing his achievements to some admixture of Saxon blood. But our present record of eminent men, when placed beside the actual status of the race in America to-day, proves that no man can represent the race. Whatever the attainments of the individual may be, unless his home has moved on *pari passu,* he can never be regarded as identical with or representative of the whole.

Not by pointing to sun-bathed mountain tops do we prove that Phoebus warms the valleys. We must point to homes, average homes, homes of the rank and file of horny handed toiling men and women of the South (where the masses are) lighted and cheered by the good, the beautiful, and the true,—then and not till then will the whole plateau be lifted into the sunlight.

Excerpt from *A Voice from the South* (New York: Oxford University Press, 1988 [1892]), pp. 28–31, 94–101, 134–135, 140–145.

Only the Black Woman can say "when and where I enter, in the quiet, undisputed dignity of my womanhood, without violence and without suing or special patronage, then and there the whole *Negro race enters with me.*" Is it not evident then that as individual workers for this race we must address ourselves with no half-hearted zeal to this feature of our mission. The need is felt and must be recognized by all. There is a call for workers, for missionaries, for men and women with the double consecration of a fundamental love of humanity and a desire for its melioration through the Gospel; but superadded to this we demand an intelligent and sympathetic comprehension of the interests and special needs of the Negro. . . .

I would eliminate also from the discussion all uncharitable reflections upon the orderly execution of laws existing in certain states of this Union, requiring persons known to be colored to ride in one car, and persons supposed to be white in another. A good citizen may use his influence to have existing laws and statutes changed or modified, but a public servant must not be blamed for obeying orders. A railroad conductor is not asked to dictate measures, nor to make and pass laws. His bread and butter are conditioned on his managing his part of the machinery as he is told to do. If, therefore, I found myself in that compartment of a train designated by the sovereign law of the state for presumable Caucasians, and for colored persons only when traveling in the capacity of nurses and maids, should a conductor inform me, as a gentleman might, that I had made a mistake, and offer to show me the proper car for black ladies; I might wonder at the expensive arrangements of the company and of the state in providing special and separate accommodations for the transportation of the various hues of humanity, but I certainly could not take it as a want of courtesy on the conductor's part that he gave the information. It is true, public sentiment precedes and begets all laws, good or bad; and on the ground I have taken, our women are to be credited largely as teachers and moulders of public sentiment. But when a law has passed and received the sanction of the land, there is nothing for our officials to do but enforce it till repealed; and I for one, as a loyal American citizen, will give those officials cheerful support and ready sympathy in the discharge of their duty. But when a great burly six feet of masculinity with sloping shoulders and unkempt beard swaggers in, and, throwing a roll of tobacco into one corner of his jaw, growls out at me over the paper I am reading, "Here gurl," (I am past thirty) "you better git out 'n dis kyar 'f yer don't, I'll put yer out,"—my mental annotation is *Here's an American citizen who has been badly trained. He is sadly lacking in both 'sweetness' and 'light';* and when in the same section of our enlightened and progressive country, I see from the car window, working on private estates, convicts from the state penitentiary, among them squads of boys from fourteen to eighteen years of age in a chain-gang, their feet chained together and heavy blocks attached—not in 1850, but in 1890, '91 and '92, I make a note on the flyleaf of my memorandum, *The women in this section should organize a Society for the Prevention of Cruelty to Human Beings, and disseminate civilizing tracts, and send throughout the region apostles of anti-barbarism for the propagation of humane and enlightened ideas.* And when farther on in the same section our train stops at a dilapidated station, rendered yet more unsightly by dozens of loafers with their hands in their pockets while a productive soil and inviting climate beckon in vain to industry; and when, looking a little more closely, I see two dingy little rooms with "FOR LADIES" swinging over one and "FOR COLORED PEOPLE" over the other; while wondering under which head I come, I notice a little way off the only hotel proprietor of the place whittling a pine stick as he sits with one leg thrown across an empty goods box; and as my eye falls on a sample room next door which seems to be driving the only wide-awake and popular business of the commonwealth, I cannot help ejaculating under my breath, "What a field for the missionary woman." I know that if by any fatality I should be obliged to lie over at that station, and, driven by hunger, should be compelled to seek refreshments or the bare necessaries of life at the only public accommodation in the town, that same stick-whittler would coolly inform me, without looking up from his pine splinter, "We doan ucommodate no niggers hyur." And yet we are so scandalized at Russia's barbarity and cruelty to the Jews! We pay a man a thousand dollars a night just to make us weep, by a recital of such heathenish inhumanity as is practiced on Sclavonic soil.

A recent writer on Eastern nations says: "If we take through the earth's temperate zone, a belt of country whose northern and southern edges are determined by certain limiting isotherms, not more than half the width of the zone apart, we shall find that we have included in a relatively small extent of surface almost all the nations of note in the world, past or present. Now, if we examine this belt and compare the different parts of it with one another, we shall be struck by a remarkable fact. *The peoples inhabiting it grow steadily more personal as we go west.* So unmistakable is this gradation, that one is almost tempted to ascribe it to cosmical rather than to human causes. It is as marked as the change in color of the human complexion observable along any meridian, which ranges from black at the equator to blonde toward the pole. In like manner the sense of self grows more intense as we follow in the wake of the setting sun, and fades steadily as we advance into the dawn. America, Europe, the Levant, India, Japan, each is less personal than the one before. . . . *That politeness should be one of the most marked results of impersonality* may appear surprising, yet a slight examination will show it to be a fact. Considered *a priori,* the connection is not far to seek. Impersonality by lessening the interest in one's self, induces one to take an interest in others. Looked at *a posteriori,* we find that where the one trait exists the other is most developed, while an absence of the second seems to prevent the full growth of the first. This is true both in general and in detail. *Courtesy increases as we travel eastward round the world, coincidently with a decrease in the sense of self.* Asia is more courteous than Europe, Europe than America. Particular races show the same concomitance of characteristics. France, the most impersonal nation of Europe, is at the same time the most polite." And by inference, Americans, the most personal, are the least courteous nation on the globe.

The Black Woman had reached this same conclusion by an entirely different route; but it is gratifying to vanity, nevertheless, to find one's self sustained by both science and philosophy in a conviction, wrought in by hard experience, and yet too apparently audacious to be entertained even as a stealthy surmise. In fact the Black Woman was emboldened some time since by a well put and timely article from an Editor's Drawer on the "Mannerless Sex," to give the world the benefit of some of her experience with the *"Mannerless Race"*; but since Mr. Lowell shows so conclusively that the entire Land of the West is a *mannerless continent,* I have determined to plead with our women, the mannerless sex on this mannerless continent, to institute a reform by placing immediately in our national curricula a department for teaching good manners.

Now, am I right in holding the American Woman responsible? Is it true that the exponents of woman's advancement, the leaders in woman's thought, the preachers and teachers of all woman's reforms, can teach this nation to be courteous, to be pitiful, having compassion one of another, not rendering evil for inoffensiveness,

and railing in proportion to the improbability of being struck back; but contrari-
wise, being *all* of one mind, to love as brethren?

I think so.

It may require some heroic measures, and like all revolutions will call for a determined front and a courageous, unwavering, stalwart heart on the part of the leaders
of the reform.

The "*all*" will inevitably stick in the throat of the Southern woman. She must be
allowed, please, to except the 'darkey' from the 'all'; it is too bitter a pill with black
people in it. You must get the Revised Version to put it, "*love all white people* as
brethren." She really could not enter any society on earth, or in heaven above, or
in—the waters under the earth, on such unpalatable conditions.

The Black Woman has tried to understand the Southern woman's difficulties; to
put herself in her place, and to be as fair, as charitable, and as free from prejudice in
judging her antipathies, as she would have others in regard to her own. She has honestly weighed the apparently sincere excuse, "But you must remember that these
people were once our slaves"; and that other, "But civility towards the Negroes will
bring us on *social equality* with them." . . .

The colored woman of to-day occupies, one may say, a unique position in this country. In a period of itself transitional and unsettled, her status seems one of the least ascertainable and definitive of all the forces which make for our civilization. She is confronted by both a woman question and a race problem, and is as yet an unknown or an
unacknowledged factor in both. While the women of the white race can with calm assurance enter upon the work they feel by nature appointed to do, while their men give
loyal support and appreciative countenance to their efforts, recognizing in most avenues of usefulness the propriety and the need of woman's distinctive co-operation,
the colored woman too often finds herself hampered and shamed by a less liberal sentiment and a more conservative attitude on the part of those for whose opinion she cares
most. That this is not universally true I am glad to admit. There are to be found both
intensely conservative white men and exceedingly liberal colored men. But as far as my
experience goes the average man of our race is less frequently ready to admit the actual
need among the sturdier forces of the world for woman's help or influence. That great
social and economic questions await her interference, that she could throw any light on
problems of national import, that her intermeddling could improve the management
of school systems, or elevate the tone of public institutions, or humanize and sanctify
the far reaching influence of prisons and reformatories and improve the treatment of
lunatics and imbeciles,—that she has a word worth hearing on mooted questions in
political economy, that she could contribute a suggestion on the relations of labor and
capital, or offer a thought on honest money and honorable trade, I fear the majority of
"Americans of the colored variety" are not yet prepared to concede. . . .

Not unfelt, then, if unproclaimed has been the work and influence of the colored
women of America. Our list of chieftains in the service, though not long, is not inferior in strength and excellence, I dare believe, to any similar list which this country
can produce.

Among the pioneers, Frances Watkins Harper could sing with prophetic exaltation in the darkest days, when as yet there was not a rift in the clouds overhanging
her people:

"Yes, Ethiopia shall stretch
Her bleeding hands abroad;

Her cry of agony shall reach the burning throne of God.
Redeemed from dust and freed from chains
Her sons shall lift their eyes,
From cloud-capt hills and verdant plains
Shall shouts of triumph rise."

Among preachers of righteousness, an unanswerable silencer of cavilers and objectors, was Sojourner Truth, that unique and rugged genius who seemed carved out without hand or chisel from the solid mountain mass; and in pleasing contrast, Amanda Smith, sweetest of natural singers and pleaders in dulcet tones for the things of God and of His Christ.

Sarah Woodson Early and Martha Briggs, planting and watering in the school room, and giving off from their matchless and irresistible personality an impetus and inspiration which can never die so long as there lives and breathes a remote descendant of their disciples and friends.

Charlotte Fortin Grimke, the gentle spirit whose verses and life link her so beautifully with America's great Quaker poet and loving reformer.

Hallie Quinn Brown, charming reader, earnest, effective lecturer and devoted worker of unflagging zeal and unquestioned power.

Fannie Jackson Coppin, the teacher and organizer, pre-eminent among women of whatever country or race in constructive and executive force.

These women represent all shades of belief and as many departments of activity; but they have one thing in common—their sympathy with the oppressed race in America and the consecration of their several talents in whatever line to the work of its deliverance and development.

Fifty years ago woman's activity according to orthodox definitions was on a pretty clearly cut "sphere," including primarily the kitchen and the nursery, and rescued from the barrenness of prison bars by the womanly mania for adorning every discoverable bit of china or canvass with forlorn looking cranes balanced idiotically on one foot. The woman of to-day finds herself in the presence of responsibilities which ramify through the profoundest and most varied interests of her country and race. Not one of the issues of this plodding, toiling, sinning, repenting, falling, aspiring humanity can afford to shut her out, or can deny the reality of her influence. No plan for renovating society, no scheme for purifying politics, no reform in church or in state, no moral, social, or economic question, no movement upward or downward in the human plane is lost on her. A man once said when told his house was afire: "Go tell my wife; I never meddle with household affairs." But no woman can possibly put herself or her sex outside any of the interests that affect humanity. All departments in the new era are to be hers, in the sense that her interests are in all and through all; and it is incumbent on her to keep intelligently and sympathetically *en rapport* with all the great movements of her time, that she may know on which side to throw the weight of her influence. She stands now at the gateway of this new era of American civilization. In her hands must be moulded the strength, the wit, the statesmanship, the morality, all the psychic force, the social and economic intercourse of that era. To be alive at such an epoch is a privilege, to be a woman then is sublime.

In this last decade of our century, changes of such moment are in progress, such new and alluring vistas are opening out before us, such original and radical suggestions for the adjustment of labor and capital, of government and the governed, of the family, the church and the state, that to be a possible factor though an infinitesimal in such a movement is pregnant with hope and weighty with responsibility. To be a woman in such an age carries with it a privilege and an opportunity never implied before. But to be a woman of the Negro race in America, and to be able to grasp the deep significance of the possibilities of the crisis, is to have a heritage, it seems to me, unique in the ages. In the first place, the race is young and full of the elasticity and hopefulness of youth. All its achievements are before it. It does not look on the masterly triumphs of nineteenth century civilization with that *blase* world-weary look which characterizes the old washed out and worn out races which have already, so to speak, seen their best days.

Said a European writer recently: "Except the Sclavonic, the Negro is the only original and distinctive genius which has yet to come to growth—and the feeling is to cherish and develop it."

Everything to this race is new and strange and inspiring. There is a quickening of its pulses and a glowing of its self-consciousness. Aha, I can rival that! I can aspire to that! I can honor my name and vindicate my race! Something like this, it strikes me, is the enthusiasm which stirs the genius of young Africa in America; and the memory of past oppression and the fact of present attempted repression only serve to gather momentum for its irrepressible powers. Then again, a race in such a stage of growth is peculiarly sensitive to impressions. Not the photographer's sensitized plate is more delicately impressionable to outer influences than is this high strung people here on the threshold of a career.

What a responsibility then to have the sole management of the primal lights and shadows! Such is the colored woman's office. She must stamp weal or woe on the coming history of this people. May she see her opportunity and vindicate her high prerogative.❖

Georg Simmel (1858–1918), though he never enjoyed a significant position in a university, was a founder (with Weber and Ferdinand Toennies) of the German Sociological Society. Simmel was a regular participant in Max and Marianne Weber's Heidelberg circle of intellectual friends. He was esteemed by many of the luminaries of German intellectual life, including Edmund Husserl and Heinrich Rickert. Yet he lived the life of an independent bourgeois intellectual, which earned him the respect denied by the university establishment. Today, his writings are read for their unusual theoretical insight into the inner workings of life in the modern world. The following selection illustrates Simmel's simple style and disarming ability to describe an important character in all social groups—the stranger—a character who became all the more important in the modern world, especially when viewed from the perspective of Europe's stranger within, the Jew.

The Stranger

Georg Simmel (1908)

If wandering, considered as a state of detachment from every given point in space, is the conceptual opposite of attachment to any point, then the sociological form of "the stranger" presents the synthesis, as it were, of both of these properties. (This is another indication that spatial relations not only are determining conditions of relationships among men, but are also symbolic of those relationships.) The stranger will thus not be considered here in the usual sense of the term, as the wanderer who comes today and goes tomorrow, but rather as the man who comes today and stays tomorrow—the potential wanderer, so to speak, who, although he has gone no further, has not quite got over the freedom of coming and going. He is fixed within a certain spatial circle—or within a group whose boundaries are analogous to spatial boundaries—but his position within it is fundamentally affected by the fact that he does not belong in it initially and that he brings qualities into it that are not, and cannot be, indigenous to it.

In the case of the stranger, the union of closeness and remoteness involved in every human relationship is patterned in a way that may be succinctly formulated as follows: the distance within this relation indicates that one who is close by is remote, but his strangeness indicates that one who is remote is near. The state of being a stranger is of course a completely positive relation; it is a specific form of interaction. The inhabitants of Sirius are not exactly strangers to us, at least not in the sociological sense of the word as we are considering it. In that sense they do not exist for us at all; they are beyond being far and near. The stranger is an element of the group itself, not unlike the poor and sundry "inner enemies"—an element whose membership within the group involves both being outside it and confronting it.

The following statements about the stranger are intended to suggest how factors of repulsion and distance work to create a form of being together, a form of union based on interaction.

In the whole history of economic activity the stranger makes his appearance everywhere as a trader, and the trader makes his as a stranger. As long as production for one's own needs is the general rule, or products are exchanged within a relatively small circle, there is no need for a middleman within the group. A trader is required only for goods produced outside the group. Unless there are people who wander out into foreign lands to buy these necessities, in which case they are themselves "strange" merchants in this other region, the trader *must* be a stranger; there is no opportunity for anyone else to make a living at it.

This position of the stranger stands out more sharply if, instead of leaving the place of his activity, he settles down there. In innumerable cases even this is possible only if he can live by trade as a middleman. Any closed economic group where land and handicrafts have been apportioned in a way that satisfies local demands will still support a livelihood for the trader. For trade alone makes possible unlimited combinations, and through it intelligence is constantly extended and applied in new areas, something that is much harder for the primary producer with his more limited mobility and his dependence on a circle of customers that can be expanded only very slowly. Trade can always absorb more men than can primary production. It is therefore the most suitable activity for the stranger, who intrudes as a supernumerary, so to speak, into a group in which all the economic positions are already occupied. The classic example of this is the history of European Jews. The stranger is by his very nature no owner of land—land not only in the physical sense but also metaphorically as a vital substance which is fixed, if not in space, then at least in an ideal position within the social environment.

Although in the sphere of intimate personal relations the stranger may be attractive and meaningful in many ways, so long as he is regarded as a stranger he is no "landowner" in the eyes of the other. Restriction to intermediary trade and often (as though sublimated from it) to pure finance gives the stranger the specific character of *mobility*. The appearance of this mobility within a bounded group occasions that synthesis of nearness and remoteness which constitutes the formal position of the stranger. The purely mobile person comes incidentally into contact with *every* single element but is not bound up organically, through established ties of kinship, locality, or occupation, with any single one.

Another expression of this constellation is to be found in the objectivity of the stranger. Because he is not bound by roots to the particular constituents and partisan dispositions of the group, he confronts all of these with a distinctly "objective" attitude, an attitude that does not signify mere detachment and nonparticipation, but is a distinct structure composed of remoteness and nearness, indifference and involvement. I refer to my analysis of the dominating positions gained by aliens, in the discussion of superordination and subordination, typified by the practice in certain Italian cities of recruiting their judges from outside, because no native was free from entanglement in family interests and factionalism.

Connected with the characteristic of objectivity is a phenomenon that is found chiefly, though not exclusively, in the stranger who moves on. This is that he often receives the most surprising revelations and confidences, at times reminiscent of a confessional, about matters which are kept carefully hidden from everybody with whom one is close. Objectivity is by no means nonparticipation, a condition that is altogether outside the distinction between subjective and objective orientations. It is rather a positive and definite kind of participation, in the same way that the objectivity of a theoretical observation clearly does not mean that the mind is a passive tabula rasa on which things inscribe their qualities, but rather signifies the full activity of a mind working according to its own laws, under conditions that exclude accidental distortions and emphases whose individual and subjective differences would produce quite different pictures of the same object.

Objectivity can also be defined as freedom. The objective man is not bound by ties which could prejudice his perception, his understanding, and his assessment of data. This freedom, which permits the stranger to experience and treat even his close relationships as though from a bird's-eye view, contains many dangerous possibilities. From earliest times, in uprisings of all sorts the attacked party has claimed that there has been incitement from the outside, by foreign emissaries and agitators. Insofar as this has happened, it represents an exaggeration of the specific role of the stranger: he is the freer man, practically and theoretically; he examines conditions with less prejudice; he assesses them against standards that are more general and more objective; and his actions are not confined by custom, piety, or precedent.

Finally, the proportion of nearness and remoteness which gives the stranger the character of objectivity also finds practical expression in the more *abstract* nature of the relation to him. That is, with the stranger one has only certain *more general* qualities in common, whereas the relation with organically connected persons is based on the similarity of just those specific traits which differentiate them from the merely universal. In fact, all personal relations whatsoever can be analyzed in terms of this scheme. They are not determined only by the existence of certain common characteristics which the individuals share in addition to their individual differences, which either influence the relationship or remain outside of it. Rather, the kind of effect which that commonality has on the relation essentially depends on whether it exists only among the participants themselves, and thus, although general within the relation, is specific and incomparable with respect to all those on the outside, or whether the participants feel that what they have in common is so only because it is common to a group, a type, or mankind in general. In the latter case, the effect of the common features becomes attenuated in proportion to the size of the group bearing the same characteristics. The commonality provides a basis for unifying the members, to be sure; but it does not specifically direct *these* particular persons to one another. A similarity so widely shared could just as easily unite each person with every possible other. This, too, is evidently a way in which a relationship includes both nearness and remoteness simultaneously. To the extent to which the similarities assume a universal nature, the warmth of the connection based on them will acquire an element of coolness, a sense of the contingent nature of precisely *this* relation—the connecting forces have lost their specific, centripetal character.

In relation to the stranger, it seems to me, this constellation assumes an extraordinary preponderance in principle over the individual elements peculiar to the relation in question. The stranger is close to us insofar as we feel between him and ourselves similarities of nationality or social position, of occupation or of general human nature. He is far from us insofar as these similarities extend beyond him and us, and connect us only because they connect a great many people.

A trace of strangeness in this sense easily enters even the most intimate relationships. In the stage of first passion, erotic relations strongly reject any thought of generalization. A love such as this has never existed before; there is nothing to compare either with the person one loves or with our feelings for that person. An estrangement is wont to set in (whether as cause or effect is hard to decide) at the moment when this feeling of uniqueness disappears from the relationship. A skepticism regarding the intrinsic value of the relationship and its value for us adheres to the very thought that in this relation, after all, one is only fulfilling a general human destiny, that one has had an experience that has occurred a thousand times before, and that, if one had not accidentally met this precise person, someone else would have acquired the same meaning for us.

Something of this feeling is probably not absent in any relation, be it ever so close, because that which is common to two is perhaps never common *only* to them but belongs to a general conception which includes much else besides, many *possibilities* of similarities. No matter how few of these possibilities are realized and how often we may forget about them, here and there, nevertheless, they crowd in like shadows between men, like a mist eluding every designation, which must congeal into solid corporeality for it to be called jealousy. Perhaps this is in many cases a more general, at least more insurmountable, strangeness than that due to differences and obscurities. It is strangeness caused by the fact that similarity, harmony, and closeness are accompanied by the feeling that they are actually not the exclusive property of this particular relation, but stem from a more general one—a relation that potentially includes us and an indeterminate number of others, and therefore prevents that relation which alone was experienced from having an inner and exclusive necessity.

On the other hand, there is a sort of "strangeness" in which this very connection on the basis of a general quality embracing the parties is precluded. The relation of the Greeks to the barbarians is a typical example; so are all the cases in which the general characteristics one takes as peculiarly and merely human are disallowed to the other. But here the expression "the stranger" no longer has any positive meaning. The relation with him is a non-relation; he is not what we have been discussing here: the stranger as a member of the group itself.

As such, the stranger is near and far *at the same time,* as in any relationship based on merely universal human similarities. Between these two factors of nearness and distance, however, a peculiar tension arises, since the consciousness of having only the absolutely general in common has exactly the effect of putting a special emphasis on that which is not common. For a stranger to the country, the city, the race, and so on, what is stressed is again nothing individual, but alien origin, a quality which he has, or could have, in common with many other strangers. For this reason strangers are not really perceived as individuals, but as strangers of a certain type. Their remoteness is no less general than their nearness.

This form appears, for example, in so special a case as the tax levied on Jews in Frankfurt and elsewhere during the Middle Ages. Whereas the tax paid by Christian citizens varied according to their wealth at any given time, for every single Jew the tax was fixed once and for all. This amount was fixed because the Jew had his social position as a *Jew,* not as the bearer of certain objective contents. With respect to taxes every other citizen was regarded as possessor of a certain amount of wealth, and his tax could follow the fluctuations of his fortune. But the Jew as taxpayer was first of all a Jew, and thus his fiscal position contained an invariable element. This appears most forcefully, of course, once the differing circumstances of individual Jews are no longer considered, limited though this consideration is by fixed assessments, and all strangers pay exactly the same head tax.

Despite his being inorganically appended to it, the stranger is still an organic member of the group. Its unified life includes the specific conditioning of this element. Only we do not know how to designate the characteristic unity of this position otherwise than by saying that it is put together of certain amounts of nearness and of remoteness. Although both these qualities are found to some extent in all relationships, a special proportion and reciprocal tension between them produce the specific form of the relation to the "stranger." ❖

Charles Horton Cooley (1864–1929) grew up at the University of Michigan, where his father taught law. There, he eventually became a presence in his own right, ascending after his studies to a professorship. From that position, he played a part in the early development of sociology in the United States. His books include *Human Nature and the Social Order* (1902), *Social Organization* (1909), and *Social Process* (1918). The following short selection presents his most famous concept, the looking-glass self, which still comes to mind when social theorists reconsider the social self.

The Looking-Glass Self
Charles Horton Cooley (1902)

I remarked above that we think of the body as "I" when it comes to have social function or significance, as when we say "I am looking well to-day," or "I am taller than you are." We bring it into the social world, for the time being, and for that reason put our self-consciousness into it. Now it is curious, though natural, that in precisely the same way we may call any inanimate object "I" with which we are identifying our will and purpose. This is notable in games, like golf or croquet, where the ball is the embodiment of the player's fortunes. You will hear a man say, "I am in the long grass down by the third tee," or "I am in position for the middle arch." So a boy flying a kite will say "I am higher than you," or one shooting at a mark will declare that he is just below the bullseye.

In a very large and interesting class of cases the social reference takes the form of a somewhat definite imagination of how one's self—that is any idea he appropriates—appears in a particular mind, and the kind of self-feeling one has is determined by the attitude toward this attributed to that other mind. A social self of this sort might be called the reflected or looking-glass self:

> "Each to each a looking-glass
> Reflects the other that doth pass."

As we see our face, figure, and dress in the glass, and are interested in them because they are ours, and pleased or otherwise with them according as they do or do not answer to what we should like them to be; so in imagination we perceive in another's mind some thought of our appearance, manners, aims, deeds, character, friends, and so on, and are variously affected by it.

A self-idea of this sort seems to have three principal elements: the imagination of our appearance to the other person; the imagination of his judgment of that appearance, and some sort of self-feeling, such as pride or mortification. The comparison with a looking-glass hardly suggests the second element, the imagined judgment, which is quite essential. The thing that moves us to pride or shame is not the mere mechanical reflection of ourselves, but an imputed sentiment, the imagined effect of this reflection upon another's mind. This is evident from the fact that the character and weight of that other, in whose mind we see ourselves, makes all the difference with our feeling. We are ashamed to seem evasive in the presence of a straightforward man, cowardly in the presence of a brave one, gross in the eyes of a refined one, and so on. We always imagine, and in imagining share, the judgments of the other mind. A man will boast to one person of an action—say some sharp transaction in trade—which he would be ashamed to own to another.❖

PART TWO

Social Theories
and World Conflict:
1919–1945

If the prevailing attitude in the West's classical age was denial, then in the interwar years it was shock. The world wars, the Holocaust, failure in the capitalist world-system, fascism, Hitler, Stalin—these were not supposed to be. It was not that the nineteenth century had been free of war, economic trouble, or political terror—hardly. But in the popular imagination, these horrors were expected to loosen their hold as time went by. That was the promise of modern society. Progress! Everything was Progress.

The very foundations of modern culture in the European world, including North America, were inspiring because they were so simple: *Man, freed from political tyranny, if he dare think for himself, will know the Truth. What is the Truth? Simply that Man, enlightened and free, will make the world better.* Though these exact words were said by no one in particular, the idea they express was everywhere from the eighteenth century well into the twentieth. You can find it in Kant and the *philosophes* in France; in and behind the American Declaration of Independence, the French Declaration of the Rights of Man, and *The Communist Manifesto;* in Adam Smith and the political economists; in the framers of early American political consciousness—Tom Paine, Thomas Jefferson, and many others; among those, like Herbert Spencer, who applied Darwinian principles to modern society; and, of course, in the writings of all the classic social theorists. Everywhere.

This new culture also inspired the practical thinking of the masses. Some picked it up from intellectual and political leaders. Others just caught it from the air of the times. In fact, few of the dramatic political or economic events in the hundred years following 1776 would have been possible without a prior conversion to this new faith by great numbers of people. One does not need to be a historian of the nineteenth century to imagine what poor and working people, as well as the bourgeoisie, must have felt in those days. Who among those who stormed the Bastille on July 14, 1789, would dare to stand against the weight of traditional authority if he did not believe truth was on his side? Who among those who migrated in the 1830s from the agrarian countryside to new industrial centers in the north of England could possibly abandon family roots in the raising of sheep's wool for the cotton-weaving factory if they did not believe in a better life? Who in the United States of the 1860s would leave her roots in the East to join a frontiersman in the Indian territories if she did not somehow believe in Progress? Who among the millions of European immigrants to Chicago, to the plains of the Northwest Territories, and to the factories of the Northeast could separate themselves from everything held dear for centuries were it not for trust in this doctrine? *Daring now to think for ourselves, let us seek a better world.* This was the popular foundation of modern culture. Deep in its intellectual bowels—below its new philosophies, its brilliant technologies, its wonderful sciences—modernity preached this simple, compelling faith. Progress was Truth.

In the 1890s, this idea predominated. The prevailing mood was expectation, and hope was strong even though the reality of life in the West had been hard. Thousands had died in revolutions that compromised original principles. Millions were degraded and exploited in the industrial centers. Women and children, as well as frontiersmen, died in the Western territories, as they did in industrial neighborhoods. Immigrants from Europe and Asia encountered miseries only marginally less acute than those they had left behind. There is no reason whatsoever to believe that life in Europe and the United States was dramatically better, or worse, for the masses than at an earlier, or later, time.

Yet at the end of the nineteenth century, people continued to look ahead, believing in Progress. The classical social theorists, many of them then at the height of their powers, were no exceptions. Yes, they understood the dark sides of modern life. But for the most part, they also shared this popular faith. Durkheim's social theory of moral life was intended to serve the modern future of France. Most of Weber's basic ideas were defined against his desire to explain the modernizing world. Whatever was wrong with it, he believed in the superiority of the rational West. The followers of Marx, an increasingly contentious lot by the 1890s, still shared his elemental faith that a final, ultimate stage of economic history was within reach. Even Freud seemed to believe that the Truth was strong enough to combat the irrational forces at war in the unconscious souls of modern people. In fact, even those who had no good reason to trust the promises of Western culture seemed to believe. In the 1890s, Frederick Douglass, Anna Julia Cooper, and W.E.B. Du Bois were chief among American Blacks who knew better than to trust the preachings, yet they, too, believed—in knowledge, in freedom, in Progress. In 1892, Cooper said, "There can be no doubt that here in America is the arena in which the next triumph of civilization is to be won."

One of Max Weber's most enduring insights came from his attempt to answer one question: Why do people obey authority? His answer: Human beings have an inner need for meaning. They will obey if the authority makes sense of their lives. In other words, people want value in return for obedience. They are, in this sense, ethical. Thus, as he explained in *The Protestant Ethic,* modern culture arose when an increasing number of people accepted the idea that meaning lay in the future, not the past. The ethical disposition of people who caught the spirit of capitalism was: Think about future goals; calculate everything to achieve those goals. In order to revolt, migrate, or brave the seas and frontiers, one had to have this ethical attitude in nearly the same measure as did the early capitalist entrepreneurs. A culture of Progress is a culture that encourages people to turn from the past, toward the future—to change their orientation in time's space. Belief in one's own rational abilities encourages a readiness to marshal energies and resources, and marshaling draws, in turn, on the storehouse of reasonable calculations.

What, *precisely,* are the means to this end? This was the ethical question that moved so many people through the nineteenth century. Trust that the answer would be evident and available was what enticed them to overlook the dark miseries all around. There is, however, a serious risk taken by those whose ethic is Progress itself. The ethical promise must eventually be kept. The payoff need not be immediate, perhaps not even in one's own time. But at least one must be able to picture the day when the children or their children will have a better life. Throughout the nineteenth century, up to World War I, enough was gained by enough people to support the doctrine that held its own well into the twentieth century.

But in the quarter century between the world wars, from 1919 or so to 1945, the world's events disturbed confidence in the original, uncomplicated version of this faith in Progress. The shock experienced in this period stemmed, in part, from the realization that what some had been saying all along had to be taken seriously. In the 1890s, all the classic social theorists understood that something was wrong—exploitation, estrangement, anomie, the bureaucratic machine, the veil, the irrational instincts. Yet none of them ever seemed to doubt that good knowledge would ultimately triumph, that moral progress would win the day. Among the canonical writers, only Weber was unready to believe that hope would overcome his gloom. He left the question open. Among the marginalized writers of the time, only Friedrich Nietzsche took serious measure of this prospect. Only he thought deeply enough about modern culture's one-sided faith in its Truth to consider the idea that the modern world was not itself an end. In 1887 in *Genealogy of Morals,* Nietzsche said:

> What would our existence amount to were it not for this, that the will to truth has been forced to examine itself? It is by this dawning self-consciousness of the will to truth that ethics must now perish. This is the great spectacle of a hundred acts that will occupy Europe for the next two centuries, the most terrible and problematical but also the most hopeful of spectacles. . . .

Were the events between the two wars that spectacle?

How can it be said, even by Nietzsche, that the political and economic crises that led to war, Hitler, and depression were theatrical displays? In what ways were they even unusual? Had not the Europeans passed the nineteenth century continuing to colonize Africa and Asia, while the Americans openly did to African slaves and their own native people something like what Hitler would do to Jewish people? Was not social evil just as evenly distributed across the nineteenth century as the twentieth? Yes, but. A spectacle, like any drama on whatever stage, depends entirely on the expectations of the audience drawn into it. The plays of Sophocles and Shakespeare pack dramatic punch into the surprise of feeling oneself not much less blind than Oedipus or Hamlet. One is led to expect something else for dramatic surprise always works in relation to what went before. World history is no different. Thus, the spectacle of the nineteenth century was that of man's fresh hopes rising above evil to meet tomorrow's dawn. For European people, at home or abroad in America, the spectacle of the twentieth century was staged against that of the nineteenth. Dawn's light was dim. Instead of spring, winter lingered. Those expecting a day, clear and warm, eventually had to reconsider the holding power of night, cold and dark.

It would be a fruitless, and inhumane, exercise to calculate a coefficient of the actual horrors of the two centuries. How exactly could one sum up the balance between the economic miseries of the new working classes in nineteenth-century industrial capitalism against the sorrows of those who lost their fortunes in the Great Depression of the twentieth century? What possible formula would one use to measure the horror wrought by Hitler against the Jews or the Soviet people in the 1930s and 1940s against the nightmare of Africans, among other peoples, enslaved and murdered throughout the nineteenth century and before? How exactly does one measure what Andrew Jackson did to the Cherokee nation in the 1830s against what Stalin did a century later? What is the worth of saying that so many more Americans died in the Civil War than in either of the two world wars? The calculation itself is cruel.

What matters to people trying to understand their worlds is beyond any calculus. They ask deeper questions: Will the present evil be overcome? What does it mean that such evil is still present after all these years? For many people through the end of the last century, it seemed right to expect if not an end to evil at least a lessening of it. This was Progress. For their counterparts in the period after 1919, this expectation seemed fragile, if not false. This, it might be said, was when the culture of the nineteenth century faded and that of the twentieth emerged. Much had to be rethought.

In social theory, what had to be rethought was the relation of the human individual to the forces of modern life. The earlier version of this moral riddle was now too simple. The forces of the modern world had to be considered against the complicated power of the state as an agent of power in world politics. The state was no longer some vague aspect of the invisible hand of modern Progress. Its capacity for good *and* evil became evident in this period. Against such a world, the enlightened individual could no longer be left to his or her own devices. Social theory had to adjust its assumptions.

John Maynard Keynes, as much as anyone, addressed the issue at just the proper moment. In 1919, having seen the irrelevance of nineteenth-century doctrine to the Versailles Peace Conference, he wrote:

> I seek only to point out that the principle of accumulation based on inequality was a vital part of the pre-war order of Society and of progress as we then understood it, and to emphasize that this principle depended on unstable psychological conditions, which it may be impossible to recreate. . . . The bluff is discovered; the laboring classes may be no longer willing to forego so largely, and the capitalist classes, no longer confident of the future, may seek to enjoy more fully their liberties of consumption so long as they last, and thus precipitate the hour of their confiscation.

This sober critique of the culture of Progress was the perfect requisite to Keynes's economic philosophy. The individualism of the previous centuries could not possibly account for the economic and social needs of the twentieth century. Political control had to be exerted in the marketplace. Smith's invisible hand magically guiding the enlightened individual had to be replaced by the hand of the state defining market and fiscal reality. Conservatives, to this day, hate Keynes's economics, just as much for his devastating attack on the simple pieties of the nineteenth century as for the welfare state that was later justified by his ideas. Apart from his influence as an economist, Keynes was an important social theorist because he was one of the first to reassess nineteenth-century laissez-faire philosophies. After him, many came to the conclusion that the rights of individuals could no longer be accorded the unexamined privilege of being the exclusive first concerns of government.

The prior assumption of all nineteenth-century laissez-faire doctrines was no longer obvious. The social world was not moving necessarily toward Progress. As a result, one of the dominant issues in social theory between the wars was how to rethink the relation of the individual to society. In one sense, this was but a variant of the original philosophical concerns of modern culture—a question of many forms: How does the subject know the objective world? How are individual rights protected against civil authorities? How is moral action responsible to, or constrained by, the social group? How is social order maintained against the demands for political and social freedom? These were the classic formulations through the end of the nineteenth century. In the period of world crisis in the twentieth century, these older questions took on a special urgency. In the process, the questions changed in ways suited to the times and in ways that would endure long after the end of World War II: How is the action of society derived from individual agents? How is the social self both an individual and a social thing? And most urgent of all, is the modern democratic state an agent of good or of evil in the lives of individuals? Though the issue necessarily had to be stated in different ways according to different specific concerns, all the questions still boiled down to a refinement of the question asked by most classic social theorists: What, precisely, is the fate of the individual in the modern world?

The crucial difference in the interwar period was that conflicts within and between world states eroded the manifest plausibility of doctrines of social hope. Progress was in doubt, for good reasons. The social fate of the individual—the subject, the agent of history, the moral self, whatever the name—had to be examined with new intellectual seriousness. In effect, looking back to the social theorists of the 1890s, one could say that the more sober estimates of Weber and Nietzsche won out in the interwar period. By contrast, the deeper cultural assumptions of Marx, Durkheim, Du Bois, and Cooper were too naive. In the earlier time, progress was the fallback. Without anyone saying it in so many words, the classic social theorists shared some version of the earlier nineteenth-century doctrine that the individual can do what needs to be done because society inclines toward progress. Weber was one of the few to voice suspicion that the constraining force of modern society was much more than a passing stage (as Marx thought) or a sometimes unreliable source of moral guidance (as Durkheim thought). The world conflicts in the early twentieth century came so late in the long story of modern life that progress counted for a great deal less. Social anxiety deepened accordingly.

If, in economic philosophy, Keynes was the prophet of a need for serious reconsideration of state action, then, in social philosophy, the period's most distinctively new school of thought prepared a similar brief for knowledge, science, and culture. The Frankfurt Institute for Social Research (later popularly known as the German School of Critical Theory) had its roots in the political and economic realities of Germany between the wars. Among the major European powers of the twentieth century, Germany had been late to enter fully into modern politics. The extended grip of Bismarckian culture and politics through the end of the nineteenth century reinforced the hold of traditionalism in politics and, to some extent, in economics. Even though France, Great Britain, and the United States struggled in this time with the contradictions between traditionalism and modernity, the conflict was distorted in Germany. By the end of the nineteenth century, Germany was, in effect, a leading industrial power resting on a foundation that was weak in the exercise of democratic politics. The Weimar Republic that governed unsuccessfully after World War I was, at best, more of a cultural experiment. Though France's Third Republic had only marginally greater staying power in the end, at least in France there had been a century-long struggle to understand the democratic basis of the modern state. Weber surely saw the differences between traditionalism and modernity, as well as the horrors of the bureaucratic state, because of his firsthand familiarity with Germany's uncertain giant steps into the modern world. These political uncertainties, joined to the worldwide economic crises in the 1920s, gave birth to fascism. If the great island cultures of the time—Great Britain and the United States—had the easier paths of relative isolation in which to learn modernity, Germany in particular among the nation-states of continental Europe had the tougher path.

Paul Tillich (1886–1965), one of the many German exiles who had been associated with the Frankfurt School, once somewhere defined sin as "a form destroying eruption of the good." Tillich spoke as a theologian, but, with minor translation, his idea fit the times and the German experience. Social evil in this period was, indeed, a form destroying eruption of the good in modern life. The destructive side of modernity was within, and part of, its good. This is what Weber the sociologist and Nietzsche the philosopher also saw at an earlier time. At some risk, one might say that Germany in the interwar period acted out the evil impulses that lay hidden within the whole of modern culture. Hitler was the manifest spectacle of those impulses. He made visible modernity's worst nightmares.

The German critical theorists were deeply shaped by their direct experiences with Hitler. Yet the brilliance of their theory lay in their courageous understanding that modern society, including its culture, had to be examined critically if one were to understand modern life. If the naive assumption of the nineteenth century had been that knowledge would set men free, then the realities of the twentieth century were that knowledge, far from being the final social good, was implicated in evil. In effect, the critical theorists were forced to take up Marx's earlier materialist critique of knowledge in order to develop a more complete, positive critique of modern culture. It was no longer enough to proclaim official science and knowledge as the ideological reverse image—the camera obscura—of economic life. Knowledge, science, and culture in the interwar years were manifestly more than passive instruments of the ruling class. They were perhaps this, but more. Hitler preached an ideology that inspired followers. Yes, he could be said to have drugged a nation, but he actually induced people to believe and act in accord with his ideas. Direct experience with the power of ideas meant knowledge could be *neither* the passive reflex of economic power *nor* the primal source of enlightened action. The ideas taken to be true knowledge had a more complicated relation to economic and political power. The German critical theorists thus began a long tradition of social theory that sought to reexamine both the assumptions of the Enlightenment and those of Marx in order to rethink the political values of knowledge itself. Eventually, theorists associated with the Frankfurt tradition came to define their view of critical social theory as the basis for human liberation from social evil. Critical theory became the social theoretical tradition most invested in defining truly emancipatory knowledge—that is, social theory with the power to free people. To fulfill the promise of modern culture, that culture had to be subjected to a thorough critique. Critical theorists were, from the beginning, radical modernists, unafraid to face the worst in modern life, prepared to define its highest realistic standard for human freedom.

Among the earliest resources of the Frankfurt School were the early, more Hegelian writings of Karl Marx, many of which were just then being taken seriously. Georg Lukács was an important early influence on the critical theorists in Germany because his thinking linked these elements in Marx to a general theory of modern culture and knowledge. His precise philosophical analysis of the subject as a reified object unable to see itself except as an abstraction harkened back to Marx's thinking in the 1844 Manuscripts. It was also a telling diagnosis of modern life in 1923 when Lukács's *History and Class Consciousness* first appeared. He was, as he said, intent on writing a social theory that could diagnose "the unhistorical and antihistorical character of bourgeois thought" as the historical problem of the present.

Max Horkheimer, like Theodor Adorno, is considered a father of the Frankfurt School. The closing words of Horkheimer's 1932 essay "Notes on Science and the Crisis" indicate the parallels between his thinking and Lukács's: "Understanding the crisis of science depends on a correct theory of the present social situation; for science as a social function reflects at present the contradictions with society." If vulgar Marxism thought of science as a mere reflection of the class interests of the bourgeoisie and if nineteenth-century versions of the Enlightenment believed Science was the final key to Progress, then Horkheimer and the other critical theorists used their situation in Germany to demand that Science, if a solution, must also be part of the problem. Erich Fromm, writing in this spirit at about the same time, was one of the first of those associated with the Frankfurt Institute to explore the relations between psychoanalysis and sociology (including Marxism). In 1929, in Germany, when Fromm wrote his short piece for his Frankfurt Institute colleagues, the usefulness of a method like psychoanalysis was evident. At the time, it alone among the developed human sciences took with utter seriousness the power of hidden, unconscious forces in the interplay between mental life and society.

This was also the theme of Karl Mannheim's sociology of knowledge. Though Mannheim was closer to Weberian sociology than to the Frankfurt theorists, his experience in Germany in the interwar years clearly affected his classic description of ideology. Like the German critical theorists, and more explicitly than Weber, Mannheim developed Marx's critique of ideology in a different direction. Like Horkheimer, he sought to show how ideas reflect the social crises of their times without being mere inversions of the true social reality, the economy. When one reads Mannheim after V. I. Lenin, the effect can be stunning. Even though Lenin's "What Is to Be Done?" was composed at the turn of the century, it is the classic source for his argument that the extremes of vulgar Marxism—economism—prevent effective political action. The revolutionary vanguard must act in relation to the total life of the working class, not just its economic circumstances. This, of course, was a theoretical move necessary for a revolutionary theory of the Socialist state. There was little in Marx's theories to guide a full social revolution, including the formation of a postrevolutionary state. Lenin's ideas, as well as his actions in the Soviet revolutionary government, demonstrated the need for a theory of governing elites. Later, Stalin's capacity for evil demonstrated the limits of Lenin's ideas. Still, the question he asked was the prevailing question of the period, and his answer to it had more actual political effect than those offered by any of the others, except perhaps for Keynes.

Some would argue that it is foolishness to suggest that the Frankfurt School be read in the same context as Keynes, to say nothing of Talcott Parsons and Robert K. Merton, much less Lenin and Mannheim. But when one keeps the focus on the social concerns of the period, their apparent differences are less acute. Parsons and Merton became the *grands hommes* of the golden age of American sociology in the 1940s and 1950s. Parsons headed the Harvard School, Merton the Columbia School. To a very large degree, they and their students represented in this later time an exaggerated revision of the old idea that Progress could, in fact, win the day with sociology as its tool. Yet in their writings in the 1930s, both Merton and Parsons could just as properly be read as critics of the nineteenth-century theories of the social individual.

In 1937, Parsons's *Structure of Social Action* was a rethinking of those he considered the classic social theorists in order to define the terms of a truly modern sociology. The omission of Marx from Parsons's list was just one of the ways in which he took the influence of Weber in an entirely different direction from that of the German critical thinkers. Had Parsons suffered in Germany, he might have thought differently. Just the same, his technical analysis of the four elements of an action system, though abstract, is sensitive to the issues of the day. Parsons saw the individual as the unit of social analysis, but his was not the freethinking individual of the nineteenth century. The Parsonian individual was lodged in a system in which individual action was constrained not just by social conditions but also by the goals of the system itself and by the complex interrelation of its structured parts. In this early writing, Parsons's individual was defined against a very complex set of social forces. Later in his career, the individual became an even more complicated unit as Parsons introduced the idea (taken from Freud) that social actors are bearers of unconsciously introjected motivational forces. Already in 1937, the individual's relation to the social system was constrained, if dynamic; situated, though motivated. The action of the individual was seen as the action of a system, not the autonomous self.

Robert K. Merton refused to write such abstract theory. Yet his views were not that different from those of Parsons. In 1938, his "Social Structure and Anomie" gave voice to the same general concerns expressed by others in this period but in a different, more elegant tone. Merton's basic assumption was that the individual is not just in a structured system of action but that his or her actions may be forced by the demands of the system. Merton argued that when the economic system fails to provide legitimate means to earn income, and status, the cultural logic of the social system may force the individual to act in ways that are culturally logical, even if illegal. Here, Merton did several things at once. He revised Durkheim's idea of anomie in ways that allowed for the real political and economic contradictions of society. (Merton, though then a functionalist, also knew his Marx.) At the same time, he offered a shrewd description of the cultural logic of American capitalism. Always understated, Merton's text can be read as much as a critique as a defense of the American way of social life. In this famous essay, Merton stood on the shoulders of Durkheim, as of Marx and Weber.

George Herbert Mead's theory of the social self is considered a classic in American social psychology and a foundation of the school of symbolic interactionism. Thus, Mead is sometimes thought to be a social theorist of limited interest. Yet his ideas of the social self represented a major advance over those of William James and Charles Horton Cooley. With Mead, the social self was more definitely a social, as opposed to a mental, thing. "The self," he said, "is essentially a social structure, and it arises in social experience." Though Mead was developing what he called a social behaviorism, his theory had radical aspects that do not meet the eye in a first reading. For example, Mead was one of the first to work out the notion, already evident in James, that the social self was, by nature, multiple. "The multiple personality is in a certain sense normal," he said. The implication is that social selves, structured by social experience in modern society, are necessarily multiple—a thinly veiled allusion to the craziness of social life. Ideas like this linked Mead to the other social theorists of the interwar years who sought to come to terms with the individual's tortured relation to social structures. Though Mead remained a philosopher throughout his life, his ideas provided a theoretical framework for many in the Chicago School of sociology—those noted particularly for the study of the urban underworld of immigrant life, gangs, urban violence, and deviant life-styles. Mead's view of the social self as a dynamic structure of multiple parts clearly supported the study of those forms of urban life in which deviant behavior was also seen as an adjustment to two or more worlds—the normal and the "abnormal." The parallels to Du Bois's idea of double-consciousness are apparent. Mead's theories thus linked the Chicago studies of his time to a post–World War II Chicago tradition that included Erving Goffman, perhaps the most famous exponent of the social study of normal deviance.

It is possible to interpret the interwar years in another way. From the inside, it was a period in which the hidden contradictions of modern culture broke out. It was, to be sure, a time of world conflict. But by the end of World War II, the world retained its form. The European dominance of world politics remained intact. The West, whatever its internal conflicts, remained the world's master. From the outside, however, one could begin to see in this period that the West was losing its grip on world politics. Though the Allies defeated both Germany and Japan, only a few years after World War II India won its independence and the Chinese Communists overthrew the nationalists allied with Western military and economic interests. A little over a decade later, the African colonies rejected European rule. Thus, though the Euro-American world kept its form at the end of this period, it began to lose its heart in the face of unavoidable and seemingly unresolvable dilemmas.

Reinhold Niebuhr was among those Americans who most clearly contended that the conflict between individual and political interests was unbridgeable. If others, like Parsons or Merton or Mead, were confident that an integrated social theory of the social individual could be constructed, Niebuhr was among those who considered this unlikely. He argued that state power is selfish and thus something entirely different from individual interests. Individual interactions can eventuate in love; state power can, at best, result in social justice. As a theologian and social ethicist, writing in 1932, Niebuhr was viewed as a radical attacking Protestant piety. It is no accident that his social theories became clear after a long tenure as pastor among the working poor in Detroit. The strangeness of urban life, particularly in the United States, bore witness to the conflicts of the twentieth century. In the working-class urban neighborhoods of Detroit and Chicago, social theorists like Niebuhr encountered not just the psychological tensions of modern life (like those described by Simmel) but also the socially structured conflicts between different people of different ethnic backgrounds.

America was trying to adjust both to new immigrant peoples and to the radically different cultures that called into question the very idea of "normal." Gunnar Myrdal's *American Dilemma* (1944) later demonstrated the structural sources of social conflict in America's long-enduring moral contradiction in its relations to the African people within its borders. If racial conflict is the most fundamental moral dilemma in the United States, then urban conflict with and among immigrant groups was the fundamental social dilemma. It was not just a matter of understanding the different habits of strangers. Far more, students of urban life in this period came to understand that the real cultural differences required a different understanding of social norms. This idea was later apparent in Merton's theory of adaptation to anomie. But earlier in the interwar period, principally in Chicago, studies of urban groups led to theories of social deviation in which illegal or deviant behavior was understood as normal to the social circumstances.

Frederic Thrasher's *The Gang* was but one of the many Chicago studies that made this point. W. I. Thomas and Florian Znaniecki's *Polish Peasant* was another. Reading these studies today, one might not be impressed by their originality. We have grown accustomed to social differences and somewhat immune to the notion that normal social behavior is nearly impossible to define. But in the 1920s, moral ideas not too different from those of today's religious right wing were much more dominant, especially in the Middle West. To the more traditional Christian people of that day, these studies of urban life must have been every bit as shocking as Niebuhr's pronouncement that Christian piety could never save the political world. One of the most famous essays to emerge from the Chicago School studies was Louis Wirth's "Urbanism as a Way of Life" (1938). It is considered a classic because Wirth (1887–1952) was one of the first to argue that cities were not just densely populated ecological zones but also the spawning ground of unique ways of life. Again, this is not news today, but it was then. The differences inherent in urban life, like those inherent in America's immoral racial conflicts, were chief among the unavoidable dilemmas that were internal to the newest of Europe's nations.

If one reads Walter Benjamin's "Art, War, and Fascism" after the writings of the American urbanists, it is possible to see a striking similarity behind the obvious differences. Benjamin was one of the Frankfurt Institute critical theorists most respected for his brilliant studies of aesthetics. Much like the other German critical theorists, he saw fascism as an extreme expression of modernity's doomed struggle to accommodate the expressive interests of the new urban masses with the property interests of the capitalist class. Though fascism was quite a different phenomenon, and Benjamin a different type of theorist, there is still a similarity with the Chicago School theorists. They, too, studied the new urban masses in order to understand the conflict between the interests of the social world as it was and the reality of the world as it was becoming. Benjamin recoiled from the aesthetics of war. The Chicago urbanists, being more traditionally scientific, stood back in appreciation of the new urban life. The perspectives were utterly at odds. The dilemmas were not.

Unless one was directly affected, it was possible not to see what was happening at home and abroad. Gandhi and Mao Tse-tung are the most notable historical figures in this period who were engaged in political lives that would eventually change the world's structure. Both were self-conscious social theorists in the sense that they developed explicit social theories to organize political action. Gandhi, first in South Africa and later in India, developed the theory of forceful nonviolence that would not only change India but also affect the American civil rights movement after World War II. Mao, in this period, organized the Chinese Communists he led after the war with evident references to a theory of world contradiction.

The failure to understand a contradiction played out in China is one thing. It is quite another when the contradiction is right at home. Virginia Woolf's "A Room of One's Own" began with a fictionalized account of male "horror and indignation" that a woman would transgress on man's preserve. Though a fiction, like Gilman's *The Yellow Wallpaper,* Woolf's 1929 lecture became a classic source of feminist social theory because it described so powerfully one of the most ubiquitous contradictions structured into daily life in the West.

It is particularly instructive to read Antonio Gramsci alongside Virginia Woolf, on the one hand, and Karl Mannheim, on the other. Gramsci's influential development of the Marxian notion of social hegemony accounts for the ways in which intellectuals, being part of the organic process of their social classes, are very often less than likely to be free-floating critics of the social order. In this respect, his notion of the intellectual is consistent with Mannheim's sociology of knowledge. Yet, though Virginia Woolf was assaulted by the prevailing intellectual culture of her day, she managed to stand firm against it. Hence the contradiction that Gramsci described from his prison cell that "every man is an intellectual"—from which arises the critical possibility.

Ruth Benedict's discussion of the differences between Japanese and American cultures was a harbinger of what would come after World War II. Her studies of Japanese culture were written, in effect, to explain the war in Asia to Americans. The Japanese were "the most alien enemy the United States has ever fought." Americans, she explained by implication, never began to understand who the Japanese were, culturally speaking, and why they fought. Had it been written today, Benedict's straightforward comparison of the two cultures would be considered multicultural. Though the essay was not self-consciously theoretical, Benedict was expressing a theoretical idea: The world is not one; social differences are real and in some cases unbridgeable. In the years following the war, Western people would encounter an increasing number of conflicts with Asians. Their inability to comprehend how little they understood of people different from themselves led the French and Americans to defeats in Vietnam that would change the course of their histories, just as Soviet Russia's defeat in Afghanistan would contribute to the collapse of the USSR. These events were still far in the postwar future, but Benedict's poignant exposition of America's ignorance of world culture hinted that the conflicts within the Euro-American world would not long be contained. It was one thing to fight Hitler, the evil within: He was a familiar force. It was quite another to fight an alien enemy without ever understanding how much one never understood.

C. L.

Notes

Page 192: Cooper, *A Voice from the South* (Oxford University Press, 1988), 12.

Page 193: Nietzsche, *Genealogy of Morals,* Third Essay, 27.

Page 196: The Tillich line must be somewhere in his *Systematic Theology,* but I cannot find it. It is possible that I heard it from Tillich himself in the early 1960s at Harvard or from his friend (and my teacher) James Luther Adams. One of the effects of reading social theory over many years is that certain things are just there, somewhere in and between what was said or written and what is remembered.

Other quotations are in the selections that follow.

❖ Action, Knowledge, Self ❖

John Maynard Keynes (1883–1946) became the dominant economist in the West between the two world wars. While serving as a senior member of Britain's delegation to the Versailles Peace Conference in 1919, he rethought in more radical terms the ideas of his teacher at Cambridge, Alfred Marshall. Keynes resigned from the delegation and wrote *Economic Consequences of the Peace* (1920), in which he attacked the prevailing orthodoxy of political and economic thinking. "The Psychology of Modern Society" is from that book. In this selection, Keynes's radical spirit is evident in his implicit statement of purpose: to state the truth of what lay hidden in "the unconscious recess of [Capitalist Society's] being." The second selection, "The New Liberalism," appeared five years later when Keynes was obviously in a somewhat less gloomy frame of mind. He borrows a popular philosophy of history to make the point that the old, nineteenth-century idea of individual freedom can no longer be trusted. Economic and social theory must recommend state policies designed to control and direct the economy. This idea influenced Franklin Roosevelt's New Deal, as well as the leading social theorists of the time (most notably Talcott Parsons), and his radical philosophy thus became established doctrine following World War II. Keynes's most important technical study was *The General Theory of Employment, Interest and Money* (1936). His ideas are particularly lucid examples of the social theoretical sentiments that arose between the wars: Given the global economic and political crises, social theory had to rethink the individual's relation to society, and the state had to be an active player in the economic world.

The Psychology of Modern Society
John Maynard Keynes (1920)

Europe was so organized socially and economically as to secure the maximum accumulation of capital. While there was some continuous improvement in the daily conditions of life of the mass of the population, Society was so framed as to throw a great part of the increased income into the control of the class least likely to consume it. The new rich of the nineteenth century were not brought up to large expenditures, and preferred the power which investment gave them to the pleasures of immediate consumption. In fact, it was precisely the *inequality* of the distribution of wealth which made possible those vast accumulations of fixed wealth and of capital

Excerpt from *The Economic Consequences of the Peace* (New York: Harcourt, Brace and Howe, 1920), pp. 18–22. Reprinted by permission of Harcourt Brace.

improvements which distinguished that age from all others. Herein lay, in fact, the main justification of the Capitalist System. If the rich had spent their new wealth on their own enjoyments, the world would long ago have found such a régime intolerable. But like bees they saved and accumulated, not less to the advantage of the whole community because they themselves held narrower ends in prospect.

The immense accumulations of fixed capital which, to the great benefit of mankind, were built up during the half century before the war, could never have come about in a Society where wealth was divided equitably. The railways of the world, which that age built as a monument to posterity, were, not less than the Pyramids of Egypt, the work of labor which was not free to consume in immediate enjoyment the full equivalent of its efforts.

Thus this remarkable system depended for its growth on a double bluff or deception. On the one hand the laboring classes accepted from ignorance or powerlessness, or were compelled, persuaded, or cajoled by custom, convention, authority, and the well-established order of Society into accepting a situation in which they could call their own very little of the cake that they and Nature and the capitalists were co-operating to produce. And on the other hand the capitalist classes were allowed to call the best part of the cake theirs and were theoretically free to consume it, on the tacit underlying condition that they consumed very little of it in practice. The duty of "saving" became nine-tenths of virtue and the growth of the cake the object of true religion. There grew round the non-consumption of the cake all those instincts of puritanism which in other ages has withdrawn itself from the world and has neglected the arts of production as well as those of enjoyment. And so the cake increased; but to what end was not clearly contemplated. Individuals would be exhorted not so much to abstain as to defer, and to cultivate the pleasures of security and anticipation. Saving was for old age or for your children; but this was only in theory,—the virtue of the cake was that it was never to be consumed, neither by you nor by your children after you.

In writing thus I do not necessarily disparage the practices of that generation. In the unconscious recesses of its being Society knew what it was about. The cake was really very small in proportion to the appetites of consumption, and no one, if it were shared all round, would be much the better off by the cutting of it. Society was working not for the small pleasures of today but for the future security and improvement of the race,—in fact for "progress." If only the cake were not cut but was allowed to grow in the geometrical proportion predicted by Malthus of population, but not less true of compound interest, perhaps a day might come when there would at last be enough to go round, and when posterity could enter into the enjoyment of *our* labors. In that day overwork, overcrowding, and underfeeding would have come to an end, and men, secure of the comforts and necessities of the body, could proceed to the nobler exercises of their faculties. One geometrical ratio might cancel another, and the nineteenth century was able to forget the fertility of the species in a contemplation of the dizzy virtues of compound interest.

There were two pitfalls in this prospect: lest, population still outstripping accumulation, our self-denials promote not happiness but numbers; and lest the cake be after all consumed, prematurely, in war, the consumer of all such hopes.

But these thoughts lead too far from my present purpose. I seek only to point out that the principle of accumulation based on inequality was a vital part of the pre-war order of Society and of progress as we then understood it, and to emphasize that this principle depended on unstable psychological conditions, which it may be impossible to recreate. It was not natural for a population, of whom so few enjoyed the comforts of life, to accumulate so hugely. The war has disclosed the possibility of consumption to all and the vanity of abstinence to many. Thus the bluff is discovered; the laboring classes may be no longer willing to forego so largely, and the capitalist classes, no longer confident of the future, may seek to enjoy more fully their liberties of consumption so long as they last, and thus precipitate the hour of their confiscation.❖

The New Liberalism
John Maynard Keynes (1925)

An eminent American economist, Professor Commons, who has been one of the first to recognise the nature of the economic transition amidst the early stages of which we are now living, distinguishes three epochs, three economic orders, upon the third of which we are entering.

The first is the Era of Scarcity, "whether due to inefficiency or to violence, war, custom, or superstition." In such a period "there is the minimum of individual liberty and the maximum of communistic, feudalistic or governmental control through physical coercion." This was, with brief intervals in exceptional cases, the normal economic state of the world up to (say) the fifteenth or sixteenth century.

Next comes the Era of Abundance. "In a period of extreme abundance there is the maximum of individual liberty, the minimum of coercive control through government, and individual bargaining takes the place of rationing." During the seventeenth and eighteenth centuries we fought our way out of the bondage of Scarcity into the free air of Abundance, and in the nineteenth century this epoch culminated gloriously in the victories of *laissez-faire* and historic Liberalism. It is not surprising or discreditable that the veterans of the party cast backward glances on that easier age.

But we are now entering on a third era, which Professor Commons calls the period of Stabilisation, and truly characterises as "the actual alternative to Marx's communism." In this period, he says, "there is a diminution of individual liberty, enforced in part by governmental sanctions, but mainly by economic sanctions through concerted action, whether secret, semi-open, open, or arbitrational, of associations, corporations, unions, and other collective movements of manufacturers, merchants, labourers, farmers, and bankers."

The abuses of this epoch in the realms of Government are Fascism on the one side and Bolshevism on the other. Socialism offers no middle course, because it also is sprung from the presuppositions of the Era of Abundance, just as much as *laissez-faire* individualism and the free play of economic forces, before which latter, almost alone amongst men, the City Editors, all bloody and blindfolded, still piteously bow down.

The transition from economic anarchy to a régime which deliberately aims at controlling and directing economic forces in the interests of social justice and social stability, will present enormous difficulties both technical and political. I suggest, nevertheless, that the true destiny of New Liberalism is to seek their solution. . . .

The idea of the old-world party, that you can, for example, alter the value of money and then leave the consequential adjustments to be brought about by the forces of supply and demand, belongs to the days of fifty or a hundred years ago when Trade Unions were powerless, and when the economic Juggernaut was allowed to crash along the highway of Progress without obstruction and even with applause.

Half the copybook wisdom of our statesmen is based on assumptions which were at one time true, or partly true, but are now less and less true day by day. We have to invent new wisdom for a new age. And in the meantime we must, if we are to do any good, appear unorthodox, troublesome, dangerous, disobedient to them that begat us.

In the economic field this means, first of all, that we must find new policies and new instruments to adapt and control the working of economic forces, so that they do not intolerably interfere with contemporary ideas as to what is fit and proper in the interests of social stability and social justice. . . . We have changed, by insensible degrees, our philosophy of economic life, our notions of what is reasonable and what is tolerable; and we have done this without changing our technique or our copybook maxims. Hence our tears and troubles.

A party programme must be developed in its details, day by day, under the pressure and the stimulus of actual events; it is useless to define it beforehand, except in the most general terms. But if the Liberal Party is to recover its forces, it must have an attitude, a philosophy, a direction. I have endeavoured to indicate my own attitude to politics, and I leave it to others to answer, in the light of what I have said, the question with which I began—Am I a Liberal?❖

Georg Lukács (1885–1971), the Hungarian Marxist philosopher, had been a visitor in Weber's Heidelberg circle before World War I. After the war, he studied at the Marx-Engels-Lenin Institute in Moscow. Lukács is considered an early contributor to the rethinking of Marx in terms suited to the twentieth century. In particular, his *History and Class Consciousness* (1923) returned explicitly to the early, somewhat Hegelian, writings of Marx in order to reformulate dialectic materialism in terms that account for the tensions within modern culture, knowledge, and literature. Yet his thinking was not so much a recovery of lost ideas as a creative reworking of Marx in light of events in the world and the history of ideas. Lukács was an important influence on the early founders of the Frankfurt Institute for Social Research and is credited with contributing to its critical theory of aesthetics. The short selection that follows, "The Irrational Chasm Between Subject and Object," is from Lukács's famous essay on reification in *History and Class Consciousness*. It illustrates the ease with which he rethought the texts of what he called vulgar Marxism to formulate a social theory of modern knowledge and modern man. The individual, he suggests, is caught in a social world in which he can see himself only as an abstraction.

The Irrational Chasm Between Subject and Object
Georg Lukács (1922)

. . . History must abolish itself. As Marx says of bourgeois economics: "Thus history existed once upon a time, but it does not exist any more." And even if this antinomy assumes increasingly refined forms in later times, so that it even makes its appear-

---

Excerpt from "Reification and the Consciousness of the Proletariat," Rodney Livingstone, trans., *History and Class Consciousness* (Cambridge, Mass.: MIT Press, 1971 [1923]), pp. 157–159. Translation 1971 by The Merlin Press Ltd. Reprinted by permission of MIT Press.

ance in the shape of historicism, of historical relativism, this does not affect the basic problem, the abolition of history, in the slightest.

We see the unhistorical and antihistorical character of bourgeois thought most strikingly when we consider *the problem of the present as a historical problem*. It is unnecessary to give examples here. Ever since the World War and the World Revolution the total inability of every bourgeois thinker and historian to see the world-historical events of the present as universal history must remain one of the most terrible memories of every sober observer. This complete failure has reduced otherwise meritorious historians and subtle thinkers to the pitiable or contemptible mental level of the worst kind of provincial journalism. But it cannot always be explained simply as the result of external pressures (censorship, conformity to 'national' class interests, etc.). It is grounded also in a theoretical approach based upon unmediated contemplation which opens up an irrational chasm between the subject and object of knowledge, the same "dark and empty" chasm that Fichte described. This murky void was also present in our knowledge of the past, though this was obscured by the distance created by time, space and historical mediation. Here, however, it must appear fully exposed.

A fine illustration borrowed from Ernst Bloch will perhaps make this theoretical limitation clearer than a detailed analysis which in any case would not be possible here. When nature becomes landscape—e.g. in contrast to the peasant's unconscious living within nature—the artist's unmediated experience of the landscape (which has of course only achieved this immediacy after undergoing a whole series of mediations) presupposes a distance (spatial in this case) between the observer and the landscape. The observer stands outside the landscape, for were this not the case it would not be possible for nature to become a landscape at all. If he were to attempt to integrate himself and the nature immediately surrounding him in space within 'nature-seen-as-landscape', without modifying his aesthetic contemplative immediacy, it would then at once become apparent that landscape only *starts* to become landscape at a definite (though of course variable) distance from the observer and that only as an observer set apart in space can he relate to nature in terms of landscape at all.

This illustration is only intended to throw light on the theoretical situation, for it is only in art that the relation to landscape is expressed in an appropriate and unproblematic way, although it must not be forgotten that even in art we find the same unbridgeable gap opening up between subject and object that we find confronting us everywhere in modern life, and that art can do no more than shape this problematic without however finding a real solution to it. But as soon as history is forced into the present—and this is inevitable as our interest in history is determined in the last analysis by our desire to understand the present—this "pernicious chasm" (to use Bloch's expression) opens up.

As a result of its incapacity to understand history, the contemplative attitude of the bourgeoisie became polarised into two extremes: on the one hand, there were the 'great individuals' viewed as the autocratic makers of history, on the other hand, there were the 'natural laws' of the historical environment. They both turn out to be equally impotent—whether they are separated or working together—when challenged to produce an interpretation of the present in all its radical novelty. The inner perfection of the work of art can hide this gaping abyss because in its perfected immediacy it does not allow any further questions to arise about a mediation no longer available to the point of view of contemplation. However, the present is a problem of history, a problem that refuses to be ignored and one which imperiously demands such mediation. It must be attempted. But in the course of these attempts we discover the truth of Hegel's remarks about one of the stages of self-consciousness that follow the definition of mediation already cited: "Therefore consciousness has become an enigma to itself as a result of the very experience which was to reveal its truth to itself; it does not regard the effects of its deeds as its own deeds: what happens to it is not the same experience *for it* as it is *in itself*; the transition is not merely a formal change of the same content and essence seen on the one hand as the content and essence of consciousness and on the other hand as the object or *intuited* essence of itself. *Abstract necessity,* therefore passes for the merely negative, uncomprehended *power of the universal* by which individuality is destroyed". ❖

Max Horkheimer (1895–1973) was born in Stuttgart and educated in Germany. Horkheimer was a founder of the school of critical theory in Germany and was director of its original institutional home, the Frankfurt Institute for Social Research. In 1932, he founded and edited the *Zeitschrift für Sozialforschung,* a principal outlet for the early writings of institute associates. (Many of Horkheimer's own contributions to the *Zeitschrift* were published in 1968 under the title *Critical Theory.*) Like many other German intellectuals of his day, he fled his native land in the early 1930s, eventually settling in the United States, where the institute was temporarily based in New York City. Horkheimer returned to Germany in 1949. Among his many books is *Dialectic of Enlightenment* (1947), written with Theodor Adorno and considered a classic philosophical text in the Frankfurt tradition. "Notes on Science and the Crisis" (1932), from *Critical Theory,* was one of Horkheimer's early contributions to the *Zeitschrift für Sozialforschung.*

Notes on Science and the Crisis

Max Horkheimer (1932)

1. In the Marxist theory of society, science is regarded as one of man's productive powers. In varying ways it has made the modern industrial system possible: as condition of the general flexibility of mind which has developed along with science over recent centuries; as a store of information on nature and the human world, which in the more developed countries is possessed even by people in the lower social classes; and, not least, as part of the intellectual equipment of the researcher, whose discoveries decisively affect the forms of social life. In so far as science is available as a means of creating social values, that is, in so far as it takes shape in methods of production, it constitutes a means of production.

2. The fact that science contributes to the social life-process as a productive power and a means of production in no way legitimates a pragmatist theory of knowledge. The fruitfulness of knowledge indeed plays a role in its claim to truth, but the fruitfulness in question is to be understood as intrinsic to the science and not as usefulness for ulterior purposes. The test of the truth of a judgment is something different

Excerpt from Matthew J. O'Connell, trans., *Critical Theory: Selected Essays* (New York: Seabury Press, 1972 [1932]), pp. 3–9.

from the test of its importance for human life. It is not for social interests to decide what is or is not true; the criteria for truth have developed, rather, in connection with progress at the theoretical level. Science itself admittedly changes in the course of history, but this fact can never stand as an argument for other criteria of truth than those which are appropriate to the state of knowledge at a given level of development. Even though science is subject to the dynamisms of history, it may not be deprived of its own proper character and misinterpreted for utilitarian ends. Of course, the reasons which justify rejecting the pragmatist theory of knowledge and relativism in general, do not lead to a positivist separation of truth and action. On the one hand, neither the direction and methods of theory nor its object, reality itself, are independent of man, and, on the other hand, science is a factor in the historical process. The separation of theory and action is itself an historical phenomenon.

3. In the general economic crisis, science proves to be one of the numerous elements within a social wealth which is not fulfilling its function. This wealth is immensely greater today than in previous eras. The world now has more raw materials, machines, and skilled workers, and better methods of production than ever before, but they are not profiting mankind as they ought. Society in its present form is unable to make effective use of the powers it has developed and the wealth it has amassed. Scientific knowledge in this respect shares the fate of other productive forces and means of production: its application is sharply disproportionate to its high level of development and to the real needs of mankind. Such a situation hinders the further development, qualitative and quantitative, of science itself. As the course of earlier crises warns us, economic balance will be restored only at the cost of great destruction of human and material resources.

4. One way of hiding the real causes of the present crisis is to assign responsibility for it to precisely those forces which are working for the betterment of the human situation, and this means, above all, rational, scientific thinking. The attempt is being made to subordinate the more intense cultivation of such thinking by individuals to the development of the "psychic" and to discredit critical reason as a decisive factor except for its professional application in industry. The view is abroad that reason is a useful instrument only for purposes of everyday life, but must fall silent in face of the great problems and give way to the more substantial powers of the soul. The result is the avoidance of any theoretical consideration of society as a whole. The struggle of contemporary metaphysics against scientism is in part a reflection of these broader social tendencies.

5. Science in the pre-War years had in fact a number of limitations. These were due, however, not to an exaggeration of its rational character but to restrictions on it which were themselves conditioned by the increasing rigidification of the social situation. The task of describing facts without respect for nonscientific considerations and of establishing the patterns of relations between them was originally formulated as a partial goal of bourgeois emancipation in its critical struggle against Scholastic restrictions upon research. But by the second half of the nineteenth century this definition had already lost its progressive character and showed itself to be, on the contrary, a limiting of scientific activity to the description, classification, and generalization of phenomena, with no care to distinguish the unimportant from the essential. In the measure that concern for a better society, which still dominated the Enlightenment, gave way to the attempt to prove that present-day society should be permanent, a deadening and disorganizing factor entered science. The result of science, at least in part, may have been usefully applied in industry, but science evaded its re-

sponsibility when faced with the problem of the social process as a whole. Yet this was the foremost problem of all even before the War, as ever more intense crises and resultant social conflicts succeeded one another. Scientific method was oriented to being and not to becoming, and the form of society at the time was regarded as a mechanism which ran in an unvarying fashion. The mechanism might be disturbed for a shorter or longer period, but in any event it did not require a different scientific approach than did the explanation of any complicated piece of machinery. Yet social reality, the development of men acting in history, has a structure. To grasp it requires a theoretical delineation of profoundly transformative processes which revolutionize all cultural relationships. The structure is not to be mastered by simply recording events as they occur, which was the method practiced in old-style natural science. The refusal of science to handle in an appropriate way the problems connected with the social process has led to superficiality in method and content, and this superficiality, in turn, has found expression in the neglect of dynamic relationships between the various areas with which science deals, while also affecting in quite varied ways the practice of the disciplines. Connected with this narrowing of scientific purview is the fact that a set of unexplicated, rigid, and fetishistic concepts can continue to play a role, when the real need is to throw light on them by relating them to the dynamic movement of events. Some examples: the concept of the self-contained consciousness as the supposed generator of science; the person and his world-positing reason; the eternal natural law, dominating all events; the unchanging relationship of subject and object; the rigid distinction between mind and nature, soul and body, and other categorical formulations. The root of this deficiency, however, is not in science itself but in the social conditions which hinder its development and are at loggerheads with the rational elements immanent in science.

6. Since around the turn of the century scientists and philosophers have pointed out the insufficiencies and unsuitability of purely mechanistic methods. The criticism has led to discussion of the principles involved in the main foundations on which research rests, so that today we may speak of a crisis within science. This inner crisis is now added to the external dissatisfaction with science as a means of production which has not been able to meet expectations in alleviating the general need. Modern physics has in large measure overcome within its own field the deficiencies of the traditional method and has revised its critical foundations. It is to the credit of postwar metaphysics, especially that of Max Scheler, that it has once again turned the attention of science as a whole to numerous neglected areas and prepared the way at many points for a method less hindered by conventional narrowness of outlook. Above all, the description of important psychic phenomena, the delineation of social types, and the founding of a sociology of knowledge have had fruitful results. Yet, leaving aside the fact that essays in metaphysics almost always presented as concrete reality something called "life," that is, a mythical essence, and not real, living society in its historical development, such essays in the last analysis did not stimulate science but were simply negative towards it. Instead of pointing out and finally breaking through the limitations science had put upon itself by its narrow concentration on classification, metaphysics identified the very inadequate science of former times with rationality as such; it denied even judgmental thinking and abandoned itself to arbitrarily chosen objects and to a method cut completely loose from science. A philosophical anthropology arose which, in its independence, absolutized certain characteristics of man; to critical reason it opposed an intuition which rejected all restraining scientific criteria and trusted unquestioningly in its own clarity

of vision. Metaphysics thereby turned its back on the causes of the social crisis and even downgraded the means of investigating it. It introduced a new confusion of its own by hypostatizing isolated, abstractly conceived man and thereby belittling the importance of a theoretical comprehension of social processes.

7. Not only metaphysics but the science it criticizes is ideological, in so far as the latter retains a form which hinders it in discovering the real causes of the crisis. To say it is ideological is not to say that its practitioners are not concerned with pure truth. Every human way of acting which hides the true nature of society, built as it is on contrarieties, is ideological, and the claim that philosophical, moral, and religious acts of faith, scientific theories, legal maxims, and cultural institutions have this function is not an attack on the character of those who originate them but only states the objective role such realities play in society. Views valid in themselves and theoretical and aesthetic works of undeniably high quality can in certain circumstances operate ideologically, while many illusions, on the contrary, are not a form of ideology. The occurrence of ideology in the members of a society necessarily depends on their place in economic life; only when relationships have so far developed and conflicts of interest have reached such an intensity that even the average eye can penetrate beyond appearances to what is really going on, does a conscious ideological apparatus in the full sense usually make its appearance. As an existing society is increasingly endangered by its internal tensions, the energies spent in maintaining an ideology grow greater and finally the weapons are readied for supporting it with violence. The more the Roman Empire was threatened by explosive inner forces, the more brutally did the Caesars try to revitalize the old cult of the State and to restore the lost sense of unity. The ages which followed the Christian persecutions and the fall of the Empire supply many other frightful examples of the same recurring pattern. In the science of such periods the ideological dimension usually comes to light less in its false judgments than in its lack of clarity, its perplexity, its obscure language, its manner of posing problems, its methods, the direction of its research, and, above all, in what it closes its eyes to.

8. At the present time, scientific effort mirrors an economy filled with contradictions. The economy is in large measure dominated by monopolies, and yet on the world scale it is disorganized and chaotic, richer than ever yet unable to eliminate human wretchedness. Science, too, shows a double contradiction. First, science accepts as a principle that its every step has a critical basis, yet the most important step of all, the setting of tasks, lacks a theoretical grounding and seems to be taken arbitrarily. Second, science has to do with a knowledge of comprehensive relationships; yet, it has no realistic grasp of that comprehensive relationship upon which its own existence and the direction of its work depend, namely, society. The two contradictions are closely connected. The process of casting light on the social life-process in its totality brings with it the discovery of the law which holds sway in the apparent arbitrariness of the scientific and other endeavors. For science, too, is determined in the scope and direction of its work not by its own tendencies alone but, in the last analysis, by the necessities of social life as well. Despite this law a wasteful dispersal of intellectual energies has characterized the course of science over the last century, and philosophers of the period have repeatedly criticized science on this score. But the situation cannot be changed by purely theoretical insight, any more than the ideological function of science can be. Only a change in the real conditions for science within the historical process can win such a victory.

9. The view that cultural disorder is connected with economic relationships and with the conflicts of interest that arise out of them says nothing about the relative

reality and importance of material and intellectual values. It does contradict, of course, the idealist thesis that the world is the product and expression of an absolute mind, for it refuses to consider mind as separable from historical being and independent of it. But we can regard idealism as essentially consisting not in such a questionable metaphysics but in the effort to develop effectively the intellectual capabilities of man. If so, the materialist thesis of the nonindependence of the ideal order corresponds better to such a conception of classical German philosophy than does a great part of modern metaphysics. For the effort to grasp the social causes of the stunting and destruction of human life and effectively to subordinate the economy to man is a more appropriate task for such striving than is the dogmatic assertion of a priority of the spiritual without heed to the course of history.

10. In so far as we can rightly speak of a crisis in science, that crisis is inseparable from the general crisis. The historical process has imposed limitations on science as a productive force, and these show in the various sectors of science, in their content and form, in their subject matter and method. Furthermore, science as a means of production has not been properly applied. Understanding of the crisis of science depends on a correct theory of the present social situation; for science as a social function reflects at present the contradictions with society.❖

Talcott Parsons (1902–1979) is considered the founder of American sociological theory. Among his many former students, Parsons's name is a virtual synonym for theoretical brilliance; among a comparable number of younger sociologists, the same name is synonymous with abstract, conservative, and incomprehensible scientism. After graduating with an economics degree from Amherst College in 1924, Parsons studied in England at the London School of Economics, then at Heidelberg from 1925 to 1926. In England, Parsons studied the economics of Alfred Marshall; in Germany, he discovered the writings of Max Weber. Parsons translated *Protestant Ethic* and other works by Weber. He first taught economics at Harvard in 1927. Later, he began teaching sociology at the invitation of the Russian émigré, Pitirim Sorokin (1889–1968), who was instrumental in establishing sociology's reputation at Harvard. Parsons came into his own with the publication of *The Structure of Social Action* in 1937. This two-volume tour de force carefully analyzed those whom Parsons considered the classical social theorists (Weber, Durkheim, Marshall, and Vilfredo Pareto) in order to renew sociological theory and research. His goal was to establish a general theory of social action that encompassed all the behavioral sciences, including biology. In the 1940s, Parsons's theoretical synthesis formed the intellectual basis for Harvard's Department of Social Relations, which, in the 1950s, was considered by many the major department in the field. Parsons chaired the department from 1946 to 1956, but the experiment at synthesis collapsed when Parsons retired and times changed.

"The Unit Act of Action Systems," from *Structure of Social Action,* may be difficult reading, but it is an important sample of Parsons's theoretical intention to define the elements in a theory of social action: the actor, the actor's ends (or goals), the social situation, and the structured relation among these elements. Though this is a different sort of writing from that of Keynes (who was also an influence on Parsons) or of Lukács or the others in this period, readers should be able to see a common theoretical concern for the fate of the individual in modern, structured society.

The Unit Act of Action Systems

Talcott Parsons (1937)

In the first chapter attention was called to the fact that in the process of scientific conceptualization concrete phenomena come to be divided into units or parts. The first salient feature of the conceptual scheme to be dealt with lies in the character of the units which it employs in making this division. The basic unit may be called the "unit act." Just as the units of a mechanical system in the classical sense, particles, can be defined only in terms of their properties, mass, velocity, location in space, direction of motion, etc., so the units of action systems also have certain basic properties without which it is not possible to conceive of the unit as "existing." Thus, to continue the analogy, the conception of a unit of matter which has mass but which cannot be located in space is, in terms of the classical mechanics, nonsensical. It should be noted that the sense in which the unit act is here spoken of as an existent entity is not that of concrete spatiality or otherwise separate existence, but of conceivability as a unit in terms of a frame of reference. There must be a minimum number of descriptive terms applied to it, a minimum number of facts ascertainable about it, before it can be spoken of at all as a unit in a system.

In this sense then, an "act" involves logically the following: (1) It implies an agent, an "actor." (2) For purposes of definition the act must have an "end," a future state of affairs toward which the process of action is oriented. (3) It must be initiated in a "situation" of which the trends of development differ in one or more important respects from the state of affairs to which the action is oriented, the end. This situation is in turn analyzable into two elements: those over which the actor has no control, that is which he cannot alter, or prevent from being altered, in conformity with his end, and those over which he has such control. The former may be termed the "conditions" of action, the latter the "means." Finally (4) there is inherent in the conception of this unit, in its analytical uses, a certain mode of relationship between these elements. That is, in the choice of alternative means to the end, in so far as the situation allows alternatives, there is a "normative orientation" of action. Within the area of control of the actor, the means employed cannot, in general, be conceived either as chosen at random or as dependent exclusively on the conditions of action, but must in some sense be subject to the influence of an independent, determinate selective factor, a knowledge of which is necessary to the understanding of the concrete course of action. What is essential to the concept of action is that there should be a normative orientation, not that this should be of any particular type. As will be seen, the discrimination of various possible modes of normative orientation is one of the most important questions with which this study will be confronted. But before entering into the definition of any of them a few of the major implications of the basic conceptual scheme must be outlined.

The first important implication is that an act is always a process in time. The time category is basic to the scheme. The concept end always implies a future reference, to a state which is either not yet in existence, and which would not come into existence if something were not done about it by the actor or, if already existent, would not remain unchanged. This process, seen primarily in terms of its relation to ends, is variously called "attainment," "realization," and "achievement."

Excerpt from *The Structure of Social Action* (New York: Free Press, 1968 [1937]), pp. 43–48.

Second, the fact of a range of choice open to the actor with reference both to ends and to means, in combination with the concept of a normative orientation of action, implies the possibility of "error," of the failure to attain ends or to make the "right" choice of means. The various meanings of error and the various factors to which it may be attributed will form one of the major themes to be discussed.

Third, the frame of reference of the schema is subjective in a particular sense. That is, it deals with phenomena, with things and events *as they appear from the point of view of the actor* whose action is being analyzed and considered. Of course the phenomena of the "external world" play a major part in the influencing of action. But in so far as they can be utilized by this particular theoretical scheme, they must be reducible to terms which are subjective in this particular sense. This fact is of cardinal importance in understanding some of the peculiarities of the theoretical structures under consideration here. The same fact introduces a further complication which must be continually kept in mind. It may be said that all empirical science is concerned with the understanding of the phenomena of the external world. Then the facts of action are, to the scientist who studies them, facts of the external world—in this sense, objective facts. That is, the symbolic reference of the propositions the scientist calls facts is to phenomena "external" to the scientist, not to the content of his own mind. But in this particular case, unlike that of the physical sciences, the phenomena being studied have a scientifically relevant subjective aspect. That is, while the social scientist is not concerned with studying the content of his own mind, he is very much concerned with that of the minds of the persons whose action he studies. This necessitates the distinction of the objective and subjective points of view. The distinction and the relation of the two to each other are of great importance. By "objective" in this context will always be meant "from the point of view of the scientific observer of action" and by "subjective," "from the point of view of the actor."

A still further consequence follows from the "subjectivity" of the categories of the theory of action. When a biologist or a behavioristic psychologist studies a human being it is as an organism, a spatially distinguishable separate unit in the world. The unit of reference which we are considering as the actor is not this organism but an "ego" or "self." The principal importance of this consideration is that the body of the actor forms, for him, just as much part of the situation of action as does the "external environment." Among the conditions to which his action is subject are those relating to his own body, while among the most important of the means at his disposal are the "powers" of his own body and, of course, his "mind." The analytical distinction between actor and situation quite definitely cannot be identified with the distinction in the biological sciences between organism and environment. It is not a question of distinctions of concrete "things," for the organism is a real unit. It is rather a matter of the analysis required by the categories of empirically useful theoretical systems.

A fourth implication of the schema of action should be noted. Certainly the situation of action includes parts of what is called in common-sense terms the physical environment and the biological organism—to mention only two points. With equal certainty these elements of the situation of action are capable of analysis in terms of the physical and biological sciences, and the phenomena in question are subject to analysis in terms of the units in use in those sciences. Thus a bridge may, with perfect truth, be said to consist of atoms of iron, a small amount of carbon, etc., and their constituent electrons, protons, neutrons and the like. Must the student of action, then, become a physicist, chemist, biologist in order to understand his subject? In a sense this is true, but for purposes of the theory of action it is not necessary or desirable to carry such analyses as far as science in general is capable of doing. A limit is set by the frame of reference with which the student of action is working. That is, he is interested in phenomena with an aspect not reducible to action terms only in so far as they impinge on the schema of action in a relevant way—in the role of conditions or means. So long as their properties, which are important in this context, can be accurately determined these may be taken as data without further analysis. Above all, atoms, electrons or cells are not to be regarded as units for purposes of the theory of action. Unit analysis of any phenomenon beyond the point where it constitutes an integral means or condition of action leads over into terms of another theoretical scheme. For the purposes of the theory of action the smallest conceivable concrete unit is the unit act, and while it is in turn analyzable into the elements to which reference has been made—end, means, conditions and guiding norms—further analysis of the phenomena of which these are in turn aspects is relevant to the theory of action only in so far as the units arrived at can be referred to as constituting such elements of a unit act or a system of them.❖

Vladimir Ilyich Ulyanov Lenin (1870–1924) was the dominant force in the Russian Revolution of 1917 and the founder of Bolshevik communism. After studying law in Saint Petersburg, he traveled throughout Russia and visited Western Europe, where he established contacts with Socialist leaders. In 1895, he began organizing working people in Saint Petersburg, for which he was arrested and exiled. In exile, he wrote *The Development of Capitalism in Russia* (1899). When the revolution began in 1917, Lenin guided action while in hiding until Aleksandr Kerensky was overthrown. Later, he led the provisional Soviet government. He suffered a stroke in 1921 and died in 1924. The selection from *What Is to Be Done?* though composed in 1901–1902, more accurately belongs to the period between the wars because of its influence on the Russian Revolution and the dilemmas of Soviet communism. Hence, the selection is dated 1917–1921, when Lenin was in power and able to practice his theory. Lenin sought to introduce the political action of the vanguard into the so-called economistic formula that limited political action to the economic needs of the working class. His social theory wed political and economic theory. Even though Stalinism was the actual and unintended consequence of his ideas, Lenin should be considered one of the first to focus social theory on the actor (as Parsons would later put it) in a structured society.

What Is to Be Done?
V. I. Lenin (1917–1921)

Without a revolutionary theory there can be no revolutionary movement. This cannot be insisted upon too strongly at a time when the fashionable preaching of opportunism is combined with absorption in the narrowest forms of practical activity. The importance of theory for Russian Social-Democrats is still greater for three reasons, which are often forgotten:

Excerpt from *What Is to Be Done? Burning Questions of Our Movement* (New York: International Publishers, 1943 [1929]), pp. 28, 75–78. Reprinted by permission.

The first is that our party is only in the process of formation, its features are only just becoming outlined, and it has not yet completely settled its reckoning with other tendencies in revolutionary thought which threaten to divert the movement from the proper path. Indeed, in very recent times we have observed (as Axelrod long ago warned the Economists would happen) a revival of non–Social-Democratic revolutionary tendencies. Under such circumstances, what at first sight appears to be an "unimportant" mistake, may give rise to most deplorable consequences, and only the shortsighted would consider factional disputes and strict distinction of shades to be inopportune and superfluous. The fate of Russian Social-Democracy for many, many years to come may be determined by the strengthening of one or the other "shade."

The second reason is that the Social-Democratic movement is essentially an international movement. This does not mean merely that we must combat national chauvinism. It means also that a movement that is starting in a young country can be successful only on the condition that it assimilates the experience of other countries. In order to assimilate this experience, it is not sufficient merely to be acquainted with it, or simply to transcribe the latest resolutions. A critical attitude is required towards this experience, and ability to subject it to independent tests. Only those who realise how much the modern labour movement has grown in strength will understand what a reserve of theoretical forces and political (as well as revolutionary) experience is required to fulfil this task.

The third reason is that the national tasks of Russian Social-Democracy are such as have never confronted any other Socialist party in the world. Farther on we shall deal with the political and organisational duties which the task of emancipating the whole people from the yoke of autocracy imposes upon us. At the moment, we wish merely to state that the *role of vanguard can be fulfilled only by a party that is guided by an advanced theory.* . . .

We have seen that the organisation of wide political agitation, and consequently, of all-sided political exposures are an absolutely necessary *and paramount* task of activity, that is, if that activity is to be truly Social-Democratic. We arrived at this conclusion *solely* on the grounds of the pressing needs of the working class for political knowledge and political training. But this ground by itself is too narrow for the presentation of the question, for it ignores the general democratic tasks of Social-Democracy as a whole, and of modern, Russian Social-Democracy in particular. In order to explain the situation more concretely we shall approach the subject from an aspect that is "nearer" to the Economist, namely, from the practical aspect. "Every one agrees" that it is necessary to develop the political consciousness of the working class. But the question arises, How is that to be done? What must be done to bring this about? The economic struggle merely brings the workers "up against" questions concerning the attitude of the government towards the working class. Consequently, *however much we may try* to "give to the economic struggle itself a political character" *we shall never be able* to develop the political consciousness of the workers (to the degree of Social-Democratic consciousness) by confining ourselves to the economic struggle, for *the limits of this task are too narrow.* . . .

The workers can acquire class political consciousness *only from without,* that is, only outside of the economic struggle, outside of the sphere of relations between workers and employers. The sphere from which alone it is possible to obtain this knowledge is the sphere of relationships between *all* classes and the state and the government—the sphere of the inter-relations between *all* classes. For that reason, the reply to the question: What must be done in order that the workers may acquire political knowledge? cannot be merely the one which, in the majority of cases, the practical workers, especially those who are inclined towards Economism, usually content themselves with, *i.e.*, "go among the workers." To bring political knowledge to the workers the Social-Democrats must *go among all classes of the population, must despatch units of their army in all directions.* . . .

The Social-Democrat's ideal should not be a trade-union secretary, but *a tribune of the people,* able to react to every manifestation of tyranny and oppression, no matter where it takes place, no matter what stratum or class of the people it affects; he must be able to group all these manifestations into a single picture of police violence and capitalist exploitation; he must be able to take advantage of every petty event in order to explain his Socialistic convictions and his Social-Democratic demands *to all,* in order to explain to *all* and every one the world historical significance of the struggle for the emancipation of the proletariat.❖

Karl Mannheim (1893–1947), like Georg Lukács, was a Hungarian social philosopher who had benefited from contact with Weber and Simmel in Germany. Mannheim would become a younger member of Lukács's circle in Budapest. In 1917, he delivered a lecture to this group, the title of which suggests his broad intellectual perspective—"Soul and Culture." In 1925, Mannheim returned to a professorship in Heidelberg. Later, he taught at Frankfurt in the days of the Institute for Social Research. In 1933, Mannheim fled to England, where he led a productive, if more English, intellectual life until his death shortly after the end of World War II. The selection "The Sociology of Knowledge and Ideology" comprises portions of Mannheim's most famous book, *Ideology and Utopia,* which was first published in Germany in 1929. The opening part of the selection ("The Sociology of Knowledge") is, however, from Mannheim's English period, during which he was drawn more toward sociology as a discipline; the latter part of the selection focuses on the theory of "ideology," stemming from Mannheim's earlier days as a general social theorist. Mannheim's *Ideology and Utopia* is considered a classic text, equally for the sociology of knowledge and for the theory of ideology as a distortion of knowledge by social and political interests.

The Sociology of Knowledge and Ideology
Karl Mannheim (1936, 1929)

The Sociology of Knowledge

Philosophers have too long concerned themselves with their own thinking. When they wrote of thought, they had in mind primarily their own history, the history of philosophy, or quite special fields of knowledge such as mathematics or physics. This type of thinking is applicable only under quite special circumstances, and what can be learned by analysing it is not directly transferable to other spheres of life. Even when it is ap-

Excerpt from Louis Wirth and Edward Shils, trans., *Ideology and Utopia: An Introduction to the Sociology of Knowledge* (New York: Harcourt Brace Jovanovich, Publishers, 1936 [1929]), pp. 1–3, 55–59. Reprinted by permission of Harcourt Brace and Co.

plicable, it refers only to a specific dimension of existence which does not suffice for living human beings who are seeking to comprehend and to mould their world.

Meanwhile, acting men have, for better or for worse, proceeded to develop a variety of methods for the experiential and intellectual penetration of the world in which they live, which have never been analysed with the same precision as the so-called exact modes of knowing. When, however, any human activity continues over a long period without being subjected to intellectual control or criticism it tends to get out of hand.

Hence it is to be regarded as one of the anomalies of our time that those methods of thought by means of which we arrive at our most crucial decisions, and through which we seek to diagnose and guide our political and social destiny, have remained unrecognized and therefore inaccessible to intellectual control and self-criticism. This anomaly becomes all the more monstrous when we call to mind that in modern times much more depends on the correct thinking through of a situation than was the case in earlier societies. The significance of social knowledge grows proportionately with the increasing necessity of regulatory intervention in the social process. This so-called pre-scientific inexact mode of thought, however (which, paradoxically, the logicians and philosophers also use when they have to make practical decisions), is not to be understood solely by the use of logical analysis. It constitutes a complex which cannot be readily detached either from the psychological roots of the emotional and vital impulses which underlie it or from the situation in which it arises and which it seeks to solve.

It is the most essential task of this book to work out a suitable method for the description and analysis of this type of thought and its changes, and to formulate those problems connected with it which will both do justice to its unique character and prepare the way for its critical understanding. The method which we will seek to present is that of the sociology of knowledge.

The principal thesis of the sociology of knowledge is that there are modes of thought which cannot be adequately understood as long as their social origins are obscured. It is indeed true that only the individual is capable of thinking. There is no such metaphysical entity as a group mind which thinks over and above the heads of individuals, or whose ideas the individual merely reproduces. Nevertheless it would be false to deduce from this that all the ideas and sentiments which motivate an individual have their origin in him alone, and can be adequately explained solely on the basis of his own life-experience.

Just as it would be incorrect to attempt to derive a language merely from observing a single individual, who speaks not a language of his own but rather that of his contemporaries and predecessors who have prepared the path for him, so it is incorrect to explain the totality of an outlook only with reference to its genesis in the mind of the individual. Only in a quite limited sense does the single individual create out of himself the mode of speech and of thought we attribute to him. He speaks the language of his group; he thinks in the manner in which his group thinks. He finds at his disposal only certain words and their meanings. These not only determine to a large extent the avenues of approach to the surrounding world, but they also show at the same time from which angle and in which context of activity objects have hitherto been perceptible and accessible to the group or the individual.

The first point which we now have to emphasize is that the approach of the sociology of knowledge intentionally does not start with the single individual and his thinking in order then to proceed directly in the manner of the philosopher to the abstract heights of "thought as such." Rather, the sociology of knowledge seeks to comprehend thought in the concrete setting of an historical-social situation out of which individually differentiated thought only very gradually emerges. Thus, it is not men in general who think, or even isolated individuals who do the thinking, but men in certain groups who have developed a particular style of thought in an endless series of responses to certain typical situations characterizing their common position.

Strictly speaking it is incorrect to say that the single individual thinks. Rather it is more correct to insist that he participates in thinking further what other men have thought before him. He finds himself in an inherited situation with patterns of thought which are appropriate to this situation and attempts to elaborate further the inherited modes of response or to substitute others for them in order to deal more adequately with the new challenges which have arisen out of the shifts and changes in his situation. Every individual is therefore in a two-fold sense predetermined by the fact of growing up in a society: on the one hand he finds a ready-made situation and on the other he finds in that situation preformed patterns of thought and of conduct. . . .

Ideology

In order to understand the present situation of thought, it is necessary to start with the problems of "ideology." For most people, the term "ideology" is closely bound up with Marxism, and their reactions to the term are largely determined by the association. It is therefore first necessary to state that although Marxism contributed a great deal to the original statement of the problem, both the word and its meaning go farther back in history than Marxism, and ever since its time new meanings of the word have emerged, which have taken shape independently of it.

There is no better introduction to the problem than the analysis of the meaning of the term "ideology": firstly we have to disentangle all the different shades of meaning which are blended here into a pseudo-unity, and a more precise statement of the variations in the meanings of the concept, as it is used to-day, will prepare the way for its sociological and historical analysis. Such an analysis will show that in general there are two distinct and separable meanings of the term "ideology"—the particular and the total.

The particular conception of ideology is implied when the term denotes that we are sceptical of the ideas and representations advanced by our opponent. They are regarded as more or less conscious disguises of the real nature of a situation, the true recognition of which would not be in accord with his interests. These distortions range all the way from conscious lies to half-conscious and unwitting disguises; from calculated attempts to dupe others to self deception. This conception of ideology, which has only gradually become differentiated from the common-sense notion of the lie is particular in several senses. Its particularity becomes evident when it is contrasted with the more inclusive total conception of ideology. Here we refer to the ideology of an age or of a concrete historico-social group, e.g. of a class, when we are concerned with the characteristics and composition of the total structure of the mind of this epoch or of this group.

The common as well as the distinctive elements of the two concepts are readily evident. The common element in these two conceptions seems to consist in the fact that neither relies solely on what is actually said by the opponent in order to reach an understanding of his real meaning and intention. Both fall back on the subject, whether individual or group, proceeding to an understanding of what is said by the indirect method of analysing the social conditions of the individual or his group. The ideas expressed by the subject are thus regarded as functions of his existence. This means that opinions, statements, propositions, and systems of ideas are not taken at their face value but are interpreted in the light of the life-situation of the one who expresses them. It signifies further that the specific character and life-situation of the subject influence his opinions, perceptions, and interpretations.

Both these conceptions of ideology, accordingly, make these so-called "ideas" a function of him who holds them, and of his position in his social milieu. Although they have something in common, there are also significant differences between them. Of the latter we mention merely the most important:—

(*a*) Whereas the particular conception of ideology designates only a part of the opponent's assertions as ideologies—and this only with reference to their content, the total conception calls into question the opponent's total *Weltanschauung* (including his conceptual apparatus), and attempts to understand these concepts as an outgrowth of the collective life of which he partakes.

(*b*) The particular conception of "ideology" makes its analysis of ideas on a purely psychological level. If it is claimed for instance that an adversary is lying, or that he is concealing or distorting a given factual situation, it is still nevertheless assumed that both parties share common criteria of validity—it is still assumed that it is possible to refute lies and eradicate sources of error by referring to accepted criteria of objective validity common to both parties. The suspicion that one's opponent is the victim of an ideology does not go so far as to exclude him from discussion on the basis of a common theoretical frame of reference. The case is different with the total conception of ideology. When we attribute to one historical epoch one intellectual world and to ourselves another one, or if a certain historically determined social stratum thinks in categories other than our own, we refer not to the isolated cases of thought-content, but to fundamentally divergent thought-systems and to widely differing modes of experience and interpretation. We touch upon the theoretical or noological level whenever we consider not merely the content but also the form, and even the conceptual framework of a mode of thought as a function of the life-situation of a thinker. "The economic categories are only the theoretical expressions, the abstractions, of the social relations of production. . . . The same men who establish social relations conformably with their material productivity, produce also the principles, the ideas, the categories, conformably with their social relations." (Karl Marx, *The Poverty of Philosophy.*) . . . These are the two ways of analysing statements as functions of their social background; the first operates only on the psychological, the second on the noological level.

(*c*) Corresponding to this difference, the particular conception of ideology operates primarily with a psychology of interests, while the total conception uses a more formal functional analysis, without any reference to motivations, confining itself to an objective description of the structural differences in minds operating in different social settings. The former assumes that this or that interest is the cause of a given lie or deception. The latter presupposes simply that there is a correspondence between a given social situation and a given perspective, point of view, or apperception mass. In this case, while an analysis of constellations of interests may often be necessary it is not to establish causal connections but to characterize the total situation. Thus interest psychology tends to be displaced by an analysis of the correspondence between the situation to be known and the forms of knowledge.

Since the particular conception never actually departs from the psychological level, the point of reference in such analyses is always the individual. This is the case even when we are dealing with groups, since all psychic phenomena must finally be reduced to the minds of individuals. The term "group ideology" occurs frequently, to be sure, in popular speech. Group existence in this sense can only mean that a group of persons, either in their immediate reactions to the same situation or as a result of direct psychic interaction, react similarly. Accordingly, conditioned by the same social situation, they are subject to the same illusions. If we confine our observations to the mental processes which take place in the individual and regard him as the only possible bearer of ideologies, we shall never grasp in its totality the structure of the intellectual world belonging to a social group in a given historical situation. Although this mental world as a whole could never come into existence without the experiences and productive responses of the different individuals, its inner structure is not to be found in a mere integration of these individual experiences. The individual members of the working-class, for instance, do not experience *all* the elements of an outlook which could be called the proletarian *Weltanschauung*. Every individual participates only in certain fragments of this thought-system, the totality of which is not in the least a mere sum of these fragmentary individual experiences. As a totality the thought-system is integrated systematically, and is no mere casual jumble of fragmentary experiences of discrete members of the group. Thus it follows that the individual can only be considered as the bearer of an ideology as long as we deal with that conception of ideology which, by definition, is directed more to detached contents than to the whole structure of thought, uncovering false ways of thought and exposing lies. As soon as the total conception of ideology is used, we attempt to reconstruct the whole outlook of a social group, and neither the concrete individuals nor the abstract sum of them can legitimately be considered as bearers of this ideological thought-system as a whole. The aim of the analysis on this level is the reconstruction of the systematic theoretical basis underlying the single judgments of the individual. Analyses of ideologies in the particular sense, making the content of individual thought largely dependent on the interests of the subject, can never achieve this basic reconstruction of the whole outlook of a social group. They can at best reveal the collective psychological aspects of ideology, or lead to some development of mass psychology, dealing either with the different behaviour of the individual in the crowd, or with the results of the mass integration of the psychic experiences of many individuals. And although the collective-psychological aspect may very often approach the problems of the total ideological analysis, it does not answer its questions exactly. It is one thing to know how far my attitudes and judgments are influenced and altered by the co-existence of other human beings, but it is another thing to know what are the theoretical implications of my mode of thought which are identical with those of my fellow members of the group or social stratum.❖

Erich Fromm (1900–1980), an early associate of the Frankfurt Institute of Social Research in the 1930s, was among those who contributed to the German critical tradition of wedding Marxism and psychoanalysis. When Fromm came to the United States, his ties with the Frankfurt School grew weak. He became a widely regarded teacher and popular writer, as well as a practicing psychoanalyst. Among his most famous books are *Escape from Freedom* (1941), *Man for Himself* (1947), and *The Art of Loving* (1956). The selection was written in 1929, during his Frankfurt days. In it, he outlines the need for a unified social theory of the individual as a socialized being in a complex society.

Psychoanalysis and Sociology

Erich Fromm (1929)

The problem of the relations between psychoanalysis and sociology, about which I will speak in the Institute's courses, has two sides. The first is the application of psychoanalysis to sociology, the second that of sociology to psychoanalysis. Of course, it is not possible even to list in a few minutes all the problems and themes that result from both sides. Therefore, I shall merely attempt to make a few fundamental remarks about the principles which seem to apply to the scientific treatment of psychoanalytic-sociological problems.

The application of psychoanalysis to sociology must definitely guard against the mistake of wanting to give psychoanalytic answers where economic, technical, or political facts provide the real and sufficient explanation of sociological questions. On the other hand, the psychoanalyst must emphasize that the subject of sociology, society, in reality consists of individuals, and that it is these human beings, rather than an abstract society as such, whose actions, thoughts, and feelings are the object of sociological research. Human beings do not have one "individual psyche," which functions when a person performs as an individual and so becomes the object of psychoanalysis, contrasted to a completely separate "mass psyche" with all sorts of mass instincts, as well as vague feelings of community and solidarity, which springs into action whenever a person performs as part of mass, and for which the sociologist creates some makeshift concepts for psychoanalytical facts unknown to him. There aren't two minds within a person's head, but only one, in which the same mechanisms and laws apply whether a person performs as an individual or people appear as a society, class, community, or what have you. What psychoanalysis can bring to sociology is the knowledge—though still imperfect—of the human psychic apparatus, which is a determinant of social development alongside technical, economic, and financial factors, and deserves no less consideration than the other factors mentioned. The common task of both sciences is to investigate in what way and to what extent the psychic apparatus of the human being causally affects or determines the development or organization of society.

Let me mention here only one essential concrete problem. It is necessary to investigate what role the instinctual and the unconscious play in the organization and development of society and in individual social facts, and to what extent the changes in mankind's psychological structure, in the sense of a growing ego-organization and thus a rational ability to cope with the instinctual and natural, is a sociologically relevant factor.

Now the other side of the problem: the application of sociological approaches to psychoanalysis. However important it may be to point out to sociologists the banal fact that society consists of living people and that psychology is one of the factors af-

---

Excerpt from Stephen Eric Bronner and Douglas MacKay Kellner, eds., *Critical Theory and Society: A Reader* (New York: Routledge, 1989), pp. 37–39.

fecting social development, it is equally important that psychology not underestimate the fact that the individual person in reality exists only as a socialized person. Psychoanalysis, in contrast to some other schools of psychology, can claim that it has understood this fact from the beginning. Indeed, the recognition that there is no *homo psychologicus,* no psychological Robinson Crusoe, is one of the foundations of its theory. Psychoanalysis is predominantly oriented to questions of genesis; it devotes its special interest to human childhood, and it teaches us to interpret a very essential part of the development of the human psychological apparatus on the basis of people's attachment to mother, father, siblings, in short to the family, and thus to society. Psychoanalysis interprets the development of individuals precisely in terms of their relationship to their closest and most intimate surroundings; it considers the psychological apparatus as formed most decisively by these relationships.

Certainly, this is only a beginning, and from it a series of further important problems result, which have so far scarcely been attacked; for instance, the question of to what extent the family is itself the product of a particular social system, and how a socially conditioned change in the family as such might influence the development of the psychic apparatus of the individual. Or there is the question of what influence the growth of technology—i.e., an ever increasing gratification, or a decreasing deprivation, or the instincts—has on the psyche of the individual.

The classification from which we proceed, into problems that result from the application of psychoanalysis to sociology and of sociology to psychoanalysis, is of course only a crude one, which corresponds to practical needs. In keeping with the reciprocal interaction of person and society, there are a whole series of further problems. Some of the most important ones are precisely those where it is impossible to apply one method to the other, but where a set of facts, which are equally psychological and social in character, can be investigated by both methods and can be understood only by employing both perspectives. It is just such a problem of how much certain concerns of psychology, which are simultaneously sociological, such as religion, depend on the material development of mankind in their appearance and decline, that constitutes the subject of the latest book by Freud.

There Freud advances the idea that religion is the psychic correlative to mankind's helplessness in the face of nature. From there he opens a perspective onto a problem which may be considered one of the most important psychologic-sociological questions: What connections exist between the social, especially the economic-technical, development of humanity, and the development of the psychic apparatus, especially the ego-organization, of the human being? In short, he raises the question of the developmental history of the psyche. Psychoanalysis has so far asked and answered this question only for the individual. Freud in his latest book has extended this genetic inquiry to the psychic development of society, and has thus given important guidance to future psychoanalytic-sociological work.

In summary, I would like to say: Psychoanalysis, which interprets the human being as a socialized being, and the psychic apparatus as essentially developed and determined through the relationship of the individual to society, must consider it a duty to participate in the investigation of sociological problems to the extent the human being or his/her psyche plays any part at all. In this effort, one may quote the words, not of a psychologist, but of (Karl Marx) the greatest sociologist of all: "History does nothing, it possesses no immense wealth, it fights no battles. It is instead the human being, the real living person, who does everything, who owns everything, and who fights all battles." ❖

George Herbert Mead (1863–1931), like Durkheim and a number of other early so-ciologists, was born to a religious family. He grew up on the campus of Oberlin Col-lege, where his father, a Protestant minister, taught preaching. Mead's mother re-turned to teaching after his father's early death and later became president of Mount Holyoke College. Mead studied at Harvard with William James a few years af-ter Du Bois had finished his studies there. Like Du Bois and W. I. Thomas (and many others), Mead also studied in Germany before beginning his teaching career. In 1891, he taught philosophy at the University of Michigan, where he encountered Charles Horton Cooley and John Dewey. One year later, he joined the philosophy faculty at the new University of Chicago, whose department of sociology was just being organized. Mead had little direct contact with the sociologists, but the social justice teachings of his father influenced his association with Jane Addams's Hull House and with other progressive activists in the city. Mead's best-known book, *Mind, Self & Society,* was compiled from lecture notes for the course in social psy-chology that he taught until his death in 1931.

"The Self, the I, and the Me" is from the portions of that book in which Mead most precisely develops his version of the social self as a double dialogue—with the social world, externally, and between the "I" and the "Me," internally. Mead's theory of the social self was an important advance over James and Cooley and is considered a classic source for subsequent social theories of the self, both normal and deviant.

The Self, the I, and the Me
George Herbert Mead (ca. 1929)

We can distinguish very definitely between the self and the body. The body can be there and can operate in a very intelligent fashion without there being a self involved in the experience. The self has the characteristic that it is an object to itself, and that characteristic distinguishes it from other objects and from the body. It is perfectly true that the eye can see the foot, but it does not see the body as a whole. We cannot see our backs; we can feel certain portions of them, if we are agile, but we cannot get an experience of our whole body. There are, of course, experiences which are some-what vague and difficult of location, but the bodily experiences are for us organized about a self. The foot and hand belong to the self. We can see our feet, especially if we look at them from the wrong end of an opera glass, as strange things which we have difficulty in recognizing as our own. The parts of the body are quite distin-guishable from the self. We can lose parts of the body without any serious invasion of the self. The mere ability to experience different parts of the body is not different from the experience of a table. The table presents a different feel from what the hand does when one hand feels another, but it is an experience of something with which we come definitely into contact. The body does not experience itself as a whole, in the sense in which the self in some way enters into the experience of the self.

It is the characteristic of the self as an object to itself that I want to bring out. This characteristic is represented in the word "self," which is a reflexive, and indicates that which can be both subject and object. This type of object is essentially different from other objects, and in the past it has been distinguished as conscious, a term which indicates an experience with, an experience of, one's self. It was assumed that consciousness in some way carried this capacity of being an object to itself. In giving a behavioristic statement of consciousness we have to look for some sort of experience in which the physical organism can become an object to itself.

When one is running to get away from someone who is chasing him, he is entirely occupied in this action, and his experience may be swallowed up in the objects about him, so that he has, at the time being, no consciousness of self at all. We must be, of course, very completely occupied to have that take place, but we can, I think, recognize that sort of a possible experience in which the self does not enter. We can, perhaps, get some light on that situation through those experiences in which in very intense action there appear in the experience of the individual, back of this intense action, memories and anticipations. Tolstoi as an officer in the war gives an account of having pictures of his past experience in the midst of his most intense action. There are also the pictures that flash into a person's mind when he is drowning. In such instances there is a contrast between an experience that is absolutely wound up in outside activity in which the self as an object does not enter, and an activity of memory and imagination in which the self is the principal object. The self is then entirely distinguishable from an organism that is surrounded by things and acts with reference to things, including parts of its own body. These latter may be objects like other objects, but they are just objects out there in the field, and they do not involve a self that is an object to the organism. This is, I think, frequently overlooked. It is that fact which makes our anthropomorphic reconstructions of animal life so fallacious. How can an individual get outside himself (experientially) in such a way as to become an object to himself? This is the essential psychological problem of selfhood or of self-consciousness; and its solution is to be found by referring to the process of social conduct or activity in which the given person or individual is implicated. The apparatus of reason would not be complete unless it swept itself into its own analysis of the field of experience; or unless the individual brought himself into the same experiential field as that of the other individual selves in relation to whom he acts in any given social situation. Reason cannot become impersonal unless it takes an objective, non-affective attitude toward itself; otherwise we have just consciousness, not *self*-consciousness. And it is necessary to rational conduct that the individual should thus take an objective, impersonal attitude toward himself, that he should become an object to himself. For the individual organism is obviously an essential and important fact or constituent element of the empirical situation in which it acts; and without taking objective account of itself as such, it cannot act intelligently, or rationally.

The individual experiences himself as such, not directly, but only indirectly, from the particular standpoints of other individual members of the same social group, or from the generalized standpoint of the social group as a whole to which he belongs. For he enters his own experience as a self or individual, not directly or immediately, not by becoming a subject to himself, but only in so far as he first becomes an object to himself just as other individuals are objects to him or in his experience; and he becomes an object to himself only by taking the attitudes of other individuals toward himself within a social environment or context of experience and behavior in which both he and they are involved.

The importance of what we term "communication" lies in the fact that it provides a form of behavior in which the organism or the individual may become an object to himself. It is that sort of communication which we have been discussing—not communication in the sense of the cluck of the hen to the chickens, or the bark of a wolf to the pack, or the lowing of a cow, but communication in the sense of significant symbols, communication which is directed not only to others but also to the individual himself. So far as that type of communication is a part of behavior it at least introduces a self. Of course, one may hear without listening; one may see things that he does not realize; do things that he is not really aware of. But it is where one does respond to that which he addresses to another and where that response of his own becomes a part of his conduct, where he not only hears himself but responds to himself, talks and replies to himself as truly as the other person replies to him, that we have behavior in which the individuals become objects to themselves.

Such a self is not, I would say, primarily the physiological organism. The physiological organism is essential to it, but we are at least able to think of a self without it. Persons who believe in immortality, or believe in ghosts, or in the possibility of the self leaving the body, assume a self which is quite distinguishable from the body. How successfully they can hold these conceptions is an open question, but we do, as a fact, separate the self and the organism. It is fair to say that the beginning of the self as an object, so far as we can see, is to be found in the experiences of people that lead to the conception of a "double." Primitive people assume that there is a double, located presumably in the diaphragm, that leaves the body temporarily in sleep and completely in death. It can be enticed out of the body of one's enemy and perhaps killed. It is represented in infancy by the imaginary playmates which children set up, and through which they come to control their experiences in their play.

The self, as that which can be an object to itself, is essentially a social structure, and it arises in social experience. After a self has arisen, it in a certain sense provides for itself its social experiences, and so we can conceive of an absolutely solitary self. But it is impossible to conceive of a self arising outside of social experience. When it has arisen we can think of a person in solitary confinement for the rest of his life, but who still has himself as a companion, and is able to think and to converse with himself as he had communicated with others. That process to which I have just referred, of responding to one's self as another responds to it, taking part in one's own conversation with others, being aware of what one is saying and using that awareness of what one is saying to determine what one is going to say thereafter—that is a process with which we are all familiar. We are continually following up our own address to other persons by an understanding of what we are saying, and using that understanding in the direction of our continued speech. We are finding out what we are going to say, what we are going to do, by saying and doing, and in the process we are continually controlling the process itself. In the conversation of gestures what we say calls out a certain response in another and that in turn changes our own action, so that we shift from what we started to do because of the reply the other makes. The conversation of gestures is the beginning of communication. The individual comes to carry on a conversation of gestures with himself. He says something, and that calls out a certain reply in himself which makes him change what he was going to say. One starts to say something, we will presume an unpleasant something, but when he starts to say it he realizes it is cruel. The effect on himself of what he is saying checks him; there is here a conversation of gestures between the individual and himself. We mean by significant speech that the action is one that affects the individual himself, and that the effect upon the individual himself is part of the intelligent carrying-out of the conversation with others. Now we, so to speak, amputate that social phase and dispense with it for the time being, so that one is talking to one's self as one would talk to another person.

This process of abstraction cannot be carried on indefinitely. One inevitably seeks an audience, has to pour himself out to somebody. In reflective intelligence one thinks to act, and to act solely so that this action remains a part of a social process. Thinking becomes preparatory to social action. The very process of thinking is, of course, simply an inner conversation that goes on, but it is a conversation of gestures which in its completion implies the expression of that which one thinks to an audience. One separates the significance of what he is saying to others from the actual speech and gets it ready before saying it. He thinks it out, and perhaps writes it in the form of a book; but it is still a part of social intercourse in which one is addressing other persons and at the same time addressing one's self, and in which one controls the address to other persons by the response made to one's own gesture. That the person should be responding to himself is necessary to the self, and it is this sort of social conduct which provides behavior within which that self appears. I know of no other form of behavior than the linguistic in which the individual is an object to himself, and, so far as I can see, the individual is not a self in the reflexive sense unless he is an object to himself. It is this fact that gives a critical importance to communication, since this is a type of behavior in which the individual does so respond to himself.

We realize in everyday conduct and experience that an individual does not mean a great deal of what he is doing and saying. We frequently say that such an individual is not himself. We come away from an interview with a realization that we have left out important things, that there are parts of the self that did not get into what was said. What determines the amount of the self that gets into communication is the social experience itself. Of course, a good deal of the self does not need to get expression. We carry on a whole series of different relationships to different people. We are one thing to one man and another thing to another. There are parts of the self which exist only for the self in relationship to itself. We divide ourselves up in all sorts of different selves with reference to our acquaintances. We discuss politics with one and religion with another. There are all sorts of different selves answering to all sorts of different social reactions. It is the social process itself that is responsible for the appearance of the self; it is not there as a self apart from this type of experience.

A multiple personality is in a certain sense normal, as I have just pointed out. There is usually an organization of the whole self with reference to the community to which we belong, and the situation in which we find ourselves. What the society is, whether we are living with people of the present, people of our own imaginations, people of the past, varies, of course, with different individuals. Normally, within the sort of community as a whole to which we belong, there is a unified self, but that may be broken up. To a person who is somewhat unstable nervously and in whom there is a line of cleavage, certain activities become impossible, and that set of activities may separate and evolve another self. Two separate "me's" and "I's," two different selves, result, and that is the condition under which there is a tendency to break up the personality. There is an account of a professor of education who disappeared, was lost to the community, and later turned up in a logging camp in the West. He freed himself of his occupation and turned to the woods where he felt, if you like, more at home. The pathological side of it was the forgetting, the leaving out of the rest of the self. This result involved getting rid of certain bodily memories which would identify the individual to himself. We often recognize the lines of cleavage that run through us. We would be glad to forget certain things, get rid of things the self is bound up with in past experiences. What we have here is a situation in which there can be different selves, and it is dependent upon the set of social reactions that is involved as to which self we are going to be. If we can forget everything involved in one set of activities, obviously we relinquish that part of the self. Take a person who is unstable, get him occupied by speech, and at the same time get his eye on something you are writing so that he is carrying on two separate lines of communication, and if you go about it in the right way you can get those two currents going so that they do not run into each other. You can get two entirely different sets of activities going on. You can bring about in that way the dissociation of a person's self. It is a process of setting up two sorts of communication which separate the behavior of the individual. For one individual it is this thing said and heard, and for the other individual there exists only that which he sees written. You must, of course, keep one experience out of the field of the other. Dissociations are apt to take place when an event leads to emotional upheavals. That which is separated goes on in its own way.

The unity and structure of the complete self reflects the unity and structure of the social process as a whole; and each of the elementary selves of which it is composed reflects the unity and structure of one of the various aspects of that process in which the individual is implicated. In other words, the various elementary selves which constitute, or are organized into, a complete self are the various aspects of the structure of that complete self answering to the various aspects of the structure of the social process as a whole; the structure of the complete self is thus a reflection of the complete social process. The organization and unification of a social group is identical with the organization and unification of any one of the selves arising within the social process in which that group is engaged, or which it is carrying on.

The phenomenon of dissociation of personality is caused by a breaking up of the complete, unitary self into the component selves of which it is composed, and which respectively correspond to different aspects of the social process in which the person is involved, and within which his complete or unitary self has arisen; these aspects being the different social groups to which he belongs within that process. . . .

Rational society, of course, is not limited to any specific set of individuals. Any person who is rational can become a part of it. The attitude of the community toward our own response is imported into ourselves in terms of the meaning of what we are doing. This occurs in its widest extent in universal discourse, in the reply which the rational world makes to our remark. The meaning is as universal as the community; it is necessarily involved in the rational character of that community; it is the response that the world made up out of rational beings inevitably makes to our own statement. We both get the object and ourselves into experience in terms of such a process; the other appears in our own experience in so far as we do take such an organized and generalized attitude.

If one meets a person on the street whom he fails to recognize, one's reaction toward him is that toward any other who is a member of the same community. He is the other, the organized, generalized other, if you like. One takes his attitude over against one's self. If he turns in one direction one is to go in another direction. One has his response as an attitude within himself. It is having that attitude within himself that makes it possible for one to be a self. That involves something beyond the mere turning to the right, as we say, instinctively, without self-consciousness. To have self-consciousness one must have the attitude of the other in one's own organism as controlling the thing that he is going to do. What appears in the immediate experience of one's self in taking that attitude is what we term the "me." It is that self which is able to maintain itself in the community, that is recognized in the community in so far as it recognizes the others. Such is the phase of the self which I have referred to as that of the "me."

Over against the "me" is the "I." The individual not only has rights, but he has duties; he is not only a citizen, a member of the community, but he is one who reacts to this community and in his reaction to it, as we have seen in the conversation of gestures, changes it. The "I" is the response of the individual to the attitude of the community as this appears in his own experience. His response to that organized attitude in turn changes it. As we have pointed out, this is a change which is not present in his own experience until after it takes place. The "I" appears in our experience in memory. It is only after we have acted that we know what we have done; it is only after we have spoken that we know what we have said. The adjustment to that organized world which is present in our own nature is one that represents the "me" and is constantly there. But if the response to it is a response which is of the nature of the conversation of gestures, if it creates a situation which is in some sense novel, if one puts up his side of the case, asserts himself over against others and insists that they take a different attitude toward himself, then there is something important occurring that is not previously present in experience.❖

Robert K. Merton (1910–) was a student at Harvard in the days of Parsons and Sorokin. It is a popular misconception that Merton had been Talcott Parsons's student; more accurately, he was the student of George Sarton, Harvard's distinguished historian of science (and father of the feminist poet and writer May Sarton). Merton's most important empirical work, *Science, Technology and Society in Seventeenth Century England* (1938), was the first of his many contributions to the sociology of science, the field of which he was the principal founder. In this regard, Merton went beyond Mannheim's preliminary definition of the sociology of knowledge to develop a branch of social studies that flourished in an era when science and technology were considered the keys to social salvation. Merton, like Parsons, is said to be a functionalist social theorist. Unlike Parsons, and in obvious response to him, Merton is known for his attempts to define researchable theories of "the middle range" between pure abstraction and mindless empiricism. With Paul Lazarsfeld, Merton made the Columbia University Department of Sociology famous for its contributions to the empirical sociology of modern American life. From 1942 to 1971, he was associate director of Columbia's Bureau of Applied Social Research, where survey research techniques were developed.

"Social Structure and Anomie" is one of the most widely read articles in the history of sociology. First published in 1938, the article reformulates Durkheim's idea of anomie to account for the unexpected ways in which social conditions force individuals to act in socially functional, if sometimes illegal, ways.

Social Structure and Anomie
Robert K. Merton (1938)

Until recently, and all the more so before then, one could speak of a marked tendency in psychological and sociological theory to attribute the faulty operation of social structures to failures of social control over man's imperious biological drives. The imagery of the relations between man and society implied by this doctrine is as clear as it is questionable. In the beginning, there are man's biological impulses which seek full expression. And then, there is the social order, essentially an apparatus for the management of impulses, for the social processing of tensions, for the "renunciation of instinctual gratifications," in the words of Freud. Nonconformity with the demands of a social structure is thus assumed to be anchored in original nature. It is the biologically rooted impulses which from time to time break through social control. And by implication, conformity is the result of an utilitarian calculus or of unreasoned conditioning.

With the more recent advancement of social science, this set of conceptions has undergone basic modification. For one thing, it no longer appears so obvious that man is set against society in an unceasing war between biological impulse and social restraint. The image of man as an untamed bundle of impulses begins to look more like a caricature than a portrait. For another, sociological perspectives have increasingly entered into the analysis of behavior deviating from prescribed patterns of conduct. For whatever the role of biological impulses, there still remains the further question of why it is that the frequency of deviant behavior varies within different social structures and how it happens that the deviations have different shapes and patterns in different social structures. Today, as then, we have still much to learn about the processes through which social structures generate the circumstances in which infringement of social codes constitutes a "normal" (that is to say, an expectable) response. This chapter is an essay seeking clarification of the problem.

The framework set out in this essay is designed to provide one systematic approach to the analysis of social and cultural sources of deviant behavior. Our primary aim is to discover how some *social structures exert a definite pressure upon certain persons in the society to engage in nonconforming rather than conforming conduct.* If we can locate groups peculiarly subject to such pressures, we should expect to find fairly high rates of deviant behavior in these groups, not because the human beings comprising them are compounded of distinctive biological tendencies but because they are responding normally to the social situation in which they find themselves. Our perspective is sociological. We look at variations in the *rates* of deviant behavior, not at its incidence. Should our quest be at all successful, some forms of deviant behavior will be found to be as psychologically normal as conforming behavior, and the equation of deviation and psychological abnormality will be put in question.

Patterns of Cultural Goals and Institutional Norms

Among the several elements of social and cultural structures, two are of immediate importance. These are analytically separable although they merge in concrete situations. The first consists of culturally defined goals, purposes and interests, held out as legitimate objectives for all or for diversely located members of the society. The goals are more or less integrated—the degree is a question of empirical fact—and roughly ordered in some hierarchy of value. Involving various degrees of sentiment and significance, the prevailing goals comprise a frame of aspirational reference. They are the things "worth striving for." They are a basic, though not the exclusive, component of what Linton has called "designs for group living." And though some, not all, of these cultural goals are directly related to the biological drives of man, they are not determined by them.

A second element of the cultural structure defines, regulates and controls the acceptable modes of reaching out for these goals. Every social group invariably couples its cultural objectives with regulations, rooted in the mores or institutions, of allowable procedures for moving toward these objectives. These regulatory norms are not necessarily identical with technical or efficiency norms. Many procedures which from the standpoint of particular individuals would be most efficient in securing desired values—the exercise of force, fraud, power—are ruled out of the institutional area of permitted conduct. At times, the disallowed procedures include some which would be efficient for the group itself—*e.g.,* historic taboos on vivisection, on medical experimentation, on the sociological analysis of "sacred" norms—since the criterion of acceptability is not technical efficiency but value-laden sentiments (supported by most members of the group or by those able to promote these sentiments through the composite use of power and propaganda). In all instances, the choice of expedients for striving toward cultural goals is limited by institutionalized norms.

Sociologists often speak of these controls as being "in the mores" or as operating through social institutions. Such elliptical statements are true enough, but they obscure the fact that culturally standardized practices are not all of a piece. They are subject to a wide gamut of control. They may represent definitely prescribed or preferential or permissive or proscribed patterns of behavior. In assessing the operation of social controls, these variations—roughly indicated by the terms *prescription, preference, permission* and *proscription*—must of course be taken into account.

To say, moreover, that cultural goals and institutionalized norms operate jointly to shape prevailing practices is not to say that they bear a constant relation to one another. The cultural emphasis placed upon certain goals varies independently of the degree of emphasis upon institutionalized means. There may develop a very heavy, at times a virtually exclusive, stress upon the value of particular goals, involving comparatively little concern with the institutionally prescribed means of striving toward these goals. The limiting case of this type is reached when the range of alternative procedures is governed only by technical rather than by institutional norms. Any and all procedures which promise attainment of the all-important goal would be permitted in this hypothetical polar case. This constitutes one type of malintegrated culture. A second polar type is found in groups where activities originally conceived as instrumental are transmuted into self-contained practices, lacking further objectives. The original purposes are forgotten and close adherence to institutionally prescribed conduct becomes a matter of ritual. Sheer conformity becomes a central value. For a time, social stability is ensured—at the expense of flexibility. Since the range of alternative behaviors permitted by the culture is severely limited, there is little basis for adapting to new conditions. There develops a tradition-bound, 'sacred' society marked by neophobia. Between these extreme types are societies which maintain a rough balance between emphases upon cultural goals and institutionalized practices, and these constitute the integrated and relatively stable, though changing, societies.

An effective equilibrium between these two phases of the social structure is maintained so long as satisfactions accrue to individuals conforming to both cultural constraints, *viz.,* satisfactions from the achievement of goals and satisfactions emerging directly from the institutionally canalized modes of striving to attain them. It is reckoned in terms of the product and in terms of the process, in terms of the outcome and in terms of the activities. Thus continuing satisfactions must derive from sheer participation in a competitive order as well as from eclipsing one's competitors if the order itself is to be sustained. If concern shifts exclusively to the outcome of competition, then those who perennially suffer defeat may, understandably enough, work for a change in the rules of the game. The sacrifices occasionally—not, as Freud assumed, invariably—entailed by conformity to institutional norms must be compensated by socialized rewards. The distribution of statuses through competition must be so organized that positive incentives for adherence to status obligations are provided *for every position* within the distributive order. Otherwise, as will soon become plain, aberrant behavior ensues. It is, indeed, my central hypothesis that aberrant behavior may be regarded sociologically as a symptom of dissociation between culturally prescribed aspirations and socially structured avenues for realizing these aspirations.

Of the types of societies that result from independent variation of cultural goals and institutionalized means, we shall be primarily concerned with the first—a society in which there is an exceptionally strong emphasis upon specific goals without a corresponding emphasis upon institutional procedures. If it is not to be misunderstood, this statement must be elaborated. No society lacks norms governing conduct. But societies do differ in the degree to which the folkways, mores and institutional controls are effectively integrated with the goals which stand high in the hierarchy of cultural values. The culture may be such as to lead individuals to center their emotional convictions upon the complex of culturally acclaimed ends, with far less emotional support for prescribed methods of reaching out for these ends. With such differential emphases upon goals and institutional procedures, the latter may be so vitiated by the stress on goals as to have the behavior of many individuals limited only by considerations of technical expediency. In this context, the sole significant question becomes: Which of the available procedures is most efficient in netting the culturally approved value? The technically most effective procedure, whether culturally legitimate or not, becomes typically preferred to institutionally prescribed conduct. As this process of attenuation continues, the society becomes unstable and there develops what Durkheim called "anomie" (or normlessness).

The working of this process eventuating in anomie can be easily glimpsed in a series of familiar and instructive, though perhaps trivial, episodes. Thus, in competitive athletics, when the aim of victory is shorn of its institutional trappings and success becomes construed as "winning the game" rather than "winning under the rules of the game," a premium is implicitly set upon the use of illegitimate but technically efficient means. The star of the opposing football team is surreptitiously slugged; the wrestler incapacitates his opponent through ingenious but illicit techniques; university alumni covertly subsidize "students" whose talents are confined to the athletic field. The emphasis on the goal has so attenuated the satisfactions deriving from sheer participation in the competitive activity that only a successful outcome provides gratification. Through the same process, tension generated by the desire to win in a poker game is relieved by successfully dealing one's self four aces or, when the cult of success has truly flowered, by sagaciously shuffling the cards in a game of solitaire. The faint twinge of uneasiness in the last instance and the surreptitious nature of public delicts indicate clearly that the institutional rules of the game are *known* to those who evade them. But cultural (or idiosyncratic) exaggeration of the success-goal leads men to withdraw emotional support from the rules.

This process is of course not restricted to the realm of competitive sport, which has simply provided us with microcosmic images of the social macrocosm. The process whereby exaltation of the end generates a literal *demoralization, i.e.,* a de-institutionalization, of the means occurs in many groups where the two components of the social structure are not highly integrated.

Contemporary American culture appears to approximate the polar type in which great emphasis upon certain success-goals occurs without equivalent emphasis upon institutional means. It would of course be fanciful to assert that accumulated wealth stands alone as a symbol of success just as it would be fanciful to deny that Americans assign it a place high in their scale of values. In some large measure, money has been consecrated as a value in itself, over and above its expenditure for articles of consumption or its use for the enhancement of power. "Money" is peculiarly well adapted to become a symbol of prestige. As Simmel emphasized, money is highly abstract and impersonal. However acquired, fraudulently or institutionally, it can be used to purchase the same goods and services. The anonymity of an urban society, in conjunction with these peculiarities of money, permits wealth, the sources of which may be unknown to the community in which the plutocrat lives or, if known, to become purified in the course of time, to serve as a symbol of high status. Moreover, in the American Dream there is no final stopping point. The measure of "monetary success" is conveniently indefinite and relative. At each income level, as H. F. Clark found, Americans want just about twenty-five per cent more (but of course this "just a bit more" continues to operate once it is obtained). In this flux of shifting standards, there is no stable resting point, or rather, it is the point which manages always to be "just ahead." An observer of a community in which annual salaries in six figures are not uncommon, reports the anguished words of one victim of the American Dream. "In this town, I'm snubbed socially because I only get a thousand a week. That hurts."

To say that the goal of monetary success is entrenched in American culture is only to say that Americans are bombarded on every side by precepts which affirm the right or, often, the duty of retaining the goal even in the face of repeated frustration. Prestigeful representatives of the society reinforce the cultural emphasis. The family, the school and the workplace—the major agencies shaping the personality structure and goal formation of Americans—join to provide the intensive disciplining required if an individual is to retain intact a goal that remains elusively beyond reach, if he is to be motivated by the promise of a gratification which is not redeemed. As we shall presently see, parents serve as a transmission belt for the values and goals of the groups of which they are a part—above all, of their social class or of the class with which they identify themselves. And the schools are of course the official agency for the passing on of the prevailing values, with a large proportion of the textbooks used in city schools implying or stating explicitly "that education leads to intelligence and consequently to job and money success." Central to this process of disciplining people to maintain their unfulfilled aspirations are the cultural proto-types of success, the living documents testifying that the American Dream can be realized if one but has the requisite abilities. Consider in this connection the following excerpts from the business journal, *Nation's Business,* drawn from a large amount of comparable materials found in mass communications setting forth the values of business class culture.

The Document *(Nation's Business, Vol. 27, No. 8, p. 7)*	*Its Sociological Implications*
'You have to be born to those jobs, buddy, or else have a good pull.'	Here is a heretical opinion, possibly born of continued frustration, which rejects the worth of retaining an apparently unrealizable goal and, moreover, questions the legitimacy of a social structure which provides differential access to this goal.
That's an old sedative to ambition.	The counter-attack, explicitly asserting the cultural value of retaining one's aspirations intact, of not losing "ambition."
Before listening to its seduction, ask these men:	A clear statement of the function to be served by the ensuing list of "successes." These men are living testimony that the social structure is such as to permit these aspirations to be achieved, *if one is worthy*. And correlatively, failure to reach these goals testifies only to one's own personal shortcomings. Aggression provoked by failure should therefore be directed inward and not outward, against oneself and not against a social structure which provides free and equal access to opportunity.
Elmer R. Jones, president of Wells-Fargo and Co., who began life as a poor boy and left school at the fifth grade to take his first job.	Success prototype I: *All* may properly have the *same* lofty ambitions, for however lowly the starting-point, true talent can reach the very heights. Aspirations must be retained intact.
Frank C. Ball, the Mason fruit jar king of America, who rode from Buffalo to Muncie, Indiana, in a boxcar along with his brother George's horse, to start a little business in Muncie that became the biggest of its kind.	Success prototype II: Whatever the present results of one's strivings, the future is large with promise; for the common man may yet become a king. Gratifications may seem forever deferred, but they will finally be realized as one's enterprise becomes "the biggest of its kind."
J. L. Bevan, present of the Illinois Central Railroad, who at twelve was a messenger boy in the freight office at New Orleans.	Success prototype III: If the secular trends of our economy seem to give little scope to small business, then one may rise within the giant bureaucracies of private enterprise. If one can no longer be a king in a realm of his own creation, he may at least become a president in one of the economic democracies. No matter what one's present station, messenger boy or clerk, one's gaze should be fixed at the top.

The symbolism of a commoner rising to the estate of economic royalty is woven deep in the texture of the American culture pattern, finding what is perhaps its ultimate expression in the words of one who knew whereof he spoke, Andrew Carnegie: "Be a king in your dreams. Say to yourself, 'My place is at the top.'"

Coupled with this positive emphasis upon the obligation to maintain lofty goals is a correlative emphasis upon the penalizing of those who draw in their ambitions. Americans are admonished "not to be a quitter" for in the dictionary of American culture, as in the lexicon of youth, "there is no such word as 'fail.'" The cultural manifesto is clear: one must not quit, must not cease striving, must not lessen his goals, for "not failure, but low aim, is crime."

Thus the culture enjoins the acceptance of three cultural axioms: First, all should strive for the same lofty goals since these are open to all; second, present seeming failure is but a way-station to ultimate success; and third, genuine failure consists only in the lessening or withdrawal of ambition.

In rough psychological paraphrase, these axioms represent, first, a symbolic secondary reinforcement of incentive; second, curbing the threatened extinction of a response through an associated stimulus; third, increasing the motive-strength to evoke continued responses despite the continued absence of reward.

In sociological paraphrase, these axioms represent, first, the deflection of criticism of the social structure onto one's self among those so situated in the society that they do not have full and equal access to opportunity; second, the preservation of a structure of social power by having individuals in the lower social strata identify themselves, not with their compeers, but with those at the top (whom they will ultimately join); and third, providing pressures for conformity with the cultural dictates of unslackened ambition by the threat of less than full membership in the society for those who fail to conform.

It is in these terms and through these processes that contemporary American culture continues to be characterized by a heavy emphasis on wealth as a basic symbol of success, without a corresponding emphasis upon the legitimate avenues on which to march toward this goal. How do individuals living in this cultural context respond? And how do our observations bear upon the doctrine that deviant behavior typically derives from biological impulses breaking through the restraints imposed by culture? What, in short, are the consequences for the behavior of people variously situated in a social structure of a culture in which the emphasis on dominant success-goals has become increasingly separated from an equivalent emphasis on institutionalized procedures for seeking these goals?

Types of Individual Adaptation

Turning from these culture patterns, we now examine types of adaptation by individuals within the culture-bearing society. Though our focus is still the cultural and social genesis of varying rates and types of deviant behavior, our perspective shifts from the plane of patterns of cultural values to the plane of types of adaptation to these values among those occupying different positions in the social structure.

We here consider five types of adaptation, as these are schematically set out in the following table, where (+) signifies "acceptance," (−) signifies "rejection," and (±) signifies "rejection of prevailing values and substitution of new values."

A Typology of Modes of Individual Adaptation

Modes of Adaptation	*Culture Goals*	*Institutionalized Means*
I. Conformity	+	+
II. Innovation	+	−
III. Ritualism	−	+
IV. Retreatism	−	−
V. Rebellion	±	±

Examination of how the social structure operates to exert pressure upon individuals for one or another of these alternative modes of behavior must be prefaced by the observation that people may shift from one alternative to another as they engage in different spheres of social activities. These categories refer to role behavior in specific types of situations, not to personality. They are types of more or less enduring response, not types of personality organization. To consider these types of adaptation in several spheres of conduct would introduce a complexity unmanageable within the confines of this chapter. For this reason, we shall be primarily concerned with economic activity in the broad sense of "the production, exchange, distribution and consumption of goods and services" in our competitive society, where wealth has taken on a highly symbolic cast.

I. Conformity

To the extent that a society is stable, adaptation type I—conformity to both cultural goals and institutionalized means—is the most common and widely diffused. Were this not so, the stability and continuity of the society could not be maintained. The mesh of expectancies constituting every social order is sustained by the modal behavior of its members representing conformity to the established, though perhaps secularly changing, culture patterns. It is, in fact, only because behavior is typically oriented toward the basic values of the society that we may speak of a human aggregate as comprising a society. Unless there is a deposit of values shared by interacting individuals, there exist social relations, if the disorderly interactions may be so called, but no society. It is thus that, at mid-century, one may refer to a Society of Nations primarily as a figure of speech or as an imagined objective, but not as a sociological reality.

Since our primary interest centers on the sources of *deviant* behavior, and since we have briefly examined the mechanisms making for conformity as the modal response in American society, little more need be said regarding this type of adaptation, at this point.

II. Innovation

Great cultural emphasis upon the success-goal invites this mode of adaptation through the use of institutionally proscribed but often effective means of attaining at least the simulacrum of success—wealth and power. This response occurs when the individual has assimilated the cultural emphasis upon the goal without equally internalizing the institutional norms governing ways and means for its attainment.

From the standpoint of psychology, great emotional investment in an objective may be expected to produce a readiness to take risks, and this attitude may be adopted by people in all social strata. From the standpoint of sociology, the question arises, which features of our social structure predispose toward this type of adaptation, thus producing greater frequencies of deviant behavior in one social stratum than in another?

On the top economic levels, the pressure toward innovation not infrequently erases the distinction between business-like strivings this side of the mores and sharp practices beyond the mores. As Veblen observed, "It is not easy in any given case—indeed it is at times impossible until the courts have spoken—to say whether it is an instance of praiseworthy salesmanship or a penitentiary offense." The history of the great American fortunes is threaded with strains toward institutionally dubious innovation as is attested by many tributes to the Robber Barons. The reluctant admiration often expressed privately, and not seldom publicly, of these "shrewd, smart and successful" men is a product of a cultural structure in which the sacrosanct goal virtually consecrates the means. This is no new phenomenon. Without assuming that Charles Dickens [in *American Notes*] was a wholly accurate observer of the American scene and with full knowledge that he was anything but impartial, we cite his perceptive remarks on the American

love of "smart" dealing: which gilds over many a swindle and gross breach of trust; many a defalcation, public and private; and enables many a knave to hold his head up with the best, who well deserves a halter. . . . The merits of a broken speculation, or a bankruptcy, or of a successful scoundrel, are not gauged by its or his observance of the golden rule, "Do as you would be done by," but are considered with reference to their smartness. . . . The following dialogue I have held a hundred times: "Is it not a very disgraceful circumstance that such a man as So-and-so should be acquiring a large property by the most infamous and odious means, and notwithstanding all the crimes of which he has been guilty, should be tolerated and abetted by your Citizens? He is a public nuisance, is he not?" "Yes, sir." "A convicted liar?" "Yes, sir." "He has been kicked and cuffed, and caned?" "Yes, sir." "And he is utterly dishonorable, debased, and profligate?" "Yes, sir." "In the name of wonder, then, what is his merit?" "Well, sir, he is a smart man."

In this caricature of conflicting cultural values, Dickens was of course only one of many wits who mercilessly probed the consequences of the heavy emphasis on financial success. . . . But perhaps most in point here was the deployment of wit by Ambrose Bierce in a form which made it evident that *wit* had not cut away from its etymological origins and still meant the power by which one knows, learns, or thinks. In his characteristically ironical and deep-seeing essay on "crime and its correctives," Bierce begins with the observation that "Sociologists have long been debating the theory that the impulse to commit crime is a disease, and the ayes appear to have it—the disease." After this prelude, he describes the ways in which the successful rogue achieves social legitimacy, and proceeds to anatomize the discrepancies between cultural values and social relations.

The good American is, as a rule, pretty hard on roguery, but he atones for his austerity by an amiable toleration of rogues. His only requirement is that he must personally know the rogues. We all "denounce" thieves loudly enough if we have not the honor of their acquaintance. If we have, why, that is different—unless they have the actual odor of the slum or the prison about them. We may know them guilty, but we meet them, shake hands with them, drink with them and, if they happen to be wealthy, or otherwise great, invite them to our houses, and deem it an honor to frequent theirs. We do not "approve their methods"—let that be understood; and thereby they are sufficiently punished. The notion that a knave cares a pin what is thought of his ways by one who is civil and friendly to himself appears to have been invented by a humorist. On the vaudeville stage of Mars it would probably have made his fortune.

[And again:] If social recognition were denied to rogues they would be fewer by many. Some would only the more diligently cover their tracks along the devious paths of unrighteousness, but others would do so much violence to their consciences as to renounce the disadvantages of rascality for those of an honest life. An unworthy person dreads nothing so much as the withholding of an honest hand, the slow, inevitable stroke of an ignoring eye.

We have rich rogues because we have "respectable" persons who are not ashamed to take them by the hand, to be seen with them, to say that they know them. In such it is treachery to censure them; to cry out when robbed by them is to turn state's evidence.

One may smile upon a rascal (most of us do many times a day) if one does not know him to be a rascal, and has not said he is; but knowing him to be, or having said he is, to smile upon him is to be a hypocrite—just a plain hypocrite or a sycophantic hypocrite, according to the station in life of the rascal smiled upon. There are more plain hypocrites than sycophantic ones, for there are more rascals of no consequence than rich and distinguished ones, though they get fewer smiles each. The American people will be plundered as long as the American character is what it is; as long as it is tolerant of successful knaves; as long as American ingenuity draws an imaginary distinction between a man's public character and his private—his commercial and his personal. In brief, the American people will be plundered as long as they deserve to be plundered. No human law can stop, none ought to stop it, for that would abrogate a higher and more salutary law: "As ye sow, ye shall reap."

Living in the age in which the American robber barons flourished, Bierce could not easily fail to observe what became later known as "white-collar crime." Nevertheless, he was aware that not all of these large and dramatic departures from institutional norms in the top economic strata are known, and possibly fewer deviations among the lesser middle classes come to light. Sutherland has repeatedly documented the prevalence of "white-collar criminality" among business men. He notes, further, that many of these crimes were not prosecuted because they were not detected or, if detected, because of "the status of the business man, the trend away from punishment, and the relatively unorganized resentment of the public against white-collar criminals." A study of some 1,700 prevalently middle-class individuals found that "off the record crimes" were common among wholly "respectable" members of society. Ninety-nine per cent of those questioned confessed to having committed one or more of 49 offenses under the penal law of the State of New York, each of these offenses being sufficiently serious to draw a maximum sentence of not less than one year. The mean number of offenses in adult years—this excludes all offenses committed before the age of sixteen—was 18 for men and 11 for women. Fully 64% of the men and 29% of the women acknowledged their guilt on one or more counts of felony which, under the laws of New York, is ground for depriving them of all rights of citizenship. One keynote of these findings is expressed by a minister, referring to false statements he made about a commodity he sold, "I tried truth first, but it's not always successful." On the basis of these results, the authors modestly conclude that "the number of acts legally constituting crimes are far in excess of those officially reported. Unlawful behavior, far from being an abnormal social or psychological manifestation, is in truth a very common phenomenon."

But whatever the differential rates of deviant behavior in the several social strata, and we know from many sources that the official crime statistics uniformly showing higher rates in the lower strata are far from complete or reliable, it appears from our analysis that the greatest pressures toward deviation are exerted upon the lower strata. Cases in point permit us to detect the sociological mechanisms involved in producing these pressures. Several researchers have shown that specialized areas of vice and crime constitute a "normal" response to a situation where the cultural emphasis upon pecuniary success has been absorbed, but where there is little access to conventional and legitimate means for becoming successful. The occupational opportunities of people in these areas are largely confined to manual labor and the lesser white-collar jobs. Given the American stigmatization of manual labor *which has been found to hold rather uniformly in all social classes,* and the absence of realistic opportunities for advancement beyond this level, the result is a marked tendency toward deviant behavior. The status of unskilled labor and the consequent low income cannot readily compete *in terms of established standards of worth* with the promises of power and high income from organized vice, rackets and crime.

For our purposes, these situations exhibit two salient features. First, incentives for success are provided by the established values of the culture, *and* second, the avenues available for moving toward this goal are largely limited by the class structure to those of deviant behavior. It is the *combination* of the cultural emphasis and the social structure which produces intense pressure for deviation. Recourse to legitimate channels for "getting in the money" is limited by a class structure which is not fully open at each level to men of good capacity. Despite our persisting open-class-ideology, advance toward the success-goal is relatively rare and notably difficult for those armed with little formal education and few economic resources. The dominant pressure leads toward the gradual attenuation of legitimate, but by and large ineffectual, strivings and the increasing use of illegitimate, but more or less effective, expedients.

Of those located in the lower reaches of the social structure, the culture makes incompatible demands. On the one hand, they are asked to orient their conduct toward the prospect of large wealth—"Every man a king," said Marden and Carnegie and Long—and on the other, they are largely denied effective opportunities to do so institutionally. The consequence of this structural inconsistency is a high rate of deviant behavior. The equilibrium between culturally designated ends and means becomes highly unstable with progressive emphasis on attaining the prestige-laden ends by any means whatsoever. Within this context, Al Capone represents the triumph of amoral intelligence over morally prescribed "failure," when channels of vertical mobility are closed or narrowed *in a society which places a high premium on economic affluence and social ascent for* all *its members.*

This last qualification is of central importance. It implies that other aspects of the social structure, besides the extreme emphasis on pecuniary success, must be considered if we are to understand the social sources of deviant behavior. A high frequency of deviant behavior is not generated merely by lack of opportunity or by this exaggerated pecuniary emphasis. A comparatively rigidified class structure, a caste order, may limit opportunities far beyond the point which obtains in American society today. It is when a system of cultural values extols, virtually above all else, certain *common* success-goals *for the population at large* while the social structure rigorously restricts or completely closes access to approved modes of reaching these goals *for a considerable part of the same population,* that deviant behavior ensues on a large scale. Otherwise said, our egalitarian ideology denies by implication the existence of non-competing individuals and groups in the pursuit of pecuniary success. Instead, the same body of success-symbols is held to apply for all. Goals are held to transcend class lines, not to be bounded by them, yet the actual social organization is such that there exist class differentials in accessibility of the goals. In this setting, a cardinal American virtue, "ambition," promotes a cardinal American vice, "deviant behavior."

This theoretical analysis may help explain the varying correlations between crime and poverty. "Poverty" is not an isolated variable which operates in precisely the same fashion wherever found; it is only one in a complex of identifiably interdependent social and cultural variables. Poverty as such and consequent limitation of opportunity are not enough to produce a conspicuously high rate of criminal behavior. Even the notorious "poverty in the midst of plenty" will not necessarily lead to this result. But when poverty and associated disadvantages in competing for the culture values approved for *all* members of the society are linked with a cultural emphasis on pecuniary success as a dominant goal, high rates of criminal behavior are the normal outcome. Thus, crude (and not necessarily reliable) crime statistics suggest that poverty is less highly correlated with crime in southeastern Europe than in the United States. The economic life-chances of the poor in these European areas would seem to be even less promising than in this country, so that neither poverty nor its association with limited opportunity is sufficient to account for the varying correlations. However, when we consider the full configuration—poverty, limited opportunity and the assignment of cultural goals—there appears some basis for explaining the higher correlation between poverty and crime in our society than in others where rigidified class structure is coupled with *differential class symbols of success.*

The victims of this contradiction between the cultural emphasis on pecuniary ambition and the social bars to full opportunity are not always aware of the structural sources of their thwarted aspirations. To be sure, they are often aware of a discrepancy between individual worth and social rewards. But they do not necessarily see how this comes about. Those who do find its source in the social structure may become alienated from that structure and become ready candidates for Adaptation V (rebellion). But others, and this appears to include the great majority, may attribute their difficulties to more mystical and less sociological sources. For as the distinguished classicist and sociologist-in-spite-of-himself, Gilbert Murray, has remarked in this general connection, "The best seed-ground for superstition is a society in which the fortunes of men seem to bear practically no relation to their merits and efforts. A stable and well-governed society does tend, speaking roughly, to ensure that the Virtuous and Industrious Apprentice shall succeed in life, while the Wicked and Idle Apprentice fails. And in such a society people tend to lay stress on the reasonable or visible chains of causation. But in [a society suffering from anomie] . . . , the ordinary virtues of diligence, honesty, and kindliness seem to be of little avail." And in such a society people tend to put stress on mysticism: the workings of Fortune, Chance, Luck.

In point of fact, both the eminently "successful" and the eminently "unsuccessful" in our society not infrequently attribute the outcome to "luck." Thus, the prosperous man of business, Julius Rosenwald, declared that 95% of the great fortunes were "due to luck." And a leading business journal, in an editorial explaining the social benefits of great individual wealth, finds it necessary to supplement wisdom with luck as the factors accounting for great fortunes: "When one man through wise investments—aided, we'll grant, by good luck in many cases—accumulates a few millions, he doesn't thereby take something from the rest of us." In much the same fashion, the worker often explains economic status in terms of chance. "The worker sees all about him experienced and skilled men with no work to do. If he is in work, he feels lucky. If he is out of work, he is the victim of hard luck. *He can see little relation between worth and consequences.*"

But these references to the workings of chance and luck serve distinctive functions according to whether they are made by those who have reached or those who have not reached the culturally emphasized goals. For the successful, it is in psychological terms, a disarming expression of modesty. It is far removed from any semblance of conceit to say, in effect, that one was lucky rather than altogether deserving of one's good fortune. In sociological terms, the doctrine of luck as expounded by the successful serves the dual function of explaining the frequent discrepancy between merit and reward while keeping immune from criticism a social structure which allows this discrepancy to become frequent. For if success is primarily a matter of luck, if it is just in the blind nature of things, if it bloweth where it listeth and thou canst not tell whence it cometh or whither it goeth, then surely it is beyond control and will occur in the same measure *whatever the social structure.*

For the unsuccessful and particularly for those among the unsuccessful who find little reward for their merit and their effort, the doctrine of luck serves the psychological function of enabling them to preserve their self-esteem in the face of failure. It may also entail the dysfunction of curbing motivation for sustained endeavor. Sociologically, as implied by Bakke, the doctrine may reflect a failure to comprehend the workings of the social and economic system, and may be dysfunctional inasmuch as it eliminates the rationale of working for structural changes making for greater equities in opportunity and reward.

This orientation toward chance and risk-taking, accentuated by the strain of frustrated aspirations, may help explain the marked interest in gambling—an institutionally proscribed or at best permitted rather than preferred or prescribed mode of activity—within certain social strata.

Among those who do not apply the doctrine of luck to the gulf between merit, effort and reward there may develop an individuated and cynical attitude toward the social structure, best exemplified in the cultural cliche that "it's not what you know, but who you know, that counts."

In societies such as our own, then, the great cultural emphasis on pecuniary success for all and a social structure which unduly limits practical recourse to approved means for many set up a tension toward innovative practices which depart from institutional norms. But this form of adaptation presupposes that individuals have been imperfectly socialized so that they abandon institutional means while retaining the success-aspiration. Among those who have fully internalized the institutional values, however, a comparable situation is more likely to lead to an alternative response in which the goal is abandoned but conformity to the mores persists.❖

❖ Unavoidable Dilemmas ❖

Reinhold Niebuhr (1892–1971), as a young man, was a Protestant minister in the reform tradition. He served a parish in an industrial area of Detroit, where his concern for social justice deepened. This experience influenced his long career as a writer and teacher of social ethics at the Union Theological Seminary in New York City (1928–1960). Niebuhr was a force in progressive politics in New York and a co-founder of the Americans for Democratic Action. His most famous book, *Moral Man and Immoral Society,* published in 1932, was an important contribution to social theory because of its then-stunning critique of the moralistic idea that good individuals filled with love for others could change the world. Nations, he argued, are concerned with power and thus with selfish interests; in politics, one strives for justice, not love. Niebuhr's thinking in 1932 was thus in line with Keynes's insistence that the era of the autonomous individual ended with the more complex political and economic crises that developed with and after World War I. Niebuhr's writings were an important influence on Martin Luther King, Jr., during his student days. King's strategy of forceful nonviolence could be said to be one part Gandhi, another Niebuhr. King certainly shared Niebuhr's idea that in the social realm, love could force justice, if not love.

Moral Man and Immoral Society

Reinhold Niebuhr (1932)

The difference between the attitudes of individuals and those of groups has been frequently alluded to, the thesis being that group relations can never be as ethical as those which characterise individual relations. In dealing with the problem of social justice, it may be found that the relation of economic classes within a state is more important than international relations. But from the standpoint of analysing the ethics of group behavior, it is feasible to study the ethical attitudes of nations first; because the modern nation is the human group of strongest social cohesion, of most undisputed central authority and of most clearly defined membership. The church may have challenged its pre-eminence in the Middle Ages, and the economic class may compete with it for the loyalty of men in our own day; yet it remains, as it has been since the seventeenth century, the most absolute of all human associations.

Nations are territorial societies, the cohesive power of which is supplied by the sentiment of nationality and the authority of the state. The fact that state and nation are not synonymous and that states frequently incorporate several nationalities, indicates that the authority of government is the ultimate force of national cohesion. The fact

Excerpt from *Moral Man and Immoral Society: A Study in Ethics and Politics* by Niebuhr, Reinhold, © 1932. Reprinted by permission of Prentice-Hall, Inc., Upper Saddle River, NJ.

that state and nation are roughly synonymous proves that, without the sentiment of nationality with its common language and traditions, the authority of government is usually unable to maintain national unity. The unity of Scotland and England within a single British state and the failure to maintain the same unity between England and Ireland, suggest both the possibilities and the limitations of transcending nationality in the formation of states. For our purposes we may think of state and nation as interchangeable terms, since our interest is in the moral attitudes of nations which have the apparatus of a state at their disposal, and through it are able to consolidate their social power and define their political attitudes and policies.

The selfishness of nations is proverbial. It was a dictum of George Washington that nations were not to be trusted beyond their own interest. "No state," declares a German author, "has ever entered a treaty for any other reason than self interest," and adds: "A statesman who has any other motive would deserve to be hung." "In every part of the world," said Professor Edward Dicey, "where British interests are at stake, I am in favor of advancing these interests even at the cost of war. The only qualification I admit is that the country we desire to annex or take under our protection should be calculated to confer a tangible advantage upon the British Empire." National ambitions are not always avowed as honestly as this, as we shall see later, but that is a fair statement of the actual facts, which need hardly to be elaborated for any student of history.

What is the basis and reason for the selfishness of nations? If we begin with what is least important or least distinctive of national attitudes, it must be noted that nations do not have direct contact with other national communities, with which they must form some kind of international community. They know the problems of other peoples only indirectly and at second hand. Since both sympathy and justice depend to a large degree upon the perception of need, which makes sympathy flow, and upon the understanding of competing interests, which must be resolved, it is obvious that human communities have greater difficulty than individuals in achieving ethical relationships. While rapid means of communication have increased the breadth of knowledge about world affairs among citizens of various nations, and the general advance of education has ostensibly promoted the capacity to think rationally and justly upon the inevitable conflicts of interest between nations, there is nevertheless little hope of arriving at a perceptible increase of international morality through the growth of intelligence and the perfection of means of communication. The development of international commerce, the increased economic interdependence among the nations, and the whole apparatus of a technological civilisation, increase the problems and issues between nations much more rapidly than the intelligence to solve them can be created.❖

Gunnar Myrdal (1898–1987), the Swedish economist, was in many ways the world statesman of social science in the post–World War II years. Myrdal was awarded the Nobel Prize in Economics in 1974. He authored over forty books in English and Swedish on a wide range of topics in economics, social theory, and social policy. Among them is *Asian Drama: An Inquiry into the Poverty of Nations* (1968). But Myrdal's most important contribution to social theory was *An American Dilemma* (1944)—his sensitive, though firm, critique of the social and economic bases of racial conflict in the United States. "The Negro Problem as a Moral Issue" is from the introduction to this book. Myrdal argues somewhat in the structural manner of

Merton's earlier essay on anomie that race is a moral issue arising out of American economic history but against its moralistic culture. Written near the end of the inter-war period, this work provides a frank assessment of conflict structured into the culture of the rising post–World War II power.

The Negro Problem as a Moral Issue
Gunnar Myrdal (1944)

There is a "Negro problem" in the United States and most Americans are aware of it, although it assumes varying forms and intensity in different regions of the country and among diverse groups of the American people. Americans have to react to it, politically as citizens and, where there are Negroes present in the community, privately as neighbors.

To the great majority of white Americans the Negro problem has distinctly negative connotations. It suggests something difficult to settle and equally difficult to leave alone. It is embarrassing. It makes for moral uneasiness. The very presence of the Negro in America; his fate in this country through slavery, Civil War and Reconstruction; his recent career and his present status; his accommodation; his protest and his aspiration; in fact his entire biological, historical and social existence as a participant American represent to the ordinary white man in the North as well as in the South an anomaly in the very structure of American society. To many, this takes on the proportion of a menace—biological, economic, social, cultural, and, at times, political. This anxiety may be mingled with a feeling of individual and collective guilt. A few see the problem as a challenge to statesmanship. To all it is a trouble.

These and many other mutually inconsistent attitudes are blended into none too logical a scheme which, in turn, may be quite inconsistent with the wider personal, moral, religious, and civic sentiments and ideas of the Americans. Now and then, even the least sophisticated individual becomes aware of his own confusion and the contradiction in his attitudes. Occasionally he may recognize, even if only for a moment, the incongruence of his state of mind and find it so intolerable that the whole organization of his moral precepts is shaken. But most people, most of the time, suppress such threats to their moral integrity together with all of the confusion, the ambiguity, and inconsistency which lurks in the basement of man's soul. This, however, is rarely accomplished without mental strain. Out of the strain comes a sense of uneasiness and awkwardness which always seems attached to the Negro problem.

The strain is increased in democratic America by the freedom left open—even in the South, to a considerable extent—for the advocates of the Negro, his rights and welfare. All "pro-Negro" forces in American society, whether organized or not, and irrespective of their wide differences in both strategy and tactics, sense that this is the situation. They all work on the national conscience. They all seek to fix everybody's attention on the suppressed moral conflict. No wonder that they are often regarded as public nuisances, or worse—even when they succeed in getting grudging concessions to Negro rights and welfare.

At this point it must be observed that America, relative to all the other branches of Western civilization, is moralistic and "moral-conscious." The ordinary American is

---

Excerpt from *An American Dilemma: The Negro Problem and Modern Democracy* (New York: Harper and Bros. Publishers, 1944), pp. xlv–xlvii.

the opposite of a cynic. He is on the average more of a believer and a defender of the faith in humanity than the rest of the Occidentals. It is a relatively important matter to him to be true to his own ideals and to carry them out in actual life. We recognize the American, wherever we meet him, as a practical idealist. Compared with members of other nations of Western civilization, the ordinary American is a rationalistic being, and there are close relations between his moralism and his rationalism. Even romanticism, transcendentalism, and mysticism tend to be, in the American culture, rational, pragmatic and optimistic. American civilization early acquired a flavor of enlightenment which has affected the ordinary American's whole personality and especially his conception of how ideas and ideals ought to "click" together. He has never developed that particular brand of tired mysticism and romanticism which finds delight in the inextricable confusion in the order of things and in ineffectuality of the human mind. He finds such leanings intellectually perverse.

These generalizations might seem venturesome and questionable to the reflective American himself, who, naturally enough, has his attention directed more on the dissimilarities than on the similarities within his culture. What is common is usually not obvious, and it never becomes striking. But to the stranger it is obvious and even striking. In the social sciences, for instance, the American has, more courageously than anywhere else on the globe, started to measure, not only human intelligence, aptitudes, and personality traits, but moral leanings and the "goodness" of communities. This man is a rationalist; he wants intellectual order in his moral set-up; he wants to pursue his own inclinations into their hidden haunts; and he is likely to expose himself and his kind in a most undiplomatic manner.

In hasty strokes we are now depicting the essentials of the American *ethos*. This moralism and rationalism are to many of us—among them the author of this book— the glory of the nation, its youthful strength, perhaps the salvation of mankind. The analysis of this "American Creed" and its implications have an important place in our inquiry. While on the one hand, to such a moralistic and rationalistic being as the ordinary American, the Negro problem and his own confused and contradictory attitudes toward it must be disturbing; on the other hand, the very mass of unsettled problems in his heterogeneous and changing culture, and the inherited liberalistic trust that things will ultimately take care of themselves and get settled in one way or another, enable the ordinary American to live on happily, with recognized contradictions around him and within him, in a kind of bright fatalism which is unmatched in the rest of the Western world. This fatalism also belongs to the national *ethos*.

The American Negro problem is a problem in the heart of the American. It is there that the interracial tension has its focus. It is there that the decisive struggle goes on. This is the central viewpoint of this treatise. Though our study includes economic, social, and political race relations, at bottom our problem is the moral dilemma of the American—the conflict between his moral valuations on various levels of consciousness and generality. The "American Dilemma," referred to in the title of this book, is the ever-raging conflict between, on the one hand, the valuations preserved on the general plane which we shall call the "American Creed," where the American thinks, talks, and acts under the influence of high national and Christian precepts, and, on the other hand, the valuations on specific planes of individual and group living, where personal and local interests; economic, social, and sexual jealousies; considerations of community prestige and conformity; group prejudice against particular persons or types of people; and all sorts of miscellaneous wants, impulses, and habits dominate his outlook.

The American philosopher, John Dewey, whose immense influence is to be explained by his rare gift for projecting faithfully the aspirations and possibilities of the culture he was born into, in the maturity of age and wisdom has written a book on *Freedom and Culture,* in which he says:

> Anything that obscures the fundamentally moral nature of the social problem is harmful, no matter whether it proceeds from the side of physical or of psychological theory. Any doctrine that eliminates or even obscures the function of choice of values and enlistment of desires and emotions in behalf of those chosen weakens personal responsibility for judgment and for action. It thus helps create the attitudes that welcome and support the totalitarian state.❖

William I. Thomas (1863–1947) and **Florian Znaniecki** (1882–1958) collaborated in the research and writing that led to the first truly classic work in American sociology. *The Polish Peasant in Europe and America* (1918–1919) remains a source of ideas, a case study for methods, and a landmark study of an immigrant population during the period when America was still attempting to redefine itself in response to the influx of European workers. "Disorganization of the Polish Immigrant," from *Polish Peasant,* illustrates their sensitive use of personal documents to define the social disorganization of the Polish immigrant in relation to the conflict of Old World and New World cultures. It is empirical social theory at its best.

Though they respected each other and worked closely over a number of years, Thomas and Znaniecki came from very different backgrounds. Thomas had been born in rural Virginia to a family of modest means and grew up in the mountains of Tennessee. At the University of Tennessee, teachers inspired his love of scholarship. He studied in Germany from 1888 to 1889, after which he taught at Oberlin. He then taught at the University of Chicago, whose department of sociology is considered the founding department of the discipline in the United States. It is said that Thomas's interest in personal documents came from the chance discovery of a personal letter in the trash in one of Chicago's Polish neighborhoods. In his subsequent work, Thomas pursued the value of personal documents in the ethnographic study of urban communities. His career was ruined when, at age fifty-five, he was dismissed from the university for unproven morals charges.

Znaniecki was born into nobility in Poland. He studied in Warsaw, Geneva, and Paris before receiving his Ph.D. in philosophy from the University of Cracow in 1909. Znaniecki first met Thomas in Poland in 1913. They renewed their relationship when Thomas fled Europe for Chicago during World War I. Znaniecki's native knowledge of the Polish people soon led to his active role in the *Polish Peasant* project. But he returned to a university position in Poland after the war, where he would define himself as a sociologist and found the Polish Sociological Institute. In the 1930s, Znaniecki visited Columbia University and eventually settled permanently in the United States after accepting a position at the University of Illinois. He was president of the American Sociological Society in 1953. Thomas, too, had been so honored in 1927 when younger members of the society pressed his candidacy, in part to rectify the injustice done him by the University of Chicago. Znaniecki died in 1958, eleven years after Thomas.

Disorganization of the Polish Immigrant

William I. Thomas and Florian Znaniecki (1918–1920)

There are from the sociological viewpoint two very different types of crime—crime within the individual's own group and crime committed by the individual outside of his group. What are the limits of the individual's own group in any particular case depends on the range within which the ties of active social solidarity are acknowledged by him as binding. Thus, for the savage these limits are those of his particular tribe; for the ignorant old-type peasant they practically coincide with his primary community; for the average modern civilized man they are those of his nation; for the conscious socialist they extend as far as the working class; for the practical Christian they include the whole human race; for the habitual criminal they are not much wider than his gang. Of course, in many cases the lines cannot be drawn exactly, for there may be several degrees of solidarity which the individual acknowledges and in a decreasing measure; for instance, the family, the community or acquaintance milieu, the city, and the nation are the individual's own groups. Nor are the two types of crime always sharply distinguishable in practice; there are complex intermediary types in which the characters of the two fundamental types are mixed in various proportions. . . .

When studying murder among other crimes in peasant communities in Poland, we had to deal chiefly with the first type of crime, i.e., with murder committed within the individual's own group. Indeed, murders of strangers are surprisingly rare among peasants. The reason is simple. The social contacts between the individual and the social world outside of his own community are relatively few and superficial, so that there is not much motive for violence, whereas, quite independently of any considerations of social solidarity, the peasant needs really strong motives for any abnormal acts because of the stable and regulated character of his habitual life and because of the strength of his desire for security. There were, indeed, many murders committed upon strangers during the period which we have investigated, . . . but these happened mainly in towns and were the outcome of the social conditions created by the revolution of 1905–6 and could be adequately understood only in connection with a study of this revolution. In peasant life a murder is usually the tragic solution of some difficult social situation involving powerful individual tendencies, a set of social conditions which make it impossible for the individual to realize these tendencies without removing the person, or persons who stand in his way, and almost always the feeling that he has been wronged and that this person or persons have broken first the principle of solidarity. Greed, fear, sexual desire, jealousy, and revenge, mostly exaggerated by long brooding, constitute the usual factors of murder, and it is clear that situations giving rise to such emotions are apt to develop only within the individual's own group.

Now, from what we know already about the weakening of all social bonds and traditions among the immigrants, we can expect that here the nature of crime in general and of murder in particular must be very different. On the one hand, most of the motives which actuated the peasant in the old country either do not exist any longer or are greatly weakened, precisely because all social ties are loosened. An individual seldom, if ever, finds himself here in a situation which seems to him insoluble except through murder, for his wishes, less determined by tradition, are less exclusive; he has

Excerpt from Eli Zaretsky, ed., *The Polish Peasant in Europe and America* (Urbana: University of Illinois Press, 1984 [1918–1920]), pp. 281–290. Reprinted by permission.

usually many ways of satisfying them, and no institutional bonds can hold him against his will. There is no need of recurring to violent means in order to get rid of one's undesirable family members, for one can simply desert them. A house or a sum of money which the individual may inherit after the death of his parents does not mean here even approximately as much as the smallest farm in the old country either in its bearing on the individual's social position or even from the purely economic standpoint relatively to his earning power. Sexual desire can be satisfied outside of the one legal way of marriage. Jealousy still exists but is in most cases weakened by the consciousness that it is possible to have many other men or women beside the unfaithful one. The fear of social opinion can hardly compel the average individual to murder as an alternative to some shameful disclosure, for social opinion has much less influence and can be easily avoided by moving away. The desire for revenge cannot be as deep as in the old country for here an individual has less chance to inflict a really serious wrong upon another, and, since the claims of solidarity have lost most of their old meaning, a break of solidarity is less resented as such.

But if thus the tragic murder, the murder with powerful motives committed within one's own group, becomes relatively rare here for lack of motives, there is a wide field for the second type of murder, the murder without internal conflict and tragedy committed outside of the criminal's group. The immigrant gets into contact with outsiders, with people not belonging to his family, community, or even race incomparably more than he ever did, and even the members of his old community living in changed conditions and no longer constituting one coherent group often become estranged from him. His usual attitude toward this social environment is not that of mere indifference. It is essentially defensive, full of mistrust, of a vague feeling of danger, of a continual expectation of wrong or offense. Mistrust toward strangers was the habitual attitude of the peasant, developed by centuries of cultural isolation and by a subordinate social status which made the peasant community often suffer from unexpected social evils whose source it could not control. The immigrant's experiences in this country, sometimes involving exploitation, often humiliation, and always full of things and happenings and human acts whose meaning he only vaguely grasps, contribute, of course, to maintain and develop this attitude of general mistrust and his first movement is usually one of apprehension or implicit hostility. Furthermore, the nervousness brought by the unsettled conditions of life makes him easily exaggerate the slightest wrong. This is the background which helps us to understand cases like the following.

Joseph Opalski, murderer of Joseph Stanczak. Joseph Opalski had been boarding with Joseph Stanczak. Stanczak was 37 years old and had been in this country 8 years. He was born in Russian Poland and married there. He had with him in Chicago his wife and 2 children, 10 and 2 years old. From the testimony at the trial of Opalski it appeared that the relations between Mrs. Stanczak and Opalski were the common gossip of the neighborhood, "but nobody wanted to interfere with him." It was well known that Stanczak wished him to leave, "but the wife wanted him to stay. Three months ago Opalski beat him up also, cutting his head. He [Opalski] had more to say in the house than the deceased." Further trouble was expected by all concerned.

One Sunday night, August 29th, Joseph Stanczak asked his brother Feliks to stay with him all night. Whether he was actually afraid of Opalski or wished his brother's help in driving the obnoxious boarder out of the house is not clear. They were all drinking beer together. Opalski said he did not drink anything but went to bed early, though he could not sleep. After he had gone to his room, where the Stanczak boy also slept, Joseph Stanczak "made two breaks to go into the room," but was stopped by his wife, who complained that she was sick and did not want any noise. Later, about 1 p.m. Stanczak went to the saloon for more beer and his brother stepped out for a moment. Mrs. Stanczak, her woman boarder, and her brother-in-law, who lived upstairs, entered Opalski's room and begged him to leave the house because Stanczak and his brother were planning to cut him up with a knife, "they were going to show him American court." He slipped quietly out of the house. When the brothers returned they went to bed, Joseph with his wife and his brother with the woman boarder—who had a husband and 2 children in the old country and an illegitimate child here.

Opalski states in his confession: "I went over to Peter Altman's house. . . . There I put on my shoes, coat, and hat, and went back to Stanczak's and entered by the rear door. Finding the two Stanczak brothers, Joe and Feliks, I said: 'If you are so strong, why, commence now.' Joseph ran towards me, struck me with his fist right by my right ear. I had a file which I carried inside with me; I pulled it out of my pocket and struck Joseph on the head with it. He fell down on his side and then Feliks ran toward me and I struck him twice on the head with the file. And he staggered against the stove and called out 'Women, help!' Feliks ran into the bedroom and Joe was about to get up. When I seen him getting up, the file slipped from my hand and I grabbed the chair and beat him with it on the head. The chair broke in pieces and he fell down again. I don't know how or when the women got out but they were gone at that time. I went into the front bedroom and got my revolver, which I had bought from a pawn man a few months before. . . . I bought it with the intention of killing Joseph Stanczak after a fight I had 3 months ago.

"I then went to Joseph Polowski at 49th St. I got there about 4 A.M. His brother-in-law opened the door and I asked him if Joe Polowski was home. He answered: 'Yes, he just came home a few minutes ago.' He let me in and I went to bed with Joe and I told him I could not sleep at home because the two brothers were fighting. Joe Polowski got up at 5.30 A.M. and went to work and I slept until about noon. Got up and ate breakfast and left there and rode to Stephen Malecki's, 26th St. I got there about 2 P.M. I changed into my Sunday clothes and left there about 4 P.M. I went downtown to see a show on State St. I left the theater at 9 P.M. and then I came home to Peter Altman's . . . and slept in the kitchen until 8 o'clock in the morning, August 31st. Then I got my revolver and went to Joseph Stanczak's. I entered by the kitchen door and went into the bedroom where Joseph Stanczak was sleeping and fired three shots at him. He was asleep. There was nobody else in the house at the time and nobody knew my intention that I know of. . . . [Went to his friends; hid the revolver; the next day went to work. The day after] I ate my supper at Stephen Weybeck's, 26th St. They mentioned that Joseph Stanczak was dead, but I didn't answer when they told me. I went down to Stanczak's place and Josephine Stanczak and Josephine Okrasina [the woman boarder] and Binkowski [Stanczak's brother-in-law] was there. And Binkowski told me that Joseph Stanczak was dead, and I answered that his time was come. The women were in bed asleep and I went to bed and slept with little John Stanczak. And no more was said about the death. The morning of September 2nd I got up at 9.30 and went to work. I worked until 1.30 P.M. At the time I was arrested. . . . "

Q. Weren't you living with her just the same as if you were married to her?
A. No, never.
Q. Why did you do this?
A. [I] done this just because I knew that this man lived long enough. He killed one in the old country. He cut a man out there with a razor.

Q. Was this man in the old country that was killed by Joseph Stanczak a relative of yours?

A. I don't know this man at all.

—From the *Records of the Cook County Criminal Court*

There is a common feature in all these cases of murder of the second type. The crime is always a reaction to some present or past act of aggression. The act may be insignificant in its outward manifestation—perhaps no more than a slighting remark or an expression of boisterousness; it may be even only a reaction to the murderer's own aggressive move. Evidently, however, it is not the objective side of the act which is important, but the meaning given to it by the man who answers by a murderous attempt. Now, this meaning is clear; the aggressive act is interpreted by the individual against whom it is directed as a provocation to fight. The psychological background of this interpretation is that general mistrust toward the social environment, the vague expectation of hostility which we have above characterized.

Even so, however, this does not explain why an apparent provocation to fight should ever lead him to a murderous assault. A socially normal individual might ignore the provocation, or appeal to his social milieu for arbitration, or have recourse to law as an instrument of struggle and redress, or indulge in a fist fight, or finally, follow the traditional code of honor of European nobility and fight a regular duel. The murderous reaction implies in the immigrant a predisposition different from those which we find in any organized society. The explanation seems to lie in the fact that the murderer does not feel himself backed in his dealings with the outside world by any strong social group of his own and is not conscious of being the member of a steadily organized society. His family is too weak and scattered to give him a safe social refuge where he could obtain all the response and recognition he needs and ignore outside provocations in the feeling of his social importance and security. The new Polish-American community is not a proper arbiter in personal struggles, since it does not have any coercive power and is in general not much interested in individual needs. The American law and police system are too different from what the peasant considers proper justice to become identified in his eyes with social order; they stand usually for a power which is often incomprehensible in its impersonal, institutional character and seems arbitrary in its applications from case to case. The Polish peasant likes to appeal to law as an instrument of fight and would very frequently do so during the first period of his stay in this country if he understood the institutions. But often by the time he begins to be able to utilize these institutions he has already forgotten the tradition of going to law in personal struggles and become accustomed to the idea of self-redress.

The Polish peasant is not and cannot be exactly the same kind of man as the native American, for his character has been molded by his social milieu and his social milieu has a set of traditions, an organization, and a form and standard of living very different in their concrete complexity from those which are familiar to the American reader. Anyone whose attitudes have evolved under the influence of the rapidly changing American life, which is full of new experiences, anyone trained to look toward unfamiliar emergencies and to meet them by his own initiative, who is accustomed and ready to be influenced in behavior as much, or more, by the indirect stimulation of the written or printed word as by direct human contact, and anyone for whom the impersonal political, legal, social, and economic institutions, with their general and abstract methods of dealing with human life are as real in their practical significance as immediately responsive personalities can neither understand the Polish peasant in Poland nor deal with him as immigrant in this country unless he realizes the full meaning of the following facts.

First, the peasant was adapted to the life of a permanent agricultural community, settled for many hundreds of years in the same locality and changing so slowly that each generation adapted itself to the changes with very little effort or abstract reflection. Secondly, the peasant was not accustomed to expect unfamiliar happenings in the course of his life within his community, and if they came he relied upon his group, which not only gave him assistance, when necessary, in accordance with the principle of solidarity, but helped him regain his mental balance and recover the feeling that life in general was normal in spite of the unexpected disturbance. Further, the peasant drew all his social stimulations, checks, and suggestions from direct social contact with his milieu, and the steadiness and efficiency of his life organization depended on the continuity of his social intercourse with his own group. Finally, he was until quite recently a member of a politically and culturally passive class and did not participate consciously, even in the slightest measure, in any of the impersonal institutions that ever existed in his country.

In view of all this it is not strange that in the different conditions which he finds in this country he becomes more or less disorganized. In fact it is surprising that there is yet so much normal life left and that as time goes on constructive forces assert themselves increasingly in Polish-American communities. This is due entirely and exclusively to the social spirit of the immigrant, to his tendency to form groups, to his traditional ability for social organization. This ability is put here to a more severe test than ever before. Scattered and isolated within a practically unknown, usually indifferent, often contemptuous, sometimes even hostile society, in poor and insecure economic conditions, with very insufficient leadership, and a partly pretentious, selfish, nationalistic . . . formulation of ideals by this leadership, these small groups of people, whose higher interests were indissolubly bound up with their old milieu and who, separated from this milieu, have lost the only real foundation of their cultural life, have already almost succeeded in uniting themselves into one cultural body and in creating institutions which are indubitably factors of progress. These institutions have not prevented a rapid demoralization of those who remain outside of their influence, for the new system is neither as rich nor as efficient in controlling the individual as was the old organization, doomed to decay in the new conditions, but this task is beyond the powers of Polish-American society as isolated from American society.

Even if the Polish-American society should maintain in general that separation which its leaders have wished, the cultural level of a *Polonia Americana* would always remain lower than that of American society, since its best men are and always will be attracted by the wider and richer field of American civilization. But as to the Polish-American institutions already created, their destruction would mean the removal of the only barrier which now stands between the mass of Polish immigrants and complete wildness. The only method which can check demoralization and make of the immigrants—and particularly of their descendants—valuable and culturally productive members of the American society, and imperceptibly and without violence lead to their real Americanization is to supplement the existing Polish-American institutions by others—many others—built on a similar foundation but in closer contact with American society.

It must be always remembered that very little can be achieved by dealing with the immigrant sporadically and individually by the case method. The Polish immigrant is an essentially social being—not "man," not "woman," not "child," in the abstract, but a group member, to be dealt with *in groups*. The only question is how to form groups, and mixed groups including a large percentage of native Americans, with really important productive purposes. There is the enormous, almost untouched field of economic cooperation. A countrywide net of thousands, hundreds of thousands of small cooperative associations, with the active participation of various nationalities, coming together on a basis of real equality and united by serious common aims would do incomparably more for economic self-dependence, for the prevention of demoralization, for the development of active solidarity, and for a genuine Americanization of the immigrant than anything that has ever been done to achieve these aims. It would, besides, contribute in a measure to the solution of many of the most difficult problems which American society itself is trying to solve at this moment.

The prevalent general social unrest and demoralization is due to the decay of the primary group organization, which gave the individual a sense of responsibility and security because he *belonged to something*. This system has given way partly to the forces making for individual efficiency, and we have developed nothing to take its place—no organization which would restore the sense of social responsibility without limiting the efficiency of the individual. This new form is apparently destined to be the cooperative society, and all immigrant groups, among them perhaps preeminently the Poles, bring to this country precisely the attitudes upon which cooperative enterprises can be built.❖

Frederic M. Thrasher (1892–1962) was one of many American sociologists trained in urban studies by the University of Chicago. *The Gang: A Study of 1,313 Gangs in Chicago* (1926), like Thomas and Znaniecki's *Polish Peasant,* is an exhaustive ethnographic study of an urban dilemma, resulting in important theoretical inventions. Also like *Polish Peasant,* Thrasher's study is one of the reasons why the Chicago School is known for its explorations of the urban underworld. In many of the studies in this tradition, one sees the early outlines of a strong theory of social deviance as a normal result of modern urban life. Here, the member's attachment to the deviant gang is explained as a normal search for social status. Though such insights are not surprising today, these early theories of deviance are important instances of social theory's willingness to study the other, darker side of modern life. Chicago was, in the interwar period, a vibrant urban center *and* a welter of social disorganization created by the conflicts of ethnic cultures, economic change, and class differences.

Personality and Status Within the Gang
Frederic M. Thrasher (1927)

The significance of the sociological conception of personality—namely, as the role of the individual in the group—comes out clearly in the study of the gang.

Every boy in the gang acquires a personality (in the sociological sense) and a name—is a person; that is, he plays a part and gets a place with reference to the other members of the group. In the developed gang he fits into his niche like a block in a puzzle box; he is formed by the discipline the gang imposes upon him. He cannot be studied intelligently or understood apart from this social role.

Excerpt from James F. Short, Jr., ed., *The Gang: A Study of 1,313 Gangs in Chicago,* abridged ed. (Chicago: University of Chicago Press, 1963 [1927]), pp. 228–231. Copyright 1927 by The University of Chicago; abridged edition copyright 1963 by The University of Chicago. Reprinted by permission.

Each gang as a whole, and other types of social groups as well, may be conceived of as possessing an action pattern. Every person in the group performs his characteristic function with reference to others, or to put it another way, fills the individual niche that previous experience in the gang has determined for him. Lacking the group, personality in the sense here used would not exist.

Yet the action pattern which characterizes each group can hardly be thought of as rigid and static; for it must be constantly changing to accommodate losses and additions of personnel, changes in its members due to growth and increasing experience, and other changes within and without the gang.

The conflicts of the gang with outsiders and the execution of its other enterprises and activities result in a sort of social stratification in its membership. There are usually three, more or less well-defined, classes of members: the "inner circle," which includes the leader and his lieutenants; the rank and file, who constitute members of the gang in good standing; and the "fringers," who are more or less hangers-on and are not considered regular members. These three groups are well illustrated in the case of Itschkie's Black Hand Society.

The inner circle is usually composed of a constellation of especially intimate pals formed about the leader. The rank and file—the less enterprising and less capable—are subordinated to the inner circle, just as it, in turn, tends to be subordinated to the leader. Most gangs are not closed corporations, however, but have a certain group of hangers-on or associates—the fringers, who may be "kid followers" or admirers. They constitute a sort of nebulous ring, not to be counted on to go the full length in any exploit and likely to disappear entirely in case of trouble. Yet the gang usually tolerates them for their applause and their occasional usefulness. A gang in embryo sometimes forms in this fringe.

Internally the gang may be viewed as a struggle for recognition. It offers the underprivileged boy probably his best opportunity to acquire status and hence it plays an essential part in the development of his personality.

This struggle in the gang takes the form of both conflict and competition, which operate to locate each individual with reference to the others. As a result the gang becomes a constellation of personal interrelationships with the leader playing the central and guiding role. It may be considered as a "unity of interacting personalities"; but it may also be regarded as an accommodation of conflicting individualities more or less definitely subordinated and superordinated with reference to each other and the leader.

It is in these very roles, subordinate though they may be, that personality is developed. Any standing in the group is better than none, and there is always the possibility of improving one's status. Participation in gang activities means everything to the boy. It not only defines for him his position in the only society he is greatly concerned with, but it becomes the basis for his conception of himself. The gang boy might well say "I would rather be a fringer in the hang-out of the gang than to dwell in the swell joints of the dukes forever."

For this reason the gang boy's conception of his role is more vivid with reference to his gang than to other social groups. Since he lives largely in the present, he conceives of the part he is playing in life as being in the gang; his status in other groups is unimportant to him, for the gang is his social world. In striving to realize the role he hopes to take he may assume a tough pose, commit feats of daring or of vandalism, or become a criminal. Thus, his conception of his essential role as being in the gang helps to explain why the larger community finds difficulty in controlling him.

If acquiring a court record, or being "put away" in an institution, gives him prestige in the gang, society is simply promoting his rise to power, rather than punishing or "reforming" him. Agencies which would attempt to redirect the boy delinquent must reach him through his vital social groups where an appeal can be made to his essential conception of himself.

There is a process of selection in the gang, as a result of the struggle for status, whereby the ultimate position of each individual is determined. The result of this process depends largely upon the individual differences—both native and acquired—which characterize the members of the group. Other things being equal, a big strong boy has a better chance than a "shrimp." Natural differences in physique are important and physical defects play a part. Natural and acquired aptitudes give certain individuals advantages. Traits of character, as well as physical differences, are significant; these include beliefs, sentiments, habits, special skills, and so on. If all members of the gang were exactly alike, status and personality could only be determined by chance differences in opportunity arising in the process of gang activity. In reality, both factors play a part.❖

Walter Benjamin (1892–1940) was one of the more mythical figures among those associated with the Frankfurt School. This is due, in part, to the acknowledged brilliance of his writings, which have enjoyed a renewed popularity among literary theorists in recent years. In addition, he died a martyr. In 1938, Benjamin refused Adorno's urging to join other members of the Frankfurt School in New York. He was committed to pursuing an intellectual and political course in Europe (at the time, in Paris) and was ambivalent about life in the United States. He was arrested by the collaborationist French government, but was later released from a Nazi internment camp through an international effort on his behalf. While trying to escape from France across the Spanish border, he was emotionally overwhelmed by a combination of ill health, the likelihood of arrest, and the impact of the tragedy that had befallen Europe. He committed suicide at age forty-eight. Though the selection "Art, War, and Fascism" is short, it reveals Benjamin's incisive mind at work analyzing the aesthetic perversions of fascism.

Art, War, and Fascism
Walter Benjamin (1936)

The growing proletarianization of modern man and the increasing formation of masses are two aspects of the same process. Fascism attempts to organize the newly created proletarian masses without affecting the property structure which the masses strive to eliminate. Fascism sees its salvation in giving these masses not their right, but instead a chance to express themselves. The masses have a right to change property relations; Fascism seeks to give them an expression while preserving property. The logical result of Fascism is the introduction of aesthetics into political life. The violation of the

Excerpt from Epilogue from "The Work of Art in the Age of Mechanical Reproduction," Hannah Arendt, ed., Harry Zohn, trans., *Illuminations*, pp. 243–244. 1955 by Suhrkamp Verlag, Frankfurt a.M., English trans. 1968 by Harcourt Brace & Co., reprinted by permission of Harcourt Brace & Co.

masses, whom Fascism, with its *Führer* cult, forces to their knees, has its counterpart in the violation of an apparatus which is pressed into the production of ritual values.

All efforts to render politics aesthetic culminate in one thing: war. War and war only can set a goal for mass movements on the largest scale while respecting the traditional property system. This is the political formula for the situation. The technological formula may be stated as follows: Only war makes it possible to mobilize all of today's technical resources while maintaining the property system. It goes without saying that the Fascist apotheosis of war does not employ such arguments. Still, Marinetti says in his manifesto on the Ethiopian colonial war: "For twenty-seven years we Futurists have rebelled against the branding of war as antiaesthetic. . . . Accordingly we state: . . . War is beautiful because it establishes man's dominion over the subjugated machinery by means of gas masks, terrifying megaphones, flame throwers, and small tanks. War is beautiful because it initiates the dreamt-of metalization of the human body. War is beautiful because it enriches a flowering meadow with the fiery orchids of machine guns. War is beautiful because it combines the gunfire, the cannonades, the cease-fire, the scents, and the stench of putrefaction into a symphony. War is beautiful because it creates new architecture, like that of the big tanks, the geometrical formation flights, the smoke spirals from burning villages, and many others. . . . Poets and artists of Futurism! . . . remember these principles of an aesthetics of war so that your struggle for a new literature and a new graphic art . . . may be illumined by them!"

This manifesto has the virtue of clarity. Its formulations deserve to be accepted by dialecticians. To the latter, the aesthetics of today's war appears as follows: If the natural utilization of productive forces is impeded by the property system, the increase in technical devices, in speed, and in the sources of energy will press for an unnatural utilization, and this is found in war. The destructiveness of war furnishes proof that society has not been mature enough to incorporate technology as its organ, that technology has not been sufficiently developed to cope with the elemental forces of society. The horrible features of imperialistic warfare are attributable to the discrepancy between the tremendous means of production and their inadequate utilization in the process of production—in other words, to unemployment and the lack of markets. Imperialistic war is a rebellion of technology which collects, in the form of "human material," the claims to which society has denied its natural material. Instead of draining rivers, society directs a human stream into a bed of trenches; instead of dropping seeds from airplanes, it drops incendiary bombs over cities; and through gas warfare the aura is abolished in a new way.

"*Fiat ars—pereat mundus,*" says Fascism, and, as Marinetti admits, expects war to supply the artistic gratification of a sense perception that has been changed by technology. This is evidently the consummation of "*l'art pour l'art.*" Mankind, which in Homer's time was an object of contemplation for the Olympian gods, now is one for itself. Its self-alienation has reached such a degree that it can experience its own destruction as an aesthetic pleasure of the first order. This is the situation of politics which Fascism is rendering aesthetic. Communism responds by politicizing art. ❖

Virginia Woolf (1882–1941), the English novelist, biographer, and literary critic, is one of the most important writers of the twentieth century. Her fiction includes *The Voyage Out* (1915), *Mrs. Dalloway* (1925), and *To the Lighthouse* (1927). "A Room of One's Own" is possibly her most famous essay. As the text indicates, it began as a lecture on women and fiction. This essay became one of the most widely used points of reference for postwar feminism, particularly among academic and literary feminists who had to balance the demands of family and work with those of the creative life. The delicately powerful description of a woman's experience on the manicured lawns of Oxbridge, like Charlotte Gilman's *The Yellow Wallpaper,* is a fictionalized but powerful attack on the not-so-subtle forces of patriarchal culture. It is theory that requires no further explanation.

A Room of One's Own

Virginia Woolf (1929)

But, you may say, we asked you to speak about women and fiction—what has that got to do with a room of one's own? I will try to explain. When you asked me to speak about women and fiction I sat down on the banks of a river and began to wonder what the words meant. They might mean simply a few remarks about Fanny Burney; a few more about Jane Austen; a tribute to the Brontës and a sketch of Haworth Parsonage under snow; some witticisms if possible about Miss Mitford; a respectful allusion to George Eliot; a reference to Mrs. Gaskell and one would have done. But at second sight the words seemed not so simple. The title women and fiction might mean, and you may have meant it to mean, women and what they are like; or it might mean women and the fiction that they write; or it might mean women and the fiction that is written about them; or it might mean that somehow all three are inextricably mixed together and you want me to consider them in that light. But when I began to consider the subject in this last way, which seemed the most interesting, I soon saw that it had one fatal drawback. I should never be able to come to a conclusion. I should never be able to fulfil what is, I understand, the first duty of a lecturer—to hand you after an hour's discourse a nugget of pure truth to wrap up between the pages of your notebooks and keep on the mantel-piece for ever. All I could do was to offer you an opinion upon one minor point—a woman must have money and a room of her own if she is to write fiction; and that, as you will see, leaves the great problem of the true nature of woman and the true nature of fiction unsolved. I have shirked the duty of coming to a conclusion upon these two questions—women and fiction remain, so far as I am concerned, unsolved problems. But in order to make some amends I am going to do what I can to show you how I arrived at this opinion about the room and the money. I am going to develop in your presence as fully and freely as I can the train of thought which led me to think this. Perhaps if I lay bare the ideas, the prejudices, that lie behind this statement you will find that they have some bearing upon women and some upon fiction. At any rate, when a subject is highly controversial—and any question about sex is that—one cannot hope to tell the truth. One can only show how one came to hold whatever opinion one does hold. One can only give one's audience the chance of drawing their own conclusions as they observe the limitations, the prejudices, the idiosyncrasies of the speaker. Fiction here is likely to contain more truth than fact. Therefore I propose, making use of all the liberties and licences of a novelist, to tell you the story of the two days that preceded my coming here—how, bowed down by the weight of the subject which you have laid upon my shoulders, I pondered it, and made it work in and out of my daily life. I need not say that what I am about to describe has no existence; Oxbridge is an invention; so is Fernham; "I" is only a convenient term for somebody who has no real being. Lies will flow from my lips, but there may perhaps be some truth mixed up with them; it is for you to seek out this truth and to decide whether any part of it is worth keeping. If not, you will of course throw the whole of it into the wastepaper basket and forget all about it.

Here then was I (call me Mary Beton, Mary Seton, Mary Carmichael or by any name you please—it is not a matter of any importance) sitting on the banks of a river a week or two ago in fine October weather, lost in thought. That collar I have spoken of, women and fiction, the need of coming to some conclusion on a subject that raises all sorts of prejudices and passions, bowed my head to the ground. To the right and left bushes of some sort, golden and crimson, glowed with the colour, even it seemed burnt with the heat, of fire. On the further bank the willows wept in perpetual lamentation, their hair about their shoulders. The river reflected whatever it chose of sky and bridge and burning tree, and when the undergraduate had oared his boat through the reflections they closed again, completely, as if he had never been. There one might have sat the clock round lost in thought. Thought—to call it by a prouder name than it deserved—had let its line down into the stream. It swayed, minute after minute, hither and thither among the reflections and the weeds, letting the water lift it and sink it, until—you know the little tug—the sudden conglomeration of an idea at the end of one's line: and then the cautious hauling of it in, and the careful laying of it out? Alas, laid on the grass how small, how insignificant this thought of mine looked; the sort of fish that a good fisherman puts back into the water so that it may grow fatter and be one day worth cooking and eating. I will not trouble you with that thought now, though if you look carefully you may find it for yourselves in the course of what I am going to say.

But however small it was, it had, nevertheless, the mysterious property of its kind—put back into the mind, it became at once very exciting, and important; and as it darted and sank, and flashed hither and thither, set up such a wash and tumult of ideas that it was impossible to sit still. It was thus that I found myself walking with extreme rapidity across a grass plot. Instantly a man's figure rose to intercept me. Nor did I at first understand that the gesticulations of a curious-looking object, in a cut-away coat and evening shirt, were aimed at me. His face expressed horror and indignation. Instinct rather than reason came to my help; he was a Beadle; I was a woman. Thus was the turf; there was the path. Only the Fellows and Scholars are allowed here; the gravel is the place for me. Such thoughts were the work of a moment. As I regained the path the arms of the Beadle sank, his face assumed its usual repose, and though turf is better walking than gravel, no very great harm was done. The only charge I could bring against the Fellows and Scholars of whatever the college might happen to be was that in protection of their turf, which has been rolled for 300 years in succession, they had sent my little fish into hiding.❖

Antonio Gramsci (1891–1937) was born in Sardinia. He studied at the University of Turin, where he became active in the Italian Socialist Party. By 1924 he became a founder and leader of the Italian Communist Party. Gramsci's literary, journalistic, and political activities eventually led to his arrest in 1926. He spent most of the balance of his life in prison, where he wrote his famous *Prison Notebooks,* from which the following selections are taken. Gramsci greatly broadened Marxist thinking on the role of intellectuals in the political process and the social hegemony, both of which would influence later social and cultural theory.

Intellectuals and Hegemony

Antonio Gramsci (1929–1936)

All men are intellectuals, one could therefore say: but not all men have in society the function of intellectuals.*

When one distinguishes between intellectuals and non-intellectuals, one is referring in reality only to the immediate social function of the professional category of the intellectuals, that is, one has in mind the direction in which their specific professional activity is weighted, whether towards intellectual elaboration or towards muscular-nervous effort. This means that, although one can speak of intellectuals, one cannot speak of non-intellectuals, because non-intellectuals do not exist. But even the relationship between efforts of intellectual-cerebral elaboration and muscular-nervous effort is not always the same, so that there are varying degrees of specific intellectual activity. There is no human activity from which every form of intellectual participation can be excluded: *homo faber* cannot be separated from *homo sapiens*. Each man, finally, outside his professional activity, carries on some form of intellectual activity, that is, he is a "philosopher", an artist, a man of taste, he participates in a particular conception of the world, has a conscious line of moral conduct, and therefore contributes to sustain a conception of the world or to modify it, that is, to bring into being new modes of thought. . . .

It is worth noting that the elaboration of intellectual strata in concrete reality does not take place on the terrain of abstract democracy but in accordance with very concrete traditional historical processes. Strata have grown up which traditionally "produce" intellectuals and these strata coincide with those which have specialised in "saving", i.e. the petty and middle landed bourgeoisie and certain strata of the petty and middle urban bourgeoisie. The varying distribution of different types of school (classical and professional) over the "economic" territory and the varying aspirations of different categories within these strata determine, or give form to, the production of various branches of intellectual specialisation. Thus in Italy the rural bourgeoisie produces in particular state functionaries and professional people, whereas the urban bourgeoisie produces technicians for industry. Consequently it is largely northern Italy which produces technicians and the South which produces functionaries and professional men.

---

* Thus, because it can happen that everyone at some time fries a couple of eggs or sews up a tear in a jacket, we do not necessarily say that everyone is a cook or a tailor.

The relationship between the intellectuals and the world of production is not as direct as it is with the fundamental social groups but is, in varying degrees, "mediated" by the whole fabric of society and by the complex of superstructures, of which the intellectuals are, precisely, the "functionaries". It should be possible both to measure the "organic quality" [*organicità*] of the various intellectual strata and their degree of connection with a fundamental social group, and to establish a gradation of their functions and of the superstructures from the bottom to the top (from the structural base upwards). What we can do, for the moment, is to fix two major superstructural "levels": the one that can be called "civil society", that is the ensemble of organisms commonly called "private", and that of "political society" or "the State". These two levels correspond on the one hand to the function of "hegemony" which the dominant group exercises throughout society and on the other hand to that of "direct domination" or command exercised through the State and "juridical" government. The functions in question are precisely organisational and connective. The intellectuals are the dominant group's "deputies" exercising the subaltern functions of social hegemony and political government. . . .

The philosophy of praxis does not tend to leave the "simple" in their primitive philosophy of common sense, but rather to lead them to a higher conception of life. If it affirms the need for contact between intellectuals and the simple, it is not in order to restrict scientific activity and preserve unity at the low level of the masses, but precisely in order to construct an intellectual moral bloc which can make politically possible the intellectual progress of the mass and not only of small intellectual groups.

The active man-in-the-mass has a practical activity, but has no clear theoretical consciousness of his practical activity, which nonetheless involves understanding the world in so far as it transforms it. His theoretical consciousness can indeed be historically in opposition to his activity. One might also say that he has two theoretical consciousnesses (or one contradictory consciousness): one which is implicit in his activity and which in reality unites him with all his fellow-workers in the practical transformation of the real world; and one, superficially explicit or verbal, which he has inherited from the past and uncritically absorbed. But this verbal conception is not without consequences. It holds together a specific social group, it influences moral conduct and the direction of will, with varying efficacity but often powerfully enough to produce a situation in which the contradictory state of consciousness does not permit of any action, any decision or any choice, and produces a condition of moral and political passivity. Critical understanding of self takes place therefore through a struggle of political "hegemonies" and of opposing directions, first in the ethical field and then in that of politics proper, in order to arrive at the working out at a higher level of one's own conception of reality. Consciousness of being part of a particular hegemonic force (that is to say, political consciousness) is the first stage towards a further progressive self-consciousness in which theory and practice will finally be one. Thus the unity of theory and practice is not just a matter of mechanical fact, but a part of the historical process, whose elementary and primitive phase is to be found in the sense of being "different" and "apart", in an instinctive feeling of independence, and which progresses to the level of real possession of a single and coherent conception of the world. This is why it must be stressed that the political development of the concept of hegemony represents a great philosophical advance as well as a politico-practical one. For it necessarily supposes an intellectual unity and an ethic in conformity with a conception of reality that has gone beyond common sense and has become, if only within narrow limits, a critical conception.

However, in the most recent developments of the philosophy of praxis the exploration and refinement of the concept of the unity of theory and practice is still only at an early stage. There still remain residues of mechanism, since people speak about theory as a "complement" or an "accessory" of practice, or as the handmaid of practice. It would seem right for this question too to be considered historically, as an aspect of the political question of the intellectuals. Critical self-consciousness means, historically and politically, the creation of an *élite* of intellectuals. A human mass does not "distinguish" itself, does not become independent in its own right without, in the widest sense, organising itself; and there is no organisation without intellectuals, that is without organisers and leaders, in other words, without the theoretical aspect of the theory-practice nexus being distinguished concretely by the existence of a group of people "specialised" in conceptual and philosophical elaboration of ideas. But the process of creating intellectuals is long, difficult, full of contradictions, advances and retreats, dispersals and regroupings, in which the loyalty of the masses is often sorely tried.❖

Mohandas Karamchand Gandhi (1869–1948) was born in India to comfortable circumstances. He married Kasturbai when both were twelve years old. After high school in India, Gandhi studied law in London. In 1893, he moved to South Africa, where he encountered the colonizing and racist attitudes against which he would struggle. While practicing before the court, he was known as one of the "coolie barristers." A formative experience was his being forcibly removed from a train, at night, for refusing to abandon first-class accommodations. According to his *Autobiography,* he said then, while sitting alone in the cold railroad waiting room, "I began to think of my duty." Thus began his commitment to nonviolence (*ahimsa*). To counter the notion of passivity in nonviolent resistance, he used the ideal of *satyagraha,* in which truth and love are considered the sources of forceful resistance to violence (*himsa*). Gandhi was assassinated in 1948, the year after the British conceded India's independence. No internal force was stronger than Gandhi's satyagraha in the decolonizing of his country.

"Nonviolent Force: A Spiritual Dilemma," though written in 1927, refers to Gandhi's South African period during the Boer War (1899–1902), in which he had sided with the British Empire. The passage indicates Gandhi's realization that nonviolence must contend with the structural sources of violence. Mr. Polak (one of Gandhi's European friends) was disturbed by Gandhi's role on the British side. The theoretical subtlety of his reply suggests why Gandhi's satyagraha had such an influence in the early stages of the American civil rights movement.

Nonviolent Force: A Spiritual Dilemma
Mohandas Karamchand Gandhi (1927)

As soon as the news reached South Africa that I along with other Indians had offered my services in the war, I received two cables. One of these was from Mr Polak who questioned the consistency of my action with my profession of *ahimsa*.

I had to a certain extent anticipated this objection, for I had discussed the question in my *Hind Swaraj (Indian Home Rule)*, and used to discuss it day in and day out with friends in South Africa. All of us recognized the immorality of war. If I was not prepared to prosecute my assailant, much less would I be willing to participate in a war, especially when I knew nothing of the justice or otherwise of the cause of the combatants. Friends of course knew that I had previously served in the Boer War, but they assumed that my views had since undergone a change.

As a matter of fact the very same line of argument that persuaded me to take part in the Boer War had weighed with me on this occasion. It was quite clear to me that participation in war could never be consistent with *ahimsa*. But it is not always given to one to be equally clear about one's duty. A votary of truth is often obliged to grope in the dark.

Ahimsa is a comprehensive principle. We are helpless mortals caught in the conflagration of *himsa*. The saying that life lives on life has a deep meaning in it. Man cannot for a moment live without consciously or unconsciously committing outward *himsa*. The very fact of his living—eating, drinking and moving about—necessarily involves some *himsa*, destruction of life, be it ever so minute. A votary of *ahimsa* therefore remains true to his faith if the spring of all his actions is compassion, if he shuns to the best of his ability the destruction of the tiniest creature, tries to save it, and thus incessantly strives to be free from the deadly coil of *himsa*. He will be constantly growing in self-restraint and compassion, but he can never become entirely free from outward *himsa*.

Then again, because underlying *ahimsa* is the unity of all life, the error of one cannot but affect all, and hence man cannot be wholly free from *himsa*. So long as he continues to be a social being, he cannot but participate in the *himsa* that the very existence of society involves. When two nations are fighting, the duty of a votary of *ahimsa* is to stop the war. He who is not equal to that duty, he who has no power of resisting war, he who is not qualified to resist war, may take part in war, and yet wholeheartedly try to free himself, his nation and the world from war.

I had hoped to improve my status and that of my people through the British Empire. Whilst in England I was enjoying the protection of the British Fleet, and taking shelter as I did under its armed might, I was directly participating in its potential violence. Therefore, if I desired to retain my connection with the Empire and to live under its banner, one of three courses was open to me: I could declare open resistance to the war and, in accordance with the law of *Satyagraha*, boycott the Empire until it changed its military policy; or I could seek imprisonment by civil disobedience of such of its laws as were fit to be disobeyed; or I could participate in the war on the side of the Empire and thereby acquire the capacity and fitness for resisting the violence of war. I lacked this capacity and fitness, so I thought there was nothing for it but to serve in the war.

I make no distinction, from the point of view of *ahimsa*, between combatants and non-combatants. He who volunteers to serve a band of dacoits [robbers], by working as their carrier, or their watchman while they are about their business, or their nurse when they are wounded, is as much guilty of dacoity [robbing] as the dacoits

Excerpt from Mahadev Desai, trans., *An Autobiography or The Story of My Experiments with Truth* (Ahmedabad: Navahivan Publishing House, 1927), pp. 291–293.

themselves. In the same way those who confine themselves to attending to the wounded in battle cannot be absolved from the guilt of war.

I had argued the whole thing out to myself in this manner, before I received Polak's cable, and soon after its receipt, I discussed these views with several friends and concluded that it was my duty to offer to serve in the war. Even today I see no flaw in that line of argument, nor am I sorry for my action, holding, as I then did, views favourable to the British connection.

I know that even then I could not carry conviction with all my friends about the correctness of my position. The question is subtle. It admits of differences of opinion, and therefore I have submitted my argument as clearly as possible to those who believe in *ahimsa* and who are making serious efforts to practise it in every walk of life. A devotee of Truth may not do anything in deference to convention. He must always hold himself open to correction, and whenever he discovers himself to be wrong he must confess it at all costs and atone for it.❖

Mao Tse-tung [Zedong] (1893–1976) was a founding leader of the Chinese Communist Party. After completing his formal studies in 1918 at the First Teachers' Training School in Changsha, Mao began a long career as writer, teacher, journalist, political organizer, and politician. He was one of the original twelve delegates to the First Congress of the Chinese Communist Party. In 1927, he led the peasant uprising in Hunan, after which he retreated into hiding. He then led the famous "long march" to Shensi Province. Thus began his role in the long Chinese revolution that culminated in the defeat of Chiang Kai-shek in 1949. After that, Mao was chairman of the People's Republic until his death in 1976. "Identity, Struggle, Contradiction" (1937) reveals Mao the theorist at his most brilliant. Here, he joins a sharp philosophical rendering of Marxist-Leninist philosophy with his direct knowledge of China's revolutionary situation. Perhaps more than anyone, including Lenin, Mao managed to unite theory and political practice into a coherent philosophy of life. In the selection, one can see the fresh meaning given to Marx's idea of contradiction in reference to China's place in the world conflicts of the interwar period.

Identity, Struggle, Contradiction

Mao Tse-tung (1937)

... The contradictory aspects in every process exclude each other, struggle with each other and are opposed to each other. Such contradictory aspects are contained without exception in the processes of all things in the world and in human thought. A simple process has only one pair of opposites, while a complex process has more than one pair. Various pairs of opposites are in turn opposed to one another. In this way all things in the objective world and human thought are formed and impelled to move.

But if this is so, there is an utter lack of identity, or unity. How then can we speak of identity or unity?

Excerpt from "On Contradiction," Anne Fremantle, ed., *Mao Tse-tung: An Anthology of His Writings* (New York: International Publishers Co., 1971 [1937]), pp. 234–238.

The reason is that a contradictory aspect cannot exist in isolation. Without the other aspect which is opposed to it, each aspect loses the condition of its existence. Just imagine, can any of the aspects of contradictory things or of contradictory concepts in the human mind exist independently? Without life, there would be no death; without death, there would also be no life. Without "above", there would be no "below"; without "below", there would also be no "above". Without misfortune, there would be no good fortune; without good fortune, there would also be no misfortune. Without facility, there would be no difficulty; without difficulty, there would also be no facility. Without landlords, there would be no tenant-peasants; without tenant-peasants, there would also be no landlords. Without the bourgeoisie, there would be no proletariat; without a proletariat, there would also be no bourgeoisie. Without imperialist oppression of the nations, there would be no colonies and semi-colonies; without colonies and semi-colonies, there would also be no imperialist oppression of the nations. All opposite elements are like this: because of certain conditions, they are on the one hand opposed to each other and on the other hand they are interconnected, interpenetrating, interpermeating and interdependent; this character is called identity. All contradictory aspects, because of certain conditions, are characterised by non-identity, hence they are spoken of as contradictory. But they are also characterised by identity, hence they are interconnected. When Lenin says that dialectics studies "how the opposites can be and how they become identical", he is referring to such a state of affairs. How can they be identical? Because of the condition of mutual sustenance of each other's existence. This is the first meaning of identity.

But is it enough to say merely that the contradictory aspects mutually sustain each other's existence, that is, there is identity between them and consequently they can coexist in an entity? No, it is not enough. The matter does not end with the interdependence of the two contradictory aspects for their existence; what is more important is the transformation of the contradictory things into each other. That is to say, each of the two contradictory aspects within a thing, because of certain conditions, tends to transform itself into the other, to transfer itself to the opposite position. This is the second meaning of the identity of contradiction.

Why is there also identity? You see, by means of revolution, the proletariat, once the ruled, becomes the ruler, while the bourgeoisie, originally the ruler, becomes the ruled, and is transferred to the position originally occupied by its opposite. This has already taken place in the Soviet Union and will take place throughout the world. I should like to ask: if there were no interconnection and identity of opposites under certain conditions, how could such a change take place?

The Kuomintang, which played a certain positive role at a certain stage in modern Chinese history, has, because of its inherent class nature and the temptations of imperialism (these being the conditions) become since 1927 a counterrevolutionary party; but, because of the intensification of the contradiction between China and Japan and the policy of the united front of the Communist Party (these being the conditions), it has been compelled to agree to resist Japan. Contradictory things change into one another, hence a certain identity is implied.

The agrarian revolution we have carried out is already and will be such a process in which the land-owning landlord class becomes a class deprived of its land, while the peasants, once deprived of their land, become small holders of land. The haves and the have-nots, gain and loss, are interconnected because of certain conditions; there is identity of the two sides. Under socialism, the system of the peasants' private ownership will in turn become the public ownership of socialist agriculture; this has already taken place in the Soviet Union and will take place throughout the world. Between private property and public property there is a bridge leading from the one to the other, which in philosophy is called identity, or transformation into each other, or interpermeation.

To consolidate the dictatorship of the proletariat or the people's dictatorship is precisely to prepare the conditions for liquidating such a dictatorship and advancing to the higher stage of abolishing all state systems. To establish and develop the Communist Party is precisely to prepare the condition for abolishing the Communist Party and all party systems. To establish the revolutionary army under the leadership of the Communist Party and to carry on the revolutionary war is precisely to prepare the condition for abolishing war for ever. These contradictory things are at the same time complementary.

As everybody knows, war and peace transform themselves into each other. War is transformed into peace; for example, the First World War was transformed into the post-war peace; the civil war in China has now also ceased and internal peace has come about. Peace is transformed into war; for example, the Kuomintang-Communist co-operation of 1927 was transformed into war, and the peaceful world situation today may also be transformed into a Second World War. Why? Because in a class society such contradictory things as war and peace are characterised by identity under certain conditions.

All contradictory things are interconnected, and they not only coexist in an entity under certain conditions, but also transform themselves into each other under certain conditions—this is the whole meaning of the identity of contradictions. . . .

Why can only an egg be transformed into a chicken but not a stone? Why is there identity between war and peace and none between war and a stone? Why can human beings give birth only to human beings but not to anything else? The reason is simply that identity of contradiction exists only under certain necessary conditions. Without certain necessary conditions there can be no identity whatever.

Why is it that in Russia the bourgeois-democratic revolution of February 1917 was directly linked with the proletarian-socialist revolution of October of the same year, while in France the bourgeois revolution was not directly linked with a socialist revolution, and the Paris Commune of 1871 finally ended in failure? Why is it, on the other hand, that the nomadic system in Mongolia and Central Asia has been directly linked with socialism? Why is it that the Chinese revolution can avoid a capitalist future and can be directly linked with socialism without traversing the old historical path of the western countries, without passing through a period of bourgeois dictatorship? The reason is none other than the concrete conditions of the time. When certain necessary conditions are present, certain contradictions arise in the process of development of things and, what is more, these contradictions and all contradictions of this kind depend upon each other for existence and transform themselves into each other; otherwise nothing is possible. . . .

All processes have a beginning and an end; all processes transform themselves into their opposites. The stability of all processes is relative, but the mutability manifested in the transformation of one process into another is absolute.

The movement of all things assumes two forms: the form of relative rest and the form of conspicuous change. Both forms of movement are caused by the struggle of the two contradictory factors contained in a thing itself. When the movement of a thing assumes the first form, it only undergoes a quantitative but not a qualitative change and consequently appears in a state of seeming rest. When the movement of a thing assumes the second form it has already reached a certain culminating point of the quantitative change of the first form, caused the dissolution of the entity, produced a qualitative change, and consequently appears as conspicuous change. Such unity, solidarity, amalgamation, harmony, balance, stalemate, deadlock, rest, stability, equilibrium, coagulation, attraction, as we see in daily life, are all the appearances of things in the state of quantitative change. On the other hand, the dissolution of the entity, the breakdown of such solidarity, amalgamation, harmony, balance, stalemate, deadlock, rest, stability, equilibrium, coagulation and attraction, and the change into their opposite states, are all the appearances of things in the state of qualitative change during the transformation of one process into another. Things are always transforming themselves from the first into the second form, while the struggle within the contradictions exists in both forms and reaches its solution through the second form. We say therefore that the unity of opposites is conditional, temporary and relative, while the struggle of mutually exclusive opposites is absolute.

When we said above that because there is identity between two opposite things, the two can coexist in an entity and can also be transformed into each other, we were referring to conditionality, that is to say, under certain conditions contradictory things can be united and can also be transformed into each other, but without such conditions, they cannot become contradictory, cannot coexist, and cannot transform themselves into one another. It is because the identity of contradiction obtains only under certain conditions that we say identity is conditional, relative. Here we add: the struggle within a contradiction runs throughout a process from beginning to end and causes one process to transform itself into another, and as the struggle within the contradiction is present everywhere, we say the struggle within the contradiction is unconditional, absolute.

Conditional, relative identity, combined with unconditional, absolute struggle, constitutes the movement of opposites in all things.

We Chinese often say, "Things opposed to each other complement each other". That is to say, there is identity of opposites. This remark is dialectical, and runs counter to metaphysics. To be "opposed to each other" means the mutual exclusion or struggle of the two contradictory aspects. To "complement each other" means that under certain conditions the two contradictory aspects become united and achieve identity. Struggle resides precisely in identity; without struggle there can be no identity.

In identity there is struggle, in particularity there is universality, in individual character there is common character. To quote Lenin, "there is an absolute even *within* the relative." ❖

Ruth Benedict (1887–1948) was one of the leading American anthropologists of the first half of the twentieth century. After graduating from Vassar College (1909), Benedict studied at the New School for Social Research, then at Columbia University. At Columbia, she studied with Franz Boas and received her Ph.D. in 1923. She was elected president of the American Anthropological Association in 1947. During World War II, Benedict served in the Office of War Information (from 1943 to 1945); in this period, she wrote her study of Japanese culture. In addition to *The Chrysanthemum and the Sword* (1946), her best-known book was *Patterns of Culture* (1936). The selection from her study of Japanese culture captures Benedict's desire to disabuse American readers of their naivete and also to present Japanese culture as filled with rich, and striking, contradictions, as the book's title suggests.

The Japanese and the Americans

Ruth Benedict (1946)

The Japanese were the most alien enemy the United States had ever fought in an all-out struggle. In no other war with a major foe had it been necessary to take into account such exceedingly different habits of acting and thinking. Like Czarist Russia before us in 1905, we were fighting a nation fully armed and trained which did not belong to the Western cultural tradition. Conventions of war which Western nations had come to accept as facts of human nature obviously did not exist for the Japanese. It made the war in the Pacific more than a series of landings on island beaches, more than an unsurpassed problem of logistics. It made it a major problem in the nature of the enemy. We had to understand their behavior in order to cope with it.

The difficulties were great. During the past seventy-five years since Japan's closed doors were opened, the Japanese have been described in the most fantastic series of 'but also's' ever used for any nation of the world. When a serious observer is writing about peoples other than the Japanese and says they are unprecedentedly polite, he is not likely to add, 'But also insolent and overbearing.' When he says people of some nation are incomparably rigid in their behavior, he does not add, 'But also they adapt themselves readily to extreme innovations.' When he says a people are submissive, he does not explain too that they are not easily amendable to control from above. When he says they are loyal and generous, he does not declare, 'But also treacherous and spiteful.' When he says they are genuinely brave, he does not expatiate on their timidity. When he says they act out of concern for others' opinions, he does not then go on to tell that they have a truly terrifying conscience. When he describes robot-like discipline in their Army, he does not continue by describing the way the soldiers in that Army take the bit in their own teeth even to the point of insubordination. When he describes a people who devote themselves with passion to Western learning, he does not also enlarge on their fervid conservatism. When he writes a book on a nation with a popular cult of aestheticism which gives high honor to actors and to artists and lavishes art upon the cultivation of chrysanthemums, that book does not ordinarily have to be supplemented by another which is devoted to the cult of the sword and the top prestige of the warrior.

All these contradictions, however, are the warp and woof of books on Japan. They are true. Both the sword and the chrysanthemum are a part of the picture. The Japanese are, to the highest degree, both aggressive and unaggressive, both militaristic and aesthetic, both insolent and polite, rigid and adaptable, submissive and resentful of being pushed around, loyal and treacherous, brave and timid, conservative and hospitable to new ways. They are terribly concerned about what other people will think of their behavior, and they are also overcome by guilt when other people know nothing of their misstep. Their soldiers are disciplined to the hilt but are also insubordinate.

When it became so important for America to understand Japan, these contradictions and many others equally blatant could not be waved aside. Crises were facing us in quick succession. What would the Japanese do? Was capitulation possible without invasion? Should we bomb the Emperor's palace? What could we expect of Japanese prisoners of war? What should we say in our propaganda to Japanese troops and to the Japanese homeland which could save the lives of Americans and lessen Japanese determination to fight to the last man? There were violent disagreements among those who knew the Japanese best. When peace came, were the Japanese a people who would require perpetual martial law to keep them in order? Would our army have to prepare to fight desperate bitter-enders in every mountain fastness of Japan? Would there have to be a revolution in Japan after the order of the French Revolution or the Russian Revolution before international peace was possible? Who would lead it? Was the alternative the eradication of the Japanese? It made a great deal of difference what our judgments were. . . .

In every cultural tradition there are orthodoxies of war and certain of these are shared in all Western nations, no matter what the specific differences. There are certain clarion calls to all-out war effort, certain forms of reassurance in case of local defeats, certain regularities in the proportion of fatalities to surrenders, and certain rules of behavior for prisoners of war which are predictable in wars between Western nations just because they have a great shared cultural tradition which covers even warfare.

All the ways in which the Japanese departed from Western conventions of war were data on their view of life and on their convictions of the whole duty of man. For the purposes of a systematic study of Japanese culture and behavior it did not matter whether or not their deviations from our orthodoxies were crucial in a military sense; any of them might be important because they raised questions about the character of the Japanese to which we needed answers.

The very premises which Japan used to justify her war were the opposite of America's. She defined the international situation differently. America laid the war to the aggressions of the Axis. Japan, Italy, and Germany had unrighteously offended against international peace by their acts of conquest. Whether the Axis had seized power in Manchukuo or in Ethiopia or in Poland, it proved that they had embarked on an evil course of oppressing weak peoples. They had sinned against an international code of 'live and let live' or at least of 'open doors' for free enterprise. Japan saw the cause of the war in another light. There was anarchy in the world as long as every nation had absolute sovereignty; it was necessary for her to fight to establish a hierarchy—under Japan, of course, since she alone represented a nation truly hierarchal from top to bottom and hence understood the necessity of taking 'one's proper place.' Japan, having attained unification and peace in her homeland, having put down banditry and built up roads and electric power and steel industries, having, according to her official figures, educated 99.5 per cent of her rising generation in her public schools, should, according to Japanese premises of hierarchy, raise her backward younger brother China. Being of the same race as Greater East Asia, she should eliminate the United States, and after her Britain and Russia, from that part of the world and 'take her proper place.' All nations were to be one world, fixed in an international hierarchy. In the next chapter we shall examine what this high value placed on hierarchy meant in Japanese culture. It was an appropriate fantasy for Japan to create. Unfortunately for her the countries she occupied did not see it in the same light. Nevertheless not even defeat has drawn from her moral repudiation of her Greater East Asia ideals, and even her prisoners of war who were least jingoistic rarely went so far as to arraign the purposes of Japan on the continent and in the Southwest Pacific. For a long, long time Japan will necessarily keep some of her in-bred attitudes and one of the most important of these is her faith and confidence in hierarchy. It is alien to equality-loving Americans but it is nevertheless necessary for us to understand what Japan meant by hierarchy and what advantages she has learned to connect with it.

Japan likewise put her hopes of victory on a different basis from that prevalent in the United States. She would win, she cried, a victory of spirit over matter. America was big, her armaments were superior, but what did that matter? All this, they said, had been foreseen and discounted. 'If we had been afraid of mathematical figures,' the Japanese read in their great newspaper, the *Mainichi Shimbun,* 'the war would not have started. The enemy's great resources were not created by this war.'

Even when she was winning, her civilian statesmen, her High Command, and her soldiers repeated that this was no contest between armaments; it was a pitting of our faith in things against their faith in spirit. When we were winning they repeated over and over that in such a contest material power must necessarily fail. This dogma became, no doubt, a convenient alibi about the time of the defeats at Saipan and Iwo Jima, but it was not manufactured as an alibi for defeats. It was a clarion call during all the months of Japanese victories, and it had been an accepted slogan long before Pearl Harbor. In the nineteen-thirties General Araki, fanatical militarist and one-time Minister of War, wrote in a pamphlet addressed 'To the whole Japanese Race' that 'the true mission' of Japan was 'to spread and glorify the Imperial way to the end of the Four Seas. Inadequacy of strength is not our worry. Why should we worry about that which is material?'

Of course, like any other nation preparing for war, they did worry. All through the nineteen-thirties the proportion of their national income which was devoted to armament grew astronomically. By the time of their attack on Pearl Harbor very nearly half the entire national income was going to military and naval purposes, and of the total expenditures of the government only 17 per cent were available for financing anything having to do with civilian administration. The difference between Japan and Western nations was not that Japan was careless about material armament. But ships and guns were just the outward show of the undying Japanese Spirit. They were symbols much as the sword of the samurai had been the symbol of his virtue.

Japan was as completely consistent in playing up nonmaterial resources as the United States was in its commitment to bigness. Japan had to campaign for all-out production just as the United States did, but her campaigns were based on her own premises. The spirit, she said, was all and was everlasting; material things were necessary, of course, but they were subordinate and fell by the way. 'There are limits to material resources,' the Japanese radio would cry: 'it stands to reason that material things cannot last a thousand years.' And this reliance on spirit was taken literally in the routine of war; their war catechisms used the slogan—and it was a traditional one, not made to order for this war—'To match our training against their numbers and our flesh against their steel.' Their war manuals began with the bold-type line, 'Read this and the war is won.' Their pilots who flew their midget planes in a suicidal crash into our warships were an endless text for the superiority of the spiritual over the material. They named them the Kamikaze Corps, for the *kamikaze* was the divine wind which had saved Japan from Genghis Khan's invasion in the thirteenth century by scattering and overturning his transports.

Even in civilian situations Japanese authorities took literally the dominance of spirit over material circumstances. Were people fatigued by twelve-hour work in the factories and all-night bombings? 'The heavier our bodies, the higher our will, our spirit, rises above them.' 'The wearier we are, the more splendid the training.' Were people cold in the bomb shelters in winter? On the radio the Dai Nippon Physical Culture Society prescribed body-warming calisthenics which would not only be a substitute for heating facilities and bedding, but, better still, would substitute for food no longer available to keep up people's normal strength. 'Of course some may say that with the present food shortages we cannot think of doing calisthenics. No! The more shortage of food there is, the more we must raise our physical strength by other means.' That is, we must increase our physical strength by expending still more of it. The American's view of bodily energy which always reckons how much strength he has to use by whether he had eight or five hours of sleep last night, whether he has eaten his regular meals, whether he has been cold, is here confronted with a calculus that does not rely on storing up energy. That would be materialistic.❖

PART THREE

The Golden Moment: 1945–1963

At the end of World War II, no one was left standing except the United States. Wherever the war had been fought, there was ruin. Germany, England, Russia, Japan, France, Italy, parts of Africa, most of Europe, and much of Asia lay wasted. Their industries were either destroyed or exhausted in the war. Their economies had long since overspent real wealth. Their people were devastated, physically and spiritually. The Soviet Union alone had lost 20 million people, compared to fewer than 300,000 by the United States. Such was the magnitude of loss and confusion, everywhere but in America.

The one power still standing stood taller than before, taller than any other in the modern era. Where the war had crushed others, the USA was lifted. Before the war, the U.S. gross national product had not yet recovered from the collapse of 1929. But in 1945, it had more than doubled predepression levels. After the war, steel production alone was four times greater than during the depression, while the other steel-producing giants (Japan, Germany, Western Europe) were crippled. By one estimate, at the end of the war, the average American enjoyed an income fifteen times greater than that of any foreigner. The United States produced half or more of the world's steel, oil, and electricity and three-quarters of the automobiles. In production sectors related to the war effort, no rivals existed. The United States possessed wealth of every kind—real capital and income, industrial capacity and know-how, spiritual self-confidence, and intellectual and technical capital developed in the war effort.

If there could be a single symbol of American might in 1945, it might be the bomb. When the United States unleashed the atomic bomb in the summer of 1945, it did more than level Hiroshima and Nagasaki. It signaled that the world had changed definitively. The older powers were less. The USA was greater. The political and economic globe was restructured. At that moment, only one nation had succeeded where others had tried. Only the United States was able to invent, produce, and deploy the ultimate weapon. Scientific knowledge, inventive genius, productive capacity, and moral force—no other nation but the United States could then lay claim to such wonderful national strengths—possessed all at once and demonstrated. To those who then admired America, its willingness to kill in such great numbers was, itself, a perverse sign of moral power. In 1945, it could have been said that the United States was the perfect fulfillment of the modern world. Knowledge set free was power. Power unleashed freed the world of war and evil. The bitter horror of those burned to death was, as always, the price of progress. There was only one flaw. The war had taught that it was too late to pretend the destructive side of progress would disappear. Still, millions pretended.

This was the Golden Age of America. This was the American Century. Everything had come together at once. It was as though all the stars and moons in the Western sky had aligned themselves—pulling the waters high, making the land shine. In this respect, the United States in its Golden Age finally seemed to have fulfilled the poetic prophecies of George Berkeley, in 1752:

> Westward the course of empire takes its way;
> The four first acts already past,
> A fifth shall close the drama with the day;
> Time's noblest offspring is the last.

For two centuries, Europeans in great numbers had seen in America the realization of their own dreams and cultures. From the first English settlers who had preceded Berkeley by a century, through Alexis de Tocqueville a century later and the millions of European immigrants through the nineteenth century, to the final reliance of the last European powers on the United States in the war, Europe had increasingly, if warily, looked to the West. It is easily forgotten that the United States had been, and had invented itself as, a new race of European people. The historical idealization of the West was, in part, an effort to redefine European culture to include its Western diaspora.

Thus, the triumphs of the United States at the end of World War II were, in some basic sense, a European triumph. It was at least possible to dream, even as Europe itself lay in tatters, that the original values of modern culture, born in Europe, were proven in and by the Americans. Not all Europeans liked this idea. Nor should they have. But as the summer of 1945 ended and Europeans had to look about for help to rebuild, there were not many choices. It was clear, in those months, to whom they must turn, like it or not. Americans in great numbers liked it, of course. But as Walter Russell Mead rightly says, George Berkeley's eighteenth-century vision of time's noblest offspring is better read against the words of a twentieth-century American skeptic, Robinson Jeffers:

> You making haste haste on decay; not blameworthy;
> life is good, be it stubbornly long or suddenly
> A mortal splendor: meteors are not needed less than
> mountains: shine, perishing republic.

If, at the end of the war, America seemed the splendid mountain built on the achievements of European culture, observers of the night sky might be forgiven for having failed to detect the meteors among the stars. They were there to be seen.

The brilliant Golden Age of European culture in the West was to last but a moment. American triumphs were real, but their exceptional qualities were exaggerated by the leveling of every rival. Economically, U.S. industry was humming at full speed; the rest of the world was its marketplace. Morally, America had triumphed; others, even the Allies, were beaten down, one way or another. But these conditions were artificial and passing. In March 1946, only months after the end of the war, Winston Churchill, speaking in the heartland of America, made public the phrase that would help define Western politics for nearly half a century: the Iron Curtain. With Franklin Roosevelt dead (he died the year before), only Churchill knew as well what Stalin and the Soviets intended. The fragile partitioning of Europe at Yalta in

February 1945 is often said to have come about due to FDR's mortal illness. The more likely cause was a world distracted by Hitler and war—a world that failed to realize the full implications of its own internal divisions. It was not even the deep ideological rivalry between the United States and the USSR—between, as they said, "freedom" and communism. We now know that the two cold war powers were built on ideologies composed out of a common culture that included modernity's willful refusal to look at itself. Each system looked to the other in order to account for the evil. Neither had the courage to consider its own complicity in the destructive forces of the modern world. The Iron Curtain stretched taut between the two powers was a prophylactic against self-examination. The Soviets attacked American imperialism and promised, in Nikita Khrushchev's word, to "bury" the United States. The Americans did much the same. Just weeks before Churchill's 1946 speech, U.S. diplomat George Kennan, in his famous long telegram from Moscow, defined the moral basis for U.S. cold war policy. The Soviets were possessed of a "neurotic view of world affairs" that drove their own imperialist impulses. In response, he said, the United States "must have courage and self-confidence to cling to our own methods and concepts of human society." This was on February 22, 1946—not even two years after Americans and Soviets had joined hands over Hitler's defeat.

How brief that golden moment had been. In late summer and early autumn 1945, nothing seemed impossible to the Americans. Now, they were advised to have courage enough to "cling" to their own ways. For good reason. Soon, they would learn that the Soviets, too, had the bomb. America was no longer the manifest exception. In 1948, Berlin was blockaded, cementing the Soviet hold on Eastern Europe. By the end of the decade, Communist parties were organized in Western Europe, China had fallen to Mao's Communist forces, and no part of the world was considered "safe" from communism. By 1950, the United States was at war again, now against communism in Korea, and Senator Joseph McCarthy had begun his crusade of domestic terror. Within a decade, in 1957, the Soviets successfully launched the first earth satellites. Sputnik seemed proof that the Soviets had surpassed the United States in the area of its greatest strength. By 1959, the year Cuba fell to Castro, Vice President Richard Nixon was in Moscow arguing with Soviet President Nikita Khrushchev that America's washing machines were the true signs of progress, that they should rather compete over the quality of their domestic economies, not their military technologies. It seemed reasonable. Today, it is evident that the Soviet system was, indeed, unable to satisfy the divergent demands of military and domestic needs. But then, at the height of the cold war, Nixon's argument was a pathetic reminder of just how far America had fallen—and how fast.

Senator McCarthy's reign of terror lasted nearly five years. He was censured by the U.S. Senate in 1954. Still, nothing so represents the frustrations of America in its Golden Age. Somehow—no one could quite say how—this splendid world society, the perfection of modern dreams, was unable to prevent communism from winning the world, abroad or at home. So, Americans attacked themselves. McCarthyism was able to exercise its threats at home because the Americans, like the Soviets, were unable to look honestly at themselves. When they did, they saw only the outsider lurking within, not their own capacity for destruction. Both nations were postwar states built squarely on the moral psychology of modernity: Progress conquers the evil without, purifying the good intentions within. The cold war, in its way, was no less a form destroying eruption of the good than was Hitler. We now know that as many died in Stalin's Gulags as in Hitler's Holocaust. No one has ever thought to count those who died in McCarthy's terrorism. But everyone who lived through it knew someone whose life was taken, or ruined, by the American fear of its own capacity for evil. In different ways, both systems destroyed their own to avoid facing what lay within. Today, the one has collapsed; the other struggles on, trying in its way to recapture its Golden Age.

The cold war was a world struggle between two systems still clinging to the most elemental of nineteenth-century doctrines. Though social theorists since World War I, at least, had begun to rethink the founding ideas of modernity, the cold war effectively wiped out much of what was gained. In the public discourse in the United States, the cold war was seen as a struggle between the basic truths of mankind: freedom versus slavery. Better dead than Red! Nineteenth-century Enlightenment and Marxist philosophies had changed by the middle of the twentieth century, but in the popular mind—and to a large extent in public policy—thinking had regressed. Then popular social theory took its rawest form and must be taken seriously as such.

In some ways, the debate during and after McCarthy's "Red Scare" could hardly be considered a serious version of the original political philosophies themselves. Rather, at least in the United States, the debate was much more the attempt of ordinary people to make some sense of the most overwhelming social fact of the day. America was supposed to have it all, but in fact, it had only a quarter section of the world's moral territory. Apart from the facts of Soviet brutality in Eastern Europe, what must have most distressed the American mind was the Socialist boast of moral superiority. Americans considered themselves exceptional, most of all because they were the moral superiors.

In 1941, Henry Luce, then publisher of *Life* and *Time* magazines, proclaimed the twentieth the American Century. He began his editorial: "In general, the issues which the American people champion revolve around their determination to make the society of men safe for the freedom, growth and increasing satisfaction of all individual men." America served the moral good of humankind! This was 1941, before the cold war. As Gunnar Myrdal would state in 1944, at the beginning of *An American Dilemma,* the Americans were always a moralistic people. Indeed, he argued, this is why their failures in race relations could be considered America's unique moral dilemma. Such a people were likely to be unnerved when others whom they considered bullies proclaimed themselves the true champions of the world's oppressed. Socialism's moral claims were, of course, central to Marx's social theory. But in the mid-twentieth century, they were particularly troubling to Americans who could not have missed the fact that, indeed, communism was making its deepest inroads among the poorer, most oppressed people of the world—not just in China and Cuba but also in Africa and the Middle East. In 1956, when Egypt's Abdel Nasser seized the Suez Canal, he struck at American wallets. Two years later, when he accepted a loan from the USSR for construction of the Aswan Dam, he struck their moral hearts. This was but the most dramatic of the moral and diplomatic struggles throughout the Third World in which the Communists were either winning or drawing even.

The cold war was far from a debate in abstracts, or a debate over who had the better rockets and kitchen tools. It reflected a deep wrenching in the guts of ordinary people. In the mid-1950s in America, many men and women just settling back into a normal life had likely been born in the early 1920s and thus brought up through the depression. Very probably, they had either fought in World War II or worked in the war effort at home. Their deepest need was to enjoy the fruits of those years of courageous suffering. People thought they had good reason to believe in the moral value of what they had done, especially in war. They believed, even more urgently, in their right to enjoy the abundant life they had earned.

Many did. Life in the 1950s was good for working and middle-class white people in the United States. But not for everyone. American Blacks returned from military service to encounter the same old story. Many suburban wives stuck out in Levit-towns and other new suburban developments, far from friends and family, won-dered just what happiness really was. Yes, they had husbands and kids and those new kitchens, but something was wrong. Yet on the surface of the life pho-tographed for *Life* and *Time* magazines, all was good. Except for those Communists. People living luxuriously middling lives could not be blamed for buying Senator Mc-Carthy's line. He told them the Reds were right there, in their schools and churches, even in the army. The Reds were the enemy within. To people who had had enough of disruption in their personal lives, it must have seemed at least a plausible claim. Whatever they *thought*, they surely *felt* that what was wrong was not far away. Then, later, there was Elvis. Clearly, something was wrong indeed.

What was wrong was that the culture they trusted to give them the good society had excised a hidden tax. Everyone had to pay the price of joining the enforced si-lence. Evil in the world did not die with Hitler. There was enough to spare. Better to think it was the Commies in the schools and churches than to face the half-truth Western culture had been built on. Progress was not a necessary condition of mod-ern life. There was plenty of the good life to go around, but this could never suffice for a people taught that, soon enough, all social evil would recede. The Red Scare was real. The Soviets did intend to win. They did their own evil to their people and to those they tried to crush with tanks. But for Americans, then the standard-bearers of European culture, it was simply too much to consider the notion that social evil was deeply structured into the American way of life. Better to blame the Reds, or Elvis's gyrating pelvis.

In early December 1955, the civil rights struggle began in Montgomery, Alabama. The yearlong Montgomery bus boycott made Martin Luther King and Rosa Parks American cultural heroes. More fundamentally, the social movements that followed Montgomery sounded an alarm that no one could fail to hear a decade later. Though it could be said that, between 1955 and 1963, the American civil rights movement failed to achieve the full social equality it sought for Blacks, it cannot be denied that this was the first and most shocking of a series of events that changed, perhaps forever, how Americans thought about their society.

Through the 1950s, those Americans with a strong determination to see the best could still believe in the virtues of their way of life. One of the most remarkable pas-sages in Ambassador Kennan's 1946 telegram conveyed the attitude perfectly:

> It was no coincidence that Marxism, which had smoldered ineffectively for half a century in Western Europe, caught hold and blazed for [the] first time in Russia. Only in this land which had never known a friendly neighbor or indeed any tolerant equilibrium of sepa-rate powers, either internal or international, could a doctrine thrive which viewed eco-nomic conflicts of society as insoluble by peaceful means.

Kennan was no McCarthy. He is a learned and cultured man. In 1946, he brought the best American wisdom to bear on the real behind the fantasy of the Soviet menace. Still, he was absolutely sure that what set the American way apart was its capacity to solve conflict by peaceful means. This was the West's hedge against communism—again, its moral superiority. But from 1955 onward, as the struggle of American Blacks moved quickly toward open confrontation, it gradually dawned that the United States might be among those world societies unable to solve conflict by peaceful means. Here, of course, lay the power of Martin Luther King's strategy, taken from Gandhi. The early movement used the force of nonviolence to expose the violence in the oppressor. But the movement eventually forced more than the hands of Bull Connor, Ross Barnett, and George Wallace. The Southern, white segregationists used all the violence of their disposition—hoses, arrest and detention, beatings, bombs, dogs, and murder. Then, force came from another quarter. The problem was not regional. When President Eisenhower, then presidents Kennedy and Johnson, reluctantly brought the force of federal law and troops down on the side of the oppressed, it was natural to hope that this would be the end of it. Again, the thought was: Put the visible evil away and progress would assert its righteous way. It was not to be.

Still, this was the reasonable hope of people of goodwill in the United States and around the world when John F. Kennedy took up the reins of world power after the 1960 elections. In passing the torch to a younger and different political leader, people believed that their Golden Age would recover its luster. It seemed, as if by some improbable miracle, that JFK had brought the stars back into line. He, the Beatles, Dr. King, and Pope John XXIII conjured up the vision of a new day dawning. Little did anyone imagine then that all three Johns would be dead before their time, or that the sweeping changes they represented would falter, weaken, or reverse themselves. But it is easy to see why people would go with the times. Perhaps the ugly contradictions of the 1950s—abundance marred by frustration—would be resolved. They were not.

After early gains culminating in the Civil Rights and Voting Rights acts of 1964 and 1965, the civil rights movement turned in a different direction. Martin Luther King took the movement beyond the South, beyond voting rights. But when he turned his eye to broader issues of social justice in a speech accepting the Nobel Prize in late 1964, he was told to keep to his specialty. The war in Vietnam started in earnest several months later, in February 1965, just days before another hero would be assassinated. One year earlier, white people began to notice Malcolm X, who took a very different line from King. In one of his most memorable speeches, Malcolm X declared the American Dream his American Nightmare. There were those— J. Edgar Hoover, director of the FBI, and others—who tried at that late date to explain away the Black uprisings as still another Communist plot. Though the accusations did damage, they did not have the force they once had. When young people who had marched with King turned in other directions—Blacks often to Black Power, whites to the antiwar movement—the crisis spread far and wide. No one could quite be convinced, however much he or she wanted to believe it, that the world and America would have been saved from the troubles of the 1960s had the Kennedys and King not been killed.

What happened between 1963 and 1968 was part of a world drama. What was wrong in the United States was structural, as Myrdal, Neibuhr, and others had been saying. What was wrong in the world was structural, too. In the latter years of the 1950s, beginning with the uprisings in Kenya, then Ghana's independence from Britain in 1957 and the Algerian revolt against French rule in 1958, African people threw off European colonial rule. In 1959, Castro threw out America's lackey, Batista—just a decade after Gandhi and Mao turned India and China away from Western control. But the most telling years were 1954 and 1955, when McCarthy was ruined and Rosa Parks refused to move any more and the French lost their colonial grip on Vietnam in a humiliating defeat at Dien Bien Phu. If only the Americans had learned the lesson from the French defeat. But then, they were still struggling with their own frustrat' ons. They were still hoping for a return to the Golden Age. As it turned out, JFK was ⸱⸳ot the beginning of a new day but the last bright glow of a meteor falling red through thick air.

Between 1945 and 1963—the Golden Age—the social theories that exerted the greatest influence fell into three categories: those affirming and developing the principles of the Golden Age; those reflecting the doubts and reservations of the time; and those openly objecting.

In the 1950s, the social sciences were brought into full partnership with the political and economic powers that were. Notwithstanding the jarring effects of the decade's contradictions, professional social scientists in all fields took up positions at or near the reins of power. These were the years when the American system of higher education grew by leaps and bounds; when the promise of a college education was seriously extended to nearly all qualified students. Following suit, European societies loosened the gates of their elite university systems to young people of working-class origins. These were the years in which, in the new universities and the research centers allied with them, the modern social sciences took the shape we recognize today. Though the emergence of the modern university goes back to the 1860s in the United States, it took a full century for that modern research university to become what it is, for better or worse, today. Only in the Golden Age was there sufficient public support for a full governmental investment in building so many costly institutions of higher learning, devoted equally to teaching the young and mastering the world through science. Between the 1940s and the 1960s, the number of Americans going to college increased at least fourfold. In 1940 the United States spent $500 million on higher education; in 1970 the figure was nearly $16 billion! There was, obviously, a happy coincidence. Veterans returning from World War II and the Korean War used the GI Bill to pay their tuition bills. The demand for college education rose sharply. At the same time, the need for social knowledge to build the postwar society was felt to be great. In real terms, however, the actual need for college graduates was artificial. There were never enough positions in U.S. or European economies to occupy all the newly educated elite.

The ideal of higher education as a necessity and a right was, no doubt, encouraged by the boost in intellectual self-confidence gained in the war. Many academics, like Ruth Benedict, had been active in the planning, administering, and informing of the war machine. After the war, there was a widespread and reasonable belief that scientific knowledge about social reality was much more than a nicety. It worked. So, in the 1950s, particularly in the United States, it was widely believed that social knowledge was the most powerful weapon. The social sciences stepped to the fore, for a while, as professional social theory enjoyed its own Golden Age, financed by the social hopes of most Americans.

George Kennan's idea that the West—the United States—was able to solve its problems without conflict was an early version of the thinking that predominated for a short while in the late 1950s and early 1960s. Daniel Bell was one of those who eloquently defended the proposition that the West had already won the struggle with Marxism, which had somehow become synonymous with the East or at least with other-than-the-West—the uncivilized. Proponents of the end of ideology in the West made a strong theoretical claim: Ideology's day was past because social knowledge's day had come. Bell announced the day of the scholar—the man of scientific objectivity, freed from the passion of the ideologue. Though Daniel Bell, like George Kennan, is a man of superior culture and refined intellectual tastes, it might still be said that his vision of the end of ideology was a quite thickly veiled version of the popular view that politically passionate intellectuals were, after all, essentially Marxists—or worse. Earlier, in his 1952 campaign against Adlai Stevenson, Dwight Eisenhower had pronounced intellectuals "eggheads." Either way, among those in power in politics and the university, room had to be made for the trustworthy use of knowledge—by scientists and scholars, not intellectuals and ideologues. The line between was that between objectivity and passion.

The writings of Daniel Bell were just one example of the conviction that social science could be the basis for better explaining the social world in order to make it better. The key was keeping it all objective. W. W. Rostow's theory of modernization's five stages was the most influential applied version of this world theory. To all appearances, Rostow's analysis of human economic history is scientific economics at its best. The elaboration of Weber's ideas is obvious: Societies can be shown to move from traditionalism to a period of readiness for change. If the conditions are right, take-off, maturity, and something like old age follow. The argument was persuasive because it was logical, comprehensive, and empirically valid—or so it seemed. The idea behind it seemed self-evident in the late 1950s. Was it not obvious that there were "mature" modern societies (of which the United States was the standard) and others that were less mature, just taking off or getting ready or still stuck in tradition? As a social scientific classification, the theory was one thing. As a master philosophy of human history, it was another. It was presented and received—for the most part in its former guise—as science. Today, one wonders if no one stopped to ask how such a philosophy might look to the African colonial people then in revolt against modernized rulers. Nor, in 1966, when Rostow was one of President Lyndon Johnson's advisers, did anyone seriously wonder how an uncritical application of a philosophy that defined America as the end of history might promote the passions that led to Vietnam. The line between science and ideology, between objective truth and political passion, was blurred—and not just in the Kremlin.

Social science, in its finest hour, moved with a bold confidence. Nothing less could explain the theoretical self-confidence of Talcott Parsons, who, in the *age d'or* of sociology, felt himself utterly free to pursue his theory of the social system into every minute detail of thinkable social space. He thus felt himself authorized to say whatever followed from the theory. One measure of just how different things are today is that it would be hard to find anyone willing to make the statements Parsons made about "dependent" and "neurotic" women in his "Sex Roles" article. People still think this way, but fewer say what they think, and fewer still would make a social theory out of gratuitous observations. But Parsons was not a man of evil intent. He was writing good sociological theory, following the unchecked lead of his scientific brilliance.

One of the surest signs that science was having its way is seen in the shifts taking place in this period in European social theory. Social science, as we know it today, was very slow to develop in Europe, where the tradition of classical learning and the effects of elitism on cultural life combined with the effects of the wars to slow progress toward modern social science. Between 1945 and 1963, European social scientists were still learning from the Americans, still necessarily borrowing to pay off the deficit in cultural capital created by the wars. But in the human sciences, it was a very different story. In France, in particular, this was another age d'or—this one in the study of human culture. It was what one commentator has called the Age of Structuralism.

Claude Lévi-Strauss, the French anthropologist, is generally considered the founder of structuralism. Borrowing from linguistics, including the ideas of Ferdinand de Saussure and Roman Jakobson, Lévi-Strauss proposed the methods he thought would establish a science of the mind. The Swiss psychologist Jean Piaget (1896–1980) was doing something similar based on laboratory observations of small children. Piaget would be one of the founders of modern developmental psychology, but Lévi-Strauss would become, as Susan Sontag put it, the intellectual hero of his day. He argued that cultural life had many of the same structural features as language. It was well known at the time that all languages were constituted as infinitely complex reservoirs of grammatical rules and semantic contents on which the speaker or writer draws while producing competent communications. Lévi-Strauss used this model of language to explain human culture. Culture was equally a vast, enduring social contract. The philosophical implication of his turn to linguistics was, in part, directed against the postwar philosophy of his day—existentialism in general, Jean-Paul Sartre (1905–1980) in particular. Structuralism, as a political theory, rejected the notion that the meaningful life was entirely dependent on real life choices made by responsible individuals. This was equivalent to suggesting that linguistic meaning was solely derived from the existential utterances of the individual speaker. Here, the linguistic model brought home the dependence of the individual on the social group. The speaker cannot say whatever he wants because communication works both ways. He or she who must listen can understand what is said only by sharing a competent grasp of the whole of the language spoken. Therefore, structuralism in its simplest terms returned the study of culture to the issues outlined by Durkheim before World War I. The important difference was that Lévi-Strauss was able to be much more precise than Durkheim about the relation between the individual event and the total structure. His advance over Durkheim was due, in large part, to the use of a linguistics model. It may have also derived from his own look at the war years. Sartre took one turn from the Nazi occupation of France, Lévi-Strauss another. Both had their reasons. Their two philosophies vied with each other in France. But clearly the day was won, for a while, by structuralism and its variants. It was more a time for rebuilding the structure of Culture. There was less evident cause to resist an occupying enemy.

Some might pause on seeing the names of Roland Barthes and Robert K. Merton in the same group. This because Merton has remained the structuralist sociologist, while Barthes changed many times over until his death in 1980. But between 1945 and 1960, when sociology came into its own in the United States and structuralism into its own in France, Merton and Barthes were not far from each other. Though in different ways, each was proposing a structural science, and each proposed to use science to uncover the latent dimensions of meaning. Merton's famous distinction between manifest and latent functions in social life is particularly interesting because it derives much more from Durkheim, even Marx, than from Freud. Barthes's outline of the structural science of human sign systems (*Elements of Semiology,* from which the selection is taken) belies his own debt to the Durkheimian tradition through Lévi-Strauss and Saussure. Later, Barthes would evolve into one of the first public proponents of a social theory based on sexual desire. But in the early 1960s, when Barthes's essay on semiology first appeared, he, like Merton and Lévi-Strauss, was proposing a structural study of cultural systems. They all relied on variants of the principle that the latent meanings in culture could best be derived by a rigorous analysis not of their surface appearances but of their deep structural elements.

In a way, Louis Althusser was doing something similar in his structuralist attempt to revise historical materialism as a science by reconstructing the intellectual biography of Marx. Althusser took from his teacher, Gaston Bachelard, his famous idea of an epistemological break in Marx's writings. This was not so much a narrow scholarly argument as a general theoretical claim with political implications. If one could show the break in Marx between the younger philosophical Hegelian in the 1840s and the mature scientist of *Capital* in the 1860s, then it was possible to justify a post-Stalinist Marxism. Why theory? The answer for many Western European Marxists in the 1960s depended on finding some key to unraveling the various strands in the history of Marxism. The idea of a structural break in a cultural or theoretical tradition permitted the leap to a Marxism that could be pure theoretical practice. Today, this seems an entirely circuitous route to a rather straightforward position. But in the days of Althusser's prominence, it was a tricky path to tread between a Left social theory and the threat of being tainted by Stalinism. In his way, Althusser was using science to clear a legitimate place for Marxism in the cold war era. American social theorists had no such struggle. Before McCarthyism, the revelations of Stalin's terrors early in the Soviet regime all but cleared the way of any manifest left-wing social theory.

All the structuralists of the time—Lévi-Strauss, Barthes, Merton, and Althusser—were, in different ways, seeking to accomplish much the same goal. They sought a new, deeper method for defining the science of social and cultural life. They had learned well the lessons of the interwar years. The individual, left alone, could not account for social action. They each pressed social theory beyond the merely visible. Surprisingly, they each were still positive in their outlook, and their method. They believed in the reasonable discovery and explanation of social facts. Others were less optimistic.

David Riesman was among the first skeptics. His *Lonely Crowd* appeared in 1950. Already, Riesman was rethinking received wisdom about modernization. He took for granted the link between individual and social character, just as he accepted the premise that the world was moving steadily along the path of economic development. Where he differed was in his judgment about what turned out to be Rostow's fifth stage of mass consumption. Though Rostow had reservations, nothing he said ten years after *Lonely Crowd* was as deeply critical of modern America. Riesman believed America had lost its original character. In place of the inner-directed entrepreneur, the ideal-type of modern man, Riesman saw in the postwar years an other-directed conformist. He was one of the first to force discussion of a topic well understood today. But then, in the Golden Age, it was yet another shock to have to consider, on top of everything else—that Americans had lost the very moral character that had set them apart.

About the same time, Erik Erikson was reporting from his studies of the psychological development of youth the outlines of a theory of social character. His argument that an identity crisis was developmentally necessary seemed to some to lend further support to Riesman's claims. Ten years later, when parents were repulsed by the politics and culture (to say nothing of the attire) of their children, identity crisis took on an even more explicit social importance. Even Erving Goffman's first writings contributed to the growing suspicion that older beliefs in the moral integrity of individuals were no longer entirely satisfactory. His first book, *Presentation of Self in Everyday Life,* gave popular culture the expression *impression-management.* Goffman held the view that individuals in social interactions were engaged in the artful management of what others thought of them. In contrast to Erikson and Riesman, however, he never said one word about his times. He wrote as though suspended in some transcendent observational space. But he introduced the radical idea that, far from being inner-directed, human beings in society were by nature oriented more to social others than to pursuing the dictates of some inner moral self. With Goffman, in the 1950s, William James's ideas—that the individual has as many selves as there are individuals who recognize him—took on a different, more historically acute meaning. In the 1890s, this was an interesting idea. In the 1950s, it was a social critique.

At about the same time, in Paris, a little-known psychoanalyst, Jacques Lacan, was already rewriting traditional Freudian theories in order to establish a similar notion. The unconscious life could only be the interplay of natural desires in the discourse of the Other in the other. As with his structuralist contemporaries, Lacan saw the powerful mystery of language as the field of human action. Not an easily decoded idea, but obviously one not entirely at odds with Goffman's social theory of the self as the management of the expressive order lying between social individuals. Later, Lacan became a celebrity in the cultural Left, which had no definite shape in the 1950s.

But in 1949, the notion that seems so hard to translate from Lacan was made perfectly clear by Simone de Beauvoir. In *The Second Sex,* the classic text of modern feminism, she left no doubt about the ways in which woman was Other to man, nor how the whole of Western culture had been built on and around this principle. Here, for the first time, was a feminist social theory that explained the situation of women with reference to Western civilization itself. Others, like Anna Julia Cooper and Charlotte Gilman, had begun this effort. But Simone de Beauvoir was the first to complete such a critique in the language of the culture she attacked. Not much later, Césaire and Fanon, who were among the first postcolonial writers to be read seriously in the West, did much the same with respect to the colonializing instincts of European cultures. It would be easy to overlook the fact that Martin Luther King's philosophy of nonviolence was itself borrowed from the first great social critic of Western culture in the twentieth century. Gandhi's ideal of satyagraha, nonviolent force, was defined by his first-hand understanding of the violent impulses of the European colonialist. King's use of that theory is therefore an implicit social theory of the colonializing instincts of the white man in the United States.

By the end of the period, Fanon was already read in the United States and Europe. In 1963, the year JFK died, Betty Friedan had given words to those millions of women trapped in little suburban houses in the 1950s. She gave the problem a name. *The Feminine Mystique* immediately became the locus classicus of American feminism. The year before, 1962, leaders of SDS began to circulate copies of a social theory of democratic society. The *Port Huron Statement* was, in its day, the manifesto of a new political generation. Its ideal was a participatory democracy in which the social structures of political life would be consistent with, and supportive of, the deepest aspirations of the human individual. In this, the *Port Huron Statement* reflected the political and social philosophy of C. Wright Mills, who was a source of inspiration and ideas for many of those who had written the statement.

In 1959, Mills's *Sociological Imagination* was the embodiment of the tensions of the age. On the one hand, he caustically denounced the pretenses of social science—mindless empiricism and abstract theorizing. To this day, his parody of Parsons remains the standard for sociological sarcasm. Yet his actual idea of the sociological imagination inspired student radicals from a place well within the culture of liberalism. Mills saw the sociologist as the new model of human liberation in that time—the individual whose sociological knowledge of the historical structures of society enhanced individual life with responsible awareness of the links between personal life and public action. Though his earlier books, particularly *Power Elite,* were sharp critical theories of American society, his ideal of the sociological imagination still held out hope that if knowledge were wrenched away from the pretenses of apolitical social science, it might find its way back as power in the lives of ordinary people.

In 1962–1963, just before the Golden Age ended, the most radical young people in the United States, in the former colonial world, and in Europe still believed in the power of knowledge. This faith would have a troubled time in the years to come.

C. L.

Notes

Page 272: The Jeffers poem, "Shine, Perishing Republic," is used by Walter Russell Mead as the theme and title for his *Mortal Splender* (Houghton Mifflin, 1987).

Page 275: The idea of linking women's experience in the suburbs to McCarthyism is from Elaine Tyler May, *Homeward Bound* (Basic Books, 1988).

Page 279: Edith Kurzweil's *The Age of Structuralism* (Columbia University Press, 1980) is the source of the phrase *Age of Structuralism.*

Other quoted material is from the selections following.

❖ The Golden Age ❖

George Kennan (1904–) was born in Wisconsin. After high school at St. John's Military Academy, he studied at Princeton. In 1926, Kennan entered the U.S. Foreign Service, where he received the training that made him an expert on Soviet affairs. After several tours of duty in the USSR, he was named ambassador in 1952. From 1953 until retirement in 1974, Kennan was permanent professor at the Institute for Advanced Studies at Princeton. He has written numerous books and articles on Russia and the Soviet Union and other subjects. "On the United States and Containment of the Soviets" is a selection from Kennan's long telegram of February 22, 1946, written while he was minister-counselor in the U.S. Embassy, Moscow. The telegram was followed (in 1947) by the equally famous article he wrote anonymously as "X" for *Foreign Affairs*, "The Sources of Soviet Conduct." These two documents were instrumental in shaping American foreign policy in the early cold war era. The telegram, in spite of its restrained good sense, reflects many of the American biases of the time. Please keep in mind that the selection is written in the sparse language of telegrams, often without the usual connectors and modifiers.

On the United States and Containment of the Soviets
George Kennan (1946)

At the bottom of the Kremlin's neurotic view of world affairs is traditional and instinctive Russian sense of insecurity. Originally, this was insecurity of a peaceful agricultural people trying to live on vast exposed plain in neighborhood of fierce nomadic peoples. To this was added, as Russia came into contact with economically advanced West, fear of more competent, more powerful, more highly organized societies in that area. But this latter type of insecurity was one which afflicted rather Russian rulers than Russian people; for Russian rulers have invariably sensed that their rule was relatively archaic in form, fragile and artificial in its psychological foundation, unable to stand comparison for contact with political systems of Western countries. For this reason they have always feared foreign penetration, feared direct contact between Western world and their own, feared what would happen if Russians learned truth about world without or if foreigners learned truth about world within. And they have learned to seek security only in patient but deadly struggle for total destruction rival power, never in compacts and compromises with it.

Excerpt from "The Long Telegram, 1946," *George F. Kennan, Memoirs 1925–1950*, pp. 549–551, 557–559. Copyright 1967 by George F. Kennan. Reprinted by permission of Little, Brown and Co.

It was no coincidence that Marxism, which had smoldered ineffectively for half a century in Western Europe, caught hold and blazed for first time in Russia. Only in this land which had never known a friendly neighbor or indeed any tolerant equilibrium of separate powers, either internal or international, could a doctrine thrive which viewed economic conflicts of society as insoluble by peaceful means. After establishment of Bolshevist regime, Marxist dogma, rendered even more truculent and intolerant by Lenin's interpretation, became a perfect vehicle for sense of insecurity with which Bolsheviks, even more than previous Russian rulers, were afflicted. In this dogma, with its basic altruism of purpose, they found justification for their instinctive fear of outside world, for the dictatorship without which they did not know how to rule, for cruelties they did not dare not to inflict, for sacrifices they felt bound to demand. In the name of Marxism they sacrificed every single ethical value in their methods and tactics. Today they cannot dispense with it. It is fig leaf of their moral and intellectual respectability. Without it they would stand before history, as best, as only the last of that long succession of cruel and wasteful Russian rulers who have relentlessly forced their country on to ever new heights of military power in order to guarantee external security for their internally weak regimes. This is why Soviet purposes must always be solemnly clothed in trappings of Marxism, and why no one should underrate the importance of dogma in Soviet affairs. Thus Soviet leaders are driven by necessities of their own past and present position to put forward a dogma which pictures the outside world as evil, hostile, and menacing, but as bearing within itself germs of creeping disease and destined to be wracked with growing internal convulsions until it is given final coup de grace by rising power of socialism and yields to new and better world. This thesis provides justification for that increase of military and police power in Russia state, for that isolation of Russian population from the outside world, and for that fluid and constant pressure to extend limits of Russian police power which are together the natural and instinctive urges of Russian rulers. Basically this is only the steady advance of uneasy Russian nationalism, a centuries-old movement in which conceptions of offense and defense are inextricably confused. But in new guise of international Marxism, with its honeyed promises to a desperate and wartorn outside world, it is more dangerous and insidious than even before.

It should not be thought from above that Soviet party line is necessarily disingenuous and insincere on part of all those who put it forward. Many of them are too ignorant of outside world and mentally too dependent to question self-hypnotism, and have no difficulty making themselves believe what they find it comforting and convenient to believe. Finally we have the unsolved mystery as to who, if anyone, in this great land actually receives accurate and unbiased information about outside world. In an atmosphere of Oriental secretiveness and conspiracy which pervades this government, possibilities for distorting or poisoning sources and currents of information are infinite. The very disrespect of Russians for objective truth—indeed, their disbelief in its existence—leads them to view all stated facts as instruments for furtherance of one ulterior purpose or another. There is good reason to suspect that this government is actually a conspiracy within a conspiracy, and it is hard to believe that Stalin himself receives anything like an objective picture of outside world. Here there is ample scope for the type of subtle intrigue at which Russians are past masters. Inability of foreign governments to place their case squarely before Russian policy makers—extent to which they are delivered up in their relations with Russia to good graces of obscure and unknown advisors whom they never see and cannot influence—this is a most disquieting feature of diplomacy in Moscow, and one which Western statesmen would do well to keep in mind if they would understand nature of difficulties encountered here. . . .

We have here a political force committed fanatically to the belief that with US there can be no permanent modus vivendi, that it is desirable and necessary that the internal harmony of our society be disrupted, our traditional way of life be destroyed, the international authority of our state be broken, if Soviet power is to be secure. This political force has complete power of disposition over energies of one of the world's greatest peoples and resources of the world's richest national territory, and is borne along by deep and powerful currents of Russian nationalism. In addition, it has an elaborate and far-flung apparatus for exertion of its influence in other countries, an apparatus of amazing flexibility and versatility, managed by people whose experience and skill in underground methods are presumable without parallel in history. Finally, it is seemingly inaccessible to considerations of reality in its basic reactions. For it, the vast fund of objective fact about human society is not, as with us, the measure against which outlook is constantly being tested and reformed, but a grab bag from which individual items are selected arbitrarily and tendentiously to bolster an outlook already preconceived. This is admittedly not a pleasant picture. Problem of how to cope with this force is undoubtedly greatest task our diplomacy has ever faced and probably the greatest it will ever have to face. It should be the point of departure from which our political general staff work at the present juncture should proceed. It should be approached with same thoroughness and care as solution of major strategic problem in war, and if necessary, with no smaller outlay in planning effort. I cannot attempt to suggest all the answers here. But I would like to record my conviction that the problem is within our power to solve—and that without recourse to any general military conflict. And in support of this conviction there are certain observations of a more encouraging nature I should like to make:

(One) Soviet power, unlike that of Hitlerite Germany, is neither schematic nor adventuristic. It does not work by fixed plans. It does not take unnecessary risks. Impervious to logic of reason, and it is highly sensitive to logic of force. For this reason it can easily withdraw—and usually does—when strong resistance is encountered at any point. Thus, if the adversary has sufficient force and makes clear his readiness to use it, he rarely has to do so. If situations are properly handled there need be no prestige-engaging showdowns.

(Two) Gauged against Western world as a whole, Soviets are still by far the weaker force. Thus, their success will really depend on degree of cohesion, firmness, and vigor which Western world can muster. And this is factor which it is within our power to influence.

(Three) Success of Soviet system, as form of internal power, is not yet finally proven. It has yet to be demonstrated that it can survive supreme test of successive transfer of power from one individual or group to another. Lenin's death was first such transfer, and its effects wracked Soviet state for fifteen years after. Stalin's death or retirement will be second. But even this will not be final test. Soviet internal system will now be subjected, by virtue of recent territorial expansions, to a series of additional strains which once proved severe tax on Tsardom. We here are convinced that never since termination of the civil war have the mass of Russian people been emotionally farther removed from doctrines of Communist Party than they are today. In Russia, party has now become a great and—for the moment—highly successful apparatus of dictatorial administration, but it has ceased to be a source of emotional inspiration. Thus, internal soundness and permanence of movement need not yet be regarded as assured.

(Four) All Soviet propaganda beyond Soviet security sphere is basically negative and destructive. It should therefore be relatively easy to combat it by any intelligent and really constructive program.

For these reasons I think we may approach calmly and with good heart the problem of how to deal with Russia. As to how this approach should be made, I only wish to advance, by way of conclusion, the following comments:

1. Our first step must be to apprehend, and recognize for what it is, the nature of the movement with which we are dealing. We must study it with the same courage, detachment, objectivity, and the same determination not to be emotionally provoked or unseated by it, with which a doctor studies unruly and unreasonable individuals.

2. We must see that our public is educated to realities of Russian situation. I cannot overemphasize the importance of this. Press cannot do this alone. It must be done mainly by government, which is necessarily more experienced and better informed on practical problems involved. In this we need not be deterred by ugliness of the picture. I am convinced that there would be far less hysterical anti-Sovietism in our country today if the realities of this situation were better understood by our people. There is nothing as dangerous or as terrifying as the unknown. It may also be argued that to reveal more information on our difficulties with Russia would reflect unfavorably on Russian-American relations. I feel that if there is any real risk here involved, it is one which we should have the courage to face, and the sooner the better. But I cannot see what we would be risking. Our stake in this country, even coming on the heels of tremendous demonstrations of our friendship for Russian people, is remarkably small. We have here no investments to guard, no actual trade to lose, virtually no citizens to protect, few cultural contacts to preserve. Our only stake lies in what we hope rather than what we have; and I am convinced we have a better chance of realizing those hopes if our public is enlightened and if our dealings with Russians are placed entirely on realistic and matter of fact basis.

3. Much depends on health and vigor of our own society. World communism is like malignant parasite which feeds only on diseased tissue. This is the point at which domestic and foreign policies meet. Every courageous and incisive measure to solve internal problems of our own society, to improve self-confidence, discipline, morale, and community spirit of our own people, is a diplomatic victory over Moscow worth a thousand diplomatic notes and joint communiques. If we cannot abandon fatalism and indifference in face of deficiencies of our own society, Moscow will profit—Moscow cannot help profiting by them in its foreign policies.

4. We must formulate and put forward for other nations a much more positive and constructive picture of the sort of world we would like to see than we have put forward in the past. It is not enough to urge the people to develop political processes similar to our own. Many foreign peoples, in Europe at least, are tired and frightened by experiences of the past, and are less interested in abstract freedom than in security. They are seeking guidance rather than responsibilities. We should be better able than the Russians to give them this. And unless we do, the Russians certainly will.

5. Finally, we must have courage and self-confidence to cling to our own methods and conceptions of human society. After all, the greatest danger that can befall us in coping with this problem of Soviet communism is that we shall allow ourselves to become like those with whom we are coping.❖

Daniel Bell (1919–) grew up on New York City's Lower East Side, the son of work-ing people. He finished high school at age sixteen and entered City College, where, like many young New York intellectuals, he was part of the anti-Communist Left. Af-ter graduating from college in 1938, he studied for his Ph.D. at Columbia University, then taught briefly at the University of Chicago. From 1948 to 1958, he wrote for *Fortune* magazine while maintaining ties with the academy. In 1959, Bell joined the faculty of Harvard University, where he has remained until the present. Bell has writ-ten numerous books and articles, including *The End of Ideology* (1960), from which the selection is taken, and *The Coming Post-Industrial Society* (1973). Though Bell de-fends the scholar against the intellectual in "The End of Ideology in the West," many would consider him every bit the intellectual by another definition—a serious, in-formed, and intelligent general social theorist of modern society. Obviously, by the time he began to write for *Fortune* in 1948, Bell had already relinquished the leftism of his youth. Yet as one can see from this text, the more centrist, even conservative instincts of his adult years were still informed by, and directed against, Marxist social theory. Bell's writings are taken seriously, for good reason, by social theorists from many points in the political spectrum.

The End of Ideology in the West
Daniel Bell (1960)

This age, too, can add appropriate citations—made all the more wry and bitter by the long period of bright hope that preceded it—for the two decades between 1930 and 1950 have an intensity peculiar in written history: world-wide economic de-pression and sharp class struggles; the rise of fascism and racial imperialism in a country that had stood at an advanced stage of human culture; the tragic self-immolation of a revolutionary generation that had proclaimed the finer ideals of man; destructive war of a breadth and scale hitherto unknown; the bureaucratized murder of millions in concentration camps and death chambers.

For the radical intellectual who had articulated the revolutionary impulses of the past century and a half, all this has meant an end to chiliastic hopes, to millenarian-ism, to apocalyptic thinking—and to ideology. For ideology, which once was a road to action, has come to be a dead end.

Whatever its origins among the French *philosophes,* ideology as a way of trans-lating ideas into action was given its sharpest phrasing by the left Hegelians, by Feuerbach and by Marx. For them, the function of philosophy was to be critical, to rid the present of the past. ("The tradition of all the dead generations weighs like a nightmare on the brain of the living," wrote Marx.) Feuerbach, the most radical of all the left Hegelians, called himself Luther II. Man would be free, he said, if we could demythologize religion. The history of all thought was a history of progressive disenchantment, and if finally, in Christianity, God had been transformed from a parochial deity to a universal abstraction, the function of criticism—using the radi-cal tool of alienation, or self-estrangement—was to replace theology by anthropol-

Excerpt from *The End of Ideology* (Glencoe, Ill.: Free Press, 1960), pp. 369–375. Reprinted by permis-sion of the author.

ogy, to substitute Man for God. Philosophy was to be directed at life, man was to be liberated from the "specter of abstractions" and extricated from the bind of the supernatural. Religion was capable only of creating "false consciousness." Philosophy would reveal "true consciousness." And by placing Man, rather than God, at the center of consciousness, Feuerbach sought to bring the "infinite into the finite."

If Feuerbach "descended into the world," Marx sought to transform it. And where Feuerbach proclaimed anthropology, Marx, reclaiming a root insight of Hegel, emphasized History and historical contexts. The world was not generic Man, but men; and of men, classes of men. Men differed because of their class position. And truths were class truths. All truths, thus, were masks, or partial truths, but the real truth was the revolutionary truth. And this real truth was rational.

Thus a dynamic was introduced into the analysis of ideology, and into the creation of a new ideology. By demythologizing religion, one recovered (from God and sin) the potential in man. By the unfolding of history, rationality was revealed. In the struggle of classes, true consciousness, rather than false consciousness, could be achieved. But if truth lay in action, one must act. The left Hegelians, said Marx, were only *litterateurs*. (For them a magazine was "practice.") For Marx, the only real action was in politics. But action, revolutionary action as Marx conceived it, was not mere social change. It was, in its way, the resumption of all the old millenarian, chiliastic ideas of the Anabaptists. It was, in its new vision, a new ideology.

Ideology is the conversion of ideas into social levers. Without irony, Max Lerner once entitled a book "Ideas Are Weapons." This is the language of ideology. It is more. It is the commitment to the consequences of ideas. . . .

A social movement can rouse people when it can do three things: simplify ideas, establish a claim to truth, and, in the union of the two, demand a commitment to action. Thus, not only does ideology transform ideas, it transforms people as well. The nineteenth-century ideologies, by emphasizing inevitability and by infusing passion into their followers, could compete with religion. By identifying inevitability with progress, they linked up with the positive values of science. But more important, these ideologies were linked, too, with the rising class of intellectuals, which was seeking to assert a place in society.

The differences between the intellectual and the scholar, without being invidious, are important to understand. The scholar has a bounded field of knowledge, a tradition, and seeks to find his place in it, adding to the accumulated, tested knowledge of the past as to a mosaic. The scholar, qua scholar, is less involved with his "self." The intellectual begins with *his* experience, *his* individual perceptions of the world, *his* privileges and deprivations, and judges the world by these sensibilities. Since his own status is of high value, his judgments of the society reflect the treatment accorded him. In a business civilization, the intellectual felt that the wrong values were being honored, and rejected the society. Thus there was a "built-in" compulsion for the free-floating intellectual to become political. The ideologies, therefore, which emerged from the nineteenth century had the force of the intellectuals behind them. They embarked upon what William James called "the faith ladder," which in its vision of the future cannot distinguish possibilities from probabilities, and converts the latter into certainties.

Today, these ideologies are exhausted. The events behind this important sociological change are complex and varied. Such calamities as the Moscow Trials, the Nazi-Soviet pact, the concentration camps, the suppression of the Hungarian workers, form one chain; such social changes as the modification of capitalism, the rise of the

Welfare State, another. In philosophy, one can trace the decline of simplistic, rationalistic beliefs and the emergence of new stoic-theological images of man, e.g. Freud, Tillich, Jaspers, etc. This is not to say that such ideologies as communism in France and Italy do not have a political weight, or a driving momentum from other sources. But out of all this history, one simple fact emerges: for the radical intelligentzia, the old ideologies have lost their "truth" and their power to persuade.

Few serious minds believe any longer that one can set down "blue-prints" and through "social engineering" bring about a new utopia of social harmony. At the same time, the older "counter-beliefs" have lost their intellectual force as well. Few "classic" liberals insist that the State should play no role in the economy, and few serious conservatives, at least in England and on the Continent, believe that the Welfare State is "the road to serfdom." In the Western world, therefore, there is today a rough consensus among intellectuals on political issues: the acceptance of a Welfare State; the desirability of decentralized power; a system of mixed economy and of political pluralism. In that sense, too, the ideological age has ended.

And yet, the extraordinary fact is that while the old nineteenth-century ideologies and intellectual debates have become exhausted, the rising states of Asia and Africa are fashioning new ideologies with a different appeal for their own people. These are the ideologies of industrialization, modernization, Pan-Arabism, color, and nationalism. In the distinctive difference between the two kinds of ideologies lies the great political and social problems of the second half of the twentieth century. The ideologies of the nineteenth century were universalistic, humanistic, and fashioned by intellectuals. The mass ideologies of Asia and Africa are parochial, instrumental, and created by political leaders. The driving forces of the old ideologies were social equality and, in the largest sense, freedom. The impulsions of the new ideologies are economic development and national power.

And in this appeal, Russia and China have become models. The fascination these countries exert is no longer the old idea of the free society, but the new one of economic growth. And if this involves the wholesale coercion of the population and the rise of new elites to drive the people, the new repressions are justified on the ground that without such coercions economic advance cannot take place rapidly enough. And even for some of the liberals of the West, "economic development" has become a new ideology that washes away the memory of old disillusionments.

It is hard to quarrel with an appeal for rapid economic growth and modernization, and few can dispute the goal, as few could ever dispute an appeal for equality and freedom. But in this powerful surge—and its swiftness is amazing—any movement that instates such goals risks the sacrifice of the present generation for a future that may see only a new exploitation by a new elite. For the newly-risen countries, the debate is not over the merits of Communism—the content of that doctrine has long been forgotten by friends and foes alike. The question is an older one: whether new societies can grow by building democratic institutions and allowing people to make choices—and sacrifices—voluntarily, or whether the new elites, heady with power, will impose totalitarian means to transform their countries. Certainly in these traditional and old colonial societies where the masses are apathetic and easily manipulated, the answer lies with the intellectual classes and their conceptions of the future.

Thus one finds, at the end of the fifties, a disconcerting caesura. In the West, among the intellectuals, the old passions are spent. The new generation, with no meaningful memory of these old debates, and no secure tradition to build upon, finds itself seeking new purposes within a framework of political society that has rejected, intellectually speaking, the old apocalyptic and chiliastic visions. In the search for a "cause," there is a deep, desperate, almost pathetic anger.❖

W. W. Rostow (1916–) studied at Yale, where he received his B.A. in 1936 and his Ph.D. in 1940. He was also a Rhodes Scholar before serving in the Office of Strategic Services during World War II. From 1950 to 1961, he was professor of economic history at MIT. Rostow was special assistant to President John F. Kennedy in 1961, then served on the Policy Planning Council in the Department of State for five years. From 1966 to 1969, during the worst years of the war in Vietnam, he again served as special assistant in the White House. After his service under President Lyndon Johnson, he became professor of economics and history at the University of Texas. Rostow has written many books, including *Process of Economic Growth* (1952) and the more popular *Stages of Economic Growth: A Non-Communist Manifesto* (1960), from which the selection is taken. His superior academic credentials, along with his years of service in government, lent particular weight to his theory of economic modernization. He was one of the best and brightest to join the Kennedy administration in 1960, bringing with him a philosophy of economic history that was perfectly consistent with Kennedy's goal of reinvigorating the American Golden Age.

Modernization: Stages of Growth

W. W. Rostow (1960)

The Traditional Society

First, the traditional society. A traditional society is one whose structure is developed within limited production functions, based on pre-Newtonian science and technology, and on pre-Newtonian attitudes towards the physical world. Newton is here used as a symbol for that watershed in history when men came widely to believe that the external world was subject to a few knowable laws, and was systematically capable of productive manipulation.

The conception of the traditional society is, however, in no sense static; and it would not exclude increases in output. Acreage could be expanded; some *ad hoc* technical innovations, often highly productive innovations, could be introduced in trade, industry and agriculture; productivity could rise with, for example, the improvement of irrigation works or the discovery and diffusion of a new crop. But the central fact about the traditional society was that a ceiling existed on the level of attainable output per head. This ceiling resulted from the fact that the potentialities which flow from modern science and technology were either not available or not regularly and systematically applied.

Both in the longer past and in recent times the story of traditional societies was thus a story of endless change. The area and volume of trade within them and between them fluctuated, for example, with the degree of political and social turbulence, the efficiency of central rule, the upkeep of the roads. Population—and,

Excerpt from *The Stages of Economic Growth* (Cambridge: Cambridge University Press, 1971), pp. 4–16.

within limits, the level of life—rose and fell not only with the sequence of the harvests, but with the incidence of war and of plague. Varying degrees of manufacture developed; but, as in agriculture, the level of productivity was limited by the inaccessibility of modern science, its applications, and its frame of mind.

Generally speaking, these societies, because of the limitation on productivity, had to devote a very high proportion of their resources to agriculture; and flowing from the agricultural system there was an hierarchical social structure, with relatively narrow scope—but some scope—for vertical mobility. Family and clan connexions played a large role in social organization. The value system of these societies was generally geared to what might be called a long-run fatalism; that is, the assumption that the range of possibilities open to one's grandchildren would be just about what it had been for one's grandparents. But this long-run fatalism by no means excluded the short-run option that, within a considerable range, it was possible and legitimate for the individual to strive to improve his lot, within his lifetime. In Chinese villages, for example, there was an endless struggle to acquire or to avoid losing land, yielding a situation where land rarely remained within the same family for a century.

Although central political rule—in one form or another—often existed in traditional societies, transcending the relatively self-sufficient regions, the centre of gravity of political power generally lay in the regions, in the hands of those who owned or controlled the land. The landowner maintained fluctuating but usually profound influence over such central political power as existed, backed by its entourage of civil servants and soldiers, imbued with attitudes and controlled by interests transcending the regions.

In terms of history then, with the phrase 'traditional society' we are grouping the whole pre-Newtonian world: the dynasties in China; the civilization of the Middle East and the Mediterranean; the world of medieval Europe. And to them we add the post-Newtonian societies which, for a time, remained untouched or unmoved by man's new capability for regularly manipulating his environment to his economic advantage.

To place these infinitely various, changing societies in a single category, on the ground that they all shared a ceiling on the productivity of their economic techniques, is to say very little indeed. But we are, after all, merely clearing the way in order to get at the subject of this book; that is, the post-traditional societies, in which each of the major characteristics of the traditional society was altered in such ways as to permit regular growth: its politics, social structure, and (to a degree) its values, as well as its economy.

The Preconditions for Take-off

The second stage of growth embraces societies in the process of transition; that is, the period when the preconditions for take-off are developed; for it takes time to transform a traditional society in the ways necessary for it to exploit the fruits of modern science, to fend off diminishing returns, and thus to enjoy the blessings and choices opened up by the march of compound interest.

The preconditions for take-off were initially developed, in a clearly marked way, in Western Europe of the late seventeenth and early eighteenth centuries as the insights of modern science began to be translated into new production functions in both agriculture and industry, in a setting given dynamism by the lateral expansion of world markets and the international competition for them. But all that lies behind the break-up of the Middle Ages is relevant to the creation of the preconditions for take-off in Western Europe. Among the Western European states, Britain, favoured by geography, natural resources, trading possibilities, social and political structure, was the first to develop fully the preconditions for take-off.

The more general case in modern history, however, saw the stage of preconditions arise not endogenously but from some external intrusion by more advanced societies. These invasions—literal or figurative—shocked the traditional society and began or hastened its undoing; but they also set in motion ideas and sentiments which initiated the process by which a modern alternative to the traditional society was constructed out of the old culture.

The idea spreads not merely that economic progress is possible, but that economic progress is a necessary condition for some other purpose, judged to be good: be it national dignity, private profit, the general welfare, or a better life for the children. Education, for some at least, broadens and changes to suit the needs of modern economic activity. New types of enterprising men come forward—in the private economy, in government, or both—willing to mobilize savings and to take risks in pursuit of profit or modernization. Banks and other institutions for mobilizing capital appear. Investment increases, notably in transport, communications, and in raw materials in which other nations may have an economic interest. The scope of commerce, internal and external, widens. And, here and there, modern manufacturing enterprise appears, using the new methods. But all this activity proceeds at a limited pace within an economy and a society still mainly characterized by traditional low-productivity methods, by the old social structure and values, and by the regionally based political institutions that developed in conjunction with them.

In many recent cases, for example, the traditional society persisted side by side with modern economic activities, conducted for limited economic purposes by a colonial or quasi-colonial power.

Although the period of transition—between the traditional society and the take-off—saw major changes in both the economy itself and in the balance of social values, a decisive feature was often political. Politically, the building of an effective centralized national state—on the basis of coalitions touched with a new nationalism, in opposition to the traditional landed regional interests, the colonial power, or both, was a decisive aspect of the preconditions period; and it was, almost universally, a necessary condition for take-off.

The Take-off

We come now to the great watershed in the life of modern societies: the third stage in this sequence, the take-off. The take-off is the interval when the old blocks and resistances to steady growth are finally overcome. The forces making for economic progress, which yielded limited bursts and enclaves of modern activity, expand and come to dominate the society. Growth becomes its normal condition. Compound interest becomes built, as it were, into its habits and institutional structure.

In Britain and the well-endowed parts of the world populated substantially from Britain (the United States, Canada etc.) the proximate stimulus for take-off was mainly (but not wholly) technological. In the more general case, the take-off awaited not only the build-up of social overhead capital and a surge of technological development in industry and agriculture, but also the emergence to political power of a group prepared to regard the modernization of the economy as serious, high-order political business.

During the take-off, the rate of effective investment and savings may rise from, say, 5% of the national income to 10% or more; although where heavy social over-head capital investment was required to create the technical preconditions for take-off the investment rate in the preconditions period could be higher than 5%, as, for example, in Canada before the 1890's and Argentina before 1914. In such cases capital imports usually formed a high proportion of total investment in the preconditions period and sometimes even during the take-off itself, as in Russia and Canada during their pre-1914 railway booms.

During the take-off new industries expand rapidly, yielding profits a large proportion of which are reinvested in new plants; and these new industries, in turn, stimulate, through their rapidly expanding requirement for factory workers, the services to support them, and for other manufactured goods, a further expansion in urban areas and in other modern industrial plants. The whole process of expansion in the modern sector yields an increase of income in the hands of those who not only save at high rates but place their savings at the disposal of those engaged in modern sector activities. The new class of entrepreneurs expands; and it directs the enlarging flows of investment in the private sector. The economy exploits hitherto unused natural resources and methods of production.

New techniques spread in agriculture as well as industry, as agriculture is commercialized, and increasing numbers of farmers are prepared to accept the new methods and the deep changes they bring to ways of life. The revolutionary changes in agricultural productivity are an essential condition for successful take-off; for modernization of a society increases radically its bill for agricultural products. In a decade or two both the basic structure of the economy and the social and political structure of the society are transformed in such a way that a steady rate of growth can be, thereafter, regularly sustained. . . .

One can approximately allocate the take-off of Britain to the two decades after 1783; France and the United States to the several decades preceding 1860; Germany, the third quarter of the nineteenth century; Japan, the fourth quarter of the nineteenth century; Russia and Canada the quarter-century or so preceding 1914; while during the 1950's India and China have, in quite different ways, launched their respective take-offs.

The Drive to Maturity

After take-off there follows a long interval of sustained if fluctuating progress, as the now regularly growing economy drives to extend modern technology over the whole front of its economic activity. Some 10–20% of the national income is steadily invested, permitting output regularly to outstrip the increase in population. The make-up of the economy changes unceasingly as technique improves, new industries accelerate, older industries level off. The economy finds its place in the international economy: goods formerly imported are produced at home; new import requirements develop, and new export commodities to match them. The society makes such terms as it will with the requirements of modern efficient production, balancing off the new against the older values and institutions, or revising the latter in such ways as to support rather than to retard the growth process.

Some sixty years after take-off begins (say, forty years after the end of take-off) what may be called maturity is generally attained. The economy, focused during the take-off around a relatively narrow complex of industry and technology, has extended its range into more refined and technologically often more complex processes; for example, there may be a shift in focus from the coal, iron, and heavy engineering industries of the railway phase to machine-tools, chemicals, and electrical equipment. This, for example, was the transition through which Germany, Britain, France, and the United States had passed by the end of the nineteenth century or shortly thereafter. . . .

Formally, we can define maturity as the stage in which an economy demonstrates the capacity to move beyond the original industries which powered its take-off and to absorb and to apply efficiently over a very wide range of its resources—if not the whole range—the most advanced fruits of (then) modern technology. This is the stage in which an economy demonstrates that it has the technological and entrepreneurial skills to produce not everything, but anything that it chooses to produce. It may lack (like contemporary Sweden and Switzerland, for example) the raw materials or other supply conditions required to produce a given type of output economically; but its dependence is a matter of economic choice or political priority rather than a technological or institutional necessity.

Historically, it would appear that something like sixty years was required to move a society from the beginning of take-off to maturity. Analytically the explanation for some such interval may lie in the powerful arithmetic of compound interest applied to the capital stock, combined with the broader consequences for a society's ability to absorb modern technology of three successive generations living under a regime where growth is the normal condition. But, clearly, no dogmatism is justified about the exact length of the interval from take-off to maturity.

The Age of High Mass-Consumption

We come now to the age of high mass-consumption, where, in time, the leading sectors shift towards durable consumers' goods and services: a phase from which Americans are beginning to emerge; whose not unequivocal joys Western Europe and Japan are beginning energetically to probe; and with which Soviet society is engaged in an uneasy flirtation.

As societies achieved maturity in the twentieth century two things happened: real income per head rose to a point where a large number of persons gained a command over consumption which transcended basic food, shelter, and clothing; and the structure of the working force changed in ways which increased not only the proportion of urban to total population, but also the proportion of the population working in offices or in skilled factory jobs—aware of and anxious to acquire the consumption fruits of a mature economy.

In addition to these economic changes, the society ceased to accept the further extension of modern technology as an overriding objective. It is in this post-maturity stage, for example, that, through the political process, Western societies have chosen to allocate increased resources to social welfare and security. The emergence of the welfare state is one manifestation of a society's moving beyond technical maturity; but it is also at this stage that resources tend increasingly to be directed to the production of consumers' durables and to the diffusion of services on a mass basis, if consumers' sovereignty reigns. The sewing-machine, the bicycle, and then the various electric-powered household gadgets were gradually diffused. Historically, however, the decisive element has been the cheap mass automobile with its quite revolutionary effects—social as well as economic—on the life and expectations of society.

For the United States, the turning point was, perhaps, Henry Ford's moving assembly line of 1913–14; but it was in the 1920's, and again in the post-war decade, 1946–56, that this stage of growth was pressed to, virtually, its logical conclusion. In the 1950's Western Europe and Japan appear to have fully entered this phase, accounting substantially for a momentum in their economies quite unexpected in the immediate post-war years. The Soviet Union is technically ready for this stage, and, by every sign, its citizens hunger for it; but Communist leaders face difficult political and social problems of adjustment if this stage is launched.

Beyond Consumption

Beyond, it is impossible to predict, except perhaps to observe that Americans, at least, have behaved in the past decade as if diminishing relative marginal utility sets in, after a point, for durable consumers' goods; and they have chosen, at the margin, larger families—behaviour in the pattern of Buddenbrooks dynamics. Americans have behaved as if, having been born into a system that provided economic security and high mass-consumption, they placed a lower valuation on acquiring additional increments of real income in the conventional form as opposed to the advantages and values of an enlarged family. But even in this adventure in generalization it is a shade too soon to create—on the basis of one case—a new stage-of-growth, based on babies, in succession to the age of consumers' durables: as economists might say, the income-elasticity of demand for babies may well vary from society to society. But it is true that the implications of the baby boom along with the not wholly unrelated deficit in social overhead capital are likely to dominate the American economy over the next decade rather than the further diffusion of consumers' durables.

Here then, in an impressionistic rather than an analytic way, are the stages-of-growth which can be distinguished once a traditional society begins its modernization: the transitional period when the preconditions for take-off are created generally in response to the intrusion of a foreign power, converging with certain domestic forces making for modernization; the take-off itself; the sweep into maturity generally taking up the life of about two further generations; and then, finally, if the rise of income has matched the spread of technological virtuosity (which, as we shall see, it need not immediately do) the diversion of the fully mature economy to the provision of durable consumers' goods and services (as well as the welfare state) for its increasingly urban— and then suburban—population. Beyond lies the question of whether or not secular spiritual stagnation will arise, and, if it does, how man might fend it off. . . .

A Dynamic Theory of Production

These stages are not merely descriptive. They are not merely a way of generalizing certain factual observations about the sequence of development of modern societies. They have an inner logic and continuity. They have an analytic bone-structure, rooted in a dynamic theory of production.

The classical theory of production is formulated under essentially static assumptions which freeze—or permit only once-over change—in the variables most relevant to the process of economic growth. As modern economists have sought to merge classical production theory with Keynesian income analysis they have introduced the dynamic variables: population, technology, entrepreneurship etc. But they have tended to do so in forms so rigid and general that their models cannot grip the essential phenomena of growth, as they appear to an economic historian. We require a dynamic theory of production which isolates not only the distribution of income between consumption, saving, and investment (and the balance of production between consumers and capital goods) but which focuses directly and in some detail on the composition of investment and on developments within particular sectors of the economy. . . .

And there are other decisions as well that societies have made as the choices open to them have been altered by the unfolding process of economic growth; and these broad collective decisions, determined by many factors—deep in history, culture, and the active political process—outside the market-place, have interplayed with the dynamics of market demand, risk-taking, technology and entrepreneurship, to determine the specific content of the stages of growth for each society.

How, for example, should the traditional society react to the intrusion of a more advanced power: with cohesion, promptness, and vigour, like the Japanese; by making a virtue of fecklessness, like the oppressed Irish of the eighteenth century; by slowly and reluctantly altering the traditional society, like the Chinese?

When independent modern nationhood is achieved, how should the national energies be disposed: in external aggression, to right old wrongs or to exploit newly created or perceived possibilities for enlarged national power; in completing and refining the political victory of the new national government over old regional interests; or in modernizing the economy?

Once growth is under way, with the take-off, to what extent should the requirements of diffusing modern technology and maximizing the rate of growth be moderated by the desire to increase consumption *per capita* and to increase welfare?

When technological maturity is reached, and the nation has at its command a modernized and differentiated industrial machine, to what ends should it be put, and in what proportions: to increase social security, through the welfare state; to expand mass-consumption into the range of durable consumers' goods and services; to increase the nation's stature and power on the world scene; or to increase leisure?

And then the question beyond, where history offers us only fragments: what to do when the increase in real income itself loses its charm? Babies, boredom, three-day week-ends, the moon, or the creation of new inner, human frontiers in substitution for the imperatives of scarcity?❖

Talcott Parsons (1902–1979) developed his social theory of action systems throughout his career. In "Action Systems and Social Systems," his summary of that theory as he worked it between 1961 and 1971, two of the most distinctive features of Parsons's social theory are illustrated. First, he understands the social system to be a distinct entity, different from but interdependent with three other action systems: culture, personality, and the behavioral organism. Second, Parsons makes explicit reference to Durkheim in his view that social systems are *sui generis* things in which values serve to maintain the patterned integrity of the system. Some have argued that these theoretical convictions were traceable to the Golden Age culture, in which it was widely believed America was *the* exemplification of society itself because of the power of its values.

"Sex Roles in the American Kinship System" (1943) is an illustration of Parsons's theory applied to an empirical topic. Here, Parsons demonstrates his remarkable ability to press deeper and deeper into the logic of his theoretical systems. In the 1940s and 1950s, when this essay was most widely studied, his ideas were not particularly remarkable; the family as he discussed it was taken for granted by social scientists. By the 1970s, however, feminist scholars began to use Parsons's theory as a point of protest against systematic, social scientific sexism. Today, of course, anyone can understand why feminists would object to being defined as dependent, neurotic, and compulsive, perhaps especially when these views are stated in so cool a scientific language.

Action Systems and Social Systems
Talcott Parsons (1961–1971)

We consider social systems to be constituents of the more general system of action, the other primary constituents being cultural systems, personality systems, and behavioral organisms; all four are abstractly defined relative to the concrete behavior of social interaction. We treat the three subsystems of actions other than the social system as constituents of its environment. This usage is somewhat unfamiliar, especially for the case of the personalities of individuals. It is justified fully elsewhere, but to understand what follows it is essential to keep in mind that neither social nor personality systems are here conceived as concrete entities.

The distinctions among the four subsystems of action are functional. We draw them in terms of the four primary functions which we impute to all systems of action, namely pattern-maintenance, integration, goal-attainment, and adaptation.

An action system's primary integrative problem is the coordination of its constituent units, in the first instance human individuals, though for certain purposes collectivities may be treated as actors. Hence, we attribute primacy of integrative function to the social system.

We attribute primacy of pattern-maintenance—and of creative pattern change—to the cultural system. Whereas social systems are organized with primary reference to the articulation of social relationships, cultural systems are organized around the

Excerpt from *The System of Modern Societies* (Englewood Cliffs, New Jersey: Prentice-Hall, 1971), pp. 4–8. Copyright 1971. Reprinted by permission of Prentice-Hall. Though this selection appeared in 1971, it represents Parsons's theory as it evolved in the post–World War II period.

characteristics of complexes of symbolic meaning—the codes in terms of which they are structured, the particular clusters of symbols they employ, and the conditions of their utilization, maintenance, and change as parts of action systems.

We attribute primacy of goal-attainment to the personality of the individual. The personality system is the primary *agency* of action processes, hence of the implementation of cultural principles and requirements. On the level of reward in the motivational sense, the optimization of gratification or satisfaction to personalities is the primary goal of action.

The behavioral organism is conceived as the adaptive subsystem, the locus of the primary human facilities which underlie the other systems. It embodies a set of conditions to which action must adapt and comprises the primary mechanism of interrelation with the physical environment, especially through the input and processing of information in the central nervous system and through motor activity in coping with exigencies of the physical environment. These relationships are presented systematically in Table 1.

TABLE 1   Action

Subsystems	Primary Functions
Social	Integration
Cultural*	Pattern Maintenance*
Personality*	Goal Attainment*
Behavioral Organism*	Adaptation*

*These are the social subsystem's environment.

There are two systems of reality which are environmental to action in general and not constituents of action in our analytical sense. The first is the *physical environment,* including not only phenomena as understandable in terms of physics and chemistry, but also the world of living organisms so far as they are not integrated into action systems. The second, which we conceive to be independent of the physical environment as well as of action systems as such, we will call "*ultimate reality,*" in a sense derived from traditions of philosophy. It concerns what Weber called "problem of meaning" for human action and is mediated into action primarily by the cultural system's structuring of meaningful orientations that include, but are not exhausted by, cognitive "answers."

In analyzing the interrelations among the four subsystems of action—and between these systems and the environments of action—it is essential to keep in mind the phenomenon of *interpenetration.* Perhaps the best-known case of interpenetration is the *internalization* of social objects and cultural norms into the personality of the individual. Learned content of experience, organized and stored in the memory apparatus of the organism, is another example, as is the *institutionalization* of normative components of cultural systems as constitutive structures of social systems. We hold that the boundary between any pair of action systems involves a "zone" of structured components or patterns which must be treated theoretically as *common* to *both* systems, not simply allocated to one system or the other. For example, it is untenable to say that norms of conduct derived from social experience, which both Freud (in the concept of the Superego) and Durkheim (in the concept of collective representations) treated as parts of the personality of the individual, must be *either* that *or* part of the social system.

It is by virtue of the zones of interpenetration that processes of interchange among systems can take place. This is especially true at the levels of symbolic meaning and generalized motivation. In order to "communicate" symbolically, individuals must have culturally organized common codes, such as those of language, which are also integrated into systems of their social interaction. In order to make information stored in the central nervous system utilizable for the personality, the behavioral organism must have mobilization and retrieval mechanisms which, through interpenetration, subserve motives organized at the personality level.

Thus, we conceived social systems to be "open," engaged in continual interchange of inputs and outputs with their environments. Moreover, we conceive them to be internally differentiated into various orders of subcomponents which are also continually involved in processes of interchange.

Social systems are those constituted by states and processes of social interaction among acting units. If the properties of interaction were derivable from properties of the acting units, social systems would be epiphenomenal, as much "individualistic" social theory has contended. Our position is sharply in disagreement: it derives particularly from Durkheim's statement that society—and other social systems—is a "reality *sui generis*."

The structure of social systems may be analyzed in terms of four types of independently variable components: values, norms, collectivities, and roles. Values take primacy in the pattern-maintenance functioning of social systems, for they are conceptions of desirable types of social systems that regulate the making of commitments by social units. Norms, which function primarily to integrate social systems, are specific to particular social functions and types of social situations. They include not only value components specified to appropriate levels in the structure of a social system, but also specific modes of orientation for acting under the functional and situational conditions of particular collectivities and roles. Collectivities are the type of structural component that have goal-attainment primacy. Putting aside the many instances of highly fluid group systems, such as crowds, we speak of a collectivity only where two specific criteria are fulfilled. First, there must be definite statuses of membership so that a useful distinction between members and nonmembers can generally be drawn, a criterion fulfilled by cases that vary from nuclear families to political communities. Second, there must be some differentiation among members in relation to their statuses and functions within the collectivity, so that some categories of members are expected to do certain things which are not expected of other members. A role, the type of structural component that has primacy in the adaptive function, we conceive as defining a class of individuals who, through reciprocal expectations, are involved in a particular collectivity. Hence, roles comprise the primary zones of interpenetration between the social system and the personality of the individual. A role is never idiosyncratic to a particular individual, however. A father is specific to his children in his fatherhood, but he is a father in terms of the role-structure of his society. At the same time, he also participates in various other contexts of interaction, filling, for example, an occupational role.

The reality *sui generis* of social systems may involve the independent variability of each of these types of structural components relative to the others. A generalized value-pattern does not legitimize the same norms, collectivities, or roles under all conditions, for example. Similarly, many norms regulate the action of indefinite numbers of collectivities and roles, but only specific sectors of their action. Hence a collectivity generally functions under the control of a large number of particular norms. It always involves a plurality of roles, although almost any major category of role is performed in a plurality of particular collectivities. Nevertheless, social systems are comprised of *combinations* of these structural components. To be institutionalized in a stable fashion, collectivities and roles must be "governed" by specific values and norms, whereas values and norms are themselves institutionalized only insofar as they are "implemented" by particular collectivities and roles.❖

Sex Roles in the American Kinship System

Talcott Parsons (1943)

Much psychological research has suggested the very great importance to the individual of his affective ties, established in early childhood, to other members of his family of orientation. When strong affective ties have been formed, it seems reasonable to believe that situational pressures which force their drastic modification will impose important strains upon the individual.

Since all known kinship systems impose an incest tabu, the transition from asexual intrafamilial relationships to the sexual relation of marriage—generally to a previously relatively unknown person—is general. But with us this transition is accompanied by a process of "emancipation" from the ties both to parents and to siblings, which is considerably more drastic than in most kinship systems, especially in that it applies to both sexes about equally, and includes emancipation from solidarity with *all* members of the family of orientation about equally, so that there is relatively little continuity with *any* kinship ties established by birth for anyone.

The effect of these factors is reinforced by two others. Since the effective kinship unit is normally the small conjugal family, the child's emotional attachments to kin are confined to relatively few persons instead of being distributed more widely. Especially important, perhaps, is the fact that no other adult woman has a role remotely similar to that of the mother. Hence the average intensity of affective involvement in family relations is likely to be high. Secondly, the child's relations outside the family are only to a small extent ascribed. Both in the play group and in the school he must to a large extent "find his own level" in competition with others. Hence the psychological significance of his security within the family is heightened.

We have then a situation where at the same time the inevitable importance of family ties is intensified and a necessity to become emancipated from them is imposed. This situation would seem to have a good deal to do with the fact that with us adolescence—and beyond—is, as has been frequently noted, a "difficult" period in the life cycle. In particular, associated with this situation is the prominence in our society of what has been called a "youth culture," a distinctive pattern of values and attitudes of the age groups between childhood and the assumption of full adult responsibilities. This youth culture, with its irresponsibility, its pleasure-seeking, its "rating and dating," and its intensification of the romantic love pattern, is not a simple matter of "apprenticeship" in adult values and responsibilities. It bears many of the marks of reaction to emotional tension and insecurity, and in all probability has among its functions that of easing the difficult process of adjustment from child-

Excerpt from "The Kinship System of the Contemporary United States," *Essays in Sociological Theory* (New York: Free Press, 1954), pp. 189–194.

hood emotional dependency to full "maturity." In it we find still a third element underlying the prominence of the romantic love complex in American society.

The emphasis which has here been placed on the multilineal symmetry of our kinship structure might be taken to imply that our society was characterized by a correspondingly striking assimilation of the roles of the sexes to each other. It is true that American society manifests a high level of the "emancipation" of women, which in important respects involves relative assimilation to masculine roles, in accessibility to occupational opportunity, in legal rights relative to property holding, and in various other respects. Undoubtedly the kinship system constitutes one of the important sets of factors underlying this emancipation since it does not, as do so many kinship systems, place a structural premium on the role of either sex in the maintenance of the continuity of kinship relations.

But the elements of sex-role assimilation in our society are conspicuously combined with elements of segregation which in many respects are even more striking than in other societies, as for instance in the matter of the much greater attention given by women to style and refinement of taste in dress and personal appearance. This and other aspects of segregation are connected with the structure of kinship, but not so much by itself as in its interrelations with the occupational system.

The members of the conjugal family in our urban society normally share a common basis of economic support in the form of money income, but this income is not derived from the co-operative efforts of the family as a unit—its principal source lies in the remuneration of occupational roles performed by individual members of the family. Status in an occupational role is generally, however, specifically segregated from kinship status—a person holds a "job" as an individual, not by virtue of his status in a family.

Among the occupational statuses of members of a family, if there is more than one, much the most important is that of the husband and father, not only because it is usually the primary source of family income, but also because it is the most important single basis of the status of the family in the community at large. To be the main "breadwinner" of his family is a primary role of the normal adult man in our society. The corollary of this role is his far smaller participation than that of his wife in the internal affairs of the household. Consequently, "housekeeping" and the care of children is still the primary functional content of the adult feminine role in the "utilitarian" division of labor. Even if the married woman has a job, it is, at least in the middle classes, in the great majority of cases not one which in status or remuneration competes closely with those held by men of her own class. Hence there is a typically asymmetrical relation of the marriage pair to the occupational structure.

This asymmetrical relation apparently both has exceedingly important positive functional significance and is at the same time an important source of strain in relation to the patterning of sex roles.

On the positive functional side, a high incidence of certain types of patterns is essential to our occupational system and to the institutional complex in such fields as property and exchange which more immediately surround this system. In relatively commonsense terms it requires scope for the valuation of personal achievement, for equality of opportunity, for mobility in response to technical requirements, for devotion to occupational goals and interests relatively unhampered by "personal" considerations. In more technical terms it requires a high incidence of technical competence, of rationality, of universalistic norms, and of functional specificity. All these are drastically different from the patterns which are dominant in the area of kinship relations, where ascription of status by birth plays a prominent part, and where roles are defined primarily in particularistic and functionally diffuse terms.

It is quite clear that the type of occupational structure which is so essential to our society requires a far-reaching structural segregation of occupational roles from the kinship roles of the *same* individuals. They must, in the occupational system, be treated primarily as individuals. This is a situation drastically different from that found in practically all non-literate societies and in many that are literate.

At the same time, it cannot be doubted that a solidary kinship unit has functional significance of the highest order, especially in relation to the socialization of individuals and to the deeper aspects of their psychological security. What would appear to have happened is a process of mutual accommodation between these two fundamental aspects of our social structure. On the one hand our kinship system is of a structural type which, broadly speaking, interferes least with the functional needs of the occupational system, above all in that it exerts *relatively* little pressure for the ascription of an individual's social status—through class affiliation, property, and of course particular "jobs"—by virtue of his kinship status. The conjugal unit can be mobile in status independently of the other kinship ties of its members, that is, those of the spouses to the members of their families of orientation.

But at the same time this small conjugal unit can be a strongly solidary unit. This is facilitated by the prevalence of the pattern that normally only *one* of its members has an occupational role which is of determinate significance for the status of the family as a whole. Minor children, that is, as a rule do not "work," and when they do, it is already a major step in the process of emancipation from the family of orientation. The wife and mother is either exclusively a "housewife" or at most has a "job" rather than a "career."

There are perhaps two primary functional aspects of this situation. In the first place, by confining the number of status-giving occupational roles of the members of the effective conjugal unit to one, it eliminates any competition for status, especially as between husband and wife, which might be disruptive of the solidarity of marriage. So long as lines of achievement are segregated and not directly comparable, there is less opportunity for jealousy, a sense of inferiority, etc., to develop. Secondly, it aids in clarity of definition of the situation by making the status of the family in the community relatively definite and unequivocal. There is much evidence that this relative definiteness of status is an important factor in psychological security.

The same structural arrangements which have this positive functional significance also give rise to important strains. What has been said above about the pressure for thoroughgoing emancipation from the family of orientation is a case in point. But in connection with the sex-role problem there is another important source of strain.

Historically, in Western culture, it may perhaps be fairly said that there has been a strong tendency to define the feminine role psychologically as one strongly marked by elements of dependency. One of the best symbols perhaps was the fact that until rather recently the married woman was not *sui juris*, could not hold property, make contracts, or sue in her own right. But in the modern American kinship system, to say nothing of other aspects of the culture and social structure, there are at least two pressures which tend to counteract this dependency and have undoubtedly played a part in the movement for feminine emancipation.

The first, already much discussed, is the multilineal symmetry of the kinship system which gives no basis of sex discrimination, and which in kinship terms favors equal rights and responsibilities for both parties to a marriage. The second is the character of the marriage relationship. Resting as it does primarily on affective attachment for the other person as a concrete human individual, a "personality," rather than on more objective considerations of status, it puts a premium on a certain kind of mutuality and equality. There is no clearly structured superordination-subordination pattern. Each is a fully responsible "partner" with a claim to a voice in decisions, to a certain human dignity, to be "taken seriously." Surely the pattern of romantic love which makes his relation to the "woman he loves" the most important single thing in a man's life, is incompatible with the view that she is an inferior creature, fit only for dependency on him.

In our society, however, occupational status has tremendous weight in the scale of prestige values. The fact that the normal married woman is debarred from testing or demonstrating her fundamental equality with her husband in competitive occupational achievement, creates a demand for a functional equivalent. At least in the middle classes, however, this cannot be found in the utilitarian functions of the role of housewife since these are treated as relatively menial functions. To be, for instance, an excellent cook, does not give a hired maid a moral claim to a higher status than that of domestic servant.

This situation helps perhaps to account for a conspicuous tendency for the feminine role to emphasize broadly humanistic rather than technically specialized achievement values. One of the key patterns is that of "good taste," in personal appearance, house furnishings, cultural things like literature and music. To a large and perhaps increasing extent the more humanistic cultural traditions and amenities of life are carried on by women. Since these things are of high intrinsic importance in the scale of values of our culture, and since by virtue of the system of occupational specialization even many highly superior men are greatly handicapped in respect to them, there is some genuine redressing of the balance between the sexes.

There is also, however, a good deal of direct evidence of tension in the feminine role. In the "glamor girl" pattern, use of specifically feminine devices as an instrument of compulsive search for power and exclusive attention are conspicuous. Many women succumb to their dependency cravings through such channels as neurotic illness or compulsive domesticity and thereby abdicate both their responsibilities and their opportunities for genuine independence. Many of the attempts to excel in approved channels of achievement are marred by garishness of taste, by instability in response to fad and fashion, by a seriousness in community or club activities which is out of proportion to the intrinsic importance of the task. In all these and other fields there are conspicuous signs of insecurity and ambivalence. Hence it may be concluded that the feminine role is a conspicuous focus of the strains inherent in our social structure, and not the least of the sources of these strains is to be found in the functional difficulties in the integration of our kinship system with the rest of the social structure. ❖

Robert K. Merton (1910–) had begun his career at Columbia University by the end of World War II. Much like Talcott Parsons at Harvard, Merton sought to establish postwar sociology on a scientific basis. For Merton, this work proceeded partly through his teaching at Columbia and his leadership of the Bureau of Applied Social Research and partly through the composition of articles, like the one selected here. "Manifest and Latent Functions" became the lead article in Merton's *Social Theory and Social Structure,* which, for his followers, was the effective textbook (in Thomas Kuhn's sense) of modern sociology. In this, as in most of the articles in that book, Merton was part teacher and part supervisor of research—always elegantly explaining his ideas, relating them to the tradition, then carefully suggesting their value to the concrete tasks of social research. In the preface to *Social Theory and Social Structure,* Merton graciously acknowledged Parsons as his teacher and friend. Yet in the book itself, he proposed a different practical direction, if not an entirely different theoretical scheme. The side-by-side development of these two masters of sociological theory in the postwar years is a compelling story of respectful scientific cooperation across differences. The Hawthorne Western Electric study that Merton mentions in the selection was one of the first and most influential studies of early industrial sociology. It was based on observations over time of men working in close quarters wiring telephone circuit banks (once used in telephone switching stations). Merton refers to the surprising results that showed efficiency was increased primarily by latent factors that were totally unexpected when the study began.

Manifest and Latent Functions

Robert K. Merton (1949)

The distinction between manifest and latent functions was devised to preclude the inadvertent confusion, often found in the sociological literature, between conscious *motivations* for social behavior and its *objective consequences.* Our scrutiny of current vocabularies of functional analysis has shown how easily, and how unfortunately, the sociologist may identify *motives* with *functions.* It was further indicated that the motive and the function vary independently and that the failure to register this fact in an established terminology has contributed to the unwitting tendency among sociologists to confuse the subjective categories of motivation with the objective categories of function. This, then, is the central purpose of our succumbing to the not-always-commendable practice of introducing new terms into the rapidly growing technical vocabulary of sociology, a practice regarded by many laymen as an affront to their intelligence and an offense against common intelligibility.

As will be readily recognized, I have adapted the terms "manifest" and "latent" from their use in another context by Freud (although Francis Bacon had long ago spoken of "latent process" and "latent configuration" in connection with processes which are below the threshold of superficial observation).

The distinction itself has been repeatedly drawn by observers of human behavior at irregular intervals over a span of many centuries. Indeed, it would be disconcerting to find that a distinction which we have come to regard as central to functional analysis had not been made by any of that numerous company who have in effect adopted a functional orientation. We need mention only a few of those who have, in recent decades, found it necessary to distinguish in their specific interpretations of behavior between the end-in-view and the functional consequences of action.

George H. Mead: ". . . that attitude of hostility toward the law-breaker has the unique advantage [read: latent function] of uniting all members of the community in the emotional solidarity of aggression. While the most admirable of humanitarian efforts are sure to run counter to the individual interests of very many in the community, or fail to touch the interest and imagination of the multitude and to leave the community divided or indifferent, the cry of thief or murderer is attuned to profound complexes, lying below the surface of competing individual efforts, and citizens who have [been] separated by divergent interests stand together against the common enemy."

Emile Durkheim's similar analysis of the social functions of punishment is also focused on its latent functions (consequences for the community) rather than confined to manifest functions (consequences for the criminal). . . .

W. I. Thomas and F. Znaniecki: "Although all the new [Polish peasant cooperative] institutions are thus formed with the definite purpose of satisfying certain specific needs, their social function is by no means limited to their explicit and conscious purpose . . . every one of these institutions—commune or agricultural circle, loan and savings bank, or theater—is not merely a mechanism for the management of certain values but also an association of people, each member of which is supposed to participate in the common activities as a living, concrete individual. Whatever is the predominant, official common interest upon which the institution is founded, the association as a concrete group of human personalities unofficially involves many other interests; the social contacts between its members are not limited to their common pursuit, though the latter, of course, constitutes both the main reason for which the association is formed and the most permanent bond which holds it together. Owing to this combination of an abstract political, economic, or rather rational mechanism for the satisfaction of specific needs with the concrete unity of a social group, the new institution is also the best intermediary link between the peasant primary-group and the secondary national system."

These and numerous other sociological observers have, then, from time to time distinguished between categories of subjective disposition ("needs, interests, purposes") and categories of generally unrecognized but objective functional consequences ("unique advantages," "never conscious" consequences, "unintended . . . service to society," "function not limited to conscious and explicit purpose").

Since the occasion for making the distinction arises with great frequency, and since the purpose of a conceptual scheme is to direct observations toward salient elements of a situation and to prevent the inadvertent oversight of these elements, it would seem justifiable to designate this distinction by an appropriate set of terms. This is the rationale for the distinction between manifest functions and latent functions; the first referring to those objective consequences for a specified unit (person, subgroup, social or cultural system) which contribute to its adjustment or adaptation and were so intended; the second referring to unintended and unrecognized consequences of the same order.

There are some indications that the christening of this distinction may serve a heuristic purpose by becoming incorporated into an explicit conceptual apparatus, thus aiding both systematic observation and later analysis. In recent years, for example, the distinction between manifest and latent functions has been utilized in analyses of racial intermarriage, social stratification, affective frustration, Veblen's sociological theories, prevailing American orientations toward Russia, propaganda as a means of social control, Malinowski's anthropological theory, Navajo witchcraft, problems in the sociology of knowledge, fashion, the dynamics of personality, national security measures, the internal social dynamics of bureaucracy, and a great variety of other sociological problems.

The very diversity of these subject-matters suggests that the theoretic distinction between manifest and latent functions is not bound up with a limited and particular range of human behavior. But there still remains the large task of ferreting out the specific uses to which this distinction can be put, and it is to this large task that we devote the remaining pages of this chapter.

Purposes of the Distinction

Clarifies the analysis of seemingly irrational social patterns. In the first place, the distinction aids the sociological interpretation of many social practices which persist even though their manifest purpose is clearly not achieved. The time-worn procedure in such instances has been for diverse, particularly lay, observers to refer to these practices as "superstitions," "irrationalities," "mere inertia of tradition," *etc.* In other words, when group behavior does not—and, indeed, often cannot—attain its ostensible purpose there is an inclination to attribute its occurrence to lack of intelligence, sheer ignorance, survivals, or so-called inertia. Thus, the Hopi ceremonials designed to produce abundant rainfall may be labelled a superstitious practice of primitive folk and that is assumed to conclude the matter. It should be noted that this in no sense accounts for the group behavior. It is simply a case of name-calling; it substitutes the epithet "superstition" for an analysis of the actual role of this behavior in the life of the group. Given the concept of latent function, however, we are reminded that this behavior *may* perform a function for the group, although this function may be quite remote from the avowed purpose of the behavior.

The concept of latent function extends the observer's attention beyond the question of whether or not the behavior attains its avowed purpose. Temporarily ignoring these explicit purposes, it directs attention *toward* another range of consequences: those bearing, for example, upon the individual personalities of Hopi involved in the ceremony and upon the persistence and continuity of the larger group. Were one to confine himself to the problem of whether the manifest (purposed) function occurs, it becomes a problem, not for the sociologist, but for the meteorologist. And to be sure, our meteorologists agree that the rain ceremonial does not produce rain; but this is hardly to the point. It is merely to say that the ceremony does not have this technological use; that this purpose of the ceremony and its actual consequences do not coincide. But with the concept of latent function, we continue our inquiry, examining the consequences of the ceremony not for the rain gods or for meteorological phenomena, but for the groups which conduct the ceremony. And here it may be found, as many observers indicate, that the ceremonial does indeed have functions—but functions which are non-purposed or latent.

Ceremonials may fulfill the latent function of reinforcing the group identity by providing a periodic occasion on which the scattered members of a group assemble to engage in a common activity. As Durkheim among others long since indicated, such ceremonials are a means by which collective expression is afforded the sentiments which, in a further analysis, are found to be a basic source of group unity. Through the systematic application of the concept of latent function, therefore, *apparently* irrational behavior may *at times* be found to be positively functional for the group. Operating with the concept of latent function, we are not too quick to conclude that if an activity of a group does not achieve its nominal purpose, then its persistence can be described only as an instance of "inertia," "survival," or "manipulation by powerful subgroups in the society."

In point of fact, some conception like that of latent function has very often, almost invariably, been employed by social scientists observing *a standardized practice designed to achieve an objective which one knows from accredited physical science cannot be thus achieved.* This would plainly be the case, for example, with Pueblo rituals dealing with rain or fertility. *But with behavior which is not directed toward a clearly unattainable objective, sociological observers are less likely to examine the collateral or latent functions of the behavior.*

Directs attention to theoretically fruitful fields of inquiry. The distinction between manifest and latent functions serves further to direct the attention of the sociologist to precisely those realms of behavior, attitude and belief where he can most fruitfully apply his special skills. For what is his task if he confines himself to the study of manifest functions? He is then concerned very largely with determining whether a practice instituted for a particular purpose does, in fact, achieve this purpose. He will then inquire, for example, whether a new system of wage-payment achieves its avowed purpose of reducing labor turnover or of increasing output. He will ask whether a propaganda campaign has indeed gained its objective of increasing "willingness to fight" or "willingness to buy war bonds," or "tolerance toward other ethic groups." Now, these are important, and complex, types of inquiry. But, so long as sociologists *confine* themselves to the study of manifest functions, their inquiry is set for them by practical men of affairs (whether a captain of industry, a trade union leader, or, conceivably, a Navaho chieftain, is for the moment immaterial), rather than by the theoretic problems which are at the core of the discipline. By dealing primarily with the realm of manifest functions, with the key problem of whether deliberately instituted practices of organizations succeed in achieving their objectives, the sociologist becomes converted into an industrious and skilled recorder of the altogether familiar pattern of behavior. *The terms of appraisal are fixed and limited by the question put to him by the non-theoretic men of affairs, e.g.,* has the new wage-payment program achieved such-and-such purposes?

But armed with the concept of latent function, the sociologist extends his inquiry in those very directions which promise most for the theoretic development of the discipline. He examines the familiar (or planned) social practice to ascertain the latent, and hence generally unrecognized, functions (as well, of course, as the manifest functions). He considers, for example, the consequences of the new wage plan for, say, the trade union in which the workers are organized or the consequences of a propaganda program, not only for increasing its avowed purpose of stirring up patriotic fervor, but also for making large numbers of people reluctant to speak their minds when they differ with official policies, *etc.* In short, it is suggested that the *distinctive* intellectual contributions of the sociologist are found primarily in the study of unintended consequences (among which are latent functions) of social practices, as well as in the study of anticipated consequences (among which are manifest functions).

There is some evidence that it is precisely at the point where the research attention of sociologists has shifted from the plane of manifest to the plane of latent functions that they have made their *distinctive* and major contributions. This can be extensively documented but a few passing illustrations must suffice.

The Hawthorne Western Electric Studies: As is well known, the early stages of this inquiry were concerned with the problem of the relations of "illumination to efficiency" of industrial workers. For some two and a half years, attention was focused on problems such as this: do variations in the intensity of lighting affect production? The initial results showed that within wide limits there was no uniform relation between illumination and output. Production output increased *both* in the experimental group where illumination was increased (or *decreased*) *and* in the control group where no changes in illumination were introduced. In short, the investigators confined themselves wholly to a search for the manifest functions. Lacking a concept of latent social function, no attention whatever was initially paid to the social consequences *of the experiment* for relations among members of the test and control groups or for relations between workers and the test room authorities. In other words, the investigators lacked a sociological frame of reference and operated merely as "engineers" (just as a group of meteorologists might have explored the "effects" upon rainfall of the Hopi ceremonial).

Only after continued investigation, did it occur to the research group to explore the consequences of the new "experimental situation" for the self-images and self-conceptions of the workers taking part in the experiment, for the interpersonal relations among members of the group, for the coherence and unity of the group. As Elton Mayo reports it, "the illumination fiasco had made them alert to the need that very careful records should be kept of everything that happened in the room in addition to the obvious engineering and industrial devices. Their observations therefore included not only records of industrial and engineering changes but also records of physiological or medical changes, and, *in a sense*, of social and anthropological. This last took the form of a 'log' that gave as full an account as possible of the actual events of every day. . . . " In short, it was only after a long series of experiments which wholly neglected the latent social functions of the experiment (as a contrived social situation) that this distinctly sociological framework was introduced. "With this realization," the authors write, "the inquiry changed its character. No longer were the investigators interested in testing for the effects of single variables. In the place of a controlled experiment, they substituted the notion of a social situation which needed to be described and understood as a system of interdependent elements." Thereafter, as is now widely known, inquiry was directed very largely toward ferreting out the latent functions of standardized practices among the workers, of informal organization developing among workers, of workers' games instituted by "wise administrators," of large programs of worker counselling and interviewing, *etc.* The new conceptual scheme entirely altered the range and types of data gathered in the ensuing research.

One has only to return to the previously quoted excerpt from Thomas and Znaniecki in their classical work of some thirty years ago, to recognize the correctness of [Edward] Shils' remark:

> . . . indeed the history of the study of primary groups in American sociology is a supreme instance of the *discontinuities of the development of this discipline:* a problem is stressed by one who is an acknowledged founder of the discipline, the problem is left

unstudied, then, some years later, it is taken up with enthusiasm as if no one had ever thought of it before.

For Thomas and Znaniecki had repeatedly emphasized the sociological view that, whatever its major purpose, "the association as a concrete group of human personalities unofficially involves many other interests; the social contacts between its members are not limited to their common pursuit. . . . " In effect, then, it had taken years of experimentation to turn the attention of the Western Electric research team to the latent social functions of primary groups emerging in industrial organizations. It should be made clear that this case is not cited here as an instance of defective experimental design; that is not our immediate concern. It is considered only as an illustration of the pertinence for *sociological* inquiry of the concept of latent function, and the associated concepts of functional analysis. It illustrates how the inclusion of this concept (whether the term is used or not is inconsequential) can sensitize sociological investigators to a range of significant social variables which are otherwise easily overlooked. The explicit ticketing of the concept may perhaps lessen the frequency of such occasions of discontinuity in future sociological research.

The discovery of latent functions represents significant increments in sociological knowledge. There is another respect in which inquiry into latent functions represents a distinctive contribution of the social scientist. It is precisely the latent functions of a practice or belief which are *not* common knowledge, for these are unintended and generally unrecognized social and psychological consequences. As a result, findings concerning latent functions represent a greater increment in knowledge than findings concerning manifest functions. They represent, also, greater departures from "common-sense" knowledge about social life. Inasmuch as the latent functions depart, more or less, from the avowed manifest functions, the research which uncovers latent functions very often produces "paradoxical" results. The seeming paradox arises from the sharp modification of a familiar popular preconception which regards a standardized practice or belief *only* in terms of its manifest functions by indicating some of its subsidiary or collateral latent functions. The introduction of the concept of latent function in social research leads to conclusions which show that "social life is not as simple as it first seems." For as long as people confine themselves to *certain* consequences (*e.g.* manifest consequences), it is comparatively simple for them to pass moral judgments upon the practice or belief in question. Moral evaluations, generally based on these manifest consequences, tend to be polarized in terms of black or white. But the perception of further (latent) consequences often complicates the picture. Problems of moral evaluation (which are not our immediate concern) and problems of social engineering (which are our concern) both take on the additional complexities usually involved in responsible social decisions.❖

Claude Lévi-Strauss (1908–) was born in Belgium. He grew up in Versailles, then studied at the University of Paris. From 1932 to 1934, he followed a normal career path for intellectual stars in France by teaching high school (*lycée*). In 1934, however, he was offered the opportunity to teach sociology at the University of São Paulo in Brazil. Though he visited Paris from time to time, he remained in Brazil until 1939. His reading and field trips to the interior led to his becoming an anthropologist. After a year's military service (1939–1940), Lévi-Strauss returned to the New

World, first to Martinique and Puerto Rico, then to the New School for Social Research in New York City. He was in the United States through the war until 1947. During this period, his interest in linguistics emerged, in large part through contact with Roman Jakobson. His first major book of structural anthropology, *Les Structures élémentaires de la parenté*, appeared in French in 1949. He had returned to France the previous year, where he taught initially at what was then the École Pratique des Hautes Etudes. In 1958, he was named to a chair of social anthropology at the Collège de France, the highest academic honor his country bestows. Among his numerous books are *Tristes tropiques* (1955), which is must reading for anyone who cares about the intellectual pleasures and challenges of anthropology; *Structural Anthropology*, two volumes of collected essays; and the three-volume *Mythologiques*.

The selection, "The Structural Study of Myth," first appeared in 1955 and is generally considered the original manifesto for the structural study of culture. Here, Lévi-Strauss performs a deep structural analysis of the Oedipal myth without any explicit reference to a concept of the unconscious. Lévi-Strauss's sources were much more Durkheimian and Saussurian than Freudian. Two terms used in the selection might require some explanation. Literally, a *chthonian being* is one who is thought to live beneath the surface of the earth (the monsters in the third column on pages 312–313). Thus, an *autochthonous origin* would be one from the soil or from beneath the earth. In the myth, monsters are considered of autochthonous origin. Thus, in the Oedipus myth, the slaying of monsters is taken as a denial of man's origins as a creature of the earth. As Lévi-Strauss shows throughout his interpretation, the method is an attempt to understand meaningful elements in their structured relation to each other. In this case, he argues that one of the natural human dilemmas resolved by the Oedipal story is concern over how we can be born both of human and of primitive natural origins. In his way, Lévi-Strauss was also dealing with existential questions.

The Structural Study of Myth

Claude Lévi-Strauss (1958)

Despite some recent attempts to renew them, it seems that during the past twenty years anthropology has increasingly turned from studies in the field of religion. At the same time, and precisely because the interest of professional anthropologists has withdrawn from primitive religion, all kinds of amateurs who claim to belong to other disciplines have seized this opportunity to move in, thereby turning into their private playground what we had left as a wasteland. The prospects for the scientific study of religion have thus been undermined in two ways. . . .

Of all the chapters of religious anthropology probably none has tarried to the same extent as studies in the field of mythology. From a theoretical point of view the situation remains very much the same as it was fifty years ago, namely, chaotic. Myths are still widely interpreted in conflicting ways: as collective dreams, as the outcome of a kind of esthetic play, or as the basis of ritual. Mythological figures are considered as personified abstractions, divinized heroes, or fallen gods. Whatever the hypothesis, the choice amounts to reducing mythology either to idle play or to a crude kind of philosophic speculation.

Excerpt from Claire Jacobson and Brooke Grundfest Schoepf, trans., *Structural Anthropology, I* (New York: Basic Books, Inc., 1963), pp. 202–212.

In order to understand what a myth really is, must we choose between platitude and sophism? Some claim that human societies merely express, through their mythology, fundamental feelings common to the whole of mankind, such as love, hate, or revenge or that they try to provide some kind of explanations for phenomena which they cannot otherwise understand—astronomical, meteorological, and the like. But why should these societies do it in such elaborate and devious ways, when all of them are also acquainted with empirical explanations? On the other hand, psychoanalysts and many anthropologists have shifted the problems away from the natural or cosmological toward the sociological and psychological fields. But then the interpretation becomes too easy: If a given mythology confers prominence on a certain figure, let us say an evil grandmother, it will be claimed that in such a society grandmothers are actually evil and that mythology reflects the social structure and the social relations; but should the actual data be conflicting, it would be as readily claimed that the purpose of mythology is to provide an outlet for repressed feelings. Whatever the situation, a clever dialectic will always find a way to pretend that a meaning has been found.

Mythology confronts the student with a situation which at first sight appears contradictory. On the one hand it would seem that in the course of a myth anything is likely to happen. There is no logic, no continuity. Any characteristic can be attributed to any subject; every conceivable relation can be found. With myth, everything becomes possible. But on the other hand, this apparent arbitrariness is belied by the astounding similarity between myths collected in widely different regions. Therefore the problem: If the content of a myth is contingent, how are we going to explain the fact that myths throughout the world are so similar?

It is precisely this awareness of a basic antinomy pertaining to the nature of myth that may lead us toward its solution. For the contradiction which we face is very similar to that which in earlier times brought considerable worry to the first philosophers concerned with linguistic problems; linguistics could only begin to evolve as a science after this contradiction had been overcome. Ancient philosophers reasoned about language the way we do about mythology. On the one hand, they did notice that in a given language certain sequences of sounds were associated with definite meanings, and they earnestly aimed at discovering a reason for the linkage between those *sounds* and that *meaning*. Their attempt, however, was thwarted from the very beginning by the fact that the same sounds were equally present in other languages although the meaning they conveyed was entirely different. The contradiction was surmounted only by the discovery that it is the combination of sounds, not the sounds themselves, which provides the significant data. . . .

To invite the mythologist to compare his precarious situation with that of the linguist in the prescientific stage is not enough. As a matter of fact we may thus be led only from one difficulty to another. There is a very good reason why myth cannot simply be treated as language if its specific problems are to be solved; myth *is* language: to be known, myth has to be told; it is a part of human speech. In order to preserve its specificity we must be able to show that it is both the same things as language, and also something different from it. Here, too, the past experience of linguists may help us. For language itself can be analyzed into things which are at the same time similar and yet different. This is precisely what is expressed in Saussure's distinction between *langue* and *parole,* one being the structural side of language, the other the statistical aspect of it, *langue* belonging to a reversible time, *parole* being nonreversible. If those two levels already exist in language, then a third one can conceivably be isolated.

We have distinguished *langue* and *parole* by the different time referents which they use. Keeping this in mind, we may notice that myth uses a third referent which combines the properties of the first two. On the one hand, a myth always refers to events alleged to have taken place long ago. But what gives the myth an operational value is that the specific pattern described is timeless; it explains the present and the past as well as the future. This can be made clear through a comparison between myth and what appears to have largely replaced it in modern societies, namely, politics. When the historian refers to the French Revolution, it is always as a sequence of past happenings, a non-reversible series of events the remote consequences of which may still be felt at present. But to the French politician, as well as to his followers, the French Revolution is both a sequence belonging to the past—as to the historian—and a timeless pattern which can be detected in the contemporary French social structure and which provides a clue for its interpretation, a lead from which to infer future developments. Michelet, for instance, was a politically minded historian. He describes the French Revolution thus: "That day . . . everything was possible. . . . Future became present . . . that is, no more time, a glimpse of eternity." It is that double structure, altogether historical and ahistorical, which explains how myth, while pertaining to the realm of *parole* and calling for an explanation as such, as well as to that of *langue* in which it is expressed, can also be an absolute entity on a third level which, though it remains linguistic by nature, is nevertheless distinct from the other two. . . .

Whatever our ignorance of the language and the culture of the people where it originated, a myth is still felt as a myth by any reader anywhere in the world. Its substance does not lie in its style, its original music, or its syntax, but in the *story* which it tells. Myth is language, functioning on an especially high level where meaning succeeds practically at "taking off" from the linguistic ground on which it keeps on rolling. . . .

Now for a concrete example of the method we propose. We shall use the Oedipus myth, which is well known to everyone. I am well aware that the Oedipus myth has only reached us under late forms and through literary transmutations concerned more with esthetic and moral preoccupations than with religious or ritual ones, whatever these may have been. But we shall not interpret the Oedipus myth in literal terms, much less offer an explanation acceptable to the specialist. We simply wish to illustrate—and without reaching any conclusions with respect to it—a certain technique, whose use is probably not legitimate in this particular instance, owing to the problematic elements indicated above. The "demonstration" should therefore be conceived, not in terms of what the scientist means by this term, but at best in terms of what is meant by the street peddler, whose aim is not to achieve a concrete result, but to explain, as succinctly as possible, the functioning of the mechanical toy which he is trying to sell to the onlookers.

The myth will be treated as an orchestra score would be if it were unwittingly considered as a unilinear series; our task is to reestablish the correct arrangement. Say, for instance, we were confronted with a sequence of the type: 1,2,4,7,8,2,3,4,6,8,1,4,5,7,8,1,2,5,7,3,4,5,6,8 . . . , the assignment being to put all the 1's together, all the 2's, the 3's, etc.; the result is a chart:

1	2		4			7	8
	2	3	4		6		8
1			4	5		7	8
1	2			5		7	
		3	4	5	6		8

We shall attempt to perform the same kind of operation on the Oedipus myth, trying out several arrangements of the mythemes until we find one which is in harmony with the principles enumerated above. Let us suppose, for the sake of argument, that the best arrangement is the following (although it might certainly be improved with the help of a specialist in Greek mythology):

Cadmos seeks his sister Europa, ravished by Zeus			
		Cadmos kills the dragon	
	The Spartoi kill one another		
			Labdacos (Laios' father) = *lame* (?)
	Oedipus kills his father, Laios		Laios (Oedipus' father) = *left-sided* (?)
		Oedipus kills the Sphinx	
			Oedipus = *swollen-foot* (?)
Oedipus marries his mother, Jocasta			
	Eteocles kills his brother, Polynices		
Antigone buries her brother, Polynices, despite prohibition			

We thus find ourselves confronted with four vertical columns, each of which includes several relations belonging to the same bundle. Were we to *tell* the myth, we would disregard the columns and read the rows from left to right and from top to bottom. But if we want to *understand* the myth, then we will have to disregard one half of the diachronic dimension (top to bottom) and read from left to right, column after column, each one being considered as a unit.

All the relations belonging to the same column exhibit one common feature which it is our task to discover. For instance, all the events grouped in the first column on the left have something to do with blood relations which are overemphasized, that is, are more intimate than they should be. Let us say, then, that the first column has as its common feature the *overrating of blood relations*. It is obvious that the second column expressed the same thing, but inverted: *underrating of blood relations*. The third column refers to monsters being slain. As to the fourth, a few words of clarification are needed. The remarkable connotation of the surnames in Oedipus' father-line has often been noticed. However, linguists usually disregard it, since to them the only way to define the meaning of a term is to investigate all the contexts in which it appears, and personal names, precisely because they are used as such, are not accompanied by any context. With the method we propose to follow the objection disappears, since the myth itself provides its own context. The significance is no longer to be sought in the eventual meaning of each name, but in the fact that all the names have a common feature: All the hypothetical meanings (which may well remain hypothetical) refer to *difficulties in walking straight and standing upright*.

What then is the relationship between the two columns on the right? Column three refers to monsters. The dragon is a chthonian being which has to be killed in order that mankind be born from the Earth; the Sphinx is a monster unwilling to permit men to live. The last unit reproduces the first one, which has to do with the *autochthonous origin* of mankind. Since the monsters are overcome by men, we may thus say that the common feature of the third column is *denial of the autochthonous origin of man*.

This immediately helps us to understand the meaning of the fourth column. In mythology it is a universal characteristic of men born from the Earth that at the moment they emerge from the depth they either cannot walk or they walk clumsily. This is the case of the chthonian beings in the mythology of the Pueblo: Muyingwu, who leads the emergence, and the chthonian Shumaikoli are lame ("bleeding-foot," "sore-foot"). The same happens to the Koskimo of the Kwakiutl after they have been swallowed by the chthonian monster, Tsiakish: When they returned to the surface of the earth "they limped forward or tripped sideways." Thus the common feature of the fourth column is *the persistence of the autochthonous origin of man*. It follows that column four is to column three as column one is to column two. The inability to connect two kinds of relationships is overcome (or rather replaced) by the assertion that contradictory relationships are identical inasmuch as they are both self-contradictory in a similar way. Although this is still a provisional formulation of the structure of mythical thought, it is sufficient at this stage.

Turning back to the Oedipus myth, we may now see what it means. The myth has to do with the inability, for a culture which holds the belief that mankind is autochthonous (see, for instance, Pausanias, VIII, xxix, 4: plants provide a *model* for humans), to find a satisfactory transition between this theory and the knowledge that human beings are actually born from the union of man and woman. Although the problem obviously cannot be solved, the Oedipus myth provides a kind of logical tool which relates the original problem—born from one or born from two?—to the derivative problem: born from different or born from same? By a correlation of this type, the overrating of blood relations is to the underrating of blood relations as the attempt to escape autochthony is to the impossibility to succeed in it. Although experience contradicts theory, social life validates cosmology by its similarity of structure. Hence cosmology is true.❖

Roland Barthes (1915–1980) was one of France's most astonishing literary critics and writers. He was a prolific author, but more significantly, like other artistic masters (Matisse, for example), Barthes was constantly experimenting and changing. After completing his education in classics and French literature at the University of Paris, he taught in France, Romania, and Egypt. He then held a research post at the prestigious National Center for Scientific Research (CNRS) in Paris. After the war, his first works were concerned with the theory of writing. These became *Writing Degree Zero* (1953), which was published in English with *Elements of Semiology* (1964). One could hardly imagine two more different texts by the same author, written within a decade of each other. The earlier was a founding text of the new critical movement in France; the latter a founding text of modern semiotics. Barthes's writing evolved through a number of phases over many topics, including: popular culture (*Mythologies,* 1957), literature (*Sur Racine,* 1963), literary criticism (*Essais critiques,* 1964), and the semiotics of the fashion industry (*Système de la mode,* 1967). In 1975, he was elected to the Collège de France, where he taught both semiotics and literature. In his last decade, beginning with *The Pleasure of the Text* (1973), then *A Lover's Discourse* (1977), he became one of the first social theorists of world reputation to write frankly and powerfully about sexuality and desire in literature and social life. Barthes died tragically in a street accident in Paris.

Semiological Prospects
Roland Barthes (1964)

In Saussure: The (dichotomic) concept of *language/speech* is central in Saussure* and was certainly a great novelty in relation to earlier linguistics which sought to find the causes of historical changes in the evolution of pronunciation, spontaneous associations and the working of analogy, and was therefore a linguistics of the individual act. In working out this famous dichotomy, Saussure started from the 'multiform and heterogeneous' nature of language, which appears at first sight as an unclassifiable reality the unity of which cannot be brought to light, since it partakes at the same time of the physical, the physiological, the mental, the individual and the social....

The language (langue): A language is therefore, so to speak, language minus speech: it is at the same time a social institution and a system of values. As a social institution, it is by no means an act, and it is not subject to any premeditation. It is the social part of language, the individual cannot by himself either create or modify it; it is essentially a collective contract which one must accept in its entirety if one wishes to communicate. Moreover, this social product is autonomous, like a game with its own rules, for it can be handled only after a period of learning. As a system of values, a language is made of a certain number of elements, each one of which is at the same time the equivalent of a given quantity of things and a term of a larger function, in which are found, in a differential order, other correlative values: from the point of view of the language, the sign is like a coin which has the value of a certain amount of goods which it allows one to buy, but also has value in relation to other coins, in a greater or lesser degree. The institutional and the systematic aspect are of course connected: it is because a language is a system of contractual values (in part arbitrary, or, more exactly, unmotivated) that it resists the modifications coming from a single individual, and is consequently a social institution.

Speech (parole): In contrast to the language, which is both institution and system, *speech* is essentially an individual act of selection and actualization; it is made in the first place of the 'combination thanks to which the speaking subject can use the code of the language with a view to expressing his personal thought' (this extended speech could be called *discourse*), and secondly by the 'psycho-physical mechanisms which allow him to exteriorize these combinations.' It is certain that phonation, for instance, cannot be confused with the language; neither the institution nor the sys-

---

Excerpt from Annette Lauers and Colin Smith, trans., *Elements of Semiology* (Hill and Wang, a division of Farrar, Strauss & Giroux, NY).

*The Saussurean notions of *langue* and *parole* present to the translator into English notorious difficulties, which their extension in the present work does nothing to alleviate. We have translated *langue* as '*a*' or '*the* language', except when the coupling with 'speech' makes the meaning clear. *Les paroles,* whether applied to several people or to several semiotic systems, has been translated by various periphrases which we hope do not obscure the identity of meaning. (Trans.)

tem are altered if the individual who resorts to them speaks loudly or softly, with slow or rapid delivery, etc. The combinative aspect of speech is of course of capital importance, for it implies that speech is constituted by the recurrence of identical signs: it is because signs are repeated in successive discourses and within one and the same discourse (although they are combined in accordance with the infinite diversity of various people's speech) that each sign becomes an element of the language; and it is because speech is essentially a combinative activity that it corresponds to an individual act and not to a pure creation.

The dialectics of language and speech: Language and speech: each of these two terms of course achieves its full definition only in the dialectical process which unites one to the other: there is no language without speech, and no speech outside language . . . On the one hand, the language is 'the treasure deposited by the practice of speech, in the subjects belonging to the same community' and, since it is a collective summa of individual imprints, it must remain incomplete at the level of each isolated individual: a language does not exist perfectly except in the 'speaking mass'; one cannot handle speech except by drawing on the language. But conversely, a language is possible only starting from speech: historically, speech phenomena always precede language phenomena (it is speech which makes language evolve), and genetically, a language is constituted in the individual through his learning from the environmental speech (one does not teach grammar and vocabulary which are, broadly speaking, the language, to babies). To sum, a language is at the same time the product and the instrument of speech: their relationship is therefore a genuinely dialectical one. . . .

The language, speech and the social sciences. The sociological scope of the *language/speech* concept is obvious. The manifest affinity of the language according to Saussure and of Durkheim's conception of a collective consciousness independent of its individual manifestations has been emphasized very early on. A direct influence of Durkheim on Saussure has even been postulated; it has been alleged that Saussure had followed very closely the debate between Durkheim and Tarde and that his conception of the language came from Durkheim while that of speech was a kind of concession to Tarde's idea on the individual element. This hypothesis has lost some of its topicality because linguistics has chiefly developed, in the Saussurean idea of the language, the 'system of values' aspect, which led to acceptance of the necessity for an immanent analysis of the linguistic institution, and this immanence is inimical to sociological research. . . .

It can be seen from these brief indications how rich in extra- or meta-linguistic developments the notion *language/speech* is. We shall therefore postulate that there exists a general category *language/speech,* which embraces all the systems of signs; since there are no better ones, we shall keep the terms *language* and *speech,* even when they are applied to communications whose substance is not verbal.

The garment system: We saw that the separation between the language and speech represented the essential feature of linguistic analysis; it would therefore be futile to propose to apply this separation straightaway to systems of objects, images or behaviour patterns which have not yet been studied from a semantic point of view. We can merely, in the case of some of these hypothetical systems, foresee that certain classes of facts will belong to the category of the *language* and others to that of *speech,* and make it immediately clear that in the course of its application to semiology, Saussure's distinction is likely to undergo modifications which it will be precisely our task to note.

Let us take the garment system for instance; it is probably necessary to subdivide it into three different systems, according to which substance is used for communication.

In clothes as *written* about, that is to say described in a fashion magazine by means of articulated language, there is practically no 'speech': the garment which is described never corresponds to an individual handling of the rules of fashion, it is a systematized set of signs and rules: it is a language in its pure state. According to the Saussurean schema, a language without speech would be impossible; what makes the fact acceptable here is, on the one hand, that the language of fashion does not emanate from the 'speaking mass' but from a group which makes the decisions and deliberately elaborates the code, and on the other hand that the abstraction inherent in any language is here materialized as written language; fashion clothes (as written about) are the language at the level of vestimentary communication and speech at the level of verbal communication.

In clothes as *photographed* (if we suppose, to simplify matters, that there is no duplication by verbal description), the language still issues from the fashion group, but it is no longer given in a wholly abstract form, for a photographed garment is always worn by an individual woman. What is given by the fashion photograph is a semi-formalized state of the garment system: for on the one hand, the language of fashion must here be inferred from a pseudo-real garment, and on the other, the wearer of the garment (the photographed model) is, so to speak, a normative individual, chosen for her canonic generality, and who consequently represents a 'speech' which is fixed and devoid of all combinative freedom.

Finally in clothes as *worn* (or real clothes), as Trubetzkoy had suggested, we again find the classic distinction between language and speech. The language, in the garment system, is made i) by the oppositions of pieces, parts of garment and 'details', the variation of which entails a change in meaning (to wear a beret or a bowler hat does not have the same meaning); ii) by the rules which govern the association of the pieces among themselves, either on the length of the body or in depth. Speech, in the garment system, comprises all the phenomena of anomic fabrication (few are still left in our society) or of individual way of wearing (size of the garment, degree of cleanliness or wear, personal quirks, free association of pieces). As for the dialectic which unites here costume (the language) and clothing (speech), it does not resemble that of verbal language; true, clothing always draws on costume (except in the case of eccentricity, which, by the way, also has its signs), but costume, at least today, *precedes* clothing, since it comes from the ready-made industry, that is, from a minority group (although more anonymous than that of Haute Couture).❖

Louis Althusser (1918–1990) was born in Algiers. During World War II, he was imprisoned in a Nazi concentration camp. After the war, in 1948, Althusser joined the French Communist Party and taught philosophy at the École Normale Supérieure in Paris. "Why Theory?" is from his best-known book, *For Marx*—a collection of essays that appeared in France in 1965. Althusser was a major influence on Left social theory with his attempts to establish the theoretical interpretation of Marxism in terms that could be considered scientific. He was the leading structuralist Marxist of his day. In many ways, Althusser's position among Marxists was comparable to that of Parsons among younger sociologists. His structuralism was, for a while, *the* theory against which every serious Marxist was required to take a stand. His productive life ended tragically when he lost his sanity, strangled his wife to death, and was committed to a mental institution in France.

Why Theory?

Louis Althusser (1963)

The problem posed by my last study—what constitutes Marx's 'inversion' of the Hegelian dialectic, what is the specific difference that distinguishes the Marxist dialectic from the Hegelian dialectic?—is a theoretical problem.

To say that it is a *theoretical* problem implies that its theoretical solution should give us a new knowledge, organically linked to the other knowledges of Marxist theory. To say that it is a theoretical *problem* implies that we are not dealing merely with an imaginary difficulty, but with a really existing difficulty posed us in the form of a *problem,* that is, in a form governed by imperative conditions: definition of the field of (theoretical) knowledges in which the problem is posed (situated), of the exact *location* of its posing, and of the concepts required to pose it.

Only the position, examination and resolution of the problem, that is, the *theoretical practice* we are about to embark on, can provide the *proof* that these conditions have been respected.

Now, in this particular case, what has to be expressed in the form of a theoretical problem and its solution *already exists in Marxist practice.* Not only has Marxist practice come up against this 'difficulty', confirmed that it was indeed real rather than imaginary, but what is more, it has, within its own limits, 'settled' it and surmounted it in fact. In the practical state, the solution to our theoretical problem has already existed for a long time in Marxist practice. So to pose and resolve our theoretical problem ultimately means to express theoretically the *'solution' existing in the practical state,* that Marxist practice has found for a real difficulty it has encountered in its development, whose existence it has noted, and, according to its own submission, settled.

So we are merely concerned with filling in a 'gap' between theory and practice on a particular point. We are not setting Marxism any imaginary or subjective problem, asking it to 'resolve' the 'problems' of 'hyperempiricism', nor even what Marx called the difficulties a philosopher has in his *personal* relations with a concept. No. The problem posed exists (and has existed) in the form of a difficulty signalled by Marxist practice. Its solution exists in Marxist practice. So we only have to express it theoretically. But this simple theoretical *expression* of a solution that exists in the practical state cannot be taken for granted: it requires a real theoretical labour, not only to work out the specific *concept* or *knowledge* of this practical resolution—but also for the real destruction of the ideological confusions, illusions or inaccuracies that may exist, by a radical critique (a critique which takes them by the root). So this *simple* theoretical 'expression' implies both the *production* of a knowledge and the *critique* of an illusion, in one movement.

And if I am asked: but why take all this trouble to express a 'truth' 'known' for such a long time?—my answer is that, if we are still using the term in its strictest sense, the existence of this truth has been *signalled, recognized* for a long time, but it has not been *known.* For the (practical) *recognition* of an existence cannot pass for a *knowledge* (that is, for *theory*) except in the imprecision of a confused thought. And if I am then asked: but what use is there in posing this problem *in theory* if its solution has already existed for a long time in the practical state? why give a theoretical expression to this practical

---

Excerpt from "On the Materialist Dialectic," Ben Brewster, trans., *For Marx* (Penguin Press, London), pp. 164–169.

solution, a theoretical expression it has so far done quite well without? what do we gain by this 'speculative' investigation that we do not possess already?

One sentence is enough to answer this question: Lenin's 'Without revolutionary theory, no revolutionary practice'. Generalizing it: theory is essential to practice, to the forms of practice that it helps bring to birth or to grow, as well as to the practice it is the theory of. But the transparency of this sentence is not enough; we must also know its *titles to validity*, so we must pose the question: what are we to understand by *theory*, if it is to be essential to *practice*?

I shall only discuss the aspects of this theme that are indispensable to our investigation. I propose to use the following definitions, as essential preliminary hypotheses.

By *practice* in general I shall mean any process of *transformation* of a determinate given raw material into a determinate *product*, a transformation effected by a determinate human labour, using determinate means (of 'production'). In any practice thus conceived, the *determinant* moment (or element) is neither the raw material nor the product, but the practice in the narrow sense: the moment of the *labour of transformation* itself, which sets to work, in a specific structure, men, means and a technical method of utilizing the means. This general definition of practice covers the possibility of particularity: there are different practices which are really distinct, even though they belong organically to the same complex totality. Thus, 'social practice', the complex unity of the practices existing in a determinate society, contains a large number of distinct practices. This complex unity of 'social practice' is structured, we shall soon see how, in such a way that in the last resort the determinant practice in it is the practice of transformation of a given nature (raw material) into useful *products* by the activity of living men working through the *methodically organized* employment of determinate *means of production* within the framework of determinate relations of production. As well as production social practice includes other essential levels: political practice—which in Marxist parties is no longer spontaneous but organized on the basis of the scientific theory of historical materialism, and which transforms its raw materials: social relations, into a determinate product (new social relations); ideological practice (ideology, whether religious, political, moral, legal or artistic, also transforms its object: men's 'consciousness'): and finally, *theoretical practice*. Ideology is not always taken seriously as an existing practice: but to recognize this is the indispensable prior condition for any theory of ideology. The existence of a *theoretical practice* is taken seriously even more rarely: but this prior condition is indispensable to an understanding of what theory itself, and its relation to 'social practice' are for Marxism.

Here we need a second definition. By theory, in this respect, I shall mean a *specific form of practice*, itself belonging to the complex unity of the 'social practice' of a determinate human society. Theoretical practice falls within the general definition of practice. It works on a raw material (representations, concepts, facts) which it is given by other practices, whether 'empirical', 'technical' or 'ideological'. In its most general form theoretical practice does not only include *scientific* theoretical practice, but also pre-scientific theoretical practice, that is, 'ideological' theoretical practice (the forms of 'knowledge' that make up the prehistory of a science, and their 'philosophies'). The theoretical practice of a science is always completely distinct from the ideological theoretical practice of its prehistory: this distinction takes the form of a 'qualitative' theoretical and historical discontinuity which I shall follow Bachelard in calling an 'epistemological break'. This is not the place to discuss the dialectic in action in the advent of this 'break': that is, the labour of specific theoretical transformation which installs it in each case, which establishes a science by detaching it from the ideology of its past and by revealing this past as ideological. Restricting myself to the essential point as far as our analysis is concerned, I shall take up a position beyond the 'break', within the constituted science, and use the following nomenclature: I shall call *theory* any theoretical practice of a *scientific* character. I shall call 'theory' (in inverted commas) the determinate *theoretical system* of a real science (its basic concepts in their more or less contradictory unity at a given time): for example, the theory of universal attraction, wave mechanics, etc. . . . or again, the '*theory*' of historical materialism. In its 'theory' any determinate science reflects within the complex unity of its concepts (a unity which, I should add, is more or less problematic) the results, which will henceforth be the conditions and means, of its own theoretical practice. I shall call Theory (with a capital T), general theory, that is, the Theory of practice in general, itself elaborated on the basis of the Theory of existing theoretical practices (of the sciences), which transforms into 'knowledges' (scientific truths) the ideological product of existing 'empirical' practices (the concrete activity of men). This Theory is the materialist *dialectic* which is none other than dialectical materialism. These definitions are necessary for us to be able to give an answer to this question: what is the use of a theoretical expression of a solution which already exists in the practical state?—an answer with a theoretical basis.

When Lenin said 'without theory, no revolutionary action', he meant one particular theory, the theory of the Marxist science of the development of social formations (historical materialism). The proposition is to be found in *What is to be Done?*, where Lenin examined the organizational methods and objectives of the Russian Social-Democratic Party in 1902. At that time he was struggling against an opportunist policy that tagged along behind the 'spontaneity' of the masses; his aim was to transform it into a revolutionary practice based on 'theory', that is, on the (Marxist) science of the development of the social formation concerned (Russian society at that time). But in expressing this thesis, Lenin was doing more than he said: by reminding Marxist political practice of the necessity for the 'theory' which is its basis, he was in fact expressing a thesis of relevance to Theory, that is, to the Theory of practice in general—the materialist dialectic.

So theory is important to practice in a double sense: for 'theory' is important to its own practice, directly. But the *relation* of a 'theory' to its practice, in so far as it is at issue, on condition that it is reflected and expressed, is also relevant to the general Theory (the dialectic) in which is theoretically expressed the essence of theoretical practice in general, through it the essence of practice in general, and through it the essence of the transformations, of the 'development' of things in general.

To return to our original problem: we find that the theoretical expression of a practical solution involves Theory, that is, the dialectic. The exact theoretical expression of the dialectic is relevant first of all to those practices in which the Marxist dialectic is active; for these practices (Marxist 'theory' and politics) need the concept of their practice (of the dialectic) in their development, if they are not to find themselves defenceless in the face of qualitatively new forms of this development (new situations, new 'problems')—or to lapse, or relapse, into the various forms of opportunism, theoretical or practical. These 'surprises' and deviations, attributable in the last resort to 'ideological errors', that is, to a *theoretical* deficiency, are always costly, and may be very costly.❖

❖ Doubts and Reservations ❖

David Riesman (1909–) was educated at Harvard College, then Harvard Law School, after which he clerked for Supreme Court Justice Louis Brandeis. After practicing law, including service as deputy assistant district attorney for New York County, Riesman began teaching social science at the University of Chicago in 1946. In 1957, he joined the Department of Social Relations at Harvard. He is now professor emeritus. In addition to his contributions to the study of American social character, Riesman is considered one of the foremost experts on higher education in the United States. The selection is from *The Lonely Crowd,* which Riesman wrote with Nathan Glazer and Reuel Denney. Since its first edition in 1950, the book has been an all-time best-seller among sociological studies. It remains the classic study of postwar American social life. Readers will note the references to Erich Fromm, with whom Riesman once had what he calls an unorthodox analysis. The range of Riesman's sources, from psychoanalysis to economic history, begins to explain the book's broad appeal.

Character and Society: The Other-directed Personality
David Riesman (1950)

What is the relation between social character and society? How is it that every society seems to get, more or less, the social character it "needs"? Erik H. Erikson writes, in a study of the social character of the Yurok Indians, that ". . . systems of child training . . . represent unconscious attempts at creating out of human raw material that configuration of attitudes which is (or once was) the optimum under the tribe's particular natural conditions and economic-historic necessities."

From "economic-historic necessities" to "systems of child training" is a long jump. Much of the work of students of social character has been devoted to closing the gap and showing how the satisfaction of the largest "needs" of society is prepared, in some half-mysterious way, by its most intimate practices. Erich Fromm succinctly suggests the line along which this connection between society and character training may be sought: "In order that any society may function well, its members must acquire the kind of character which makes them *want* to act in the way they *have* to act as members of the society or of a special class within it. They have to *desire* what objectively is *necessary* for them to do. *Outer force* is replaced by *inner compulsion,* and by the particular kind of human energy which is channeled into character traits."

Excerpt from *The Lonely Crowd: A Study of the Changing American Character* (New Haven, Conn.: Yale University Press, 1969 [1961]), pp. 4–8, 19–22, 24–25. Reprinted with permission of Yale University Press. Copyright 1950, 1961 by Yale University Press.

Thus, the link between character and society—certainly not the only one, but one of the most significant, and the one I choose to emphasize in this discussion—is to be found in the way in which society ensures some degree of conformity from the individuals who make it up. In each society, such a mode of ensuring conformity is built into the child, and then either encouraged or frustrated in later adult experience. (No society, it would appear, is quite prescient enough to ensure that the mode of conformity it has inculcated will satisfy those subject to it in every stage of life.) I shall use the term "mode of conformity" interchangeably with the term "social character"—though certainly conformity is not all of social character: "mode of creativity" is as much a part of it. However, while societies and individuals may live well enough—if rather boringly—without creativity, it is not likely that they can live without some mode of conformity—even be it one of rebellion.

My concern in this book is with two revolutions and their relation to the "mode of conformity" or "social character" of Western man since the Middle Ages. The first of these revolutions has in the last four hundred years cut us off pretty decisively from the family- and clan-oriented traditional ways of life in which mankind has existed throughout most of history; this revolution includes the Renaissance, the Reformation, the Counter-Reformation, the Industrial Revolution, and the political revolutions of the seventeenth, eighteenth, and nineteenth centuries. This revolution is, of course, still in process, but in the most advanced countries of the world, and particularly in America, it is giving way to another sort of revolution—a whole range of social developments associated with a shift from an age of production to an age of consumption.

The first revolution we understand moderately well; it is, under various labels, in our texts and our terminology; this book has nothing new to contribute to its description, but perhaps does contribute something to its evaluation. The second revolution, which is just beginning, has interested many contemporary observers, including social scientists, philosophers, and journalists. Both description and evaluation are still highly controversial; indeed, many are still preoccupied with the first set of revolutions and have not invented the categories for discussing the second set. In this book I try to sharpen the contrast between, on the one hand, conditions and character in those social strata that are today most seriously affected by the second revolution, and, on the other hand, conditions and character in analogous strata during the earlier revolution; in this perspective, what is briefly said about the traditional and feudal societies which were overturned by the first revolution is in the nature of backdrop for these later shifts.

One of the categories I make use of is taken from demography, the science that deals with birth rates and death rates, with the absolute and relative numbers of people in a society, and their distribution by age, sex, and other variables, for I tentatively seek to link certain social and characterological developments, as cause and effect, with certain population shifts in Western society since the Middle Ages.

It seems reasonably well established, despite the absence of reliable figures for earlier centuries, that during this period the curve of population growth in the Western countries has shown an S-shape of a particular type (as other countries are drawn more closely into the net of Western civilization, their populations also show a tendency to develop along the lines of this S-shaped curve). The bottom horizontal line of the S represents a situation where the total population does not increase or does so very slowly, for the number of births equals roughly the number of deaths, and both are very high. In societies of this type, a high proportion of the population is young, life expectancy is low, and the turnover of generations is extremely rapid.

Such societies are said to be in the phase of "high growth potential"; for should something happen to decrease the very high death rate (greater production of food, new sanitary measures, new knowledge of the causes of disease, and so on), a "population explosion" would result, and the population would increase very rapidly. This in effect is what happened in the West, starting with the seventeenth century. This spurt in population was most marked in Europe, and the countries settled by Europeans, in the nineteenth century. It is represented by the vertical bar of the S. Demographers call this the stage of "transitional growth," because the birth rate soon begins to follow the death rate in its decline. The rate of growth then slows down, and demographers begin to detect in the growing proportion of middle-aged and aged in the population the signs of a third stage, "incipient population decline." Societies in this stage are represented by the top horizontal bar of the S, again indicating, as in the first stage, that total population growth is small—but this time because births and deaths are low.

The S-curve is not a theory of population growth so much as an empirical description of what has happened in the West and in those parts of the world influenced by the West. After the S runs its course, what then? The developments of recent years in the United States and other Western countries do not seem to be susceptible to so simple and elegant a summing up. "Incipient population decline" has not become "population decline" itself, and the birth rate has shown an uncertain tendency to rise again, which most demographers think is temporary.

It would be very surprising if variations in the basic conditions of reproduction, livelihood, and chances for survival, that is, in the supply of and demand for human beings, with all these imply for change in the spacing of people, the size of markets, the role of children, the society's feeling of vitality or senescence, and many other intangibles, failed to influence character. My thesis is, in fact, that each of these three different phases on the population curve appears to be occupied by a society that enforces conformity and molds social character in a definably different way.

The society of high growth potential develops in its typical members a social character whose conformity is insured by their tendency to follow tradition: these I shall term *tradition-directed* people and the society in which they live *a society dependent on tradition-direction*.

The society of transitional population growth develops in its typical members a social character whose conformity is insured by their tendency to acquire early in life an internalized set of goals. These I shall term *inner-directed* people and the society in which they live *a society dependent on inner-direction*.

Finally, the society of incipient population decline develops in its typical members a social character whose conformity is insured by their tendency to be sensitized to the expectations and preferences of others. These I shall term *other-directed* people and the society in which they live one *dependent on other-direction*. . . .

A definition of other-direction.   The type of character I shall describe as other-directed seems to be emerging in very recent years in the upper middle class of our larger cities: more prominently in New York than in Boston, in Los Angeles than in Spokane, in Cincinnati than Chillicothe. Yet in some respects this type is strikingly similar to the American, whom Tocqueville and other curious and astonished visitors from Europe, even before the Revolution, thought to be a new kind of man. Indeed, travelers' reports on America impress us with their unanimity. The American is said to be shallower, freer with his money, friendlier, more uncertain of himself and his values, more demanding of approval than the European. It all adds up to a pattern which, without stretching matters too far, resembles the kind of character that a number of social scientists have seen as developing in contemporary, highly industrialized, and bureaucratic America: [Erich] Fromm's "marketer," [C. Wright] Mills's "fixer," Arnold Green's "middle class male child."

It is my impression that the middle-class American of today is decisively different from those Americans of Tocqueville's writings who nevertheless strike us as so contemporary, and much of this book will be devoted to discussing these differences. It is also my impression that the conditions I believe to be responsible for other-direction are affecting increasing numbers of people in the metropolitan centers of the advanced industrial countries. My analysis of the other-directed character is thus at once an analysis of the American and of contemporary man. Much of the time I find it hard or impossible to say where one ends and the other begins. Tentatively, I am inclined to think that the other-directed type does find itself most at home in America, due to certain unique elements in American society, such as its recruitment from Europe and its lack of any feudal past. As against this, I am also inclined to put more weight on capitalism, industrialism, and urbanization—these being international tendencies—than on any character-forming peculiarities of the American scene.

Bearing these qualifications in mind, it seems appropriate to treat contemporary metropolitan America as our illustration of a society—so far, perhaps, the only illustration—in which other-direction is the dominant mode of insuring conformity. It would be premature, however, to say that it is already the dominant mode in America as a whole. But since the other-directed types are to be found among the young, in the larger cities, and among the upper income groups, we may assume that, unless present trends are reversed, the hegemony of other-direction lies not far off.

If we wanted to cast our social character types into social class molds, we could say that inner-direction is the typical character of the "old" middle class—the banker, the tradesman, the small entrepreneur, the technically oriented engineer, etc.—while other-direction is becoming the typical character of the "new" middle class—the bureaucrat, the salaried employee in business, etc. Many of the economic factors associated with the recent growth of the "new" middle class are well known. They have been discussed by James Burnham, Colin Clark, Peter Drucker, and others. There is a decline in the numbers and in the proportion of the working population engaged in production and extraction—agriculture, heavy industry, heavy transport—and an increase in the numbers and the proportion engaged in white-collar work and the service trades. People who are literate, educated, and provided with the necessities of life by an ever more efficient machine industry and agriculture, turn increasingly to the "tertiary" economic realm. The service industries prosper among the people as a whole and no longer only in court circles.

Education, leisure, services, these go together with an increased consumption of words and images from the new mass media of communications. While societies in the phase of transitional growth step up the process of distributing words from urban centers, the flow becomes a torrent in the societies of incipient population decline. This process, while modulated by profound national and class differences, connected with differences in literacy and loquacity, takes place everywhere in the industrialized lands. Increasingly, relations with the outer world and with oneself are mediated by the flow of mass communication. For the other-directed types political events are likewise experienced through a screen of words by which the events are habitually atomized and personalized—or pseudo-personalized. For the inner-directed person who remains still extant in this period the tendency is rather to systematize and moralize this flow of words.

These developments lead, for large numbers of people, to changes in paths to success and to the requirement of more "socialized" behavior both for success and for marital and personal adaptation. Connected with such changes are changes in the family and in child-rearing practices. In the smaller families of urban life, and with the spread of "permissive" child care to ever wider strata of the population, there is a relaxation of older patterns of discipline. Under these newer patterns the peer-group (the group of one's associates of the same age and class) becomes much more important to the child, while the parents make him feel guilty not so much about violation of inner standards as about failure to be popular or otherwise to manage his relations with these other children. Moreover, the pressures of the school and the peer-group are reinforced and continued—in a manner whose inner paradoxes I shall discuss later—by the mass media: movies, radio, comics, and popular culture media generally. Under these conditions types of character emerge that we shall here term other-directed. To them much of the discussion in the ensuing chapters is devoted. *What is common to all the other-directed people is that their contemporaries are the source of direction for the individual—either those known to him or those with whom he is indirectly acquainted, through friends and through the mass media. This source is of course "internalized" in the sense that dependence on it for guidance in life is implanted early. The goals toward which the other-directed person strives shift with that guidance: it is only the process of striving itself and the process of paying close attention to the signals from others that remain unaltered throughout life.* This mode of keeping in touch with others permits a close behavioral conformity, not through drill in behavior itself, as in the tradition-directed character, but rather through an exceptional sensitivity to the actions and wishes of others. . . .

The three types compared. One way to see the structural differences that mark the three types is to see the differences in the emotional sanction or control in each type.

The tradition-directed person feels the impact of his culture as a unit, but it is nevertheless mediated through the specific, small number of individuals with whom he is in daily contact. These expect of him not so much that he be a certain type of person but that he behave in the approved way. Consequently the sanction for behavior tends to be the fear of being *shamed.*

The inner-directed person has early incorporated a psychic gyroscope which is set going by his parents and can receive signals later on from other authorities who resemble his parents. He goes through life less independent than he seems, obeying this internal piloting. Getting off course, whether in response to inner impulses or to the fluctuating voices of contemporaries, may lead to the feeling of *guilt.*

Since the direction to be taken in life has been learned in the privacy of the home from a small number of guides and since principles, rather than details of behavior, are internalized, the inner-directed person is capable of great stability. Especially so when it turns out that his fellows have gyroscopes too, spinning at the same speed and set in the same direction. But many inner-directed individuals can remain stable even when the reinforcement of social approval is not available—as in the upright life of the stock Englishman isolated in the tropics.

Contrasted with such a type as this, the other-directed person learns to respond to signals from a far wider circle than is constituted by his parents. The family is no longer a closely knit unit to which he belongs but merely part of a wider social environment to which he early becomes attentive. In these respects the other-directed person resembles the tradition-directed person: both live in a group milieu and lack the inner-directed person's capacity to go it alone. The nature of this group milieu, however, differs radically in the two cases. The other-directed person is cosmopolitan. For him the border between the familiar and the strange—a border clearly marked in the societies depending on tradition-direction—has broken down. As the family continuously absorbs the strange and reshapes itself, so the strange becomes familiar. While the inner-directed person could be "at home abroad" by virtue of his relative insensitivity to others, the other-directed person is, in a sense, at home everywhere and nowhere, capable of a rapid if sometimes superficial intimacy with and response to everyone.

The tradition-directed person takes his signals from others, but they come in a cultural monotone; he needs no complex receiving equipment to pick them up. The other-directed person must be able to receive signals from far and near; the sources are many, the changes rapid. What can be internalized, then, is not a code of behavior but the elaborate equipment needed to attend to such messages and occasionally to participate in their circulation. As against guilt-and-shame controls, though of course these survive, one prime psychological lever of the other-directed person is a diffuse *anxiety*. This control equipment, instead of being like a gyroscope, is like a radar.❖

Erik H. Erikson (1902–1994) was born of Danish parents in Germany. After completing school in 1927, Erikson lived in Vienna, where he taught school and began analytic training. He was analyzed by Anna Freud and finished his training in 1933. He later fled Europe for Boston, becoming that city's first child analyst. He was associated with Massachusetts General Hospital and Harvard, where he began (but never completed) doctoral studies. In 1936, Erikson taught at Yale; three years later, he moved to San Francisco, where he held a research position at the University of California at Berkeley. In 1950, he refused to sign a loyalty oath and left Berkeley. Erikson taught at Harvard for many years, retiring in 1970. He was recognized as a pioneer psychoanalyst for his clinical work, his research, and his writing. His studies of children were the basis for his contributions to the psychology of emotional development. Erikson was generally considered the founder of psychohistorical studies and one of the few ever able to use psychology to interpret history in a way that balances the different demands of the two fields. In addition to *Childhood and Society*, published in 1950 (the same year as *The Lonely Crowd*), his many writings include *Gandhi's Truth* (1969) and *Young Man Luther* (1958).

Youth and American Identity
Erik H. Erikson (1950)

Youth

With the establishment of a good initial relationship to the world of skills and tools, and with the advent of puberty, childhood proper comes to an end. Youth begins.

Excerpt from *Childhood and Society* (New York: W. W. Norton and Co., 1963 [1950]), pp. 261–263, 285–287. Copyright 1950, 1963 by W. W. Norton and Company, Inc. Reprinted by permission of W. W. Norton and Co. and Hogarth Press, Ltd.

But in puberty and adolescence all samenesses and continuities relied on earlier are more or less questioned again, because of a rapidity of body growth which equals that of early childhood and because of the new addition of genital maturity. The growing and developing youths, faced with this physiological revolution within them, and with tangible adult tasks ahead of them, are now primarily concerned with what they appear to be in the eyes of others as compared with what they feel they are, and with the question of how to connect the roles and skills cultivated earlier with the occupational prototypes of the day. In their search for a new sense of continuity and sameness, adolescents have to refight many of the battles of earlier years, even though to do so they must artificially appoint perfectly well-meaning people to play the roles of adversaries; and they are ever ready to install lasting idols and ideals as guardians of a final identity.

The integration now taking place in the form of ego identity is, as pointed out, more than the sum of the childhood identifications. It is the accrued experience of the ego's ability to integrate all identifications with the vicissitudes of the libido, with the aptitudes developed out of endowment, and with the opportunities offered in social roles. The sense of ego identity, then, is the accrued confidence that the inner sameness and continuity prepared in the past are matched by the sameness and continuity of one's meaning for others, as evidenced in the tangible promise of a "career."

The danger of this stage is role confusion. Where this is based on a strong previous doubt as to one's sexual identity, delinquent and outright psychotic episodes are not uncommon. If diagnosed and treated correctly, these incidents do not have the same fatal significance which they have at other ages. In most instances, however, it is the inability to settle on an occupational identity which disturbs individual young people. To keep themselves together they temporarily overidentify, to the point of apparent complete loss of identity, with the heroes of cliques and crowds. This initiates the stage of "falling in love," which is by no means entirely, or even primarily, a sexual matter—except where the mores demand it. To a considerable extent adolescent love is an attempt to arrive at a definition of one's identity by projecting one's diffused ego image on another and by seeing it thus reflected and gradually clarified. This is why so much of young love is conversation.

Young people can also be remarkably clannish, and cruel in their exclusion of all those who are "different," in skin color or cultural background, in tastes and gifts, and often in such petty aspects of dress and gesture as have been temporarily selected as *the* signs of an in-grouper or out-grouper. It is important to understand (which does not mean condone or participate in) such intolerance as a defense against a sense of identity confusion. For adolescents not only help one another temporarily through much discomfort by forming cliques and by stereotyping themselves, their ideals, and their enemies; they also perversely test each other's capacity to pledge fidelity. The readiness for such testing also explains the appeal which simple and cruel totalitarian doctrines have on the minds of the youth of such countries and classes as have lost or are losing their group identities (feudal, agrarian, tribal, national) and face world-wide industrialization, emancipation, and wider communication.

The adolescent mind is essentially a mind of the *moratorium,* a psychosocial stage between childhood and adulthood, and between the morality learned by the child, and the ethics to be developed by the adult. It is an ideological mind—and, indeed, it is the ideological outlook of a society that speaks most clearly to the adolescent who is eager to be affirmed by his peers, and is ready to be confirmed by rituals, creeds, and programs which at the same time define what is evil, uncanny, and inimical. In searching for the social values which guide identity, one therefore confronts the problems of *ideology* and *aristocracy*, both in their widest possible sense which connotes that within a defined world image and a predestined course of history, the best people will come to rule and rule develops the best in people. In order not to become cynically or apathetically lost, young people must somehow be able to convince themselves that those who succeed in their anticipated adult world thereby shoulder the obligation of being the best. We will discuss later the dangers which emanate from human ideals harnessed to the management of super-machines, be they guided by nationalistic or international, communist or capitalist ideologies. In the last part of this book we shall discuss the way in which the revolutions of our day attempt to solve and also to exploit the deep need of youth to redefine its identity in an industrialized world. . . .

American Identity

It is a commonplace to state that whatever one may come to consider a truly American trait can be shown to have its equally characteristic opposite. This, one suspects, is true of all "national characters," or (as I would prefer to call them) national identities—so true, in fact that one may begin rather than end with the proposition that a nation's identity is derived from the ways in which history has, as it were, counterpointed certain opposite potentialities; the ways in which it lifts this counterpoint to a unique style of civilization, or lets it disintegrate into mere contradiction.

This dynamic country subjects its inhabitants to more extreme contrasts and abrupt changes during a lifetime or a generation than is normally the case with other great nations. Most of her inhabitants are faced, in their own lives or within the orbit of their closest relatives, with alternatives presented by such polarities as: open roads of immigration and jealous islands of tradition; outgoing internationalism and defiant isolationism; boisterous competition and self-effacing co-operation; and many others. The influence of the resulting contradictory slogans on the development of an individual ego probably depends on the coincidence of nuclear ego stages with critical changes in the family's geographic and economic vicissitudes.

The process of American identity formation seems to support an individual's ego identity as long as he can preserve a certain element of deliberate tentativeness of autonomous choice. The individual must be able to convince himself that the next step is up to him and that no matter where he is staying or going he always has the choice of leaving or turning in the opposite direction if he chooses to do so. In this country the migrant does not want to be told to move on, nor the sedentary man to stay where he is; for the life style (and the family history) of each contains the opposite element as a potential alternative which he wishes to consider his most private and individual decision.

Thus the functioning American, as the heir of a history of extreme contrasts and abrupt changes, bases his final ego identity on some tentative combination of dynamic polarities such as migratory and sedentary, individualistic and standardized, competitive and co-operative, pious and freethinking, responsible and cynical, etc.

While we see extreme elaborations of one or the other of these poles in regional, occupational, and characterological types, analysis reveals that this extremeness (of rigidity or of vacillation) contains an inner defense against the always implied, deeply feared, or secretly hoped-for opposite extreme.

To leave his choices open, the American, on the whole, lives with two sets of "truths": a set of religious principles or religiously pronounced political principles of a highly puritan quality, and a set of shifting slogans, which indicate what, at a given time, one may get away with on the basis of not more than a hunch, a mood, or a notion. Thus, the same child may have been exposed in succession or alternately to sudden decisions expressing the slogans "Let's get the hell out of here" and again, "Let's stay and keep the bastards out"—to mention only two of the most sweeping ones. Without any pretense of logic or principle, slogans are convincing enough to those involved to justify action whether within or just outside of the lofty law (in so far as it happens to be enforced or forgotten, according to changing local climate). Seemingly shiftless slogans contain time and space perspectives as ingrained as those elaborated in the Sioux or Yurok system; they are experiments in collective time-space to which individual ego defenses are co-ordinated. But they change, often radically, during one and the same childhood.

A true history of the American identity would have to correlate Parrington's observations on the continuity of formulated thought with the rich history of discontinuous American slogans which pervade public opinion in corner stores and in studies, in the courts and in the daily press. For in principles and concepts too, an invigorating polarity seems to exist on the one hand between the intellectual and political aristocracy which, always mindful of precedent, guards a measure of coherent thought and indestructible spirit, and, on the other hand, a powerful mobocracy which seems to prefer changing slogans to self-perpetuating principles. This native polarity of aristocracy and mobocracy (so admirably synthesized in Franklin D. Roosevelt) pervades American democracy more effectively than the advocates and the critics of the great American middle class seem to realize. This American middle class, decried by some as embodying an ossification of all that is mercenary and philistine in this country, may represent only a transitory series of overcompensatory attempts at settling tentatively around some Main Street, fireplace, bank account, and make of car; it does not, as a class should, preclude high mobility and a cultural potential unsure of its final identity. Status expresses a different relativity in a more mobile society: it resembles an escalator more than a platform; it is a vehicle, rather than a goal.

All countries, and especially large ones, complicate their own progress in their own way with the very premises of their beginnings. We must try to formulate the way in which self-contradictions in American history may expose her youth to an emotional and political short circuit and thus endanger her dynamic potential.❖

Erving Goffman (1922–1982) was born in Canada and took a B.A. from the University of Toronto in 1945. He then studied at the University of Chicago, receiving his Ph.D. in 1953. His thesis research was an observational study of social networks in a small Scottish island community. This study formed the basis for his first important book, *The Presentation of Self in Everyday Life* (1956). In 1961, Goffman began teaching at the University of California, Berkeley, until 1968 when he moved to the University of Pennsylvania. He died of cancer at age sixty. Goffman is noted for having been brilliantly inscrutable. He refused to write what others called theory, yet his ideas have had a major impact on social theory. He is considered a Chicago School field researcher, yet his methods were multiple and idiosyncratic. He seemed to have mastered completely the professional literature on his subjects, yet he wrote entirely from his own, unique literary space. His writings include *Asylums* (1961), *Stigma* (1964), *Interaction Ritual* (1967), *Gender Advertisements* (1969), and an important but not yet well understood article, "Felicity's Condition," published posthumously in 1983. He was once called sociology's Kafka for his uncanny, and disturbing, insights into human nature. In "On Face-Work," for example, he says that "universal human nature is not a very human thing." Though Goffman's writings have been used to justify the idea that social interaction is an arbitrary drama, this selection from early in his career shows his attempt to relate interaction to widely shared, if not truly universal, interaction rituals.

On Face-Work
Erving Goffman (1955)

Every person lives in a world of social encounters, involving him either in face-to-face or mediated contact with other participants. In each of these contacts, he tends to act out what is sometimes called a *line*—that is, a pattern of verbal and nonverbal acts by which he expresses his view of the situation and through this his evaluation of the participants, especially himself. Regardless of whether a person intends to take a line, he will find that he has done so in effect. The other participants will assume that he has more or less willfully taken a stand, so that if he is to deal with their response to him he must take into consideration the impression they have possibly formed of him.

Face

The term *face* may be defined as the positive social value a person effectively claims for himself by the line others assume he has taken during a particular contact. Face is an image of self delineated in terms of approved social attributes—albeit an image that others may share, as when a person makes a good showing for his profession or religion by making a good showing for himself.

A person tends to experience an immediate emotional response to the face which a contact with others allows him; he cathects his face; his "feelings" become attached to it. If the encounter sustains an image of him that he has long taken for granted, he probably will have few feelings about the matter. If events establish a face for him that is better than he might have expected, he is likely to "feel good"; if his ordinary expectations are not fulfilled, one expects that he will "feel bad" or "feel hurt." In general, a person's attachment to a particular face, coupled with the ease with which disconfirming information can be conveyed by himself and others, provides one reason why he finds that participation in any contact with others is a commitment. A person will also have feelings about the face sustained for the other participants, and while these feelings may differ in quantity and direction from those he has for his own face, they constitute an involvement in the face of others that is as immedi-

---

Excerpt from *Interaction Ritual* (Garden City, New York: Anchor Books, 1967 [1955]), pp. 5–9, 41–45.

ate and spontaneous as the involvement he has in his own face. One's own face and the face of others are constructs of the same order; it is the rules of the group and the definition of the situation which determine how much feeling one is to have for face and how this feeling is to be distributed among the faces involved.

A person may be said to *have*, or *be in*, or *maintain* face when the line he effectively takes presents an image of him that is internally consistent, that is supported by judgments and evidence conveyed by other participants, and that is confirmed by evidence conveyed through impersonal agencies in the situation. At such times the person's face clearly is something that is not lodged in or on his body, but rather something that is diffusely located in the flow of events in the encounter and becomes manifest only when these events are read and interpreted for the appraisals expressed in them.

The line maintained by and for a person during contact with others tends to be of a legitimate institutionalized kind. During a contact of a particular type, an interactant of known or visible attributes can expect to be sustained in a particular face and can feel that it is morally proper that this should be so. Given his attributes and the conventionalized nature of the encounter, he will find a small choice of lines will be open to him and a small choice of faces will be waiting for him. Further, on the basis of a few known attributes, he is given the responsibility of possessing a vast number of others. His coparticipants are not likely to be conscious of the character of many of these attributes until he acts perceptibly in such a way as to discredit his possession of them; then everyone becomes conscious of these attributes and assumes that he willfully gave a false impression of possessing them.

Thus while concern for face focuses the attention of the person on the current activity, he must, to maintain face in this activity, take into consideration his place in the social world beyond it. A person who can maintain face in the current situation is someone who abstained from certain actions in the past that would have been difficult to face up to later. In addition, he fears loss of face now partly because the others may take this as a sign that consideration for his feelings need not be shown in the future. There is nevertheless a limitation to this interdependence between the current situation and the wider social world: an encounter with people whom he will not have dealings with again leaves him free to take a high line that the future will discredit, or free to suffer humiliations that would make future dealings with them an embarrassing thing to have to face.

A person may be said to *be in wrong face* when information is brought forth in some way about his social worth which cannot be integrated, even with effort, into the line that is being sustained for him. A person may be said to *be out of face* when he participates in a contact with others without having ready a line of the kind participants in such situations are expected to take. The intent of many pranks is to lead a person into showing a wrong face or no face, but there will also be serious occasions, of course, when he will find himself expressively out of touch with the situation.

When a person senses that he is in face, he typically responds with feelings of confidence and assurance. Firm in the line he is taking, he feels that he can hold his head up and openly present himself to others. He feels some security and some relief—as he also can when the others feel he is in wrong face but successfully hide these feelings from him.

When a person is in wrong face or out of face, expressive events are being contributed to the encounter which cannot be readily woven into the expressive fabric of the occasion. Should he sense that he is in wrong face or out of face, he is likely to

feel ashamed and inferior because of what has happened to the activity on his account and because of what may happen to his reputation as a participant. Further,
he may feel bad because he had relied upon the encounter to support an image of
self to which he has become emotionally attached and which he now finds threatened. Felt lack of judgmental support from the encounter may take him aback, confuse him, and momentarily incapacitate him as an interactant. His manner and
bearing may falter, collapse, and crumble. He may become embarrassed and chagrined; he may become shamefaced. The feeling, whether warranted or not, that he
is perceived in a flustered state by others, and that he is presenting no usable line,
may add further injuries to his feelings, just as his change from being in wrong face
or out of face to being shamefaced can add further disorder to the expressive organization of the situation. Following common usage, I shall employ the term *poise* to
refer to the capacity to suppress and conceal any tendency to become shamefaced
during encounters with others.

In our Anglo-American society, as in some others, the phrase "to lose face" seems
to mean to be in wrong face, to be out of face, or to be shamefaced. The phrase "to
save one's face" appears to refer to the process by which the person sustains an impression for others that he has not lost face. Following Chinese usage, one can say
that "to give face" is to arrange for another to take a better line than he might otherwise have been able to take, the other thereby gets face given him, this being one way
in which he can gain face. . . .

Face and Social Relationships

When a person begins a mediated or immediate encounter, he already stands in
some kind of social relationship to the others concerned, and expects to stand in a
given relationship to them after the particular encounter ends. This, of course, is one
of the ways in which social contacts are geared into the wider society. Much of the
activity occurring during an encounter can be understood as an effort on everyone's
part to get through the occasion and all the unanticipated and unintentional events
that can cast participants in an undesirable light, without disrupting the relationships of the participants. And if relationships are in the process of change, the object
will be to bring the encounter to a satisfactory close without altering the expected
course of development. This perspective nicely accounts, for example, for the little
ceremonies of greeting and farewell which occur when people begin a conversa-
tional encounter or depart from one. Greetings provide a way of showing that a relationship is still what it was at the termination of the previous coparticipation, and,
typically, that this relationship involves sufficient suppression of hostility for the
participants temporarily to drop their guards and talk. Farewells sum up the effect of
the encounter upon the relationship and show what the participants may expect of
one another when they next meet. The enthusiasm of greetings compensates for the
weakening of the relationship caused by the absence just terminated, while the enthusiasm of farewells compensates the relationship for the harm that is about to be
done to it by separation.

It seems to be a characteristic obligation of many social relationships that each of
the members guarantees to support a given face for the other members in given situations. To prevent disruption of these relationships, it is therefore necessary for each
member to avoid destroying the others' face. At the same time, it is often the person's

social relationship with others that leads him to participate in certain encounters with them, where incidentally he will be dependent upon them for supporting his face. Furthermore, in many relationships, the members come to share a face, so that in the presence of third parties an improper act on the part of one member becomes a source of acute embarrassment to the other members. A social relationship, then, can be seen as a way in which the person is more than ordinarily forced to trust his self-image and face to the tact and good conduct of others.

The Nature of the Ritual Order

The ritual order seems to be organized basically on accommodative lines, so that the imagery used in thinking about other types of social order is not quite suitable for it. For the other types of social order a kind of schoolboy model seems to be employed: if a person wishes to sustain a particular image of himself and trust his feelings to it, he must work hard for the credits that will buy this self-enhancement for him; should he try to obtain ends by improper means, by cheating or theft, he will be punished, disqualified from the race, or at least made to start all over again from the beginning. This is the imagery of a hard, dull game. In fact, society and the individual join in one that is easier on both of them, yet one that has dangers of its own.

Whatever his position in society, the person insulates himself by blindnesses, half-truths, illusions, and rationalizations. He makes an "adjustment" by convincing himself, with the tactful support of his intimate circle, that he is what he wants to be and that he would not do to gain his ends what the others have done to gain theirs. And as for society, if the person is willing to be subject to informal social control—if he is willing to find out from hints and glances and tactful cues what his place is, and keep it—then there will be no objection to his furnishing this place at his own discretion, with all the comfort, elegance, and nobility that his wit can muster for him. To protect this shelter he does not have to work hard, or join a group, or compete with anybody; he need only be careful about the expressed judgments he places himself in a position to witness. Some situations and acts and persons will have to be avoided; others, less threatening, must not be pressed too far. Social life is an uncluttered, orderly thing because the person voluntarily stays away from the places and topics and times where he is not wanted and where he might be disparaged for going. He cooperates to save his face, finding that there is much to be gained from venturing nothing.

Facts are of the schoolboy's world—they can be altered by diligent effort but they cannot be avoided. But what the person protects and defends and invests his feelings in is an idea about himself, and ideas are vulnerable not to facts and things but to communications. Communications belong to a less punitive scheme than do facts, for communications can be by-passed, withdrawn from, disbelieved, conveniently misunderstood, and tactfully conveyed. And even should the person misbehave and break the truce he has made with society, punishment need not be the consequence. If the offense is one that the offended persons can let go by without losing too much face, then they are likely to act forbearantly, telling themselves that they will get even with the offender in another way at another time, even though such an occasion may never arise and might not be exploited if it did. If the offense is great, the offended persons may withdraw from the encounter, or from future similar ones, allowing their withdrawal to be reinforced by the awe they may feel toward someone who breaks the ritual code. Or they may have the offender withdrawn, so that no further communication can occur. But since the offender can salvage a good deal of face from such operations, withdrawal is often not so much an informal punishment for an offense as it is merely a means of terminating it. Perhaps the main principle of the ritual order is not justice but face, and what any offender receives is not what he deserves but what will sustain for the moment the line to which he has committed himself, and through this the line to which he has committed the interaction.

Throughout this paper it has been implied that underneath their differences in culture, people everywhere are the same. If persons have a universal human nature, they themselves are not to be looked to for an explanation of it. One must look rather to the fact that societies everywhere, if they are to be societies, must mobilize their members as self-regulating participants in social encounters. One way of mobilizing the individual for this purpose is through ritual; he is taught to be perceptive, to have feelings attached to self and a self expressed through face, to have pride, honor, and dignity, to have considerateness, to have tact and a certain amount of poise. These are some of the elements of behavior which must be built into the person if practical use is to be made of him as an interactant, and it is these elements that are referred to in part when one speaks of universal human nature.

Universal human nature is not a very human thing. By acquiring it, the person becomes a kind of construct, built up not from inner psychic propensities but from moral rules that are impressed upon him from without. These rules, when followed, determine the evaluation he will make of himself and of his fellow-participants in the encounter, the distribution of his feelings, and the kinds of practices he will employ to maintain a specified and obligatory kind of ritual equilibrium. The general capacity to be bound by moral rules may well belong to the individual, but the particular set of rules which transforms him into a human being derives from requirements established in the ritual organization of social encounters. And if a particular person or group or society seems to have a unique character all its own, it is because its standard set of human-nature elements is pitched and combined in a particular way. Instead of much pride, there may be little. Instead of abiding by the rules, there may be much effort to break them safely. But if an encounter or undertaking is to be sustained as a viable system of interaction organized on ritual principles, then these variations must be held within certain bounds and nicely counterbalanced by corresponding modifications in some of the other rules and understandings. Similarly, the human nature of a particular set of persons may be specially designed for the special kind of undertakings in which they participate, but still each of these persons must have within him something of the balance of characteristics required of a usable participant in any ritually organized system of social activity.❖

Jacques Lacan (1901–1981) was born in Paris. After studying medicine there, he specialized in psychiatry and psychoanalysis. In 1963, he began teaching at the École Pratique des Hautes Etudes. He founded his own school of psychoanalysis, the École Freudienne de Paris, which has been the major psychoanalytic school in Paris since the 1960s. It is typical of psychoanalytic training centers to combine intense clinical experience with the study and interpretation of the Freudian tradition. Lacan's was no exception. In his lecturing and writing, Lacan sought to wrest psychoanalysis away from the traditionalists by introducing his own, often quite independent, understandings of the social theories of desire, language, and literature that were coming into their own in Paris in the 1960s and 1970s. Beyond his impact on psychoanalytic practice, Lacan is the psychoanalyst most closely identified with post-structuralism.

The Eccentric Self and the Discourse of the Other

Jacques Lacan (1957)

Who, then, is this other to whom I am more attached than to myself, since, at the heart of my assent to my own identity it is still he who agitates me?

His presence can be understood only at a second degree of otherness, which already places him in the position of mediating between me and the double of myself, as it were with my counterpart.

If I have said that the unconscious is the discourse of the Other (with a capital O), it is in order to indicate the beyond in which the recognition of desire is bound up with the desire for recognition.

In other words this other is the Other that even my lie invokes as a guarantor of the truth in which it subsists.

By which we can also see that it is with the appearance of language the dimension of truth emerges. . . .

Madness, you are no longer the object of the ambiguous praise with which the sage decorated the impregnable burrow of his fear; and if after all he finds himself tolerably at home there, it is only because the supreme agent forever at work digging its tunnels is none other than reason, the very Logos that he serves.

So how do you imagine that a scholar with so little talent for the 'commitments' that solicited him in his age (as they do in all ages), that a scholar such as Erasmus held such an eminent place in the revolution of a Reformation in which man has as much of a stake in each man as in all men?

The answer is that the slightest alteration in the relation between man and the signifier, in this case in the procedures of exegesis, changes the whole course of history by modifying the moorings that anchor his being.

It is precisely in this that Freudianism, however misunderstood it has been, and however confused its consequences have been, to anyone capable of perceiving the changes we have lived through in our own lives, is seen to have founded an intangible but radical revolution. There is no point in collecting witnesses to the fact: everything involving not just the human sciences, but the destiny of man, politics, metaphysics, literature, the arts, advertising, propaganda, and through these even economics, everything has been affected.

Is all this anything more than the discordant effects of an immense truth in which Freud traced for us a clear path? What must be said, however, is that any technique that bases its claim on the mere psychological categorization of its object is not following this path, and this is the case of psychoanalysis today except in so far as we return to the Freudian discovery.

Furthermore, the vulgarity of the concepts by which it recommends itself to us, the embroidery of pseudo-Freudianism (*frofreudisme*) which is no longer anything but decoration, as well as the bad repute in which it seems to prosper, all bear witness to its fundamental betrayal of its founder.

By his discovery, Freud brought within the circle of science the boundary between the object and being that seemed to mark its outer limit.

That this is the symptom and the prelude of a re-examination of the situation of man in the existent such as has been assumed up to the present by all our postulates of knowledge—don't be content, I beg of you, to write this off as another case of Heideggerianism, even prefixed by a neo- that adds nothing to the dustbin style in which currently, by the use of his ready-made mental jetsam, one excuses oneself from any real thought.

When I speak of Heidegger, or rather when I translate him, I at least make the effort to leave the speech he proffers us its sovereign significance.

If I speak of being and the letter, if I distinguish the other and the Other, it is because Freud shows me that they are the terms to which must be referred the effects of resistance and transference against which, in the twenty years I have engaged in what we all call after him the impossible practice of psychoanalysis, I have done unequal battle. And it is also because I must help others not to lose their way there.

It is to prevent the field of which they are the inheritors from becoming barren, and for that reason to make it understood that if the symptom is a metaphor, it is not a metaphor to say so, any more than to say that man's desire is a metonymy. For the symptom *is* a metaphor whether one likes it or not, as desire *is* a metonymy, however funny people may find the idea.

Finally, if I am to rouse you to indignation over the fact that, after so many centuries of religious hypocrisy and philosophical bravado, nothing has yet been validly articulated as to what links metaphor to the question of being and metonymy to its lack, there must be an object there to answer to that indignation both as its instigator and its victim: that object is humanistic man and the credit, hopelessly affirmed, which he has drawn over his intentions.❖

❖ Others Object ❖

Simone de Beauvoir (1908–1986) was born in Paris to a bourgeois family. Much of her early life was spent in rebellion against the constraints of bourgeois manners. Though her public life with Jean-Paul Sartre is often considered the symbol of that rebellion, it is much more accurate to say that, from her youth, Simone de Beauvoir focused her intelligence and energy on the problem of defining, and living, the authentic human life. This was the real-life foundation of her feminism. She and Sartre met at the École Normale Supérieure, from which both graduated with distinction in 1929. They were companions, occasional lovers, and coworkers until the last years before Sartre's death in 1980. Some are inclined to fault de Beauvoir's feminist credentials because of her relation to Sartre, to whom she seemed, at times, to have ceded too much. Their relationship was, however, complicated. Hurt ran in both directions. The important thing is that they lived an honest and engaged life of politics, letters, intimacy, and friendship. De Beauvoir wrote fiction, autobiography and memoirs, and philosophy. Her *Prime of Life* (1960) is one of the best narrative descriptions both of her relation with Sartre and of life in Paris before, during, and after World War II. *The Mandarins* (1954), one of her fictional works, won the Prix Goncourt. She and Sartre were founding editors of *Les Temps modernes*. Her most enduring philosophical work is *The Second Sex*. However history may treat the philosophy of Sartre, it is virtually certain that *Second Sex* will always be remembered as a classic of feminist social theory and, thus, of modern philosophy.

Woman as Other

Simone de Beauvoir (1949)

Thus humanity is male and man defines woman not in herself but as relative to him; she is not regarded as an autonomous being. Michelet writes: "Woman, the relative being. . . . " And Benda is most positive in his *Rapport d'Uriel*: "The body of man makes sense in itself quite apart from that of woman, whereas the latter seems wanting in significance by itself. . . . Man can think of himself without woman. She cannot think of herself without man." And she is simply what man decrees; thus she is called "the sex," by which is meant that she appears essentially to the male as a sexual being. For him she is sex—absolute sex, no less. She is defined and differentiated with reference to man and not he with reference to her; she is the incidental, the

---

Excerpt from H. M. Parshley, trans., *The Second Sex* (Random House UK Ltd., Jonathan Cape, publisher).

inessential as opposed to the essential. He is the Subject, he is the Absolute—she is the Other.

The category of the *Other* is as primordial as consciousness itself. In the most primitive societies, in the most ancient mythologies, one finds the expression of a duality—that of the Self and the Other. This duality was not originally attached to the division of the sexes; it was not dependent upon any empirical facts. It is revealed in such works as that of Granet on Chinese thought and those of Dumézil on the East Indies and Rome. The feminine element was at first no more involved in such pairs as Varuna-Mitra, Uranus-Zeus, Sun-Moon, and Day-Night than it was in the contrasts between Good and Evil, lucky and unlucky auspices, right and left, God and Lucifer. Otherness is a fundamental category of human thought.

Thus it is that no group ever sets itself up as the One without at once setting up the Other over against itself. If three travelers chance to occupy the same compartment, that is enough to make vaguely hostile "others" out of all the rest of the passengers on the train. In small-town eyes all persons not belonging to the village are "strangers" and suspect; to the native of a country all who inhabit other countries are "foreigners"; Jews are "different" for the anti-Semite, Negroes are "inferior" for American racists, aborigines are "natives" for colonists, proletarians are the "lower class" for the privileged.

Lévi-Strauss, at the end of a profound work on the various forms of primitive societies, reaches the following conclusion: "Passage from the state of Nature to the state of Culture is marked by man's ability to view biological relations as a series of contrasts; duality, alternation, opposition, and symmetry, whether under definite or vague forms, constitute not so much phenomena to be explained as fundamental and immediately given data of social reality." These phenomena would be incomprehensible if in fact human society were simply a *Mitsein* or fellowship based on solidarity and friendliness. Things become clear, on the contrary, if, following Hegel, we find in consciousness itself a fundamental hostility toward every other consciousness; the subject can be posed only in being opposed—he sets himself up as the essential, as opposed to the other, the inessential, the object.

But the other consciousness, the other ego, sets up a reciprocal claim. The native traveling abroad is shocked to find himself in turn regarded as a "stranger" by the natives of neighboring countries. As a matter of fact, wars, festivals, trading, treaties, and contests among tribes, nations, and classes tend to deprive the concept *Other* of its absolute sense and to make manifest its relativity; willy-nilly, individuals and groups are forced to realize the reciprocity of their relations. How is it, then, that this reciprocity has not been recognized between the sexes, that one of the contrasting terms is set up as the sole essential, denying any relativity in regard to its correlative and defining the latter as pure otherness? Why is it that women do not dispute male sovereignty? No subject will readily volunteer to become the object, the inessential; it is not the Other who, in defining himself as the Other, establishes the One. The Other is posed as such by the One in defining himself as the One. But if the Other is not to regain the status of being the One, he must be submissive enough to accept this alien point of view. Whence comes this submission in the case of woman?

There are, to be sure, other cases in which a certain category has been able to dominate another completely for a time. Very often this privilege depends upon inequality of numbers—the majority imposes its rule upon the minority or persecutes it. But women are not a minority, like the American Negroes or the Jews; there are as many women as men on earth. Again, the two groups concerned have often been originally independent; they may have been formerly unaware of each other's existence, or perhaps they recognized each other's autonomy. But a historical event has resulted in the subjugation of the weaker by the stronger. The scattering of the Jews, the introduction of slavery into America, the conquests of imperialism are examples in point. In these cases the oppressed retained at least the memory of former days; they possessed in common a past, a tradition, sometimes a religion or a culture.

The parallel drawn by Bebel between women and the proletariat is valid in that neither ever formed a minority or a separate collective unit of mankind. And instead of a single historical event it is in both cases a historical development that explains their status as a class and accounts for the membership of *particular individuals* in that class. But proletarians have not always existed, whereas there have always been women. They are women in virtue of their anatomy and physiology. Throughout history they have always been subordinated to men, and hence their dependency is not the result of a historical event or a social change—it was not something that *occurred*. The reason why otherness in this case seems to be an absolute is in part that it lacks the contingent or incidental nature of historical facts. A condition brought about at a certain time can be abolished at some other time, as the Negroes of Haiti and others have proved; but it might seem that a natural condition is beyond the possibility of change. In truth, however, the nature of things is no more immutably given, once for all, than is historical reality. If woman seems to be the inessential which never becomes the essential, it is because she herself fails to bring about this change. Proletarians say "We"; Negroes also. Regarding themselves as subjects, they transform the bourgeois, the whites, into "others." But women do not say "We," except at some congress of feminists or similar formal demonstration; men say "women," and women use the same word in referring to themselves. They do not authentically assume a subjective attitude. The proletarians have accomplished the revolution in Russia, the Negroes in Haiti, the Indo-Chinese are battling for it in Indo-China; but the women's effort has never been anything more than a symbolic agitation. They have gained only what men have been willing to grant; they have taken nothing, they have only received.

The reason for this is that women lack concrete means for organizing themselves into a unit which can stand face to face with the correlative unit. They have no past, no history, no religion of their own; and they have no such solidarity of work and interest as that of the proletariat. They are not even promiscuously herded together in the way that creates community feeling among the American Negroes, the ghetto Jews, the workers of Saint-Denis, or the factory hands of Renault. They live dispersed among the males, attached through residence, housework, economic condition, and social standing to certain men—fathers or husbands—more firmly than they are to other women. If they belong to the bourgeoisie, they feel solidarity with men of that class, not with proletarian women; if they are white, their allegiance is to white men, not to Negro women. The proletariat can propose to massacre the ruling class, and a sufficiently fanatical Jew or Negro might dream of getting sole possession of the atomic bomb and making humanity wholly Jewish or black; but woman cannot even dream of exterminating the males. The bond that unites her to her oppressors is not comparable to any other. The division of the sexes is a biological fact, not an event in human history. Male and female stand opposed within a primordial *Mitsein,* and woman has not broken it. The couple is a fundamental unity which its two halves riveted together, and the cleavage of society along the line of sex is impossible. Here is to be found the basic trait of woman: she is the Other in a totality of which the two components are necessary to one another.❖

Aimé Césaire (1913–) was born in Martinique, where he attended school. He then studied at the École Normale Supérieure in Paris, before returning to Martinique. Throughout his life, Césaire has been active in political life and government in Martinique. He is known as much for his poetry and drama as for *Discourse on Colonialism* (1955), from which the selection is taken. "Between Colonizer and Colonized" represents the early thinking of social theorists in the late-colonial world: The text's systematic critique of colonialism expresses the distinctive view of the colonial subject in the colonialist's language. Albert Memmi's *The Colonizer and the Colonized* (1959) is another important example of the early social theory of those who became postcolonial subjects. One of the unique features of this perspective is that it resists categorization as either a race- or class-based point of view. Many today would consider theories written from the postcolonial point of view as those most completely sensitive to the many factors at play in the systematic oppression of people anywhere.

Between Colonizer and Colonized

Aimé Césaire (1955)

But let us speak about the colonized.

I see clearly what colonization has destroyed: the wonderful Indian civilizations—neither Deterding nor Royal Dutch nor Standard Oil will ever console me for the Aztecs and the Incas.

I see clearly the civilizations, condemned to perish at a future date, into which it has introduced a principle of ruin: the South Sea islands, Nigeria, Nyasaland. I see less clearly the contributions it has made.

Security? Culture? The rule of law? In the meantime, I look around and wherever there are colonizers and colonized face to face, I see force, brutality, cruelty, sadism, conflict, and, in a parody of education, the hasty manufacture of a few thousand subordinate functionaries, "boys," artisans, office clerks, and interpreters necessary for the smooth operation of business.

I spoke of contact.

Between colonizer and colonized there is room only for forced labor, intimidation, pressure, the police, taxation, theft, rape, compulsory crops, contempt, mistrust, arrogance, self-complacency, swinishness, brainless elites, degraded masses.

No human contact, but relations of domination and submission which turn the colonizing man into a classroom monitor, an army sergeant, a prison guard, a slave driver, and the indigenous man into an instrument of production.

My turn to state an equation: colonization = "thingification."

I hear the storm. They talk to me about progress, about "achievements," diseases cured, improved standards of living.

I am talking about societies drained of their essence, cultures trampled underfoot, institutions undermined, lands confiscated, religions smashed, magnificent artistic creations destroyed, extraordinary *possibilities* wiped out.

They throw facts at my head, statistics, mileages of roads, canals, and railroad tracks.

I am talking about thousands of men sacrificed to the Congo-Océan.*

I am talking about those who, as I write this, are digging the harbor of Abidjan by hand. I am talking about millions of men torn from their gods, their land, their habits, their life—from life, from the dance, from wisdom.

I am talking about millions of men in whom fear has been cunningly instilled, who have been taught to have an inferiority complex, to tremble, kneel, despair, and behave like flunkeys.

They dazzle me with the tonnage of cotton or cocoa that has been exported, the acreage that has been planted with olive trees or grapevines.

I am talking about natural *economies* that have been disrupted—harmonious and viable *economies* adapted to the indigenous population—about food crops destroyed, malnutrition permanently introduced, agricultural development oriented solely toward the benefit of the metropolitan countries, about the looting of products, the looting of raw materials.

They pride themselves on abuses eliminated.

I too talk about abuses, but what I say is that on the old ones—very real—they have superimposed others—very detestable. They talk to me about local tyrants brought to reason; but I note that in general the old tyrants get on very well with the new ones, and that there has been established between them, to the detriment of the people, a circuit of mutual services and complicity.

They talk to me about civilization, I talk about proletarianization and mystification.

For my part, I make a systematic defense of the non-European civilizations.

Every day that passes, every denial of justice, every beating by the police, every demand of the workers that is drowned in blood, every scandal that is hushed up, every punitive expedition, every police van, every gendarme and every militiaman, brings home to us the value of our old societies.

They were communal societies, never societies of the many for the few.

They were societies that were not only ante-capitalist, as has been said, but also *anti-capitalist.*

They were democratic societies, always.

They were cooperative societies, fraternal societies.

I make a systematic defense of the societies destroyed by imperialism.

They were the fact, they did not pretend to be the idea; despite their faults, they were neither to be hated nor condemned. They were content to be. In them, neither the word *failure* nor the word *avatar* had any meaning. They kept hope intact.

Whereas those are the only words that can, in all honesty, be applied to the European enterprises outside Europe. My only consolation is that periods of colonization pass, that nations sleep only for a time, and that peoples remain.

This being said, it seems that in certain circles they pretend to have discovered in me an "enemy of Europe" and a prophet of the return of the ante-European past.

For my part, I search in vain for the place where I could have expressed such views; where I ever underestimated the importance of Europe in the history of human thought; where I ever preached a *return* of any kind; where I ever claimed that there could be a *return.*

---

*A railroad line connecting Brazzaville with the port of Pointe-Noire. (Trans.)

The truth is that I have said something very different: to wit, that the great historical tragedy of Africa has been not so much that it was too late in making contact
with the rest of the world, as the manner in which that contact was brought about;
that Europe began to "propagate" at a time when it had fallen into the hands of the
most unscrupulous financiers and captains of industry; that it was our misfortune
to encounter that particular Europe on our path, and that Europe is responsible before the human community for the highest heap of corpses in history.

In another connection, in judging colonization, I have added that Europe has gotten on very well indeed with all the local feudal lords who agreed to serve, woven a
villainous complicity with them, rendered their tyranny more effective and more efficient, and that it has actually tended to prolong artificially the survival of local
pasts in their most pernicious aspects.

I have said—and this is something very different—that colonialist Europe has
grafted modern abuse onto ancient injustice, hateful racism onto old inequality.

That if I am attacked on the grounds of intent, I maintain that colonialist Europe
is dishonest in trying to justify its colonizing activity *a posteriori* by the obvious
material progress that has been achieved in certain fields under the colonial
regime—since *sudden change* is always possible, in history as elsewhere; since no one
knows at what stage of material development these same countries would have been
if Europe had not intervened; since the technical outfitting of Africa and Asia, their
administrative reorganization, in a word, their "Europeanization," was (as is proved
by the example of Japan) in no way tied to the European *occupation;* since the Europeanization of the non-European continents could have been accomplished otherwise than under the heel of Europe; since this movement of Europeanization *was in
progress;* since it was even slowed down; since in any case it was distorted by the European takeover.

The proof is that at present it is the indigenous peoples of Africa and Asia who are
demanding schools, and colonialist Europe which refuses them; that it is the African
who is asking for ports and roads, and colonialist Europe which is niggardly on this
score; that it is the colonized man who wants to move forward, and the colonizer
who holds things back.❖

Martin Luther King, Jr. (1929–1968) was born in Atlanta, Georgia. His father, the
Reverend Martin Luther King, Sr., was pastor of one of the two most prestigious
black churches in that city. King, Jr., studied theology at the Crozer Theological
School in Chester, Pennsylvania, then at Boston University, where he received his
Ph.D. in 1955. One year earlier, he had become pastor of the Dexter Avenue Baptist
Church in Montgomery, Alabama. In the events following December 1955, when
Rosa Parks spontaneously refused to step to the back of the bus, King was elected
leader of the Montgomery Improvement Association, which directed the yearlong,
successful bus boycott. In 1957, he founded the Southern Christian Leadership Conference, which was the institutional base from which he became the leader of the
early civil rights movement. In 1964, King was awarded the Nobel Peace Prize.

In the mid-1960s, the movement changed. Young people shifted away from the
policy of nonviolence. Whites were less welcome, and women began to protest the
dominance of men in the movement. When King tried to march in the North, particularly in Chicago in 1966, the resistance was ugly, and the march unsuccessful. If

the most memorable event in the movement was the march on Washington in August 1963, the last great triumph was the Selma march to Montgomery in April 1965, ten years after the movement began in the same city. King was murdered in Memphis in 1968 as he was organizing the "poor people's march" on Washington. The selection explains his nonviolent philosophy and his differing debts to Niebuhr and Gandhi (described as a recollection from his student days, probably over Christmas vacation in 1949).

The Power of Nonviolent Action

Martin Luther King, Jr. (1958)

During this period I had about despaired of the power of love in solving social problems. Perhaps my faith in love was temporarily shaken by the philosophy of Nietzsche. I had been reading parts of *The Genealogy of Morals* and the whole of *The Will to Power*. Nietzsche's glorification of power—in his theory all life expressed the will to power—was an outgrowth of his contempt for ordinary morals. He attacked the whole of the Hebraic-Christian morality—with its virtues of piety and humility, its other-worldiness and its attitude toward suffering—as the glorification of weakness, as making virtues out of necessity and impotence. He looked to the development of a superman who would surpass man as man surpassed the ape.

Then one Sunday afternoon I traveled to Philadelphia to hear a sermon by Dr. Mordecai Johnson, president of Howard University. He was there to preach for the Fellowship House of Philadelphia. Dr. Johnson had just returned from a trip to India, and, to my great interest, he spoke of the life and teachings of Mahatma Gandhi. His message was so profound and electrifying that I left the meeting and bought a half-dozen books on Gandhi's life and works.

Like most people, I had heard of Gandhi, but I had never studied him seriously. As I read I became deeply fascinated by his campaigns of nonviolent resistance. I was particularly moved by the Salt March to the Sea and his numerous fasts. The whole concept of "Satyagraha" (*Satya* is truth which equals love, and *agraha* is force; "Satyagraha," therefore, means truth-force or love force) was profoundly significant to me. As I delved deeper into the philosophy of Gandhi my skepticism concerning the power of love gradually diminished, and I came to see for the first time its potency in the area of social reform. Prior to reading Gandhi, I had about concluded that the ethics of Jesus were only effective in individual relationship. The "turn the other cheek" philosophy and the "love your enemies" philosophy were only valid, I felt, when individuals were in conflict with other individuals; when racial groups and nations were in conflict a more realistic approach seemed necessary. But after reading Gandhi, I saw how utterly mistaken I was.

Gandhi was probably the first person in history to lift the love ethic of Jesus above mere interaction between individuals to a powerful and effective social force on a large scale. Love for Gandhi was a potent instrument for social and collective transformation. It was in this Gandhian emphasis on love and nonviolence that I discovered the method for social reform that I had been seeking for so many months. The intellectual and moral satisfaction that I failed to gain from the utilitarianism of Bentham and Mill, the revolutionary methods of Marx and Lenin, the social-contracts theory of Hobbes, the "back to nature" optimism of Rousseau, and the superman philosophy of Nietzsche, I found in the nonviolent resistance philosophy of Gandhi. I came to feel that this was the only morally and practically sound method open to oppressed people in their struggle for freedom.

But my intellectual odyssey to nonviolence did not end here. During my last year in theological school. I began to read the works of Reinhold Niebuhr. The prophetic and realistic elements in Niebuhr's passionate style and profound thought were appealing to me, and I became so enamored of his social ethics that I almost fell into the trap of accepting uncritically everything he wrote.

About this time I read Niebuhr's critique of the pacifist position. Niebuhr had himself once been a member of the pacifist ranks. For several years, he had been national chairman of the Fellowship of Reconciliation. His break with pacifism came in the early thirties, and the first full statement of his criticism of pacifism was in *Moral Man and Immoral Society.* Here he argued that there was no intrinsic moral difference between violent and nonviolent resistance. The social consequences of the two methods were different, he contended, but the differences were in degree rather than kind. Later Niebuhr began emphasizing the irresponsibility of relying on non-violent resistance when there was no ground for believing that it would be successful in preventing the spread of totalitarian tyranny. It could only be successful, he argued, if the groups against whom the resistance was taking place had some degree of moral conscience, as was the case in Gandhi's struggle against the British. Niebuhr's ultimate rejection of pacifism was based primarily on the doctrine of man. He argued that pacifism failed to do justice to the reformation doctrine of justification by faith, substituting for it a sectarian perfectionism which believes "that divine grace actually lifts men out of the sinful contradictions of history and establishes him above the sins of the world." . . .

Violence as a way of achieving racial justice is both impractical and immoral. It is impractical because it is a descending spiral ending in destruction for all. The old law of an eye for an eye leaves everybody blind. It is immoral because it seeks to humiliate the opponent rather than win his understanding; it seeks to annihilate rather than to convert. Violence is immoral because it thrives on hatred rather than love. It destroys community and makes brotherhood impossible. It leaves society in monologue rather than dialogue. Violence ends by defeating itself. It creates bitterness in the survivors and brutality in the destroyers. A voice echoes through time saying to every potential Peter, "Put up your sword." History is cluttered with the wreckage of nations that failed to follow this command.

If the American Negro and other victims of oppression succumb to the temptation of using violence in the struggle for freedom, future generations will be the recipients of a desolate night of bitterness, and our chief legacy to them will be an endless reign of meaningless chaos. Violence is not the way.

The third way open to oppressed people in their quest for freedom is the way of nonviolent resistance. Like the synthesis in Hegelian philosophy, the principle of nonviolent resistance seeks to reconcile the truths of two opposites—acquiescence and violence—while avoiding the extremes and immoralities of both. The nonviolent resister agrees with the person who acquiesces that one should not be physically aggressive toward his opponent; but he balances the equation by agreeing with the person of violence that evil must be resisted. He avoids the nonresistance of the former and the violent resistance of the latter. With nonviolent resistance, no individual or group need submit to any wrong, nor need anyone resort to violence in order to right a wrong.

It seems to me that this is the method that must guide the actions of the Negro in the present crisis in race relations. Through nonviolent resistance the Negro will be able to rise to the noble height of opposing the unjust system while loving the perpetrators of the system. The Negro must work passionately and unrelentingly for full stature as a citizen, but he must not use inferior methods to gain it. He must never come to terms with falsehood, malice, hate, or destruction.

Nonviolent resistance makes it possible for the Negro to remain in the South and struggle for his rights. The Negro's problem will not be solved by running away. He cannot listen to the glib suggestion of those who would urge him to migrate en masse to other sections of the country. By grasping his great opportunity in the South he can make a lasting contribution to the moral strength of the nation and set a sublime example of courage for generations yet unborn.

By nonviolent resistance, the Negro can also enlist all men of good will in his struggle for equality. The problem is not a purely racial one, with Negroes set against whites. In the end, it is not a struggle between people at all, but a tension between justice and injustice. Nonviolent resistance is not aimed against oppressors but against oppression. Under its banner consciences, not racial groups, are enlisted.

If the Negro is to achieve the goal of integration, he must organize himself into a militant and nonviolent mass movement. All three elements are indispensable. The movement for equality and justice can only be a success if it has both a mass and militant character; the barriers to be overcome require both. Nonviolence is an imperative in order to bring about ultimate community.

A mass movement of a militant quality that is not at the same time committed to nonviolence tends to generate conflict, which in turn breeds anarchy. The support of the participants and the sympathy of the uncommitted are both inhibited by the threat that bloodshed will engulf the community. This reaction in turn encourages the opposition to threaten and resort to force. When, however, the mass movement repudiates violence while moving resolutely toward its goal, its opponents are revealed as the instigators and practitioners of violence if it occurs. Then public support is magnetically attracted to the advocates of nonviolence, while those who employ violence are literally disarmed by overwhelming sentiment against their stand.

Only through a nonviolent approach can the fears of the white community be mitigated. A guilt-ridden white minority lives in fear that if the Negro should ever attain power, he would act without restraint or pity to revenge the injustices and brutality of the years. It is something like a parent who continually mistreats a son. One day that parent raises his hand to strike the son, only to discover that the son is now as tall as he is. The parent is suddenly afraid—fearful that the son will use his new physical power to repay his parent for all the blows of the past.

The Negro, once a helpless child, has now grown up politically, culturally, and economically. Many white men fear retaliation. The job of the Negro is to show them that they have nothing to fear, that the Negro understands and forgives and is ready to forget the past. He must convince the white man that all he seeks is justice, *for both himself and the white man.* A mass movement exercising nonviolence is an object lesson in power under discipline, a demonstration to the white community that if such a movement attained a degree of strength, it would use its power creatively and not vengefully.

Nonviolence can touch men where the law cannot reach them. When the law regulates behavior it plays an indirect part in molding public sentiment. The enforcement of the law is itself a form of peaceful persuasion. But the law needs help. The courts can order desegregation of the public schools. But what can be done to mitigate the fears, to disperse the hatred, violence, and irrationality gathered around school integration, to take the initiative out of the hands of racial demagogues, to release respect for the law? In the end, for laws to be obeyed, men must believe they are right.

Here nonviolence comes in as the ultimate form of persuasion. It is the method which seeks to implement the just law by appealing to the conscience of the great decent majority who through blindness, fear, pride, or irrationality have allowed their consciences to sleep.

The nonviolent resisters can summarize their message in the following simple terms: We will take direct action against injustice without waiting for other agencies to act. We will not obey unjust laws or submit to unjust practices. We will do this peacefully, openly, cheerfully because our aim is to persuade. We adopt the means of nonviolence because our end is a community at peace with itself. We will try to persuade with our words, but if our words fail, we will try to persuade with our acts. We will always be willing to talk and seek fair compromise, but we are ready to suffer when necessary and even risk our lives to become witnesses to the truth as we see it.

The way of nonviolence means a willingness to suffer and sacrifice. It may mean going to jail. If such is the case the resister must be willing to fill the jail houses of the South. It may even mean physical death. But if physical death is the price that a man must pay to free his children and his white brethren from a permanent death of the spirit, then nothing could be more redemptive.

What is the Negro's best defense against acts of violence inflicted upon him? As Dr. Kenneth Clark has said so eloquently, "His only defense is to meet every act of barbarity, illegality, cruelty and injustice toward an individual Negro with the fact that 100 more Negroes will present themselves in his place as potential victims." Every time one Negro school teacher is fired for believing in integration, a thousand others should be ready to take the same stand. If the oppressors bomb the home of one Negro for his protest, they must be made to realize that to press back the rising tide of the Negro's courage they will have to bomb hundreds more, and even then they will fail.

Faced with this dynamic unity, this amazing self-respect, this willingness to suffer, and this refusal to hit back, the oppressor will find, as oppressors have always found, that he is glutted with his own barbarity. Forced to stand before the world and his God splattered with the blood of his brother, he will call an end to his self-defeating massacre.

American Negroes must come to the point where they can say to their white brothers, paraphrasing the words of Gandhi: "We will match your capacity to inflict suffering with our capacity to enduring suffering. We will meet your physical force with soul force. We will not hate you, but we cannot in all good conscience obey your unjust laws. Do to us what you will and we will still love you. Bomb our homes and threaten our children; send your hooded perpetrators of violence into our communities and drag us out on some wayside road, beating us and leaving us half dead, and we will still love you. But we will soon wear you down by our capacity to suffer. And in winning our freedom we will so appeal to your heart and conscience that we will win you in the process."

Realism impels me to admit that many Negroes will find it difficult to follow the path of nonviolence. Some will consider it senseless; some will argue that they have neither the strength nor the courage to join in such a mass demonstration of nonviolent action. As E. Franklin Frazier points out in *Black Bourgeoisie,* many Negroes are occupied in a middle-class struggle for status and prestige. They are more concerned about "conspicuous consumption" than about the cause of justice, and are probably not prepared for the ordeals and sacrifices involved in nonviolent action. Fortunately, however, the success of this method is not dependent on its unanimous acceptance. A few Negroes in every community, unswervingly committed to the nonviolent way, can persuade hundreds of others at least to use nonviolence as a technique and serve as the moral force to awaken the slumbering national conscience. Thoreau was thinking of such a creative minority when he said: "I know this well, that if one thousand, if one hundred, if ten men whom I could name—if ten honest men only—aye, if one honest man, in the state of Massachusetts, ceasing to hold slaves, were actually to withdraw from the copartnership, and be locked up in the county jail therefore, it would be the abolition of slavery in America. For it matters not how small the beginning may seem to be, what is once well done is done forever."

Mahatma Gandhi never had more than one hundred persons absolutely committed to his philosophy. But with this small group of devoted followers, he galvanized the whole of India, and through a magnificent feat of nonviolence challenged the might of the British Empire and won freedom for his people.

This method of nonviolence will not work miracles overnight. Men are not easily moved from their mental ruts, their prejudiced and irrational feelings. When the underprivileged demand freedom, the privileged first react with bitterness and resistance. Even when the demands are couched in nonviolent terms, the initial response is the same. Nehru once remarked that the British were never so angry as when the Indians resisted them with nonviolence, that he never saw eyes so full of hate as those of the British troops to whom he turned the other cheek when they beat him with laths. But nonviolent resistance at least changed the minds and hearts of the Indians, however impervious the British may have appeared. "We cast away our fear," says Nehru. And in the end the British not only granted freedom to India but came to have a new respect for the Indians. Today a mutual friendship based on complete equality exists between these two peoples within the Commonwealth.

In the South too, the initial white reaction to Negro resistance has been bitter. I do not predict that a similar happy ending will come to Montgomery in a few months, because integration is more complicated than independence. But I know that the Negroes of Montgomery are already walking straighter because of the protest. And I expect that this generation of Negro children throughout the United States will grow up stronger and better because of the courage, the dignity, and the suffering of the nine children of Little Rock, and their counterparts in Nashville, Clinton, and Sturges. And I believe that the white people of this country are being affected too, that beneath the surface this nation's conscience is being stirred.

The nonviolent approach does not immediately change the heart of the oppressor. It first does something to the hearts and souls of those committed to it. It gives them new self-respect; it calls up resources of strength and courage that they did not know they had. Finally it reaches the opponent and so stirs his conscience that reconciliation becomes a reality. . . .

This is a great hour for the Negro. The challenge is here. To become the instruments of a great idea is a privilege that history gives only occasionally. Arnold

Toynbee says in *A Study of History* that it may be the Negro who will give the new spiritual dynamic to Western civilization that it so desperately needs to survive. I hope this is possible. The spiritual power that the Negro can radiate to the world comes from love, understanding, good will, and nonviolence. It may even be possible for the Negro, through adherence to nonviolence, so to challenge the nations of the world that they will seriously seek an alternative to war and destruction. In a day when Sputniks and Explorers dash through outer space and guided ballistic missiles are carving highways of death through the stratosphere, nobody can win a war. Today the choice is no longer between violence and nonviolence. It is either nonviolence or nonexistence. The Negro may be God's appeal to this age—an age drifting rapidly to its doom. The eternal appeal takes the form of a warning: "All who take the sword will perish by the sword."❖

C. Wright Mills (1916–1962) was born in Waco, Texas. After undergraduate studies at the University of Texas, Mills did his doctoral work at the University of Wisconsin. There, he met Hans Gerth, with whom he edited, translated, and introduced *From Max Weber,* a still-important collection of Weber's writings. After teaching in what he considered a provincial exile at the University of Maryland, Mills moved to Columbia and the Bureau of Applied Social Research in 1945. His earliest days at Columbia were spent in empirical social research. Yet he never became an accepted member or even a full professor in Columbia's department. In the 1950s, Mills became much more the public intellectual, while teaching primarily undergraduates at Columbia. Works like *Power Elite, Listen Yankee! White Collar,* and *The Causes of World War Three*—all written in this period—brought him much public acclaim and informal membership in New York's Left, intellectual elite. Mills was considered arrogant by many colleagues and a hero by many of his readers. He dressed and played the part of the young intellectual radical—complete with leather jacket and motorcycle. However, he suffered from a chronic heart condition that killed him at age forty-five in 1962, the year of SDS's *Port Huron Statement.* Mills was a source of intellectual inspiration to younger radicals and social theorists because, true to his ideal of the sociological imagination, his writings based strong critical ideas on careful empirical work. He read Weber in relation to Marx *and* the American pragmatists. He sought to unite the best of European and American classical theory into a social philosophy for the New Left.

The Sociological Imagination
C. Wright Mills (1959)

The sociological imagination enables its possessor to understand the larger historical scene in terms of its meaning for the inner life and the external career of a variety of individuals. It enables him to take into account how individuals, in the welter of their daily experience, often become falsely conscious of their social positions. Within that welter, the framework of modern society is sought, and within that framework the psychologies of a variety of men and women are formulated. By such means the personal uneasiness of individuals is focused upon explicit troubles and the indifference of publics is transformed into involvement with public issues.

The first fruit of this imagination—and the first lesson of the social science that embodies it—is the idea that the individual can understand his own experience and gauge his own fate only by locating himself within his period, that he can know his own chances in life only by becoming aware of those of all individuals in his circumstances. In many ways it is a terrible lesson; in many ways a magnificent one. We do not know the limits of man's capacities for supreme effort or willing degradation, for agony or glee, for pleasurable brutality or the sweetness of reason. But in our time we have come to know that the limits of 'human nature' are frighteningly broad. We have come to know that every individual lives, from one generation to the next, in some society; that he lives out a biography, and that he lives it out within some historical sequence. By the fact of his living he contributes, however minutely, to the shaping of this society and to the course of its history, even as he is made by society and by its historical push and shove.

The sociological imagination enables us to grasp history and biography and the relations between the two within society. That is its task and its promise. To recognize this task and this promise is the mark of the classic social analyst. It is characteristic of Herbert Spencer—turgid, polysyllabic, comprehensive; of E. A. Ross—graceful, muckraking, upright; of Auguste Comte and Emile Durkheim; of the intricate and subtle Karl Mannheim. It is the quality of all that is intellectually excellent in Karl Marx; it is the clue to Thorstein Veblen's brilliant and ironic insight, to Joseph Schumpeter's many-sided constructions of reality; it is the basis of the psychological sweep of W.E.H. Lecky no less than of the profundity and clarity of Max Weber. And it is the signal of what is best in contemporary studies of man and society.

No social study that does not come back to the problems of biography, of history and of their intersections within a society has completed its intellectual journey. Whatever the specific problems of the classic social analysts, however limited or however broad the features of social reality they have examined, those who have been imaginatively aware of the promise of their work have consistently asked three sorts of questions:

(1) What is the structure of this particular society as a whole? What are its essential components, and how are they related to one another? How does it differ from other varieties of social order? Within it, what is the meaning of any particular feature for its continuance and for its change?

(2) Where does this society stand in human history? What are the mechanics by which it is changing? What is its place within and its meaning for the development of humanity as a whole? How does any particular feature we are examining affect, and how is it affected by, the historical period in which it moves? And this period—what are its essential features? How does it differ from other periods? What are its characteristic ways of history-making?

(3) What varieties of men and women now prevail in this society and in this period? And what varieties are coming to prevail? In what ways are they selected and formed, liberated and repressed, made sensitive and blunted? What kinds of 'human nature' are revealed in the conduct and character we observe in this society in this period? And what is the meaning for 'human nature' of each and every feature of the society we are examining?

Whether the point of interest is a great power state or a minor literary mood, a family, a prison, a creed—these are the kinds of questions the best social analysts have asked. They are the intellectual pivots of classic studies of man in society—and they are the questions inevitably raised by any mind possessing the sociological imagination. For that imagination is the capacity to shift from one perspective to another—from the political to the psychological; from examination of a single family to comparative assessment of the national budgets of the world; from the theological school to the military establishment; from considerations of an oil industry to studies of contemporary poetry. It is the capacity to range from the most impersonal and remote transformations to the most intimate features of the human self— and to see the relations between the two. Back of its use there is always the urge to know the social and historical meaning of the individual in the society and in the period in which he has his quality and his being.

That, in brief, is why it is by means of the sociological imagination that men now hope to grasp what is going on in the world, and to understand what is happening in themselves as minute points of the intersections of biography and history within society. In large part, contemporary man's self-conscious view of himself as at least an outsider, if not a permanent stranger, rests upon an absorbed realization of social relativity and of the transformative power of history. The sociological imagination is the most fruitful form of this self-consciousness. By its use men whose mentalities have swept only a series of limited orbits often come to feel as if suddenly awakened in a house with which they had only supposed themselves to be familiar. Correctly or incorrectly, they often come to feel that they can now provide themselves with adequate summations, cohesive assessments, comprehensive orientations. Older decisions that once appeared sound now seem to them products of a mind unaccountably dense. Their capacity for astonishment is made lively again. They acquire a new way of thinking, they experience a transvaluation of values: in a word, by their reflection and by their sensibility, they realize the cultural meaning of the social sciences.

Perhaps the most fruitful distinction with which the sociological imagination works is between 'the personal troubles of milieu' and 'the public issues of social structure.' This distinction is an essential tool of the sociological imagination and a feature of all classic work in social science.

Troubles occur within the character of the individual and within the range of his immediate relations with others; they have to do with his self and with those limited areas of social life of which he is directly and personally aware. Accordingly, the statement and the resolution of troubles properly lie within the individual as a biographical entity and within the scope of his immediate milieu—the social setting that is directly open to his personal experience and to some extent his willful activity. A trouble is a private matter: values cherished by an individual are felt by him to be threatened.

Issues have to do with matters that transcend these local environments of the individual and the range of his inner life. They have to do with the organization of many such milieux into the institutions of an historical society as a whole, with the ways in which various milieux overlap and interpenetrate to form the larger structure of social and historical life. An issue is a public matter: some value cherished by publics is felt to be threatened. Often there is a debate about what that value really is and about what it is that really threatens it. This debate is often without focus if only because it is the very nature of an issue, unlike even widespread trouble, that it cannot very well be defined in terms of the immediate and everyday environments of ordinary men. An issue, in fact, often involves a crisis in institutional arrangements, and often too it involves what Marxists call 'contradictions' or 'antagonisms.' . . .

In every intellectual age some one style of reflection tends to become a common denominator of cultural life. Nowadays, it is true, many intellectual fads are widely taken up before they are dropped for new ones in the course of a year or two. Such enthusiasms may add spice to cultural play, but leave little or no intellectual trace. That is not true of such ways of thinking as 'Newtonian physics' or 'Darwinian biology.' Each of these intellectual universes became an influence that reached far beyond any special sphere of idea and imagery. In terms of them, or in terms derived from them, unknown scholars as well as fashionable commentators came to re-focus their observations and re-formulate their concerns.

During the modern era, physical and biological science has been the major common denominator of serious reflection and popular metaphysics in Western societies. 'The technique of the laboratory' has been the accepted mode of procedure and the source of intellectual security. That is one meaning of the idea of an intellectual common denominator: men can state their strongest convictions in its terms; other terms and other styles of reflection seem mere vehicles of escape and obscurity.

That a common denominator prevails does not of course mean that no other styles of thought or modes of sensibility exist. But it does mean that more general intellectual interests tend to slide into this area, to be formulated there most sharply, and when so formulated, to be thought somehow to have reached, if not a solution, at least a profitable way of being carried along.

The sociological imagination is becoming, I believe, the major common denominator of our cultural life and its signal feature. This quality of mind is found in the social and psychological sciences, but it goes far beyond these studies as we now know them. Its acquisition by individuals and by the cultural community at large is slow and often fumbling; many social scientists are themselves quite unaware of it. They do not seem to know that the use of this imagination is central to the best work that they might do, that by failing to develop and to use it they are failing to meet the cultural expectations that are coming to be demanded of them and that the classic traditions of their several disciplines make available to them.

Yet in factual and moral concerns, in literary work and in political analysis, the qualities of this imagination are regularly demanded. In a great variety of expressions, they have become central features of intellectual endeavor and cultural sensibility. Leading critics exemplify these qualities as do serious journalists—in fact the work of both is often judged in these terms. Popular categories of criticism—high, middle, and low-brow, for example—are now at least as much sociological as aesthetic. Novelists—whose serious work embodies the most widespread definitions of human reality—frequently possess this imagination, and do much to meet the demand for it. By means of it, orientation to the present as history is sought. As images of 'human nature' become more problematic, an increasing need is felt to pay closer yet more imaginative attention to the social routines and catastrophes which reveal (and which shape) man's nature in this time of civil unrest and ideological conflict. Although fashion is often revealed by attempts to use it, the sociological imagination is not merely a fashion. It is a quality of mind that seems most dramatically to promise an understanding of the intimate realities of ourselves in connection with larger social realities. It is not merely one quality of mind among the contemporary range of cultural sensibilities—it is *the* quality whose wider and more adroit use offers the promise that all such sensibilities—and in fact, human reason itself—will come to play a greater role in human affairs.❖

Students for a Democratic Society (SDS) was the first important national organization in the U.S. student movement of the 1960s. Its home initially was the University of Michigan, where many of its early leaders were students. One of them, Tom Hayden, was the author of the first draft of the *Port Huron Statement,* submitted for discussion to a national conference of SDS members in June 1962. The meeting, held at a labor movement conference center on the shores of Lake Huron, attracted a small but intense group. Among those present was Richard Flacks, who is usually considered the intellectual-scholar of the early student movement, just as Hayden was its most flamboyant activist. Today, Hayden is a politician in California. Flacks now teaches sociology at the University of California at Santa Barbara and continues actively to participate in and write about the political principles of the New Left. Flacks's book *Making History* (1988) is an elegant elaboration of the social theory of C. Wright Mills and SDS. After the 1960s, the student movement faded, even though—like Hayden and Flacks—most of its members are still pursuing lives of political responsibility. In its earliest days, SDS was active in the civil rights movement (especially in the Mississippi Freedom Summer voter drive in 1964) and, later, in the antiwar movement.

Participatory Democracy (from The Port Huron Statement*)*
Students for a Democratic Society (1962)

We are people of this generation, bred in at least modest comfort, housed now in universities, looking uncomfortably to the world we inherit.

When we were kids the United States was the wealthiest and strongest country in the world; the only one with the atom bomb, the least scarred by modern war, an initiator of the United Nations that we thought would distribute Western influence throughout the world. Freedom and equality for each individual, government of, by, and for the people—these American values we found good, principles by which we could live as men. Many of us began maturing in complacency.

As we grew, however, our comfort was penetrated by events too troubling to dismiss. First, the permeating and victimizing fact of human degradation, symbolized by the Southern struggle against racial bigotry, compelled most of us from silence to activism. Second, the enclosing fact of the Cold War, symbolized by the presence of the Bomb, brought awareness that we ourselves, and our friends, and millions of abstract "others" we knew more directly because of our common peril, might die at any time. We might deliberately ignore, or avoid, or fail to feel all other human problems, but not these two, for these were too immediate and crushing in their impact, too challenging in the demand that we as individuals take the responsibility for encounter and resolution.

Excerpt from Judith Clavir Albert and Steward Edward Albert, eds., *The Sixties Papers: Documents of a Rebellious Decade* (New York: Praeger Publishers, 1984), pp. 176–178, 180–182. Reprinted by permission of Greenwood Publishing Group.

While these and other problems either directly oppressed us or rankled our consciences and became our own subjective concerns, we began to see complicated and disturbing paradoxes in our surrounding America. The declaration "all men are created equal . . ." rang hollow before the facts of Negro life in the South and the big cities of the North. The proclaimed peaceful intentions of the United States contradicted its economic and military investments of the Cold War status quo.

We witnessed, and continue to witness, other paradoxes. With nuclear energy whole cities can easily be powered, yet the dominant nation-states seem more likely to unleash destruction greater than that incurred in all wars of human history. Although our own technology is destroying old and creating new forms of social organization, men still tolerate meaningless work and idleness. While two thirds of mankind suffers undernourishment, our own upper classes revel amidst superfluous abundance. Although world population is expected to double in forty years, the nations still tolerate anarchy as a major principle of international conduct and uncontrolled exploitation governs the sapping of the earth's physical resources. Although mankind desperately needs revolutionary leadership, America rests in national stalemate, its goals ambiguous and tradition-bound instead of informed and clear, its democratic system apathetic and manipulated rather than "of, by, and for the people."

Not only did tarnish appear on our image of American virtue, not only did disillusion occur when the hypocrisy of American ideals was discovered, but we began to sense that what we had originally seen as the American Golden Age was actually the decline of an era. The worldwide outbreak of revolution against colonialism and imperialism, the entrenchment of totalitarian states, the menace of war, overpopulation, international disorder, supertechnology—these trends were testing the tenacity of our own commitment to democracy and freedom and our abilities to visualize their application to a world in upheaval.

Our work is guided by the sense that we may be the last generation in the experiment with living. But we are a minority—the vast majority of our people regard the temporary equilibriums of our society and world as eternally-functional parts. In this is perhaps the outstanding paradox: we ourselves are imbued with urgency, yet the message of our society is that there is no viable alternative to the present. Beneath the reassuring tones of the politicians, beneath the common opinion that America will "muddle through," beneath the stagnation of those who have closed their minds to the future, is the pervading feeling that there simply are no alternatives, that our times have witnessed the exhaustion not only of Utopias, but of any new departures as well. Feeling the press of complexity upon the emptiness of life, people are fearful of the thought that at any moment things might be thrust out of control. They fear change itself, since change might smash whatever invisible framework seems to hold back chaos for them now. For most Americans, all crusades are suspect, threatening. The fact that each individual sees apathy in his fellows perpetuates the common reluctance to organize for change. The dominant institutions are complex enough to blunt the minds of their potential critics, and entrenched enough to swiftly dissipate or entirely repel the energies of protest and reform, thus limiting human expectancies. Then, too, we are a materially improved society, and by our own improvements we seem to have weakened the case for further change.

Some would have us believe that Americans feel contentment amidst prosperity—but might it not be better called a glaze above deeply-felt anxieties about their role in the new world? And if these anxieties produce a developed indifference to human affairs, do they not as well produce a yearning to believe there is an alternative to the present, that something *can* be done to change circumstances in the school, the workplaces, the bureaucracies, the government? It is to this latter yearning, at once the spark and engine of change, that we direct our present appeal. The search for truly democratic alternatives to the present, and a commitment to social experimentation with them, is a worthy and fulfilling human enterprise, one which moves us and, we hope, others today. On such a basis do we offer this document of our convictions and analysis: as an effort in understanding and changing the conditions of humanity in the late twentieth century, an effort rooted in the ancient, still unfulfilled conception of man attaining determining influence over his circumstances of life. . . .

In suggesting social goals and values, therefore, we are aware of entering a sphere of some disrepute. Perhaps matured by the past, we have no sure formulas, no closed theories—but that does not mean values are beyond discussion and tentative determination. A first task of any social movement is to convince people that the search for orienting theories and the creation of human values is complex but worthwhile. We are aware that to avoid platitudes we must analyze the concrete conditions of social order. But to direct such an analysis we must use the guideposts of basic principles. Our own social values involve conceptions of human beings, human relationships, and social systems.

We regard *men* as infinitely precious and possessed of unfulfilled capacities for reason, freedom, and love. In affirming these principles we are aware of countering perhaps the dominant conceptions of man in the twentieth century: that he is a thing to be manipulated, and that he is inherently incapable of directing his own affairs. We oppose the depersonalization that reduces human beings to the status of things—if anything, the brutalities of the twentieth century teach that means and ends are intimately related, that vague appeals to "posterity" cannot justify the mutilations of the present. We oppose, too, the doctrine of human incompetence because it rests essentially on the modern fact that men have been "competently" manipulated into incompetence—we see little reason why men cannot meet with increasing skill the complexities and responsibilities of their situation, if society is organized not for minority, but for majority, participation in decision-making.

Men have unrealized potential for self-evaluation, self-direction, self-understanding, and creativity. It is this potential that we regard as crucial and to which we appeal, not to the human potentiality for violence, unreason, and submission to authority. The goal of man and society should be human independence; a concern not with image of popularity but with finding meaning in life that is personally authentic; a quality of mind not compulsively driven by a sense of powerlessness, nor one which unthinkingly adopts status values, nor one which represses all threats to its habits, but one which has full, spontaneous access to present and past experiences, one which easily unites the fragmented parts of personal history, one which openly faces problems which are troubling and unresolved; one with an intuitive awareness of possibilities, an active sense of curiosity, an ability and willingness to learn.

This kind of independence does not mean egotistic individualism—the object is not to have one's way so much as it is to have a way that is one's own. Nor do we deify man—we merely have faith in his potential.

Human relationships should involve fraternity and honesty. Human interdependence is contemporary fact; human brotherhood must be willed, however, as a condition of future survival and as the most appropriate form of social relations. Personal links between man and man are needed, especially to go beyond the partial and fragmentary bonds of function that bind men only as worker to worker, employer to employee, teacher to student, American to Russian.

Loneliness, estrangement, isolation describe the vast distance between man and man today. These dominant tendencies cannot be overcome by better personnel management, nor by improved gadgets, but only when a love of man overcomes the idolatrous worship of things by man. As the individualism we affirm is not egoism, the selflessness we affirm is not self-elimination. On the contrary, we believe in generosity of a kind that imprints one's unique individual qualities in the relation to other men, and to all human activity. Further, to dislike isolation is not to favor the abolition of privacy; the latter differs from isolation in that it occurs or is abolished according to individual will.

We would replace power rooted in possession, privilege, or circumstance by power and uniqueness rooted in love, reflectiveness, reason, and creativity. As a *social system* we seek the establishment of a democracy of individual participation, governed by two central aims: that the individual share in those social decisions determining the quality and direction of his life; that society be organized to encourage independence in men and provide the media for their common participation.

In a participatory democracy, the political life would be based in several root principles:

> that decision-making of basic social consequence be carried on by public groupings;
> that politics be seen positively, as the art of collectively creating an acceptable pattern of social relations;
> that politics have the function of bringing people out of isolation and into community, thus being a necessary, though not sufficient, means of finding meaning in personal life;
> that the political order should serve to clarify problems in a way instrumental to their solution; it should provide outlets for the expression of personal grievance and aspiration; opposing views should be organized so as to illuminate choices and facilitate the attainment of goals; channels should be commonly available to relate men to knowledge and to power so that private problems—from bad recreation facilities to personal alienation—are formulated as general issues.

The economic sphere would have as its basis the principles:

> that the economic experience is so personally decisive that the individual must share in its full determination;
> that the economy itself is of such social importance that its major resources and means of production should be open to democratic participation and subject to democratic social regulation.

Like the political and economic ones, major social institutions—cultural, educational, rehabilitative, and others—should be generally organized with the well-being and dignity of man as the essential measure of success.

In social change or interchange, we find violence to be abhorrent because it requires generally the transformation of the target, be it a human being or a community of people, into a depersonalized object of hate. It is imperative that the means of violence be abolished and the institutions—local, national, international—that encourage nonviolence as a condition of conflict be developed.

These are our central values, in skeletal form. It remains vital to understand their denial or attainment in the context of the modern world.❖

Betty Friedan (1921–) was born and grew up in Illinois, where she experienced the marginalization of being Jewish in the provincial Midwest. She felt immediately liberated on entering Smith College, where she edited the school paper. She graduated in 1942. In 1963, *Feminine Mystique* became an immediate best-seller (well over one million copies were soon sold). Three years later, Friedan founded NOW, the National Organization for Women, based on the organizational ideals of the NAACP. Although NOW was soon considered too centrist as more radical feminisms emerged, it remains a powerful force in public politics. Today, Friedan is an influential speaker, writer, and activist on women's issues.

The Problem That Has No Name

Betty Friedan (1963)

The problem lay buried, unspoken, for many years in the minds of American women. It was a strange stirring, a sense of dissatisfaction, a yearning that women suffered in the middle of the twentieth century in the United States. Each suburban wife struggled with it alone. As she made the beds, shopped for groceries, matched slipcover material, ate peanut butter sandwiches with her children, chauffeured Cub Scouts and Brownies, lay beside her husband at night—she was afraid to ask even of herself the silent question—"Is this all?"

For over fifteen years there was no word of this yearning in the millions of words written about women, for women, in all the columns, books and articles by experts telling women their role was to seek fulfillment as wives and mothers. Over and over women heard in voices of tradition and of Freudian sophistication that they could desire no greater destiny than to glory in their own femininity. Experts told them how to catch a man and keep him, how to breastfeed children and handle their toilet training, how to cope with sibling rivalry and adolescent rebellion; how to buy a dishwasher, bake bread, cook gourmet snails, and build a swimming pool with their own hands; how to dress, look, and act more feminine and make marriage more exciting; how to keep their husbands from dying young and their sons from growing into delinquents. They were taught to pity the neurotic, unfeminine, unhappy women who wanted to be poets or physicists or presidents. They learned that truly feminine women do not want careers, higher education, political rights—the independence and the opportunities that the old-fashioned feminists fought for. Some women, in their forties and fifties, still remembered painfully giving up those dreams, but most of the younger women no longer even thought about them. A thousand expert voices applauded their femininity, their adjustment, their new maturity. All they had to do was devote their lives from earliest girlhood to finding a husband and bearing children.

Excerpt from *The Feminine Mystique* (New York: W. W. Norton and Co., 1963), pp. 15–19, 32. Copyright 1963 by Betty Friedan. Reprinted by permission of W. W. Norton and Co. and Curtis Brown Ltd.

By the end of the nineteen-fifties, the average marriage age of women in America dropped to 20, and was still dropping, into the teens. Fourteen million girls were engaged by 17. The proportion of women attending college in comparison with men dropped from 47 per cent in 1920 to 35 per cent in 1958. A century earlier, women had fought for higher education; now girls went to college to get a husband. By the mid-fifties, 60 per cent dropped out of college to marry, or because they were afraid too much education would be a marriage bar. Colleges built dormitories for "married students," but the students were almost always the husbands. A new degree instituted for the wives—"Ph.T." (Putting Husband Through).

Then American girls began getting married in high school. And the women's magazines, deploring the unhappy statistics about these young marriages, urged that courses on marriage, and marriage counselors, be installed in the high schools. Girls started going steady at twelve and thirteen, in junior high. Manufacturers put out brassieres with false bosoms of foam rubber for little girls of ten. And an advertisement for a child's dress, sizes 3–6x, in the *New York Times* in the fall of 1960, said: "She Too Can Join the Man-Trap Set."

By the end of the fifties, the United States birthrate was overtaking India's. The birth-control movement, renamed Planned Parenthood, was asked to find a method whereby women who had been advised that a third or fourth baby would be born dead or defective might have it anyhow. Statisticians were especially astounded at the fantastic increase in the number of babies among college women. Where once they had two children, now they had four, five, six. Women who had once wanted careers were now making careers out of having babies. So rejoiced *Life* magazine in a 1956 paean to the movement of American women back to the home.

In a New York hospital, a woman had a nervous breakdown when she found she could not breastfeed her baby. In other hospitals, women dying of cancer refused a drug which research had proved might save their lives: its side effects were said to be unfeminine. "If I have only one life, let me live it as a blonde," a larger-than-life-sized picture of a pretty, vacuous woman proclaimed from newspaper, magazine, and drugstore ads. And across America, three out of every ten women dyed their hair blonde. They ate a chalk called Metrecal, instead of food, to shrink to the size of the thin young models. Department-store buyers reported that American women, since 1939, had become three and four sizes smaller. "Women are out to fit the clothes, instead of vice-versa," one buyer said.

Interior decorators were designing kitchens with mosaic murals and original paintings, for kitchens were once again the center of women's lives. Home sewing became a million-dollar industry. Many women no longer left their homes, except to shop, chauffeur their children, or attend a social engagement with their husbands. Girls were growing up in America without ever having jobs outside the home. In the late fifties, a sociological phenomenon was suddenly remarked: a third of American women now worked, but most were no longer young and very few were pursuing careers. They were married women who held part-time jobs, selling or secretarial, to put their husbands through school, their sons through college, or to help pay the mortgage. Or they were widows supporting families. Fewer and fewer women were entering professional work. The shortages in the nursing, social work, and teaching professions caused crises in almost every American city. Concerned over the Soviet Union's lead in the space race, scientists noted that America's greatest source of unused brain-power was women. But girls would not study physics: it was "unfeminine." A girl refused a science fellowship at Johns Hopkins to take a job in a real-estate office. All she wanted, she said, was what every other American girl wanted—to get married, have four children and live in a nice house in a nice suburb.

The suburban housewife—she was the dream image of the young American women and the envy, it was said, of women all over the world. The American housewife—freed by science and labor-saving appliances from the drudgery, the dangers of childbirth and the illnesses of her grandmother. She was healthy, beautiful, educated, concerned only about her husband, her children, her home. She had found true feminine fulfillment. As a housewife and mother, she was respected as a full and equal partner to man in his world. She was free to choose automobiles, clothes, appliances, supermarkets; she had everything that women ever dreamed of.

In the fifteen years after World War II, this mystique of feminine fulfillment became the cherished and self-perpetuating core of contemporary American culture. Millions of women lived their lives in the image of those pretty pictures of the American suburban housewife, kissing their husbands goodbye in front of the picture window, depositing their stationwagonsful of children at school, and smiling as they ran the new electric waxer over the spotless kitchen floor. They baked their own bread, sewed their own and their children's clothes, kept their new washing machines and dryers running all day. They changed the sheets on the beds twice a week instead of once, took the rug-hooking class in adult education, and pitied their poor frustrated mothers, who had dreamed of having a career. Their only dream was to be perfect wives and mothers; their highest ambition to have five children and a beautiful house, their only fight to get and keep their husbands. They had no thought for the unfeminine problems of the world outside the home; they wanted the men to make the major decisions. They gloried in their role as women, and wrote proudly on the census blank: "Occupation: housewife."

For over fifteen years, the words written for women, and the words women used when they talked to each other, while their husbands sat on the other side of the room and talked shop or politics or septic tanks, were about problems with their children, or how to keep their husbands happy, or improve their children's school, or cook chicken or make slipcovers. Nobody argued whether women were inferior or superior to men; they were simply different. Words like "emancipation" and "career" sounded strange and embarrassing; no one had used them for years. When a Frenchwoman named Simone de Beauvoir wrote a book called *The Second Sex,* an American critic commented that she obviously "didn't know what life was all about," and besides, she was talking about French women. The "woman problem" in America no longer existed.

If a woman had a problem in the 1950's and 1960's, she knew that something must be wrong with her marriage, or with herself. Other women were satisfied with their lives, she thought. What kind of a woman was she if she did not feel this mysterious fulfillment waxing the kitchen floor? She was so ashamed to admit her dissatisfaction that she never knew how many other women shared it. If she tried to tell her husband, he didn't understand what she was talking about. She did not really understand it herself. For over fifteen years women in America found it harder to talk about this problem than about sex. Even the psychoanalysts had no name for it. When a woman went to a psychiatrist for help, as many women did, she would say, "I'm so ashamed," or "I must be hopelessly neurotic." "I don't know what's wrong with women today," a suburban psychiatrist said uneasily. "I only know something is wrong because most of my patients happen to be women. And their problem isn't sexual." Most women with this problem did not go to see a psychoanalyst, however. "There's nothing wrong really," they kept telling themselves. "There isn't any problem." . . .

If I am right, the problem that has no name stirring in the minds of so many American women today is not a matter of loss of femininity or too much education, or the demands of domesticity. It is far more important than anyone recognizes. It is the key to these other new and old problems which have been torturing women and their husbands and children, and puzzling their doctors and educators for years. It may well be the key to our future as a nation and a culture. We can no longer ignore that voice within women that says: "I want something more than my husband and my children and my home."❖

Frantz Fanon (1925–1961) was born in Martinique. He studied medicine in France and became a psychiatrist. During the French-Algerian war, Fanon served in a hospital in Algeria—an experience that deepened his native sympathy for and understanding of those subject to colonial oppressions. He died of cancer at thirty-six, yet his works endure. Both *Black Skin, White Masks* (1952) and *The Wretched of the Earth* (1961) were among the most widely read books in Europe and the United States in the 1960s, as well as early classics in the emerging literature of the late- and post-colonial world.

Decolonizing, National Culture, and the Negro Intellectual

Frantz Fanon (1961)

National liberation, national renaissance, the restoration of nationhood to the people, commonwealth: whatever may be the headings used or the new formulas introduced, decolonization is always a violent phenomenon. At whatever level we study it—relationships between individuals, new names for sports clubs, the human admixture at cocktail parties, in the police, on the directing boards of national or private banks—decolonization is quite simply the replacing of a certain "species" of men by another "species" of men. Without any period of transition, there is a total, complete, and absolute substitution. It is true that we could equally well stress the rise of a new nation, the setting up of a new state, its diplomatic relations, and its economic and political trends. But we have precisely chosen to speak of that kind of *tabula rasa* which characterizes at the outset all decolonization. Its unusual importance is that it constitutes, from the very first day, the minimum demands of the colonized. To tell the truth, the proof of success lies in a whole social structure being changed from the bottom up. The extraordinary importance of this change is that it is willed, called for, demanded. The need for this change exists in its crude state, impetuous and compelling, in the consciousness and in the lives of the men and women who are colonized. But the possibility of this change is equally experienced in the form of a terrifying future in the consciousness of another "species" of men and women: the colonizers.

Excerpt from Constance Farrington, trans., *The Wretched of the Earth* (New York: Grove Press, Inc., 1968 [1963]), pp. 35–38, 215–222. Copyright 1963 by Presence Africaine, renewed 1991 by Presence Africaine. Used with permission of Grove/Atlantic Monthly Press.

Decolonization, which sets out to change the order of the world, is, obviously, a program of complete disorder. But it cannot come as a result of magical practices, nor of a natural shock, nor of a friendly understanding. Decolonization, as we know, is a historical process: that is to say that it cannot be understood, it cannot become intelligible nor clear to itself except in the exact measure that we can discern the movements which give it historical form and content. Decolonization is the meeting of two forces, opposed to each other by their very nature, which in fact owe their originality to that sort of substantification which results from and is nourished by the situation in the colonies. Their first encounter was marked by violence and their existence together—that is to say the exploitation of the native by the settler—was carried on by dint of a great array of bayonets and cannons. The settler and the native are old acquaintances. In fact, the settler is right when he speaks of knowing "them" well. For it is the settler who has brought the native into existence and who perpetuates his existence. The settler owes the fact of his very existence, that is to say, his property, to the colonial system.

Decolonization never takes place unnoticed, for it influences individuals and modifies them fundamentally. It transforms spectators crushed with their inessentiality into privileged actors, with the grandiose glare of history's floodlights upon them. It brings a natural rhythm into existence, introduced by new men, and with it a new language and a new humanity. Decolonization is the veritable creation of new men. But this creation owes nothing of its legitimacy to any supernatural power; the "thing" which has been colonized becomes man during the same process by which it frees itself.

In decolonization, there is therefore the need of a complete calling in question of the colonial situation. If we wish to describe it precisely, we might find it in the well-known words: "The last shall be first and the first last." Decolonization is the putting into practice of this sentence. That is why, if we try to describe it, all decolonization is successful.

The naked truth of decolonization evokes for us the searing bullets and blood-stained knives which emanate from it. For if the last shall be first, this will only come to pass after a murderous and decisive struggle between the two protagonists. That affirmed intention to place the last at the head of things, and to make them climb at a pace (too quickly, some say) the well-known steps which characterize an organized society, can only triumph if we use all means to turn the scale, including, of course, that of violence.

You do not turn any society, however primitive it may be, upside down with such a program if you have not decided from the very beginning, that is to say from the actual formulation of that program, to overcome all the obstacles that you will come across in so doing. The native who decides to put the program into practice, and to become its moving force, is ready for violence at all times. From birth it is clear to him that this narrow world, strewn with prohibitions, can only be called in question by absolute violence.

The colonial world is a world divided into compartments. It is probably unnecessary to recall the existence of native quarters and European quarters, of schools for natives and schools for Europeans; in the same way we need not recall apartheid in South Africa. Yet, if we examine closely this system of compartments, we will at least be able to reveal the lines of force it implies. This approach to the colonial world, its ordering and its geographical layout will allow us to mark out the lines on which a decolonized society will be reorganized.

The colonial world is a world cut in two. The dividing line, the frontiers are shown by barracks and police stations. In the colonies it is the policeman and the soldier who are the official, instituted go-betweens, the spokesmen of the settler and his rule of oppression. In capitalist societies the educational system, whether lay or clerical, the structure of moral reflexes handed down from father to son, the exemplary honesty of workers who are given a medal after fifty years of good and loyal service, and the affection which springs from harmonious relations and good behavior—all these aesthetic expressions of respect for the established order serve to create around the exploited person an atmosphere of submission and of inhibition which lightens the task of policing considerably. In the capitalist countries a multitude of moral teachers, counselors and "bewilderers" separate the exploited from those in power. In the colonial countries, on the contrary, the policeman and the soldier, by their immediate presence and their frequent and direct action maintain contact with the native and advise him by means of rifle butts and napalm not to budge. It is obvious here that the agents of government speak the language of pure force. The intermediary does not lighten the oppression, nor seek to hide the domination; he shows them up and puts them into practice with the clear conscience of an upholder of the peace; yet he is the bringer of violence into the home and into the mind of the native. . . .

The Negroes who live in the United States and in Central or Latin America in fact experience the need to attach themselves to a cultural matrix. Their problem is not fundamentally different from that of the Africans. The whites of America did not mete out to them any different treatment from that of the whites who ruled over the Africans. We have seen that the whites were used to putting all Negroes in the same bag. During the first congress of the African Cultural Society which was held in Paris in 1956, the American Negroes of their own accord considered their problems from the same standpoint as those of their African brothers. Cultured Africans, speaking of African civilizations, decreed that there should be a reasonable status within the state for those who had formerly been slaves. But little by little the American Negroes realized that the essential problems confronting them were not the same as those that confronted the African Negroes. The Negroes of Chicago only resemble the Nigerians or the Tanganyikans in so far as they were all defined in relation to the whites. But once the first comparisons had been made and subjective feelings were assuaged, the American Negroes realized that the objective problems were fundamentally heterogeneous. The test cases of civil liberty whereby both whites and blacks in America try to drive back racial discrimination have very little in common in their principles and objectives with the heroic fight of the Angolan people against the detestable Portuguese colonialism. Thus, during the second congress of the African Cultural Society the American Negroes decided to create an American society for people of black cultures.

Negritude therefore finds its first limitation in the phenomena which take account of the formation of the historical character of men. Negro and African-Negro culture broke up into different entities because the men who wished to incarnate these cultures realized that every culture is first and foremost national, and that the problems which kept Richard Wright or Langston Hughes on the alert were fundamentally different from those which might confront Leopold Senghor or Jomo Kenyatta. In the same way certain Arab states, though they had chanted the marvelous hymn of Arab renaissance, had nevertheless to realize that their geographical position and the economic ties of their region were stronger even than the past that they wished to revive. Thus we find today the Arab states organically linked once more with societies which are Mediterranean in their culture. The fact is that these states are submitted to modern pressure and to new channels of trade while the network of trade relations which was dominant during the great period of Arab history has disappeared. But above all there is the fact that the political regimes of certain Arab states are so different, and so far away from each other in their conceptions, that even a cultural meeting between these states is meaningless.

Thus we see that the cultural problem as it sometimes exists in colonized countries runs the risk of giving rise to serious ambiguities. The lack of culture of the Negroes, as proclaimed by colonialism, and the inherent barbarity of the Arabs ought logically to lead to the exaltation of cultural manifestations which are not simply national but continental, and extremely racial. In Africa, the movement of men of culture is a movement toward the Negro-African culture or the Arab-Moslem culture. It is not specifically toward a national culture. Culture is becoming more and more cut off from the events of today. It finds its refuge beside a hearth that glows with passionate emotion, and from there makes its way by realistic paths which are the only means by which it may be made fruitful, homogeneous, and consistent.

If the action of the native intellectual is limited historically, there remains nevertheless the fact that it contributes greatly to upholding and justifying the action of politicians. It is true that the attitude of the native intellectual sometimes takes on the aspect of a cult or of a religion. But if we really wish to analyze this attitude correctly we will come to see that it is symptomatic of the intellectual's realization of the danger that he is running in cutting his last moorings and of breaking adrift from his people. This stated belief in a national culture is in fact an ardent, despairing turning toward anything that will afford him secure anchorage. In order to ensure his salvation and to escape from the supremacy of the white man's culture the native feels the need to turn backward toward his unknown roots and to lose himself at whatever cost in his own barbarous people. Because he feels he is becoming estranged, that is to say because he feels that he is the living haunt of contradictions which run the risk of becoming insurmountable, the native tears himself away from the swamp that may suck him down and accepts everything, decides to take all for granted and confirms everything even though he may lose body and soul. The native finds that he is expected to answer for everything, and to all comers. He not only turns himself into the defender of his people's past; he is willing to be counted as one of them, and henceforward he is even capable of laughing at his past cowardice.

This tearing away, painful and difficult though it may be, is however necessary. If it is not accomplished there will be serious psycho-affective injuries and the result will be individuals without an anchor, without a horizon, colorless, stateless, rootless—a race of angels. It will be also quite normal to hear certain natives declare, "I speak as a Senegalese and as a Frenchman . . . " "I speak as an Algerian and as a Frenchman. . . . " The intellectual who is Arab and French, or Nigerian and English, when he comes up against the need to take on two nationalities, chooses, if he wants to remain true to himself, the negation of one of these determinations. But most often, since they cannot or will not make a choice, such intellectuals gather together all the historical determining factors which have conditioned them and take up a fundamentally "universal standpoint."

This is because the native intellectual has thrown himself greedily upon Western culture. Like adopted children who only stop investigating the new family framework at the moment when a minimum nucleus of security crystallizes in their psyche, the native intellectual will try to make European culture his own. He will not be content to get to know Rabelais and Diderot, Shakespeare and Edgar Allen Poe; he will bind them to his intelligence as closely as possible. . . .

But at the moment when the nationalist parties are mobilizing the people in the name of national independence, the native intellectual sometimes spurns these acquisitions which he suddenly feels make him a stranger in his own land. It is always easier to proclaim rejection than actually to reject. The intellectual who through the medium of culture has filtered into Western civilization, who has managed to become part of the body of European culture—in other words who has exchanged his own culture for another—will come to realize that the cultural matrix, which now he wishes to assume since he is anxious to appear original, can hardly supply any figureheads which will bear comparison with those, so many in number and so great in prestige, of the occupying power's civilization. History, of course, though nevertheless written by the Westerners and to serve their purposes, will be able to evaluate from time to time certain periods of the African past. But, standing face to face with his country at the present time, and observing clearly and objectively the events of today throughout the continent which he wants to make his own, the intellectual is terrified by the void, the degradation, and the savagery he sees there. Now he feels that he must get away from the white culture. He must seek his culture elsewhere, anywhere at all; and if he fails to find the substance of culture of the same grandeur and scope as displayed by the ruling power, the native intellectual will very often fall back upon emotional attitudes and will develop a psychology which is dominated by exceptional sensitivity and susceptibility. This withdrawal, which is due in the first instance to a begging of the question in his internal behavior mechanisms and his own character, brings out, above all, a reflect and contradiction which is muscular.

This is sufficient explanation of the style of those native intellectuals who decide to give expression to this phase of consciousness which is in the process of being liberated. It is a harsh style, full of images, for the image is the drawbridge which allows unconscious energies to be scattered on the surrounding meadows. It is a vigorous style, alive with rhythms, struck through and through with bursting life; it is full of color, too, bronzed, sunbaked, and violent. This style, which in its time astonished the peoples of the West, has nothing racial about it, in spite of frequent statements to the contrary; it expresses above all a hand-to-hand struggle and it reveals the need that man has to liberate himself from a part of his being which already contained the seeds of decay. Whether the fight is painful, quick, or inevitable, muscular action must substitute itself for concepts.

If in the world of poetry this movement reaches unaccustomed heights, the fact remains that in the real world the intellectual often follows up a blind alley. When at the height of his intercourse with his people, whatever they were or whatever they are, the intellectual decides to come down into the common paths of real life, he only brings back from his adventuring formulas which are sterile in the extreme. He sets a high value on the customs, traditions, and the appearances of his people; but his inevitable, painful experience only seems to be a banal search for exoticism. The sari becomes sacred, and shoes that come from Paris or Italy are left off in favor of pampooties, while suddenly the language of the ruling power is felt to burn your lips. Finding your fellow countrymen sometimes means in this phase to will to be a nigger, not a nigger like all other niggers but a real nigger, a Negro cur, just the sort of nigger that the white man wants you to be. Going back to your own people means to become a dirty wog, to go native as much as you can, to become unrecognizable, and to cut off those wings that before you had allowed to grow.

The native intellectual decides to make an inventory of the bad habits drawn from the colonial world, and hastens to remind everyone of the good old customs of the people, that people which he has decided contains all truth and goodness. The scandalized attitude with which the settlers who live in the colonial territory greet this new departure only serves to strengthen the native's decision. When the colonialists, who had tasted the sweets of their victory over these assimilated people, realize that these men whom they considered as saved souls are beginning to fall back into the ways of niggers, the whole system totters. Every native won over, every native who had taken the pledge not only marks a failure for the colonial structure when he decides to lose himself and to go back to his own side, but also stands as a symbol for the uselessness and the shallowness of all the work that has been accomplished. Each native who goes back over the line is a radical condemnation of the methods and of the regime; and the native intellectual finds in the scandal he gives rise to a justification and an encouragement to persevere in the path he has chosen.❖

PART FOUR

Will the Center Hold?
1963–1979

Americans sometimes confuse *their* Sixties with *the* Sixties. This is not entirely unreasonable. Certainly, the American 1960s had many dramatic moments, tragic and not, that drew world attention—the civil rights march on Washington, John Kennedy's assassination, Malcolm X's, the Black Power revolts, Stokely Carmichael, Martin Luther King's assassination, Robert Kennedy's, the student rebellions at Berkeley and Columbia, Bob Dylan, People's Park, the Chicago conspiracy trial, the antiwar movement, Jerry Rubin and Abbie Hoffman, early feminist rebellions in homes and in public, Woodstock, the Stonewall rebellion, Altamont, Kent State, and so on. These were events worthy of world attention.

But if one is to speak of "the Sixties," as if to condense a long and complex series of disjointed events into something "everyone understands," then it is necessary to speak of a world event. Because the United States was the virtual center of the world at the time of these disruptions, "the Sixties" were American in the sense that the disjointing of America was a phenomenon of world importance. This is why the whole world was watching. The world was affecting what it was watching, and being affected. When all was said and done, this is what underlay the question of the period.

Will the Center hold? The question was drawn from a line in William Butler Yeats's "The Second Coming." It may have been Joan Didion's widely read essay, "Slouching Toward Bethlehem," that brought new meaning to this famous poem. In any case, by the spring and summer of 1968, Yeats's words expressed what many (perhaps most) people, nearly everywhere, felt:

> *Turning and turning in the widening gyre*
> *The falcon cannot hear the falconer;*
> *Things fall apart; the centre cannot hold;*
> *Mere anarchy is loosed upon the world,*
> *The blood-dimmed tide is loosed, and everywhere*
> *The ceremony of innocence is drowned;*
> *The best lack all convictions, while the worst*
> *Are full of passionate intensity.*

Those closest to the Center, either by devotion or dependence, were most struck. It was not, of course, the West's first encounter with a world spinning out of control. But for reasons then not at all obvious, the spin of political events wrenched moral culture against its grain. This time, Euro-American innocence was lost. And of all that happened, nothing disturbed the West's long dreams as much as Vietnam. Startled, people awoke confused, angry, frightened.

Those who had the most to lose from the loosening of world order hated the best and the worst. Throughout the presidency of Lyndon B. Johnson, the best and brightest Kennedy had brought to Washington were still in charge. They invented the War on Poverty, and the war in Vietnam. They managed the government, the military, the universities, and much of the culture. And as events unfolded after the death of JFK, it became clear that the brightness of men like W. W. Rostow, John Kenneth Galbraith, Robert McNamara, McGeorge Bundy, and Arthur Schlesinger, Jr., was part of the problem, however good their intentions. They, more than others, directly and indirectly sponsored the war in Southeast Asia. But after it became evident that massive bombing and burning made little difference, these same men could not make up their minds. To this day, they are hated by some for not having had the political will to win; by others for having abandoned morality and good sense for getting involved in the first place. Against them, those who considered themselves the saving middle remnant of society saw the worst. Unkempt youth. Strange music. Drugs. Radical protesters. Priests spilling blood on draft files. Open disobedience of authority. Abuse of the flag. Draft dodging. On the one side, there was no compelling conviction; on the other, a dirty, drug-ridden, sexual mess—or so it seemed. Whichever way they turned, those longing for a moral Center were without comfort.

Bizarre slogans defined an unfamiliar spiritual terrain. The best could say, as they sank deeper and deeper into the jungles of Vietnam, "We had to destroy it to save it." In the technical reasoning of the best and brightest, this was logic. The best of the West was its rationality applied to the technology of war. The moral force of history was on their side. The words referred to a village in Vietnam. But many of those who heard them felt they could have been referring to the world itself.

Against the best, the worst shouted: "Hey, hey, LBJ. How many kids did you kill today?" Perhaps unwittingly, they attacked the authority of the land—a man whose persona was Authority itself—at his most vulnerable point. Whatever could have rightly been said against Lyndon Johnson, he was not a child killer. He was a schoolteacher and author of the War on Poverty—a man of compassion for the weak in mass society. Yet the passionate intensity of the slogan suggested the extent to which the Center was deteriorating. The cohesive center of social life first starts to come unglued whenever members of the same family can no longer contact one another's reality. The best and the worst were not, after all, natural enemies. They were kin. The young people who shouted in protest were the intellectual and cultural children of LBJ's best, bright administrators of the war. Literally, some of those marching in the streets could have been students of W. W. Rostow at MIT or Arthur Schlesinger and McGeorge Bundy at Harvard—special assistants to the president in the early and middle 1960s.

This was a struggle *within* the most liberal sectors of American and European culture. To this, the excluded middle responded: "America: Love It or Leave It." In the absence of an intelligent Center, the silent majority's native logic prevailed. Those who had never had any palpable contact with the centers of power and persuasion were able to assert the logic of the excluded middle. To them, America was the transcendent, self-evident Truth that required no techniques and deserved no abuse. This saving principle moved more than enough voters out of the Democratic column in 1968 to defeat presidential candidate Hubert H. Humphrey, the most thoroughly decent liberal in postwar American politics. Richard M. Nixon was elected to restore law and order. Concerning America's place in the world, he exclaimed: "We are number one!" "Peace with Honor!"

Political language, on all sides, had become hollow. Incantations without moral feet filled the air. The West had raised the idea of a Center to the level of historical axiom. The Sixties brought the Center down to earth, where, under mundane conditions, it had lost its power. This was a world event, something much more than yet another rejection of Euro-American authority. The entire world was implicated in the spectacle of the then great power of the West losing its grip in the absence of a ready successor. Though the meaning of all this did not become clear for a long time, by 1968 one sensed that the West's failures in Southeast Asia belonged to some new and different series of events. They were not just rebellions but the early shifts in a reconfiguration of world power and culture. Whatever was to be was making itself evident both in the United States and in the world.

In the world, the collapse of the European colonial system and the defeat of the United States in Southeast Asia were followed in the early 1970s by the birth of the Organization of Petroleum Exporting Countries (OPEC) and the world oil crisis of 1973–1974. For the first time since World War II, the Euro-American powers faced a nonwhite, alien world opponent. This time, however, the so-called Third World forces yielded neither to Westernization nor to occupation. World politics since have been different. If America remained the world superpower, it was on terms fundamentally different from those after World War II. OPEC forced the United States to borrow. As it became a debtor nation, its moral credit, though still good, was devalued. Others—in Europe, the Middle East, the Pacific Basin—now held the better hand in world capital markets, leaving the holders of world resources (usually countries poorer in capital) with a stronger card to play. Now, regional forces like Iran, Cuba, Iraq, and Afghanistan could resist, if not deter, the power of the Center, thus weakening its might. In this sense, the world lost not just the United States as Center but also the prospect that any new Center would organize the world into a system in service to the West's interest.

Meanwhile, in the United States, the civil rights movement was one thing, as was the rise of Black Power after 1966. White people, whether in the excluded middle or near the centers of power, could think of these as a problem with "those" people. But when, beginning at Berkeley in 1964, the student movement turned against the university, then against the war, then seemingly against all that was normal and sacred, it was no longer an alien force within. "They," then, were "us."

If, in the Golden Age, the university was America's most distinctive institutional promise of the good society for which brilliant government offered to be the servant, then the postwar family was the moral basis of that ideal society. But as Elaine Tyler May shows in *Homeward Bound: American Families in the Cold War Era,* the postwar American family was an unstable invention of Golden Age culture. May demonstrates that the ideal suburban family—husband, wife, kids, dishwashers—was, as much as anything, part of the culture's strategy of domestic containment. May's study of personal reports by suburban housewives supports her claim that the family was also a means to contain the society's ambivalence toward feminine sexuality. Female sexual power was, perhaps, the domestic equivalent of international communism. If the Communists threatened America's masculinity abroad, female sex threatened it at home. Women's power therefore had to be kept from invading the male consciousness or escaping the bounds of the domestic wage-based family. Men's fear of Woman, including fear of their own female urges and feelings, was considered every bit as much a threat to American character as was the prospect that women might want (as indeed they did) to keep the jobs they had held of necessity in World War II. Though Elaine Tyler May did not state it in just this way, it would seem that, deep in the recess of the cultural logic of America in the 1950s, Man felt an urgency to control *his* female desires as much as "his" woman. Somehow, American might depended more or less equally on keeping women at home, homosexuals out of the army, and the Communists behind the Iron Curtain.

The so-called American family *may* have been invented at this late day, in the 1940s and 1950s, when abundance could support it and politics required it. In any case, after 1963, these three institutions—the university, government, the family—became vectors of discontent intersecting where the Center had been. Once protest arose within and against these institutions, Yeats's beast seemed nearer. No longer could it be said that the problem was "those" people—American Blacks, the PLO, the Viet Cong, Castro, colonial rebels—all incited by the Communists.

When the rebellions in the United States turned on the university, against the government, within the families, against the prevailing culture of contained sexuality, then the rough, slouching beast threatened to be born. Vietnam was, indeed, another extravagant attack of the white world against its well-defined other. But it was *not* just another international event in a series of aggressions in world politics. Soon, it became a crisis within American moral culture and thus within the West's sense of itself. It was a crisis of many parts, each eventually turning on the other in "widening gyre." America, like the British and other European colonizing powers, fought enemies abroad to protect the culture. This was official policy. But in Vietnam, it was never clear who the enemy was. Those with whom the United States sided were a worse lot than the Communists that U.S. troops were fighting. And, whoever they were, the enemies were nowhere to be seen after they disappeared into the jungles. To many, there was no enemy. Muhammad Ali (after JFK, the man most widely recognized around the world) refused induction to fight in Vietnam, saying, "No Viet Cong ever called me Nigger." Then, American ground troops began fragging officers in the dark jungles. The unreal images near the end of the film *Apocalypse Now* were real: America had entered the Heart of Darkness. By the time of the Tet Offensive early in 1968, Vietnam no longer had much to do with the traditional principles of war and politics. It was a confusion within the moral Center of the West. The world had somehow shifted. The new enemy was not the stealthy, yellow-skinned Communists who disappeared into the jungle, who rebuilt bombed bridges within days, who refused to cower. Those people were doing nothing more than what colonial people throughout the world had been doing since the late 1940s—resisting to the point of throwing out the Euro-American colonizers. The real enemy was within—the worst who so confounded the best, giving power to the excluded middle.

Between 1963, when Kennedy died, and 1968, when the Center failed to hold, everything changed in the United States and the world. In America, what Stokely Carmichael later called Black Power made its first, noncommercial appearance before white people. One of Malcolm X's early speeches before a racially mixed audience after his departure from the nation of Islam—his famous "Ballot or the Bullet" speech of April 1964—included these chilling lines: "I'm not an American. I'm one of 22 million black people who are the victims of Americanism. . . . I see America through the eyes of the victim. I don't see any American dream. I see an American nightmare." This was less than a year after Martin Luther King, Jr., roused Americans, white and Black, to a new integrated dream. Malcolm was responding to King, to the civil rights movement, to the myth that the white-dominated world-system would work. If King had brought the nonviolent force of Gandhi to his dream, Malcolm brought the culturally separate and morally stern principles of other parts of the non-Western world to his. Later, after Malcolm X was killed in February 1965, the civil rights movement started to dissolve. The Student Nonviolent Coordinating Committee (SNCC) eventually adopted a position on the use of force in self-defense that was not much different from Malcolm X's. Stokely Carmichael and H. Rap Brown, the best-known spokesmen for Black Power, became international representatives of the rising tide of color against the Center.

At the same time, the women's movement moved in two directions. It worked against the restraints and abuses women suffered within the family. Consciousness-raising groups invited women to talk and understand themselves apart from the culture of patriarchal families. Men were as unsettled and angered by the separatism of wives and lovers as whites generally were by the separatism of Blacks. The movement also worked against the dominant structures, as feminists began to organize politically. NOW took the centrist approach. Other groups were more radical. One heard of SCUM (Society for Cutting Up Men), WAR (Women of the American Revolution), and WITCH. WITCH and the others were not so much organizations as manifestos of a movement. "There is no 'joining' WITCH. If you are a woman and dare to look within yourself, you are a WITCH." Most men, and many righteous women, were furious. They complained about the outrages of bra-burning at the 1968 protest against the Miss America Pageant in Atlantic City. But bras were never burned. They were thrown off and out. Clearly, millions simply assumed that uncontained female breasts were incendiary to the political order. They seemed to have understood that the entrance into politics of women with a feminist consciousness would change everything. Which it did. Outrages against the abandonment of "femininity" were, certainly, subtle displays of the deeper fear that, in addition to the risks these feminists posed for the family-wage system, their apparent refusal of the culture of contained femininity would unleash sexuality. To those who hated feminism, uncontained breasts could mean nothing but sex. To a culture that required the strictest possible control of sex, the very idea that there could be such a thing as sexuality was unimaginable. Sexuality means that sex was more than God's procreative will or, if you must, fucking. Sexuality means that people are sexual beings and that they draw their sense of themselves in part from their sexual lives. During this time, two words gained new meanings in Western languages: *woman* and *gender*. *Woman* was newly constructed in part on the understanding that a gender is not exhausted by sex. Thus, feminist consciousness constructed a new political force based on the denial of a natural essence behind the feminine. This set loose sex itself.

In June 1969, in New York's Greenwich Village, the Stonewall rebellion was the first historic, public protest of gays and lesbians against the straight world. The long-standing practice of official police abuse against gays, lesbians, and bisexuals was met with a violent revolt, setting 400 police against a crowd of 2,000 gays and their supporters. Though gay and lesbian people had been organizing politically since at least the beginning of World War II, this was the event associated with organized, public resistance to the culture's silent insistence on official heterosexuality. The appearance of a militant gay movement at more or less the same time as a militant feminism aggravated the crisis. Together, they signified that the family was not what it was supposed to be.

Actually, there had already been a storm of controversy over the family, incited by another of Washington's best and brightest. Daniel Patrick Moynihan's 1965 report on the Negro family was intelligent and well intended. But its evidence, and argument, that the problem of American Blacks was linked to the disappearance of the Black man as head of family was read by many Blacks as white society's racist ignorance of Black life. More than a few whites read it as a confirmation of what they believed, or feared, was true of Black people: Blacks would not, or could not, sustain responsible lives necessary for good family life. Somewhere, surely, white assumptions about Black sexuality lurked not far behind.

If the family was threatened by these movements, then the civil order was threatened by another. The student protests against the university, beginning with the free speech movement at Berkeley in 1964, seemed to be the worst kind of ingratitude. The new universities had been built, at great cost, to assure the futures of the very children who now protested them. To some in the student movement, the universities were factories in the machinery of an inhumane society. After the riots at Columbia in the spring of 1968, the independent report of a commission headed by Archibald Cox of Harvard Law School came very close to agreeing.

But in the public mind, the superficial similarities between legitimate political protest on campus and the counterculture's rejection of everything accepted as decent only added to the terror. Middle-class, suburban whites in conservative Cincinnati could hardly be expected to detect the fine, but evident, line distinguishing protests at the 1968 Democratic Convention in Chicago and Woodstock the following August. Jerry Rubin, once a nice boy from Cincinnati's Walnut Hills High School, was now something beyond comprehension. Yet his book with a title that needs no explanation—*Do It!*—condensed everything objectionable about students, youth, counterculture, the new attitudes, sex, and more into one volume.

All this came to a terrible denouement on May 4, 1970, at Kent State University in Ohio. Though President Nixon had begun to withdraw troops from Vietnam, students protested the continuing war. National Guard troops, called to restore order, were commanded to fire into a crowd. Four students were killed. This time, however, white, working-class kids from the industrial belt murdered their own. Now, those on the margins of the silent middle were sucked into the vortex. No one was spared. Ten days later, two Black students were killed in a similar situation at Jackson State University in Mississippi. Naturally, the public was less anguished at the latter event. The death of Blacks was considered familiar. The political slaying of whites by whites—of "good" young people *by* good young people—was something else. It marked the full turn of that gyre set in motion when the old values that centered the world gave way.

The Kent State incident occurred five years before the final pullout from Vietnam. Watergate and the OPEC oil crisis were still to come. One could say that the 1960s began in 1955, when Rosa Parks refused to move to the back of the bus, and ended some twenty years later, with the pictures of those desperate Americans clinging to the last helicopter lifting off from the U.S. Embassy in Saigon, leaving the Vietnamese they had intended to save to an expected slaughter. What Rosa Parks did led to events that changed the United States forever. What the war did not do in Vietnam changed America's place in the world forever. The two, and everything in between, were not unrelated.

One of the strangest happenstances of the 1960s is that they also gave birth to new social theories that, at first, seemed to be about as remote from the protests and war and turmoil as anything could be. They were not.

In 1966, at an international meeting of scholars on a very technical subject, Jacques Derrida made public the words already quoted in the introduction to this book:

This was the moment when language invaded the universal problematic, the moment when, in the absence of a center or origin, everything became discourse—provided we can agree on this word—that is to say, a system in which the central signified, is never absolutely present outside a system of differences.

In 1966 in Derrida's Paris, as in the United States where this talk was presented, events leading to the collapse of the Center two years later were well under way. Whether Derrida had them specifically in mind is hard to say, though it would seem that he did. Certainly, the movement associated with him and others, like Michel Foucault, was later connected to those events in the minds of those who found the new social theories compelling. Whatever it is that may link, in some hidden way, the abstract thinking of professional social theorists with the concrete notions of practical political people, they were indeed linked in this time. At first, the name of the theoretical movement was *poststructuralism*. It was initially a matter of interest only to those who customarily followed current intellectual and cultural events in France, then to a growing number of philosophers and literary theorists abroad. Eventually, under various names, it became the most current line of social thinking in the universities and colleges, especially in the United States. Not everyone was pleased.

One of the reasons so many names are used to define this strange turn in social thinking is that it seems to have been not so much a refinement of arguments within a philosophical tradition as one of a number of explorations of the idea that modern culture had its limits. In the short passage from Derrida, one should take seriously the key phrases: "absence of a center," "language invaded the universal problematic," "a system of differences." Without paying any attention to the precise theoretical argument, it is fair to say that the slogans that would define the end of modernity are suggested here: decentering, discourse, and differences. In short, this was one of the first technical summaries of what became of social theory of the world. Simply put (in my words):

In the absence of a Center (whether intellectual or political), one cannot trust reality. In the absence of a trustable reality, one can only rely on language. What a person says is sufficiently true. No one person's saying is more true. Thus, the world is a world of differences. In the absence of a Center, there is difference.

Though this attitude was initially viewed with great suspicion, it soon began to make its way into the varieties of social theories that were emerging in the late 1960s (from about 1966 to 1970). Amazingly, many of them, in spite of being at considerable odds with each other, were directly or indirectly preoccupied with language. This free talk about talk itself, much like the free speech movement at Berkeley in 1964, used and explored language in order to shock and rethink the social world. It both came out of a changing world and, in time, became part of change. If this was not the end of the old cultural order, as Derrida's line suggests, it was at least the beginning of a major withdrawal of belief in its plausibility.

Michel Foucault, if anything, came to be better known than Derrida because he wrote about historically concrete subjects—madness, prisons, hospitals, sexuality. In his inaugural address in 1970 at the Collège de France, "Discourse of Language," Foucault noted precisely the public fear of what was going on culturally and politically:

There is undoubtedly in our society, and I would not be surprised to see it in others, . . . a sort of dumb fear of these events, of this mass of spoken things, of everything that could possibly be violent, discontinuous, querulous, disordered even and perilous in it, of the incessant, disorderly buzzing of discourse.

It is not by accident that Foucault's address begins with reference to the charming myth of the West that Europe's culture is universal. This was a central theme behind all of Foucault's studies.

C.L.R. James, the great Caribbean writer and social theorist from Trinidad, wrote at about the same time of the importance of the Black Power movement to the freedom of the world's oppressed. He begins with a defense of the slogan, "Black Power," then moves to a defense of the world importance of the politics of Stokeley Carmichael and others. In the mid-1960s, this and other radical slogans held most of their power *as* slogans. Like the speeches of Martin Luther King, Jr., and Malcolm X, Black Power proponents possessed very little power in real economic, political, or military terms. It was enough for Black people, feminists, and students to say something to alarm those who felt the Center was weak. This was one of the senses in which language had invaded the universal problematic.

Elsewhere, writers as different in temperament and orientation as Alvin Gouldner, Herbert Marcuse, Harold Garfinkel, and Pierre Bourdieu wrote social theories that took well-established traditions of thought in new directions. Though they were not poststructuralists, or even necessarily critics of modernity, all went deep to the heart of modern culture's way of thinking. Gouldner, in *The Coming Crisis of Western Sociology,* dared to take himself—that is, the personal life of the social theorist—seriously. Though he may not have intended it, this was a move that pushed C. Wright Mills's sociological imagination beyond the traditional categories of the subject and the object. Gouldner's reflexive sociologist was meant to transform the very idea of sociology. He was, in part, responding to the political experience of the many new students attracted to the field by the events of the Sixties. He, the reflexive sociologist, is one who transforms self in order to know the world differently and thus to change it. Though the deeper sentiments of Gouldner's theory were quite the opposite of Marcuse's skepticism, what Gouldner was trying to rethink about sociology was at least consistent with Marcuse's critique of one-dimensional man. Both sought to generate some transcendent critical attitude from which individuals could escape the mind-numbing effects of modernity. Gouldner's critiques of sociology and Marxism were similar to Marcuse's famous critique of modern culture. Both saw a world that stimulated in order to contain the best human instincts. Social science and sex had both turned against humanity. Both required liberation.

Pierre Bourdieu's idea of reflexive sociology bears comparison to Gouldner's, as David Swartz has shown. Bourdieu, one might add, actually went beyond Gouldner in his attempt to reinvent sociology without relying on modernity's epistemological doublet: subject/object. While Gouldner remained somewhat closer to the cautious framework of Mills by proposing a sociological self able to stretch to grasp objective structures, Bourdieu's famous concept *habitus* aimed for a new beginning point without subjects and objects. In this same period, Harold Garfinkel published the classic text of ethnomethodology. Again, the parallels are striking. Bourdieu wanted to convey the way in which enduring social things achieve spontaneous expression in practical life by focusing on the disposition (or habitus) of individuals in collective action. Garfinkel did something similar in studying ordinary people's methods (literally, ethnomethods) for constructing regularity in a world of infinite reflexivities. Though in other ways they are worlds apart, Bourdieu and Garfinkel focused social theory on the practices of everyday life, from which both sought to derive, in one way or another, the world's larger structures. Reading them against their times and what has happened since, it is possible to see that they were developing theories that, if taken seriously, put enormous strain on anyone's naive faith that the social world was ordered by progress from a center toward some end. This was the time when the world was taken apart without any great concern to put it back together as it had been.

Audre Lorde's well-known attack on academic thinking, including academic feminism, came near the end of this period; it could just as well be considered part of the next. Yet she was one of those voices from the margins of the academy that reminded social theorists of the origins of the new social theorists in political and cultural life. Like Derrida and Foucault in the mid-1960s, Lorde declared the need for new tools, new concepts. "The Master's Tools Will Never Dismantle the Master's House" rests on the prior assumption that the house must be dismantled. By 1979, this was no longer shocking or even surprising. Rethinking the world was increasingly what one did.

Just the same, there were many in this same period who still believed in the basic assumptions of modern culture, however skeptical they were. Jürgen Habermas, for one, took social theory's interest in language in quite a different direction from Derrida's. He aimed to find in language the universal principles of ideal democratic society and thus the critical principles sufficient to revise and save modernity. Habermas is his generation's leading representative of the Frankfurt tradition. Though less overtly skeptical, he, like Adorno and Horkheimer, still believed that somehow the best values of the Enlightenment were adequate to a radical reformation of modern society. The tone, if not the philosophy, of Habermas's original discussion of the ideal speech situation is not far from John Kenneth Galbraith's discussion of the new industrial state. Galbraith accepted the planning system, acknowledged its limitations, yet believed it could, and must, serve. As he says: "The planning system . . . brings into existence to serve its intellectual and scientific needs the community that, all should hope, will reject its monopoly of social purpose." Like those who broke with modernity in this period, Habermas and Galbraith held deep reservations with respect to the inherent capacity of society to serve humanity's best interests. Unlike believers in the Golden Age, they had learned the lessons of the interwar period, without completely absorbing the lessons of the Sixties. They still believed the world, with healthy skepticism, could use its reason to free mankind.

Others straddled the same fence. Peter Berger and Thomas Luckmann dazzled the world of professional social theorists with *The Social Construction of Reality*. Not only did the book seem to bring together all the strains of European and American theory, it also defined the outlines of a new philosophy of social reality. The social world was no longer a given, an objective imprint on subjective consciousness. It was, rather, a constructed human product. From one angle, this was radical stuff; from another, it was conservative. Berger and Luckmann still believed in, and assumed, an orderly world. In 1966, when their book first appeared, that order was much in doubt. Theirs was the most successful of a number of attempts in the mid- and late 1960s to produce a grand synthesis of social theory's essential terms. It was already too late. Most of those who wrote in the 1970s turned away from systematic theorizing toward social theories of important aspects of social life—women's reality, the world economic system, the state, and the family.

Dorothy Smith's first statements of a woman's standpoint as a critique of sociology were ignored, until recently, by everyone but feminists in and outside sociology.

Though she kept faith with the basic terms of modern social theory, she aimed to invert their traditional order. The woman's standpoint is not just another view on social life; it is a surer way to clear and powerful knowledge. Immanuel Wallerstein's multi-volume study of the capitalist world-system first appeared in 1974, the same year as Smith's first statement of her theory of women's perspective. Just as Smith's feminist standpoint position was a forthright attack on traditional social knowledge, so Wallerstein's world-systems theory was an attack on modernization theory and, in a way, on modernity itself. Though their concerns were different, both Smith and Wallerstein could be said to have attacked the master's house with the master's tools, though this is more true in Wallerstein's case. His studies of the emergence of the capitalist world-system since the sixteenth century provided what was then the most comprehensive description of the economic and historical foundations of the modern world centered in Europe. Like Smith's feminism, Wallerstein's theory attacked by describing. One learns a great deal about patriarchically inspired sociology in reading Smith, much as one learns about the world aspirations of capitalism in reading Wallerstein. Yet neither quite escapes the criticism of participating in that which they seek to criticize. Wallerstein is sometimes called a functionalist with Marxist intents. Smith can be said to have wanted to recenter sociology in a woman's perspective and, in so doing, to keep social knowledge bound to a center. The debates on the limits of Wallerstein's theory of economic development and Smith's feminist standpoint have contributed to subsequent changes in thinking in both areas.

When it first appeared in 1979, Theda Skocpol's *States and Social Revolutions* stood out among many reconsiderations of the state as an independent force in world political action. Her theory shows a willingness both to learn from and to move beyond structuralist, Marxist, and liberal theories of political action. In this sense, Skocpol was, and is, representative of the social theory since the 1960s that brought Left-liberal concerns to academic subjects, seeking to reformulate traditional assumptions. However, her supple regard for the state's Janus-like qualities—one face turned to the world, the other to its society—somewhat contradicts her readiness to accept the available methods and terms of social science. The result is a powerful argument, certainly one richer and more compelling than the abstract Marxist theories of the state popular in the early 1970s. Yet she remains for her own good reasons within the language of modernity. In a similar way, Nancy Chodorow's influential discussion of mothering as a dual structure—partly fixed by early childhood experience, partly fixed by the social structure of kinship—is a radical development of the respective insights of psychoanalytic and sociological reasoning.

When Chodorow is read against Christopher Lasch's discussion of the Moynihan report and Skocpol is read in relation to Wallerstein's structural theory of world economies, it is possible to get a sense of the extent to which social theory had changed in this period. Even where belief in the categories of modern culture remained constant, the subjects selected for study reflected the conditions in the world. In those days, from the mid-1960s through their aftermath in the 1970s, it was very difficult *not* to have something to say about the world and its structures, on the one hand, and engendered personal life and its structures, on the other. Though the social theorists who began to break with modernity reached into new theoretical territory, those who did not still reflected the general conditions of the world at the time. Once the Center either failed or faltered (however one chooses to frame it), there was considerable pressure, and motivation, to have something to say about one question above all others: If the world's structures are different, how do those differences affect personal life? In one sense, this is the same question C. Wright Mills asked in 1959. But a generation later, it was put differently. At the later time, it was harder to believe uncritically in a straightforward relation of biography and structure. Between the individual with his or her troubles and the world's structured issues, a disturbing presence had intervened. For some, it was the presence of new theoretical problems requiring the best thinking. For others, it was the presence of an absence—that which remained when everything moderns had believed for two centuries was in doubt. The years from about 1963 to 1979 were not, in reality, the end of anything. Yet after, some began to see them as the beginning of an end.

C. L.

Notes

Page 368: Malcolm X, "Ballot or the Bullet," *Malcolm X Speaks* (Grove Press, 1966), 26.

Page 369: The WITCH quote is from a New York Covens pamphlet, in Robin Morgan, ed., *Sisterhood Is Powerful* (Vintage, 1970), 605. WITCH was an acronym of multiple definitions varying from coven to coven and issue to issue.

Other quoted material is from the selections following.

Experiments at Renewal ❖ and Reconstruction

❖

John Kenneth Galbraith (1908–) was born in Ontario, Canada. He came to the United States in 1931, becoming a naturalized citizen in 1937. Until his retirement in 1975, he taught economics at Harvard. During World War II, Galbraith was director of the Strategic Bombing Survey (1945). Later, he was ambassador to India in the Kennedy administration (1961–1963). His many books include *A Theory of Price Control* (1952), *The Affluent Society* (1958), and *Age of Uncertainty* (1967), as well as *The New Industrial State* (1967), from which the selection is taken. Though trained and respected as an economist, Galbraith is known as an elegantly clever and broad-thinking writer, as the lead sentence in the selection suggests. No one of his generation was better able to see and state the social and economic conditions of the postwar era in widely accessible terms. Where others were caught in the enthusiasms of the Golden Age, Galbraith was more circumspect.

Change and the Planning System

John Kenneth Galbraith (1967)

I venture to think that modern economic life is seen much more clearly when, as here, there is such effort to see it whole.

I am also concerned to show how, in this larger context of change, the forces inducing human effort have changed. This assaults the most majestic of all economic assumptions, namely that man, in his economic activities, is subject to the authority of the market. Instead we have an economic system which, whatever its formal ideological billing, is, in substantial part, a planned economy. The initiative in deciding what is to be produced comes not from the sovereign consumer who, through the market, issues the instructions that bend the productive mechanism to his ultimate will. Rather it comes from the great producing organization which reaches forward to control the markets that it is presumed to serve and, beyond, to bend the customer to its needs. And, in so doing, it deeply influences his values and beliefs—including not a few that will be mobilized in resistance to the present argument. One of the conclusions that follows from this analysis is that there is a broad convergence between industrial systems. The imperatives of technology and organization, not the images of ideology, are what determine the shape of economic society. This, on the whole, is fortunate, although it will not necessarily be welcomed by those whose intellectual capital and moral fervor are invested in the present image of the market economy as the antithesis of social planning. Nor will it be welcomed by their disciples, who, with even smaller intellectual investment, carry the banners of free markets and free enterprise and therewith, by definition, of the free nations into political, diplomatic or military battle. Nor will it be welcomed by those who identify planning exclusively with socialism. The ideas here offered have, in one form or another, been gaining ground. There has been visible movement since they were first offered in the present form in 1967. But they are not yet the ideas of the consensus.

The continuing subordination of belief to industrial necessity and convenience is not in accordance with the greatest vision of man. Nor is it entirely safe. . . .

The two questions most asked about an economic system are whether it serves man's physical needs and whether it is consistent with his liberty. There is little doubt as to the ability of the planning system to serve man's needs. As we have seen, it is able to manage these needs only because it serves them abundantly. It requires a mechanism for making men want what it provides. But this mechanism would not work—wants would not be subject to manipulation—had not these wants been dulled by sufficiency.

The prospects for liberty involve far more interesting questions. It has always been imagined, especially by conservatives, that to associate all, or a large part, of economic activity with the state is to endanger freedom. The individual and his preferences, in one way or another, will be sacrificed to the needs and conveniences of the apparatus created ostensibly to serve him. As the planning system evolves into a penumbra of the state, the question of its relation to liberty thus arises in urgent form. In recent years, in the Soviet-type economies, there has been an ill-concealed conflict between the state and the intellectuals. In essence, this has been a conflict between those for whom the needs of the government, including above all its needs as economic planner and producer of goods, are preeminent and those who assert the high but inconvenient claims of uninhibited intellectual and artistic expression. Is this a warning?

The instinct which warns of dangers in this association of economic and public power is sound. It comes close to being the subject of this book. But conservatives have looked in the wrong direction for the danger. They have feared that the state might reach out and destroy the vigorous, money-making entrepreneur. They have not noticed that, all the while, the successors to the entrepreneur were uniting themselves ever more closely with the state and rejoicing in the result. They were also, and with enthusiasm, accepting abridgment of their freedom. Part of this is implicit in the subordination of individual personality to the needs of organization. Some of it is in the exact pattern of the classical business expectation. The president of McDonnell Douglas is no more likely in public to speak critically, or even candidly, of the Air Force than is the head of a Soviet *combinat* of the ministry to which he reports. No modern head of the Ford Motor Company will ever react with the same pristine vigor to the presumed foolishness of Washington as did its founder. No head of Montgomery Ward will ever again breathe defiance of a President of the United States as did Sewell Avery, who was once carried by the police from the company offices for resisting a demand that he do business with a union. Manners may be involved. But it would also now be said that "too much is at stake."

The problem, however, is not the freedom of the businessman. Business orators have spoken much about freedom in the past. But it can be laid down as a rule that those who speak most of liberty are least inclined to use it. The high executive who speaks fulsomely of personal freedom carefully submits his speeches on the subject for review by the experts in public imagery for elimination of controversial words, phrases and ideas, as befits a good organization man. The general who tells his troops and the world that they are in the forefront of the fight for freedom is a man who has always submitted happily to army discipline. The pillar of the foreign policy establishment who adverts most feelingly to the values of the free world is the man who extravagantly admires the orthodoxy of his own views.

The danger to liberty lies in the subordination of belief to the needs of the planning system. In this the state and the planning system will be partners. This threat has already been assessed, as also the means for minimizing it.

If we continue to believe that the goals of the planning system—the expansion of output, the companion increase in consumption, technological advance, the public images that sustain it—are coordinate with life, then all of our lives will be in the service of these goals. What is consistent with these ends we shall have or be allowed; all else will be off limits. Our wants will be managed in accordance with the needs of the planning system; the policies of the state will be subject to similar influence; education will be adapted to industrial need; the disciplines required by the planning system will be the conventional morality of the community. All other goals will be made to seem precious, unimportant or antisocial. We will be bound to the ends of the system. The state will add its moral, and perhaps some of its legal, power to their enforcement. What will eventuate, on the whole, will be the benign servitude of the household retainer who is taught to love her mistress and see her interests as her own, and not the compelled servitude of the field hand. But it will not be freedom.

If, on the other hand, the planning system is only a part, and relatively a diminishing part, of life, there is much less occasion for concern. Aesthetic goals will have pride of place; those who serve them will not be subject to the goals of the technostructure; the planning system itself will be subordinate to the claims of these dimensions of life. Intellectual preparation will be for its own sake and not for better service to the planning system. Men will not be entrapped by the belief that apart from the goals of the planning system—apart from the production of goods and income by progressively more advanced technical methods—there is nothing important in life.

The foregoing being so, we may, over time, come to see the planning system in fitting light as an essentially technical arrangement for providing convenient goods and services in adequate volume. Those who rise through its bureaucracy will so see themselves. And the public consequences will be in keeping, for if economic goals are the only goals of the society, it is natural that the planning system should dominate the state and the state should serve its ends. If other goals are strongly asserted, the planning system will, one can hope, fall into its place as a detached and autonomous arm of the state but one responsive to the larger purposes of the society.

We have seen wherein the chance for salvation lies. The planning system, in contrast with its economic antecedents, is intellectually demanding. It brings into existence to serve its intellectual and scientific needs the community that, all should hope, will reject its monopoly of social purpose. ❖

Jürgen Habermas (1929–) was born in Düsseldorf. After studies at Göttigen and Bonn, he taught at Heidelberg, then Frankfurt. From 1971 to 1983, he was director of the Max Planck Institute in Frankfurt. He is considered heir to the tradition of philosophically based critical social theory in the Frankfurt tradition. Habermas's writings include *Theory and Practice* (1971), *Toward a Rational Society: Student Protest, Science and Politics* (1970), *Communication and the Evolution of Society* (1979), *Theory of Communicative Action* (1984, 2 vols.), and *Moral Consciousness and Communicative Action* (1990).

"Emancipatory Knowledge" is from the conclusion to Habermas's 1968 book, *Knowledge and Human Interests*. Though a tightly written summary, the selection illustrates Habermas's theoretical debt to the great critical theorists Adorno and Horkheimer and represents the basis for his theory of communicative competence that evolved over the years. It suggests the outlines of a critical theory of society that frankly admits that knowledge is never pure, always founded in universal human interests, of which emancipation is the most fundamental. "Social Analysis and Communicative Competence" is one of Habermas's earliest statements of his general theory of communication. The selection clearly shows his concern to link social analysis to language. Here, he develops that link from a technical discussion of the ideal speech situation derived by philosophical analysis from the social implications of discourse. Language performance, he argues (following a prominent school of language philosophy), rests on the assumption of the possibility of dialogue—an assumption that must be universal in language and thus in social life. Though the theory was developed in great detail over the years, this remains a reliable guide to Habermas's attempt to found a theory of social life on a theory of communication.

Emancipatory Knowledge

Jürgen Habermas (1968)

The sciences have retained one characteristic of philosophy: the illusion of pure theory. This illusion does not determine the practice of scientific research but only its self-understanding. And to the extent that this self-understanding reacts back upon scientific practice, it even has its point.

The glory of the sciences is their unswerving application of their methods without reflecting on knowledge-constitutive interests. From knowing not what they do methodologically, they are that much surer of their discipline, that is of methodical progress within an unproblematic framework. False consciousness has a protective function. For the sciences lack the means of dealing with the risks that appear once the connection of knowledge and human interest has been comprehended on the level of self-reflection. It was possible for fascism to give birth to the freak of a national physics and Stalinism to that of a Soviet Marxist genetics (which deserves to be taken more seriously than the former) only because the illusion of objectivism was lacking. It would have been able to provide immunity against the more dangerous bewitchments of misguided reflection.

But the praise of objectivism has its limits. Husserl's critique was right to attack it, if not with the right means. As soon as the objectivist illusion is turned into an affirmative *Weltanschauung*, methodologically unconscious necessity is perverted to the dubious virtue of a scientific profession of faith. Objectivism in no way prevents the sciences from intervening in the conduct of life, as Husserl thought it did. They are integrated into it in any case. But they do not of themselves develop their practical efficacy in the direction of a growing rationality of action.

Instead, the positivist self-understanding of the *nomological sciences* lends countenance to the substitution of technology for enlightened action. It directs the utilization of scientific information from an illusory viewpoint, namely that the practical mastery of history can be reduced to technical control of objectified processes. The objectivist self-understanding of the *hermeneutic sciences* is of no lesser consequence. It defends sterilized knowledge against the reflected appropriation of active traditions and locks up history in a museum. Guided by the objectivist attitude of theory as the image of facts, the nomological and hermeneutical sciences reinforce each other with regard to their practical consequences. The latter displace our connection with tradition into the realm of the arbitrary, while the former, on the levelled-off basis of the repression of history, squeeze the conduct of life into the behavioral system of instrumental action. The dimension in which acting subjects could arrive rationally at agreement about goals and purposes is surrendered to the obscure area of mere decision among reified value systems and irrational beliefs. When this dimension, abandoned by all men of good will, is subjected to reflection that relates to history objectivistically, as did the philosophical tradition, then positivism triumphs at the highest level of thought, as with Comte. This happens when critique uncritically abdicates its own connection with the emancipatory knowledge-constitutive interest in favor of pure theory. This sort of high-flown critique projects the undecided process of the evolution of the human species onto the level of a philosophy of history that dogmatically issues instructions for action. A *delusive philosophy of history, however, is only the obverse of deluded decisionism.* Bureaucratically prescribed partisanship goes only too well with contemplatively misunderstood value freedom.

These practical consequences of a restricted, scientistic consciousness of the sciences can be countered by a critique that destroys the illusion of objectivism. Contrary to Husserl's expectations, objectivism is eliminated not through the power of renewed *theoria* but through demonstrating what it conceals: the connection of knowledge and interest. Philosophy remains true to its classic tradition by renouncing it. The insight that the truth of statements is linked in the last analysis to the intention of the good and true life can be preserved today only on the ruins of ontology. However even this philosophy remains a specialty alongside of the sciences and outside public consciousness as long as the heritage that it has critically abandoned lives on in the positivistic self-understanding of the sciences.❖

Social Analysis and Communicative Competence
Jürgen Habermas (1970)

If one thus analyzes the structure which we generate and describe by pure dialogue constitutive universals, one arrives at a number of symmetrical relations for the ideal speech situation. Pure intersubjectivity is determined by a symmetrical relation between I and You (We and You), I and He (We and They). An unlimited inter-

Excerpt from "Toward a Theory of Communicative Competence," Hans Peter Dreitzel, ed., *Recent Sociology No. 2: Patterns of Communicative Behavior* (New York: Macmillan Co., 1970), pp. 143–146.

changeability of dialogue roles demands that no side be privileged in the performance of these roles: pure intersubjectivity exists only when there is complete symmetry in the distribution of assertion and disputation, revelation and hiding, prescription and following among the partners of communication. As long as these symmetries exist, communication will not be hindered by constraints arising from its own structure: (1) In the case of unrestricted discussion (in which no prejudiced opinion can continually avoid being made thematic and being criticized) it is possible to develop strategies for reaching unconstrained consensus; (2) based on the mutuality of unimpaired self-representation (which includes the acknowledgment of the self-representation of the Other as well), it is possible to achieve subtle nearness along with inviolable distance among the partners and that means communication under conditions of extreme individuation; (3) in the case of full complementation of expectations (which excludes one-sided obliging norms), the claim of universal understanding exists as well as the necessity of universalized norms. These three symmetries represent, by the way, a linguistic conceptualization for that which we traditionally apprehend as the ideas of truth, freedom, and justice.

The speech situation, which is determined by pure intersubjectivity, is an idealization. The mastery of dialogue-constitutive universals is not synonymous to the capability of actually establishing the ideal speech situation. But communicative competence does mean the mastery of the means of construction necessary for the establishment of an ideal speech situation. No matter how the intersubjectivity of mutual understanding may be deformed, the design of an ideal speech situation is necessarily implied with the structure of potential speech; for every speech, even that of intentional deception, is oriented towards the idea of truth. This idea can only be analyzed with regard to a consensus achieved in unrestraint and universal discourse. Insofar as we master the means for the construction of an ideal speech situation, we can conceive the ideas of truth, freedom, and justice—which interpret each other—only as ideas of course. For on the strength of communicative competence we can by no means really produce the ideal speech situation independent of the empirical structures of the social system to which we belong; we can only anticipate this situation.

One must be able to demonstrate the deformations of pure intersubjectivity which are induced by the social structure on the basis of asymmetries in the performance of dialogue rules. The uneven distribution of dialogue constitutive universals in standard communication between individuals and social groups indicates the particular form and deformation of the intersubjectivity of mutual understanding which is built into the social structure. At this place I have to interrupt these considerations which can only claim to be a first attempt to grasp communicative competence in terms of linguistic theory. Let me, however, draw two conclusions, the first of which will lead back to the problem of general semantics.

I imagine that the particular form of intersubjectivity is of mutual understanding; that means: the particular structure of potential speech is the basic linguistic framework, which also determines the scope and structure of corresponding world views. Then, the classification of semantic fields is predetermined by the question of how far the net of intersubjectivity must be spread in order to stabilize the identity of the individuals as well as that of the social group in a given culture or subculture at a given time. The structural differences between the animistic, the mythical, the religious, the philosophical, and the scientific views of life lie clearly in this dimension. The range of those global interpretations of nature and society extend from the case of total mediation of the individual and his group with all nonhuman phenomena, within an all-embracing association of motivated actions, to the case of total reification of all intersubjective relationships within the framework of objectifying sciences. At this time I cannot further pursue this topic. However, one consequence seems to me to be important for our context. If we could succeed, namely, in describing deformations of pure intersubjectivity in the dimension in which dialogue constitutive universals are applied; and if it were possible, moreover, to distinguish the categorical frameworks of potential views of life in terms of distribution of dialogue constitutive universals—then general semantics could be developed on the basis of a theory of communicative competence.

The . . . final point is how that theory of communicative competence might be employed for social analysis.

As already mentioned, the idealization of the concept of the ideal speech situation is comprised not only in the fact that we disregard contingent empirical limitations. The idealization consists rather of the supposition . . . that the motivational base of all actions is organized linguistically, *i.e.*, within the structure of potential speech. By this very idealization we imagine the actual motivations of the action as being identical with the linguistically apprehensible intentions of the speaker. This model of pure communicative actions is included in the design of pure intersubjectivity. Now we have reason enough to assume however, that social action is not only—and perhaps not even primarily—controlled by motives which coincide with the intentions of the actor-speaker, but rather by motives excluded from public communication and fixed to a prelinguistic symbol organization. The greater the share of prelinguistically fixed motivations which cannot be freely converted in public communication, the greater the deviance from the model of pure communicative action. I would propose to make the empirical assumptions that these deviations increase correspondingly to the varying degrees of repression which characterize the institutional system within a given society; and that in turn, the degree of repression depends on the developmental stage of the productive forces and on the organization of authority, that is of the institutionalization of political and economic power.❖

Peter Berger (1929–) was born in Vienna and now teaches at Boston University. In addition to authoring numerous works in sociology, including *An Invitation to Sociology* (1963), Berger writes as a lay theologian, as in the recent book *A Far Glory: The Quest for Faith in an Age of Credulity* (1992). **Thomas Luckmann** (1927–), after teaching for a period in Frankfurt, is now at Konstanz. He has written *Invisible Religion* (1967) and is the editor and coauthor of Alfred Schutz's *Structure of the Lifeworld,* a systematic social theory from a phenomenological point of view.

Berger and Luckmann wrote *The Social Construction of Reality* at a time when both were interested in the sociology of religion. They thus worked somewhat in the spirit of the classic social theorists, who derived much of their theoretical positions from assessments of, or reaction to, religion. Berger and Luckmann both felt that religion continued as an important force in modern life. This conviction underlay their argument that the social world was orderly, even though constructed in human process. Their book, from which the selection is taken, represents the most successful attempt since Schutz to construct an explicitly phenomenological social theory.

Society as a Human Product

Peter Berger and Thomas Luckmann (1966)

It should be clear from the foregoing that the statement that man produces himself in no way implies some sort of Promethean vision of the solitary individual. Man's self-production is always, and of necessity, a social enterprise. Men *together* produce a human environment, with the totality of its socio-cultural and psychological formations. None of these formations may be understood as products of man's biological constitution, which, as indicated, provides only the outer limits for human productive activity. Just as it is impossible for man to develop as man in isolation, so it is impossible for man in isolation to produce a human environment. Solitary human being is being on the animal level (which, of course, man shares with other animals). As soon as one deserves phenomena that are specifically human, one enters the realm of the social. Man's specific humanity and his sociality are inextricably intertwined. *Homo sapiens* is always, and in the same measure, *homo socius*.

The human organism lacks the necessary biological means to provide stability for human conduct. Human existence, if it were thrown back on its organismic resources by themselves, would be existence in some sort of chaos. Such chaos is, however, empirically unavailable, even though one may theoretically conceive of it. Empirically, human existence takes place in a context of order, direction, stability. The question then arises: From what does the empirically existing stability of human order derive? An answer may be given on two levels. One may first point to the obvious fact that a given social order precedes any individual organismic development. That is, world-openness, while intrinsic to man's biological make-up, is always preempted by social order. One may say that the biologically intrinsic world-openness of human existence is always, and indeed must be, transformed by social order into a relative world-closedness. While this reclosure can never approximate the closedness of animal existence, if only because of its humanly produced and thus "artificial" character, it is nevertheless capable, most of the time, of providing direction and stability for the greater part of human conduct. The question may then be pushed to another level. One may ask in what manner social order itself arises.

The most general answer to this question is that social order is a human product, or, more precisely, an ongoing human production. It is produced by man in the course of his ongoing externalization. Social order is not biologically given or derived from any biological *data* in its empirical manifestations. Social order, needless to add, is also not given in man's natural environment, though particular features of this may be factors in determining certain features of a social order (for example, its economic or technological arrangements). Social order is not part of the "nature of things," and it cannot be derived from the "laws of nature." Social order exists *only* as a product of human activity. No other ontological status may be ascribed to it without hopelessly obfuscating its empirical manifestations. Both in its genesis (social order is the result of past human activity) and its existence in any instant of time (social order exists only and insofar as human activity continues to produce it) it is a human product.

While the social products of human externalization have a character *sui generis* as against both their organismic and their environmental context, it is important to stress that externalization as such is an anthropological necessity. Human being is impossible in a closed sphere of quiescent interiority. Human being must ongoingly externalize itself in activity. This anthropological necessity is grounded in man's biological equipment. The inherent instability of the human organism makes it imperative that man himself provide a stable environment for his conduct. Man himself must specialize and direct his drives. These biological facts serve as a necessary presupposition for the production of social order. In other words, although no existing social order can be derived from biological *data*, the necessity for social order as such stems from man's biological equipment.

To understand the causes, other than those posited by the biological constants, for the emergence, maintenance and transmission of a social order one must undertake an analysis that eventuates in a theory of institutionalization.

Origins of Institutionalization

All human activity is subject to habitualization. Any action that is repeated frequently becomes cast into a pattern, which can then be reproduced with an economy of effort and which, *ipso facto*, is apprehended by its performer *as* that pattern. Habitualization further implies that the action in question may be performed again in the future in the same manner and with the same economical effort. This is true of non-social as well as of social activity. Even the solitary individual on the proverbial desert island habitualizes his activity. When he wakes up in the morning and resumes his attempts to construct a canoe out of matchsticks, he may mumble to himself, "There I go again," as he starts on step one of an operating procedure consisting of, say, ten steps. In other words, even solitary man has at least the company of his operating procedures.

Habitualized actions, of course, retain their meaningful character for the individual although the meanings involved become embedded as routines in his general stock of knowledge, taken for granted by him and at hand for his projects into the future. Habitualization carries with it the important psychological gain that choices are narrowed. While in theory there may be a hundred ways to go about the project of building a canoe out of matchsticks, habitualization narrows these down to one. This frees the individual from the burden of "all those decisions," providing a psychological relief that has its basis in man's undirected instinctual structure. Habitualization provides the direction and the specialization of activity that is lacking in man's biological equipment, thus relieving the accumulation of tensions that result from undirected drives. And by providing a stable background in which human activity may proceed with a minimum of decision-making most of the time, it frees energy for such decisions as may be necessary on certain occasions. In other words, the background of habitualized activity opens up a foreground for deliberation and innovation.

In terms of the meanings bestowed by man upon his activity, habitualization makes it unnecessary for each situation to be defined anew, step by step. A large variety of situations may be subsumed under its predefinitions. The activity to be undertaken in these situations can then be anticipated. Even alternatives of conduct can be assigned standard weights.

These processes of habitualization precede any institutionalization, indeed can be made to apply to a hypothetical solitary individual detached from any social interaction. The fact that even such a solitary individual, assuming that he has been formed as a self (as we would have to assume in the case of our matchstick-canoe builder), will habitualize his activity in accordance with biographical experience of a world of social institutions preceding his solitude need not concern us at the moment. Empirically, the more important part of the habitualization of human activity is coextensive with the latter's institutionalization. The question then becomes how do institutions arise.

Institutionalization occurs whenever there is a reciprocal typification of habitualized actions by types of actors. Put differently, any such typification is an institution. What must be stressed is the reciprocity of institutional typifications and the typicality of not only the actions but also the actors in institutions. The typifications of habitualized actions that constitute institutions are always shared ones. They are *available* to all the members of the particular social group in question, and the institution itself typifies individual actors as well as individual actions. The institution posits that actions of type X will be performed by actors of type X. For example, the institution of the law posits that heads shall be chopped off in specific ways under specific circumstances, and that specific types of individuals shall do the chopping (executioners, say, or members of an impure caste, or virgins under a certain age, or those who have been designated by an oracle).

Institutions further imply historicity and control. Reciprocal typifications of actions are built up in the course of a shared history. They cannot be created instantaneously. Institutions always have a history, of which they are the products. It is impossible to understand an institution adequately without an understanding of the historical process in which it was produced. Institutions also, by the very fact of their existence, control human conduct by setting up predefined patterns of conduct, which channel it in one direction as against the many other directions that would theoretically be possible. It is important to stress that this controlling character is inherent in institutionalization as such, prior to or apart from any mechanisms of sanctions specifically set up to support an institution. These mechanisms (the sum of which constitute what is generally called a system of social control) do, of course, exist in many institutions and in all the agglomerations of institutions that we call societies. Their controlling efficacy, however, is of a secondary or supplementary kind. As we shall see again later, the primary social control is given in the existence of an institution as such. To say that a segment of human activity has been institutionalized is already to say that this segment of human activity has been subsumed under social control. Additional control mechanisms are required only insofar as the processes of institutionalization are less than completely successful. Thus, for instance, the law may provide that anyone who breaks the incest taboo will have his head chopped off. This provision may be necessary because there have been cases when individuals offended against the taboo. It is unlikely that this sanction will have to be invoked continuously (unless the institution delineated by the incest taboo is itself in the course of disintegration, a special case that we need not elaborate here). It makes little sense, therefore, to say that human sexuality is socially controlled by beheading certain individuals. Rather, human sexuality is socially controlled by its institutionalization in the course of the particular history in question. One may add, of course, that the incest taboo itself is nothing but the negative side of an assemblage of typifications, which define in the first place which sexual conduct is incestuous and which is not.

In actual experience institutions generally manifest themselves in collectivities containing considerable numbers of people. It is theoretically important, however, to emphasize that the institutionalizing process of reciprocal typification would occur even if two individuals began to interact *de novo*. . . . *A* and *B* alone are responsible for having constructed this world. *A* and *B* remain capable of changing or abolishing it. What is more, since they themselves have shaped this world in the course of a shared biography which they can remember, the world thus shaped appears fully transparent to them. They understand the world that they themselves have made. All this changes in the process of transmission to the new generation. The objectivity of the institutional world "thickens" and "hardens," not only for the children, but (by a mirror effect) for the parents as well. The "There we go again" now becomes "This is how these things are done." A world so regarded attains a firmness in consciousness; it becomes real in an ever more massive way and it can no longer be changed so readily. For the children, especially in the early phase of their socialization into it, it becomes *the* world. For the parents, it loses its playful quality and becomes "serious." For the children, the parentally transmitted world is not fully transparent. Since they had no part in shaping it, it confronts them as a given reality that, like nature, is opaque in places at least.

Only at this point does it become possible to speak of a social world at all, in the sense of a comprehensive and given reality confronting the individual in a manner analogous to the reality of the natural world. Only in this way, *as* an objective world, can the social formations be transmitted to a new generation. In the early phases of socialization the child is quite incapable of distinguishing between the objectivity of natural phenomena and the objectivity of the social formations. To take the most important item of socialization, language appears to the child as inherent in the nature of things, and he cannot grasp the notion of its conventionality. A thing *is* what it is called, and it could not be called anything else. All institutions appear in the same way, as given, unalterable and self-evident. Even in our empirically unlikely example of parents having constructed an institutional world *de novo*, the objectivity of this world would be increased for them by the socialization of their children, because the objectivity experienced by the children would reflect back upon their own experience of this world. Empirically, of course, the institutional world transmitted by most parents already has the character of historical and objective reality. The process of transmission simply strengthens the parents' sense of reality, if only because, to put it crudely, if one says, "This is how these things are done," often enough one believes it oneself.

An institutional world, then, is experienced as an objective reality. It has a history that antedates the individual's birth and is not accessible to his biographical recollection. It was there before he was born, and it will be there after his death. This history itself, as the tradition of the existing institutions, has the character of objectivity. The individual's biography is apprehended as an episode located within the objective history of the society. The institutions, as historical and objective facticities, confront the individual as undeniable facts. The institutions are *there*, external to him, persistent in their reality, whether he likes it or not. He cannot wish them away. They resist his attempts to change or evade them. They have coercive power over him, both in themselves, by the sheer force of their facticity, and through the control mechanisms that are usually attached to the most important of them. The objective reality of institutions is not diminished if the individual does not understand their purpose or their mode of operation. He may experience large sectors of the social world as incomprehensible, perhaps oppressive in their opaqueness, but real nonetheless. Since institutions exist as external reality, the individual cannot understand them by introspection.

He must "go out" and learn about them, just as he must to learn about nature. This remains true even though the social world, as a humanly produced reality, is potentially understandable in a way not possible in the case of the natural world.

It is important to keep in mind that the objectivity of the institutional world, however massive it may appear to the individual, is a humanly produced, constructed objectivity. The process by which the externalized products of human activity attain the character of objectivity is objectivation. The institutional world is objectivated human activity, and so is every single institution. In other words, despite the objectivity that marks the social world in human experience, it does not thereby acquire an ontological status apart from the human activity that produced it. The paradox that man is capable of producing a world that he then experiences as something other than a human product will concern us later on. At the moment, it is important to emphasize that the relationship between man, the producer, and the social world, his product, is and remains a dialectical one. That is, man (not, of course, in isolation but in his collectivities) and his social world interact with each other. The product acts back upon the producer. Externalization and objectivation are moments in a continuing dialectical process. The third moment in this process, which is internalization (by which the objectivated social world is retrojected into consciousness in the course of socialization), will occupy us in considerable detail later on. It is already possible, however, to see the fundamental relationship of these three dialectical moments in social reality. Each of them corresponds to an essential characterization of the social world. *Society is a human product. Society is an objective reality. Man is a social product.* It may also already be evident than an analysis of the social world that leaves out any one of these three moments will be distortive. One may further add that only with the transmission of the social world to a new generation (that is, internalization as effectuated in socialization) does the fundamental social dialectic appear in its totality. To repeat, only with the appearance of a new generation can one properly speak of a social world.❖

Dorothy Smith (1926–) studied in the 1960s at the University of California at Berkeley, from which she received her Ph.D. in sociology (1963). A resident and citizen of Canada, Smith taught at Berkeley, the University of British Columbia, and the University of Essex before joining the Ontario Institute for Studies in Education in Toronto, Canada, in 1977. She is the author of numerous articles and books on such topics as the family, teaching, gender, suicide, and mental illness, in relation to which she has developed her feminist social theory. Recently, Smith's work has enjoyed renewed attention among general social theorists as well as feminist theorists. Her books include *The Conceptual Practices of Power: A Feminist Sociology of Knowledge* (1990) and *Everyday World as Problematic: A Feminist Sociology* (1987).

Knowing a Society from Within: A Woman's Standpoint
Dorothy Smith (1974)

Women's standpoint, as I am analyzing it here, discredits sociology's claim to constitute an objective knowledge independent of the sociologist's situation. Sociology's

---

Excerpt from "Women's Experience as a Radical Critique of Sociology," *The Conceptual Practices of Power: A Feminist Sociology of Knowledge* (Boston: Northeastern University Press, 1990 [1974]), pp. 21–24. Copyright 1990 by Dorothy E. Smith. Reprinted with the permission of Northeastern University Press.

conceptual procedures, methods, and relevances organize its subject matter from a determinate position in society. This critical disclosure is the basis of an alternative way of thinking sociology. If sociology cannot avoid being situated, then it should take that as its beginning and build it into its methodological and theoretical strategies. As it is now, these strategies separate a sociologically constructed world from that of direct experience; it is precisely that separation that must be undone.

I am not proposing an immediate and radical transformation of the subject matter and methods of the discipline nor the junking of everything that has gone before. What I am suggesting is more in the nature of a reorganization of the relationship of sociologists to the object of our knowledge and of our problematic. This reorganization involves first placing sociologists where we are actually situated, namely, at the beginning of those acts by which we know or will come to know, and second, making our direct embodied experience of the everyday world the primary ground of our knowledge.

A sociology worked on in this way would not have as its objective a body of knowledge subsisting in and of itself; inquiry would not be justified by its contribution to the heaping up of such a body. We would reject a sociology aimed primarily at itself. We would not be interested in contributing to a body of knowledge whose uses are articulated to relations of ruling in which women participate only marginally, if at all. The professional sociologist is trained to think in the objectified modes of sociological discourse, to think sociology as it has been and is thought; that training and practice has to be discarded. Rather, as sociologists we would be constrained by the actualities of how things come about in people's direct experience, including our own. A sociology for women would offer a knowledge of the social organization and determinations of the properties and events of our directly experienced world. Its analyses would become part of our ordinary interpretations of the experienced world, just as our experience of the sun's sinking below the horizon is transformed by our knowledge that the world turns away from a sun that seems to sink.

The only way of knowing a socially constructed world is knowing it from within. We can never stand outside it. A relation in which sociological phenomena are objectified and presented as external to and independent of the observer is itself a special social practice also known from within. The relation of observer and object of observation, of sociologist to "subject," is a specialized social relationship. Even to be a stranger is to enter a world constituted from within as strange. The strangeness itself is the mode in which it is experienced.

When Jean Briggs made her ethnographic study of the ways in which an Eskimo people structure and express emotion, what she learned emerged for her in the context of the actual developing relations between her and the family with whom she lived and other members of the group. Her account situates her knowledge in the context of those relationships and in the actual sites in which the work of family subsistence was done. Affections, tensions, and quarrels, in some of which she was implicated, were the living texture in which she learned what she describes. She makes it clear how this context structured her learning and how what she learned and can speak of became observable to her.

Briggs tells us what is normally discarded in the anthropological or sociological telling. Although sociological inquiry is necessarily a social relation, we have learned to dissociate our own part in it. We recover only the object of our knowledge as if it stood all by itself. Sociology does not provide for seeing that there are always two terms to this relation. An alternative sociology must preserve in it the presence, concerns, and experience of the sociologist as knower and discoverer.

To begin from direct experience and to return to it as a constraint or "test" of the adequacy of a systematic knowledge is to begin from where we are located bodily. The actualities of our everyday world are already socially organized. Settings, equipment, environment, schedules, occasions, and so forth, as well as our enterprises and routines, are socially produced and concretely and symbolically organized prior to the moment at which we enter and at which inquiry begins. By taking up a standpoint in our original and immediate knowledge of the world, sociologists can make their discipline's socially organized properties first observable and then problematic.

When I speak of *experience* I do not use the term as a synonym for *perspective*. Nor in proposing a sociology grounded in the sociologist's actual experience am I recommending the self-indulgence of inner exploration or any other enterprise with self as sole focus and object. Such subjectivist interpretations of *experience* are themselves an aspect of that organization of consciousness that suppresses the locally situated side of the bifurcated consciousness and transports us straight into mind country, stashing away the concrete conditions and practices upon which it depends. We can never escape the circles of our own heads if we accept that as our territory. Rather, sociologists' investigation of our directly experienced world as a problem is a mode of discovering or rediscovering the society from within. We begin from our own original but tacit knowledge and from within the acts by which we bring it into our grasp in making it observable and in understanding how it works. We aim not at a reiteration of what we already (tacitly) know, but at an exploration of what passes beyond that knowledge and is deeply implicated in how it is.

Our knowledge of the world is given to us in the modes by which we enter into relations with the object of knowledge. But in this case the object of our knowledge is or originates in the co-ordering of activities among "subjects." The constitution of an objective sociology as an authoritative version of how things are is done from a position in and as a part of the practices of ruling in our kind of society. Our training as sociologists teaches us to ignore the uneasiness at the junctures where multiple and diverse experiences are transformed into objectified forms. That juncture shows in the ordinary problems respondents have of fitting their experience of the world to the questions in the interview schedule. The sociologist who is a woman finds it hard to preserve this exclusion, for she discovers, if she will, precisely that uneasiness in her relation to her discipline as a whole. The persistence of the privileged sociological version (or versions) relies upon a substructure that has already discredited and deprived of authority to speak the voices of those who know the society differently. The objectivity of a sociological version depends upon a special relationship with others that makes it easy for sociologists to remain outside the others' experience and does not require them to recognize that experience as a valid contention.❖

Immanuel Wallerstein (1930–) was a prominent supporter of the students during the riots at Columbia University in 1968. For many years, he has been director of the Fernand Braudel Center and Distinguished Professor of Sociology at the State University of New York at Binghamton. He is also the founding editor of *Review,* a journal devoted largely to studies in world development and world-system theory. His major work is *The Modern World-System* (1974, 1980, 1989; 3 vols.). The selection is from the first volume of this study. It summarizes Wallerstein's now-famous argument that the modern world-system is distinguished from empires by its reliance on economic control of the world order by a dominating capitalist Center in systemic economic and political relation to peripheral and semiperipheral world areas. In developing these concepts, Wallerstein clearly intended to supplant modernization theory's ideological notions of a progressively developing world economy.

The Modern World-System

Immanuel Wallerstein (1976)

In order to describe the origins and initial workings of a world system, I have had to argue a certain conception of a world-system. A world-system is a social system, one that has boundaries, structures, member groups, rules of legitimation, and coherence. Its life is made up of the conflicting forces which hold it together by tension, and tear it apart as each group seeks eternally to remold it to its advantage. It has the characteristics of an organism, in that it has a life-span over which its characteristics change in some respects and remain stable in others. One can define its structures as being at different times strong or weak in terms of the internal logic of its functioning.

What characterizes a social system in my view is the fact that life within it is largely self-contained, and that the dynamics of its development are largely internal. The reader may feel that the use of the term "largely" is a case of academic weaseling. I admit I cannot quantify it. Probably no one ever will be able to do so, as the definition is based on a counterfactual hypothesis: If the system, for any reason, were to be cut off from all external forces (which virtually never happens), the definition implies that the system would continue to function substantially in the same manner. Again, of course, substantially is difficult to convert into hard operational criteria. Nonetheless the point is an important one and key to many parts of the empirical analyses of this book. Perhaps we should think of self-containment as a theoretical absolute, a sort of social vacuum, rarely visible and even more implausible to create artificially, but still and all a socially-real asymptote, the distance from which is somehow measurable.

Using such a criterion, it is contended here that most entities usually described as social systems—"tribes," communities, nation-states—are not in fact total systems. Indeed, on the contrary, we are arguing that the only real social systems are, on the one hand, those relatively small, highly autonomous subsistence economies not part of some regular tribute-demanding system and, on the other hand, world-systems. These latter are to be sure distinguished from the former because they are relatively large; that is, they are in common parlance "worlds." More precisely, however, they are defined by the fact that their self-containment as an economic-material entity is based on extensive division of labor and that they contain within them a multiplicity of cultures.

It is further argued that thus far there have only existed two varieties of such world-systems: world-empires, in which there is a single political system over most of the area, however attenuated the degree of its effective control; and those systems in which such a single political system does not exist over all, or virtually all, of the space. For convenience and for want of a better term, we are using the term "world-economy" to describe the latter.

Finally, we have argued that prior to the modern era, world-economies were highly unstable structures which tended either to be converted into empires or to disintegrate. It is the peculiarity of the modern world-system that a world-economy has survived for 500 years and yet has not come to be transformed into a world-empire—a peculiarity that is the secret of its strength.

This peculiarity is the political side of the form of economic organization called capitalism. Capitalism has been able to flourish precisely because the world-economy has had within its bounds not one but a multiplicity of political systems.

I am not here arguing the classic case of capitalist ideology that capitalism is a system based on the noninterference of the state in economic affairs. Quite the contrary! Capitalism is based on the constant absorption of economic loss by political entities, while economic gain is distributed to "private" hands. What I am arguing rather is that capitalism as an economic mode is based on the fact that the economic factors operate within an arena larger than that which any political entity can totally control. This gives capitalists a freedom of maneuver that is structurally based. It has made possible the constant economic expansion of the world-system, albeit a very skewed distribution of its rewards. The only alternative world-system that could maintain a high level of productivity and change the system of distribution would involve the reintegration of the levels of political and economic decision-making. This would constitute a third possible form of world-system, a socialist world government. This is not a form that presently exists, and it was not even remotely conceivable in the sixteenth century.

The historical reasons why the European world-economy came into existence in the sixteenth century and resisted attempts to transform it into an empire have been expounded at length. We shall not review them here. It should however be noted that the size of a world-economy is a function of the state of technology, and in particular of the possibilities of transport and communication within its bounds. Since this is a constantly changing phenomenon, not always for the better, the boundaries of a world-economy are ever fluid.

We have defined a world-system as one in which there is extensive division of labor. This division is not merely functional—that is, occupational—but geographical. That is to say, the range of economic tasks is not evenly distributed throughout the world-system. In part this is the consequence of ecological considerations, to be sure. But for the most part, it is a function of the social organization of work, one which magnifies and legitimizes the ability of some groups within the system to exploit the labor of others, that is, to receive a larger share of the surplus.

While, in an empire, the political structure tends to link culture with occupation, in a world-economy the political structure tends to link culture with spatial location. The reason is that in a world-economy the first point of political pressure available to groups is the local (national) state structure. Cultural homogenization tends to serve the interests of key groups and the pressures build up to create cultural-national identities.

This is particularly the case in the advantaged areas of the world-economy—what we have called the core-states. In such states, the creation of a strong state machinery coupled with a national culture, a phenomenon often referred to as integration, serves both as a mechanism to protect disparities that have arisen within the world-system, and as an ideological mask and justification for the maintenance of these disparities.

World-economies then are divided into core-states and peripheral areas. I do not say peripheral *states* because one characteristic of a peripheral area is that the indigenous state is weak, ranging from its nonexistence (that is, a colonial situation) to one with a low degree of autonomy (that is, a neo-colonial situation).

There are also semiperipheral areas which are in between the core and the periphery on a series of dimensions, such as the complexity of economic activities, strength of the state machinery, cultural integrity, etc. Some of these areas had been core-areas of earlier versions of a given world-economy. Some had been peripheral areas that were later promoted, so to speak, as a result of the changing geopolitics of an expanding world-economy.

The semiperiphery, however, is not an artifice of statistical cutting points, nor is it a residual category. The semiperiphery is a necessary structural element in a world-economy. These areas play a role parallel to that played, *mutatis mutandis,* by middle trading groups in an empire. They are collection points of vital skills that are often politically unpopular. These middle areas (like middle groups in an empire) partially deflect the political pressures which groups primarily located in peripheral areas might otherwise direct against core-states and the groups which operate within and through their state machineries. On the other hand, the interests primarily located in the semiperiphery are located outside the political arena of the core-states, and find it difficult to pursue the ends in political coalitions that might be open to them were they in the same political arena.

The division of a world-economy involves a hierarchy of occupational tasks, in which tasks requiring higher levels of skill and greater capitalization are reserved for higher-ranking areas. Since a capitalist world-economy essentially rewards accumulated capital, including human capital, at a higher rate than "raw" labor power, the geographical maldistribution of these occupational skills involves a strong trend toward self-maintenance. The forces of the marketplace reinforce them rather than undermine them. And the absence of a central political mechanism for the world-economy makes it very difficult to intrude counteracting forces to the maldistribution of rewards.

Hence, the ongoing process of a world-economy tends to expand the economic and social gaps among its varying areas in the very process of its development. One factor that tends to mask this fact is that the process of development of a world-economy brings about technological advances which make it possible to expand the boundaries of a world-economy. In this case, particular regions of the world may change their structural role in the world-economy, to their advantage, even though the disparity of reward between different sectors of the world-economy as a whole may be simultaneously widening. It is in order to observe this crucial phenomenon clearly that we have insisted on the distinction between a peripheral area of a given world-economy and the external arena of the world-economy. The external arena of one century often becomes the periphery of the next—or its semiperiphery. But then too core-states can become semiperipheral and semiperipheral ones peripheral.

While the advantages of the core-states have not ceased to expand throughout the history of the modern world-system, the ability of a particular state to remain in the core sector is not beyond challenge. The hounds are ever to the hares for the position of top dog. Indeed, it may well be that in this kind of system it is not structurally possible to avoid, over a long period of historical time, a circulation of the elites in the sense that the particular country that is dominant at a given time tends to be replaced in this role sooner or later by another country.

We have insisted that the modern world-economy is, and only can be, a capitalist world-economy. It is for this reason that we have rejected the appellation of "feudalism" for the various forms of capitalist agriculture based on coerced labor which grow up in a world-economy. Furthermore, although this has not been discussed in this volume, it is for this same reason that we will, in future volumes, regard with great circumspection and prudence the claim that there exist in the twentieth century socialist national economies within the framework of the world-economy (as opposed to socialist movements controlling certain state-machineries within the world-economy).

If world-systems are the only real social systems (other than truly isolated subsistence economies), then it must follow that the emergence, consolidation, and political roles of classes and status groups must be appreciated as elements of this *world-*system. And in turn it follows that one of the key elements in analyzing a class or a status-group is not only the state of its self-consciousness but the geographical scope of its self-definition.

Classes always exist potentially (*an sich*). The issue is under what conditions they become class-conscious (*für sich*), that is, operate as a group in the politico-economic arenas and even to some extent as a cultural entity. Such self-consciousness is a function of conflict situations. But for upper strata open conflict, and hence overt consciousness, is always *faute de mieux*. To the extent that class boundaries are not made explicit, to that extent it is more likely that privileges be maintained.

Since in conflict situations, multiple factions tend to reduce to two by virtue of the forging of alliances, it is by definition not possible to have three or more (conscious) classes. There obviously can be a multitude of occupational interest groups which may organize themselves to operate within the social structure. But such groups are really one variety of status-groups, and indeed often overlap heavily with other kinds of status-groups such as those defined by ethnic, linguistic, or religious criteria.

To say that there cannot be three or more classes is not however to say that there are always two. There may be none, though this is rare and transitional. There may be one, and this is most common. There may be two, and this is most explosive.

We say there may be only one class, although we have also said that classes only actually exist in conflict situations, and conflicts presume two sides. There is no contradiction here. For a conflict may be defined as being between one class, which conceives of itself as the universal class, and all the other strata. This has in fact been the usual situation in the modern world-system. The capitalist class (the *bourgeoisie*) has claimed to be the universal class and sought to organize political life to pursue its objectives against two opponents. On the one hand, there were those who spoke for the maintenance of traditional rank distinctions despite the fact that these ranks might have lost their original correlation with economic function. Such elements preferred to define the social structure as a non-class structure. It was to counter this ideology that the bourgeoisie came to operate as a class conscious of itself. . . .

The European world-economy of the sixteenth century tended overall to be a one-class system. It was the dynamic forces profiting from economic expansion and the capitalist system, especially those in the core-areas, who tended to be class-conscious, that is to operate within the political arena as a group defined primarily by their common role in the economy. This common role was in fact defined somewhat broadly from a twentieth-century perspective. It included persons who were farmers, merchants, and industrialists. Individual entrepreneurs often moved back and forth between these activities in any case, or combined them. The crucial distinction was between these men, whatever their occupation, principally oriented to obtaining profit in the world market, and the others not so oriented.

The "others" fought back in terms of their status privileges—those of the traditional aristocracy, those which small farmers had derived from the feudal system, those resulting from guild monopolies that were outmoded. Under the cover of cultural similarities, one can often weld strange alliances. Those strange alliances can take a very activist form and force the political centers to take account of them. We pointed to such instances in our discussion of France. Or they can take a politically passive form that serves well the needs of the dominant forces in the world-system. The triumph of Polish Catholicism as a cultural force was a case in point.

The details of the canvas are filled in with the panoply of multiple forms of status-groups, their particular strengths and accents. But the grand sweep is in terms of the process of class formation. And in this regard, the sixteenth century was indecisive. The capitalist strata formed a class that survived and gained *droit de cité*, but did not yet triumph in the political arena.

The evolution of the state machineries reflected precisely this uncertainty. Strong states serve the interests of some groups and hurt those of others. From however the standpoint of the world-system as a whole, if there is to be a multitude of political entities (that is, if the system is not a world-empire), then it cannot be the case that all these entities be equally strong. For if they were, they would be in the position of blocking the effective operation of transnational economic entities whose locus were in another state. And obviously certain combinations of these groups control the state. It would then follow that the world division of labor would be impeded, the world-economy decline, and eventually the world-system fall apart.

It also cannot be that *no* state machinery is strong. For in such a case, the capitalist strata would have no mechanisms to protect their interests, guaranteeing their property rights, assuring various monopolies, spreading losses among the larger population, etc.

It follows then that the world-economy develops a pattern where state structures are relatively strong in the core areas and relatively weak in the periphery. Which areas play which roles is in many ways accidental. What is necessary is that in some areas the state machinery be far stronger than in others.

What do we mean by a strong state-machinery? We mean strength vis-à-vis other states within the world-economy including other core-states, and strong vis-à-vis local political units within the boundaries of the state. In effect, we mean a sovereignty that is *de facto* as well as *de jure*. We also mean a state that is strong vis-à-vis any particular social group within the state. Obviously, such groups vary in the amount of pressure they can bring to bear upon the state. And obviously certain combinations of these groups control the state. It is not that the state is a neutral arbiter. But the state is more than a simple vector of given forces, if only because many of these forces are situated in more than one state or are defined in terms that have little correlation with state boundaries.

A strong state then is a partially autonomous entity in the sense that it has a margin of action available to it wherein it reflects the compromises of multiple interests, even if the bounds of these margins are set by the existence of some groups of primordial strength. To be a partially autonomous entity, there must be a group of people whose direct interests are served by such an entity: state managers and a state bureaucracy.

Such groups emerge within the framework of a capitalist world-economy because a strong state is the best choice between difficult alternatives for the two groups that are strongest in political, economic, and military terms: the emergent capitalist strata, and the old aristocratic hierarchies.

For the former, the strong state in the form of the "absolute monarchies" was a prime customer, a guardian against local and international brigandage, a mode of social legitimation, a preemptive protection against the creation of strong state barriers elsewhere. For the latter, the strong state represented a brake on these same capitalist strata, an upholder of status conventions, a maintainer of order, a promoter of luxury.

No doubt both nobles and bourgeois found the state machineries to be a burdensome drain of funds, and a meddlesome unproductive bureaucracy. But what options did they have? Nonetheless they were always restive and the immediate politics of the world-system was made up of the pushes and pulls resulting from the efforts of both groups to insulate themselves from what seemed to them the negative effects of the state machinery.

A state machinery involves a tipping mechanism. There is a point where strength creates more strength. The tax revenue enables the state to have a larger and more efficient civil bureaucracy and army which in turn leads to greater tax revenue—a process that continues in spiral form. The tipping mechanism works in other direction too—weakness leading to greater weakness. In between these two tipping points lies the politics of state-creation. It is in this arena that the skills of particular managerial groups make a difference. And it is because of the two tipping mechanisms that at certain points a small gap in the world-system can very rapidly become a larger one.

In those states in which the state machinery is weak, the state managers do not play the role of coordinating a complex industrial-commercial-agricultural mechanism. Rather they simply become one set of landlords amidst others, with little claim to legitimate authority over the whole.

These tend to be called traditional rulers. The political struggle is often phrased in terms of tradition versus change. This is of course a grossly misleading and ideological terminology. It may in fact be taken as a general sociological principle that, at any given point of time, what is thought to be traditional is of more recent origin than people generally imagine it to be, and represents primarily the conservative instincts of some group threatened with declining social status. Indeed, there seems to be nothing which emerges and evolves as quickly as a "tradition" when the need presents itself.

In a one-class system, the "traditional" is that in the name of which the "others" fight the class-conscious group. If they can encrust their values by legitimating them widely, even better by enacting them into legislative barriers, they thereby change the system in a way favorable to them.

The traditionalists may win in some states, but if a world-economy is to survive, they must lose more or less in the others. Furthermore, the gain in one region is the counterpart of the loss in another.

This is not quite a zero-sum game, but it is also inconceivable that all elements in a capitalist world-economy shift their values in a given direction simultaneously. The social system is built on having a multiplicity of value systems within it, reflecting the specific functions groups and areas play in the world division of labor.

We have not exhausted here the theoretical problems relevant to the functioning of a world-economy. We have tried only to speak to those illustrated by the early period of the world-economy in creation, to wit, sixteenth-century Europe. Many other problems emerged at later stages and will be treated, both empirically and theoretically, in later volumes.

In the sixteenth century, Europe was like a bucking bronco. The attempt of some groups to establish a world-economy based on a particular division of labor, to create national states in the core areas as politico-economic guarantors of this system, and to get the workers to pay not only the profits but the costs of maintaining the system was not easy. It was to Europe's credit that it was done, since without the thrust of the sixteenth century the modern world would not have been born and, for all its cruelties, it is better that it was born than that it had not been.

It is also to Europe's credit that it was not easy, and particularly that it was not easy because the people who paid the short-run costs screamed lustily at the unfairness of it all. The peasants and workers in Poland and England and Brazil and Mexico were all rambunctious in their various ways. As R. H. Tawney says of the agrarian disturbances of sixteenth-century England: "Such movements are a proof of blood and sinew and of a high and gallant spirit. . . . Happy the nation whose people has not forgotten how to rebel."

The mark of the modern world is the imagination of its profiteers and the counter-assertiveness of the oppressed. Exploitation and the refusal to accept exploitation as either inevitable or just constitute the continuing antinomy of the modern era, joined together in a dialectic which was far from reached its climax in the twentieth century.❖

Theda Skocpol (1947–) teaches at Harvard University, where she had been a student in the 1970s (receiving her Ph.D. in sociology in 1975). She was initially denied tenure at Harvard on the superficial grounds that her widely acclaimed book, *States and Social Revolutions*, was not sufficiently original. Skocpol brought sex discrimination charges and fought the denial. Eventually, after much embarrassment to the Department of Sociology and to Harvard, she was awarded tenure. Some believe that the attempt to deny tenure also involved a dispute over the role of secondary analysis and historical data (as opposed to quantitative studies) in sociology. While away from Harvard, Skocpol taught at the University of Chicago. She is considered a leader in the revival of interest in the sociology of the state. She is also the author of *Protecting Soldiers and Mothers: The Political Origins of Social Policy in the United States* (1992), which, like her first book, has been widely acclaimed as a classic in political sociology.

The selection presents the key elements in Skocpol's theory of the state. She takes up and revises earlier arguments for the relative autonomy of state from class power. The subtlety of her structural interpretation is seen in the way she relates the state to the structured world-system, on the one hand, and, as she puts it, the "class-divided socioeconomic structures," on the other. The study for which she devises this theory is an attempt to explain the phenomenon of social revolution with reference to the classic revolutions in eighteenth-century France and to Russia and China in the twentieth century. She explains that in none of these cases could the revolution be accounted for without accounting for changes in state structures in relation to world events *and* class-based pressures from below in the societies.

The State as a Janus-faced Structure
Theda Skocpol (1979)

We can make sense of social-revolutionary transformations only if we take the state seriously as a macro-structure. The state properly conceived is no mere arena in

Excerpt from *States and Social Revolutions: A Comparative Analysis of France, Russia, and China* (Cambridge: Cambridge University Press, 1979), pp. 29–32. Reprinted with the permission of Cambridge University Press.

which socioeconomic struggles are fought out. It is, rather, a set of administrative, policing, and military organizations headed, and more or less well coordinated by, an executive authority. Any state first and fundamentally extracts resources from society and deploys these to create and support coercive and administrative organizations. Of course, these basic state organizations are built up and must operate within the context of class-divided socioeconomic relations, as well as within the context of national and international economic dynamics. Moreover, coercive and administrative organizations are only parts of overall political systems. These systems also may contain institutions through which social interests are represented in state policy-making as well as institutions through which nonstate actors are mobilized to participate in policy implementation. Nevertheless, the administrative and coercive organizations are the basis of state power as such.

Where they exist, these fundamental state organizations are at least potentially autonomous from direct dominant-class control. The extent to which they *actually* are autonomous, and to what effect, varies from case to case. It is worth emphasizing that the actual extent and consequences of state autonomy can only be analyzed and explained in terms specific to particular types of sociopolitical systems and to particular sets of historical international circumstances. . . . Also, the likely lines of conflict between landed dominant classes and state rulers in such agrarian states [as prerevolutionary France, Russia, and China] will be indicated. There is no need to go into this discussion now. For the purposes of the argument at hand, it is enough to note that states are potentially autonomous and to explore what distinct interests they *might* pursue.

State organizations necessarily compete to some extent with the dominant class(es) in appropriating resources from the economy and society. And the objectives to which the resources, once appropriated, are devoted may very well be at variance with existing dominant-class interests. Resources may be used to strengthen the bulk and autonomy of the state itself—something necessarily threatening to the dominant class unless the greater state power is indispensably needed and actually used to support dominant-class interests. But the use of state power to support dominant-class interests is not inevitable. Indeed, attempts of state rulers merely to perform the state's "own" functions may create conflicts of interest with the dominant class. The state normally performs two basic sets of tasks: It maintains order, and it competes with other actual or potential states. As Marxists have pointed out, states usually do function to preserve existing economic and class structures, for that is normally the smoothest way to enforce order. Nevertheless, the state has its own distinct interests vis-à-vis subordinate classes. Although both the state and the dominant class(es) share a broad interest in keeping the subordinate classes in place in society and at work in the existing economy, the state's own fundamental interest in maintaining sheer physical order and political peace may lead it—especially in periods of crisis—to enforce concessions to subordinate-class demands. These concessions may be at the expense of the interests of the dominant class, but not contrary to the state's own interests in controlling the population and collecting taxes and military recruits.

Moreover, we should not forget that states also always exist in determinant geopolitical environments, in interaction with other actual or potential states. An existing economy and class structure condition and influence a given state structure and the activities of the rulers. So, too, do geopolitical environments create tasks and opportunities for states and place limits on their capacities to cope with either external or internal tasks or crises. As the German historian Otto Hintze once wrote, two phenomena above all condition "the real organization of the state. These are, first, the structure of social classes, and second, the external ordering of the states—their position relative to each other, and their over-all position in the world." Indeed, a state's involvement in an international network of states is a basis for potential autonomy of action over and against groups and economic arrangements within its jurisdiction—even including the dominant class and existing relations of production. For international military pressures and opportunities can prompt state rulers to attempt policies that conflict with, and even in extreme instances contradict, the fundamental interests of a dominant class. State rulers may, for example, undertake military adventures abroad that drain resources from economic development at home, or that have the immediate or ultimate effect of undermining the position of dominant socioeconomic interests. And, to give a different example, rulers may respond to foreign military competition or threats of conquest by attempting to impose fundamental socioeconomic reforms or by trying to reorient the course of national economic development through state intervention. Such programs may or may not be successfully implemented. But even if they are not carried through, the sheer attempt may create a contradictory clash of interests between the state and the existing dominant class.

The perspective on the state advanced here might appropriately be labeled "organizational" and "realist." In contrast to most (especially recent) Marxist theories, this view refuses to treat states as if they were mere analytic aspects of abstractly conceived modes of production, or even political aspects of concrete class relations and struggles. Rather it insists that states are actual organizations controlling (or attempting to control) territories and people. Thus the analyst of revolutions must explore not only class relations but also relations of states to one another and relations of states to dominant and subordinate classes. For the historical cases of social revolutions to be discussed in the core chapters of this book, the analysis of old-regime contradictions and the emergence of revolutionary crises will center especially upon the relationships of states to military competitors abroad and to dominant classes and existing socioeconomic structures at home. And the analysis of the emergence and structure of new regimes will focus especially on the relationships of state-building revolutionary movements to international circumstances and to those subordinate classes, invariably including the peasantry, who were key insurrectionary participants in the conflicts of the revolutions. The state organizations of both old and new regimes will have a more central and autonomous place in the analysis than they would in a straightforward Marxist explanation.

Yet not only does an organizational, realist perspective on the state entail differences from Marxist approaches, it also contrasts with non-Marxist approaches that treat the *legitimacy* of political authorities as an important explanatory concept. If state organizations cope with whatever tasks they already claim smoothly and efficiently, legitimacy—either in the sense of moral approval or in the probably much more usual sense of sheer acceptance of the status quo—will probably be accorded to the state's form and rulers by most groups in society. In any event, what matters most is always the support or acquiescence not of the popular majority of society but of the politically powerful and mobilized groups, invariably including the regime's own cadres. Loss of legitimacy, especially among these crucial groups, tends to ensue with a vengeance if and when (for reasons that are always open to sociological and historical explanation) the state fails consistently to cope with existing tasks, or proves unable to cope with new tasks suddenly thrust upon it by crisis circumstances. Even after great loss of legitimacy has occurred, a state can remain quite stable—and certainly invulnerable to internal mass-based revolts—especially if its coercive organizations remain coherent and effective. Consequently, the structure of those organizations, their place within the state apparatus as a whole, and their linkages to class forces and to politically mobilized groups in society are all important issues for the analyst of states in revolutionary situations, actual or potential. Such an analytic focus seems certain to prove more fruitful than any focus primarily or exclusively upon political legitimation. The ebbing of a regime's legitimacy in the eyes of its own cadres and other politically powerful groups may figure as a mediating variable in an analysis of regime breakdown. But the basic causes will be found in the structure and capacities of state organizations, as these are conditioned by developments in the economy and class structure and also by developments in the international situation.

The state, in short, is fundamentally Janus-faced, with an intrinsically dual anchorage in class-divided socioeconomic structures and an international system of states. If our aim is to understand the breakdown and building-up of state organizations in revolutions, we must look not only at the activities of social groups. We must also focus upon the points of intersection between international conditions and pressures, on the one hand, and class-structured economies and politically organized interests, on the other hand. State executives and their followers will be found maneuvering to extract resources and build administrative and coercive organizations precisely at this intersection. Here, consequently, is the place to look for the political contradictions that help launch social revolutions. Here, also, will be found the forces that shape the rebuilding of state organizations within social-revolutionary crises.❖

Christopher Lasch (1932–1994) was born in Omaha. He studied at Harvard (B.A., 1954), then Columbia (Ph.D., 1961). He taught at Bard, Hobart, and Williams colleges and Roosevelt, Iowa, and Northwestern universities. From 1979 until his death in 1994, Lasch taught at the University of Rochester. His books included *The Culture of Narcissism* (1979), which attracted considerable attention from many people, including U.S. President Jimmy Carter. He also wrote *True and Only Heaven* (1991), *Minimal Self* (1984), and *Haven in a Heartless World* (1977), the source of the following selection. The book as a whole diagnosed the extreme pressure put on family life in American society. "The Moynihan Report: Rethinking Family" both summarizes the original report and the reaction to it and frames the debate in relation to larger issues of family in American life.

The Moynihan Report: Rethinking Family

Christopher Lasch (1977)

Recent studies of the black family show, more clearly than any other example, the disintegrating impact on the family of a dangerous social environment, in which the struggle to survive creates an atmosphere of chronic antagonism, and friendship, love, and marriage are sustained only with great difficulty.

Excerpt from *Haven in a Heartless World: The Family Besieged* (New York: Basic Books, 1977), pp. 157–166. Copyright 1978 by Basic Books, Inc. Reprinted by permission of Basic Books, a division of HarperCollins Publishers, Inc.

The sociology of the black family, because it touches so many sensitive issues, has given rise to bitter debates, especially since the publication of the Moynihan Report, widely accused of diverting attention from racism and poverty to the false issue of the "matriarchal" family. In March 1965, the U.S. Department of Labor sent to President Johnson and a few of his advisers a seventy-five-page report, "The Negro Family: The Case for National Action." The anonymous author of this document, Daniel Patrick Moynihan, personified the union of social science and federal policy. A political scientist with a special interest in urban sociology, Moynihan went to Washington in the great influx of intellectuals in 1961. Like other New Frontiersmen, he seems to have shared John F. Kennedy's belief that the complicated problems of modern government defied the understanding of the ordinary citizen. Just as the makers of American foreign policy sought to base decisions on systems analysis and game theory, so Moynihan proposed to recast the race problem, the central domestic issue of the sixties, in the light of academic social science. His report drew on the work of E. Franklin Frazier, Frank Tannenbaum, Stanley Elkins, and other scholars, summarizing a long tradition of inquiry into the peculiarly debilitating effects of American Negro slavery. It also drew on a long tradition of social work, according to which social pathology originates in "broken homes."

Brimming with graphs, charts, and tables, the Moynihan Report argued that "the Negro family in the urban ghettos is crumbling" and that the "deterioration" of the family is "the fundamental source of the weakness of the Negro community at the present time." Even the removal of arbitrary forms of discrimination would not promote racial equality, according to Moynihan, so long as weaknesses in the structure of ghetto life prevented blacks from taking advantage of their new opportunities. Poverty had forced the ghetto into a matriarchal and highly unstable pattern of family life, which, perpetuating itself over the generations, gave rise to a complicated "tangle of pathology." For reasons that Moynihan did not explore, "Negro children without fathers flounder—and fail." Statistical correlations appeared to connect juvenile delinquency, crime, academic failure, and the "inability to delay gratification" with fatherless or otherwise "disorganized" homes. Although patrifocal families "presumably" enjoyed no intrinsic advantage over "matriarchal" families, "it is clearly a disadvantage"—for reasons, once again, that Moynihan failed to clarify—"for a minority group to be operating on one principle, while the great majority . . . is operating on another." The federal government should therefore make it an object of policy to bring Negro family patterns into harmony with the dominant pattern: "to strengthen the Negro family so as to enable it to raise and support its members as do other families."

The Moynihan Report exemplified the medicalization of politics: it was this above all that stamped it as a typical product of academic social science. Moynihan did not ignore the effects of poverty and racism, as his critics unfairly charged; nor did he argue that broken homes "caused" poverty. His insistence on the "pathology" of the matrifocal family, however, left the impression that the problem, whatever it was, required some form of therapeutic intervention. Herbert Gans feared that the Moynihan Report would "lead to a clamor for pseudo-psychiatric programs that attempt to change the Negro family through counseling and other therapeutic methods." But the point is not that Moynihan proposed to substitute therapy for social action, or in the words of another critic, that he thought "it's the individual's fault when it's the damned system that really needs changing," but rather that Moynihan saw the "system" itself as an organism understood only by social pathologists and proceeded to redefine social action as a form of therapy by its very nature. Thus the struggle for racial equality—which now had to take precedence, in Moynihan's view, over struggles for political freedom or a mere equality of opportunity—had to be waged not by the victims of racial inequality but by the federal government: this was the underlying import of his analysis. He sought to channel the ghetto revolt into acceptable forms and to bring it under federal leadership, and his interpretation of its origins— a diagnosis of ghetto "pathology" that would enable the right kind of doctors to cure it—admirably suited that end.

In singling out the family for special emphasis, however, Moynihan by no means diverted attention from the "real issue," as his critics charged. On the contrary, he addressed a central problem in the black revolt, addressed in quite different language by the Black Muslims and later by the advocates of Black Power: the restoration of black manhood. In effect, Moynihan proposed to forestall more radical solutions of this problem, in which a militant and deliberately exaggerated male chauvinism supported other forms of militancy, with a program of federal intervention designed, in the words of President Johnson at Howard University, "to strengthen the family, to create conditions under which most parents will stay together."

Unfortunately for Moynihan, the intensification of racial conflict after the Watts riot made his report a convenient target of radicals and would-be radicals. His critics misrepresented Moynihan's views, often in a thoroughly opportunistic fashion, while leaving uncriticized his overriding concern with health and disease. Indeed they adopted his medical imagery as their own. "What may seem to be a disease to the white middle class," wrote Bayard Rustin of the matrifocal family, "may be a healthy adaptation to the Negro lower class."

Moynihan's opponents pursued one or another of two strategies, both of which disclose widely held misconceptions about the family and its significance—the only reason for rehearsing a controversy so devoid of intellectual merit on either side. The first strategy denied the importance of the family altogether, reducing the plight of the ghetto to purely economic oppression or to "white racism." Poverty and racism, not the family, determined the structure of ghetto life, according to this view, whereas Moynihan's emphasis on the family encouraged the illusion that "the weaknesses and defects of the Negro himself . . . account for the present status of inequality between Negro and white." Laura Carper, after announcing that she was "not prepared to argue an economic determinist thesis," argued precisely that poverty, not the matriarchal organization of the family, explained the Negro's lack of social progress.

Such interpretations ignore the family's mediation between social conditions and individual experience. Few would deny that social conditions shape the structure of the family, but the family in turn shapes the individual's perceptions of the world and the psychic mechanisms by means of which he attempts to deal with it. Poverty is undoubtedly the overriding fact of ghetto life, and all interpreters of the ghetto family agree that its special characteristics originate in the father's inability to support his household. Nevertheless, the growing child experiences poverty through the intermediary of his parents, and the quality of that mediation unavoidably influences his psychic development. Although the blacks of the ghetto subscribe to a middle-class norm of marriage in which the husband "oughta be out makin' a livin'" while his wife stays home with the children, they find it impossible to sustain this ideal in the face of poverty. The male, unable to find steady work, often leaves his family for the more agreeable, easygoing society of his peers. Even when he stays at home, he hesitates to make an emotional investment in relations in which he is almost certain to fail.

Even when both father and mother are present, black parents find it difficult to insulate their children against the dangers and temptations of the street. Parents complain that children "see too much" and become prematurely wise to the ways of the world. Children then use this knowledge to negotiate their independence from parents. At first, when children are young, parents seek to imprison them in the house, but as these efforts inevitably fail, the parents become resigned to their own lack of influence. The sense of impotence further undermines their attempt to teach the child what he needs to know in order to master his surroundings. Elders retreat from painful confrontations by not enforcing their own standards on the young. The child learns to fend for himself and to get what he wants by manipulating, seducing, or exploiting the emotions of others. He perfects what Lee Rainwater calls an expressive style of adaptation, which depends on skill in social interaction, "competitive self-enhancement," and "dramatic self-presentation." He learns to get what he wants by taking it rather than by waiting for what he is entitled to receive.

These strategies ensure survival but at the same time perpetuate the victimization of blacks by other blacks. Although the ghetto subculture—an amalgam of middle-class norms and situational responses to poverty and exploitation—serves the black community as a means of coping with everyday hardships, it also contributes in its own right to the harsh and oppressive quality of the environment. The family and other agencies of socialization toughen the young, but in doing so they not only disable the young for life in other surroundings but prevent them from mastering, instead of being mastered by, their own. Those who argue that study of the black family diverts attention from poverty and racism fail to notice the ways in which poverty and racism reverberate in every area of life, embedding themselves in cultural patterns and personality and thus perpetuating themselves from one generation to the next. The view that presents itself as clear-sighted realism about the economic basis of culture closes its eyes to the very desperation it pretends to reveal.

A second type of criticism of the Moynihan Report, instead of ignoring the family, defends the matrifocal household as a "healthy adaptation" to ghetto conditions. Herbert Gans wrote that "instability, illegitimacy, and matriarchy" may be "the most positive adaptations . . . to the conditions which most Negroes must endure." Other interpreters have reminded us that two parents in conflict make "little positive contribution to the household" and that "some women with stormy marriages behind them feel that they are better off alone."

According to Ray L. Birdwhistell, an authority much quoted by critics of the Moynihan Report, psychiatrists and other students of the family have set up a "sentimental model" of the family, a middle-class suburban norm which they try to impose on others by treating deviations from the model as pathological. Drawing on Birdwhistell's work, critics of Moynihan argue that culture-bound assumptions about the family prevent the middle-class observer from seeing that the ghetto has its own distinctive culture, which admirably serves its needs. "Divorce, illegitimacy, and female-headed households," according to Robert Staples, "are not necessarily dysfunctional except in the context of western, middle-class, white values." The black family appears "unstable" only "when judged by the white ideals of the husband-wife-child relationship-complex." Feminists condemn Moynihan for assuming that "leadership is necessarily male," Negro activists for thinking that "everyone should have a family structure like his own." Instead of recognizing that Negroes "have a culture of their own," according to one scholar, critics of the black family judge it against "the nuclear family of a generalized American culture" and judge it a failure, whereas in fact "Negro families, whether headed by males or females, provide secure groups for child raising."

The trouble with this line of argument is that blacks themselves regard the male-centered household as the most desirable form of the family. Far from upholding the matrifocal arrangement as a "healthy adaptation" or a "secure group for child raising," black mothers condemn their husbands for their failure to provide support. Indeed, they go so far as to blame this failure on laziness rather than on the unavailability of jobs. Most of the evidence supports Rainwater's conclusion that poor black people find it almost impossible to develop a sense of family solidarity. "They did not regard themselves," Rainwater writes of one St. Louis family, ". . . as a solitary unit separate from the outside world. Instead, their home territory was readily invaded by anyone who established a relationship with one of them, and the children were ready to derogate and demean other family members." The defenders of the matrifocal family, posing as critics of cultural parochialism, have unthinkingly absorbed the rising middle-class dissatisfaction with the isolated, "privatized" suburban family, a dissatisfaction that has become especially pervasive in the very suburbs in which the "sentimental model of the family" is said to originate. Claiming to have liberated themselves from the assumptions of their own class, these writers share the fashionable concern with "alternatives to the nuclear family" and project the search for alternate life-styles onto the ghetto. They idealize the matrifocal family, exaggerate the degree to which it is embedded in a rich network of kinship relations, and ignore evidence which plainly shows that blacks themselves prefer a family in which the male earns the money and the mother rears the young.

In a study of ghetto life-styles, Ulf Hannerz attacks the "sentimental model" and its Freudian underpinnings, which allegedly assume that if the father does not serve as an example to his son, the son identifies with his mother and then develops "compulsive masculinity" as a defense against effeminacy. But the concept of compulsive masculinity derives from Parsons, not from Freud, and it rests, as we have seen, on a debased version of the theory of identification—one that confuses internalization of lost love-objects with imitation of "role models." Hannerz sets up this simplified "Freudian" interpretation and then tries to refute it with a still more simpleminded interpretation of his own. The "Freudian" view, he argues, rests on "mainstream assumptions about what a man should be like." Thus a Freudian interpretation of "joning" or the "dozens"—the ritualized verbal aggression in which ghetto adolescents claim to have had sexual intercourse, under bizarre and imaginative circumstances, with the opponent's mother—would insist that "the boys have supposedly just found out that they have identified with the wrong person, the mother. Now they must do their utmost to ridicule her and thus convince everybody . . . of their masculinity." In reality, according to Hannerz, the aggressive banter of the ghetto functions as a "rite of passage" whereby adolescent boys train for the roles they will play as adults. Even without fathers, they learn masculinity from the men of the street, and verbal "motherfucking" initiates them into the culture of the grown-up world.

This interpretation fails to explain why ghetto masculinity depends to such a large degree on sexual intercourse with mothers, and why the term "motherfucker" pervades ghetto speech, both as a term of praise and as a term of contempt. The concept of compulsive masculinity at least addresses this issue, but it does so crudely and with little feeling for nuance. Indeed, the problem of "motherfucking" demonstrates more clearly than any other the inadequacy of the Parsonian theory of socialization. Far from signifying a declaration of independence from the mother, the term directs against her the aggression typically experienced by infants, an aggression associated with dependence and helpless rage. It also embodies a recognition, by no means unrealistic in a world of poverty and exploitation, that dependence is the common fate and that "the individual is not strong enough or adult enough to achieve his goal in a legitimate way, but is rather like a child, dependent on others who tolerate his childish maneuvers." The term reminds those who use it that even adult males often depend on women for support and nurture; that many of them have to "pimp" for a living, ingratiating themselves with a woman in order to pry money from her; that sexual relations thus become manipulative and predatory; and that satisfaction depends on taking what you want (fucking someone's mother) instead of earning what is rightfully yours to receive.

The premature toughness of ghetto youth, like the toughness of middle-class adolescents, conceals a deeper dependence. Detailed analysis of the psychic origins of this need would take us beyond the bounds of the present inquiry, but the failure to internalize parental authority clearly lies at the heart of the problem. The well-known distinction between "shame-cultures" and "guilt-cultures" helps to locate the culture of the ghetto, to characterize the personality structure it tends to produce, and to clarify, if only in a preliminary fashion, the psychological processes at work. Shame—the fear of ridicule and ostracism—originates in a primitive fear of the loss of nurture, whereas guilt fears the loss of parental approval and its heir, self-approval. Guilt, as Rainwater reminds us, arises only when "individuals have the opportunity to develop (in fantasy if not in reality) an orderly, predictable and loving relationship with their parents, and to regard the parents as themselves capable of living up to the norms which they proffer." In the absence of such experience, early dependence on the mother dominates later development. The immediate satisfaction of wants takes precedence over future gratifications; strategies for day-to-day survival take precedence over investments in a future that presents itself as menacing and unpredictable. Expressive styles of interaction predominate over instrumental styles. A dramatic presentation of the self helps to seduce and manipulate others, even as it undermines the capacity for sustained activity and for long-term friendships and love relations. Interpersonal intercourse, at the same time that it monopolizes attention, becomes increasingly manipulative, fragile, and precarious.

These observations describe, in a schematic and tentative fashion, the personality structure produced not just by the dangerous world of the ghetto but, increasingly, by the conditions of middle-class life as well. The real objection to the Moynihan Report is that it exaggerates the distance between the ghetto and the rest of American culture, which in some ways has come to resemble a pale copy of the black ghetto. Without minimizing the poverty of the ghetto or the suffering inflicted by whites on blacks, we can see that the increasingly dangerous and unpredictable conditions of middle-class life give rise to similar strategies for survival, a similar search for non-binding commitments, and a similar toughness (combined with an underlying dependence) in the young. Indeed, the attraction of black culture for disaffected whites suggests that it now speaks to a general condition, the most striking feature of which is a widespread loss of confidence in the future.

Middle-class "Momism," a muted version of black "matriarchy," can be understood as a product of the general deterioration of the social environment. In a dangerous world from which the family can no longer protect its members—a world, moreover, in which exploitation dominates even friendship, love, and marriage—children find it more and more difficult to form secure and loving ties to their parents. In the absence of such ties, early impressions of the mother remain the basis of personality structure. Fear of maternal abandonment underlies the frantic search for psychic survival, which has replaced the traditional virtues of work, thrift, and achievement as the essence of the bourgeois ethic. The dependence on the mother which Bateson found in schizophrenics, and which so many others have identified as a characteristic pattern in all American males (revealing itself in the cult of large breasts, a fixation on oral sex, and a tendency to regard all women as mothers)—this dependence, the key to the post-protestant personality, originates in the changes that have transformed domestic life. More precisely, it originates in the invasion of the family by the marketplace and the street, the crumbling of the walls that once provided a protected space in which to raise children, and the perversion of the most intimate relationships by the calculating, manipulative spirit that has long been ascendant in business life.❖

Nancy Chodorow (1944–) teaches at the University of California at Berkeley. She did her doctoral studies at Brandeis University at a time when its Department of Sociology's exceptional openness encouraged the early intellectual development of many of America's most important feminist sociologists. Chodorow's use of psychoanalysis and sociology is indicative of the creative and interdisciplinary approach of many academic feminists who—especially in the 1970s and 1980s—have been required, and encouraged, to work between and on the margins of the traditional disciplines. Some would say that Chodorow's *Reproduction of Mothering* (1978), apart from its important contributions to the study of gender relations, is the most successfully balanced integration of psychoanalytic and sociological perspectives to date. One need only compare Chodorow's work to, say, Erich Fromm's earlier, more programmatic essay on the two fields to get an idea of how her attempt to resolve a concrete problem—mothering—has led to a more complex use of ideas from both sides. Some consider Chodorow's argument a standpoint feminism. In this respect, her work is often compared to Carol Gilligan's *In a Different Voice*. Because the selection summarizes the key theoretical points in the argument, readers can judge this for themselves. In any case, *Reproduction of Mothering* is a classic text for contemporary feminist theory, as well as for the sociology of gender relations and family. Chodorow is also the author of *Feminism and Psychoanalytic Theory* (1989).

Gender Personality and the Reproduction of Mothering

Nancy Chodorow (1978)

In spite of the apparently close tie between women's capacities for childbearing and lactation on the one hand and their responsibilities for child care on the other, and in spite of the probable prehistoric convenience (and perhaps survival necessity) of a sexual division of labor in which women mothered, biology and instinct do not

Excerpt from *Reproduction of Mothering: Psychoanalysis and the Sociology of Gender* (Berkeley, Calif.: University of California Press, 1978), pp. 205–209. Reprinted by permission of the Regents of the University of California and the University of California Press.

provide adequate explanations for how women come to mother. Women's mothering as a feature of social structure requires an explanation in terms of social structure. Conventional feminist and social psychological explanations for the genesis of gender roles—girls and boys are "taught" appropriate behaviors and "learn" appropriate feelings—are insufficient both empirically and methodologically to account for how women become mothers.

Methodologically, socialization theories rely inappropriately on individual intention. Ongoing social structures include the means for their own reproduction—in the regularized repetition of social processes, in the perpetuation of conditions which require members' participation, in the genesis of legitimating ideologies and institutions, and in the psychological as well as physical reproduction of people to perform necessary roles. Accounts of socialization help to explain the perpetuation of ideologies about gender roles. However, notions of appropriate behavior, like coercion, cannot in themselves produce parenting. Psychological capacities and a particular object-relational stance are central and definitional to parenting in a way that they are not to many other roles and activities.

Women's mothering includes the capacities for its own reproduction. This reproduction consists in the production of women with, and men without, the particular psychological capacities and stance which go into primary parenting. Psychoanalytic theory provides us with a theory of social reproduction that explains major features of personality development and the development of psychic structure, and the differential development of gender personality in particular. Psychoanalysts argue that personality both results from and consists in the ways a child appropriates, internalizes, and organizes early experiences in their family—from the fantasies they have, the defenses they use, the ways they channel and redirect drives in this object-relational context. A person subsequently imposes this intrapsychic structure, and the fantasies, defenses, and relational modes and preoccupations which go with it, onto external social situations. This reexternalization (or mutual reexternalization) is a major constituting feature of social and interpersonal situations themselves.

Psychoanalysis, however, has not had an adequate theory of the reproduction of mothering. Because of the teleological assumption that anatomy is destiny, and that women's destiny includes primary parenting, the ontogenesis of women's mothering has been largely ignored, even while the genesis of a wide variety of related disturbances and problems has been accorded widespread clinical attention. Most psychoanalysts agree that the basis for parenting is laid for both genders in the early relationship to a primary caretaker. Beyond that, in order to explain why *women* mother, they tend to rely on vague notions of a girl's subsequent identification with her mother, which makes her and not her brother a primary parent, or on an unspecified and uninvestigated innate femaleness in girls, or on logical leaps from lactation or early vaginal sensations to caretaking abilities and commitments.

The psychoanalytic account of male and female development, when reinterpreted, gives us a developmental theory of the reproduction of women's mothering. Women's mothering reproduces itself through differing object-relational experiences and differing psychic outcomes in women and men. As a result of having been parented by a woman, women are more likely than men to seek to be mothers, that is, to relocate themselves in a primary mother-child relationship, to get gratification from the mothering relationship, and to have psychological and relational capacities for mothering.

The early relation to a primary caretaker provides in children of both genders both the basic capacity to participate in a relationship with the features of the early parent-child one, and the desire to create this intimacy. However, because women mother, the early experience and preoedipal relationship differ for boys and girls. Girls retain more concern with early childhood issues in relation to their mother, and a sense of self involved with these issues. Their attachments therefore retain more preoedipal aspects. The greater length and different nature of their preoedipal experience, and their continuing preoccupation with the issues of this period, mean that women's sense of self is continuous with others and that they retain capacities for primary identification, both of which enable them to experience the empathy and lack of reality sense needed by a cared-for infant. In men, these qualities have been curtailed, both because they are early treated as an opposite by their mother and because their later attachment to her must be repressed. The relational basis for mothering is thus extended in women, and inhibited in men, who experience themselves as more separate and distinct from others.

The different structure of the feminine and masculine oedipal triangle and process of oedipal experience that results from women's mothering contributes further to gender personality differentiation and the reproduction of women's mothering. As a result of this experience, women's inner object world, and the affects and issues associated with it, are more actively sustained and more complex than men's. This means that women define and experience themselves relationally. Their heterosexual orientation is always in internal dialogue with both oedipal and preoedipal mother-child relational issues. Thus, women's heterosexuality is triangular and requires a third person—a child—for its structural and emotional completion. For men, by contrast, the heterosexual relationship alone recreates the early bond to their mother; a child interrupts it. Men, moreover, do not define themselves in relationship and have come to suppress relational capacities and repress relational needs. This prepares them to participate in the affect-denying world of alienated work, but not to fulfill women's needs for intimacy and primary relationships.

The oedipus complex, as it emerges from the asymmetrical organization of parenting, secures a psychological taboo on parent-child incest and pushes boys and girls in the direction of extrafamilial heterosexual relationships. This is one step toward the reproduction of parenting. The creation and maintenance of the incest taboo and of heterosexuality in girls and boys are different, however. For boys, superego formation and identification with their father, rewarded by the superiority of masculinity, maintain the taboo on incest with their mother, while heterosexual orientation continues from their earliest love relation with her. For girls, creating them as heterosexual in the first place maintains the taboo. However, women's heterosexuality is not so exclusive as men's. This makes it easier for them to accept or seek a male substitute for their fathers. At the same time, in a male-dominant society, women's exclusive emotional heterosexuality is not so necessary, nor is her repression of love for her father. Men are more likely to initiate relationships, and women's economic dependence on men pushes them anyway into heterosexual marriage.

Male dominance in heterosexual couples and marriage solves the problem of women's lack of heterosexual commitment and lack of satisfaction by making women more reactive in the sexual bonding process. At the same time, contradictions in heterosexuality help to perpetuate families and parenting by ensuring that women will seek relations to children and will not find heterosexual relationships alone satisfactory. Thus, men's lack of emotional availability and women's less exclusive heterosexual commitment help ensure women's mothering.

Women's mothering, then, produces psychological self-definition and capacities appropriate to mothering in women, and curtails and inhibits these capacities and this self-definition in men. The early experience of being cared for by a woman produces a fundamental structure of expectations in women and men concerning mothers' lack of separate interests from their infants and total concern for their infants' welfare. Daughters grow up identifying with these mothers, about whom they have such expectations. This set of expectations is generalized to the assumption that women naturally take care of children of all ages and the belief that women's "maternal" qualities can and should be extended to the nonmothering work that they do. All these results of women's mothering have ensured that women will mother infants and will take continuing responsibility for children.

The reproduction of women's mothering is the basis for the reproduction of women's location and responsibilities in the domestic sphere. This mothering, and its generalization to women's structural location in the domestic sphere, links the contemporary social organization of gender and social organization of production and contributes to the reproduction of each. That women mother is a fundamental organizational feature of the sex-gender system: It is basic to the sexual division of labor and generates a psychology and ideology of male dominance as well as an ideology about women's capacities and nature. Women, as wives and mothers, contribute as well to the daily and generational reproduction, both physical and psychological, of male workers and thus to the reproduction of capitalist production.

Women's mothering also reproduces the family as it is constituted in male-dominated society. The sexual and familial division of labor in which women mother creates a sexual division of psychic organization and orientation. It produces socially gendered women and men who enter into asymmetrical heterosexual relationships; it produces men who react to, fear, and act superior to women, and who put most of their energies into the nonfamilial work world and do not parent. Finally, it produces women who turn their energies toward nurturing and caring for children—in turn reproducing the sexual and familial division of labor in which women mother.

Social reproduction is thus asymmetrical. Women in their domestic role reproduce men and children physically, psychologically, and emotionally. Women in their domestic role as houseworkers reconstitute themselves physically on a daily basis and reproduce themselves as mothers, emotionally and psychologically, in the next generation. They thus contribute to the perpetuation of their own social roles and position in the hierarchy of gender.

Institutionalized features of family structure and the social relations of reproduction reproduce themselves. A psychoanalytic investigation shows that women's mothering capacities and commitments, and the general psychological capacities and wants which are the basis of women's emotional work, are built developmentally into feminine personality. Because women are themselves mothered by women, they grow up with the relational capacities and needs, and psychological definition of self-in-relationship, which commits them to mothering. Men, because they are mothered by women, do not. Women mother daughters who, when they become women, mother.❖

❖ Breaking with Modernity ❖

Jacques Derrida (1930–) was born in Algiers. He studied in Paris at the École Normale Supérieure and at Harvard (1956–1957). From 1960 to 1964, he taught at the Sorbonne. The following year, he became professor of the history of philosophy at the École Normale Supérieure. Derrida has lectured and taught around the world and is particularly well regarded in the United States, where he has held irregular professorships at Yale, Johns Hopkins, New York University, and the University of California at Irvine. Derrida's many writings include *Speech and Phenomena and Other Essays on Husserl's Theory of Signs, Writing and Difference,* and *Of Grammatology*—all three appeared in France in 1967, the year following his famous 1966 presentation at Johns Hopkins, "Structure, Sign and Play in the Discourse of the Human Sciences." He has written many books since, but these were the texts in which the first and clearest outlines of deconstructionism appeared. The 1966 paper, from which the selection is taken, is sometimes considered, in retrospect, the event Derrida referred to in the work's first sentence—an event in the history of structuralism, the beginning of poststructuralism; an event in the history of world structures. Given his clear critique of the philosophy of the Center, it is unlikely that he meant that he himself caused this event. Even if he did, that is not the point. Deconstructionism concerns itself with problems of this sort.

The Decentering Event in Social Thought
Jacques Derrida (1966)

Perhaps something has occurred in the history of the concept of structure that could be called an "event," if this loaded word did not entail a meaning which it is precisely the function of structural—or structuralist—thought to reduce or to suspect. Let us speak of an "event," nevertheless, and let us use quotation marks to serve as a precaution. What would this event be then? Its exterior form would be that of a *rupture* and a redoubling.

It would be easy enough to show that the concept of structure and even the word "structure" itself are as old as the *epistémé*—that is to say, as old as Western science and Western philosophy—and that their roots thrust deep into the soil of ordinary language, into whose deepest recesses the *epistémé* plunges in order to gather them up and to make them part of itself in a metaphorical displacement. Nevertheless, up

---

Excerpt from "Structure, Sign and Play in the Discourse of the Human Sciences," Alan Bass, trans., *Writing and Difference* (Chicago: University of Chicago Press, 1978 [1966]), pp. 278–282.

to the event which I wish to mark out and define, structure—or rather the structurality of structure—although it has always been at work, has always been neutralized or reduced, and this by a process of giving it a center or of referring it to a point of presence, a fixed origin. The function of this center was not only to orient, balance, and organize the structure—one cannot in fact conceive of an unorganized structure—but above all to make sure that the organizing principle of the structure would limit what we might call the play of the structure. By orienting and organizing the coherence of the system, the center of a structure permits the play of its elements inside the total form. And even today the notion of a structure lacking any center represents the unthinkable itself.

Nevertheless, the center also closes off the play which it opens up and makes possible. As center, it is the point at which the substitution of contents, elements, or terms is no longer possible. At the center, the permutation or the transformation of elements (which may of course be structures enclosed within a structure) is forbidden. At least this permutation has always remained *interdicted* (and I am using this word deliberately). Thus it has always been thought that the center, which is by definition unique, constituted that very thing within a structure which while governing the structure, escapes structurality. This is why classical thought concerning structure could say that the center is, paradoxically, *within* the structure and *outside it.* The center is at the center of the totality, and yet, since the center does not belong to the totality (is not part of the totality), the totality *has its center elsewhere.* The center is not the center. The concept of centered structure—although it represents coherence itself, the condition of the *epistémé* as philosophy or science—is contradictorily coherent. And as always, coherence in contradiction expresses the force of a desire. The concept of centered structure is in fact the concept of a play based on a fundamental ground, a play constituted on the basis of a fundamental immobility and a reassuring certitude, which itself is beyond the reach of play. And on the basis of this certitude anxiety can be mastered, for anxiety is invariably the result of a certain mode of being implicated in the game, of being caught by the game, of being as it were at stake in the game from the outset. And again on the basis of what we call the center (and which, because it can be either inside or outside, can also indifferently be called the origin or end, *arché* or telos), repetitions, substitutions, transformations, and permutations are always taken from a history of meaning [sens]—that is, in a word, a history—whose origin may always be reawakened or whose end may always be anticipated in the form of presence. This is why one perhaps could say that the movement of any archaeology, like that of any eschatology, is an accomplice of this reduction of the structurality of structure and always attempts to conceive of structure on the basis of a full presence which is beyond play.

If this is so, the entire history of the concept of structure, before the rupture of which we are speaking, must be thought of as a series of substitutions of center for center, as a linked chain of determinations of the center. Successively, and in a regulated fashion, the center receives different forms or names. The history of metaphysics, like the history of the West, is the history of these metaphors and metonymies. Its matrix—if you will pardon me for demonstrating so little and for being so elliptical in order to come more quickly to my principal theme—is the determination of Being as *presence* in all senses of this word. It could be shown that all the names related to fundamentals, to principles, or to the center have always designated an invariable presence—*eidos, arché, telos, energeia, ousia* (essence, existence, substance, subject) *alétheia,* transcendentality, consciousness, God, man, and so forth.

The event I called a rupture, the disruption I alluded to at the beginning of this paper, presumably would have come about when the structurality of structure had to begin to be thought, that is to say, repeated, and this is why I said that this disruption was repetition in every sense of the word. Henceforth, it became necessary to think both the law which somehow governed the desire for a center in the constitution of structure, and the process of signification which orders the displacements and substitutions for this law of central presence—but a central presence which has never been itself, has always already been exiled from itself into its own substitute. The substitute does not substitute itself for anything which has somehow existed before it. Henceforth, it was necessary to begin thinking that there was no center, that the center could not be thought in the form of a present-being, that the center had no natural site, that it was not a fixed locus but a function, a sort of nonlocus in which an infinite number of sign-substitutions came into play. This was the moment when language invaded the universal problematic, the moment when, in the absence of a center or origin, everything became discourse—provided we can agree on this word—that is to say, a system in which the central signified, the original or transcendental signified, is never absolutely present outside a system of differences. The absence of the transcendental signified extends the domain and the play of signification infinitely.

Where and how does this decentering, this thinking the structurality of structure, occur? It would be somewhat naive to refer to an event, a doctrine, or an author in order to designate this occurrence. It is no doubt part of the totality of an era, our own, but still it has always already begun to proclaim itself and begun to *work*. Nevertheless, if we wished to choose several "names," as indications only, and to recall those authors in whose discourse this occurrence has kept most closely to its most radical formulation, we doubtless would have to cite the Nietzschean critique of metaphysics, the critique of the concepts of Being and truth, for which were substituted the concepts of play, interpretation, and sign (sign without present truth); the Freudian critique of self-presence, that is, the critique of consciousness, of the subject, of self-identity and of self-proximity or self-possession; and, more radically, the Heideggerean destruction of metaphysics, of onto-theology, of the determination of Being as presence. But all these destructive discourses and all their analogues are trapped in a kind of circle. This circle is unique. It describes the form of the relation between the history of metaphysics and the destruction of the history of metaphysics. There is no sense in doing without the concepts of metaphysics in order to shake metaphysics. We have no language—no syntax and no lexicon—which is foreign to this history; we can pronounce not a single destructive proposition which has not already had to slip into the form, the logic, and the implicit postulations of precisely what it seeks to contest. To take one example from many: the metaphysics of presence is shaken with the help of the concept of *sign*. But, as I suggested a moment ago, as soon as one seeks to demonstrate in this way that there is no transcendental or privileged signified and that the domain or play of signification henceforth has no limit, one must reject even the concept and word "sign" itself—which is precisely what cannot be done. For the signification "sign" has always been understood and determined, in its meaning, as sign-of, a signifier referring to a signified, a signifier different from its signified. If one erases the radical difference between signifier and signified, it is the word "signifier" itself which must be abandoned as a metaphysical concept. When Lévi-Strauss says in the preface to *The Raw and the Cooked* that he has "sought to transcend the opposition between the sensible and the intelligible by operating from the outset at the level of signs," the necessity, force, and legitimacy of his act cannot make us forget that the concept of the sign cannot in itself surpass this opposition between the sensible and the intelligible. The concept of the sign, in each of its aspects, has been determined by this opposition throughout the totality of its history. It has lived only on this opposition and its system. But we cannot do without the concept of the sign, for we cannot give up this metaphysical complicity without also giving up the critique we are directing against this complicity, or without the risk of erasing difference in the self-identity of a signified reducing its signifier into itself or, amounting to the same thing, simply expelling its signifier outside itself. For there are two heterogeneous ways of erasing the difference between the signifier and the signified: one, the classic way, consists in reducing or deriving the signifier, that is to say, ultimately in *submitting* the sign to thought; the other, the one we are using here against the first one, consists in putting into question the system in which the preceding reduction functioned: first and foremost, the opposition between the sensible and the intelligible. For the *paradox* is that the metaphysical reduction of the sign needed the opposition it was reducing. The opposition is systematic with the reduction. And what we are saying here about the sign can be extended to all the concepts and all the sentences of metaphysics, in particular to the discourse on "structure." But there are several ways of being caught in this circle. They are all more or less naïve, more or less empirical, more or less systematic, more or less close to the formulation—that is, to the formalization, of this circle. It is these differences which explain the multiplicity of destructive discourses and the disagreement between those who elaborate them. Nietzsche, Freud, and Heidegger, for example, worked within the inherited concepts of metaphysics. Since these concepts are not elements or atoms, and since they are taken from a syntax and a system, every particular borrowing brings along with it the whole of metaphysics. This is what allows these destroyers to destroy each other reciprocally—for example, Heidegger regarding Nietzsche, with as much lucidity and rigor as bad faith and misconstruction, as the last metaphysician, the last "Platonist." One could do the same for Heidegger himself, for Freud, or for a number of others. And today no exercise is more widespread.

What is the relevance of this formal schema when we turn to what are called the "human sciences"? One of them perhaps occupies a privileged place—ethnology. In fact one can assume that ethnology could have been born as a science only at the moment when a decentering had come about: at the moment when European culture—and, in consequence, the history of metaphysics and of its concepts—had been *dislocated,* driven from its locus, and forced to stop considering itself as the culture of reference. This moment is not first and foremost a moment of philosophical or scientific discourse. It is also a moment which is political, economic, technical, and so forth. One can say with total security that there is nothing fortuitous about the fact that the critique of ethnocentrism—the very condition for ethnology—should be systematically and historically contemporaneous with the destruction of the history of metaphysics. Both belong to one and the same era. Now, ethnology—like any science—comes about within the element of discourse. And it is primarily a European science employing traditional concepts, however much it may struggle against them. Consequently, whether he wants to or not—and this does not depend on a decision on his part—the ethnologist accepts into his discourse the premises of ethnocentrism at the very moment when he denounces them. This necessity is irreducible; it is not a historical contingency. We ought to consider all its implications very carefully. But if no one can escape this necessity, and if no one is therefore responsible for giving in to it, however little he may do so, this does not mean that all the ways of giving in to it are of equal pertinence. The quality and fecundity of a discourse are perhaps measured by the critical rigor with which this relation to the history of metaphysics and to inherited concepts is thought. Here it is a question both of a critical relation to the language of the social sciences and a critical responsibility of the discourse itself. It is a question of explicitly and systematically posing the problem of the status of a discourse which borrows from a heritage the resources necessary for the deconstruction of that heritage itself. A problem of *economy* and *strategy.*❖

Michel Foucault (1926–1984) was born in Poitiers and studied at the École Normale Supérieure, where Louis Althusser was one of his teachers. He completed his state doctorate in 1960. Foucault lived and worked outside France—in Uppsala, Warsaw, and Hamburg early in his career—and was a frequent visitor to the United States (particularly Berkeley) in his later years. From 1964 to 1968, he was head of the Department of Philosophy at the University of Clermont-Ferrand. He was on the faculty at Vincennes in Paris during the events of 1968. Foucault became professor of history and systems of thought at the Collège de France in 1970; the selection is from his inaugural address there. Foucault's first writings were on mental illness and madness in Western history. *Madness and Civilization* is the English version of his French work *Folie et deraison* (1961). Other books include *Birth of the Clinic* (1963), *The Order of Things* (1966), *The Archaeology of Knowledge* (1971), *Discipline and Punish* (1975), and the series of historical studies of sexuality written at the end of his life. The inaugural address (published with *Archaeology* in the American edition) is a broad theoretical statement, one of the very few Foucault made. After 1970, he returned to specific historical studies, each with an evident political concern. His studies of sexuality are considered important contributions to current social theories of sexuality. Foucault died of AIDS in 1984.

Discourse on the West

Michel Foucault (1971)

Here, I would like to recount a little story so beautiful I fear it may well be true. It encompasses all the constraints of discourse: those limiting its powers, those controlling its chance appearances and those which select from among speaking subjects. At the beginning of the seventeenth century, the Shogun heard tell of European superiority in navigation, commerce, politics and the military arts, and that this was due to their knowledge of mathematics. He wanted to obtain this precious knowledge. When someone told him of an English sailor possessed of this marvelous discourse, he summoned him to his palace and kept him there. The Shogun took lessons from the mariner in private and familiarised himself with mathematics,

---

Excerpt from "Discourse on Language," Rupert Swyer, trans., *The Archaeology of Knowledge* (New York: Pantheon Books, 1972), pp. 225–229. Copyright 1971 by Éditions Gallimard. English translation copyright 1972 by Tavistock Publications Limited. Reprinted by permission of Georges Borchardt, Inc.

after which he retained power and lived to a very old age. It was not until the nine-teenth century that there were *Japanese* mathematicians. But that is not the end of the anecdote, for it has its European aspect as well. The story has it that the English sailor, Will Adams, was a carpenter and an autodidact. Having worked in a shipyard he had learnt geometry. Can we see in this narrative the expression of one of the great myths of European culture? To the monopolistic, secret knowledge of oriental tyranny, Europe opposed the universal communication of knowledge and the infi-nitely free exchange of discourse.

This notion does not, in fact, stand up to close examination. Exchange and com-munication are positive forces at play within complex but restrictive systems; it is probable that they cannot operate independently of these. The most superficial and obvious of these restrictive systems is constituted by what we collectively refer to as ritual; ritual defines the qualifications required of the speaker (of who in dialogue, interrogation or recitation, should occupy which position and formulate which type of utterance); it lays down gestures to be made, behaviour, circumstances and the whole range of signs that must accompany discourse; finally, it lays down the sup-posed, or imposed significance of the words used, their effect upon those to whom they are addressed, the limitations of their constraining validity. Religious discourse, juridical and therapeutic as well as, in some ways, political discourse are all barely dissociable from the functioning of a ritual that determines the individual proper-ties and agreed roles of the speakers.

A rather different function is filled by 'fellowships of discourse', whose function is to preserve or to reproduce discourse, but in order that it should circulate within a closed community, according to strict regulations, without those in possession being dispossessed by this very distribution. An archaic model of this would be those groups of Rhapsodists, possessing knowledge of poems to recite or, even, upon which to work variations and transformations. But though the ultimate object of this knowledge was ritual recitation, it was protected and preserved within a deter-minate group, by the, often extremely complex, exercises of memory implied by such a process. Apprenticeship gained access both to a group and to a secret which recitation made manifest, but did not divulge. The roles of speaking and listening were not interchangeable.

Few such 'fellowships of discourse' remain, with their ambiguous interplay of se-crecy and disclosure. But do not be deceived; even in true discourse, even in the or-der of published discourse, free from all ritual, we still find secret-appropriation and non-interchangeability at work. It could even be that the act of writing, as it is insti-tutionalised today, with its books, its publishing system and the personality of the writer, occurs within a diffuse, yet constraining, 'fellowship of discourse'. The sepa-rateness of the writer, continually opposed to the activity of all other writing and speaking subjects, the intransitive character he lends to his discourse, the fundamen-tal singularity he has long accorded to 'writing', the affirmed dissymmetry between 'creation' and any use of linguistic systems—all this manifests in its formulation (and tends moreover to accompany the interplay of these factors in practice) the ex-istence of a certain 'fellowship of discourse'. But there are many others, functioning according to entirely different schemas of exclusivity and disclosure: one has only to think of technical and scientific secrets, of the forms of diffusion and circulation in medical discourse, of those who have appropriated economic or political discourse.

At first sight, 'doctrine' (religious, political, philosophical) would seem to consti-tute the very reverse of a 'fellowship of discourse'; for among the latter, the number of speakers were, if not fixed, at least limited, and it was among this number that discourse was allowed to circulate and be transmitted. Doctrine, on the other hand, tends to diffusion: in the holding in common of a single ensemble of discourse that individuals, as many as you wish, could define their reciprocal allegiance. In appearance, the sole requisite is the recognition of the same truths and the acceptance of a certain rule—more or less flexible—of conformity with validated discourse. If it were a question of just that, doctrines would barely be any different from scientific disciplines, and discursive control would bear merely on the form or content of what was uttered, and not on the speaker. Doctrinal adherence, however, involves both speaker and the spoken, the one through the other. The speaking subject is involved through, and as a result of, the spoken, as is demonstrated by the rules of exclusion and the rejection mechanism brought into play when a speaker formulates one, or many, inassimilable utterances; questions of heresy and unorthodoxy in no way arise out of fanatical exaggeration of doctrinal mechanisms; they are a fundamental part of them. But conversely, doctrine involves the utterances of speakers in the sense that doctrine is, permanently, the sign, the manifestation and the instrument of a prior adherence—adherence to a class, to a social or racial status, to a nationality or an interest, to a struggle, a revolt, resistance or acceptance. Doctrine links individuals to certain types of utterance while consequently barring them from all others. Doctrine effects a dual subjection, that of speaking subjects to discourse, and that of discourse to the group, at least virtually, of speakers.

Finally, on a much broader scale, we have to recognize the great cleavages in what one might call the social appropriation of discourse. Education may well be, as of right, the instrument whereby every individual, in a society like our own, can gain access to any kind of discourse. But we well know that in its distribution, in what it permits and in what it prevents, it follows the well-trodden battle-lines of social conflict. Every educational system is a political means of maintaining or of modifying the appropriation of discourse, with the knowledge and the powers it carries with it.

I am well aware of the abstraction I am performing when I separate, as I have just done, verbal rituals, 'fellowships of discourse', doctrinal groups and social appropriation. Most of the time they are linked together, constituting great edifices that distribute speakers among the different types of discourse, and which appropriate those types of discourse to certain categories of subject. In a word, let us say that these are the main rules for the subjection of discourse. What is an educational system, after all, if not a ritualisation of the word; if not a qualification of some fixing of roles for speakers; if not the constitution of a (diffuse) doctrinal group; if not a distribution and an appropriation of discourse, with all its learning and its powers? What is 'writing' (that of 'writers') if not a similar form of subjection, perhaps taking rather different forms, but whose main stresses are nonetheless analogous? May we not also say that the judicial system, as well as institutionalised medicine, constitute similar systems for the subjection of discourse?

I wonder whether a certain number of philosophical themes have not come to conform to this activity of limitation and exclusion and perhaps even to reinforce it.

They conform, first of all, by proposing an ideal truth as a law of discourse, and an immanent rationality as the principle of their behaviour. They accompany, too, an ethic of knowledge, promising truth only to the desire for truth itself and the power to think it.

They then go on to reinforce this activity by denying the specific reality of discourse in general.

Ever since the exclusion of the activity and commerce of the sophists, ever since their paradoxes were muzzled, more or less securely, it would seem that Western thought has seen to it that discourse be permitted as little room as possible between thought and words. It would appear to have ensured that *to discourse* should appear merely as a certain interjection between speaking and thinking; that it should constitute thought, clad in its signs and rendered visible by words or, conversely, that the structures of language themselves should be brought into play, producing a certain effect of meaning.

This very ancient elision of the reality of discourse in philosophical thought has taken many forms in the course of history. We have seen it quite recently in the guise of many themes now familiar to us.

It seems to me that the theme of the founding subject permits us to elide the reality of discourse. The task of the founding subject is to animate the empty forms of language with his objectives; through the thickness and inertia of empty things, he grasps intuitively the meanings lying within them. Beyond time, he indicates the field of meanings—leaving history to make them explicit—in which propositions, sciences, and deductive ensembles ultimately find their foundation. In this relationship with meaning, the founding subject has signs, marks, tracks, letters at his disposal. But he does not need to demonstrate these passing through the singular instance of discourse.

The opposing theme, that of originating experience, plays an analogous role. This asserts, in the case of experience, that even before it could be grasped in the form of a *cogito,* prior significations, in some ways already spoken, were circulating in the world, scattering it all about us, and from the outset made possible a sort of primitive recognition. Thus, a primary complicity with the world founds, for us, a possibility of speaking of experience, in it, to designate and name it, to judge it and, finally, to know it in the form of truth. If there is discourse, what could it legitimately be if not a discrete reading? Things murmur meanings our language has merely to extract; from its most primitive beginnings, this language was already whispering to us of a being of which it forms the skeleton.

The theme of universal mediation is, I believe, yet another manner of eliding the reality of discourse. And this despite appearances. At first sight it would seem that, to discover the movement of a logos everywhere elevating singularities into concepts, finally enabling immediate consciousness to deploy all the rationality in the world, is certainly to place discourse at the centre of speculation. But, in truth, this logos is really only another discourse already in operation, or rather, it is things and events themselves which *insensibly* become discourse in the unfolding of the essential secrets. Discourse is no longer much more than the shimmering of a truth about to be born in its own eyes; and when all things come eventually to take the form of discourse, when everything may be said and when anything becomes an excuse for pronouncing a discourse, it will be because all things having manifested and exchanged meanings, they will then all be able to return to the silent interiority of self-consciousness.

Whether it is the philosophy of a founding subject, a philosophy of originating experience or a philosophy of universal mediation, discourse is really only an activity, of writing in the first case, of reading in the second and exchange in the third. This exchange, this writing, this reading never involve anything but signs. Discourse thus nullifies itself, in reality, in placing itself at the disposal of the signifier.

What civilization, in appearance, has shown more respect towards discourse than our own? Where has it been more and better honoured? Where have men depended more radically, apparently, upon its constraints and its universal character? But, it seems to me, a certain fear hides behind this apparent supremacy accorded, this apparent logophilia. It is as though these taboos, these barriers, thresholds and limits were deliberately disposed in order, at least partly, to master and control the great proliferation of discourse, in such a way as to relieve its richness of its most dangerous elements; to organise its disorder so as to skate round its most uncontrollable aspects. It is as though people had wanted to efface all trace of its irruption into the activity of our thought and language. There is undoubtedly in our society, and I would not be surprised to see it in others, though taking different forms and modes, a profound logophobia, a sort of dumb fear of these events, of this mass of spoken things, of everything that could possibly be violent, discontinuous, querulous, disordered even and perilous in it, of the incessant, disorderly buzzing of discourse.

If we wish—I will not say to efface this fear—but to analyse it in its conditions, its activity and its effects, I believe we must resolve ourselves to accept three decisions which our current thinking rather tends to resist, and which belong to the three groups of function I have just mentioned: to question our will to truth; to restore to discourse its character as an event; to abolish the sovereignty of the signifier.❖

C.L.R. James (1901–1989) was born in Trinidad. From a very young age, he was a voracious reader and keen observer of social life. Under British teachers in Trinidad, he mastered the style and substance of European culture, without letting it master him. Still in his twenties, James published two novels, *La Divinia Pastora* (1927) and *Triumph* (1929). At thirty-one, he moved to London, where he soon became a prominent intellectual figure in the Trotskyist movement. In this period, he wrote the play *Toussaint L'Ouverture,* based on the great Haitian revolutionary, as well as *Black Jacobins* (1938) and *World Revolution* (1937). Throughout his life thereafter, James lived and worked as a world figure—always putting himself at a principled distance from European civilization. In his writing and lecturing, he applied Marxist ideas to his vast cultural and political knowledge of Africa, America, the Caribbean, and Europe. As the selection shows, James was quick to respond to world events (the lecture on Stokely Carmichael was given when the Black Power leaders in the United States were at risk) and to frame his response in world perspective. The essay reveals James's broad appreciation of the historical roots of Black Power. Few before or since have been able to maintain James's evenhanded sense of Booker T. Washington, Du Bois, and Marcus Garvey—who were, themselves, at odds. Yet James saw Pan-African principles partly through Marxist social theory—that is, somewhat from a European perspective, somewhat as a Black Pan-Africanist. In this sense, James was in the tradition of Du Bois. He spent the last years of his life in London, where he died in 1989 just as the Socialist states of Eastern Europe were collapsing.

Black Power and Stokely

C.L.R. James (1967)

Black Power. I believe that this slogan is destined to become one of the great political slogans of our time. Of course, only time itself can tell that. Nevertheless, when we see how powerful an impact this slogan has made it is obvious that it touches very sensi-

---

Excerpt from "Black Power," Anna Grimshaw, ed., *The C.L.R. James Reader* (Oxford: Basil Blackwell, 1991), pp. 362–370, 372, 374.

tive nerves in the political consciousness of the world today. This evening I do not intend to tell you that it is your political duty to fight against racial consciousness in the
British people; or that you must seek ways and means to expose and put an end to the
racialist policies of the present Labour government. If you are not doing that already I
don't see that this meeting will help you to greater political activity. That is not the particular purpose of this meeting though, as you shall hear, there will be specific aims
and concrete proposals. What I aim to do this evening is to make clear to all of us what
this slogan Black Power means, what it does *not* mean, *cannot* mean; and I say quite
plainly, we must get rid, once and for all, of a vast amount of confusion which is arising, copiously, both from the right and also from the left. . . .

But before I outline, so to speak, the premises on which I will build, I want to say a
few words about Stokely Carmichael: I think I ought to say Stokely because everybody, everywhere, calls him Stokely which I think is a political fact of some importance. The slogan Black Power, beginning in the United States and spreading from
there elsewhere, is undoubtedly closely associated with him and with those who are
fighting with him. But for us in Britain his name, whether we like it or not, means
more than that. It is undoubtedly his presence here, and the impact that he has made
in his speeches and his conversations, that have made the slogan Black Power reverberate in the way that it is doing in political Britain, and even outside of that, in
Britain in general. And I want to begin by making a particular reference to Stokely
which, fortunately, I am in a position to make. And I do this because on the whole in
public speaking, in writing (and also to a large degree in private conversation), I usually avoid, take great care to avoid placing any emphasis on a personality in politics.

I was reading the other day Professor Lévi-Strauss and in a very sharp attack on
historical conceptions prevalent today, I saw him say that the description of personality, or of the anecdote (which so many people of my acquaintance historically and
politically live by) were the lowest forms of history. With much satisfaction I agreed;
I have been saying so for nearly half a century. But then he went on to place the political personality within a context that I thought was misleading, and it seemed to
me that in avoiding it as much as I have done, I was making a mistake, if not so
much in writing, certainly in public speech. And that is why I begin what I have to
say, and will spend a certain amount of time, on one of the most remarkable personalities of contemporary politics. And I am happy to say that I did not have to wait
until Stokely came here to understand the force which he symbolizes.

I heard him speak in Canada at Sir George Williams University in March of this
year. There were about one thousand people present, chiefly white students, about
sixty or seventy Negro people, and I was so struck by what he was saying and the way
he was saying it (a thing which does not happen to me politically very often) that I
sat down immediately and took the unusual step of writing a letter to him, a political letter. After all, he was a young man of twenty-three or twenty-four and I was old
enough to be his grandfather and, as I say, I thought I had a few things to tell him
which would be of use to him and, through him, the movement he represented. I
will now read to you parts of this letter:

> I was glad to hear you because I wanted to know for myself what had lifted you up to the
> pinnacle on which you now stand. It is a pinnacle and one that is very rare in my experi-
> ence or even historically. You are just twenty-four and you are not only one of the people
> on the American continent who is to be reckoned with, but you are a world-famous figure.
> At twenty-four. That fact is something very special and seems to offer immense possibili-

ties both for the cause and the advancement, or rather I should say the development, of the personality. I am profoundly aware of the dangers of being in such a position at such an early age. I propose therefore in this letter to deal of course with the movement, because everything depends on that, but also with the specific dangers that beset you as a leader, perhaps the most prominent leader today, of this great movement in the United States.

I then explained why in particular I had been so struck by him. The letter continues:

One of my most important and pregnant experiences is my experience both personal and otherwise of West Indians and people of West Indian origin who have made their way on the broad stage of Western civilization. Some of them I knew very well personally and others I have studied, am very familiar with their work, and have systematically added to my information and knowledge about them from people who knew them well. They are Marcus Garvey, George Padmore, Aimé Césaire, Frantz Fanon. These are West Indians who have played a role on the world political stage that is not even properly understood by their own people. One of the tasks I have set myself is to make people understand what these men have done and their significance in world politics. In a substantial respect I am one of them, although I have not played the concrete role that they have played: I say that I am one of them because it means that I understand the type very well. And you are one. I suspected it when I was reading some of your writings and having heard you I am absolutely certain of it. Let me briefly state at once some of the points that brought this home to me with extreme force, particularly at that meeting.

We need not go further into that now. I went on to say (it was a rather lengthy letter) that there were certain doubtful points in his speech which he should bear in mind. I went on further to indicate in the letter that there were grave weaknesses in the whole Negro struggle in the United States; for one, that it lacked a sound historical and theoretical basis. And I suggested to him, that if he did not see his way to initiate this study himself, he should see to it that others take it up and take it up seriously. *So large and far-reaching a struggle needed to know where it was, where it had come from, and where it was going.*

I received a reply in which he took up the points I had made and said he recognized their importance. That was in March and April of this year, 1967. The year has not ended and now he speaks with a scope and a depth and range of political understanding that astonishes me. That the Stokely whom I heard in March and whose conspicuous political ability and character I recognized (that is why I wrote to him) in less than a year should have developed into the political leader we are hearing and seeing, this to me is a testimony not merely to him but to the speed with which the modern world is moving politically. I have to add that much that I shall now say to you I knew before, but I could never have said it in the way that you will hear, unless I had been able to listen and to talk to the new Stokely, the Stokely that we have been hearing.

Now, Black Power. A political slogan and yet not a political slogan: rather a banner. We see that at once the moment we look at previous statements which have captured the political imagination and guided the activity of people all over the world during past centuries and up to today. I shall take some of the best known ones and that will enable us to put Black Power in the proper place to which it belongs.

You remember about the middle of the eighteenth century Rousseau's statement with which he began his famous book *The Social Contract?* "Man was born free and is everywhere in chains." Listen to it again: "Man was born free and is everywhere in

chains." It was written two hundred years ago and yet today, in classes in political philosophy, in universities all over the world, in articles and books that are daily published, the debate rages: what did Rousseau mean by saying that man was born free
and is everywhere in chains? Some people draw the conclusion about Rousseau that he
was the originator of the totalitarian state, others that we have not yet reached the kind
of democracy which he had in mind. It is not our business this evening to come to any
decision about that (although I know where I stand). The point is that the phrase has
been a banner under which men have struggled for liberty and freedom, a phrase under which that struggle goes on today. Without Rousseau's "Man was born free and is
everywhere in chains," the world would be a poorer place.

Let us take another statement almost two hundred years old, the statement by Jefferson that "We hold these truths to be self-evident, that all men are created equal
. . . that they are endowed by their Creator with certain inalienable rights . . ." the
beginning of one of the most famous documents in history, the Declaration of Independence of the United States, declared in Congress on the fourth of July 1776. Self-
evident! Jefferson had a nerve. Nothing like that was "self-evident" anywhere. In
Britain, all over Europe, all over Asia, all over the known world, people were being
governed by kings who were supposed to have been placed on the throne by God;
there were nobles, aristocrats; there were the clergy with special rights, in every part
of the known globe. In the United States itself there was a solid mass of people who
did not believe that even in the United States all men were created equal. Yet Jefferson had the nerve to begin the famous document by saying that this was a truth that
he held to be self-evident, i.e. everybody could see it. At the time there were very few
people who accepted it. To this day there are vast numbers of people who don't believe it. Nevertheless it is one of the greatest political statements ever made. It is a
banner by which and under which tremendous struggles have been waged for liberty, for democracy, for democratic freedom. I hope that you are following me in my
view that it is only by placing it historically that we can begin to see what Black
Power signifies and avoid gross and dangerous blunders. In fact, it is not a slogan at
all. Rather it is a banner for people with certain political aims, needs and attitudes, a
banner around which they can rally, a banner which I believe many millions already
today see and in the not too distant future will see, as the symbol of a tremendous
change in life and society as they have known it.

Let us now leave these slogans (I prefer to think of them as banners) and go directly
to the origin and ancestry of this world-shaking movement, Booker T. Washington.
For, yes, it is with Booker T. Washington that we have to begin. Today the name of
Booker T. is not often mentioned in regard to the development of Negro struggles.
Most often people mention with a certain disdain his famous concession, or I can call
it his infamous capitulation to race prejudice in the South. It is part of the history of
the Negro and of the history of the United States that Booker T., in a famous speech in
Atlanta, Georgia, told the South: "In all things purely social we can be as separate as the
five fingers, and yet one as the hand in all things essential to mutual progress."

Today we ought to be able to see first that Booker T. Washington faced a situation
in which he was seeking desperately for a way out, and he could see no way out except capitulation. But Booker T. did something else. He said that Negroes should
prepare themselves for the work of artisans and labourers; everybody could not be a
scholar or do a skilled clerical job; the Negro had to prepare himself for manual labor. But, added Booker T., he should also seek to educate himself in the humanities.
So it was that Tuskegee, which was the centre of Negro education in the South for

many years, became a great pioneer of modern education, i.e. education for the members of a modern community, education of body and mind for manual and intellectual labor. So that today Booker T. Washington's *method* of education, *forced upon him by race prejudice,* has become an educational ideal which is more and more widely accepted as a necessity for the world in which we live.

But Booker T. is also remembered for the fact that he drew upon himself a devastating attack by another great pioneer in Negro struggles, Dr W.E.B. Du Bois. Du Bois marked a great stage in the history of Negro struggles when he said that Negroes could no longer accept the subordination which Booker T. Washington had preached. On it Booker T. had built a base not only for himself but for a certain type of Negro educator and social functionary. Dr Du Bois declared the absolute right of the Negro for whatever task he was fitted. And we can see how history changes in that, looking at the qualifications and weaknesses of American Negroes in his day, Du Bois championed specifically the Negroes of "the talented tenth," that tenth of the Negro community which he believed was already fitted to exercise fully the qualifications it had already attained. We can see how history moves when we understand that this, which was a legitimate demand by one of the great pioneers of Negro emancipation, would today be repudiated by Stokely and all supporters of Black Power. They do not seek to advance claims, rights for one-tenth of the present Negro population of the United States. They say that it is this tenth of the Negro population which has been and is being given special positions which corrupt it and act as a deadweight on the development of the great mass of the Negro people as a whole. So that "the talented tenth" in the days of Du Bois fifty years ago represented an advance, while today it is the main enemy of all those who fight under the banner of Black Power.

But if we wish properly to understand *the advanced position which Stokely Carmichael and the advocates of Black Power hold today,* we have only to see that Dr Du Bois was not a man whose reputation rested only on the fact that he was one of the great leaders of Negro emancipation. Not only white journalists have thus circumscribed him. I have had to protest to leading people in the coloured community in the United States about what they said when Du Bois died. I am glad to say that I had had the opportunity to point out that in organizing the National Association for the Advancement of Coloured People and founding its periodical *The Crisis,* Dr Du Bois took the lead in making the United States and the world recognize that racial prejudice was not a mere matter of Negroes being persecuted but was a cancer which poisoned the whole civilization of the United States. Secondly, in the Pan-African Conferences that he organized all over the world, he first made people in the United States and elsewhere recognize that Africa could not be left in the state of stagnation and exploitation in which it had entered the twentieth century. Thirdly, in his study of the American slave trade and in his studies of the Civil War he was undoubtedly one of the most penetrating and effective historians of his time: there is no noteworthy American historian writing today and during the last fifty years who does not owe a tremendous debt to Du Bois's work in history. So that in all these respects he was far more than "a leader of our people." In fundamental respects he was a generation in advance of most American thinking of his time and he is one of the great citizens of the United States in the twentieth century. We must bear that mistake in mind and not make it again as we are on the way to doing in regard to the advocates of Black Power. *Think of this seriously, please.*

Now the foundation having been firmly laid, we can move a little faster. Next on the list is Marcus Garvey, of whom we need say only a few sentences. Before Garvey the great millions of Africans and people of African descent simply did not exist in the political consciousness of the world in general, of the general public, and of politicians in particular. After less than a decade this Jamaican had placed them there. He had placed them there in a manner that they could never be removed again. Garvey had placed them not only in the consciousness of the oppressors but as a constituent part of the minds and aims of the great mass of Africans and people of African descent.

We can now go still faster. After Garvey came Padmore, who added a new dimension. Padmore was the originator of the movement to achieve the political independence of the African countries and people of African descent. That is why he is increasingly known as the Father of African Emancipation. So that a certain stage of African emancipation had arrived, very soon after the independence of Ghana, by actually achieving political independence, i.e. rule by local and native politicians over large areas.

There follows automatically the rise and significance of the activities and writings of Frantz Fanon. We must see Fanon as the political activist and writer who is saying that now we have actually achieved independence we have to fight against not only the old imperialism creeping back: we have to carry on a desperate all-out struggle against those native leaders who may have fought for independence. Many do not represent the forward movement of the underdeveloped peoples to some new stage of economic and political progress. Says Fanon: after independence those become the enemy. We do not see Fanon correctly if we do not see him as a natural development after what Padmore represented, and Padmore as the political stage of the wide avenue opened by Du Bois and Marcus Garvey.

It is only now that we are able to see what Stokely and the advocates of Black Power represent. They stand on the shoulder of their ancestors. I have not mentioned all. For example, I have had to leave out Aimé Césaire, the man of Négritude, and I have had to leave out Malcolm X, that great fighter whose potentialities were growing so fast that his opponents had to get rid of him by plain murder. So then, it is now that we can see what Stokely and the concept of Black Power represent.

Stokely and the advocates of Black Power stand on the shoulders of all that has gone before. To too many people here in England, and unfortunately to people in the United States too (you remember I had mentioned this in my letter to Stokely), too many people see Black Power and its advocates as some sort of portent, a sudden apparition, as some racist eruption from the depths of black oppression and black backwardness. It is nothing of the kind. It represents the high peak of thought on the Negro question which has been going on for over half a century. That much we have to know, and that much we have to be certain other people get to know.

Now, as in any political manifestation on a world scale, there is involved not only a general principle. As far as any particular country is concerned, we have to see it not only in its general but in its particular application. Now you notice that Booker T. Washington was from the South of the United States. W.E.B. Du Bois was South and North, everywhere, and in the world outside: his was a universal mind. But the West Indies, Garvey, Césaire, Padmore and Fanon, all worked abroad, away from home, and much of their work, in fact most of it, was concerned with Africa. And taking advantage of this immense political experience which has been accumulated, and the advanced stage of American society, we find that it is in the United States that the Negro struggle has advanced and is now taken to the highest peak it has ever reached. For note that whereas the others on the whole concentrated on Africa and peoples of African descent, in the voice of Stokely we can hear that they are laying the basis of a mortal struggle to the death for what black people believe to be their rights.

They have further extended that struggle to what they call the Third World. By that phrase, the Third World, they embrace what is today the majority of mankind. There are people who say that the Stokely they heard in England here, and the Stokely they have read about, is racist. The falsity of that, or if not falsity, its dishonesty, can be easily exposed. You all have heard him say that as far as he is concerned Tshombe is a white man. Black though his skin may be, he is the servant of what Malcolm X called the white power structure. He tells us specifically that the concept of the Third World includes the population of Latin America. He says specifically that they are not in the majority coloured but he includes them in the Third World. How can one call this racism except through ignorance or malice? And he embraces the concept of the Third World under the slogan Black Power because blacks are the ones who have suffered longest and most from the crimes of imperialism.

Furthermore, there are special conditions in the United States to some of which I shall now draw your attention. First there are districts in the South where Negroes are prevented from exercising the elementary rights of parliamentary democracy by the guns which the white racists keep pointed at their heads. The advocates of Black Power say that they intend (if necessary by using guns) to restore to the blacks in these areas the political power which is theirs by right. Secondly, they say what has long been noted and commented upon in the United States, that as the whites have moved out to the suburbs, the centers of all the big cities of the United States are increasingly populated by Negro majorities. This is a source of power which they propose to organize, and use as key positions in the struggle for Negro rights in the United States as a whole. Note and note well how precise is their concrete use of the term Black Power. And finally, the Negro people in the United States are not a people of a backward colonial area; they are Americans in what is in many ways the most advanced country in the world. The kind of impact the Negroes are making is due to the fact that they constitute a vanguard not only to the Third World, but constitute also that section of the United States which is most politically advanced.

So for the time being, that is what we know. I hope we know it. That is what Black Power means, and when we consider where that banner is being advanced and held aloft, and the kind of people who are carrying it, we can recognize that it is a banner which has come to stay, a banner which the twentieth century will need in the great efforts it will need to overcome the crisis that imperialist domination has imposed upon the whole world. Not only upon the Third.

So far I have been dealing with what we know *or what we ought to know*. That is, I now inform you, the answer to the first of the three famous questions asked by Kant: "What do I know?" The second question is "What must I do?", and here I will take the liberty of reminding you of another profound warning by a famous philosopher: *every determination is negation*. That is to say: every time you do something, every time you *determine* on something, you *do not do* something else. That is very important for us here. The things that I believe we ought to do are very much in opposition to the things we ought not to do. They are, I would suggest, two in number.

Number one, we support the fighters for Negro rights and for Black Power in the United States. That means we *do not* apologize or seek to explain, particularly to British people (and in particular to British Marxists), or give any justification or apologize for whatever forms the struggle in the United States may take.

It is over one hundred years since the abolition of slavery. The Negro people in the United States have taken plenty and they have reached a stage where they have decided that they are not going to take any more. Who are we here to stand, or rather to sit in judgment over what they decide to do or what they decide not to do? I want to take in particular Mr Rap Brown, who makes the most challenging statements. He is prepared to challenge American racial prejudice to the utmost limit of his strength and the strength of the Negroes who will follow him. Who are we to say, "Yes, you are entitled to say this but not to say that; you are entitled to do this but not to do that"? If we know the realities of Negro oppression in the USA (and if we don't we should keep our mouths shut until we do), then we should guide ourselves by a West Indian expression which I recommend to you: *what he do, he well do.* Let me repeat that: what the American Negroes do is, as far as we are concerned, well done. They will take their chances, they will risk their liberty, they risk their lives if need be. *The decisions are theirs.* . . .

They will decide and we support. But if we do that we do not do something else. We do not go around seeking to explain away what they have done, or to prove that they are not good Marxists in that they are not waiting for the American proletariat to move. We know the first thing we must do, and that tells us what we do not do.

The second thing is that we miss no opportunity to make the British public and the public at large know that we consider the life and safety of Stokely Carmichael to be in the greatest danger in the United States. A number of people here, and all over the world, realize that the simple way out for the racists in the United States (or the men of peace, peace at any price) is to murder him out of hand. They did it to Malcolm X, and today the progress of the struggle, building on what Malcolm X began, makes Stokely a person who is a mortal danger to those who wish to preserve the old way of life of the United States. We have not only to let the people in the United States know what we think, but we have to let the people know, and understand, that Stokely is not a person to be shot at by trigger-happy racists, or by deep thinkers who believe that the best black man is a dead black man. Let us, therefore, to personal friends and acquaintances, to unions, to whatever political parties we belong, let us tell them that it is their duty to register, by resolution and motion, the fears that all have for Stokely's safety; and so make those in the United States who want to kill him realize that such an action will make the public opinion of the world question not only the attitude of America to the coloured races, but the American attitude to elementary democracy and respect for the human person. We can do no better than take note of what Fidel Castro said about Stokely's safety at the closing of the OLAS Conference:

> And our people admire Stokely for the courageous statements he has made in the OLAS Conference, because we know that it takes courage to do this, because we know what it means to make such statements when you are going to return to a society that applies the most cruel and brutal procedures of repression, that constantly practices the worst crimes against the Negro sector of the population, and we know the hatred that his statements will arouse among the oppressors.
>
> And for this reason, we believe that the revolutionary movements all over the world must give Stokely their utmost support as protection against the repression of the imperialists, in such a way that everyone will know that any crime committed against this leader will have serious repercussions throughout the world. And our solidarity can help to protect Stokely's life.

Castro is a revolutionary, one of the greatest revolutionaries history has ever known, but the sentiment that he there expresses, you can participate in and take action upon even though you may be a Liberal or, it is not impossible, a Conservative. . . .

Now we come to Kant's last question. The first one, you remember, was: what do I know? Second: what must I do? And now, third: what may I hope? And here I have to deal with a personal experience which I shall share with you. Needless to say, it is completely political. I went to the US from England in 1938 and found them in a rare confusion as to what a Marxist policy should be on the Negro question. What for them, as Marxists, was a difficult social situation was further complicated by the fact that the Stalinists for years had been preaching that Marxism demanded the advocacy of an independent Negro state within the confines of the US. And the Trotskyist movement from top to bottom, at home and abroad, simply did not know where it stood in regard to this fundamental question for a socialist party in the US. I had no difficulty whatever in telling them what I was quite certain was the correct policy. And this I knew not because I was a Negro, not because I have studied closely the situation in the US. No. From the very beginning I put forward what I conceived to be a very simple, straightforward Leninist policy.

I had studied Lenin in order to write *The Black Jacobins,* the analysis of a revolution for self-determination in a colonial territory. I had studied Lenin to be able to write my book on *World Revolution.* I had studied Lenin to be able to take part with George Padmore in his organization that worked for the independence of all colonial territories, but particularly the territories of Africa. I therefore was in a position from the very beginning to state my position and to state it in a discussion that some of us had with Trotsky on the Negro question [in] 1939.

The position was this: the independent struggle of the Negro people for their democratic rights and equality with the rest of the American nation not only had to be defended and advocated by the Marxist movement. The Marxist movement had to understand that *such independent struggles were a contributory factor to the socialist revolution.* Let me restate that as crudely as possible: the American Negroes in fighting for their democratic rights were making an indispensable addition to the struggle for socialism in the US. . . .

I began by telling you that early this year I listened to Stokely Carmichael and was immediately struck by the enormous revolutionary potential which was very clear to me. But I had no idea that before the end of the year I would hear from him the following:

> We speak with you, comrades, because we wish to make clear that we understand that our destinies are intertwined. Our world can only be the third world; our only struggle for the third world; our only vision, of the third world.

Stokely is speaking at the OLAS Conference, and the Negro movement in the US, being what it is, he makes very clear that this movement sees itself as a part of the Third World. But before very long he says what I knew was always inherent in his thoughts, if not always totally plain in his words. I wish you to appreciate the gravity and the weight which a man who speaks as Stokely has been speaking must give to the following words:

> But we do not seek to create communities where, in place of white rules, black rulers control the lives of black masses and where black money goes into a few black pockets: we want to see it go into the communal pocket. The society we seek to build among black people is not an oppressive capitalist society—for capitalism by its very nature cannot create structures free from exploitation. We are fighting for the redistribution of wealth and for the end of private property inside the United States.

In the opinion of myself and many of my friends no clearer or stronger voice for socialism has ever been raised in the US. It is obvious that for him, based as he is and fighting for a future of freedom for the Negro people of the US, the socialist society is not a hope, *not what we may hope,* but a compelling necessity. *What he or any other Negro leader may say tomorrow, I do not know.* But I have followed fairly closely the career of this young man, and I leave you with this very deeply based philosophical conception of political personality. He is far away out, in a very difficult position, and I am sure there are those in his own camp who are doubtful of the positions he is taking, but I believe his future and the future of the policies which he is now advocating does not depend upon him as an individual. It depends upon the actions and reactions of those surrounding him and, to a substantial degree, not only on what you who are listening to me may hope, but also on what you do. ❖

Alvin W. Gouldner (1920–1980) grew up in the Bronx, where he fashioned himself as a street tough, a self-image he maintained through his life. Gouldner was also a brilliant student in the New York City schools and eventually at Columbia University, where, as a student of Robert K. Merton, he did his doctoral studies in sociology. His thesis was published in two parts, *Wildcat Strike* (1954) and *Patterns of Industrial Bureaucracy* (1954). The latter became a classic in industrial sociology. Though Gouldner would later become one of the world's foremost critical interpreters of Marxism, in his early career he expressed his radical views in a more Weberian form. In the mid-1960s, Gouldner began a major multivolume rethinking of social theory, beginning with *Enter Plato* (1965). He always challenged narrow boundaries. Some classicists hated him for daring to write on the Greeks without a knowledge of the ancient language. He was undaunted. *The Coming Crisis of Western Sociology,* the source of the selection, appeared in 1970. In many respects, it had an influence similar to Mills's *Sociological Imagination* a decade earlier. *Crisis* was a kind of textbook for many young radicals pursuing careers in sociology as the 1960s came to an end. His ideas on reflexive sociology are clearly consistent with the New Left ideal of taking seriously the personal as well as the political. Gouldner's other books include *The Dialectic of Ideology and Technology* (1976), *The Future of Intellectuals and the Rise of the New Class* (1979), and *The Two Marxisms* (1980). Underneath a rough and abrasive manner, Gouldner was a sensitive soul. These differing personal attributes contributed to his remarkable willingness and ability to see the weakness and strength of his resources. *Coming Crisis,* like most of what he wrote thereafter, is an attempt to define a third force in social theory—part sociology, part Marxism; part academic, part political. With Gouldner, nothing was ever simple.

Toward a Reflexive Sociology
Alvin W. Gouldner (1970)

Sociologists are no more ready than other men to cast a cold eye on their own doings. No more than others are they ready, willing, or able to tell us what they are really doing and to distinguish this firmly from what they *should* be doing. Professional courtesy stifles intellectual curiosity; guild interests frown upon the washing of dirty linen in public; the teeth of piety bite the tongue of truth. Yet, first and fore-

---

Excerpt from *The Coming Crisis of Western Sociology* (New York: Basic Books, 1970), pp. 488–495. Reprinted by permission of Basic Books, a Member of the Perseus Books Group.

most, a Reflexive Sociology is concerned with what sociologists want to do and with what, in fact, they actually do in the world.

The intellectual development of sociology during the last two decades or so, especially the growth of the sociologies of occupations and of science, is, when fused with the larger perspectives of the older sociology of knowledge, one promising basis for the development of a Reflexive Sociology. We have already seen some of the first stirrings of a Reflexive Sociology, in one form or another. Indeed, I believe we have already also seen the emergence of defensive reactions that, in effect, seek to contain the impact of a Reflexive Sociology by defining it as just one other technical specialty within sociology.

What sociologists now most require from a Reflexive Sociology, however, is not just one more specialization, not just another topic for panel meetings at professional conventions, and not just another burbling little stream of technical reports about the sociological profession's origins, educational characteristics, patterns of productivity, political preferences, communication networks, nor even about its fads, foibles, and phonies. For there are ways and ways of conducting and reporting such studies. There are ways that do not touch and quicken us but may, instead, deaden us to the disorders we bear; by allowing us to talk about them with a ventriloquist's voice, they only create an illusion of self-confrontation that serves to disguise a new form of self-celebration. The historical mission of a Reflexive Sociology as I conceive it, however, would be to *transform* the sociologist, to penetrate deeply into his daily life and work, enriching them with new sensitivities, and to raise the sociologist's self-awareness to a new historical level.

To the extent that it succeeds in this, and in order to succeed in it, a Reflexive Sociology is and would need to be a radical sociology. Radical, because it would recognize that knowledge of the world cannot be advanced apart from the sociologist's knowledge of himself and his position in the social world, or apart from his efforts to change these. Radical, because it seeks to transform as well as to know the alien world outside the sociologist as well the alien world inside of him. Radical, because it would accept the fact that the roots of sociology pass through the sociologist as a total man, and that the question he must confront, therefore, is not merely how to *work* but how to *live.*

The historical mission of a Reflexive Sociology is to transcend sociology as it now exists. In deepening our understanding of our own sociological selves and of our position in the world, we can, I believe, simultaneously help to produce a new breed of sociologists who can also better understand other men and their social worlds. A Reflexive Sociology means that we sociologists must—at the very least—acquire the ingrained *habit* of viewing our own beliefs as we now view those held by others.

It will be difficult for many sociologists to accept that we presently know little or nothing about ourselves or other sociologists or, in point of fact, that we know little about how one piece of social research, or one sociologist, comes to be esteemed while another is disparaged or ignored. The temptation is great to conceal our ignorance of this process behind a glib affirmation of the proprieties and to pretend that there is no one here but us scientists. In other words, one of the basic reasons we deceive ourselves and lie to others is because we are moral men. Sociologists, like other men, confuse the moral answer with the empirical and, indeed, often prefer it to the empirical. Much of our noble talk about the importance of "truth for its own sake" is often a tacit way of saying that we want the truth about *others,* at whatever cost it may be to *them.* A Reflexive Sociology, however, implies that sociologists must surrender the assumption, as wrongheaded as it is human, that others believe out of need while we believe—only or primarily—because of the dictates of logic and evidence.

A systematic and dogged insistence upon seeing ourselves as we see others would, I have suggested, transform not only our view of ourselves but also our view of others. We would increasingly recognize the depth of our kinship with those whom we study. They would no longer be viewable as alien others or as mere objects for our superior technique and insight; they could, instead, be seen as brother sociologists, each attempting with his varying degree of skill, energy, and talent to understand social reality. In this respect, all men are basically akin to those whom we usually acknowledge as professional "colleagues," who are no less diversified in their talents and competence. With the development of a Reflexive Sociology that avoids becoming molded into just another technical specialty, such rigor as sociology attains may be blended with a touch of mercy, and such skills as sociologists possess may come to yield not only information but perhaps even a modest measure of wisdom.

The development of a Reflexive Sociology, in sum, requires that sociologists cease acting as if they thought of subjects and objects, sociologists who study and "laymen" who are studied, as two distinct breeds of men. There is only one breed of man. But so long as we are without a Reflexive Sociology, we will act upon the tacit dualistic premise that there are two, regardless of how monistic our professions of methodological faith.

I conceive of Reflexive Sociology as requiring an empirical dimension which might foster a large variety of researches about sociology and sociologists, their occupational roles, their career "hangups," their establishments, power systems, subcultures, and their place in the larger social world. Indeed, my emphasis on the empirical character of a Reflexive Sociology and my insistence that the methodological morality of social science not be confused with the description of its social system and cultures, may seem to express a Positivistic bias. Yet while I believe that a Reflexive Sociology must have an empirical dimension. I do not conceive of this as providing a factual basis that determines the character of its guiding theory. Which is to say that I do not conceive of the theory of a Reflexive Sociology merely as an induction from researches or from "facts." And more important, I do not conceive of these researches or their factual output as being "value-free," for I would hope that their originating motives and terminating consequences would embody and advance certain specific *values*. A Reflexive Sociology would be a moral sociology.

Perhaps this can be adumbrated by clarifying my conception of the ultimate objective or goal of a Reflexive Sociology, in regard to both its theory and its researches. The nominal objective of any scientific enterprise is to extend knowledge of some part of the world. The difficulty with this conception, however, resides in the ambiguity of its core notion, namely, "knowledge." This ambiguity is of long standing, especially in the social sciences, where it has been particularly acute. Although expressible in different ways, this ambiguity will be formulated here as meaning that knowledge may be, and has been, conceived of as either "information" or "awareness."

Since the nineteenth century, when a distinction was formulated between the natural sciences, on the one hand, and the cultural or human sciences, on the other, this implicit ambiguity in the meaning of "knowledge" was imported into the social sciences and has remained at the core of certain of its fundamental controversies. Those believing that the social sciences were a "natural" science, like physics or biology, took an essentially Positivistic view, holding that they should be pursued with the same methods and objectives as the physical sciences. They largely conceived of knowledge as "information," as empirically confirmed assertions about "reality," whose scientific value derived from their implications for rational theory and whose larger social value derived from technologies based upon them. In short, science thus construed aimed at producing information, either for its own sake or to enhance power over the surrounding world: to know in order to control.

So long as this was a conception of the physical (as distinct from the social) sciences, it was an ideology (1) behind which all "humanity" might unite in a common effort to subdue a "nature" that was implicitly regarded as external to man, and (2) with which to promote technologies that could transform the universe into the usable resource of mankind as a whole. Such a conception of science was based upon an assumption of the essential unity and the common interests of mankind as a species. It was also a tacitly parochial conception of the relationship of the human species to others; it postulated humanity's lordship over the rest of the universe and its right to use the entire universe for its own benefit, a right tempered only by the species' expedient concern for its own long-range welfare. If such a view of science was an expression of the unthinking ethnocentrism of an expanding animal species, it was also an historical summit of this species' idealism; limitations were ignored in the flush of an optimistic sense that the newly realized universalism of science constituted an advance over narrower and more ancient parochialisms—and so it was.

The humanistic parochialism of science, with its premised unity of mankind, created problems, however, when the effort was made to apply science to the study of mankind itself. It did so partly because national or class differences then became acutely visible, but also, and perhaps more important, because men now expected to use social science to "control" men themselves, as they were already using physical science to control "nature." Such a view of social science premised that a man might be known, used, and controlled like any other thing: it "thingafied" man. The use of the physical sciences as a model fostered just such a conception of the social sciences, all the more so as they were developing in the context of an increasingly utilitarian culture.

This view of the social sciences was fostered by French Positivism. In opposition to it, largely under German auspices and the Romantic Movement with its full-scale critique of utilitarian culture, there emerged a different conception of social science. This required a different method, for example, *verstehen*, clinical intuition, or historical empathy—an inward closeness to the object studied rather than an antiseptic distance from it, an inward communion with it rather than an external manipulation of it. This conception of social science held that its ultimate goal was not neutral "information" about social reality, but rather such knowledge as was relevant to men's own changing interests, hopes, and values and as would enhance men's awareness of their *place* in the social world rather than simply facilitating their *control* over it.

In this conception of social science both the inquiring subject and the studied object are seen not only as mutually interrelated but also as mutually constituted. The entire world of social objects is seen as constituted by men, by the shared meanings bestowed and confirmed by men themselves, rather than as substances eternally fixed and existent apart from them. The social world, therefore, is to be known not simply by "discovery" of some external fact, not only by looking outward, but also by opening oneself inward. Awareness of the *self* is seen as an indispensable avenue to awareness of the social world. For there is no knowledge of the world that is not a knowledge of our own experience with it and our relation to it.

In a knowing conceived as awareness, the concern is not with "discovering" the truth about a social world regarded as external to the knower, but with seeing truth as growing out of the knower's encounter with the world and his effort to order his experience with it. The knower's knowing of himself—of who, what, and where he is—on the one hand, and of others and their social worlds, on the other, are two sides of a single process.

Insofar as social reality is seen as contingent in part on the effort, the character, and the position of the knower, the search for knowledge about social worlds is also contingent upon the knower's *self-awareness.* To know others he cannot simply study *them,* but must also listen to and confront *himself.* Knowing as awareness involves not a simple impersonal effort of segmented "role players," but a personalized effort by whole, embodied men. The character and quality of such knowing is molded not only by a man's technical skills or even by his intelligence alone, but also by all that he is and wants, by his courage no less than his talent, by his passion no less than his objectivity. It depends on all that a man does and lives. In the last analysis, if a man wants to change what he knows he must change how he lives; he must change his *praxis* in the world.

Knowing as the pursuit of information, however, conceives of the resultant knowledge as depersonalized; as a product that can be found in a card file, a book, a library, a colleague, or some other "storage bank." Such knowledge does not have to be recallable by a specific knower and, indeed, does not have to be in the mind of any person; all that need be known about it is its "location." Knowledge as information, then, is the attribute of a *culture* rather than of a person; its meaning, pursuit, and consequence are all depersonalized. Knowledge as awareness, however, is quite another matter, for it has no existence, apart from the persons that pursue and express it. Awareness is an attribute of persons, even though it is influenced by the location of these persons in specific cultures or in parts of a social structure. A culture may assist or hinder in attaining awareness, but a culture as such cannot be aware.

Awareness entails a relationship between persons and information; yet information, while necessary to, is not sufficient for awareness. Awareness turns on the *attitude* of persons toward information and is related to their ability to hold onto and to use information. The crux of the matter is that information is rarely neutral in its implication for men's purposes, hopes, or values. Information, therefore, tends to be experienced—even if not expressly defined—as either "friendly" or "hostile," as consonant or dissonant with man's purposes. It is the relation of information to a man's purposes, not what it is "in itself," that makes information hostile or friendly. News of the stability of a government is hostile information to a revolutionary but friendly to a conservative. An openness to and a capacity to use hostile information is awareness. Awareness is an openness to bad news, and is born of a capacity to overcome resistance to its acceptance or use. This is inevitably linked, at some vital point, with an ability to know and to control the self in the face of threat. The pursuit of awareness, then, even in the world of modern technology, remains rooted in the most ancient of virtues. The quality of a social scientist's work remains dependent upon the quality of his manhood.

Whether "hostile information" refers directly to some state of the larger world itself, or, rather, to the deficiencies of an established, perhaps technical, system of *information* about the world, an openness to it always requires a measure of self-knowledge and courage. The self of a scholar may be as deeply and personally invested in his work on information systems as is a revolutionary's on a political system. Both have conceptions of their work that may, at some point, be maintained only through the blunting of their awareness. A politician's capacity to accept and use hostile information about his own political efforts and situation is often referred to as his "realism." A scholar's ability to accept and use hostile information about his own view of social reality, and his efforts to know it, is part of what is usually called his "objectivity."

As a program for a Reflexive Sociology, then, this implies that: (1) The conduct of researches is only a necessary but not a sufficient condition for the maturation of the sociological enterprise. What is needed is a new *praxis* that transforms the person of the sociologist. (2) The ultimate goal of a Reflexive Sociology is the deepening of the sociologist's own awareness, of who and what he is, in a specific society at any given time, and of how both his social role and his personal praxis affect his work as a sociologist. (3) Its work seeks to deepen the sociologist's self-awareness as well as his ability to produce valid-reliable bits of information about the social world of others. (4) Therefore, a Reflexive Sociology requires not only valid-reliable bits of information about the world of sociology, and not only a methodology or a set of technical skills for procuring this. It also requires a persistent commitment to the *value* of that awareness which expresses itself through all stages of work, as well as auxiliary skills or arrangements that will enable the sociologist's self to be open to hostile information.

Conventional Positivism premises that the self is treacherous and that, so long as it remains in contact with the information system, its primary effect is to bias or distort it. It is assumed, therefore, that the way to defend the information system is to insulate it from the scholar's self by generating distance and by stressing impersonal detachment from the objects studied. From the standpoint of a Reflexive Sociology, however, the assumption that the self can be sealed off from information systems is mythological. The assumption that the self affects the information system solely in a distorting manner is one-sided: it fails to see that the self may also be a source both of valid insight that enriches study and of motivation that energizes it. A Reflexive Sociology looks, therefore, to the deepening of the self's capacity to recognize that it views certain information as hostile, to recognize the various dodges that it uses to deny, ignore, or camouflage information that is hostile to it, and to the strengthening of its capacity to accept and to use hostile information. In short, what Reflexive Sociology seeks is not an insulation but a *transformation* of the sociologist's self, and hence of his praxis in the world.

A Reflexive Sociology, then, is not characterized by *what* it studies. It is distinguished neither by the persons and the problems studied nor even by the techniques and instruments used in studying them. It is characterized, rather, by the *relationship* it establishes between being a sociologist and being a person, between the role and the man performing it. A Reflexive Sociology embodies a critique of the conventional conception of segregated scholarly roles and has a vision of an alternative. It aims at transforming the sociologist's relation to his work.❖

Herbert Marcuse (1898–1979) was born in Berlin. He studied in Germany and received a Ph.D. from Freiburg University. From 1922 to 1933, he was actively associated with the Frankfurt Institute. After emigrating from Germany for the United States in 1934, Marcuse continued his association with the Frankfurt School-in-exile in its Columbia University days. He taught at Brandeis (1954–1965) and at the University of California at San Diego (1965–1969). His books include *Eros and Civiliza-*

tion (1955), *Counter-revolution and Revolt* (1972), and *The Aesthetic Dimension* (1978). It is plain from the titles alone that Marcuse was faithful to the original theoretical interests of critical theory by working in and on the relations among Marxist theory, culture and aesthetics, and psychoanalysis. In the 1960s, Marcuse's *One-Dimensional Man* (1964), from which the selection is taken, was considered must reading by intellectually serious student radicals. His famous concept *repressive desublimation* refers to his argument that postwar mass culture, with its profusion of sexual provocations, serves to reinforce political repression. If people are preoccupied with unauthentic sexual stimulation, their political energy will be "desublimated"; instead of acting constructively to change the world, they remain repressed and uncritical. Obviously, Marcuse advanced the prewar thinking of critical theory toward a critical account of the "one-dimensional" nature of bourgeois life in Europe and America. His thinking could, therefore, also be considered an advance of the concerns of earlier liberal critics like David Riesman.

Repressive Desublimation

Herbert Marcuse (1964)

Today's novel feature is the flattening out of the antagonism between culture and social reality through the obliteration of the oppositional, alien, and transcendent elements in the higher culture by virtue of which it constituted *another dimension* of reality. This liquidation of *two-dimensional* culture takes place not through the denial and rejection of the "culture values," but through their wholesale incorporation into the established order, through their reproduction and display on a massive scale.

In fact, they serve as instruments of social cohesion. The greatness of a free literature and art, the ideals of humanism, the sorrows and joys of the individual, the fulfillment of the personality are important items in the competitive struggle between East and West. They speak heavily against the present forms of communism, and they are daily administered and sold. The fact that they contradict the society which sells them does not count. Just as people know or feel that advertisements and political platforms must not be necessarily true or right, and yet hear and read them and even let themselves be guided by them, so they accept the traditional values and make them part of their mental equipment. If mass communications blend together harmoniously, and often unnoticeably, art, politics, religion, and philosophy with commercials, they bring these realms of culture to their common denominator—the commodity form. The music of the soul is also the music of salesmanship. Exchange value, not truth value counts. On it centers the rationality of the status quo, and all alien rationality is bent to it.

As the great words of freedom and fulfillment are pronounced by campaigning leaders and politicians, on the screens and radios and stages, they turn into meaningless sounds which obtain meaning only in the context of propaganda, business, discipline, and relaxation. This assimilation of the ideal with reality testifies to the extent to which the ideal has been surpassed. It is brought down from the sublimated realm of the soul or the spirit or the inner man, and translated into opera-

---

Excerpt from *One-Dimensional Man: Studies in the Ideology of Advanced Industrial Society* (Boston: Beacon Press, 1964), pp. 57–58, 71–74. Copyright 1964 by Herbert Marcuse. Reprinted by permission of Beacon Press.

tional terms and problems. Here are the progressive elements of mass culture. The perversion is indicative of the fact that advanced industrial society is confronted with the possibility of a materialization of ideals. The capabilities of this society are progressively reducing the sublimated realm in which the condition of man was represented, idealized, and indicted. Higher culture becomes part of the material culture. In this transformation, it loses the greater part of its truth. . . .

It is a rational universe which, by the mere weight and capabilities of its apparatus, blocks all escape. In its relation to the reality of daily life, the high culture of the past was many things—opposition and adornment, outcry and resignation. But it was also the appearance of the realm of freedom: the refusal to behave. Such refusal cannot be blocked without a compensation which seems more satisfying than the refusal. The conquest and unification of opposites, which finds its ideological glory in the transformation of higher into popular culture, takes place on a material ground of increased satisfaction. This is also the ground which allows a sweeping *desublimation*.

Artistic alienation is sublimation. It creates the images of conditions which are irreconcilable with the established Reality Principle but which, as cultural images, become tolerable, even edifying and useful. Now this imagery is invalidated. Its incorporation into the kitchen, the office, the shop; its commercial release for business and fun is, in a sense, desublimation—replacing mediated by immediate gratification. But it is desublimation practiced from a "position of strength" on the part of society, which can afford to grant more than before because its interests have become the innermost drives of its citizens, and because the joys which it grants promote social cohesion and contentment.

The Pleasure Principle absorbs the Reality Principle; sexuality is liberated (or rather liberalized) in socially constructive forms. This notion implies that there are repressive modes of desublimation, compared with which the sublimated drives and objectives contain more deviation, more freedom, and more refusal to heed the social taboos. It appears that such repressive desublimation is indeed operative in the sexual sphere, and here, as in the desublimation of higher culture, it operates as the by-product of the social controls of technological reality, which extend liberty while intensifying domination. The link between desublimation and technological society can perhaps best be illuminated by discussing the change in the social use of instinctual energy.

In this society, not all the time spent on and with mechanisms is labor time (i.e., unpleasurable but necessary toil), and not all the energy saved by the machine is labor power. Mechanization has also "saved" libido, the energy of the Life Instincts—that is, has barred it from previous modes of realization. This is the kernel of truth in the romantic contrast between the modern traveler and the wandering poet or artisan, between assembly line and handicraft, town and city, factory-produced bread and the home-made loaf, the sailboat and the outboard motor, etc. True, this romantic pre-technical world was permeated with misery, toil, and filth, and these in turn were the background of all pleasure and joy. Still, there was a "landscape," a medium of libidinal experience which no longer exists.

With its disappearance (itself a historical prerequisite of progress), a whole dimension of human activity and passivity has been de-eroticized. The environment from which the individual could obtain pleasure—which he could cathect as gratifying almost as an extended zone of the body—has been rigidly reduced. Consequently, the "universe" of libidinous cathexis is likewise reduced. The effect is a localization and contraction of libido, the reduction of erotic to sexual experience and satisfaction.

For example, compare love-making in a meadow and in an automobile, on a lovers' walk outside the town walls and on a Manhattan street. In the former cases, the environment partakes of and invites libidinal cathexis and tends to be eroticized. Libido transcends beyond the immediate erotogenic zones—a process of nonrepressive sublimation. In contrast, a mechanized environment seems to block such self-transcendence of libido. Impelled in the striving to extend the field of erotic gratification, libido becomes less "polymorphous," less capable of eroticism beyond localized sexuality, and the *latter* is intensified.

Thus diminishing erotic and intensifying sexual energy, the technological reality *limits the scope of sublimation.* It also reduces the *need* for sublimation. In the mental apparatus, the tension between that which is desired and that which is permitted seems considerably lowered, and the Reality Principle no longer seems to require a sweeping and painful transformation of instinctual needs. The individual must adapt himself to a world which does not seem to demand the denial of his innermost needs—a world which is not essentially hostile.

The organism is thus being preconditioned for the spontaneous acceptance of what is offered. Inasmuch as the greater liberty involves a contraction rather than extension and development of instinctual needs, it works *for* rather than *against* the status quo of general repression—one might speak of "institutionalized desublimation." The latter appears to be a vital factor in the making of the authoritarian personality of our time.❖

Harold Garfinkel (1917–) is the inventor of the term *ethnomethodology* and the cofounder of the movement of that name. When it first came to public attention in the late 1960s, ethnomethodology was the brunt of dismissive jokes: a "cult," "California sociology," and the like. Such complaints were partly due to the confusion readers experienced both at Garfinkel's strange language and at his even more upsetting notion that social analysis begins with the fact that language itself is an attempt to repair the social problems created in human communication. Ethnomethodology, however, remained a steady force in social theory and made significant contributions. Most importantly, ethnomethodology has worked out an empirical method for taking seriously the complex properties of common, everyday social action. In the 1940s, Garfinkel was a student of Talcott Parsons at Harvard. It is increasingly accepted that Parsons's theory of action was nearly as important an influence on Garfinkel's thinking as the phenomenology of Alfred Schutz. Certainly, he went beyond both in inventing his version of ethnomethodology. The selection is from *Studies in Ethnomethodology,* the locus classicus of the movement. It includes a sample of ethnomethodological reasoning applied to empirical data through observations taken from the study of the Los Angeles Suicide Prevention Center. Garfinkel's argument that the center's work was largely an attempt to turn suicide deaths into rationally accountable—hence, normally recognizable—events suggests both ethnomethodology's unique interpretive attitude and why some find it troubling. Garfinkel is professor emeritus at UCLA.

Reflexive Properties of Practical Sociology
Harold Garfinkel (1967)

Virtually unanimous agreement exists among students of practical sociological reasoning, laymen and professionals, about the properties of indexical expressions and indexical actions. Impressive agreement exists as well (1) that although indexical expressions "are of enormous utility" they are "awkward for formal discourse"; (2) that a distinction between objective expressions and indexical expressions is not only procedurally proper but unavoidable for whosoever would do science; (3) that without the distinction between objective and indexical expressions, and without the preferred use of objective expressions the victories of generalizing, rigorous, scientific inquiries—logic, mathematics, some of the physical sciences—are unintelligible, the victories would fail, and the inexact sciences would have to abandon their hopes; (4) that the exact sciences are distinguishable from the inexact sciences by the fact that in the case of the exact sciences the distinction between and substitution of objective for indexical expressions for problem formulation, methods, findings, adequate demonstration, adequate evidence and the rest is both an actual task and an actual achievement, whereas in the case of the inexact sciences the availability of the distinction and substitutability to actual tasks, practices, and results remains unrealizably programmatic; (5) that the distinction between objective and indexical expressions, insofar as the distinction consists of inquirers' tasks, ideals, norms, resources, achievements, and the rest describes the difference between sciences and arts—e.g., between biochemistry and documentary filming; (6) that terms and sentences can be distinguished as one or the other in accordance with an assessment procedure that makes decidable their character as indexical or objective expressions; and (7) that in any particular case only practical difficulties prevent the substitution by an objective expression for an indexical expression.

Features of indexical expressions motivate endless methodological studies directed to their remedy. Indeed, attempts to rid the practices of a science of these nuisances lends to each science its distinctive character of preoccupation and productivity with methodological issues. Research practitioners' studies of practical activities of a science, whatever their science, afford them endless occasions to deal rigorously with indexical expressions.

Areas in the social sciences where the promised distinction and promised substitutability occurs are countless. The promised distinction and substitutability are supported by and themselves support immense resources directed to developing methods for the strong analysis of practical actions and practical reasoning. Promised applications and benefits are immense.

Nevertheless, *wherever practical actions are topics of study* the promised distinction and substitutability of objective for indexical expressions remains programmatic in every *particular* case and in every *actual* occasion in which the distinction or substitutability must be demonstrated. In every actual case without exception, conditions will be cited that a competent investigator will be required to recognize, such that in *that* particular case the terms of the demonstration can be relaxed and nevertheless the demonstration be counted an adequate one.

We learn from logicians and linguists, who are in virtually unanimous agreement about them, what some of these conditions are. For "long" texts, or "long" courses of action, for events where members' actions are features of the events their actions are accomplishing, or wherever tokens are not used or are not suitable as proxies for indexical expressions, the program's claimed demonstrations are satisfied as matters of practical social management.

Under such conditions indexical expressions, by reason of their prevalence and other properties, present immense, obstinate, and irremediable nuisances to the tasks of dealing rigorously with the phenomena of structure and relevance in theories of consistency proofs and computability, and in attempts to recover actual as compared with supposed common conduct and common talk with full structural particulars. Drawing upon their experience in the uses of sample surveys, and the design and application of measurements of practical actions, statistical analyses, mathematical models, and computer simulations of social processes, professional sociologists are able to document endlessly the ways in which the programmatic distinction and substitutability is satisfied in, and depends upon, professional practices of socially managed demonstration.

In short, wherever studies of practical actions are involved, the distinction and substitutability is always accomplished *only* for all practical purposes. Thereby, the first problematic phenomenon is recommended to consist of the reflexivity of the practices and attainments of sciences in and of the organized activities of everyday life, which is an essential reflexivity.

The "Uninteresting" Essential Reflexivity of Accounts

For members engaged in practical sociological reasoning—as we shall see in later studies, for staff personnel at the Los Angeles Suicide Prevention Center, for staff users of psychiatric clinic folders at U.C.L.A., for graduate student coders of psychiatric records, for jurors, for an intersexed person managing a sex change, for professional sociological researchers—their concerns are for what is decidable "for practical purposes," "in light of this situation," "given the nature of actual circumstances," and the like. Practical circumstances and practical actions refer for them to many organizationally important and serious matters: to resources, aims, excuses, opportunities, tasks, and of course to grounds for arguing or foretelling the adequacy of procedures and of the findings they yield. One matter, however, is excluded from their interests: practical actions and practical circumstances are not in themselves *a* topic, let alone a sole topic of their inquiries; nor are their inquiries, addressed to the tasks of sociological theorizing, undertaken to formulate what these tasks consist of as practical actions. In no case is the investigation of practical actions undertaken in order that personnel might be able to recognize and describe what they are doing in the first place. Least of all are practical actions investigated in order to explain to practitioners their own talk about what they are doing. For example personnel at the Los Angeles Suicide Prevention Center found it altogether incongruous to consider seriously that they be so engaged in the work of certifying mode of death that a person seeking to commit suicide and they could concert their efforts to assure the unequivocal recognition of "what really happened."

To say they are "not interested" in the study of practical actions is not to complain, nor to point to an opportunity they miss, nor is it a disclosure of error, nor is it an ironic comment. Neither is it the case that because members are "not interested" that they are "precluded" from sociological theorizing. Nor do their inquiries preclude the use of the rule of doubt, nor are they precluded from making the organized activities of everyday life scientifically problematical, nor does the comment insinuate a difference between "basic" and "applied" interests in research and theorizing.

What does it mean then to say that they are "not interested" in studying practical actions and practical sociological reasoning? And what is the import of such a statement?

There is a feature of members' accounts that for them is of such singular and prevailing relevance that it controls other features in their specific character as recognizable, rational features of practical sociological inquiries. The feature is this. With respect to the problematic character of practical actions and to the practical adequacy of their inquiries, members take for granted that a member must at the outset "know" the settings in which he is to operate if his practices are to serve as measures to bring particular, located features of these settings to recognizable account. They treat as the most passing matter of fact that members' accounts, of every sort, in all their logical modes, with all of their uses, and for every method for their assembly are constituent features of the settings they make observable. Members know, require, count on, and make use of this reflexivity to produce, accomplish, recognize, or demonstrate rational-adequacy-for-all-practical-purposes of their procedures and findings.

Not only do members—the jurors and the others—take that reflexivity for granted, but they recognize, demonstrate, and make observable for each other the rational character of their actual, and that means their occasional, practices while respecting that reflexivity as an unalterable and unavoidable condition of their inquiries.

When I propose that members are "not interested" in studying practical actions, I do not mean that members will have none, a little, or a lot of it. That they are "not interested" has to do with reasonable practices, with plausible argument, and with reasonable findings. It has to do with treating "accountable-for-all-practical-purposes" as a discoverable matter, exclusively, only, and entirely. For members to be "interested" would consist of their undertaking to make the "reflexive" character of practical activities observable; to examine the artful practices of rational inquiry as organizational phenomena without thought for correctives or irony. Members of the Los Angeles Suicide Prevention Center are like members wherever they engage in practical sociological inquiries: though they would, they *can* have none of it.

The Analyzability of Actions-in-Context as a Practical Accomplishment

In indefinitely many ways members' inquiries are constituent features of the settings they analyze. In the same ways, their inquiries are made recognizable to members as adequate-for-all-practical-purposes. For example, at the Los Angeles Suicide Prevention Center, that deaths are made accountable-for-all-practical-purposes are practical organizational accomplishments. Organizationally, the Suicide Prevention Center consists of practical procedures for accomplishing the rational accountability of suicidal deaths as recognizable features of the settings in which that accountability occurs.

In the actual occasions of interaction that accomplishment is for members omnipresent, unproblematic, and commonplace. For members doing sociology, to make that accomplishment a topic of practical sociological inquiry seems unavoidably to require that they treat the rational properties of practical activities as "anthropologically strange." By this I mean to call attention to "reflexive" practices such as the following: that by his accounting practices the member makes familiar, commonplace activities of everyday life recognizable *as* familiar, commonplace activities; that on each occasion that an account of common activities is used, that they be recognized for "another first time"; that the member treat the processes and attainments of "imagination" as continuous with the *other* observable features of the settings in which they occur; and of proceeding in such a way that at the same time that the member "in the midst" of witnessed actual settings recognizes that witnessed settings have an *accomplished* sense, an accomplished facticity, an accomplished objectivity, an accomplished familiarity, an accomplished accountability, for the member the organizational hows of these accomplishments are unproblematic, are known vaguely, and are known only in the doing which is done skillfully, reliably, uniformly, with enormous standardization and as an unaccountable matter.

That accomplishment consists of members doing, recognizing, and using ethnographies. In unknown ways that accomplishment is for members a commonplace phenomenon. And in the unknown ways that the accomplishment is commonplace it is for our interests, an awesome phenomenon, for in its unknown ways it consists (1) of members' uses of concerted everyday activities as methods with which to recognize and demonstrate the isolatable, typical, uniform, potential repetition, connected appearance, consistency, equivalence, substitutability, directionality, anonymously describable, planful—in short, the rational properties of indexical expressions and indexical actions. (2) The phenomenon consists, too, of the analyzability of actions-in-context given that not only does no concept of context-in-general exist, but every use of "context" without exception is itself essentially indexical.

The *recognizedly* rational properties of their common sense inquiries—their recognizedly consistent, or methodic, or uniform, or planful, etc. character—are *somehow* attainments of members' concerted activities. For Suicide Prevention Center staff, for coders, for jurors the rational properties of their practical inquiries *somehow* consist in the concerted work of making evident from fragments, from proverbs, from passing remarks, from rumors, from partial descriptions, from "codified" but essentially vague catalogues of experience and the like how a person died in society, or by what criteria patients were selected for psychiatric treatment, or which among the alternative verdicts was correct. *Somehow* is the problematic crux of the matter.

What Is Ethnomethodology?

The earmark of practical sociological reasoning, wherever it occurs, is that it seeks to remedy the indexical properties of members' talk and conduct. Endless methodological studies are directed to the tasks of providing members a remedy for indexical expressions in members' abiding attempts, with rigorous uses of ideals to demonstrate the observability of organized activities in actual occasions with situated particulars of talk and conduct.

The properties of indexical expressions and indexical actions are ordered properties. These consist of organizationally demonstrable sense, or facticity, or methodic use, or agreement among "cultural colleagues." Their ordered properties consist of organizationally demonstrable rational properties of indexical expressions and in-dexical actions. Those ordered properties are ongoing achievements of the con-certed commonplace activities of investigators. The demonstrable rationality of in-dexical expressions and indexical actions retains over the course of its managed production by members the character of ordinary, familiar, routinized practical cir-cumstances. As process and attainment the produced rationality of indexical expres-sions consists of practical tasks subject to every exigency of organizationally situated conduct.

I use the term "ethnomethodology" to refer to the investigation of the rational properties of indexical expressions and other practical actions as contingent ongo-ing accomplishments of organized artful practices of everyday life.❖

Pierre Bourdieu (1930–) studied at the Lycée Louis le Grand in Paris, then at the École Normale Supérieure, where he was a student of philosophy. He came into so-ciology with the support of Raymond Aron and soon became one of the dominant forces in French sociology. Today, he is considered one of the world's leading social theorists and students of culture. For many years, Bourdieu has taught at the École Pratique des Hautes Etudes. In 1975, he founded the journal he continues to edit—*Actes de la récherche en sciences sociales*—in which appear the brilliant empirical stud-ies of French culture Bourdieu does with coworkers like Monique de St. Martin. In 1982, Bourdieu was elected to a chair in sociology at the Collège de France. His many books include *Outline of a Theory of Practice* (1972), *Distinction* (1979), *Homo Academicus* (1984), and *The Logic of Practice* (1990). The selection is from the last of these. It presents Bourdieu's famous idea of *habitus*—that is, the notion that objec-tive structures never work in the abstract but exert themselves in the habitual dispo-sitions of individuals. In habits, subjective consciousness meets objective reality in practical human action that is both enduring and unique. This is clearly one of the most inventive attempts to work through the dilemma of modern social theory: How do structures affect actions? A comparison with earlier thinkers reveals just how far social thinking had advanced since Niebuhr and Keynes saw, in the 1920s and 1930s, that individuals and structures were not easy companions.

Structures, Habitus, *Practices*
Pierre Bourdieu (1974, 1980)

Objectivism constitutes the social world as a spectacle offered to an observer who takes up a 'point of view' on the action and who, putting into the object the principles of his relation to the object, proceeds as if it were intended solely for knowledge and as if all the interactions within it were purely symbolic exchanges. This viewpoint is the one taken from high positions in the social structure, from which the social world is seen as a representation (as the word is used in idealist philosophy, but also as in painting) or a performance (in the theatrical or musical sense), and practices are seen as no

Excerpt from Richard Nice, trans., *The Logic of Practice* (Stanford: Stanford University Press, 1990), pp. 52–58. Reprinted with the permission of the publishers, Stanford University Press, Polity Press, and Basil Blackwell.

more than the acting-out of roles, the playing of scores or the implementation of plans. The theory of practice as practice insists, contrary to positivist materialism, that the objects of knowledge are constructed, not passively recorded, and, contrary to intellectualist idealism, that the principle of this construction is the system of structured, structuring dispositions, the *habitus*, which is constituted in practice and is always oriented towards practical functions. It is possible to step down from the sovereign viewpoint from which objectivist idealism orders the world, as Marx demands in the *Theses on Feuerbach,* but without having to abandon to it the 'active aspect' of apprehension of the world by reducing knowledge to a mere recording. To do this, one has to situate oneself *within* 'real activity as such,' that is, in the practical relation to the world, the preoccupied, active presence in the world through which the world imposes its presence, with its urgencies, its things to be done and said, things made to be said, which directly govern words and deeds without ever unfolding as a spectacle. One has to escape from the realism of the structure, to which objectivism, a necessary stage in breaking with primary experience and constructing the objective relationships, necessarily leads when it hypostatizes these relations by treating them as realities already constituted outside of the history of the group—without falling back into subjectivism, which is quite incapable of giving an account of the necessity of the social world. To do this, one has to return to practice, the site of the dialectic of the *opus operatum* and the *modus operandi;* of the objectified products and the incorporated products of historical practice; of structures and *habitus.*

> The bringing to light of the presuppositions inherent in objectivist construction has paradoxically been delayed by the efforts of all those who, in linguistics as in anthropology, have sought to 'correct' the structuralist model by appealing to 'context' or 'situation' to account for variations, exceptions and accidents (instead of making them simple variants, absorbed into the structure, as the structuralists do). They have thus avoided a radical questioning of the objectivist mode of thought, when, that is, they have not simply fallen back on to the free choice of a rootless, unattached, pure subject. Thus, the method known as 'situational analysis,' which consists of 'observing people in a variety of social situations' in order to determine 'the way in which individuals are able to exercise choices within the limits of a specified social structure' (Gluckman 1961) remains locked within the framework of the rule and the exception, which Edmund Leach (often invoked by the exponents of this method) spells out explicitly: 'I postulate that structural systems in which all avenues of social action are narrowly institutionalized are impossible. In all viable systems, there must be an area where the individual is free to make choices so as to manipulate the system to his advantage.'

The conditionings associated with a particular class of conditions of existence produce *habitus,* systems of durable, transposable dispositions, structured structures predisposed to function as structuring structures, that is, as principles which generate and organize practices and representations that can be objectively adapted to their outcomes without presupposing a conscious aiming at ends or an express mastery of the operations necessary in order to attain them. Objectively 'regulated' and 'regular' without being in any way the product of obedience to rules, they can be collectively orchestrated without being the product of the organizing action of a conductor.

It is, of course, never ruled out that the responses of the *habitus* may be accompanied by a strategic calculation tending to perform in a conscious mode the operation that the *habitus* performs quite differently, namely an estimation of chances presupposing transformation of the past effect into an expected objective. But these responses are first defined, without any calculation, in relation to objective potentialities, immediately inscribed in the present, things to do or not to do, things to say or not to say, in relation to a probable, 'upcoming' future (*un à venir*), which—in contrast to the future seen as 'absolute possibility' (*absolute Möglichkeit*) in Hegel's (or Sartre's) sense, projected by the pure project of a 'negative freedom'—puts itself forward with an urgency and a claim to existence that excludes all deliberation. Stimuli do not exist for practice in their objective truth, as conditional, conventional triggers, acting only on condition that they encounter agents conditioned to recognize them. The practical world that is constituted in the relationship with the *habitus,* acting as a system of cognitive and motivating structures, is a world of already realized ends—procedures to follow, paths to take—and of objects endowed with a 'permanent teleological character,' in Husserl's phrase, tools or institutions. This is because the regularities inherent in an arbitrary condition ('arbitrary' in Saussure's and Mauss's sense) tend to appear as necessary, even natural, since they are the basis of the schemes of perception and appreciation through which they are apprehended.

If a very close correlation is regularly observed between the scientifically constructed objective probabilities (for example, the chances of access to a particular good) and agents' subjective aspirations ('motivations' and 'needs'), this is not because agents consciously adjust their aspirations to an exact evaluation of their chances of success, like a gambler organizing his stakes on the basis of perfect information about his chances of winning. In reality, the dispositions durably inculcated by the possibilities and impossibilities, freedoms and necessities, opportunities and prohibitions inscribed in the objective conditions (which science apprehends through statistical regularities such as the probabilities objectively attached to a group or class) generate dispositions objectively compatible with these conditions and in a sense pre-adapted to their demands. The most improbable practices are therefore excluded, as unthinkable, by a kind of immediate submission to order that inclines agents to make a virtue of necessity, that is, to refuse what is anyway denied and to will the inevitable. The very conditions of production of the *habitus,* a virtue made of necessity, mean that the anticipations it generates tend to ignore the restriction to which the validity of calculation of probabilities is subordinated, namely that the experimental conditions should not have been modified. Unlike scientific estimations, which are corrected after each experiment according to rigorous rules of calculation, the anticipations of the *habitus,* practical hypotheses based on past experience, give disproportionate weight to early experiences. Through the economic and social necessity that they bring to bear on the relatively autonomous world of the domestic economy and family relations, or more precisely, through the specifically familial manifestations of this external necessity (forms of the division of labour between the sexes, household objects, modes of consumption, parent-child relations, etc.), the structures characterizing a determinate class of conditions of existence produce the structures of the *habitus,* which in their turn are the basis of the perception and appreciation of all subsequent experiences.

The *habitus,* a product of history, produces individual and collective practices—more history—in accordance with the schemes generated by history. It ensures the active presence of past experiences, which, deposited in each organism in the form of schemes of perception, thought and action, tend to guarantee the 'correctness' of practices and their constancy over time, more reliably than all formal rules and explicit norms. This system of dispositions—a present past that tends to perpetuate itself into the future by reactivation in similarly structured practices, an internal law through which the law of external necessities, irreducible to immediate constraints, is constantly exerted—is the principle of the continuity and regularity which objectivism sees in social practices without being able to account for it; and also of the regulated transformations that cannot be explained either by the extrinsic, instantaneous determinisms of mechanistic sociologism or by the purely internal but equally instantaneous determination of spontaneist subjectivism. Overriding the spurious opposition between the forces inscribed in an earlier state of the system, outside the body, and the internal forces arising instantaneously as motivations springing from free will, the internal dispositions—the internalization of externality—enable the external forces to exert themselves, but in accordance with the specific logic of the organisms in which they are incorporated, i.e., in a durable, systematic and non-mechanical way. As an acquired system of generative schemes, the *habitus* makes possible the free production of all the thoughts, perceptions and actions inherent in the particular conditions of its production—and only those. Through the *habitus,* the structure of which it is the product governs practice, not along the paths of a mechanical determinism, but within the constraints and limits initially set on its inventions. This infinite yet strictly limited generative capacity is difficult to understand only so long as one remains locked in the usual antinomies— which the concept of the *habitus* aims to transcend—of determinism and freedom, conditioning and creativity, consciousness and the unconscious, or the individual and society. Because the *habitus* is an infinite capacity for generating products— thoughts, perceptions, expressions and actions—whose limits are set by the historically and socially situated conditions of its production, the conditioned and conditional freedom it provides is as remote from creation of unpredictable novelty as it is from simple mechanical reproduction of the original conditioning.

Nothing is more misleading than the illusion created by hindsight in which all the traces of a life, such as the works of an artist or the events at a biography, appear as the realization of an essence that seems to preexist them. Just as a mature artistic style is not contained, like a seed, in an original inspiration but is continuously defined and redefined in the dialectic between the objectifying intention and the already objectified intention, so too the unity of meaning which, after the event, may seem to have preceded the acts and works announcing the final significance, retrospectively transforming the various stages of the temporal series into mere preparatory sketches, is constituted through the confrontation between questions that only exist in and for a mind armed with a particular type of schemes and the solutions obtained through application of these same schemes. The genesis of a system of works or practices generated by the same *habitus* (or homologous *habitus,* such as those that underlie the unity of the life-style of a group or a class) cannot be described either as the autonomous development of a unique and always self-identical essence, or as a continuous creation of novelty, because it arises from the necessary yet unpredictable confrontation between the *habitus* and an event that can exercise a pertinent incitement on the *habitus* only if the latter snatches it from the contingency of the accidental and constitutes it as a problem by applying to it the very principles of its solution; and also because the *habitus,* like every 'art of inventing,' is what makes it possible to produce an infinite number of practices that are relatively unpredictable (like the corresponding situations) but also limited in their diversity.

In short, being the product of a particular class of objective regularities, the *habitus* tends to generate all the 'reasonable,' 'common-sense,' behaviours (and only these) which are possible within the limits of these regularities, and which are likely to be positively sanctioned because they are objectively adjusted to the logic characteristic of a particular field, whose objective future they anticipate. At the same time, 'without violence, art or argument,' it tends to exclude all 'extravagances' ('not for the likes of us'), that is, all the behaviours that would be negatively sanctioned because they are incompatible with the objective conditions.

Because they tend to reproduce the regularities immanent in the conditions in which their generative principle was produced while adjusting to the demands inscribed as objective potentialities in the situation as defined by the cognitive and motivating structures that constitute the *habitus,* practices cannot be deduced either from the present conditions which may seem to have provoked them or from the past conditions which have produced the *habitus,* the durable principle of their production. They can therefore only be accounted for by relating the social conditions in which the *habitus* that generated them was constituted, to the social conditions in which it is implemented, that is, through the scientific work of performing the interrelationship of these two states of the social world that the *habitus* performs, while concealing it, in and through practice. The 'unconscious,' which enables one to dispense with this interrelating, is never anything other than the forgetting of history which history itself produces by realizing the objective structures that it generates in the quasi-natures of *habitus.* . . .

The *habitus*—embodied history, internalized as a second nature and so forgotten as history—is the active presence of the whole past of which it is the product. As such, it is what gives practices their relative autonomy with respect to external determinations of the immediate present. This autonomy is that of the past, enacted and acting, which, functioning as accumulated capital, produces history on the basis of history and so ensures the permanence in change that makes the individual agent a world within the world. The *habitus* is a spontaneity without consciousness or will, opposed as much to the mechanical necessity of things without history in mechanistic theories as it is to the reflexive freedom of subjects 'without inertia' in rationalist theories.

Thus the dualistic vision that recognizes only the self-transparent act of consciousness or the externally determined thing has to give way to the real logic of action, which brings together two objectifications of history, objectification in bodies and objectification in institutions or, which amounts to the same thing, two states of capital, objectified and incorporated, through which a distance is set up from necessity and its urgencies. This logic is seen in paradigmatic form in the dialectic of expressive dispositions and instituted means of expression (morphological, syntactic and lexical instruments, literary genres, etc.) which is observed in the intentionless invention of regulated improvisation. Endlessly overtaken by his own words, with which he maintains a relation of 'carry and be carried,' as Nicolai Hartmann put it, the virtuoso finds in his discourse the triggers for his discourse, which goes along like a train laying its own rails. In other words, being produced by a *modus operandi* which is not consciously mastered, the discourse contains an 'objective intention,' as the Scholastics put it, which outruns the conscious intentions of its apparent author and constantly offers new pertinent stimuli to the *modus operandi* of which it is the product and which functions as a kind of 'spiritual automaton.' If witticisms strike as much by their unpredictability as by their retrospective necessity, the reason is that the *trouvaille* that brings to light long buried resources presupposes a *habitus* that so perfectly possesses the objectively available means of expression that it is possessed by them, so much so that it asserts its freedom from them by realizing the rarest of the possibilities that they necessarily imply. The dialectic of the meaning of the language and the 'sayings of the tribe' is a particular and particularly significant case of the dialectic between *habitus* and institutions, that is, between two modes of objectification of past history, in which there is constantly created a history that inevitably appears, like witticisms, as both original and inevitable.

This durably installed generative principle of regulated improvisations is a practical sense which reactivates the sense objectified in institutions. Produced by the work of inculcation and appropriation that is needed in order for objective structures, the products of collective history, to be reproduced in the form of the durable, adjusted dispositions that are the condition of their functioning, the *habitus*, which is constituted in the course of an individual history, imposing its particular logic on incorporation, and through which agents partake of the history objectified in institutions, is what makes it possible to inhabit institutions, to appropriate them practically, and so to keep them in activity, continuously pulling them from the state of dead letters, reviving the sense deposited in them, but at the same time imposing the revisions and transformations that reactivation entails. Or rather, the *habitus* is what enables the institution to attain full realization: it is through the capacity for incorporation, which exploits the body's readiness to take seriously the performative magic of the social, that the king, the banker or the priest are hereditary monarchy, financial capitalism or the Church made flesh. Property appropriates its owner, embodying itself in the form of a structure generating practices perfectly conforming with its logic and its demands. If one is justified in saying, with Marx, that 'the lord of an entailed estate, the first-born son, belongs to the land,' that 'it inherits him,' or that the 'persons' of capitalists are the 'personification' of capital, this is because the purely social and quasi-magical process of socialization, which is inaugurated by the act of marking that institutes an individual as an eldest son, an heir, a successor, a Christian, or simply as a man (as opposed to a woman), with all the corresponding privileges and obligations, and which is prolonged, strengthened and confirmed by social treatments that tend to transform instituted difference into natural distinction, produces quite real effects, durably inscribed in the body and in belief. An institution, even an economy, is complete and fully viable only if it is durably objectified not only in things, that is, in the logic, transcending individual agents, of a particular field, but also in bodies, in durable dispositions to recognize and comply with the demands immanent in the field.❖

Audre Lorde (1934–1992) was born in Manhattan and graduated from Hunter College and Columbia University. She was an acclaimed poet whose poetry and other writings are classic texts to contemporary feminism, particularly to Black lesbian feminisms. Lorde traveled and lectured across the world and was a founder of the Women of Color Press. Between 1968 and 1992, Lorde published at least seventeen books of poetry, essays, and memoirs. She was the poet laureate of the State of New York in 1991. Her book of essays, *A Burst of Light,* won an American Book Award in 1989, and an earlier collection, *From the Land Where Other People Live* (1973), was nominated for a National Book Award. Lorde's last book was *Undersong: Chosen Po-*

ems, Old and New (1992). The selection is a 1979 essay from her collection of feminist essays and talks, *Sister Outsider* (1984). Here, Lorde frames an earlier version of the fractured identities perspective as a critique of white, academic feminism. This and her famous open letter to Mary Daly of the same year are early statements of the distance women of color sometimes felt, and continue to feel, from white-dominated academic feminism. Implicitly, Lorde's argument is a critique of stand-point feminism in that she affirms that her identity is not simply that of her gender but also of her race and sexuality. Audre Lorde died in 1992 after many years struggling with cancer, about which she wrote in *Cancer Journals* (1980).

The Master's Tools Will Never Dismantle the Master's House
Audre Lorde (1979)

I agreed to take part in a New York University Institute for the Humanities conference a year ago, with the understanding that I would be commenting upon papers dealing with the role of difference within the lives of American women: difference of race, sexuality, class, and age. The absence of these considerations weakens any feminist discussion of the personal and the political.

It is a particular academic arrogance to assume any discussion of feminist theory without examining our many differences, and without a significant input from poor women, Black and Third World women, and lesbians. And yet, I stand here as a Black lesbian feminist, having been invited to comment within the only panel at this conference where the input of Black feminists and lesbians is represented. What this says about the vision of this conference is sad, in a country where racism, sexism, and homophobia are inseparable. To read this program is to assume that lesbian and Black women have nothing to say about existentialism, the erotic, women's culture and silence, developing feminist theory, or heterosexuality and power. And what does it mean in personal and political terms when even the two Black women who did present here were literally found at the last hour? What does it mean when the tools of a racist patriarchy are used to examine the fruits of that same patriarchy? It means that only the most narrow perimeters of change are possible and allowable.

The absence of any consideration of lesbian consciousness or the consciousness of Third World women leaves a serious gap within this conference and within the papers presented here. For example, in a paper on material relationships between women, I was conscious of an either/or model of nurturing which totally dismissed my knowledge as a Black lesbian. In this paper there was no examination of mutuality between women, no systems of shared support, no interdependence as exists between lesbians and women-identified women. Yet it is only in the patriarchal model of nurturance that women "who attempt to emancipate themselves pay perhaps too high a price for the results," as this paper states.

For women, the need and desire to nurture each other is not pathological but redemptive, and it is within that knowledge that our real power is rediscovered. It is this real connection which is so feared by a patriarchal world. Only within a patriarchal structure is maternity the only social power open to women.

Interdependency between women is the way to a freedom which allows the *I* to *be*, not in order to be used, but in order to be creative. This is a difference between the passive *be* and the active *being*.

Advocating the mere tolerance of difference between women is the grossest reformism. It is a total denial of the creative function of difference in our lives. Difference must be not merely tolerated, but seen as a fund of necessary polarities between which our creativity can spark like a dialectic. Only then does the necessity for interdependency become unthreatening. Only within that interdependency of different strengths, acknowledged and equal, can the power to seek new ways of being in the world generate, as well as the courage and sustenance to act where there are no charters.

Within the interdependence of mutual (nondominant) differences lies that security which enables us to descend into the chaos of knowledge and return with true visions of our future, along with the concomitant power to effect those changes which can bring that future into being. Difference is that raw and powerful connection from which our personal power is forged.

As women, we have been taught either to ignore our differences, or to view them as causes for separation and suspicion rather than as forces for change. Without community there is no liberation, only the most vulnerable and temporary armistice between an individual and her oppression. But community must not mean a shedding of our differences, nor the pathetic pretense that these differences do not exist.

Those of us who stand outside the circle of this society's definition of acceptable women; those of us who have been forged in the crucibles of difference—those of us who are poor, who are lesbians, who are Black, who are older—know that *survival is not an academic skill*. It is learning how to stand alone, unpopular and sometimes reviled, and how to make common cause with those others identified as outside the structures in order to define and seek a world in which we can all flourish. It is learning how to take our differences and make them strengths. *For the master's tools will never dismantle the master's house.* They may allow us temporarily to beat him at his own game, but they will never enable us to bring about genuine change. And this fact is only threatening to those women who still define the master's house as their only source of support.

Poor women and women of Color know there is a difference between the daily manifestations of marital slavery and prostitution because it is our daughters who line 42nd Street. If white American feminist theory need not deal with the differences between us, and the resulting difference in our oppressions, then how do you deal with the fact that the women who clean your houses and tend your children while you attend conferences on feminist theory are, for the most part, poor women and women of Color? What is the theory behind racist feminism?

In a world of possibility for us all, our personal visions help lay the groundwork for political action. The failure of academic feminists to recognize difference as a crucial strength is a failure to reach beyond the first patriarchal lesson. In our world, divide and conquer must become define and empower.

Why weren't other women of Color found to participate in this conference? Why were two phone calls to me considered a consultation? Am I the only possible source of names of Black feminists? And although the Black panelist's paper ends on an important and powerful connection of love between women, what about interracial cooperation between feminists who don't love each other?

In academic feminist circles, the answer to these questions is often, "We did not know who to ask." But that is the same evasion of responsibility, the same cop-out, that keeps Black women's art out of women's exhibitions, Black women's work out of most feminist publications except for the occasional "Special Third World Women's Issue," and Black women's texts off your reading lists. But as Adrienne Rich pointed out in a recent talk, white feminists have educated themselves about such an enormous amount over the past ten years, how come you haven't also educated yourselves about Black women and the differences between us—white and Black—when it is key to our survival as a movement?

Women of today are still being called upon to stretch across the gap of male ignorance and to educate men as to our existence and our needs. This is an old and primary tool of all oppressors to keep the oppressed occupied with the master's concerns. Now we hear that it is the task of women of Color to educate white women—in the face of tremendous resistance—as to our existence, our differences, our relative roles in our joint survival. This is a diversion of energies and a tragic repetition of racist patriarchal thought.

Simone de Beauvoir once said: "It is in the knowledge of the genuine conditions of our lives that we must draw our strength to live and our reasons for acting."

Racism and homophobia are real conditions of all our lives in this place and time. *I urge each one of us here to reach down into that deep place of knowledge inside herself and touch that terror and loathing of any difference that lives there. See whose face it wears.* Then the personal as the political can begin to illuminate all our choices. ❖

PART FIVE

After Modernity,
Since 1979

Each of the previous periods began in years the meaning of which is evident: 1848, 1919, 1945, 1963. Reasonable people might disagree over whether historical periods actually began in those years. Just the same, the years are meaningful. Nothing similar could be said of 1980 or 1979 or any particular year thereabout.

The late 1970s and early 1980s were, historically speaking, a sloppy, indefinite time. Much happened, but hardly anyone today can say what it all meant. In the two years 1979 and 1980, the following notable events occurred in the United States: gasoline rationing; U.S. inflation was 13 percent; Chrysler Corporation was bailed out by taxpayers; Tom Wolfe's *Right Stuff* was published; Christopher Lasch's *The Culture of Narcissism* became a best-seller; Francis Ford Coppola directed *Apocalypse Now;* the Three-Mile Island nuclear reactor was damaged; Walter Cronkite retired. Interesting, but hard to figure. In the world, in the same two years, the following events transpired: the Ayatollah Khomeini led a successful revolution in Iran; the Sandinistas chased Anastasio Somoza from Managua; Panama took control of the Canal Zone; Egypt and Israel entered into a peace treaty; Rhodesia became Zimbabwe; the Soviets invaded Afghanistan; Iraq invaded Iran; Mother Teresa won the Nobel Peace Prize; Leonid Brezhnev won the Lenin Peace Prize. Though the events on both lists may suggest trends developing from the events of the 1960s, no large event defined the historical moment as in 1945 or 1963 or 1968. The late 1970s and 1980s just were whatever they were.

Yet there are those who would claim that sometime around these years, the most momentous event of the last 500 years may have occurred: the end of modernity itself. Or, more modestly, it can be said this was when people began to talk seriously about postmodernism. Why, then, is unclear. One might say, however, that the very indefiniteness of the nonevent (in contrast to the event of which Derrida spoke in 1966) is typical of postmodernism, whatever it might be.

This, of course, was not the first time social commentators spoke of a "post-something." Beginning in 1945, "postwar" meant something was changed, hopefully forever. In the late 1950s, Daniel Bell and others who wrote of the end of ideology had in mind a new era of democratic freedoms. Later, about the time John Kenneth Galbraith wrote *The New Industrial State,* many were talking seriously of a postindustrial world order. In the early 1990s, U.S. President George Bush spoke of a new world order. Such ventures to define the end of one thing and the beginning of the next were, in one sense, little more than the natural tendency of modern people to feel the upward-rising trajectory of progress. Modernity's foremost logical dilemma is that it must always project a next stage (thus, a post-the-previous-stage)—or it must prove that the present is, in fact, the final fulfillment of history. Because the lat-

ter is almost impossible to prove, modernity has always pressed on to the next envelope of time.

But prophecies of a postmodern time, or culture, are different. Generally, they do
not claim to be progress of any kind. Nor do they prophesy a reversal of history's lin-
ear fortunes, a kind of progressive devolution. From time to time in the modern era,
cyclical theories of the rise and fall of civilization offered this sort of interpretation.
Some, even now, say that America is the falling civilization, with the expectation
that another (Europe or Japan) will inevitably rise. But these, too, are variants on the
theme of modern progress; that is, when things go bad, one way to account for the
absence of progress is to say it has temporarily turned back, as if to clear the way for
the rise of the next, better civilization. But theories of the postmodern do not make
this sort of claim.

Those who believe in the postmodern, different as they are, tend to believe it is a
surprising, sometimes humorous, and always disconcerting mixture of present, past,
and future—or of cultural and spatial elements from these different times. Probably
the most famous architectural symbol of the postmodern is the AT&T building in
midtown New York City. Physically, the building rises from a classic base of Greco-
Roman arches and columns to a Chippendale pediment decorating the top of a
modernist skyscraper. At least three design features, from at least as many different
periods of time, seem to be saying that history is not a straight, progressive line. History is not real and simple but complicated and perverse. The Chippendale decoration is clearly a joke of some kind. Is it to say, "This building is really a piece of furniture"? Or, as some suggest, is the Chippendale design a mockery of AT&T's
product—a cradle for old-fashioned telephones? Impossible to say, but it is a joke,
even if one cannot get it. Then, of course, one must wonder why one of the world's
most visibly powerful American corporations wanted a building that made a joke of
the idea that history makes sense. When, in the early 1990s, AT&T sold the building
to one of Japan's most visible corporations, Sony, it only added to the confusion, the
joke, the disruption of normal cultural and economic sense.

In "Postmodernity or Radicalized Modernity?" Anthony Giddens conveys the popular impression that the postmodern is about fragmentation, the dissolution of the
self, the uncertainty of any theory of knowledge. Those, like Giddens, who are skeptical of postmodernism tend to picture it just so: a kind of ongoing drama of 1968,
the ever-augmenting disappearance of the Center into a sea of relativism. Some proponents of the postmodern find this impression too overwrought. They would point
out, for example, that whatever is going on designwise, the AT&T building is still a
building that works, complete with rest rooms, offices, real telephones, and working
people. A controversy like this, one without an evidently strong solution, at least
helps clarify the questions being asked:

Are modern times at their end? Has the world changed, in the last generation, in
such a way that the culture of the modern world that took shape in the eighteenth
century is no longer viable? Is the new world order somehow different? Put this way,
the debate makes better sense. Those who believe in the postmodern could argue
that the world is, indeed, more fragmented, without a single powerful political and
economic Center. The notion that things are progressing steadily and obviously toward some definitely better state is far from clear, they would add. On the other
side, proponents of the modern (like Habermas or Giddens and many others) would
argue: Obviously, the modern world has changed since the nineteenth or even mid-
twentieth century. Social life is less well tied together in the older sense: some would

AT&T Building

contend it is better integrated in other ways. Electronic media (CNN, fax machines, computer networks) are the tools of extra-governmental forces (corporations, terrorist groups, new political movements) that integrate the world in new ways. The fall of the European powers, some modernists would say, does not mean the modern world is not advancing. In Giddens's words, radicalized modernity "sees high modernity as a set of circumstances in which dispersal is dialectically connected to profound tendencies towards global integration." In simpler terms, other modernists believe that, as bad as things are, it is still possible to gather the world's people around common principles of human aspiration. The old Enlightenment doctrines need revision, they insist, but the principles still work. In this view, the hand we've been dealt may not be great, but it is good enough to effect human liberation from all that oppresses. Modernists tend to assume that postmodernists have given up on humanity, that their jokes and frivolity take the world too lightly. Serious modernists will refer to writers like Jean Baudrillard, who seem to say that the real world is no more real than Disneyland. They find this an absurdly apolitical attitude. On the other hand, postmodernists, even those who would never say that Disneyland is reality, might argue that the trouble with modernists of all kinds is that they take themselves and history far too seriously.

Each point of view has something to recommend it. It is true that modernity, whether traditional or radical, has proven itself ponderous, self-important, and largely unable to support its claims that things are getting better. On the other hand, proponents of the postmodern seem to be tricksters far too ready to throw out the best hopes for human freedom and fulfillment, without a ready explanation as to what we will do in a fragmented world without moral centers or values of any kind. Choosing between the two alternatives is mostly a matter of taste. Pick the one that appeals to your sensibilities. This is, itself, a kind of postmodern dilemma. If one side cannot win the argument, if there is no final authority (as Richard Rorty puts it) to which we can refer to resolve the debate, then are we not in something like a postmodern time, whatever we might call it? It turns out that recognition of this dilemma is the only (admittedly weak) reason to select a date like 1979 as the beginning of a *possible* postmodern period. This was when Jean-François Lyotard, a French philosopher, and Richard Rorty, an American, published two very different books, *The Postmodern Condition* and *Philosophy and the Mirror of Nature.* For some, these books, provided explanations for the commonsense experience that no one seemed to agree on what, if anything, was real—and that no one had any final argument or wonderful story to tell on which people might agree.

It is, of course, more than a little outrageous to suggest that two very technical academic books could serve as defining moments. But because enthusiasts for the postmodern tend to be in the cultural elite (many of them are academics), this is not surprising. It would be wrong, however, to leave the impression that the idea of a postmodern condition is nothing more than the fad of certain paid social theorists. The issue of the postmodern is, in part, a debate among intellectuals. But it is also a debate about the history of the world and its culture. For every unsettling book about Disneyland that says there is no real world, one can find "real" world events to support the postmodern claim. Vietnam was somehow like a Francis Ford Coppola movie. Richard Nixon's Watergate was, as they said, "unreal." It was unbelievable that the Americans would become involved in Vietnam after what happened to the French—and the Soviets would make the same unreal mistake in Afghanistan. Moreover, there really are buildings like the AT&T. One finds them in most cities of any size. There is such a thing as MTV, and Madonna and Public Enemy—musicalized performances that invite one into a world in which music, culture, sex, politics, everything is without any stable distinction, a world in which reality is focused fragments. Even those who say they hate Madonna somehow "know" what she is saying—like it or not.

So, though it is a very un-postmodern thing to say, one could conclude that, whatever the cultural elite writes or produces, there is still something "out there" that corresponds to their ideas. Postmodernism—that is, the idea that we are now in a state of postmodernity—is not just an idea. It *might* be real, so to speak. Therefore, whether one believes in it or not, it is possible to reconstruct, in general terms, the historical markers (if not events) on which the belief in postmodernity is founded.

If there is such a thing as the postmodern, then the years 1979 and 1980 must be thought of much like the quantum rings vibrating around the unstable energy nucleus of all elemental atoms in the universe. These years are, in such a sense, arbitrary points of reference between two very extreme high-energy points: 1968, on the one hand, and 1989–1990, on the other. These were the quantum limits between the year things collapsed in the 1960s to the years the cold war era ended with the dramatic changes in Eastern Europe and the former Soviet Union. In 1968, while all the Western capitals were under a state of siege, the Soviets crushed the first clear signs of internal rebellion in Prague. A little more than twenty years later, Prague broke out again—in Berlin, in Moscow, in Bucharest—everywhere in the East of the West. The end of the 1960s and the end of the 1980s seem now to be defining limits in the same series of events. True, there are those in the West who claim that the fall of communism was really the triumph of the West. But the enormous financial crises within the West, from Berlin to Tokyo (not to mention the United States), make such a claim less than self-evident. That the only remaining superpower, the USA, is, in fact, *only* a military superpower and (at best) first among near equals economically makes the term *superpower* mean something different. The United States "won" the war in Iraq with superior military technology, paid for by borrowing from its "allies." In the end, no one won anything. Not much is changed, after all the expense, death, and destruction. Operation Desert Storm changed the meaning of *super* in ways consistent with a world that has no stable, positive power center.

It is as though the end of the cold war undermined the culture of the West, which always defined itself against a barbarian other. Without the Communists, the West lacks a defining evil. No one has yet been able to inflate the Iraqis into a threat of sufficient scale to keep the West believing in itself. This is largely because most Western societies are dependent on world conditions. None can stand alone. The stronger economies require world labor, resources, and commodity markets. Nothing is local, or even regional. Economic growth means constantly chasing the last few remaining profit markets. Most of the American and European economies were forced to open their borders to foreign labor over the past twenty-five years. To undercut the high wage demands of indigenous skilled workers, they all liberalized immigration laws, admitting workers who gave the word *stranger* a new meaning. In the United States since the mid-1960s, internal (or border) labor is increasingly provided by people from the Caribbean, Latin America, Mexico, Vietnam, and elsewhere in Asia. Just as Germany imported workers from Turkey, France and Britain imported them from former African or Far Eastern colonies. These workers, who built buildings, cleaned streets, guarded doorways, and the like, eventually became major forces in the host countries. It is well known that by the end of the century, the populations of most American cities will be predominantly minority. But this time the minorities are not Irish, Italian, or other European peoples. Many are from parts of the world where none of the European languages are spoken. Eventually, the United States will not be merely bilingual (English and variants of Spanish) but multilingual. This, in part, is why there is so much fear and anger over multiculturalism today.

Those who object to multiculturalism pretend they are only concerned with "political correctness"—that is, bad political manners. They say they do not object to

African-Americans living their own lives in their own cultures. They object only to African-Americans who, as Arthur Schlesinger puts it in "E Pluribus Unum," are unwilling to take "one step at a time." Schlesinger is among those who object to Afrocentrism and other instances of multiculturalism on the grounds that people who believe in their cultures *over* the dominant culture thereby display "disdain for the other cultures." It is true, of course, that strong internal cultures, like the African-American, include elements who disdain the long history of abuses to which they have been subject. But it is also true that most of the "multicultural" cultures, especially the African-Americans, are strongly committed in other ways to American society. African-American voters, for example, tend to be among the more conservative on many social issues. But what unnerves those who see a suddenly different America (or Germany, or England, or France, etc.) is that the traditionally white, European peoples who dominated throughout the modern era are no longer the only players in the cultural game. They invited new people into their labor markets to do the dirty work. When these people stayed, then insisted they had not only rights but also viable cultural and economic terms of their own, the formerly dominant people found the strangers less welcome. The problem is that the original Euro-Americans in the West depend on the very people whose manners they now despise. Let a white, middle-class visitor from Illinois try getting a cab or a bagel and coffee at three o'clock in the morning in New York City without dealing with someone who is "different." When the world changes, it never changes in theory alone. Theories always reflect something. It is far from clear that the multiculturalization of European and North American societies means the end of the modern world. It is not even clear what it all means. But it means something, and this is what the supposition of a postmodern world is based on. Clearly, enough people take it with enough seriousness to fight cultural wars over it.

Postmodernism can be made to look naive and foolish when it is a matter of social theorists debating Disneyland or Madonna or other cultural phenomena—fads, as the critics think of them. It is a more serious matter when it involves the destructive fury of right-wing talk-show hosts and camera-ready politicians directed against "those feminists"; or that of Alan Bloom and others directed against the young people too influenced by rock and roll and sex; or even the fury of the skinheads in Germany directed against the Turkish foreigners. These are real wars in which real people get hurt. Though the epistemological meaning of "real" may be in doubt, the political and personal reality of these injuries is not. The reality of Western societies no longer dominated by the traditional European peoples, and the anger this condition inspires, points to a world newly structured since the 1960s. How much these changes derived directly from the decentering world events of the 1960s is somewhat more difficult to assess. That they seem to be connected, more or less directly, is enough to establish as fact that the mythical West, the home of Modern Times, has a different set of conditions on its hands. However the world turns out, the talk of a postmodern, multicultural world that started in earnest around 1979 is a reality that requires consideration. This is why, since then, most social theory has had something to say in support of, in opposition to, or in response to various theories of the postmodern.

One of the surest signs that *something* was different in the 1980s was the variety of responses to the new cultural circumstances. Not all of them were framed as responses to postmodernity. In fact, many were outright defenses of modernity or, at least, attempts to revise its culture or philosophy. But it would be hard for anyone to identify any point on the cultural or political spectrum that was *not* affected by the controversy over the state of culture. The 1980s were when people first started to speak of the cultural wars. Even more, this was the period when "culture" super-seded "politics" or, at least, when the two were thought of as so complexly related that a person's politics were assumed to be his or her culture as well. Then, in the words of Cornel West, one could speak of the "new cultural politics" or, in the phrase given currency by Henry Louis Gates, Jr., of the cultural Left. In several of his writings, Gates defined the cultural Left as a loose mixture of positions drawn from feminism, poststructuralism, Marxism, African-American studies and culture, and gay-lesbian studies (or, later, queer theory), among other activities more or less asso-ciated with the universities. It was to the cultural Left that a seemingly endless num-ber of journalistic, and a few academic, books responded. The most famous was the late Alan Bloom's *Closing of the American Mind* (1987). Bloom's subtitle captures the position he took in the cultural wars: *How Higher Education Has Failed Democracy and Impoverished the Souls of Today's Students.* Thus began the cultural Right. Thereafter, William Bennett, Lynne Chenney, Dinesh D'Souza, Roger Kimball, former vice presi-dent Dan Quayle, Patrick Buchanan, and the Reverend Pat Robertson would claim, or be given, a cultural Right identity. Between the cultural Right and the Left, virtu-ally everyone with an academic reputation to maintain was forced to take a position, even if only to say they were both ridiculous.

What remains a curiosity to this day, and what may never be fully explained, is how exactly it happened that political struggle came to be so closely identified with a struggle over who controls the right to determine what is the mainstream culture in American society. There is only one, frankly speculative, explanation readily avail-able: *Everyone* (or virtually everyone) understood that the older cultural ways of Modern Times no longer had the power they once had. Indeed, in some quarters, they were becoming, in Schlesinger's words, objects of disdain. If there is any fact in all this, it is this: We do not know who will win the war, but everyone can have a po-sition. And most do. Whenever "everyone" assumes they need a position in a de-bate, something is at stake, and that something is not likely to be abstract. The cul-tural wars are about how we are to view the world that is thought to have changed—too much for some, too little for others.

Cornel West's "The New Cultural Politics of Difference" is the clearest available statement of the cultural Left's interpretation of the history of the West's culture—how it came to be, what it thought, and how it fell apart. And Henry Louis Gates, Jr.'s introduction to an important 1986 collection of essays, *"Race," Writing and Dif-ference,* was itself an event in the cultural wars. Then, for the first time, most of the leading figures of the cultural Left lent their views to a special issue of an academic journal, *Critical Inquiry;* they made a statement of their understanding of the neces-sity of seeing world politics as defined largely by cultural differences. Gates's own in-troduction was one of the most important essays in the collection. He summarized in clear terms what many had understood: that the very idea of the West was founded, arbitrarily, on a massive cultural figure of speech that served to sort every-thing culturally European into the category of civilization and everything else into the category "other." The West, Gates explained, just happened to be white; the other was of color. Gates was not the first to draw this connection. But much like Derrida in 1966, Gates in 1986 was able to put the argument together at the right time with the right cultural authority. The fact that he and Cornel West are African-Americans and considered leaders in both African-American studies and Black culture not only added to their public authority but also solidified the claim that the wars over culture were political.

This was 1986, the year before Alan Bloom's *The Closing of the American Mind.* Bloom's book actually confused everyone. While Gates's *"Race," Writing and Difference* never became a best-seller, Bloom's book did. Hardly anyone on either side can say exactly why, or even pretend to have fully understood Bloom's argument. There was, of course, a good bit of posturing. Yet Bloom was a reputably trained and respected philosopher who knew his stuff. What unnerved many people was that his expositions of his philosophy of modernity were interspersed with hateful attacks on students in the 1960s, the trouble caused by Black rebels on campus, sex, and popular music. *Closing* was taken to be the definitive cultural Right attack on the culture of the Left, which the Right (correctly) understood to have come from the 1960s. Bloom argued, among other things, that since the 1960s, students have been taught to read too much Nietzsche, which made them too "relativistic," which made American culture weak.

Others who would not normally be identified with Bloom and others in the political or cultural Right took positions that, nonetheless, were in keeping with Bloom's. Arthur Schlesinger, lifelong liberal and former adviser to President Kennedy, is said to have been chagrined that his book, *The Disuniting of America,* was associated with Bloom's book and the Right. What Schlesinger, the historian, may have forgotten is that when a massive civil war occurs within a society, there are few safe havens between camps. Schlesinger argued that America had to be one and that "the attack on the common American identity is the culmination of the cult of ethnicity." He had in mind Afrocentrists and all other multiculturalists who defined themselves first with reference to their group identity and only second (if at all) with respect to their nation. Here, again, the intrusion of world events on thinking about culture is obvious. Schlesinger, no more than Bloom, seemed unable to consider that many, many people worldwide and many within American society no longer believed in America, or even the West, as the one true path to the good society. Some people associated Schlesinger, against his will, with the cultural Right because he, like they, still believed in a world cultural Center. Those on the other side, the side with which Schlesinger had been identified in his youth, now considered such thinking a thing of the past.

Though nothing in all this is ever simple, the reader of texts like those in this section would do well to keep one question in mind: What does this author believe about the Center? Authors who believe the world is, or can be, organized around one or a few cultural or political principles will move in one direction; those who don't move in another. For example, Donna Haraway's 1985 essay "The Cyborg Manifesto" belongs to the postmodern or multicultural camp. But (as Andreas Huyssen might suggest) a first reading of this essay could lead one to think of it as avant-gardism, a kind of theater of the absurd within modernity. The writing is circular, the figure of the cyborg is duplicitous, the theory is a mixture of socialism and feminism—or neither, but rather something beyond. There are people who have read this essay time and time again without ever quite getting inside it, so to speak. Yet whatever else one concludes, it is clear that Haraway is arguing that the world is a challenging mixture of identities, and realities, in which the normal boundaries between human, mechanical, and natural things are utterly blurred and inverted. "The Cyborg Manifesto" was an opening in the debate over fractured identities—the idea that many people in the world do not believe their identity can be reduced to any one essence. Far from being "American" or "European," these people are not even simply "feminist," "Black," "lesbian," "working-class," "postcolonial," "subaltern," or *any* one thing. They are, rather, varying combinations of several fracturing, yet integrating, political and cultural identities. For example, Haraway was among the first to call the attention of white, middle-class intellectuals to the importance of the figure of the "woman of color":

> "Women of color," a name contested at its origins by those whom it would incorporate, as well as a historical consciousness marking systematic breakdown of all the signs of Man in "Western" traditions, constructs a kind of postmodernist identity out of otherness, difference, specificity.

Haraway's essay first began to circulate after publication in *Socialist Review* in 1985, the year before Gates's collection was completely published. Soon after, an increasing number of members of the cultural Left began to discover other writings by women of color, some of which are represented in the selections that follow. Gloria Anzaldúa, Gayatri Chakravorty Spivak, Patricia Hill Collins, Trinh T. Minh-ha, and Paula Gunn Allen are among those whose social theoretical positions are adequately characterized by Haraway's statement. Each represents (a word that itself is open to debate) a woman-of-color position; each takes a position that sees the world, including the world of people's self-understanding, as one of multiple elements; each understands culture and politics, and thus the politics of culture, to be an ongoing process of defining and living according to one's several affinities. Eventually, by the early 1990s, queer theory came into public notice as gay and lesbian social theorists developed the importance of sexuality in political and cultural identification. Judith Butler and Jeffrey Weeks are among the foremost theorists in this tradition. But one need only read Gloria Anzaldúa's statements on the importance of her lesbian identity to see that gay, lesbian, and bisexual identity had already been an important option, and resource, in the politics of culture.

These writers may or may not allow themselves to be labeled postmodern. But each trades on a similar intellectual and cultural tradition, and each shares some version of the historical judgment that the world is no longer one—or even unifiable. To them, the world is many, and culture, like politics, is the differences individuals encounter whenever they step into the world as it is. Whether they are looking for bagels and coffee or for a way to explain themselves to themselves and others, people in such a world are forced to face differences. Postmodernists do not find this a tragic loss. They do not worry over the decline of the West or of America or of the British Empire. Rather, they rejoice and occasionally make poetry or jokes about the fresh air of a world that may not, after all, be heading toward some final, progressive End.

It is sometimes difficult to distinguish postmodernists from those who might better be described as radical or Left modernists. But keeping that test question in mind, the reader can figure out which authors still somehow take a modernist, or modernist-like, position. The question, again, is: Who believes in a Center of whatever kind? Molefi Kete Asante, for example, is to Afrocentrism what Gates is to postmodern African-American social theory. From one angle, they seem to take a similar position. Asante has argued that African-American culture is deeply shaped by traces of African culture. Gates argued this idea (somewhat in the tradition of Du Bois's twoness theory) in *The Signifying Monkey,* his book on African-American literary theory. In *The Afrocentric Idea,* Asante makes a similar argument, referring (as did Gates) to the striking similarity between African forms of discourse (*Nommo*) and the prevalence of call-and-response in African-American public discourse. In both, language possesses its own power. In contrast to European beliefs about discourse, African cultures, according to Asante, believe language is not the product of the speaker so much as that of the community. In *Signifying Monkey,* Gates made comparable references to these facts of public rhetoric. So, what is the difference? It is a fine line, but Asante aims to attack and supplant Eurocentric discourse, while Gates wants to work and think within a criticized (one might say "deconstructed") Eurocentric discourse. It is the difference between a position that would stand outside European culture and one willing to stand in and against the West. The former stance, of which Asante's Afrocentrism is a striking example, may not be modernist in the usual sense, but it certainly is not Eurocentric. Like some standpoint feminisms, Asante's theory takes the general form of seeking to invert the world. If a standpoint feminist *may* seek to replace a patriarchal principle with Woman's perspective, then certain Afrocentrists want to replace Eurocentric principles with an African standpoint.

As it is within feminist theory, the debate over the Center is of crucial importance in framing the theoretical attitude of the social theorists. Nancy Hartsock's critique of Michel Foucault's theory of power bears some comparison to Asante's Afrocentric idea. Hartsock is respectfully critical of Foucault's view that power is dispersed throughout the micropolitics of a society and is never simply a matter of those in the ruling elite crushing the oppressed. Central to Foucault's theory of power was his prior argument that one of the ways modernity exerted its force on individuals was by shaping their subjecthood. By encouraging individuals to believe in their subjective authority, modern culture actually weakened their political convictions. Foucault was, therefore, among those who argued that a critique of modern culture also required a critique of the modernist ideal of the strong moral subject. Hartsock is among those who consider this a dangerous move. In making her case, she has authored one of the most memorable lines in recent social theory:

> Why is it just when so many of us who have been silenced begin to demand the right to name ourselves, to act as subjects rather than objects of history, that just then the concept of subjecthood becomes problematic?

Hartsock's powerful, and subtle, argument is one of the most compelling attacks on postmodernism. In effect, she says: Postmodernism may be right about the world and right about all the evils encouraged by modernist culture and philosophy, but what does it put in the place of modernity's most liberating values? Like many others on the cultural and political Left, she does not want to throw the baby out with the bath water. This is a question that must be taken seriously, especially when it is posed by members of social groups who have, over time, been silenced. The ironic lightness of some postmodernisms can, indeed, be justification to avoid the deadly seriousness of reality. However much the world has changed, people suffer, in real ways. It is said that, sometime before he died of AIDS, Michel Foucault stated that AIDS was a discursive phenomenon. There are some realities. The question is, what to make of them and how? This is what the cultural wars are about. There is no certain agreement as to how, if at all, one can settle the matter.

In fact, one must read and listen closely just to determine where a writer stands. This is largely due to the pervasive effect of world events on social theory. For example, Ernesto LaClau and Chantal Mouffe's analysis of radical democracy is a frank attempt to revitalize New Left politics using postmodern philosophical assumptions.

With considerable sophistication, they assert the primacy of differences and the illusion of reality. Yet in the end, they also believe in such a reality as the Left, a definite political position capable of deepening and expanding itself in more radically democratic ways. This, like Hartsock's critique of Foucault, is a responsible position. Ultimately, it may or may not make a difference whether it is postmodern or not, even though it still represents the world as politically recentered around a Left founded on democratic principles.

It is even more controversial to situate Stuart Hall's short intellectual memoir among the reacting modernists rather than among the postmodernists. A good argument could be made for the opposite choice. Yet as Hall makes clear, the cultural studies movement can best be characterized as a constant "struggle with the angels," one of which is Marxism. Somewhat in the fashion of LaClau and Mouffe, Hall's position seeks both to aggress and to maintain the terms of Marxism. The very idea of a partly Marxist theory of culture is, obviously, an assault on vulgar materialist Marxisms, a paradox of sorts. Yet there is a fine, but certain, difference between a postmodernism that accepts the differences of world reality, even to the point of enjoying them, and a position like Stuart Hall's that sees the reality to which the cultural Left refers as an ongoing struggle or, in one of the words of the movement, a "contestation." During its brief period of institutional success at the University of Birmingham, England, in the 1960s and 1970s, cultural studies was, indeed, a site of struggle. Those associated with the school—and the texts they wrote (Paul Willis's *Learning to Labor,* Paul Gilroy's *There Ain't No Black in the Union Jack,* and many others)—were, and are, brilliant examples of bold, empirical studies that showed the way toward a new path of cultural study between the formal disciplines. On the one hand, cultural studies remains an unstable site of theoretical contestation in a world of difference; on the other, it aspires in its own way to live within the terms of the modern university, as a kind of new, undisciplined discipline.

But whatever one might think of the postmodernism in cultural studies, there are numerous positions that are not the least postmodern, yet avoid the reactionary qualities of the cultural Right. James Coleman, in his scientific work, comes just short of the cultural Right positions he seems to recommend in his political life. The fact that he can draw a line between his politics and his science illustrates just how much he remains a modernist without embarrassment. His book *Foundations of Social Theory* is to be admired for its attempt to build an exhaustive, and theoretically concrete, system of social theory based on the astonishing view that social action in society can be explained as a series of rational choices. Rational choice theory is often taken by cultural Left sociologists as the very essence of social theoretical reaction to postmodernity. Yet what is evident in Coleman's argument is that he does not settle for simple answers. In a way, his rational choice theory can be seen as heroic modernism, at least in its attempt to work through a theory of the corporate actor that explains the new social structures of late- (if not post-) modern society. In his own way, Coleman is working through the terms of social theory's classic dilemma: What is the relation between individual actors and acting structures?

There are many social theorists who find themselves in still another position on the spectrum of cultural politics—neither postmodern nor modernist in the usual sense; certainly not cultural Right but also not cultural Left. These are writers who are willing and able to respond constructively to the "Whither Postmodernism?" debate without accepting one of the obvious settled positions. If Habermas's critical theoretical defense of modernity is the most ambitious attempt to keep modernity as a source of Left principles, then Anthony Giddens's structuration theory is one of the most imaginative attempts to stretch modernist social theory to a limit just shy of postmodernism. Somewhere between Habermas and Giddens, one might situate Jeffrey Alexander's postpositivist social theory. Both in his defense and revision of classical social theory and in his constructive social theory of civil society, Alexander frankly defends liberal culture, for which he is often rebuked. His first major book, the four-volume *Theoretical Logic in Sociology,* was the brunt of wiseguy jokes from those who considered it too much in the form of Talcott Parsons's *Structure of Social Action.* Since then, Alexander has shown himself ready to read and think widely in order to rework liberal values in relation to the categories, and writings, of postliberal thinking. The Alexander selection illustrates his use of the language and concepts of poststructuralism in order to establish a postpositivist case for reading the classic social theorists. Here, Alexander adroitly avoids the naivete of rational choice theories like Coleman's, while reflecting a robust respect for the varieties of professional social theories that have surfaced because of the postmodernism controversy.

In the end, wherever one stands in the cultural wars, the controversy sooner or later comes down, as I have said, to a question of how one views the political world. In the words of one postmodernist:

> Sooner or later politics will be faced with the task of finding a new, postmodern face. A politician must become a persona again, someone who trusts not only a scientific representation and analysis of the world, but also the world itself. . . . He must trust not only an objective interpretation of reality, but also his own soul; not only an adopted ideology, but also his own thoughts; not only the summary reports he receives each morning, but also his own feeling.

These, of course, are the words of a member of his country's cultural elite, a philosopher and playwright who, in addition, had suffered as a political prisoner. They were written while he was still president of Czechoslovakia, when there still *was* a Czechoslovakia. When postmodernism is explained by a real cultural and political hero like Vaclav Havel, it seems more human, less of a joke.

In any case, the question of the day in the early 1990s and probably through the end of the twentieth century remains: What can the human individual know and trust in his or her own feelings that encourages a more human story of life in society? Whether postmodern or not, today's world seems to be a place in which, in the absence of Progress and Final Truths, people must tell the stories they have to tell. In so doing, they tell themselves and their worlds into reality. It is possible that all men and women are social theorists in this sense.

C. L.

Note

Page 457: Bloom, *Closing of the American Mind* (Simon and Schuster, 1987). Other quoted material is from selections following.

❖ The Idea of the Postmodern ❖

Andreas Huyssen (1942–) was born in Germany. He taught at the University of Wisconsin, then in 1986 moved to Columbia University, where he is professor of German. Huyssen is an editor of *New German Critique,* in which the selection first appeared in 1984, and author of *After the Great Divide* (1986) and other books. "Whither Postmodernism?" (from the longer article "Mapping Postmodernism") is one of the more balanced assessments of postmodernism available. Huyssen clearly distinguishes postmodernism from avant-gardism, on the one hand, while acknowledging some of the peculiar extremes of postmodern cultural fads, on the other. The elegance of this text lies in the author's sensitivity to postmodernism as a series of movements in world culture that threaten Western culture's period of dominance; thus, it is a movement with evident links to political and economic changes in world history in the last generation.

Whither Postmodernism?

Andreas Huyssen (1984)

The cultural history of the 1970s still has to be written, and the various postmodernisms in art, literature, dance, theater, architecture, film, video, and music will have to be discussed separately and in detail. All I want to do now is to offer a framework for relating some recent cultural and political changes to postmodernism, changes which already lie outside the conceptual network of "modernism/avantgardism" and have so far rarely been included in the postmodernism debate.

I would argue that the contemporary arts—in the widest possible sense, whether they call themselves postmodernist or reject that label—can no longer be regarded as just another phase in the sequence of modernist and avantgardist movements which began in Paris in the 1850s and 1860s and which maintained an ethos of cultural progress and vanguardism through the 1960s. On this level, postmodernism cannot be regarded simply as a sequel to modernism, as the latest step in the neverending revolt of modernism against itself. The postmodern sensibility of our time is different from both modernism and avantgardism precisely in that it raises the question of cultural tradition and conservation in the most fundamental way as an aesthetic and a political issue. It doesn't always do it successfully, and it often does it exploitatively. And yet, my main point about contemporary postmodernism is that

---

Excerpt from "Mapping the Postmodern," Linda Nicholson, ed., *Feminism/Postmodernism* (New York: Routledge, 1990), pp. 267–271.

it operates in a field of tension between tradition and innovation, conservation and renewal, mass culture and high art, in which the second terms are no longer automatically privileged over the first; a field of tension which can no longer be grasped in categories such as progress vs. reaction, Left vs. Right, present vs. past, modernism vs. realism, abstraction vs. representation, avantgarde vs. Kitsch. The fact that such dichotomies, which after all are central to the classical accounts of modernism, have broken down is part of the shift in the following terms: Modernism and the avantgarde were always closely related to social and industrial modernization. They were related to it as an adversary culture, yes, but they drew their energies, not unlike Poe's *Man of the Crowd,* from their proximity to the crises brought about by modernization and progress. Modernization—such was the widely held belief, even when the word was not around—had to be traversed. There was a vision of emerging on the other side. The modern was a world-scale drama played out on the European and American stage, with mythic modern man as its hero and with modern art as a driving force, just as Saint-Simon had envisioned it already in 1825. Such heroic visions of modernity and of art as a force of social change (or, for that matter, resistance to undesired change) are a thing of the past, admirable for sure, but no longer in tune with current sensibilities, except perhaps with an emerging apocalyptic sensibility as the flip side of modernist heroism.

Seen in this light, postmodernism at its deepest level represents not just another crisis within the perpetual cycle of boom and bust, exhaustion and renewal, which has characterized the trajectory of modernist culture. It rather represents a new type of crisis of that modernist culture itself. Of course, this claim has been made before, and fascism indeed was a formidable crisis of modernist culture. But fascism was never the alternative to modernity it pretended to be, and our situation today is very different from that of the Weimar Republic in its agony. It was only in the 1970s that the historical limits of modernism, modernity and modernization came into sharp focus. The growing sense that we are not bound to *complete* the project of modernity (Habermas' phrase) and still do not necessarily have to lapse into irrationality or into apocalyptic frenzy, the sense that art is not exclusively pursuing some telos of abstraction, nonrepresentation and sublimity—all of this has opened up a host of possibilities for creative endeavors today. And in certain ways it has altered our views of modernism itself. Rather than being bound to a one-way history of modernism, which interprets it as a logical unfolding toward some imaginary goal, and which thus is based on a whole series of exclusions, we are beginning to explore its contradictions and contingencies, its tensions and internal resistances to its own "forward" movement. Postmodernism is far from making modernism obsolete. On the contrary, it casts a new light on it and appropriates many of its aesthetic strategies and techniques inserting them and making them work in new constellations. What has become obsolete, however, are those codifications of modernism in critical discourse which, however subliminally, are based on a teleological view of progress and modernization. Ironically, these normative and often reductive codifications have actually prepared the ground for that repudiation of modernism which goes by the name of the postmodern. Confronted with the critic who argues that this or that novel is not up to the latest in narrative technique, that it is regressive, behind the times and thus uninteresting, the postmodernist is right in rejecting modernism. But such rejection affects only that trend within modernism which has been codified into a narrow dogma, not modernism as such. In some ways, the story of modernism and postmodernism is like the story of the hedgehog and the hare: the hare could not win because there always was more than just one hedgehog. But the hare was still the better runner. . . .

The crisis of modernism is more than just a crisis of those trends within it which tie it to the ideology of modernization. In the age of late capitalism, it is also a new crisis of art's relationship to society. At their most emphatic, modernism and avant-gardism attributed to art a privileged status in the processes of social change. Even the aestheticist withdrawal from the concern of social change is still bound to it by virtue of its denial of the status quo and the construction of an artificial paradise of exquisite beauty. When social change seemed beyond grasp or took an undesired turn, art was still privileged as the only authentic voice of critique and protest, even when it seemed to withdraw into itself. The classical accounts of high modernism attest to that fact. To admit that these were heroic illusions—perhaps even necessary illusions in art's struggle to survive in dignity in a capitalist society—is not to deny the importance of art in social life.

But modernism's running feud with mass society and mass culture as well as the avantgarde's attack on high art as a support system of cultural hegemony always took place on the pedestal of high art itself. And certainly that is where the avantgarde has been installed after its failure, in the 1920s, to create a more encompassing space for art in social life. To continue to demand today that high art leave the pedestal and relocate elsewhere (wherever that might be) is to pose the problem in obsolete terms. The pedestal of high art and high culture no longer occupies the privileged space it used to, just as the cohesion of the class which erected its monuments on that pedestal is a thing of the past; recent conservative attempts in a number of Western countries to re-store the dignity of the classics of Western Civilization, from Plato via Adam Smith to the high modernists, and to send students back to the basics, prove the point. I am not saying here that the pedestal of high art does not exist any more. Of course it does, but it is not what it used to be. Since the 1960s, artistic activities have become much more diffuse and harder to contain in safe categories or stable institutions such as the acad-emy, the museum or even the established gallery network. To some, this dispersal of cultural and artistic practices and activities will involve a sense of loss and disorienta-tion; others will experience it as a new freedom, a cultural liberation. Neither may be entirely wrong, but we should recognize that it was not only recent theory or criticism that deprived the univalent, exclusive and totalizing accounts of modernism of their hegemonic role. It was the activities of artists, writers, film makers, architects, and per-formers that have propelled us beyond a narrow vision of modernism and given us a new lease on modernism itself.

In political terms, the erosion of the triple dogma modernism/modernity/avant-gardism can be contextually related to the emergence of the problematic of "other-ness," which has asserted itself in the socio-political sphere as much as in the cultural sphere. I cannot discuss here the various and multiple forms of otherness as they emerge from differences in subjectivity, gender and sexuality, race and class, tempo-ral *Ungleichzeitigkeiten* and spatial geographic locations and dislocations. But I want to mention at least four recent phenomena which, in my mind, are and will remain constitutive of postmodern culture for some time to come.

Despite all its noble aspirations and achievements, we have come to recognize that the culture of enlightened modernity has also always (though by no means exclu-sively) been a culture of inner and outer imperialism, a reading already offered by Adorno and Horkheimer in the 1940s and an insight not unfamiliar to those of our ancestors involved in the multitude of struggles against rampant modernization.

Such imperialism, which works inside and outside, on the micro and macro levels, no longer goes unchallenged either politically, economically or culturally. Whether these challenges will usher in a more habitable, less violent and more democratic world remains to be seen, and it is easy to be skeptical. But enlightened cynicism is as insufficient an answer as blue-eyed enthusiasm for peace and nature.

The women's movement has led to some significant changes in social structure and cultural attitudes which must be sustained even in the face of the recent grotesque revival of American machismo. Directly and indirectly, the women's movement has nourished the emergence of women as a self-confident and creative force in the arts, in literature, film and criticism. The ways in which we now raise questions of gender and sexuality, reading and writing, subjectivity and enunciation, voice and performance are unthinkable without the impact of feminism, even though many of these activities may take place on the margin or even outside the movement proper. Feminist critics have also contributed substantially to revisions of the history of modernism, not just by unearthing forgotten artists, but also by approaching the male modernists in novel ways. This is true also of the "new French feminists" and their theorization of the feminine in modernist writing, even though they often insist on maintaining a polemical distance from an American-type feminism.

During the 1970s, questions of ecology and environment have deepened from single-issue politics to a broad critique of modernity and modernization, a trend which is politically and culturally much stronger in West Germany than in the U.S. A new ecological sensibility manifests itself not only in political and regional subcultures, in alternative life-styles and the new social movements in Europe, but it also affects art and literature in a variety of ways: the work of Joseph Beuys, certain land art projects, Christo's California running fence, the new nature poetry, the return to local traditions, dialects, and so on. It was especially due to the growing ecological sensibility that the link between certain forms of modernism and technological modernization has come under critical scrutiny.

There is a growing awareness that other cultures, non-European, non-Western cultures must be met by means other than conquest or domination, as Paul Ricoeur put it more than twenty years ago, and that the erotic and aesthetic fascination with "the Orient"—so prominent in Western culture, including modernism—is deeply problematic. This awareness will have to translate into a type of intellectual work different from that of the modernist intellectual who typically spoke with the confidence of standing at the cutting edge of time and of being able to speak for others. Foucault's notion of the local and specific intellectual as opposed to the "universal" intellectual of modernity may provide a way out of the dilemma of being locked into our own culture and traditions while simultaneously recognizing their limitations.

In conclusion, it is easy to see that a postmodernist culture emerging from these political, social and cultural constellations will have to be a postmodernism of resistance, including resistance to that easy postmodernism of the "anything goes" variety. Resistance will always have to be specific and contingent upon the cultural field within which it operates. It cannot be defined simply in terms of negativity or nonidentity à la Adorno, nor will the litanies of a totalizing, collective project suffice. At the same time, the very notion of resistance may itself be problematic in its simple opposition to affirmation. After all, there are affirmative forms of resistance and resisting forms of affirmation. But this may be more a semantic problem than a problem of practice. And it should not keep us from making judgments. How such resistance can be articulated in art works in ways that would satisfy the needs of the political and those of the aesthetic, of the producers and of the recipients, cannot be prescribed, and it will remain open to trial, error and debate. But it is time to abandon that dead-end dichotomy of politics and aesthetics which for too long has dominated accounts of modernism, including the aestheticist trend within poststructuralism. The point is not to eliminate the productive tension between the political and the aesthetic, between history and the text, between engagement and the mission of art. The point is to heighten that tension, even to rediscover it and to bring it back into focus in the arts as well as in criticism. No matter how troubling it may be, the landscape of the postmodern surrounds us. It simultaneously delimits and opens our horizons. It's our problem and our hope.❖

Jean-François Lyotard (1926–1998) was born in Versailles and was educated in Paris at the prestigious Lycée Louis le Grand and the University of Paris. After completing his studies, he held a research post with France's National Center for Scientific Research, which (unlike the National Science Foundation [NSF] in the United States) frequently grants research positions to philosophers as well as scientists. He taught at Nanterre, where the events of 1968 are generally said to have started, from 1966 to 1970; he then taught at Vincennes from 1970 to 1972, before teaching at various branches of the University of Paris. At the time of his death in 1998, Lyotard was teaching at Emory University in Atlanta. Lyotard wrote numerous books, including *Economie libidinale* (1974), *Le Differend* (1983), and *Le Postmoderne expliqué aux enfants* (1986)—some of which are translated in excerpted form. He was best known, however, for the 1979 book *The Postmodern Condition*, a work commissioned by the Province of Quebec on the modest topic "A Report on Knowledge." Even though the book is small and parts of it quite straightforward philosophical discourse on discourse, *Postmodern Condition* was an immediate sensation—so much so that it could itself be considered a beginning point in the history of postmodernism, much as Derrida's 1966 lecture was the beginning of poststructuralism. The selection from that book presents Lyotard's most enduring idea—that postmodernity arises with the collapse of the *grand narrative* of the Enlightenment. This figure of a deflated grand narrative elegantly condenses the idea that modernity was, after all, more a narrative than the Truth; once revealed as such, modernity loses its power. No one has better captured the assumptions and language of postmodernity.

The Postmodern Condition

Jean-François Lyotard (1979)

In contemporary society and culture—postindustrial society, postmodern culture—the question of the legitimation of knowledge is formulated in different terms. The grand narrative has lost its credibility, regardless of what mode of unification it uses, regardless of whether it is a speculative narrative or a narrative of emancipation.

The decline of narrative can be seen as an effect of the blossoming of techniques and technologies since the Second World War, which has shifted emphasis from the

---

Excerpt from Geoff Bennington and Brian Massumi, trans., *The Postmodern Condition: A Report on Knowledge* (Minneapolis: University of Minneapolis Press, 1984 [1979]), pp. 37–41.

ends of action to its means; it can also be seen as an effect of the redeployment of advanced liberal capitalism after its retreat under the protection of Keynesianism during the period 1930–60, a renewal that has eliminated the communist alternative and valorized the individual enjoyment of goods and services.

Anytime we go searching for causes in this way we are bound to be disappointed. Even if we adopted one or the other of these hypotheses, we would still have to detail the correlation between the tendencies mentioned and the decline of the unifying and legitimating power of the grand narratives of speculation and emancipation.

It is, of course, understandable that both capitalist renewal and prosperity and the disorienting upsurge of technology would have an impact on the status of knowledge. But in order to understand how contemporary science could have been susceptible to those effects long before they took place, we must first locate the seeds of "delegitimation" and nihilism that were inherent in the grand narratives of the nineteenth century.

First of all, the speculative apparatus maintains an ambiguous relation to knowledge. It shows that knowledge is only worthy of that name to the extent that it reduplicates itself ("lifts itself up," *hebt sich auf;* is sublated) by citing its own statements in a second-level discourse (autonymy) that functions to legitimate them. This is as much as to say that, in its immediacy, denotative discourse bearing on a certain referent (a living organism, a chemical property, a physical phenomenon, etc.) does not really know what it thinks it knows. Positive science is not a form of knowledge. And speculation feeds on its suppression. The Hegelian speculative narrative thus harbors a certain skepticism toward positive learning, as Hegel himself admits.

A science that has not legitimated itself is not a true science; if the discourse that was meant to legitimate it seems to belong to a prescientific form of knowledge, like a "vulgar" narrative, it is demoted to the lowest rank, that of an ideology or instrument of power. And this always happens if the rules of the science game that discourse denounces as empirical are applied to science itself.

Take for example the speculative statement: "A scientific statement is knowledge if and only if it can take its place in a universal process of engendering." The question is: Is this statement knowledge as it itself defines it? Only if it can take its place in a universal process of engendering. Which it can. All it has to do is to presuppose that such a process exists (the Life of spirit) and that it is itself an expression of that process. This presupposition, in fact, is indispensable to the speculative language game. Without it, the language of legitimation would not be legitimate; it would accompany science in a nosedive into nonsense, at least if we take idealism's word for it.

But this presupposition can also be understood in a totally different sense, one which takes us in the direction of postmodern culture: we could say, in keeping with the perspective we adopted earlier, that this presupposition defines the set of rules one must accept in order to play the speculative game. Such an appraisal assumes first that we accept that the "positive" sciences represent the general mode of knowledge and second, that we understand this language to imply certain formal and axiomatic presuppositions that it must always make explicit. This is exactly what Nietzsche is doing, though with a different terminology, when he shows that "European nihilism" resulted from the truth requirement of science being turned back against itself."

There thus arises an idea of perspective that is not far removed, at least in this respect, from the idea of language games. What we have here is a process of delegitimation fueled by the demand for legitimation itself. The "crisis" of scientific knowledge, signs of which have been accumulating since the end of the nineteenth century, is not born of a chance proliferation of sciences, itself an effect of progress in technology and the expansion of capitalism. It represents, rather, an internal erosion of the legitimacy principle of knowledge. There is erosion at work inside the speculative game, and by loosening the weave of the encyclopedic net in which each science was to find its place, it eventually sets them free.

The classical dividing lines between the various fields of science are thus called into question—disciplines disappear, overlappings occur at the borders between sciences, and from these new territories are born. The speculative hierarchy of learning gives way to an immanent and, as it were, "flat" network of areas of inquiry, the respective frontiers of which are in constant flux. The old "faculties" splinter into institutes and foundations of all kinds, and the universities lose their function of speculative legitimation. Stripped of the responsibility for research (which was stifled by the speculative narrative), they limit themselves to the transmission of what is judged to be established knowledge, and through didactics they guarantee the replication of teachers rather than the production of researchers. This is the state in which Nietzsche finds and condemns them.

The potential for erosion intrinsic to the other legitimation procedure, the emancipation apparatus flowing from the *Aufklärung* [Enlightenment], is no less extensive than the one at work within speculative discourse. But it touches a different aspect. Its distinguishing characteristic is that it grounds the legitimation of science and truth in the autonomy of interlocutors involved in ethical, social, and political praxis. As we have seen, there are immediate problems with this form of legitimation: the difference between a denotative statement with cognitive value and a prescriptive statement with practical value is one of relevance, therefore of competence. There is nothing to prove that if a statement describing a real situation is true, it follows that a prescriptive statement based upon it (the effect of which will necessarily be a modification of that reality) will be just.

Take, for example, a closed door. Between "The door is closed" and "Open the door" there is no relation of consequence as defined in propositional logic. The two statements belong to two autonomous sets of rules defining different kinds of relevance, and therefore of competence. Here, the effect of dividing reason into cognitive or theoretical reason on the one hand, and practical reason on the other, is to attack the legitimacy of the discourse of science. Not directly, but indirectly, by revealing that it is a language game with its own rules (of which the a priori conditions of knowledge in Kant provide a first glimpse) and that it has no special calling to supervise the game of praxis (nor the game of aesthetics, for that matter). The game of science is thus put on a par with the others.

If this "delegitimation" is pursued in the slightest and if its scope is widened (as Wittgenstein does in his own way, and thinkers such as Martin Buber and Emmanuel Lévinas in theirs) the road is then open for an important current of postmodernity: science plays its own game; it is incapable of legitimating the other language games. The game of prescription, for example, escapes it. But above all, it is incapable of legitimating itself, as speculation assumed it could.

The social subject itself seems to dissolve in this dissemination of language games. The social bond is linguistic, but is not woven with a single thread. It is a fabric formed by the intersection of at least two (and in reality an indeterminate number) of language games, obeying different rules. Wittgenstein writes: "Our language can be seen as an ancient city: a maze of little streets and squares, of old and new houses, and of houses with additions from various periods; and this surrounded by a multitude of new boroughs with straight regular streets and uniform houses." And to drive home that the principle of unitotality—or synthesis under the authority of a metadiscourse of knowledge—is inapplicable, he subjects the "town" of language to the old sorites paradox by asking: "how many houses or streets does it take before a town begins to be a town?"

New languages are added to the old ones, forming suburbs of the old town: "the symbolism of chemistry and the notation of the infinitesimal calculus." Thirty-five years later we can add to the list: machine languages, the matrices of game theory, new systems of musical notation, systems of notation for nondenotative forms of logic (temporal logics, deontic logics, modal logics), the language of the genetic code, graphs of phonological structures, and so on.

We may form a pessimistic impression of this splintering: nobody speaks all of those languages, they have no universal metalanguage, the project of the system-subject is a failure, the goal of emancipation has nothing to do with science, we are all stuck in the positivism of this or that discipline of learning, the learned scholars have turned into scientists, the diminished tasks of research have become compartmentalized and no one can master them all. Speculative or humanistic philosophy is forced to relinquish its legitimation duties, which explains why philosophy is facing a crisis wherever it persists in arrogating such functions and is reduced to the study of systems of logic or the history of ideas where it has been realistic enough to surrender them.

Turn-of-the-century Vienna was weaned on this pessimism: not just artists such as Musil, Kraus, Hofmannsthal, Loos, Schönberg, and Broch, but also the philosophers Mach and Wittgenstein. They carried awareness of and theoretical and artistic responsibility for delegitimation as far as it could be taken. We can say today that the mourning process has been completed. There is no need to start all over again. Wittgenstein's strength is that he did not opt for the positivism that was being developed by the Vienna Circle, but outlined in his investigation of language games a kind of legitimation not based on performativity. That is what the postmodern world is all about. Most people have lost the nostalgia for the lost narrative. It in no way follows that they are reduced to barbarity. What saves them from it is their knowledge that legitimation can only spring from their own linguistic practice and communicational interaction. Science "smiling into its beard" at every other belief has taught them the harsh austerity of realism.❖

Richard Rorty (1931–) was born in New York City, then educated at Berkeley and Yale (Ph.D. in philosophy, 1956). He has taught at Yale, Wellesley, Princeton, and (since 1982) the University of Virginia. Where Lyotard is sometimes opaque, Rorty is satisfyingly clear. Where Lyotard seems to enjoy being a postmodernist, Rorty claims nothing more than that he is a philosopher, explicitly in the modest American tradition of pragmatism. Yet differences aside, Rorty makes clear the full philosophical implications of Lyotard's dead narrative figure. In the selection, from *Contingency, Irony, and Solidarity,* Rorty discusses both his political philosophy and his two most compelling ideas: (1) that there is no longer a final authority to judge the truth of philosophical discourse, and (2) that the Plato-Kant canon is dead, leaving philosophy with literary criticism. Irony, in effect, is the philosophical attitude of postmodernity. This thinking was anticipated in Rorty's important critique of foundationalism in the philosophy of knowledge, *Philosophy and the Mirror of Nature,* which appeared in 1979, the year that Lyotard's book was published. The conjunction of these two books is one of the more or less arbitrary reasons for suggesting that, although post-modernity is an uncertain thing historically, 1979 was the year in which it became clear that the postmodern had to be taken seriously. Ironically, one could argue that neither of the two books is postmodern, strictly speaking. This is the way postmodernism is.

Private Irony and Liberal Hope
Richard Rorty (1989)

All human beings carry about a set of words which they employ to justify their actions, their beliefs, and their lives. These are the words in which we formulate praise of our friends and contempt for our enemies, our long-term projects, our deepest self-doubts and our highest hopes. They are the words in which we tell, sometimes prospectively and sometimes retrospectively, the story of our lives. I shall call these words a person's "final vocabulary."

It is "final" in the sense that if doubt is cast on the worth of these words, their user has no noncircular argumentative recourse. Those words are as far as he can go with language; beyond them there is only helpless passivity or a resort to force. A small part of a final vocabulary is made up of thin, flexible, and ubiquitous terms such as "true," "good," "right," and "beautiful." The larger part contains thicker, more rigid, and more parochial terms, for example, "Christ," "England," "professional standards," "decency," "kindness," "the Revolution," "the Church," "progressive," "rigorous," "creative." The more parochial terms do most of the work.

I shall define an "ironist" as someone who fulfills three conditions: (1) She has radical and continuing doubts about the final vocabulary she currently uses, because she has been impressed by other vocabularies, vocabularies taken as final by people or books she has encountered; (2) she realizes that argument phrased in her present vocabulary can neither underwrite nor dissolve these doubts; (3) insofar as she philosophizes about her situation, she does not think that her vocabulary is closer to reality than others, that it is in touch with a power not herself. Ironists who are inclined to philosophize see the choice between vocabularies as made neither within a neutral and universal metavocabulary nor by an attempt to fight one's way past appearances to the real, but simply by playing the new off against the old.

I call people of this sort "ironists" because their realization that anything can be made to look good or bad by being redescribed, and their renunciation of the attempt to formulate criteria of choice between final vocabularies, puts them in the position which Sartre called "meta-stable": never quite able to take themselves seriously because always aware that the terms in which they describe themselves are subject to change, always aware of the contingency and fragility of their final vocabularies, and thus of their selves. Such people take naturally to the line of thought developed in the first two chapters of this book. If they are also liberals—people for whom (to use Judith Shklar's definition) "cruelty is the worst thing they do"—they will take naturally to the views offered in the third chapter.

Excerpt from *Contingency, Irony, and Solidarity* (Cambridge: Cambridge University Press, 1989), pp. 73–74, 79–80, 84–85, 86–88. Reprinted with permission from Cambridge University Press.

The opposite of irony is common sense. For that is the watchword of those who un-selfconsciously describe everything important in terms of the final vocabulary to which they and those around them are habituated. To be commonsensical is to take for granted that statements formulated in that final vocabulary suffice to describe and judge the beliefs, actions and lives of those who employ alternative final vocabularies. . . .

We ironists treat these people not as anonymous channels for truth but as abbre-viations for a certain final vocabulary and for the sorts of beliefs and desires typical of its users. The older Hegel became a name for such a vocabulary, and Kierkegaard and Nietzsche have become names for others. If we are told that the actual lives such men lived had little to do with the books and the terminology which attracted our attention to them, we brush this aside. We treat the names of such people as the names of the heroes of their own books. We do not bother to distinguish Swift from *saeva indignatio*, Hegel from Geist, Nietzsche from Zarathustra, Marcel Proust from Marcel the narrator, or Trilling from The Liberal Imagination. We do not care whether these writers managed to live up to their own self-images. What we want to know is whether to adopt those images—to re-create ourselves, in whole or in part, in these people's image. We go about answering this question by experimenting with the vocabularies which these people concocted. We redescribe ourselves, our situa-tion, our past, in those terms and compare the results with alternative redescriptions which use the vocabularies of alternative figures. We ironists hope, by this continual redescription, to make the best selves for ourselves that we can.

Such comparison, such playing off of figures against each other, is the principal activity now covered by the term "literary criticism." Influential critics, the sort of critics who propose new canons—people like Arnold, Pater, Leavis, Eliot, Edmund Wilson, Lionel Trilling, Frank Kermode, Harold Bloom—are not in the business of explaining the real meaning of books, nor of evaluating something called their "lit-erary merit." Rather, they spend their time placing books in the context of other books, figures in the context of other figures. This placing is done in the same way as we place a new friend or enemy in the context of old friends and enemies. In the course of doing so, we revise our opinions of both the old and the new. Simultane-ously, we revise our own moral identity by revising our own final vocabulary. Liter-ary criticism does for ironists what the search for universal moral principles is sup-posed to do for metaphysicians.

For us ironists, nothing can serve as a criticism of a final vocabulary save another such vocabulary; there is no answer to a redescription save a re-re-redescription. Since there is nothing beyond vocabularies which serves as a criterion of choice between them, criticism is a matter of looking on this picture and on that, not of comparing both pictures with the original. Nothing can serve as a criticism of a person save an-other person, or of a culture save an alternative culture—for persons and cultures are, for us, incarnated vocabularies. So our doubts about our own characters or our own culture can be resolved or assuaged only by enlarging our acquaintance. The easiest way of doing that is to read books, and so ironists spend more of their time placing books than in placing real live people. Ironists are afraid that they will get stuck in the vocabulary in which they were brought up if they only know the people in their own neighborhood, so they try to get acquainted with strange people (Alcibiades, Julien Sorel), strange families (the Karamazovs, the Casaubons), and strange communities (the Teutonic Knights, the Nuer, the mandarins of the Sung). . . .

The social glue holding together the ideal liberal society described in the previous chapter consists in little more than a consensus that the point of social organization is to let everybody have a chance at self-creation to the best of his or her abilities, and that that goal requires, besides peace and wealth, the standard "bourgeois freedoms." This conviction would not be based on a view about universally shared human ends, human rights, the nature of rationality, the Good for Man, nor anything else. It would be a conviction based on nothing more profound than the historical facts which suggest that without the protection of something like the institutions of bourgeois liberal society, people will be less able to work out their private salvations, create their private self-images, reweave their webs of belief and desire in the light of whatever new people and books they happen to encounter. In such an ideal society, discussion of public affairs will revolve around (1) how to balance the needs for peace, wealth, and freedom when conditions require that one of these goals be sacrificed to one of the others and (2) how to equalize opportunities for self-creation and then leave people alone to use, or neglect, their opportunities.

The suggestion that this is all the social glue liberal societies need is subject to two main objections. The first is that as a practical matter, this glue is just not thick enough—that the (predominantly) metaphysical rhetoric of public life in the democracies is essential to the continuation of free institutions. The second is that it is psychologically impossible to be a liberal ironist—to be someone for whom "cruelty is the worst thing we do," and to have no metaphysical beliefs about what all human beings have in common. . . .

If you tell someone whose life is given meaning by this hope that philosophers are waxing ironic over real essence, the objectivity of truth, and the existence of an ahistorical human nature, you are unlikely to arouse much interest, much less do any damage. The idea that liberal societies are bound together by philosophical beliefs seems to me ludicrous. What binds societies together are common vocabularies and common hopes. The vocabularies are, typically, parasitic on the hopes—in the sense that the principal function of the vocabularies is to tell stories about future outcomes which compensate for present sacrifices.

Modern, literate, secular societies depend on the existence of reasonably concrete, optimistic, and plausible *political* scenarios, as opposed to scenarios about redemption beyond the grave. To retain social hope, members of such a society need to be able to tell themselves a story about how things might get better, and to see no insuperable obstacles to this story's coming true. If social hope has become harder lately, this is not because the clerks have been committing treason but because, since the end of World War II, the course of events has made it harder to tell a convincing story of this sort. The cynical and impregnable Soviet Empire, the continuing shortsightedness and greed of the surviving democracies, and the exploding, starving populations of the Southern Hemisphere make the problems our parents faced in the 1930s—Fascism and unemployment—look almost manageable. People who try to update and rewrite the standard social democratic scenario about human equality, the scenario which their grandparents wrote around the turn of the century, are not having much success. The problems which metaphysically inclined social thinkers believe to be caused by our failure to find the right sort of theoretical glue—a philosophy which can command wide assent in an individualistic and pluralistic society—are, I think, caused by a set of historical contingencies. These contingencies are making it easy to see the last few hundred years of European and American history—centuries of increasing public hope and private ironism—as an island in time, surrounded by misery, tyranny, and chaos. As Orwell put it, "The democratic vistas seem to end in barbed wire." . . .

In the ideal liberal society, the intellectuals would still be ironists, although the nonintellectuals would not. The latter would, however, be commonsensically nominalist and historicist. So they would see themselves as contingent through and through, without feeling any particular doubts about the contingencies they happened to be. They would not be bookish, nor would they look to literary critics as moral advisers. But they would be commonsensical nonmetaphysicians, in the way in which more and more people in the rich democracies have been commonsensical nontheists. They would feel no more need to answer the questions "*Why* are you a liberal? Why do you *care* about the humiliation of strangers?" than the average sixteenth-century Christian felt to answer the question "Why are you a Christian?" or than most people nowadays feel to answer the question "Are you saved?" Such a person would not need a justification for her sense of human solidarity, for she was not raised to play the language game in which one asks and gets justifications for that sort of belief. Her culture is one in which doubts about the public rhetoric of the culture are met not by Socratic requests for definitions and principles, but by Deweyan requests for concrete alternatives and programs. Such a culture could, as far as I can see, be every bit as self-critical and every bit as devoted to human equality as our own familiar, and still metaphysical, liberal culture—if not more so.

But even if I am right in thinking that a liberal culture whose public rhetoric is nominalist and historicist is both possible and desirable, I cannot go on to claim that there could or ought to be a culture whose public rhetoric is *ironist*. I cannot imagine a culture which socialized its youth in such a way as to make them continually dubious about their own process of socialization. Irony seems inherently a private matter. On my definition, an ironist cannot get along without the contrast between the final vocabulary she inherited and the one she is trying to create for herself. Irony is, if not intrinsically resentful, at least reactive. Ironists have to have something to have doubts about, something from which to be alienated.

This brings me to the second of the two objections I listed above, and thus to the idea that there is something about being an ironist which unsuits one for being a liberal, and that a simple split between private and public concerns is not enough to overcome the tension.

One can make this claim plausible by saying that there is at least a prima facie tension between the idea that social organization aims at human equality and the idea that human beings are simply incarnated vocabularies. The idea that we all have an overriding obligation to diminish cruelty, to make human beings equal in respect to their liability to suffering, seems to take for granted that there is something within human beings which deserves respect and protection quite independently of the language they speak. It suggests that a nonlinguistic ability, the ability to feel pain, is what is important, and that differences in vocabulary are much less important.

Metaphysics—in the sense of a search for theories which will get at real essence—tries to make sense of the claim that human beings are something more than centerless webs of beliefs and desires. The reason many people think such a claim essential to liberalism is that if men and women were, indeed, nothing more than sentential attitudes—nothing more than the presence or absence of dispositions toward the use of sentences phrased in some historically conditioned vocabulary—then not only human nature, but human *solidarity*, would begin to seem an eccentric and dubious idea. For solidarity with all possible vocabularies seems impossible. Metaphysicians tell us that unless there is some sort of common ur-vocabulary, we have no "reason" not to be cruel to those whose final vocabularies are very unlike ours. A universalistic ethics seems incompatible with ironism, simply because it is hard to imagine stating such an ethic without some doctrine about the nature of man. Such an appeal to real essence is the antithesis of ironism.❖

Michel Foucault (1926–1984), near the end of his life, took on a major, four-volume study of the history of sexuality. The selection is from the first volume, a theoretical introduction to the larger project. Published in 1976, it represents an excellent summary of his social theory of power/knowledge in modernity. Soon, however, he had misgivings about the original plan for the sexuality series, leading to a complete revision of his thinking on the subject. At the time of his death in 1984, two of the remaining three volumes were complete (*The Uses of Pleasure* and *The Care of the Soul*), but the project was left open. Throughout his life, Foucault explored the various ways in which political power was subtly invested in the mechanisms of knowledge in the modern world. His studies of sexuality make him a classic source for the history and social theory of sexualities, just as his earlier work had established his importance in other historical fields—penality, medicine, science, madness.

Power as Knowledge
Michel Foucault (1976)

Hence the objective is to analyze a certain form of knowledge regarding sex, not in terms of repression or law, but in terms of power. But the word *power* is apt to lead to a number of misunderstandings—misunderstandings with respect to its nature, its form, and its unity. By power, I do not mean "Power" as a group of institutions and mechanisms that ensure the subservience of the citizens of a given state. By power, I do not mean, either, a mode of subjugation which, in contrast to violence, has the form of the rule. Finally, I do not have in mind a general system of domination exerted by one group over another, a system whose effects, through successive derivations, pervade the entire social body. The analysis, made in terms of power, must not assume that the sovereignty of the state, the form of the law, or the over-all unity of a domination are given at the outset; rather, these are only the terminal forms power takes. It seems to me that power must be understood in the first instance as the multiplicity of force relations immanent in the sphere in which they operate and which constitute their own organization; as the process which, through ceaseless struggles and confrontations, transforms, strengthens, or reverses them; as the support which these force relations find in one another, thus forming a chain or a system, or on the contrary, the disjunctions and contradictions which isolate them from one another; and lastly, as the strategies in which they take effect, whose general design or institutional crystallization is embodied in the state apparatus, in the formulation of the law, in the various social hegemonies. Power's condition of possibility, or in any case the viewpoint which permits one to understand its exercise, even in its more "peripheral" effects, and which also makes it possible to use its mechanisms as a grid of intelligibility of the social order, must not be sought in the primary existence of a central power, in a unique source of sovereignty from which secondary and descendent forms would emanate; it is the moving substrate of force relations which, by virtue of their inequality, constantly engender states of power, but the latter are always local and unstable. The omnipresence of power: not because it has the privilege of consolidating everything under its invincible unity, but because it is produced from one moment to the next, at every point, or rather in every relation from one point to another. Power is everywhere; not because it embraces everything, but because it comes from everywhere. And "Power," insofar as it is permanent, repetitious, inert, and self-reproducing, is simply the over-all effect that emerges from all these mobilities, the concatenation that rests on each of them and seeks in turn to arrest their movement. One needs to be nominalistic, no doubt: power is not an institution, and not a structure; neither is it a certain strength we are endowed with; it is the name that one attributes to a complex strategical situation in a particular society.

Should we turn the expression around, then, and say that politics is war pursued by other means? If we still wish to maintain a separation between war and politics, perhaps we should postulate rather that this multiplicity of force relations can be coded—in part but never totally—either in the form of "war," or in the form of "politics"; this would imply two different strategies (but the one always liable to switch into the other) for integrating these unbalanced, heterogeneous, unstable, and tense force relations.

Continuing this line of discussion, we can advance a certain number of propositions:

- Power is not something that is acquired, seized, or shared, something that one holds on to or allows to slip away; power is exercised from innumerable points, in the interplay of nonegalitarian and mobile relations.
- Relations of power are not in a position of exteriority with respect to other types of relationships (economic processes, knowledge relationships, sexual relations), but are immanent in the latter; they are the immediate effects of the divisions, inequalities, and disequilibriums which occur in the latter, and conversely they are the internal conditions of these differentiations; relations of power are not in superstructural positions, with merely a role of prohibition or accompaniment; they have a directly productive role, wherever they come into play.
- Power comes from below; that is, there is no binary and all-encompassing opposition between rulers and ruled at the root of power relations, and serving as a general matrix—no such duality extending from the top down and reacting on more and more limited groups to the very depths of the social body. One must suppose rather that the manifold relationships of force that take shape and come into play in the machinery of production, in families, limited groups, and institutions, are the basis for wide-ranging effects of cleavage that run through the social body as a whole. These then form a general line of force that traverses the local oppositions and links them together; to be sure, they also bring about redistributions, realignments, homogenizations, serial arrangements, and convergences of the force relations. Major dominations are the hegemonic effects that are sustained by all these confrontations.

- Power relations are both intentional and nonsubjective. If in fact they are intelligible, this is not because they are the effect of another instance that "explains" them, but rather because they are imbued, through and through, with calculation: there is no power that is exercised without a series of aims and objectives. But this does not mean that it results from the choice or decision of an individual subject; let us not look for the headquarters that presides over its rationality; neither the caste which governs, nor the groups which control the state apparatus, nor those who make the most important economic decisions direct the entire network of power that functions in a society (and makes *it* function); the rationality of power is characterized by tactics that are often quite explicit at the restricted level where they are inscribed (the local cynicism of power), tactics which, becoming connected to one another, attracting and propagating one another, but finding their base of support and their condition elsewhere, end by forming comprehensive systems: the logic is perfectly clear, the aims decipherable, and yet it is often the case that no one is there to have invented them, and few who can be said to have formulated them: an implicit characteristic of the great anonymous, almost unspoken strategies which coordinate the loquacious tactics whose "inventors" or decisionmakers are often without hypocrisy.
- Where there is power, there is resistance, and yet, or rather consequently, this resistance is never in a position of exteriority in relation to power. Should it be said that one is always "inside" power, there is no "escaping" it, there is no absolute outside where it is concerned, because one is subject to the law in any case? Or that, history being the ruse of reason, power is the ruse of history, always emerging the winner? This would be to misunderstand the strictly relational character of power relationships. Their existence depends on a multiplicity of points of resistance: these play the role of adversary, target, support, or handle in power relations. These points of resistance are present everywhere in the power network. Hence there is no single locus of great Refusal, no soul of revolt, source of all rebellions, or pure law of the revolutionary. Instead there is a plurality of resistances, each of them a special case: resistances that are possible, necessary, improbable; others that are spontaneous, savage, solitary, concerted, rampant, or violent; still others that are quick to compromise, interested, or sacrificial; by definition, they can only exist in the strategic field of power relations. But this does not mean that they are only a reaction or rebound, forming with respect to the basic domination an underside that is in the end always passive, doomed to perpetual defeat. Resistances do not derive from a few heterogeneous principles; but neither are they a lure or a promise that is of necessity betrayed. They are the odd term in relations of power; they are inscribed in the latter as an irreducible opposite. Hence they too are distributed in irregular fashion; the points, knots, or focuses of resistance are spread over time and space at varying densities, at times mobilizing groups or individuals in a definitive way, inflaming certain points of the body, certain moments in life, certain types of behavior. Are there no great radical ruptures, massive binary divisions, then? Occasionally, yes. But more often one is dealing with mobile and transitory points of resistance, producing cleavages in a society that shift about, fracturing unities and effecting regroupings, furrowing across individuals themselves, cutting them up and

remolding them, marking off irreducible regions in them, in their bodies and minds. Just as the network of power relations ends by forming a dense web that passes through apparatuses and institutions, without being exactly localized in them, so too the swarm of points of resistance traverses social stratifications and individual unities. And it is doubtless the strategic codification of these points of resistance that makes a revolution possible, somewhat similar to the way in which the state relies on the institutional integration of power relationships.

It is in this sphere of force relations that we must try to analyze the mechanisms of power. In this way we will escape from the system of Law-and-Sovereign which has captivated political thought for such a long time. And if it is true that Machiavelli was among the few—and this no doubt was the scandal of his "cynicism"—who conceived the power of the Prince in terms of force relationships, perhaps we need to go one step further, do without the persona of the Prince, and decipher power mechanisms on the basis of a strategy that is immanent in force relationships.

To return to sex and the discourses of truth that have taken charge of it, the question that we must address, then, is not: Given a specific state structure, how and why is it that power needs to establish a knowledge of sex? Neither is the question: What overall domination was served by the concern, evidenced since the eighteenth century, to produce true discourses on sex? Nor is it: What law presided over both the regularity of sexual behavior and the conformity of what was said about it? It is rather: In a specific type of discourse on sex, in a specific form of extortion of truth, appearing historically and in specific places (around the child's body, apropos of women's sex, in connection with practices restricting births, and so on), what were the most immediate, the most local power relations at work? How did they make possible these kinds of discourses, and conversely, how were these discourses used to support power relations: How was the action of these power relations modified by their very exercise, entailing a strengthening of some terms and a weakening of others, with effects of resistance and counterinvestments, so that there has never existed one type of stable subjugation, given once and for all? How were these power relations linked to one another according to the logic of a great strategy, which in retrospect takes on the aspect of a unitary and voluntarist politics of sex? In general terms: rather than referring all the infinitesimal violences that are exerted on sex, all the anxious gazes that are directed at it, and all the hiding places whose discovery is made into an impossible task, to the unique form of a great Power, we must immerse the expanding production of discourses on sex in the field of multiple and mobile power relations.

Which leads us to advance, in a preliminary way, four rules to follow. But these are not intended as methodological imperatives; at most they are cautionary prescriptions.

Rule of Immanence

One must not suppose that there exists a certain sphere of sexuality that would be the legitimate concern of a free and disinterested scientific inquiry were it not the object of mechanisms of prohibition brought to bear by the economic or ideological requirements of power. If sexuality was constituted as an area of investigation, this was only because relations of power had established it as a possible object; and conversely, if power was able to take it as a target, this was because techniques of knowledge and procedures of discourse were capable of investing it. Between techniques of knowledge and strategies of power, there is no exteriority, even if they have specific roles and are linked together on the basis of their difference. We will start, therefore, from what might be called "local centers" of power-knowledge: for example, the relations that obtain between penitents and confessors, or the faithful and their directors of conscience. Here, guided by the theme of the "flesh" that must be mastered, different forms of discourse—self-examination, questionings, admissions, interpretations, interviews—were the vehicle of a kind of incessant back-and-forth movement of forms of subjugation and schemas of knowledge. Similarly, the body of the child, under surveillance, surrounded in his cradle, his bed, or his room by an entire watch-crew of parents, nurses, servants, educators, and doctors, all attentive to the least manifestations of his sex, has constituted, particularly since the eighteenth century, another "local center" of power-knowledge.

Rules of Continual Variations

We must not look for who has the power in the order of sexuality (men, adults, parents, doctors) and who is deprived of it (women, adolescents, children, patients); nor for who has the right to know and who is forced to remain ignorant. We must seek rather the pattern of the modifications which the relationships of force imply by the very nature of their process. The "distributions of power" and the "appropriations of knowledge" never represent only instantaneous slices taken from processes involving, for example, a cumulative reinforcement of the strongest factor, or a reversal of relationship, or again, a simultaneous increase of two terms. Relations of power-knowledge are not static forms of distribution, they are "matrices of transformations." The nineteenth-century grouping made up of the father, the mother, the educator, and the doctor, around the child and his sex, was subjected to constant modifications, continual shifts. One of the more spectacular results of the latter was a strange reversal: whereas to begin with the child's sexuality had been problematized within the relationship established between doctor and parents (in the form of advice, or recommendations to keep the child under observation, or warnings of future dangers), ultimately it was in the relationship of the psychiatrist to the child that the sexuality of adults themselves was called into question.

Rule of Double Conditioning

No "local center," no "pattern of transformation" could function if, through a series of sequences, it did not eventually enter into an over-all strategy. And inversely, no strategy could achieve comprehensive effects if it did not gain support from precise and tenuous relations serving, not as its point of application or final outcome, but as its prop and anchor point. There is no discontinuity between them, as if one were dealing with two different levels (one microscopic and the other macroscopic); but neither is there homogeneity (as if the one were only the enlarged projection or the miniaturization of the other); rather, one must conceive of the double conditioning of a strategy by the specificity of possible tactics, and of tactics by the strategic envelope that makes them work. Thus the father in the family is not the "representative" of the sovereign or the state; and the latter are not projections of the father on a different scale. The family does not duplicate society, just as society does not imitate the family. But the family organization, precisely to the extent that it was insular and heteromorphous with respect to the other power mechanisms, was used to support the great "maneuvers" employed for the Malthusian control of the birthrate, for the populationist incitements, for the medicalization of sex and the psychiatrization of its nongenital forms.

Rule of the Tactical Polyvalence of Discourses

What is said about sex must not be analyzed simply as the surface of projection of these power mechanisms. Indeed, it is in discourse that power and knowledge are joined together. And for this very reason, we must conceive discourse as a series of discontinuous segments whose tactical function is neither uniform nor stable. To be more precise, we must not imagine a world of discourse divided between accepted discourse and excluded discourse, or between the dominant discourse and the dominated one; but as a multiplicity of discursive elements that can come into play in various strategies. It is this distribution that we must reconstruct, with the things said and those concealed, the enunciations required and those forbidden, that it comprises; with the variants and different effects—according to who is speaking, his position of power, the institutional context in which he happens to be situated—that it implies; and with the shifts and reutilizations of identical formulas for contrary objectives that it also includes. Discourses are not once and for all subservient to power or raised up against it, any more than silences are. We must make allowance for the complex and unstable process whereby discourse can be both an instrument and an effect of power, but also a hindrance, a stumbling-block, a point of resistance and a starting point for an opposing strategy. Discourse transmits and produces power; it reinforces it, but also undermines and exposes it, renders it fragile and makes it possible to thwart it. In like manner, silence and secrecy are a shelter for power, anchoring its prohibitions; but they also loosen its holds and provide for relatively obscure areas of tolerance. Consider for example the history of what was once "the" great sin against nature. The extreme discretion of the texts dealing with sodomy—that utterly confused category—and the nearly universal reticence in talking about it made possible a twofold operation: on the one hand, there was an extreme severity (punishment by fire was meted out well into the eighteenth century, without there being any substantial protest expressed before the middle of the century), and on the other hand, a tolerance that must have been widespread (which one can deduce indirectly from the infrequency of judicial sentences, and which one glimpses more directly through certain statements concerning societies of men that were thought to exist in the army or in the courts). There is no question that the appearance in nineteenth-century psychiatry, jurisprudence, and literature of a whole series of discourses on the species and subspecies of homosexuality, inversion, pederasty, and "psychic hermaphrodism" made possible a strong advance of social controls into this area of "perversity"; but it also made possible the formation of a "reverse" discourse: homosexuality began to speak in its own behalf, to demand that its legitimacy or "naturality" be acknowledged, often in the same vocabulary, using the same categories by which it was medically disqualified. There is not, on the one side, a discourse of power, and opposite it, another discourse that runs counter to it. Discourses are tactical elements or blocks operating in the field of force relations; there can exist different and even contradictory discourses within the same strategy; they can, on the contrary, circulate without changing their form from one strategy to another, opposing strategy. We must not expect the discourses on sex to tell us, above all, what strategy they derive from, or what moral divisions they accompany, or what ideology—dominant or dominated—they represent; rather we must question them on the two levels of their tactical productivity (what reciprocal effects of power and knowledge they ensure) and their strategical integration (what conjunction and what force relationship make their utilization necessary in a given episode of the various confrontations that occur).

In short, it is a question of orienting ourselves to a conception of power which replaces the privilege of the law with the viewpoint of the objective, the privilege of prohibition with the viewpoint of tactical efficacy, the privilege of sovereignty with the analysis of a multiple and mobile field of force relations, wherein far-reaching, but never completely stable, effects of domination are produced. The strategical model, rather than the model based on law. And this, not out of a speculative choice or theoretical preference, but because in fact it is one of the essential traits of Western societies that the force relationships which for a long time had found expression in war, in every form of warfare, gradually became invested in the order of political power.❖

Jean Baudrillard (1929–) is one of France's most flamboyant social commentators and intellectuals in the fashion that dominated in Paris in the 1960s and 1970s. His explorations of the social reality of simulated worlds, like Disneyland, lead some to dismiss Baudrillard. Yet his writing, like the selection on simulacra, is deadly serious in an ironic way. Baudrillard is perhaps the most representative of the postmodern cultural leftists, who argue (as he does in the selection) that the line between reality and simulation is false. By implication, only modernity maintained the distinction; by inference, today's world has erased it, both in philosophy and, so to speak, in "reality." Baudrillard's early writings, in the years following 1968, were much more in the tradition of Marxism. At that point, Baudrillard was primarily concerned with developing a social theory of mass society based on Marx and Saussure—a critique of political economy and a semiotics. To this day, his *For a Critique of Political Economy* (1972) is rightly considered the most perspicacious interpretation of the close similarity of Marx's and Saussure's theories of social values. In this early period, he also wrote *The System of Objects* (1968) and *Consumer Society* (1970). The selection is obviously from a later period, when Baudrillard had left behind all visible traces of Marxism and his interest in semiotics had been fully transformed into a general, discursive theory of culture. *Cool Memories* (1987) is also from this later phase.

Simulacra and Simulations: Disneyland
Jean Baudrillard (1983)

> *The simulacrum is never that which conceals the truth—it is the truth which conceals that there is none.*
> *The simulacrum is true.*
>
> —Ecclesiastes

If we were able to take as the finest allegory of simulation the Borges tale where the cartographers of the Empire draw up a map so detailed that it ends up exactly covering the territory (but where, with the decline of the Empire this map becomes frayed and finally ruined, a few shreds still discernible in the deserts—the metaphysical beauty of this ruined abstraction, bearing witness to an imperial pride and rotting like a carcass, returning to the substance of the soil, rather as an aging double ends up being confused with the real thing), this fable would then have come full circle for us, and now has nothing but the discrete charm of second-order simulacra.

Abstraction today is no longer that of the map, the double, the mirror or the concept. Simulation is no longer that of a territory, a referential being or a substance. It is the generation by models of a real without origin or reality: a hyperreal. The territory no longer precedes the map, nor survives it. Henceforth, it is the map that precedes the territory—*precession of simulacra*—it is the map that engenders the territory and if we were to revive the fable today, it would be the territory whose shreds are slowly rotting across the map. It is the real, and not the map, whose vestiges subsist here and there, in the deserts which are no longer those of the Empire, but our own. *The desert of the real itself.*

In fact, even inverted, the fable is useless. Perhaps only the allegory of the Empire remains. For it is with the same imperialism that present-day simulators try to make the real, all the real, coincide with their simulation models. But it is no longer a question of either maps or territory. Something has disappeared: the sovereign difference between them that was the abstraction's charm. For it is the difference which forms the poetry of the map and the charm of the territory, the magic of the concept and the charm of the real. This representational imaginary, which both culminates in and is engulfed by the cartographer's mad project of an ideal coextensivity between the map and the territory, disappears with simulation, whose operation is nuclear and genetic, and no longer specular and discursive. With it goes all of metaphysics. No more mirror of being and appearances, of the real and its concept; no more imaginary coextensivity: rather, genetic miniaturization is the dimension of simulation. The real is produced from miniaturized units, from matrices, memory banks and command models—and with these it can be reproduced an indefinite number of times. It no longer has to be rational, since it is no longer measured against some ideal or negative instance. It is nothing more than operational. In fact, since it is no longer enveloped by an imaginary, it is no longer real at all. It is a hyperreal: the product of an irradiating synthesis of combinatory models in a hyperspace without atmosphere.

In this passage to a space whose curvature is no longer that of the real, nor of truth, the age of simulation thus begins with a liquidation of all referentials—worse: by their artificial resurrection in systems of signs, which are a more ductile material than meaning, in that they lend themselves to all systems of equivalence, all binary oppositions and all combinatory algebra. It is no longer a question of imitation, nor of reduplication, nor even of parody. It is rather a question of substituting signs of the real for the real itself; that is, an operation to deter every real process by its operational double, a metastable, programmatic, perfect descriptive machine which provides all the signs of the real and short-circuits all its vicissitudes. Never again will the real have to be produced: this is the vital function of the model in a system of death, or rather of anticipated resurrection which no longer leaves any chance even in the event of death. A hyperreal henceforth sheltered from the imaginary, and from any distinction between the real and the imaginary, leaving room only for the orbital recurrence of models and the simulated generation of difference.

The Divine Irreference of Images

To dissimulate is to feign not to have what one has. To simulate is to feign to have what one hasn't. One implies a presence, the other an absence. But the matter is more complicated, since to simulate is not simply to feign: "Someone who feigns an illness can simply go to bed and pretend he is ill. Someone who simulates an illness produces in himself some of the symptoms" (Littre). Thus, feigning or dissimulating leaves the reality principle intact: the difference is always clear, it is only masked; whereas simulation threatens the difference between "true" and "false," between "real" and "imaginary." Since the simulator produces "true" symptoms, is he or she ill or not? The simulator cannot be treated objectively either as ill, or as not ill. Psychology and medicine stop at this point, before a thereafter undiscoverable truth of the illness. For if any symptom can be "produced," and can no longer be accepted as a fact of nature, then every illness may be considered as simulatable and simulated, and medicine loses its meaning since it only knows how to treat "true" illnesses by their objective causes. Psychosomatics evolves in a dubious way on the edge of the illness principle. As for psychoanalysis, it transfers the symptom from the organic to the unconscious order: once again, the latter is held to be real, more real than the former; but why should simulation stop at the portals of the unconscious? Why couldn't the "work" of the unconscious be "produced" in the same way as any other symptom in classical medicine? Dreams already are.

The alienist, of course, claims that "for each form of the mental alienation there is a particular order in the succession of symptoms, of which the simulator is unaware and in the absence of which the alienist is unlikely to be deceived." This (which dates from 1865) in order to save at all cost the truth principle, and to escape the specter raised by simulation: namely that truth, reference and objective causes have ceased to exist. What can medicine do with something which floats on either side of illness, on either side of health, or with the reduplication of illness in a discourse that is no longer true or false? What can psychoanalysis do with the reduplication of the discourse of the unconscious in a discourse of simulation that can never be unmasked, since it isn't false either?

What can the army do with simulators? Traditionally, following a direct principle of identification, it unmasks and punishes them. Today, it can reform an excellent simulator as though he were equivalent to a "real" homosexual, heart-case or lunatic. Even military psychology retreats from the Cartesian clarities and hesitates to draw the distinction between true and false, between the "produced" symptom and the authentic symptom. "If he acts crazy so well, then he must be mad." Nor is it mistaken: in the sense that all lunatics are simulators, and this lack of distinction is the worst form of subversion. Against it, classical reason armed itself with all its categories. But it is this today which again outflanks them, submerging the truth principle.

Outside of medicine and the army, favored terrains of simulation, the affair goes back to religion and the simulacrum of divinity: "I forbade any simulacrum in the temples because the divinity that breathes life into nature cannot be represented." Indeed it can. But what becomes of the divinity when it reveals itself in icons, when it is multiplied in sumulacra? Does it remain the supreme authority, simply incarnated in images as a visible theology? Or is it volatilized into simulacra which alone deploy their pomp and power of fascination—the visible machinery of icons being substituted for the pure and intelligible Idea of God? This is precisely what was feared by the Iconoclasts, whose millennial quarrel is still with us today. Their rage to destroy images rose pre-

cisely because they sensed this omnipotence of simulacra, this facility they have of erasing God from the consciousnesses of people, and the overwhelming, destructive truth
which they suggest: that ultimately there has never been any God; that only simulacra
exist; indeed that God himself has only ever been his own simulacrum. Had they been
able to believe that images only occulted or masked the Platonic idea of God, there
would have been no reason to destroy them. One can live with the idea of a distorted
truth. But their metaphysical despair came from the idea that the images concealed
nothing at all, and that in fact they were not images, such as the original model would
have made them, but actually perfect simulacra forever radiant with their own fascination. But this death of the divine referential has to be exorcised at all cost.

It can be seen that the iconoclasts, who are often accused of despising and denying images, were in fact the ones who accorded them their actual worth, unlike the
iconolaters, who saw in them only reflections and were content to venerate God at
one remove. But the converse can also be said, namely that the iconolaters possessed
the most modern and adventurous minds, since, underneath the idea of the apparition of God in the mirror of images, they already enacted his death and his disappearance in the epiphany of his representations (which they perhaps knew no longer
represented anything, and that they were purely a game, but that this was precisely
the greatest game—knowing also that it is dangerous to unmask images, since they
dissimulate the fact that there is nothing behind them).

This was the approach of the Jesuits, who based their politics on the virtual disappearance of God and on the worldly and spectacular manipulation of consciences—
the evanescence of God in the epiphany of power—the end of transcendence, which
no longer serves as alibi for a strategy completely free of influences and signs. Behind the baroque of images hides the grey eminence of politics.

Thus perhaps at stake has always been the murderous capacity of images: murderers of the real; murderers of their own model as the Byzantine icons could murder
the divine identity. To this murderous capacity is opposed the dialectical capacity of
representations as a visible and intelligible mediation of the real. All of Western faith
and good faith was engaged in this wager on representation: that a sign could refer
to the depth of meaning, that a sign could *exchange* for meaning and that something
could guarantee this exchange—God, of course. But what if God himself can be
simulated, that is to say, reduced to the signs which attest his existence? Then the
whole system becomes weightless; it is no longer anything but a gigantic simulacrum: not unreal, but a simulacrum, never again exchanging for what is real, but
exchanging in itself, in an uninterrupted circuit without reference or circumference.

So it is with simulation, insofar as it is opposed to representation. Representation
starts from the principle that the sign and the real are equivalent (even if this equivalence is Utopian, it is a fundamental axiom). Conversely, simulation starts from the
Utopia of this principle of equivalence, *from the radical negation of the sign as value,*
from the sign as reversion and death sentence of every reference. Whereas representation tries to absorb simulation by interpreting it as false representation, simulation
envelops the whole edifice of representation as itself a simulacrum.

These would be the successive phases of the image:

1. It is the reflection of a basic reality.
2. It masks and perverts a basic reality.
3. It masks the *absence* of a basic reality.
4. It bears no relation to any reality whatever: it is its own pure simulacrum.

In the first case, the image is a *good* appearance: the representation is of the order of sacrament. In the second, it is an *evil* appearance: of the order of malefice. In the third, it *plays at being* an appearance: it is of the order of sorcery. In the fourth, it is no longer in the order of appearance at all, but of simulation.

The transition from signs which dissimulate something to signs which dissimulate that there is nothing, marks the decisive turning point. The first implies a theology of truth and secrecy (to which the notion of ideology still belongs). The second inaugurates an age of simulacra and simulation, in which there is no longer any God to recognize his own, nor any last judgement to separate truth from false, the real from its artificial resurrection, since everything is already dead and risen in advance.

When the real is no longer what it used to be, nostalgia assumes its full meaning. There is a proliferation of myths of origin and signs of reality; of second-hand truth, objectivity and authenticity. There is an escalation of the true, of the lived experience; a resurrection of the figurative where the object and substance have disappeared. And there is a panic-stricken production of the real and the referential, above and parallel to the panic of material production. This is how simulation appears in the phase that concerns us: a strategy of the real, neo-real and hyperreal, whose universal double is a strategy of deterrence.

Hyperreal and Imaginary

Disneyland is a perfect model of all the entangled orders of simulation. To begin with it is a play of illusions and phantasms: pirates, the frontier, future world, etc. This imaginary world is supposed to be what makes the operation successful. But, what draws the crowds is undoubtedly much more the social microcosm, the miniaturized and *religious* revelling in real America, in its delights and drawbacks. You park outside, queue up inside, and are totally abandoned at the exit. In this imaginary world the only phantasmagoria is in the inherent warmth and affection of the crowd, and in that sufficiently excessive number of gadgets used there to specifically maintain the multitudinous affect. The contrast with the absolute solitude of the parking lot—a veritable concentration camp—is total. Or rather: inside, a whole range of gadgets magnetize the crowd into direct flows; outside, solitude is directed onto a single gadget: the automobile. By an extraordinary coincidence (one that undoubtedly belongs to the peculiar enchantment of this universe), this deep-frozen infantile world happens to have been conceived and realized by a man who is himself now cryogenized; Walt Disney, who awaits his resurrection at minus 180 degrees centigrade.

The objective profile of the United States, then, may be traced throughout Disneyland, even down to the morphology of individuals and the crowd. All its values are exalted here, in miniature and comic-strip form. Embalmed and pacified. Whence the possibility of an ideological analysis of Disneyland: . . . digest of the American way of life, panegyric to American values, idealized transposition of a contradictory reality. To be sure. But this conceals something else, and that "ideological" blanket exactly serves to cover over a *third-order simulation:* Disneyland is there to conceal the fact that it is the "real" country, all of "real" America, which *is* Disneyland (just as prisons are there to conceal the fact that it is the social in its entirety, in its banal omnipotence, which is carceral). Disneyland is presented as imaginary in order to make us believe that the rest is real, when in fact all of Los Angeles and the

America surrounding it are no longer real, but of the order of the hyperreal and of simulation. It is no longer a question of a false representation of reality (ideology), but of concealing the fact that the real is no longer real, and thus of saving the reality principle.

The Disneyland imaginary is neither true nor false: it is a deterrence machine set up in order to rejuvenate in reverse the fiction of the real. Whence the debility, the infantile degeneration of this imaginary. It is meant to be an infantile world, in order to make us believe that the adults are elsewhere, in the "real" world, and to conceal the fact that real childishness is everywhere, particularly among those adults who go there to act the child in order to foster illusions of their real childishness.

Moreover, Disneyland is not the only one. Enchanted Village, Magic Mountain, Marine World: Los Angeles is encircled by these "imaginary stations" which feed reality, reality-energy, to a town whose mystery is precisely that it is nothing more than a network of endless, unreal circulation: a town of fabulous proportions, but without space or dimensions. As much as electrical and nuclear power stations, as much as film studios, this town, which is nothing more than an immense script and a perpetual motion picture, needs this old imaginary made up of childhood signals and faked phantasms for its sympathetic nervous system.❖

❖ Reactions and Alternatives ❖

Anthony Giddens (1938–) taught for many years at King's College, Cambridge, where he was professor of sociology in the Faculty of Economics and Politics. He is now director of the London School of Economics. Giddens is also a founder, publisher, and editor of Polity Press, one of the most ambitious and interesting publishers of books in social theory. His first widely read book was *New Rules of Sociological Methods* (1976). As the title's play on Durkheim suggests, the book is an attempt to reformulate sociological reasoning, in this instance by reexamining the idea of interpretative, or hermeneutic, sociology. This was Giddens's first statement of structuration theory, which is systematically worked out in *Constitution of Society* (1984). Giddens has written on many subjects, from war to sexual intimacy. The selection is from *Consequences of Modernity* (1989), which is his defense of what he calls radicalized modernity. The selection offers a particularly clear illustration of his understanding of the complexity of modern life, stated in his own discursive theoretical style. The tabular presentation of modernity (RM) and postmodernity (PM), though it reflects Giddens's radicalized preferences for RM over PM, offers a useful comparison of theories of the two cultural types. More importantly, the selection presents what is perhaps the crucial idea behind Giddens's structuration theory: that the individual lives in an ongoing recursive relation with the complex structures of modern society. Structures create the individual, while they are being created and held by individuals. Giddens, like others (Gouldner, Bourdieu), views reflexivity as the fundamental feature of modern life arising in the relation of individuals to structures—a relation that creates the series of paradoxes he discusses. In effect, Giddens argues that modernity opens new and different opportunities for human fulfillment. Moderns may be displaced from local communities, but they are reembedded in world culture in ways that can be liberating. This is an example of a reflexive social theory recursively producing a theory of the world as reflexive.

Post-Modernity or Radicalized Modernity?

Anthony Giddens (1990)

A Phenomenology of Modernity

Two images of what it feels like to live in the world of modernity have dominated the sociological literature, yet both of them seem less than adequate. One is that of Weber, according to which the bonds of rationality are drawn tighter and tighter, im-

---

Excerpt from *The Consequences of Modernity* (Stanford, Calif.: Stanford University Press, 1990), pp. 137–150. Reprinted with the permission of the publishers, Stanford University Press. 1990 by the Board of Trustees of the Leland Stanford Junior University. Reprinted by permission of Polity Press and Basil Blackwell.

prisoning us in a featureless cage of bureaucratic routine. Among the three major founders of modern sociology, Weber saw most clearly the significance of expertise in modern social development and used it to outline a phenomenology of modernity. Everyday experience, according to Weber, retains its colour and spontaneity, but only on the perimeter of the "steel-hard" cage of bureaucratic rationality. The image has a great deal of power and has, of course, featured strongly in fictional literature in the twentieth century as well as in more directly sociological discussions. There are many contexts of modern institutions which are marked by bureaucratic fixity. But they are far from all-pervasive, and even in the core settings of its application, namely, large-scale organisations, Weber's characterisation of bureaucracy is inadequate. Rather than tending inevitably towards rigidity, organisations produce areas of autonomy and spontaneity—which are actually often less easy to achieve in smaller groups. We owe this counterinsight to Durkheim, as well as to subsequent empirical study of organisations. The closed climate of opinion within some small groups and the modes of direct sanction available to its members fix the horizons of action much more narrowly and firmly than in larger organisational settings.

The second is the image of Marx—and of many others, whether they regard themselves as Marxist or not. According to this portrayal, modernity is seen as a monster. More limpidly perhaps than any of his contemporaries, Marx perceived how shattering the impact of modernity would be, and how irreversible. At the same time, modernity was for Marx what Habermas has aptly called an "unfinished project." The monster can be tamed, since what human beings have created they can always subject to their own control. Capitalism, simply, is an irrational way to run the modern world, because it substitutes the whims of the market for the controlled fulfilment of human need.

For these images I suggest we should substitute that of the juggernaut*—a runaway engine of enormous power which, collectively as human beings, we can drive to some extent but which also threatens to rush out of our control and which could rend itself asunder. The juggernaut crushes those who resist it, and while it sometimes seems to have a steady path, there are times when it veers away erratically in directions we cannot foresee. The ride is by no means wholly unpleasant or unrewarding; it can often be exhilarating and charged with hopeful anticipation. But, so long as the institutions of modernity endure, we shall never be able to control completely either the path or the pace of the journey. In turn, we shall never be able to feel entirely secure, because the terrain across which it runs is fraught with risks of high consequence. Feelings of ontological security and existential anxiety will coexist in ambivalence.

The juggernaut of modernity is not all of one piece, and here the imagery lapses, as does any talk of a single path which it runs. It is not an engine made up of integrated machinery, but one in which there is a tensionful, contradictory, push-and-pull of different influences. Any attempt to capture the experience of modernity must begin from this view, which derives ultimately from the dialectics of space and time, as expressed in the time-space constitution of modern institutions. I shall sketch a phenomenology of modernity in terms of four dialectically related frameworks of experience, each of which connects in an integral way with the preceding discussion in this study:

---

*The term comes from the Hindi *Jagannath*, "lord of the world," and is a title of Krishna; an idol of this deity was taken each year through the streets on a huge car, which followers are said to have thrown themselves under, to be crushed beneath the wheels.

Displacement and reembedding: the intersection of estrangement and familiarity.
Intimacy and impersonality: the intersection of personal trust and impersonal ties.
Expertise and reappropriation: the intersection of abstract systems and day-to-day knowledgeability.
Privatism and engagement: the intersection of pragmatic acceptance and activism.

Modernity "dis-places" in the sense previously analysed—place becomes phantas-magoric. Yet this is a double-layered, or ambivalent, experience rather than simply a loss of community. We can see this clearly only if we keep in mind the contrasts between the pre-modern and the modern described earlier. What happens is not simply that localised influences drain away into the more impersonalised relations of abstract systems. Instead, the very tissue of spatial experience alters, conjoining proximity and distance in ways that have few close parallels in prior ages. There is a complex relation here between familiarity and estrangement. Many aspects of life in local contexts continue to have a familiarity and ease to them, grounded in the day-to-day routines individuals follow. But the sense of the familiar is one often mediated by time-space distanciation. It does not derive from the particularities of localised place. And this experience, so far as it seeps into general awareness, is simultaneously disturbing and rewarding. The reassurance of the familiar, so important to a sense of ontological security, is coupled with the realisation that what is comfortable and nearby is actually an expression of distant events and was "placed into" the local environment rather than forming an organic development within it. The local shopping mall is a milieu in which a sense of ease and security is cultivated by the layout of the buildings and the careful planning of public places. Yet everyone who shops there is aware that most of the shops are chain stores, which one might find in any city, and indeed that innumerable shopping malls of similar design exist elsewhere.

A feature of displacement is our insertion into globalised cultural and information settings, which means that familiarity and place are much less consistently connected than hitherto. This is less a phenomenon of estrangement from the local than one of integration within globalised "communities" of shared experience. The boundaries of concealment and disclosure become altered, since many erstwhile quite distinct activities are juxtaposed in unitary public domains. The newspaper and the sequence of television programmes over the day are the most obvious concrete examples of this phenomenon, but it is generic to the time-space organisation of modernity. We are all familiar with events, with actions, and with the visible appearance of physical settings thousands of miles away from where we happen to live. The coming of electronic media has undoubtedly accentuated these aspects of displacement, since they override presence so instantaneously and at such distance. As Joshua Meyrowitz points out, a person on the telephone to another, perhaps on the opposite side of the world, is more closely bound to that distant other than to another individual in the same room (who may be asking, "Who is it? What's she saying?" and so forth).

The counterpart of displacement is reembedding. The disembedding mechanisms lift social relations and the exchange of information out of specific time-space contexts, but at the same time provide new opportunities for their reinsertion. This is another reason why it is a mistake to see the modern world as one in which large, impersonal systems increasingly swallow up most of personal life. The self-same processes that lead to the destruction of older city neighbourhoods and their replacement by towering office-blocks and skyscrapers often permit the gentrification of other areas and a recreation of locality. Although the picture of tall, impersonal clusters of city-centre buildings is often presented as the epitome of the landscape of modernity, this is a mistake. Equally characteristic is the recreation of places of relative smallness and informality. The very means of transportation which help to dissolve the connection between locality and kinship provide the possibility for reembedding, by making it easy to visit "close" relatives who are far away.

Parallel comments can be made about the intersection of intimacy and impersonality in modern contexts of action. It is simply not true that in conditions of modernity we live increasingly in a "world of strangers." We are not required more and more to exchange intimacy for impersonality in the contacts with others we routinely make in the course of our day-to-day lives. Something much more complex and subtle is involved. Day-to-day contacts with others in pre-modern settings were normally based upon a familiarity stemming in part from the nature of place. Yet contacts with familiar others probably rarely facilitated the level of intimacy we associate with personal and sexual relations today. The "transformation of intimacy" of which I have spoken is contingent upon the very distancing which the disembedding mechanisms bring about, combined with the altered environments of trust which they presuppose. There are some very obvious ways in which intimacy and abstract systems interact. Money, for example, can be spent to purchase the expert services of a psychologist who guides the individual in an exploration of the inner universe of the intimate and the personal.

A person walks the streets of a city and encounters perhaps thousands of people in the course of a day, people she or he has never met before—"strangers" in the modern sense of that term. Or perhaps that individual strolls along less crowded thoroughfares, idly scrutinising passersby and the diversity of products for sale in the shops—Baudelaire's *flâneur*. Who could deny that these experiences are an integral element of modernity? Yet the world "out there"—the world that shades off into indefinite time-space from the familiarity of the home and the local neighbourhood—is not at all a purely impersonal one. On the contrary, intimate relationships can be sustained at distance (regular and sustained contact can be made with other individuals at virtually any point on the earth's surface—as well as some below and above), and personal ties are continually forged with others with whom one was previously unacquainted. We live in a *peopled* world, not merely one of anonymous, blank faces, and the interpolation of abstract systems into our activities is intrinsic to bringing this about.

In relations of intimacy of the modern type, trust is always ambivalent, and the possibility of severance is more or less ever present. Personal ties can be ruptured, and ties of intimacy returned to the sphere of impersonal contacts—in the broken love affair, the intimate suddenly becomes again a stranger. The demand of "opening oneself up" to the other which personal trust relations now presume, the injunction to hide nothing from the other, mix reassurance and deep anxiety. Personal trust demands a level of self-understanding and self-expression which must itself be a source of psychological tension. For mutual self-revelation is combined with the need for reciprocity and support; yet the two are frequently incompatible. Torment and frustration interweave themselves with the need for trust in the other as the provider of care and support.

Deskilling and Reskilling in Everyday Life

Expertise is part of intimacy in conditions of modernity, as is shown not just by the huge variety of forms of psychotherapy and counseling available, but by the plurality of books, articles, and television programmes providing technical information about "relationships." Does this mean that, as Habermas puts it, abstract systems "colonise" a pre-existing "life-world," subordinating personal decisions to technical expertise? It does not. The reasons are twofold. One is that modern institutions do not just implant themselves into a "life-world," the residues of which remain much the same as they always were. Changes in the nature of day-to-day life also affect the disembedding mechanisms, in a dialectical interplay. The second reason is that technical expertise is continuously reappropriated by lay agents as part of their routine dealings with abstract systems. No one can become an expert, in the sense of the possession either of full expert knowledge or of the appropriate formal credentials, in more than a few small sectors of the immensely complicated knowledge systems which now exist. Yet no one can interact with abstract systems without mastering some of the rudiments of the principles upon which they are based.

Sociologists often suppose that, in contrast to the pre-modern era, where many things were mysteries, today we live in a world from which mystery has retreated and where the way "the world works" can (in principle) be exhaustively known. But this is not true for either the lay person or the expert, if we consider their experience as individuals. To all of us living in the modern world things are specifically *opaque,* in a way that was not the case previously. In pre-modern environments the "local knowledge," to adapt a phrase from Clifford Geertz, which individuals possessed was rich, varied, and adapted to the requirements of living in the local milieu. But how many of us today when we switch on the light know much about where the electricity supply comes from or even, in a technical sense, what electricity actually is?

Yet, although "local knowledge" cannot be of the same order as it once was, the sieving off of knowledge and skill from everyday life is not a one-way process. Nor are individuals in modern contexts less knowledgeable about their local milieux than their counterparts in pre-modern cultures. Modern social life is a complex affair, and there are many "filter-back" processes whereby technical knowledge, in one shape or another, is reappropriated by lay persons and routinely applied in the course of their day-to-day activities. As was mentioned earlier, the interaction between expertise and reappropriation is strongly influenced, among other things, by experiences at access points. Economic factors may decide whether a person learns to fix her or his car engine, rewire the electrical system of the house, or fix the roof; but so do the levels of trust that an individual vests in the particular expert systems and known experts involved. Processes of reappropriation relate to all aspects of social life—for example, medical treatment, child-rearing, or sexual pleasure.

For the ordinary individual, all this does not add up to feelings of secure control over day-to-day life circumstances. Modernity expands the arenas of personal fulfilment and of security in respect of large swathes of day-to-day life. But the lay person—and *all* of us are lay persons in respect of the vast majority of expert systems—must ride the juggernaut. The lack of control which many of us feel about some of the circumstances of our lives in real.

It is against this backdrop that we should understand patterns of privatism and engagement. A sense of "survival," in Lasch's use of this term, cannot be absent from our thoughts all of the time in a world in which, for the indefinite future, survival is a real and inescapable issue. On the level of the unconscious—even, and perhaps especially, among those whose attitude is one of pragmatic acceptance towards high-consequence risks—the relation to survival probably exists as existential dread. For basic trust in the continuity of the world must be anchored in the simple conviction that it will continue, and this is something of which we cannot be entirely sure. Saul Bellow remarks in the novel *Herzog,* "The revolution of nuclear terror returns the metaphysical dimension to us. All practical activity has reached this culmination: everything may go now, civilisation, history, nature. Now to recall Mr. Kierkegaard's question . . . " "Mr. Kierkegaard's question" is, how do we avoid the dread of nonexistence, considered not just as individual death but as an existential void? The possibility of global calamity, whether by nuclear war or other means, prevents us from reassuring ourselves with the assumption that the life of the species inevitably surpasses that of the individual.

How remote that possibility is, literally no one knows. So long as there is deterrence, there must be the chance of war, because the notion of deterrence only makes sense if the parties involved are in principle prepared to use the weaponry they hold. Once again, no one, no matter how "expert" about the logistics of weapons and military organisation or about world politics, can say whether deterrence "works," because the most that can be said is that so far there has been no war. Awareness of these inherent uncertainties does not escape the lay population, however vague that awareness might be.

Balanced against the deep anxieties which such circumstances must produce in virtually everyone is the psychological prop of the feeling that "there's nothing that I as an individual can do," and that at any rate the risk must be very slight. Business-as-usual, as I have pointed out, is a prime element in the stabilising of trust and ontological security, and this no doubt applies in respect of high-consequence risks just as it does in other areas of trust relations.

Yet obviously even high-consequence risks are not only remote contingencies, which can be ignored in daily life, albeit at some probable psychological cost. Some such risks, and many others which are potentially life-threatening for individuals or otherwise significantly affect them, intrude right into the core of day-to-day activities. This is true, for example, of any pollution damage which affects the health of adults or children, and anything which produces toxic contents in food or affects its nutritional properties. It is also true of a multitude of technological changes that influence life chances, such as reproductive technologies. The mix of risk and opportunity is so complex in many of the circumstances involved that it is extremely difficult for individuals to know how far to vest trust in particular prescriptions or systems, and how far to suspend it. How can one manage to eat "healthily," for example, when all kinds of food are said to have toxic qualities of one sort or another and when what is held to be "good for you" by nutritional experts varies with the shifting state of scientific knowledge?

Trust and risk, opportunity and danger—these polar, paradoxical features of modernity permeate all aspects of day-to-day life, once more reflecting an extraordinary interpolation of the local and the global. Pragmatic acceptance can be sustained towards most of the abstract systems that impinge on individuals' lives, but by its very nature such an attitude cannot be carried on all the while and in respect of all areas of activity. For incoming expert information is often fragmentary or inconsistent, as is the recycled knowledge which colleagues, friends, and intimates pass on to one another. On a personal level, decisions must be taken and policies forged. Privatism, the avoidance of contestatory engagement—which can be supported by attitudes of basic optimism, pessimism, or pragmatic acceptance—can serve the purposes of day-to-day "survival" in many respects. But it is likely to be interspersed with phases of active engagement, even on the part of those most prone to attitudes of indifference or cynicism. For, to repeat, in respect of the balance of security and danger which modernity introduces into our lives, there are no longer "others"—no one can be completely outside. Conditions of modernity, in many circumstances, provoke activism rather than privatism, because of modernity's inherent reflexivity and because there are many opportunities for collective organisation within the polyarchic systems of modern nation-states.

TABLE [1]   A Comparison of Conceptions
of "Post-Modernity" (PM) and "Radicalised Modernity" (RM)

PM	RM
1. Understands current transitions in epistemological terms or as dissolving epistemology altogether.	1. Identifies the institutional developments which create a sense of fragmentation and dispersal.
2. Focuses upon the centrifugal tendencies of current social transformations and their dislocating character.	2. Sees high modernity as a set of circumstances in which dispersal is dialectically connected to profound tendencies towards global integration.
3. Sees the self as dissolved or dismembered by the fragmenting of experience.	3. Sees the self as more than just a site of intersecting forces; active processes of reflexive self-identity are made possible by modernity.
4. Argues for the contextuality of truth claims or sees them as "historical."	4. Argues that the universal features of truth claims force themselves upon us in an irresistible way given the primacy of problems of a global kind. Systematic knowledge about these developments is not precluded by the reflexivity of modernity.
5. Theorises powerlessness which individuals feel in the face of globalising tendencies.	5. Analyses a dialectic of powerlessness and empowerment, in terms of both experience and action.
6. Sees the "emptying" of day-to-day life as a result of the intrusion of abstract systems.	6. Sees day-to-day life as an active complex of reactions to abstract systems, involving appropriation as well as loss.
7. Regards coordinated political engagement as precluded by the primacy of contextuality and dispersal.	7. Regards coordinated political engagement as both possible and necessary, on a global level as well as locally.
8. Defines post-modernity as the end of epistemology/the individual/ethics.	8. Defines post-modernity as possible transformations moving "beyond" the institutions of modernity.

Objections to Post-Modernity

Let me at this point return briefly to issues raised near the beginning of the book and at the same time look ahead to the closing sections. I have sought to develop an interpretation of the current era which challenges the usual views of the emergence of post-modernity. As ordinarily understood, conceptions of post-modernity— which mostly have their origin in post-structuralist thought—involve a number of distinct strands. I compare this conception of post-modernity (PM) with my alternative position, which I shall call radicalised modernity (RM), in Table [1].❖

Ernesto LaClau studied both in Buenos Aires and at Oxford University. Since 1973, he has taught government at the University of Essex. LaClau has lectured in the United States, Canada, and Latin America, as well as in Europe. He is also the author of *Politics and Ideology in Marxist Theory* (1977). **Chantal Mouffe** studied in Belgium, France, and England. She has taught at the National University of Colombia and the University of London. She is editor of and contributor to *Gramsci and Marxist Theory* (1979) and *Dimensions of Radical Democracy* (1992), as well as an author and lecturer on numerous subjects in political and feminist theory.

Radical Democracy: Alternative for a New Left

Ernesto LaClau and Chantal Mouffe (1985)

The conservative reaction thus has a clearly hegemonic character. It seeks a profound transformation of the terms of political discourse and the creation of a new 'definition of reality,' which under the cover of the defence of 'individual liberty' would legitimize inequalities and restore the hierarchical relations which the struggles of previous decades had destroyed. What is at stake here is in fact the creation of a new historic bloc. Converted into organic ideology, liberal-conservatism would construct a new hegemonic articulation through a system of equivalences which would unify multiple subject positions around an individualist definition of rights and a negative conception of liberty. We are once again faced, then, with the displacement of the frontier of the social. A series of subject positions which were accepted as *legitimate differences* in the hegemonic formation corresponding to the Welfare State are expelled from the field of social positivity and construed as negativity—the parasites on social security (Mrs Thatcher's 'scroungers'), the inefficiency associated with union privileges, and state subsidies, and so on.

It is clear, therefore, that a left alternative can *only* consist of the construction of a different system of equivalents, which establishes social division on a new basis. In the face of the project for the reconstruction of a hierarchic society, the alternative of the Left should consist of locating itself fully in the field of the democratic revolution and expanding the chains of equivalents between the different struggles against oppression. *The task of the Left therefore cannot be to renounce liberal-democratic ideology, but on the contrary, to deepen and expand it in the direction of a radical and plural democracy.* We shall explain the dimensions of this task in the following pages, but the very fact that it is possible arises out of the fact that the *meaning* of liberal discourse on individual rights is not definitively fixed; and just as this unfixity permits their articulation with elements of conservative discourse, it also permits different forms of articulation and redefinition which accentuate the democratic movement. That is to say, as with any other social element, the elements making up the liberal discourse never appear as crystallized, and may be the field of hegemonic struggle. It is not in the abandonment of the democratic terrain but, on the contrary, in the extension of the field of democratic struggles to the whole of civil society and the state, that the possibility resides for a hegemonic strategy of the Left. It is nevertheless important to understand the radical extent of the changes which are necessary in the political imaginary of the Left, if it

---

Excerpt from *Hegemony and Socialist Strategy: Towards a Radical Democratic Politics* (London: Verso, 1985), pp. 176–180.

wishes to succeed in founding a political practice fully located in the field of the democratic revolution and conscious of the depth and variety of the hegemonic articulations which the present conjuncture requires. The fundamental obstacle in this task is the one to which we have been drawing attention from the beginning of this book: essentialist apriorism, the conviction that the social is sutured at some point, from which it is possible to fix the meaning of any event independently of any articulatory practice. This has led to a failure to understand the constant displacement of the nodal points structuring a social formation, and to an organization of discourse in terms of a logic of 'a priori privileged points' which seriously limits the Left's capacity for action and political analysis. This logic of privileged points has operated in a variety of directions. From the point of view of the determining of the fundamental antagonisms, the basic obstacle, as we have seen, has been *classism:* that is to say, the idea that the working class represents the privileged agent in which the fundamental impulse of social change resides—without perceiving that the very orientation of the working class depends upon a political balance of forces and the radicalization of a plurality of democratic struggles which are decided in good part *outside* the class itself. From the point of view of the *social levels* at which the possibility of implementing changes is concentrated, the fundamental obstacles have been *statism*—the idea that the expansion of the role of the state is the panacea for all problems; and *economism* (particularly in its technocratic version)—the idea that from a successful economic strategy there necessarily follows a continuity of political effects which can be clearly specified.

But if we look for the ultimate core of this essentialist fixity, we shall find it in the fundamental nodal point which has galvanized the political imagination of the Left: the classic concept of 'revolution,' cast in the Jacobin mould. Of course, there would be nothing in the concept of 'revolution' to which objection could be made if we understood by it the overdetermination of a set of struggles in a point of political rupture, from which there follow a variety of effects spread across the whole of the fabric of society. If this were all that was involved, there is no doubt that in many cases the violent overthrow of a repressive regime is the condition of every democratic advance. But the classic concept of revolution implied much more than this: it implied the *foundational* character of the revolutionary act, the institution of a point of concentration of power from which society could be 'rationally' reorganized. This is the perspective which is incompatible with the plurality and the opening which a radical democracy requires. Once again radicalizing certain of Gramsci's concepts, we find the theoretical instruments which allow us to redimension the revolutionary act itself. The concept of a 'war of position' implies precisely the *process* character of every radical transformation— the revolutionary act is, simply, an internal moment of this process. The multiplication of political spaces and the preventing of the concentration of power in one point are, then, preconditions of every truly democratic transformation of society. The classic conception of socialism supposed that the disappearance of private ownership of the means of production would set up a chain of effects which, over a whole historical epoch, would lead to the extinction of all forms of subordination. Today we know that this is not so. *There are not,* for example, necessary links between anti-sexism and anti-capitalism, and a unity between the two can only be the result of a hegemonic articulation. It follows that it is only possible to construct this articulation on the basis of separate struggles, which only exercise their equivalential and overdetermining effects in *certain* spheres of the social. This requires the autonomization of the spheres of struggle and the multiplication of political spaces, which is incompatible with the concentration of power and knowledge that classic Jacobinism and its different socialist variants imply. Of course, every project for radical democracy implies a socialist dimension, as it is necessary to put an end to capitalist relations of production, which are at the root of numerous relations of subordination; but socialism is *one* of the components of a project for radical democracy, not vice versa. For this very reason, when one speaks of the socialization of the means of production as one element in the strategy for a radical and plural democracy, one must insist that this cannot mean only workers' self-management, as what is at stake is true participation by all subjects in decisions about what is to be produced, how it is to be produced, and the forms in which the product is to be distributed. Only in such conditions can there be *social appropriation* of production. To reduce the issue to a problem of workers' self-management is to ignore the fact that the workers' 'interests' can be constructed in such a way that they do not take account of ecological demands or demands of other groups which, without being producers, are affected by decisions taken in the field of production.

From the point of view of a hegemonic politics, then, the crucial limitation of the traditional left perspective is that it attempts to determine *a priori* agents of change, levels of effectiveness in the field of the social, and privileged points and moments of rupture. All these obstacles come together into a common core, which is the refusal to abandon the assumption of a sutured society. Once this is discarded, however, there arises a whole set of new problems which we should now tackle. . . .

It is impossible to define *a priori* the surfaces on which antagonisms will be constituted. Thus, although several left politics may be conceived and specified in certain contexts, there is not *one* politics of the Left whose *contents* can be determined in isolation from all contextual reference. It is for this reason that all attempts to proceed to such determination *a priori* have necessarily been unilateral and arbitrary, with no validity in a great number of circumstances. The exploding of the uniqueness of meaning of the political—which is linked to the phenomena of combined and uneven development—dissolves every possibility of fixing the signified in terms of a division between left and right. Say we try to define an ultimate content of the left which underlies all the contexts in which the word has been used: we shall never find one which does not present exceptions. We are exactly in the field of Wittgenstein's language games: the closest we can get is to find 'family resemblances.' Let us examine a few examples. In recent years much has been talked about the need to deepen the line of separation between state and civil society. It is not difficult to realize, however, that this proposal does not furnish the Left with any theory of the surface of emergence of antagonisms which can be generalized beyond a limited number of situations. It would appear to imply that every form of domination is incarnated in the state. But it is clear that civil society is also the seat of numerous relations of oppression, and, in consequence, of antagonisms and democratic struggles. With a greater or lesser clarity in their results, theories such as Althusser's analysis of 'ideological state apparatuses' sought to create a conceptual framework with which to think these phenomena of displacement in the field of domination. In the case of the feminist struggle, the state is an important means for effecting an advance, frequently *against* civil society, in legislation which combats sexism. In numerous underdeveloped countries the expansion of the functions of the central state is a means of establishing a frontier in the struggle against extreme forms of exploitation by landowning oligarchies. Furthermore, the state is not a homogeneous medium, separated from civil society by a ditch, but an uneven set of branches and functions, only relatively integrated by the hegemonic practices which take place within it. Above all, it should not be forgotten that the state can be the seat of numerous democratic antagonisms, to the extent that a set of functions within it—professional or technical, for example—can enter into relations of antagonism with centres of power, within the state itself, which seek to restrict and deform them. None of this means to say, of course, that in certain cases the division between state and civil society *cannot* constitute the fundamental political line of demarcation: this is what happens when the state has been transformed into a bureaucratic excrescence imposed by force upon the rest of society, as in Eastern Europe, or in the Nicaragua of the Somozas, which was a dictatorship sustained by a military apparatus. At any event, it is clearly impossible to identify either the state or civil society *a priori* as *the* surface of emergence of democratic antagonisms. The same can be said when it is a question of determining the positive or negative character, from the point of view of the politics of the Left, of certain organizational forms. Let us consider, for example, the 'party' form. The party as a political institution can, in certain circumstances, be an instance of bureaucratic crystallization which acts as a brake upon mass movements; but in others it can be the organizer of dispersed and politically virgin masses, and can thus serve as an instrument for the expansion and deepening of democratic struggles. The important point is that inasmuch as the field of 'society in general' has disappeared as a valid framework of political analysis, there has also disappeared the possibility of establishing a *general* theory of politics on the basis of topographic categories—that is to say, of categories which fix in a permanent manner the meaning of certain contents as differences which can be located within a relational complex.❖

Nancy Hartsock teaches political science and women's studies at the University of Washington. Among her writings is *Money, Sex, and Power: Toward a Feminist Historical Materialism* (1984) and the important article "The Feminist Standpoint: Developing the Ground for a Specifically Feminist Historical Materialism" (1983). The selection is from her essay "Foucault on Power: A Theory for Women?" Here, Hartsock presents a nuanced standpoint response to Foucault, who has been a particularly troubling theorist for feminists. On the one hand, Foucault's deep critique of modernity and his theory of the diffusion of power throughout the micropolitics of modern society are thought to weaken the basis for informed political action. On the other, few social theorists have done more than Foucault to open consideration of sex and sexuality in social theory and research. Hence, he is sometimes considered a dangerous ally. Another well-known feminist response to Foucault is Nancy Fraser's *Unruly Practices: Power, Discourse and Gender in Contemporary Social Theory* (1989). Hartsock's essay is in Linda Nicholson (ed.), *Feminism/Postmodernism,* which (along with *Feminists Theorize the Political,* edited by Judith Butler and Joan Scott in 1992) is an excellent source for the feminist debate on postmodernism.

Foucault on Power: A Theory for Women?
Nancy Hartsock (1987)

To mention the power of women leads immediately to the problem of what is meant by "women." The problem of differences among women has been very prominent in the United States in recent years. We face the task of developing our understanding

Excerpt from Linda J. Nicholson, ed., *Feminism/Postmodernism* (New York: Routledge, 1990), pp. 158–160, 161–168, 170–172.

of difference as part of the theoretical task of developing a theory of power for women. Issues of difference reminds us as well that many of the factors which divide women also unite some women with men—factors such as racial or cultural differences. Perhaps theories of power for women will also be theories of power for others groups as well. We need to develop our understanding of difference by creating a situation in which hitherto marginalized groups can name themselves, speak for themselves, and participate in defining the terms of interaction, a situation in which we can construct an understanding of the world that is sensitive to difference.

What might such a theory look like? Can we develop a general theory, or should we abandon the search for such a theory in favor of making space for a number of heterogeneous voices to be heard? What kinds of common claims can be made about the situations of women and men of color? About those of white women and women and men of color? About the situations of Western peoples and those they have colonized? For example, is it ever legitimate to say "women" without qualification? These kinds of questions make it apparent that the situation we face involves not only substantive claims about the world, but also raises questions about how we come to know the world, about what we can claim for our theories and ultimately about who "we" are. I want to ask what kinds of knowledge claims are required for grounding political action by different groups. Should theories produced by "minorities" rest on different epistemologies than those of the "majority?" Given the fact that the search for theory has been called into question in majority discourse and has been denounced as totalizing, do we want to ask similar questions of minority proposals or set similar standards?

In our efforts to find ways to include the voices of marginalized groups, one might expect helpful guidance from those who have argued against totalizing and universalistic theories such as those of the Enlightenment. Many radical intellectuals have been attracted to a compilation of diverse writings ranging from literary criticism to the social sciences, generally termed postmodern. The writers, among them figures such as Foucault, Derrida, Rorty, and Lyotard, argue against the faith in a universal reason we have inherited from Enlightenment European philosophy. They reject stories that claim to encompass all of human history: As Lyotard puts it, "let us wage war on totality." In its place they propose a social criticism that is *ad hoc,* contextual, plural, and limited. A number of feminist theorists have joined in the criticism of modernity put forward by these writers. They have endorsed their claims about what can and cannot be known or said or read into/from texts.

Despite their apparent congruence with the project I am proposing, I will argue these theories would hinder rather than help its accomplishment. Despite their own desire to avoid universal claims and despite their stated opposition to these claims, some universalistic assumptions creep back into their work. Thus, postmodernism, despite its stated efforts to avoid the problems of European modernism of the eighteenth and nineteenth centuries, at best manages to criticize these theories without putting anything in their place. For those of us who want to understand the world systematically in order to change it, postmodern theories at their best give little guidance. (I should note that I recognize that some postmodernist theorists are committed to ending injustice. But this commitment is not carried through in their theories.) Those of us who are not part of the ruling race, class, or gender, not a part of the minority which controls our world, need to know how it works. Why are we—in all our variousness—systematically excluded and marginalized? What systematic changes would be required to create a more just society? At worst, postmodernist theories can recapitulate the effects of Enlightenment theories which deny the right to participate in defining the terms of interaction. Thus, I contend, in broad terms, that postmodernism represents a dangerous approach for any marginalized group to adopt.

The Construction of the Colonized Other

In thinking about how to think about these issues, I found that the work of Albert Memmi in *The Colonizer and the Colonized* was very useful as a metaphor for understanding both our situation with regard to postmodernist theorists and the situation of some postmodernist theorists themselves: Those of us who have been marginalized enter the discussion from a position analogous to that which the colonized holds in relation to the colonizer. Most fundamentally, I want to argue that the philosophical and historical creation of a devalued "Other" was the necessary precondition for the creation of the transcendental rational subject outside of time and space, the subject who is the speaker in Enlightenment philosophy. Simone de Beauvoir has described the essence of the process in a quite different context: "Evil is necessary to Good, Matter to Idea, and Darkness to Light." While this subject is clearest in the work of bourgeois philosophers such as Kant, one can find echoes of this mode of thought in some of Marx's claims about the proletariat as the universal subject of history.

Memmi described the bond that creates both the colonizer and the colonized as one which destroys both parties, although in different ways. As he draws a portrait of the Other as described by the colonizer, the colonized emerges as the image of everything the colonizer is not. Every negative quality is projected onto her/him. The colonized is said to be lazy, and the colonizer becomes practically lyrical about it. Moreover, the colonized is both wicked and backward, a being who is in some important ways not fully human. As he describes the image of the colonized, feminist readers of de Beauvoir's *Second Sex* cannot avoid a sense of familiarity. We recognize a great deal of this description.

Memmi points to several conclusions drawn about this artificially created Other. First, the Other is always seen as "Not," as a lack, a void, as lacking in the valued qualities of the society, whatever those qualities may be. Second, the humanity of the Other becomes "opaque." Colonizers can frequently be heard making statements such as "you never know what they think. Do they think? Or do they instead operate according to intuition?" (Feminist readers may be reminded of some of the arguments about whether women had souls, or whether they were capable of reason or of learning Latin.) Memmi remarks ironically that the colonized must indeed by very strange, if he remains so mysterious and opaque after years of living with the colonizer. Third, the Others are not seen as fellow individual members of the human community, but rather as part of a chaotic, disorganized, and anonymous collectivity. They carry, Memmi states, "the mark of the plural." In more colloquial terms, they all look alike.

I want to stress once again that I am not claiming that women are a unitary group or that Western white women have the same experiences as women or men of color or as colonized peoples. Rather, I am pointing to a way of looking at the world characteristic of the dominant white, male, Eurocentric ruling class, a way of dividing up the world that puts an omnipotent subject at the center and constructs marginal Others as sets of negative qualities.

What is left of the Other after this effort to dehumanize her or him? She/he is pushed toward becoming an object. As an end, in the colonizer's supreme ambition, she/he should exist only as a function of the needs of the colonizer, that is, be transformed into a pure colonized. An object for himself or herself as well as for the colonizer. The colonized ceases to be a subject of history and becomes only what the colonizer is not. After having shut the colonized out of history and having forbidden him all development, the colonizer asserts his fundamental immobility. Confronted with this image as it is imposed by every institution and in every human contact, the colonized cannot be indifferent to this picture. Its accusations worry the colonized even more because she/he admires and fears the powerful colonizing accuser.

We can expand our understanding of the way this process works by looking briefly at Edward Said's account of the European construction of the Orient. He makes the political dimensions of this ideological move very clear: Said describes the creation of the Orient as an outgrowth of a will to power. "Orientalism," he states, "is a Western style for dominating, restructuring, and having authority over the Orient."

Interestingly enough, in the construction of these power relations, the Orient is often feminized. There is, however, the creation—out of this same process of the opposite of the colonized, the opposite of the Oriental, the opposite of women—of a being who sees himself as located at the center and possessed of all the qualities valued in his society (I use the masculine pronoun here purposely). Memmi describes this process eloquently:

> . . . the colonialist stresses those things that keep him separate rather than emphasizing that which might contribute to the foundation of a joint community. In those differences, the colonized is always degraded and the colonialist finds justification for rejecting his subjectivity. But perhaps the most important thing is that once the behavioral feature or historical or geographical factor which characterizes the colonialist and contrasts him with the colonized has been isolated, this gap must be kept from being filled. The colonialist removes the factor from history, time and therefore possible evolution. What is actually a sociological point becomes labeled as being biological, or preferably, metaphysical. It is attached to the colonized's basic nature. Immediately the colonial relationship between colonized and colonizer, founded on the essential outlook of the two protagonists, becomes a definitive category. It is what it is because they are what they are, and neither one nor the other will ever change.

Said points to something very similar. He argues that "European culture gained in strength and identity by setting itself off against the Orient as a sort of surrogate and even underground self." Orientalism is part of the European identity that defines "us" versus the nonEuropeans. To go further, the studied object becomes another being with regard to whom the studying subject becomes transcendent. Why? Because, unlike the Oriental, the European observer is a true human being.

But what does all this have to do with theory and the search for a theory of power for women? I want to suggest that in each of these cases—and the examples could be multiplied—what we see is the construction of the social relations, the power relations, which form the basis of the transcendent subject of Enlightenment theories— he (and I mean *he*) who theorizes. Put slightly differently, the political and social as well as ideological/intellectual creation of the devalued Other was at the same time the creation of the universalizing and totalizing voice postmodernists denounce as the voice of theory. . . .

Foucault's Resistance and Refusal

Foucault represents one of the several figures in Memmi's landscape. I have so far spoken only of the colonizer and the colonized, and these are indeed the basic structural positions. But Memmi makes an important distinction between the colonizer who accepts and the colonizer who refuses. If, as a group, modernist theories represent the views of the colonizer who accepts, postmodernist ideas can be divided between those who, like Richard Rorty, ignore the power relations involved, and those, like Foucault, who resist these relations. Foucault, I would argue, represents Memmi's colonizer who refuses and thus exists in a painful ambiguity. He is, therefore, a figure who also fails to provide an epistemology which is usable for the task of revolutionizing, creating, and constructing.

Memmi states that as a Jewish Tunisian he knew the colonizer as well as the colonized, and so "understood only too well (the difficulty of the colonizer who refuses) their inevitable ambiguity and the resulting isolation; more serious still, their inability to act." He notes that it is difficult to escape from a concrete situation and to refuse its ideology while continuing to live in the midst of the concrete relations of a culture. The colonizer who attempts it is a traitor, but he is still not the colonized. The political ineffectiveness of the Left Colonizer comes from the nature of his position in the colony. Has one, Memmi asks, ever seen a serious political demand which did not rest on concrete supports of people or money or force? The colonizer who refuses to become a part of his group [of] fellow citizens faces the difficult political question of who might he be.

This lack of certainty and power infuses Foucault's work most profoundly in his methodological texts. He is clearly rejecting any form of totalizing discourse: Reason, he argues, must be seen as born from chaos, truth as simply an error hardened into unalterable form in the long process of history. He argues for a glance that disperses and shatters the unity of man's being through which he sought to extend his sovereignty. That is, Foucault appears to endorse a rejection of modernity. Moreover, he has engaged in social activism around prisons. His sympathies are obviously with those over whom power is exercised, and he suggests that many struggles can be seen as linked to the revolutionary working-class movement.

In addition, his empirical critiques in works such as *Discipline and Punish* powerfully unmask coercive power. Yet, they do so on the one hand by making use of the values of humanism that he claims to be rejecting: That is, as Nancy Fraser points out, the project gets its political force from "the reader's familiarity with and commitment to modern ideals of autonomy, dignity, and human rights. Moreover, Foucault explicitly attempts to limit the power of his critique by arguing that unmasking power can have only destabilizing rather than transformative effects. But the sense of powerlessness and the isolation of the colonial intellectual resurfaces again and again. Thus, Foucault argues that:

> Humanity does not gradually progress from combat to combat until it arrives at universal reciprocity, where the rule of law finally replaces warfare; humanity installs each of its violences in a system of rules and thus proceeds from domination to domination.

Moreover, Foucault sees intellectuals as working only alongside rather than as those who struggle for power, working locally and regionally. Finally, in opposition to modernity, he calls for a history that is parodic, dissociative, and satirical. These must be seen as positive steps. Foucault is attempting to oppose the establishment of the relations of the colonizer to the colonized. But what is the positive result? . . .

. . . Foucault makes a number of important contributions to our understanding of contemporary social relations. One can cite his accounts of the development of the confession as a means of producing power by requiring those who are to be dominated to take the initiative. One can note as well his substitution of domination/subjugation for the traditional problem of sovereignty/obedience. In addition, his development of the concept of disciplinary power, a power which possesses, in a sense, the same possibilities for expansion as capital itself, marks a major advance. One might continue to enumerate his contributions, but I will leave that to his disciples. Instead, what I want to argue here is that Foucault reproduces in his work the situation of the colonizer who resists [and in so doing renders his work inadequate and even irrelevant to the needs of the colonized or the dominated]. So, let me return to the two central points I want to make.

Foucault's Perspective

In sum, reading Foucault persuades me that Foucault's world is not my world but is instead a world in which I feel profoundly alien. Indeed, when he argues that this is our world, I am reminded of a joke told about two U.S. comic book figures—the Lone Ranger and Tonto, "his faithful Indian companion" (and subordinate). As the story goes, the two are chased and then surrounded by hostile Indians. As he comes to recognize their danger, the Lone Ranger turns to Tonto and asks, "What do we do now?" To which Tonto replies, "What do you mean, 'we,' white boy?" Foucault's is a world in which things move, rather than people, a world in which subjects become obliterated or, rather, recreated as passive objects, a world in which passivity or refusal represent the only possible choices. Thus, Foucault writes, the confession "detached itself" from religion and "emigrated" toward pedagogy, or he notes that "hypotheses offer themselves." Moreover, he argues that subjects not only cease to be sovereign but also that external forces such as power are given access even to the body and thus are the forces which constitute the subject as a kind of effect. . . .

Perhaps this stress on resistance rather than transformation is due to Foucault's profound pessimism. Power appears to him as ever expanding and invading. It may even attempt to "annex" the counter-discourses that have developed. The dangers of going beyond resistance to power are nowhere more clearly stated than in Foucault's response to one interviewer who asked what might replace the present system. He responded that to even imagine another system is to extend our participation in the present system. Even more sinister, he added that perhaps this is what happened in the Soviet Union, thus suggesting that Stalinism might be the most likely outcome of efforts at social transformation. Foucault's insistence on simply resisting power is carried even further in his arguments that one must avoid claims to scientific knowledge. In particular, one should not claim Marxism as a science because to do so would invest it with the harmful effects of the power of science in modern culture. Foucault then, despite his stated aims of producing an account of power which will enable and facilitate resistance and opposition, instead adopts the position of what he has termed official knowledge with regard to the knowledge of the dominated and reinforces the relations of domination in our society by insisting that those of us who have been marginalized remain at the margins. . . .

Toward Theories for Women

Those of us who have been marginalized by the transcendental voice of universalizing theory need to do something other than ignore power relations as Rorty does or resist them as figures such as Foucault and Lyotard suggest. We need to transform them, and to do so, we need a revised and reconstructed theory (indebted to Marx among others) with several important features.

First, rather than getting rid of subjectivity or notions of the subject, as Foucault does and substituting his notion of the individual as an effect of power relations, we need to engage in the historical, political, and theoretical process of constituting ourselves as subjects as well as objects of history. We need to recognize that we can be the makers of history as well as the objects of those who have made history. Our nonbeing was the condition of being of the One, the center, the taken-for-granted ability of one small segment of the population to speak for all; our various efforts to constitute ourselves as subjects (through struggles for colonial independence, racial and sexual liberation struggles, and so on) were fundamental to creating the preconditions for the current questioning of universalist claims. But, I believe, we need to sort out who we really are. Put differently, we need to dissolve the false "we" I have been using into its real multiplicity and variety and out of this concrete multiplicity build an account of the world as seen from the margins, an account which can expose the falseness of the view from the top and can transform the margins as well as the center. The point is to develop an account of the world which treats our perspectives not as subjugated or disruptive knowledges, but as primary and constitutive of a different world. . . .

Second, we must do our work on an epistemological base that indicates that knowledge is possible—not just conversation or a discourse on how it is that power relations work. Conversation as a goal is fine; understanding how power works in oppressive societies is important. But if we are to construct a new society, we need to be assured that some systematic knowledge about our world and ourselves is possible. Those (simply) critical of modernity can call into question whether we ever really knew the world (and a good case can be made that "they" at least did not). They are in fact right that they have not known the world as it is rather than as they wished and needed it to be; they created their world not only in their own image but in the image of their fantasies. To create a world that expresses our own various and diverse images, we need to understand how it works.

Third, we need a theory of power that recognizes that our practical daily activity contains an understanding of the world—subjugated perhaps, but present. Here I am reaffirming Gramsci's argument that everyone is an intellectual and that each of us has an epistemology. The point, then, for "minority" theories is to "read out" the epistemologies in our various practices. I have argued elsewhere for a "standpoint" epistemology—an account of the world with great similarities to Marx's fundamental stance. While I would modify some of what I argued there, I would still insist that we must not give up the claim that material life (class position in Marxist theory) not only structures but sets limits on the understanding of social relations, and that, in systems of domination, the vision available to the rulers will be both partial and will reverse the real order of things.

Fourth, our understanding of power needs to recognize the difficulty of creating alternatives. The ruling class, race, and gender actively structure the material-social relations in which all the parties are forced to participate; their vision, therefore, cannot be dismissed as simply false or misguided. In consequence, the oppressed groups must struggle for their own understandings which will represent achievements requiring both theorizing and the education which grows from political struggle.

Fifth, as an engaged vision, the understanding of the oppressed exposes the relations among people as inhuman and thus contains a call to political action. That is, a theory of power for women, for the oppressed, is not one that leads to a turning away from engagement but rather one that is a call for change and participation in altering power relations.

The critical steps are, first, using what we know about our lives as a basis for critique of the dominant culture and, second, creating alternatives. When the various "minority" experiences have been described and when the significance of these experiences as a ground for critique of the dominant institutions and ideologies of society is better recognized, we will have at least the tools to begin to construct an account of the world sensitive to the realities of race and gender as well as class. To paraphrase Marx, the point is to change the world, not simply to redescribe ourselves or reinterpret the world yet again.❖

Molefi Kete Asante (1942–) is professor and, until 1996, chair of the Department of African-American studies at Temple University, which is considered the foremost center for graduate training in the Afrocentric perspective. Asante is an influential speaker, editor, columnist, and author. His many books include *Afrocentricity* (1988) and *The Afrocentric Idea* (1987), from which the selection is taken.

The Afrocentric Idea

Molefi Kete Asante (1987)

The critic's chief problem is finding a place to stand—so to speak—in relation to Western standards, imposed as interpretative measures on other cultures. I have familiarized myself with the leading proponents of the logic of scientific discovery, only to find their reductionist views of the world incapable of adequately dealing with African cultural data. In fact, it is questionable whether they are able to examine any data that are dynamic and transformational. Since the time-space domain is not stationary, and has not been considered to be so since the Newtonian view was shattered by the quantum theory's evidence of particle-wave behavior, there needs to be an accommodating, flexible frame of reference that permits the dynamic. . . .

While the contributions of the Eurocentric philosophers and scientists have been important and valuable, they have not been fully expressive of the extent or power of human ways of knowing. The arguments that have been advanced for the Western formulation of science are not convincing. . . . Afrocentricity expands the repertoire of human perspectives on knowledge.

Excerpt from *The Afrocentric Idea* (Philadelphia, Pa.: Temple University Press, 1987), pp. 11–17, 59–60, 78–80.

The Afrocentric View

The term *Afrology,* coined in *Afrocentricity: The Theory of Social Change,* denotes the Afrocentric study of African concepts, issues, and behaviors. It includes research on African themes in the Americas and the West Indies, as well as the African continent. Most of the relevant research involves the systematic exploration of relationships, social codes, cultural and commercial customs, and oral traditions and proverbs, although interpretation of communicative behaviors, as expressed in discourse, spoken or written, and techniques found in jazz studies and urban street-vernacular signifying, is also included. Human beings tend to recognize three fundamental existential postures one can take with respect to the human condition: feeling, knowing, and acting. Afrology recognizes these three stances as interrelated, not separate. Europeans normally call these categories *affective, cognitive,* and *conative.*

The affective component deals with a person's feelings, of liking or disliking, about an object or idea. The cognitive refers to how an object is perceived, its conceptual connotation. Conative is the person's behavioral tendencies regarding an object. However, in Afrology, the study of an object or idea is best performed when all three components are interrelated....

Any interpretation of African culture must begin at once to dispense with the notion that, in all things, Europe is teacher and Africa is pupil. This is the central point of my argument. To raise the question of an imperialism of the intellectual tradition is to ask a most meaningful question as we pursue African rhetoric, because Western theorists have too often tended to generalize from a Eurocentric base. What I seek to demonstrate is the existence of an African concept of communication rooted in traditional African philosophies....

African Public Discourse

Public speaking as practice predates the development of theory, whether in Africa, Asia, or Europe. Both speaking and writing are forms of human interaction. What purpose is served by these forms of communication? The answer to this question speaks of the complex problem of cultural evaluation. For example, writing is used for communication and historical preservation. In some traditional African societies those two ends have been admirably satisfied by the drum. Communication was swift and the range was great; in the event that the first drummer was unable to reach all the persons he wanted to reach, another drummer, at the outer fringes, could take up the message for further transmission. Thus the drummer, along with the village sage, became a repository of all the necessary historical data relating to the village.

In some African societies, such as ancient Meroe, Kemet, and Abyssinia, written documents are extensive. However, in the whole of Africa and the African world, both past and present, there is a vocal-expressive modality that dominates all communication culture. This modality is part of the continuity with the ancient African past. What is of importance to us is that Africans in America maintained an expressive sense that manifested itself as life force in dance, music, and speech. Expression, therefore, is not the captive of the written word; it is the word revealed in life. I use the term *orature* to refer to this phenomenon as the sum total of oral tradition, which includes vocality, drumming, storytelling, praise singing, and naming....

Towards Concrete Images in Discourse

I have discussed the place of the spoken word, the function of speaker, and the character of the audiences in an African concept of rhetoric. But, one will ask, what is the substance of African public discourse? The questioner who poses such a query would be a Euro-American or a Eurocentric African, exercising the contextual criteria provided by Western thought. To ask, What is the *substance?* is to see a dichotomy between form and substance that does not plague most African thought. Since form and content are *activity, force* unifies what is called form and content in creative expression. The speech is meant to be alive and moving in all of its aspects so that separation of the members becomes impossible, because the creative production is "an experience" or a happening occurring within and outside the speaker's soul. Thus, unlike the Euro-American, the African seeks the totality of an experience, concept, or system. Traditional African society looked for unity of the whole rather than specifics of the whole; such a concentration, which also emphasized synthesis more than analysis, contributed to community stability because considerations in the whole were more productive than considerations in detail. Now it is clear that this has a very real bearing upon the making of a public discourse.

The public discourse convinces an audience not merely through attention to logical substance but through the power to fascinate, to generate creative energy. Yet this does not preclude the materials of composition, or the arrangement and structure of those materials; it simply expresses a belief that when images are arranged according to their power and chosen because of their power, the speaker's ability to convince is greater than if he attempted to employ a formal logic. When a speaker possesses visionary ecstasy, vivid but controlled, his audiences' participation is more assured than if he exercised only syllogistic reasoning. Perhaps that is drawing the choices too sharply, inasmuch as few neo-Aristotelians would argue for a dichotomy of emotion and logic. However, it is necessary to state the polar positions to illustrate the emphasis of the traditional African speaker. The African speaker means to be poet, not lecturer; indeed, the rhythmic equipment of the two will always be different. So now it is possible to say that traditional African public discourse is given to concrete images that are capable of producing compulsive relationships and invoking the inner needs of audiences because of the inherent power of the images. A mastery of proverbs is a good resource for the speaker who invokes tradition. Additionally, the more powerful the speaker, the more fascinated the audiences will be. And power is derived from the experience of the "orality" and spirituality of the presentation.

To maintain that fascination, the African American speaker seeks to appeal to the principal myths. The African, with an unbroken link to the traditions, maintains that linkage organically. For the African American, the task is to find the myths that have developed in our American history. These are the driving forces of our sanity. High John de Conqueror, the Flying African, Shine, John Henry, Stagolee, and others inform the communicative dimension of our lives. ❖

Jeffrey Alexander (1947–) teaches sociology at the University of California at Los Angeles, having chaired the department for a number of years. After studying at Harvard, Alexander did graduate work at Berkeley, where he began his four-volume study *Theoretical Logic in Sociology*. He has written and edited many books and articles on theory, culture, and politics, including *Neofunctionalism* (1985), *Twenty Lectures: Social Theory Since World War II* (1987), *Action and Its Environments* (1988), *Fin-de-siècle Social Theory* (1995), and *Neo-Functionalism and Beyond* (1998).

Postpositivist Case for the Classics

Jeffrey Alexander (1987)

The ratio between exemplars and classics is so much different in social science because in its social application science produces so much more disagreement. Because there is persistent and widespread disagreement, the more general background assumptions which remain implicit and relatively invisible in natural science here come vividly into play. The conditions which Kuhn defines for paradigm crisis in the natural sciences are routine in the social. I am not suggesting that there is no 'objective' knowledge in the social sciences, nor even that there is no possibility for successful predictions or covering laws. It is possible, it seems to me, to gain real cumulative knowledge about the world from within different and competing points of view, and even to sustain relatively predictive covering laws from within general orientations which differ in substantial ways. What I am suggesting, however, is that the conditions of social science make consistent agreement about the precise nature of empirical knowledge—let alone agreement about explanatory covering laws—highly unlikely. In social science, therefore, arguments about scientific truth do not refer only to the empirical level. They cut across the full range of non-empirical commitments which sustain competing points of view.

There are cognitive and evaluative reasons for the vast differences in the level of consensus. I will mention here only the most fundamental.

1. In so far as the objects of a science are located in the physical world outside of the human mind, its empirical referents can, in principle, more easily be verified through interpersonal communication. In social science, where the objects are either mental states or conditions in which mental states are embedded, the possibility for confusing mental states of the scientific observer with mental states of those observed is endemic.

2. Resistance to simple agreement on empirical referents also emerges from the distinctive evaluative nature of social science. There is a symbiotic relationship between description and evaluation. The findings of social science often carry significant implications for the desirable organization and reorganization of social life. In natural science, by contrast, 'changes in the content of science do not usually imply changes in social structures' (Hagstrom)....

3. Needless to say, in so far as it is difficult, for cognitive and evaluative reasons, to gain consensus about even the simple empirical referents of social science, there will be even less about the abstractions from such concrete referents which form the substance of social theory....

Excerpt from "The Centrality of the Classics," Anthony Giddens and Jonathan H. Turner, eds., *Social Theory Today* (Stanford, Calif.: Stanford University Press, 1987), pp. 20–28. Reprinted with the permission of the publishers, Stanford University Press. 1987 Polity Press.

4. In so far as neither empirical referents nor covering laws generate agreement, the full range of non-empirical inputs to empirical perception become objects of debate. Because there is such endemic disagreement, moreover, social science will invariably be differentiated by traditions (Shils) and schools (Tiryakian). . . .

For all of these reasons, discourse—not just explanation—becomes a major feature of the social science field. By discourse, I refer to modes of argument which are more consistently generalized and speculative than are normal scientific discussions. The latter are directed in a more disciplined manner to specific pieces of empirical evidence, to inductive and deductive logics, to explanation through covering laws and to the methods by which these laws can be verified or falsified. Discourse, by contrast, is ratiocinative. It focuses on the process of reasoning rather than the results of immediate experience, and it becomes significant when there is no plain and evident truth. Discourse seeks persuasion through argument rather than prediction. Its persuasiveness is based on such qualities as logical coherence, expansiveness of scope, interpretive insight, value relevance, rhetorical force, beauty, and texture of argument.

Foucault identifies intellectual, scientific and political practices as 'discourses' in order to deny their merely empirical, inductive status. In this way, he insists that practical activities are historically constituted and shaped by metaphysical understandings that can define an entire epoch. Sociology, too, is a discursive field. Still, one finds here little of the homogeneity that Foucault attributes to such fields; in social science, there are discourses, not a discourse. These discourses are not, moreover, closely linked to the legitimation of power, as Foucault in his later work increasingly claimed. Social scientific discourses are aimed at truth, and they are constantly subjected to rational stipulations about how truth can be arrived at and what truth might be. Here I draw upon Habermas' understanding of discourse as part of an effort that speakers make at achieving undistorted communication. If Habermas underestimates the irrational qualities of communication, let alone action, he certainly has provided a way to conceptualize its rational aspirations. His systematic attempts to identify modes of argument and criteria for arriving at persuasive justification show how rational commitments and the recognition of supraempirical arguments can be combined. Between the rationalizing discourse of Habermas and the arbitrary discourse of Foucault, this is where the actual field of social science discourse uneasily lies.

It is because of the centrality of discourse that theory in the social sciences is so multivalent and that compulsive efforts to follow the logic of natural science are so misguided. Those of the positivist persuasion sense the tension between such a multivalent conception and their empiricist point of view. To resolve it they try to privilege 'theory' over 'metatheory,' indeed, to exclude theory in favour of 'explanation' narrowly conceived. Thus, complaining that 'far too much social theory consists of the history of ideas and general hero worship of Marx, Weber, [and] Durkheim,' [J.] Turner argues for 'doing theory as opposed to . . . providing yet another metatheoretical analysis of the early theoretical masters.' And Stinchcombe describes Marx, Durkheim and Weber as 'those great *empirical* analysts . . . who did not work mainly at what we now call *theory*.' He insists that they 'worked out *explanations* of the growth of capitalism, or of class conflict, or of primitive religion'. . . .

These distinctions, however, seem more like 'utopian' efforts to escape from social science than efforts really to understand it. Generalized discourse is central, and theory is inherently multivalent. Indeed, the centrality of discourse and the conditions which produce it make for the overdetermination of social science by theory and its underdetermination by fact. Because there is no clear, indisputable reference for the elements which compose social science, there is no neat translatability between different levels of generality. Formulations at one level do not ramify in clear-cut ways for the other levels of scientific concern. For example, while precise empirical measurements of two variable correlations can sometimes be established, it is rarely possible for such a correlation to prove or disprove a proposition about this interrelationship that is stated in more general terms. The reason is that the existence of empirical and ideological dissensus allows social scientists to operationalize propositions in a variety of different ways. . . .

. . . [T]he proportion of classics to contemporaries is so much greater in social than natural science because endemic disagreement makes the background assumptions of social science more explicit. It is this obvious quality of background assumptions, in turn, that makes discourse so central a quality of social scientific debate. What remains is to explain why this discursive form of argument so often takes a 'classical' turn. The existence of generalized, non-empirical debate does not logically imply any privileged position for earlier works. None the less, the very conditions which make discourse so prominent also make the classics central. There are two reasons for this centrality: the functional, and the intellectual or scientific.

Because disagreement is so rife in social science, serious problems of mutual understanding arise. Without some baseline of minimal understanding, however, communication is impossible. For disagreement to be possible in a coherent, ongoing and consistent way, there must be some basis for a cultural relationship. This can exist only if the participants in a disagreement have a fair idea of what one another is talking about.

This is where the classics come in. The functional necessity for classics develops because of the need for integrating the field of theoretical discourse. By integration, I do not mean cooperation and equilibrium but rather the boundary maintenance, or closure, which allows systems to exist (Luhmann). It is this functional demand that explains the formation of disciplinary boundaries which from an intellectual standpoint often seem arbitrary. It is the disciplines of social science, and the schools and traditions of which they are composed, which have classics.

To mutually acknowledge a classic is to have a common point of reference. A classic reduces complexity (cf. Luhmann). It is a symbol which condenses—'stands for'—a range of diverse general commitments. Condensation, it seems to me, has at least four functional advantages.

In the first place, of course, it simplifies, and thereby facilitates, theoretical discussion. It does so by allowing a very small number of works to substitute for—to represent by a stereotyping or standardizing process—the myriad of finely-graded formulations which are produced in the course of contingent intellectual life. When we discuss the central issues which affect social science in classical terms, we are sacrificing the ability to embrace this finely-graded specificity. We gain, however, something very important. By speaking in terms of the classics, we can be relatively confident that those whom we address will at least know whereof we speak, even if they do not recognize in our discussion their own particular and unique position. It is for this reason that if we wish to make a critical analysis of capitalism we will be more than likely to draw from Marx's work. Similarly, if we wish to evaluate the variety of critical analyses of capitalism which exist today, we will probably typify them by comparing them to Marx's original. Only by so doing can we be relatively confident that others will be able to follow, and perhaps be persuaded by, our ideological and cognitive judgements.

The second functional advantage is that classics allow generalized commitments to be argued without the necessity for making the criteria for their adjudication explicit. Since such criteria are very difficult to formulate, and virtually impossible to gain agreement upon, this concretizing function of the classics is very important. Rather than having to define equilibrium and the nature of systems, one can argue about Parsons, about the relative 'functionality' of his early and later works, about whether his theory (whatever that may be precisely) can actually explain conflict in the real world. Or, rather than explicitly exploring the advantages of an affective or normative perspective on human action, one can argue that such a perspective was, in fact, actually taken by Durkheim's most important works.

The third functional advantage is an ironic one. Because a common classical medium of communication is taken for granted, it becomes possible not to acknowledge the existence of generalized discourse at all. Thus, because the importance of the classics is accepted without argument, it is possible for a social scientist to begin an empirical study—in, for example, industrial sociology—by discussing the treatment of labour in Marx's early writings. While it would be quite illegitimate for him to suggest that non-empirical considerations about human nature, let alone utopian speculations about human possibility, form the baseline for industrial sociology, this is precisely what he has implicitly acknowledged by referring to Marx's work.

Finally, because the condensation provided by the classics gives them such privileged power, reference to the classics becomes important for purely strategic and instrumental reasons. It is in the immediate self-interest of every ambitious social scientist and every rising school to be legitimated *vis-à-vis* the classical founders. Even if no genuine concern for the classics exists, they still must be criticized, re-read, or rediscovered if the discipline's normative criteria for evaluation are to be challenged anew.❖

James S. Coleman (1926–1995) was born in Bedford, Indiana. After a brief career as a chemist, Coleman went to Columbia University in 1951 to study sociology when the Columbia department was at its strongest. Like many Columbia sociology students in those days, Coleman went on to a distinguished career in the field. After teaching at Johns Hopkins, Coleman went to the University of Chicago, where he was university professor until his death in 1995. Coleman was a president of the American Sociological Association. His books include *Community Conflict* (1957), *The Adolescent Society* (1961), *Introduction to Mathematical Sociology* (1961), and *Foundations of Social Theory* (1990), from which the selection is taken.

The New Social Structure and the New Social Science

James S. Coleman (1990)

Nation-States Versus Multinational Corporations

... The nation-state is a corporate actor of intermediate form, exhibiting some properties of premodern corporate actors based on primordial bonds and some properties of modern purposive corporate actors. Many nation-states evolved from

Excerpt from *Foundations of Social Theory* (Cambridge, Mass.: Harvard University Press, 1990), pp. 660–664. Reprinted by permission of the publishers. Copyright 1990 by the President and Fellows of Harvard College.

an ethnically homogeneous people or nation, and some remain ethnically homogeneous. Many have a single religion or culture. A shared religion or culture has been responsible for many acts of oppression or hostility toward religious or ethnic minorities, as well as for wars of aggression in the name of religion or nation.

Even when nations are not ethnically or religiously homogeneous, they retain many characteristics of premodern corporate actors. The elements of which they are composed are persons, not positions. They take responsibility for the person as a whole and claim authority over the person as a whole. Yet many are organized through an explicit constitution, which is conceived of as a social contract among independent individuals who are joining together with a common purpose. This constitutional basis of a nation-state is conceptually in opposition to the primordial basis (ethnic, religious, or cultural), and the nation-state is often in uneasy tension between these two bases.

Multinational corporations are prototypically modern purposive corporate actors. They are composed of positions as elements, and persons are merely occupants of positions and agents of the corporation. Corporate purposes are embodied in products, and the corporations can reasonably be described as acting to maximize some objective function (such as profit or size).

Nation-states and multinational corporations are in fundamental conflict, as two modes of organizing the global social system. As the economic division of labor becomes international, the conflict between these two modes intensifies. Multinational corporations seek to move persons and goods with as little regard for national borders as possible. Nations have a monopoly over legitimate coercive power within their borders, which they exercise through police and military forces. Multinational corporations control economic power, although without a comparable partitioning into exclusive domains.

The contrast between multinationals' interests and nations' interests is illustrated by a quotation from a brochure of a multinational hotel chain that has several hundred hotels throughout Europe: "As we see it, Europe is a single vast nation made up of a number of regions—Germany, Italy, France, Austria, Great Britain, the Netherlands, Belgium, Luxembourg, and Switzerland." If this quotation does not seem to call into question national autonomy, suppose the chain expanded throughout Asia and put out a brochure which read: "As we see it, Eurasia constitutes a single vast nation made up of a number of regions—Germany, Turkey, Italy, the Soviet Union, France, Iran, . . . "

The conflict between nation-states and multinational corporations is not an overt one. Unlike struggles between nation-states or competition between corporations, it is not a conflict between particular corporate bodies for dominance; it is a conflict for dominance of a *form.* The first question, then, is whether the two forms are truly in conflict, rather than being complementary. Can nation-states continue to exist as sovereign entities when their economic systems merge into a single international economy? Or, can a single international economy come into existence as long as nation-states are dominant?

The principal points on which the two forms are in conflict have to do with movements of persons and goods. Corporations move goods and induce people to move for economic gain. For example, corporations in Northern Europe in the 1950s and 1960s relocated people from the Mediterranean rim (Greeks, Yugoslavs, Italians, Spaniards, Turks, and Algerians) to work in their factories, changing irrevocably the population distributions within nation-states. But nation-states maintain barriers to such movements, designed to preserve economic inequalities across nations and to maintain territorial sovereignty. As rich nations, which are part of the international economic system, become richer and poor nations largely outside that system remain poor, and as the system becomes more international, the pressures to break down barriers to immigration increase. If these barriers disappear completely, will national sovereignty continue to exist? If not, what will happen to persons' self-identification? Will they become detached from the now mythical nation? Will they become detached from place altogether? Will they become attached to the corporation? But how could that happen, since persons are merely temporary occupants of positions within the corporation?

All these questions arise from the fundamentally different bases of organization on which nation-states have developed and multinational corporations have been constructed. Answers to these questions will require greater knowledge of the way the conflict between nations and multinationals is resolved in the minds and actions of persons—for it will be the choices of persons, individually and collectively, that will give dominance to one or the other form.

These questions may be examined from a somewhat different perspective, that is, the way individual preferences affect corporate action. Insofar as persons exercise control over the actions of nations, they do so through voicing their preferences via some democratic institution of collective decision. Elections of legislatures and chief executive officers and rights of petition and referendum exemplify these institutions. But insofar as persons exercise control over the actions of multinational corporations, they do so through exiting. . . . As customers, they shift their custom to another supplier; as employees, they leave and go to work for another firm. There are some modifications of these pure types: Collective bargaining and industrial democracy introduce voice into the corporation, and emigration from a nation-state can affect its government's policies.

Thus the conflict between nation-states and multinational corporations as modes of organizing the world corresponds roughly to a conflict between voice and exit, or a conflict between democracy and the market as ways of translating individual-level preferences into macro-level outcomes. In these terms the conflict is one between two systems of rights allocation. The two systems differ not in their approximation to equality of rights, but in the way rights are partitioned. Democratic voice assumes that rights of control over corporate actions are collectively held, with each member having some fraction of those rights. Individual exit assumes that rights of control over individual actions (that is, the exercise of choice) are individually held, with the organization affected slightly and independently by each action.

It is obvious, of course, that not all corporate actions can be organized according to democracy (or collective control) or according to the market (individual control). Yet the latitude for substitution between voice and exit is very great, and one mode or the other can come to dominate—manifested in the dominance of nation-states or multinationals.

The New Social Science

As primordial corporate actors wither away and the social capital on which societal functioning has depended is eroded, the purposive social structure that replaces them presents both opportunities and problems. The three preceding sections have sketched the kinds of changes occurring, in order to provide some idea of these opportunities and problems. Those sections should also have given a sense of the necessity for the development of social theory and the pursuit of social research if society is to realize the opportunities and avoid the problems.

This is not the way institutional change has ordinarily been approached. The implicit assumption on which decision making in democratic societies has proceeded is that legislatures composed of responsible persons from various walks of life can design institutions that will satisfactorily cope with social change. Such an assumption may be valid when the social changes constitute minor adjustments within a stable structural form. But when the structural form itself is changing, as is currently the case, the assumption is no longer valid.

The assumption is invalidated for several reasons. The issues discussed here illustrate three of these. First, the change in structural form, from primordial to purposive, means that purposive organization replaces those functions that can be bought and sold in a market but not those which cannot. In other words, purposive organization reorganizes the production and distribution of private goods in such a way that the spillover benefits (or positive externalities, or by-products) for other activities are lost. The most prominent example is childrearing as a by-product of the production and consumption activities of the family.

The loss of these nonmarketable functions as a result of the replacement of primordial by purposive organization is what I have called a loss of social capital; and in this chapter I have described some of the consequences of that loss. It is improbable that legislatures (or government agencies) will effectively address this loss of social capital because legislators know no organizations other than formal organizations, which buy services on a market and resell them. Legislatures cannot buy sustained attention and have no organizational means to bring it about. Knowledge about such matters derived from social theory would use organizational forms not merely as a way of organizing and targeting services, but as a way of creating social capital to fill in the interstices left by the market.

A second reason for the invalidity of the assumption that legislatures can design a replacement for the social structure that has been lost is illustrated by the shift from household economies to a single interdependent economy. Legislatures, concerned only with global viability of a nation's economy, have no conceptual tools for making the transition from household economies to a single interdependent economy in a way that preserves the virtues of independent viability. Some progress toward developing such tools has been made in organization theory as applied to the internal economy of business firms; but to extend and reshape the tools for use on the economies of nation-states is a task that requires dedicated development of social and economic theory.

A third reason why legislatures cannot create a structure to replace the functions of that which is vanishing lies in the fact that some social changes tend to make national legislatures irrelevant. Multinational corporations, as prototypical purposive corporate actors, are representatives of an organizational form that is in conflict with that of nation-states. If the multinationals win, national legislatures will have lost control of the decision making that affects the organizational structure of society. In that circumstance the very question of how national legislatures can best further the reconstruction of society becomes irrelevant. Then the question goes up one level: What is the means, in a worldwide social system, by which the movement from primordial to purposive social organization can be carried out without sacrificing all the virtues of the former?

These questions, posed by changes in the very basis of social organization, consti-tute a demand for a new social science. The demand increases as the transformation of social organization continues, a demand for knowledge and ideas that will help realize the opportunities created by this transformation and avoid the problems it generates. The new social science must consist of both applied research and theory. The theory, if it is to be of value for this task, must cross the traditional bounds of the disciplines within which knowledge is ordered, for the transformation of society has changed the linkages among these institutional areas. In so doing, it becomes the new social science, appropriate to the new social structure.❖

Arthur M. Schlesinger, Jr. (1917–) was born in Columbus, Ohio. After completing his B.A. at Harvard in 1938, Schlesinger was a Harvard Society of Fellows scholar un-til 1942. He taught at Harvard from 1946 to 1954. From 1961 to 1964, he was spe-cial assistant to presidents Kennedy and Johnson. Since 1966, Schlesinger has been Schweitzer Professor of Humanities at the City University of New York. His books in-clude *The Age of Jackson* (1945), *The Vital Center* (1949), *Politics of Hope* (1963), and *A Thousand Days* (1965). The selection is from *The Disuniting of America* (1991), which Schlesinger wrote at the height of the multiculturalism controversy in the United States. *Disuniting* was written soon after his service on a State of New York special committee on the teaching of history, in which connection he had direct ex-perience with the debate over the Afrocentrism in school curricula.

E Pluribus Unum?

Arthur M. Schlesinger, Jr. (1991)

The attack on the common American identity is the culmination of the cult of ethnic-ity. That attack was mounted in the first instance by European Americans of non-British origin ("unmeltable ethnics") against the British foundations of American cul-ture; then, latterly and massively, by Americans of non-European origin against the European foundations of that culture. As Theodore Roosevelt's foreboding suggests, the European immigration itself palpitated with internal hostilities, everyone at every-body else's throats—hardly the "monocultural" crowd portrayed by ethnocentric sep-aratists. After all, the two great "world" wars of the 20th century began as fights among European states. Making a single society out of this diversity of antagonistic European peoples is a hard enough job. The new salience of non-European, nonwhite stocks compounds the challenge. And the non-Europeans, or at least their self-appointed spokesmen, bring with them a resentment, in some cases a hatred, of Europe and the West provoked by generations of Western colonialism, racism, condescension, con-tempt, and cruel exploitation. . . .

Will not this rising flow of non-European immigrants create a "minority majority" that will make Eurocentrism obsolete by the 21st century? This is the fear of some white Americans and the hope (and sometimes the threat) of some nonwhites. . . .

One of the oddities of the situation is that the assault on the Western tradition is conducted very largely with analytical weapons forged in the West. What are the

---

Excerpt from *The Disuniting of America* (Knoxville, Tenn.: Whittle Direct Books, 1991), pp. 70, 72–73, 76–77, 80–83.

names invoked by the coalition of latter-day Marxists, deconstructionists, poststructuralists, radical feminists, Afrocentrists? Marx, Nietzsche, Gramsci, Derrida, Foucault, Lacan, Sartre, de Beauvoir, Habermas, the Frankfurt "critical theory" school—Europeans all. The "unmasking," "demythologizing," "decanonizing," "dehegemonizing" blitz against Western culture depends on methods of critical analysis unique to the West—which surely testifies to the internally redemptive potentialities of the Western tradition.

Even Afrocentrists seem to accept subliminally the very Eurocentric standards they think they are rejecting. "Black intellectuals condemn Western civilization," Professor Pearce Williams says, "yet ardently wish to prove it was founded by their ancestors." And, like Frantz Fanon and Léopold Senghor, whose books figure prominently on their reading lists, Afrocentric ideologues are intellectual children of the West they repudiate. Fanon, the eloquent spokesman of the African wretched of the earth, had French as his native tongue and based his analyses on Freud, Marx, and Sartre. Senghor, the prophet of Negritude, wrote in French, established the Senegalese educational system on the French model and, when he left the presidency of Senegal, retired to France.

Western hegemony, it would seem, can be the source of protest as well as of power. Indeed, the invasion of American schools by the Afrocentric curriculum, not to mention the conquest of university departments of English and comparative literature by deconstructionists, poststructuralists, etc., are developments that by themselves refute the extreme theory of "cultural hegemony." Of course, Gramsci had a point. Ruling values do dominate and permeate any society; but they do not have the rigid and monolithic grip on American democracy that academic leftists claim.

Radical academics denounce the "canon" as an instrument of European oppression enforcing the hegemony of the white race, the male sex, and the capitalist class, designed, in the words of one professor, "to rewrite the past and construct the present from the perspective of the privileged and the powerful." Or in the elegant words of another—and a professor of theological ethics at that: "The canon of great literature was created by high Anglican assholes to underwrite their social class."

The poor old canon is seen not only as conspiratorial but as static. Yet nothing changes more regularly and reliably than the canon: compare, for example, the canon in American poetry as defined by Edmund Clarence Stedman in his *Poets of America* (1885) with the canon of 1935 or of 1985 (whatever happened to Longfellow and Whittier?); or recall the changes that have overtaken the canonical literature of American history in the last half-century (who reads Beard and Parrington now?). And the critics clearly have no principled objection to the idea of the canon. They simply wish to replace an old gang by a new gang. After all, a canon means only that because you can't read everything, you give some books priority over others.

Oddly enough, serious Marxists—Marx and Engels, Lukács, Trotsky, Gramsci—had the greatest respect for what Lukács called "the classical heritage of mankind." Well they should have, for most great literature and much good history are deeply subversive in their impact on orthodoxies. Consider the present-day American literary canon: Emerson, Jefferson, Melville, Whitman, Hawthorne, Thoreau, Lincoln, Twain, Dickinson, William and Henry James, Henry Adams, Holmes, Dreiser, Faulkner, O'Neill. Lackeys of the ruling class? Apologists for the privileged and the powerful? Agents of American imperialism? Come on!

It is time to adjourn the chat about hegemony. If hegemony were as real as the cultural radicals pretend, Afrocentrism would never have got anywhere, and the heirs of William Lyon Phelps would still be running the Modern Language Association.

*   *   *

Is the Western tradition a bar to progress and a curse on humanity? Would it really do America and the world good to get rid of the European legacy?

No doubt Europe has done terrible things, not least to itself. But what culture has not? History, said Edward Gibbon, is little more than the register of the crimes, follies, and misfortunes of mankind. The sins of the West are no worse than the sins of Asia or of the Middle East or of Africa.

There remains, however, a crucial difference between the Western tradition and the others. The crimes of the West have produced their own antidotes. They have provoked great movements to end slavery, to raise the status of women, to abolish torture, to combat racism, to defend freedom of inquiry and expression, to advance personal liberty and human rights.

Whatever the particular crimes of Europe, that continent is also the source—the *unique* source—of those liberating ideas of individual liberty, political democracy, the rule of law, human rights, and cultural freedom that constitute our most precious legacy and to which most of the world today aspires. These are *European* ideas, not Asian, nor African, nor Middle Eastern ideas, except by adoption.

The freedoms of inquiry and of artistic creation, for example, are Western values. Consider the differing reactions to the case of Salman Rushdie: what the West saw as an intolerable attack on individual freedom the Middle East saw as a proper punishment for an evildoer who had violated the mores of his group. Individualism itself is looked on with abhorrence and dread by collectivist cultures in which loyalty to the group overrides personal goals—cultures that, social scientists say, comprise about 70 percent of the world's population.

There is surely no reason for Western civilization to have guilt trips laid on it by champions of cultures based on despotism, superstition, tribalism, and fanaticism. In this regard the Afrocentrists are especially absurd. The West needs no lectures on the superior virtue of those "sun people" who sustained slavery until Western imperialism abolished it (and, it is reported, sustain it to this day in Mauritania and the Sudan), who still keep women in subjection and cut off their clitorises, who carry out racial persecutions not only against Indians and other Asians but against fellow Africans from the wrong tribes, who show themselves either incapable of operating a democracy or ideologically hostile to the democratic idea, and who in their tyrannies and massacres, their Idi Amins and Boukassas, have stamped with utmost brutality on human rights.

Certainly the European overlords did little enough to prepare Africa for self-government. But democracy would find it hard in any case to put down roots in a tribalist and patrimonial culture that, long before the West invaded Africa, had sacralized the personal authority of chieftains and ordained the submission of the rest. What the West would call corruption is regarded through much of Africa as no more than the prerogative of power. Competitive political parties, an independent judiciary, a free press, the rule of law are alien to African traditions.

It was the French, not the Algerians, who freed Algerian women from the veil (much to the irritation of Frantz Fanon, who regarded deveiling as symbolic rape); as in India it was the British, not the Indians, who ended (or did their best to end) the horrible custom of *suttee*—widows burning themselves alive on their husbands' funeral pyres. And it was the West, not the non-Western cultures, that launched the crusade to abolish slavery—and in doing so encountered mighty resistance, especially in the Islamic world (where Moslems, with fine impartiality, enslaved whites as well as blacks).

Those many brave and humane Africans who are struggling these days for decent societies are animated by Western, not by African, ideals. White guilt can be pushed too far.

The Western commitment to human rights has unquestionably been intermittent and imperfect. Yet the ideal remains—and movement toward it has been real, if sporadic. Today it is the *Western* democratic tradition that attracts and empowers people of all continents, creeds, and colors. When the Chinese students cried and died for democracy in Tiananmen Square, they brought with them not representations of Confucius or Buddha but a model of the Statue of Liberty. . . .

The ethnic revolt against the melting pot has reached the point, in rhetoric at least, though not I think in reality, of a denial of the idea of a common culture and a single society. If large numbers of people really accept this, the republic would be in serious trouble. The question poses itself: how to restore the balance between *unum* and *pluribus?*

The old American homogeneity disappeared well over a century ago, never to return. Ever since, we have been preoccupied in one way or another with the problem, as Herbert Croly phrased it 80 years back in *The Promise of American Life,* "of preventing such divisions from dissolving the society into which they enter—of keeping such a highly differentiated society fundamentally sound and whole." This required, Croly believed, an "ultimate bond of union." There was only one way by which solidarity could be restored, "and that is by means of a democratic social ideal . . . "

The genius of America lies in its capacity to forge a single nation from peoples of remarkably diverse racial, religious, and ethnic origins. It has done so because democratic principles provide both the philosophical bond of union and practical experience in civic participation. The American Creed envisages a nation composed of individuals making their own choices and accountable to themselves, not a nation based on inviolable ethnic communities. The Constitution turns on individual rights, not on group rights. Law, in order to rectify past wrongs, has from time to time (and in my view often properly so) acknowledged the claims of groups; but this is the exception, not the rule.

Our democratic principles contemplate an open society founded on tolerance of differences and on mutual respect. In practice, America has been more open to some than to others. But it is more open to all today than it was yesterday and is likely to be even more open tomorrow than today. The steady movement of American life has been from exclusion to inclusion.

Historically and culturally this republic has an Anglo-Saxon base; but from the start the base has been modified, enriched, and reconstituted by transfusions from other continents and civilizations. The movement from exclusion to inclusion causes a constant revision in the texture of our culture. The ethnic transfusions affect all aspects of American life—our politics, our literature, our music, our painting, our movies, our cuisine, our customs, our dreams.

Black Americans in particular have influenced the ever-changing national culture in many ways. They have lived here for centuries, and, unless one believes in racist mysticism, they belong far more to American culture than to the culture of Africa. Their history is part of the Western democratic tradition, not an alternative to it. No one does black Americans more disservice than those Afrocentric ideologues who would define them out of the West.

The interplay of diverse traditions produces the America we know. "Paradoxical though it may seem," Diane Ravitch has well said, "the United States has a common culture that is multicultural." That is why unifying political ideals coexist so easily and cheerfully with diversity in social and cultural values. Within the overarching political commitment, people are free to live as they choose, ethnically and otherwise. Differences will remain; some are reinvented; some are used to drive us apart. But as we renew our allegiance to the unifying ideals, we provide the solvent that will prevent differences from escalating into antagonism and hatred.

One powerful reason for the movement from exclusion to inclusion is that the American Creed facilitates the appeal from the actual to the ideal. When we talk of the American democratic faith, we must understand it in its true dimensions. It is not an impervious, final, and complacent orthodoxy, intolerant of deviation and dissent, fulfilled in flag salutes, oaths of allegiance, and hands over the heart. It is an ever-evolving philosophy, fulfilling its ideals through debate, self-criticism, protest, disrespect, and irreverence; a tradition in which all have rights of heterodoxy and opportunities for self-assertion. The Creed has been the means by which Americans have haltingly but persistently narrowed the gap between performance and principle. It is what all Americans should learn, because it is what binds all Americans together.

Let us by all means in this increasingly mixed-up world learn about those other continents and civilizations. But let us master our own history first. Lamentable as some may think it, we inherit an American experience, as America inherits a European experience. To deny the essentially European origins of American culture is to falsify history.

Americans of whatever origin should take pride in the distinctive inheritance to which they have all contributed, as other nations take pride in their distinctive inheritances. Belief in one's own culture does not require disdain for other cultures. But one step at a time: no culture can hope to ingest other cultures all at once, certainly not before it ingests its own. As we begin to master our own culture, then we can explore the world.

Our schools and colleges have a responsibility to teach history for its own sake—as part of the intellectual equipment of civilized persons—and not to degrade history by allowing its contents to be dictated by pressure groups, whether political, economic, religious, or ethnic. The past may sometimes give offense to one or another minority; that is no reason for rewriting history. Giving pressure groups vetoes over textbooks and courses betrays both history and education. Properly taught, history will convey a sense of the variety, continuity, and adaptability of cultures, of the need for understanding other cultures, of the ability of individuals and peoples to overcome obstacles, of the importance of critical analysis and dispassionate judgment in every area of life.

Above all, history can give a sense of national identity. We don't have to believe that our values are absolutely better than the next fellow's or the next country's, but we have no doubt that they are better *for us,* reared as we are—and are worth living by and worth dying for. For our values are not matters of whim and happenstance. History has given them to us. They are anchored in our national experience, in our great national documents, in our national heroes, in our folkways, traditions, and standards. People with a different history will have differing values. But we believe that our own are better for us. They work for us; and, for that reason, we live and die by them.

It has taken time to make the values real for all our citizens, and we still have a good distance to go, but we have made progress. If we now repudiate the quite marvelous inheritance that history bestows on us, we invite the fragmentation of the national community into a quarrelsome spatter of enclaves, ghettos, tribes. The bonds of cohesion in our society are sufficiently fragile, or so it seems to me, that it makes no sense to strain them by encouraging and exalting cultural and linguistic apartheid.

The American identity will never be fixed and final; it will always be in the making. Changes in the population have always brought changes in the national ethos and will continue to do so; but not, one must hope, at the expense of national integration. The question America confronts as a pluralistic society is how to vindicate cherished cultures and traditions without breaking the bonds of cohesion—common ideals, common political institutions, common language, common culture, common fate—that hold the republic together.

Our task is to combine due appreciation of the splendid diversity of the nation with due emphasis on the great unifying Western ideas of individual freedom, political democracy, and human rights. These are the ideas that define the American nationality—and that today empower people of all continents, races, and creeds.

"What then is the American, this new man?" asked Crèvecoeur, . . . "Here individuals of all nations are melted into a new race of men." Still a good answer—still the best hope.❖

❖ After Modernity ❖

Cornel West (1953–) was born in Tulsa, Oklahoma. It is said that the two important influences on West in his youth were the Baptist church and the Black Panthers. He studied at Harvard (where he earned magna cum laude honors), then at Princeton, where he encountered Richard Rorty during his doctoral studies. West taught at Union Theological Seminary in New York City, then at Yale. He now teaches at Princeton, where he continues to be a leader in making its African-American studies program one of the best in the country. West's books include *Prophesy Deliverance! An Afro-American Revolutionary Christianity* (1982), *Prophetic Fragments* (1988), *The American Invasion of Philosophy* (1989), and *Race Matters* (1993). The selection is from his contribution to *Out There: Marginalization and Contemporary Cultures* (1990), which he edited with Trinh T. Minh-ha and others.

The New Cultural Politics of Difference
Cornel West (1990)

In these last few years of the 20th century, there is emerging a significant shift in the sensibilities and outlooks of critics and artists. In fact, I would go so far as to claim that a new kind of cultural worker is in the making, associated with a new politics of difference. These new forms of intellectual consciousness advance reconceptions of the vocation of critic and artist, attempting to undermine the prevailing disciplinary divisions of labor in the academy, museum, mass media and gallery networks, while preserving modes of critique within the ubiquitous commodification of culture in the global village. Distinctive features of the new cultural politics of difference are to trash the monolithic and homogeneous in the name of diversity, multiplicity and heterogeneity; to reject the abstract, general and universal in light of the concrete, specific and particular; and to historicize, contextualize and pluralize by highlighting the contingent, provisional, variable, tentative, shifting and changing. Needless to say, these gestures are not new in the history of criticism or art, yet what makes them novel—along with the cultural politics they produce—is how and what constitutes difference, the weight and gravity it is given in representation and the way in which highlighting issues like exterminism, empire, class, race, gender, sexual orientation, age, nation, nature, and region at this historical moment acknowledges some discontinuity and disruption from previous forms of cultural critique. To put it

---

Excerpt from Russell Ferguson, Martha Gever, Trinh T. Minh-ha, Cornel West, eds., *Out There: Marginalization and Contemporary Cultures* (Cambridge, Mass.: MIT Press, 1990), pp. 19–32.

bluntly, the new cultural politics of difference consists of creative responses to the precise circumstances of our present moment—especially those of marginalized First World agents who shun degraded self-representations, articulating instead their sense of the flow of history in light of the contemporary terrors, anxieties and fears of highly commercialized North Atlantic capitalist cultures (with their escalating xenophobias against people of color, Jews, women, gays, lesbians and the elderly). The thawing, yet still rigid, Second World ex-communist cultures (with increasing nationalist revolts against the legacy of hegemonic party henchmen), and the diverse cultures of the majority of inhabitants on the globe smothered by international communication cartels and repressive postcolonial elites (sometimes in the name of communism, as in Ethiopia) or starved by austere World Bank and IMF policies that subordinate them to the North (as in free-market capitalism in Chile) also locate vital areas of analysis in this new cultural terrain.

The new cultural politics of difference are neither simply oppositional in contesting the mainstream (or *male*stream) for inclusion, nor transgressive in the avant-gardist sense of shocking conventional bourgeois audiences. Rather, they are distinct articulations of talented (and usually privileged) contributors to culture who desire to align themselves with demoralized, demobilized, depoliticized and disorganized people in order to empower and enable social action and, if possible, to enlist collective insurgency for the expansion of freedom, democracy and individuality. This perspective impels these cultural critics and artists to reveal, as an integral component of their production, the very operations of power within their immediate work contexts (i.e., academy, museum, gallery, mass media). This strategy, however, also puts them in an inescapable double bind—while linking their activities to the fundamental, structural overhaul of these institutions, they often remain financially dependent on them (so much for "independent" creation). For these critics of culture, theirs is a gesture that is simultaneously progressive *and* co-opted. Yet without social movement or political pressure from outside these institutions (extra-parliamentary and extra-curricular actions like the social movements of the recent past), transformation degenerates into mere accommodation or sheer stagnation, and the role of the "co-opted progressive"—no matter how fervent one's subversive rhetoric—is rendered more difficult. There can be no artistic breakthrough or social progress without some form of crisis in civilization—a crisis usually generated by organizations or collectivities that convince ordinary people to put their bodies and lives on the line. There is, of course, no guarantee that such pressure will yield the result one wants, but there is a guarantee that the status quo will remain or regress if no pressure is applied at all.

The new cultural politics of difference faces three basic challenges—intellectual, existential and political. The intellectual challenge—usually cast as methodological debate in these days in which academicist forms of expression have a monopoly on intellectual life—is how to think about representational practices in terms of history, culture and society. How does one understand, analyze and enact such practices today? An adequate answer to this question can be attempted only after one comes to terms with the insights and blindnesses of earlier attempts to grapple with the question in light of the evolving crisis in different histories, cultures and societies. I shall sketch a brief genealogy—a history that highlights the contingent origins and often ignoble outcomes—of exemplary critical responses to the question. This genealogy sets forth a historical framework that characterizes the rich yet deeply flawed Eurocentric traditions which the new cultural politics of difference build upon yet go beyond.

*   *   *

An appropriate starting point is the ambiguous legacy of the Age of Europe. Between 1492 and 1945, European breakthroughs in oceanic transportation, agricultural production, state-consolidation, bureaucratization, industrialization, urbanization and imperial dominion shaped the makings of the modern world. Precious ideals like the dignity of persons (individuality) or the popular accountability of institutions (democracy) were unleashed around the world. Powerful critiques of illegitimate authorities—of the Protestant Reformation against the Roman Catholic Church, the Enlightenment against state churches, liberal movements against absolutist states and feudal guild constraints, workers against managerial subordination, people of color and Jews against white and gentile supremacist decrees, gays and lesbians against homophobic sanctions—were fanned and fuelled by these precious ideals refined within the crucible of the Age of Europe. Yet the discrepancy between sterling rhetoric and lived reality, glowing principles and actual practices loomed large.

By the last European century—the last epoch in which European domination of most of the globe was uncontested and unchallenged in a substantive way—a new world seemed to be stirring. At the height of England's reign as the major imperial European power, its exemplary cultural critic, Matthew Arnold, painfully observed in his "Stanzas From the Grand Chartreuse" that he felt some sense of "wandering between two worlds, one dead / the other powerless to be born." Following his Burkean sensibilities of cautious reform and fear of anarchy, Arnold acknowledged that the old glue—religion—that had tenuously and often unsuccessfully held together the ailing European regimes could not do so in the mid-19th century. Like Alexis de Tocqueville in France, Arnold saw that the democratic temper was the wave of the future. So he proposed a new conception of culture—a secular, humanistic one—that could play an integrative role in cementing and stabilizing an emerging bourgeois civil society and imperial state. His famous castigation of the immobilizing materialism of the declining aristocracy, the vulgar philistinism of the emerging middle classes and the latent explosiveness of the working-class majority was motivated by a desire to create new forms of cultural legitimacy, authority and order in a rapidly changing moment in 19th century Europe.

For Arnold, (in *Culture and Anarchy*, [1869]) this new conception of culture

> . . . seeks to do away with classes; to make the best that has been thought and known in the world current everywhere; to make all men live in an atmosphere of sweetness and light. . . .
>
> This is the *social idea* and the men of culture are the true apostles of equality. The great men of culture are those who have had a passion for diffusing, for making prevail, for carrying from one end of society to the other, the best knowledge, the best ideas of their time, who have laboured to divest knowledge of all that was harsh, uncouth, difficult, abstract, professional, exclusive; to humanize it, to make it efficient outside the clique of the cultivated and learned, yet still remaining the best knowledge and thought of the time, and a true source, therefore, of sweetness and light.

As an organic intellectual of an emergent middle class—as the inspector of schools in an expanding educational bureaucracy, Professor of Poetry at Oxford (the first non-cleric and the first to lecture in English rather than Latin) and an active participant in a thriving magazine network—Arnold defined and defended a new secular culture of critical discourse. For him, this discursive strategy would be lodged in the educational and periodical apparatuses of modern societies as they contained and incorporated the frightening threats of an arrogant aristocracy and especially of an "anarchic" working-class majority. His ideals of disinterested, dispassionate and objective inquiry would regulate this new secular cultural production, and his justifications for the use of state power to quell any threats to the survival and security of this culture were widely accepted. He aptly noted, "Through culture seems to lie our way, not only to perfection, but even to safety."

This sentence is revealing in two ways. First, it refers to "our way" without explicitly acknowledging who constitutes the "we." This move is symptomatic among many bourgeois, male Eurocentric critics whose universalizing gestures exclude (by guarding a silence around) or explicitly degrade women and peoples of color. Second, the sentence links culture to safety—presumably the safety of the "we" against the barbaric threats of the "them," i.e., those viewed as different in some debased manner. Needless to say, Arnold's negative attitudes toward British working-class people, women and especially Indians and Jamaicans in the Empire clarify why he conceives of culture as, in part, a weapon for bourgeois male European "safety."

For Arnold the best of the Age of Europe—modeled on a mythological melange of Periclean Athens, late Republican/early Imperial Rome and Elizabethan England— could be promoted only if there was an interlocking affiliation among the emerging middle classes, a homogenizing of cultural discourse in the educational and university networks, and a state advanced enough in its policing techniques to safeguard it. The candidates for participation and legitimation in this grand endeavor of cultural renewal and revision would be detached intellectuals willing to shed their parochialism, provincialism and class-bound identities for Arnold's middle-class-skewed project: ". . . Aliens, if we may so call them—persons who are mainly led, not by their class spirit, but by a general *humane* spirit, by the love of human perfection." Needless to say, this Arnoldian perspective still informs much of the academic practices and secular cultural attitudes today—dominant views about the canon, admission procedures and collective self-definitions of intellectuals. Yet Arnold's project was disrupted by the collapse of 19th century Europe—World War I. This unprecedented war brought to the surface the crucial role and violent potential not of the masses Arnold feared but of the state he heralded. Upon the ashes of this wasteland of human carnage— some of it the civilian European population—T.S. Eliot emerged as the grand cultural spokesman. . . .

Eliot's image of Europe as a wasteland, a culture of fragments with no cementing center, predominated in postwar Europe. And though his early poetic practices were more radical, open and international than his Eurocentric criticism, Eliot posed a return to and revision of tradition as the only way of regaining European cultural order and political stability. . . .

Eliot found this tradition in the Church of England, to which he converted in 1927. Here was a tradition that left room for his Catholic cast of mind, Calvinistic heritage, puritanical temperament and ebullient patriotism for the old American South (the place of his upbringing). Like Arnold, Eliot was obsessed with the idea of civilization and the horror of barbarism (echoes of Joseph Conrad's Kurtz in *Heart of Darkness*) or more pointedly, the notion of the decline and decay of European civilization. With the advent of World War II, Eliot's obsession became a reality. Again unprecedented human carnage (50 million dead)—including an indescribable genocidal attack on Jewish people—throughout Europe as well as around the globe, put the last nail in the coffin of the Age of Europe. After 1945, Europe consisted of a devastated and divided continent, crippled by a humiliating dependency on and deference to the USA and USSR.

The second historical coordinate of my genealogy is the emergence of the USA as *the* world power. The USA was unprepared for world power status. However, with the recovery of Stalin's Russia (after losing 20 million dead), the USA felt compelled to make its presence felt around the globe. Then with the Marshall plan to strengthen Europe against Russian influence (and provide new markets for U.S. products), the 1948 Russian takeover of Czechoslovakia, the 1948 Berlin blockade, the 1950 beginning of the Korean War and the 1952 establishment of NATO forces in Europe, it seemed clear that there was no escape from world power obligations.

The post–World War II era in the USA, or the first decades of what Henry Luce envisioned as "The American Century," was not only a period of incredible economic expansion but of active cultural ferment. In the classical Fordist formula, mass production required mass consumption. With unchallenged hegemony in the capitalist world, the USA took economic growth for granted. Next to exercising its crude, anti-communist, McCarthyist obsessions, buying commodities became the primary act of civic virtue for many American citizens at this time. The creation of a mass middle class—a prosperous working class with a bourgeois identity—was countered by the first major emergence of subcultures of American non-WASP intellectuals: the so-called New York intellectuals in criticism, the Abstract Expressionists in painting and the BeBop artists in jazz music. This emergence signaled a vital challenge to an American male WASP elite loyal to an older and eroding European culture.

The first significant blow was dealt when assimilated Jewish Americans entered the higher echelons of the cultural apparatuses (academy, museums, galleries, mass media). Lionel Trilling is an emblematic figure. This Jewish entree into the anti-Semitic and patriarchal critical discourse of the exclusivistic institutions of American culture initiated the slow but sure undoing of the male WASP cultural hegemony and homogeneity. Lionel Trilling's project was to appropriate Matthew Arnold for his own political and cultural purposes—thereby unraveling the old male WASP consensus, while erecting a new post–World War II liberal academic consensus around cold war, anti-communist renditions of the values of complexity, difficulty, variousness and modulation. In addition, the post-war boom laid the basis for intense professionalization and specialization in expanding institutions of higher education—especially in the natural sciences that were compelled to somehow respond to Russia's successful ventures in space. Humanistic scholars found themselves searching for new methodologies that could buttress self-images of rigor and scientific seriousness. For example, the close reading techniques of New Criticism (severed from their conservative, organicist, anti-industrialist ideological roots), the logical precision of reasoning in analytic philosophy and the jargon of Parsonian structural-functionalism in sociology helped create such self-images. Yet towering cultural critics like C. Wright Mills, W.E.B. Du Bois, Richard Hofstadter, Margaret Mead and Dwight MacDonald bucked the tide. . . .

This threat is partly associated with the third historical coordinate of my genealogy—the decolonization of the Third World. It is crucial to recognize the importance of this world-historical process if one wants to grasp the significance of the end of the Age of Europe and the emergence of the USA as a world power. With the first defeat of a western nation by a non-western nation—in Japan's victory over Russia (1905), revolutions in Persia (1905), Turkey (1908), China (1912), Mexico

(1911–12) and much later the independence of India (1947) and China (1948) and the triumph of Ghana (1957)—the actuality of a decolonized globe loomed large. Born of violent struggle, consciousness-raising and the reconstruction of identities, decolonization simultaneously brings with it new perspectives on that long festering underside of the Age of Europe (of which colonial domination represents the *costs* of "progress," "order" and "culture"), as well as requiring new readings of the economic boom in the USA (wherein the Black, Brown, Yellow, Red, female, elderly, gay, lesbian and White working class live the same *costs* as cheap labor at home as well as in US-dominated Latin American and Pacific rim markets).

The impetuous ferocity and moral outrage that motors the decolonization process is best captured by Frantz Fanon in *The Wretched of the Earth* (1961).

> Decolonization, which sets out to change the order of the world, is obviously, a program of complete disorder . . . Decolonization is the meeting of two forces, opposed to each other by their very nature, which in fact owe their originality to that sort of substantification which results from and is nourished by the situation in the colonies. Their first encounter was marked by violence and their existence together—that is to say the exploitation of the native by the settler—was carried on by dint of a great array of bayonets and cannons . . .
>
> In decolonization, there is therefore the need of a complete calling in question of the colonial situation. If we wish to describe it precisely, we might find it in the well-known words: "The last shall be first and the first last." Decolonization is the putting into practice of this sentence.
>
> The naked truth of decolonization evokes for us the searing bullets and bloodstained knives which emanate from it. For if the last shall be first, this will only come to pass after a murderous and decisive struggle between the two protagonists.

Fanon's strong words, though excessively Manichean, still describe the feelings and thoughts between the occupying British Army and colonized Irish in Northern Ireland, the occupying Israeli Army and subjugated Palestinians on the West Bank and Gaza Strip, the South African Army and oppressed Black South Africans in the townships, the Japanese Police and Koreans living in Japan, the Russian Army and subordinated Armenians and others in the Southern and Eastern USSR. His words also partly invoke the sense many Black Americans have toward police departments in urban centers. In other words, Fanon is articulating century-long heartfelt human responses to being degraded and despised, hated and hunted, oppressed and exploited, marginalized and dehumanized at the hands of powerful xenophobic European, American, Russian and Japanese imperial countries.

During the late '50s, '60s and early '70s in the USA, these decolonized sensibilities fanned and fueled the Civil Rights and Black Power movements, as well as the student anti-war, feminist, gray, brown, gay, and lesbian movements. In this period we witnessed the shattering of male WASP cultural homogeneity and the collapse of the short-lived liberal consensus. The inclusion of African Americans, Latino/a Americans, Asian Americans, Native Americans and American women into the culture of critical discourse yielded intense intellectual polemics and inescapable ideological polarization that focused principally on the exclusions, silences and blindnesses of male WASP cultural homogeneity and its concomitant Arnoldian notions of the canon.

In addition, these critiques promoted three crucial processes that affected intellectual life in the country. First is the appropriation of the theories of post-war Europe—especially the work of the Frankfurt school (Marcuse, Adorno, Horkheimer), French/Italian Marxisms (Sartre, Althusser, Lefebvre, Gramsci), structuralisms (Lévi-Strauss, Todorov) and post-structuralisms (Deleuze, Derrida, Foucault). These diverse and disparate theories—all preoccupied with keeping alive radical projects after the end of the Age of Europe—tend to fuse versions of transgressive European modernisms with Marxist or post-Marxist left politics and unanimously shun the term "post-modernism." Second, there is the recovery and revisioning of American history in light of the struggles of white male workers, women, African Americans, Native Americans, Latino/a Americans, gays and lesbians. Third is the impact of forms of popular culture such as television, film, music videos and even sports, on highbrow literate culture. The Black-based hip-hop culture of youth around the world is one grand example.

After 1973, with the crisis in the international world economy, America's slump in productivity, the challenge of OPEC nations to the North Atlantic monopoly of oil production, the increasing competition in hi-tech sectors of the economy from Japan and West Germany and the growing fragility of the international debt structure, the USA entered a period of waning self-confidence (compounded by Watergate) and a nearly contracting economy. As the standards of living for the middle classes declined, owing to runaway inflation, and the quality of living fell for most, due to escalating unemployment, underemployment and crime, religious and secular neo-conservatism emerged with power and potency. This fusion of fervent neo-nationalism, traditional cultural values and "free market" policies served as the ground work for the Reagan-Bush era.

The ambiguous legacies of the European Age, American preeminence and decolonization continue to haunt our postmodern movement as we come to terms with both the European, American, Japanese, Soviet, and Third World *crimes against* and *contributions to* humanity. The plight of Africans in the New World can be instructive in this regard.

By 1914 European maritime empires had dominion over more than half of the land and a third of the peoples in the world—almost 72 million square kilometers of territory and more than 560 million people under colonial rule. Needless to say, this European control included brutal enslavement, institutional terrorism and cultural degradation of Black diaspora people. The death of roughly seventy-five million Africans during the centuries-long transatlantic slave trade is but one reminder, among others, of the assault on Black humanity. The Black diaspora condition of New World servitude—in which they were viewed as mere commodities with production value, who had no proper legal status, social standing or public worth—can be characterized as, following Orlando Patterson, natal alienation. This state of perpetual and inheritable domination that diaspora Africans had at birth produced the *modern Black diaspora problematic of invisibility and namelessness.* White supremacist practices—enacted under the auspices of the prestigious cultural authorities of the churches, printed media and scientific academics—promoted Black inferiority and constituted the European background against which Black diaspora struggles for identity, dignity (self-confidence, self-respect, self-esteem) and material resources took place.

An inescapable aspect of this struggle was that the Black diaspora peoples' quest for validation and recognition occurred on the ideological, social and cultural terrains of other non-Black peoples. White supremacist assaults on Black intelligence, ability, beauty and character required persistent Black efforts to hold self-doubt, self-contempt and even self-hatred at bay. Selective appropriation, incorporation and re-articulation of European ideologies, cultures and institutions alongside an African heritage—a heritage more or less confined to linguistic innovation in rhetorical practices, stylizations of the body in forms of occupying an alien social space (hair styles, ways of walking, standing, hand expressions, talking) and means of constituting and sustaining comraderie and community (e.g. antiphonal, call-and-response styles, rhythmic repetition, risk-ridden syncopation in spectacular modes in musical and rhetorical expressions)—were some of the strategies employed.

The modern Black diaspora problematic of invisibility and namelessness can be understood as the condition of *relative lack of Black power to represent themselves to themselves and others as complex human beings, and thereby to contest the bombardment of negative, degrading stereotypes put forward by White supremacist ideologies.* The initial Black response to being caught in this whirlwind of Europeanization was to resist the misrepresentation and caricature of the terms set by uncontested non-Black norms and models and fight for self-representation and recognition. Every modern Black person, especially cultural disseminators, encounters this problematic of invisibility and namelessness. The initial Black diaspora response was a mode of resistance that was *moralistic in content* and *communal in character.* That is, the fight for representation and recognition highlighted moral judgments regarding Black "positive" images over and against White supremacist stereotypes. These images "represented" monolithic and homogeneous Black communities, in a way that could displace past misrepresentations of these communities. Stuart Hall has talked about these responses as attempts to change "the relations of representation."

These courageous yet limited Black efforts to combat racist cultural practices uncritically accepted non-Black conventions and standards in two ways. First, they proceeded in an *assimilationist manner* that set out to show that Black people were really like White people—thereby eliding differences (in history, culture) between Whites and Blacks. Black specificity and particularity was thus banished in order to gain White acceptance and approval. Second, these Black responses rested upon a *homogenizing impulse* that assumed that all Black people were really alike—hence obliterating differences (class, gender, region, sexual orientation) between Black peoples. I submit that there are elements of truth in both claims, yet the conclusions are unwarranted owing to the basic fact that non-Black paradigms set the terms of the replies.

The insight in the first claim is that Blacks and Whites are in some important sense alike—i.e., in their positive capacities for human sympathy, moral sacrifice, service to others, intelligence and beauty, or negatively, in their capacity for cruelty. Yet the common humanity they share is jettisoned when the claim is cast in an assimilationist manner that subordinates Black particularity to a false universalism, i.e., non-Black rubrics or prototypes. Similarly, the insight in the second claim is that all Blacks are in some significant sense "in the same boat"—that is, subject to White supremacist abuse. Yet this common condition is stretched too far when viewed in a *homogenizing* way that overlooks how racist treatment vastly differs owing to class, gender, sexual orientation, nation, region, hue and age.

The moralistic and communal aspects of the initial Black diaspora responses to social and psychic erasure were not simply cast into simplistic binary oppositions of positive/negative, good/bad images that privileged the first term in light of a White norm so that Black efforts remained inscribed within the very logic that dehumanized them. They were further complicated by the fact that these responses were also advanced principally by anxiety-ridden, middle-class Black intellectuals, (predominantly male and heterosexual) grappling with their sense of double-consciousness—namely their own crisis of identity, agency and audience—caught between a quest for White approval and acceptance and an endeavor to overcome the internalized association of Blackness with inferiority. . . .

One crucial lesson of this decolonization process remains the manner in which most Third World authoritarian bureaucratic elites deploy essentialist rhetorics about "homogeneous national communities" and "positive images" in order to repress and regiment their diverse and heterogeneous populations. Yet in the diaspora, especially among First World countries, this critique has emerged not so much from the Black male component of the left but rather from the Black women's movement. The decisive push of postmodern Black intellectuals toward a new cultural politics of difference has been made by the powerful critiques and constructive explorations of Black diaspora women (e.g. Toni Morrison). The coffin used to bury the innocent notion of the essential Black subject was nailed shut with the termination of the Black male monopoly on the construction of the Black subject. In this regard, the Black diaspora womanist critique has had a greater impact than the critiques that highlight exclusively class, empire, age, sexual orientation or nature.

This decisive push toward the end of Black innocence—though prefigured in various degrees in the best moments of W.E.B. DuBois, Anna Cooper, C.L.R. James, James Baldwin, Claudia Jones, the later Malcolm X, Frantz Fanon, Amiri Baraka and others—forces Black diaspora cultural workers to encounter what Hall has called the "politics of representation." The main aim now is not simply access to representation in order to produce positive images of homogeneous communities—though broader access remains a practical and political problem. Nor is the primary goal here that of contesting stereotypes—though contestation remains a significant though limited venture. Following the model of the Black diaspora traditions of music, athletics and rhetoric, Black cultural workers must constitute and sustain discursive and institutional networks that deconstruct earlier modern Black strategies for identity-formation, demystify power relations that incorporate class, patriarchal and homophobic biases, and construct more multi-valent and multi-dimensional responses that articulate the complexity and diversity of Black practices in the modern and postmodern world.

Furthermore, Black cultural workers must investigate and interrogate the other of Blackness-Whiteness. One cannot deconstruct the binary oppositional logic of images of Blackness without extending it to the contrary condition of Blackness/Whiteness itself. However, a mere dismantling will not do—for the very notion of a deconstructive social theory is oxymoronic. Yet social theory is what is needed to examine and *explain* the historically specific ways in which "Whiteness" is a politically constructed category parasitic on "Blackness," and thereby to conceive of the profoundly hybrid character of what we mean by "race," "ethnicity," and "nationality." For instance, European immigrants arrived on American shores perceiving themselves as "Irish," "Sicilian," "Lithuanian," etc. They had to learn that they were "White" principally by adopting an American discourse of positively-valued Whiteness and negatively-charged Blackness. This process by which people define themselves physically, socially, sexually and even politically in terms of Whiteness or Blackness has much bearing not only on constructed notions of race and ethnicity but also on how we understand the changing character of U.S. nationalities. And given the Americanization of the world, especially in the sphere of mass culture, such inquiries—encouraged by the new cultural politics of difference—raise critical issues of "hybridity," "exilic status" and "identity" on an international scale. Needless to say, these inquiries must traverse those of "male/female," "colonizer/colonized," "heterosexual/homosexual," et al., as well.

In light of this brief sketch of the emergence of our present crisis—and the turn toward history and difference in cultural work—four major historicist forms of theoretical activity provide resources for how we understand, analyze and enact our representational practices: Heideggerian *destruction* of the western metaphysical tradition, Derridean *deconstruction* of the western philosophical tradition, Rortian *demythologization* of the western intellectual tradition and Marxist, Foucaultian, feminist, antiracist or anti-homophobic *demystification* of western cultural and artistic conventions.

Despite his abominable association with the Nazis, Martin Heidegger's project is useful in that it discloses the suppression of temporality and historicity in the dominant metaphysical systems of the West from Plato to Rudolph Carnap. This is noteworthy in that it forces one to understand philosophy's representational discourses as thoroughly historical phenomena. Hence, they should be viewed with skepticism as they are often flights from the specific, concrete, practical and particular. The major problem with Heidegger's project—as noted by his neo-Marxist student, Herbert Marcuse—is that he views history in terms of fate, heritage and destiny. He dramatizes the past and present as if it were a Greek tragedy with no tools of social analyses to relate cultural work to institutions and structures or antecedent forms and styles.

Jacques Derrida's version of deconstruction is one of the most influential schools of thought among young academic critics. It is salutary in that it focuses on the political power of rhetorical operations—of tropes and metaphors in binary oppositions like white/black, good/bad, male/female, machine/nature, ruler/ruled, reality/appearance—showing how these operations sustain hierarchal world views by devaluing the second terms as something subsumed under the first. Most of the controversy about Derrida's project revolves around this austere epistemic doubt that unsettles binary oppositions while undermining any determinate meaning of a text, i.e., book, art-object, performance, building. Yet, his views about skepticism are no more alarming than those of David Hume, Ludwig Wittgenstein or Stanley Cavell. He simply revels in it for transgressive purposes, whereas others provide us with ways to dissolve, sidestep or cope with skepticism. None, however, slide down the slippery, crypto-Nietzschean slope of sophomoric relativism as alleged by old-style humanists, be they Platonists, Kantians or Arnoldians.

The major shortcoming of Derrida's deconstructive project is that it puts a premium on a sophisticated ironic consciousness that tends to preclude and foreclose analyses that guide action with purpose. And given Derrida's own status as an Algerian-born, Jewish leftist marginalized by a hostile French academic establishment (quite different from his reception by the youth in the American academic establishment), the sense of political impotence and hesitation regarding the efficacy of moral action is understandable—but not justifiable. His works and those of his followers too often become rather monotonous, Johnny-one-note rhetorical readings that disassemble texts with little attention to the effects and consequences these dismantlings have in relation to the operations of military, economic and social powers.

Richard Rorty's neo-pragmatic project of demythologization is insightful in that it provides descriptive mappings of the transient metaphors—especially the ocular and specular ones—that regulate some of the fundamental dynamics in the construction of self-descriptions dominant in highbrow European and American philosophy. His perspective is instructive because it discloses the crucial role of narrative as the background for rational exchange and critical conversation. To put it crudely, Rorty shows why we should speak not of History, but histories, not of Reason, but historically constituted forms of rationality, not of Criticism or Art, but of socially constructed notions of criticism and art—all linked but not reducible to political purposes, material interests and cultural prejudices.

Rorty's project nonetheless leaves one wanting owing to its distrust of social analytical explanation. Similar to the dazzling new historicism of Stephen Greenblatt, Louis Montrose and Catherine Gallagher—inspired by the subtle symbolic-cum-textual anthropology of Clifford Geertz and the powerful discursive materialism of Michel Foucault—Rorty gives us mappings and descriptions with no explanatory accounts for change and conflict. In this way, it gives us an aestheticized version of historicism in which the provisional and variable are celebrated at the expense of highlighting who gains, loses or bears what costs.

Demystification is the most illuminating mode of theoretical inquiry for those who promote the new cultural politics of difference. Social structural analyses of empire, exterminism, class, race, gender, nature, age, sexual orientation, nation and region are the springboards—though not landing grounds—for the most desirable forms of critical practice that take history (and herstory) seriously. Demystification tries to keep track of the complex dynamics of institutional and other related power structures in order to disclose options and alternatives for transformative praxis; it also attempts to grasp the way in which representational strategies are creative responses to novel circumstances and conditions. In this way, the central role of human agency (always enacted under circumstances not of one's choosing)—be it in the critic, artist or constituency and audience—is accented.

I call demystificatory criticism "prophetic criticism"—the approach appropriate for the new cultural politics of difference—because while it begins with social structural analyses it also makes explicit its moral and political aims. It is partisan, partial, engaged and crisis-centered, yet always keeps open a skeptical eye to avoid dogmatic traps, premature closures, formulaic formulations or rigid conclusions. In addition to social structural analyses, moral and political judgments, and sheer critical consciousness, there indeed is evaluation. Yet the aim of this evaluation is neither to pit art-objects against one another like racehorses nor to create eternal canons that dull, discourage or even dwarf contemporary achievements. We listen to Ludwig Beethoven, Charlie Parker, Luciano Pavarotti, Laurie Anderson, Sarah Vaughan, Stevie Wonder or Kathleen Battle, read William Shakespeare, Anton Chekhov, Ralph Ellison, Doris Lessing, Thomas Pynchon, Toni Morrison or Gabriel García Márquez, see works of Pablo Picasso, Ingmar Bergman, Le Corbusier, Martin Puryear, Barbara Kruger, Spike Lee, Frank Gehry or Howardena Pindell—not in order to undergird bureaucratic assents or enliven cocktail party conversations, but rather to be summoned by the styles they deploy for their profound insight, pleasures and challenges. Yet all evaluation—including a delight in Eliot's poetry despite his reactionary politics, or a love of Zora Neale Hurston's novels despite her Republican party affiliations—is inseparable from, though not identical or reducible to, social structural analyses, moral and political judgments and the workings of a curious critical consciousness.

The deadly traps of demystification—and any form of prophetic criticism—are those of reductionism, be it of the sociological, psychological, or historical sort. By reductionism I mean either one factor analyses (i.e., crude Marxisms, feminisms, racialisms, etc.) that yield a one-dimensional functionalism, or a hyper-subtle analytical perspective that loses touch with the specificity of an art work's form and the context of its reception. Few cultural workers of whatever stripe can walk the tightrope between the Scylla of reductionism and the Charybdis of aestheticism—yet demystificatory (or prophetic) critics must.❖

Henry Louis Gates, Jr. (1950–) was born in Keyser, West Virginia. After completing undergraduate studies at Yale in 1973, Gates studied at Cambridge University, where he received his Ph.D. in 1979. He has taught at Cornell (1985–1990), Duke (1990–1991), and Harvard, where he is director of the W.E.B. Du Bois Institute and professor of humanities. Gates moved to Harvard with the clear intent that he would revive its African-American studies program. He is the author and editor of numerous books, series, and collections, including *Our Nig: Sketches in the Life of a Free Black* (1983), *Signifying Monkey* (1988), *Loose Canons* (1991), *Colored People* (1994), and the multivolume *Schomburg Library of Nineteenth-Century Black Women Writers*.

"Race" as the Trope of the World

Henry Louis Gates, Jr. (1986)

Race, as a meaningful criterion within the biological sciences, has long been recognized to be a fiction. When we speak of "the white race" or "the black race," "the Jewish race" or "the Aryan race," we speak in biological misnomers and, more generally, in metaphors. Nevertheless, our conversations are replete with usages of race which have their sources in the dubious pseudoscience of the eighteenth and nineteenth centuries. One need only flip through the pages of the *New York Times* to find headlines such as "Brown University President Sees School Racial Problems" or "Sensing Racism, Thousands March in Paris." In "The Lost White Tribe," a lead editorial in the 29 March 1985 issue, the *New York Times* notes that while "racism is not unique to South Africa," we must condemn that society because in "betraying the religious tenets underlying Western culture, it has made race the touchstone of political rights." The *Times* editorial echoes Eliot's "dissociation of sensibility," which he felt had been caused in large part by the fraternal atrocities of the First World War. (For many people with non-European origins, however, dissociation of sensibility resulted from colonialism and human slavery.) Race, in these usages, pretends to be an objective term of classification, when in fact it is a dangerous trope.

The sense of difference defined in popular usages of the term "race" has both described and *inscribed* differences of language, belief system, artistic tradition, and gene pool, as well as all sorts of supposedly natural attributes such as rhythm, athletic ability, cerebration, usury, fidelity, and so forth. The relation between "racial character" and these sorts of characteristics has been inscribed through tropes of race, lending the sanction of God, biology, or the natural order to even presumably unbiased descriptions of cultural tendencies and differences. "Race consciousness," Zora Neale Hurston wrote, "is a deadly explosive on the tongues of men." In 1973 I

---

was amazed to hear a member of the House of Lords describe the differences between Irish Protestants and Catholics in terms of their "distinct and clearly definable differences of race." "You mean to say that you can tell them apart?" I asked incredulously. "Of course," responded the lord. "Any Englishman can."

Race has become a trope of ultimate, irreducible difference between cultures, linguistic groups, or adherents of specific belief systems which—more often than not—also have fundamentally opposed economic interests. Race is the ultimate trope of difference because it is so very arbitrary in its application. The biological criteria used to determine "difference" in sex simply do not hold when applied to "race." Yet we carelessly use language in such a way as to *will* this sense of *natural* difference into our formulations. To do so is to engage in a pernicious act of language, one which exacerbates the complex problem of cultural or ethnic difference, rather than to assuage or redress it. This is especially the case at a time when, once again, racism has become fashionable. The extreme "otherness" of the black African continues to surface as a matter of controversy even in such humanitarian and cosmopolitan institutions as the Roman Catholic Church. On a visit to west Africa in August, Pope John Paul II sailed across Lake Togo to face Aveto, "supreme priest" of Togo's traditional African religion, on the edge of the sacred forest at Togoville, the historical meeting point of the Roman Catholic and traditional black religions. It was a confrontation of primal dimensions: the Pope, accompanied by the Vatican Secretary of State and other top officials, and Aveto, accompanied by five of his chief priests and priestesses, exchanged blessings and then discussed the compatibility of their belief systems. The Pope, however, a rather vocal critic of the creative African integration of traditional black ("animist") beliefs with those received from Rome, emerged from his confrontation with the mystical black Other in the heart of darkness, still worried about "great confusions in ideas," "syncretistic mysticism incompatible with the Church," and customs "contrary to the will of God," thereby denying Africans the right to remake European religion in their own images, just as various Western cultures have done.

Scores of people are killed every day in the name of differences ascribed only to race. This slaughter demands the gesture in which the contributors to this volume are collectively engaged: to deconstruct, if you will, the ideas of difference inscribed in the trope of race, to explicate discourse itself in order to reveal the hidden relations of power and knowledge inherent in popular and academic usages of "race." But when, on 31 March 1985, twenty-five thousand people felt compelled to gather on the rue de Rivoli in support of the antiracist "Ne touche pas à mon pote" movement, when thousands of people willingly risk death to protest apartheid, when Iran and Iraq each feel justified in murdering the other's citizens because of their "race," when Beirut stands as a monument of shards and ruins, the gesture that we make here seems local and tiny.

I have edited this volume of *Critical Inquiry* to explore, from a variety of methodological perspectives and formal concerns, the curious dialectic between formal language use and the inscription of metaphorical racial differences. At times, as Nancy Stepan expertly shows in *The Idea of Race in Science,* these metaphors have sought a universal and transcendent sanction in biological science. Western writers in French, Spanish, German, Portuguese, and English have tried to mystify these rhetorical figures of race, to make them natural, absolute, essential. In doing so, they have *inscribed* these differences as fixed and finite categories which they merely report or draw upon for authority. It takes little reflection, however, to recognize that these pseudoscientific categories are themselves figures. Who has seen a black or red person, a white, yellow, or brown? These terms are arbitrary constructs, not reports of reality. But language is not only the medium of this often insidious tendency; it is its *sign*. Current language use signifies the difference between cultures and their possession of power, spelling out the distance between subordinate and superordinate, between bondsman and lord in terms of their "race." These usages develop simultaneously with the shaping of an economic order in which the cultures of color have been dominated in several important senses by Western Judeo-Christian, Greco-Roman cultures and their traditions. To use contemporary theories of criticism to explicate these modes of inscription is to demystify large and obscure ideological relations and, indeed, theory itself. Before discussing the essays gathered here, it would be useful to consider a typical example of Western culture's use of writing as a commodity to confine and delimit a culture of color. For literacy, as I hope to demonstrate, is the emblem that links racial alienation with economic alienation.

Where better to test this thesis than in the example of the black tradition's first poet in English, the African slave girl Phillis Wheatley. Let us imagine the scene.

One bright morning in the spring of 1772, a young African girl walked demurely into the courthouse at Boston to undergo an oral examination, the results of which would determine the direction of her life and work. Perhaps she was shocked upon entering the appointed room. For there, gathered in a semicircle, sat eighteen of Boston's most notable citizens. Among them was John Erving, a prominent Boston merchant; the Reverend Charles Chauncey, pastor of the Tenth Congregational Church; and John Hancock, who would later gain fame for his signature on the Declaration of Independence. At the center of this group would have sat His Excellency, Thomas Hutchinson, governor of the colony, with Andrew Oliver, his lieutenant governor, close by his side.

Why had this august group been assembled? Why had it seen fit to summon this young African girl, scarcely eighteen years old, before it? This group of "the most respectable characters in *Boston*," as it would later define itself, had assembled to question closely the African adolescent on the slender sheaf of poems that she claimed to have written by herself. We can only speculate on the nature of the questions posed to the fledgling poet. Perhaps they asked her to identify and explain—for all to hear—exactly who were the Greek and Latin gods and poets alluded to so frequently in her work. Perhaps they asked her to conjugate a verb in Latin, or even to translate randomly selected passages from the Latin, which she and her master, John Wheatley, claimed that she "had made some progress in." Or perhaps they asked her to recite from memory key passages from the texts of John Milton and Alexander Pope, the two poets by whom the African claimed to be most directly influenced. We do not know.

We do know, however, that the African poet's responses were more than sufficient to prompt the eighteen august gentlemen to compose, sign, and publish a two-paragraph "Attestation," an open letter "To the Publick" that prefaces Phillis Wheatley's book, and which reads in part:

> We whose Names are underwritten, do assure the World, that the poems specified in the following Page, were (as we veribly believe) written by Phillis, a young Negro Girl, who was but a few Years since, brought an uncultivated Barbarian from *Africa*, and has ever since been, and now is, under the Disadvantage of serving as a Slave in a Family in this Town. She has been examined by some of the best judges, and is thought qualified to write them.

So important was this document in securing a publisher for Phillis Wheatley's poems that it forms the signal element in the prefatory matter printed in the opening pages of her *Poems on Various Subjects, Religious and Moral,* published at London in 1773.

Without the published "Attestation," Phillis Wheatley's publisher claimed, few would believe that an African could possibly have written poetry all by herself. As the eighteen put the matter clearly in their letter, "Numbers would be ready to suspect they were not really the Writings of Phillis." Phillis Wheatley and her master, John Wheatley, had attempted to publish a similar volume in 1770 at Boston, but Boston publishers had been incredulous. Three years later, "Attestation" in hand, Phillis Wheatley and her master's son, Nathaniel Wheatley, sailed for England, where they completed arrangements for the publication of a volume of her poems with the aid of the countess of Huntington and the earl of Dartmouth.

This curious anecdote, surely one of the oddest oral examinations on record, is only a tiny part of a larger, and even more curious, episode in the Enlightenment. Since the beginning of the seventeenth century, Europeans had wondered aloud whether or not the African "species of men," as they most commonly put it, *could* ever create formal literature, could ever master "the arts and sciences." If they could, the argument ran, then the African variety of humanity and the European variety were fundamentally related. If not, then it seemed clear that the African was destined by nature to be a slave.

Why was the creative writing of the African of such importance to the eighteenth century's debate over slavery? I can briefly outline one thesis: after René Descartes, *reason* was privileged, or valorized, above all other human characteristics. Writing, especially after the printing press became so widespread, was taken to be the *visible* sign of reason. Blacks were "reasonable," and hence "men," if—and only if—they demonstrated mastery of "the arts and sciences," the eighteenth century's formula for writing. So, while the Enlightenment is characterized by its foundation on man's ability to reason, it simultaneously used the absence and presence of reason to delimit and circumscribe the very humanity of the cultures and people of color which Europeans had been "discovering" since the Renaissance. The urge toward the systematization of all human knowledge (by which we characterize the Enlightenment) led directly to the relegation of black people to a lower place in the great chain of being, an ancient construct that arranged all of creation on a vertical scale from plants, insects, and animals through man to the angels and God himself.

By 1750, the chain had become minutely calibrated; the human scale rose from "the lowliest Hottentot" (black South Africans) to "glorious Milton and Newton." If blacks could write and publish imaginative literature, then they could, in effect, take a few "giant steps" up the chain of being in an evil game of "Mother, May I?" For example, scores of reviews of Wheatley's book argued that the publication of her poems meant that the African was indeed a human being and should not be enslaved. Indeed, Wheatley herself was manumitted soon after her poems were published. That which was only implicit in Wheatley's case would become explicit fifty years later. George Moses Horton had, by the middle of the 1820s, gained a considerable reputation at Chapel Hill as "the slave-poet." His master printed full-page advertisements in Northern newspapers soliciting subscriptions for a book of Horton's poems and promising to exchange the slave's freedom for a sufficient return on sales of the book. Writing, for these slaves, was not an activity of mind; rather, it was a commodity which they were forced to trade for their humanity.

Blacks and other people of color could not write.

Writing, many Europeans argued, stood alone among the fine arts as the most salient repository of "genius," the visible sign of reason itself. In this subordinate role, however, writing, although secondary to reason, is nevertheless the *medium* of reason's expression. We *know* reason by its writing, by its representations. Such representations could assume spoken or written form. And while several superb scholars give priority to the *spoken* as the privileged of the pair, most Europeans privileged *writing*—in their writings about Africans, at least—as the principal measure of the Africans' humanity, their capacity for progress, their very place in the great chain of being.

The direct correlation between economic and political alienation, on the one hand, and racial alienation, on the other, is epitomized in the following 1740 South Carolina statute that attempted to make it almost impossible for black slaves to acquire, let alone master, literacy:

> *And whereas* the having slaves taught to write, or suffering them to be employed in writing, may be attending with great inconveniences;
>
> *Be it enacted*, that all and every person and persons whatsoever, who shall hereafter teach, or cause any slave or slaves to be taught to write, or shall use or employ any slave as a scribe in any manner of writing whatsoever, hereafter taught to write; every such person or persons shall, for every offense, forfeith the sum of one hundred pounds current money.

Learning to read and to write, then, was not only difficult, it was a violation of a law.

As early as 1705, a Dutch explorer, William Bosman, had encased the commodity function of writing and its relation to racial and economic alienation in a myth which the Africans he "discovered" had purportedly related to him. According to Bosman, the blacks

> tell us, that in the beginning God created Black as well as White men; thereby . . . giving the Blacks the first Election, who chose Gold, and left the Knowledge of Letters to the White. God granted their Request, but being incensed at their Avarice, resolved that the Whites should for ever be their masters, and they obliged to wait on them as their slaves.

Bosman's fabrication, of course, was a claim of origins designed to sanction through mythology a political order created by Europeans. But it was Hume, writing midway through the eighteenth century, who gave to Bosman's myth the sanction of Enlightenment philosophical reasoning.

In a major essay, "Of National Characters" (1748), Hume discusses the "characteristics" of the world's major division of human beings. In a footnote added in 1753 to his original text (the margins of his discourse), Hume posited with all of the authority of philosophy the fundamental identity of complexion, character, and intellectual capacity:

> I am apt to suspect the negroes, and in general all the other species of men (for there are four or five different kinds) to be naturally inferior to the whites. There never was a civilized nation of any other complexion than white, nor even any individual eminent either in action or speculation. No ingenious manufactures amongst them, *no arts, no sciences* . . . Such a uniform and constant difference could not happen, in so many countries and ages, if *nature* had not made an original distinction betwixt these breeds

of men. Not to mention our colonies, there are Negroe slaves dispersed all over Europe, of which none ever discovered any symptoms and ingenuity.... In Jamaica indeed they talk of one negroe as a man of parts and learning [Francis Williams, the Cambridge-educated poet who wrote verse in Latin]; but 'tis likely he is admired for very slender accomplishments, like a parrot, who speaks a few words plainly.

Hume's opinion on the subject, as we might expect, became prescriptive.

In his *Observations on the Feeling of the Beautiful and Sublime* (1764), Kant elaborates on Hume's essay in section 4, entitled "Of National Characteristics, So Far as They Depend upon the Distinct Feeling of the Beautiful and Sublime." Kant first claims that "so fundamental is the difference between [the black and white] races of man, ... it appears to be as great in regard to mental capacities as in color." Kant, moreover, is one of the earliest major European philosophers to conflate color with intelligence, a determining relation he posits with dictatorial surety:

Father Labat reports that a Negro carpenter, whom he reproached for haughty treatment toward his wives, answered: "You whites are indeed fools, for first you make great concessions to your wives, and afterward you complain when they drive you mad." And it might be that there were something in this which perhaps deserved to be considered; but in short, this fellow was *quite black* from head to foot, a clear proof that what he said was stupid.

The correlation of "black" and "stupid" Kant posits as if it were self-evident.

Hegel, echoing Hume and Kant, claimed that Africans had no history, because they had developed no systems of writing and had not mastered the art of writing in European languages. In judging civilizations, Hegel's strictures with respect to the absence of written history presume a crucial role for *memory,* a collective, cultural memory. Metaphors of the childlike nature of the slaves, of the masked, puppetlike personality of the black, all share this assumption about the absence of memory. Mary Langdon, in her novel *Ida May: A Story of Things Actual and Possible* (1854), writes that "they *are* mere children.... You seldom hear them say much about anything that's past, if they only get enough to eat and drink at the present moment." Without writing, no *repeatable* sign of the workings of reason, of mind, could exist. Without memory or mind, no history could exist. Without history, no humanity, as defined consistently from Vico to Hegel, could exist.

Ironically, Anglo-African writing arose as a response to allegations of its absence, Black people responded to these profoundly serious allegations about their "nature" as directly as they could: they wrote books, poetry, autobiographical narratives. Political and philosophical discourse were the predominant forms of writing. Among these, autobiographical "deliverance" narratives were the most common and the most accomplished. Accused of lacking a formal and collective history, blacks published individual histories which, taken together, were intended to narrate in segments the larger yet fragmented history of blacks in Africa, now dispersed throughout a cold New World. The narrated, descriptive "eye" was put into service as a literary form to posit both the individual "I" of the black author as well as the collective "I" of the race. Text created author; and black authors, it was hoped, would create, or re-create, the image of the race in European discourse. The very *face* of the race was contingent upon the recording of the black *voice.* Voice presupposed a face, but also seems to have been thought to determine the very contours of the black face.

The recording of an authentic black voice—a voice of deliverance from the deafening discursive silence which an enlightened Europe cited to prove the absence of the African's humanity—was the millennial instrument of transformation through which the African would become the European, the slave become the ex-slave, brute animal become the human being. So central was this idea to the birth of the black literary tradition in the eighteenth century that five of the earliest slave narratives draw upon the figure of the voice in the text—of the talking book—as crucial "scenes of instruction" in the development of the slave on the road to freedom.

These five authors, linked by revision of a trope into the very first chain of black signifiers, implicitly signify upon another chain, the metaphorical great chain of being. Blacks were most commonly represented on the chain either as the lowest of the human races or as first cousin to the ape. Because writing, according to Hume, was the ultimate sign of difference between animal and human, these writers implicitly were signifyin(g) upon the figure of the chain itself. Simply by publishing autobiographies, they indicted the received order of Western culture, of which slavery was to them the most salient sign. The writings of James Gronniosaw, John Marrant, Olaudah Equiano, Ottabah Cugoano, and John Jea served to criticize the sign of the chain of being and the black person's figurative "place" on the chain. This chain of black signifiers, regardless of their intent or desire, made the first political gesture in the Anglo-African literary tradition "simply" by the act of writing. Their collective act gave birth to the black literary tradition and defined it as the "Other's chain," the chain of black being as black people themselves would have it. Making the book speak, then, constituted a motivated and political engagement with and condemnation of Europe's fundamental sign of domination, the commodity of writing, the text and technology of reason. We are justified, however, in wondering aloud if the sort of subjectivity which these writers seek through the act of writing can be realized through a process which is so very ironic from the outset: how can the black subject posit a full and sufficient self in a language in which blackness is a sign of absence? Can writing, with the very difference it makes and marks, mask the blackness of the black face that addresses the text of Western letters, in a voice that speaks English through an idiom which contains the irreducible element of cultural difference that will always separate the white voice from the black? Black people, we know, have not been liberated from racism by our writings. We accepted a false premise by assuming that racism would be destroyed once white racists became convinced that we were human, too. Writing stood as a complex "certificate of humanity," as Paulin Hountondji put it. Black writing, and especially the literature of the slave, served not to obliterate the difference of race; rather, the inscription of the black voice in Western literatures has preserved those very cultural differences to be repeated, imitated, and revised in a separate Western literary tradition, a tradition of black difference.

We black people tried to write ourselves out of slavery, a slavery even more profound than mere physical bondage. Accepting the challenge of the great white Western tradition, black writers wrote as if their lives depended upon it—and, in a curious sense, their lives did, the "life of the race" in Western discourse.❖

Donna Haraway (1944–) was trained in the history and philosophy of science. She holds a Ph.D. in biology from Yale. Haraway teaches in the History of Consciousness Program at the University of California at Santa Cruz. Her writings include *Primate Visions: Gender, Race, and Nature in the World of Modern Science* (1989), *Modest-Witness@Second-Millennium FemaleMale-Meets-Onco-Mouse* (1997), and *Simians, Cyborgs, and Women: The Reinvention of Nature* (1991), which is a collection of many of her most important essays in social theory and feminism—all (like "The Cyborg Manifesto") informed by her training in biology.

The Cyborg Manifesto and Fractured Identities

Donna Haraway (1985)

This chapter is an effort to build an ironic political myth faithful to feminism, socialism, and materialism. Perhaps more faithful as blasphemy is faithful, than as reverent worship and identification. Blasphemy has always seemed to require taking things very seriously. I know no better stance to adopt from within the secular-religious, evangelical traditions of United States politics, including the politics of socialist feminism. Blasphemy protects one from the moral majority within, while still insisting on the need for community. Blasphemy is not apostasy. Irony is about contradictions that do not resolve into larger wholes, even dialectically, about the tension of holding incompatible things together because both or all are necessary and true. Irony is about humour and serious play. It is also a rhetorical strategy and a political method, one I would like to see more honoured within socialist-feminism. At the centre of my ironic faith, my blasphemy, is the image of the cyborg.

A cyborg is a cybernetic organism, a hybrid of machine and organism, a creature of social reality as well as a creature of fiction. Social reality is lived social relations, our most important political construction, a world-changing fiction. The international women's movements have constructed 'women's experience', as well as uncovered or discovered this crucial collective object. This experience is a fiction and fact of the most crucial, political kind. Liberation rests on the construction of the consciousness, the imaginative apprehension, of oppression, and so of possibility. The cyborg is a matter of fiction and lived experience that changes what counts as women's experience in the late twentieth century. This is a struggle over life and death, but the boundary between science fiction and social reality is an optical illusion.

Contemporary science fiction is full of cyborgs—creatures simultaneously animal and machine, who populate worlds ambiguously natural and crafted. Modern medicine is also full of cyborgs, of couplings between organism and machine, each conceived as coded devices, in an intimacy and with a power that was not generated in the history of sexuality. Cyborg 'sex' restores some of the lovely replicative baroque of ferns and invertebrates (such nice organic prophylactics against heterosexism). Cyborg replication is uncoupled from organic reproduction. Modern production seems like a dream of cyborg colonization work, a dream that makes the nightmare of Taylorism seem idyllic. And modern war is a cyborg orgy, coded by C^3I, command-control-communication-intelligence, an $84 billion item in 1984's US defence budget. I am

Excerpt from *Simians, Cyborgs, and Women: The Reinvention of Nature* (New York: Routledge, 1991), pp. 149–151, 154–161.

making an argument for the cyborg as a fiction mapping our social and bodily reality and as an imaginative resource suggesting some very fruitful couplings. Michel Foucault's biopolitics is a flaccid premonition of cyborg politics, a very open field. . . .

The cyborg is resolutely committed to partiality, irony, intimacy, and perversity. It is oppositional, utopian, and completely without innocence. No longer structured by the polarity of public and private, the cyborg defines a technological polis based partly on a revolution of social relations in the *oikos,* the household. Nature and culture are reworked; the one can no longer be the resource for appropriation or incorporation by the other. The relationships for forming wholes from parts, including those of polarity and hierarchical domination, are at issue in the cyborg world. Unlike the hopes of Frankenstein's monster, the cyborg does not expect its father to save it through a restoration of the garden; that is, through the fabrication of a heterosexual male, through its completion in a finished whole, a city and cosmos. The cyborg does not dream of community on the model of the organic family, this time without the oedipal project. The cyborg would not recognize the Garden of Eden; it is not made of mud and cannot dream of returning to dust. Perhaps that is why I want to see if cyborgs can subvert the apocalypse of returning to nuclear dust in the manic compulsion to name the Enemy. Cyborgs are not reverent; they do not re-member the cosmos. They are wary of holism, but needy for connection—they seem to have a natural feel for united front politics, but without the vanguard party. The main trouble with cyborgs, of course, is that they are the illegitimate offspring of militarism and patriarchal capitalism, not to mention state socialism. But illegitimate offspring are often exceedingly unfaithful to their origins. Their fathers, after all, are inessential. . . .

So my cyborg myth is about transgressed boundaries, potent fusions, and dangerous possibilities which progressive people might explore as one part of needed political work. One of my premises is that most American socialists and feminists see deepened dualisms of mind and body, animal and machine, idealism and materialism in the social practices, symbolic formulations, and physical artefacts associated with 'high technology' and scientific culture. From *One-Dimensional Man* (Marcuse, 1964) to *The Death of Nature* (Merchant, 1980), the analytic resources developed by progressives have insisted on the necessary domination of technics and recalled us to an imagined organic body to integrate our resistance. Another of my premises is that the need for unity of people trying to resist world-wide intensification of domination has never been more acute. But a slightly perverse shift of perspective might better enable us to contest for meanings, as well as for other forms of power and pleasure in technologically mediated societies. . . .

Fractured Identities

It has become difficult to name one's feminism by a single adjective—or even to insist in every circumstance upon the noun. Consciousness of exclusion through naming is acute. Identities seem contradictory, partial, and strategic. With the hard-won recognition of their social and historical constitution, gender, race, and class cannot provide the basis for belief in 'essential' unity. There is nothing about being 'female' that naturally binds women. There is not even such a state as 'being' female, itself a highly complex category constructed in contested sexual scientific discourses and other social practices. Gender, race, or class consciousness is an achievement forced on us by the terrible historical experience of the contradictory social realities of patriarchy, colonialism, and capitalism. And who counts as 'us' in my own rhetoric? Which identities are available to ground such a potent political myth called 'us,' and what could motivate enlistment in this collectivity? Painful fragmentation among feminists (not to mention among women) along every possible fault line has made the concept of *woman* elusive, an excuse for the matrix of women's dominations of each other. For me—and for many who share a similar historical location in white, professional middle-class, female, radical, North American, mid-adult bodies—the sources of a crisis in political identity are legion. The recent history for much of the US left and US feminism has been a response to this kind of crisis by endless splitting and searches for a new essential unity. But there has also been a growing recognition of another response through coalition—affinity, not identity.

Chela Sandoval, from a consideration of specific historical moments in the formation of the new political voice called women of colour, has theorized a hopeful model of political identity called 'oppositional consciousness,' born of the skills for reading webs of power by those refused stable membership in the social categories of race, sex, or class. 'Women of color,' a name contested at its origins by those whom it would incorporate, as well as a historical consciousness marking systematic breakdown of all the signs of Man in 'Western' traditions, constructs a kind of postmodernist identity out of otherness, difference, and specificity. This postmodernist identity is fully political, whatever might be said about other possible postmodernisms. Sandoval's oppositional consciousness is about contradictory locations and heterochronic calendars, not about relativisms and pluralisms.

Sandoval emphasizes the lack of any essential criterion for identifying who is a woman of colour. She notes that the definition of the group has been by conscious appropriation of negation. For example, a Chicana or US black woman has not been able to speak as a woman or as a black person or as a Chicano. Thus, she was at the bottom of a cascade of negative identities, left out of even the privileged oppressed authorial categories called 'women and blacks,' who claimed to make the important revolutions. The category 'woman' negated all non-white women; 'black' negated all non-black people, as well as all black women. But there was also no 'she,' no singularity, but a sea of differences among US women who have affirmed their historical identity as US women of colour. This identity marks out a self-consciously constructed space that cannot affirm the capacity to act on the basis of natural identification, but only on the basis of conscious coalition, of affinity, of political kinship. Unlike the 'woman' of some streams of the white women's movement in the United States, there is no naturalization of the matrix, or at least this is what Sandoval argues is uniquely available through the power of oppositional consciousness.

Sandoval's argument has to be seen as one potent formulation for feminists out of the world-wide development of anti-colonialist discourse; that is to say, discourse dissolving the 'West' and its highest product—the one who is not animal, barbarian, or woman; man, that is, the author of a cosmos called history. As orientalism is deconstructed politically and semiotically, the identities of the occident destabilize, including those of feminists. Sandoval argues that 'women of colour' have a chance to build an effective unity that does not replicate the imperializing, totalizing revolutionary subjects of previous Marxisms and feminisms which had not faced the consequences of the disorderly polyphony emerging from decolonization. . . .

The theoretical and practical struggle against unity-through-domination or unity-through-incorporation ironically not only undermines the justifications for patriarchy, colonialism, humanism, positivism, essentialism, scientism, and other unlamented -isms, but *all* claims for an organic or natural standpoint. I think that radical and socialist/Marxist-feminisms have also undermined their/our own epistemological strategies and that this is a crucially valuable step in imagining possible unities. It remains to be seen whether all 'epistemologies' as Western political people have known them fail us in the task to build effective affinities.

It is important to note that the effort to construct revolutionary standpoints, epistemologies as achievements of people committed to changing the world, has been part of the process showing the limits of identification. The acid tools of postmodernist theory and the constructive tools of ontological discourse about revolutionary subjects might be seen as ironic allies in dissolving Western selves in the interests of survival. We are excruciatingly conscious of what it means to have a historically constituted body. But with the loss of innocence in our origin, there is no expulsion from the Garden either. Our politics lose the indulgence of guilt with the *naïveté* of innocence. But what would another political myth for socialist-feminism look like? What kind of politics could embrace partial, contradictory, permanently unclosed constructions of personal and collective selves and still be faithful, effective—and, ironically, socialist-feminist?

I do not know of any other time in history when there was greater need for political unity to confront effectively the dominations of 'race,' 'gender,' 'sexuality,' and 'class.' I also do not know of any other time when the kind of unity we might help build could have been possible. None of 'us' have any longer the symbolic or material capability of dictating the shape of reality to any of 'them.' Or at least 'we' cannot claim innocence from practising such dominations. White women, including socialist feminists, discovered (that is, were forced kicking and screaming to notice) the non-innocence of the category 'woman.' That consciousness changes the geography of all previous categories; it denatures them as heat denatures a fragile protein. Cyborg feminists have to argue that 'we' do not want any more natural matrix of unity and that no construction is whole. Innocence, and the corollary insistence on victimhood as the only ground for insight, has done enough damage. But the constructed revolutionary subject must give late-twentieth-century people pause as well. In the fraying of identities and in the reflexive strategies for constructing them, the possibility opens up for weaving something other than a shroud for the day after the apocalypse that so prophetically ends salvation history.

Both Marxist/socialist-feminisms and radical feminisms have simultaneously naturalized and denatured the category 'woman' and consciousness of the social lives of 'women.' . . . [N]either Marxist nor radical feminist points of view have tended to embrace the status of a partial explanation; both were regularly constituted as totalities. Western explanation has demanded as much; how else could the 'Western' author incorporate its others? Each tried to annex other forms of domination by expanding its basic categories through analogy, simple listing, or addition. Embarrassed silence about race among white radical and socialist feminists was one major, devastating political consequence. History and polyvocality disappear into political taxonomies that try to establish genealogies. There was no structural room for race (or for much else) in theory claiming to reveal the construction of the category woman and social group women as a unified or totalizable whole. The structure of my caricature looks like this:

> socialist feminism—structure of class//wage labour//alienation
> labour, by analogy reproduction, by extension sex, by addition race
> radical feminism—structure of gender//sexual appropriation//objectification
> sex, by analogy labour, by extension reproduction, by addition race

In another context, the French theorist, Julia Kristeva, claimed women appeared as a historical group after the Second World War, along with groups like youth. Her dates are doubtful; but we are now accustomed to remembering that as objects of knowledge and as historical actors, 'race' did not always exist, 'class' has a historical genesis, and 'homosexuals' are quite junior. It is no accident that the symbolic system of the family of man—and so the essence of woman—breaks up at the same moment that networks of connection among people on the planet are unprecedentedly multiple, pregnant, and complex. 'Advanced capitalism' is inadequate to convey the structure of this historical moment. In the 'Western' sense, the end of man is at stake. It is no accident that woman disintegrates into women in our time. Perhaps socialist feminists were not substantially guilty of producing essentialist theory that suppressed women's particularity and contradictory interests. I think we have been, at least through unreflective participation in the logics, languages, and practices of white humanism and through searching for a single ground of domination to secure our revolutionary voice. Now we have less excuse. But in the consciousness of our failures, we risk lapsing into boundless difference and giving up on the confusing task of making partial, real connection. Some differences are playful; some are poles of world historical systems of domination. 'Epistemology' is about knowing the difference.❖

Trinh T. Minh-ha (1952–) is a filmmaker and composer, as well as a social theorist and writer. She teaches at San Francisco State University. Her films include *Reassemblage* (1982), *Naked Spaces—Living Is Round* (1985), and *Surname Viet, Given Name Nam* (1989). The selection is from her best-known written work, *Woman, Native, Other: Writing Postcoloniality and Feminism* (1989). Along with Cornel West and others, she is also editor of *Out There*.

Infinite Layers/Third World?
Trinh T. Minh-ha (1989)

Infinite Layers: I am not i can be you and me

A critical difference from myself means that I am not i, am within and without i. I/i can be I or i, you and me both involved. We (with capital W) sometimes include(s), other times exclude(s) me. You and I are close, we intertwine; you may stand on the other side of the hill once in a while, but you may also be me, while remaining what you are and what i am not. The differences made *between* entities comprehended as absolute presences—hence the notions of *pure origin* and *true self*—are an outgrowth of a dualistic system of thought peculiar to the Occident (the "onto-theology" which characterizes Western metaphysics). They should be distinguished from the differences grasped *both between* and *within* entities, each of these being understood as multiple presence. Not One, not two either. "I" is, therefore, not a unified subject, a fixed identity, or that solid mass covered with layers of superficialities one has gradually to peel off before one can see its true face. "I" is, itself, *infinite layers*. Its complex-

---

Excerpt from *Woman, Native, Other: Writing, Postcoloniality, and Feminism* (Bloomington: Indiana University Press, 1989), pp. 90–100.

ity can hardly be conveyed through such typographic conventions as I, i, or I/i. Thus, I/i am compelled by the will to say/unsay, to resort to the entire gamut of personal pronouns to stay near this fleeing *and* static essence of Not-I. Whether I accept it or not, the natures of *I, i, you, s/he, We, we, they,* and *wo/man* constantly overlap. They all display a necessary ambivalence, for the line dividing *I* and *Not-I, us* and *them,* or *him* and *her* is not (cannot) always (be) as clear as we would like it to be. Despite our desperate, eternal attempt to separate, contain, and mend, categories always leak. Of all the layers that form the open (never finite) totality of "I," which is to be filtered out as superfluous, fake, corrupt, and which is to be called pure, true, real, genuine, original, authentic? Which, indeed, since all interchange, revolving in an endless process? (According to the context in which they operate, the superfluous can become the real; the authentic can prove fake; and so on.) *Authenticity* as a need to rely on an "undisputed origin," is prey to an obsessive *fear:* that of *losing a connection.* Everything must hold together. In my craving for a logic of being, I cannot help but loathe the threats of interruptions, disseminations, and suspensions. To begin, to develop to a climax, then, to end. To fill, to join, to unify. The order and the links create an illusion of continuity, which I highly prize for fear of nonsense and emptiness. Thus, a clear origin will give me a connection back through time, and I shall, by all means, search for that genuine layer of myself to which I can always cling. To abolish it in such a perspective is to remove the basis, the prop, the overture, or the finale—giving thereby free rein to indeterminancy: the result, forefeared, is either an anarchic succession of climaxes or a de(inex)pressive, uninterrupted monotony—and to enter into the limitless process of interactions and changes that nothing will stop, not even death. In other words, things may be said to be what they are, not exclusively in relation to what was and what will be (they should not solely be seen as clusters chained together by the temporal sequence of cause and effect), but also in relation to each other's immediate presences and to themselves as non/presences. The *real,* nothing else than a *code of representation,* does not (cannot) coincide with the lived or the performed. This is what Vine Deloria, Jr. accounts for when he exclaims: "Not even Indians can relate themselves to this type of creature who, to anthropologists, is the 'real' Indian." A realistic identification with such a code has, therefore, no reality whatsoever: it is like "stopping the ear while trying to steal the bell" (Chinese saying). . . .

The Female Identity Enclosure

Difference as uniqueness or special identity is both limiting and deceiving. If identity refers to the whole pattern of sameness within a human life, the style of a continuing me that permeates all the changes undergone, then difference remains within the boundary of that which distinguishes one identity from another. This means that *at heart,* X must be X, Y must be Y, and Y *cannot* be Y. Those who run around yelling that X is not X and X *can* be Y usually land in a hospital, a "rehabilitation" center, a concentration camp, or a res-er-va-tion. All deviations from the dominant stream of thought, that is to say, the belief in a permanent essence of wo/man and in an invariant but fragile identity, whose "loss" is considered to be a "specifically human danger," can easily fit into the categories of the "mentally ill" or the "mentally underdeveloped." It is probably difficult for a "normal," probing mind to recognize that to seek is to lose, for seeking presupposes a separation between the seeker and the sought, the continuing me and the changes it undergoes. What if the popularized story of the identity crisis proves to be only a story and nothing else? Can identity, indeed, be viewed other than as a by-product of a "manhandling" of life, one that, in fact, refers no more to a consistent "pattern of sameness" than to an inconsequential process of otherness? How am I to lose, maintain, or gain an (fe/male) identity when it is impossible to me to take up a position outside this identity from which I presumably reach in and feel for it? Perhaps a way to portray it is to borrow these verses from the *Cheng-tao-ke:*

> You cannot take hold of it,
> But you cannot lose it.
> In not being able to get it, you get it.
> When you are silent, it speaks;
> When you speak, it is silent.

Difference in such an insituable context is *that which undermines the very idea of identity,* deferring to infinity the layers whose totality forms "I." It subverts the foundations of any affirmation or vindication of value and cannot, thereby, ever bear in itself an absolute value. The difference (within) between *difference* itself and *identity* has so often been ignored and the use of the two terms so readily confused, that claiming a female/ethnic identity/difference is commonly tantamount to reviving a kind of naive "male-tinted" romanticism. If feminism is set forth as a demystifying force, then it will have to question thoroughly the belief in its own identity. To suppose, like Judith Kegan Gardiner, that "the concept of female identity provides a key to understanding the *special qualities* of contemporary writing by women . . . , the diverse ways in which writing by women *differs* from writing by men," and to "propose the preliminary metaphor 'female identity is a process' for the most fundamental of these differences" does not, obviously, allow us to radically depart from the master's logic. Such a formulation endeavors to "reach a theory of female identity . . . that *varies from the male model,*" and to demonstrate that:

> primary identity for women is more flexible and relational *than for men*. Female gender identity is *more* stable *than male gender identity*. Female infantile identifications are *less* predictable *than male ones* . . . the *female counterpart* of the male identity crisis may occur more diffusely, at a different stage, or not at all. (my italics)

It seems quite content with reforms that, at best, contribute to the improvement and/or enlargement of the identity enclosure, but do not, in any way, attempt to remove its fence. The constant need to refer to the "male model" for comparisons unavoidably maintains the subject under tutelage. For the point is not to carve one's space in "identity theories that ignore women" and describe some of the faces of female identity, saying, like Gardiner: "I picture female identity as typically less fixed, less unitary, and more flexible than male individuality, both in its primary core and in the entire maturational complex developed from this core," but patiently to dismantle the very notion of core (be it static or not) and identity.

Woman can never be defined. Bat, dog, chick, mutton, tart. Queen, madam, lady of pleasure. MISTRESS. *Belle-de-nuit,* woman of the streets, fruitwoman, fallen woman. Cow, vixen, bitch. Call girl, joy girl, working girl. Lady and whore are both bred to please. The old Woman image-repertoire says She is a Womb, a mere baby's pouch, or "nothing but sexuality." She is a passive substance, a parasite, an enigma whose mystery proves to be a snare and a delusion. She wallows in night, disorder, and immanence and is at the same time the "disturbing factor (between men)" and the key to the beyond. The further the repertoire unfolds its images, the more entangled it gets in its attempts at capturing Her. "Truth, Beauty, Poetry—she is All: once more all under the form of the Other. All except herself," Simone De Beauvoir wrote. Yet, even with or because of Her capacity to embody All, Woman is the lesser man, and among male athletes, to be called a woman is still resented as the worst of insults. "Wo-" appended to "man" in sexist contexts is not unlike "Third World," "Third," "minority," or "*color*" affixed to *woman* in pseudo-feminist contexts. Yearning for universality, the generic "woman," like its counterpart, the generic "man," tends to efface difference within itself. Not every female is "a real woman," one knows this through hearsay . . . Just as "man" provides an example of how the part played by women has been ignored, undervalued, distorted, or omitted through the use of terminology presumed to be generic, "woman" more often than not reflects the subtle power of linguistic exclusion, for its set of referents rarely includes those relevant to Third World "female persons." "All the Women Are White, All the Blacks are Men, But Some of Us Are Brave" is the title given to an anthology edited by Gloria T. Hull, Patricia Bell Scott, and Barbara Smith. It is, indeed, somehow devious to think that WOMAN also encompasses the Chinese with bound feet, the genitally mutilated Africans, and the one thousand Indians who committed *suttee* for one royal male. Sister Cinderella's foot is also enviably tiny but never crooked! And, European witches were also burnt to purify the body of Christ, but they do not pretend to "self-immolation." "Third World," therefore, belongs to a category apart, a "special" one that is meant to be both complimentary and complementary, for First and Second went out of fashion, leaving a serious Lack behind to be filled.

Third World?

To survive, "Third World" must necessarily have negative *and* positive connotations: negative when viewed in a vertical ranking system—"underdeveloped" compared to over-industrialized, "underprivileged" within the already Second sex—and positive when understood sociopolitically as a subversive, "non-aligned" force. Whether "Third World" sounds negative or positive also depends on *who* uses it. Coming from you Westerners, the word can hardly mean the same as when it comes from Us members of the Third World. Quite predictably, you/we who condemn it most are both we who buy in and they who deny any participation in the bourgeois mentality of the West. For it was in the context of such mentality that "Third World" stood out as a new semantic finding to designate what was known as "the savages" before the Independences. Today, hegemony is much more subtle, much more pernicious than the form of blatant racism once exercised by the colonial West. I/i always find myself asking, in this one-dimension society, where I/i should draw the line between tracking down the oppressive mechanisms of the system and aiding their spread. "Third World" commonly refers to those states in Africa, Asia and Latin America which called themselves "non-aligned," that is to say, affiliated with neither the Western (capitalist) nor the Eastern (communist) power blocs. Thus, if "Third World" is often rejected for its judged-to-be-derogative connotations, it is not so much because of the hierarchical, first-second-third order implied, as some invariably repeat, but because of the growing threat "Third World" consistently presents to the Western

bloc the last few decades. The emergence of repressed voices into the worldwide political arena has already prompted her (Julia Kristeva) to ask: "How will the West
greet the awakening of the 'third world' as the Chinese call it? Can we [Westerners]
participate, actively and lucidly, in this awakening when the center of the planet is in
the process of moving toward the East?" Exploited, looked down upon, and lumped
together in a convenient term that denies their individualities, a group of "poor"
(nations), having once sided with neither of the dominating forces, has slowly
learned to turn this denial to the best account. "The Third World to Third World
peoples" thus becomes an empowering tool, and one which politically includes all
non-whites in their solidarist struggle against all forms of Western dominance. And
since "Third World" now refers to more than the geographically and economically
determined nations of the "South"(versus "North"), since the term comprises such
"developed" countries as Japan and those which have opted for socialist reconstruction of their system (China, Cuba, Ethiopia, Angola, Mozambique) as well as those
which have favored a capitalist mode of development (Nigeria, India, Brazil), there
no longer exists such a thing as a unified unaligned Third World bloc. Moreover,
Third World has moved West (or North, depending on where the dividing line falls)
and has expanded so as to include even the remote parts of the First World. What is
at stake is not only the hegemony of Western cultures, but also their identities as
unified cultures. Third World dwells on diversity; so does First World. This is our
strength and our misery. The West is painfully made to realize the existence of a
Third World in the First World, and vice versa. The Master is bound to recognize
that His Culture is not as homogeneous, as monolithic as He believed it to be. He
discovers, with much reluctance, He is just an other among others.

Thus, whenever it is a question of "Third World women" or, more disquietingly, of
"Third World Women in the U.S.," the reaction provoked among many whites almost
never fails to be that of annoyance, irritation, or vexation. "Why Third World in the
U.S.?" they say angrily; "You mean those who still have relatives in South East Asia?"
"Third World! I don't understand how one can use such a term, it doesn't mean anything." Or even better, "Why use such a term to defeat yourself?" Alternatives like
"Western" and "non-Western" or "Euro-American" and "non-Euro-American" may
sound a bit less charged, but they are certainly neither neutral nor satisfactory, for they
still take the dominant group as point of reference, and they reflect well the West's ideology of dominance (it is as if we were to use the term "non-Afro-Asian," for example,
to designate all white peoples). More recently, we have been hearing of the Fourth
World which, we are told, "is a world populated by indigenous people who still continue to bear a spiritual relationship to their traditional lands." The colonialist creed
"Divide and Conquer" is here again, alive and well. Often ill at ease with the outspoken
educated natives who represent the Third World in debates and paternalistically scornful of those who remain reserved, the dominant thus decides to weaken this term of
solidarity, both by invalidating it as empowering tool and by inciting divisiveness
within the Third World—a Third World within the Third World. Aggressive Third
World (educated "savages") with its awareness and resistance to domination must
therefore be classified apart from gentle Fourth World (uneducated "savages"). Every
unaligned voice should necessarily/consequently be either a personal or a minority
voice. The (impersonal) majority, as logic dictates, has to be the (aligned) dominant.

It is, apparently, inconvenient, if not downright mind stretching [notes Alice Walker],
for white women scholars to think of black women as women, perhaps because

"woman" (like "man" among white males) is a name they are claiming for themselves, and themselves alone. Racism decrees that if they are now women (years ago they were ladies, but fashions change) then black women must, perforce, be something else. (While they were "ladies" black women could be "women" and so on.)

Another revealing example of this separatist majority mentality is the story Walker relates of an exhibit of women painters at the Brooklyn Museum: when asked "Are there no black women painters represented here?" (none of them is, apparently), a white woman feminist simply replies "It's a *women's* exhibit!" Different historical contexts, different semantic contents . . . ❖

Gayatri Chakravorty Spivak (1942–) was born in Calcutta, India. After undergraduate studies in English at the University of Calcutta, she did graduate work at Cornell (Ph.D., 1967) in comparative literature. She has taught at many universities, including Iowa, Texas, Wesleyan, Emory, and Pittsburgh. Spivak first came to wide attention with her translation of and remarkable introduction to Derrida's *Of Grammatology* (1976). Her first book was *Myself Must I Remake: Life and Poetry of W. B. Yeats* (1974). She has lectured and written on numerous subjects in and around issues in feminism, literary theory, Marxism, deconstructionism, and subaltern studies. Among her many books and collected essays is *In Other Worlds: Essays in Cultural Politics* (1987).

Can the Subaltern Speak?

Gayatri Chakravorty Spivak (1988)

The first part of my proposition—that the phased development of the subaltern is complicated by the imperialist project—is confronted by a collective of intellectuals who may be called the "Subaltern Studies" group. They *must* ask, Can the subaltern speak? Here we are within Foucault's own discipline of history and with people who acknowledge his influence. Their project is to rethink Indian colonial historiography from the perspective of the discontinuous chain of peasant insurgencies during the colonial occupation. This is indeed the problem of "the permission to narrate" discussed by Said. As Ranajit Guha argues,

> The historiography of Indian nationalism has for a long time been dominated by elitism—colonialist elitism and bourgeois-nationalist elitism . . . shar[ing] the prejudice that the making of the Indian nation and the development of the consciousness—nationalism—which confirmed this process were exclusively or predominantly elite achievements. In the colonialist and neo-colonialist historiographies these achievements are credited to British colonial rulers, administrators, policies, institutions, and culture; in the nationalist and neo-nationalist writings—to Indian elite personalities, institutions, activities and ideas.

Excerpt from Cary Nelson and Lawrence Grossberg, eds., *Marxism and the Interpretation of Culture* (Urbana: University of Illinois Press, 1988), pp. 283–284, 294–298.

Certain varieties of the Indian elite are at best native informants for first-world intellectuals interested in the voice of the Other. But one must nevertheless insist that the colonized subaltern *subject* is irretrievably heterogeneous. . . .

Can the subaltern speak? What must the elite do to watch out for the continuing construction of the subaltern? The question of "woman" seems most problematic in this context. Clearly, if you are poor, black, and female you get it in three ways. If, however, this formulation is moved from the first-world context into the postcolonial (which is not identical with the third-world) context, the description "black" or "of color" loses persuasive significance. The necessary stratification of colonial subject-constitution in the first phase of capitalist imperialism makes "color" useless as an emancipatory signifier. Confronted by the ferocious standardizing benevolence of most U.S. and Western European human-scientific radicalism (recognition by assimilation), the progressive though heterogeneous withdrawal of consumerism in the comprador periphery, and the exclusion of the margins of even the center-periphery articulation (the "true and differential subaltern"), the analogue of class-consciousness rather than race-consciousness in this area seems historically, disciplinarily, and practically forbidden by Right and Left alike. It is not just a question of a *double* displacement, as it is not simply the problem of finding a psychoanalytic allegory that can accommodate the third-world woman with the first.

The cautions I have just expressed are valid only if we are speaking of the subaltern woman's consciousness—or, more acceptably, subject. Reporting on, or better still, participating in, antisexist work among women of color or women in class oppression in the First World or the Third World is undeniably on the agenda. We should also welcome all the information retrieval in these silenced areas that is taking place in anthropology, political science, history, and sociology. Yet the assumption and construction of a consciousness or subject sustains such work and will, in the long run, cohere with the work of imperialist subject-constitution, mingling epistemic violence with the advancement of learning and civilizations. And the subaltern woman will be as mute as ever.

In so fraught a field, it is not easy to ask the question of the consciousness of the subaltern woman; it is thus all the more necessary to remind pragmatic radicals that such a question is not an idealist red herring. Though all feminist or antisexist projects cannot be reduced to this one, to ignore it is an unacknowledged political gesture that has a long history and collaborates with a masculine radicalism that renders the place of the investigator transparent. In seeking to learn to speak to (rather than listen to or speak for) the historically muted subject to the subaltern woman, the postcolonial intellectual *systematically* "unlearns" female privilege. This systematic unlearning involves learning to critique postcolonial discourse with the best tools it can provide and not simply substituting the lost figure of the colonized. Thus, to question the unquestioned muting of the subaltern woman even within the anti-imperialist project of subaltern studies is not, as Jonathan Culler suggests, to "produce difference by differing" or to "appeal . . . to a sexual identity defined as essential and privilege experiences associated with that identity."

Culler's version of the feminist project is possible within what Elizabeth Fox-Genovese has called "the contribution of the bourgeois-democratic revolutions to the social and political individualism of women." Many of us were obliged to understand the feminist project as Culler now describes it when we were still agitating as U.S. academics. It was certainly a necessary stage in my own education in "unlearning" and has consolidated the belief that the mainstream project of Western femi-

nism both continues and displaces the battle over the right to individualism between women and men in situations of upward class mobility. One suspects that the
debate between U.S. feminism and European "theory" (as theory is generally represented by women from the United States or Britain) occupies a significant corner of
that very terrain. I am generally sympathetic with the call to make U.S. feminism
more "theoretical." It seems, however, that the problem of the muted subject of the
subaltern woman, though not solved by an "essentialist" search for lost origins, cannot be served by the call for more theory in Anglo-America either.

That call is often given in the name of a critique of "positivism," which is seen
here as identical with "essentialism." Yet Hegel, the modern inaugurator of "the work
of the negative," was not a stranger to the notion of essences. For Marx, the curious
persistence of essentialism within the dialectic was a profound and productive problem. Thus, the stringent binary opposition between positivism/essentialism (read,
U.S.) and "theory" (read, French or Franco-German via Anglo-American) may be
spurious. Apart from repressing the ambiguous complicity between essentialism
and critiques of positivism (acknowledged by Derrida in "Of Grammatology As a
Positive Science"), it also errs by implying that positivism is not a theory. This move
allows the emergence of a proper name, a positive essence, Theory. Once again, the
position of the investigator remains unquestioned. And, if this territorial debate
turns toward the Third World, no change in the question of method is to be dis-
cerned. This debate cannot take into account that, in the case of the woman as subaltern, no ingredients for the constitution of the itinerary of the trace of a sexed subject can be gathered to locate the possibility of dissemination.

Yet I remain generally sympathetic in aligning feminism with the critique of positivism and the defetishization of the concrete. I am also far from averse to learning
from the work of Western theorists, though I have learned to insist on marking their
positionality as investigating subjects. Given these conditions, and as a literary critic,
I tactically confronted the immense problem of the consciousness of the woman as
subaltern. I reinvented the problem in a sentence and transformed it into the object
of a simple semiosis. What does this sentence mean? The analogy here is between the
ideological victimization of a Freud and the positionality of the postcolonial intellectual as investigating subject.

As Sarah Kofman has shown, the deep ambiguity of Freud's use of women as a
scapegoat is a reaction-formation to an initial and continuing desire to give the hysteric a voice, to transform her into the *subject* of hysteria. The masculine-imperialist
ideological formation that shaped that desire into "the daughter's seduction" is part of
the same formation that constructs the monolithic "third-world woman." As a postcolonial intellectual, I am influenced by that formation as well. Part of our "unlearning" project is to articulate that ideological formation—by *measuring* silences, if necessary—into the *object* of investigation. Thus, when confronted with the questions, Can
the subaltern speak? and Can the subaltern (as woman) speak?, our efforts to give the
subaltern a voice in history will be doubly open to the dangers run by Freud's discourse. As a product of these considerations, I have put together the sentence "White
men are saving brown women from brown men" in a spirit not unlike the one to be
encountered in Freud's investigations of the sentence "A child is being beaten."

The use of Freud here does not imply an isomorphic analogy between subject-
formation and the behavior of social collectives, a frequent practice, often accompanied by a reference to Reich, in the conversation between Deleuze and Foucault. So I
am not suggesting that "White men are saving brown women from brown men" is a

sentence indicating a *collective* fantasy symptomatic of a *collective* itinerary of sado-masochistic repression in a *collective* imperialist enterprise. There is a satisfying symmetry in such an allegory, but I would rather invite the reader to consider it a problem in "wild psychoanalysis" than a clinching solution. Just as Freud's insistence on making the woman the scapegoat in "A child is being beaten" and elsewhere discloses his political interests, however imperfectly, so my insistence on imperialist subject-production as the occasion for this sentence discloses my politics.

Further, I am attempting to borrow the general methodological aura of Freud's strategy toward the sentence he constructed *as a sentence* out of the many similar substantive accounts his patients gave him. This does not mean I will offer a case of transference-in-analysis as an isomorphic model for the transaction between reader and text (my sentence). The analogy between transference and literary criticism or historiography is no more than a productive catachresis. To say that the subject is a text does not authorize the converse pronouncement: the verbal text is a subject.

I am fascinated, rather, by how Freud predicates a *history* of repression that produces the final sentence. It is a history with a double origin, one hidden in the amnesia of the infant, the other lodged in our archaic past, assuming by implication a pre-originary space where human and animal were not yet differentiated. We are driven to impose a homologue of this Freudian strategy on the Marxist narrative to explain the ideological dissimulation of imperialist political economy and outline a history of repression that produces a sentence like the one I have sketched. This history also has a double origin, one hidden in the maneuverings behind the British abolition of widow sacrifice in 1829, the other lodged in the classical and Vedic past of Hindu India, the *Rg-Veda* and the *Dharmasastra*. No doubt there is also an undifferentiated preoriginary space that supports this history.

The sentence I have constructed is one among many displacements describing the relationship between brown and white men (sometimes brown and white women worked in). It takes its place among some sentences of "hyperbolic admiration" or of pious guilt that Derrida speaks of in connection with the "hieroglyphist prejudice." The relationship between the imperialist subject and the subject of imperialism is at least ambiguous.

The Hindu widow ascends the pyre of the dead husband and immolates herself upon it. This is widow sacrifice. (The conventional transcription of the Sanskrit word for the widow would be *sati*. The early colonial British transcribed it *suttee*.) The rite was not practiced universally and was not caste- or class-fixed. The abolition of this rite by the British has been generally understood as a case of "White men saving brown women from brown men." White women—from the nineteenth-century British Missionary Registers to Mary Daly—have not produced an alternative understanding. Against this is the Indian nativist argument, a parody of the nostalgia for lost origins: "The women actually wanted to die."

The two sentences go a long way to legitimize each other. One never encounters the testimony of the women's voice-consciousness. Such a testimony would not be ideology-transcendent or "fully" subjective, of course, but it would have constituted the ingredients for producing a countersentence. As one goes down the grotesquely mistranscribed names of these women, the sacrificed widows, in the police reports included in the records of the East India Company, one cannot put together a "voice." The most one can sense is the immense heterogeneity breaking through even such a skeletal and ignorant account (castes, for example, are regularly described as tribes). Faced with the dialectically interlocking sentences that are constructible as "White men are saving brown women from brown men" and "The women wanted to die," the postcolonial woman intellectual asks the question of simple semiosis—What does this mean?—and begins to plot a history.

To mark the moment when not only a civil but a good society is born out of domestic confusion, singular events that break the letter of the law to instill its spirit are often invoked. The protection of women by men often provides such an event. If we remember that the British boasted of their absolute equity toward and noninterference with native custom/law, an invocation of this sanctioned transgression of the letter for the sake of the spirit may be read in J. M. Derrett's remark: "The very first legislation upon Hindu Law was carried through without the assent of a single Hindu." The legislation is not named here. The next sentence, where the measure is named, is equally interesting if one considers the implications of the survival of a colonially established "good" society after decolonization: "The recurrence of *sati* in independent India is probably an obscurantist revival which cannot long survive even in a very backward part of the country."

Whether this observation is correct or not, what interests me is that the protection of woman (today the "third-world woman") becomes a signifier for the establishment of a *good* society which must, at such inaugurative moments, transgress mere legality, or equity of legal policy. In this particular case, the process also allowed the redefinition as a crime of what had been tolerated, known, or adulated as ritual. In other words, this one item in Hindu law jumped the frontier between the private and the public domain.

Although Foucault's *historical narrative,* focusing solely on Western Europe, sees merely a tolerance for the criminal antedating the development of criminology in the late eighteenth century, his *theoretical description* of the "episteme" is pertinent here: "The *episteme* is the 'apparatus' which makes possible the separation not of the true from the false, but of what may not be characterized as scientific"—ritual as opposed to crime, the one fixed by superstition, the other by legal science.

The leap of *suttee* from private to public has a clear and complex relationship with the changeover from a mercantile and commercial to a territorial and administrative British presence; it can be followed in correspondence among the police stations, the lower and higher courts, the courts of directors, the prince regent's court, and the like. (It is interesting to note that, from the point of view of the native "colonial subject," also emergent from the feudalism-capitalism transition, *sati* is a signifier with the reverse social charge: "Groups rendered psychologically marginal by their exposure to Western impact . . . had come under pressure to demonstrate, to others as well as to themselves, their ritual purity and allegiance to traditional high culture. To many of them *sati* became an important proof of their conformity to older norms at a time when these norms had become shaky within."❖

Patricia Hill Collins (1948–) teaches African-American studies at the University of Cincinnati, having held a similar position at Tufts University. Her book *Black Feminist Thought* (1990) has been widely praised for combining a deep personal and historical understanding of African-American women with pathbreaking theoretical analysis. In addition to representing social theory in the tradition of Black feminism, the book is capable of transforming social theoretical analysis generally. The selection, for example, reworks the fractured identity perspective in terms that are more explicitly sociological, thus contributing to feminist theory as well as to sociological theory's concerns with the individual's relation to macrostructures. *Black Feminist Thought* is the first book to integrate the literature of and by African-American women. (The selection necessarily omits Collins's numerous references to those works.)

Black Feminist Thought in the Matrix of Domination
Patricia Hill Collins (1990)

Black feminist thought demonstrates Black women's emerging power as agents of knowledge. By portraying African-American women as self-defined, self-reliant individuals confronting race, gender, and class oppression, Afrocentric feminist thought speaks to the importance that oppression, Afrocentric feminist thought speaks to the importance that knowledge plays in empowering oppressed people. One distinguishing feature of Black feminist thought is its insistence that both the changed consciousness of individuals and the social transformation of political and economic institutions constitute essential ingredients for social change. New knowledge is important for both dimensions of change.

Knowledge is a vitally important part of the social relations of domination and resistance. By objectifying African-American women and recasting our experiences to serve the interests of elite white men, much of the Eurocentric masculinist worldview fosters Black women's subordination. But placing Black women's experiences at the center of analysis offers fresh insights on the prevailing concepts, paradigms, and epistemologies of this worldview and on its feminist and Afrocentric critiques. Viewing the world through a both/and conceptual lens of the simultaneity of race, class, and gender oppression and of the need for a humanist vision of community creates new possibilities for an empowering Afrocentric feminist knowledge. Many Black feminist intellectuals have long thought about the world in this way because this is the way we experience the world.

Afrocentric feminist thought offers two significant contributions toward furthering our understanding of the important connections among knowledge, consciousness, and the politics of empowerment. First, Black feminist thought fosters a fundamental paradigmatic shift in how we think about oppression. By embracing a paradigm of race, class, and gender as interlocking systems of oppression, Black feminist thought reconceptualizes the social relations of domination and resistance. Second, Black feminist thought addresses ongoing epistemological debates in feminist theory and in the sociology of knowledge concerning ways of assessing "truth." Offering subordinate groups new knowledge about their own experiences can be empowering. But revealing new ways of knowing that allow subordinate groups to define their own reality has far greater implications.

Reconceptualizing Race, Class, and Gender as Interlocking Systems of Oppression

"What *I* really feel is radical is trying to make coalitions with people who are different from you," maintains Barbara Smith. "I feel it is radical to be dealing with race and

---

sex and class and sexual identity all at one time. I think *that* is really radical because it has never been done before." Black feminist thought fosters a fundamental paradigmatic shift that rejects additive approaches to oppression. Instead of starting with gender and then adding in other variables such as age, sexual orientation, race, social class, and religion, Black feminist thought sees these distinctive systems of oppression as being part of one overarching structure of domination. Viewing relations of domination for Black women for any given sociohistorical context as being structured via a system of interlocking race, class, and gender oppression expands the focus of analysis from merely describing the similarities and differences distinguishing these systems of oppression and focuses greater attention on how they interconnect. Assuming that each system needs the others in order to function creates a distinct theoretical stance that stimulates the rethinking of basic social science concepts.

Afrocentric feminist notions of family reflect this reconceptualization process. Black women's experiences as bloodmothers, othermothers, and community othermothers reveal that the mythical norm of a heterosexual, married couple, nuclear family with a nonworking spouse and a husband earning a "family wage" is far from being natural, universal, and preferred but instead is deeply embedded in specific race and class formations. Placing African-American women in the center of analysis not only reveals much-needed information about Black women's experiences but also questions Eurocentric masculinist perspectives on family.

Black women's experiences and the Afrocentric feminist thought rearticulating them also challenge prevailing definitions of community. Black women's actions in the struggle for group survival suggest a vision of community that stands in opposition to that extant in the dominant culture. The definition of community implicit in the market model sees community as arbitrary and fragile, structured fundamentally by competition and domination. In contrast, Afrocentric models of community stress connections, caring, and personal accountability. As cultural workers, African-American women have rejected the generalized ideology of domination advanced by the dominant group in order to conserve Afrocentric conceptualizations of community. Denied access to the podium, Black women have been unable to spend time theorizing about alternative conceptualizations of community. Instead, through daily actions African-American women have *created* alternative communities that empower.

This vision of community sustained by African-American women in conjunction with African-American men addresses the larger issue of reconceptualizing power. The type of Black women's power discussed here does resemble feminist theories of power which emphasize energy and community. However, in contrast to this body of literature whose celebration of women's power is often accompanied by a lack of attention to the importance of power as domination, Black women's experiences as mothers, community othermothers, educators, church leaders, labor union centerwomen, and community leaders seem to suggest that power as energy can be fostered by creative acts of resistance.

The spheres of influence created and sustained by African-American women are not meant solely to provide a respite from oppressive situations or a retreat from their effects. Rather, these Black female spheres of influence constitute potential sanctuaries where individual Black women and men are nurtured in order to confront oppressive social institutions. Power from this perspective is a creative power used for the good of the community, whether that community is conceptualized as one's family, church community, or the next generation of the community's children. By making the community stronger, African-American women become empowered, and that same community can serve as a source of support when Black women encounter race, gender, and class oppression. . . .

Approaches that assume that race, gender, and class are interconnected have immediate practical applications. For example, African-American women continue to be inadequately protected by Title VII of the Civil Rights Act of 1964. The primary purpose of the statute is to eradicate all aspects of discrimination. But judicial treatment of Black women's employment discrimination claims has encouraged Black women to identify race *or* sex as the so-called primary discrimination. "To resolve the inequities that confront Black women," counsels Scarborough, "the courts must first correctly conceptualize them as 'Black women,' a distinct class protected by Title VII." Such a shift, from protected categories to protected classes of people whose Title VII claims might be based on more than two discriminations, would work to alter the entire basis of current antidiscrimination efforts.

Reconceptualizing phenomena such as the rapid growth of female-headed households in African-American communities would also benefit from a race-, class-, and gender-inclusive analysis. Case studies of Black women heading households must be attentive to racially segmented local labor markets and community patterns, to changes in local political economies specific to a given city or region, and to established racial and gender ideology for a given location. This approach would go far to deconstruct Eurocentric, masculinist analyses that implicitly rely on controlling images of the matriarch or the welfare mother as guiding conceptual premises. . . . Black feminist thought that rearticulates experiences such as these fosters an enhanced theoretical understanding of how race, gender, and class oppression are part of a single, historically created system.

The Matrix of Domination

Additive models of oppression are firmly rooted in the either/or dichotomous thinking of Eurocentric, masculinist thought. One must be either Black or white in such thought systems—persons of ambiguous racial and ethnic identity constantly battle with questions such as "what are you, anyway?" This emphasis on quantification and categorization occurs in conjunction with the belief that either/or categories must be ranked. The search for certainty of this sort requires that one side of a dichotomy be privileged while its other is denigrated. Privilege becomes defined in relation to its other.

Replacing additive models of oppression with interlocking ones creates possibilities for new paradigms. The significance of seeing race, class, and gender as interlocking systems of oppression is that such an approach fosters a paradigmatic shift of thinking inclusively about other oppressions, such as age, sexual orientation, religion, and ethnicity. Race, class, and gender represent the three systems of oppression that most heavily affect African-American women. But these systems and the economic, political, and ideological conditions that support them may not be the most fundamental oppressions, and they certainly affect many more groups than Black women. Other people of color, Jews, the poor, white women, and gays and lesbians have all had similar ideological justifications offered for their subordination. All categories of humans labeled Others have been equated to one another, to animals, and to nature.

Placing African-American women and other excluded groups in the center of analysis opens up possibilities for a both/and conceptual stance, one in which all groups possess varying amounts of penalty and privilege in one historically created system. In this system, for example, white women are penalized by their gender but privileged by their race. Depending on the context, an individual may be an oppressor, a member of an oppressed group, or simultaneously oppressor and oppressed.

Adhering to a both/and conceptual stance does not mean that race, class, and gender oppression are interchangeable. For example, whereas race, class, and gender oppression operate on the social structural level of institutions, gender oppression seems better able to annex the basic power of the erotic and intrude in personal relationships via family dynamics and within individual consciousness. This may be because racial oppression has fostered historically concrete communities among African-Americans and other racial/ethnic groups. These communities have stimulated cultures of resistance. While these communities segregate Blacks from whites, they simultaneously provide counter-institutional buffers that subordinate groups such as African-Americans use to resist the ideas and institutions of dominant groups. Social class may be similarly structured. Traditionally conceptualized as a relationship of *individual* employees to their employers, social class might be better viewed as a relationship of *communities* to capitalist political economies. Moreover, significant overlap exists between racial and social class oppression when viewing them through the collective lens of family and community. Existing community structures provide a primary line of resistance against racial and class oppression. But because gender cross-cuts these structures, it finds fewer comparable institutional bases to foster resistance.

Embracing a both/and conceptual stance moves us from additive, separate systems approaches to oppression and toward what I now see as the more fundamental issue of the social relations of domination. Race, class, and gender constitute axes of oppression that characterize Black women's experiences within a more generalized matrix of domination. Other groups may encounter different dimensions of the matrix, such as sexual orientation, religion, and age, but the overarching relationship is one of domination and the types of activism it generates.

Bell hooks labels this matrix a "politic of domination" and describes how it operates along interlocking axes of race, class, and gender oppression. This politic of domination

> refers to the ideological ground that they share, which is a belief in domination, and a belief in the notions of superior and inferior, which are components of all of those systems. For me it's like a house, they share the foundation, but the foundation is the ideological beliefs around which notions of domination are constructed.

Johnella Butler claims that new methodologies growing from this new paradigm would be "non-hierarchical" and would "refuse primacy to either race, class, gender, or ethnicity, demanding instead a recognition of their matrix-like interaction." Race, class, and gender may not be the most fundamental or important systems of oppression, but they have most profoundly affected African-American women. One significant dimension of Black feminist thought is its potential to reveal insights about the social relations of domination organized along other axes such as religion, ethnicity, sexual orientation, and age. Investigating Black women's particular experiences thus promises to reveal much about the more universal process of domination.

Multiple Levels of Domination

In addition to being structured along axes such as race, gender, and social class, the matrix of domination is structured on several levels. People experience and resist oppression on three levels: the level of personal biography; the group or community level of the cultural context created by race, class, and gender; and the systemic level of social institutions. Black feminist thought emphasizes all three levels as sites of domination and as potential sites of resistance.

Each individual has a unique personal biography made up of concrete experiences, values, motivations, and emotions. No two individuals occupy the same social space; thus no two biographies are identical. Human ties can be freeing and empowering, as is the case with Black women's heterosexual love relationships or in the power of motherhood in African-American families and communities. Human ties can also be confining and oppressive. Situations of domestic violence and abuse or cases in which controlling images foster Black women's internalized oppression represent domination on the personal level. The same situation can look quite different depending on the consciousness one brings to interpret it.

This level of individual consciousness is a fundamental area where new knowledge can generate change. Traditional accounts assume that power as domination operates from the top down by forcing and controlling unwilling victims to bend to the will of more powerful superiors. But these accounts fail to account for questions concerning why, for example, women stay with abusive men even with ample opportunity to leave or why slaves did not kill their owners more often. The willingness of the victim to collude in her or his own victimization becomes lost. They also fail to account for sustained resistance by victims, even when chances for victory appear remote. By emphasizing the power of self-definition and the necessity of a free mind, Black feminist thought speaks to the importance African-American women thinkers place on consciousness as a sphere of freedom. Black women intellectuals realize that domination operates not only by structuring power from the top down but by simultaneously annexing the power as energy of those on the bottom for its own ends. In their efforts to rearticulate the standpoint of African-American women as a group, Black feminist thinkers offer individual African-American women the conceptual tools to resist oppression.

The cultural context formed by those experiences and ideas that are shared with other members of a group or community which give meaning to individual biographies constitutes a second level at which domination is experienced and resisted. Each individual biography is rooted in several overlapping cultural contexts—for example, groups defined by race, social class, age, gender, religion, and sexual orientation. The cultural component contributes, among other things, the concepts used in thinking and acting, group validation of an individual's interpretation of concepts, the "thought models" used in the acquisition of knowledge, and standards used to evaluate individual thought and behavior. The most cohesive cultural contexts are those with identifiable histories, geographic locations, and social institutions. For Black women African-American communities have provided the location for an Afrocentric group perspective to endure.

Subjugated knowledges, such as a Black women's culture of resistance, develop in cultural contexts controlled by oppressed groups. Dominant groups aim to replace subjugated knowledge with their own specialized thought because they realize that gaining control over this dimension of subordinate groups' lives simplifies control.

While efforts to influence this dimension of an oppressed group's experiences can be partially successful, this level is more difficult to control than dominant groups would have us believe. For example, adhering to externally derived standards of beauty leads many African-American women to dislike their skin color or hair texture. Similarly, internalizing Eurocentric gender ideology leads some Black men to abuse Black women. These are cases of the successful infusion of the dominant group's specialized thought into the everyday cultural context of African-Americans. But the long-standing existence of a Black women's culture of resistance as expressed through Black women's relationships with one another, the Black women's blues tradition, and the voices of contemporary African-American women writers all attest to the difficulty of eliminating the cultural context as a fundamental site of resistance.

Domination is also experienced and resisted on the third level of social institutions controlled by the dominant group: namely, schools, churches, the media, and other formal organizations. These institutions expose individuals to the specialized thought representing the dominant group's standpoint and interests. While such institutions offer the promise of both literacy and other skills that can be used for individual empowerment and social transformation, they simultaneously require docility and passivity. Such institutions would have us believe that the theorizing of elites constitutes the whole of theory. The existence of African-American women thinkers such as Maria Stewart, Sojourner Truth, Zora Neale Hurston, and Fannie Lou Hamer who, though excluded from and/or marginalized within such institutions, continued to produce theory effectively opposes this hegemonic view. Moreover, the more recent resurgence of Black feminist thought within these institutions, the case of the outpouring of contemporary Black feminist thought in history and literature, directly challenges the Eurocentric masculinist thought pervading these institutions.

Resisting the Matrix of Domination

Domination operates by seducing, pressuring, or forcing African-American women and members of subordinated groups to replace individual and cultural ways of knowing with the dominant group's specialized thought. As a result, suggests Audre Lorde, "the true focus of revolutionary change is never merely the oppressive situations which we seek to escape, but that piece of the oppressor which is planted deep within each of us." Or as Toni Cade Bambara succinctly states, "revolution begins with the self, in the self."

Lorde and Bambara's suppositions raise an important issue for Black feminist intellectuals and for all scholars and activists working for social change. Although most individuals have little difficulty identifying their own victimization within some major system of oppression—whether it be by race, social class, religion, physical ability, sexual orientation, ethnicity, age or gender—they typically fail to see how their thoughts and actions uphold someone else's subordination. Thus white feminists routinely point with confidence to their oppression as women but resist seeing how much their white skin privileges them. African-Americans who possess eloquent analyses of racism often persist in viewing poor white women as symbols of white power. The radical left fares little better. "If only people of color and women could see their true class interests," they argue, "class solidarity would eliminate racism and sexism." In essence, each group identifies the oppression with which it feels most comfortable as being fundamental and classifies all others as being of lesser importance. Oppression is filled with such contradictions because these approaches fail to recognize that a matrix of domination contains few pure victims or oppressors. Each individual derives varying amounts of penalty and privilege from the multiple systems of oppression which frame everyone's lives.

A broader focus stresses the interlocking nature of oppressions that are structured on multiple levels, from the individual to the social structural, and which are part of a larger matrix of domination. Adhering to this inclusive model provides the conceptual space needed for each individual to see that she or he is *both* a member of multiple dominant groups *and* a member of multiple subordinate groups. Shifting the analysis to investigating how the matrix of domination is structured along certain axes—race, gender, and class being the axes of investigation for African-American women—reveals that different systems of oppression may rely in varying degrees on systemic versus interpersonal mechanisms of domination.

Empowerment involves rejecting the dimensions of knowledge, whether personal, cultural, or institutional, that perpetuate objectification and dehumanization. African-American women and other individuals in subordinate groups become empowered when we understand and use those dimensions of our individual, group, and disciplinary ways of knowing that foster our humanity as fully human subjects. This is the case when Black women value our self-definitions, participate in a Black women's activist tradition, invoke an Afrocentric feminist epistemology as central to our worldview, and view the skills gained in schools as part of a focused education for Black community development. C. Wright Mills identifies this holistic epistemology as the "sociological imagination" and identifies its task and its promise as a way of knowing that enables individuals to grasp the relations between history and biography within society. Using one's standpoint to engage the sociological imagination can empower the individual. "My fullest concentration of energy is available to me," Audre Lorde maintains, "only when I integrate all the parts of who I am, openly, allowing power from particular sources of my living to flow back and forth freely through all my different selves, without the restriction of externally imposed definition."

Black Women as Agents of Knowledge

Living life as an African-American woman is a necessary prerequisite for producing Black feminist thought because within Black women's communities thought is validated and produced with reference to a particular set of historical, material, and epistemological conditions. African-American women who adhere to the idea that claims about Black women must be substantiated by Black women's sense of our own experiences and who anchor our knowledge claims in an Afrocentric feminist epistemology have produced a rich tradition of Black feminist thought.

Traditionally such women were blues singers, poets, autobiographers, storytellers, and orators validated by everyday Black women as experts on a Black women's standpoint. Only a few unusual African-American feminist scholars have been able to defy Eurocentric masculinist epistemologies and explicitly embrace an Afrocentric feminist epistemology. Consider Alice Walker's description of Zora Neal Hurston:

> In my mind, Zora Neale Hurston, Billie Holiday, and Bessie Smith form a sort of unholy trinity. Zora *belongs* in the tradition of black women singers, rather than among "the

literati." . . . Like Billie and Bessie she followed her own road, believed in her own gods, pursued her own dreams, and refused to separate herself from "common" people.

Zora Neal Hurston is an exception for prior to 1950, few African-American women earned advanced degrees and most of those who did complied with Eurocentric masculinist epistemologies. Although these women worked on behalf of Black women, they did so within the confines of pervasive race and gender oppression. Black women scholars were in a position to see the exclusion of African-American women from scholarly discourse, and the thematic content of their work often reflected their interest in examining a Black women's standpoint. However, their tenuous status in academic institutions led them to adhere to Eurocentric masculinist epistemologies so that their work would be accepted as scholarly. As a result, while they produced Black feminist thought, those African-American women most likely to gain academic credentials were often least likely to produce Black feminist thought that used an Afrocentric feminist epistemology.

An ongoing tension exists for Black women as agents of knowledge, a tension rooted in the sometimes conflicting demands of Afrocentricity and feminism. Those Black women who are feminists are critical of how Black culture and many of its traditions oppress women. For example, the strong pronatal beliefs in African-American communities that foster early motherhood among adolescent girls, the lack of self-actualization that can accompany the double-day of paid employment and work in the home, and the emotional and physical abuse that many Black women experience from their fathers, lovers, and husbands all reflect practices opposed by African-American women who are feminists. But these same women may have a parallel desire as members of an oppressed racial group to affirm the value of that same culture and traditions. Thus strong Black mothers appear in Black women's literature, Black women's economic contributions to families is lauded, and a curious silence exists concerning domestic abuse.

As more African-American women earn advanced degrees, the range of Black feminist scholarship is expanding. Increasing numbers of African-American women scholars are explicitly choosing to ground their work in Black women's experiences, and, by doing so, they implicitly adhere to an Afrocentric feminist epistemology. Rather than being restrained by their both/and status of marginality, these women make creative use of their outsider-within status and produce innovative Afrocentric feminist thought. The difficulties these women face lie less in demonstrating that they have mastered white male epistemologies than in resisting the hegemonic nature of these patterns of thought in order to see, value, and use existing alternative Afrocentric feminist ways of knowing.

In establishing the legitimacy of their knowledge claims, Black women scholars who want to develop Afrocentric feminist thought may encounter the often conflicting standards of three key groups. First, Black feminist thought must be validated by ordinary African-American women who, in the words of Hannah Nelson, grow to womanhood "in a world where the saner you are, the madder you are made to appear." To be credible in the eyes of this group, scholars must be personal advocates for their material, be accountable for the consequences of their work, have lived or experienced their material in some fashion, and be willing to engage in dialogues about their findings with ordinary, everyday people. Second, Black feminist thought also must be accepted by the community of Black women scholars. These scholars place varying amounts of importance on rearticulating a Black women's standpoint using an Afrocentric feminist epistemology. Third, Afrocentric feminist thought within academia must be prepared to confront Eurocentric masculinist political and epistemological requirements.

The dilemma facing Black women scholars engaged in creating Black feminist thought is that a knowledge claim that meets the criteria of adequacy for one group and thus is judged to be an acceptable knowledge claim may not be translatable into the terms of a different group. Using the example of Black English, June Jordan illustrates the difficulty of moving among epistemologies:

> You cannot "translate" instances of Standard English preoccupied with abstraction or with nothing/nobody evidently alive into Black English. That would warp the language into uses antithetical to the guiding perspective of its community of users. Rather you must first change those Standard English sentences, themselves, into ideas consistent with the person-centered assumptions of Black English.

Although both worldviews share a common vocabulary, the ideas themselves defy direct translation.

For Black women who are agents of knowledge, the marginality that accompanies outsider-within status can be the source of both frustration and creativity. In an attempt to minimize the differences between the cultural context of African-American communities and the expectations of social institutions, some women dichotomize their behavior and become two different people. Over time, the strain of doing this can be enormous. Others reject their cultural context and work against their own best interests by enforcing the dominant group's specialized thought. Still others manage to inhabit both contexts but do so critically, using their outsider-within perspectives as a source of insights and ideas. But while outsiders within can make substantial personal cost. "Eventually it comes to you," observes Lorraine Hansberry, "the thing that makes you exceptional, if you are at all, is inevitably that which must also make you lonely."

Once Black feminist scholars face the notion that, on certain dimensions of a Black women's standpoint, it may be fruitless to try and translate ideas from an Afrocentric feminist epistemology into a Eurocentric masculinist framework, then other choices emerge. Rather than trying to uncover universal knowledge claims that can withstand the translation from one epistemology to another (initially, at least), Black women intellectuals might find efforts to rearticulate a Black women's standpoint especially fruitful. Rearticulating a Black women's standpoint refashions the concrete and reveals the more universal human dimensions of Black women's everyday lives. "I date all my work," notes Nikki Giovanni, "because I think poetry, or any writing, is but a reflection of the moment. The universal comes from the particular." Bell Hooks maintains, "my goal as a feminist thinker and theorist is to take that abstraction and articulate it in a language that renders it accessible—not less complex or rigorous—but simply more accessible." The complexity exists; interpreting it remains the unfulfilled challenge for Black women intellectuals.

Situated Knowledge, Subjugated Knowledge, and Partial Perspectives

"My life seems to be an increasing revelation of the intimate face of universal struggle," claims June Jordan:

You begin with your family and the kids on the block, and next you open your eyes to what you call your people and that leads you into land reform into Black English into Angola leads you back to your own bed where you lie by yourself, wondering if you deserve to be peaceful, or trusted or desired or left to the freedom of your own unfaltering heart. And the scale shrinks to the use of a skull: your own interior cage.

Lorraine Hansberry expresses a similar idea: "I believe that one of the most sound ideas in dramatic writing is that in order to create the universal, you must pay very great attention to the specific. Universality, I think, emerges from the truthful identity of what is." Jordan and Hansberry's insights that universal struggle and truth may wear a particularistic, intimate face suggest a new epistemological stance concerning how we negotiate competing knowledge claims and identify "truth."

The context in which African-American women's ideas are nurtured or suppressed matters. Understanding the content and epistemology of Black women's ideas as specialized knowledge requires attending to the context from which those ideas emerge. While produced by individuals, Black feminist thought as situated knowledge is embedded in the communities in which African-American women find ourselves.

A Black women's standpoint and those of other oppressed groups is not only embedded in a context but exists in a situation characterized by domination. Because Black women's ideas have been suppressed, this suppression has stimulated African-American women to create knowledge that empowers people to resist domination. Thus Afrocentric feminist thought represents a subjugated knowledge. A Black women's standpoint may provide a preferred stance from which to view the matrix of domination because, in principle, Black feminist thought as specialized thought is less likely than the specialized knowledge produced by dominant groups to deny the connection between ideas and the vested interests of their creators. However, Black feminist thought as subjugated knowledge is not exempt from critical analysis, because subjugation is not grounds for an epistemology.

Despite African-American women's potential power to reveal new insights about the matrix of domination, a Black women's standpoint is only one angle of vision. Thus Black feminist thought represents a partial perspective. The overarching matrix of domination houses multiple groups, each with varying experiences with penalty and privilege that produce corresponding partial perspectives, situated knowledges, and, for clearly identifiable subordinate groups, subjugated knowledges. No one group has a clear angle of vision. No one group possesses the theory or methodology that allows it to discover the absolute "truth" or, worse yet, proclaim its theories and methodologies as the universal norm evaluating other groups' experiences. Given that groups are unequal in power in making themselves heard, dominant groups have a vested interest in suppressing the knowledge produced by subordinate groups. Given the existence of multiple and competing knowledge claims to "truth" produced by groups with partial perspectives, what epistemological approach offers the most promise?

Dialogue and Empathy

Western social and political thought contains two alternative approaches to ascertaining "truth." The first, reflected in positivist science, has long claimed that absolute truths exist and that the task of scholarship is to develop objective, unbiased tools of science to measure these truths. . . . Relativism, the second approach, has been forwarded as the antithesis of and inevitable outcome of rejecting a positivist science. From a relativist perspective all groups produce specialized thought and each group's thought is equally valid. No group can claim to have a better interpretation of the "truth" than another. In a sense, relativism represents the opposite of scientific ideologies of objectivity. As epistemological stances, both positivist science and relativism minimize the importance of specific location in influencing a group's knowledge claims, the power inequities among groups that produce subjugated knowledges, and the strengths and limitations of partial perspective.

The existence of Black feminist thought suggests another alternative to the ostensibly objective norms of science and to relativism's claims that groups with competing knowledge claims are equal. . . . This approach to Afrocentric feminist thought allows African-American women to bring a Black women's standpoint to larger epistemological dialogues concerning the nature of the matrix of domination. Eventually such dialogues may get us to a point at which, claims Elsa Barkley Brown, "all people can learn to center in another experience, validate it, and judge it by its own standards without need of comparison or need to adopt that framework as their own." In such dialogues, "one has no need to 'decenter' anyone in order to center someone else; one has only to constantly, appropriately, 'pivot the center.'"

Those ideas that are validated as true by African-American women, African-American men, Latina lesbians, Asian-American women, Puerto Rican men, and other groups with distinctive standpoints, with each group using the epistemological approaches growing from its unique standpoint, thus become the most "objective" truths. Each group speaks from its own standpoint and shares its own partial, situated knowledge. But because each group perceives its own truth as partial, its knowledge is unfinished. Each group becomes better able to consider other groups' standpoints without relinquishing the uniqueness of its own standpoint or suppressing other groups' partial perspectives. "What is always needed in the appreciation of art, or life," maintains Alice Walker, "is the larger perspective. Connections made, or at least attempted, where none existed before, the straining to encompass in one's glance at the varied world the common thread, the unifying theme through immense diversity." Partiality and not universality is the condition of being heard; individuals and groups forwarding knowledge claims without owning their position are deemed less credible than those who do.

Dialogue is critical to the success of this epistemological approach, the type of dialogue long extant in the Afrocentric call-and-response tradition whereby power dynamics are fluid, everyone has a voice, but everyone must listen and respond to other voices in order to be allowed to remain in the community. Sharing a common cause fosters dialogue and encourages groups to transcend their differences. . . .

African-American women have been victimized by race, gender, and class oppression. But portraying Black women solely as passive, unfortunate recipients of racial and sexual abuse stifles notions that Black women can actively work to change our circumstances and bring about changes in our lives. Similarly, presenting African-American women solely as heroic figures who easily engage in resisting oppression on all fronts minimizes the very real costs of oppression and can foster the perception that Black women need no help because we can "take it."

Black feminist thought's emphasis on the ongoing interplay between Black women's oppression and Black women's activism presents the matrix of domination as responsive to human agency. Such thought views the world as a dynamic place where the goal is not merely to survive or to fit in or to cope; rather, it becomes a place where we feel ownership and accountability. The existence of Afrocentric feminist thought suggests that there is always choice, and power to act, no matter how bleak the situation may appear to be. Viewing the world as one in the making raises the issue of individual responsibility for bringing about change. It also shows that while individual empowerment is key, only collective action can effectively generate lasting social transformation of political and economic institutions.❖

Gloria Anzaldúa (1942–) writes fiction and nonfiction, including social theory, with intentional reference to her multiple identities—Chicana, *tejana* (Indian), lesbian, feminist, poet. She has taught and lectured at many institutions, including the University of Texas, San Francisco State, and Vermont College. The selections are from *Borderlands/La Frontera: The New Mestiza* (1987), a blend of poetry and autobiography in which the reader can readily discern her social theory. She is the editor of *Making Face, Making Soul/Haciendo Cara* (1990) and coeditor (with Cherríe Moraga) of *This Bridge Called My Back* (1981), which together are the best available resources for writings in the women-of-color tradition.

The New Mestiza
Gloria Anzaldúa (1987)

> El otro México que acá hemos construido
> el espacio es lo que ha sido
> territorio nacional.
> Esté el esfuerzo de todos nuestros hermanos
> y latinoamericanos que han sabido
> progressar.
>   —Los Tigres del Norte

"The *Aztecas del norte* . . . compose the largest single tribe or nation of Anishinabeg (Indians) found in the United States today. . . . Some call themselves Chicanos and see themselves as people whose true homeland is Aztlán [the U.S. Southwest]."

> Wind tugging at my sleeve
> feet sinking into the sand
> I stand at the edge where earth touches ocean
> where the two overlap
> a gentle coming together
> at other times and places a violent clash.

Excerpt from *Borderlands/La Frontera: The New Mestiza* (San Francisco: Spinsters/Aunt Lute, 1987), pp. 1–8. 1987 by Gloria Anzaldúa. Reprinted by permission of Aunt Lute Books.

Across the border in Mexico
stark silhouette of houses gutted by waves,
cliffs crumbling into the sea,
silver waves marbled with spume
gashing a hole under the border fence.

Miro el mar atacar
la cerca en Border Field Park
con sus buchones de agua,
an Easter Sunday resurrection
of the brown blood in my veins.

Oigo el llorido del mar, el respiro del aire,
my heart surges to the beat of the sea.
In the gray haze of the sun
the gulls' shrill cry of hunger,
the tangy smell of the sea seeping into me.

I walk   through the hole in the fence
to the other side.
Under my fingers I feel the gritty wire
rusted by 139 years
of the salty breath of the sea.

Beneath the iron sky
Mexican children kick their soccer ball across,
run after it, entering the U.S.

I press my hand to the steel curtain—
chainlink fence crowned with rolled barbed wire
rippling from the sea where Tijuana touches San Diego
unrolling over mountains
and plains
and deserts,
this "Tortilla Curtain" turning into *el río Grande*
flowing down to the flatlands
of the Magic Valley of South Texas
its mouth emptying into the Gulf.

1,950 mile-long open wound
dividing a *pueblo,* a culture,
running down the length of my body,
staking fence rods in my flesh,
splits me   splits me
me raja   me raja

This is my home
this thin edge of
barbwire.

But the skin of the earth is seamless.
The sea cannot be fenced,
el mar does not stop at borders.
To show the white man what she thought of his
arrogance.
Yemaya blew that wire fence down.

This land was Mexican once,
was Indian always
and is.
And   will be again.

Yo soy un puente tendido
del mundo gabacho al del mojado,
lo pasado me estirá pa' 'trás
y lo presente pa' 'delante.
Que la Virgen de Guadalupe me cuide
Ay ay ay, soy mexicana de este lado.

The U.S.-Mexican border *es una herida abierta* where the Third World grates against the first and bleeds. And before a scab forms it hemorrhages again, the lifeblood of two worlds merging to form a third country—a border culture. Borders are set up to define the places that are safe and unsafe, to distinguish *us* from *them*. A border is a dividing line, a narrow strip along a steep edge. A borderland is a vague and undetermined place created by the emotional residue of an unnatural boundary. It is in a constant state of transition. The prohibited and forbidden are its inhabitants. *Los atravesados* live here: the squint-eyed, the perverse, the queer, the troublesome, the mongrel, the mulato, the half-breed, the half dead; in short, those who cross over, pass over, or go through the confines of the "normal." Gringos in the U.S. Southwest consider the inhabitants of the borderlands transgressors, aliens— whether they possess documents or not, whether they're Chicanos, Indians or Blacks. Do not enter, trespassers will be raped, maimed, strangled, gassed, shot. The only "legitimate" inhabitants are those in power, the whites and those who align themselves with whites. Tension grips the inhabitants of the borderlands like a virus. Ambivalence and unrest reside there and death is no stranger.

In the fields, *la migra.* My aunt saying, "*No corran,* don't run. They'll think you're *del otro lao.*" In the confusion, Pedro ran, terrified of being caught. He couldn't speak English, couldn't tell them he was fifth generation American. *Sin papeles*—he did not carry his birth certificate to work in the fields. *La migra* took him away while we watched. *Se lo llevaron.* He tried to smile when he looked back at us, to raise his fist. But I saw the shame pushing his head down, I saw the terrible weight of shame hunch his shoulders. They deported him to Guadalajara by plane. The furthest he'd ever been to Mexico was Reynosa, a small border town opposite Hidalgo, Texas, not far from McAllen. Pedro walked all the way to the Valley. *Se lo llevaron sin un centavo al pobre. Se vino andando desde Guadalajara.*

During the original peopling of the Americas, the first inhabitants migrated across the Bering Straits and walked south across the continent. The oldest evidence of humankind in the U.S.—the Chicanos' ancient Indian ancestors—was found in Texas and has been dated to 35,000 b.c. In the Southwest United States archeologists have found 20,000-year-old campsites of the Indians who migrated through, or permanently occupied, the Southwest, Aztlán—land of the herons, land of whiteness, the Edenic place of origin of the Azteca.

In 1000 B.C., descendants of the original Cochise people migrated into what is now Mexico and Central America and became the direct ancestors of many of the Mexican people. (The Cochise culture of the Southwest is the parent culture of the Aztecs. The Uto-Aztecan languages stemmed from the language of the Cochise people.) The Aztecs (the Nahuatl word for people of Aztlán) left the Southwest in 1168 A.D.

> Now let us go.
> *Tihueque, tihueque,*
> *Vámonos, vámonos.*
> *Un pájaro cantó.*
> *Con sus ocho tribus salieron*
> *de la "cueva del origen."*
> *los aztecas siguieron al dios*
> *Huitzilopochtli.*

Huitzilopochtli, the God of War, guided them to the place (that later became Mexico City) where an eagle with a writhing serpent in its beak perched on a cactus. The eagle symbolizes the spirit (as the sun, the father); the serpent symbolizes the soul (as the earth, the mother). Together, they symbolize the struggle between the spiritual/celestial/male and the underworld/earth/feminine. The symbolic sacrifice of the serpent to the "higher" masculine powers indicates that the patriarchal order had already vanquished the feminine and matriarchal order in pre-Columbian America.

At the beginning of the 16th century, the Spaniards and Hernán Cortés invaded Mexico and, with the help of tribes that the Aztecs had subjugated, conquered it. Before the Conquest, there were twenty-five million Indian people in Mexico and the Yucatan. Immediately after the Conquest, the Indian population had been reduced to under seven million. By 1650, only one-and-a-half-million pure-blooded Indians remained. The *mestizos* who were genetically equipped to survive small pox, measles, and typhus (Old World diseases to which the natives had no immunity), founded a new hybrid race and inherited Central and South America. *En 1521 nació una nueva raza, el mestizo, el mexicano* (people of mixed Indian and Spanish blood), a race that had never existed before. Chicanos, Mexican-Americans, are the offspring of those first matings.

Our Spanish, Indian, and *mestizo* ancestors explored and settled parts of the U.S. Southwest as early as the sixteenth century. For every gold-hungry *conquistador* and soul-hungry missionary who came north from Mexico, ten to twenty Indians and *mestizos* went along as porters or in other capacities. For the Indians, this constituted a return to the place of origin, Aztlán, thus making Chicanos originally and secondarily indigenous to the Southwest. Indians and *mestizos* from central Mexico intermarried with North American Indians. The continual intermarriage between Mexican and American Indians and Spaniards formed an even greater *mestizaje.* . . .

In the 1800s, Anglos migrated illegally into Texas, which was then part of Mexico, in greater and greater numbers and gradually drove the *tejanos* (native Texans of

Mexican descent) from their lands, committing all manner of atrocities against them. Their illegal invasion forced Mexico to fight a war to keep its Texas territory. The Battle of the Alamo, in which the Mexican forces vanquished the whites, became, for the whites, the symbol for the cowardly and villainous character of the Mexicans. It became (and still is) a symbol that legitimized the white imperialist takeover. With the capture of Santa Anna later in 1836, Texas became a republic. *Tejanos* lost their land and, overnight, became the foreigners. . . .

In 1846, the U.S. incited Mexico to war. U.S. troops invaded and occupied Mexico, forcing her to give up almost half of her nation, what is now Texas, New Mexico, Arizona, Colorado and California.

With the victory of the U.S. forces over the Mexican in the U.S.-Mexican War, *los norteamericanos* pushed the Texas border down 100 miles, from *el río Nueces* to *el río Grande.* South Texas ceased to be part of the Mexican state of Tamaulipas. Separated from Mexico, the Native Mexican-Texan no longer looked toward Mexico as home; the Southwest became our homeland once more. The border fence that divides the Mexican people was born on February 2, 1848 with the signing of the Treaty of Guadalupe-Hidalgo. It left 100,000 Mexican citizens on this side, annexed by conquest along with the land. The land established by the treaty as belonging to Mexicans was soon swindled away from its owners. The treaty was never honored and restitution, to this day, has never been made.

> *The justice and benevolence of God*
> *will forbid that . . . Texas should again*
> *become a howling wilderness*
> *trod only by savages, or . . . benighted*
> *by the ignorance and superstition,*
> *the anarchy and rapine of Mexican misrule.*
> *The Anglo-American race are destined*
> *to be forever the proprietors of*
> *this land of promise and fulfillment.*
> *Their laws will govern it,*
> *their learning will enlighten it,*
> *their enterprise will improve it.*
> *Their flocks range its boundless pastures,*
> *for them its fertile lands will yield . . .*
> *luxuriant harvests . . .*
> *The wilderness of Texas has been redeemed*
> *by Anglo-American blood & enterprise.*
> —William H. Wharton

The Gringo, locked into the fiction of white superiority, seized complete political power, stripping Indians and Mexicans of their land while their feet were still rooted in it. *Con el destierro y el exilo fuimos desuñados, destroncados, destripados*—we were jerked out by the roots, truncated, disemboweled, dispossessed, and separated from our identity and our history. Many, under the threat of Anglo terrorism, abandoned homes and ranches and went to Mexico. Some stayed and protested. But as the courts, law enforcement officials, and government officials not only ignored their pleas but penalized them for their efforts, *tejanos* had no other recourse but armed retaliation. . . .

Fear of Going Home: Homophobia

For the lesbian of color, the ultimate rebellion she can make against her native culture is through her sexual behavior. She goes against two moral prohibitions: sexuality and homosexuality. Being lesbian and raised Catholic, indoctrinated as straight, I *made the choice to be queer* (for some it is genetically inherent). It's an interesting path, one that continually slips in and out of the white, the Catholic, the Mexican, the indigenous, the instincts. In and out of my head. It makes for *loquería,* the crazies. It is a path of knowledge—one of knowing (and of learning) the history of oppression of our *raza.* It is a way of balancing, of mitigating duality.

In a New England college where I taught, the presence of a few lesbians threw the more conservative heterosexual students and faculty into a panic. The two lesbian students and we two lesbian instructors met with them to discuss their fears. One of the students said, "I thought homophobia meant fear of going home after a residency."

And I thought, how apt. Fear of going home. And of not being taken in. We're afraid of being abandoned by the mother, the culture, *la Raza,* for being unacceptable, faulty, damaged. Most of us unconsciously believe that if we reveal this unacceptable aspect of the self our mother/culture/race will totally reject us. To avoid rejection, some of us conform to the values of the culture, push the unacceptable parts into the shadows. Which leaves only one fear—that we will be found out and that the Shadow-Beast will break out of its cage. Some of us take another route. We try to make ourselves conscious of the Shadow-Beast, stare at the sexual lust and lust for power and destruction we see on its face, discern among its features the under-shadow that the reining order of heterosexual males project on our Beast. Yet still others of us take it another step: we try to waken the Shadow-Beast inside us. Not many jump at the chance to confront the Shadow Beast in the mirror without flinching at her lidless serpent eyes, her cold clammy moist hand dragging us underground, fangs barred and hissing. How does one put feathers on this particular serpent? But a few of us have been lucky—on the face of the Shadow-Beast we have seen not lust but tenderness; on its face we have uncovered the lie.

Intimate Terrorism: Life in the Borderlands

The world is not a safe place to live in. We shiver in separate cells in enclosed cities, shoulders hunched, barely keeping the panic below the surface of the skin, daily drinking shock along with our morning coffee, fearing the torches being set to our buildings, the attacks on the streets. Shutting down. Woman does not feel safe when her own culture, and white culture, are critical of her; when the males of all races hunt her as prey.

Alienated from her mother culture, "alien" in the dominant culture, the woman of color does not feel safe within the inner life of her Self. Petrified, she can't respond, her face caught between *los intersticios,* the spaces between the different worlds she inhabits.

The ability to respond is what is meant by responsibility, yet our cultures take away our ability to act—shackle us in the name of protection. Blocked, immobilized, we can't move forward, can't move backwards. That writhing serpent movement, the very movement of life, swifter than lightning, frozen.

We do not engage fully. We do not make full use of our faculties. We abnegate. And there in front of us is the crossroads therefore responsible and to blame (being a victim and transferring the blame on culture, mother, father, ex-lover, friend, absolves me of responsibility), or to feel strong, and, for the most part, in control.

My Chicana identity is grounded in the Indian woman's history of resistance. The Aztec female rites of mourning were rites of defiance protesting the cultural changes which disrupted the equality and balance between female and male, and protesting their demotion to a lesser status, their denigration. Like *la Llorona*, the Indian woman's only means of protest was wailing.

So *mamá, Raza,* how wonderful, *no tener que rendir cuentas a nadie.* I feel perfectly free to rebel and to rail against my culture. I fear no betrayal on my part because, unlike Chicanas and other women of color who grew up white or who have only recently returned to their native cultural roots, I was totally immersed in mine. It wasn't until I went to high school that I "saw" whites. Until I worked on my master's degree I had not gotten within an arm's distance of them. I was totally immersed *en lo mexicano,* a rural, peasant, isolated, *mexicanismo.* To separate from my culture (as from my family) I had to feel competent enough on the outside and secure enough inside to live life on my own. Yet in leaving home I did not lose touch with my origins because *lo mexicano* is in my system. I am a turtle, wherever I go I carry "home" on my back.

Not me sold out my people but they me. So yes, though "home" permeates every sinew and cartilage in my body, I too am afraid of going home. Though I'll defend my race and culture when they are attacked by non-*mexicanos, conosco el malestar de mi cultura.* I abhor some of my culture's ways, how it cripples its women, *como burras,* our strengths used against us, lowly *burras* bearing humility with dignity. The ability to serve, claim the males, is our highest virtue. I abhor how my culture makes *macho* caricatures of its men. No, I do not buy all the myths of the tribe into which I was born. I can understand why the more tinged with Anglo blood, the more adamantly my colored and colorless sisters glorify their colored culture's values—to offset the extreme devaluation of it by the white culture. It's a legitimate reaction. But I will not glorify those aspects of my culture which have injured me and which have injured me in the name of protecting me.

So, don't give me your tenets and your laws. Don't give me your lukewarm gods. What I want is an accounting with all three cultures—white, Mexican, Indian. I want the freedom to carve and chisel my own face, to stanch the bleeding with ashes, to fashion my own gods out of my entrails. And if going home is denied me then I will have to stand and claim my space, making a new culture—*una cultura mestiza*—with my own lumber, my own bricks and mortar and my own feminist architecture.❖

Jeffrey Weeks (1945–) teaches at Bristol Polytechnic. He is one of the leading contributors to the emerging field of gay and lesbian social theory. His books include *Coming Out* (1977), *Sex, Politics and Society* (1981), and *Sexuality and Its Discontents* (1985). The selection is from *Against Nature* (1991).

Sexual Identification Is a Strange Thing

Jeffrey Weeks (1991)

One difficulty is that not all homosexually inclined people want to identify their minority status—or even see themselves as homosexual. Sexologists, at least since Kinsey, have pointed out that there is no necessary connection between sexual behaviour and sexual identity. According to Kinsey's best-known statistic, some 37 per cent of men had homosexual experiences to orgasm. But perhaps less than 4 per cent were exclusively homosexual—and even they did not necessarily express a homosexual identity, a concept of which, in any case, Kinsey disapproved.

Sexual identification is a strange thing. There are some people who identify as gay and participate in the gay community but do not experience or wish for homosexual activity. And there are homosexually active people who do not identify as gay. Many black homosexuals, for example, prefer to identify primarily as "black" rather than "gay" and align themselves with black rather than gay political positions. Obviously, as Barry Dank has argued, "the development of a homosexual identity is dependent on the meanings that the actor attaches to the concepts of homosexual and homosexuality". These processes in turn depend on the person's environment and wider community. Many people, it has been argued, "drift" into identity, battered by contingency rather than guided by will. Four characteristic stages have been identified by Plummer: "sensitization", when the individual becomes aware of the possibility of being different; "signification", when he or she attributes a developing meaning to these differences; "subculturalization", the stage of recognizing oneself through involvement with others; and "stabilization", the stage of full acceptance of one's feelings and way of life. There is no automatic progression through these stages; each transition is dependent as much on chance as on decision; and there is no necessary acceptance of a final destiny, in an explicit identity. Some choices are forced on individuals, whether through stigmatization and public obloquy or through political necessity. But the point that needs underlining is that *identity* is a choice. It is not *dictated* by internal imperatives.

The implication of this is that "desire" is one thing, while subject position, that is identification with a particular social position and organizing sense of self, is another. This means that labels such as "gay" and "lesbian" increasingly become *political* choices, and in that process the sexual connotations can all but disappear. This is clearest in recent debates about a lesbian identity. Among gay men the issue has fundamentally concerned sex, validating a denied sexuality. In debates on lesbianism, on the other hand, there have been heated exchanges about the necessary connection of a lesbian identity to sexual practices. Conventional wisdom and, even more stringently, sexological expertise, have defined lesbianism as a sexual category. But increasingly it has been proposed by feminists as primarily a political definition, in which sexuality

Excerpt from *Against Nature: Essays on History, Sexuality and Identity* (London: Rivers Oram Press, 1991), pp. 79–85.

plays a problematic role. As Lillian Faderman puts it, "Women who identify themselves as lesbians generally do not view lesbianism as a sexual phenomenon first and foremost". It is instead a relationship in which two women's strongest emotions and affection are directed towards one another. It becomes a synonym for sisterhood, solidarity, and affection, and as such a fundamental attribute of feminism.

Recent lesbian-feminist writers have understandably largely rejected the social-science and sexological definitions of lesbianism. Traditionally female homosexuality has been seen almost exclusively in terms derived from the experience or study of males. Male homosexuality has invariably been more closely observed and researched than lesbianism, partly because of its greater public salience, partly because it challenged the dominant definitions of male sexuality, and partly because female sexuality has usually been studied only in so far as it was responsive to male sexuality, and lesbianism was hardly understandable in those terms. More recently, ethnographies of female homosexuality have tended to adopt research techniques honed in investigation of male behaviour, concentrating, for example, on "coming out", contact patterns, sexual expression, and duration of relationships. The impact of this has been to conceptualize lesbianism, like male homosexuality, as a specific minority experience little different in its implications from male patterns. This has been criticized in turn by some lesbian feminists as inevitably having the effect of establishing male homosexuality as the norm, while ignoring the implications of lesbianism for feminism.

The most powerful exponent of a "political lesbianism" position has been Adrienne Rich. In her influential essay "Compulsory Heterosexuality and Lesbian Existence" she argues that a distinction has to be made between the "lesbian continuum" and "lesbian existence". The latter is equivalent to a lesbian identity but its character is not defined by sexual practice. It is the sense of self of women bonded primarily to women who are sexually and emotionally independent of men. In turn this is the expression of the "lesbian continuum", the range through women's lives of woman-identified experience. Such experiences go beyond the possibility of genital sex, to embrace many forms of primary intensity, including the sharing of inner life, the bonding against male tyranny, practical and political support, marriage resistance, female support networks and communities. Such possibilities of bonding between women are denied by "compulsory heterosexuality". Rich speaks of "the rendering invisible of the lesbian possibility, an engulfed continent which rises fragmentedly to view from time to time only to become submerged again". "Compulsory heterosexuality" is the key mechanism of control of women, ensuring in its tyranny definition the perpetuation of male domination. Lesbianism is the point of resistance to this heterosexual dominance, its central antagonistic force.

Lesbianism is thus about the realization of the male-free potential of women, and in drawing on this essence, male definitions are cast aside. Rich sharply dissociates lesbianism from male homosexuality because of the latter's presumed relationship, *inter alia*, to pederasty, anonymous sex, and ageism. Lesbianism, on the other hand, she argues, is a profoundly *female* experience, like motherhood, and she looks forward to a powerful new female eroticism.

Against the passion and conviction of Rich's position three fundamental criticisms have been made. In the first place it is based on a romantic naturalization of female bonds. It is not always clear whether Rich sees the "lesbian continuum" as a powerful solidarity that is there but constantly suppressed, or as a potentiality that could be realized in a mythical future, but in either case it stretches towards an essentialism about femininity which can distort the complexities of the construction of women, and ob-

scure the necessary politics. As Cora Kaplan has noted, in Rich's scenario, "female heterosexuality is socially constructed and female homosexuality is natural. . . . Political
lesbianism becomes more than a strategic position for feminism, it is a return to nature". Nature is now benign, female and affectionate, sensual and creative, revolutionary and transcendent—and lesbian. But all the problems in naturalistic explanations
of sex still come to the fore: its untheorized and untheorizable claims to truth, its
transhistorical pretensions, and its strong moralism: this is how you must behave because nature tells us so. The result is a narrowing in political focus, and this is the second major objection. The view that attributes all women's oppression to "compulsory
heterosexuality" suggests that somehow women are always socially controlled by men.
Women are, in consequence, inevitably presented as perpetual sufferers and victims,
beyond the possibility of resistance.

Finally, the political lesbian position tends to deny the specifics of lesbian sexuality.
Lesbian activists such as Pat Califia have suggested that there is a history of a specific
lesbian eroticism which has been historically denied, and which has produced its own
forms of struggle and institutionalization. According to Ann Ferguson, Rich's view:

> undermines the important historical development of an explicit identity connected to
> genital sexuality. My own view is that the development of such an identity, and with it the
> development of a sexuality valued and accepted in a community of peers, extended
> women's life options and degree of independence from men.

For such feminists, the elevation of female sexuality in general into a semi-mystical
bonding, where bodily contact and genital pleasure are secondary or even non-existent,
denies the possibilities of female eroticism, including the real potentiality of lesbianism.

This is not the place to enter a full discussion of these differing positions. The point
that requires emphasizing here is that like the gay male identity, the lesbian identity
has a political as well as a social and personal implication. That means that there need
be no necessary relationship between sexual practice and sexual identity. On the other
hand the existence of a specific identity testifies to the historic denial of a particular
form of female desire—and the struggle necessary to affirm it. As with the homosexual
male, the lesbian identity—whatever its "true" meaning—is historically contingent
but seemingly inevitable; potentially limiting—but apparently politically essential.

Identity is not a destiny but a choice. But in a culture where homosexual desires, female or male, are still execrated and denied, the adoption of lesbian or gay identities
inevitably constitutes a *political* choice. These identities are not expressions of secret
essences. They are self-creations, but they are creations on ground not freely chosen
but laid out by history. So homosexual identities illustrate the play of constraint and
opportunity, necessity and freedom, power and pleasure. Sexual identities seem necessary in the contemporary world as starting-points for a politics around sexuality. But
the form they take is not pre-determined. In the end, therefore, they are not so much
about who we really are, what our sex dictates. They are about what we want to be and
could be. But this means they are also about the morality of acts and the quality of relations. We live in a world of proliferating "sexual identities" as specific desires (pae-
dophile, sado-masochistic, bisexual) become the focus either for minute subdivisions
of well-established notions (gayness or lesbianism) or spin off into wholly new ones.
Can we therefore say that all identities are of equal value, and that minute subdivisions of desire, however apparently bizarre and esoteric, deserve social recognition
on the basis of the right to erotic difference and sexual identity?

Such questions have led to the development of what may be termed a "relationship paradigm" as opposed to the traditional "identity paradigm" as a way of thinking through some of the conceptual—and political—issues. If, as many advocates of gay politics have suggested, identity is a constraint, a limitation on the flux of possibilities and the exploration of desires, if it is only an historical acquisition, then surely its assertion should be historically junked or at least modified. The difficulty is to find a replacement that would equally satisfactorily provide a basis for personal coherence and social recognition. One possibility is to celebrate the flux, to indulge in a glorification of the "polysexualities" to which, on a radical reading of the Freudian tradition, we are all heirs. The unfortunate difficulty with this is that most individuals do not feel "polymorphously perverse". On the contrary they feel their sexual desires are fairly narrowly organized, whatever use they make of those desires in real life. Moreover, a social identity is no less real for being historically formed. Sexual identities are no longer arbitrary divisions of the field of possibilities; they are encoded in a complex web of social practices—legal, pedagogic, medical, moral, and personal. They cannot be willed away.

The aim of the "relationship paradigm", in contrast, is not to ignore questions of identity but to displace them, by stressing instead the need to examine relationships. If this is done we can look again both at our sexual history and our sexual presence. Historically, we need no longer look for the controversial emergence of identities. Instead we can see the complicated net of relationships through which sexuality is always expressed, changing over time. Looked at from a contemporary point of view, we see not the culmination of a process of identity development but the formation of new types of relationships, validating hitherto execrated sexualities, in complex communities of interest around sex.

This is a very tempting position to adopt. In particular it potentially allows sexual thinking to move away from a "morality of acts", where all debate is about the merits of this form of sexuality as opposed to that, to an "ethics of choice", where the question becomes one of the quality of involvement and the freedom of relationships. This puts the whole debate on quite a new footing, allowing questions of power, diversity and sexual pluralism to be brought in.

The difficulty with the "relationship paradigm" is that it is offered as an alternative to questions of identity. This is a false antinomy. Identities are always "relational" in the general sense that they only exist in relation to other potential identities. More crucially, identities must always be about relationships: to ourselves, precarious unities of conflicting desires and social commitments, "composed of heterogeneous fragments of fossilized cultures", and to others, who address us and call upon our recognition in diverse ways and through whom our sense of self is always negotiated. A sense of identity is essential for the establishment of relationships. As Foucault has argued, "sex is not a fatality, it's a possibility for creative life". For a variety of historical reasons that possibility is mediated through a recognition of identity. Identity may well be a historical fiction, a controlling myth, a limiting burden. But it is at the same time a necessary means of weaving our way through a hazard-strewn world and a complex web of social relations. Without it, it seems, the possibilities of sexual choice are not increased but diminished.❖

Judith Butler (1957–) teaches in the Humanities Center at Johns Hopkins University. She is the author of *Gender Trouble: Feminism and the Subversion of Identity* (1990). The selection is from her contribution to *Inside/Out: Lesbian Theories, Gay Theories* (edited by Diana Fuss, 1991), an excellent and important collection of the writings of gay and lesbian social theorists.

Imitation and Gender Insubordination
Judith Butler (1991)

To Theorize as a Lesbian?

At first I considered writing a different sort of essay, one with a philosophical tone: the "being" of being homosexual. The prospect of *being* anything, even for pay, has always produced in me a certain anxiety, for "to be" gay, "to be" lesbian seems to be more than a simple injunction to become who or what I already am. And in no way does it settle the anxiety for me to say that this is "part" of what I am. To write or speak *as a lesbian* appears a paradoxical appearance of this "I," one which feels neither true nor false. For it is a production, usually in response to a request, to come out or write in the name of an identity which, once produced, sometimes functions as a politically efficacious phantasm. I'm not at ease with "lesbian theories, gay theories," for as I've argued elsewhere, identity categories tend to be instruments of regulatory regimes, whether as the normalizing categories of oppressive structures or as the rallying points for a liberatory contestation of that very oppression. This is not to say that I will not appear at political occasions under the sign of lesbian, but that I would like to have it permanently unclear what precisely that sign signifies. So it is unclear how it is that I can contribute to this book and appear under its title, for it announces a set of terms that I propose to contest. One risk I take is to be recolonized by the sign under which I write, and so it is this risk that I seek to thematize. To propose that the invocation of identity is always a risk does not imply that resistance to it is always or only symptomatic of a self-inflicted homophobia. Indeed, a Foucaultian perspective might argue that the affirmation of "homosexuality" is itself an extension of a homophobic discourse. And yet "discourse," he writes on the same page, "can be both an instrument and an effect of power, but also a hindrance, a stumbling-block, a point of resistance and a starting point for an opposing strategy."

So I am skeptical about how the "I" is determined as it operates under the title of the lesbian sign, and I am no more comfortable with its homophobic determination than with those normative definitions offered by other members of the "gay or lesbian community." I'm permanently troubled by identity categories, consider them to be invariable stumbling-blocks, and understand them, even promote them, as sites of necessary trouble. In fact, if the category were to offer no trouble, it would cease to be interesting to me: it is precisely the *pleasure* produced by the instability of those categories which sustains the various erotic practices that make me a candidate for the category to begin with. To install myself within the terms of an identity category would be to turn against the sexuality that the category purports to de-

Excerpt from Diana Fuss, ed., *Inside/Out: Lesbian Theories, Gay Theories* (New York: Routledge, 1991), pp. 13–31.

scribe; and this might be true for any identity category which seeks to control the very eroticism that it claims to describe and authorize, much less "liberate."

And what's worse, I do not understand the notion of "theory," and am hardly interested in being cast as its defender, much less in being signified as part of an elite gay/lesbian theory crowd that seeks to establish the legitimacy and domestication of gay/lesbian studies within the academy. Is there a pregiven distinction between theory, politics, culture, media? How do those divisions operate to quell a certain intertextual writing that might well generate wholly different epistemic maps? But I am writing here now: is it too late? Can this writing, can any writing, refuse the terms by which it is appropriated even as, to some extent, that very colonizing discourse enables or produces this stumbling block, this resistance? How do I relate the paradoxical situation of this dependency and refusal?

If the political task is to show that theory is never merely *theoria,* in the sense of disengaged contemplation, and to insist that it is fully political (*phronesis* or even *praxis*), then why not simply call this operation *politics,* or some necessary permutation of it?

I have begun with confessions of trepidation and a series of disclaimers, but perhaps it will become clear that *disclaiming,* which is no simple activity, will be what I have to offer as a form of affirmative resistance to a certain regulatory operation of homophobia. The discourse of "coming out" has clearly served its purposes, but what are its risks? And here I am not speaking of unemployment or public attack or violence, which are quite clearly and widely on the increase against those who are perceived as "out" whether or not of their own design. Is the "subject" who is "out" free of its subjection and finally in the clear? Or could it be that the subjection that subjectivates the gay or lesbian subject in some ways continues to oppress, or oppresses most insidiously, once "outness" is claimed? What or who is it that is "out," made manifest and fully disclosed, when and if I reveal myself as lesbian? What is it that is now known, anything? What remains permanently concealed by the very linguistic act that offers up the promise of a transparent revelation of sexuality? Can sexuality even remain sexuality once it submits to a criterion of transparency and disclosure, or does it perhaps cease to be sexuality precisely when the semblance of full explicitness is achieved? Is sexuality of any kind even possible without that opacity designated by the unconscious, which means simply that the conscious "I" who would reveal its sexuality is perhaps the last to know the meaning of what it says?

To claim that this is what I *am* is to suggest a provisional totalization of this "I." But if the I can so determine itself, then that which it excludes in order to make that determination remains constitutive of the determination itself. In other words, such a statement presupposes that the "I" exceeds its determination, and even produces that very excess in and by the act which seeks to exhaust the semantic field of that "I." In the act which would disclose the true and full content of that "I," a certain radical *concealment* is thereby produced. For it is always finally unclear what is meant by invoking the lesbian-signifier, since its signification is always to some degree out of one's control, but also because its *specificity* can only be demarcated by exclusions that return to disrupt its claim to coherence. What, if anything, can lesbians be said to share? And who will decide this question, and in the name of whom? If I claim to be a lesbian, I "come out" only to produce a new and different "closet." The "you" to whom I come out now has access to a different region of opacity. Indeed, the locus of opacity has simply shifted: before, you did not know whether I "am," but now you do not know what that means, which is to say that the copula is empty, that it cannot be substituted for with a set of descriptions. And perhaps that is a situation to be valued. Conventionally, one comes out *of* the closet (and yet, how often is it the case that we are "outted" when we are young and without resources?); so we are out of the closet, but into what? what new unbounded spatiality? the room, the den, the attic, the basement, the house, the bar, the university, some new enclosure whose door, like Kafka's door, produces the expectation of a fresh air and a light of illumination that never arrives? Curiously, it is the figure of the closet that produces this expectation, and which guarantees its dissatisfaction. For being "out" always depends to some extent on being "in"; it gains its meaning only within that polarity. Hence, being "out" must produce the closet again and again in order to maintain itself as "out." In this sense, *outness* can only produce a new opacity; and *the closet* produces the promise of a disclosure that can, by definition, never come. Is this infinite postponement of the disclosure of "gayness," produced by the very act of "coming out," to be lamented? Or is this very deferral of the signified *to be valued,* a site for the production of values, precisely because the term now takes on a life that cannot be, can never be, permanently controlled?

It is possible to argue that whereas no transparent or full revelation is afforded by "lesbian" and "gay," there remains a political imperative to use these necessary errors or category mistakes, as it were (what Gayatri Spivak might call "catachrestic" operations: to use a proper name improperly), to rally and represent an oppressed political constituency. Clearly, I am not legislating against the use of the term. My question is simply: which use will be legislated, and what play will there be between legislation and use such that the instrumental uses of "identity" do not become regulatory imperatives? If it is already true that "lesbians" and "gay men" have been traditionally designated as impossible identities, errors of classification, unnatural disasters within juridico-medical discourses, or, what perhaps amounts to the same, the very paradigm of what calls to be classified, regulated, and controlled, then perhaps these sites of disruption, error, confusion, and trouble can be the very rallying points for a certain resistance to classification and to identity as such.

The question is not one of *avowing* or *disavowing* the category of lesbian or gay, but, rather, why it is that the category becomes the site of this "ethical" choice? What does it mean to *avow* a category that can only maintain its specificity and coherence by performing a prior set of *disavowals?* Does this make "coming out" into the avowal of disavowal, that is, a return to the closet under the guise of an escape? And it is not something like heterosexuality or bisexuality that is disavowed by the category, but a set of identificatory and practical crossings between these categories that renders the discreteness of each equally suspect. Is it not possible to maintain and pursue heterosexual identifications and aims within homosexual practice, and homosexual identifications and aims within heterosexual practices? If a sexuality is to be disclosed, what will be taken as the true determinant of its meaning: the phantasy structure, the act, the orifice, the gender, the anatomy? And if the practice engages a complex interplay of all of those, which one of this erotic dimensions will come to stand for the sexuality that requires them all? Is it the *specificity* of a lesbian experience or lesbian desire or lesbian sexuality that lesbian theory needs to elucidate? Those efforts have only and always produced a set of contests and refusals which should by now make it clear that there is no necessarily common element among lesbians, except perhaps that we all know something about how homophobia works against women—although, even then, the language and the analysis we use will differ.

To argue that there might be a *specificity* to lesbian sexuality has seemed a necessary counterpoint to the claim that lesbian sexuality is just heterosexuality once removed, or that it is derived, or that it does not exist. But perhaps the claim of specificity, on the one hand, and the claim of derivativeness or non-existence, on the other, are not as contradictory as they seem. Is it not possible that lesbian sexuality is a process that reinscribes the power domains that it resists, that it is constituted in part from the very heterosexual matrix that it seeks to displace, and that its specificity is to be established, not *outside* or *beyond* that reinscription or reiteration, but in the very modality and effects of that reinscription. In other words, the negative constructions of lesbianism as a fake or a bad copy can be occupied and reworked to call into question the claims of heterosexual priority. In a sense I hope to make clear in what follows, lesbian sexuality can be understood to redeploy its 'derivativeness' in the service of displacing hegemonic heterosexual norms. Understood in this way, the political problem is not to establish the specificity of lesbian sexuality over and against its derivativeness, but to turn the homophobic construction of the bad copy against the framework that privileges heterosexuality as origin, and so 'derive' the former from the latter. This description requires a reconsideration of imitation, drag, and other forms of sexual crossing that affirm the internal complexity of a lesbian sexuality constituted in part within the very matrix of power that it is compelled both to reiterate and to oppose.

On the Being of Gayness as Necessary Drag

The professionalization of gayness requires a certain performance and production of a "self" which is the *constituted effect* of a discourse that nevertheless claims to "represent" that self as a prior truth. When I spoke at the conference on homosexuality in 1989, I found myself telling my friends beforehand that I was off to Yale to be a lesbian, which of course didn't mean that I wasn't one before, but that somehow then, as I spoke in that context, I *was* one in some more thorough and totalizing way, at least for the time being. So I *am* one, and my qualifications are even fairly unambiguous. Since I was sixteen, being a lesbian is what I've been. So what's the anxiety, the discomfort? Well, it has something to do with that redoubling, the way I can say, I'm going to Yale to be a lesbian; a lesbian is what I've been being for so long. How is it that I can both "be" one, and yet endeavor to be one at the same time? When and where does my being a lesbian come into play, when and where does this playing a lesbian constitute something like what I am? To say that I "play" at being one is not to say that I am not one "really"; rather, how and where I play at being one is the way in which that "being" gets established, instituted, circulated, and confirmed. This is not a performance from which I can take radical distance, for this is deep-seated play, psychically entrenched play, *and this "I" does not play its lesbianism as a role.* Rather, it is through the repeated play of this sexuality that the "I" is insistently reconstituted as a lesbian "I"; paradoxically, it is precisely the *repetition* of that play that establishes as well the *instability* of the very category that it constitutes. For if the "I" is a site of repetition, that is, if the "I" only achieves the semblance of identity through a certain repetition of itself, then the I is always displaced by the very repetition that sustains it. In other words, does or can the "I" ever repeat itself, cite itself, faithfully, or is there always a displacement from its former moment that establishes the permanently non-self-identical status of that "I" or its "being lesbian"? What "performs" does not exhaust the "I"; it does not lay out in visible terms the comprehensive content of that "I," for if the performance is "repeated," there is always the question of what differentiates from each other the moments of identity that are repeated. And if the "I" is the effect of a certain repetition, one which produces the semblance of a continuity or coherence, then there is no "I" that precedes the gender that it is said to perform; the repetition, and the failure to repeat, produce a string of performances that constitute and contest the coherence of that "I."

But *politically,* we might argue, isn't it quite crucial to insist on lesbian and gay identities precisely because they are being threatened with erasure and obliteration from homophobic quarters? Isn't the above theory *complicitous* with those political forces that would obliterate the possibility of gay and lesbian identity? Isn't it "no accident" that such theoretical contestations of identity emerge within a political climate that is performing a set of similar obliterations of homosexual identities through legal and political means?

The question I want to raise in return is this: ought such threats of obliteration dictate the terms of the political resistance to them, and if they do, do such homophobic efforts to that extent win the battle from the start? There is no question that gays and lesbians are threatened by the violence of public erasure, but the decision to counter that violence must be careful not to reinstall another in its place. Which version of lesbian or gay ought to be rendered visible, and which internal exclusions will that rendering visible institute? Can the visibility of identity *suffice* as a political strategy, or can it only be the starting point for a strategic intervention which calls for a transformation of policy? Is it not a sign of despair over public politics when identity becomes its own policy, bringing with it those who would 'police' it from various sides? And this is not a call to return to silence or invisibility, but, rather, to make use of a category that can be called into question, made to account for what it excludes. That any consolidation of identity requires some set of differentiations and exclusions seems clear. But which ones ought to be valorized? That the identity-sign I use now has its purposes seems right, but there is no way to predict or control the political uses to which that sign will be put in the future. And perhaps this is a kind of openness, regardless of its risks, that ought to be safeguarded for political reasons. If the rendering visible of lesbian/gay identity now presupposes a set of exclusions, then perhaps part of what is necessarily excluded is *the future uses of the sign.* There is a political necessity to use some sign now, and we do, but how to use it in such a way that its futural significations are not *foreclosed?* How to use the sign and avow its temporal contingency at once?

In avowing the sign's strategic provisionality (rather than its strategic essentialism), that identity can become a site of contest and revision, indeed, take on a future set of significations that those of us who use it now may not be able to foresee. It is in the safeguarding of the future of the political signifiers—preserving the signifier as a site of rearticulation—that Laclau and Mouffe discern its democratic promise.

Within contemporary U.S. politics, there are a vast number of ways in which lesbianism in particular is understood as precisely that which cannot or dare not *be.* In a sense, Jesse Helms's attack on the NEA for sanctioning representations of "homoeroticism" focuses various homophobic fantasies of what gay men are and do on the work of Robert Mapplethorpe. In a sense, for Helms, gay men exist as objects of prohibition; they are, in his twisted fantasy, sadomasochistic exploiters of children, the paradigmatic exemplars of "obscenity"; in a sense, the lesbian is not even produced within this discourse as a prohibited object. Here it becomes important to recognize that oppression works not merely through acts of overt prohibition, but covertly, through the constitution of viable subjects and through the corollary constitution of a domain of unviable (un)subjects—*abjects,* we might call them—who are neither named nor prohibited within the economy of the law. Here oppression works through the production of a domain of unthinkability and unnameability. Lesbianism is not explicitly prohibited in part because it has not even made its way into the thinkable, the imaginable, that grid of cultural intelligibility that regulates the real and the nameable. How, then, to "be" a lesbian in a political context in which the lesbian does not exist? That is, in a political discourse that wages its violence against lesbianism in part by excluding lesbianism from discourse itself? To be prohibited explicitly is to occupy a discursive site from which something like a reverse-discourse can be articulated; to be implicitly proscribed is not even to qualify as an object of prohibition. And through homosexualities of all kinds in this present climate are being erased, reduced, and (then) reconstituted as sites of radical homophobic fantasy, it is important to retrace the different routes by which the unthinkability of homosexuality is being constituted time and again.

It is one thing to be erased from discourse, and yet another to be present within discourse as an abiding falsehood. Hence, there is a political imperative to render lesbianism visible, but how is that to be done outside or through existing regulatory regimes? Can the exclusion from ontology itself become a rallying point for resistance?

Here is something like a confession which is meant merely to thematize the impossibility of confession: As a young person, I suffered for a long time, and I suspect many people have, from being told, explicitly or implicitly, that what I "am" is a copy, an imitation, a derivative example, a shadow of the real. Compulsory heterosexuality sets itself up as the original, the true, the authentic; the norm that determines the real implies that "being" lesbian is always a kind of miming, a vain effort to participate in the phantasmatic plenitude of naturalized heterosexuality which will always and only fail. And yet, I remember quite distinctly when I first read in Esther Newton's *Mother Camp: Female Impersonators in America* that drag is not an imitation or a copy of some prior and true gender; according to Newton, drag enacts the very structure of impersonation by which *any gender* is assumed. Drag is not the putting on of a gender that belongs properly to some other group, i.e. an act of *ex*-propriation or *ap*propriation that assumes that gender is the rightful property of sex, that "masculine" belongs to "male" and "feminine" belongs to "female." There is no "proper" gender, a gender proper to one sex rather than another, which is in some sense that sex's cultural property. Where that notion of the "proper" operates, it is always only *improperly* installed as the effect of a compulsory system. Drag constitutes the mundane way in which genders are appropriated, theatricalized, worn, and done; it implies that all gendering is a kind of impersonation and approximation. If this is true, it seems, there is no original or primary gender that drag imitates, but *gender is a kind of imitation for which there is no original;* in fact, it is a kind of imitation that produces the very notion of the original as an *effect* and consequence of the imitation itself. In other words, the naturalistic effects of heterosexualized genders are produced through imitative strategies; what they imitate is a phantasmatic ideal of heterosexual identity, one that is produced by the imitation as its effect. In this sense, the "reality" of heterosexual identities is performatively constituted through an imitation that sets itself up as the origin and the ground of all imitations. In other words, heterosexuality is always in the process of imitating and approximating its own phantasmatic idealization of itself—*and failing.* Precisely because it is bound to fail, and yet endeavors to succeed, the project of heterosexual identity is propelled into an endless repetition of itself. Indeed, in its efforts to naturalize itself as the original, heterosexuality must be understood as a compulsive and compulsory repetition that can only produce the *effect* of its own originality; in other words, compulsory heterosexual identities, those ontologically consolidated phantasms of "man" and "woman," are theatrically produced effects that posture as grounds, origins, the normative measure of the real.

Reconsider then the homophobic charge that queens and butches and femmes are imitations of the heterosexual real. Here "imitation" carries the meaning of "derivative" or "secondary," a copy of an origin which is itself the ground of all copies, but which is itself a copy of nothing. Logically, this notion of an "origin" is suspect, for how can something operate as an origin if there are no secondary consequences which retrospectively confirm the originality of that origin? The origin requires its derivatives in order to affirm itself as an origin, for origins only make sense to the extent that they are differentiated from that which they produce as derivatives. Hence, if it were not for the notion of the homosexual *as* copy, there would be no construct of heterosexuality *as* origin. Heterosexuality here presupposes homosexuality. And if the homosexual *as* copy *precedes* the heterosexual as *origin*, then it seems only fair to concede that the copy comes before the origin, and that homosexuality is thus the origin, and heterosexuality the copy.

But simple inversions are not really possible. For it is only *as* a copy that homosexuality can be argued to *precede* heterosexuality as the origin. In other words, the entire framework of copy and origin proves radically unstable as each position inverts into the other and confounds the possibility of any stable way to locate the temporal or logical priority of either term.

But let us then consider this problematic inversion from a psychic/political perspective. If the structure of gender imitation is such that the imitat*ed* is to some degree produced—or, rather, *re*produced—by imitation (see again Derrida's inversion and displacement of mimesis in "The Double Session"), then to claim that gay and lesbian identities are implicated in heterosexual norms or in hegemonic culture generally is not to *derive* gayness from straightness. On the contrary, *imitation* does not copy that which is prior, but produces and *inverts* the very terms of priority and derivativeness. Hence, if gay identities are implicated in heterosexuality, that is not the same as claiming that they are determined or derived from heterosexuality, and it is not the same as claiming that that heterosexuality is the only cultural network in which they are implicated. These are, quite literally, *inverted* imitations, ones which invert the order of imitated and imitation, and which, in the process, expose the fundamental dependency of "the origin" on that which it claims to produce as its secondary effect.

What follows if we concede from the start that gay identities as derivative inversions are in part defined in terms of the very heterosexual identities from which they are differentiated? If heterosexuality is an impossible imitation of itself, an imitation that performatively constitutes itself as the original, then the imitative parody of "heterosexuality"—when and where it exists in gay cultures—is always and only an imitation of an imitation, a copy of a copy, for which there is no original. Put in yet a different way, the parodic or imitative effect of gay identities works neither to copy nor to emulate heterosexuality, but rather, to expose heterosexuality as an incessant and *panicked* imitation of its own naturalized idealization. That heterosexuality is always in the act of elaborating itself is evidence that it is perpetually at risk, that is, that it "knows" its own possibility of becoming undone: hence, its compulsion to repeat which is at once a foreclosure of that which threatens its coherence. That it can never eradicate that risk attests to its profound dependency upon the homosexuality that it seeks fully to eradicate and never can or that it seeks to make second, but which is always already there as a prior possibility. Although this failure of naturalized heterosexuality might constitute a source of pathos for heterosexuality itself— what its theorists often refer to as its constitutive malaise—it can become an occasion for a subversive and proliferating parody of gender norms in which the very claim to originality and to the real is shown to be the effect of a certain kind of naturalized gender mime.

It is important to recognize the ways in which heterosexual norms reappear within gay identities, to affirm that gay and lesbian identities are not only structured in part by dominant heterosexual frames, but that they are *not* for that reason *determined* by them. They are running commentaries on those naturalized positions as well, parodic replays and resignifications of precisely those heterosexual structures that would consign gay life to discursive domains of unreality and unthinkability. But to be constituted or structured in part by the very heterosexual norms by which gay people are oppressed is not, I repeat, to be claimed or determined by those structures. And it is not necessary to think of such heterosexual constructs as the pernicious intrusion of "the straight mind," one that must be rooted out in its entirety. In a way, the presence of heterosexual constructs and positionalities in whatever form in gay and lesbian identities presupposes that there is a gay and lesbian repetition of straightness, a recapitulation of straightness—which is itself a repetition and recapitulation of its own ideality—within its own terms, a site in which all sorts of resignifying and parodic repetitions become possible. The parodic replication and resignification of heterosexual constructs within non-heterosexual frames brings into relief the utterly constructed status of the so-called original, but it shows that heterosexuality only constitutes itself as the original through a convincing act of repetition. The more that "act" is expropriated, the more the heterosexual claim to originality is exposed as illusory.

Although I have concentrated in the above on the reality-effects of gender practices, performances, repetitions, and mimes, I do not mean to suggest that drag is a "role" that can be taken on or taken off at will. There is no volitional subject behind the mime who decides, as it were, which gender it will be today. On the contrary, the very possibility of becoming a viable subject requires that a certain gender mime be already underway. The "being" of the subject is no more self-identical than the "being" of any gender; in fact, coherent gender, achieved through an apparent repetition of the same, produces as its *effect* the illusion of a prior and volitional subject. In this sense, gender is not a performance that a prior subject elects to do, but gender is *performative* in the sense that it constitutes as an effect the very subject it appears to express. It is a *compulsory* performance in the sense that acting out of line with heterosexual norms brings with it ostracism, punishment, and violence, not to mention the transgressive pleasures produced by those very prohibitions.

To claim that there is no performer prior to the performed, that the performance is performative, that the performance constitutes the appearance of a "subject" as its effect is difficult to accept. This difficulty is the result of a predisposition to think of sexuality and gender as "expressing" in some indirect or direct way a psychic reality that precedes it. The denial of the *priority* of the subject, however, is not the denial of the subject; in fact, the refusal to conflate the subject with the psyche marks the psychic as that which exceeds the domain of the conscious subject. This psychic excess is precisely what is being systematically denied by the notion of a volitional "subject" who elects at will which gender and/or sexuality to be at any given time and place. It is this excess which erupts within the intervals of those repeated gestures and acts that construct the apparent uniformity of heterosexual positionalities, indeed which compels the repetition itself, and which guarantees its perpetual failure. In this sense, it is this excess which, within the heterosexual economy, implicitly includes homosexuality, that perpetual threat of a disruption which is quelled through a reenforced repetition of the same. And yet, if repetition is the way in which power works to construct the illusion of a seamless heterosexual identity, if heterosexuality is compelled to *repeat itself* in order to establish the illusion of its own uniformity and identity, then this is an identity permanently at risk, for what if it fails to repeat, or if the very exercise of repetition is redeployed for a very different performative purpose? If there is, as it were, always a compulsion to repeat, repetition never fully accomplishes identity. That there is a need for a repetition at all is a sign that identity is not self-identical. It requires to be instituted again and again, which is to say that it runs the risk of becoming *de*-instituted at every interval.

So what is this psychic excess, and what will constitute a subversive or *de*-instituting repetition? First, it is necessary to consider that sexuality always exceeds any given performance, presentation, or narrative which is why it is not possible to derive or read off a sexuality from any given gender presentation. And sexuality may be said to exceed any definitive narrativization. Sexuality is never fully "expressed" in a performance or practice; there will be passive and butchy femmes, femmy and aggressive butches, and both of those, and more, will turn out to describe more or less anatomically stable "males" and "females." There are no direct expressive or causal lines between sex, gender, gender presentation, sexual practice, fantasy and sexuality. None of those terms captures or determines the rest. Part of what constitutes sexuality is precisely that which does not appear and that which, to some degree, can never appear. This is perhaps the most fundamental reason why sexuality is to some degree always closeted, especially to the one who would express it through acts of self-disclosure. That which is excluded for a given gender presentation to "succeed" may be precisely what is played out sexually, that is, an "inverted" relation, as it were, between gender and gender presentation, and gender presentation and sexuality. On the other hand, both gender presentation and sexual practices may corollate such that it appears that the former "expresses" the latter, and yet both are jointly constituted by the very sexual possibilities that they exclude.

This logic of inversion gets played out interestingly in versions of lesbian butch and femme gender stylization. For a butch can present herself as capable, forceful, and all-providing, and a stone butch may well seek to constitute her lover as the exclusive site of erotic attention and pleasure. And yet, this "providing" butch who seems *at first* to replicate a certain husband-like role, can find herself caught in a logic of inversion whereby that "providingness" turns to a self-sacrifice, which implicates her in the most ancient trap of feminine self-abnegation. She may well find herself in a situation of radical need, which is precisely what she sought to locate, find, and fulfill in her femme lover. In effect, the butch inverts into the femme or remains caught up in the specter of that inversion, or takes pleasure in it. On the other hand, the femme who, as Amber Hollibaugh has argued, "orchestrates" sexual exchange, may well eroticize a certain dependency only to learn that the very power to orchestrate that dependency exposes her own incontrovertible power, at which point she inverts into a butch or becomes caught up in the specter of that inversion, or perhaps delights in it.

Psychic Mimesis

Whether loss or mimetism is primary (perhaps an undecidable problem), the psychic subject is nevertheless constituted internally by differentially gendered Others and is, therefore, never, as a gender, self-identical.

In my view, the self only becomes a self on the condition that it has suffered a separation (grammar fails us here, for the "it" only becomes differentiated through that separation), a loss which is suspended and provisionally resolved through a melancholic incorporation of some "Other." That "Other" installed in the self thus establishes the permanent incapacity of that "self" to achieve self-identity; it is as it were always already disrupted by that Other; the disruption of the Other at the heart of the self is the very condition of that self's possibility.

Such a consideration of psychic identification would vitiate the possibility of any stable set of typologies that explain or describe something like gay or lesbian identities. And any effort to supply one—as evidenced in Kaja Silverman's recent inquiries into male homosexuality—suffer from simplification, and conform, with alarming ease, to the regulatory requirements of diagnostic epistemic regimes. If incorporation in Freud's sense in 1914 is an effort to *preserve* a lost and loved object and to refuse or postpone the recognition of loss and, hence, of grief, then to become *like* one's mother or father or sibling or other early "lovers" may be an act of love and/or a hateful effort to replace or displace. How would we "typologize" the ambivalence at the heart of mimetic incorporations such as these?

How does this consideration of psychic identification return us to the question, what constitutes a subversive repetition? How are troublesome identifications apparent in cultural practices? Well, consider the way in which heterosexuality naturalizes itself through setting up certain illusions of continuity between sex, gender, and desire. When Aretha Franklin sings, "you make me feel like a natural woman," she seems at first to suggest that some natural potential of her biological sex is actualized by her participation in the cultural position of "woman" as object of heterosexual recognition. Something in her "sex" is thus expressed by her "gender" which is then fully known and consecrated within the heterosexual scene. There is no breakage, no discontinuity between "sex" as biological facticity and essence, or between gender and sexuality. Although Aretha appears to be all too glad to have her naturalness confirmed, she also seems fully and paradoxically mindful that that confirmation is never guaranteed, that the effect of naturalness is only achieved as a consequence of that moment of heterosexual recognition. After all, Aretha sings, you make me feel *like* a natural woman, suggesting that this is a kind of metaphorical substitution, an act of imposture, a kind of sublime and momentary participation in an ontological illusion produced by the mundane operation of heterosexual drag.

But what if Aretha were singing to me? Or what if she were singing to a drag queen whose performance somehow confirmed her own?

How do we take account of these kinds of identifications? It's not that there is some kind of *sex* that exists in hazy biological form that is somehow *expressed* in the gait, the posture, the gesture; and that some sexuality then expresses both that apparent gender or that more or less magical sex. If gender is drag, and if it is an imitation that regularly produces the ideal it attempts to approximate, then gender is a performance that *produces* the illusion of an inner sex or essence or psychic gender core; it *produces* on the skin, through the gesture, the move, the gait (that array of corporeal theatrics understood as gender presentation), the illusion of an inner depth. In effect, one way that gender gets naturalized is through being constructed as an inner psychic or physical *necessity*. And yet, it is always a surface sign, a signification on and with the public body that produces this illusion of an inner depth, necessity or essence that is somehow magically, causally expressed.

To dispute the psyche as *inner depth*, however, is not to refuse the psyche altogether. On the contrary, the psyche calls to be rethought precisely as a compulsive repetition, as that which conditions and disables the repetitive performance of identity. If every performance repeats itself to institute the effect of identity, then every repetition requires an interval between the acts, as it were, in which risk and excess threaten to disrupt the identity being constituted. The unconscious is this excess that enables and contests every performance, and which never fully appears within the performance itself. The psyche is not "in" the body, but in the very signifying process through which that body comes to appear; it is the lapse in repetition as well as its compulsion, precisely what the performance seeks to deny, and that which compels it from the start.

To locate the psyche within this signifying chain as the instability of all iterability is not the same as claiming that it is inner core that is awaiting its full and liberatory expression. On the contrary, the psyche is the permanent failure of expression, a failure that has its values, for it impels repetition and so reinstates the possibility of disruption. What then does it mean to pursue disruptive repetition within compulsory heterosexuality?

Although compulsory heterosexuality often presumes that there is first a sex that is expressed through a gender and then through a sexuality, it may now be necessary fully to invert and displace that operation of thought. If a regime of sexuality mandates a compulsory performance of sex, then it may be only through that performance that the binary system of gender and the binary system of sex come to have intelligibility at all. It may be that the very categories of sex, of sexual identity, of gender are produced or maintained in the *effects* of this compulsory performance, effects which are disingenuously renamed as causes, origins, disingenuously lined up within a causal or expressive sequence that the heterosexual norm produces to legitimate itself as the origin of all sex. How then to expose the causal lines as retrospectively and performatively produced fabrications, and to engage gender itself as an inevitable fabrication, to fabricate gender in terms which reveal every claim to the origin, the inner, the true, and the real as nothing other than the effects of *drag*, whose subversive possibilities ought to be played and replayed to make the "sex" of gender into site of insistent political play? Perhaps this will be a matter of working sexuality *against* identity, even against gender, and of letting that which cannot fully appear in any performance persist in its disruptive promise.❖

Paula Gunn Allen (1939–) was born on the Cubero land grant in New Mexico into Laguna, Sioux, Pueblo, and Chicano family cultures. Although she holds a Ph.D. and has taught at Berkeley, Allen is principally known for her many writings about native American life. Among her five books of poetry are *The Blind Lion* (1974), *A Cannon Between My Knees* (1981), and *Shadow Country* (1982). Her fiction includes *The Woman Who Owns the Shadows* (1983), and her principal nonfiction publications are *The Sacred Hoop: Recovering the Feminine in American Indian Traditions* (1986) and *Grandmothers of the Light: A Medicine Woman's Source Book* (1991).

Who Is Your Mother? Red Roots of White Feminism

Paula Gunn Allen (1986)

At Laguna Pueblo in New Mexico, "Who is your mother?" is an important question. At Laguna, one of several of the ancient Keres gynocratic societies of the region, your mother's identity is the key to your own identity. Among the Keres, every individual has a place within the universe—human and nonhuman—and that place is defined by clan membership. In turn, clan membership is dependent on matrilineal descent. Of course, your mother is not only that woman whose womb formed and released you—the term refers in every individual case to an entire generation of women whose psychic, and consequently physical, "shape" made the psychic existence of the following generation possible. But naming your own mother (or her equivalent) enables people to place you precisely within the universal web of your life, in each of its dimensions: cultural, spiritual, personal, and historical.

Among the Keres, "context" and "matrix" are equivalent terms, and both refer to approximately the same thing as knowing your derivation and place. Failure to know your mother, that is, your position and its attendant traditions, history, and place in the scheme of things, is failure to remember your significance, your reality, your right relationship to earth and society. It is the same thing as being lost—isolated, abandoned, self-estranged, and alienated from your own life. This importance of tradition in the life of every member of the community is not confined to Keres Indians; all American Indian Nations place great value on traditionalism.

The Native American sense of the importance of continuity with one's cultural origins runs counter to contemporary American ideas: in many instances, the immigrants to America have been eager to cast off cultural ties, often seeing their antecedents as backward, restrictive, even shameful. Rejection of tradition constitutes one of the major features of American life, an attitude that reaches far back into American colonial history and that now is validated by virtually every cultural institution in the country. Feminist practice, at least in the cultural artifacts the community values most, follows this cultural trend as well.

The American idea that the best and the brightest should willingly reject and repudiate their origins leads to an allied idea—that history, like everything in the past, is of little value and should be forgotten as quickly as possible. This all too often causes us to reinvent the wheel continually. We find ourselves discovering our collective pasts over and over, having to retake ground already covered by women in the preceding decades and centuries. The Native American view, which highly values maintenance of traditional customs, values, and perspectives, might result in slower societal change and in quite a bit less social upheaval, but it has the advantage of providing a solid sense of identity and lowered levels of psychological and interpersonal conflict.

Contemporary Indian communities value individual members who are deeply connected to the traditional ways of their people, even after centuries of concerted and brutal effort on the part of the American government, the churches, and the corporate system to break the connections between individuals and their tribal

---

world. In fact, in the view of the traditionals, rejection of one's culture—one's traditions, language, people—is the result of colonial oppression and is hardly to be applauded. They believe that the roots of oppression are to be found in the loss of tradition and memory because that loss is always accompanied by a loss of positive sense of self. In short, Indians think it is important to remember, while Americans believe it is important to forget.

The traditional Indians' view can have a significant impact if it is expanded to mean that the sources of social, political, and philosophical thought in the Americas not only should be recognized and honored by Native Americans but should be embraced by American society. If American society judiciously modeled the traditions of the various Native Nations, the place of women in society would become central, the distribution of goods and power would be egalitarian, the elderly would be respected, honored, and protected as a primary social and cultural resource, the ideals of physical beauty would be considerably enlarged (to include "fat," strong-featured women, gray-haired, and wrinkled individuals, and others who in contemporary American culture are viewed as "ugly"). Additionally, the destruction of the biota, the life sphere, and the natural resources of the planet would be curtailed, and the spiritual nature of human and nonhuman life would become a primary organizing principle of human society. And if the traditional tribal systems that are emulated included pacifist ones, war would cease to be a major method of human problem solving.

Re-membering Connections and Histories

The belief that rejection of tradition and of history is a useful response to life is reflected in America's amazing loss of memory concerning its origins in the matrix and context of Native America. America does not seem to remember that it derived its wealth, its values, its food, much of its medicine, and a large part of its "dream" from Native America. It is ignorant of the genesis of its culture in this Native American land, and that ignorance helps to perpetuate the long-standing European and Middle Eastern monotheistic, hierarchical, patriarchal cultures' oppression of women, gays, and lesbians, people of color, working class, unemployed people, and the elderly. Hardly anyone in America speculates that the constitutional system of government might be as much a product of American Indian ideas and practices as of colonial American and Anglo-European revolutionary fervor.

Even though Indians are officially and informally ignored as intellectual movers and shapers in the United States, Britain, and Europe, they are peoples with ancient tenure on this soil. During the ages when tribal societies existed in the Americas largely untouched by patriarchal oppression, they developed elaborate systems of thought that included science, philosophy, and government based on a belief in the central importance of female energies, autonomy of individuals, cooperation, human dignity, human freedom, and egalitarian distribution of status, goods, and services. Respect for others, reverence for life, and as a by-product, pacifism as a way of life; importance of kinship ties in the customary ordering social interaction; a sense of the sacredness and mystery of existence; balance and harmony in relationships both sacred and secular were all features of life among the tribal confederacies and nations. And in those that lived by the largest number of these principles, gynarchy was the norm rather than the exception. Those systems are as yet unmatched in any contemporary industrial, agrarian, or postindustrial society on earth.

There are many female gods recognized and honored by the tribes and Nations. Femaleness was highly valued, both respected and feared, and all social institutions reflected this attitude. Even modern sayings, such as the Cheyenne statement that a people is not conquered until the hearts of the women are on the ground, express the Indians' understanding that without the power of woman the people will not live, but with it, they will endure and prosper.

Indians did not confine this belief in the central importance of female energy to matters of worship. Among many of the tribes (perhaps as many as 70 percent of them in North America alone), this belief was reflected in all of their social institutions. The Iroquois Constitution or White Roots of Peace, also called the Great Law of the Iroquois, codified the Matrons' decision-making and economic power:

> The lineal descent of the people of the Five Fires (the Iroquois Nations) shall run in the female line. Women shall be considered the progenitors of the Nation. They shall own the land and the soil. Men and women shall follow the status of their mothers. (Article 44)
>
> The women heirs of the chieftainship titles of the League shall be called Oiner or Otinner [Noble] for all time to come. (Article 45)
>
> If a disobedient chief persists in his disobedience after three warnings [by his female relatives, by his male relatives, and by one of his fellow council members, in that order], the matter shall go to the council of War Chiefs. The Chiefs shall then take way the title of the erring chief *by order of the women in whom the title is vested.* When the chief is deposed, the women shall notify the chiefs of the League . . . and the chiefs of the League shall sanction the act. The women will then select another of their sons as a candidate and the chiefs shall elect him. (Article 19) (Emphasis mine)

The Matrons held so much policy-making power traditionally that once, when their position was threatened they demanded its return, and consequently the power of women was fundamental in shaping the Iroquois Confederation sometime in the sixteenth or early seventeenth century. It was women

> who fought what may have been the first successful feminist rebellion in the New World. The year was 1600, or thereabouts, when these tribal feminists decided that they had had enough of unregulated warfare by their men. Lysistratas among the Indian women proclaimed a boycott on lovemaking and childbearing. Until the men conceded to them the power to decide upon war and peace, there would be no more warriors. Since the men believed that the women alone knew the secret of childbirth, the rebellion was instantly successful.
>
> In the Constitution of Deganawidah the founder of the Iroquois Confederation of Nations had said: "He caused the body of our mother, the woman, to be of great worth and honor. He purposed that she shall be endowed and entrusted with the birth and upbringing of men, and that she shall have the care of all that is planted by which life is sustained and supported and the power to breathe is fortified: *and moreover that the warriors shall be her assistants.*"
>
> The footnote of history was curiously supplied when Susan B. Anthony began her "Votes for Women" movement two and a half centuries later. Unknowingly the feminists chose to hold their founding convention of latter-day suffragettes in the town of Seneca [Falls], New York. The site was just a stone's throw from the old council house where the Iroquois women had plotted their feminist rebellion. (Emphasis mine)

Beliefs, attitudes, and laws such as these became part of the vision of American feminists and of other human liberation movements around the world. Yet feminists too often believe that no one has ever experienced the kind of society that empowered women and made that empowerment the basis of its rules of civilization. The price the feminist community must pay because it is not aware of the recent presence of gynarchical societies on this continent is unnecessary confusion, division, and much lost time.

The Root of Oppression Is Loss of Memory

An odd thing occurs in the minds of Americans when Indian civilization is mentioned: little or nothing. As I write this, I am aware of how far removed my version of the roots of American feminism must seem to those steeped in either mainstream or radical versions of feminism's history. I am keenly aware of the lack of image Americans have about our continent's recent past. I am intensely conscious of popular notions of Indian women as beasts of burden, squaws, traitors, or, at best, vanished denizens of a long-lost wilderness. How odd, then, must my contention seem that the gynocratic tribes of the American continent provided the basis for all the dreams of liberation that characterize the modern world.

We as feminists must be aware of our history on this continent. We need to recognize that the same forces that devastated the gynarchies of Britain and the Continent also devastated the ancient African civilizations, and we must know that those same materialistic, antispiritual forces are presently engaged in wiping out the same gynarchical values, along with the peoples who adhere to them, in Latin America. I am convinced that those wars were and continue to be about the imposition of patriarchal civilization over the holistic, pacifist, and spirit-based gynarchies they supplant. To that end the wars of imperial conquest have not been solely or even mostly waged over the land and its resources, but they have been fought within the bodies, minds, and hearts of the people of the earth for dominion over them. I think this is the reason traditionals say we must remember our origins, our cultures, our histories, our mothers and grandmothers, for without that memory, which implies continuance rather than nostalgia, we are doomed to engulfment by a paradigm that is fundamentally inimical to the vitality, autonomy, and self-empowerment essential for satisfying, high-quality life.

The vision that impels feminists to action was the vision of the Grandmothers' society, the society that was captured in the words of the sixteenth-century explorer Peter Martyr nearly five hundred years ago. It is the same vision repeated over and over by radical thinkers of Europe and America, from François Villon to John Locke, from William Shakespeare to Thomas Jefferson, from Karl Marx to Friedrich Engels, from Benito Juarez to Martin Luther King, from Elizabeth Cady Stanton to Judy Grahn, from Harriet Tubman to Audre Lorde, from Emma Goldman to Bella Abzug, from Malinalli to Cherríe Moraga, and from Iyatiku to me. That vision as Martyr told it is of a country where there are "no soldiers, no gendarmes or police, no nobles, kings, regents, prefects, or judges, no prisons, no lawsuits . . . All are equal and free," or so Friedrich Engels recounts Martyr's words.

Columbus wrote:

Nor have I been able to learn whether they [the inhabitants of the islands he visited on his first journey to the New World] held personal property, for it seemed to me that whatever one had, they all took shares of . . . They are so ingenuous and free with all they have, that no one would believe it who has not seen it; of anything that they possess, if it be asked of them, they never say no; on the contrary, they invite you to share it and show as much love as if their hearts went with it.

At least that's how the Native Caribbean people acted when the whites first came among them; American Indians are the despair of social workers, bosses, and missionaries even now because of their deeply ingrained tendency to spend all they have, mostly on others. In any case, as the historian William Brandon notes,

the Indian *seemed* free, to European eyes, gloriously free, to the European soul shaped by centuries of toil and tyranny, and this impression operated profoundly on the process of history and the development of America. Something in the peculiar character of the Indian world gave an impression of classlessness, of propertylessness, and that in turn led to an impression, as H. H. Bancroft put it, of "humanity unrestrained . . . in the exercise of liberty absolute."

A Feminist Heroine

Early in the women's suffrage movement, Eva Emery Dye, an Oregon suffragette, went looking for a heroine to embody her vision of feminism. She wanted a historical figure whose life would symbolize the strengthened power of women. She found Sacagawea (or Sacajawea) buried in the journals of Lewis and Clark. The Shoshoni teenager had traveled with the Lewis and Clark expedition, carrying her infant son, and on a small number of occasions acted as translator.

Dye declared that Sacagawea, whose name is thought to mean Bird Woman, had been the guide to the historic expedition, and through Dye's work Sacagawea became enshrined in American memory as a moving force and friend of the whites, leading them in the settlement of western North America.

But Native American roots of white feminism reach back beyond Sacagawea. The earliest white women on this continent were well acquainted with tribal women. They were neighbors to a number of tribes and often shared food, information, child care, and health care. Of course little is made of these encounters in official histories of colonial America, the period from the Revolution to the Civil War, or on the evermoving frontier. Nor, to my knowledge, has either the significance or incidence of intermarriage between Indian and white or between Indian and Black been explored. By and large, the study of Indian-white relations has been focused on government and treaty relations, warfare, missionization, and education. It has been almost entirely documented in terms of formal white Christian patriarchal impacts and assaults on Native Americans, though they are not often characterized as assaults but as "civilizing the savages." Particularly in organs of popular culture and miseducation, the focus has been on what whites imagine to be degradation of Indian women ("squaws"), their equally imagined love of white government and white conquest ("princesses"), and the horrifyingly misleading, fanciful tales of "blood-thirsty, backward primitives" assaulting white Christian settlers who were looking for life, liberty, and happiness in their chosen land.

But, regardless of official versions of relations between Indians and whites or other segments of the American population, the fact remains that great numbers of apparently "white" or "Black" Americans carry notable degrees of Indian blood. With that blood has come the culture of the Indians, informing the lifestyles, attitudes, and values of their descendants. Somewhere along the line—and often quite recently—an Indian woman was giving birth to and raising the children of a family both officially and informally designated as white or Black—not Indian. In view of this, it should be evident that one of the major enterprises of Indian women in America has been the transfer of Indian values and culture to as large and influential a segment of American immigrant populations as possible. Their success in this endeavor is amply demonstrated in the Indian values and social styles that increasingly characterize American life. Among these must be included "permissive" childrearing practices, for imprisoning, torturing, caning, strapping, starving, or verbally abusing children was considered outrageous behavior. Native Americans did not believe that physical or psychological abuse of children would result in their edification. They did not believe that children are born in sin, are congenitally predisposed to evil, or that a good parent who wishes the child to gain salvation, achieve success, or earn the respect of her or his fellows can be helped to those ends by physical or emotional torture.

The early Americans saw the strongly protective attitude of the Indian people as a mark of their "savagery"—as they saw the Indian's habit of bathing frequently, their sexual openness, their liking for scant clothing, their raucous laughter at most things, their suspicion and derision of authoritarian structures, their quick pride, their genuine courtesy, their willingness to share what they had with others less fortunate than they, their egalitarianism, their ability to act as if various lifestyles were a normal part of living, and their granting that women were of equal or, in individual cases, of greater value than men.

Yet the very qualities that marked Indian life in the sixteenth century have, over the centuries since contact between the two worlds occurred, come to mark much of contemporary American life. And those qualities, which I believe have passed into white culture from Indian culture, are the very ones that fundamentalists, immigrants from Europe, the Middle East, and Asia often find the most reprehensible. Third- and fourth-generation Americans indulge in growing nudity, informality in social relations, egalitarianism, and the rearing of women who value autonomy, strength, freedom, and personal dignity—and who are often derided by European, Asian, and Middle Eastern men for those qualities. Contemporary Americans value leisure almost as much as tribal people do. They find themselves increasingly unable to accept child abuse as a reasonable way to nurture. They bathe more than any other industrial people on earth—much to the scorn of their white cousins across the Atlantic, and they sometimes enjoy a good laugh even at their own expense (though they still have a less developed sense of the ridiculous than one might wish).

Contemporary Americans find themselves more and more likely to adopt a "live and let live" attitude in matters of personal sexual and social styles. Two-thirds of their diet and a large share of their medications and medical treatments mirror or are directly derived from Native American sources. Indianization is not a simple concept, to be sure, and it is one that Americans often find themselves resisting; but it is a process that has taken place, regardless of American resistance to recognizing the source of many if not most of American's vaunted freedoms in our personal, family, social, and political arenas.

This is not to say that Americans have become Indian in every attitude, value, or social institution. Unfortunately, Americans have a way to go in learning how to live in the world in ways that improve the quality of life for each individual while doing minimal damage to the biota, but they have adapted certain basic qualities of perception and certain attitudes that are moving them in that direction.

An Indian-focused Version of American History

American colonial ideas of self-government came as much from the colonists' observations of tribal governments as from their Protestant or Greco-Roman heritage. Neither Greece nor Rome had the kind of pluralistic democracy as that concept has been understood in the United States since Andrew Jackson, but the tribes, particularly the gynarchical tribal confederacies, did. It is true that the *oligarchic* form of government that colonial Americans established was originally based on Greco-Roman systems in a number of important ways, such as its restriction of citizenship to propertied white males over twenty-one years of age, but it was never a form that Americans as a whole have been entirely comfortable with. Politics and government in the United States during the Federalist period also reflected the English common-law system as it had evolved under patriarchal feudalism and monarchy—hence the United States' retention of slavery and restriction of citizenship to propertied white males.

The Federalists did make one notable change in the feudal system from which their political system derived on its Anglo side. They rejected blooded aristocracy and monarchy. This idea came from the Protestant Revolt to be sure, but it was at least reinforced by colonial America's proximity to American Indian nonfeudal confederacies and their concourse with those confederacies over the two hundred years of the colonial era. It was this proximity and concourse that enabled the revolutionary theorists to "dream up" a system in which all local polities would contribute to and be protected by a central governing body responsible for implementing policies that bore on the common interest of all. It should also be noted that the Reformation followed Columbus's contact with the Americas and that his and Martyr's reports concerning Native Americans' free and easy egalitarianism were in circulation by the time the Reformation took hold.

The Iroquois federal system, like that of several in the vicinity of the American colonies, is remarkably similar to the organization of the federal system of the United States. It was made up of local, "state," and federal bodies composed of executive, legislative, and judicial branches. The Council of Matrons was the executive: it instituted and determined general policy. The village, tribal (several villages), and Confederate councils determined and implemented policies when they did not conflict with the broader Council's decisions or with theological precepts that ultimately determined policy at all levels. The judicial was composed of the men's councils and the Matron's council, who sat together to make decisions. Because the matrons were the ceremonial center of the system, they were also the prime policymakers.

Obviously, there are major differences between the structure of the contemporary American government and that of the Iroquois. Two of those differences were and are crucial to the process of just government. The Iroquois system is spirit-based, while that of the United States is secular, and the Iroquois Clan Matrons formed the executive. The female executive function was directly tied to the ritual nature of the Iroquois politic, for the executive was lodged in the hands of the Matrons of particular clans across village, tribe, and national lines. The executive office was hereditary, and only sons of eligible clans could serve, at the behest of the Matrons of their clans, on the councils at the three levels. Certain daughters inherited the office of Clan Matron through their clan affiliations. No one could impeach or disempower a Matron, though her violation of certain laws could result in her ineligibility for the Matron's council. For example, a woman who married *and took her husband's name* could not hold the title Matron.

American ideals of social justice came into sharp focus through the commentaries of Iroquois observers who traveled in France in the colonial period. These observers expressed horror at the great gap between the lifestyles of the wealthy and the poor, remarking to the French philosopher Montaigne, who would heavily influence the radical communities of Europe, England, and America, that "they had noticed that in Europe there seemed to be two moities, consisting of the rich 'full gorged' with wealth, and the poor, starving 'and bare with need and povertie.' The Indian tourists not only marveled at the division, but marveled that the poor endured 'such an injustice, and that they took not the others by the throte, or set fire on their house.' " It must be noted that the urban poor eventually did just that in the French Revolution. The writings of Montaigne and of those he influenced provided the theoretical framework and the vision that propelled the struggle for liberty, justice, and equality on the Continent and later throughout the British empire.

The feminist idea of power as it ideally accrues to women stems from tribal sources. The central importance of the clan Matrons in the formulation and determination of domestic and foreign policy as well as in their primary role in the ritual and ceremonial life of their respective Nations was the single most important attribute of the Iroquois, as of the Cherokee and Muskogee, who traditionally inhabited the southern Atlantic region. The latter peoples were removed to what is now Oklahoma during the Jackson administration, but prior to the American Revolution they had regular and frequent communication with and impact on both the British colonizers and later the American people, including the African peoples brought here as slaves.

Ethnographer Lewis Henry Morgan wrote an account of Iroquoian matriarchal culture, published in 1877, that heavily influenced Marx and the development of communism, particularly lending it the idea of the liberation of women from patriarchal dominance. The early socialists in Europe, especially in Russia, saw women's liberation as a central aspect of the socialist revolution. Indeed, the basic ideas of socialism, the egalitarian distribution of goods and power, the peaceful ordering of society, and the right of every member of society to participate in the work and benefits of that society, are ideas that pervade American Indian political thought and action. And it is through various channels—the informal but deeply effective Indianization of Europeans, and christianizing Africans, the social and political theory of the confederacies feuding and then intertwining with European dreams of liberty and justice, and, more recently, the work of Morgan and the writings of Marx and Engels—that the age-old gynarchical systems of egalitarian government found their way into contemporary feminist theory.

When Eva Emery Dye discovered Sacagawea and honored her as the guiding spirit of American womanhood, she may have been wrong in bare historical fact, but she was quite accurate in terms of deeper truth. The statues that have been erected depicting Sacagawea as a Matron in her prime signify an understanding in the American mind, however unconscious, that the source of just government, of right order ing of social relationships, the dream of "liberty and justice for all" can be gained only by following the Indian Matrons' guidance. For, as Dr. Anna Howard Shaw said of Sacagawea at the National American Woman's Suffrage Association in 1905:

> Forerunner of civilization, great leader of men, patient and motherly woman, we bow our hearts to do you honor! . . . May we the daughters of an alien race . . . learn the lessons of calm endurance, of patient persistence and unfaltering courage exemplified in your life, in our efforts to lead men through the Pass of justice, which goes over the mountains of prejudice and conservatism to the broad land of the perfect freedom of a true republic; one in which men and women together shall in perfect equality solve the problems of a nation that knows no caste, no race, no sex in opportunity, in responsibility or in justice! May 'the eternal womanly' ever lead us on!❖

Vaclav Havel (1936–) is a philosopher, playwright, and political leader. He was a moral force behind Czechoslovakia's velvet revolution, after which he became president of the country until the federation dissolved on January 1, 1993, at which time he was elected president of the Czech Republic.

The End of the Modern Era

Vaclav Havel (1992)

The end of Communism is, first and foremost, a message to the human race. It is a message we have not yet fully deciphered and comprehended. In its deepest sense, the end of Communism has brought a major era in human history to an end. It has brought an end not just to the nineteenth and twentieth centuries, but to the modern age as a whole.

The modern era has been dominated by the culminating belief, expressed in different forms, that the world—and Being as such—is a wholly knowable system governed by a finite number of universal laws that man can grasp and rationally direct for his own benefit. This era, beginning in the Renaissance and developing from the Enlightenment to socialism, from positivism to scientism, from the Industrial Revolution to the information revolution, was characterized by rapid advances in rational, cognitive thinking.

This, in turn, gave rise to the proud belief that man, as the pinnacle of everything that exists, was capable of objectively describing, explaining and controlling everything that exists, and of possessing the one and only truth about the world. It was an era in which there was a cult of depersonalized objectivity, an era in which objective knowledge was amassed and technologically exploited, an era of belief in automatic progress brokered by the scientific method. It was an era of systems, institutions, mechanisms and statistical averages. It was an era of ideologies, doctrines, interpretations of reality, an era in which the goal was to find a universal theory of the world, and thus a universal key to unlock its prosperity.

Communism was the perverse extreme of this trend. It was an attempt, on the basis of a few propositions masquerading as the only scientific truth, to organize all of

---

"The End of the Modern Era," *The New York Times* (March 1, 1992).

life according to a single model, and to subject it to central planning and control regardless of whether or not that was what life wanted.

The fall of Communism can be regarded as a sign that modern thought—based on the premise that the world is objectively knowable, and that the knowledge so obtained can be absolutely generalized—has come to a final crisis. This era has created the first global, or planetary, technical civilization, but it has reached the limit of its potential, the point beyond which the abyss begins. The end of Communism is a serious warning to all mankind. It is a signal that the era of arrogant, absolutist reason is drawing to a close and that it is high time to draw conclusions from that fact.

Communism was not defeated by military force, but by life, by the human spirit, by conscience, by the resistance of Being and man to manipulation. It was defeated by a revolt of color, authenticity, history in all its variety and human individuality against imprisonment within a uniform ideology.

This powerful signal is coming at the 11th hour. We all know civilization is in danger. The population explosion and the greenhouse effect, holes in the ozone and AIDS, the threat of nuclear terrorism and the dramatically widening gap between the rich north and the poor south, the danger of famine, the depletion of the biosphere and the mineral resources of the planet, the expansion of commercial television culture and the growing threat of regional wars—all these, combined with thousands of other factors, represent a general threat to mankind.

The large paradox at the moment is that man—a great collector of information—is well aware of all this, yet is absolutely incapable of dealing with the danger. Traditional science, with its usual coolness, can describe the different ways we might destroy ourselves, but it cannot offer us truly effective and practicable instructions on how to avert them. There is too much to know; the information is muddled or poorly organized; these processes can no longer be fully grasped and understood, let alone contained or halted.

We are looking for new scientific recipes, new ideologies, new control systems, new institutions, new instruments to eliminate the dreadful consequences of our previous recipes, ideologies, control systems, institutions and instruments. We treat the fatal consequences of technology as though they were a technical defect that could be remedied by technology alone. We are looking for an objective way out of the crisis of objectivism.

Everything would seem to suggest that this is not the way to go. We cannot devise, within the traditional modern attitude to reality, a system that will eliminate all the disastrous consequences of previous systems. We cannot discover a law or theory whose technical application will eliminate all the disastrous consequences of the technical application of earlier laws and technologies.

What is needed is something different, something larger. Man's attitude to the world must be radically changed. We have to abandon the arrogant belief that the world is merely a puzzle to be solved, a machine with instructions for use waiting to be discovered, a body of information to be fed into a computer in the hope that, sooner or later, it will spit out a universal solution.

It is my profound conviction that we have to release from the sphere of private whim such forces as a natural, unique and unrepeatable experience of the world, an elementary sense of justice, the ability to see things as others do, a sense of transcendental responsibility, archetypal wisdom, good taste, courage, compassion and faith in the importance of particular measures that do not aspire to be a universal key to salvation. Such forces must be rehabilitated.

Things must once more be given a chance to present themselves as they are, to be perceived in their individuality. We must see the pluralism of the world, and not bind it by seeking common denominators or reducing everything to a single common equation.

We must try harder to understand than to explain. The way forward is not in the mere construction of universal systemic solutions, to be applied to reality from the outside; it is also in seeking to get to the heart of reality through personal experience. Such an approach promotes an atmosphere of tolerant solidarity and unity in diversity based on mutual respect, genuine pluralism and parallelism. In a word, human uniqueness, human action and the human spirit must be rehabilitated.

The world today is a world in which generality, objectivity and universality are in crisis. This world presents a great challenge to the practice of politics, which, it seems to me, still has a technocratic, utilitarian approach to Being, and therefore to political power as well. Many of the traditional mechanisms of democracy created and developed and conserved in the modern era are so linked to the cult of objectivity and statistical average that they can annul human individuality. We can see this in political language, where cliché often squeezes out a personal tone. And when a personal tone does crop up, it is usually calculated, not an outburst of personal authenticity.

Sooner or later politics will be faced with the task of finding a new, postmodern face. A politician must become a person again, someone who trusts not only a scientific representation and analysis of the world, but also the world itself. He must believe not only in sociological statistics, but also in real people. He must trust not only an objective interpretation of reality, but also his own soul; not only an adopted ideology, but also his own thoughts; not only the summary reports he receives each morning, but also his own feeling.

Soul, individual spirituality, first-hand personal insight into things, the courage to be himself and go the way his conscience points, humility in the face of the mysterious order of Being, confidence in its natural direction and, above all, trust in his own subjectivity as his principal link with the subjectivity of the world—these are the qualities that politicians of the future should cultivate.

Looking at politics "from the inside," as it were, has if anything confirmed my belief that the world of today—with the dramatic changes it is going through and in its determination not to destroy itself—presents a great challenge to politicians.

It is not that we should simply seek new and better ways of managing society, the economy and the world. The point is that we should fundamentally change how we behave. And who but politicians should lead the way? Their changed attitude toward the world, themselves and their responsibility can give rise to truly effective systemic and institutional changes.❖

PART SIX

Searching for
the Millennium

As I write, it is early January 1998. At a definite instant in the near future—a moment for which some people have already begun the countdown—the clocks and calendars will flip from one millennium to another. Some who read this edition of this book will read it after that much-talked-about second. They will know whether something truly amazing transpired at midnight on December 31, 1999. Why is it that so rare an event makes such a difference in the fantasy life of so many people? It is as if the calendrical event has an inherent force of its own, acting powerfully on the social imagination.

It is impossible, of course, to study the phenomenon of millennium frenzy by the usual methods. None of us was around when this sort of thing last occurred, so we cannot make a very exact historical comparison. It is, I recently discovered, a devilish task to try to unearth even one thing that transpired at the end of the previous millennium. Before turning to the reference works, I thought there must have been something salient about the year 1000 C.E. I had been thus disposed by my own cultural bias about events occurring near the year we now call 0 C.E. (or, is it 0 B.C.E.?). I had expected that something remarkable happens as one millennium ends and another begins. In 1000 C.E., there must have been, I thought, something similar to, if not exactly the same as, the events that gave birth to what some of us call the Christian Era. But I could find nothing of particular interest,—only stray facts: On or about the year 1000 C.E., in the area we have since come to call Europe, the last Frankish king (Charles the Fat!) had been dead for over a century, and the dominant German king was then Otto the Third. At about the same time in China, the northern Sung dynasty was enjoying sufficient prosperity to strike a major peace treaty in 1004, which perhaps, in turn, gave impetus to the invention of the world's first paper currency in 1024. In the Islamic world, the Fatimids had built the Mosque-university of al-Azhar in Cairo, while elsewhere in Africa, things seemed pretty stable so far as I could determine in several hours of research. I am sure that experts can come up with something that happened on the late evening of December 31, 999, but it is a little shocking to the sincere amateur that nothing noteworthy presented itself. Then again, I remember from a systematic study I once did of the early Christian era that the events of the year 0 C.E. were at the time of interest only to a small group of provincials in a remote corner of Mesopotamia. Elsewhere in the Roman Empire everyone was busy writing laws, building aqueducts, conquering foreigners. Pretty much business as usual.

These painfully imprecise comparisons of our own millennium frenzy with the apparent lack of such like in the previous eras do not mean that those who lived in those times did not find the calendrical changes exciting. Still, we can be certain that they were not hounded by television and other media attempting to increase their market share by, among other sordid affairs, cheerleading for the new millennium.

Since social theory is a heightened expression of the sociological imagination, it is not surprising that so much social theory after, especially, 1995 or so has been preoccupied with dreams of a new age. Though the postmodernism controversy that dominated a good bit of social thought through the 1980s and early 1990s led to no conclusive results, as I believe it could not have, this does not mean that something big and important might not be changing in the world, whether because of or in spite of the millennium frenzy.

In fact, there is good reason to believe that some very important, and decidedly real, changes in the world *have* taken place in recent years. What is different, first of all, about the world today is that most people understand very well that their economic hopes are tied to the economic success or failure of strangers in other parts of the world. Last night, for example, a new alarm clock my wife had purchased kept me awake because it made a most irregular noise. Early this morning before the sun rose I complained about the stupid thing. My wife's response was: "It should be okay, it was made in China." I said, stupidly: "Don't buy clocks that aren't made in Switzerland." She said, "They don't make clocks in Switzerland anymore." The truth is that neither of us had any idea where the best clocks are made, but we did not hesitate to argue the point of a sleepless night with reference to our respective, similarly uninformed, attitudes toward the world economy. Though I hate to admit it, I really did have in mind poor Chinese laborers smoking cigarettes and working long hours in some smog-filled city like Shanghai and, by contrast, a neatly shaven white man with a long beard making cuckoo clocks in the pristine Alps of Switzerland. I would be the first to admit that these are prejudices of the collective unconscious. I don't like them. They may have little to do with the facts of the world productive system. But the interesting thing about this little story is that at a very early hour while still in bed, my wife and I were thinking globally. Somehow talk of the new millennium is mixed up with talk of globalization. How, or if, the two are connected is hard to say.

What can be said for certain is that globalization is one of the ways in which the world is changing. But what is globalization? On this there is little agreement. Some say it is principally an effect of the new economic order in which, as Manuel Castells explains in "The Global Network," the capital funds that drive the economy are no longer the sole property of a capitalist class or even of a select number of banks in London, New York, or Tokyo. A global economy is one in which the economic goods and services that determine the life-chances of individuals and their families are now part of a worldwide market. The capital funds necessary to produce products like new basketball shoes or pay wages to workers (most of them impoverished women) in the *maquiladoras* on the U.S.-Mexican border flow freely and at amazing speeds to anywhere in the world where the cheapest labor—hence, best profits—can be found. If a decline in, say, the South Korean stock market or a precipitous rise in the cost of Iranian oil can affect the price of my daily bread, then it cannot be said that whoever legally owns the Korean stocks or the Iranian oil, much less my daily bread, really controls the economic values of what they own. In a world where no one controls even what they own, economic values—and thus economic hopes—are determined by terribly complicated events occurring in strange corners of the world we may never visit even though they visit us each day.

Now to be sure, such a change as this could not have occurred in the flash of the last decade or so. Though the economic realities have shifted over a much longer time, what has begun to change very quickly, and most acutely by the mid-1990s, is the worldwide *recognition* that the fate of individuals is determined by global events. You can be certain that if my wife and I, a very comfortable middle-class couple, start our day with talk of global events, those who suffer ever so much more than we begin and end their days with such talk. Today, thousands upon thousands of people in every part of the world are migrating from traditional villages to wherever they can find paid work that will improve their economic chances. Many of these people are women with small children; many others are victims of civil strife or the hopeless poverty of their peasant villages. They migrate in desperate search of work along the Mexican border or in the recovering cities of Vietnam or across the sprawling slums of urban India or Brazil. These are people whose hopes are almost always disappointed. When construction or assembly work is available, it is often poorly paid and living conditions are miserable. Their children suffer. Some are forced into the degradations of sex work or the drug trade. Some, like those who live in the squalor of the *maquiladoras* along Mexico's border with Texas, remain because, however awful the conditions and disappointing the pay, the alternatives back home are worse. For them, the making of even bad alarm clocks is no joke. They wake early to the stirrings of hungry babies in shantytowns. They must work if they can— for whoever will pay for whatever work under whichever available conditions. You can be certain that people living and working in these conditions are well aware that they live in a global economy. They know that what few chances they have for a decent life depend entirely on the comings and goings of the large multinational corporations that may be here today and gone tomorrow.

When, exactly, the world's well-off began to understand what the world's poor have known for a long time is hard to say. Some Europeans may have understood as long ago as the 1940s and 1950s, when their financial interests in plantations and gold mines in colonial Africa were threatened by rebellion and independence movements. For Americans of comfortable circumstances, the realization may have come in the 1960s when their poorly paid maids and workers joined the civil rights protests or, a little later, when the terrible war in Vietnam started going sour. After 1968, more and more poor people in the United States and across the world refused any longer to see the Americans as the brave and morally innocent defenders of freedom that their fathers may well have been in the Second World War against imperial evil in Germany and Asia. The war in Vietnam, whatever it was about, was about anything but the nice American pilots defending good against evil. This war caused many more people than the radicals and hippies back home to sit up and take notice. Just as Europeans had earlier, in the years after the Second World War, been forced to face decolonizing challenges to their colonial empires, so then, a generation later, Americans were confronted by the fast-fading innocence of their arrogant adventures in Vietnam.

The comfortable people of Europe and America soon had no choice but to accept the reality that the world was globally complicated. By the early 1970s, the already well-organized oil-producing states of the Middle East and parts of South America became an economic force they could not ignore. For the thoughtlessly comfortable, the Organization of Oil Exporting Countries (OPEC) came quickly to be the very symbol of a change for the worse in the world. The images of men dressed in the fashion of the ancient desert nomads, or of recent revolutionary heroes, disturbed Americans of good repute—and for good reason. These new economic and political powers that emerged on the world scene in the 1960s and early 1970s were, with rare exception, veterans of struggles to overcome Euro-American economic imperialism. They had determined, by the rights and the realities of the world oil markets, that they could control the flow of crude oil from their petroleum-rich areas and thus fix the price of crude oil at the highest possible level. They did nothing other that what the large oil corporations had done for years, except perhaps that they did it in public before the unbelieving eyes of those hitherto innocent of the dark side of capitalism.

By early 1974, especially in the United States, where the price of gasoline had been artificially low, the cost of driving the family car for fun and games became prohibitive, at least in relative terms. For a while, since the crude oil was being hoarded in reserve in the Middle East, there simply wasn't enough gasoline to go around at the pumps in downstate Illinois or far west Wyoming. This led to a degree of scarcity that Americans had not experienced since the hard times of World War II. For a while even those who would pay any price for a fill-up could not get the gas that once was all but free for the asking.

But this first pinch of global reality on the middle class did not ease up. It was not just the crimp that fuel prices put in the fun and games of the comfortable that caused them to think differently about the global economy. As it turns out, we eventually realized what everyone knows today—that virtually everything we have come to count on for the good life is made from one or another derivative of crude oil. Plastics for housing construction, artificial fibers for clothing, fuel for light and electricity—these, and much else, are by-products of oil that suddenly was crude in name only. As a result of the new world market in oil, aggravated by real natural scarcities, the cost of life in the industrial world was higher. Everything cost more. People had to work longer and harder just to keep up with their previous standard of living. And even as the rich got richer in the 1980s, the vast majority of once-comfortable people got poorer in relative terms.

It was during this period from the mid-1970s to the mid-1990s that people of relative comfort began to realize that something was different and that that something had to do with the global economy. This was the span of time during which the well-off began to get the message the poor had long understood. We live in a world in which what happens in the neighborhood is somehow, often quite directly, if mysteriously, connected to what is going on in neighborhoods and cities a world away. Villagers whose children were slaughtered in My Lai, South Vietnam, understood this fact of global life in 1968. It took many of those who lived in the comfortable villages of America and Switzerland many more years. But today, there are very few people anywhere who do not understand that we live in a global economy.

It is important, nonetheless, to distinguish between the reality of the global economy and the *understanding* of that reality. It is obvious that people are very often unable to understand what is happening in the larger world about them, even when it affects their lives in important ways. There would be no need of social theory, or the sociological imagination, were it the case that people generally understood the larger structures of their worlds. So even while exploring the economic causes and effects of a globalizing world, social theory must explore the explorations of that world—or in other words, attempt to understand the precise social forms in which people come to live with, and thus practice, their understandings of the global economic reality. Both—the reality and the social forms by which it is understood—are important; and both must be thought through.

This, therefore, is why as the world searches for the new millennium, social theory has increasingly concerned itself with both globalization and the new social formations that are coming into their own as a result of the global process. As social theory has attempted to understand the new world, it has been forced increasingly to reconsider not just the facts of global reality but the methods by which theory thinks through those facts. This may sound to some like an indication that the postmodernists have won the day. But the situation is not so simple as that. The postmodernism controversy has had its effects and it has had them because, to a large extent, the more reasonable disputants in the debate have realized that because the changing world requires it, something must be done about how social theory does its work. Curiously, even a good number of those who would still deny that the world is changing have been disputants in the cultural wars so often associated with postmodernism and multiculturalism. At the same time, as the postmodernism arguments lose their curiosity value, many of the issues they provoke remain to be dealt with.

One striking case of this surprising effect is Charles Tilly's already, and justly, famous essay "The Invisible Elbow," part of which follows. Over the past quarter-century no social theorist has done more than Charles Tilly to demonstrate the importance of taking seriously the careful historical study of social change. His studies of political rebellions, revolutions, and economic process have taught an entire generation of social theorists always to look at the larger picture, including the larger economic scene. Tilly could well have rested on his scientific laurels. Yet in "The Invisible Elbow," an essay first published as late as 1996, Tilly declares that it is time to set aside all comforting illusions. He has in mind, in particular, the famous nineteenth-century utilitarian belief in an invisible hand rationally guiding the marketplace. He proposes, by contrast to an older economic world in which everything has its proper place, that our actions in the world, and therefore world processes themselves, operate more according to the figure of the invisible elbow. Things get done, but sometimes because of, other times in spite of, the accidents we make with clumsy elbows while carrying too many bags of groceries from car to kitchen. The world is filled with, and moved by, false starts and foolish errors. The task of social theory is to make sense as much of these as of the apparent conformities that occasionally calm the surface of things.

Tilly's way of rethinking the basic ethical attitude of social science at the end of the millennium is in sharp contrast to the upbeat expectations of Bill Gates about the "information age." Gates, the founder and chairman of Microsoft Corporation, is said to be the richest man in the world. He may also be one of its most powerful, at least for as long as his Microsoft products serve as the brains that drive virtually every personal computer and electronic workstation in the world. Curiously, however, though he beats optimistic drums for the possibilities of the new information age, Gates admits that electronic technologies will change the face of the world. Yet he sees nothing wrong, for example, with the prospect that "advanced communication systems promise to make countries more alike and reduce the importance of national boundaries." His world sounds at times much like the nicer neighborhoods of Seattle, Washington, where he lives and where, for those well employed, life could not be better.

Quite (again) by contrast to Bill Gates's information age utopia, David Harvey, in "The City in a Globalizing World," believes that for many, life in the coming millennium will be a "dystopian nightmare." Harvey, a geographer with strong affinities to Marxist social theory, has written thoughtfully on the postmdernism question. His book *The Postmodern Condition* is one of the most widely read academic books on the subject. Yet in part because of his roots in Marxist social theory and its concerns for universal social justice, Harvey is as skeptical of the sometimes naive celebrations of many postmodernists as he is of the wide-eyed, good-for-business optimism of cybercapitalists like Bill Gates. As Harvey says in "The City in a Globalizing World," globalization has come about systematically through economic processes within world capitalism that have produced quite specific social effects, many of them devastating to those marginalized by their poverty. Harvey's account of global reality is a bracing antidote to the Microsoft chairman's optimism. Global communications may reduce some differences among nations, but there remain painful differences between the realities of the posh suburbs of Seattle and the world of AIDS victims suffering against the global odds in parts of urbanized West Africa.

Among the familiar categories of social thought that must be rethought in the face of globalization is the nineteenth-century habit of considering economic realities as of an entirely different order of things from cultural ones. The distinction made some sense in nineteenth- and early-twentieth-century cities in which the capitalist classes, because of their wealth, were also the principal possessors of a society's culture. In the early days of industrialization, laborers were grindingly poor, seldom educated, and thus deprived of any real opportunity to participate in the higher culture of a society. It was perfectly reasonable for Marx in the 1840s to insist that all the glamorous forms of nineteenth-century bourgeois culture—art and entertainment, religion, higher education, political ideals—were nothing more than instruments for the oppression of the impoverished working class. Even, over the decades of the twentieth century, as the working classes gained better economic rights and advantages, there remained an evident difference between the culture of the symphony orchestras and art museums generally serving the better-off and the minstrel-show foolishness of the television sitcoms serving the so-called masses of the, if not poor, less well off.

Of course, I am referring here to culture in its more narrow sense, deriving from the nineteenth-century bourgeois ideal of the "cultured" individual who was known by her attendance at the best churches, the finest museums, or the most exclusive salons. But even then, and certainly in the writings of critics in the tradition of Marx, "culture" was always meant to include, directly or indirectly, the broad effects of the so-called noneconomic world of a society's collected ideals, values, myths, rituals, art and ethics, and the like. One of the most important intellectual movements to survive the postmodernism debate in the 1980s is cultural studies. For many, the most important new form of social studies, cultural studies, was established in an effort to understand the counterintuitive fact of the global world that the cultural sphere is no longer sharply distinguishable from the economic. We may have to think of culture and economics as different, but in the truth of how things work, they are very much mixed up with each other.

Stuart Hall, the founder and leader of the British school of cultural studies, has been notable among his many colleagues and followers for having advanced a more subtle idea of culture such that its roots in, effects on, and relations to the economic order of things are more clearly evident. In part because of cultural studies, social theory today thinks about culture differently, more subtly—as indeed it must in an age of globalized information. In "The Global, the Local, and the Return of Ethnicity," Hall provides still another kind of retort to those who trust the information age with foolhardy optimism. If the differences among nations are disappearing, that may be because the very idea of the modern nation was a studied effect of modern culture to create the ideal of the nation as an "imagined community" of free and good men and women. (Hall here refers to the important work of the English social historian

Benedict Anderson.) Hall goes on to describe the social differences, most notably the return of ethnicities and other forms of identity politics. Though globalization has a homogenizing effect, it has also unleashed a world of combative social differences. As global processes reduce the sway of the nation over the hearts and minds of people, they return to and uncover the ethnic traditions that have long been suppressed by the ideal of the national community. Once the Soviet nationalist ideal collapsed in Russia, Russia too began to unravel along the lines of its many, long-repressed ethnic traditions. In this the events in Russia are not all that different from the emergence of new social movements in Western Europe, the United States, and other nationalized places in which the political struggles of the 1960s introduced a deep suspicion of the value of the nation. Feminists, queers, Blacks, and Native Americans in the United States are chief among those who withdrew allegiance from the national ideal in order to stake their political claims on the prior fates of their respective social groups, from which they very often take what might be called their postnationalist identities. Today, the very mention of identity politics gives fits to those who remain loyal to older nationalist or modernist values. Yet, it is impossible to deny that the return to ethnicity as a source of political identity in the world is here to stay, at least for the time being. Stuart Hall illustrates the more powerful ways in which social theorists have come to think about these surprisingly local effects in a globalizing world.

One of the most important reasons it is no longer as convincing as it once was to think of cultural and economic things as different, even antithetical, spheres of social life is that the global economy depends upon culture to do its work. In the broadest possible sense of the word, "culture" must include all the varieties of *information* by which people convey to each other and themselves a sense of what is going on in the world and what it means. Clearly, insofar as globalization of the world economy is promoted by the new information age of the Worldwide Web, the new economic realities are made possible by new cultural, or informational, realities. These are the realities spawned by the Web and the personal computer, not to exclude still important media like television and its electronic variants—video games, VCRs, home shopping, talk shows, and the like; and they are very much more than fast machines for processing information.

The tools of the information age are widely available, even in many places to the poor. Because they are, the ploughshares of technology are very often beaten into weapons of political power, shaping the hopes of people and thereby how they actually live, or try to live. In an account of his travels around the poorer regions of the world, journalist Robert Kaplan reported just this effect:

> India is a world of cellular phones and primitive public sanitation. Not only is poverty destablizing, but so is fast economic growth. The poor in India's cities are increasingly migrants from the villages, often fleeing land scarcity and erosion, uprooted from many of their traditions. Though they have insufficient food in their bellies, they often have transistor radios and are surrounded by Western billboard advertisements. Like the inhabitants of the Chinese and Egyptian shantytowns that I had seen, with television antennas rising above their mudhuts, these poor know temptation. They are less fatalistic, perhaps more prone to revolt than before. And their numbers are growing as fast as those of the middle class.

Though the social differences between the wired-poor and the wealthy are considerable, they inhabit the same world in part because of the new media. The poor in

Calcutta who never come into direct contact with slick bonds brokers in Bombay now understand that such a cultural type exists. So also, even the well-suited capitalist road warriors already faxing away from their well-cushioned first-class seats as the ordinary are rushed along to economy class cannot help but look out the windows upon takeoff and see the sprawling slums of Cairo or East New York. Both the poor and fancy know that their fortunes, different as they are, are somehow linked. This may be the only proper social theoretical use of the abused expression "interface." The poor and the well-off are indeed interfaced through the invisible cables of the worldwide communications web.

One of the more intriguing possibilities of the new cultural links between the strong and the weak is the leverage the new communications networks make available to the traditionally oppressed who now are struggling, on various fronts, to overcome what had once been impossible political or military odds. Feminists and others working in what Patricia Clough, following Nancy Fraser, calls "subaltern publics" today have a stronger purchase on political power because they have access through telecommunications to new publics shaped by new cultural knowledges. Clough's "Cultural Criticism and Communications" is an important contribution to the rethinking of politics in today's technological environment. Many social historians have thought for some time that, beginning with the decolonizing and civil rights movements of the 1950s and 1960s, new social movements of all kinds have proven so potent a force for social change because television and other media, by providing access to wider audiences, allow them to shape new cultural understandings and new public attitudes. Televised images of police dogs attacking children in the American South in the 1960s or of innocent villagers murdered by the American napalm attacks in Vietnam certainly gave public impetus to both the civil rights and the antiwar movements. Similarly, and much more recently, rebels against very strong odds can and do use the new world communications networks in their struggles. In their failed revolt in 1989, Chinese students on opposite corners of Tiananmen Square were cut off by the blockades of the state militia. But the tanks and troops could not blockade their communications. They simply faxed messages to allies in Los Angeles, who refaxed tactical plans to rebels across the square in Beijing. Similarly, when, not long ago, UN troops attempted to control a local warlord in Somalia, they were greeted as they disembarked at water's edge by the bright lights of CNN television crews. Their local enemy had to do nothing more than flip on a TV set in Mogadishu. In such a world, political power is redistributed, for better or worse. Those on both sides of barricades and battlegrounds are, today, closer than opponents or enemies ever could have imagined just a half-century ago during the Second World War. It is one thing to hear the rain-soaked enemy cry himself to sleep in his foxhole just a few meters across the western front, still another to observe his actions as they take place in the course of the struggle.

Globalization is thus a process in which, yes, people's economic destinies are linked, but so too are their cultural understandings. Hence, while we must still speak of culture as a crucial aspect of social life, globalization means that we can no longer speak of culture as though it were a sphere entirely different from, independent of, or even inferior to the economic realities of the global world. Hence a second surprising feature of the globalizing world. Just as globalization has undercut the nation-state with the curious effect of encouraging not like-mindedness but ethnic differences, so, in sharpening the terrible disparities of economic opportunity, the global economy has, against every reasonable expectation, lessened the cultural gap between the powerful rich and the politically vulnerable poor—thereby lessening also the very difference between the economic and the cultural.

One of the concrete effects of these changes on social theory has been an increased commitment to new strategies for studying and thinking about social life. Though the writers represented under the caption "The New Social Formations" may be classified as professional sociologists (with two important and obvious exceptions), they all represent a new kind of social theory that crashes the gates of traditional social science in order to open the way to new ideas. What each of them studies, though from remarkably different points of view, is not so much a stable field of scientific objects as one or several new social formations emerging even as they, and the rest of us, watch.

The new social formations are, thus, evidently different, if hard to figure, forms of prior existing social structures. They cannot be said to be institutions, or even particularly definite structures, if only because what is emerging has not yet been instituted in a fixed way, and may never be. A new social formation is, thus, an unusual, but increasingly well-organized, way of practicing the necessary habits of daily life. To speak of new social formations is, therefore, to attempt to understand the ways in which the new structural conditions of the globalizing world have forced people to adjust and adapt, thus to make new forms for their lives. These formations may be good for human life or destructive, just as some may endure and others disappear as rapidly as they came.

One of the obvious areas of new social formation, and one that is likely to endure, is new patterns and problems associated with work and employment. How work is organized in order to distribute income has been, perhaps, the most unique and essential feature of modern societies. Over the past two centuries, as industrialization took over the economic centrality of agriculture and small commercial enterprises, work in the form of regular employment in an industrial or business establishment became the principal, if not exclusive, social mechanism by which ordinary people earned their income and thus organized their lives.

Yet, one of the most disturbing effects of the global economy is that the information age produces goods and generates services at such blindingly efficient speeds that, in many sectors of the economy, workers are no longer needed in the numbers they once were. In the decades just after World War II, the once poor working class enjoyed improved economic chances because the industrial economy of that time offered millions of new construction, assembly, factory, transportation, and low-level administrative jobs. In many cases, members of the new working class of the 1950s in the United States and 1960s in Europe were very well paid relative to the subsistence wages on which their grandparents struggled to survive early in the industrial era.

Then, sometime no later than the 1970s, all this began to change. As the global process took over, workers were replaced by machines. When the cheapest labor was required, the high-flying managers of the global corporations moved their assembly or manufacturing plants to wherever they could find it—first, Mississippi; then, Taiwan; then, Indonesia; now, Vietnam or Mexico; tomorrow, far provincial China. Just as your grandmother's dress was once sewn by East European workers in sweatshops on the Lower East Side (as some of yours are today by immigrant workers from the Caribbean or Asia), so today your new Nikes are stitched, most likely, in no-longer-rural Vietnam. As the capitalists, well aware that they cannot forever control the cash they own, speed about the world in search of cheap labor and high profit margins, so too do jobs fly away from neighborhoods in the United States and parts of Western Europe, where not so long ago work was readily available. The job market (and thus the availability of reliable incomes) has changed dramatically since the 1970s. Today, at the end of the 1990s, even in a prosperous society like the United States, the very poor are great in number for want of jobs. Their relative social circumstances are increasingly like those of the poor at the beginning of the industrial age a century before. Hence, another of the odd effects of globalization has been that, with respect to work, the rich and the poor now again live in a two-class economy divided between those with the cultural capital that allows them to work in the jobs of the information age and those, often barely educated at all, who work in the petty service jobs cleaning toilets or serving hamburgers, or those with no job or hope of finding one.

In his book *When Work Disappears*, William Julius Wilson describes some of the most devastating effects of the changing global economy. As in his previous studies, Wilson has focused his research on the black neighborhoods, principally of Chicago. In the 1950s, he points out, the black neighborhoods of the South and West Sides of Chicago were safe, vital, and growing communities. Today these same areas are no longer neighborhoods but wastelands of dangerous public housing, scant employment, crime, and decay. Why the difference in so short a time? Wilson says it is because work has disappeared from these neighborhoods into the global economy. Wilson, a former president of the American Sociological Association and one of professional sociology's most respected empirical researchers, has been the subject of often bitter denunciations by fellow blacks who are outraged that he seems to downgrade the role of race in favor of class in his accounts of the black urban underclass. One of Wilson's books was, in pointed fact, entitled *The Declining Significance of Race*. Yet, however one feels about this issue, Wilson is a striking example of an empirical social scientist who has insisted on rethinking his field's theoretical categories. While he clearly believes that race and thus racism are among the causes of the declining fortunes of the urban poor, he does not believe that race alone explains enough. In effect, he is describing a new social formation in which the urban poor are utterly without hope of jobs because there are no jobs and no prospect of any. Where the well-satisfied are inclined to see welfare and the drug trade as the evil, immoral outcomes of the culture of poverty, Wilson sees them as the appalling but only remaining alternatives for the poor in a society where work has disappeared. Thus, he proposes in "What to Do When Work Disappears" once unimaginable social policies such as the return of a form of the depression-era Works Project Administration (WPA), which provided government-invented, socially useful jobs for the poor in order to provide them work-based income.

Social theory began in the late nineteenth century with attempts to come to terms with the apparent necessity of work as the foundation of both economic and moral life. Karl Marx, Max Weber, Charlotte Gilman, and W.E.B. Du Bois are among those of that era who were preoccupied with work as a fundamental principle of modern society. But, what are we to do in a global economy where work is disappearing, not just for the most poor but increasingly for the once middle classes? Some economists predict that early in the first century of the new millennium the economy will be so transformed as to be able to provide paid work, as we now understand it, for no more than 20 percent of the world's population. Even if things do not turn out all that badly, we know that job-based employment as the means to income and self-worth is now a social problem of uncertain solution, and one that will be with us for years to come. All the pious speeches of the politicians and other self-interested moralists about putting the poor back to work will not change the facts of the global economy. As a result, many social theorists have begun to rethink the world without work.

Stanley Aronowitz, once himself a labor organizer, joins three other social theorists in announcing the "Post-Work Manifesto." One of the manifesto's most intriguing features is the underlying theme that in the absence of jobs the society as a whole (if not the weakened national state) must provide guaranteed incomes to all people in return for which they offer not demeaning work in hamburger joints but social service, political participation, commitment to learning and teaching. Again, it is obvious that as jobs disappear, one of the theories that must be reconsidered is culture. In the absence of work, people will not be able to derive their sense of personal or collective self-worth from a career or job. This will have to come from a new formation of culture in which work takes on an entirely new social value divorced from the job and linked now to other socially and culturally valued activities.

Those whose moral sensibilities are shocked by the idea of a postwork society are no less disturbed by social theories of the dramatic changes in family life. The talk-radio furor over family values is vicious in direct proportion to the evidence that supports theories of the new social formations in family life. These deep feelings may fill the airwaves because, under the covers of domestic life, those upset by the changing world might hope to find solace at home from the brutal degradations of the new economy. Instead, when they find that their family relations are changing just as markedly—and usually because of the changing economy—their discouragement very often breaks into outrage. Feeling thus deprived, they find it difficult to imagine that the ideal of a family in which Mom stays home to tend to her knitting and the kids is fading away because Mom now must work to keep the family afloat. Thus, though men feel the assault in their way, the stronger consequence of the globalizing economy is that the majority of those who suffer its negative effects directly are women, especially women in the poorest regions of the world. But, even in the once-stable middle classes, the relations between men and women in families are drastically altered because of changes in the global economy.

In "The Post-Modern Family," Judith Stacey reflects on the fate of working and middle-class women in new forms of family life. For *Brave New Families*, a book published in 1990, Stacey engaged in field research with two female-headed households in the Silicon Valley in California. The site was not chosen by chance. The Silicon Valley is, of course, thus named because of its global importance in research and development for the electronic advancements of the new information age. As one would expect, and as Stacey found, the new patterns of work associated with this advanced level of the global marketplace altered family life. In "The Post-Modern Family," a selection from her 1996 book (*In the Name of the Family*), Stacey summarizes her findings in the earlier book but also comments on the public reaction to her argument that family and gender relations have taken on a postmodern form. Judith Stacey is among a good many social theorists today who, like most of those introduced in this section, have returned to classic sociology's commitment to participate in public debates over the political and ethical issues underlying societal change. It is not surprising, therefore, that she has been attacked in particular by those who are nostalgic for the older, father-dominated family form. Stacey defends her arguments particularly well when she refers convincingly not just to her own ethnographic research but to the demographic evidence that the so-called traditional family is fast fading from the social scene.

Arlie Hochschild, a sociologist who (in marked contrast to Judith Stacey) would not use the word "postmodern" in a favorable sense, also demonstrates how the changed conditions of economic life affect family life. In her earlier book, *The Second Shift* (1989), Hochschild offered evidence that, public impressions to the contrary, a woman's work in the home (on her second shift) was *not* diminished by her work on the first shift, the job. To the chagrin of many so-called new men, Hochschild gave good reason to suspect that, though there are some differences now, women still did the major share of domestic work even as they worked full time outside the home. In "Working Women in the Time Bind," from her 1997 book *The Time Bind*, Hochschild explains how the effects of the first- and second-shift activities of working mothers have important consequences for their children. The time bind arises because the schedules of children and their parents are not ever quite in synch. The kids are not always ready for Mom's quality time at the end of her long day. Hochschild's research is still another instance of the new social formation between the workplace (for those who have jobs) and the home—and of how the modern (or postmodern—as you wish) corporation and families must rethink the structuring of social time between work and family.

Both Stacey and Hochschild, by careful empirical work, have uncovered surprising—one might even say revolutionary—developments just under the surface of life in the global society. Work and family life are close to the conservative heart of modern social life, just as the homosexual life is traditionally conceived by reactionary forces as the very antithesis of the old work-ethic-based family values. To the heteronormative horror of most social conservatives, queer politics have come to be, at least in the more European and American regions of the globalizing world, one of the most revolutionary of the new social movements. As Steven Seidman, one of American sociology's leading queer theorists, explains, queer politics are those based on a radical coming out of the closet in which forbidden sexual desires were once hidden. Seidman's current research, briefly reported in "The Productivity of the Closet," shows that, as time has gone by since the famous Stonewall Rebellion in Greenwich Village in 1969, the closet seems to have emerged from the shadows of shame into a new form of constructive social production. The closet thus takes its place for gays and lesbians as the virtual as well as real social space that serves for a new formation of gay and lesbian social life, just as the churches did for blacks and local women's shelters have done for feminists since a somewhat early time.

With all these changes, social theory must never lose living contact with its experiential roots in the practical world of political and social struggle. The book concludes with selections from two of the globalizing world's most visible and revered cultural heroes. Neither Wei Jingsheng nor Toni Morrison can be called social theorists in the usual sense of the word, yet their words inspire the highest reach of social thought.

Wei is China's most famous political prisoner and one of the world's most admired voices for democratic reforms. Until his release in 1997, Wei had spent all but a few years since the early 1970s in prison. Like other political exiles and prisoners represented in this book—Du Bois, Marx, Gandhi, King, Gramsci, Havel—Wei has spoken out courageously against the moral corruption of those who would attempt to imprison the voices of social change. In "The Courage to Stand Alone," Wei reminds us that in today's world millions of people suffer not just economic poverty but the spiritual impoverishment that is bred when people are deprived of their political rights. He writes of democracy in a disarmingly simple yet powerful way and thus speaks to those who might forget that there would be no social theory, and no effective sociological imagination, without the freedom to speak and write of what one sees.

It cannot yet be known exactly what the globalizing world has to do with the millennium frenzy. Still, the spaces of global reality and the time of its clocks and calendars do seem to be hurtling toward some near warp that confuses the common sense of social differences. Toni Morrison's "Reach Toward the Ineffable" is a poetic glimpse of what is possible, and necessary, even in the global world. One of the great literary geniuses of our time, a poet laureate of the social imagination, Toni Morrison reminds us all that social thought withers and dies when it grasps too harshly for the simplifying truth. She moves us to trust that, even against the worst in a changing world, there is an ineffable human possibility toward which we must reach.

Notes

Page 603: Robert Kaplan, *The Ends of the Earth* (Random House, 1996), 351.

❖ Rethinking the Globalizing World ❖

Charles Tilly (1929–) is currently the Joseph L. Buttenwieser Professor of Social Science at Columbia University. He has taught at Harvard, the University of Toronto, the University of Michigan, and the New School for Social Research. Tilly is respected worldwide for his historical studies, the empirical rigor of which accounts, in part, for the influence of his social theories of political and economic change. Tilly's books include *The Vendeé* (1964), *Strikes in France, 1930–1968* (1974, with Edward Shorter), *From Mobilization to Revolution* (1978), *The Contentious French* (1986), *Popular Contention in Great Britain, 1758–1834*, and *Roads from the Past to Future* (1997).

Future Social Science and the Invisible Elbow
Charles Tilly (1996)

For the Invisible Hand, let's substitute the Invisible Elbow. Coming home from the grocery store, arms overflowing with food-filled bags, you wedge yourself against the doorjamb, somehow free a hand to open the kitchen door, enter the house, then nudge the door closed with your elbow. Because elbows are not prehensile and, in this situation, not visible either, you sometimes slam the door smartly, sometimes swing the door halfway closed, sometimes miss completely on the first pass, sometimes bruise your arm on the wood, sometimes shatter the glass, and sometimes—responding to one of these earlier calamities—spill groceries all over the kitchen floor.

You, your elbow, the groceries, and the kitchen have systematic properties that strongly limit the likely consequences of your attempted nudge. Over many trips to the grocery store, which of these outcomes occurs forms a frequency distribution with stable probabilities modified by learning. With practice, you may get your door-closing average up to .900. After a calamitous elbow shot, however, you tell a story not of frequency distributions, but of good intentions frustrated by bad circumstances: the floor was wet, children left toys just inside the door, the grocery bagger put heavy items on top, or something of the sort. Thus we . . . save the belief in rational action, at least our own.

Don't hear my analysis as an irrationalist model of social life. Despite the fact that batters rationally aim to hit safely on almost every swing, over the long run, few major-league baseball players ever maintain batting averages even a third of the way to .900. As Herbert Simon has taught us to understand, instead of true maximizing,

---

Excerpt from *Roads From the Future* (Lanham, MD: Roman & Littlefield, 1997). Copyright © 1997. Reprinted by permission of Roman & Littlefield.

most of us mostly "satisfice" by settling for the first outcome of our efforts that falls within an acceptable zone. Despite the appeal of solipsism to postmodernists and paranoids, faulty everyday talk contains enough redundancy and error correction to convey meanings from one person to another. Even great dancers make constant adjustments to their own and their partners' almost imperceptible deviations from choreographed movements. Life is like that. The big differences among persons and groups lie not in the frequency with which they make mistakes, but in the speed, frequency, and manner of their correction. Smart people correct their many errors fast and well.

All life, I am claiming, fills with erroneous interactions, therefore with unanticipated consequences. But life also teems with error correction and responses, sometimes almost instantaneous, to unexpected outcomes. In conversation, we incessantly utter mistakes, receive signals from ourselves or others that mark our errors, then repair them so quickly and well that no one notices unless a witness replays the tape. Erving Goffman delighted in collecting errors and repairs in radio announcing, for example:

> Disk Jockey: "And now a record by Little Willie John . . . here's 'Sleep-Sleep-Sleep' . . . By the way, did you get any last night? . . . (*pause*) . . . SLEEP, that is!

Or the more subtle:

> So all you do when you are on your way home is, stop by at Korvette's and leave your odor . . . ORDER!!!

Only transcription of the text, or replay of the tape, captures the odor of the disorder. . . .

When working in Toronto, I asked my three eldest children to draw maps of the city from memory. Seven-year-old Laura drew an area bounded on the west (left) and the north (up) by the closest major thoroughfares to our house, placed the block containing our house prominently in the lower left (southwest) corner, displayed two more adjacent blocks (one with major areas marked "playground," "grass," and "working"), and sketched in a few other schematic streets, both vertical and horizontal. Nine-year-old Kit bounded her map vertically with the southward-flowing Humber and Don Rivers, placed the McDonald-Cartier Freeway at the northern limits, and limned in a gridwork of vertical and horizontal streets centering almost precisely on our home block. Chris, then eleven, produced a wondrously detailed map of the metropolis, complete with north, east, south, and west compass points. In Lake Ontario, he placed a presentable outline of Toronto Island, then next to it a blob labeled "this represents all other islands." All three children innovated delightfully. But all three also followed conventions of mapmaking they had somehow absorbed from schooling and everyday practice: north to the top, streets horizontal and vertical within that frame, major boundaries defined by waterways and big thoroughfares.

Of course, my children were responding not just to convention, but to verifiable features of the Toronto cityscape, all of which they had observed piecemeal even if they had never regarded all of them simultaneously. Indeed, their maps identified common features of Toronto, Cleveland, Chicago, Milwaukee, and other lakeside cities—features that themselves resulted from the interplay of topography, city-building conventions, and the incremental error-filled interactions of local residents. At all these levels, innovation, error, and conformity alike operate within constraints set by previous understandings and practices; they thereby produce intelligible structure.

Here, we encounter another paradox, for those very regularities define possibilities that could occur, but do not—at least not yet. Sound social science concerns counterfactuals: explaining what actually occurs, which ironically requires specifying what did *not* occur but could have occurred, then comparing factual with counterfactual. The central work of social science consists of specifying nonexistent social structures and processes that were possible, that are now possible, that under specifiable circumstances will be possible. Strong explanations do just that, comparing observed states with other possible states, using known causes to account for the differences. Game theory and Markov processes gain some of their intuitive appeal as representations of social life because they explicitly represent choice points, hence counterfactuals.

Counterfactual explanation makes social science a powerful complement to ethics and politics. In his renowned lecture "Science as a Vocation," Max Weber touched on this realization, but reduced it to the observation that if you choose a certain end, scientific experience can teach "you have to use such and such a *means* in order to carry out your conviction practically." If actors could actually anticipate consequences of their chosen actions and then produce the actions without error, we would indeed only need to sort intentions and preferences.

Much more, however, lies beyond that point. Every ethical or political proposal imports, however covertly, a theory of the possible, a selection among alternative actions that theory names as possible, and causal arguments relating actions to outcomes. To advocate turning away aspiring immigrants in order to protect your country's existing workers against unfair competition invokes a theory of competition, an argument concerning the probable effects of immigration and suppositions about the efficacy of anti-migration controls.

Even short of adjudicating fairness, social scientists have much to say about ethically implicated theories of possibility, selections among possible actions, and causal arguments. However one comes down on the question, to the extent that it generates reliable knowledge of causes and possibilities, social science obviously bears on ethical and political choices. For that very reason, assertions of social science's explanatory power regularly stir passions rarely seen in discussions of astronomy and geology: they constitute claims to pronounce on the possibility assumptions of religious, moral, and political doctrines.

Incessant error intersects with counterfactual explanation at two different points. First, the order-producing imbrication of error-filled interaction in shared understandings and interpersonal networks constitutes a causal domain requiring explanation of what actually happens along with what else might have happened. Second, the implicit computation of possible interaction and their possible outcomes that inheres in every initiation of interaction, erroneous or otherwise, takes place within limits set by the actor's social location and the previous history of the interaction in question. That constraint on decisionmaking itself requires counterfactual explanation. Any explanation of social processes worth its salt must account both for social interaction and for its consequences in the face of omnipresent constraint and error.

I certainly didn't discover these principles. Merton's analysis of unanticipated consequences more or less implies them. Camouflaged, they frequently enter literary territory as might-have-beens, as speculations on other available choices one could have made, other possible outcomes of choices actually made. In a self-congratulatory mode, Robert Frost told the story of having to decide between two roads that branched in the woods, never to know the other one's itinerary:

> *I shall be telling this with a sigh,*
> *Somewhere ages and ages hence:*
> *Two roads diverged in a wood, and I—*
> *I took the one less traveled by,*
> *And that has made all the difference.*
>   ("The Road Not Taken")

But grimmer variants also recur, reducing competing possibilities to chance or questioning whether one trajectory has any more meaning than another. Poet-novelist Paul Auster voices the despairing version powerfully:

> It comes down to this: that everything should count, that everything should be a part of it, even the things I do not or cannot understand. The desire, for example, to destroy everything I have written so far. Not from any revulsion at the inadequacy of these words (although that remains a distinct possibility), but rather from the need to remind myself, at each moment, that things do not have to happen this way, that there is always another way, neither better nor worse, in which things might take shape. I realize in the end that I am probably powerless to affect the outcome of even the least thing that happens, but nevertheless, and in spite of myself, as if in an act of blind faith, I want to assume full responsibility.

Somewhere between boastful Frost and despairing Auster we hear the music of chance, the counterfactual canticle of modest successful persons, pleading for contradiction: "I've just been lucky; I was in the right place at the right time," which implies strongly that something else could just as easily have happened and that someone else in the same location would have done as well. Joseph Conrad put it well:

> I follow the instincts of vainglory and humility natural to all mankind. For it can hardly be denied that it is not their own deserts that men are most proud of, but rather of their prodigious luck, of their marvellous fortune, of that in their lives for which thanks and sacrifices must be offered on the altars of the inscrutable gods.

To challenge such self-deprecation does not necessarily deny the other possibilities; the heroine gains even more credit if her grit, wit, or resourcefulness explains why she did not fall into the counterfactuals. (Although fear of having to explain what I do for a living and why has always kept me away from school reunions, they fascinate me as occasions for observing what other paths one might have followed from the same point of origin.) In social science itself, the idea of alternative possibilities spreads far beyond game theory and Markov chains. It appears in the recurrent impulse to contrast meaningful but fallible human agency with both random behavior and instrumental rationality.

Responses to error, in any case, are neither instinctual nor random; they draw on historically accumulated shared understandings, on culture. They also take place within constraining webs of previously established social relations and, in the process, alter those webs incrementally. Culture and social relations, however, do not alter unpredictably; they interact, and they obey strong constraints as they interact.❖

Bill Gates (1955–) was born and grew up in Seattle, Washington. He is sometimes considered the world's most famous college dropout. He left Harvard to found the Microsoft Corporation in 1976. Today, Gates is the chairman and chief executive officer of Microsoft, which is a dominant force in the marketplace of software products. Gates is among the wealthiest individuals in the world. His fortune owes to the power and ingenious simplicity of the software tools he envisaged and then created soon after leaving school. The selection is from *The Road Ahead*, his bestselling book

---

The Information Age
Bill Gates (1996)

This is an exciting time in the Information Age. It is the very beginning. Almost everywhere I go, whether to speak to a group or have dinner with friends, questions come up about how information technology will change our lives. People want to understand how it will make the future different, whether it will make our lives better or worse.

It should be obvious by now that I'm an optimist about the impact of the new technology. It will enhance our leisure time and enrich our culture by expanding the distribution of information. It will help relieve pressures on urban areas by enabling people to work from home or remote-site offices. It will relieve pressures on natural resources because increasing numbers of products will take the form of bits rather than manufactured goods. It will give us more control over our lives, enabling us to tailor our experiences and the products we use to our interests. Citizens of the information society will enjoy new opportunities for productivity, learning, and entertainment. Countries that move boldly and in concert with each other will enjoy economic rewards. Whole new markets will emerge, and a myriad of new opportunities for employment will be created.

For the past few hundred years every generation has found more efficient ways of getting work done, and the cumulative benefits have been enormous. The average person today enjoys a much better life than the nobility did a few centuries ago. It would be great to have a medieval king's land, but what about his lice? Medical advances alone have greatly increased life spans and improved standards of living.

In the first part of the twentieth century, Henry Ford *was* the automotive industry, but your car is superior to anything he ever drove. It's safer and more reliable, and it certainly has a better sound system. This pattern of improvement isn't going to change. Advancing productivity propels societies forward, and it's only a matter of time before the average person in a developed country will be "richer" in many ways than anyone is today.

Just because I'm optimistic doesn't mean that I don't have concerns about what's going to happen to all of us. Major changes always involve tradeoffs, and the benefits of the information society will carry costs. Societies are going to be asked to make hard choices about the universal availability of technology, investment in education, regulation, and the balance between individual privacy and community security. We'll confront tough new problems, only a few of which we can foresee. In some business sectors, dislocations will create a need for worker retraining. The availability of virtually free communications and computing will alter the relationships of nations and of socioeconomic groups within nations. The power and versatility of digital technology will raise new concerns about individual privacy, commercial confidentiality, and national security. There are equity issues that will have to be addressed because the information society should serve all of its citizens, not just the technically sophisticated and the economically privileged. I don't necessarily have the solutions to the many issues and problems we'll confront, but as I said at the beginning of this book, now is a good time for a broad debate to begin. . . .

The presence of advanced communications systems promises to make countries more alike and reduce the importance of national boundaries. The fax machine, the portable videocamera, and Cable News Network are among the forces that brought about the end of communist regimes and the Cold War because they enabled news to pass both ways through the Iron Curtain. Most sites on the World Wide Web are in English so far, which confers economic and entertainment benefits on people around the world who speak English. English-speaking people will enjoy this advantage until a great deal more content is posted in a variety of languages—or until software does a first-rate job of translating text on the fly.

The new access to information can draw people together by increasing their understanding of other cultures. But commercial satellite broadcasts to countries such as China and Iran offer citizens glimpses of the outside world that are not necessarily sanctioned by their governments. Some governments are afraid that such exposure will cause discontent and worse, a "revolution of expectations" when disenfranchised people get enough information about another lifestyle to contrast it with their own. Within individual societies, the balance between traditional and modern experiences is bound to shift as people use the network to expose themselves to a greater range of possibilities. Some cultures may feel under assault as people pay greater attention to global issues and cultures and less to their traditional local ones.

"The fact that the same ad can appeal to someone in a New York apartment and on an Iowa farm and in an African village does not prove these situations are alike," commented Bill McKibben, a critic of what he sees as television's tendency to override local diversity with homogenized common experiences. "It is merely evidence that the people living in them have a few feelings in common, and it is these barest, most minimal commonalities that are the content of the global village."

Yet if people want to watch the ad, or the program the ad supports, should they be denied that privilege? This is a political question for every country to answer individually.

American popular culture is so potent that outside the United States some countries now try to ration exposure to it. They hope to guarantee the viability of domestic content producers by permitting only a certain number of hours of foreign television to be aired each week, for instance. In Europe, the availability of satellite and cable-delivered programming has made it harder for governments to control what people watch. The Internet is going to break down boundaries and may promote a world culture, or at least a greater sharing of cultural activities and values. But the network will also make it easy for people who are deeply involved in their own ethnic communities at home or abroad to reach out to other people who share their preoccupations no matter where they are. This may strengthen cultural diversity and counter the tendency toward a single, homogenized world culture. It's hard to predict what the net effect will be—a strengthening or a weakening of local cultural values.❖

Manuel Castells (1942–) was born in Spain but lived in exile, mostly in France, during the last years of the repressive Franco regime in his native land. He has taught in universities in every part of the world, including Paris, Madrid, Hong Kong, Singapore, Moscow, and throughout Latin America. Since 1979 he has been professor of sociology and urban planning at the University of California at Berkeley. He has written numerous books including *The Economic Crisis and American Society* (1980), *The Information City* (1989), and *The Rise of the Network Society* (1996), which is the first book in a trilogy, *The Information Age: Economy, Society and Culture.*

The Global Network
Manuel Castells (1996)

I shall first define the concept of network, since it plays such a central role in my characterization of society in the information age. A network is a set of interconnected nodes. A node is the point at which a curve intersects itself. What a node is, concretely speaking, depends on the kind of concrete networks of which we speak. They are stock exchange markets, and their ancillary advanced services centers, in the network of global financial flows. They are national councils of ministers and European Commissioners in the political network that governs the European Union. They are coca fields and poppy fields, clandestine laboratories, secret landing strips, street gangs, and money-laundering financial institutions, in the network of drug traffic that penetrates economies, societies, and states throughout the world. They are television systems, entertainment studios, computer graphics milieux, news teams, and mobile devices generating, transmitting, and receiving signals, in the global network of the new media at the roots of cultural expression and public opinion in the information age. The topology defined by networks determines that the distance (or intensity and frequence of interaction) between two points (or social positions) is shorter (or more frequent, or more intense) if both points are nodes in a network than if they do not belong to the same network. On the other hand, within a given network flows have no distance, or the same distance, between nodes. Thus, distance (physical, social, economic, political, cultural) for a given point or position varies between zero (for any node in the same network) and infinite (for any point external to the network). The inclusion/exclusion in networks, and the architecture of relationships between networks, enacted by light-speed operating information technologies, configurate dominant processes and functions in our societies.

Networks are open structures, able to expand without limits, integrating new nodes as long as they are able to communicate within the network, namely as long as they share the same communication codes (for example, values or performance goals). A

network-based social structure is a highly dynamic, open system, susceptible to inno-
vating without threatening its balance. Networks are appropriate instruments for a
capitalist economy based on innovation, globalization, and decentralized concentration; for work, workers, and firms based on flexibility, and adaptability; for a culture of
endless deconstruction and reconstruction; for a polity geared towards the instant
processing of new values and public moods; and for a social organization aiming at
the supersession of space and the annihilation of time. Yet the network morphology is
also a source of dramatic reorganization of power relationships. Switches connecting
the networks (for example, financial flows taking control of media empires that influence political processes) are the privileged instruments of power. Thus, the switchers
are the power holders. Since networks are multiple, the interoperating codes and
switches between networks become the fundamental sources in shaping, guiding, and
misguiding societies. The convergence of social evolution and information technologies has created a new material basis for the performance of activities throughout the
social structure. This material basis, built in networks, earmarks dominant social
processes, thus shaping social structure itself.

So observations and analyses presented in this volume seem to indicate that the
new economy is organized around global networks of capital, management, and information, whose access to technological know-how is at the roots of productivity
and competitiveness. Business firms and, increasingly, organizations and institutions are organized in networks of variable geometry whose intertwining supersedes
the traditional distinction between corporations and small business, cutting across
sectors, and spreading along different geographic clusters of economic units. Accordingly, the work process is increasingly individualized, labor is disaggregated in
its performance, and reintegrated in its outcome through a multiplicity of interconnected tasks in different sites, ushering in a new division of labor based on the at-
tributes/capabilities of each worker rather than on the organization of the task.

However, this evolution towards networking forms of management and production does not imply the demise of capitalism. The network society, in its various institutional expressions, is, for the time being, a capitalist society. Furthermore, for
the first time in history, the capitalist mode of production shapes social relationships over the entire planet. But this brand of capitalism is profoundly different
from its historical predecessors. It has two fundamental distinctive features: it is
global, and it is structured to a large extent, around a network of financial flows.
Capital works globally as a unit in real time; and it is realized, invested, and accumulated mainly in the sphere of circulation, that is as finance capital. While finance
capital has generally been among the dominant fractions of capital, we are witness-
ing the emergence of something different: capital accumulation proceeds, and its
value-making is generated, increasingly, in the global financial markets enacted by
information networks in the timeless space of financial flows. From these networks,
capital is invested, globally, in all sectors of activity: information industries, media
business, advanced services, agricultural production, health, education, technology,
old and new manufacturing, transportation, trade, tourism, culture, environmental
management, real estate, war-making and peace-selling, religion, entertainment,
and sports. Some activities are more profitable than others, as they go through cycles, market upswings and downturns, and segmented global competition. Yet whatever is extracted as profit (from producers, consumers, technology, nature, and institutions) is reverted to the meta-network of financial flows, where all capital is
equalized in the commodified democracy of profit-making. In this electronically

operated global casino specific capitals boom or bust, settling the fate of corporations, household savings, national currencies, and regional economies. The net result sums to zero: the losers pay for the winners. But who are the winners and the losers changes by the year, the month, the day, the second, and permeates down to the world of firms, jobs, salaries, taxes, and public services. To the world of what is sometimes called "the real economy," and of what I would be tempted to call the "unreal economy," since in the age of networked capitalism the fundamental reality, where money is made and lost, invested or saved, is in the financial sphere. All other activities (except those of the dwindling public sector) are primarily the basis to generate the necessary surplus to invest in global flows, or the result of investment originated in these financial networks. . . .

What happens to labor, and to the social relationships of production, in this brave new world of informational, global capitalism? Workers do not disappear in the space of flows, and, down to earth, work is plentiful. Indeed, belying apocalyptic prophecies of simplistic analyses, there are more jobs and a higher proportion of working-age people employed than at any time in history. This is mainly because of the massive incorporation of women in paid work in all industrialized societies, an incorporation that has generally been absorbed, and to a large extent induced, by the labor market without major disruptions. So the diffusion of information technologies, while certainly displacing workers and eliminating some jobs, has not resulted, and it does not seem that it will result in the foreseeable future, in mass unemployment. This in spite of the rise of unemployment in European economies, a trend that is related to social institutions rather than to the new production system. But, if work, workers, and working classes exist, and even expand, around the world, the social relationships between capital and labor are profoundly transformed. At its core, capital is global. As a rule, labor is local. Informationalism, in its historical reality, leads to the concentration and globalization of capital, precisely by using the decentralizing power of networks. Labor is disaggregated in its performance, fragmented in its organization, diversified in its existence, divided in its collective action. Networks converge toward a meta-network of capital that integrates capitalist interests at the global level and across sectors and realms of activity: not without conflict, but under the same overarching logic. Labor loses its collective identity, becomes increasingly individualized in its capacities, in its working conditions, and in its interests and projects. Who are the owners, who the producers, who the managers, and who the servants, becomes increasingly blurred in a production system of variable geometry, of teamwork, of networking, outsourcing, and subcontracting. Can we say that the producers of value are the computer nerds who invent new financial instruments to be dispossessed from their work by corporate brokers? who is contributing to value creation in the electronics industry: the Silicon Valley chip designer, or the young woman on the assembly line of a South-East Asian factory? Certainly both, albeit in quite substantially different proportions. Thus, are they jointly the new working class? Why not include in it the Bombay computer consultant subcontracted to program this particular design? Or the flying manager who commutes or telecommutes between California and Singapore customizing chip production and electronics consumption? There is unity of the work process throughout the complex, global networks of interaction. But there is at the same time differentiation of work, segmentation of workers, and disaggregation of labor on a global scale. So while capitalist relationships of production still persist (indeed, in many economies the dominant logic is more strictly capitalist than ever before), capital and labor increasingly tend to exist in different spaces and times: the space of flows and the space of places, instant time of computerized networks versus clock time of everyday life. Thus, they live by each other, but do not relate to each other, as the life of global capital depends less and less on specific labor, and more and more on accumulated, generic labor, operated by a small brains trust inhabiting the virtual palaces of global networks. Beyond this fundamental dichotomy a great deal of social diversity still exists, made up of investors' bids, workers' efforts, human ingenuity, human suffering, hirings and layoffs, promotions and demotions, conflicts and negotiations, competition and alliances: working life goes on. Yet, at a deeper level of the new social reality, social relationships of production have been disconnected in their actual existence. Capital tends to escape in its hyperspace of pure circulation, while labor dissolves its collective entity into an infinite variation of individual existences. Under the conditions of the network society, capital is globally coordinated, labor is individualized. The struggle between diverse capitalists and miscellaneous working classes is subsumed into the more fundamental opposition between the bare logic of capital flows and the cultural values of human experience.

Processes of social transformation summarized under the ideal type of the network society go beyond the sphere of social and technical relationships of production: they deeply affect culture and power as well. Cultural expressions are abstracted from history and geography, and become predominantly mediated by electronic communication networks that interact with the audience by the audience in a diversity of codes and values, ultimately subsumed in a digitized, audiovisual hypertext. Because information and communication circulate primarily through the diversified, yet comprehensive media system, politics becomes increasingly played out in the space of media. Leadership is personalized, and image-making is power-making. Not that all politics can be reduced to media effects, or that values and interests are indifferent to political outcomes. But whoever the political actors and whatever their orientations, they exist in the power game through and by the media, in the whole variety of an increasingly diverse media system, that includes computer-mediated communication networks. The fact that politics has to be framed in the language of electronically based media has profound consequences on the characteristics, organization, and goals of political processes, political actors, and political institutions. Ultimately, the powers that are in the media networks take second place to the power of flows embodied in the structure and language of these networks.

At a deeper level, the material foundations of society, space and time are being transformed, organized around the space of flows and timeless time. Beyond the metaphorical value of these expressions, supported by a number of analyses and illustrations in preceding chapters, a major hypothesis is put forward: dominant functions are organized in networks pertaining to a space of flows that links them up around the world, while fragmenting subordinate functions, and people, in the multiple space of places, made of locales increasingly segregated and disconnected from each other. Timeless time appears to be the result of the negation of time, past and future, in the networks of the space of flows. Meanwhile clock time, measured and valued differentially for each process according to its position in the network, continues to characterize subordinate functions and specific locales. The end of history, enacted in the circularity of computerized financial flows or in the instantaneity of surgical wars, overpowers the biological time of poverty or the mechanical time of industrial work. The social construction of new dominant forms of space and time develops a meta-network that switches off nonessential functions, subordinate social groups, and devalued territories. By so doing, infinite social distance is created between this meta-network and most individuals, activities, and locales around the world. Not that people, locales, or activities disappear. But their structural meaning does, subsumed in the unseen logic of the meta-network where value is produced, cultural codes are created, and power is decided. The new social order, the network society, increasingly appears to most people as a meta-social disorder. Namely, as an automated, random sequence of events, derived from the uncontrollable logic of markets, technology, geopolitical order, or biological determination.

In a broader historical perspective, the network society represents a qualitative change in the human experience. If we refer to an old sociological tradition according to which social action at the most fundamental level can be understood as the changing pattern of relationships between Nature and Culture, we are indeed in a new era.

The first model of relationship between these two fundamental poles of human existence was characterized for millennia by the domination of Nature over Culture. The codes of social organization almost directly expressed the struggle for survival under the uncontrolled harshness of Nature, as anthropology taught us by tracing the codes of social life back to the roots of our biological entity.

The second pattern of the relationship established at the origins of the Modern Age, and associated with the Industrial Revolution and with the triumph of Reason, saw the domination of Nature by Culture, making society out of the process of work by which Humankind found both its liberation from natural forces and its submission to its own abysses of oppression and exploitation.

We are just entering a new stage in which Culture refers to Culture, having superseded Nature to the point that Nature is artificially revived ("preserved") as a cultural form: this is in fact the meaning of the environmental movement, to reconstruct Nature as an ideal cultural form. Because of the convergence of historical evolution and technological change we have entered a purely cultural pattern of social interaction and social organization. This is why information is the key ingredient of our social organization and why flows of messages and images between networks constitute the basic thread of our social structure. This is not to say that history has ended in a happy reconciliation of Humankind with itself. It is in fact quite the opposite: history is just beginning, if by history we understand the moment when, after millennia of a prehistoric battle with Nature, first to survive, then to conquer it, our species has reached the level of knowledge and social organization that will allow us to live in a predominantly social world. It is the beginning of a new existence, and indeed the beginning of a new age, the information age, marked by the autonomy of culture *vis-à-vis* the material bases of our existence. But this is not necessarily an exhilarating moment. Because, alone at last in our human world, we shall have to look at ourselves in the mirror of historical reality. And we may not like the vision.

To be continued.❖

David Harvey (1935–) currently teaches geography at the Johns Hopkins University. He was previously the Halford Mackinder Professor of Geography at Oxford University. His writing on urban life is recognized worldwide for its probing reinterpretation of the late-modern society. His books include *Social Justice and the City* (1973), *The Limits to Capital* (1982), *The Condition of Postmodernity* (1989), and *Justice, Nature and the Geography of Difference* (1996).

The City in a Globalizing World

David Harvey (1996)

At the beginning of this century, there were just 16 cities in the world with more than a million people. Most were in the advanced capitalist countries and London, by far the largest of them all, had just under seven million. At the beginning of this century, too, no more than 7 percent of the world's population could reasonably be classified as "urban." By the year 2000 there may well be as many as 500 cities with more than a million inhabitants while the largest of them, Tokyo, São Paulo, Bombay, and possibly Shanghai (although the list is perpetually being revised both upwards and downwards), will perhaps boast populations of more than 20 million trailed by a score of cities, mostly in the so-called developing countries, with upwards of ten million. Sometime early next century, if present trends continue, more than half of the world's population will be classified as urban rather than rural.

The twentieth century has been, then, *the* century of urbanization. Before 1800 the size and numbers of urban concentrations in all social formations seem to have been strictly limited. The nineteenth century saw the breach of those barriers in a few advanced capitalist countries, but the latter half of the twentieth century has seen that localized breach turned into a universal flood of massive urbanizaton. The future of the most of humanity now lies, for the first time in history, fundamentally in urbanizing areas. The qualities of urban living in the twenty-first century will define the qualities of civilization itself.

But judging superficially by the present state of the world's cities, future generations will not find that civilization particularly congenial. Every city now has its share (often increasing and in some instances predominant) of concentrated impoverishment and human hopelessness, of malnourishment and chronic diseases, of crumbling or stressed out infrastructures, of senseless and wasteful consumerism, of ecological degradation and excessive pollution, of congestion, of seemingly stymied economic and human development, and of sometimes bitter social strife, varying from individualized violence on the streets to organized crime (often an alternative form of urban governance), through police-state exercises in social control to occasional massive civic protest movements (sometimes spontaneous) demanding political-economic change. For many, then, to talk of the city of the twenty-first century is to conjure up a dystopian nightmare in which all that is judged worst in the fatally flawed character of humanity collects together in some hell-hole of despair.

In some of the advanced capitalist countries, that dystopian vision has been strongly associated with the long-cultivated habit on the part of those with power and privilege of running as far from the city centers as possible. Fueled by a permissive car culture, the urge to get some money and get out has taken command. Liverpool's population fell by 40 percent between 1961 and 1991, for example, and Baltimore city's fell from close to a million to under 700,000 in the same three decades. But the upshot has been not only to create endless suburbanization, so-called "edge cities," and sprawling megalopoli, but also to make every village and every rural retreat in the advanced cap-italist world part of a complex web of urbanization that defies any simple categoriza-tion of populations into "urban" and "rural" in that sense which once upon a time could reasonably be accorded to those terms. The hemorrhaging of wealth, popula-tion, and power from central cities has left many of them languishing in limbo. Needy populations have been left behind as the rich and influential have moved out. Add to this the devastating loss of jobs (particularly in manufacturing) in recent years and the parlous state of the older cities becomes all too clear. Nearly 250,000 manufacturing jobs were lost in Manchester in two decades while 40,000 disappeared from Sheffield's steel industry alone in just three short catastrophic years in the mid-1980s. Baltimore likewise lost nearly 200,000 manufacturing jobs from the late 1960s onwards and there is hardly a single city in the United States that has not been the scene of similar devas-tation through deindustrialization.

The subsequent train of events has been tragic for many. Communities built to service now defunct manufacturing industries have been left high and dry, wracked with long-term structural unemployment. Disenchantment, dropping out, and quasi-legal means to make ends meet follow. Those in power rush to blame the vic-tims, the police powers move in (often insensitively), and the politician-media com-plex has a field day stigmatizing and stereotyping an underclass of idle wrong-doers, irresponsible single parents and feckless fathers, debasement of family values, wel-fare junkies, and much worse. If those marginalized happen to be an ethnic or racially marked minority, as is all-too often the case, then the stigmatization amounts to barely concealed racial bigotry. The only available response on the part of those left marginalized is urban rage, making the actual state of social and even more emphatically race relations (for all the campus rhetoric on political correct-ness) far worse now than it has been for several decades. . . .

There is a strong predilection these days to regard the future of urbanization as al-ready determined by the powers of globalization and of market competition. Urban possibilities are limited to mere competitive jockeying of individual cities for position within a global urban system. There seems then to be no place within the urbanization process from which to launch any kind of militant particularism capable of grounding the drive for systemic transformations. In the last 20 years in particular, the rhetoric of "globalization" has become particularly important, even replacing within segments of radical thought the more politicized concepts of imperialism, colonialism, and neo-colonialism. The ideological effect of this discursive shift has been extraordinarily dis-empowering with respect to all forms of local, urban, and even national political action.

Yet, the process of globalization is not new. Certainly from 1492 onwards, and even before (cf. the Hanseatic league system), the globalization of capitalism was well under way in part through the production of a network of urban places. Marx and Engels emphasized the point in *The Communist Manifesto*. Modern industry not only creates the world market, they wrote, but the need for a constantly expanding market "chases the bourgeoisie over the whole surface of the globe" so that it "must nestle every-where, settle everywhere, establish connections everywhere." They continue:

The bourgeoisie has through its exploitation of the world market given a cosmopolitan character to production and consumption in every country. . . . All old established national industries have been destroyed or are daily being destroyed. They are dislodged by new industries, whose introduction becomes a life and death question for all civilized nations, by industries that no longer work up indigenous raw material, but raw material drawn from the remotest zones; industries whose products are consumed, not only at home, but in every quarter of the globe. In place of the old wants, satisfied by the production of the country, we find new wants, requiring for their satisfaction the products of distant lands and climes. In place of the old local and national seclusion and self-sufficiency, we have intercourse in every direction, universal interdependence of nations. And as in material, so also in intellectual production. The intellectual creations of individual nations become common property. National one-sidedness and narrow-mindedness become more and more impossible, and from the numerous national and local literatures, there arises a world literature. . . .

If this is not a good description of globalization then what is? And from this Marx and Engels derived the global imperative "working men of all nations unite" as a necessary condition for an anti-capitalist and socialist revolution.

The bourgeoisie's quest for class domination has always been and continues to be a very geographical affair. "Globalization" is a long-standing *process* always implicit in capital accumulation rather than a political-economic condition that has recently come into being. This does not preclude saying that the process has changed or worked itself out to a particular or even "final" state. But a process-based definition makes us concentrate on *how* globalization has occurred and is occurring. So what kind of process is it and, more importantly, how has it changed in recent years? Some major shifts stand out. To describe them is to describe some of the key forces at work that have changed within the complex dynamic of urbanization, in particular the extraordinary growth of urbanization in many developing countries.

(*a*) *Financial deregulation* began in the United States in the early 1970s as a forced response to stagflation and the breakdown of the Bretton Woods system of international trade and exchange. Bretton Woods was a global system so this meant a shift from one global system (largely controlled politically by the United States) to another that was more decentralized, coordinated through the market and resting on fluxes and flows of money. The effect was to make the financial conditions of capitalism far more temporally volatile and spatially unstable. The term "globalization" was, I note, largely promoted by the financial press in the early 1970s as a necessary virtue of this process of financial deregulation, as something progressive and inevitable, opening up whole new fields of opportunity for capital. It was a term embedded in the language of money and the commodity that then entered into public and academic discourses (including my own) without too much attention being paid to its class origins and ideological functions. It describes a spatial condition in which a Singapore bank can finance a local development in Baltimore with scarcely any mediation from other levels of territorial control (such as the nation state). The connection between urbanization processes and finance capital has become, as a consequence, much more direct. It is unmediated by other institutional forms of control and much more prone to rapid and ephemeral geographical dispersal across the globe. Ideologically, it makes it appear as if all urban places must submit to the discipline of free-floating finance.

(*b*) *The cost and time of moving commodities, people, and particularly information ratcheted downwards* (cf. above). This brought some significant changes to the organization of production and consumption as well as to the definition of wants and needs.

The ultimate "dematerialization of space" in the communication field permitted all sorts of geographical adjustments in the location of industry, consumption, and the like. It is, however, easy to make too much of the so-called information revolution. The newness of it all impresses, but then the newness of the railroad and the telegraph, the automobile, the radio and the telephone in their day impressed equally. These earlier examples are instructive, since each in their own way did change the way globalization worked, the ways in which production and consumption could be organized, politics conducted, and the ways in which social relations between people could become converted on an ever widening scale into social relations between things. Urbanization and the connectivity of urban places through networking across space is indeed changing very rapidly through the use of informational technology.

(c) *Production and organizational forms changed.* The effect was an increasing geographical dispersal and fragmentation of production systems, divisions of labor, specialization of tasks, albeit in the midst of an increasing centralization of corporate power through mergers, takeovers, or joint production agreements that transcended national boundaries. The global television set, the global car, became an everyday aspect of political-economic life as did the so-called "global cities." The closing down of production in one place and the opening up of production somewhere else became a familiar story—some large-scale production operations have moved four or five times in the last 20 years. Corporations have more power to command space, making individual places much more vulnerable to their whims but the whole network of urbanization more open to rapid shifts and flows of manufacturing capital.

(d) *The world proletariat has almost doubled* in the last 30 years. This occurred in part through rapid population growth but also through mobile capital mobilizing more and more of the world's population (including women) as wage laborers in, for example, South Korea, Taiwan, Africa, as well as most recently in the former Soviet bloc. Much of this huge global proletariat is working under conditions of gross exploitation and political oppression. But it is geographically dispersed across a variety of massive urban concentrations. It is consequently hard to organize even though its conditions would indicate a favorable terrain for widespread anti-capitalist struggle.

(e) *The territorialization of the world has changed.* State operations have become much more strongly disciplined by money capital and finance. Structural adjustment and fiscal austerity have become the name of the game and the state has to some degree been reduced to the role of finding ways to promote a favorable business climate, which frequently means exercising strong discipline over the labor force. The "globalization thesis" here functions as a powerful capitalist ideology to beat upon socialists, welfare statists, nationalists, etc. Welfare for the poor has largely been replaced, therefore, by public subventions to capital (Mercedes-Benz recently received one-quarter billion dollars of subventions in a package from the state of Alabama in order to persuade it to locate there).

(f) *While individual states lost some of their power, geopolitical democratization created new opportunities.* It became harder for any core power to exercise discipline over others and easier for peripheral powers to insert themselves into the capitalist competitive game. Money power is a "leveler and cynic" empowering whoever commands it wherever they are. Competitive states could do well in global competition—and this meant low-wage states with strong labor discipline often did better than others. Labor control became, therefore, a vital ideological issue within the globalization argument, again pushing socialist arguments onto the defensive.

All of these quantitative changes taken together have been synergistic enough to transform processes of urbanization. But there has been no revolution in the mode of production and its associated social relations. If there is any real qualitative trend it is towards the reassertion of early nineteenth-century capitalist laissez-faire and social Darwinian values coupled with a twenty-first-century penchant for pulling everyone (and everything that can be exchanged) into the orbit of capital. The effect is to render ever larger segments of the world's population permanently redundant in relation to capital accumulation while severing them from any alternative means of support.

But the political objection to the globalization thesis, is that it denies the possibility for meaningful action within any one of the places of capitalism (be it the nation state or the city as a political milieu for anti-capitalist mobilization). It undialectically presumes the unalloyed powers of spatial processes of capital flow to dominate places. In response, there are many who now try to put the shoe on the other foot.❖

Stuart Hall (1932–) was born in Jamaica and studied at Jamaica College. In 1951 he became a Rhodes scholar at Oxford University. Hall has been professor of sociology at the Open University in England since 1979. He was director of the Center for Cultural Studies at Birmingham in the 1970s, where he was a leader in the founding of cultural studies as an academic discipline. Hall was also an editor of the *New Left Review* from 1957 to 1961. His many books and writings include *Resisting Through Rituals* (1974), *Politics and Ideology* (1986), *Culture, Media, Language* (1986), and *Modernity: An Introduction to Modern Societies* (1996, with David Held, Dan Hubert, and Kenneth Thompson).

The Global, the Local, and the Return of Ethnicity
Stuart Hall (1996)

Narrating the Nation: An Imagined Community

National cultures are composed not only of cultural institutions, but of symbols and representations. A national culture is a *discourse*—a way of constructing meanings which influences and organizes both our actions and our conception of ourselves. National cultures construct identities by producing meanings about "the nation" with which we can *identify*; these are contained in the stories which are told about it, memories which connect its present with its past, and images which are constructed of it. As Benedict Anderson has argued, national identity is an "imagined community."

Anderson argues that the differences between nations lie in the different ways in which they are imagined. Or, as Enoch Powell put it, "the life of nations no less than that of men is lived largely in the imagination." But how is the modern nation imagined? What representational strategies are deployed to construct our common-sense views of national belonging or identity? What are the representations of, say, "England" which win the identifications and define the identities of "English" people? "Nations," Homi Bhabha has remarked, "like narratives, lose their origins in the myths of time and only fully realize their horizons in the mind's eye." How is the narrative of the national culture told?

Excerpt from Hall, ed., *Modernity: An Introduction to Modern Societies* (Oxford: Blackwell Publishers, 1996), pp. 613–619, 626–628. Copyright © 1996. Reprinted by permission of Blackwell Publishers.

Of the many aspects which a comprehensive answer to that question would include, I have selected *five* main elements.

1. First, there is the *narrative of the nation,* as it is told and retold in national histories, literatures, the media, and popular culture. These provide a set of stories, images, landscapes, scenarios, historical events, national symbols, and rituals which stand for, or *represent,* the shared experiences, sorrows, and triumphs and disasters which give meaning to the nation. As members of such an "imagined community," we see ourselves in our mind's eye sharing in this narrative. It lends significance and importance to our humdrum existence, connecting our everyday lives with a national destiny that pre-existed us and will outlive us. From England's green and pleasant land, its gentle, rolling countryside, rose-trellised cottages and country-house gardens—Shakespeare's "sceptered isle"—to public ceremonials like Royal weddings, the discourse of "Englishness" represents what "England" *is,* gives meaning to the identity of "being English," and fixes "England" as a focus of identification in English (and Anglophile) hearts. . . .

2. Secondly, there is the emphasis on *origins, continuity, tradition, and timelessness.* National identity is represented as primordial—"there, in the very nature of things," sometimes slumbering, but ever ready to be "awoken" from its "long, persistent and mysterious somnolence" to resume its unbroken existence. The essentials of the national character remain unchanged through all the vicissitudes of history. It is there from birth, unified and continuous, "changeless" throughout all the changes, eternal. Prime Minister Margaret Thatcher remarked at the time of the Falklands War that there were some people "who thought we could no longer do the great things which we once did . . . that Britain was no longer the nation that had built an Empire and ruled a quarter of the world. . . . Well they were wrong . . . Britain has not changed."

3. A third discursive strategy is what Hobsbawm and Ranger call *the invention of tradition:* "Traditions which appear or claim to be old are often quite recent in origin and sometimes invented. . . . 'Invented tradition' [means] a set of practices, . . . of a ritual or symbolic nature which seek to inculcate certain values and norms of behaviours by repetition which automatically implies continuity with a suitable historical past." For example, "Nothing appears more ancient, and linked to an immemorial past, than the pageantry which surrounds British monarchy and its public ceremonial manifestations. Yet . . . in its modern form it is the product of the late nineteenth and twentieth centuries."

4. A fourth example of the narrative of national culture is that of a *foundational myth:* a story which locates the origin of the nation, the people, and their national character so early that they are lost in the mists of, not "real," but "mythic" time. Invented traditions make the confusions and disasters of history intelligible, converting disarray into "community" and disasters into triumphs. Myths of origin also help disenfranchised peoples to "conceive and express their resentment and its contents in intelligible terms." They provide a narrative in terms of which an alternative history or counter-narrative, which pre-dates the ruptures of colonization, can be constructed (e.g. Rastafarianism for the dispossessed poor of Kingston, Jamaica). New nations are then founded on these myths. (I say "myths" because, as was the case with many African nations which emerged after decolonization, what preceded colonization was not "one nation, one people," but many different tribal cultures and societies.)

5. National identity is also often symbolically grounded on the idea of a *pure, original people or "folk."* But, in the realities of national development, it is rarely this pri-

mordial folk who persist or exercise power. As Gellner wryly observes, "When [simple people] donned folk costume and trekked over the hills, composing poems in the forest clearings, they did not also dream of one day becoming powerful bureaucrats, ambassadors and ministers."

The discourse of national culture is thus not as modern as it appears to be. It constructs identities which are ambiguously placed between past and future. It straddles the temptation to return to former glories and the drive to go forwards ever deeper into modernity. Sometimes national cultures are tempted to turn the clock back, to retreat defensively to that "lost time" when the nation was "great," and to restore past identities. This is the regressive, the anachronistic, element in the national cultural story. But often this very return to the past conceals a struggle to mobilize "the people" to purify their ranks, to expel the "others" who threaten their identity, and to gird their loins for a new march forwards. In Britain during the 1980s, the rhetoric of Thatcherism sometimes inhabited both these aspects of what Tom Nairn calls the "Janus-face" of nationalism: looking back to past imperial glories and "Victorian values" while simultaneously undertaking a kind of modernization in preparation for a new stage of global capitalist competition. Something of the same kind may be going on now in Eastern Europe. Areas breaking away from the old Soviet Union reaffirm their essential ethnic identities and claim nationhood, buttressed by (sometimes extremely dubious) "stories" of mythic origins, religious orthodoxy, and racial purity. Yet they may be also using the nation as the form in which to compete with other ethnic "nations," and so to gain entry to the rich "club" of the West. As Immanuel Wallerstein has acutely observed, "the nationalisms of the modern world are the ambiguous expression [of a desire] for . . . assimilation into the universal . . . and simultaneously for . . . adhering to the particular, the reinvention of differences. Indeed it is a universalism through particularism and particularism through universalism."

Deconstructing the "National Culture": Identity and Difference

This section now turns to the question of whether national cultures and the national identities they construct are actually *unified*. In his famous essay on the topic, Ernest Renan said that three things constitute the spiritual principle of the unity of a nation: ". . . the possession in common of a rich legacy of memories, . . . the desire to live together, [and] the will to perpetuate the heritage that one has received in an undivided form." You should bear in mind these three resonant concepts of what constitutes a national culture as an "imagined community": *memories* from the past; the *desire* to live together; the perpetuation of the *heritage*.

Timothy Brennan reminds us that the word *nation* refers "both to the modern nation-state and to something more ancient and nebulous—the *natio*—a local community, domicile, family, condition of belonging." National identities represented precisely the result of bringing these two halves of the national equation together— offering both membership of the political nation-state and identification with the national culture: "to make culture and polity congruent" and to endow "reasonably homogeneous cultures, each with its own political roof . . . . "

To put it crudely, however different its members may be in terms of class, gender, or race, a national culture seeks to unify them into one cultural identity, to

represent them all as belonging to the same great national family. But is national identity a unifying identity of this kind, which cancels or subsumes cultural difference?

Such an idea is open to doubt, for several reasons. A national culture has never
been simply a point of allegiance, bonding and symbolic identification. It is also a
structure of cultural power. Consider the following points:

1. Most modern nations consist of disparate cultures which were only unified by
a lengthy process of violent conquest—that is, by the forcible suppression of cultural difference. "The British people" are the product of a series of such conquests—Celtic, Roman, Saxon, Viking, and Norman. Throughout Europe the
story is repeated *ad nauseam*. Each conquest subjugated conquered peoples and
their cultures, customs, languages, and traditions and tried to impose a more unified cultural hegemony. As Ernest Renan has remarked, these violent beginnings
which stand at the origins of modern nations have first to be "forgotten" before allegiance to a more unified, homogeneous national identity could begin to be
forged. Thus "British" culture still does not consist of an equal partnership between the component cultures of the UK, but of the effective hegemony of "English," a southern-based culture which represents itself as the essential British culture, over Scottish, Welsh, and Irish and, indeed, other regional cultures. Matthew
Arnold, who tried to fix the essential character of the English people from their
literature, claimed when considering the Celts that such "provincial nationalisms
had to be swallowed up at the level of the political and licensed as cultural contributors to English culture."

2. Secondly, nations are always composed of different social classes, and gender
and ethnic groups. Modern British nationalism was the product of a very concerted effort, in the late Victorian and high imperial period, to unify the classes
across social divisions by providing them with an alternative point of identification—common membership of "the family of the nation." The same point can be
made about gender. National identities are strongly gendered. The meanings and
values of "Englishness" have powerful masculine associations. Women play a secondary role as guardians of hearth, kith, and kin, and as "mothers" of the nation's
"sons."

3. Thirdly, modern western nations were also the centers of empires or of neo-
imperial spheres of influence, exercising cultural hegemony over the cultures of
the colonized. Some historians now argue that it was in this process of comparison
between the "virtues" of "Englishness" and the negative features of other cultures
that many of the distinctive characteristics of English identities were first defined.

Instead of thinking of national cultures as unified, we should think of them as
constituting a *discursive device* which represents difference as unity or identity.
They are cross-cut by deep internal divisions and differences, and "unified" only
through the exercise of different forms of cultural power. Yet—as in the fantasies
of the "whole" self of which Lacanian psychoanalysis speaks—national identities
continue to be represented as *unified*.

One way of unifying them has been to represent them as the expression of the underlying culture of "one people." Ethnicity is the term we give to cultural features—
language, religion, custom, traditions, feeling for "place"—which are shared by a
people. It is therefore tempting to try to use ethnicity in this "foundational" way. But
this belief turns out, in the modern world, to be a myth. Western Europe has no nations which are composed of only one people, one culture or ethnicity. *Modern nations are all cultural hybrids. . . .*

Globalization

The previous section qualified the idea that national identities have ever been as unified or homogeneous as they are represented to be. Nevertheless, in modern history, national cultures have dominated "modernity" and national identities have tended to win out over other, more particularistic sources of cultural identification.

What, then, is so powerfully dislocating national cultural identities now, at the end of the twentieth century? The answer is a complex of processes and forces of change, which for convenience can be summed up under the term "globalization." [As] Anthony McGrew . . . argued, "globalization" refers to those processes, operating on a global scale, which cut across national boundaries, integrating and connecting communities and organizations in new space–time combinations, making the world in reality and in experience more interconnected. Globalization implies a movement away from the classical sociological idea of a "society" as a well-bounded system, and its replacement by a perspective which concentrates on "how social life is ordered across time and space." These new temporal and spatial features, resulting in the compression of distances and time-scales, are among the most significant aspects of globalization affecting cultural identities, and they are discussed in greater detail below.

Remember that globalization is not a recent phenomenon: "Modernity is inherently globalizing." As David Held argues, nation-states were never as autonomous or as sovereign as they claimed to be. And, as Wallerstein reminds us, capitalism "was from the beginning an affair of the world economy and not of nation states. Capital has never allowed its aspirations to be determined by national boundaries." *So both* the trend towards national autonomy and the trend towards globalization are deeply rooted in modernity.

You should bear in mind these two contradictory tendencies within globalization. Nevertheless, it is generally agreed that, since the 1970s, both the scope and pace of global integration have greatly increased, accelerating the flows and linkages between nations. In this and the next section, I shall attempt to track the consequences of these aspects of globalization on cultural identities, examining *three* possible consequences:

1. National identities are being *eroded* as a result of the growth of cultural homogenization and "the global post-modern."
2. National and other "local" or particularistic identities are being *strengthened* by the resistance to globalization.
3. National identities are declining but *new* identities of hybridity are taking their place. . . .

"The Rest" in "the West"

The preceding pages have presented three qualifications to the first of the three possible consequences of globalization: i.e. the homogenization of global identities. These are that:

1. Globalization can go hand in hand with a strengthening of local identities, though this is still within the logic of time–space compression;
2. Globalization is an uneven process and has its own "power geometry";

3. Globalization retains some aspects of western global domination, but cultural identities everywhere are being relativized by the impact of time–space compression.

Perhaps the most striking example of this third point is the phenomenon of migration. After World War II, the decolonizing European powers thought they could pull out of their colonial spheres of influence, leaving the consequences of imperialism behind them. But global interdependence now works both ways. The movements of western styles, images, commodities, and consumer identities outwards has been matched by a momentous movement of peoples from the peripheries to the center in one of the largest and most sustained periods of "unplanned" migration in recent history. Driven by poverty, drought, famine, economic under-development and arbitrary changes of political regime, the accumulating foreign indebtedness of their governments to western banks, very large numbers of the poorer peoples of the globe have taken the "message" of global consumerism at face value, and moved towards the places where "the goodies" come from and where the chances of survival are higher. In the era of global communications, the West is only a one-way airline charter ticket away.

There have been continuous, large-scale, legal and "illegal" migrations into the US from many poor countries of Latin America and the Caribbean basin (Cuba, Haiti, Puerto Rico, the Dominican Republic, the islands of the British Caribbean), as well as substantial numbers of "economic migrants" and political refugees from South-East Asia and the Far East—Chinese, Koreans, Vietnamese, Cambodians, Indians, Pakistanis, Japanese. Canada has a substantial minority Caribbean population. One consequence is a dramatic shift in the "ethnic mix" of the US population—the first since the mass migrations of the early part of this century. In 1980, one in every five Americans came from an African-American, Asian-American, or American-Indian background. In 1990, the figure was one in four. In many major cities (including Los Angeles, San Francisco, New York, Chicago, and Miami), whites are now a minority. In the 1980s, the population of California grew by 5.6 million, 43 percent of which were people of color—that is, including Hispanics and Asians, as well as African-Americans (compared to 33 percent in 1980)—and one-fifth are foreign born. By 1995 one-third of American public school students were expected to be "non-white" (US Census, 1991, quoted in Platt, 1991).

Over the same period, there has been a parallel "migration" into Europe of Arabs from the Maghreb (Morocco, Algeria, Tunisia), and Africans from Senegal and Zaire into France and Belgium; of Turks and North Africans into Germany; of Asians from the ex-Dutch East and West Indies and Surinam into the Netherlands; of North Africans into Italy; and, of course, of people from the Caribbean and from India, Pakistan, Bangladesh, Kenya, Uganda, and Sri Lanka into the United Kingdom. There are political refugees from Somalia, Ethiopia, the Sudan, and Sri Lanka and other places in small numbers everywhere.

This formation of ethnic-minority "enclaves" within the nation-states of the West has led to a "pluralization" of national cultures and national identities.

The Dialectic of Identities

We can look at how this situation has played itself out in Britain in terms of identity. The first effect has been to contest the settled contours of national identity, and to expose its closures to the pressures of difference, "otherness," and cultural diversity. This is happening, to different degrees, in all the western national cultures and as a consequence it has brought the whole issue of national identity and the cultural "centeredness" of the West into the open.

> Older certainties and hierarchies of British identity have been called into question in a world of dissolving boundaries and disrupted continuities. In a country that is now a container of African and Asian cultures, the sense of what it is to be British can never again have the old confidence and surety. Other sources of identity are no less fragile. What does it mean to be European in a continent coloured not only by the cultures of its former colonies, but also by American and now Japanese cultures? Is not the very category of identity itself problematical? Is it at all possible, in global times, to regain a coherent and integral sense of identity? Continuity and historicity of identity are challenged by the immediacy and intensity of global cultural confrontations. The comforts of Tradition are fundamentally challenged by the imperative to forge a new self-interpretation based upon the responsibilities of cultural Translation.

Another effect has been to trigger a widening of the field of identities, and a proliferation of new identity-positions together with a degree of polarization among and between them. These developments constitute the second and third possible consequences of globalization I referred to earlier—the possibility that globalization might lead to a *strengthening* of local identities, or to the production of *new identities*.

The strengthening of local identities can be seen in the strong defensive reaction of those members of dominant ethnic groups who feel threatened by the presence of other cultures. In the UK, for example, such defensiveness has produced a revamped Englishness, and a retreat to ethnic absolutism in an attempt to shore up the nation and rebuild "an identity that coheres, is unified and filters out threats in social experience." This is often grounded in what I have earlier called "cultural racism," and is evident now in legitimate political parties of both Left and Right, and in more extremist political movements throughout Western Europe.

It is sometimes matched by a strategic retreat to more defensive identities among the minority communities themselves in response to the experience of cultural racism and exclusion. Such strategies include re-identification with cultures of origin (in the Caribbean, India, Bangladesh, Pakistan); the construction of strong counter-ethnicities—as in the symbolic identification of second-generation Afro-Caribbean youth, through the symbols and motifs of Rastafarianism, with their African origin and heritage; or the revival of cultural traditionalism, religious orthodoxy, and political separatism, for example, among *some* sections of the Muslim community.

There is also some evidence of the third possible consequence of globalization—the production of *new* identities. A good example is those new identities which have emerged in the 1970s, grouped around the signifier "black," which in the British context provides a new focus of identification for *both* Afro-Caribbean and Asian communities. What these communities have in common, which they represent through taking on the "black" identity, is not that they are culturally, ethnically, linguistically, or even physically the same, but that they are seen and treated as "the same" (i.e. non-white, "other") by the dominant culture. It is their exclusion which provides what Laclau and Mouffe call the common "axis of equivalence" of this new identity. However, despite the fact that efforts are made to give this "black" identity a single or unified content, it continues to exist as an identity *alongside a wide range of other differences*. Afro-Caribbean and Indian people continue to maintain different cultural traditions. "Black" is thus an example, not only of the *political* character of new identities—i.e. their *positional* and conjunctural character (their formation in and for specific times and places)—but also of the way identity and difference are inextricably articulated or knitted together in different identities, the one never wholly obliterating the other.

As a tentative conclusion it would appear, then, that globalization *does* have the effect of contesting and dislocating the centered and "closed" identities of a national culture. It does have a pluralizing impact on identities, producing a variety of possibilities and new positions of identification, and making identities more positional, more political, more plural and diverse; less fixed, unified or trans-historical. However, its general impact remains contradictory.❖

❖ The New Social Formations ❖

Stanley Aronowitz (1933–) is professor of sociology at the Graduate Center, City University of New York. His many books include *False Promises: The Shaping of American Working-Class Consciousness* (1974), *Historical Materialism* (1981), *Roll Over Beethoven* (1993), *Post-Work* (1998, with Jonathan Cutler), and *From the Ashes of the Old: American Labor and America's Future* (1998). **Dawn Esposito** (1949–) teaches sociology at St. John's University in New York. She works in feminist and film studies. **William DiFazio** (1947–) is professor of sociology at St. John's University. His books include *The Jobless Future: Sci-Tech and the Dogma of Work* (1995, with Stanley Aronowitz). **Margaret Yard** (1943–) has taught sociology and nursing at several medical centers in New York City, in addition to having served as associate director of the Center for Cultural Studies at the CUNY Graduate Center.

The Post-Work Manifesto

Stanley Aronowitz, Dawn Esposito,
William DiFazio, Margaret Yard (1998)

The bottom is falling out and with it our sense of well-being. For two centuries, despite depressions and wars, America was the "golden door" behind which beckoned the call of the Good Life. Yet, as the twenty-first century approaches, the United States is more accurately characterized as the home of downsizing jobs and lost security, of disappointed hopes and expectations. For many, recent economic and political developments point to the withering away of comfortable full-time jobs "with a future." With jobless futures have also come deteriorating and lost benefits, from quality health care to assurances like social security that were once guaranteed—if only minimally in the United States—by the employment contract.

If the current situation is allowed to continue on its present course, only the few will be able to enjoy life without the constant stress of economic worries. The rest of us will be so buried in work without end, anxious about procuring or simply sustaining our livelihoods, that even the freedom to imagine a different kind of life will seem more and more like a luxury. It has become increasingly difficult to find the time just to reflect, to write, to feel—to change. Ours is a moment when private and public employers regularly demand "give-backs," from health benefits to pensions and holidays. It is anxiety—certainly not the economy—which becomes democratized as the quest for secure paid labor consumes more and more of our time, uniting people in divergent job and class strata from blue-collar to middle and upper managements as perhaps not for centuries before. For no one is immune as these distinctions themselves commence to collapse, and are rendered increasingly meaningless by the immensity of socioeconomic transformations emblematic of our age.

Most people are likely to understand that industrial workers suffer an ever-present threat of runaway shops and technological change. Thirty years ago many working people fought against employers' efforts to get more work out of them for the same or less money and less free time. But at the end of the twentieth century, fearful of losing jobs, this group of working people now silently suffers more speedup, compulsory overtime and work accidents (lest the boss pull up stakes and leave). Even as statistics show economic growth, legal factory jobs continue to shrink while illegal factory labor has grown. Moreover, in the past decade, we have seen the return of what we thought had been banished forever: the sweatshop. Many people are working "off the books" in the underground economy, translating into ten- and twelve-hour days at wages below legal minimums. In these sweatshops, which make more of our clothing and toys than ever, child labor has reappeared. Children work next to their parents or alone and are often beaten by the bosses, chained to machines and locked in poorly ventilated rooms.

It is not just industrial or blue-collar workers who have been profoundly affected. Doctors are working for salaries in health maintenance organizations (HMOs) and in the relentless drive for cost-cutting are losing control over their own work. In the new world of the HMOs the manager, not the doctor, decides who is sick and who is not, who deserves treatment and who doesn't. And many other professionals are being subordinated to the steady drumbeat of downsizing. For example, as a group, academics are freer than most people in the sense of having time to do one's own work and to speak one's mind in a classroom. Yet tenure itself is no longer secure: as a form of guaranteed income, a kind of entitlement, it is not surprising to find this—like any little security offered most of us is—beginning to be threatened. And just at the moment when a college education seems to be a ticket to a better chance for steady work, tuition at public and private colleges has skyrocketed. Many students can no longer afford to go to school, for pleasure or to pursue careers more instrumentally oriented, because student aid is also rapidly disappearing. Tuition costs in public institutions have increased so rapidly that working-class students, many of whom are minorities, need to work at one or more part-time or full-time jobs while having little time to study. Colleges are once more becoming the province of the privileged.

But an alternative direction to the one in which we are now headed is also possible. This other road would lead to shorter working hours, higher wages, and best of all, our ability to control much more of our own time. In such a different and improved world, we would still produce the goods and services that society needs but we would spend less time doing it. There's plenty to produce: we need millions of homes at rents people can afford. Our environment needs to be cleaned, improved and maintained; depleted drinking water supplies need to be restored and pollution levels reduced. There's also plenty to do: kids need child-care and recreation activities. Ordinary people might run television channels and, together with independent film and video makers, become more genuinely involved with contemporary media. Neighborhoods would have their theaters, concert halls, sports facilities, and collective meeting spaces. Libraries would become full-time again. And people would have time to use them. And, as in much of Europe, many of these services would be free or offered at small prices. The seemingly impossible dream of shorter hours may lead to a life where we are relatively freed from the oppressiveness of time as we now commonly experience it.

Are we headed for freedom or hell? Are current trends towards corporate, government and educational "downsizing" a natural event or are they produced by real people for specific purposes? Can we afford the "free" market which puts two million people on the street without shelter, produces poverty for more than a quarter of Americans, and puts a million more children under the poverty line each year? Do we want an economy which depresses wages for about 80 percent of the working population and continues to ship jobs to low-wage countries? Whose market is it anyway? The middle class does not really benefit when the poor lose with the ending of "welfare as we know it" and the looming privatization of Medicare and Social Security. Those employees shed by the welfare state simply flood the labor market, undermining the bargaining leverage of middle-class workers in the private sector. Only the multimillion dollar salaries and stock options of corporate executives remain in place—and then, not even for these men all that securely—as the rest of our jobs are cut or cut back. . . .

The new world of post-work is a rupture with both the economic and cultural assumptions of work without end. What has been called utopian in the past is now a practical necessity. The world of post-work doesn't have to mean a world of massive poverty, drudgery and want but it can be a world of limitless individual and social potential where everyone is guaranteed "the good life." Work that is personally absorbing and satisfying and expressing creativity and freedom is now possible if a movement is formed and a struggle conducted.

We argue here that the moment of post-work is entirely justified. It is time for a movement that struggles for increased wages with less work. We argue here that everyone must be guaranteed a decent standard of living as a minimum. Our proposals assume the goal of assuring the possibility of the full development of individual and social capacities.

We dare to imagine a world beyond scarcity and thus a world where the jobless future is not about misery and desperation but a future in which time would be liberated and freedom made possible. To imagine is to entertain not only the possibility of a future, but to acknowledge that indeed the present has the potential to be shaped as we dream. To imagine means to dream, to move beyond the boundaries of what is routine and practical. Imagination is lodged not only in the individual creative dream, but in cultural movements that create new ways, new dreams enacted in social solidarity, hope and trust.

Too often this benign act of reflection, this spark of daring imagination, floods an individual with tension ranging from vague uneasiness to high anxiety. To imagine a different way is always a risk. But in the world where work is destroyed by global capital and computer-aided technologies, *not* to imagine an alternative is to take the greater risk. Not to imagine alternatives makes individuals and collectivities dependent on those in power without any possibility of escape. In this situation the Right endorses capital's hegemony while the Left only wants room to maneuver, to make little changes to maintain some social justice and a semblance of equality.

We disagree with both sides and propose a world where work is not without end. We propose a world of self-managed time where radical participatory democracy is possible. Our new technologies managed differently can lead not to more surveillance and less freedom but to a world of less required labor. Under these conditions we now have the time to shape our own lives: family, community and polity. For this to be achieved a different control system is needed for both production and distribution. The basic necessities of life would be determined by participatory democratic means, for we can no longer have individual and social requirements decided by corporate interests and the profit motive. Not just profitable housing but good housing for all. We would emphasize environmental considerations like clean air and water before the profit considerations of the marketplace. Education must be made available for all, not just for those who can afford to pay for it. In this newly imagined world we consider these as human rights. Rights are not the end of a struggle but the beginning demands, as the very minimum. Ruptures created by the new technologies and global capitalism's hegemony demand that we imagine a world where what was once utopian is now practical. Our very survival requires that our demands are more than the reforms of the system. We demand a world where ordinary people are at the very center. We demand a world where radical, participatory democracy and thus universal freedom is at the heart of any new social movement. . . .

For a world beyond compulsory labor and where human freedom is the measure of social life we propose the following program:

1. Guaranteed Income: Everyone would be guaranteed a minimum annual income sufficient for a decent standard of living. This would include nutrition, housing, clothing, transportation and recreational requirements. Everyone would assume the responsibilities of producing and maintaining the community. Able-bodied women and men would share the tasks associated with a clean and healthy environment and one that affords its members amenities such as education, recreation and cultural development. If adequate income were guaranteed for all, the private sector would have to pay wages above the income guarantee to motive workers in this sector. (After all, this was the original idea of minimum wage legislation: to raise the general living standard by raising the bottom. Even if most people earned more, the floor on the incomes was measured by a basic, adequate income level.) In order to reduce their costs corporations would be induced to further develop labor-saving technologies. Savings would be shared in the form of more public services and shorter hours.

There would be no welfare sector—with its cycle of dependency and degradation—because of the income guarantee. Services such as health care, education and social work would expand and be paid for through the progressive income tax. As a result there would be a new perspective on jobs and the emphasis would shift from work done for the purchase of consumer goods to work done for problem solving, exploring possibilities and for finding new ethical, social and individual ways of life.

2. Radical Participatory Democracy: With the end of endless work, which binds our time to the demands of profit, we will finally have time to truly participate in the governance of our social world. We will finally have the time to imagine alternatives to the present and the possibility of a better future. With the progressive reduction of work time will come the possibility of all of the people to participate in democratic decision-making. One example: using e-mail and the Net for providing information in order to expand decision-making to wider constituencies. This is contingent on the availability of computers and training for all people. With this form of enhanced face-to-face communication we can bring to birth a truly democratic civil society in which all members could participate in the discourse on political, eco-

nomic, cultural, environmental and recreational issues. Decisions would be made by a free association of individuals in popular assemblies. This would amount to the creation of a popular politics.

The liberation of time from endless work and the new power of ordinary people to participate daily in politics and community affairs is the precondition for the emancipation of the individual, who would gain the freedom of a self-managed life. But there is more than participation in civic affairs. The slogan for the eight-hour movement was "eight hours labor, eight hours rest and eight hours for what we will." "What we will" remains a goal for most of us. Our time seems crowded with imposed obligations. While some of these are both necessary and pleasurable, many are not. Cutting working hours would increase time to develop our capacities or simply to do what most pleases us, including things which provide private enjoyment without the impositions of external authority.

3. A New Labor Policy: We need to consider the pace of technological change and the effects of corporate reorganization that have shed tens of thousands of employees. We have to gauge these developments in terms of the impact that they have on individuals and communities. Though we aren't against the development of technological innovations or forms of work reorganization which lighten our burdens, these should be open to public scrutiny, and planning should be open to public participation. Democratic decision-making in the workplace can have important outcomes for human survival at the individual, social and environmental levels. The costs of these new technological developments must be paid for by the corporations who have a responsibility to the public. These costs are measured by job and wage loss but also their effects on neighborhood and regional institutions and services and by potential environmental hazards associated with conducting business and abandoning production sites. A sustainable biosphere with stable ecosystems is as important to human survival as is a sustainable economy. In order to achieve a sustainable economy we foresee the need to reregulate many aspects of production, commerce and technological innovation by subjecting them to ecological and democratic criteria. In this respect, the bureaucratic regulatory agencies would not remain the court of last resort. As in AIDS policy—where those affected by the disease have played an active role in negotiating the size of the research budget, its priorities and policies affecting the introduction of new drugs—workers and their unions, community groups and individuals would have a substantial voice in various aspects of economic policy at both the enterprise level and regulatory agencies.

4. The Reduction of Working Hours: There has been no significant legal reduction in working hours in the United States since 1938. On the contrary, working hours have lengthened as many employers require overtime hours on penalty of discharge or inadequate income. The distribution of benefits of the new technologies has been one-sided. Only corporations and some professionals and entrepreneurs have benefitted. For most workers the new technologies have only created job insecurity and tens of thousands of workers have suffered job loss, wage loss and part-time or temporary work. It is time that the population at large benefit from the progressive reduction of working hours. Thus we call for a six-hour day without a reduction in pay and for the abolition of overtime except under special conditions that, in any case, would not be compulsory. This will cause anxiety for many who have depended on overtime for their survival. The income guarantee and the decommodification of costs such as health care and education may alleviate problems associated with income losses for some. Equally important, we believe there can be

no genuine improvement in general living standards until the standards enjoyed by the minority are shared by the vast majority. Unless the scourge of unemployment and underemployment is removed for all, the relative privileges which some have achieved will remain at risk.

5. Higher Education as a Form of Life: The new technologies require an increase in knowledge work. The education required to perform this work should be continuously available to all. At the same time the thrust towards multiculturalism and the emergence of new identities means that we must be educated for a global world. This requires a global curriculum that isn't only Eurocentric. This doesn't mean that we no longer read *Hamlet* and Greek philosophy but that we read Shakespeare as well as African folktales and Indian and Chinese philosophy. A global curriculum requires more time for education as it does for new developments in science and philosophy. For the first time in human history everyone may be able to pursue their own educational ends at any age and for the goal of individual development. When we have freed ourselves from work without end, education isn't required to be only vocationland. In the post-work world intellectual and aesthetic interests of students are primary. Students will enter and leave education according to their needs and not just the requirements of jobs.

6. There is Still Work to be Done: Despite labor-saving technologies, our roads, bridges, water systems, schools and parks need rebuilding and repair. We need to create an effective mass transit system in every urban community and nationally which can gradually reduce the use of automobiles. We need to maintain and refurbish the environment and public spaces. We need to care medically and emotionally for our population. Cancer, heart disease, AIDS, and other diseases require both research and massive care facilities.

7. People do not live on bread alone: There have been periods in the twentieth century when an effort was made to publicly finance the arts in a fairly substantial way: the Depression and the 1960s. The New Deal's arts program was killed when some reactionary politicians discovered radicals among the program's employees. In the 1990s another generation of reactionaries have all but killed a much more modestly funded National Endowment for the Arts because it gave grants to dissenting artists, especially those who broke puritanical sexual codes. Creating visual, written and musical arts are an important part of the new public responsibility because, typically, the market does not support most people who produce culture, especially those who challenge us to think differently. We need a well-funded national program for artists and intellectuals who recognize their duty to speak to us freely and which opposes all forms of censorship masked as morality.

8. We favor a universal public service in which all tasks are shared including those tasks that are most unpleasant: In fact we suggest public service jobs be paid on the principle of reverse remuneration. This means paying more for jobs that are more unpleasant but enhance public goods, such as garbage collection, street cleaning, heavy industrial tasks, repetitive bureaucratic work, caring for children and the disabled. As the values of shared work are enhanced and new technologies are developed the amount of time required for these jobs will diminish. These are the requirements of public service in a world of participatory democracy and in which the individual has been liberated from work in a post-work world.❖

William Julius Wilson (1935–) was professor of sociology at the University of Chicago until 1996, when he became the Malcolm Wiener Professor of Social Policy at Harvard University. In the Chicago years he did much of the empirical work for his three controversial books—*The Declining Significance of Race* (1980), *The Truly Disadvantaged: The Inner City, the Underclass, and Public Policy* (1987), and *When Work Disappears: The World of the Urban Poor* (1996). By focusing attention on the urban underclass, Wilson has forcibly altered both the academic and public debates over the respective roles of race and class in urban poverty. He has been widely honored for his work, including election as president of the American Sociological Association, as member of the National Academy of Science, and as recipient of a MacArthur Foundation fellowship.

What to Do When Work Disappears

William Julius Wilson (1996)

The problems of joblessness and social dislocation in the inner city are, in part, related to the processes in the global economy that have contributed to greater inequality and insecurity among American workers in general, and to the failure of U.S. social policies to adjust to these processes. It is therefore myopic to view the problems of jobless ghettos as if they were separate from those that plague the larger society.

In using this cross-cultural perspective I am not suggesting that we can or even should simply import the social policies of the Japanese, Germans, or other West Europeans. As Ray Marshall has appropriately pointed out, the approaches in these other countries are embedded in their own cultures and have their "own flaws and deficiencies, as well as strengths." We should instead "learn from the approaches used in other countries and adapt the best aspects into our own home-grown solutions."

The strengths of some of the approaches in other countries are apparent. For example, in Japan and Germany most high school and college graduates leave school with skills in keeping with the demands of the highly technological marketplace in the global economy. In the United States, by contrast, only college graduates and those few with extra-specialized post–high school training acquire such skills. Those with only high school diplomas or less do not.

The flaws and deficiencies of some of the approaches in the other countries are also apparent. Except for Germany, European countries have the same gap in worker skills. Because of the generous unemployment benefits, however, the low-skilled European workers tend to be less willing to accept the lower-paying jobs that their counterparts in the United States are often forced to take. Therefore, the problems of unskilled European workers are not only restricted to low wages, they also include high levels of unemployment. . . . The growing problems of unemployment among low-skilled European workers is placing a strain on the welfare state. Immigrant minorities are disproportionately represented among the jobless population, and therefore tend to be publicly identified with the problem of maintaining welfare costs. These perceptions contribute to growing intergroup tensions. Accordingly, the problems of race, unemployment, and concentration of urban poverty that have traditionally plagued the United States are now surfacing in various countries in Europe.

Just as the United States can learn from some of the approaches in the other countries, the Europeans could learn from the United States how to make their workforces more flexible instead of paying them to stay unemployed indefinitely. In particular, they could learn how to get unskilled workers into low-wage jobs that would be buttressed by maintaining certain desirable aspects of the safety net, such as universal health insurance, that prevent workers from slipping into the depths of poverty, as so often happens to their American counterparts. . . .

The mismatch between residence and the location of jobs is a special problem for some workers in America because, unlike in Europe, the public transportation system is weak and expensive. This presents a special problem for inner-city blacks because they have less access to private automobiles and, unlike Mexicans, do not have a network system that supports organized car pools. Accordingly, they depend heavily on public transportation and therefore have difficulty getting to the suburbs, where jobs are more plentiful and employment growth is greater. Until public transit systems are improved in metropolitan areas, the creation of privately subsidized car-pool and van-pool networks to carry inner-city residents to the areas of employment, particularly suburban areas, would be a relatively inexpensive way to increase work opportunities.

In the inner-city ghettos, the problems of spatial mismatch have been aggravated by the breakdown in the informal job information network. In neighborhoods in which a substantial number of adults are working, people are more likely to learn about job openings or be recommended for jobs by working kin, relatives, friends, and acquaintances. Job referrals from current employees are important in the American labor market, as our discussion of employer interviews so clearly revealed. Individuals in jobless ghettos are less likely to gain employment through this process. But the creation of for-profit or not-for-profit job information and placement centers in various parts of the inner city not only could significantly improve awareness of the availability of employment in the metropolitan area but could also serve to refer workers to employers.

These centers would recruit or accept inner-city workers and try to place them in jobs. One of their main purposes would be to make persons who have been persistently unemployed or out of the labor force "job-ready" so that a prospective employer would be assured that a worker understands and appreciates employer expectations such as showing up for work on time and on a regular basis, accepting the orders of supervisors, and so on. When an information and placement center is satisfied that a worker is job-ready, then and only then would the worker be referred to an employer who has a job vacancy. Moreover, information and placement centers could coordinate efforts with the car-pool and van-pool networks to get those job applicants who lack private transportation to the employment sites. . . .

The central problem facing inner-city workers is not improving the flow of information about the availability of jobs, or getting to where the jobs are, or becoming job-ready. The central problem is that the demand for labor has shifted away from low-skilled workers because of structural changes in the economy. During certain periods, this problem can be offset to some extent by appropriate macroeconomic levers that can act to enhance economic growth and reduce unemployment, including fiscal policies that regulate government spending and taxation and monetary policies that influence interest rates and control the money supply. But given the fundamental structural decline in the demand for low-skilled workers, such policies will have their greatest impact in the higher-wage sectors of the economy. Many low-wage workers, especially those in high-jobless inner-city neighborhoods who are not in or have dropped out of the labor force and who also face the problem of negative employer attitudes, will not experience any improvement in their job prospects because of fiscal or monetary policies. Despite some claims that low-skilled workers fail to take advantage of labor-market opportunities, available evidence strongly suggests not only that the jobs for such workers carry lower real wages and fewer benefits than did comparable jobs in the early 1970s, but that it is harder for certain low-skilled workers, especially low-skilled males who are not being absorbed into the expanding service sector to find employment today. As the economists Sheldon Danziger and Peter Gottschalk put it:

> In our view, the problem is not that more people have chosen not to work, but rather that demand by employers for less-skilled workers, even those who are willing to work at low wages, has declined. We find it paradoxical that so much attention has been focused on changing the labor-supply behavior of welfare recipients and so little has been given to changing the demand side of a labor market that has been increasingly unable to employ less-skilled and less-experienced workers.

If firms in the private sector cannot use or refuse to hire low-skilled adults who are willing to take minimum-wage or subminimum-wage jobs, then the jobs problem for inner-city workers cannot be adequately addressed without considering a policy of public-sector employment of last resort. . . .

Programs proposed to increase employment opportunities, such as the creation of WPA-style jobs, should be aimed at broad segments of the U.S. population, not just inner-city workers, in order to provide the needed solid political base of support. In the new, highly integrated global economy, an increasing number of Americans across racial, ethnic, and income groups are experiencing declining real incomes, increasing job displacement, and growing economic insecurity. The unprecedented level of inner-city joblessness represents one important aspect of the broader economic dislocations that cut across racial and ethnic groups in the United States. Accordingly, when promoting economic and social reforms, it hardly seems politically wise to focus mainly on the most disadvantaged groups while ignoring other segments of the population that have also been adversely affected by global economic changes.

Yet, just when bold new comprehensive initiatives are urgently needed to address these problems, the U.S. Congress has retreated from using public policy as an instrument with which to fight social inequality. Failure to deal with this growing social inequality, including the rise of joblessness in U.S. inner cities, could seriously worsen the economic life of urban families and neighborhoods.

Groups ranging from the inner-city poor to those working- and middle-class Americans who are struggling to make ends meet will have to be effectively mobilized in order to change the current course and direction taken by policymakers. Perhaps the best way to accomplish this is through coalition politics that promote race-neutral programs such as jobs creation, further expansion of the earned income tax credit, public school reform, child care programs, and universal health insurance. A broad-based political coalition is needed to successfully push such programs through the political process.

Because an effective political coalition in part depends upon how the issues to be addressed are defined, it is imperative that the political message underscore the need for economic and social reform that benefits all groups, not just America's minority poor. The framers of this message should be cognizant of the fact that changes in the global economy are creating growing social inequality and situations which intensify antagonisms between different racial and ethnic groups, and that these groups, although often seen as adversaries, are potential allies in a reform coalition because they suffer from a common problem—economic distress caused by forces outside their own control.

In the absence of an effective political coalition, priorities will be established that do not represent the interests of disadvantaged groups. For example, in the [U.S.] House of Representatives, 67 percent of proposed spending cuts from the federal budget for the year 2000 would come from low-income programs, even though these programs represent only 21 percent of the current federal budget. Without an effective political coalition it is unlikely that Congress would be willing to finance the kinds of reforms that are needed to combat the new social inequality. . . .

The solutions I have outlined were developed with the idea of providing a policy framework that would be suitable for and could be easily adopted by a reform coalition. The long-term solutions, which include the development of a system of national performance standards in public schools, family policies to reinforce the learning system in the schools, a national system of school-to-work transition, and ways to promote city-suburban integration and cooperation, would be beneficial to and could draw the support of a broad range of groups in America. The short-term solutions, which range from the development of job information and placement centers and subsidized car pools in the ghetto to the creation of WPA-style jobs, are more relevant to low-income Americans, but they are the kinds of opportunity-enhancing programs that Americans of all racial and class backgrounds tend to support.

Although my policy framework is designed to appeal to broad segments of the population, I firmly believe that if adopted, it would alleviate a good deal of the economic and social distress currently plaguing the inner cities. The immediate problem of the disappearance of work in many inner-city neighborhoods would be confronted. The employment base in these neighborhoods would be increased immediately by the creation of WPA-style jobs, and income levels would rise because of the expansion of the earned income tax credit. Programs such as universal health care and day care would increase the attractiveness of low-wage jobs and "make work pay."

Increasing the employment base would have an enormous positive impact on the social organization of ghetto neighborhoods. As more people become employed, crime, including violent crime, and drug use will subside; families will be strengthened and welfare receipt will decline significantly; ghetto-related culture and behavior, no longer sustained and nourished by persistent joblessness, will gradually fade. As more people become employed and gain work experience, they will have a better chance of finding jobs in the private sector when they become available. The attitudes of employers toward inner-city workers will undergo change, in part because they would be dealing with job applicants who have steady work experience and would furnish references from their previous supervisors.

This is not to suggest that all the jobless individuals from the inner-city ghetto would take advantage of these employment opportunities. Some have responded to persistent joblessness by abusing alcohol and drugs, and these handicaps will affect their overall job performance, including showing up for work on time or on a consistent basis. But they represent only a small segment of the worker population in the inner city. Most workers in the inner city are ready, willing, able, and anxious to hold a steady job.

The long-term solutions that I have advanced would reduce the likelihood that a new generation of jobless workers would be produced from the youngsters now in school and preschool. We must break the cycle of joblessness and improve the youngsters' preparation for the new labor market in the global economy.

My framework for long-term and immediate solutions is based on the notion that the problems of jobless ghettos cannot be separated from those of the rest of the nation. Although these solutions have wide-ranging application and would alleviate the economic distress of many Americans, their impact on jobless ghettos would be profound. Their most important contribution would be their effect on the children of the ghetto, who would be able to anticipate a future of economic mobility and share the hopes and aspirations that so many of their fellow citizens experience as part of the American way of life.❖

Patricia Clough (1945–) was born in Corona in Queens, New York City, and educated at the University of Illinois, where in addition to studying sociology and cultural criticism, she studied cybernetics at the world-famous Biological Computer Lab. During the 1960s, Clough was a nun in the Roman Catholic Order of the Sisters of Mercy; yet, she broke the traditional silence of the convent to participate in political and social movements in Brooklyn. Her books include *The End(s) of Ethnography* (1992), *Feminist Thought* (1994), and *Auto-affection: The Unconscious in the Age of Teletechnology* (1999).

Cultural Criticism and Telecommunications
Patricia Clough (1997)

Since the 1980s, deregulation has led to intense competition in the development of telecommunications. Cable services, satellite systems, interactive CD and video games, VCR innovation, and camcorders all have moved the apparatus of television beyond a broadcast model. Zapping, time shifting, multiple forms of storage and replay, have become reference points of a vision to interface the so-called passivity of television watching with the Net in the production of what is referred to as push-pull programming. Push programming means making the activity of browsing the net a machine function, moving it further from the user's consciousness. It means cascades of information across various sites—phone, PC, wristwatch, miniature TV monitors. Without waiting for the user's prompt, these devices will provide the user with updated traffic reports, the stock market's ups and downs, shopping opportunities, and updates on personalized information needs. There still will be pull programming, which the user is invited to choose; pull programming is the option to turn to old movies, reruns of TV sitcoms, video games, and sources of various abstract knowledges. Part of this vi-

Reprinted by permission of the author. A version of this essay originally appeared in *Perspectives*, the newsletter of the American Sociological Association's Theory Section.

sion is the availability of banks of information about each of us—not only demographics of all sorts but also the more general treatment of individuals as ontologically specific databases of genetic information that can be exchanged among agents that may just as easily be computer programs as people.

Such a vision is part of the accumulation of capital based on the speed of information transfer, connected to the globalized, flexible production of postmodernity. But the vision of telecommunications is not only a matter of capital. It also is a re-visioning of the subject in relationship to representation. As such, telecommunications raises questions about the assumptions informing the sociological project *tout court*. For example, questions arise about the assumptions underlying our discourse on democracy.

In modern Western thought, the discourse on democracy has leaned on the assumption that private needs of family members are socialized through the public sphere; the public sphere is thought to be distinct from state and civil society, such that public discourse can be both sensitive to private needs and shape them into a social consensus in terms of which the individual subject is educated and enabled to stand against what is judged to be illegitimate deployments of force by the state. With the development of mass-mediated cultures and mass consumption, the discourse on democracy was theoretically reshaped. The educative function was given over to civil society in keeping with a "consumerist-humanism." This reformulation of theoretical discourse involved rethinking the socialization of the working class for participation in the state, as expressed in Gramsci's work on one hand and Foucault's on the other. Whereas Gramsci theorized that the educative function of civil society would lead to extended democratic processes, Foucault imagined the state's power reaching each individual through disciplining institutions of civil society—the family, the labor union, the school. But, both of these elaborations seem politically ineffectual today, when information rather than labor is central to accumulation of capital and the socialization of labor is no longer urgent. Furthermore, telecommunications makes it possible for there to be many points for the application of power/knowledge with something other than socialization as the aim.

Telecommunications is not a subject system. Telecommunications no longer allows technology to be perceived only as a perfecting of the human being while maintaining the intentional, knowing subject at its center as its agency; the subject is only one node in the network, and not necessarily the central node. Whatever its ideological function, telecommunications is no longer thought to be functioning ideologically by interpellating the subject to idealized versions of a culture or personal identity.

Even recent treatments of multiple public spheres, or "subaltern publics," to use Nancy Fraser's term, do not seem to deconstruct enough the configuration that has informed Western discourse on democracy. The thought of subaltern publics hurries to address the unequal distribution of resources for self-representation without taking into account the effects of telecommunications on the configuration of family, private and public spheres, state and civil society, and on the privilege given the individual subject in this configuration. Especially where political presents are being (re)structured in the wake of colonialism, it may not be enough to think that a certain configuration of family, private and public spheres, states and civil society, has been frustrated and needs only to be encouraged for there to be democracy. Instead, other ways of thinking about freedom, rights, self-determination, and resistance may be altogether necessary. The point is that just when telecommunications may make questions about democracy pressing, the configuration assumed in the discourse on democracy seems both too rigid and too fragile a standard for assessing political institutions locally and globally.❖

Judith Stacey (1943–) studied at Brandeis University, after which she taught for many years at the University of California at Davis. Stacey currently holds the Barbra Streisand chair in gender studies at the University of Southern California. She lives in Los Angeles as well as Oakland, which allowed her access to the families she studied for her controversial and influential book *Brave New Families: Stories of Domestic Upheaval in Late Twentieth Century America* (1990). Stacey's writings also include *Patriarchy and the Socialist Revolution* (1983) as well as *In the Name of the Family: Rethinking Family Values in the Postmodern Age* (1996), from which the following selection is taken.

The Post-Modern Family
Judith Stacey (1996)

The past half-century of postindustrial social and economic transformations in the United States and Europe have rung down the historic curtain on the modern family regime. In 1950, three-fifths of U.S. households contained a male breadwinner and a full-time female homemaker, whether children resided with the couples or not. Now, more than three-fifths of married women with dependent children are in the labor force, as well as a majority of mothers of infants, while there are more than twice as many single-mother families as married, homemaker-mom families. By the middle of the 1970s, moreover, divorce had outstripped death as the key source of marital dissolutions, generating in its wake a complex array of new kinship ties and tribulations. While here too the United States leads most of the globe, the same demographic and social trends pervade the postindustrial world. The diversity of our contemporary kinship relationships undermines Tolstoy's famous contrast between happy and unhappy families; even happy families no longer are all alike. No longer is there a single culturally dominant family pattern, like the "modern" one, to which a majority of citizens conform and most of the rest aspire. Instead, postindustrial conditions have compelled and encouraged us to craft a wide array of family arrangements which we inhabit uneasily and reconstitute frequently as our occupational and personal circumstances shift.

We have been living through a tumultuous and fractious period of family history, a period after the modern family order, but before what we cannot foretell. When Shorter employed the term "the postmodern family" in 1975, he did so to underscore three emergent trends of Western family life that he considered unprecedented—peer influence surpassing parental influence over the young, marital instability, and women's departure from the nest. Although I agree that these are important features of contemporary family life, I use the term postmodern family instead to signal the contested, ambivalent, and undecided character of our contemporary family cultures. The postmodern, as art historian Clive Dilnot has suggested, "is first, an uncertainty, an insecurity, a doubt." Most of the "post" words provoke uneasiness because they imply "both the end, or at least the radical transformation, of a familiar pattern of activity or group of ideas," and the emergence of "new fields of cultural activity whose contours are still unclear and whose meanings and implications . . . cannot yet be fathomed."

Like postmodern culture, contemporary Western family arrangements are diverse, fluid, and unresolved. Like postmodern cultural forms, our families today admix unlikely elements in an improvisational pastiche of old and new. The postmodern family condition is not a new model of family life equivalent to that of the modern family; it is not the next stage in an orderly progression of stages of family history; rather the postmodern family condition signals the moment in that history when our belief in a logical progression of stages has broken down. Modernization narratives about "the family," like the one in Shorter's *The Making of the Modern Family,* once portrayed Western family life steadily evolving toward a more democratic and progressive form. Rupturing this self-congratulatory and reassuring logic, the postmodern family condition incorporates both experimental and nostalgic dimensions as it lurches forward and backward into an uncertain future.

In 1990, I published *Brave New Families,* a book about this postmodern family condition that was based upon three years of fieldwork I had conducted during the height of the Reagan-Bush era among (not always) working people in California's Silicon Valley. *Brave New Families* depicts people struggling heroically and creatively, but with mixed success, to navigate the new gender, family and work conditions of postindustrial dislocations. Two years after its publication, defenders of "family values" attacked my book in the pages of the *New York Times* and elsewhere, portraying (in my view, misportraying) it as uncritically celebrating the postmodern family condition and an "anything goes" approach to family life. Social scientists James Q. Wilson and David Popenoe both identified my stance with the misguided school of "family optimism, since it stresses that changes in the contemporary family are really nothing to worry about." More pointedly, the late historian Christopher Lasch chided me for feminist "ideological preconceptions" that produced "cheery conclusions" to which "Stacey's research does not lend much support." . . .

Two challenges to my class and gender prejudices provoked my turn to ethnographic research and the selection of the two kin groups who became its focus. Pamela Gama, an administrator of social services for women at a Silicon Valley antipoverty agency when I met her in July of 1984, became central to my study when she challenged my secular feminist preconceptions by "coming out" to me as a recent born-again Christian convert. Pamela was the 47-year-old bride at the Christian wedding ceremony I attended two years later. There she exchanged vows with her second husband, Albert Gama, a construction worker, with whom she had previously cohabited. Pamela's first marriage in 1960 to Don Franklin, the father of her three children, lasted fifteen years, spanning the headiest days of Silicon Valley development and the period of Don's successful rise from telephone repairman to electronics packaging engineer.

In contrast, Dotty Lewison, my central contact in the second kin network I studied, challenged my class prejudices. The physical appearance and appurtenances of the worn and modest Lewison abode, Dotty's polyester attire and bawdy speech, her husband's heavily tattooed body, and the geographic and occupational details of her family's history satisfied all of my stereotypic notions of an authentic working-class family. But the history of feminist activism Dotty recounted proudly, as she unpacked a newly purchased bible, demonstrated the serious limitations of my tacit understandings. When I met Dotty in October of 1984, she was the veteran of an intact and reformed marriage of thirty years' duration to her disabled husband, Lou, formerly an electronics maintenance mechanic and supervisor, as well as, I would later learn, a wife and child abuser.

Pamela, Dotty, and several of their friends whom I came to know during my study were members of Betty Friedan's *Feminine Mystique* generation, but not of her social class. Unlike the more affluent members of Friedan's intended audience, Pam and Dotty were "beneficiaries" of the late, ephemeral achievement of a male family wage and homeownership won by privileged sectors of the working class. This was a pyrrhic victory, as it turned out, that had allowed this population a brief period of access to the modern family system just as it was decomposing. Pam and Dotty, like most white women of their generation, were young when they married in the 1950s and early 1960s. They entered their first marriages with gender expectations about family and work responsibilities that were conventional for their era. For a significant period of time, they and their husbands conformed, as best they could, to the culturally prescribed pattern of male breadwinner and female homemaker. Assuming primary responsibility for rearing the children they began to bear immediately after marriage, Pam and Dotty supported their husbands' successful efforts to progress from working-class to middle- and upper-middle-class careers in the electronics industry. Their experiences with the modern family, however, were always more tenuous, less pure, than those women to whom, and for whom, Betty Friedan spoke.

The insecurities and inadequacies of their husbands' earnings made itinerant labor force participation by Dotty and Pam both necessary and resented by their husbands before feminism made female employment a badge of pride. Dotty alternated frequent childbearing with recurrent forays in the labor force in a wide array of low-wage jobs. In fact, Dotty herself assembled semiconductors before her husband, Lou, entered the electronics industry, but she did not perceive or desire significant opportunities for her own occupational mobility at that point. Pamela's husband began his career ascent earlier than Dotty's, but Pamela still found his earnings insufficient, and his spending habits too profligate, to balance the household budget. To make the ends of their beyond-their-means, middle-class lifestyle meet without undermining her husband's pride, Pam shared childcare and a clandestine housecleaning occupation with her African-American neighbor and friend, Lorraine. Thus Pam and Dotty did not manage to suffer the full effects of what Friedan had termed the "problem without a name" until feminism had begun to name it, and in terms both women found compelling.

In the early 1970s, while their workaholic husbands were increasingly absent from their families, Pam and Dotty each joined friends taking women's reentry courses in local community colleges. There they encountered feminism, and their lives and their modern families were never the same. Feminism provided an analysis and rhetoric for their discontent, and it helped each develop the self-esteem she needed to exit or reform her unhappy modern marriage. Both women left their husbands, became welfare mothers and experimented with the single life. Pam divorced, pursued a college degree, and developed a social service career. Dotty, with lesser educational credentials and employment options, took her husband back, but on her own terms, after his disabling heart attack (and after a lover left her). Disabled, Lou ceased his physical abuse and performed most of the housework, while Dotty had control over her time, some of which she devoted to community activism in anti-battering work.

By the time I met Pamela and Dotty a decade later, at a time when my own feminist-inspired joint household of the prior eight years was failing, national and local feminist ardor had cooled. Pam was then a recent convert to born-again Christianity, receiving Christian marriage counseling to buttress and enhance her second marriage to construction worker Al. Certainly this represented a retreat from feminist family ideology, but, as Pamela gradually taught me, a far less dramatic retreat than I at first imagined. Like other women active in the contemporary evangelical Christian revival, Pam was making creative use of its surprisingly flexible patriarchal ideology to reform her husband in her own image. She judged it "not so bad a deal" to cede Al nominal family headship in exchange for substantial improvements in his conjugal behavior. Indeed, few contemporary feminists would find fault with the Christian marital principles that Al identified as his goals: "I just hope that we can come closer together and be more honest with each other. Try to use God as a guideline. The goals are more openness, a closer relationship, be more loving both verbally and physically, have more concern for the other person's feelings."

Nor did Pamela's conversion return her to a modern family pattern. Instead she collaborated with her first husband's live-in Jewish lover, Shirley Moskowitz, to build a remarkably harmonious and inclusive divorce-extended kin network whose constituent households swapped resources, labor, and lodgers in response to shifting family circumstances and needs.

Dotty Lewison was also no longer a political activist when we met in 1984. Instead she was supplementing Lou's disability pension with part-time paid work in a small insurance office and pursuing spiritual exploration more overtly postmodern in form than Pam's in a metaphysical Christian church. During the course of my fieldwork, however, an overwhelming series of tragedies claimed the lives of Dotty's husband and two of the Lewison's five adult children. Dotty successfully contested her abusive son-in-law for custody of her four motherless grandchildren. Struggling to support them, she formed a joint household with her only occupationally successful child, Kristina, an electronics drafter-designer and a single mother of one child. While Dotty and Pamela both had moved partway back from feminist fervor, at the same time both had moved further away from the (no-longer) modern family.

Between them, Pamela and Dotty had eight children—five daughters and three sons—children of modern families disrupted by postindustrial developments and feminist challenges. All were in their twenties when I first met them in 1984 and 1985, members of the quintessential postfeminist generation. Although all five daughters distanced themselves from feminist identity and ideology, all too had semiconsciously incorporated feminist principles into their gender and kin expectations and practices. They took for granted, and, at times eschewed, the gains in women's work opportunities, sexual autonomy and male participation in childrearing and domestic work for which feminists of their mothers' generation struggled. Ignorant or disdainful of the political efforts feminists had expended to secure such gains, they were preoccupied instead coping with the expanded opportunities and burdens women now encounter. They came of age in a period that expected a successful woman to combine marriage to a communicative, egalitarian man with motherhood and an engaging, rewarding career. All but one of these daughters of successful white working-class fathers had absorbed these postfeminist expectations, the firstborns most fully. Yet none found such a pattern attainable. Only Pam's younger daughter, Katie, the original source of the evangelical conversions in her own marriage and her mother's, explicitly rejected such a vision. At fourteen, Katie joined the Christian revival, where, I believe, she found an effective refuge from the disruptions of parental divorce and adolescent drug culture that had threatened her more rebellious siblings. Ironically, however, Katie's total involvement in a Pentecostal ministry led her to practice the most alternative family arrangement of all. Katie, with her husband and young children, lived "in community" in various joint households (occasionally interracial households) whose accordian structures and shared childrearing, ministry labors, and expenses enabled her to integrate her family, work, and spiritual life to an exceptional, and enviable, degree.

At the outset of my fieldwork, none of Pam's or Dotty's daughters inhabited a modern family. However, over the next few years, discouraging experiences with the jobs available to them led three to retreat from the world of paid work and to attempt a modified version of the modern family strategy that their mothers had practiced earlier. All demanded, and two received, substantially greater male involvement in childcare and domestic work than had their mothers (or mine) in the prefeminist past. Only one, however, seemed to have reasonable prospects for succeeding in her modern gender strategy, and these she had secured through unacknowledged benefits feminism helped her to enjoy. Dotty's second daughter, Polly, had left the Silicon Valley when the electronics company she worked for opened a branch in a state with lower labor and housing costs. Legalized abortion and liberalized sexual norms for women allowed Polly to become heterosexually active while deferring marriage and childbearing until she was able to negotiate a marriage whose domestic labor arrangements represented a distinct improvement over that of the prefeminist modern family. Nonetheless, Polly scorned feminism and political activism. . . .

While economic pressures have always encouraged expansionary kin work among working-class women, these have often weakened men's family ties. Men's muted family voices whisper of a masculinity crisis among blue-collar men. As working-class men's access to breadwinner status has receded, so too has their confidence in their masculinity. The decline of the family wage and the escalation of women's involvement in paid work has generated profound ambivalence about the eroding breadwinner ethic. Pam's and Dotty's male kin, like many postfeminist men, appeared uncertain whether a man who provides sole support to his family is a hero or a chump. Two avoided domestic commitments entirely, while several embraced these wholeheartedly. Two vacillated between romantic engagements and the unencumbered single life. Too many of the men I met expressed their masculinity in antisocial, self-destructive, and violent forms.

Women continue to strive, meanwhile, as they always have, to buttress and reform their male kin. Responding to the extraordinary diffusion of feminist ideology as well as to sheer overwork, working-class women, like middle-class women, have struggled to transfer some of their domestic burdens to men. My fieldwork led me to believe that they had achieved more success in the daily trenches than some of the research on the politics of housework indicates. Working-class women have had more success, I suspect, than most middle-class women. While only a few of the women in my study expected, or desired, men to perform an equal share of housework and child care, none was willing to exempt men from domestic labor. Almost all of the men I observed or heard about routinely performed domestic tasks that my own blue-collar father and his friends never deigned to contemplate. Some did so with reluctance and resentment, but most did so willingly. Although the division of household labor remains profoundly inequitable, a major gender norm has shifted here. . . .

One glimpses the ironies of class and gender history here. For decades, industrial unions struggled heroically to achieve a socially recognized male breadwinner wage that would allow working-class families to participate in the modern gender order. These struggles, however, contributed to the very cheapening of female labor that later made women workers so attractive to postindustrial employers who became free to operate outside a union context. This, in turn, fostered the massive entry of married women into the workforce that has done so much to undermine the modern family regime. Escalating consumption standards, the expansion of mass collegiate coeducation, and the persistence of high divorce rates then gave more and more women ample cause to invest a portion of their identities in the sphere of paid labor. In retrospect, we can see that middle-class women began to abandon their confinement in the modern family just as working-class women were approaching its access ramps. The former did so, however, only after African-American women and the wives of white, working-class men had pioneered the twentieth-century revolution in women's paid work. As working-class wives took whatever jobs they could find during the catastrophic 1930s, participated in defense industries in the 1940s, and raised their family incomes to middle-class standards by returning to the labor force rapidly after childrearing in the 1950s, they quietly modeled and normalized the postmodern family standard of employment for married mothers. Whereas in 1950 the less a man earned, the more likely his wife was employed, by 1968 it was the wives of middle-income men who were the most likely to be in the labor force.

African-American women have always had to work and to devise alternative, cooperative kin ties in order to sustain their vulnerable families. They and white, working-class women have been the genuine postmodern family pioneers, even though they also suffer the most from its most negative effects. Long denied the mixed benefits that the modern family order offered middle-class women, less privileged women quietly forged alternative models of femininity to full-time domesticity and mother-intensive childrearing. Struggling creatively, often heroically, to sustain oppressed families and to escape the most oppressive ones, they drew on "traditional," premodern kinship resources and crafted untraditional ones. In the process, they created postmodern family strategies.

Rising divorce and cohabitation rates, working mothers, two-earner households, single and unwed parenthood, along with inter-generational female-linked extended kin support networks appeared earlier and more extensively among poor and working-class people. Economic pressures, rather than ideological principles, governed many of these departures from domesticity, but many working women found additional reasons to appreciate paid employment. Eventually white, middle-class women, sated and even sickened by our modern family privileges, began to emulate, elaborate, and celebrate many of these alternative family practices. How ironic and unfortunate it seems, therefore, that feminism's antimodern family ideology should come to offend many women from the social groups whose gender and kinship strategies helped to foster it. . . .

Recently, however, politicians, journalists, and much of the public have become increasingly preoccupied with the problem of what David Blankenhorn terms "fatherlessness." The National Fatherhood Initiative which he directs, the Christian men's Promise Keepers movement, and the 1995 Million Man March of African-Americans all reflect this partial shift in public attention from the plight of motherless to that of fatherless children. I certainly welcome signs of awareness that, if there is a family crisis, it is primarily a male family crisis, just as I welcome serious efforts to encourage men to assume greater responsibility for children and family bonds. After all, the vast majority of women, like Pam and Dotty, have amply demonstrated a continuing commitment to sustaining kin ties. Unfortunately, however, too much of the new public concern with "fatherlessness" actually holds women and feminism largely responsible for men's absence from the lives of children. Women are now blamed for developing unreasonable familial expectations of men that frighten men away—particularly in regard to equal treatment and shared responsibility for children and housework. Women also are blamed for rejecting paternal participation in favor of rearing children on their own. Blankenhorn devotes a scornful chapter in *Fatherless America* to treating what he regards as emasculating, androgynous visions of "The New Father," that he attributes to feminists and their liberal cultural allies. "As a cultural proposition," Blankenhorn warns, "much of the New Father model depends upon denigrating or ignoring the historical meaning of fatherhood in America. Indeed, much of the New Father ideal is based explicitly upon belittling our own fathers."

The historical meaning of fatherhood that Blankenhorn celebrates with the greatest nostalgia pays homage to the sort of 1950s suburban, breadwinner dads that Pam's first husband and Lou Lewison once had seemed to represent.... Thus, *in the name of The Father and of The Family,* Blankenhorn, Farrakhan, and a mounting crescendo of advocates of family values urge women to gratefully settle for a modified version of the modern family gender regime. In light of the increasingly difficult and dangerous familial conditions of the postindustrial, anti-welfare state regime, many women might readily agree with Pam that such a compromise would be, "not so bad a deal," were it genuinely available to them.

For most women, or men for that matter, even "such a deal" is beyond their reach. Nostalgia for the modern family order deflects public attention from the social sources of many of our most pervasive family troubles. Supply-side economics, governmental deregulation, and the right-wing assault on social welfare programs that began in the 1980s and has escalated in the 1990s have magnified the destabilizing effects of postindustrial occupational shifts not only on flagging modern families but also on emergent postmodern ones. Surveys suggest that providing financial security is the chief family concern reported by parents in the postindustrial United States. Responding to economic and social insecurities at least as much as to feminism, higher percentages of families in almost all income groups have adopted a multiple-earner strategy. Thus, the household form which has come closer than any other to replacing the modern family as a new cultural and statistical norm consists of a two-earner, heterosexual married couple with children.

It is not likely, however, that any singular household type will soon achieve the measure of normalcy that the modern family long enjoyed. Indeed, the postmodern "success" of the voluntary principle of the modern family system precludes this, assuring a fluid, unstable familial culture. The routinization of divorce and remarriage generates a diversity of family patterns even greater than was characteristic of the premodern period when death prevented family stability or household homogeneity. Even cautious demographers judge the new family diversity to be, "an intrinsic feature ... rather than a temporary aberration," of contemporary family life.❖

Arlie Hochschild (1940–) teaches sociology at the University of California at Berkeley. Her academic work has attracted respectful notice from media commentators because of her thoughtful attention to the emotional and domestic consequences of the changing economic world. Two of Hochschild's earlier books—*The Managed Heart: Commercialization of Human Feeling* (1983) and *The Second Shift: Working Parents and the Revolution at Home* (1989)—were mentioned as notable books by the *New York Times.* The selection below is from *The Time Bind: When Work Becomes Home and Home Becomes Work* (1997), based on Hochschild's study of the effects of the family-friendly worktime policies of a Fortune 500 corporation to which she gave the fictitious name Amerco.

Working Women in the Time Bind

Arlie Hochschild (1997)

Amerco, a highly profitable, innovative company, had the budget and the will to experiment with new ways to organize its employees' lives. Its Work-Life Balance program could have become a model, demonstrating to other corporations that workforce talents can be used effectively without wearing down workers and their families. But that did not happen. The question I have asked is: Why not? The answer, as we have seen, is complex. Some working parents, especially on the factory floor, were disinclined to work shorter hours because they needed the money or feared losing their jobs. Though not yet an issue at Amerco, in some companies workers may also fear that "good" shorter-hour jobs could at any moment be converted into "bad" ones, stripped of benefits or job security. Even when such worries were absent, pressure from peers or supervisors to be a "serious player" could cancel out any desire to cut back on work hours. The small number of employees who resolved to actually reduce their hours risked coming up against a company Balashev. But all these sources of inhibition did not fully account for the lack of resistance Amerco's working parents showed to the encroachments of work time on family life.

Much of the solution to the puzzle of work-family balance appeared to be present at Amerco—the pieces were there, but they remained unassembled. Many of those pieces lay in the hands of the powerful men at the top of the company hierarchy, who had the authority and skill to engineer a new family-friendly work culture but lacked any deep interest in doing so. Other pieces were held by the advocates of family-friendly policies lower down the corporate ladder, who had a strong interest in such changes but little authority to implement them. And the departmental supervisors and managers, whose assent was crucial to solving the puzzle, were sometimes overtly hostile to anything that smacked of work-family balance. So even if the workers who could have benefited from such programs had demanded them, resistance from above would still have stymied their efforts.

But why *weren't* Amerco working parents putting up a bigger fight for family time, given the fact that most said they needed more? Many of them may have been responding to a powerful process that is devaluing what was once the essence of family life. The more women and men do what they do in exchange for money and the more their work in the public realm is valued or honored, the more, almost by definition, private life is devalued and its boundaries shrink. For women as well as men, work in the marketplace is less often a simple economic fact than a complex cultural value. If in the early part of the century it was considered unfortunate that a woman had to work, it is now thought surprising when she doesn't.

People generally have the urge to spend more time on what they value most and on what they are most valued for. This tendency may help explain the historic decline in time devoted to private social relations, a decline that has taken on a distinctive cultural form at Amerco. The valued realm of work is registering its gains in part by incorporating the best aspects of home. The devalued realm, the home, is meanwhile taking on what were once considered the most alienating attributes of work. However one explains the failure of Amerco to create a good program of work–family balance, though, the fact is that in a cultural contest between work and home, working parents are voting with their feet, and the work-place is winning. . . .

A Third Shift: Time Work

As the first shift (at the workplace) takes more time, the second shift (at home) becomes more hurried and rationalized. The longer the workday at the office or plant, the more we feel pressed at home to hurry, to delegate, to delay, to forgo, to segment, to hyperorganize the precious remains of family time. Both their time deficit and what seem like solutions to it (hurrying, segmenting, and organizing) force parents . . . to engage in a third shift—noticing, understanding, and coping with the emotional consequences of the compressed second shift.

Children respond to the domestic work-bred cult of efficiency in their own ways. Many, as they get older, learn to protest it. Parents at Amerco and elsewhere then have to deal with their children, as they act out their feelings about the sheer scarcity of family time. For example, Dennis Long, an engineer at Amerco, told me about what happened with his son from a previous marriage when he faced a project dead-line at work. Whenever Dennis got home later than usual, four-year-old Joshua greeted him with a tantrum. As Dennis ruefully explained,

> Josh gets really upset when I'm not home. He's got it in his head that the first and third weeks of every month, he's with me, not with his mom. He hasn't seen me for a while, and I'm supposed to be there. When a project deadline like this one comes up and I come home late, he gets to the end of his rope. He gives me hell. I understand it. He's frustrated. He doesn't know what he can rely on.

This father did his "third shift" by patiently sitting down on the floor to "receive" Josh's tantrum, hearing him out, soothing him, and giving him some time. For a period of six months, Joshua became upset at almost any unexpected delay or rapid shift in the pace at which events were, as he saw it, supposed to happen. Figuring out what such delays or shifts in pace meant to Joshua became another part of Dennis Long's third shift.

Such episodes raise various questions: If Josh's dad keeps putting off their dates to play together, does it mean he doesn't care about Josh? Does Josh translate the language of time the same way his father does? What if time symbolizes quite different things to the two of them? Whose understanding counts the most? Sorting out such emotional tangles is also part of the third shift.

Ironically, many Amerco parents were challenged to do third-shift work by their children's reactions to "quality time." As one mother explained,

> Quality time is seven-thirty to eight-thirty at night, and then it's time for bed. I'm ready at seven-thirty, but Melinda has other ideas. As soon as quality time comes she wants to have her bath or watch TV; *no way* is she going to play with Mommy. Later, when I'm ready to drop, *then* she's ready for quality time. . . .

In such situations, pressed parents often don't have time to sort through their children's responses. They have no space to wonder what their gift of time means. Or whether a parent's visit to daycare might seem to a child like a painfully pro-longed departure. Is a gift of time what a parent wants to give, or what a child wants to receive? Such questions are often left unresolved. . . .

Women's Uneasy Love Affair with Capitalism

A second way of trying to evade the time bind is to buy oneself out of it, an ap-proach that puts women, in particular, at the heart of a contradiction. Like men, women absorb the work-family speedup far more than they resist it; but unlike men, women are the ones who shoulder most of the workload at home. Naturally, then, they are more starved for time than men. It is women who feel more acutely the need to save time and women who are more tempted by the goods and services of the growing "time industry." They are the ones who shop for time. What the speedup takes away, the new time industry sells back in time-saving goods and ser-vices, many of which are geared to appeal to eager working women, especially of the urban middle and upper classes. But at what point does this infatuation with con-sumerism become a problem?

There are many substitutes for family services—summer camp for children or re-tirement homes for the elderly, to mention two—that have already become accept-able features of modern life. Increasingly, though, new products and concepts are being developed to extract smaller and smaller bits of time and effort from family life and return them to the family—for a price—as ready-made goods and services.

Some of these replace the practical activities of a 1950s housewife. In some parts of the country, a family can now phone in a dinner order to a child's daycare center in the morning and pick up both the child and the meal (in an ovenproof container) in the evening. Bright Horizons offers dry-cleaning services based on the same principle. Ac-cording to one news report, some daycare centers will schedule your child's extra time, arranging for and making sure that children get to swimming or gymnastics classes, for example. As the president of Bright Horizons notes, "At Christmas we even have vendors come in and set up displays so parents can buy gifts."

A mail-order company called Extended Family Food From Hane allows people to order a week's worth of dinners, $64.95 plus shipping. Meals are cooked, flash-frozen, and delivered two days later in an insulated box. A week's worth of prepared breakfasts can be shipped out in brown paper bags. Merry Maids, an Omaha-based company with six hundred franchise offices nationwide, will regularly clean the house, or for a special price do the annual spring cleaning. . . .

This trend toward the commodification of home life appears to be reinforcing itself. The fastest-growing sector of the American economy is the self-employed, a majority of whom are now women. Many of their small businesses have been set up to take various tasks out of the hands of busy working mothers. So some of the women consuming items produced by the time-industry do so in order to go to work selling more of the same to other women in similar situations. . . .

Any successful movement for social change begins with a vision of life as it could be, with the notion that something potential could become real. So let's imagine Gwen Bell picking up her daughter Cassie at childcare twice a week at 3 P.M. instead of 6 P.M. and saving those fudge bars for late afternoon treats. Picture John Bell working a half-day Fridays and volunteering at Cassie's center. And what if Vicky King arranged with the eight male executives in her office for "coverage" and took Wednesdays off? Let's imagine PTA meetings to which a large majority of the parents come, libraries where working parents can afford to devote their spare time to reading or literacy programs, and community gardens in which they and their children have the leisure to grow fresh vegetables. Picture voting booths in which parents choose candidates who make flexible work time possible. Finally, let's imagine Janey King turning the music back on and finishing her dance.

But vision alone will not be enough. A time movement will not succeed without change in many of the underlying social conditions that make it necessary. The rising power of global capitalism, the relative decline of labor unions, and the erosion of civil society will all test the resolve of such a movement. Such trends tighten the time bind we live with, of course, but they also highlight the driving need for a way to gain release from it. Job scarcity can make people "work scared" (and thus work longer hours), but it can also force corporations and unions to look at ways to share more lower-hour jobs. Under the right political and social conditions, the growth of technology, which is extending the "anywhere, anytime" work-place into the home, might help people balance work and family even as it squeezes nonwork time even harder.

Finally, I believe that the rising number of working women—and their partners— are a growing constituency for a time movement. At all levels in the workforce, there are women and men whose potential selves are clamoring for more time at home. At a hypothetical future meeting of time activists, a unionized auto worker who wants to cut down on overtime in order to give hours back to laid-off comrades may yet join together with an upper-middle-class, working mom who wants to job share.

The two could find common cause in their children. In fact, the most ardent constituency for a solution to the time bind are those too young as yet to speak up. Fifteen years from now, ten-year-old Janet, home alone in the afternoons, and four-year-old Cassie, waiting to be picked up at the Spotted Deer Childcare Center, will have passed through a childhood of long waits for absent parents. They may say "enough" to the family equivalent of Charlie Chaplin's automatic feeding device. It is they who could form the core of a movement to reclaim private time. But if that would be a good thing in the future, why leave it as an angel of an idea now?❖

Steven Seidman (1948–) is professor of sociology at the State University of New York at Albany. Seidman is recognized worldwide for his writings on social theory, queer theory, and sexualities. His reputation is founded on an astonishing list of books, of which some are *Liberalism and the Origins of European Social Theory* (1983), *Romantic Longings: Love in America, 1830–1980* (1991), *Embattled Eros* (1992), *Contested Knowledge: Social Theory in the Postmodern Era* (1994), *Queer Theory/Sociology* (1996), and *Difference Troubles: Queering Social Theory and Sexual Politics* (1997). The selection is from Seidman's 1998 essay "Are We All in the Closet?"

The Productivity of the Closet

Steven Seidman (1998)

The concept of the homosexual closet is a core category of knowledge and politics in postwar American public culture. More specifically, it has been integral to the discourses of homosexual life that are associated with what I'll call Stonewall culture, that is, the lesbian and gay culture that took shape roughly in the early seventies and eighties in the United States . The category of the closet has been the chief way individuals who identify as lesbian and gay—and individuals who analyze those who identify as lesbian and gay—narrate homosexual experience. Stonewall culture fashioned a romantic narrative of the homosexual heroically struggling to be free of the oppression of the closet. "Out of the closets and into the streets" was the rallying cry of liberationist politics in the 1970s and, as the politics of "outing" in the 1990s suggests, a politics of visibility or coming out remains at the center of the lesbian and gay movement. . . .

[Yet,] I intend to raise some questions about the implicit sociology and politics of the closet that have dominated Stonewall culture. . . . I outline a perspective that underscores the "productive" aspects of the closet, that emphasizes its limited sociohistorical applicability, and that underscores the limits of the politics of visibility or recognition. The theme of the closet as an organizing principle of American life is used to explore some reservations regarding recent queer theory. In this regard, I make the case, in fact only propose the contours of an argument, for a stronger sociological and cultural turn in queer studies. . . .

The dominant discourses of Stonewall culture framed the closet in a way that assumes an already formed homosexual self. Repressed in the closet, the homosexual would be liberated by the act of coming out. However, a queer critique, that is, a perspective that makes the making of the subject into a problem, opened up a line of inquiry that has been unthinkable in Stonewall culture—namely, the role of the closet in the formation of a homosexual self. Part of what I want to consider is to what extent the closet—or the condition of concealment and confinement that it refers to—is productive of homosexual selves. Let me explain.

The dominant Stonewall narrative frames the closet as signifying the concealment of homosexual desire and identity—to the extent that desire functions as a cultural marker of identity. The closet is said to describe a state of self-alienation and inauthenticity. However, the experience of concealment implies not only repression but the formation of a desire and self around homosexuality. The interiority forced upon the individual by closeting makes it possible for same-sex desire to become an object of overdetermined investment and cathexis. To what extent does the closet indicate a condition where homosexual desires are imagined and cultivated, and where a self is formed around this desire? Doesn't the concept of the closet presume [that] the individual invests homosexual desire not only with shame but with pleasure and the longing for an imaginary integrated, whole self? . . .

Proposing a notion of the productivity of the closet parallels, I think, the way many thinkers now approach the concept of a woman's sphere, the colonized other, and the ghetto. Each of these concepts were initially pivotal for analyzing dynamics of oppression. Feminists and critical race theorists, for example, analyzed how the power to enforce a certain social invisibility works internally to produce dominated selves. But also, feminists and postcolonial theorists, for example, have inquired into how this very same condensation of the self around a particular identity might be productive of new subaltern subjects who resist domination. In this regard, I might add parenthetically that a study of the closet that inquires into the conditions making possible the formation of a homosexual subject would necessarily draw on a psychoanalytical language of unconscious processes.

I have come to believe that the social texture of American lesbian and gay life in the 1990s is considerably different from the way it is represented in the dominant discourses of Stonewall culture. By investigating the social conditions that make the closet narrative central to Stonewall culture, we can perhaps begin to delineate its outer historical boundaries. Specifically, to what extent is it plausible to speak of the emergence of at least the contours of a post-Stonewall culture—one where the closet, coming out, and declaring a public sexual identity are no longer the key narrative figures in terms of which homosexuality is understood?

My argument in this regard turns on a conjecture based, however, on a wide range of documentary evidence and interviews to the effect that there is occurring a trend toward the "normalization" (internal acceptance) and social routinization (social acceptance) of homosexuality. Homosexuals are becoming an integrated, visible part of American life—in politics, popular culture, law, and everyday life.

To my surprise, I found strong support for this claim in interviews I conducted in 1996–1997. My initial aim was to research what it means to be "in" the closet. How did social domination shape a homosexual subject? How did concealment and sequestration make possible a resisting homosexual subject? However, from the very first interview I found that many of those I interviewed reported lives that were in a significant sense "beyond the closet." When I interviewed individuals who lived in small towns or mid-sized cities, and who were not strongly integrated into—or did not identify with—a lesbian and gay subculture (and therefore, we would expect, likely to be "closeted"), many of them described an incomplete achievement of an internally normalized, socially routinized, homosexual life.

Typical in many ways is the case of Lenny, a 40-year-old gay man. Until recently, Lenny lived in a small upstate New York town, the place where he grew up and where his working-class, religious family still lives. Coming of age at the very beginning of the making of a public gay culture (mid-1970s), Lenny's only ideas about homosexuality were very negative. He recalls hearing words like "fag" and "queer" from peers and family as derogatory and shaming—a message reinforced by his church. He grew up being aware of, yet suppressing, his homosexuality. Lenny lived an almost classically defined "closeted" life until he was about 30. The suppression of his homosexuality, in other words, shaped key life decisions such as getting married, joining the marines, and drinking heavily. Concealment, moreover, meant disassociating his inner and outer life and maintaining a vigilant, intense self-management, driven by extreme fear, to avoid exposure. No one knew of his homosexuality, except those few men with whom he had anonymous, guilt-ridden sex.

This changed when he turned 30. Lenny "came out"—initially to a lesbian friend, then to gay men at bars and community events, and finally to family, friends, and co-workers. For example, Lenny reports that today his supervisor and co-workers know about his homosexuality. More important as an indicator of normalization and social routinization, they know about his homosexuality not merely as an abstract identity but as something that is interwoven into his life. That is, his co-workers know about his homosexuality as it relates to his friends, dates or lovers, gay community events and politics, and so on. When I pressed further into the extent to which his homosexuality had become normalized and routinized, Lenny reported that he talks about his life to his co-workers in an open, easy way that is no different than if he were heterosexual. Like heterosexually identified individuals, Lenny doesn't tell everyone everything about the homosexual aspects of his life. Disclosure decisions are determined by a series of factors including feeling safe, the closeness or intimacy of the relationship, a determination of whether the other can handle it, and a judgment about whether disclosure will result in being treated as a mere label or as a complex, multidimensional person.

> I just feel everybody out, one at a time. I think first of all would they be supportive and more importantly was it any of their business. I would ask myself that. And in a lot of cases, I feel like its more important that they get to know me, who I am, you know without that aspect, so that they really won't be so prejudiced when they do find out. I try to prepare people and I try to feel them out, because some people just can't handle it and don't want to know it.

Make no mistake—heterosexuality remains very definitely normative, and homosexuality and the homosexual are still freighted with connotations of moral pollution. As the statement by Lenny indicates, and as many interviews make clear, concealment, disclosure decisions, and sexual-identity management are still part of the lives of lesbians and gay men in America. Homosexuals still suffer and, for many, the closet and coming out remains not merely a phase of their lives but its center. Yet, whether the evidence is individual reports of the normalization and routinization of homosexuality or shifts in popular culture (e.g., television, novels, news coverage) and politics, a trend toward normalization and social routinization seems at least a credible claim even if the extent and meaning remain very much unclear.❖

Wei Jingsheng (1950–) was released from prison in 1997 by the Chinese authorities after having spent most of the previous twenty years in confinement. Once a member of the Red Guard and an apparently loyal worker during Mao's Cultural Revolution, Wei broke onto the world scene in 1978 as a leader of the Democracy Wall Movement in Beijing, for which he was arrested after posting his defiant "The Fifth Modernization" declaration. While in prison he continued to write eloquently and courageously, often ridiculing his captors. Wei has been honored worldwide for his courage as a nominee for the Nobel Prize, a recipient of the Olof Palme Award, and a winner of the European Parliament's Sakharov Prize for Freedom of Thought. "The Courage to Stand Alone" is taken from a book of the same title that is a collection of Wei's prison and other political writings. This selection is from one of his many open letters to the president and premier of the People's Republic of China. The selection comprises two of the seven fallacies in the full letter.

The Courage to Stand Alone
Wei Jingsheng (1997)

Dear Jiang Zemin and Li Peng:

Human rights have become a popular topic of conversation lately and even the Party line on the issue seems to have softened somewhat. It has declared that it intends to "study human rights theories and questions in order to deal with the peaceful evolution of hostile forces," and so on. These very words prove that the basic theories of the Communist Party as they currently exist do not cover the issue of human rights, and that people are no more than tools for production and struggle within its theoretical framework. Tools, naturally, do not have any rights. All they have is the "right" to be submissive and to be used. When "peaceful evolution of hostile forces" comes into the picture and the tools are no longer as docile and useful, then it becomes necessary to find out what to do to make them docile once again. At least, this is the stand and attitude revealed in your Party's newspaper. . . .

But what is the use of saying all this nonsense anyway? Let us take a serious look at human rights theories and practices, how they stand in relation to socialism, and in particular why Marxist societies often turn out to be political structures that do not respect human rights. These questions are matters of primary importance for modern China. They may seem very far removed from us, but actually they are very close to home; they might appear as merely abstract concepts, but they are, in fact, very concrete. The lack of human rights is the principal cause for many of the concrete problems confronting Chinese society. Human rights are also a problem about which fallacies and confusion abound. . . .

FALLACY: *"Looking after the interests of the majority of people is our major point of departure on the issue of human rights."*

On the surface, these words sound fine, but in fact there are often things that need to be examined beneath the surface. When talking about the rights that every person should enjoy, the claim that "the majority is the point of departure" is an act of deceptive sophistry and excuse-making. It occurs when faced with a situation which one cannot deny but in which one is unwilling to admit fault. This is because even if we talk about "gross violations of human rights," the phrase still refers to the violation of the rights belonging to every individual—in other words, the violation of an individual's internal affairs. It does not refer to a matter of contention that may or may not belong to a particular individual, and does not refer to public matters in the political, economic, or environmental domains. These are expressed by other concepts. Rather, it refers to rights that should belong to every individual. This has nothing to do with "the majority," and the majority has no right to curtail the basic right to freedom of even a small minority. Although parts of their concepts can be duplicated and may overlap, we cannot thus say that chemistry equals physics, that energy equals transport, that grain equals smelly night soil, and so on. This is the same sort of sophistry as using the majority as an excuse to confuse the issue of the human rights that belong to every individual.

Perhaps these words indicate that in our country's society, there exists a majority that enjoys rights and a small minority that does not enjoy basic rights. Who, then, is this majority, and who is the small minority? Do we need to redraw class divisions? Or are some minority nationalities going to serve as the antithesis, as was the case in the 1950s and 1960s? Regardless, juggling with terms such as "the majority" on the question of basic human rights proves that this society is an unequal one and that the Constitution and laws that talk of "all persons being equal" are nothing more than waste paper. This, then, produces a dilemma. Either the Constitution and the laws have been cleverly juggled by people so that some enjoy full rights and others enjoy fewer rights or none at all, and the surface and content of the laws and the Constitution are different or even meaningless; or else some people have usurped the rights that should belong to every person rather than to only some of the people and therefore there has been a large-scale violation of human rights. Which of the two situations do you think is the most likely? Or do both exist simultaneously?

South Africa is a country in which a small number of white people violate the rights of the majority of the people, including some white people. This certainly cannot be tolerated and it is certainly valid to openly attack such abuses. However, people of your age should remember that the Nazis and some "socialist comrades" who were not Nazis used the pretext of "the majority" to eliminate the "inferior races"—the Jews, the Tartars, and the blacks. Is it the case that because some persons constituted "the majority" in Germany, the Soviet Union, and the United States they had the right to violate the rights and freedoms of other people? Was it the case that because such violations did not violate the laws of these countries at that time, and were tolerated, supported, and implemented by the governments, that they were reasonable and should not have been denounced, since as you say, "interference in internal affairs is impermissible"? While the violation of human rights based on race and national differences is obviously a barbarous act, is not the violation of human rights within a single race or nation, based on artificial differences or even with no basis at all, even more barbarous and intolerable? If the people allow those who hold power in the people's name to violate and ignore the rights of some of the people, then at the same time they are giving them the power to violate the rights of all the people. This is especially so in a society where there are no racial or cultural differences.

FALLACY: Marx had a famous popular definition: "Man's nature is the sum of his social relations." Some people, on this basis, infer that as different societies have social relations and the sums of such relations are different, there are also different human natures. Thus, the different views on and practices of human rights are suited to different types of human natures and the rationality of all of these should be fully recognized. It would be an abnormal phenomenon to have uniform requirements.

Man is not a product of his social relations, nor indeed of any relations. He is not a robot, nor is he a product created by other people based on a pattern for man. Rather, he is a product of nature. Thus, his essential qualities are likewise a product of nature. These are "instinctive" and very basic and they constitute a human "commonality" which is inborn and possessed by all and on which all other human natures and social relations are based. Human rights and basic freedoms refer to the satisfying or realizing of this part of human nature. They are the sum of hopes and aspirations that emerge naturally and do not need to be taught.

Human rights are themselves a type of social relation. The respect and protection of human rights and basic freedoms is in itself a social institution, a social system, and a mechanism to ensure its own effectiveness. However, this refers to primary-level social relations, which emerge from man's basic nature or, put another way, are the foundation of all social relations. These are basically different from those social relations that are derived and that are stipulated or manufactured by man.

Wherever a great amount of social injustice is enshrined in law, that is to say, where the cornerstone of a legal system is social injustice maintained through violence, the social models are societies of enslavement such as slavery and fascism. These societies can be distinguished by determining the degree of human rights existing in them. We need to look at whether or not within these societies the basic freedoms and rights of a part or the majority of the people have actually been expropriated "by law." Law is people's social nature and is not the sole or most basic standard for social relations. Human rights are a more basic standard.

In order to have progressed to its present stage, Western civilization has had to safeguard outstanding elements of its culture and tradition and learn many things from the remarkable achievements of the civilizations of China and elsewhere. This has enabled it to maintain appropriate development for itself at pace with an increasingly rapid global development. Chinese civilization has begun a similar process of study and assimilation. At the present time, is it really necessary that we continue to enshrine and worship "isms" that Western civilization has already spit out?

Wei Jingsheng ❖

Toni Morrison (1931–) was born in Lorain, Ohio, from which she took many of the depictions in her novels. She was educated at Howard and Cornell Universities. After working as a book editor in New York City, Morrison turned full time to her life as an artist. Her novels include *The Bluest Eye* (1970), *Sula* (1973), *Song of Solomon* (1977), *Tar Baby* (1981), *Beloved* (1988)—for which she won the Pulitzer Prize—and *Paradise* (1998). Toni Morrison teaches at Princeton University. The selection is from her acceptance address on being awarded the 1993 Nobel Prize for literature.

Reach Toward the Ineffable
Toni Morrison (1993)

The conventional wisdom of the Tower of Babel story is that the collapse was a misfortune. That it was the distraction or the weight of many languages that precipitated the tower's failed architecture. That one monolithic language would have expedited the building, and heaven would have been reached. Whose heaven, she wonders? And what kind? Perhaps the achievement of Paradise was premature, a little hasty if no one could take the time to understand other languages, other views, other narratives. Had they, the heaven they imagined might have been found at their feet. Complicated, demanding, yes, but a view of heaven as life; not heaven as post-life. . . .

The vitality of language lies in its ability to limn the actual, imagined and possible lives of its speakers, readers, writers. Although its poise is sometimes in displacing experience, it is not a substitute for it. It arcs toward the place where meaning may lie. When a President of the United States thought about the graveyard his country had become, and said, "The world will little note nor long remember what we say here. But it will never forget what they did here," his simple words were exhilarating in their life-sustaining properties because they refused to encapsulate the reality of 600,000 dead men in a cataclysmic race war. Refusing to monumentalize, disdaining the "final word," the precise "summing up," acknowledging their "poor power to add or detract," his words signal deference to the uncapturability of the life it mourns. It is the deference that moves her, that recognition that language can never live up to life once and for all. Nor should it. Language can never "pin down" slavery, genocide, war. Nor should it yearn for the arrogance to be able to do so. Its force, its felicity, is in its reach toward the ineffable.❖

Final Notes:
Where Does Reading End?

Just last Sunday, I read as we rode the E train uptown. Having lost interest in the ads for hemorrhoid laser surgeries, I had brought along a collection of Raymond Carver's short stories, *What We Talk About When We Talk About Love*. I finished the first story in the few stops between Canal Street and Penn Station. I paused only a moment. My wife said, "Amazing, isn't it?" I just nodded. It was.

Later, while we were walking in the park, on the Eastside just north of the zoo, a jogger lunged toward us at a good pace. His stride was strong but broken. He was crippled. Cerebral palsy, we thought, saying little else. After, we took the shortcut to the Westside. Soon, he came again, having already circled most of the six-mile circuit. Then, my wife said, "I've seen him running here for years. Think of what it takes." I did. I imagined a solitary life, ordered around chaotic limbs, a life he ran with dignity among hundreds of beautiful bodies on roller blades. She had her thoughts too. We said a little, but less than you would suppose.

Reading is like that. A relatively few abstracted marks or events evoke worlds others already know. But how does it work? When I was a little boy, I asked such a question about the radio. How was it that each weekday evening at 6:15 I could tune in *Tom Mix* on the Magnavox console in the safe, far corner of the living room? Though I have since learned many theories about reading, I still do not understand either it or the radio. Somehow, something is broadcast in the air. We get it. Others do, too, even those with whom we share no intimacies at all. In a blurb on the back of the book of stories I read on the subway, Frank Kermode says, "Carver's fiction is so spare in manner that it takes a time before one realizes how completely a whole culture and a whole moral condition is represented by even the most seemingly slight sketch." Though Raymond Carver was among the masters of this sort of writing, much the same can be said of all writing. It succeeds at whatever it does in spite of the sparseness of its means relative to the worlds evoked.

The difference between reading and radio listening, though, is that reading seems to have become an activity of no necessary limits. Among the people I talk to in the school where I teach, it is common to refer to the analysis of many different sorts of situations as a "reading." I once heard a little story in which the term was used in such a way: At a dinner party several years before, a guest had delivered a crude ethnic insult that angered and embarrassed most of those at the table. In a response calculated to set things straight without disrupting the dinner, the hostess gave him what the teller of the story described as "a postmodern reading of the anti-Semitism in his remark." Apparently, that reading did little of its intended good. The old insult was still raw. Just the same, in this case a "reading" is a vastly more complex communication than whatever it was that allowed my wife to understand what I was feeling about a story we had both read and a man we saw. If "reading" is an activity inclusive not just of books and events in the park but even of delicate retorts to gratuitous insults, then it is possible that there is no end to what reading might be. Nor should there be.

However it works, reading does seem to be an accurate way to describe what happens when different people discover a similar sense in an event as spare as that of a crippled man running well. In the same way that there is not an infinite number of meanings to be derived from a written text like one of Carver's short stories, neither is it that the true nature of that man's world is likely to be much different from what most people might imagine. Different, surely, but certainly not random. Otherwise, nothing we read would make sense. However it works, on whatever events or marks, reading cannot work all too differently from the radio. Somehow, in Kermode's words, "a whole culture" is out there. Reading is what is done with it in order to make worlds for ourselves.

Reading, in this expanded sense, is the natural corollary to social theory. If, as I said at the beginning, the least common denominator of social theory is telling one's world into being, then reading must be the means by which others recognize that story as somehow familiar to them. Many will disagree with this view. One of the anonymous readers of my introduction was particularly irritated at the suggestion I make that scientific social theory is no different from the theories people produce in ordinary life. There is a difference, of course. But, however people may cherish and defend that difference, I do not think that the possibility that professional social theories might enjoy common ground with ordinary human activity degrades them in any way. On the contrary.

Nor is it the case that social theory and reading, whether lay or professional, are uncomplicated practices. In fact, if there is a sense in which the professional sciences are at a relative disadvantage, it is in their less subtle relation to social worlds. Professional standards, like scientific protocols, are intended to ensure a degree of stability (some would say universality) to a theory of the world. So long as one has reason to believe that the world to which the theory applies is, in fact, stable, this is all to the good. But, for better or worse, the worlds in which most people live today are not. As a result, what is said and read in ordinary life is likely to be as sure a truth as what is found in the professional journals. Different; not necessarily better, but, perhaps, as sure.

If the world in which many worlds are spoken of is well named when people call it *multicultural,* then such a world requires a certain change of attitude among its inhabitants. Were the world one for all persons, then all could be held to a universal standard for its truths, and there would be no coherent justification for multiple readings of it. If, on the contrary, one experiences different truths in different stories of the world, there are many worlds to tell and many readings to enjoy. Though there is a philosophic beauty to the former, the personal and historical evidence for the latter is, in my opinion, stronger. A world of multiple cultures requires not just that people tolerate differences. They must, like it or not, tolerate in the sense of enduring the effect of those differences. This may seem a slight difference, but it turns out to require an extraordinarily difficult change of attitude, especially for those accustomed to the assumption that their world is all that matters. At the least, one experiences irritation and frustration—and possibly more, depending on one's social position in such a world. The same may well apply to reading any book that attempts to collect or speak of it.

Social Theory: The Multicultural and Classic Readings has been composed with such a world of worlds in mind. It is expected, as a matter of principle, that different readers will read it differently. Nothing would please me more than if this collection were to find its way into the homes of the reading public. Though it was planned, in large part, with students and teachers in mind, the editors at Westview Press readily shared my ambition that such a book ought to appeal to those who are no longer (or, perhaps, never were) students or teachers. My own experience as a teacher is that my work as a professional social theorist too often distracts me from the obvious fact that students are also people. Some of them may choose to become sociologists or professional social theorists of some other sort, but all of them want, above all else, to live well. They undergo the demands of student work to learn, but they learn in order to acquire the power to make and enjoy the worlds they imagine. Whatever the presumed differences among the colleges and universities, high schools and boarding schools, that make up an educational system, it seems to me untrue that students of varying abilities or social and economic circumstances differ significantly on this simple hope. This is what makes the student, first and foremost, a member of the reading public. The book is designed to appeal, most of all, to them as readers. By this I do not mean that the selections are merely accessible. They will be readable to different people to different degrees. What I do intend is that the collection, as a whole, invites the reader into the worlds made possible by good social theory over the years.

Teachers will come to this book with interests made more complex as much by their sense of responsibility for students as for their particular professional convictions. For myself, I imagine I would ask students to supplement this collection by reading the whole of some books. Weber's *Protestant Ethic* or Du Bois's *Souls of Black Folk*, for example. But I also imagine that the book could be used comfortably on its own, or with a minimum of supplementing according to taste. Certainly, I understand that different teachers, whatever the professional pressures on them, are also readers and that, in this regard, some will be disappointed by the selections I have made. Some would prefer more, and different kinds, of feminism. Others will regret, perhaps, the absence of more and later Habermas. One person has already said that he does not understand why I have chosen so many writers who are so well known. At first, I thought the answer was obvious, until I came back to the realization that a few years ago, hardly anyone had heard of Anna Julia Cooper or Charlotte Perkins Gilman. I realize, for example, that there is little representation from Asia and less from Eastern Europe. I can only trust that readers will know for themselves how to supply what is lacking, at least as time goes by.

If, in the end, the book establishes enough of an interest in reading social theory and thus encourages readers to think and speak of their worlds from some or several unusual perspectives, then it will have served the purposes intended. If some or many also find pleasure in the book, then all the better.

Though it may seem a strange place to do it, I would like to thank those who, in different ways, have helped with this book. I do it here, rather than separately, because, having now done the book, I know for certain that it could not ever have been done alone. The readings included here were selected out of a series of relations, and thus readings, more complex but just as mysterious as those that allow two people in the park to make similar sense of the same event.

The following people read parts of the outline and introduction: Jeffrey Alexander, Patricia Clough, Indira Karamchetti, Michael Kennedy, Richard Lachman, Barbara Laslett, and Steve Seidman. Each made excellent suggestions, some of which I used with appreciation. I also wish to thank present and former faculty and students in the sociology department at Wesleyan University, in particular Ann Branaman, Mary Ann Clawson, Alex Dupuy, Sue Fisher, Elizabeth Friedman, Chris Krauss, Peter Levin, Lucinda Mendez, Joy Rhoden, Rob Rosenthal, Kassandra Salmon, David Swartz, Sandra Wong, and John Yoo. With them, I have shared, in different ways and times, the pleasures and pains of teaching and learning. Elizabeth Traube and I invented and taught the core course on social theory in the anthropology-sociology joint program. Much of what I think, especially about the nineteenth-century theorists, is influenced by this work with her. Elisa Istueta helped prepare the manuscript. Dean Birkenkamp has been a wonderful editor. I thank also friends who have influenced my thinking in important ways pertinent to this book: Sandy Becker, Patricia Clough (again), Julie Doar, Michael Harris, and Claire Shea. Matthew, Noah, and Geri know what they need to know about how I feel. They, too, are helpful readers.

Charles Lemert
January 28, 1993

Acknowledgments/1999 Edition

Between the first and second editions, Florence Brown Lyons died. The dedication of the first edition gave her much pleasure. The dedication of the second edition to her memory gives me pleasure of another kind, though one tinged with feeling for the loss of her.

Elaine Markson, my agent, is beloved among those she represents because she represents us with such loving force. Thank you, Elaine—for this and so much else.

I wish also to acknowledge the student and faculty colleagues who have written to me about this book. Many wrote of the ways this book, or some parts of it, touched them personally as well as intellectually. I take very little credit for this, since what touched them were the good words of the complex traditions of social theory. I, in turn, am pleased that *Social Theory* has provoked so much long overdue discussion in classrooms and wherever else readers talk about their worlds.

Charles Lemert
January 30, 1998

Index